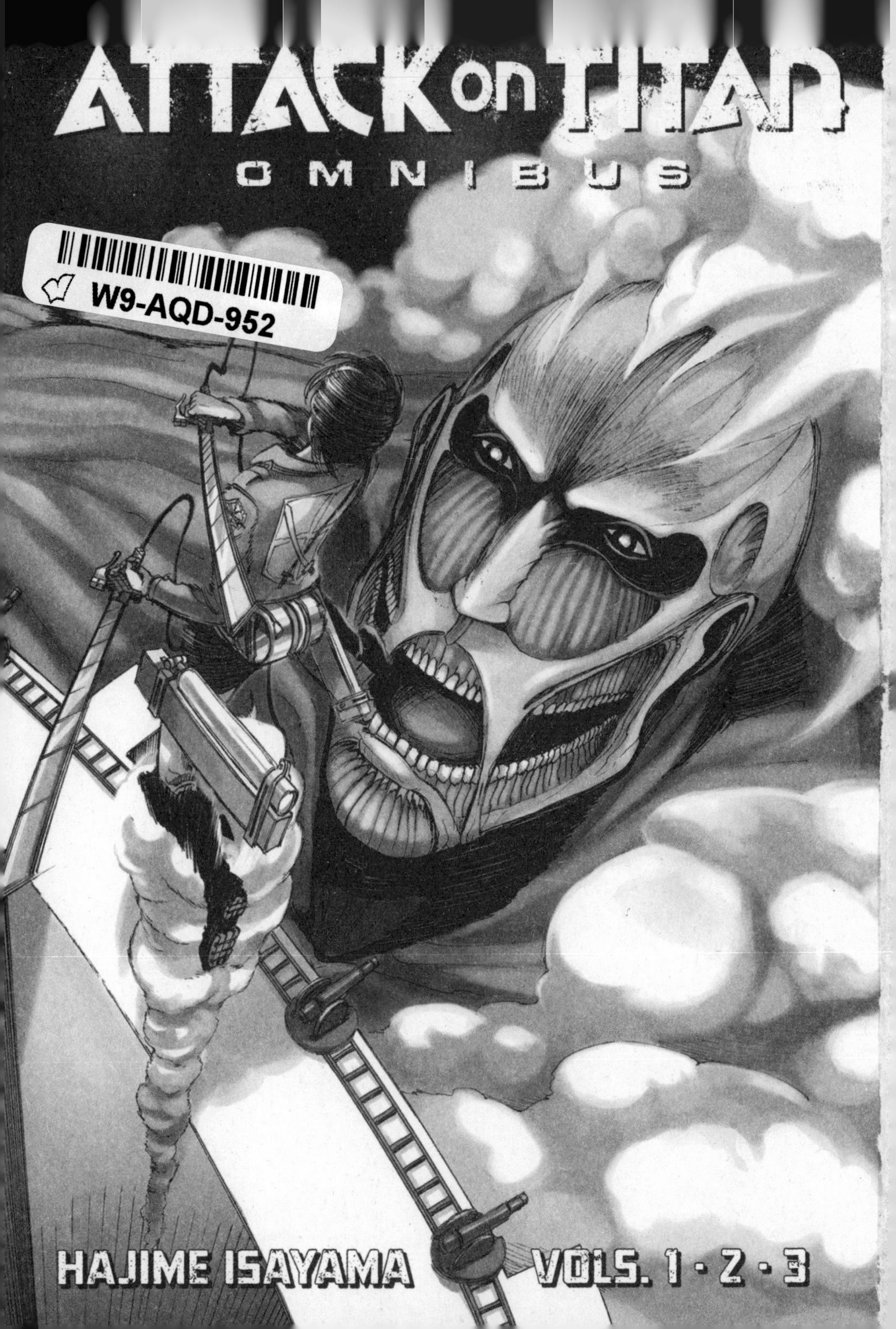
ATTACK on TITAN
OMNIBUS
W9-AQD-952
HAJIME ISAYAMA
VOLS. 1 · 2 · 3

ATTACK on TITAN

OMNIBUS 1 (VOL. 1-3)

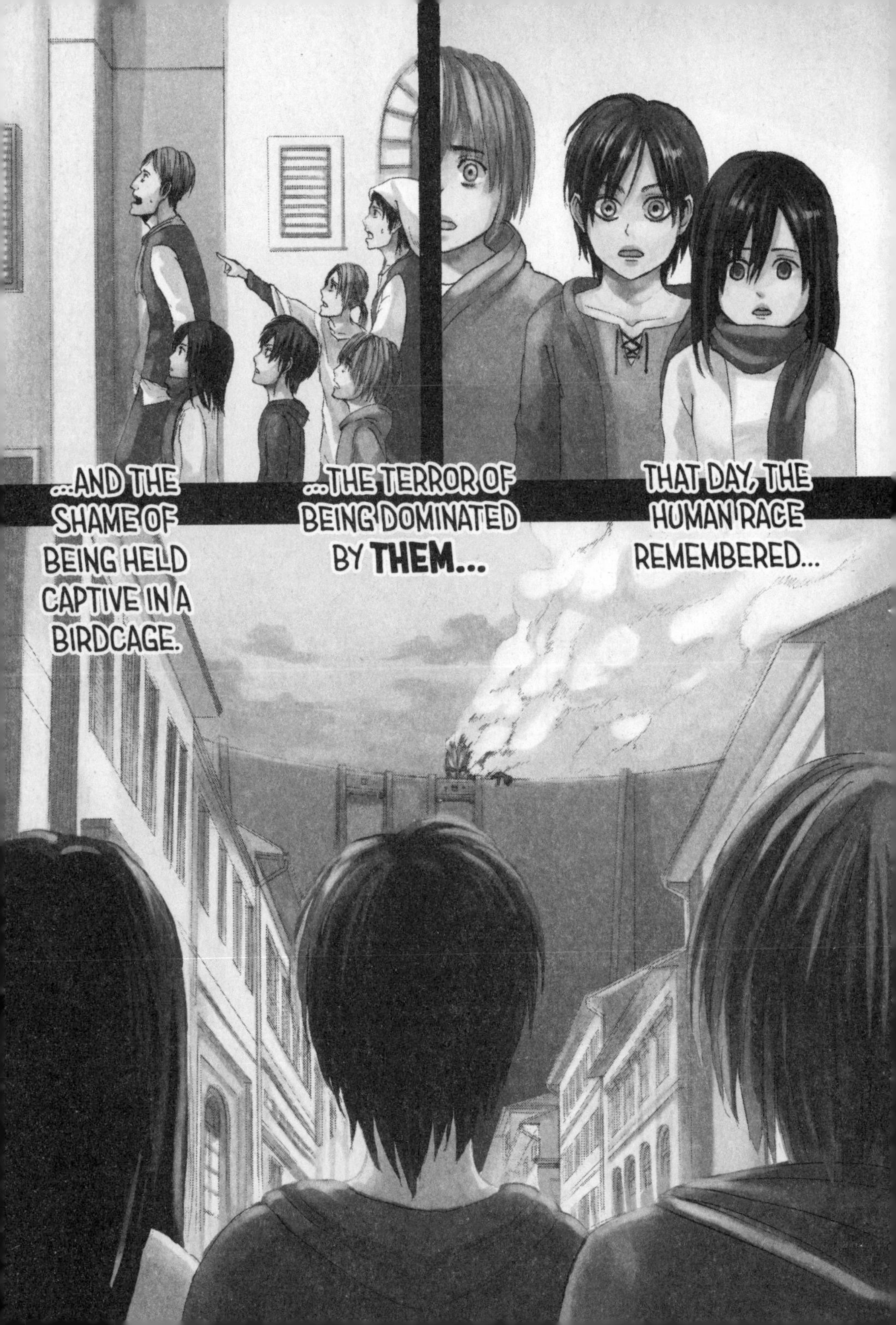
THAT DAY, THE HUMAN RACE REMEMBERED...
...THE TERROR OF BEING DOMINATED BY THEM...
...AND THE SHAME OF BEING HELD CAPTIVE IN A BIRDCAGE.

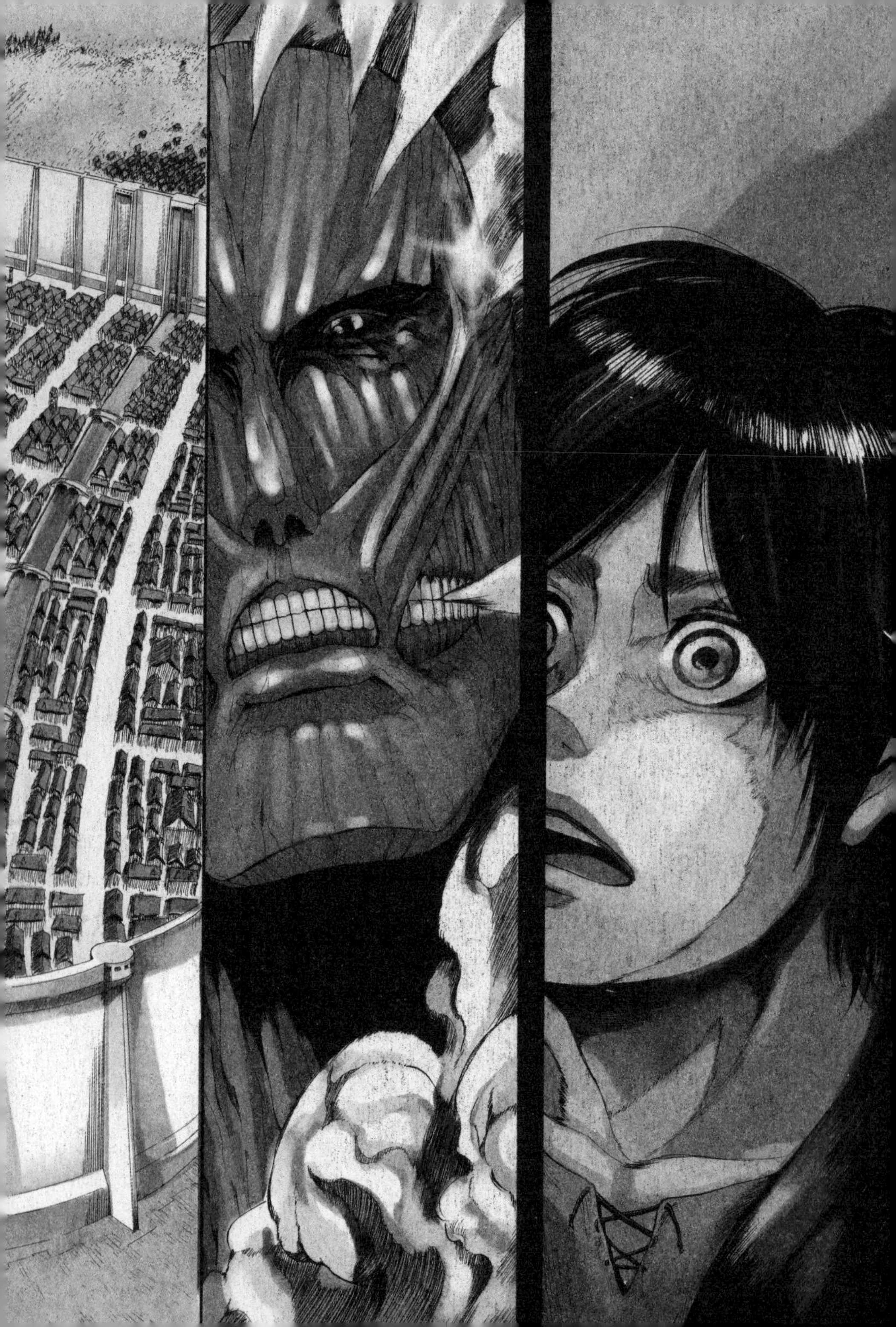

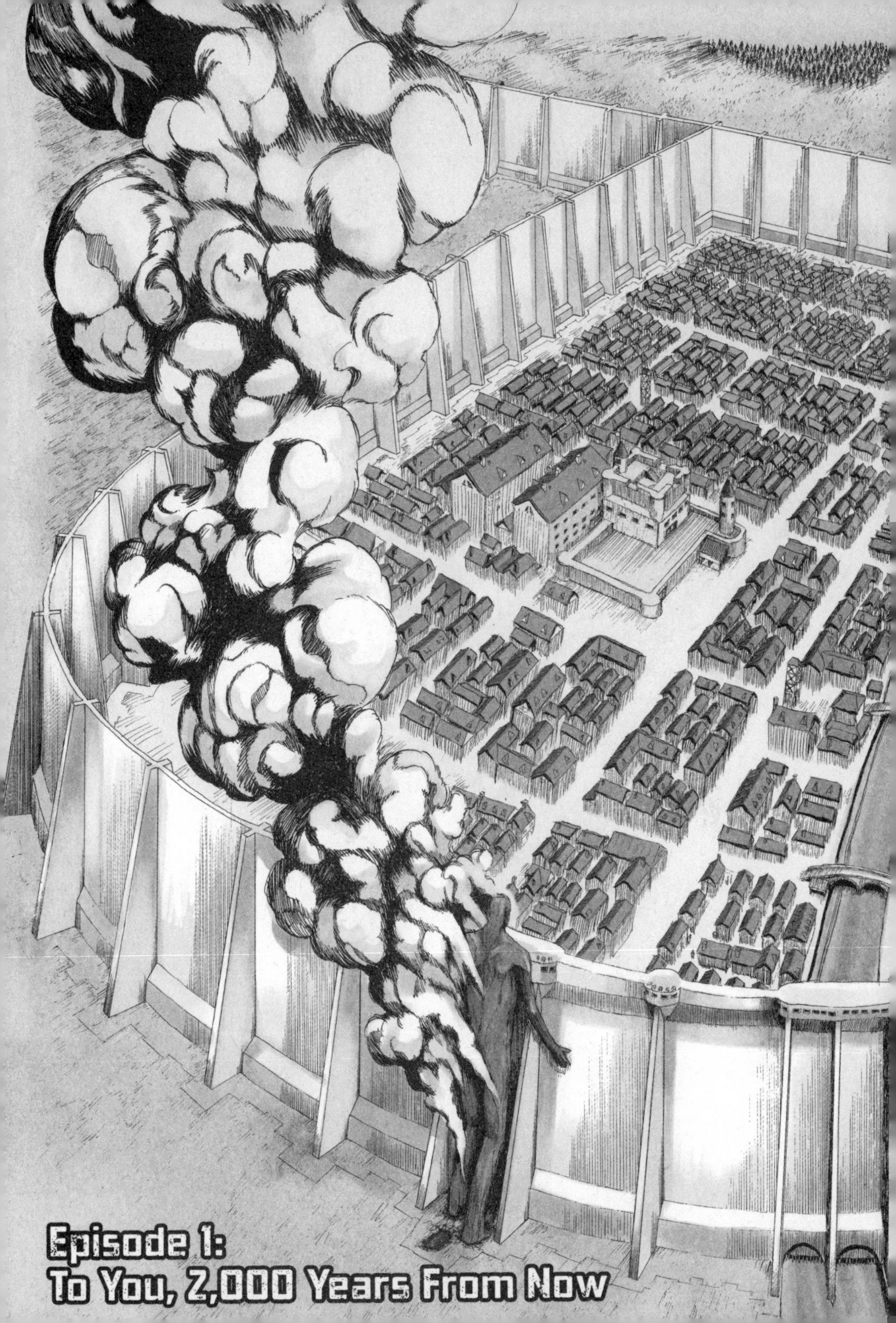

Episode 1:
To You, 2,000 Years From Now

ATTACK ON TITAN

1

HAJIME ISAYAMA

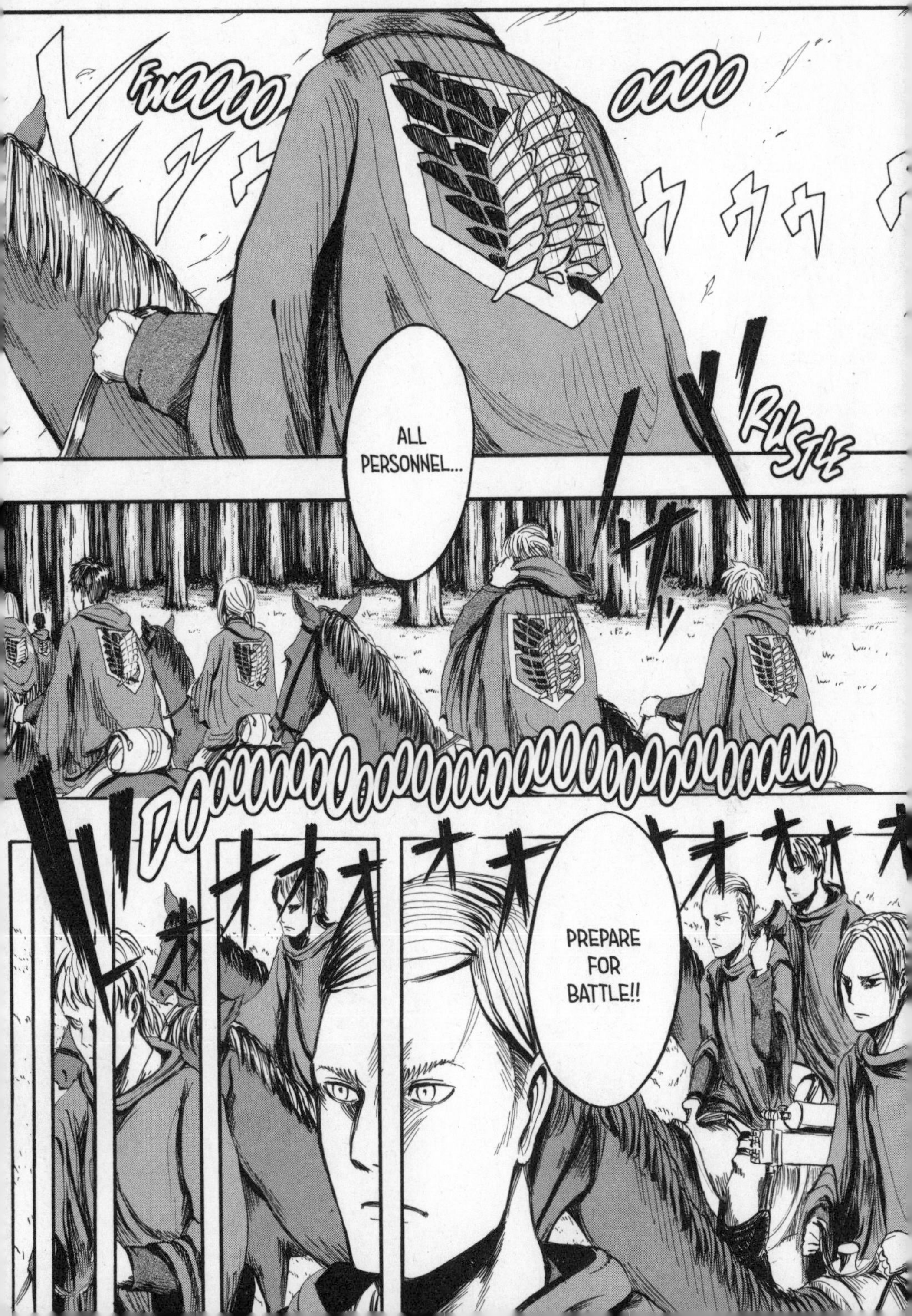
FWOOOOO
OOOOO
ALL PERSONNEL...
RUSTLE
DOOOOOOOOOOOOOOOOOOOOOOOOOOOOOOOOOOO
PREPARE FOR BATTLE!!

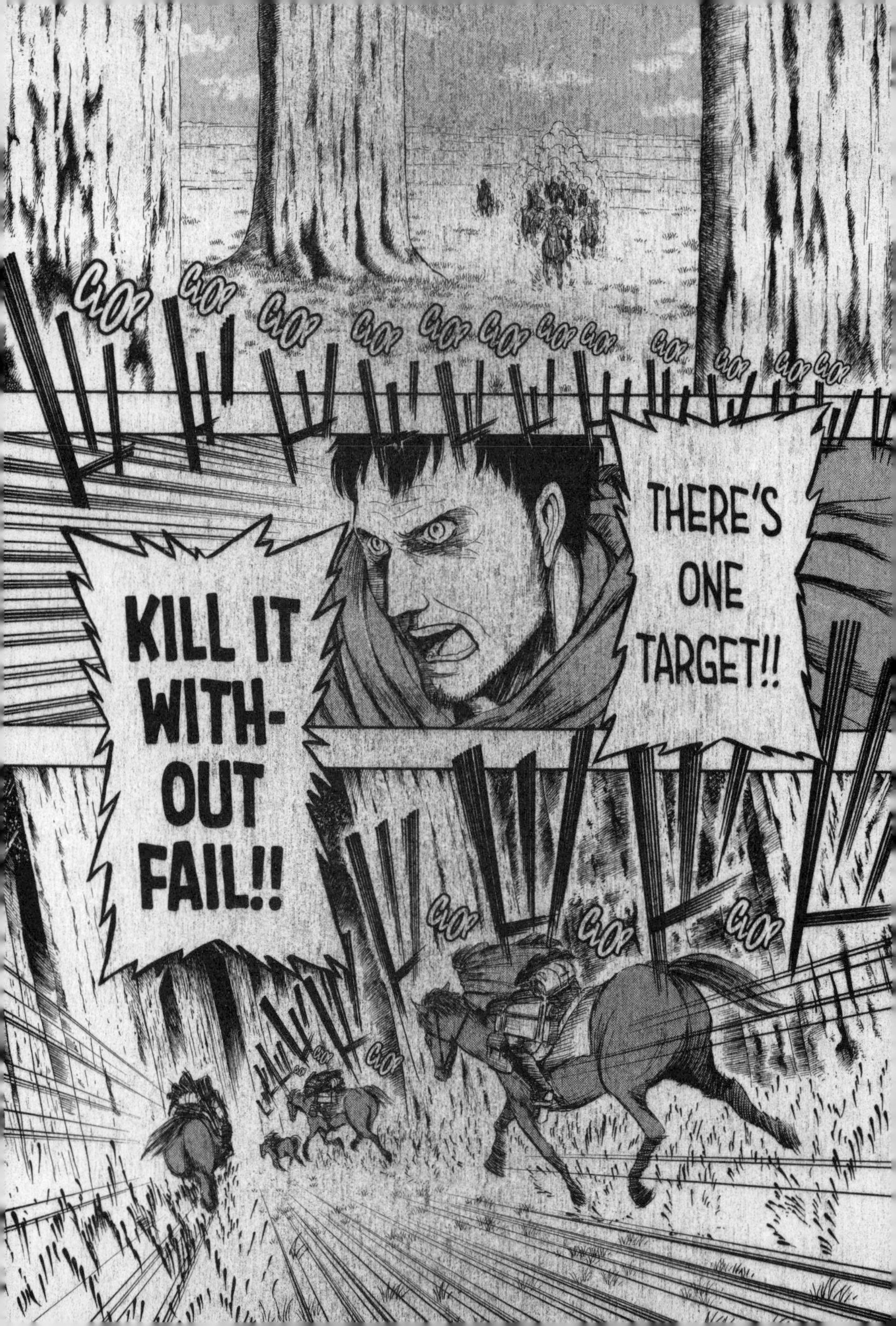
CLOP CLOP CLOP CLOP CLOP CLOP CLOP CLOP CLOP CLOP CLOP CLOP
THERE'S ONE TARGET!!
KILL IT WITH-OUT FAIL!!
CLOP CLOP CLOP
CLOP

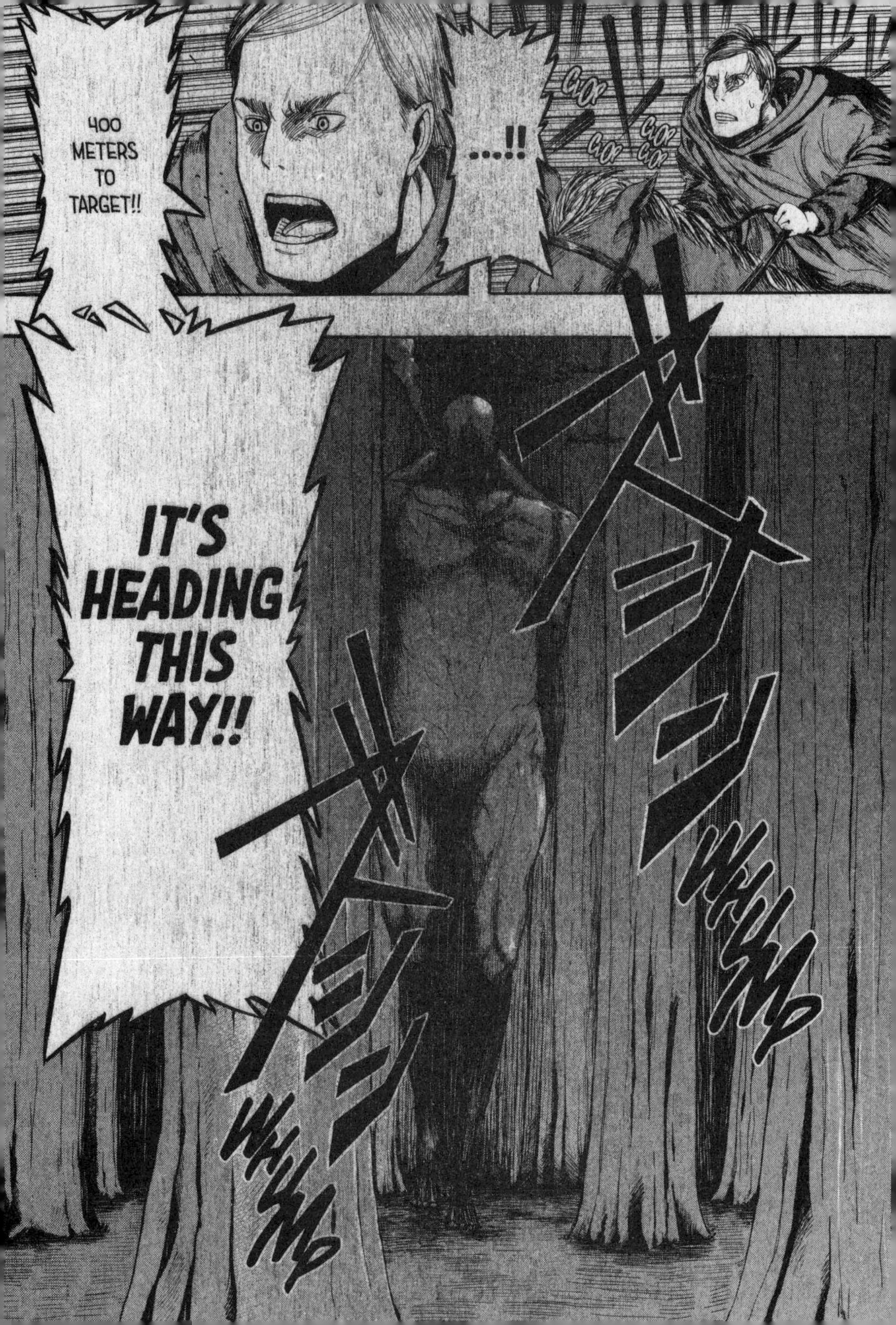
CLOP
CLOP CLOP
CLOP CLOP
...!!
400 METERS TO TARGET!!
IT'S HEADING THIS WAY!!
WHUMP
WHUMP

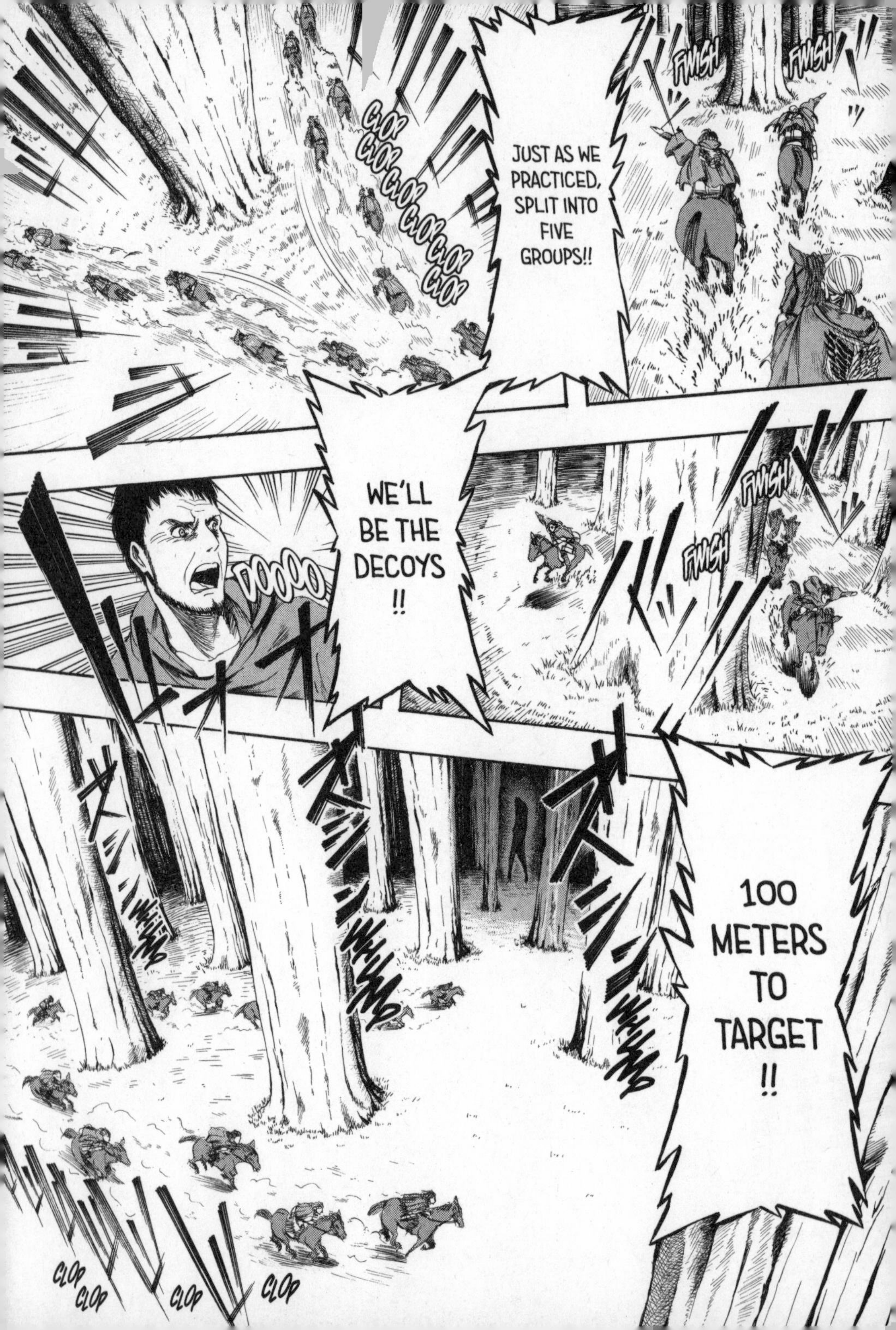
FWISH
FWISH
JUST AS WE PRACTICED, SPLIT INTO FIVE GROUPS!!
CLOP CLOP CLOP CLOP CLOP CLOP
FWISH
FWISH
WE'LL BE THE DECOYS!!
DOOOO
100 METERS TO TARGET!!
CLOP CLOP
CLOP
CLOP

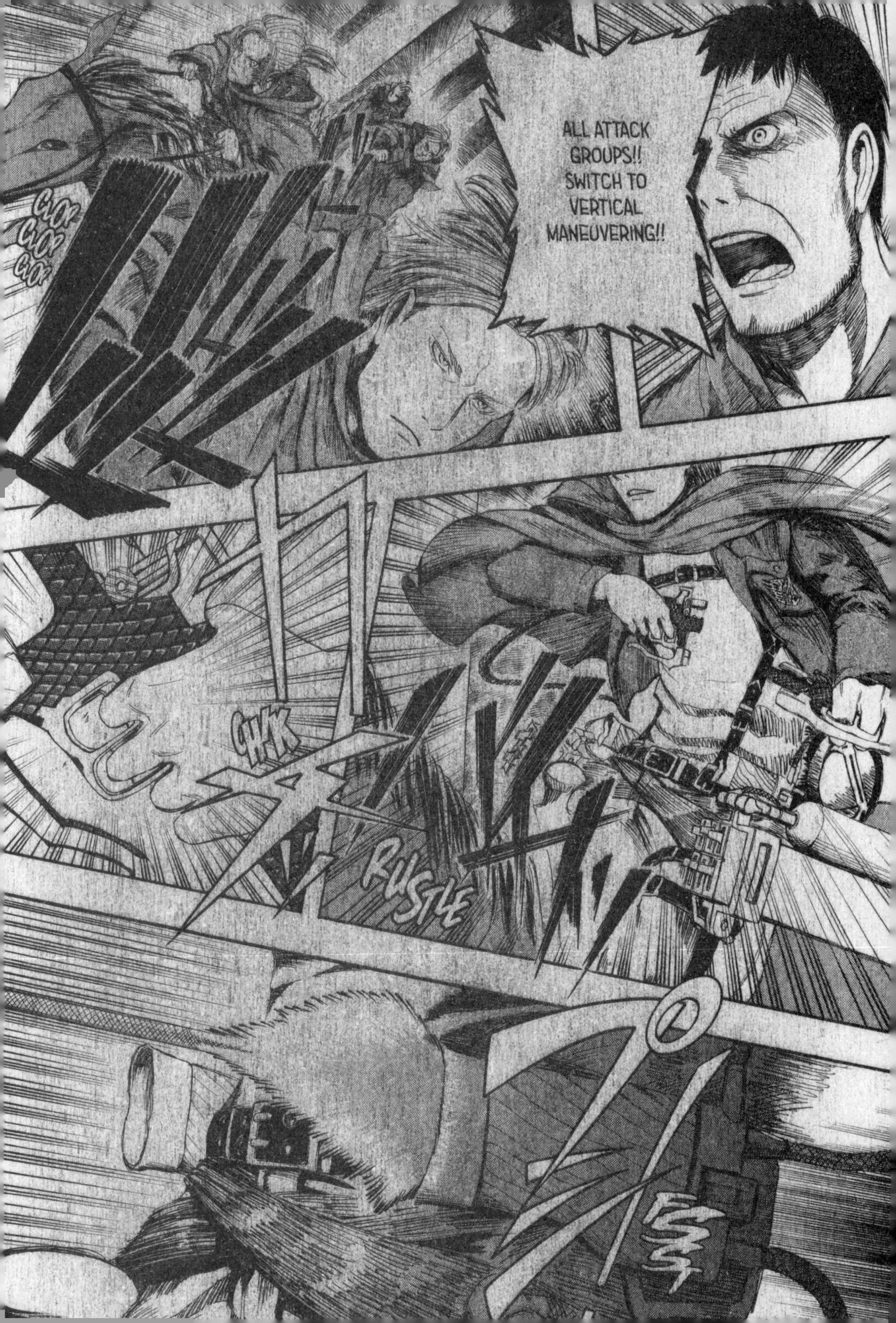
ALL ATTACK GROUPS!! SWITCH TO VERTICAL MANEUVERING!!
CLOP CLOP CLOP
CHAK
RUSTLE
FSST

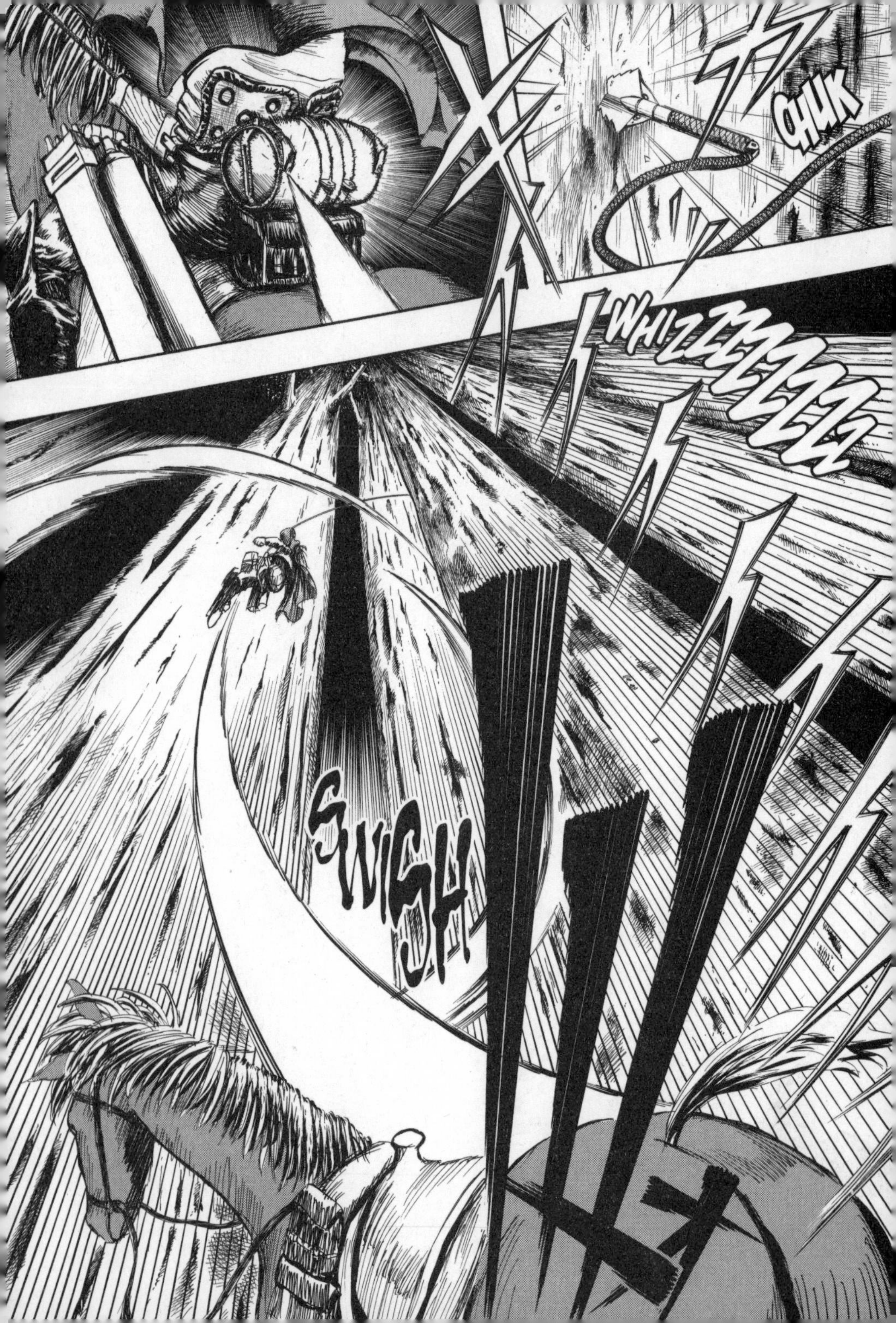
CHUK
WHIZZZZZZZZ
SWISH

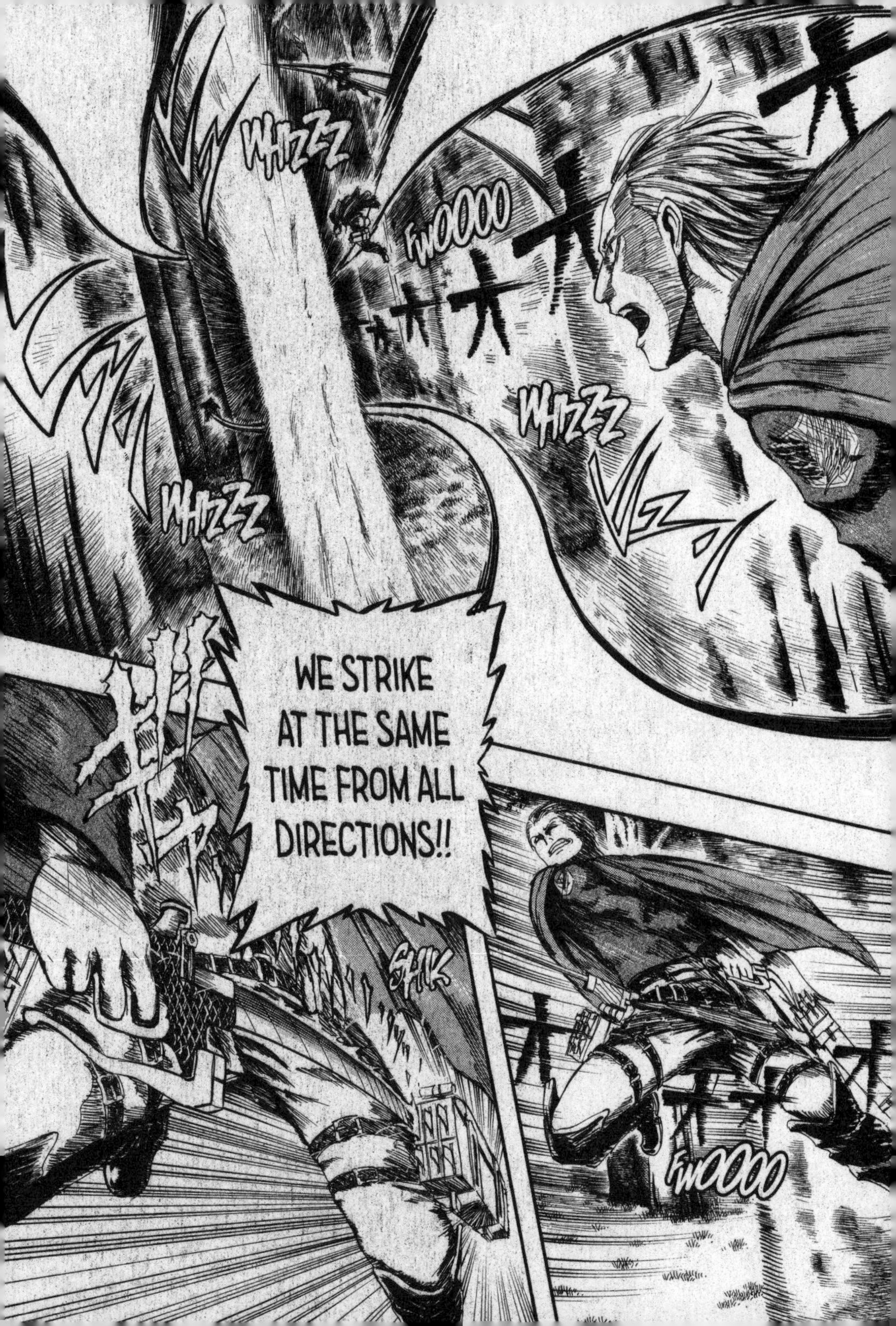
WHIZZZ
FWOOOO
WHIZZZ
WHIZZZ
WE STRIKE AT THE SAME TIME FROM ALL DIRECTIONS!!
FWOOOO
SHIK

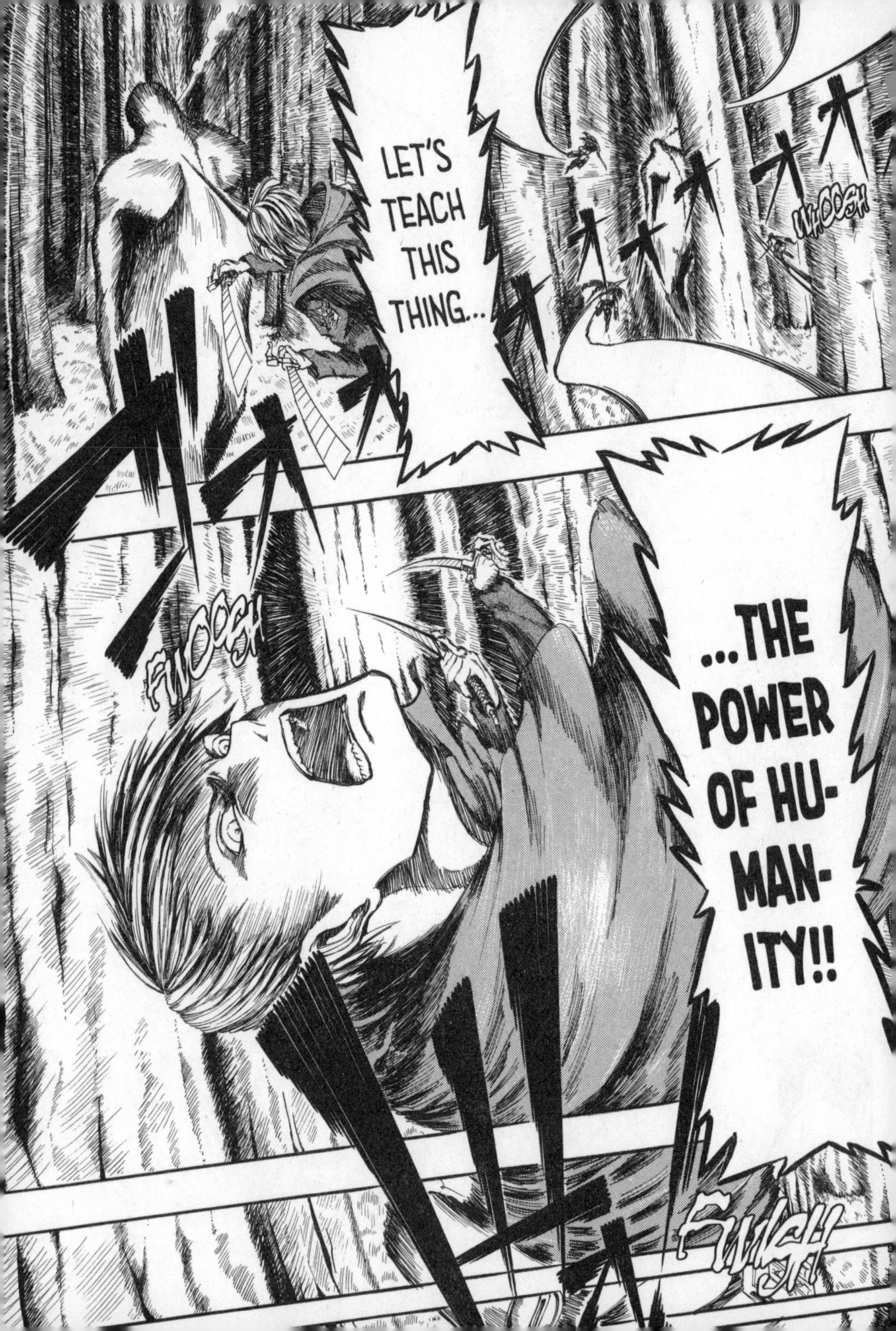
WHOOSH
LET'S TEACH THIS THING...
...THE POWER OF HU-MAN-ITY!!
FWOOSH
FWISH

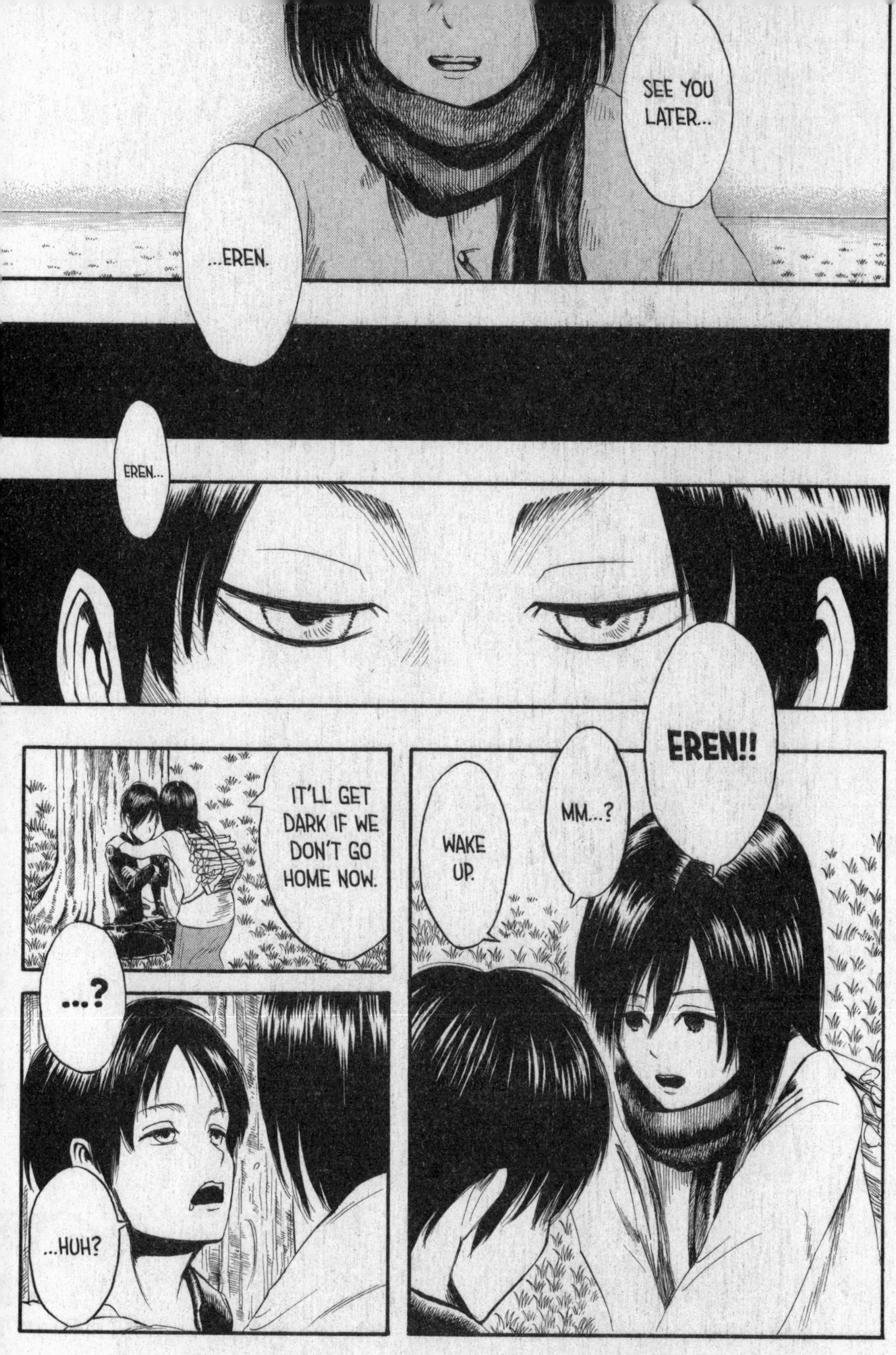
SEE YOU LATER...
...EREN.
EREN...
EREN!!
MM...?
WAKE UP.
IT'LL GET DARK IF WE DON'T GO HOME NOW.
...?
...HUH?

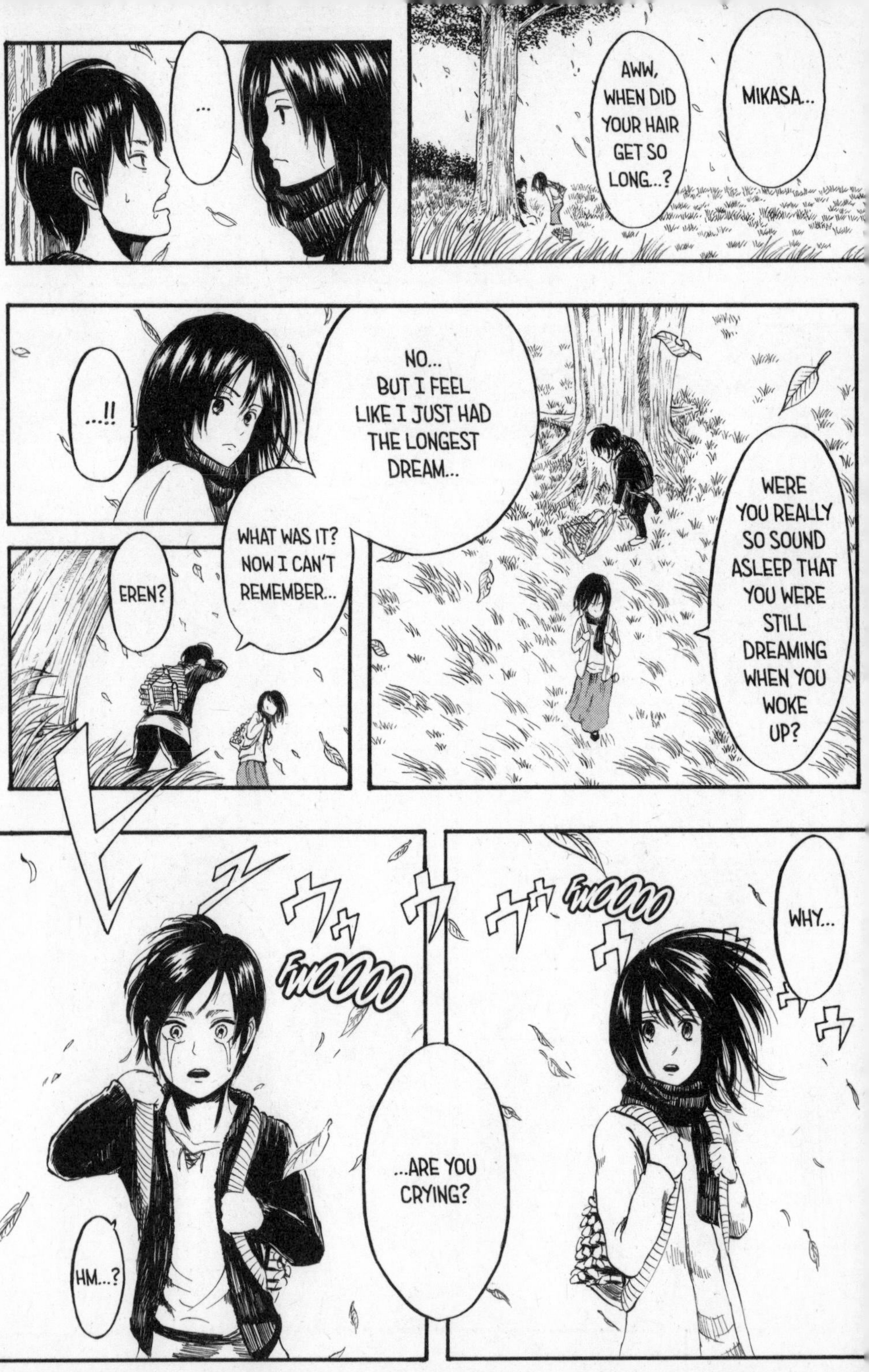
MIKASA...
AWW, WHEN DID YOUR HAIR GET SO LONG...?
...
WERE YOU REALLY SO SOUND ASLEEP THAT YOU WERE STILL DREAMING WHEN YOU WOKE UP?
NO... BUT I FEEL LIKE I JUST HAD THE LONGEST DREAM...
...!!
WHAT WAS IT? NOW I CAN'T REMEMBER...
EREN?
WHY...
FWOOOO
...ARE YOU CRYING?
FWOOOO
HM...?

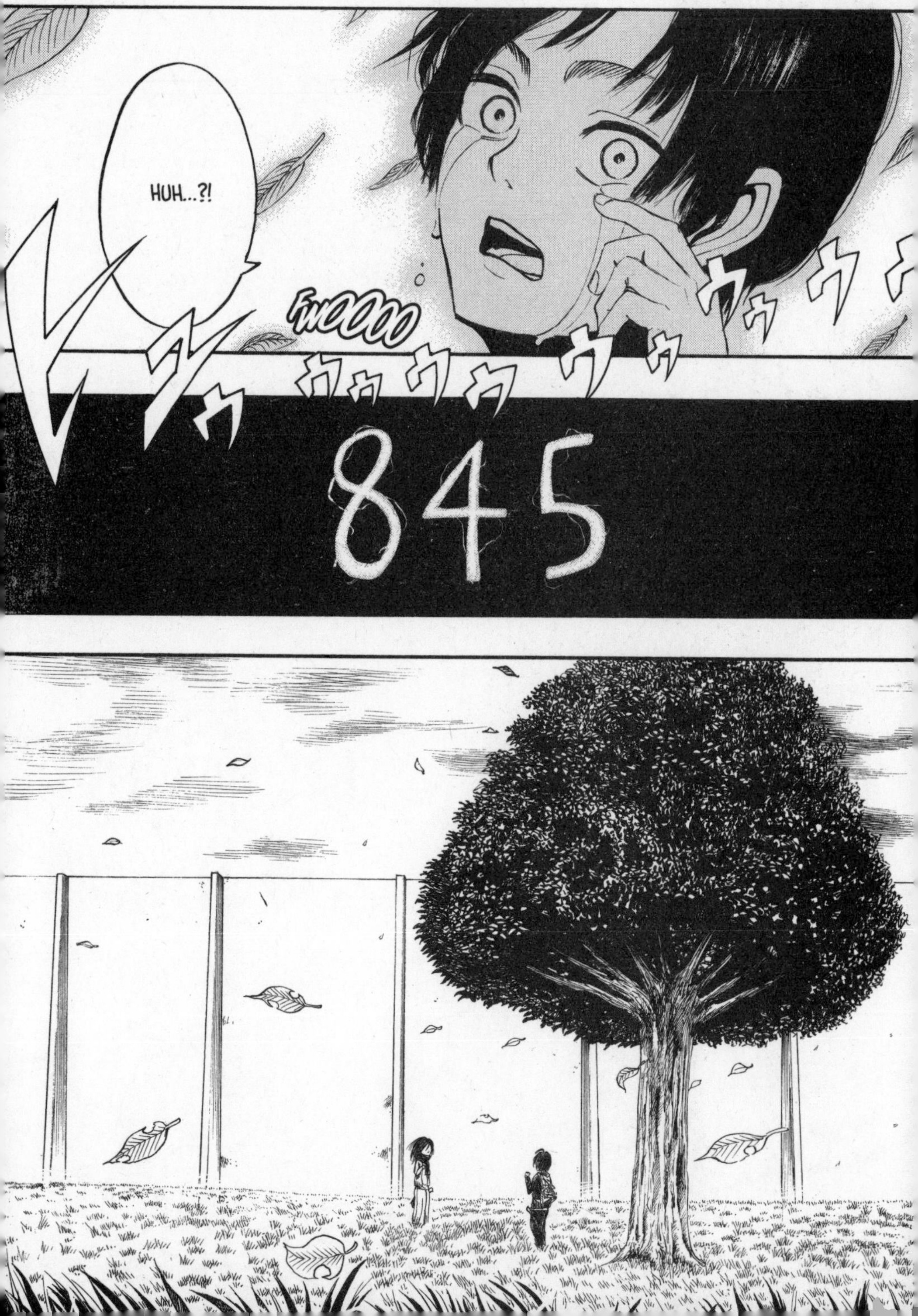
HUH...?!
FWOOOO
845

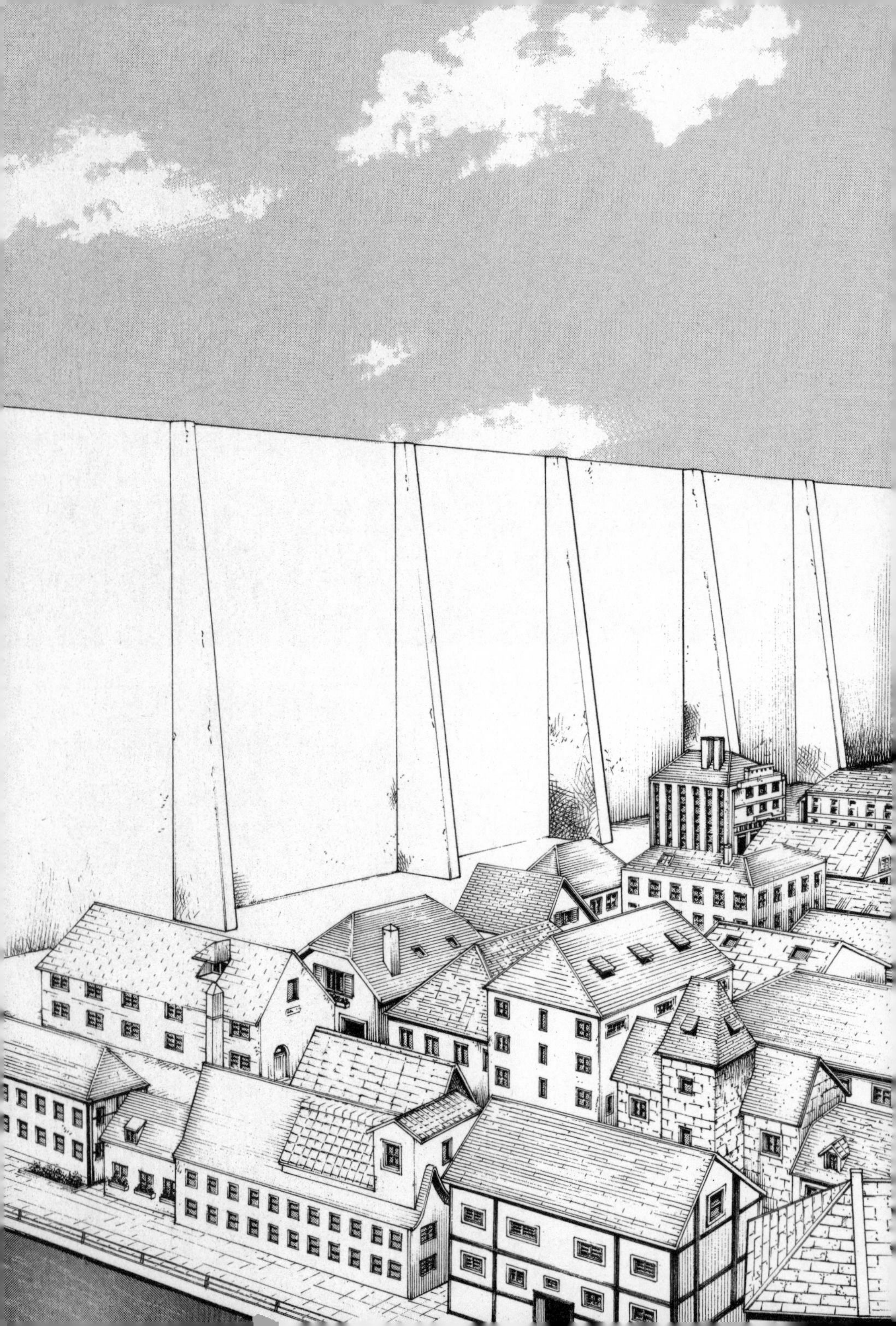

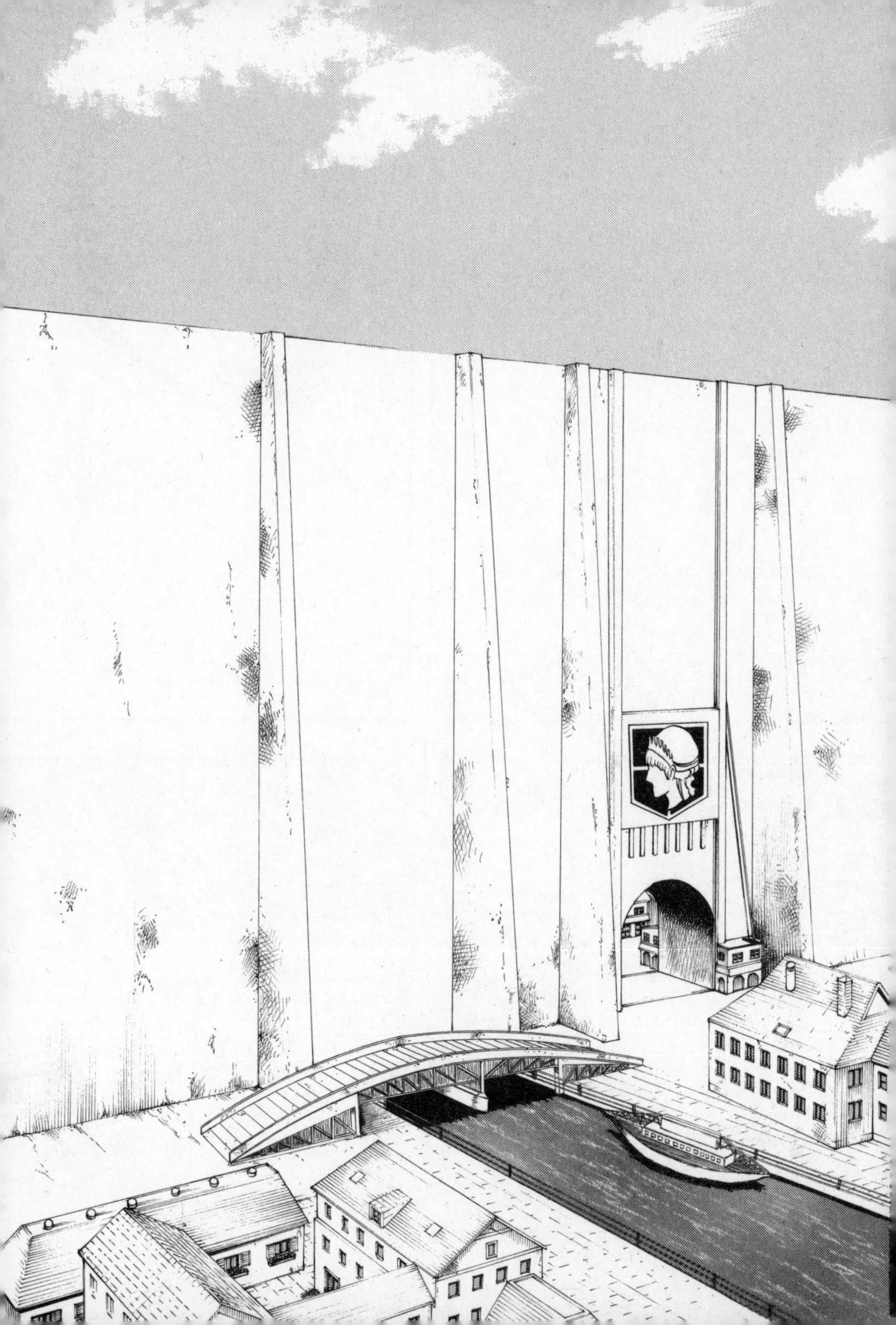

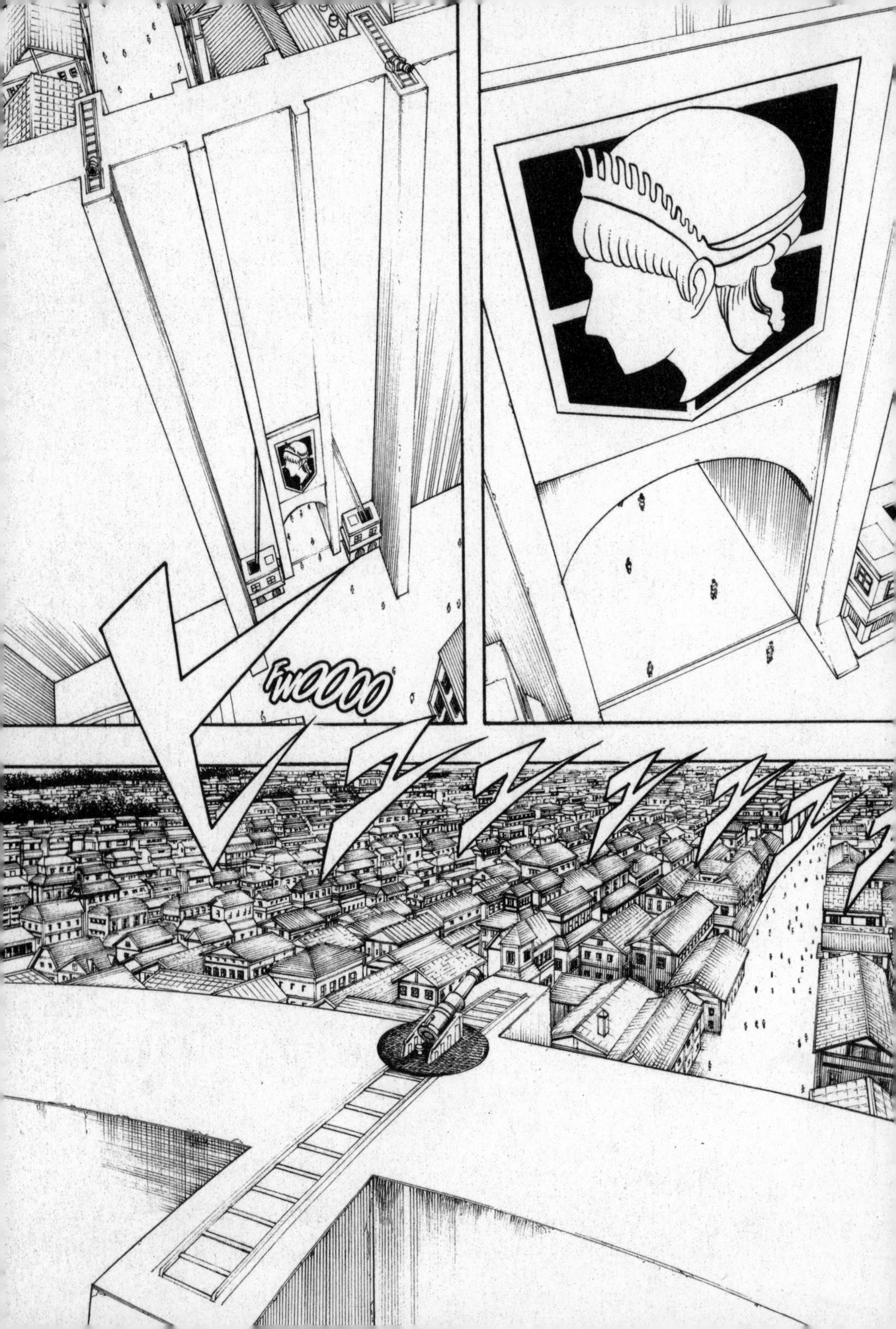
FWOOOO

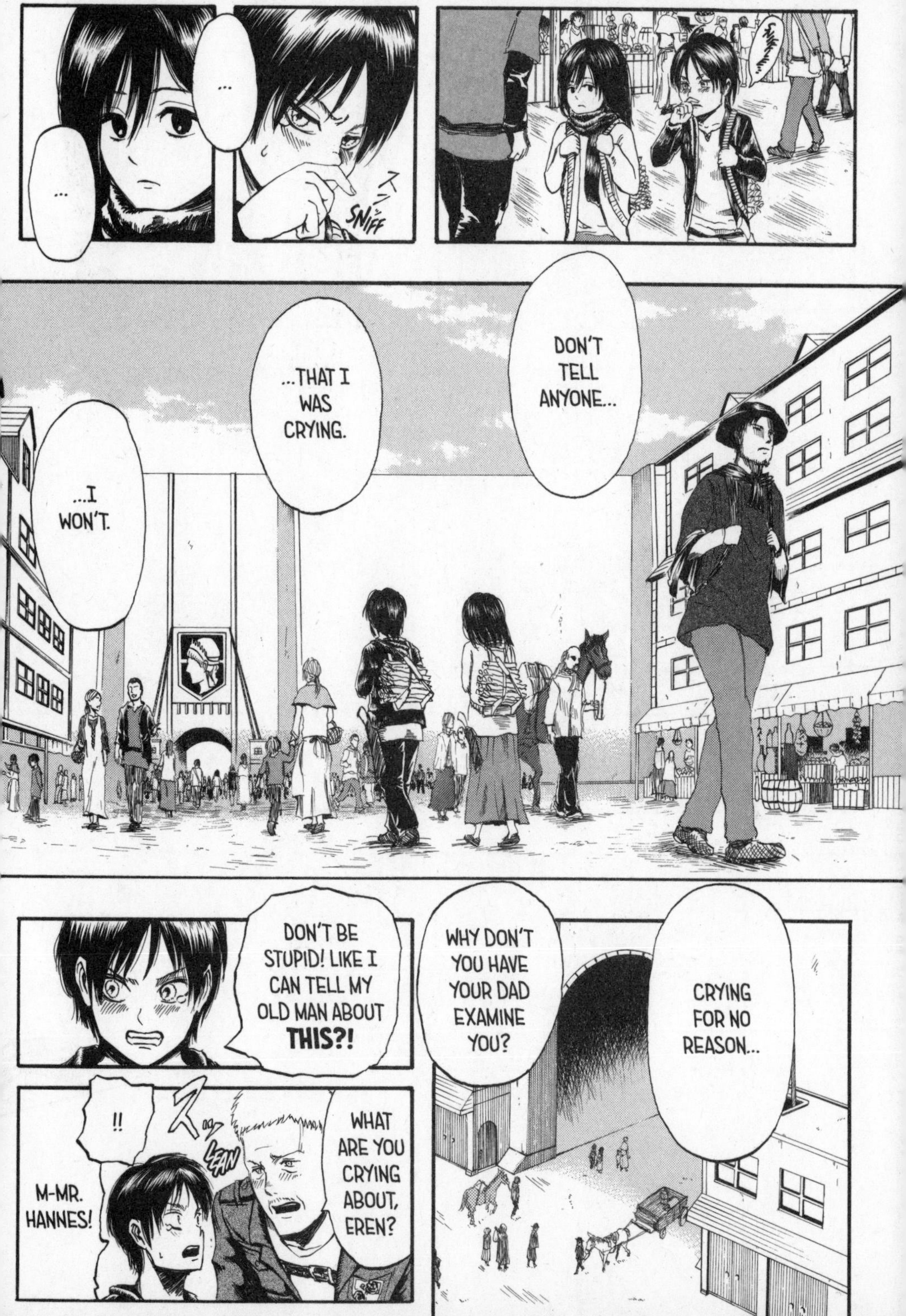
...
SNIFF
...
DON'T TELL ANYONE...
...THAT I WAS CRYING.
...I WON'T.
CRYING FOR NO REASON...
WHY DON'T YOU HAVE YOUR DAD EXAMINE YOU?
DON'T BE STUPID! LIKE I CAN TELL MY OLD MAN ABOUT THIS?!
LEAN
WHAT ARE YOU CRYING ABOUT, EREN?
!!
M-MR. HANNES!

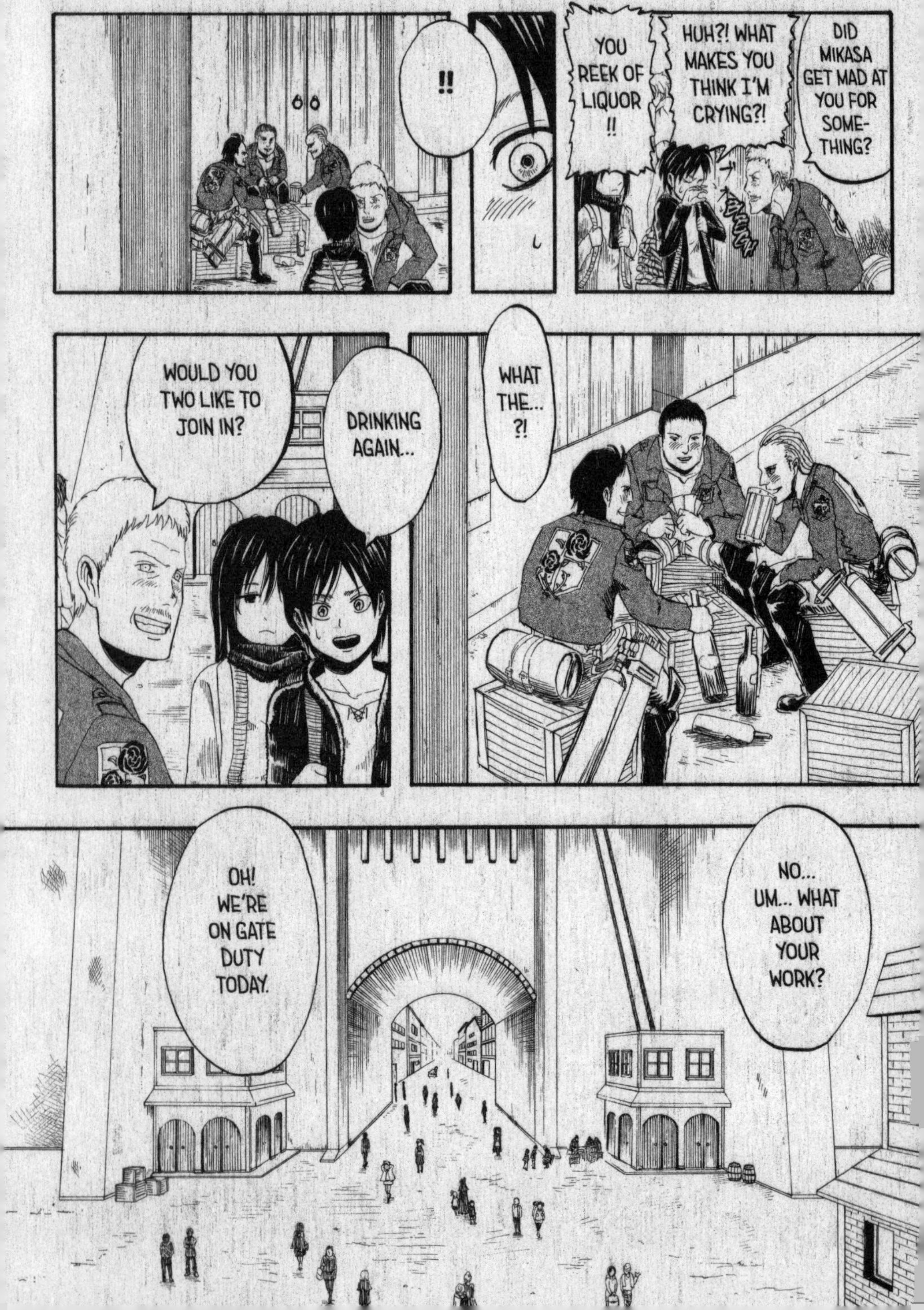
DID MIKASA GET MAD AT YOU FOR SOME-THING?
HUH?! WHAT MAKES YOU THINK I'M CRYING?!
YOU REEK OF LIQUOR !!
!!
WHAT THE... ?!
DRINKING AGAIN...
WOULD YOU TWO LIKE TO JOIN IN?
NO... UM... WHAT ABOUT YOUR WORK?
OH! WE'RE ON GATE DUTY TODAY.

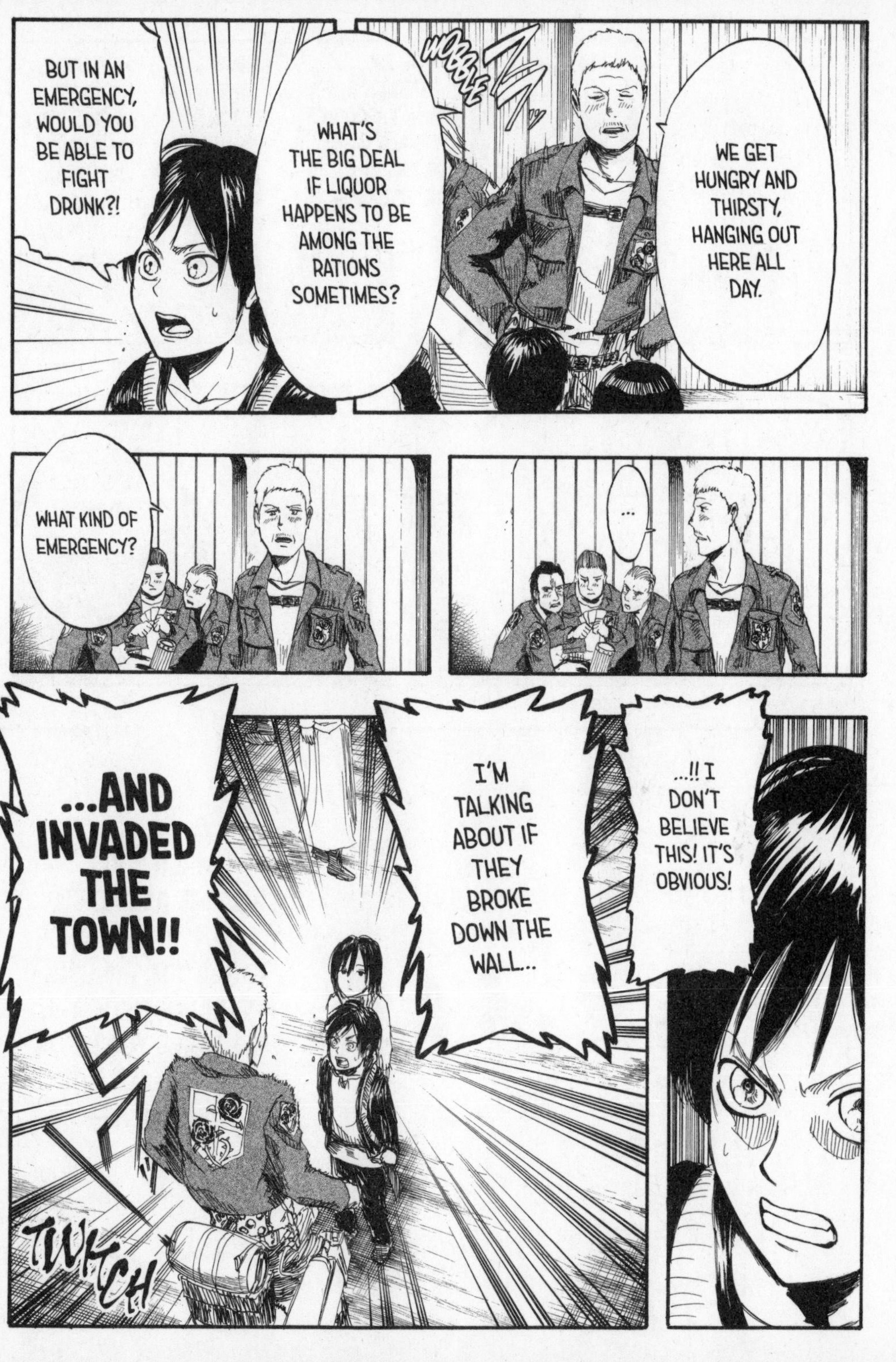
WOBBLE
WE GET HUNGRY AND THIRSTY, HANGING OUT HERE ALL DAY.
WHAT'S THE BIG DEAL IF LIQUOR HAPPENS TO BE AMONG THE RATIONS SOMETIMES?
BUT IN AN EMERGENCY, WOULD YOU BE ABLE TO FIGHT DRUNK?!
...
WHAT KIND OF EMERGENCY?
...!! I DON'T BELIEVE THIS! IT'S OBVIOUS!
I'M TALKING ABOUT IF THEY BROKE DOWN THE WALL...
...AND INVADED THE TOWN!!
TWITCH

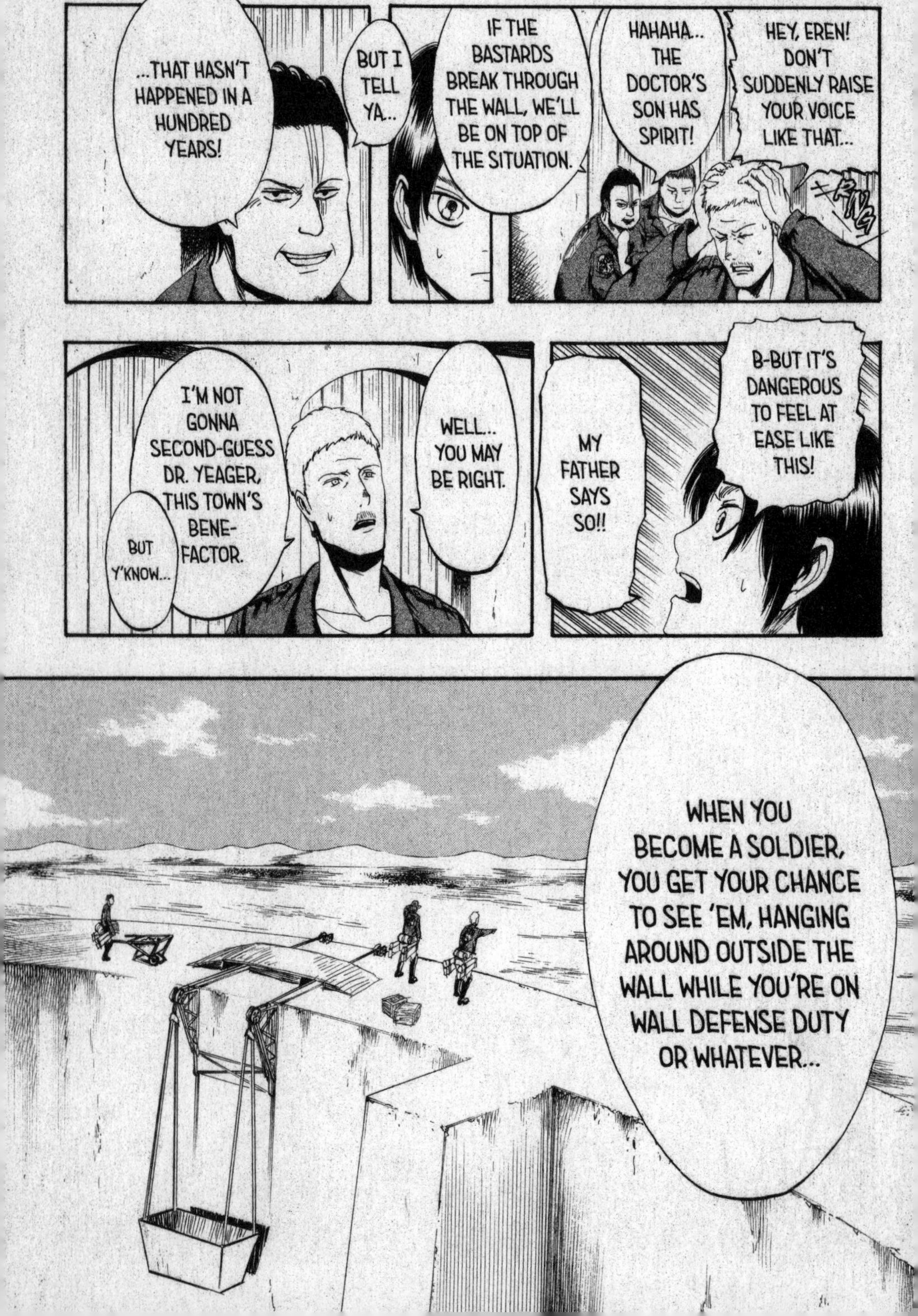
HEY, EREN! DON'T SUDDENLY RAISE YOUR VOICE LIKE THAT...
RING
HAHAHA... THE DOCTOR'S SON HAS SPIRIT!
IF THE BASTARDS BREAK THROUGH THE WALL, WE'LL BE ON TOP OF THE SITUATION.
BUT I TELL YA...
...THAT HASN'T HAPPENED IN A HUNDRED YEARS!
B-BUT IT'S DANGEROUS TO FEEL AT EASE LIKE THIS!
MY FATHER SAYS SO!!
WELL... YOU MAY BE RIGHT.
I'M NOT GONNA SECOND-GUESS DR. YEAGER, THIS TOWN'S BENE-FACTOR.
BUT Y'KNOW...
WHEN YOU BECOME A SOLDIER, YOU GET YOUR CHANCE TO SEE 'EM, HANGING AROUND OUTSIDE THE WALL WHILE YOU'RE ON WALL DEFENSE DUTY OR WHATEVER...

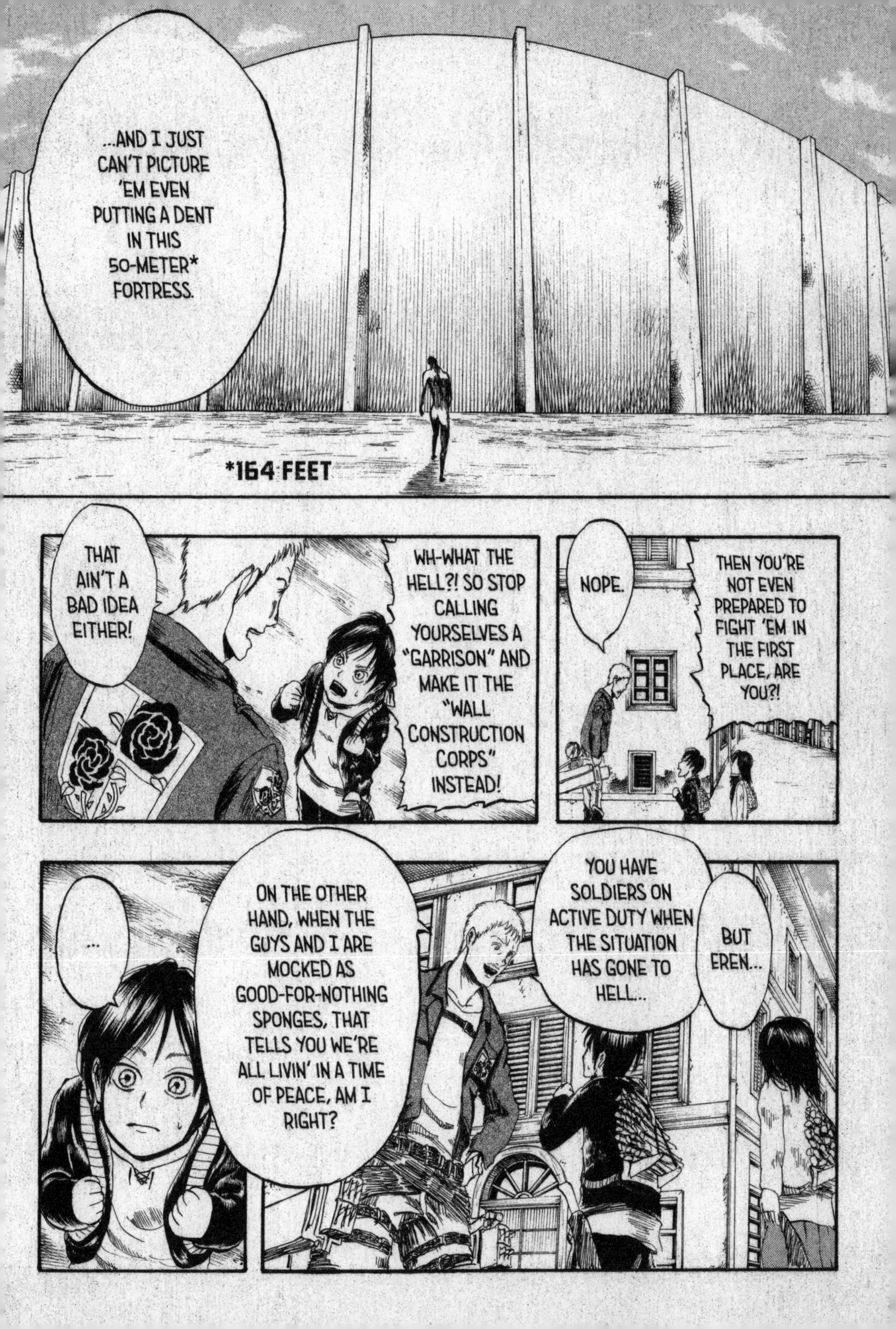
...AND I JUST CAN'T PICTURE 'EM EVEN PUTTING A DENT IN THIS 50-METER* FORTRESS.
*164 FEET
THEN YOU'RE NOT EVEN PREPARED TO FIGHT 'EM IN THE FIRST PLACE, ARE YOU?!
NOPE.
WH-WHAT THE HELL?! SO STOP CALLING YOURSELVES A "GARRISON" AND MAKE IT THE "WALL CONSTRUCTION CORPS" INSTEAD!
THAT AIN'T A BAD IDEA EITHER!
BUT EREN...
YOU HAVE SOLDIERS ON ACTIVE DUTY WHEN THE SITUATION HAS GONE TO HELL...
ON THE OTHER HAND, WHEN THE GUYS AND I ARE MOCKED AS GOOD-FOR-NOTHING SPONGES, THAT TELLS YOU WE'RE ALL LIVIN' IN A TIME OF PEACE, AM I RIGHT?
...

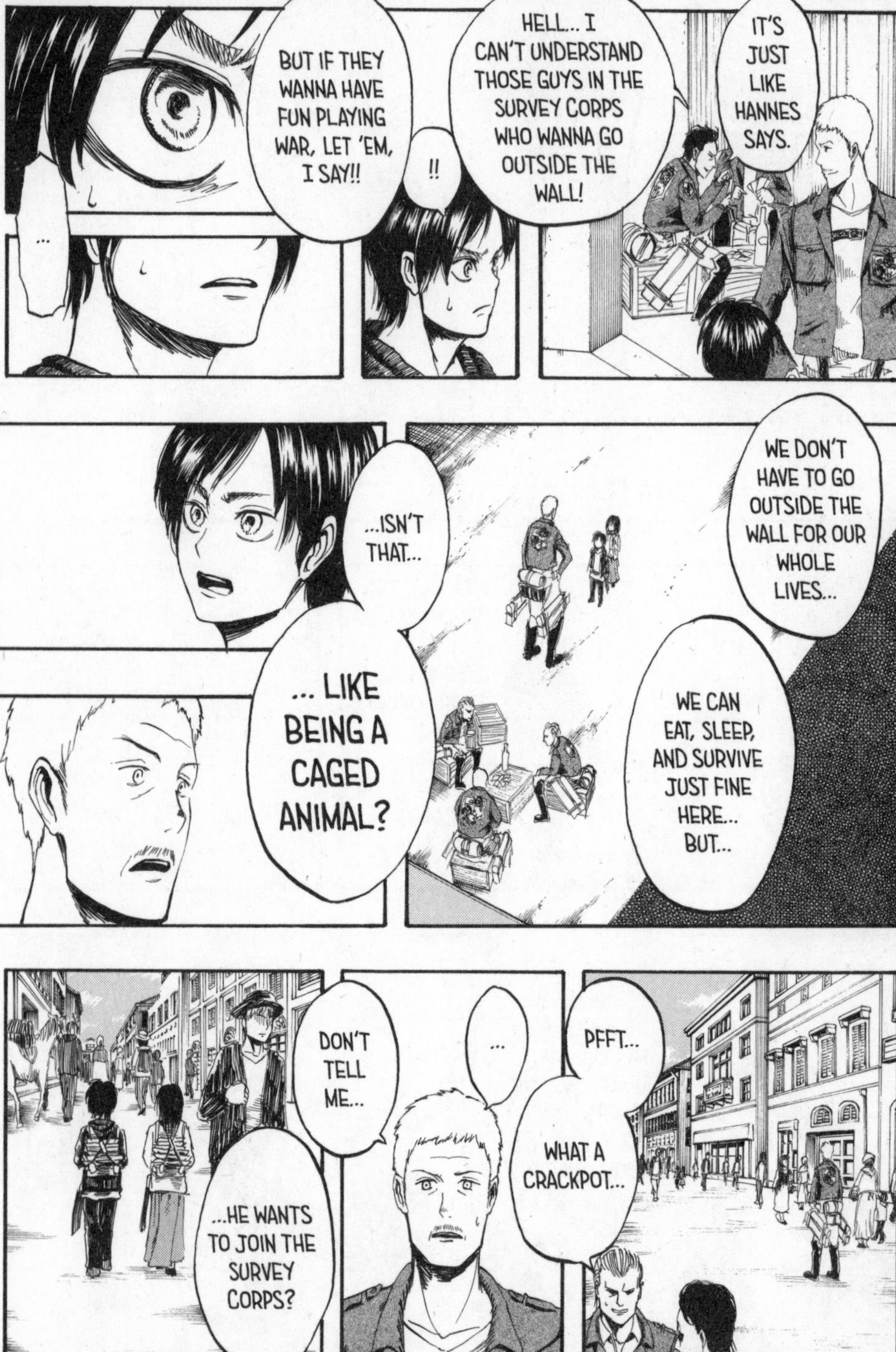
IT'S JUST LIKE HANNES SAYS.
HELL... I CAN'T UNDERSTAND THOSE GUYS IN THE SURVEY CORPS WHO WANNA GO OUTSIDE THE WALL!
!!
BUT IF THEY WANNA HAVE FUN PLAYING WAR, LET 'EM, I SAY!!
...
WE DON'T HAVE TO GO OUTSIDE THE WALL FOR OUR WHOLE LIVES...
WE CAN EAT, SLEEP, AND SURVIVE JUST FINE HERE... BUT...
...ISN'T THAT...
... LIKE BEING A CAGED ANIMAL?
PFFT...
WHAT A CRACKPOT...
...
DON'T TELL ME...
...HE WANTS TO JOIN THE SURVEY CORPS?

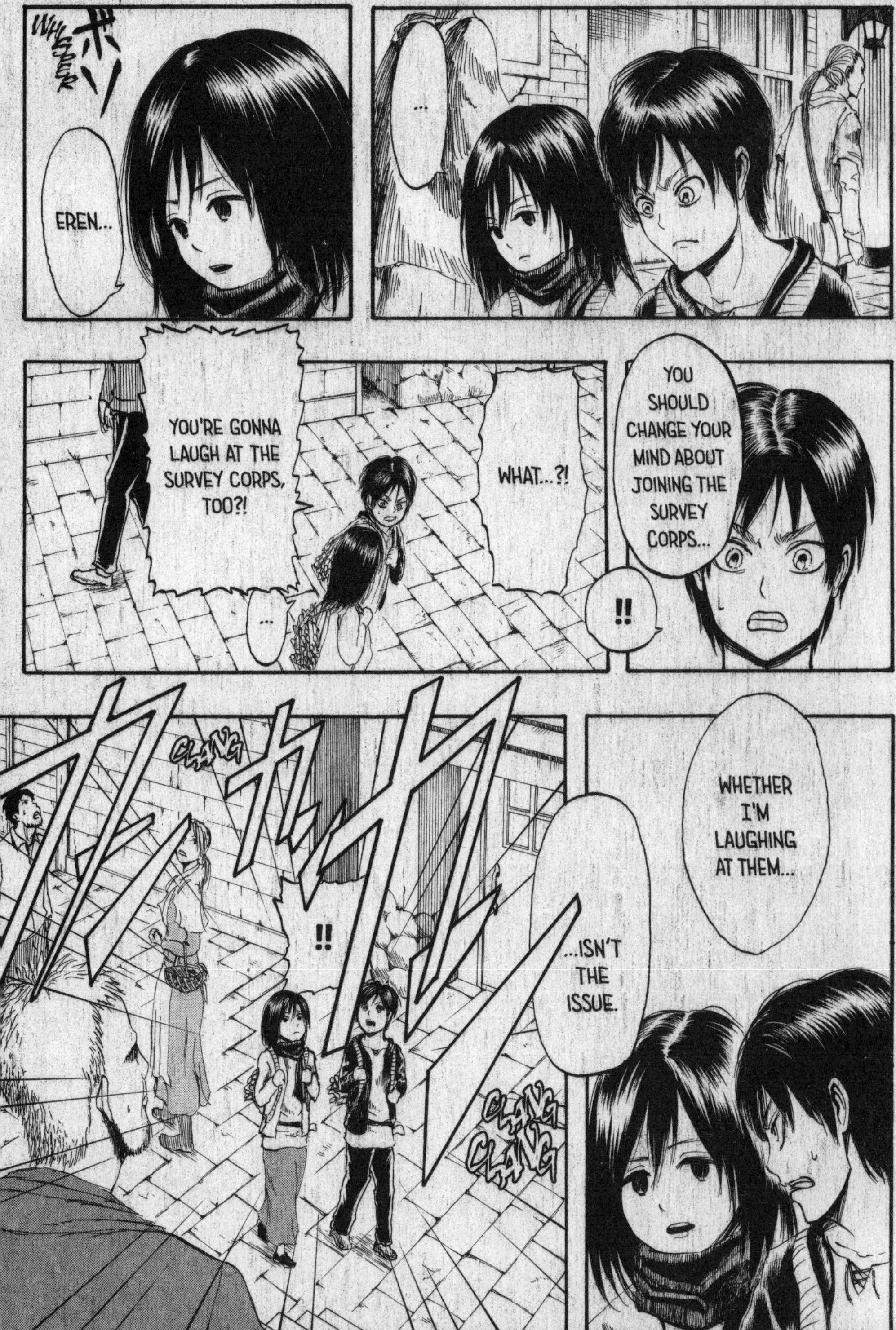
...
ボソ
WHISPER
EREN...
YOU SHOULD CHANGE YOUR MIND ABOUT JOINING THE SURVEY CORPS...
!!
WHAT...?!
YOU'RE GONNA LAUGH AT THE SURVEY CORPS, TOO?!
...
WHETHER I'M LAUGHING AT THEM...
...ISN'T THE ISSUE.
CLANG
!!
CLANG CLANG

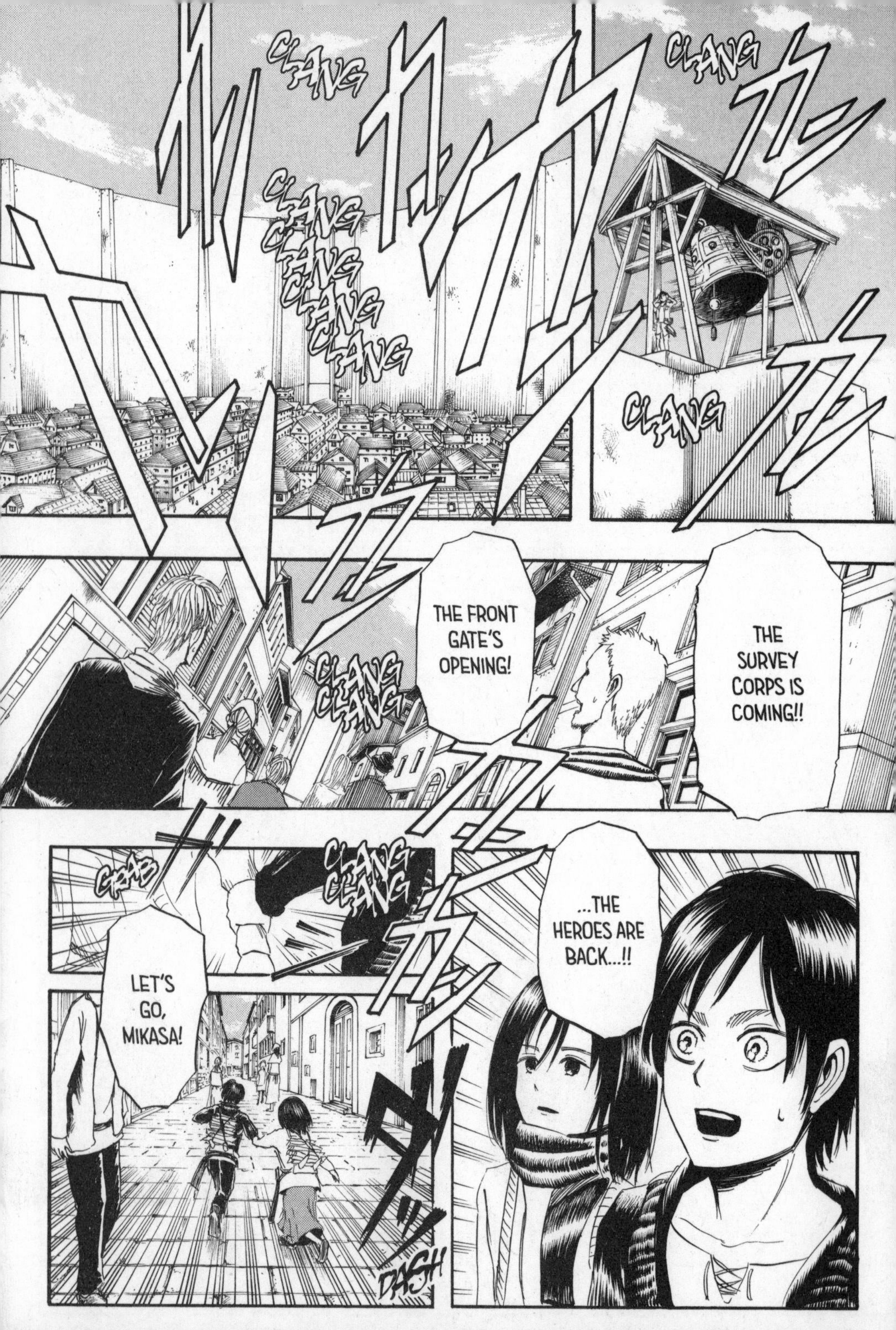
CLANG
CLANG
CLANG
CLANG
CLANG
CLANG
CLANG
CLANG
THE SURVEY CORPS IS COMING!!
THE FRONT GATE'S OPENING!
CLANG
CLANG
...THE HEROES ARE BACK...!!
CLANG
CLANG
GRAB
LET'S GO, MIKASA!
DASH

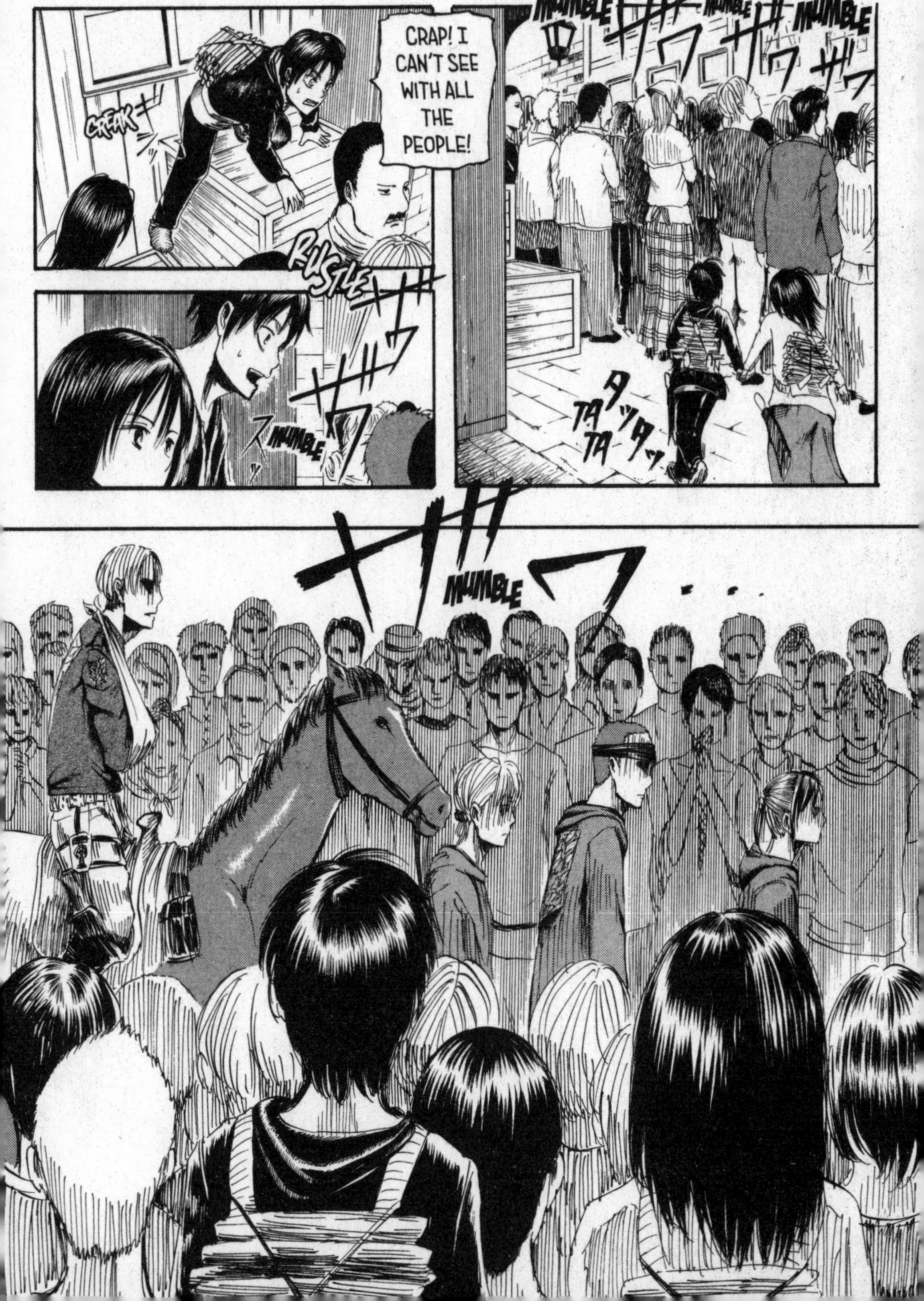
MUMBLE
MUMBLE
MUMBLE
TA
TA
CREAK
CRAP! I CAN'T SEE WITH ALL THE PEOPLE!
RUSTLE
MUMBLE
MUMBLE

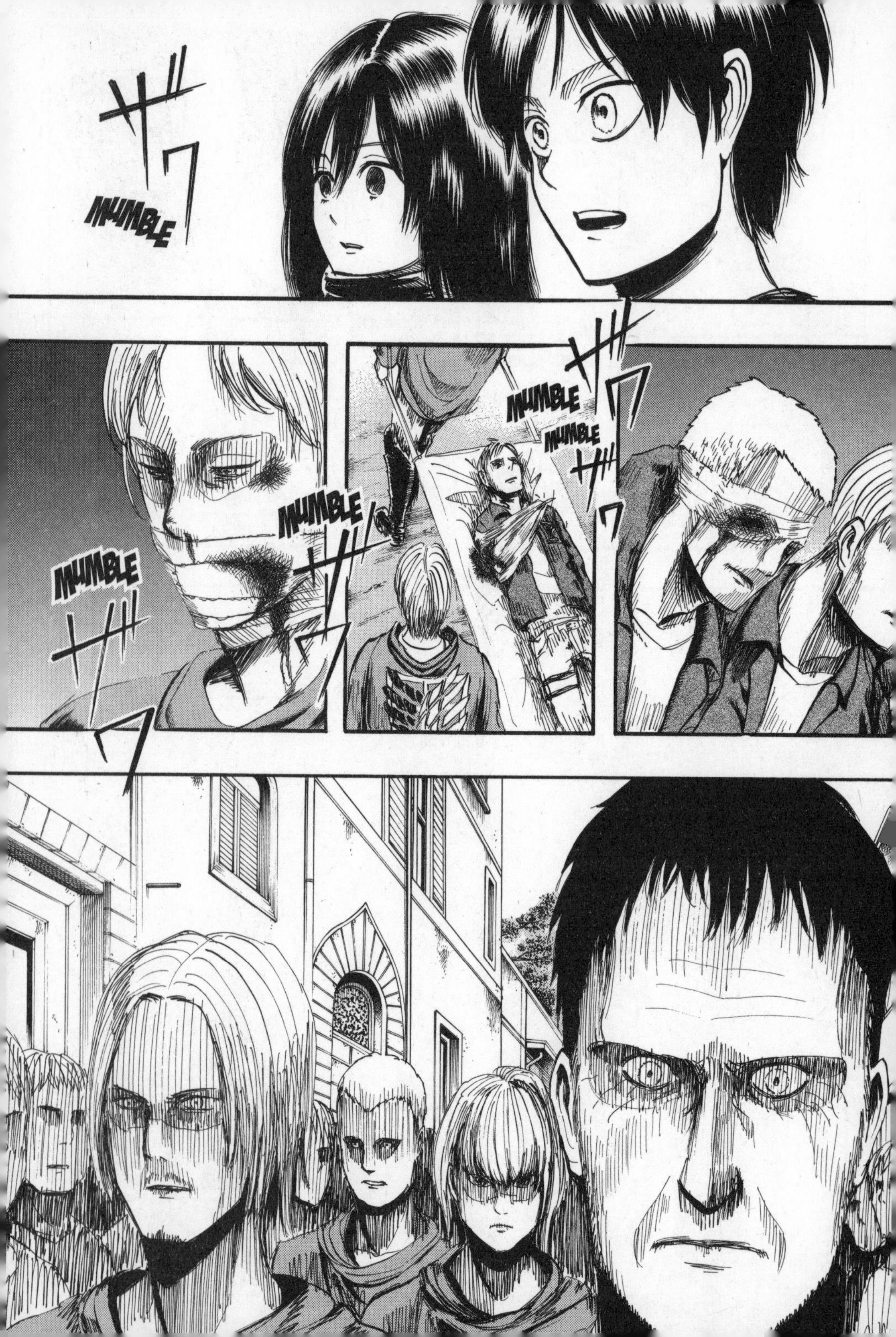
ザワ
MUMBLE
ザワ
MUMBLE
MUMBLE
ザワ
MUMBLE
ザワ
MUMBLE
ザワ

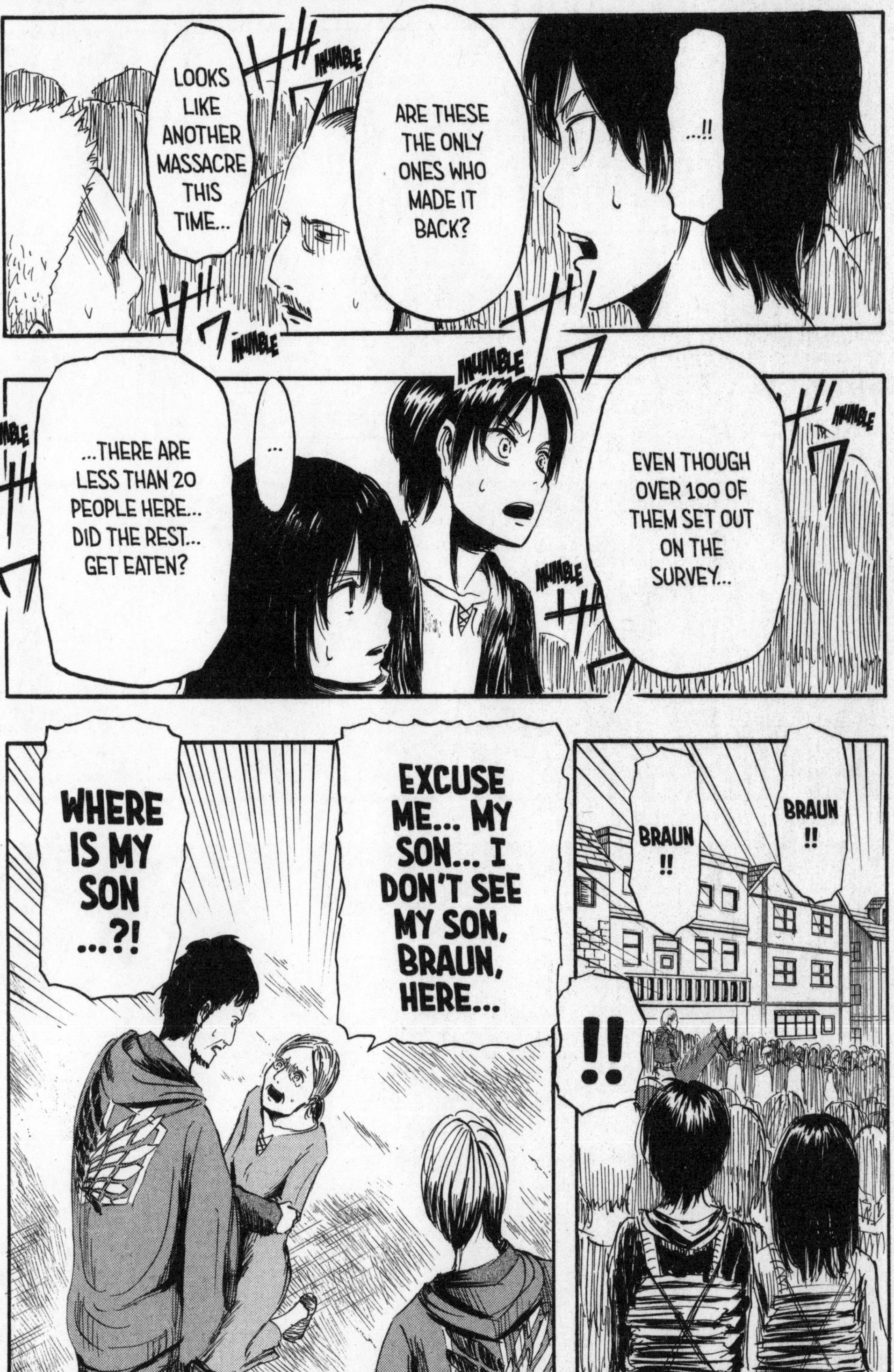
MUMBLE
...!!
ARE THESE THE ONLY ONES WHO MADE IT BACK?
LOOKS LIKE ANOTHER MASSACRE THIS TIME...
MUMBLE
MUMBLE
MUMBLE
EVEN THOUGH OVER 100 OF THEM SET OUT ON THE SURVEY...
MUMBLE
...
...THERE ARE LESS THAN 20 PEOPLE HERE... DID THE REST... GET EATEN?
MUMBLE
BRAUN!!
BRAUN!!
!!
EXCUSE ME... MY SON... I DON'T SEE MY SON, BRAUN, HERE...
WHERE IS MY SON...?!

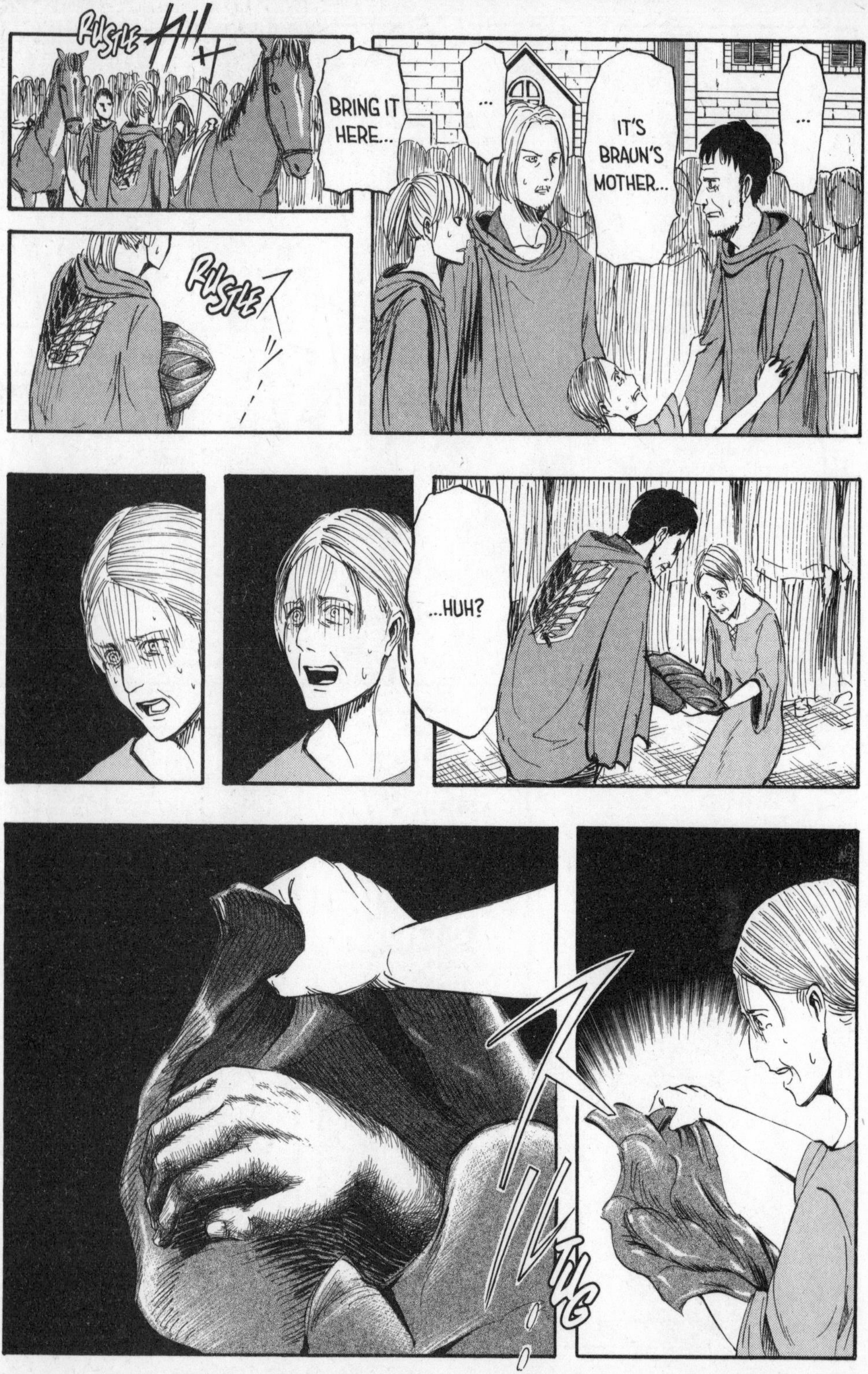
...
IT'S BRAUN'S MOTHER...
...
BRING IT HERE...
RUSTLE
RUSTLE
...HUH?
TUG

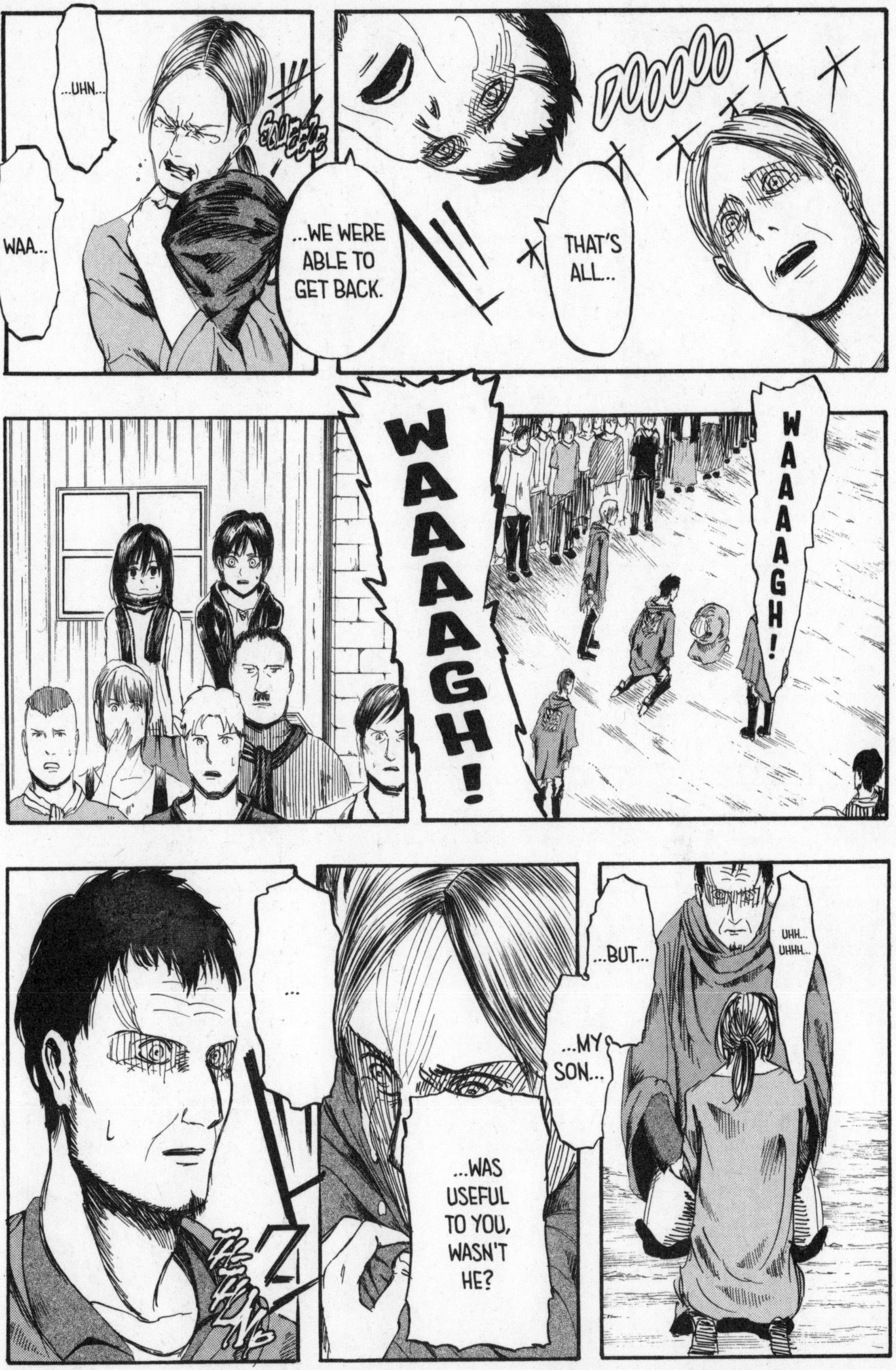
DOOOOO
THAT'S ALL...
...WE WERE ABLE TO GET BACK.
...UHN...
WAA...
WAAAAAGH!
WAAAAGH!
UHH... UHHH...
...BUT...
...MY SON...
...WAS USEFUL TO YOU, WASN'T HE?
...

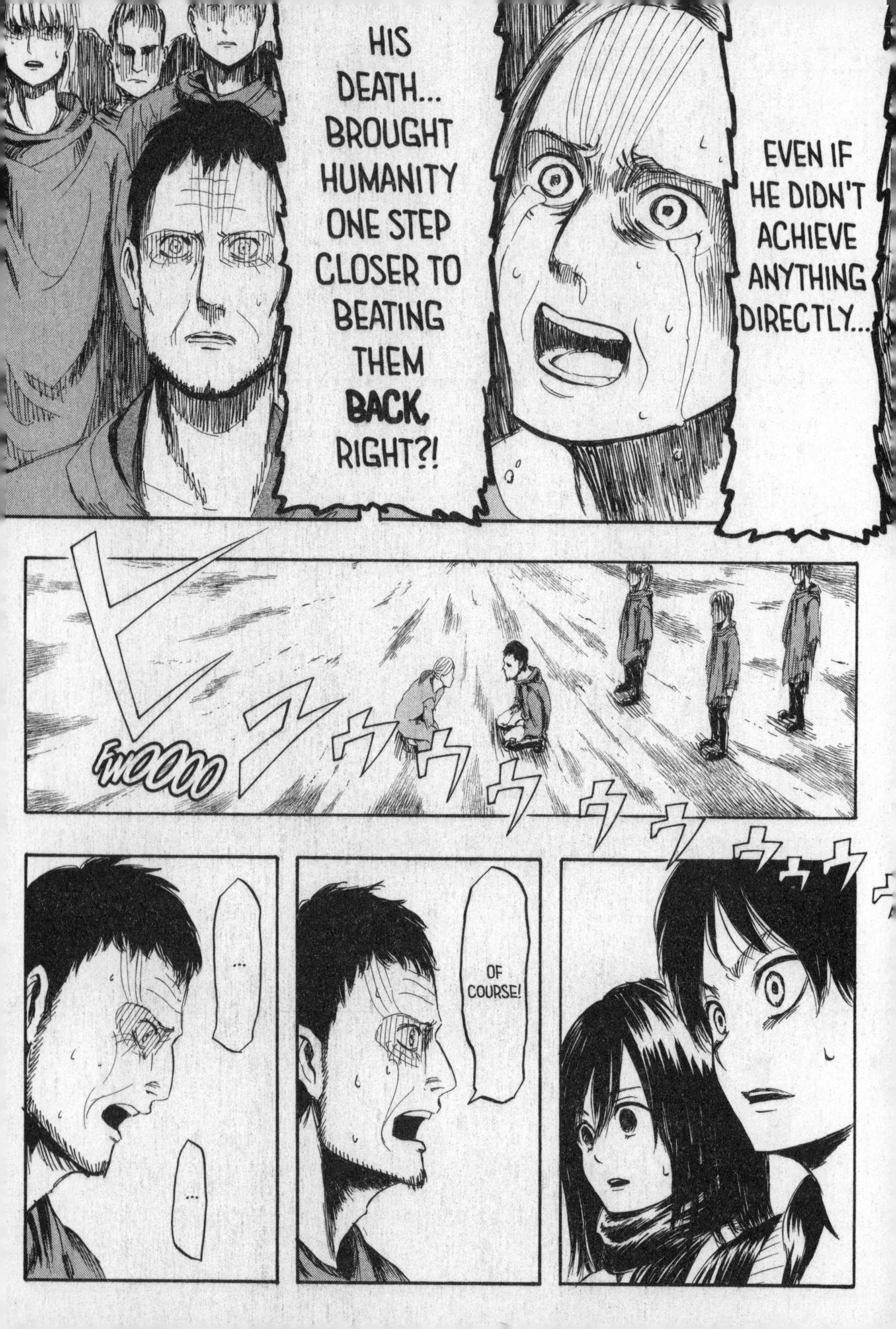
EVEN IF HE DIDN'T ACHIEVE ANYTHING DIRECTLY...
HIS DEATH... BROUGHT HUMANITY ONE STEP CLOSER TO BEATING THEM BACK. RIGHT?!
FWOOOOO
OF COURSE!
...
...

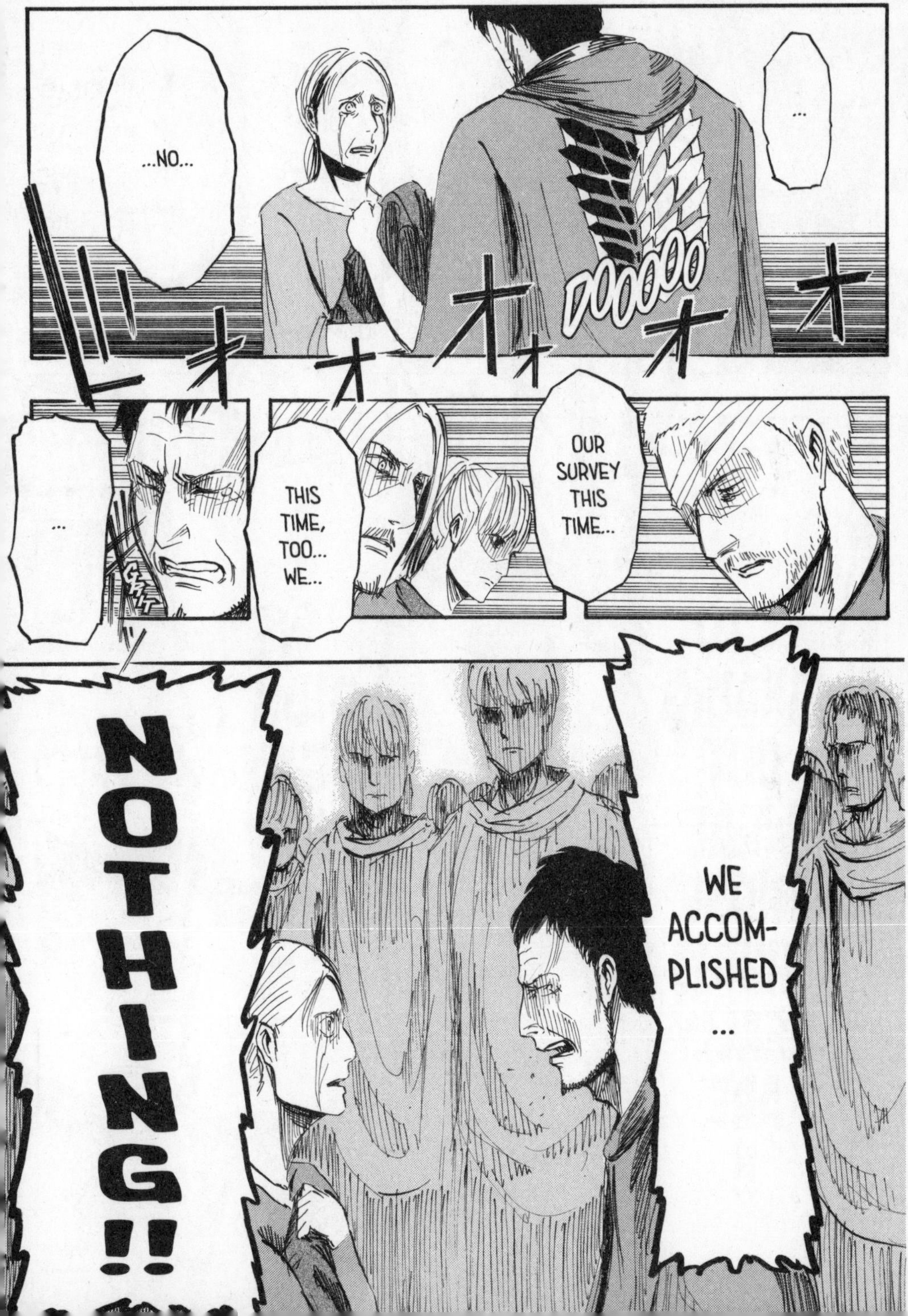
...
...NO...
DOOOOO
OUR SURVEY THIS TIME...
THIS TIME, TOO... WE...
...
GRIT
WE ACCOM-PLISHED ...
NOTHING!!

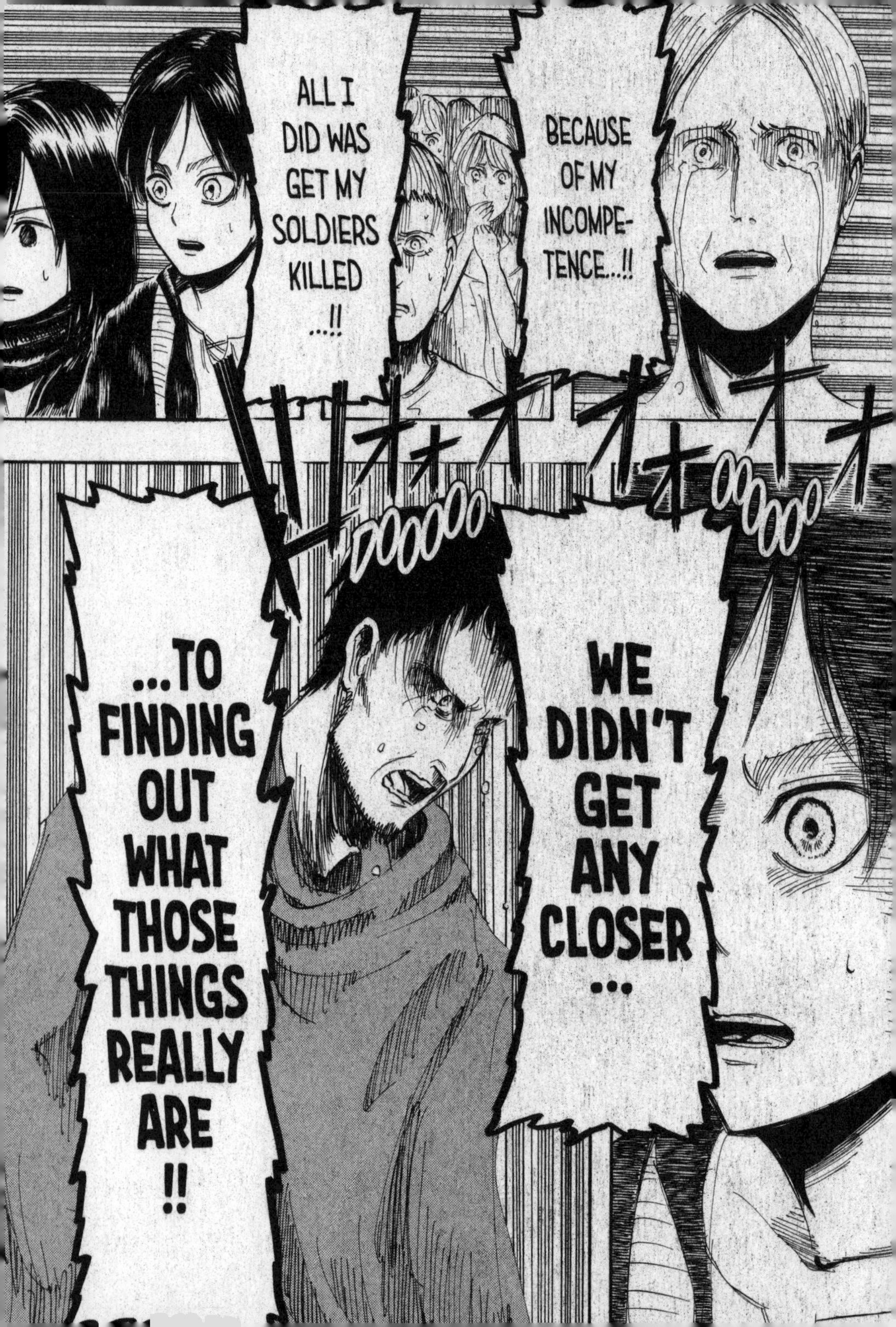
BECAUSE OF MY INCOMPE-TENCE...!!
ALL I DID WAS GET MY SOLDIERS KILLED ...!!
DOOOOOOOOOOOOO
WE DIDN'T GET ANY CLOSER ...
...TO FINDING OUT WHAT THOSE THINGS REALLY ARE !!

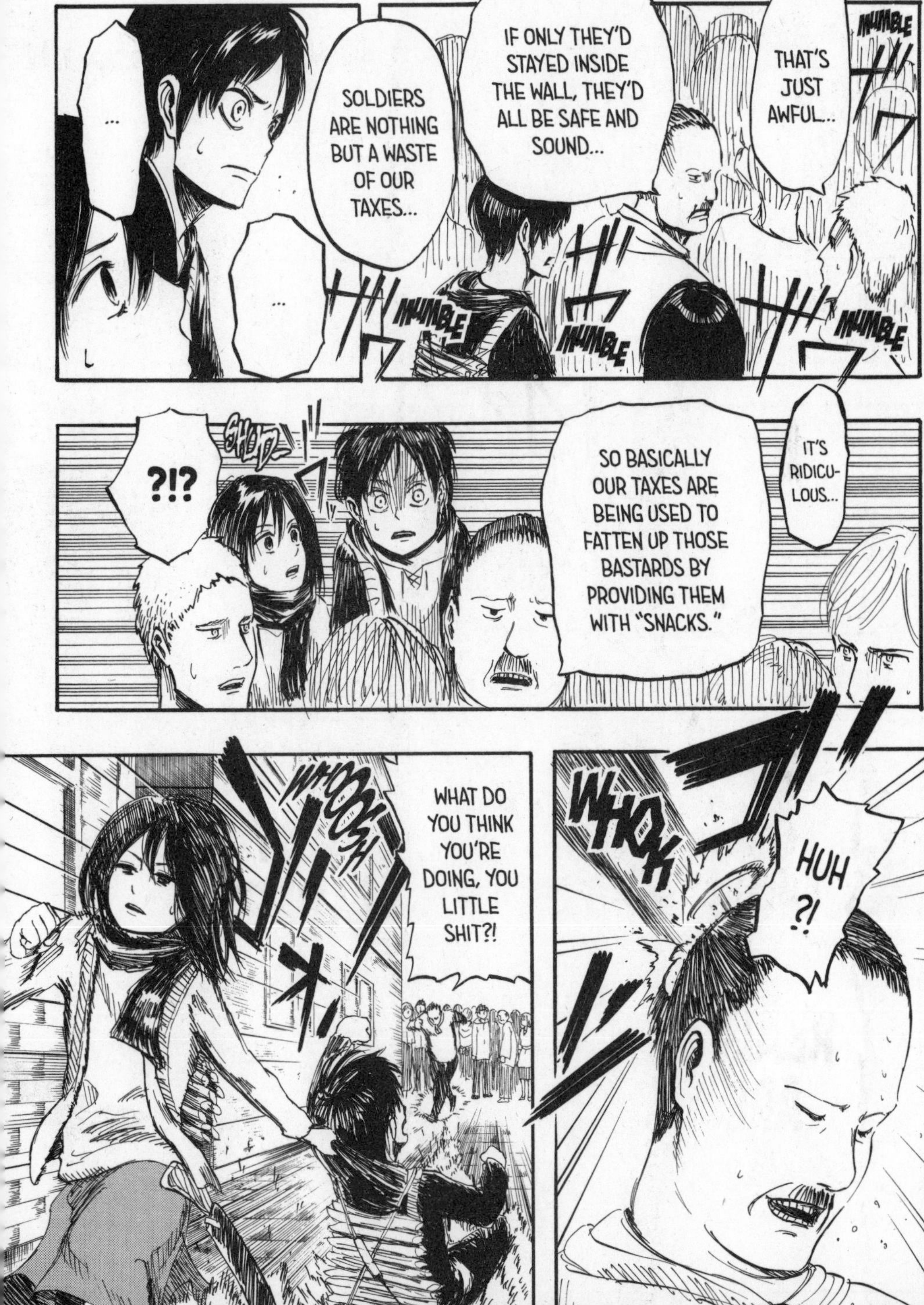
MUMBLE
THAT'S JUST AWFUL...
IF ONLY THEY'D STAYED INSIDE THE WALL, THEY'D ALL BE SAFE AND SOUND...
SOLDIERS ARE NOTHING BUT A WASTE OF OUR TAXES...
MUMBLE
MUMBLE
MUMBLE
...
...
IT'S RIDICU-LOUS...
SO BASICALLY OUR TAXES ARE BEING USED TO FATTEN UP THOSE BASTARDS BY PROVIDING THEM WITH "SNACKS."
?!?
WHOK
HUH ?!
WHAT DO YOU THINK YOU'RE DOING, YOU LITTLE SHIT?!
WHOOSH

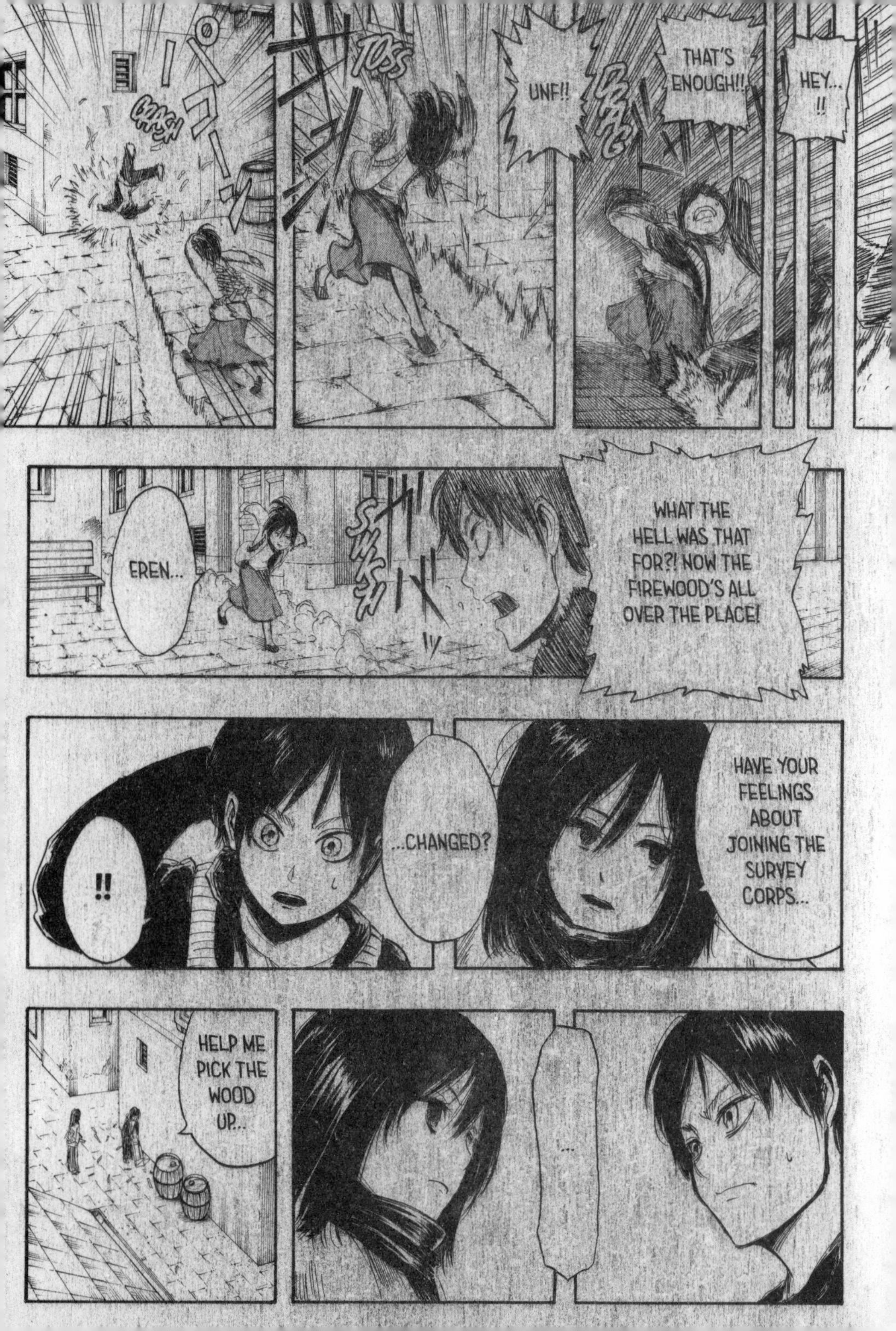
HEY... !!
THAT'S ENOUGH!!
UNF!!
TOSS
WHAT THE HELL WAS THAT FOR?! NOW THE FIREWOOD'S ALL OVER THE PLACE!
EREN...
HAVE YOUR FEELINGS ABOUT JOINING THE SURVEY CORPS...
...CHANGED?
!!
...
HELP ME PICK THE WOOD UP...

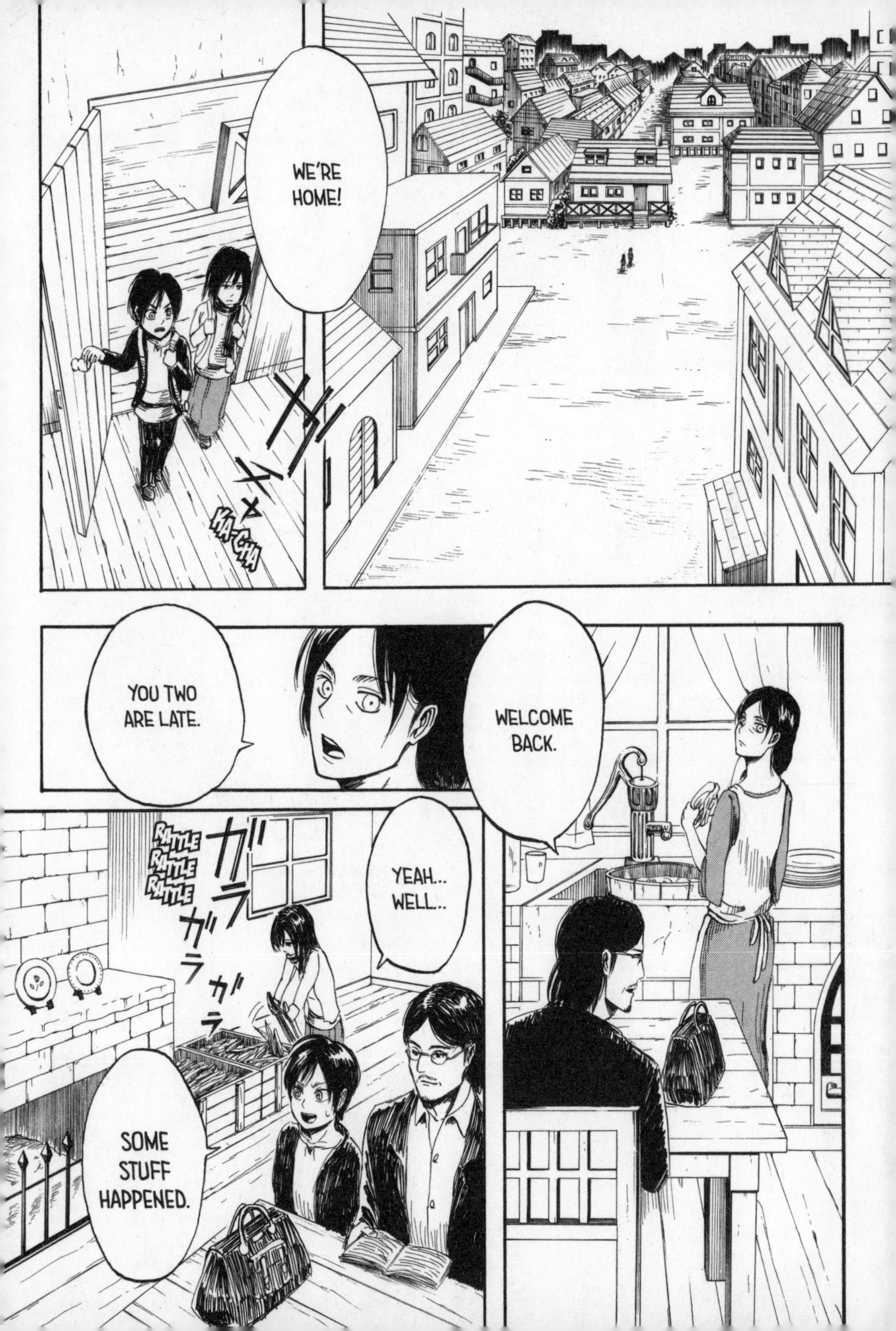
WE'RE HOME!
KA-CHA
WELCOME BACK.
YOU TWO ARE LATE.
YEAH... WELL...
RATTLE RATTLE RATTLE
SOME STUFF HAPPENED.

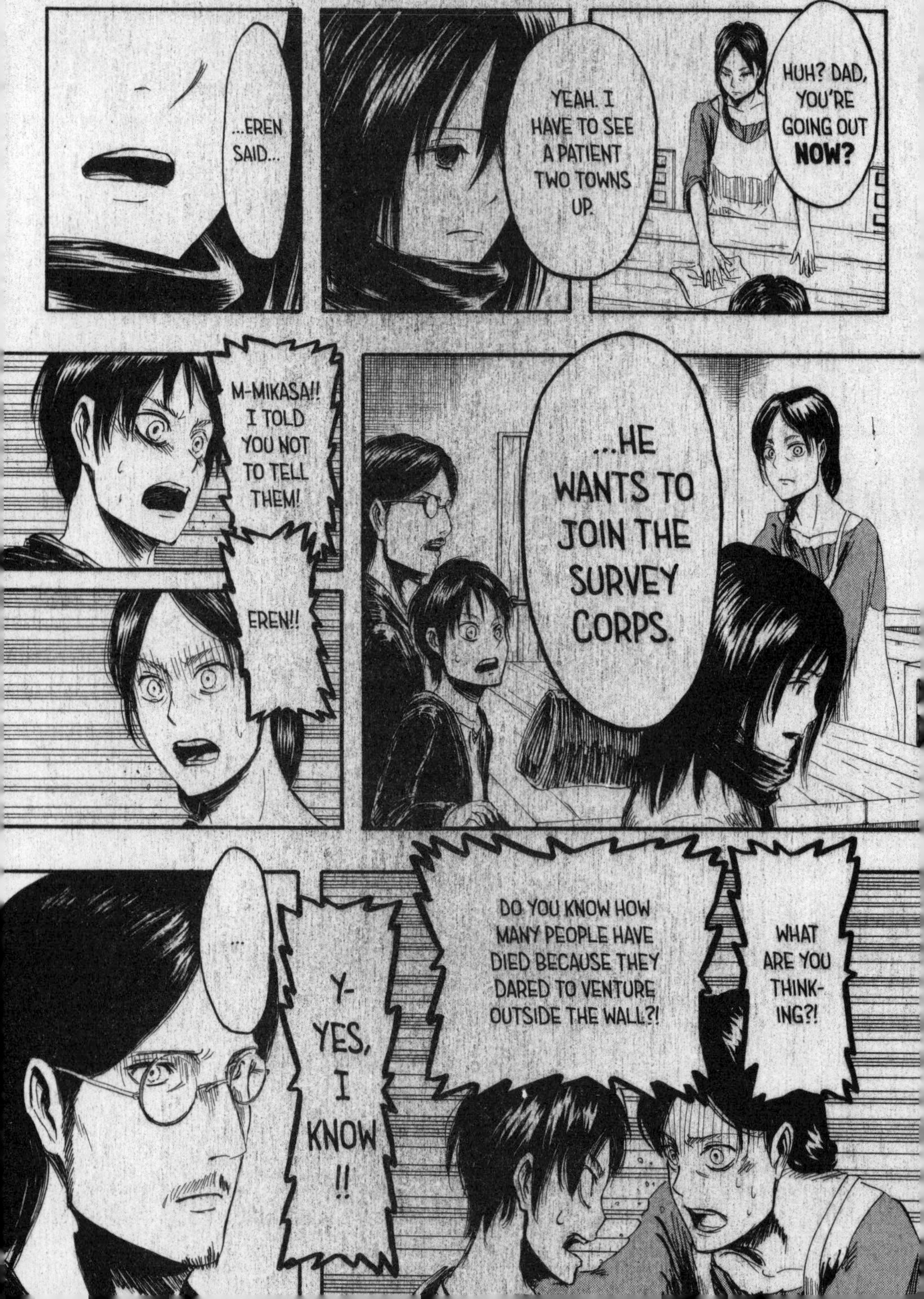
HUH? DAD, YOU'RE GOING OUT **NOW?**
YEAH. I HAVE TO SEE A PATIENT TWO TOWNS UP.
...EREN SAID...
...HE WANTS TO JOIN THE SURVEY CORPS.
M-MIKASA!! I TOLD YOU NOT TO TELL THEM!
EREN!!
WHAT ARE YOU THINK-ING?!
DO YOU KNOW HOW MANY PEOPLE HAVE DIED BECAUSE THEY DARED TO VENTURE OUTSIDE THE WALL?!
Y-YES, I KNOW!!
...

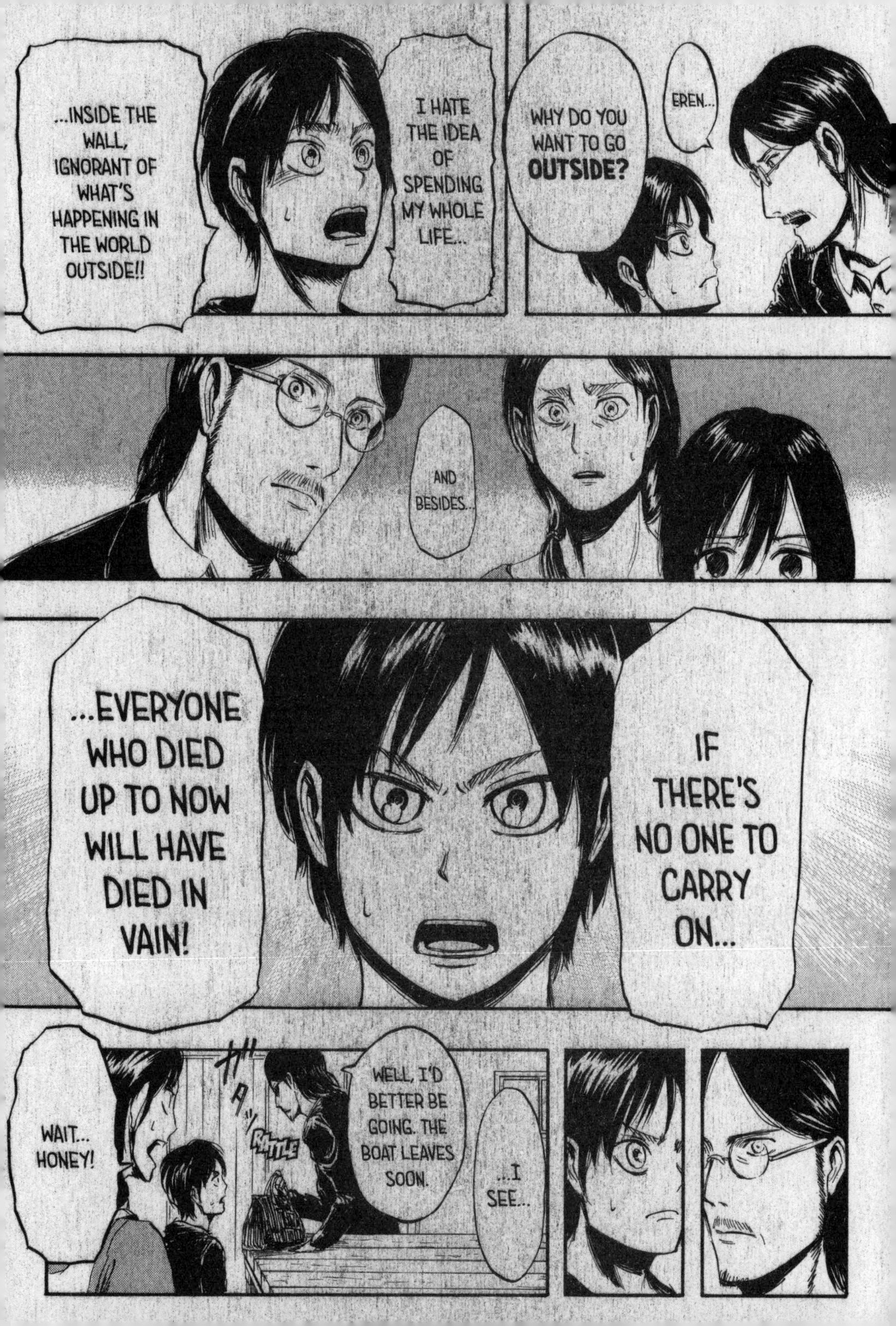
EREN...
WHY DO YOU WANT TO GO OUTSIDE?
I HATE THE IDEA OF SPENDING MY WHOLE LIFE...
...INSIDE THE WALL, IGNORANT OF WHAT'S HAPPENING IN THE WORLD OUTSIDE!!
AND BESIDES...
IF THERE'S NO ONE TO CARRY ON...
...EVERYONE WHO DIED UP TO NOW WILL HAVE DIED IN VAIN!
...I SEE...
WELL, I'D BETTER BE GOING. THE BOAT LEAVES SOON.
RATTLE
WAIT... HONEY!

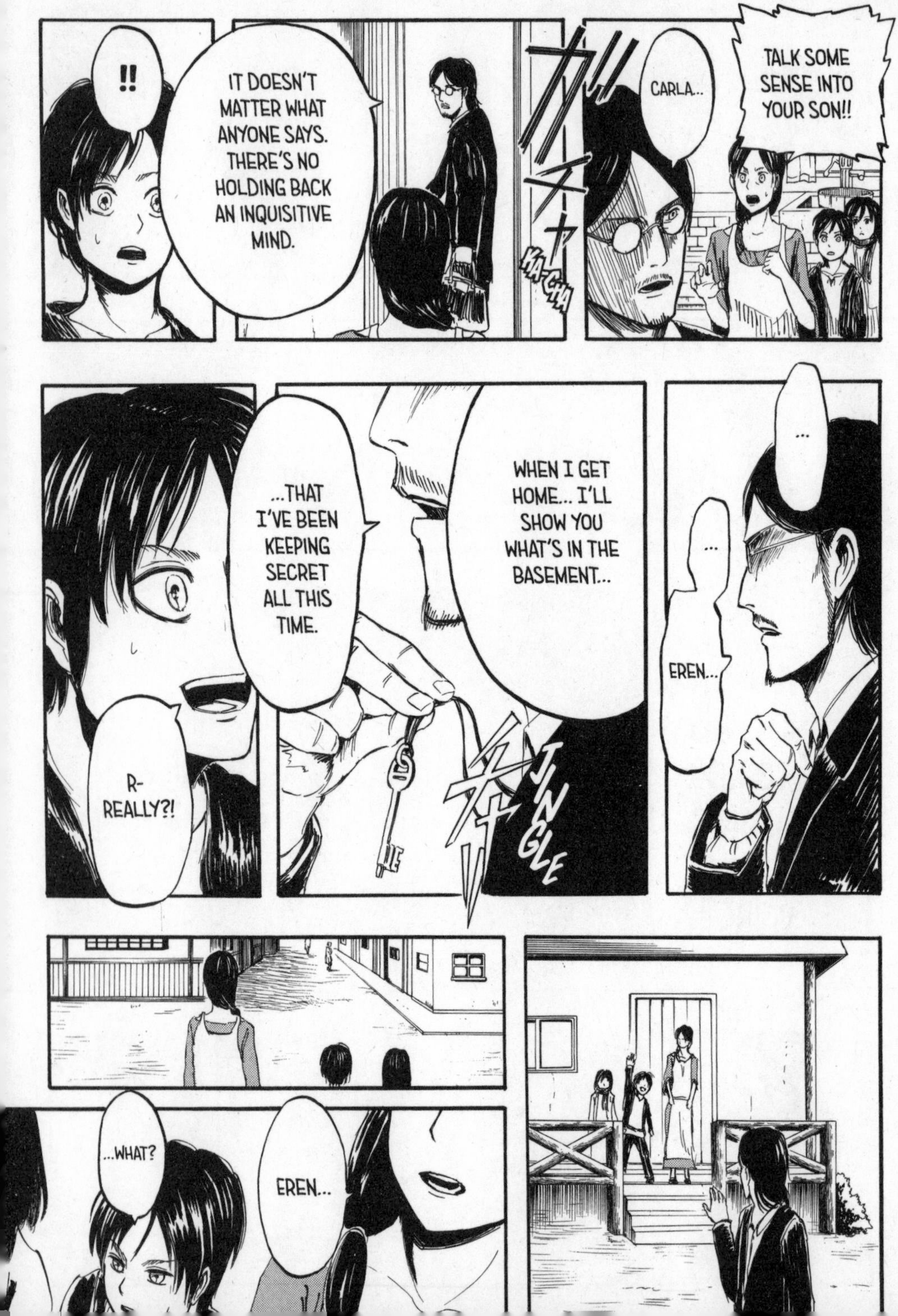
TALK SOME SENSE INTO YOUR SON!!
CARLA...
KA-CHA
IT DOESN'T MATTER WHAT ANYONE SAYS. THERE'S NO HOLDING BACK AN INQUISITIVE MIND.
!!
...
...
EREN...
WHEN I GET HOME... I'LL SHOW YOU WHAT'S IN THE BASEMENT...
...THAT I'VE BEEN KEEPING SECRET ALL THIS TIME.
JINGLE
R-REALLY?!
EREN...
...WHAT?

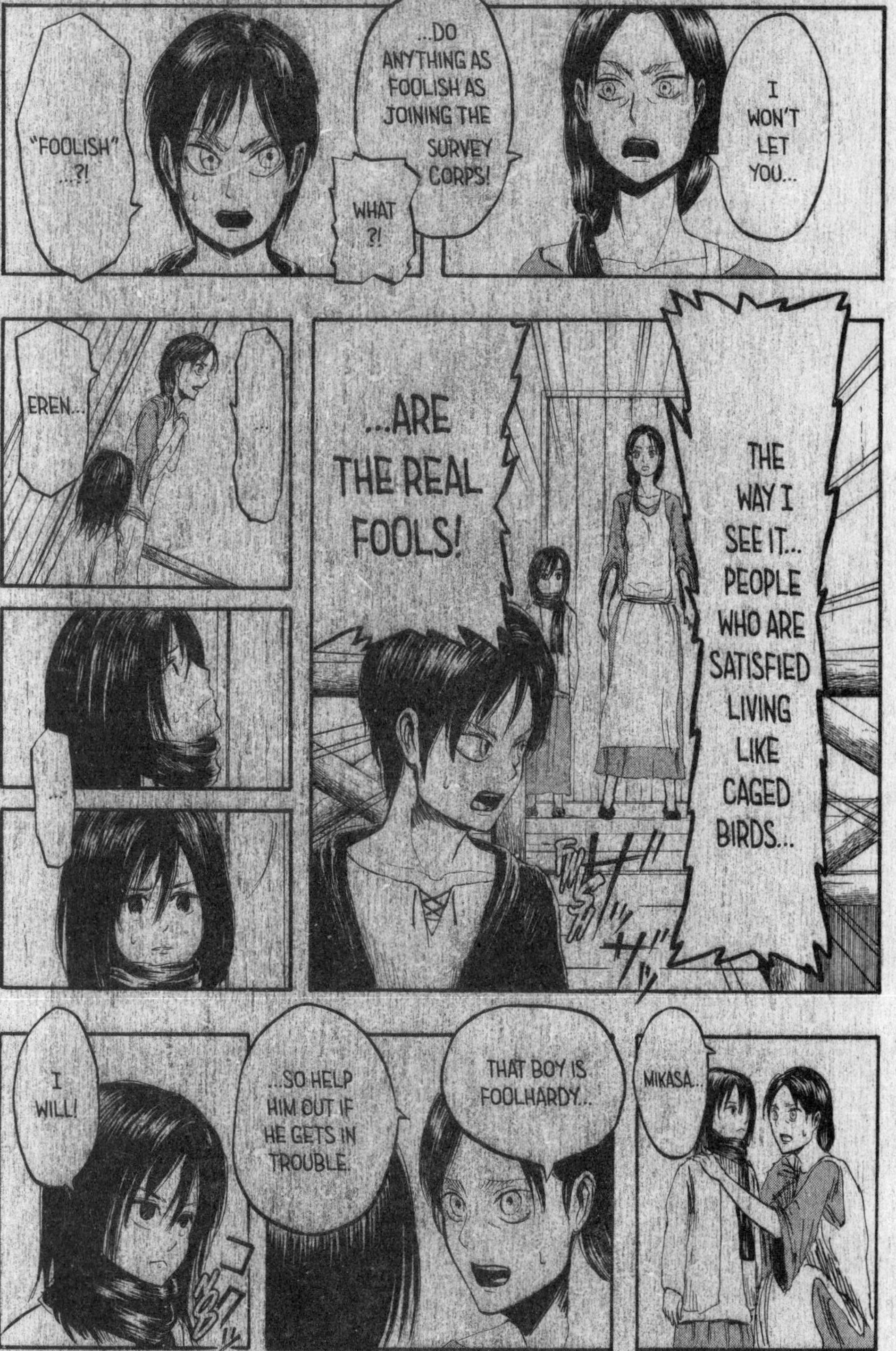
I WON'T LET YOU...
...DO ANYTHING AS FOOLISH AS JOINING THE SURVEY CORPS!
WHAT?!
"FOOLISH"...?!
THE WAY I SEE IT... PEOPLE WHO ARE SATISFIED LIVING LIKE CAGED BIRDS...
...ARE THE REAL FOOLS!
...
EREN...
...
MIKASA...
THAT BOY IS FOOLHARDY...
...SO HELP HIM OUT IF HE GETS IN TROUBLE.
I WILL!

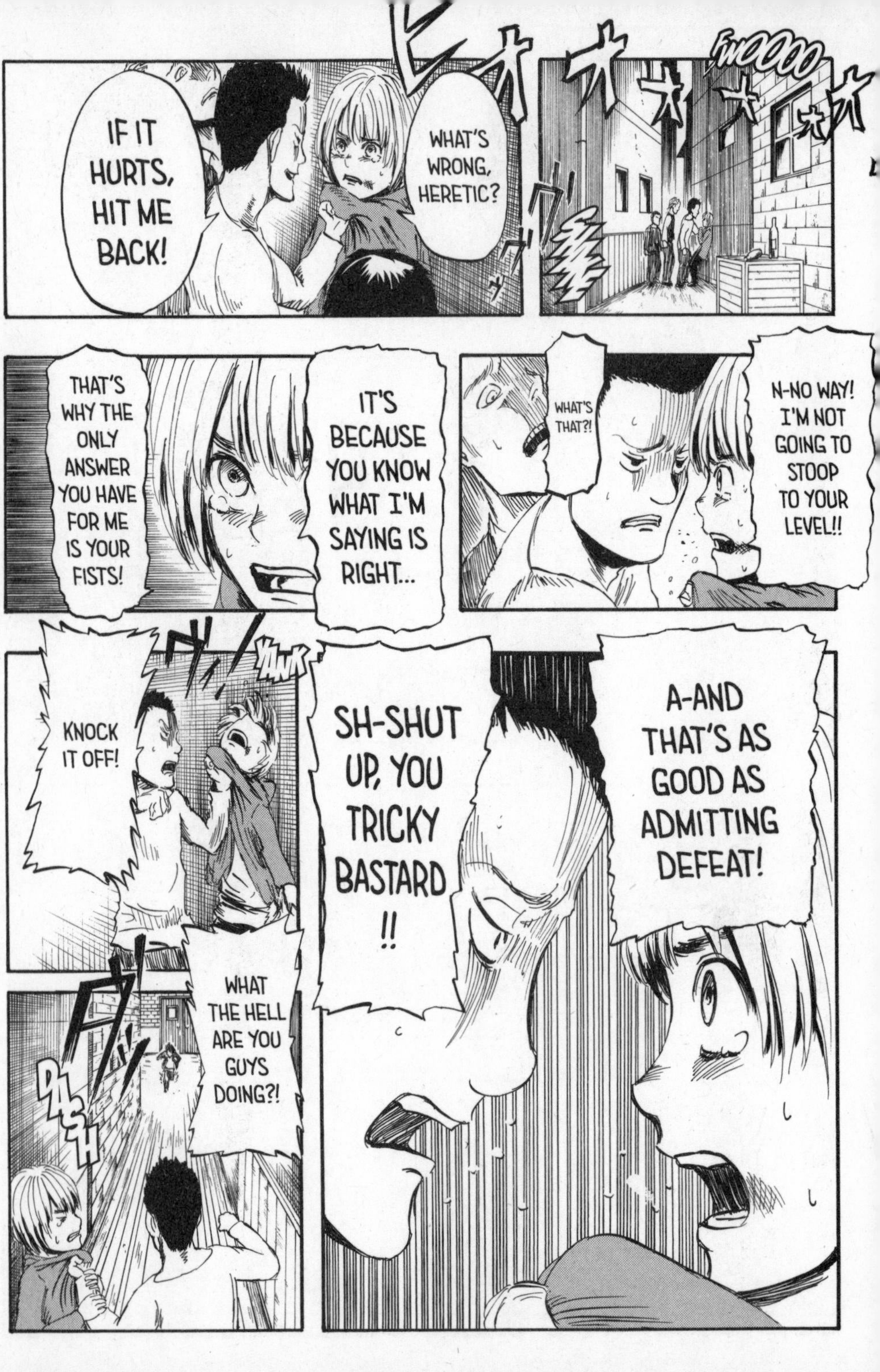
FWOOOO
WHAT'S WRONG, HERETIC?
IF IT HURTS, HIT ME BACK!
N-NO WAY! I'M NOT GOING TO STOOP TO YOUR LEVEL!!
WHAT'S THAT?!
IT'S BECAUSE YOU KNOW WHAT I'M SAYING IS RIGHT...
THAT'S WHY THE ONLY ANSWER YOU HAVE FOR ME IS YOUR FISTS!
A-AND THAT'S AS GOOD AS ADMITTING DEFEAT!
SH-SHUT UP, YOU TRICKY BASTARD!!
YANK
KNOCK IT OFF!
WHAT THE HELL ARE YOU GUYS DOING?!
DASH

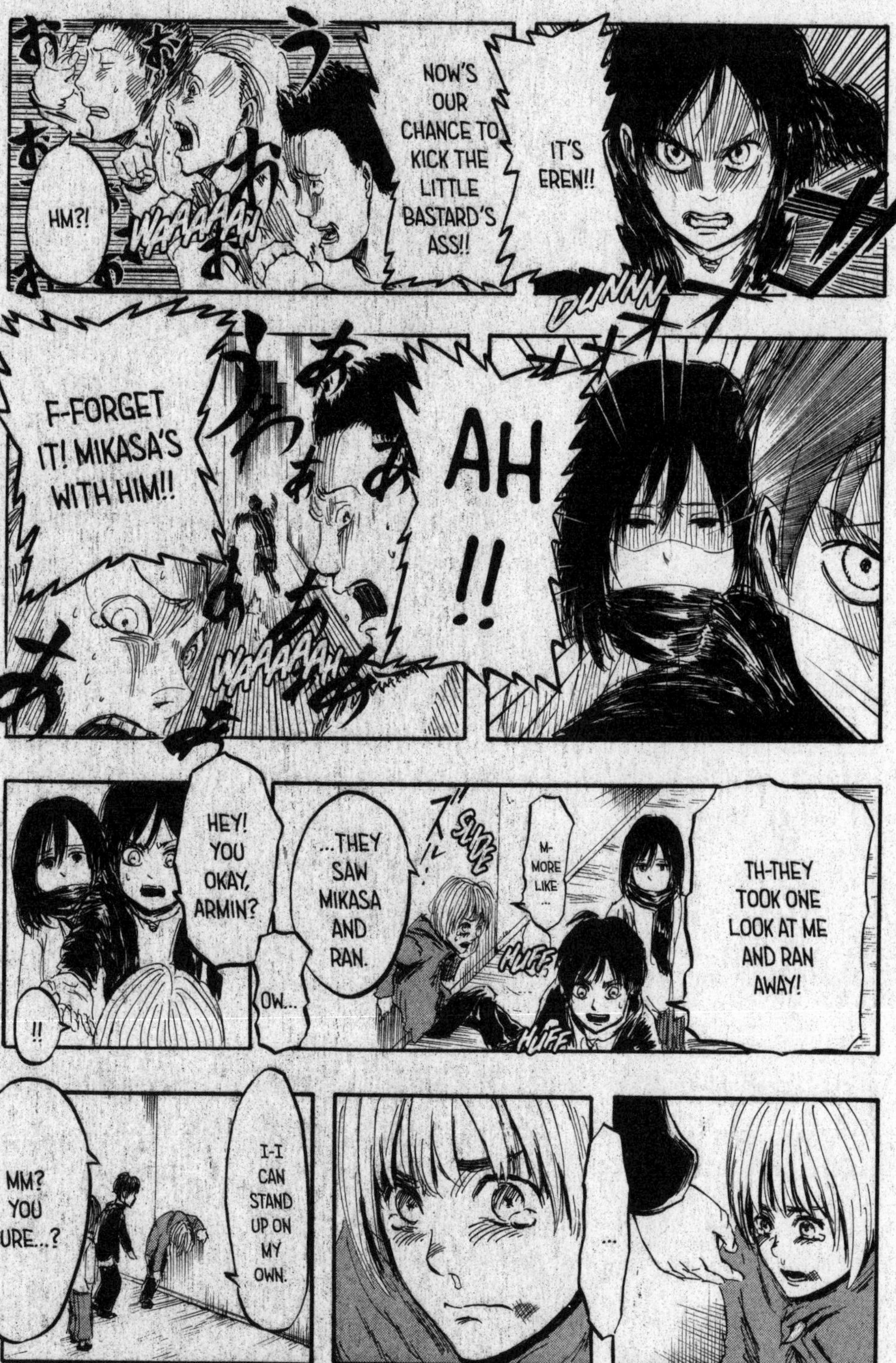
IT'S EREN!!
DUNNN
NOW'S OUR CHANCE TO KICK THE LITTLE BASTARD'S ASS!!
WAAAAAH
HM?!
AH!!
F-FORGET IT! MIKASA'S WITH HIM!!
WAAAAAH
TH-THEY TOOK ONE LOOK AT ME AND RAN AWAY!
M-MORE LIKE ...
HUFF
HUFF
SLIDE
...THEY SAW MIKASA AND RAN.
OW...
HEY! YOU OKAY, ARMIN?
!!
...
I-I CAN STAND UP ON MY OWN.
MM? YOU SURE...?

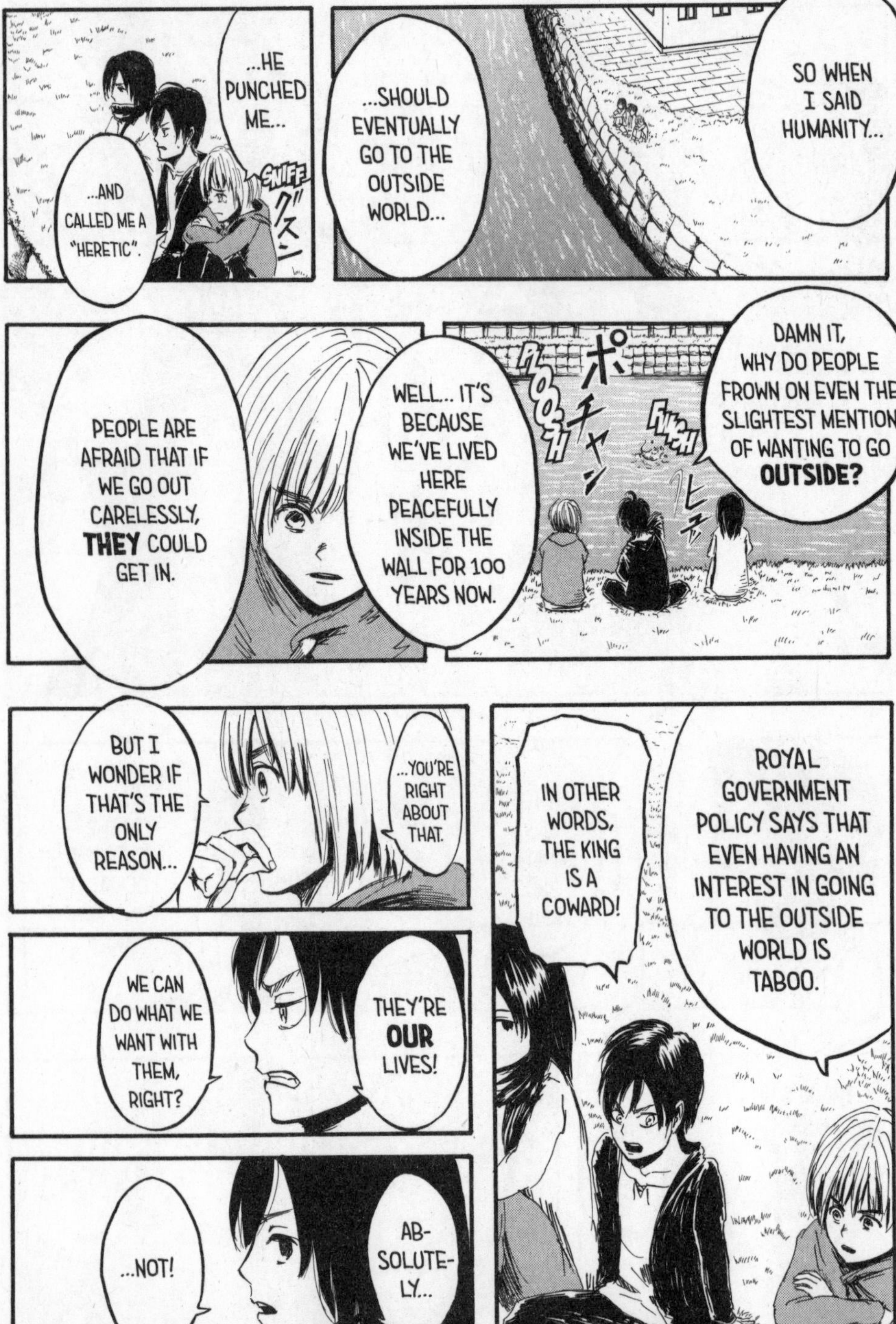
SO WHEN I SAID HUMANITY...
...SHOULD EVENTUALLY GO TO THE OUTSIDE WORLD...
...HE PUNCHED ME...
SNIFF
グスン
...AND CALLED ME A "HERETIC".
DAMN IT, WHY DO PEOPLE FROWN ON EVEN THE SLIGHTEST MENTION OF WANTING TO GO **OUTSIDE?**
FWSH
PLOOSH
ポチャン
WELL... IT'S BECAUSE WE'VE LIVED HERE PEACEFULLY INSIDE THE WALL FOR 100 YEARS NOW.
PEOPLE ARE AFRAID THAT IF WE GO OUT CARELESSLY, **THEY** COULD GET IN.
ROYAL GOVERNMENT POLICY SAYS THAT EVEN HAVING AN INTEREST IN GOING TO THE OUTSIDE WORLD IS TABOO.
IN OTHER WORDS, THE KING IS A COWARD!
...YOU'RE RIGHT ABOUT THAT.
BUT I WONDER IF THAT'S THE ONLY REASON...
THEY'RE **OUR** LIVES!
WE CAN DO WHAT WE WANT WITH THEM, RIGHT?
AB-SOLUTE-LY...
...NOT!

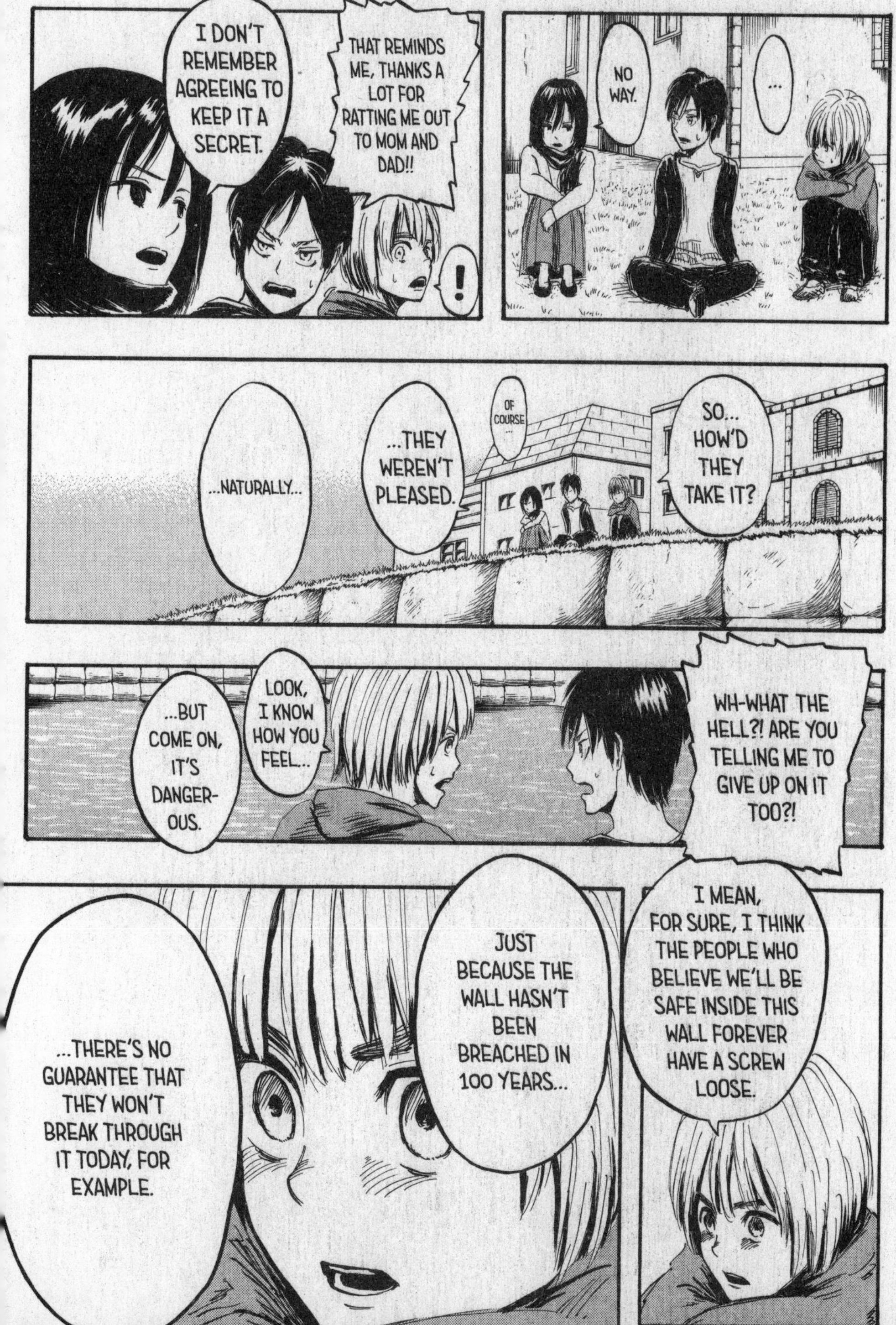
...
NO WAY.
THAT REMINDS ME, THANKS A LOT FOR RATTING ME OUT TO MOM AND DAD!!
I DON'T REMEMBER AGREEING TO KEEP IT A SECRET.
!
SO... HOW'D THEY TAKE IT?
OF COURSE...
...THEY WEREN'T PLEASED.
...NATURALLY...
WH-WHAT THE HELL?! ARE YOU TELLING ME TO GIVE UP ON IT TOO?!
LOOK, I KNOW HOW YOU FEEL...
...BUT COME ON, IT'S DANGER-OUS.
I MEAN, FOR SURE, I THINK THE PEOPLE WHO BELIEVE WE'LL BE SAFE INSIDE THIS WALL FOREVER HAVE A SCREW LOOSE.
JUST BECAUSE THE WALL HASN'T BEEN BREACHED IN 100 YEARS...
...THERE'S NO GUARANTEE THAT THEY WON'T BREAK THROUGH IT TODAY, FOR EXAMPLE.

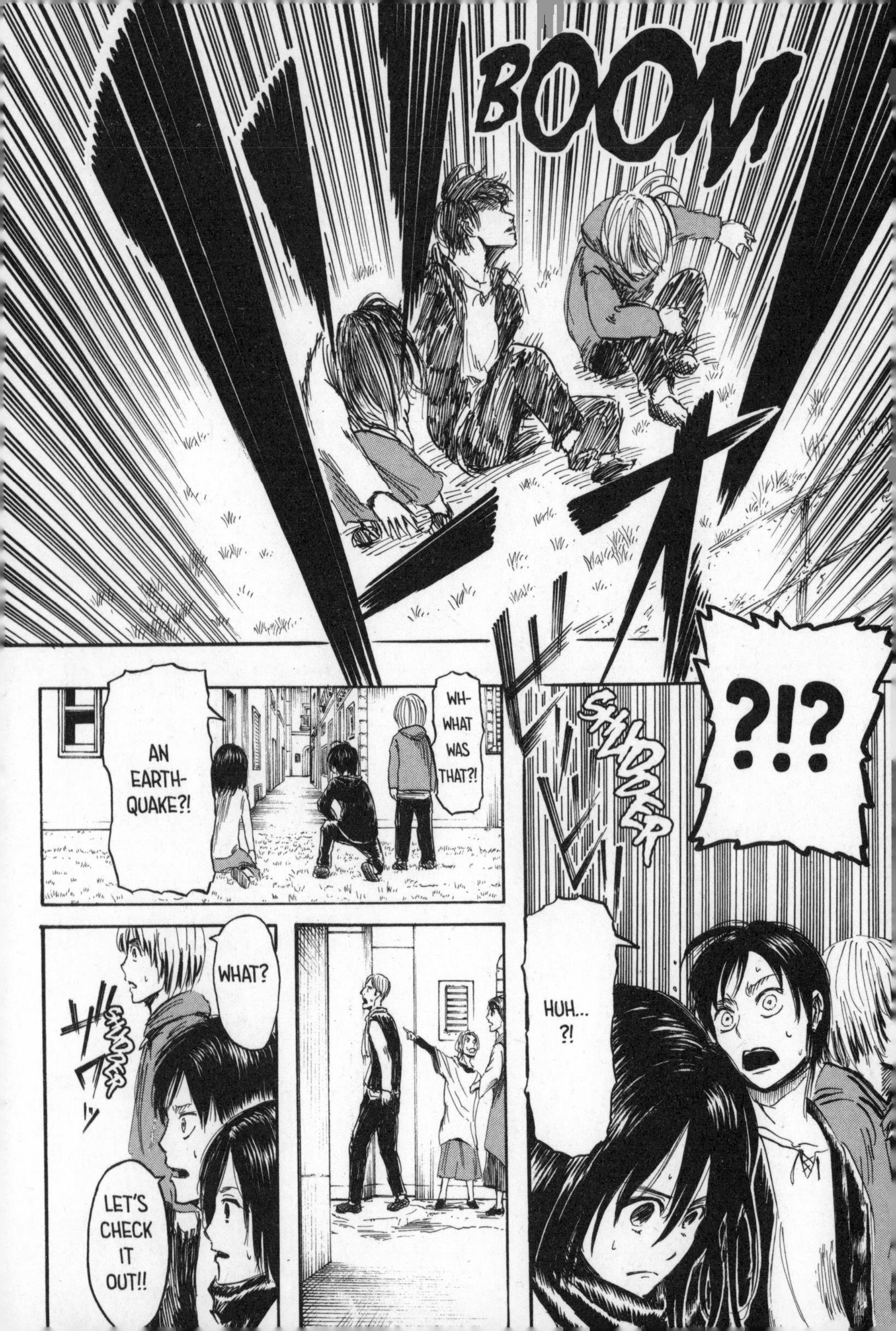
BOOM
?!?
SHUDDER
WH- WHAT WAS THAT?!
AN EARTH- QUAKE?!
HUH... ?!
WHAT?
LET'S CHECK IT OUT!!

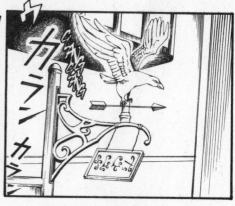

ARMIN, WHAT IS IT...?!

H-HEY... WHAT THE HECK ARE YOU LOOKING AT?!

DASH

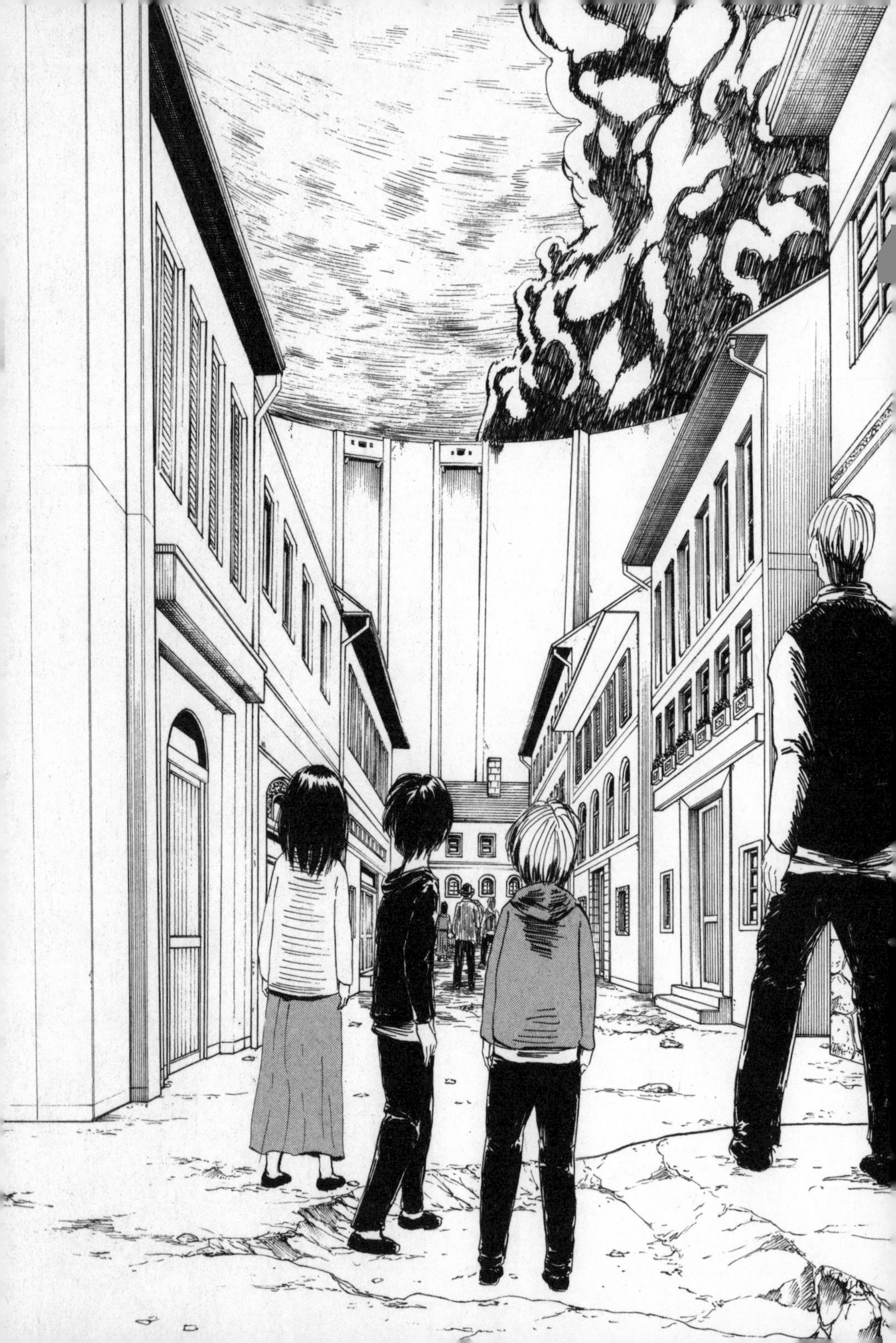

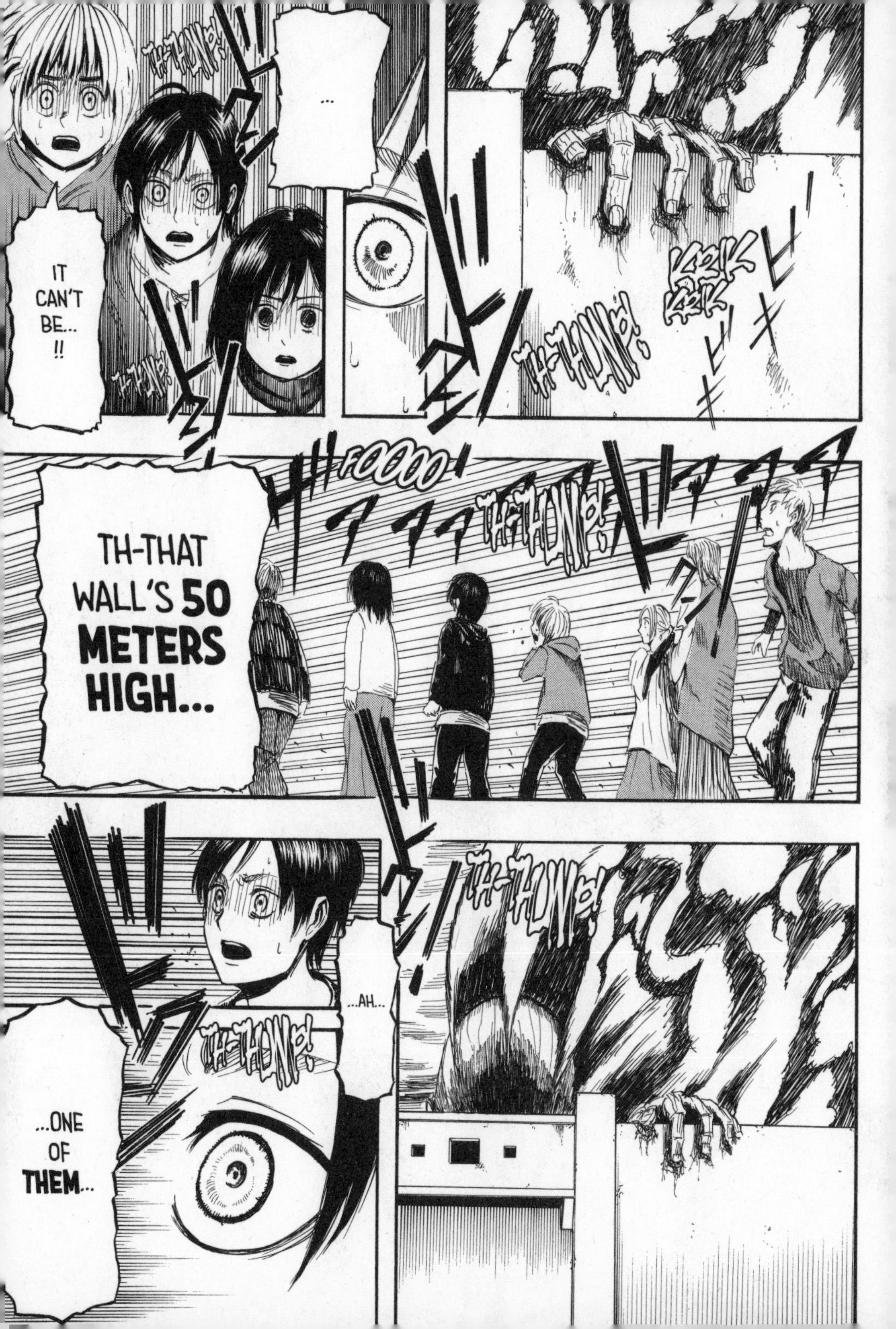
TH-THUMP!
KRRK KRRK
TH-THUMP!
...
IT CAN'T BE... !!
TH-THUMP!
FOOOO
TH-THUMP!
TH-THAT WALL'S 50 METERS HIGH...
TH-THUMP!
...AH...
TH-THUMP!
...ONE OF THEM...

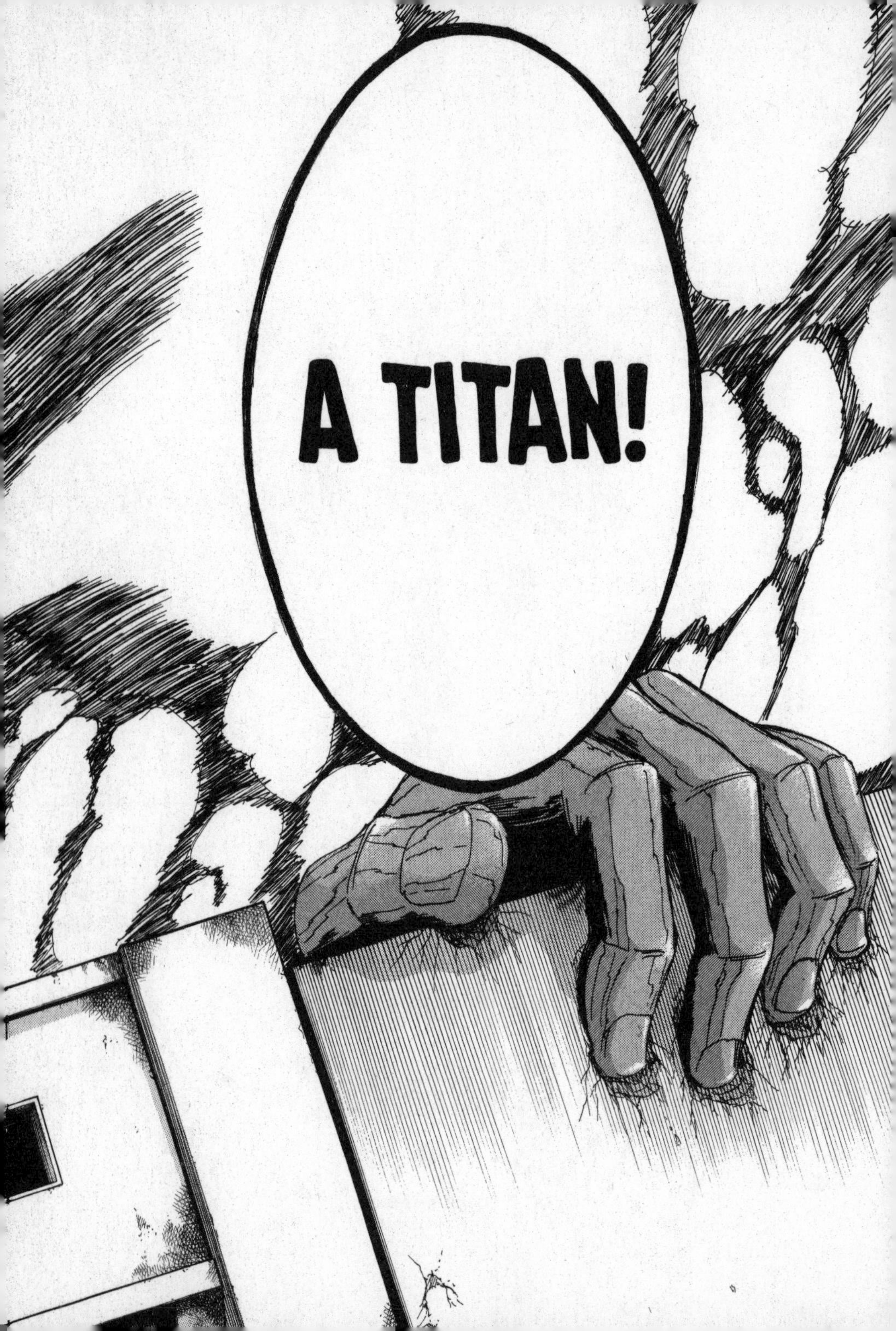
A TITAN!

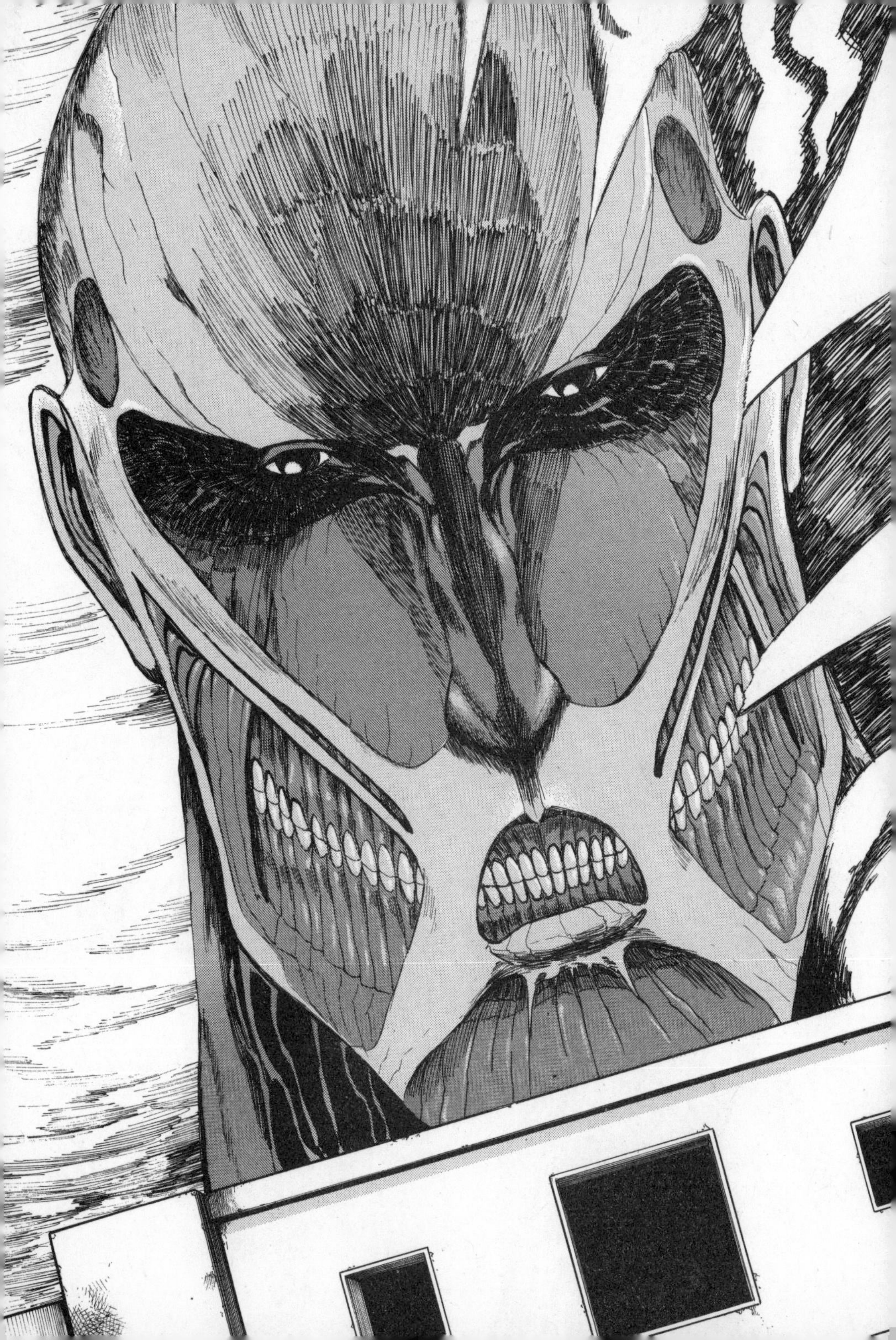

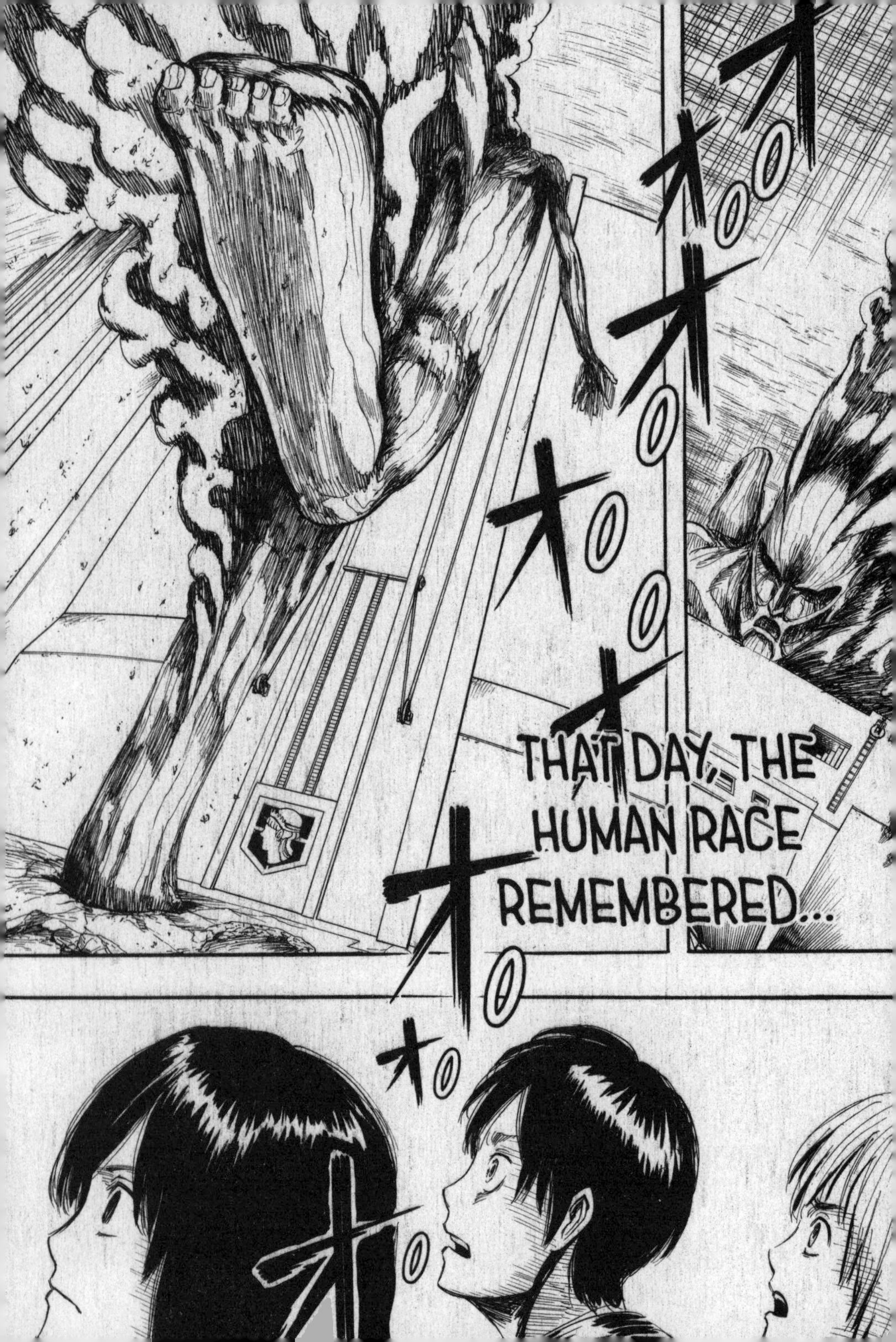
THAT DAY, THE HUMAN RACE REMEMBERED...

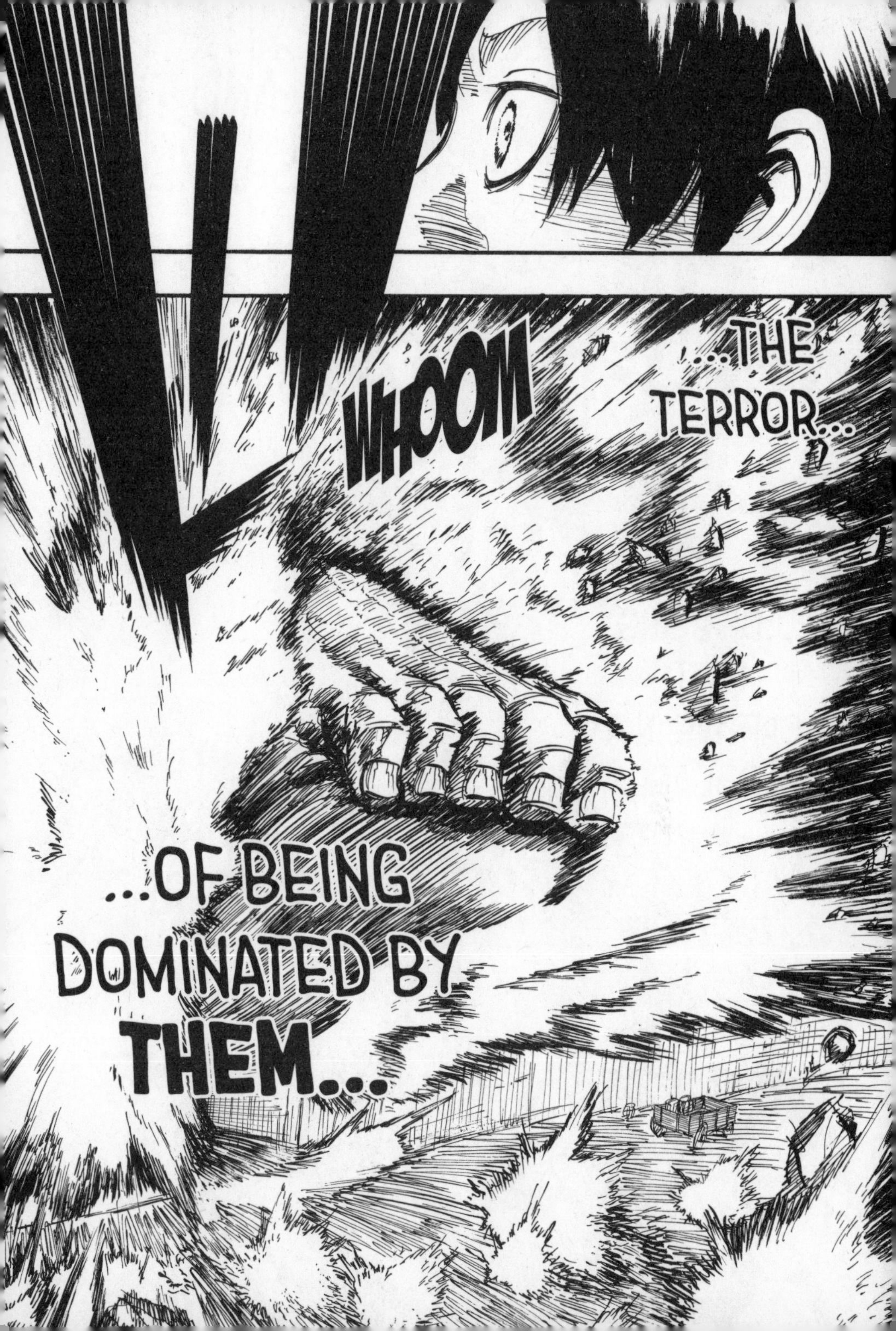
WHOOM
...THE TERROR...
...OF BEING DOMINATED BY THEM...

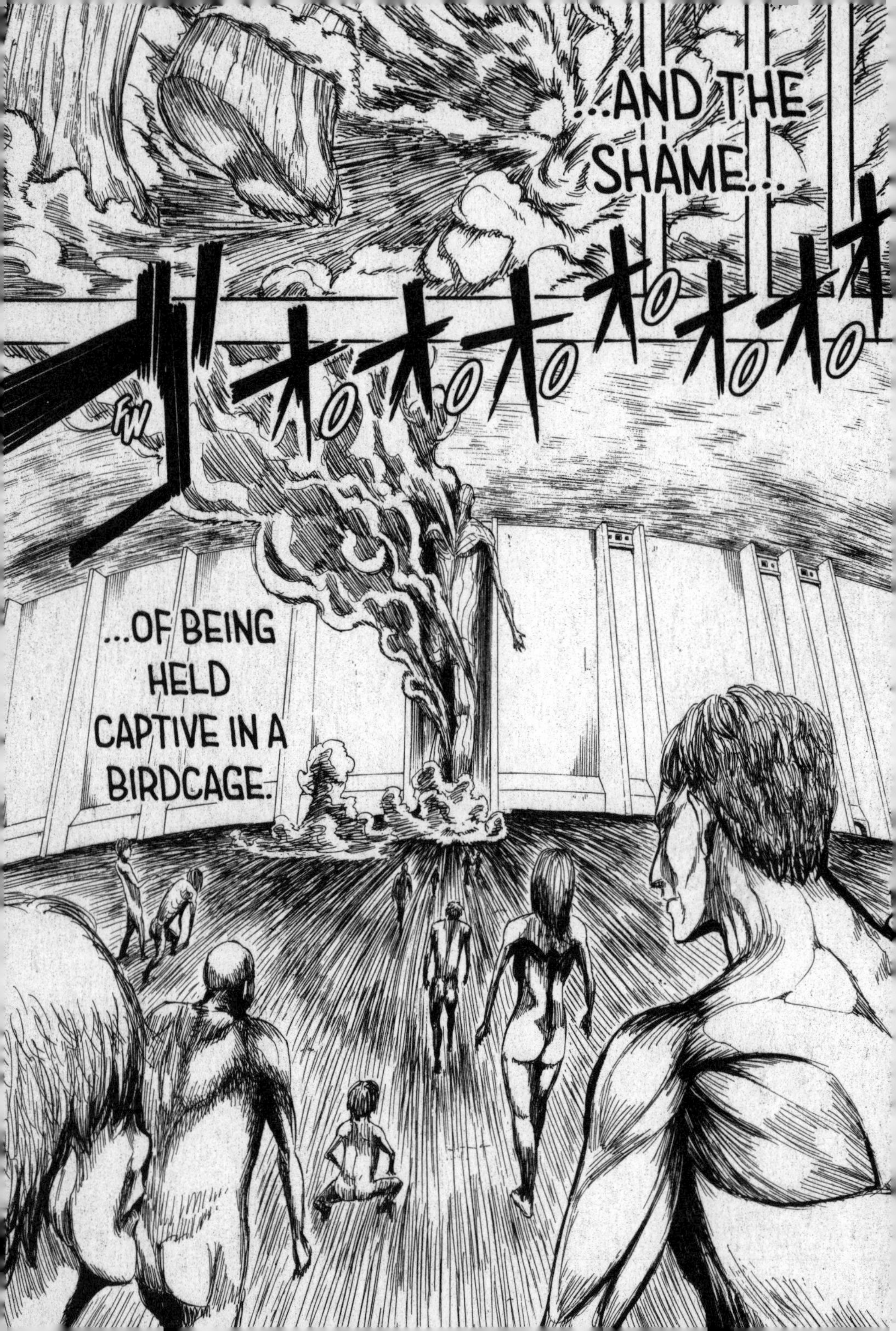
...AND THE SHAME...
FW
...OF BEING HELD CAPTIVE IN A BIRDCAGE.

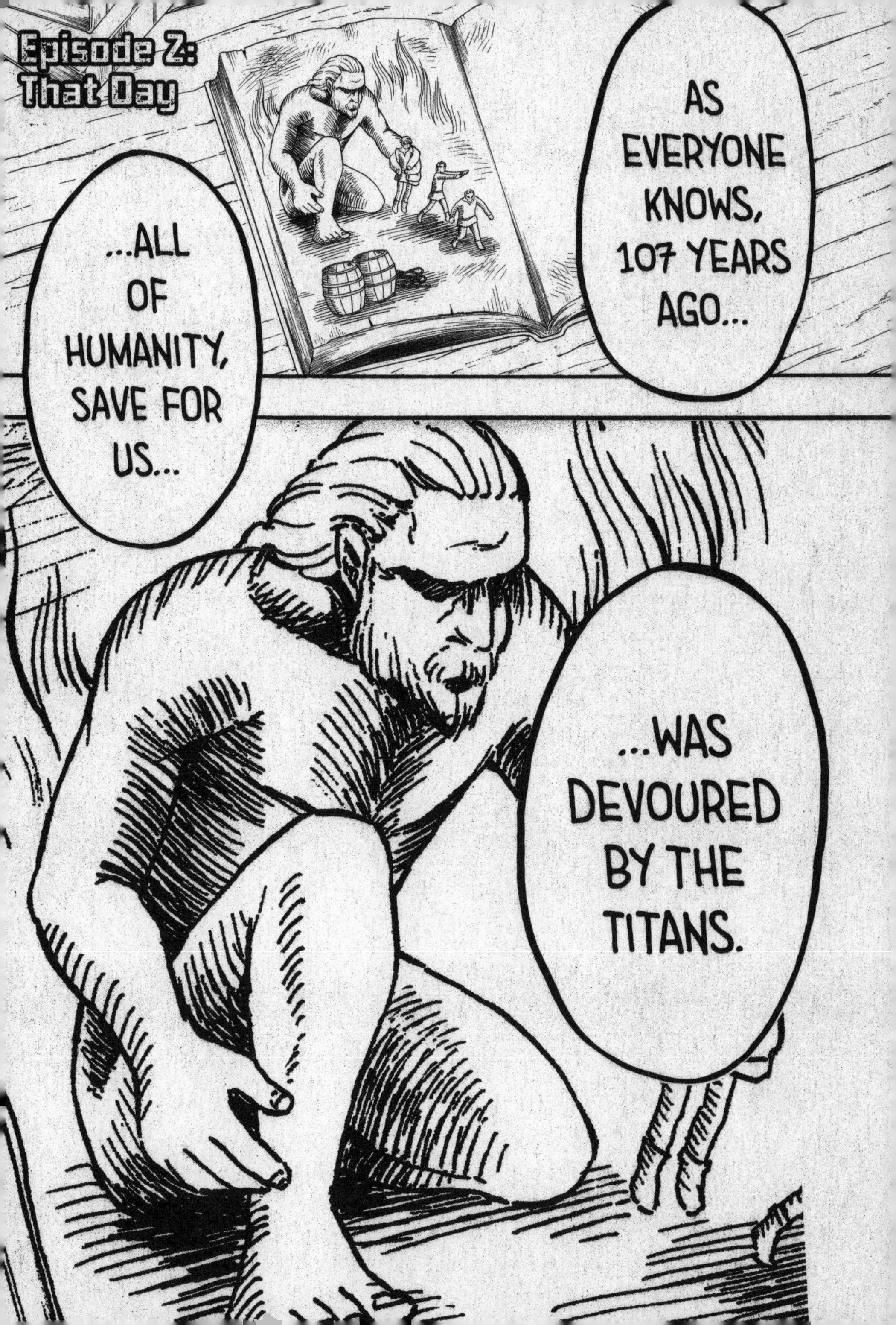
Episode 2: That Day
AS EVERYONE KNOWS, 107 YEARS AGO...
...ALL OF HUMANITY, SAVE FOR US...
...WAS DEVOURED BY THE TITANS.

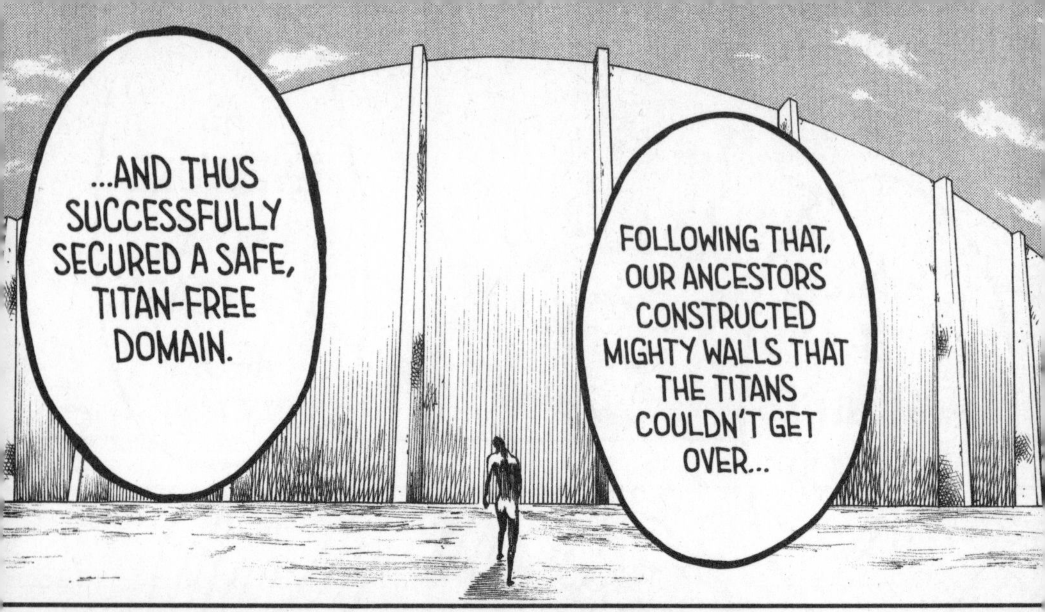
FOLLOWING THAT, OUR ANCESTORS CONSTRUCTED MIGHTY WALLS THAT THE TITANS COULDN'T GET OVER...
...AND THUS SUCCESSFULLY SECURED A SAFE, TITAN-FREE DOMAIN.

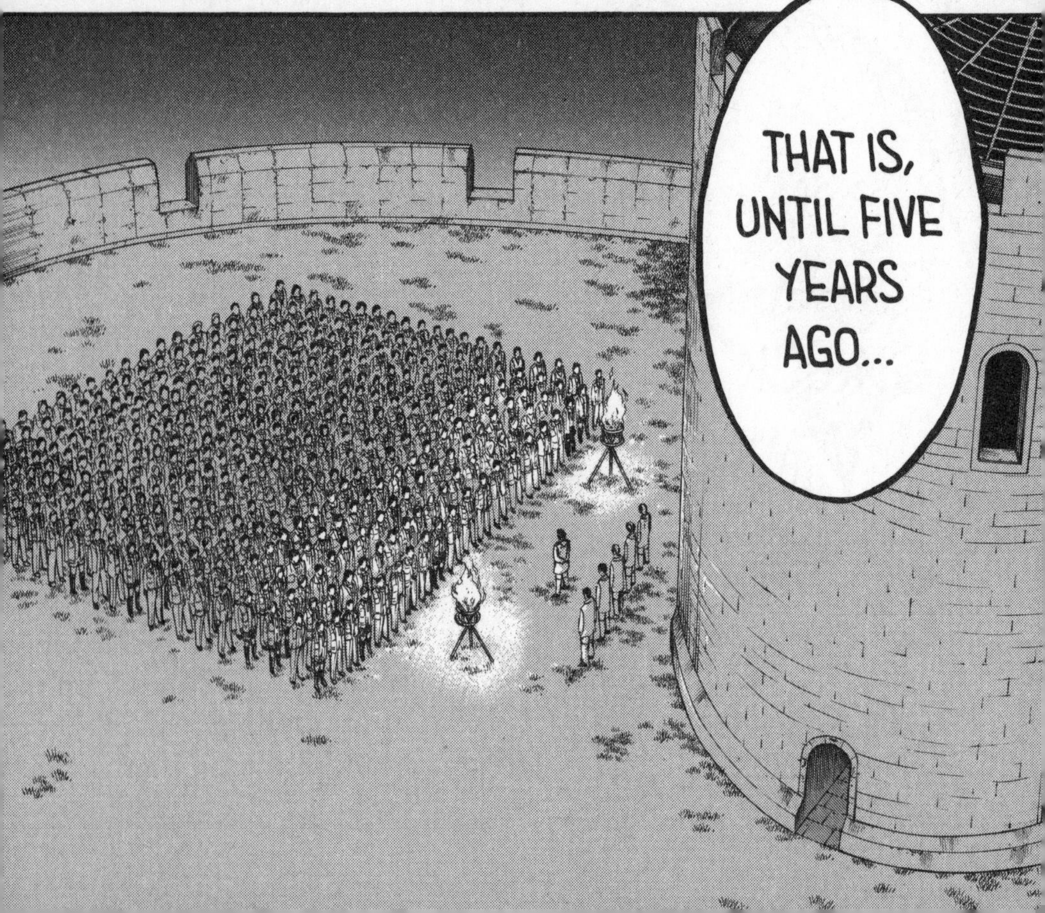
THAT IS, UNTIL FIVE YEARS AGO...

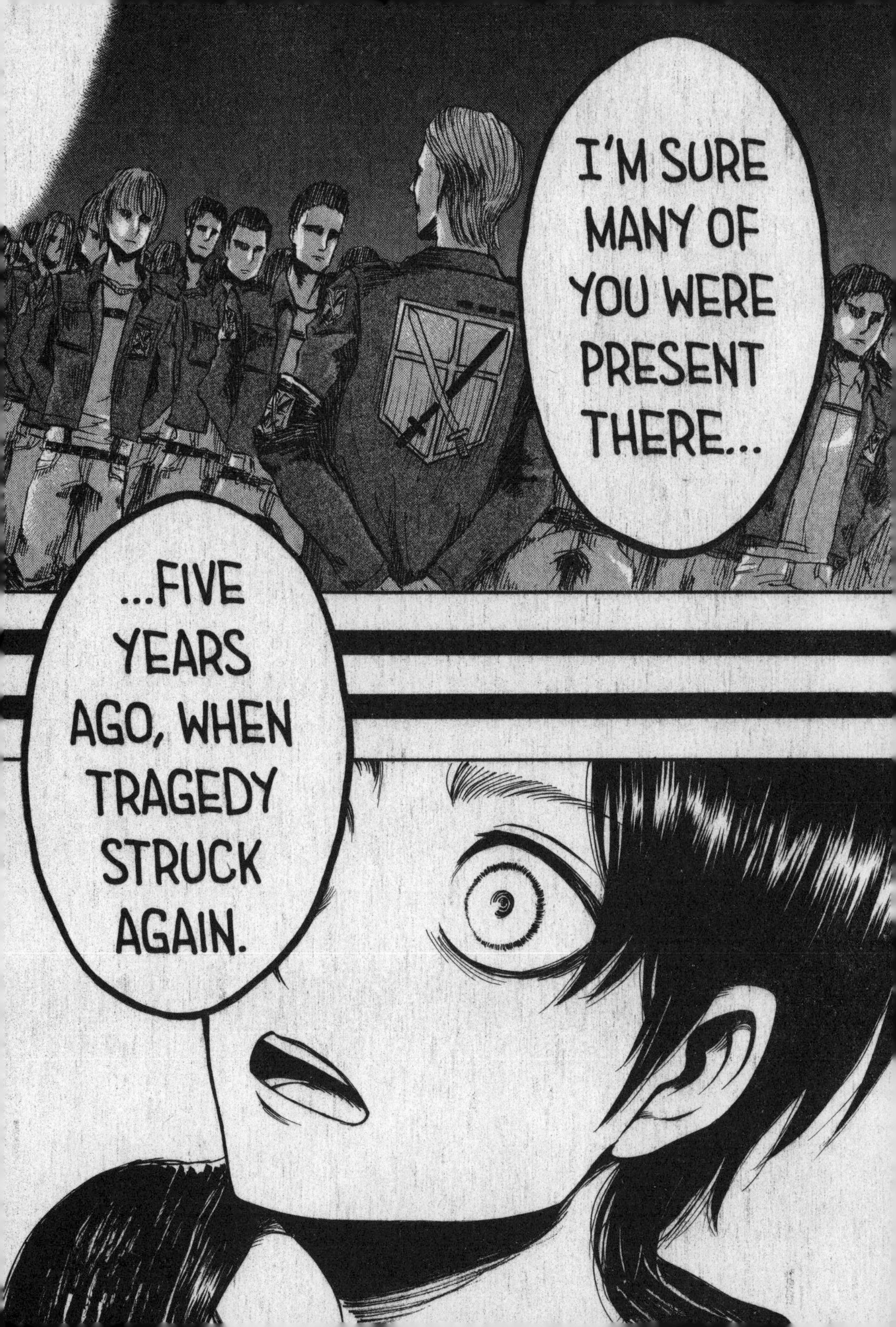
I'M SURE MANY OF YOU WERE PRESENT THERE...
...FIVE YEARS AGO, WHEN TRAGEDY STRUCK AGAIN.

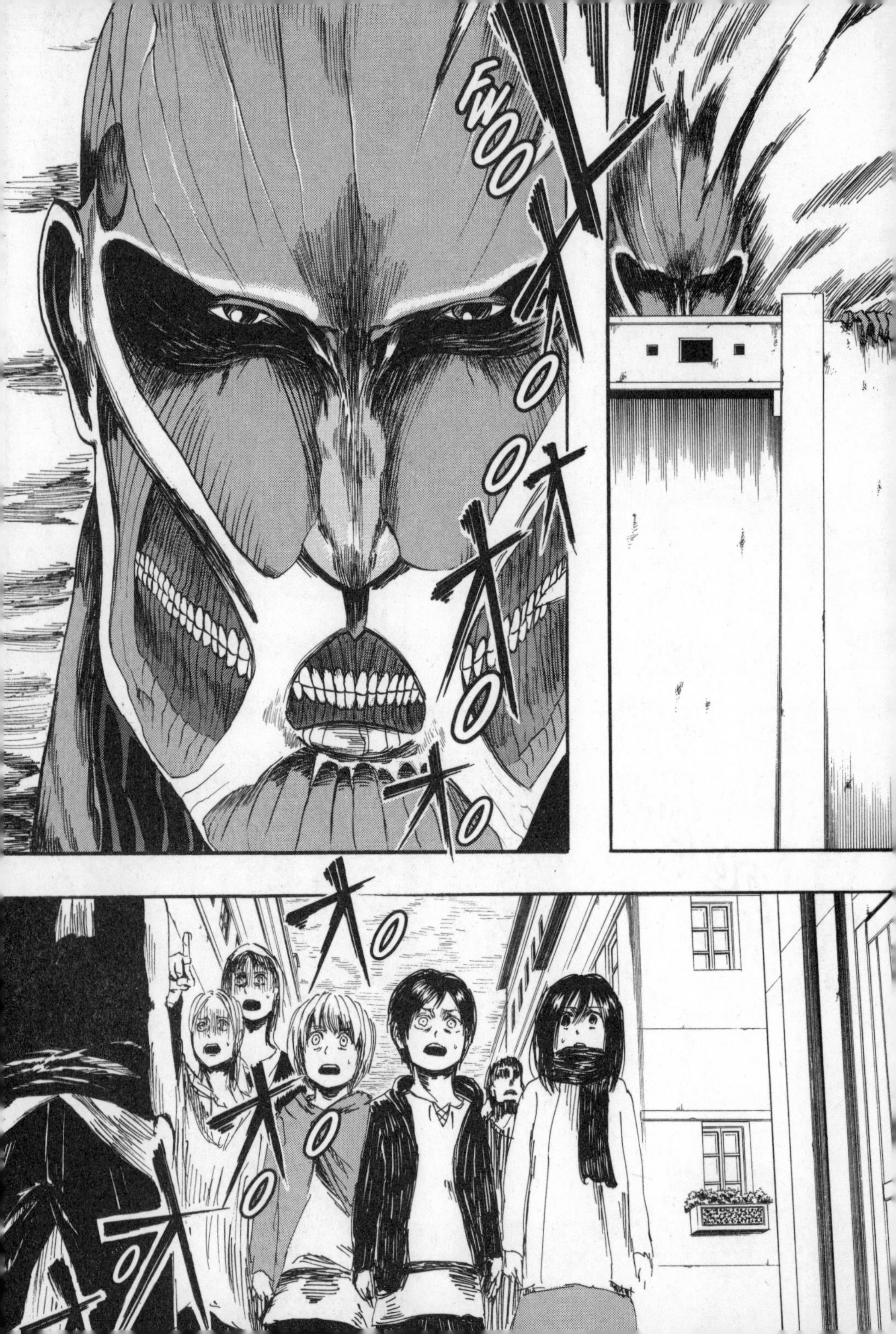
FWOOO

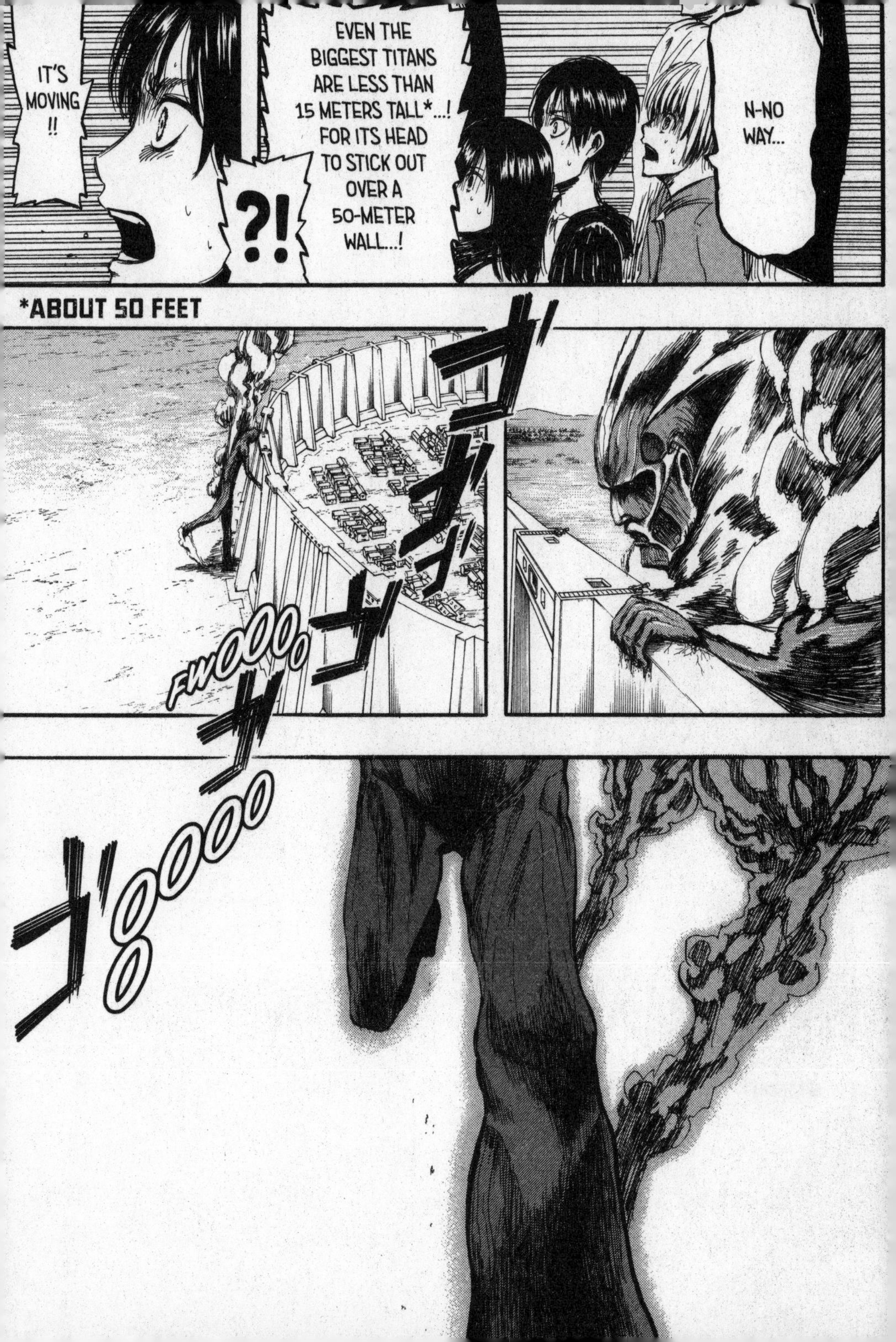
N-NO WAY...
EVEN THE BIGGEST TITANS ARE LESS THAN 15 METERS TALL*...! FOR ITS HEAD TO STICK OUT OVER A 50-METER WALL...!
?!
IT'S MOVING !!
*ABOUT 50 FEET
FWOOOO
GOOOO

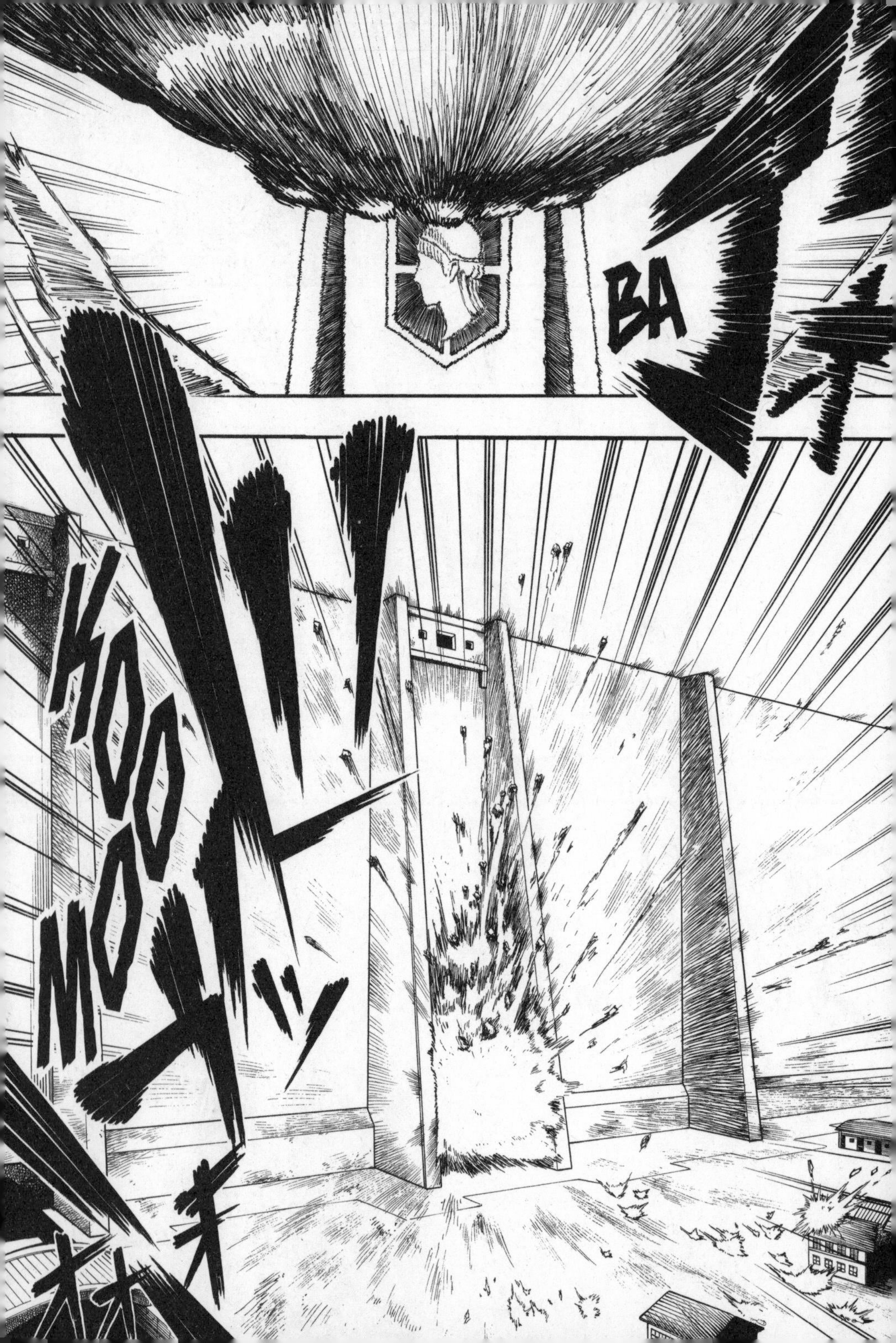
BA
KOOOM

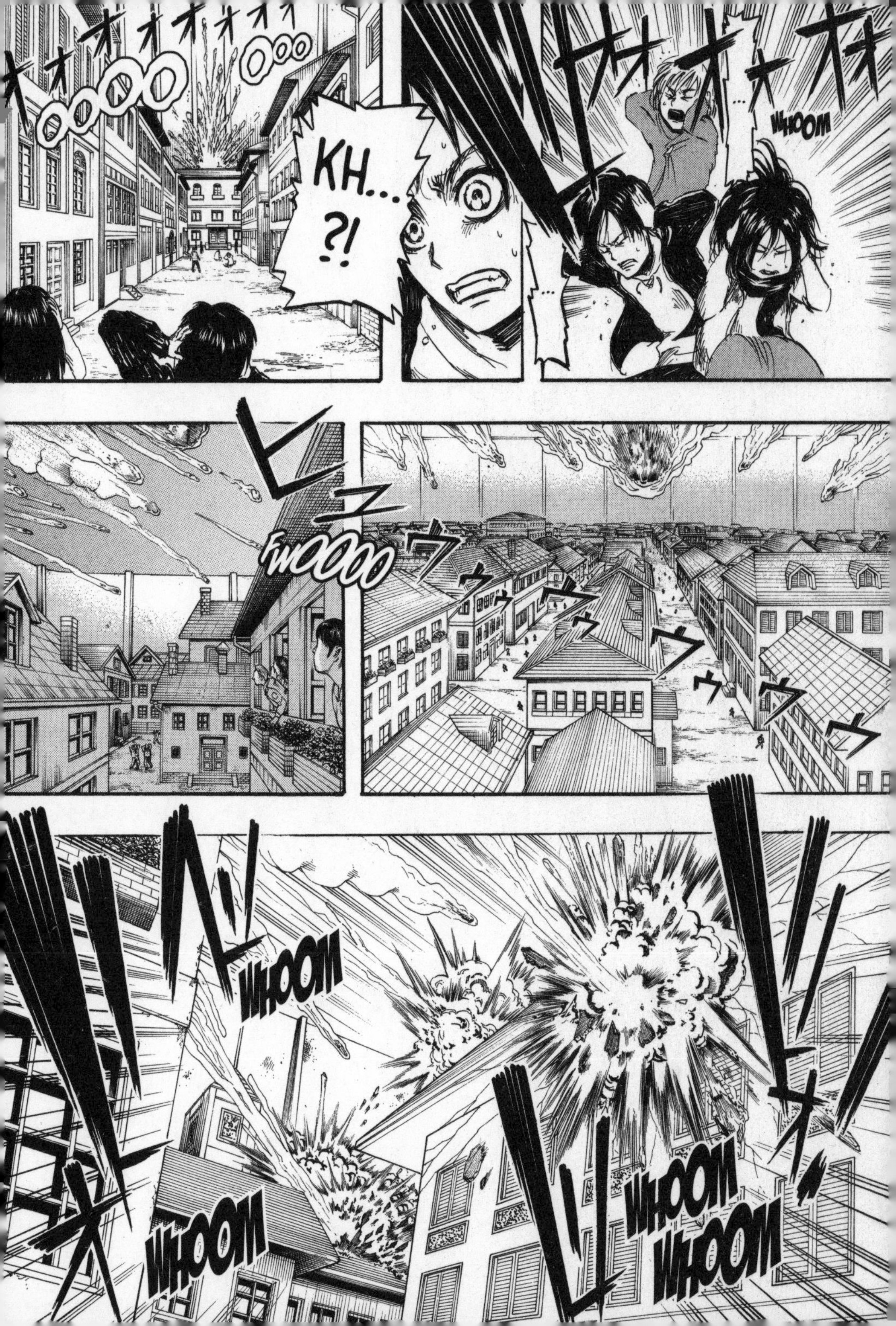

...
WHOOM
...
KH...
?!
OOOOO
Ooo
FWOOOO
WHOOM
WHOOM
WHOOM
WHOOM

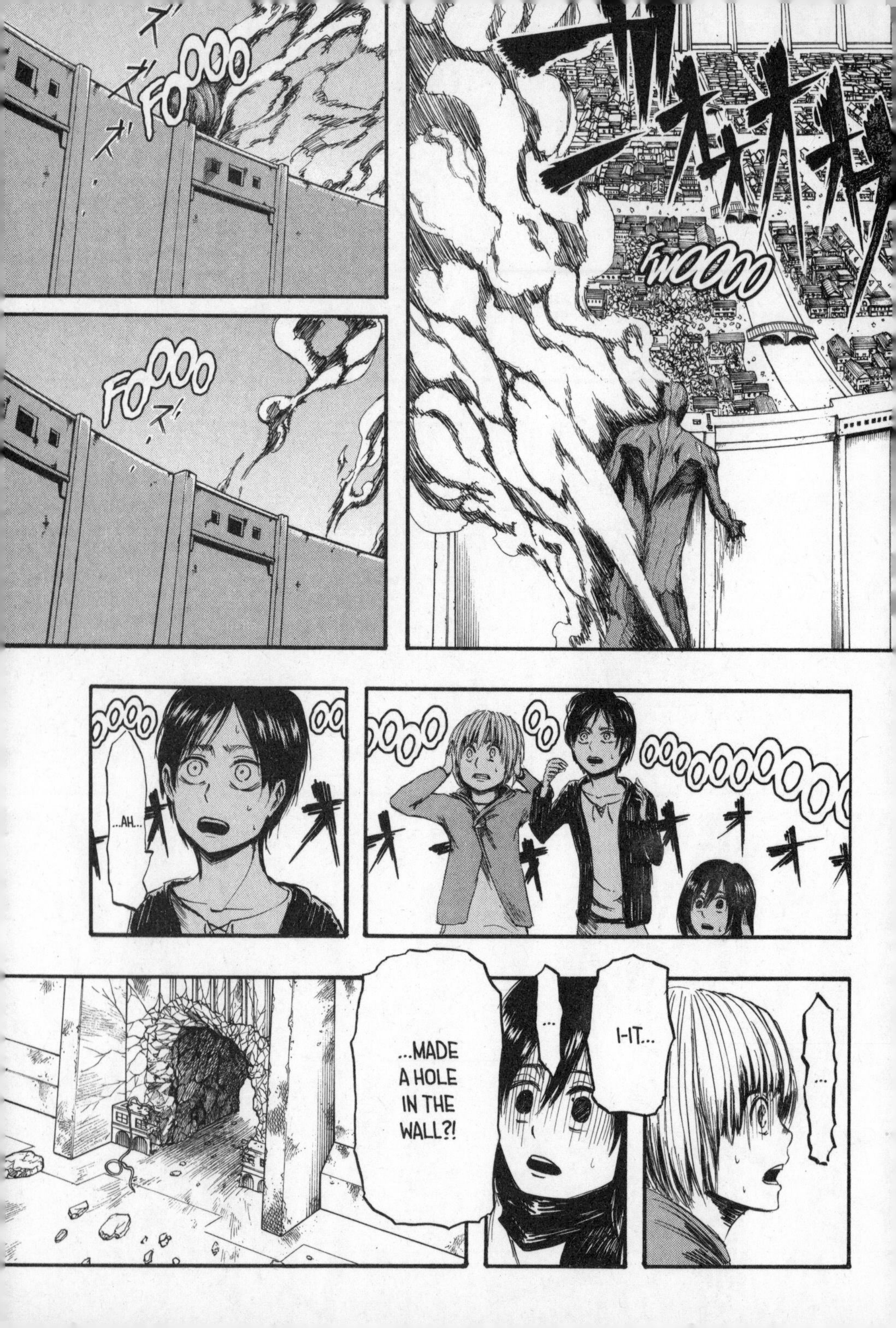

FWOOOO
FOOOO
FOOOO
...AH...
...
I-IT...
...
...MADE A HOLE IN THE WALL?!

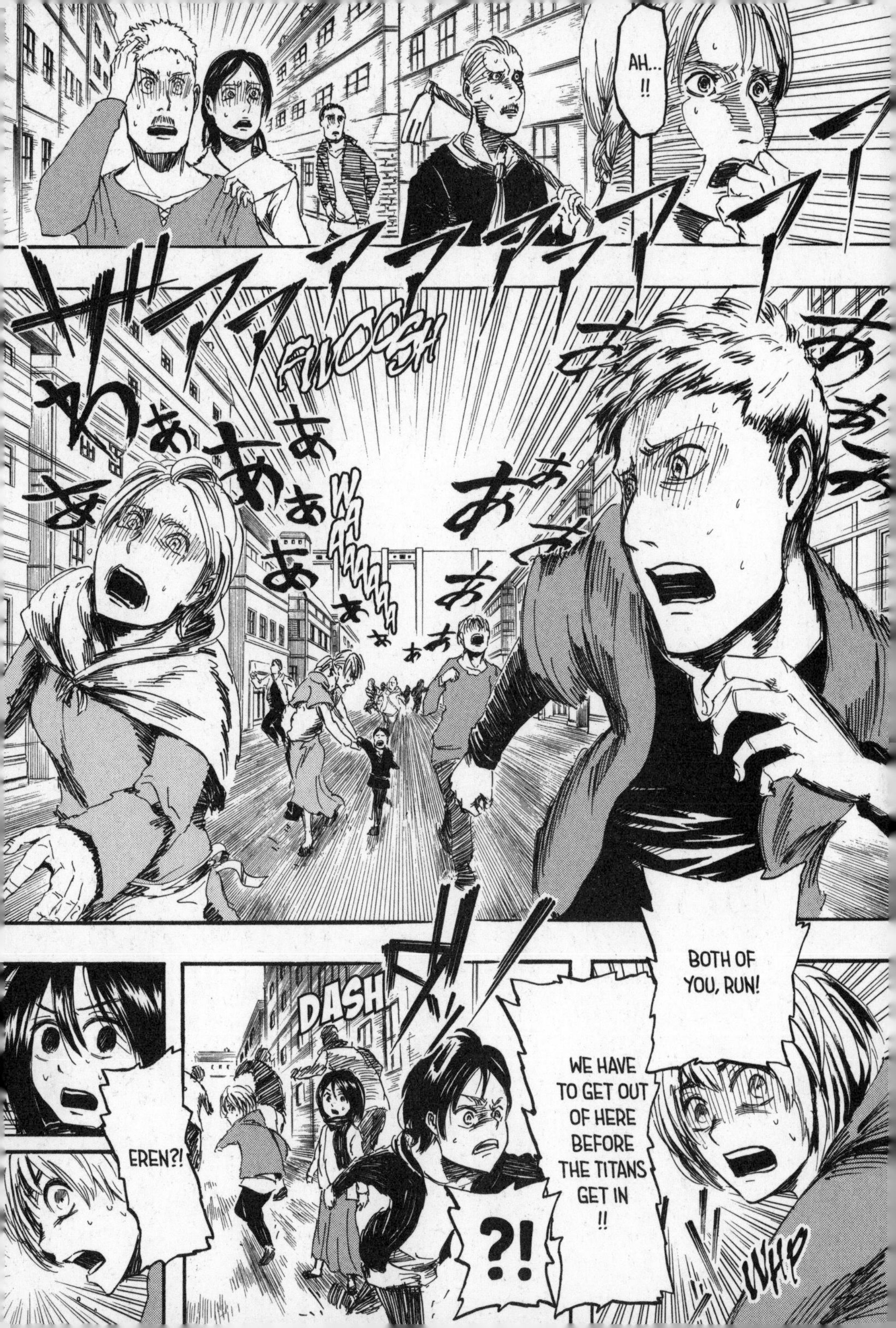

AH... !!
FWOOSH
WAAAAAAAAA
BOTH OF YOU, RUN!
WE HAVE TO GET OUT OF HERE BEFORE THE TITANS GET IN !!
WHIP
DASH
?!
EREN?!

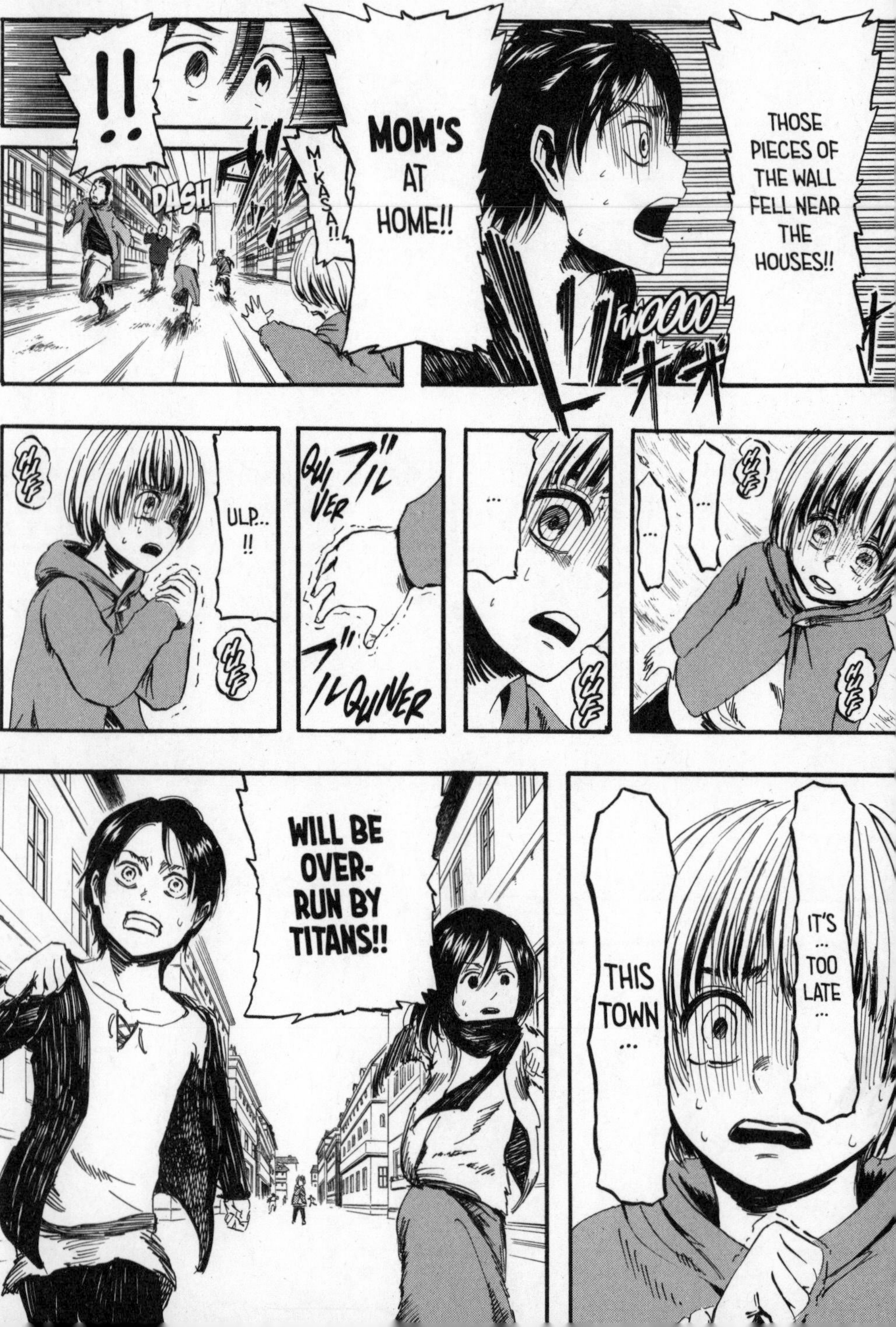
THOSE PIECES OF THE WALL FELL NEAR THE HOUSES!!
FWOOOO
MOM'S AT HOME!!
!!
MIKASA!!
DASH
...
...
...
...
QUIVER
QUIVER
ULP... !!
IT'S... TOO LATE...
THIS TOWN...
WILL BE OVER-RUN BY TITANS!!

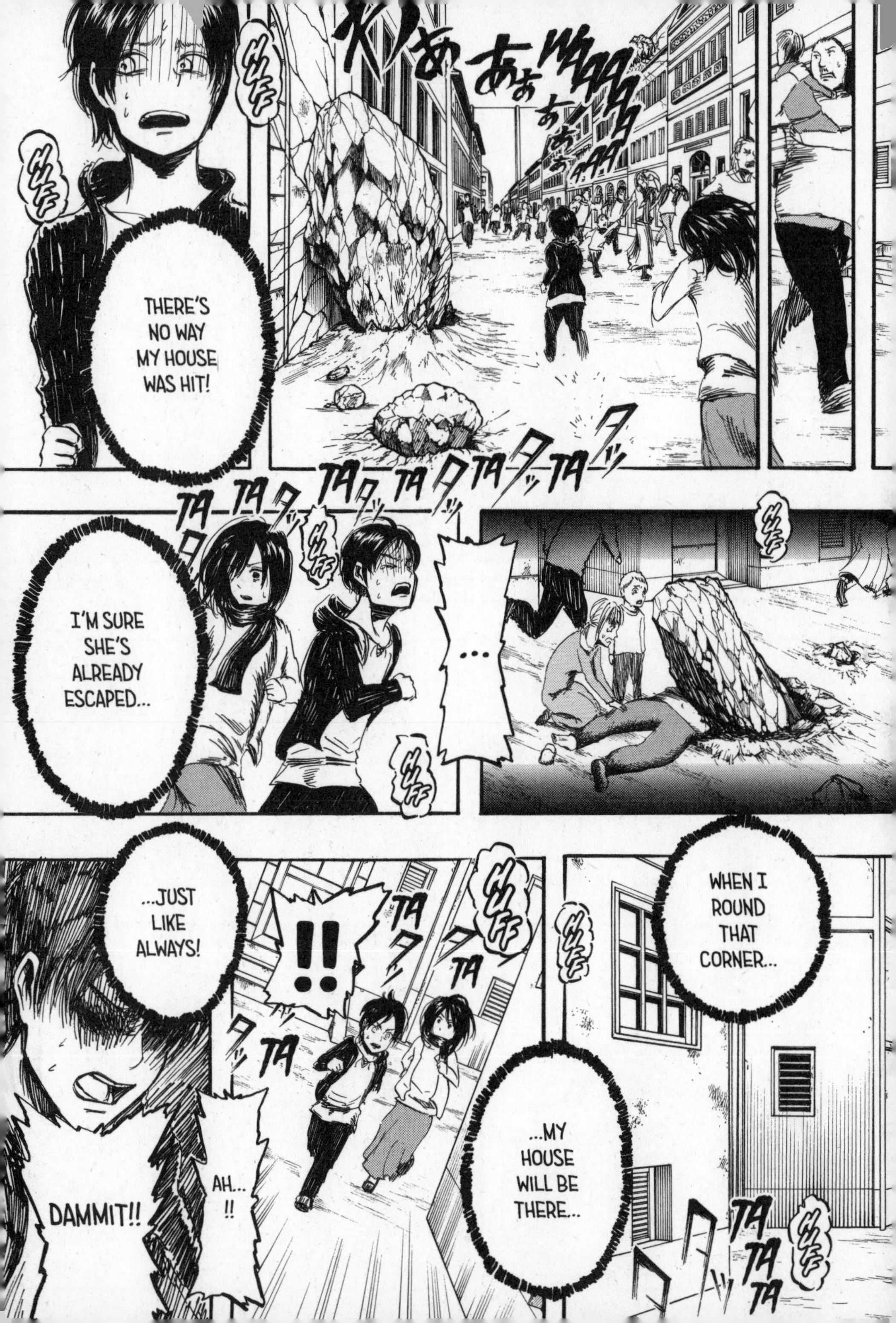
HUFF
HUFF
THERE'S NO WAY MY HOUSE WAS HIT!
TA TA TA TA TA TA
HUFF
HUFF
...
I'M SURE SHE'S ALREADY ESCAPED...
HUFF
HUFF
WHEN I ROUND THAT CORNER...
...MY HOUSE WILL BE THERE...
TA TA TA
HUFF
HUFF
TA TA
!!
...JUST LIKE ALWAYS!
TA
AH... !!
DAMMIT!!

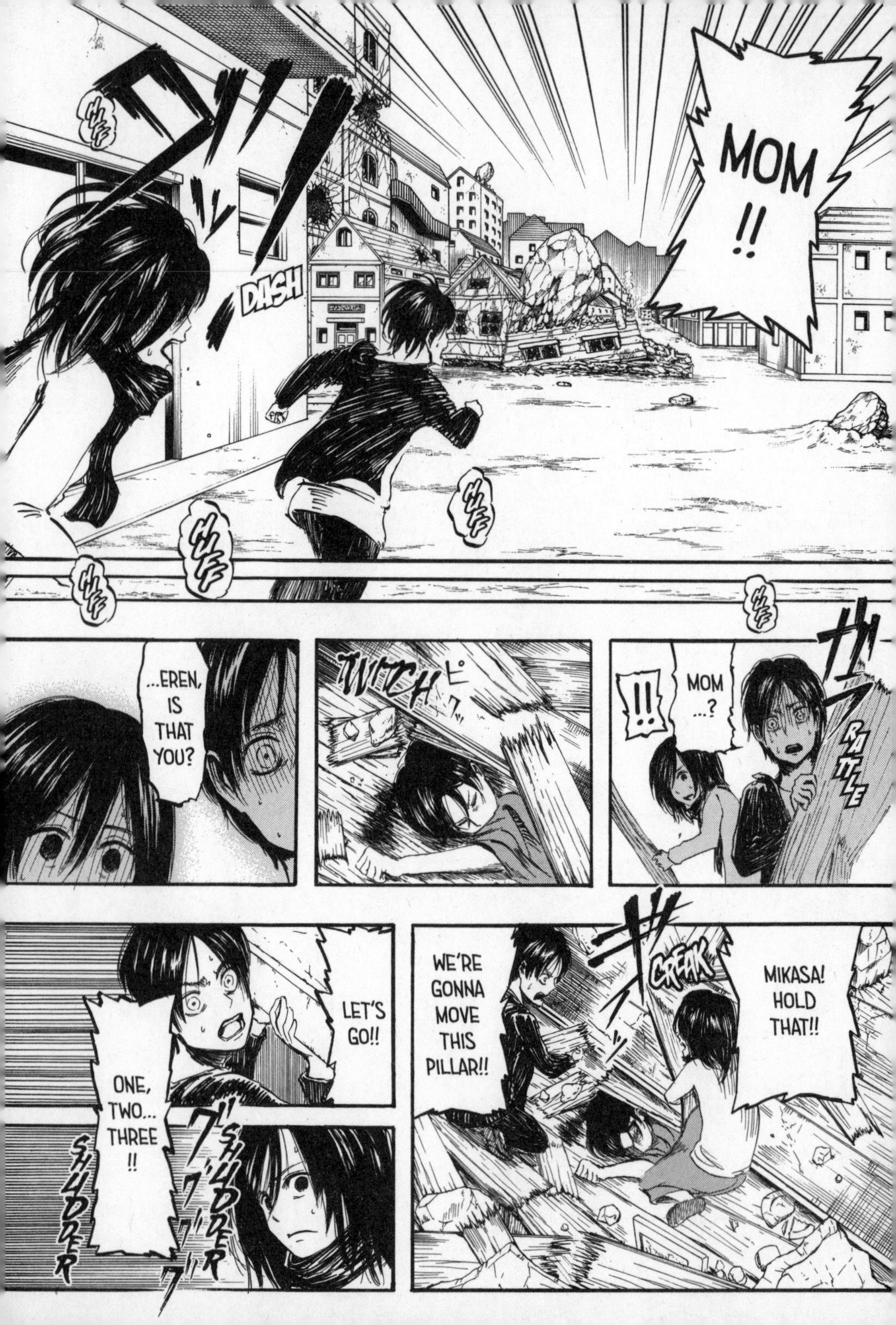
MOM !!
DASH
HUFF
HUFF
HUFF
HUFF
HUFF
RATTLE
MOM ...?
!!
TWITCH
...EREN, IS THAT YOU?
MIKASA! HOLD THAT!!
CREAK
WE'RE GONNA MOVE THIS PILLAR!!
LET'S GO!!
ONE, TWO... THREE !!
SHUDDER
SHUDDER

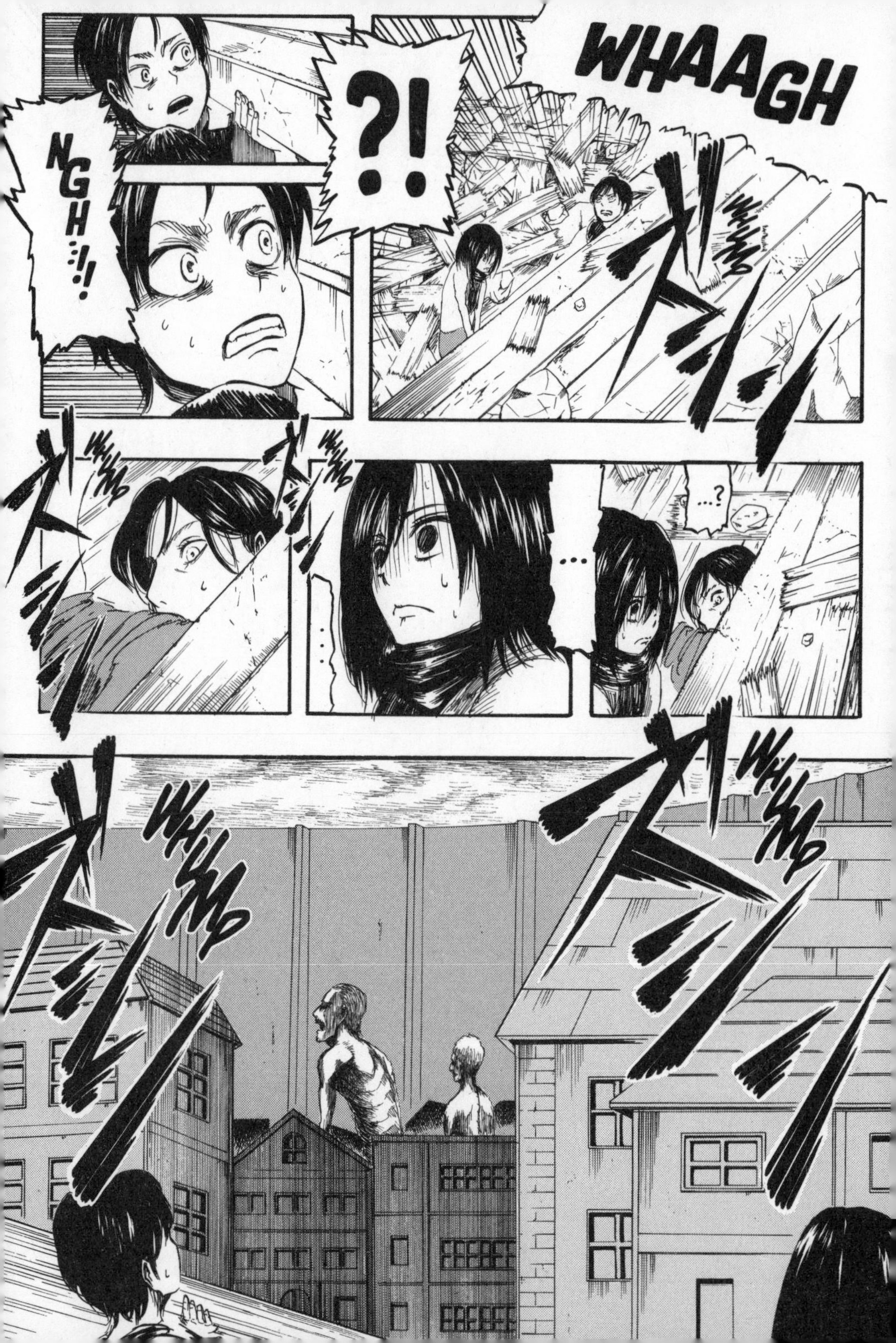
WHAAGH
WHUNG
?!
NGH...!!
...?
...
...
WHUNG
WHUNG
WHUNG
WHUNG

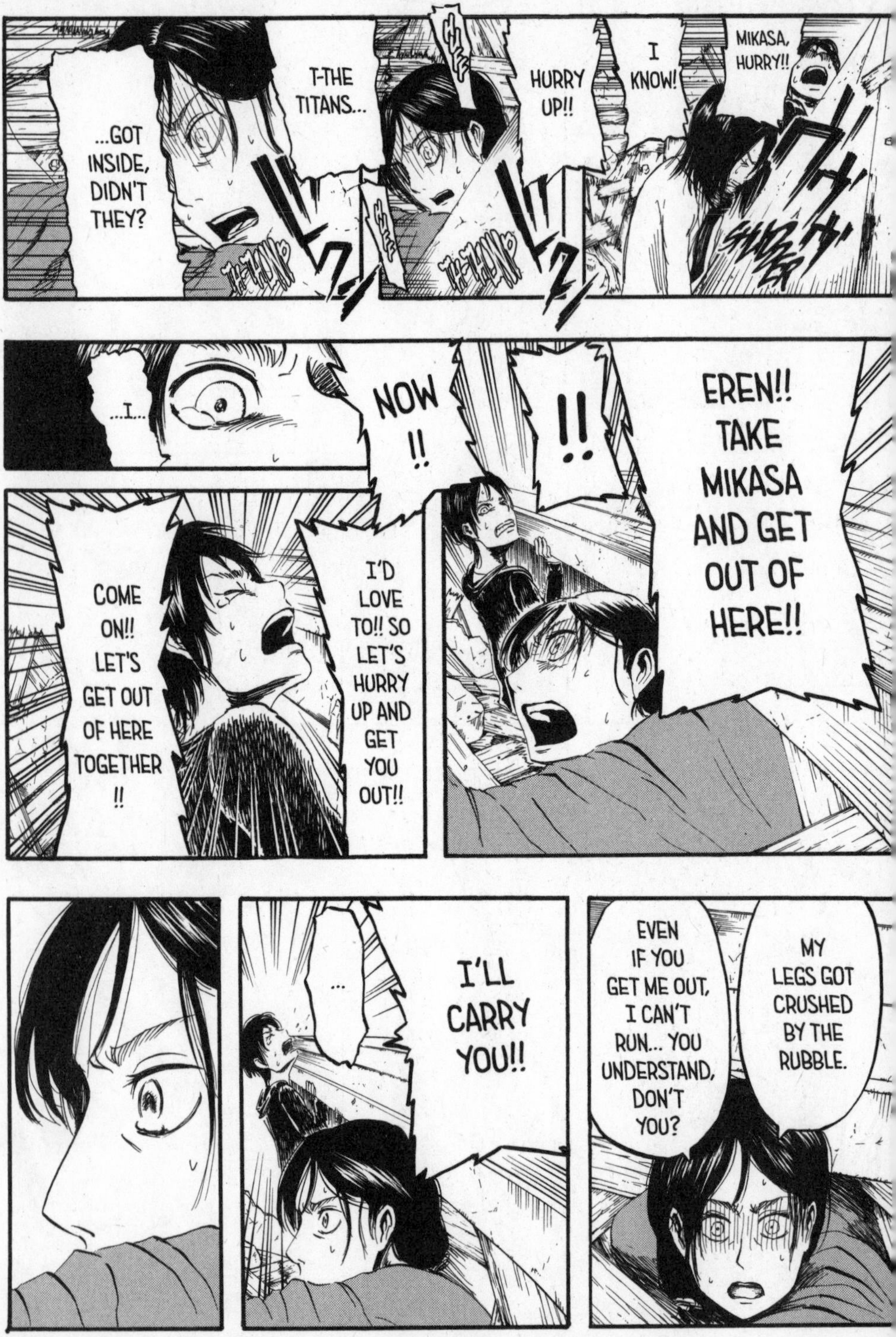
MIKASA, HURRY!!
I KNOW!
HURRY UP!!
T-THE TITANS...
...GOT INSIDE, DIDN'T THEY?
EREN!! TAKE MIKASA AND GET OUT OF HERE!!
!!
NOW!!
...I...
I'D LOVE TO!! SO LET'S HURRY UP AND GET YOU OUT!!
COME ON!! LET'S GET OUT OF HERE TOGETHER!!
MY LEGS GOT CRUSHED BY THE RUBBLE.
EVEN IF YOU GET ME OUT, I CAN'T RUN... YOU UNDERSTAND, DON'T YOU?
I'LL CARRY YOU!!
...

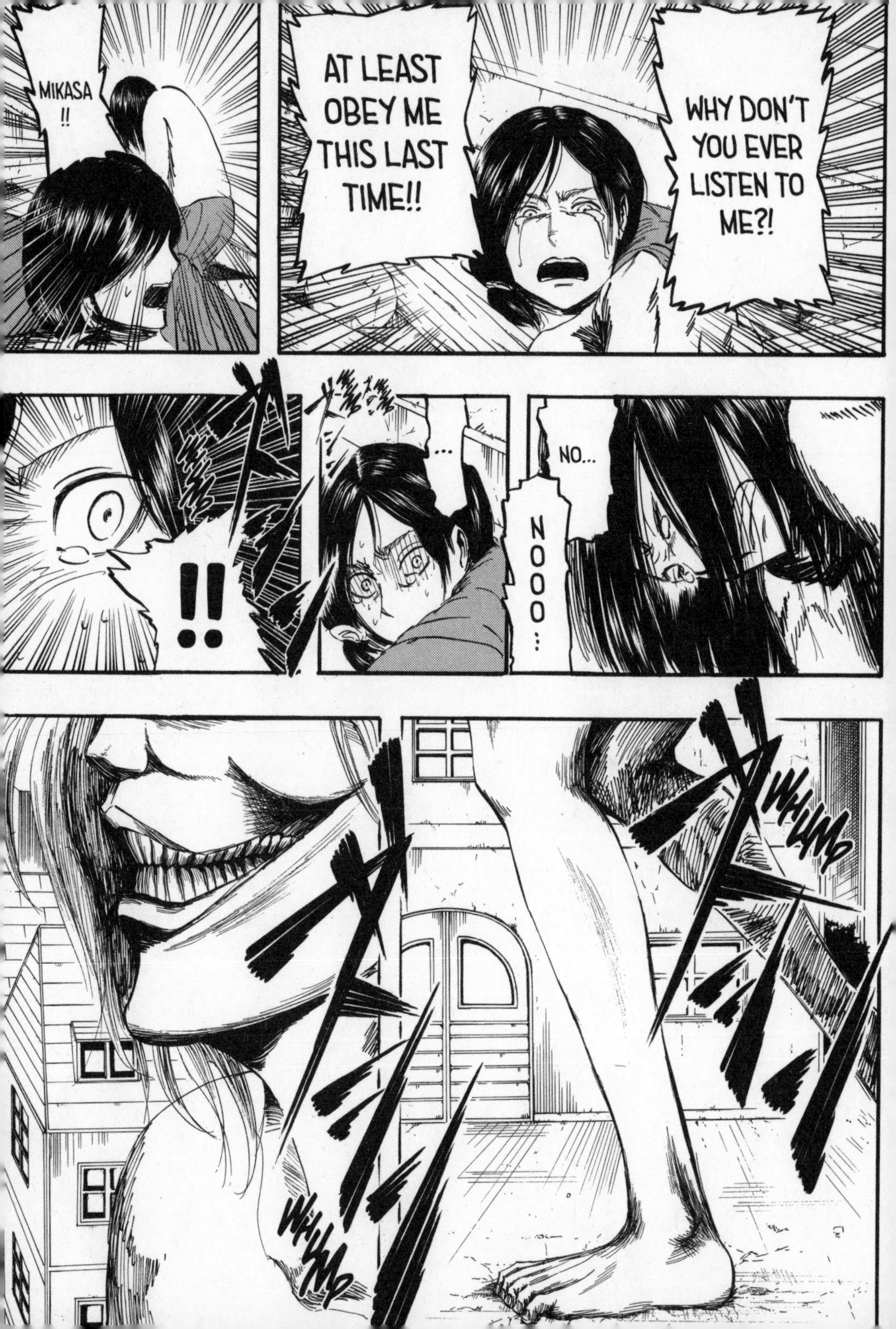
WHY DON'T YOU EVER LISTEN TO ME?!
AT LEAST OBEY ME THIS LAST TIME!!
MIKASA !!
NO...
NOOO...
...
!!
WHUMP
WHUMP

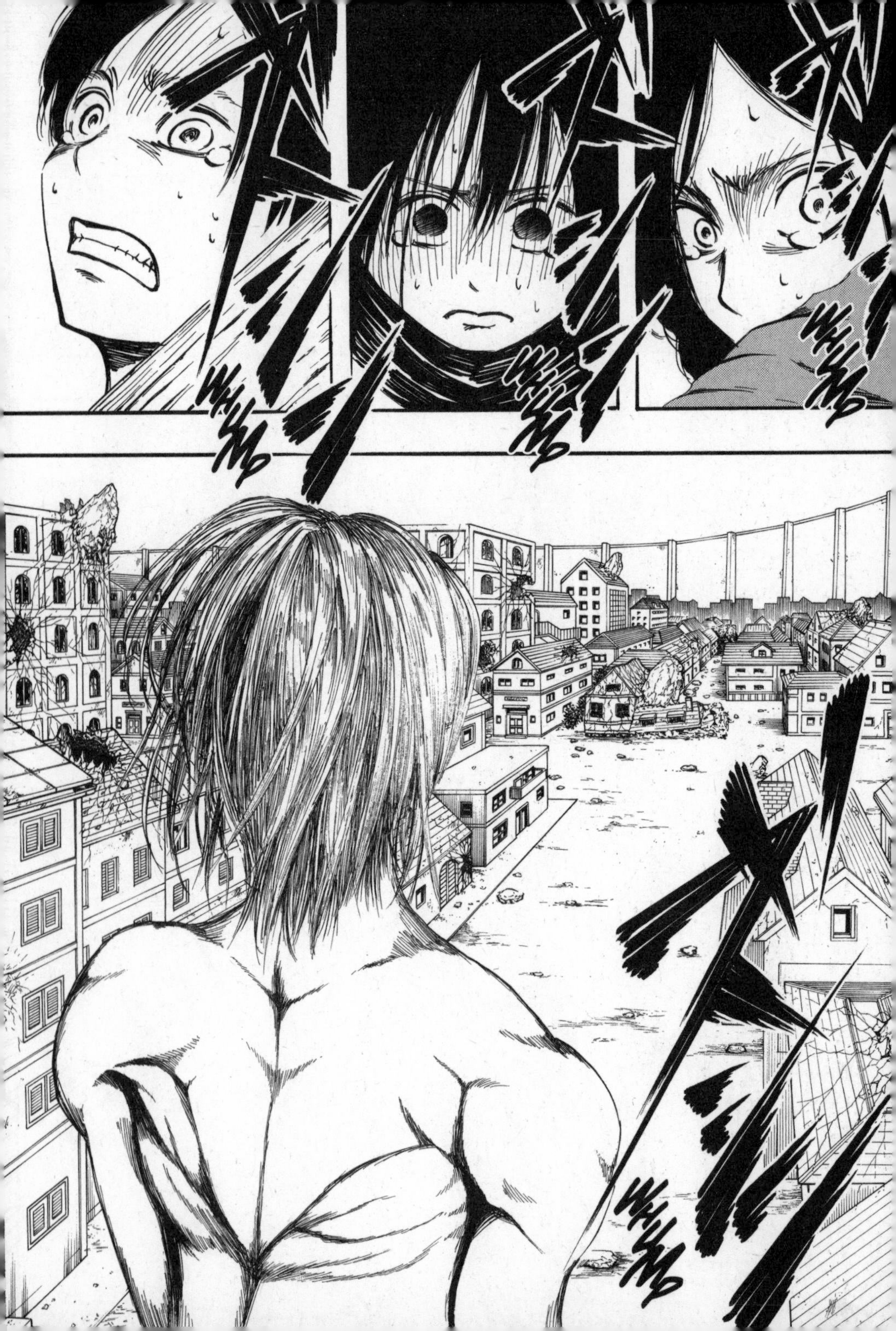
WHUMP
WHUMP
WHUMP
WHUMP

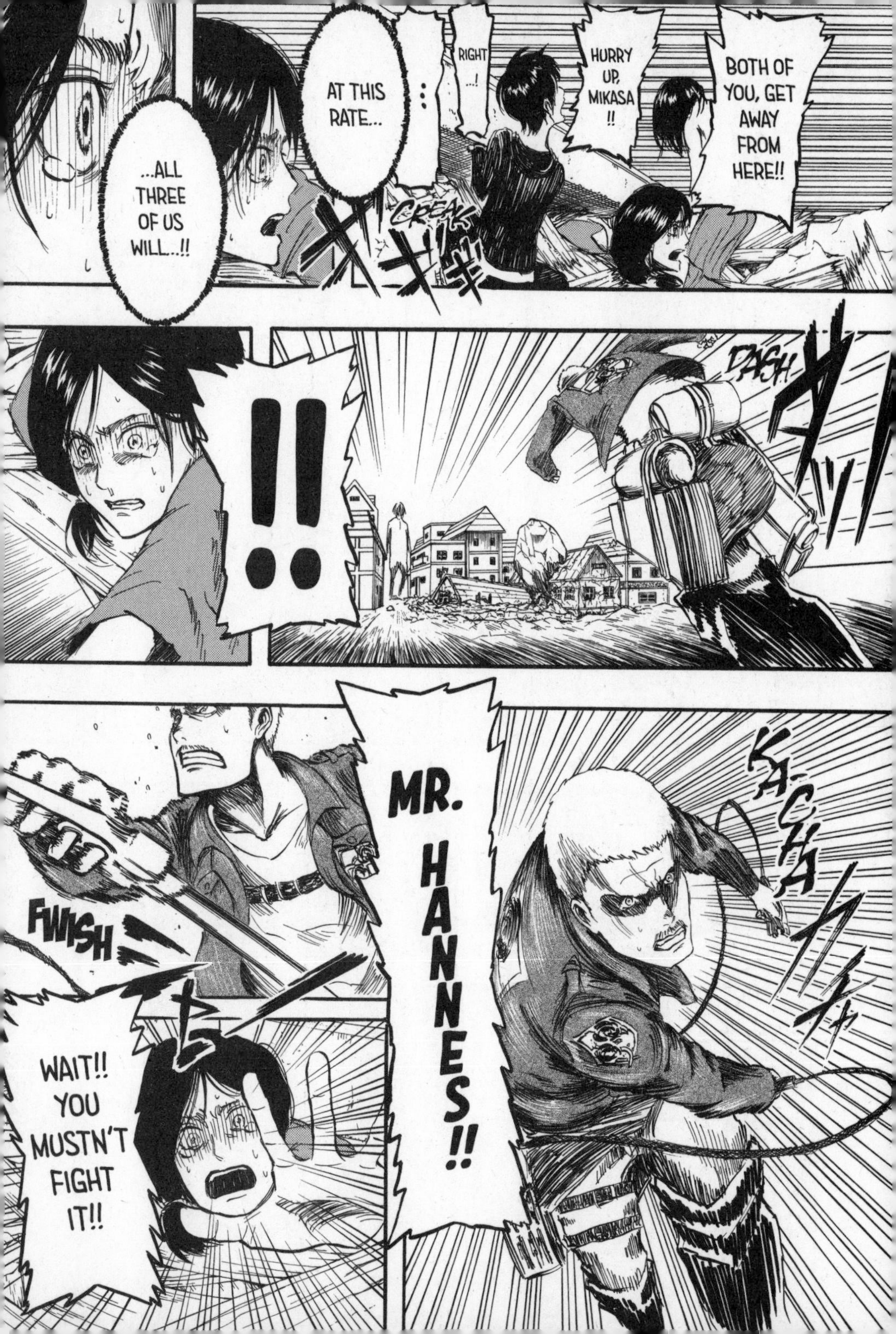
BOTH OF YOU, GET AWAY FROM HERE!!
HURRY UP, MIKASA!!
RIGHT ...!
CREAK
AT THIS RATE...
...ALL THREE OF US WILL...!!
DASH
!!
KA-CHA
MR. HANNES!!
FWISH
WAIT!! YOU MUSTN'T FIGHT IT!!

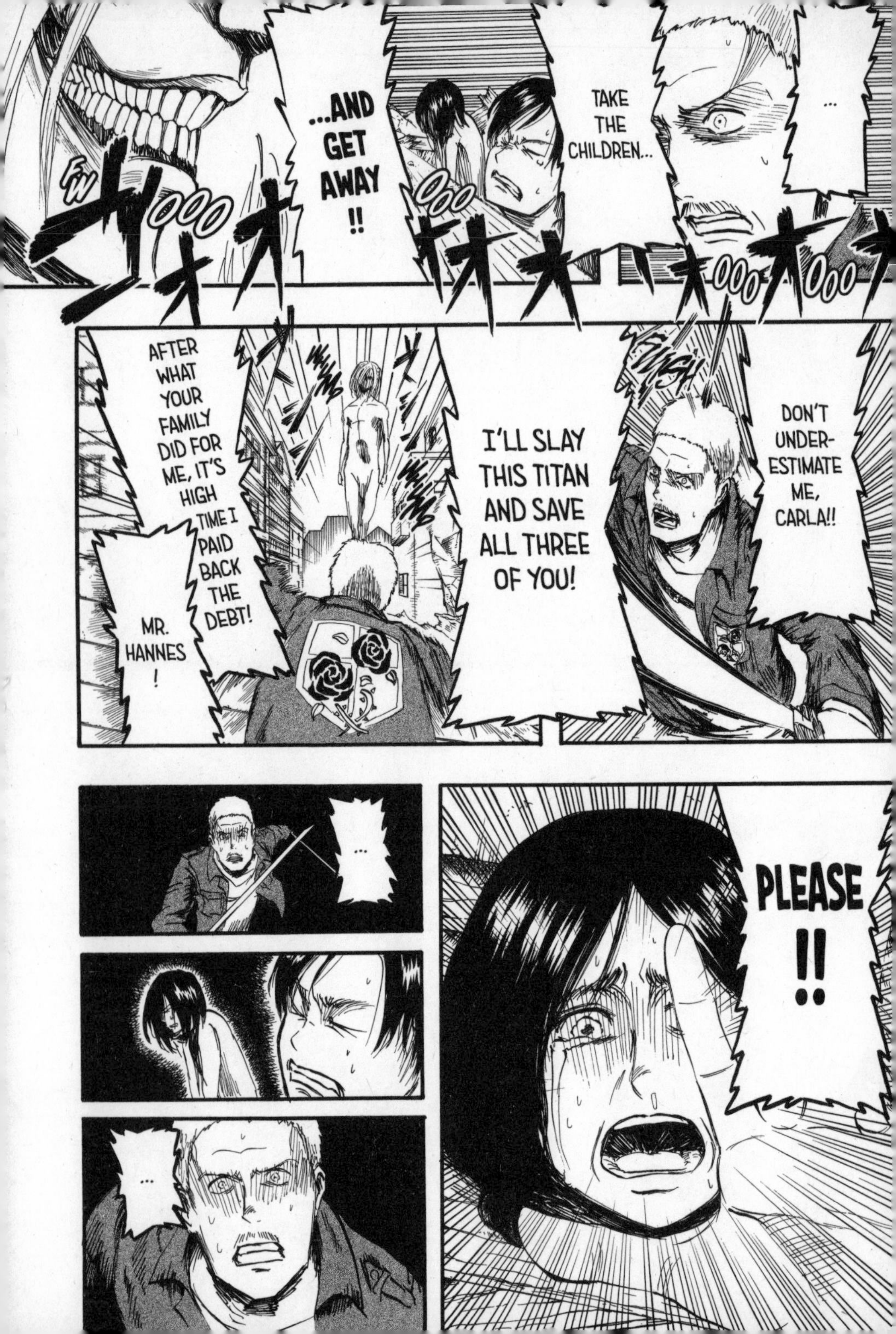
...
TAKE THE CHILDREN...
...AND GET AWAY!!
FWOOO
OOO
OOO
OOO
SHING
DON'T UNDER-ESTIMATE ME, CARLA!!
I'LL SLAY THIS TITAN AND SAVE ALL THREE OF YOU!
AFTER WHAT YOUR FAMILY DID FOR ME, IT'S HIGH TIME I PAID BACK THE DEBT!
MR. HANNES!
PLEASE!!
...
...

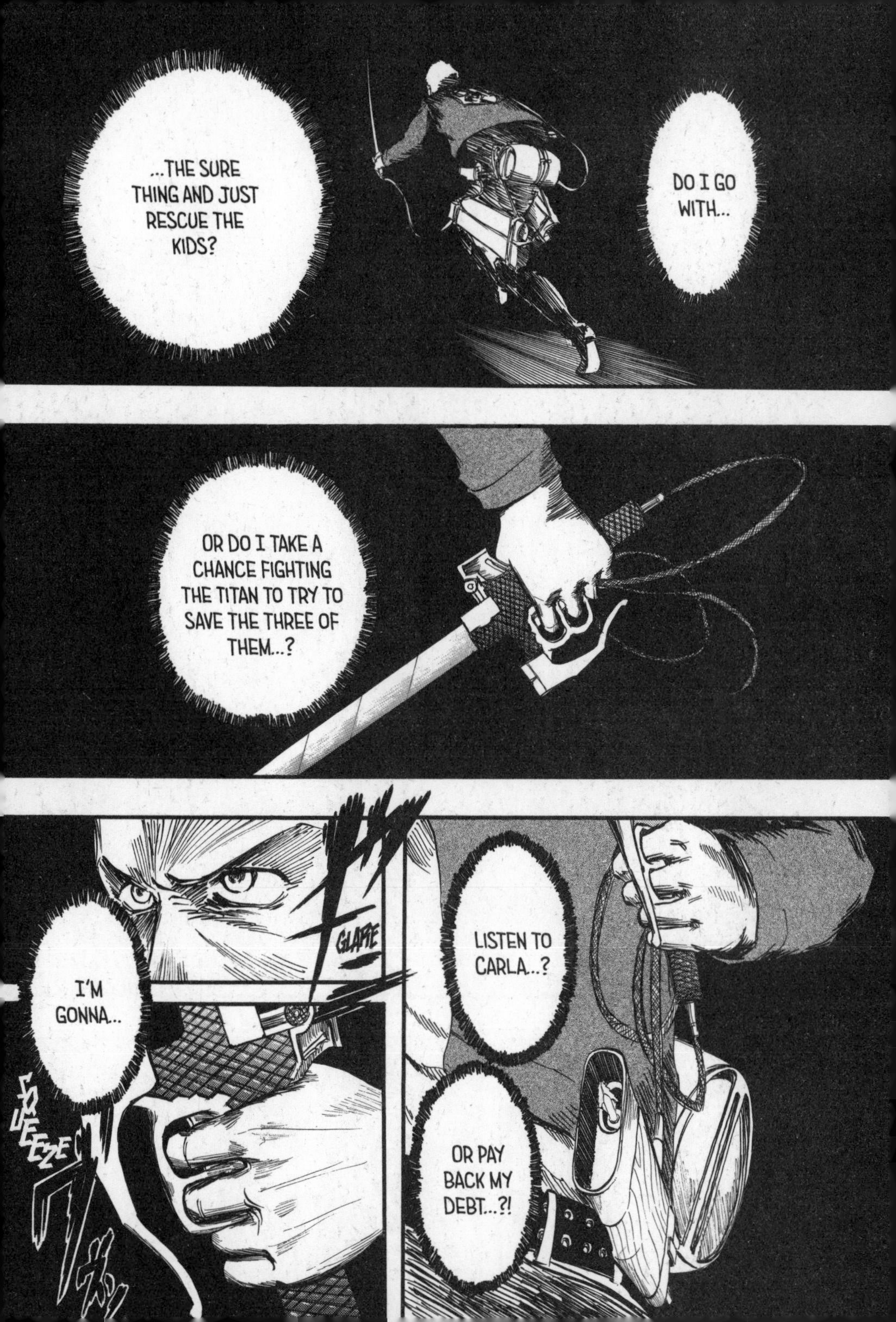
DO I GO WITH...
...THE SURE THING AND JUST RESCUE THE KIDS?
OR DO I TAKE A CHANCE FIGHTING THE TITAN TO TRY TO SAVE THE THREE OF THEM...?
GLARE
I'M GONNA...
LISTEN TO CARLA...?
OR PAY BACK MY DEBT...?!
SQUEEZE

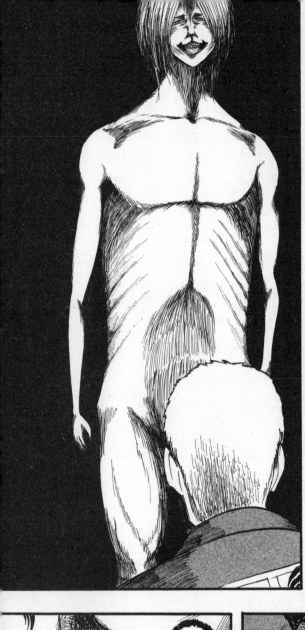
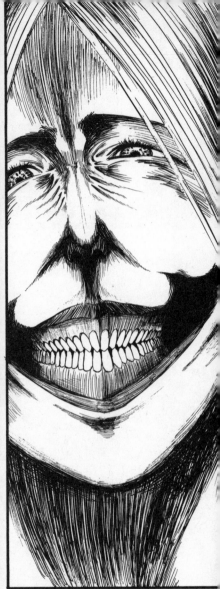

I...

QUIVER ブルル

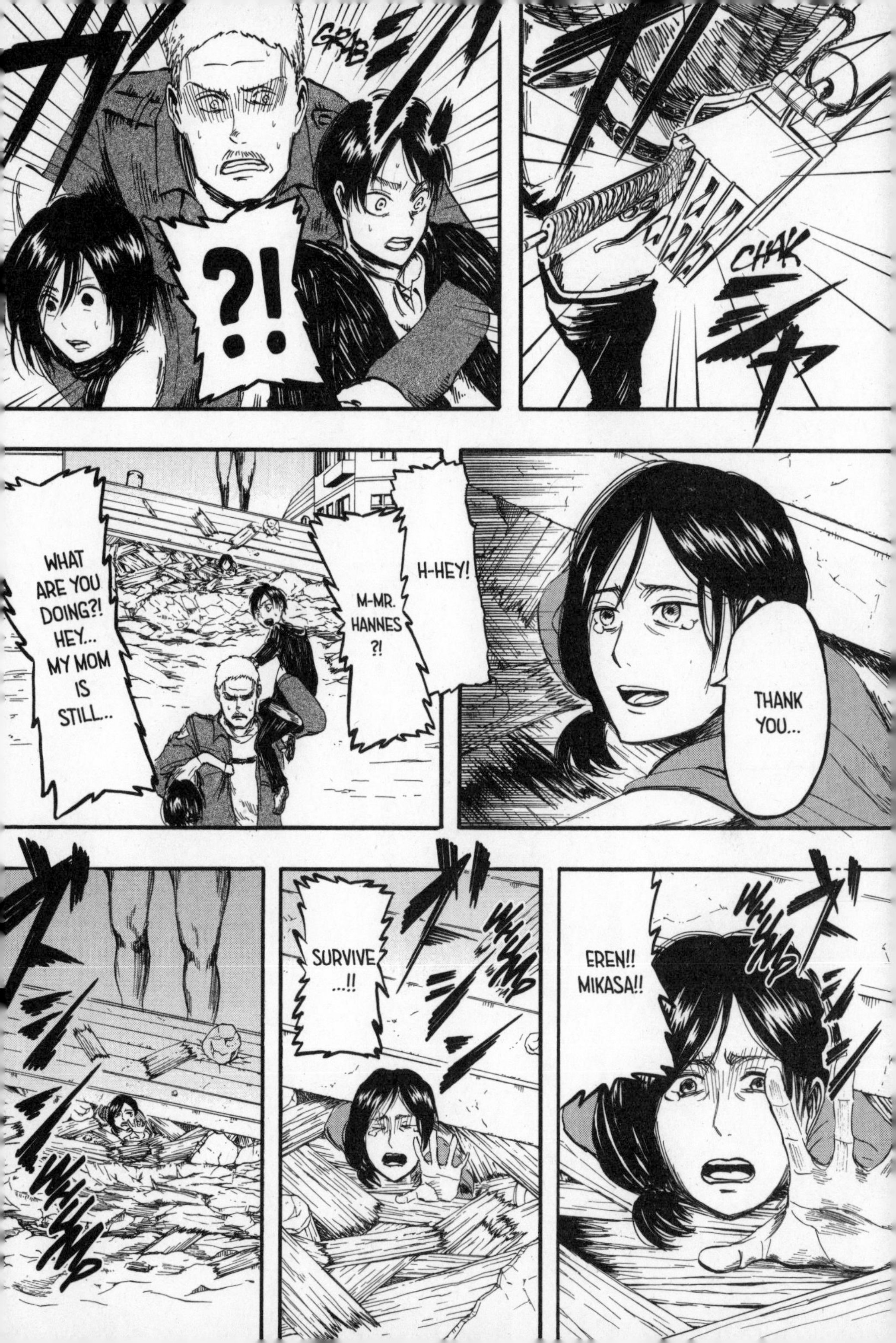
CHAK
GRAB
?!
THANK YOU...
H-HEY!
M-MR. HANNES ?!
WHAT ARE YOU DOING?! HEY... MY MOM IS STILL...
EREN!! MIKASA!!
WHUMP
SURVIVE ...!!
WHUMP
WHUMP

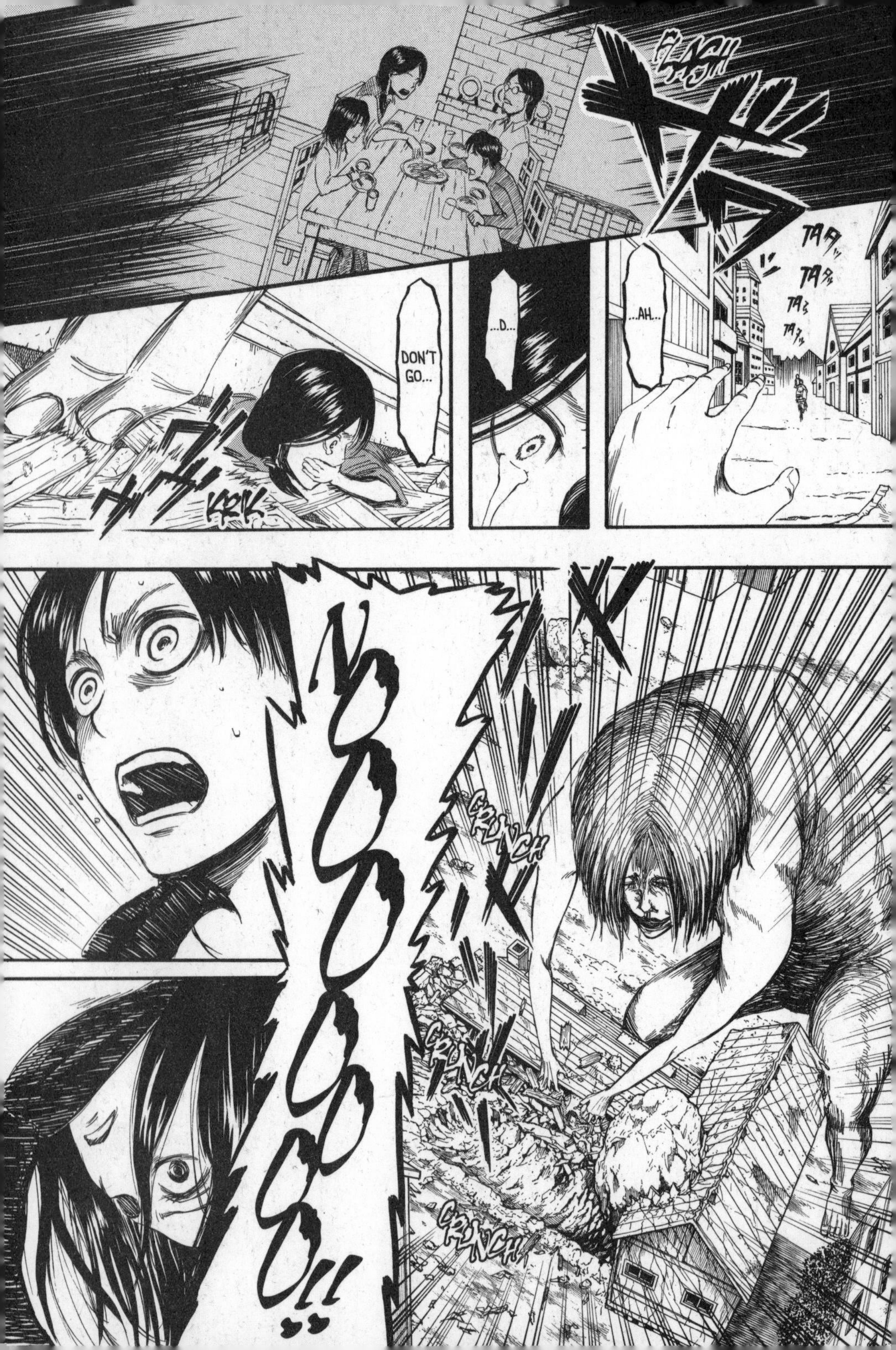

…AH…
TA
TA
TA
TA
…D…
DON'T GO…
KRIK
NOOOOOOOO!!
CRUNCH
CRUNCH
CRUNCH

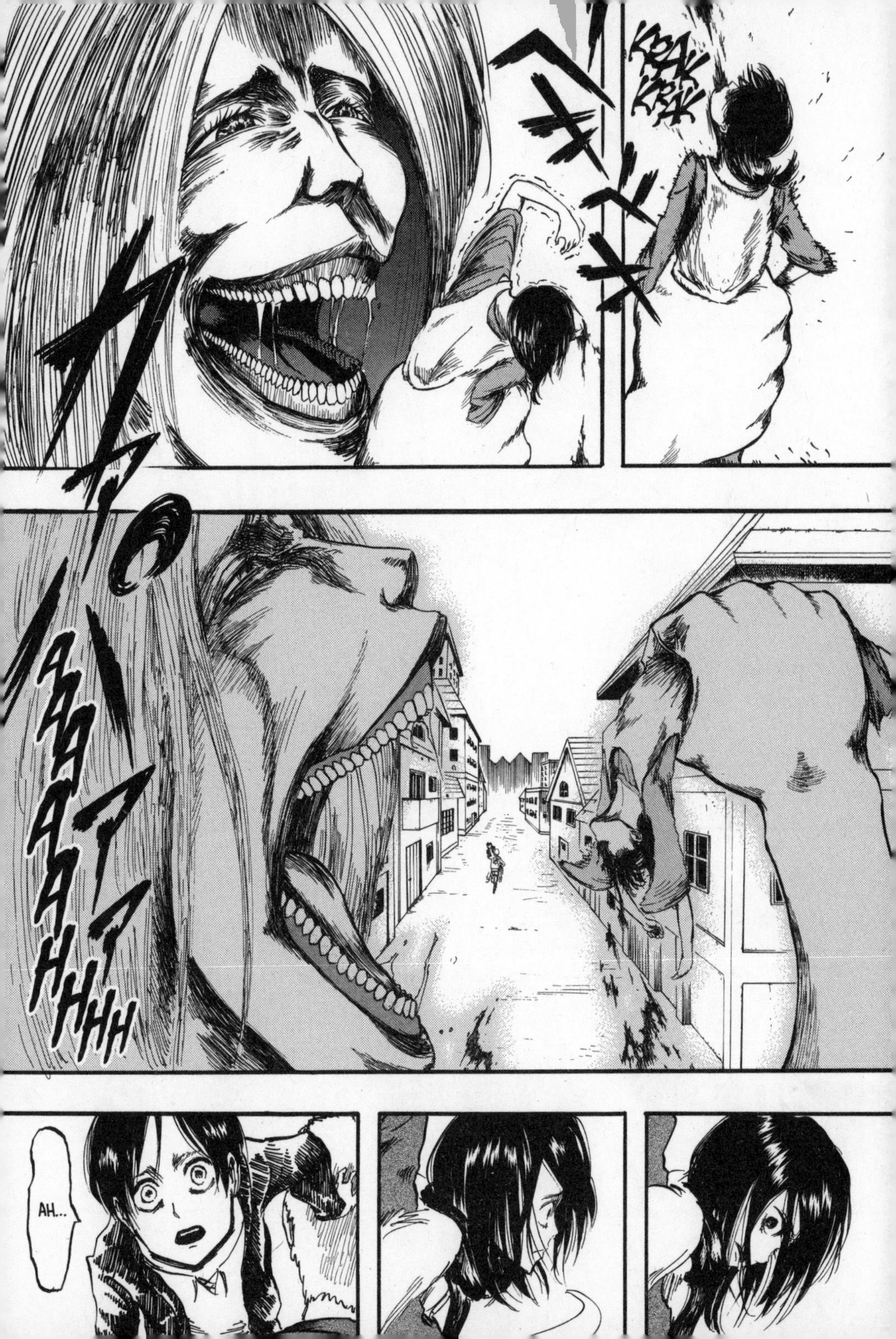
KRAK KRAK
AAAAAHHHH
AH...

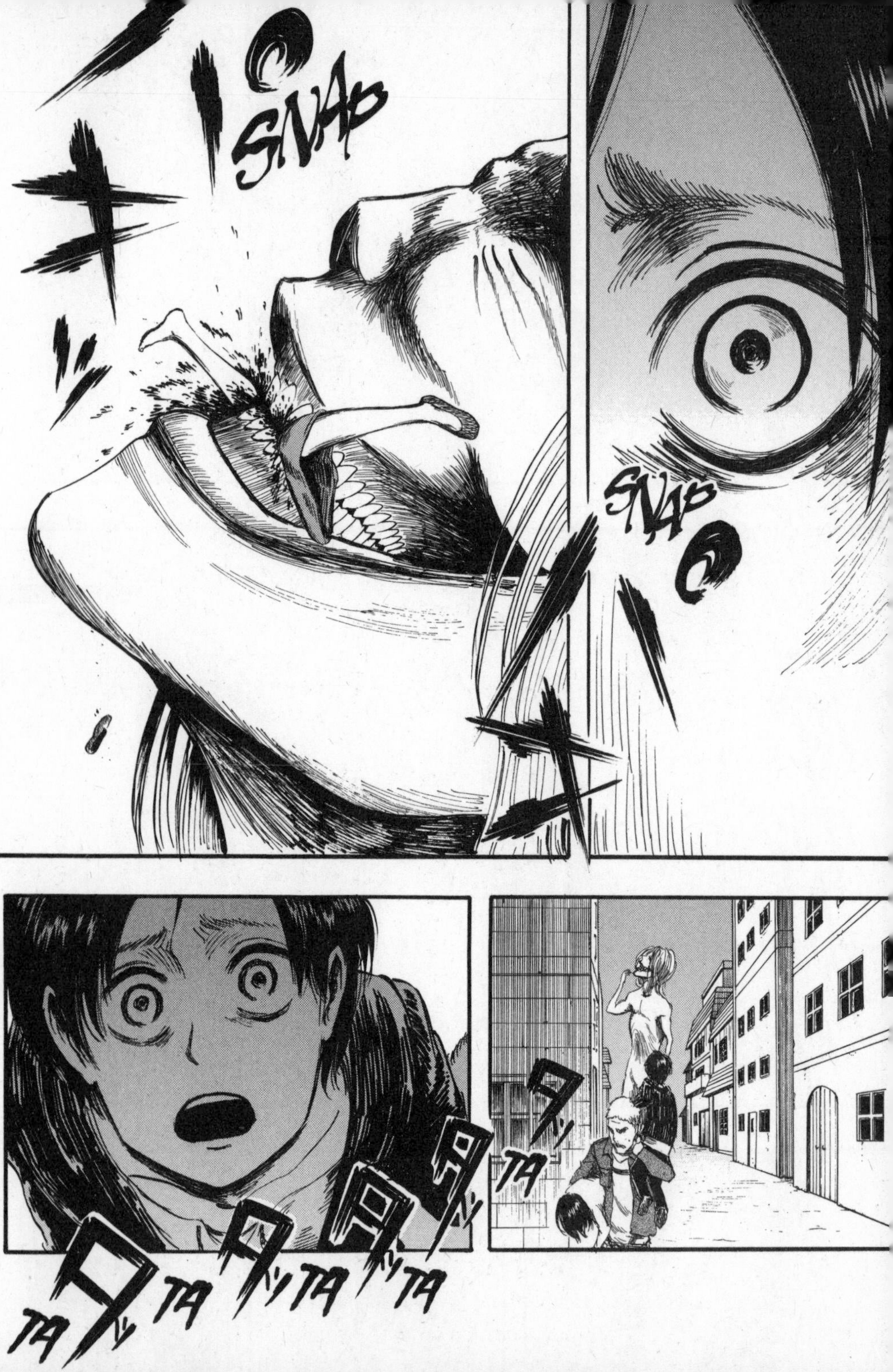
SNAP
SNAP
TA
TA TA TA TA TA

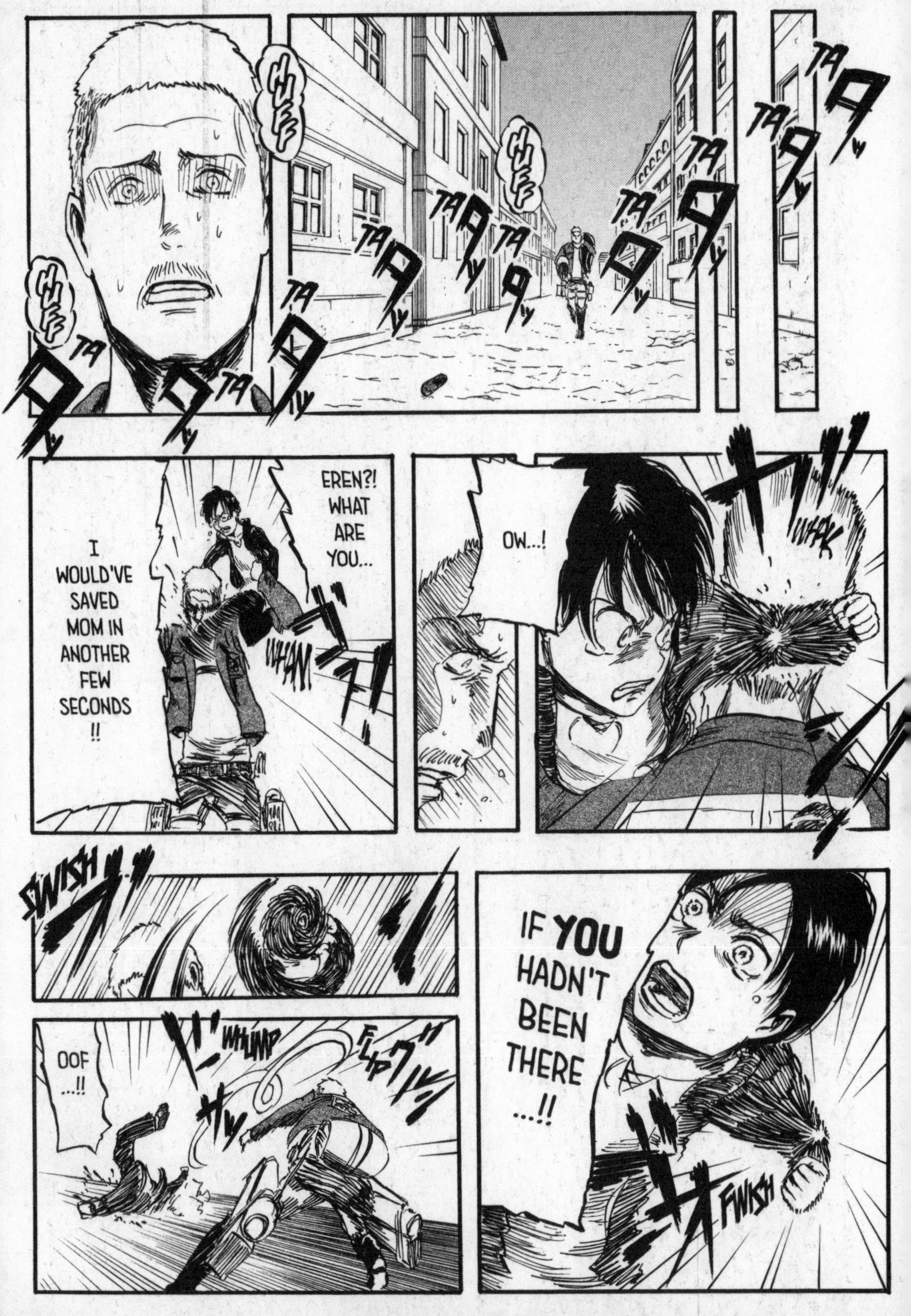
TA
TA
TA
TA
HUFF
TA
TA
TA
TA
HUFF
HUFF
TA
TA
TA
OW...!
WHAK
EREN?! WHAT ARE YOU...
I WOULD'VE SAVED MOM IN ANOTHER FEW SECONDS !!
WHAM
IF YOU HADN'T BEEN THERE ...!!
FWISH
SWISH
WHUMP
FLIP
OOF ...!!

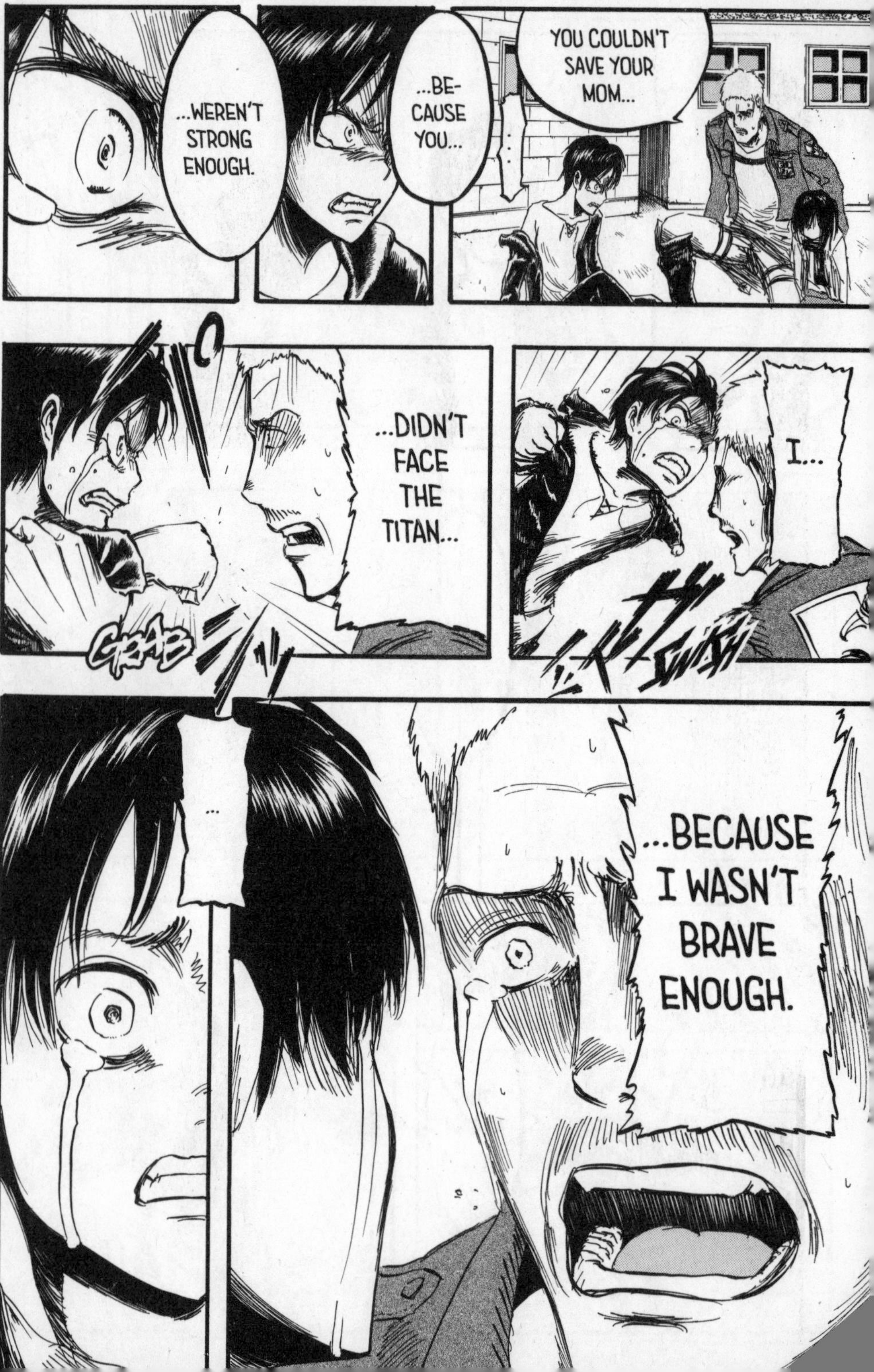
YOU COULDN'T SAVE YOUR MOM...
...BE- CAUSE YOU...
...WEREN'T STRONG ENOUGH.
I...
SWISH
...DIDN'T FACE THE TITAN...
GRAB
...BECAUSE I WASN'T BRAVE ENOUGH.
...

UHN...

...

I'M SORRY...

I'M SORRY...

FWOOOO

THIS AGAIN...

OH...

THROB

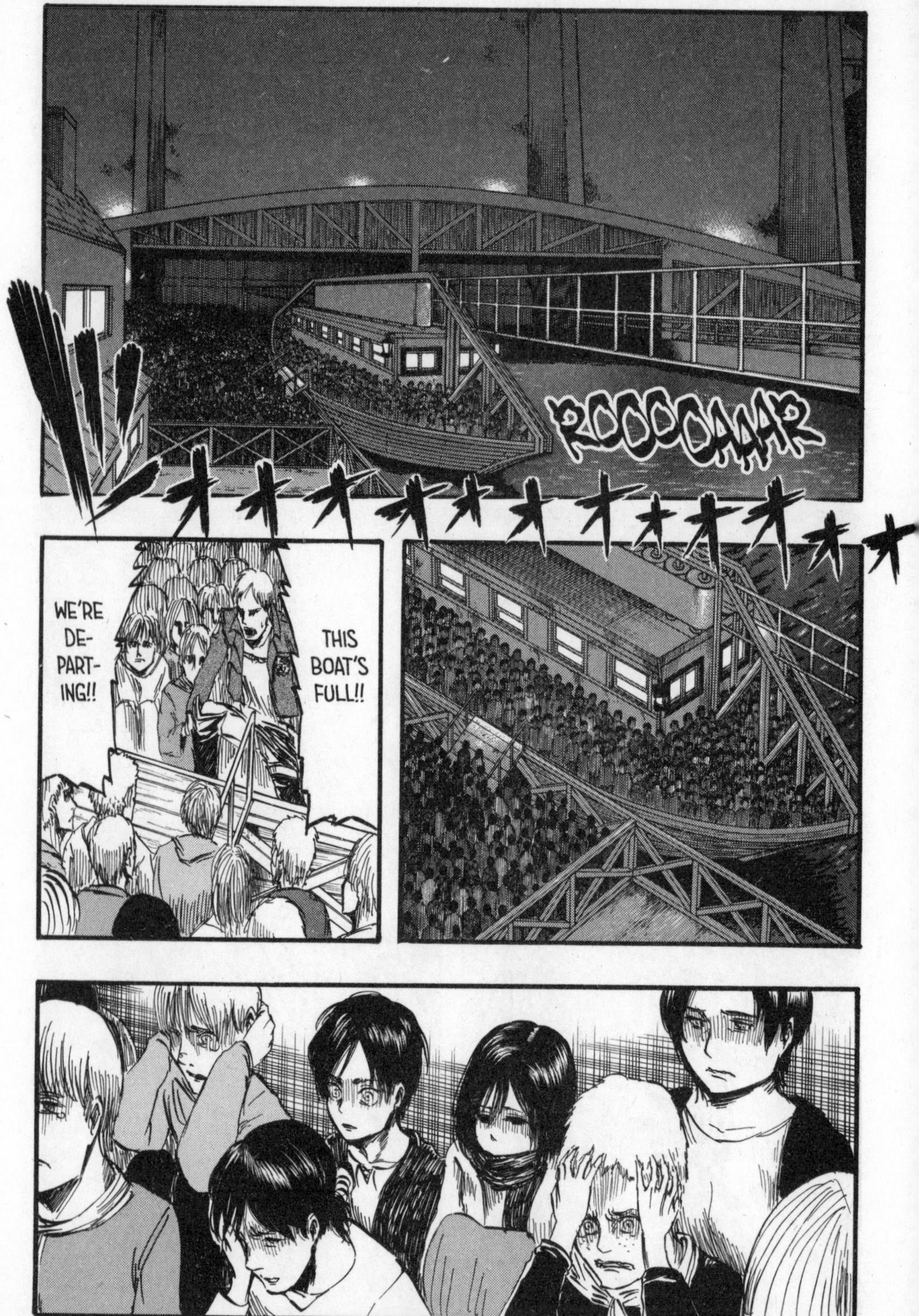
ROOOOAAR
THIS BOAT'S FULL!!
WE'RE DE-PART-ING!!

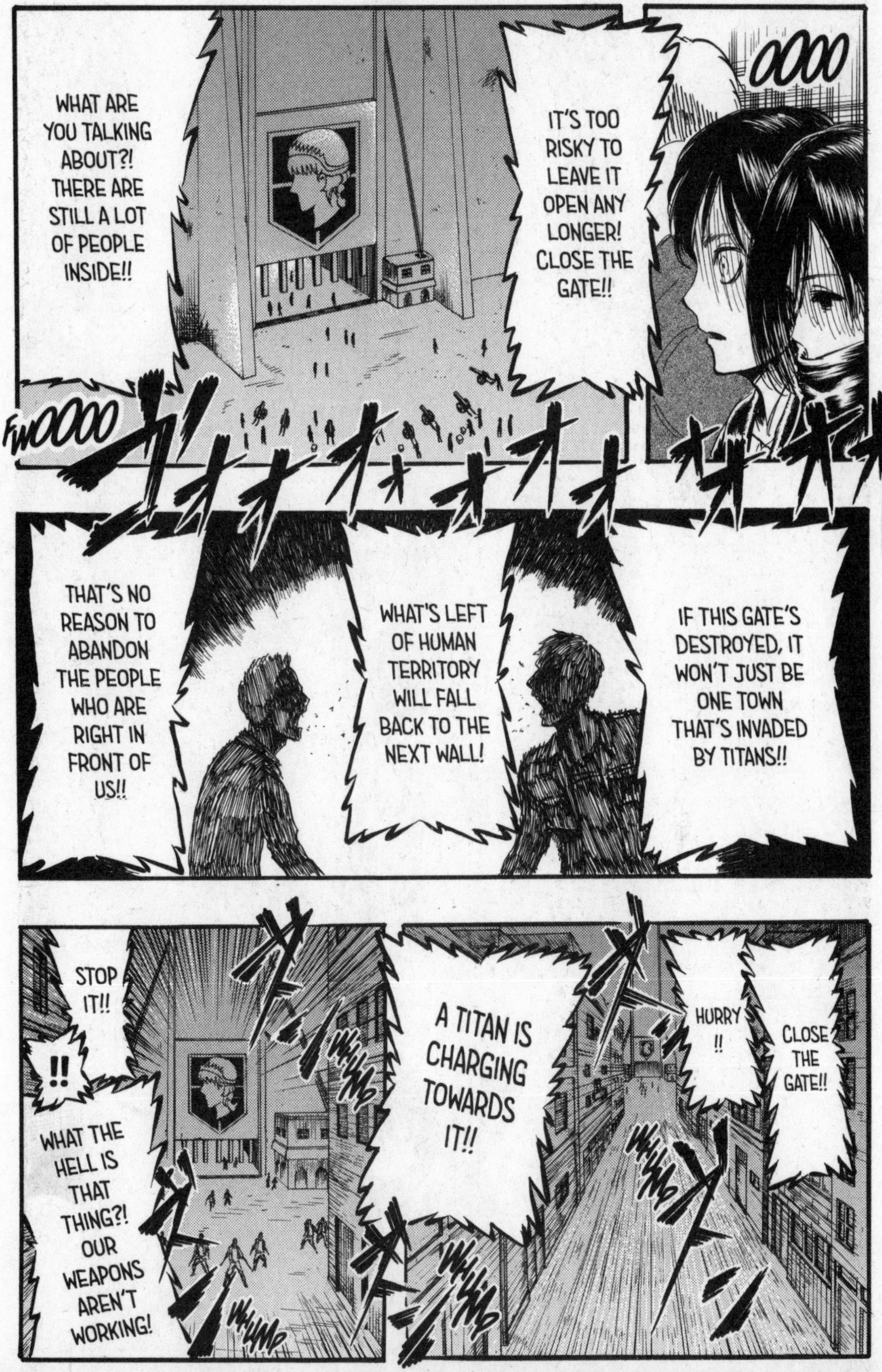
OOOO
IT'S TOO RISKY TO LEAVE IT OPEN ANY LONGER! CLOSE THE GATE!!
WHAT ARE YOU TALKING ABOUT?! THERE ARE STILL A LOT OF PEOPLE INSIDE!!
FWOOOO
IF THIS GATE'S DESTROYED, IT WON'T JUST BE ONE TOWN THAT'S INVADED BY TITANS!!
WHAT'S LEFT OF HUMAN TERRITORY WILL FALL BACK TO THE NEXT WALL!
THAT'S NO REASON TO ABANDON THE PEOPLE WHO ARE RIGHT IN FRONT OF US!!
CLOSE THE GATE!!
HURRY!!
A TITAN IS CHARGING TOWARDS IT!!
WHUMP
STOP IT!!
!!
WHAT THE HELL IS THAT THING?! OUR WEAPONS AREN'T WORKING!
WHUMP

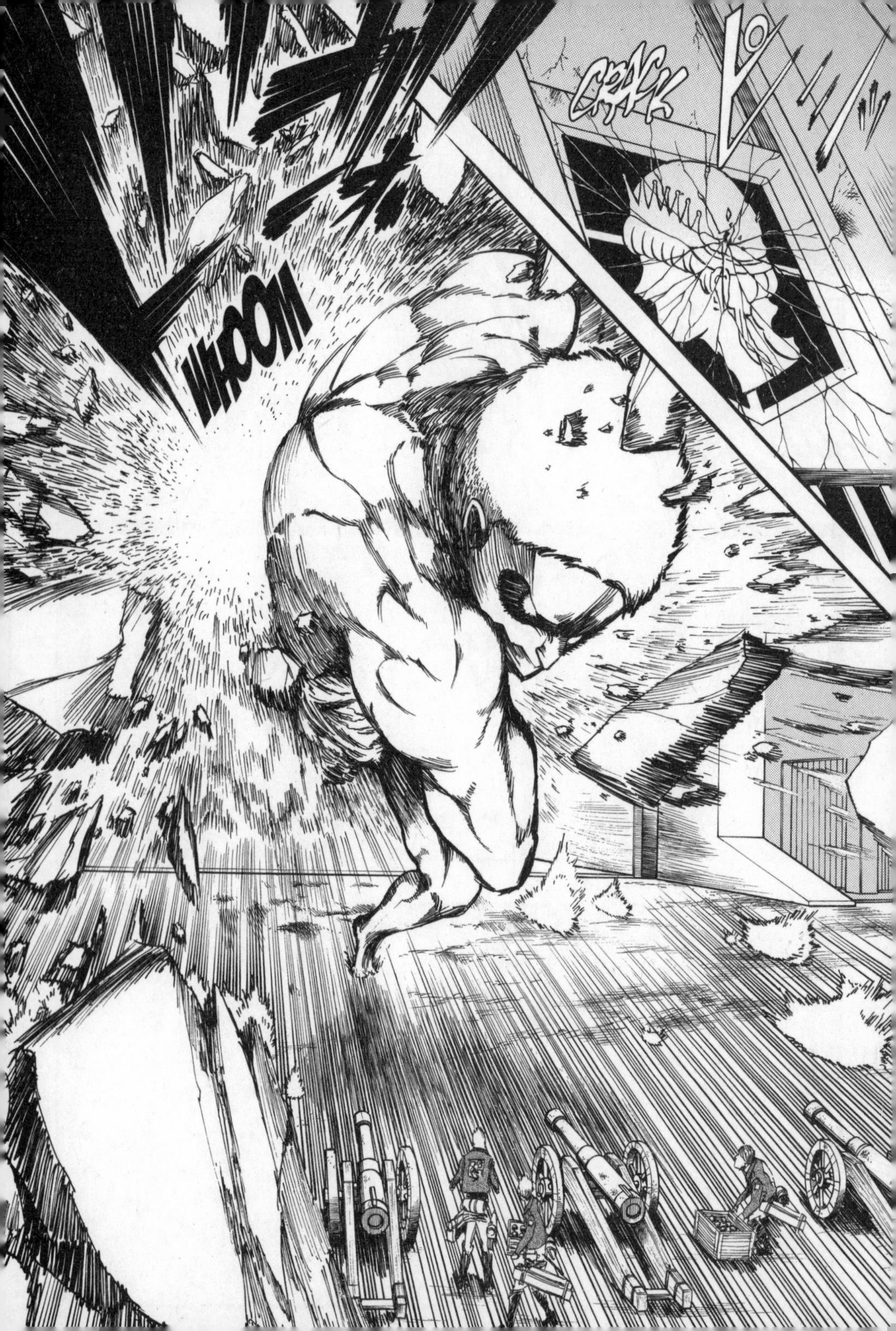
CRACK
WHOOM

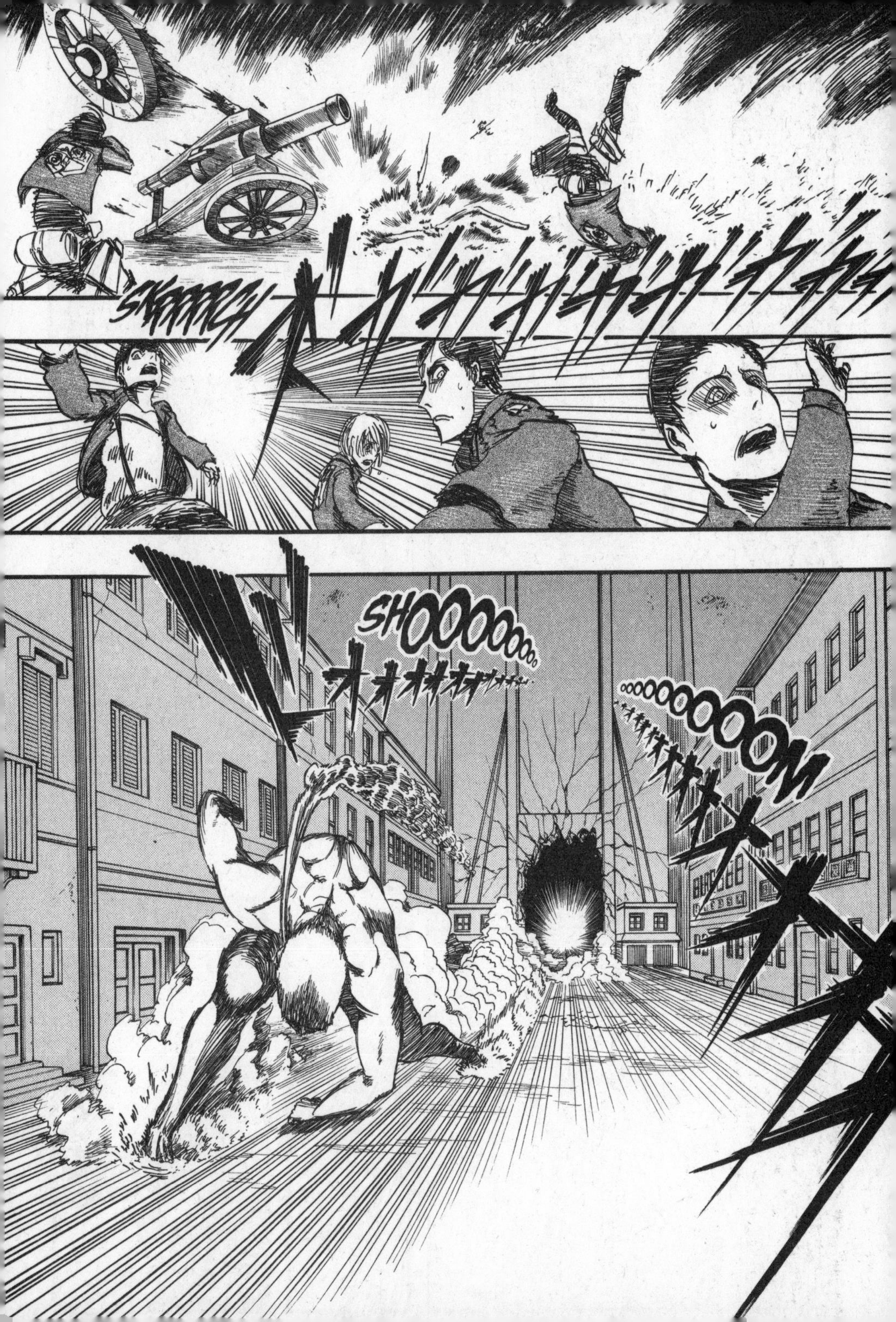
SKRRRRCH
SHOOOOOooo
oooooOOOOOOM

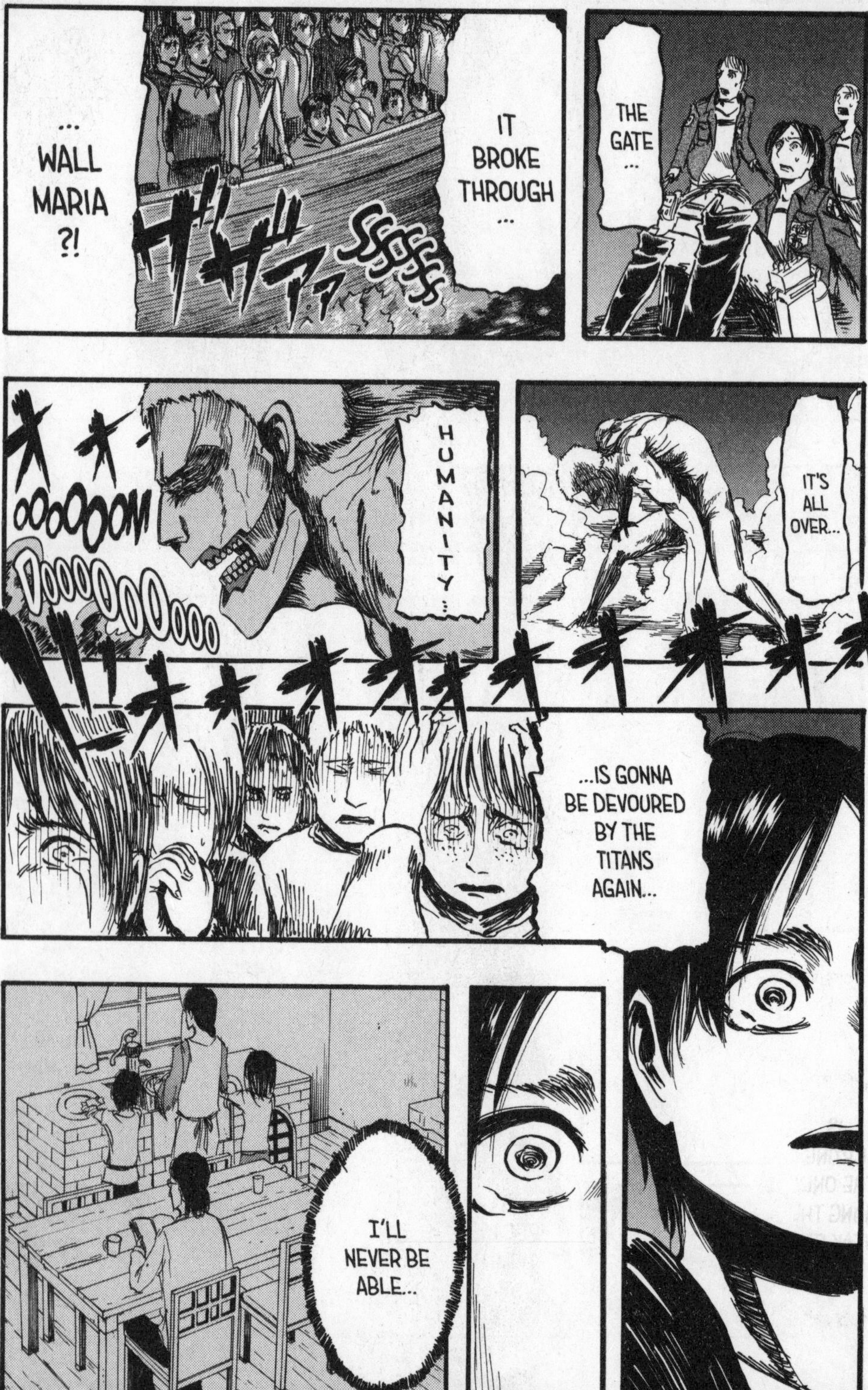
THE GATE ...
IT BROKE THROUGH ...
... WALL MARIA ?!
IT'S ALL OVER...
HUMANITY...
OOOOOOM
DOOOOOOOooo
...IS GONNA BE DEVOURED BY THE TITANS AGAIN...
I'LL NEVER BE ABLE...

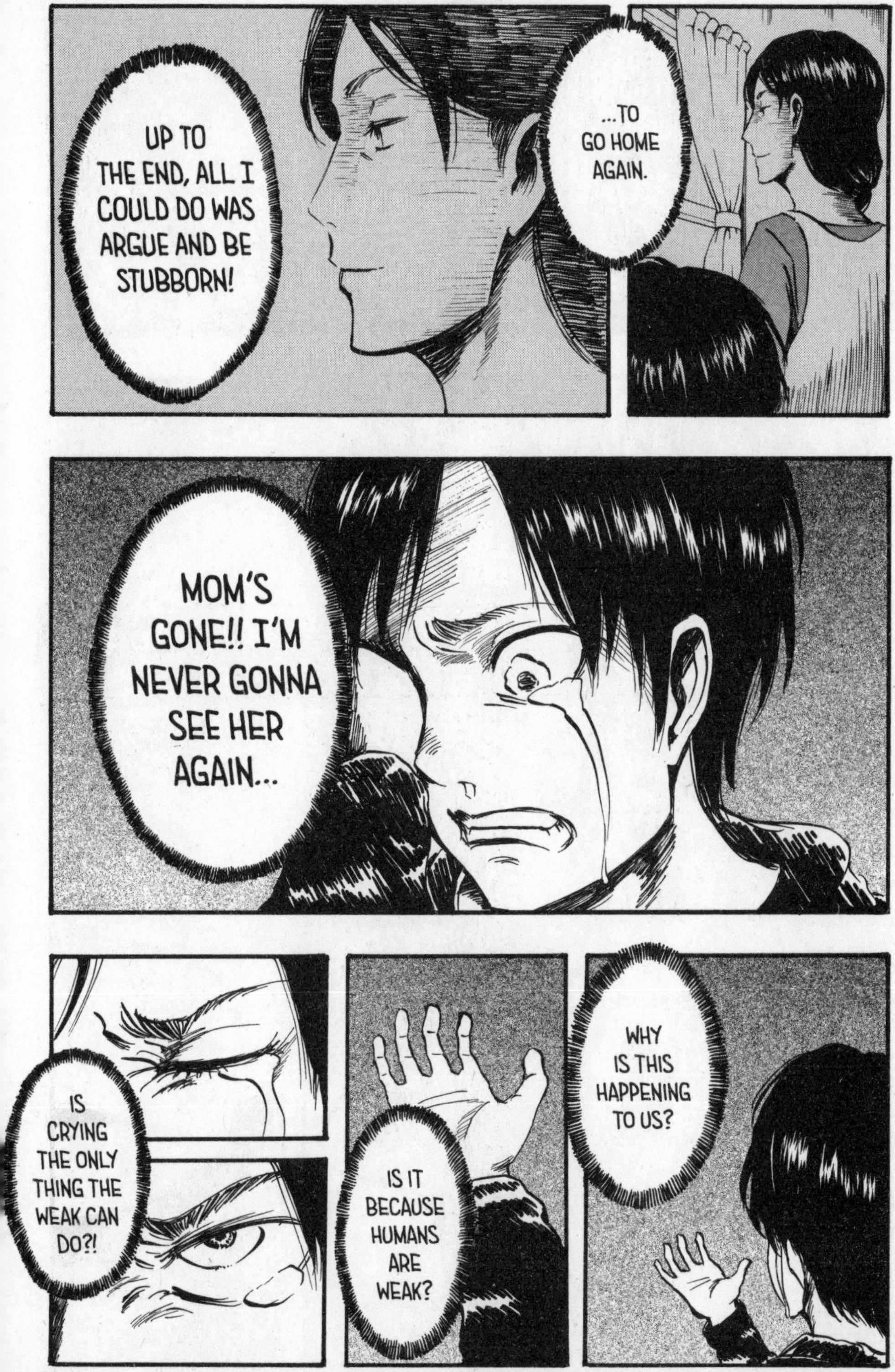
...TO GO HOME AGAIN.
UP TO THE END, ALL I COULD DO WAS ARGUE AND BE STUBBORN!
MOM'S GONE!! I'M NEVER GONNA SEE HER AGAIN...
WHY IS THIS HAPPENING TO US?
IS IT BECAUSE HUMANS ARE WEAK?
IS CRYING THE ONLY THING THE WEAK CAN DO?!

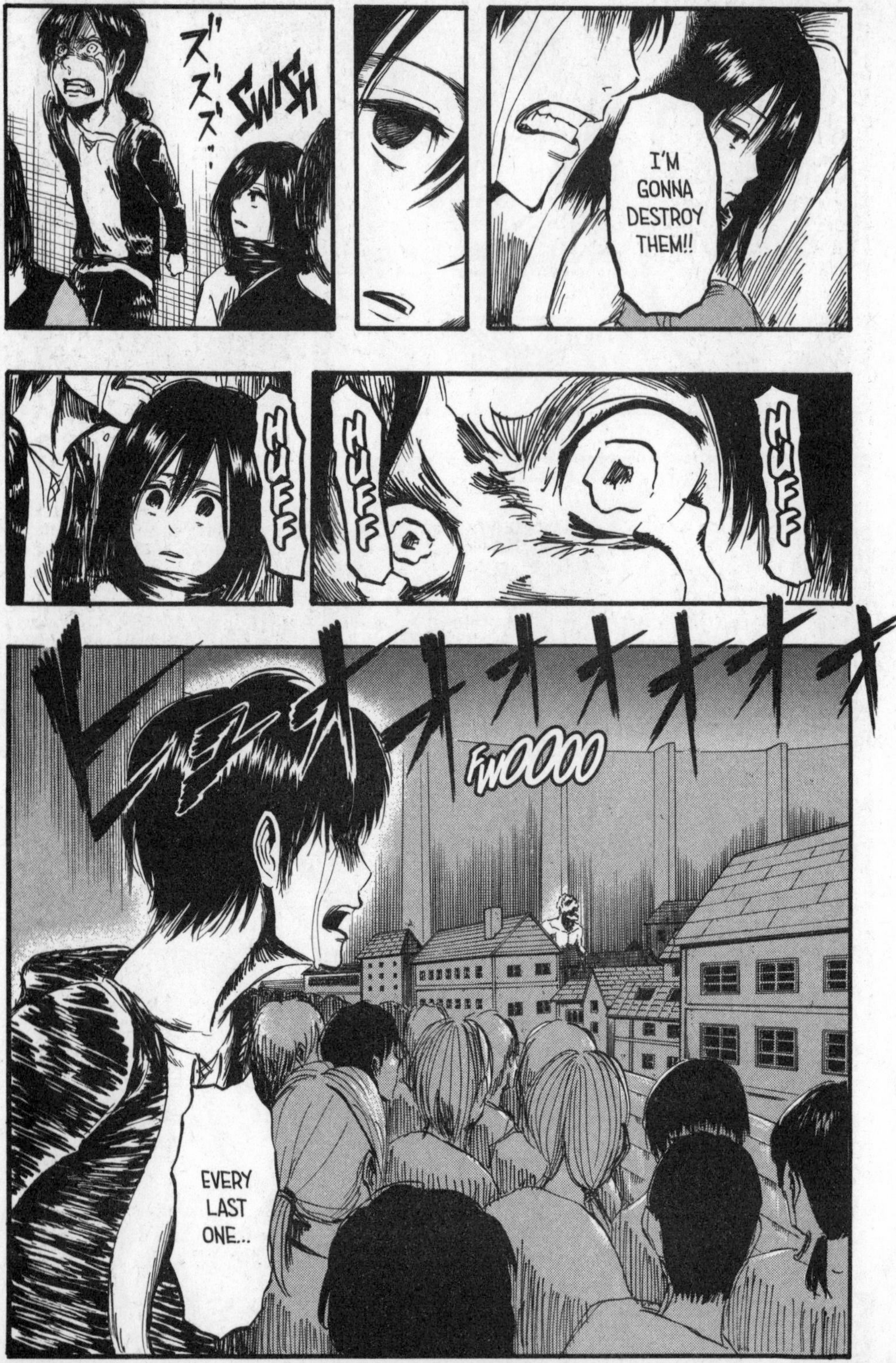
I'M GONNA DESTROY THEM!!
SWISH
ズズズ…
HUFF
HUFF
HUFF
FWOOOO
EVERY LAST ONE...

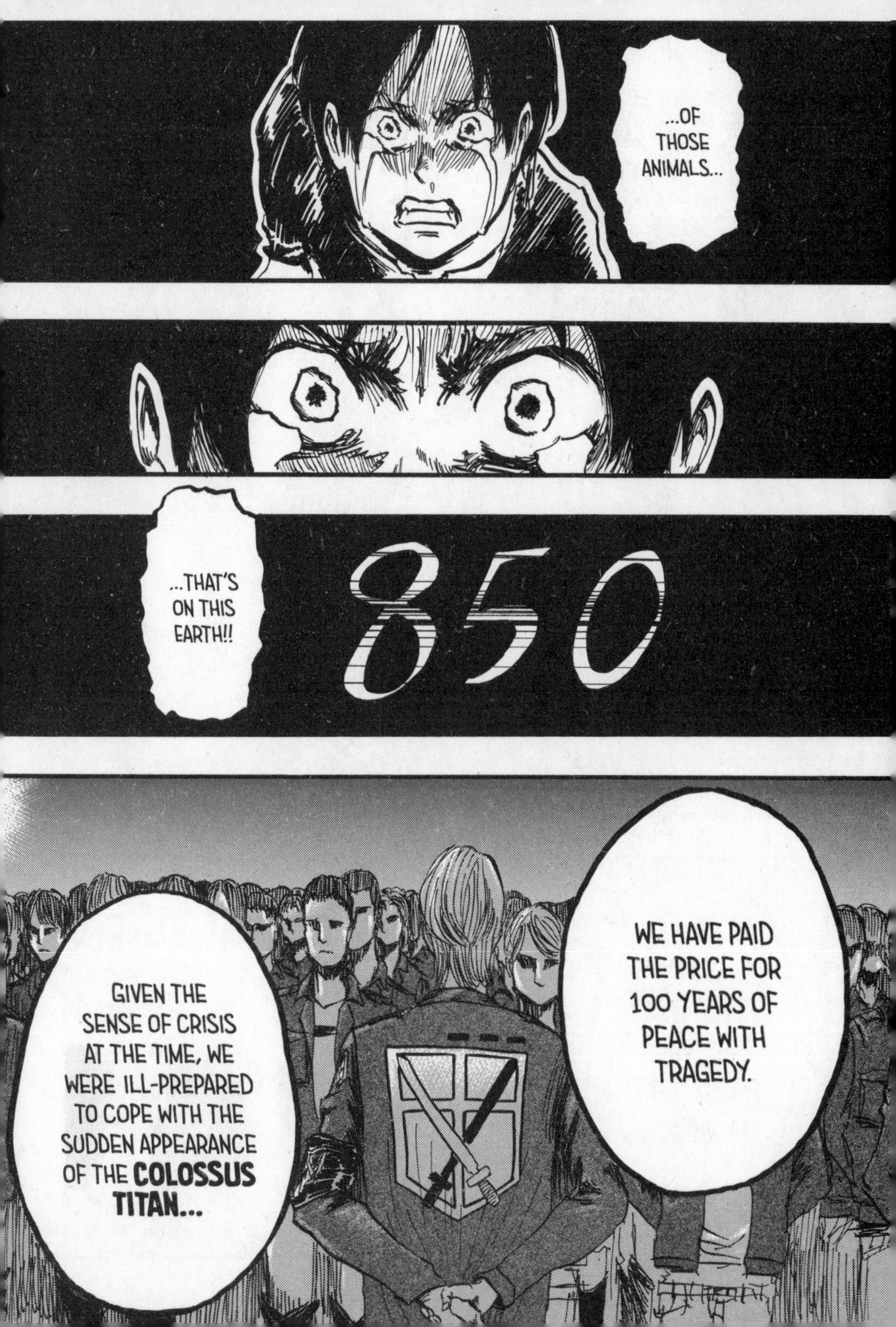
...OF THOSE ANIMALS...
...THAT'S ON THIS EARTH!!
850
WE HAVE PAID THE PRICE FOR 100 YEARS OF PEACE WITH TRAGEDY.
GIVEN THE SENSE OF CRISIS AT THE TIME, WE WERE ILL-PREPARED TO COPE WITH THE SUDDEN APPEARANCE OF THE **COLOSSUS TITAN...**

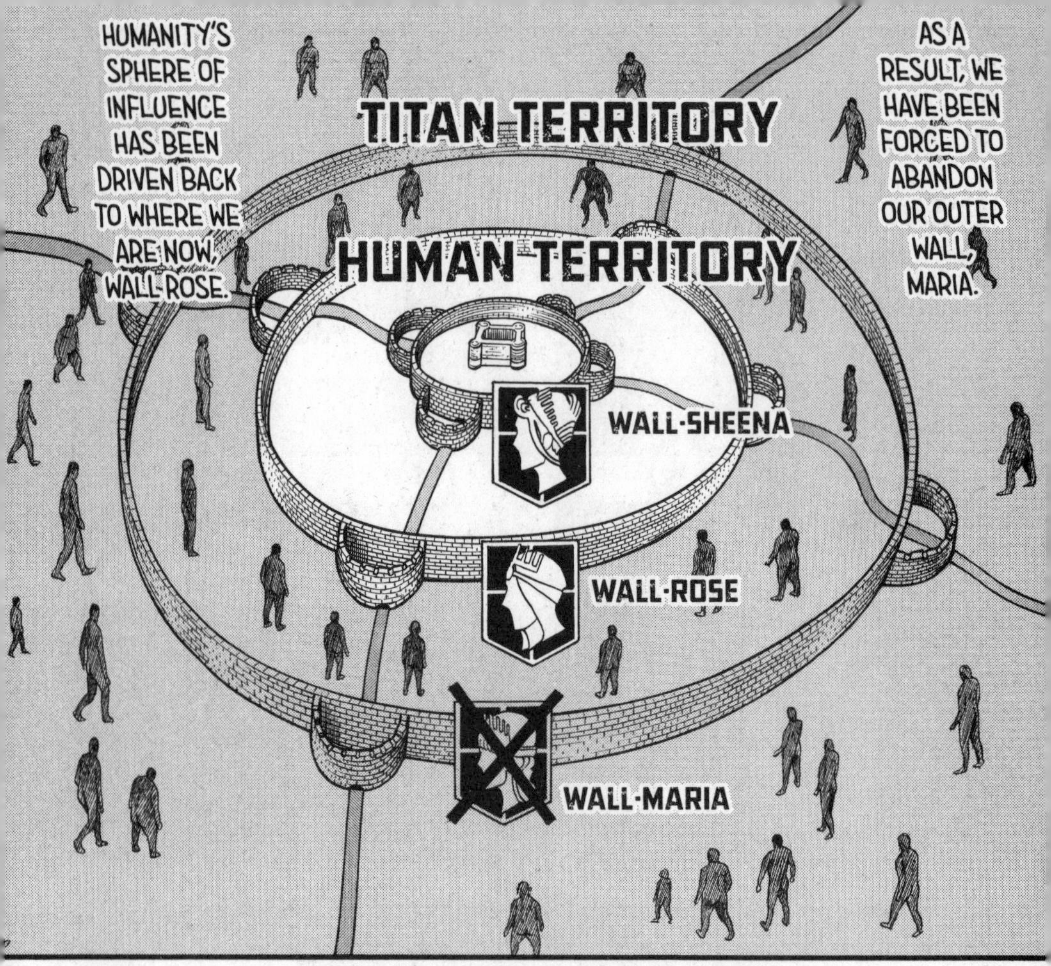
AS A RESULT, WE HAVE BEEN FORCED TO ABANDON OUR OUTER WALL, MARIA.
HUMANITY'S SPHERE OF INFLUENCE HAS BEEN DRIVEN BACK TO WHERE WE ARE NOW, WALL ROSE.
TITAN TERRITORY
HUMAN TERRITORY
WALL-SHEENA
WALL-ROSE
WALL-MARIA
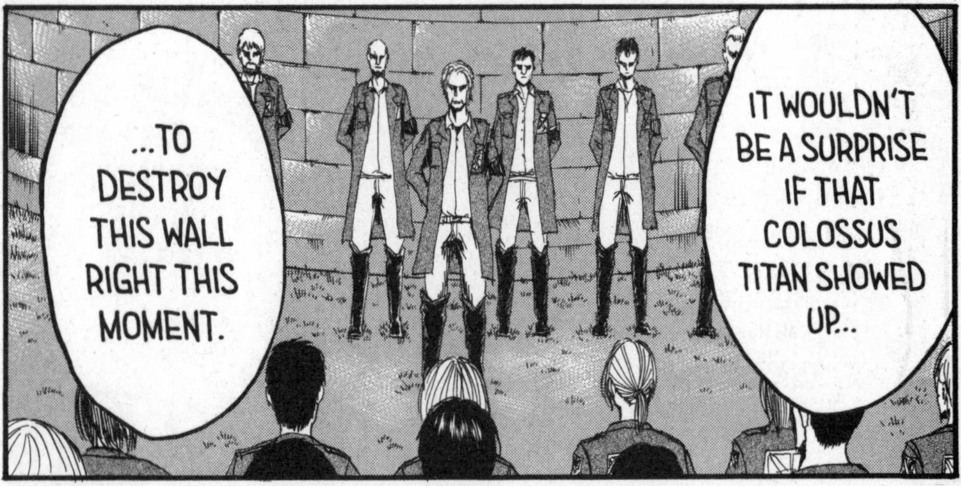
IT WOULDN'T BE A SURPRISE IF THAT COLOSSUS TITAN SHOWED UP...
...TO DESTROY THIS WALL RIGHT THIS MOMENT.

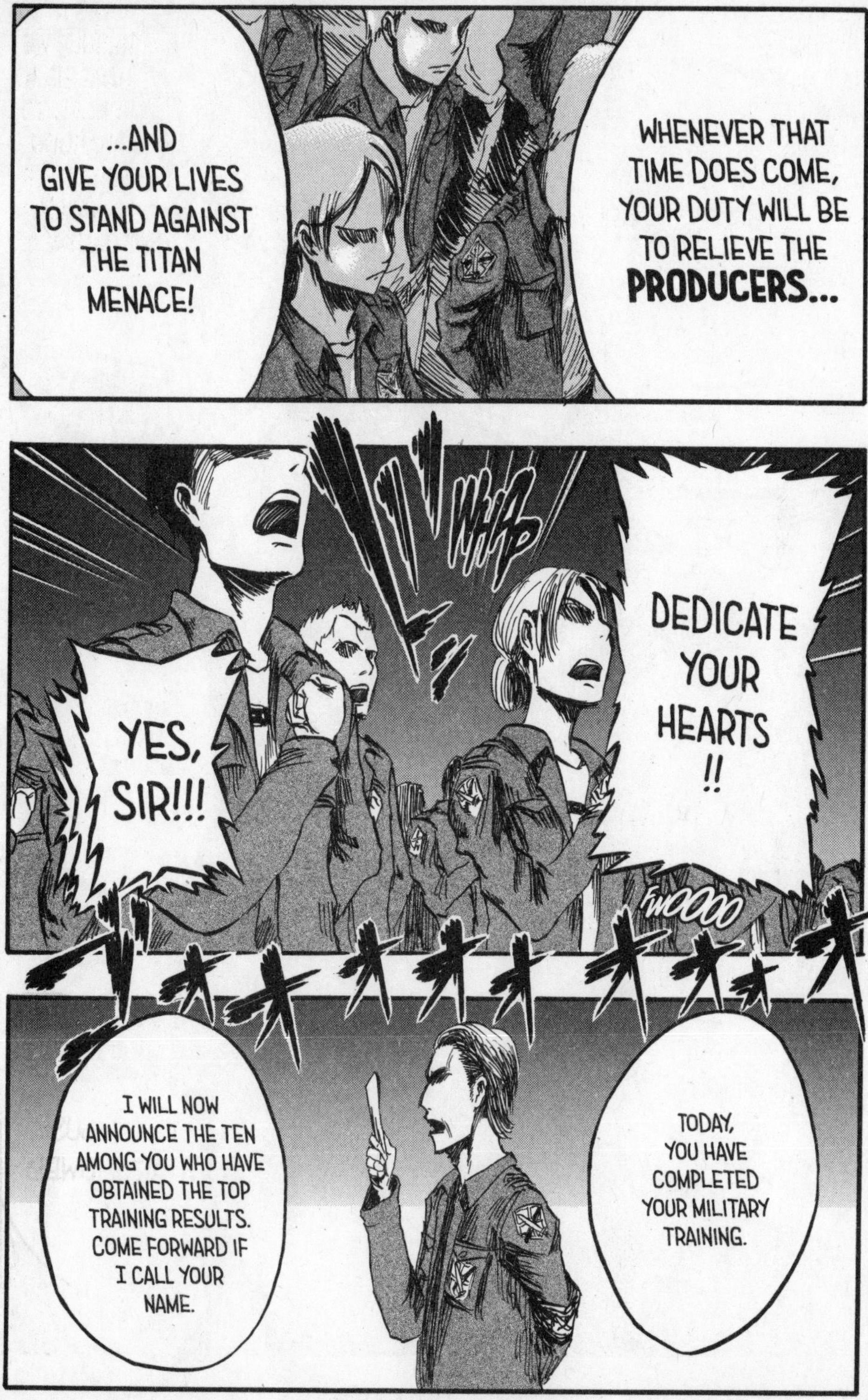
WHENEVER THAT TIME DOES COME, YOUR DUTY WILL BE TO RELIEVE THE **PRODUCERS...**
...AND GIVE YOUR LIVES TO STAND AGAINST THE TITAN MENACE!
WHIP
DEDICATE YOUR HEARTS !!
YES, SIR!!!
FWOOOO
TODAY, YOU HAVE COMPLETED YOUR MILITARY TRAINING.
I WILL NOW ANNOUNCE THE TEN AMONG YOU WHO HAVE OBTAINED THE TOP TRAINING RESULTS. COME FORWARD IF I CALL YOUR NAME.

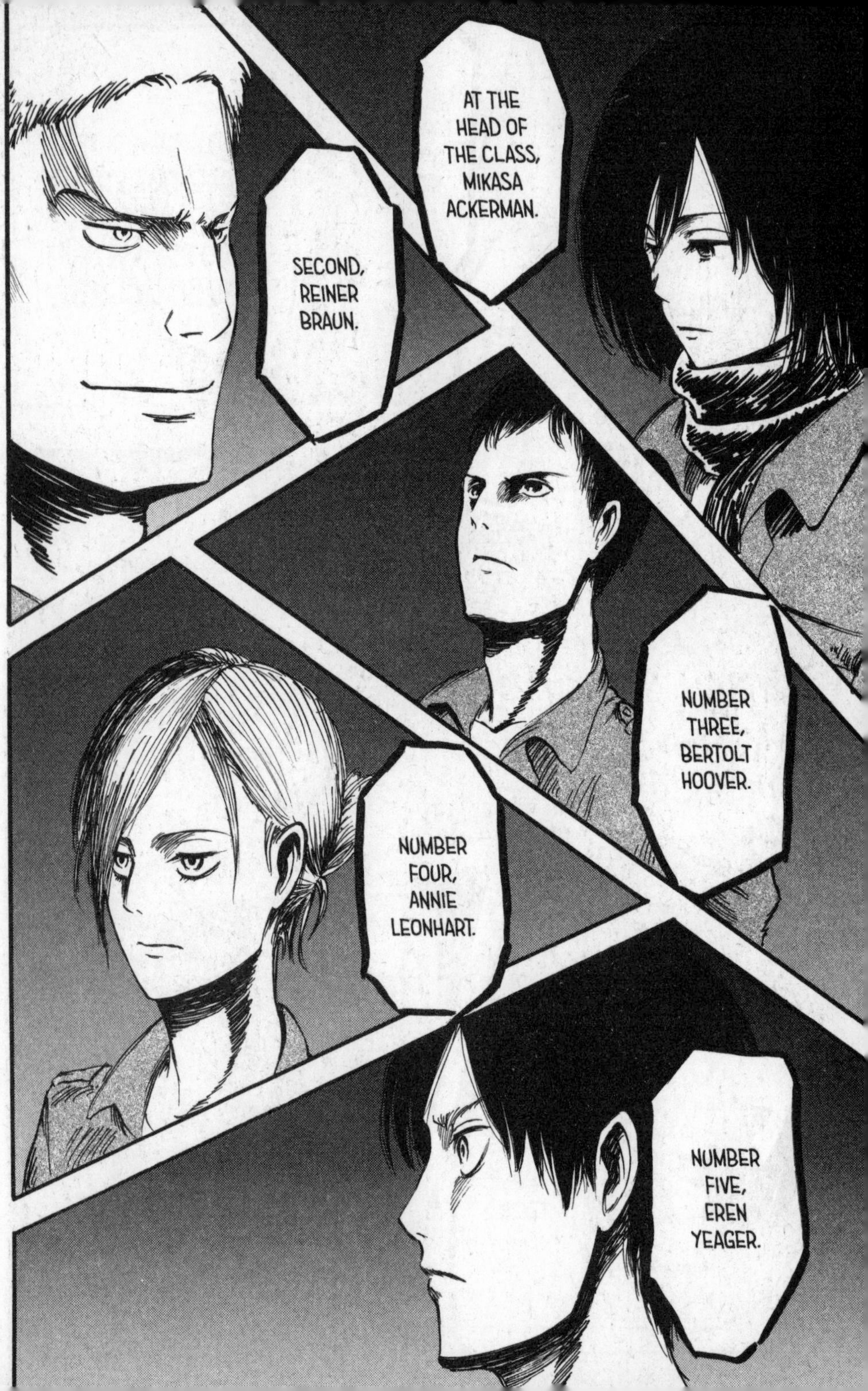
AT THE HEAD OF THE CLASS, MIKASA ACKERMAN.
SECOND, REINER BRAUN.
NUMBER THREE, BERTOLT HOOVER.
NUMBER FOUR, ANNIE LEONHART.
NUMBER FIVE, EREN YEAGER.

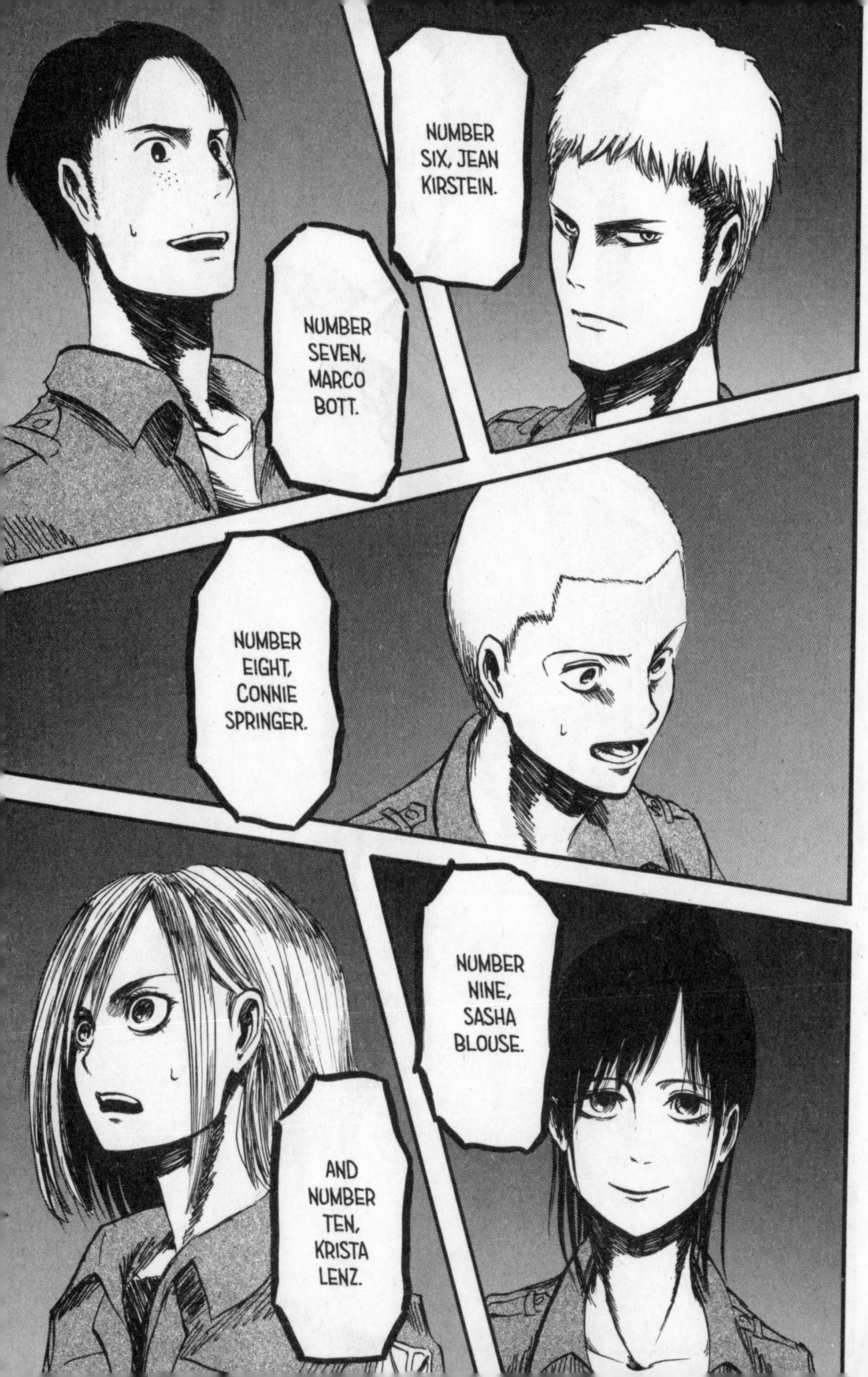
NUMBER SIX, JEAN KIRSTEIN.
NUMBER SEVEN, MARCO BOTT.
NUMBER EIGHT, CONNIE SPRINGER.
NUMBER NINE, SASHA BLOUSE.
AND NUMBER TEN, KRISTA LENZ.

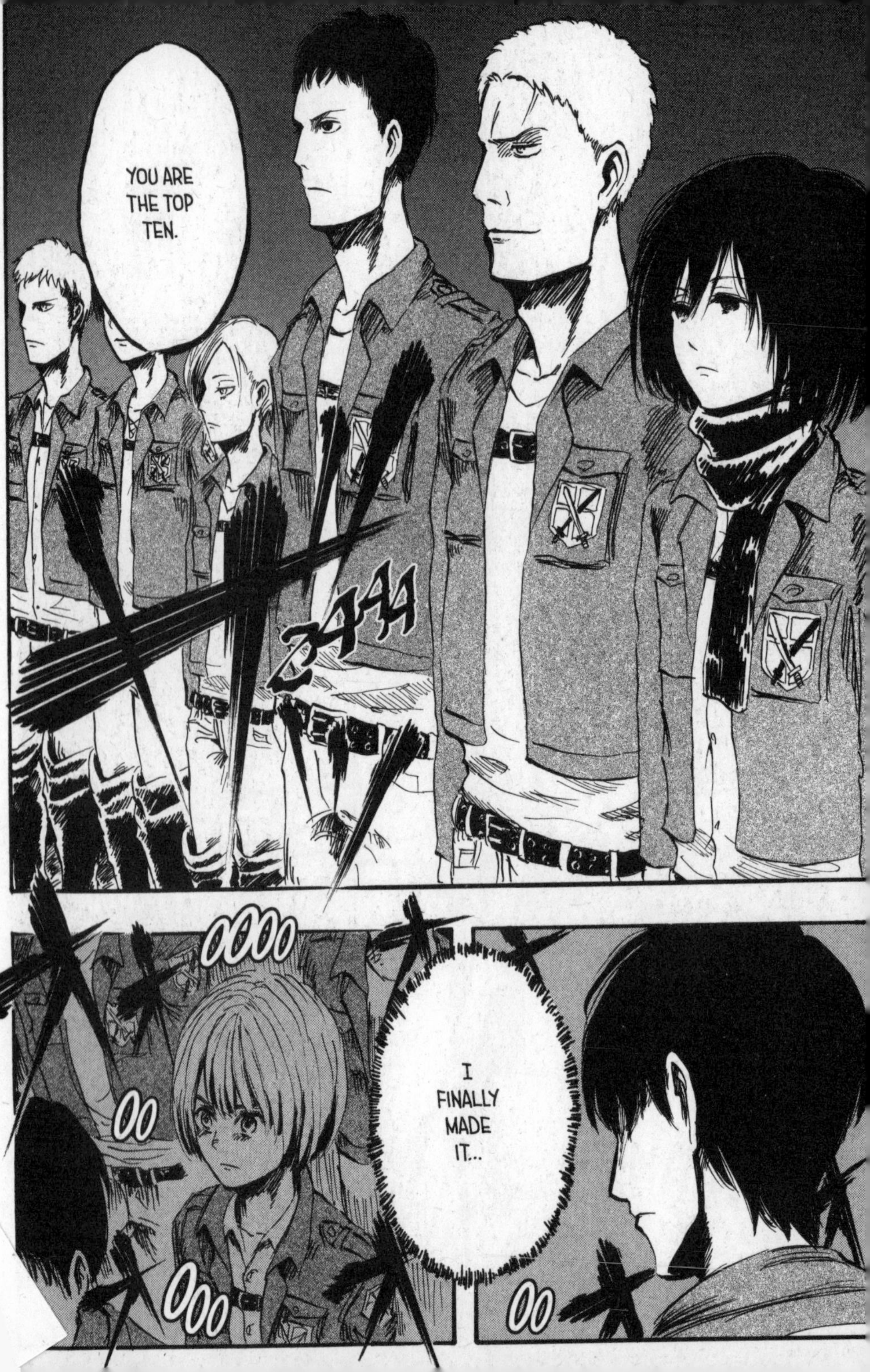
YOU ARE THE TOP TEN.
ZAAA
OOOO
OO
OOO
I FINALLY MADE IT...
OO

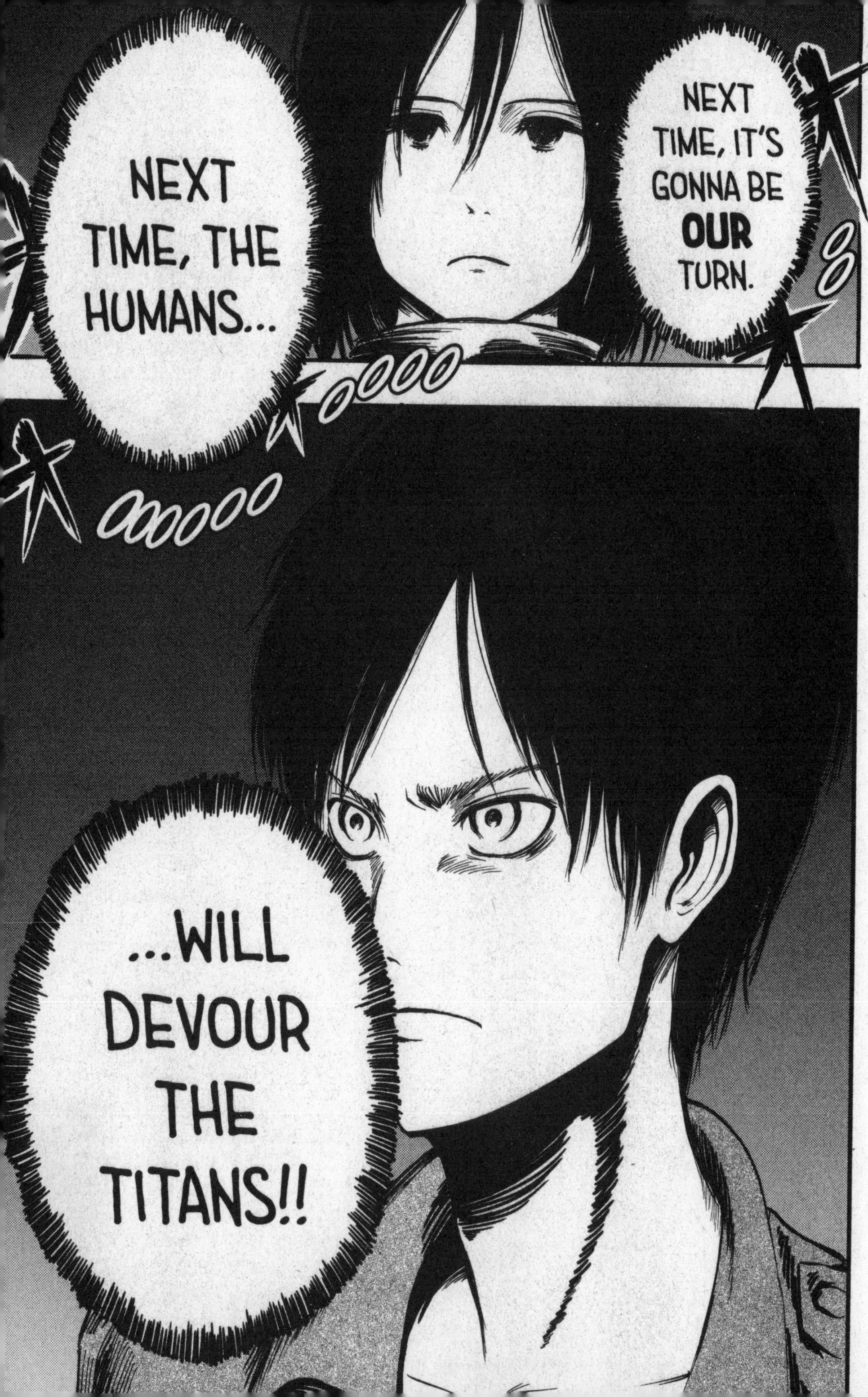
NEXT TIME, IT'S GONNA BE **OUR** TURN.
NEXT TIME, THE HUMANS...
AOOOOO
...WILL DEVOUR THE TITANS!!

Current Publicly Available Information

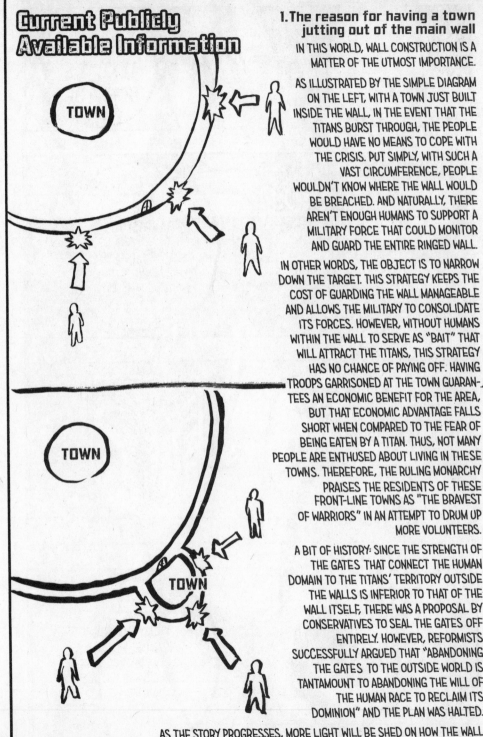

1. The reason for having a town jutting out of the main wall

IN THIS WORLD, WALL CONSTRUCTION IS A MATTER OF THE UTMOST IMPORTANCE.

AS ILLUSTRATED BY THE SIMPLE DIAGRAM ON THE LEFT, WITH A TOWN JUST BUILT INSIDE THE WALL, IN THE EVENT THAT THE TITANS BURST THROUGH, THE PEOPLE WOULD HAVE NO MEANS TO COPE WITH THE CRISIS. PUT SIMPLY, WITH SUCH A VAST CIRCUMFERENCE, PEOPLE WOULDN'T KNOW WHERE THE WALL WOULD BE BREACHED. AND NATURALLY, THERE AREN'T ENOUGH HUMANS TO SUPPORT A MILITARY FORCE THAT COULD MONITOR AND GUARD THE ENTIRE RINGED WALL.

IN OTHER WORDS, THE OBJECT IS TO NARROW DOWN THE TARGET. THIS STRATEGY KEEPS THE COST OF GUARDING THE WALL MANAGEABLE AND ALLOWS THE MILITARY TO CONSOLIDATE ITS FORCES. HOWEVER, WITHOUT HUMANS WITHIN THE WALL TO SERVE AS "BAIT" THAT WILL ATTRACT THE TITANS, THIS STRATEGY HAS NO CHANCE OF PAYING OFF. HAVING TROOPS GARRISONED AT THE TOWN GUARAN- TEES AN ECONOMIC BENEFIT FOR THE AREA, BUT THAT ECONOMIC ADVANTAGE FALLS SHORT WHEN COMPARED TO THE FEAR OF BEING EATEN BY A TITAN. THUS, NOT MANY PEOPLE ARE ENTHUSED ABOUT LIVING IN THESE TOWNS. THEREFORE, THE RULING MONARCHY PRAISES THE RESIDENTS OF THESE FRONT-LINE TOWNS AS "THE BRAVEST OF WARRIORS" IN AN ATTEMPT TO DRUM UP MORE VOLUNTEERS.

A BIT OF HISTORY: SINCE THE STRENGTH OF THE GATES THAT CONNECT THE HUMAN DOMAIN TO THE TITANS' TERRITORY OUTSIDE THE WALLS IS INFERIOR TO THAT OF THE WALL ITSELF, THERE WAS A PROPOSAL BY CONSERVATIVES TO SEAL THE GATES OFF ENTIRELY. HOWEVER, REFORMISTS SUCCESSFULLY ARGUED THAT "ABANDONING THE GATES TO THE OUTSIDE WORLD IS TANTAMOUNT TO ABANDONING THE WILL OF THE HUMAN RACE TO RECLAIM ITS DOMINION" AND THE PLAN WAS HALTED.

AS THE STORY PROGRESSES, MORE LIGHT WILL BE SHED ON HOW THE WALL WAS INITIALLY BUILT AND THE SITUATION AT THE TIME OF ITS CONSTRUCTION.

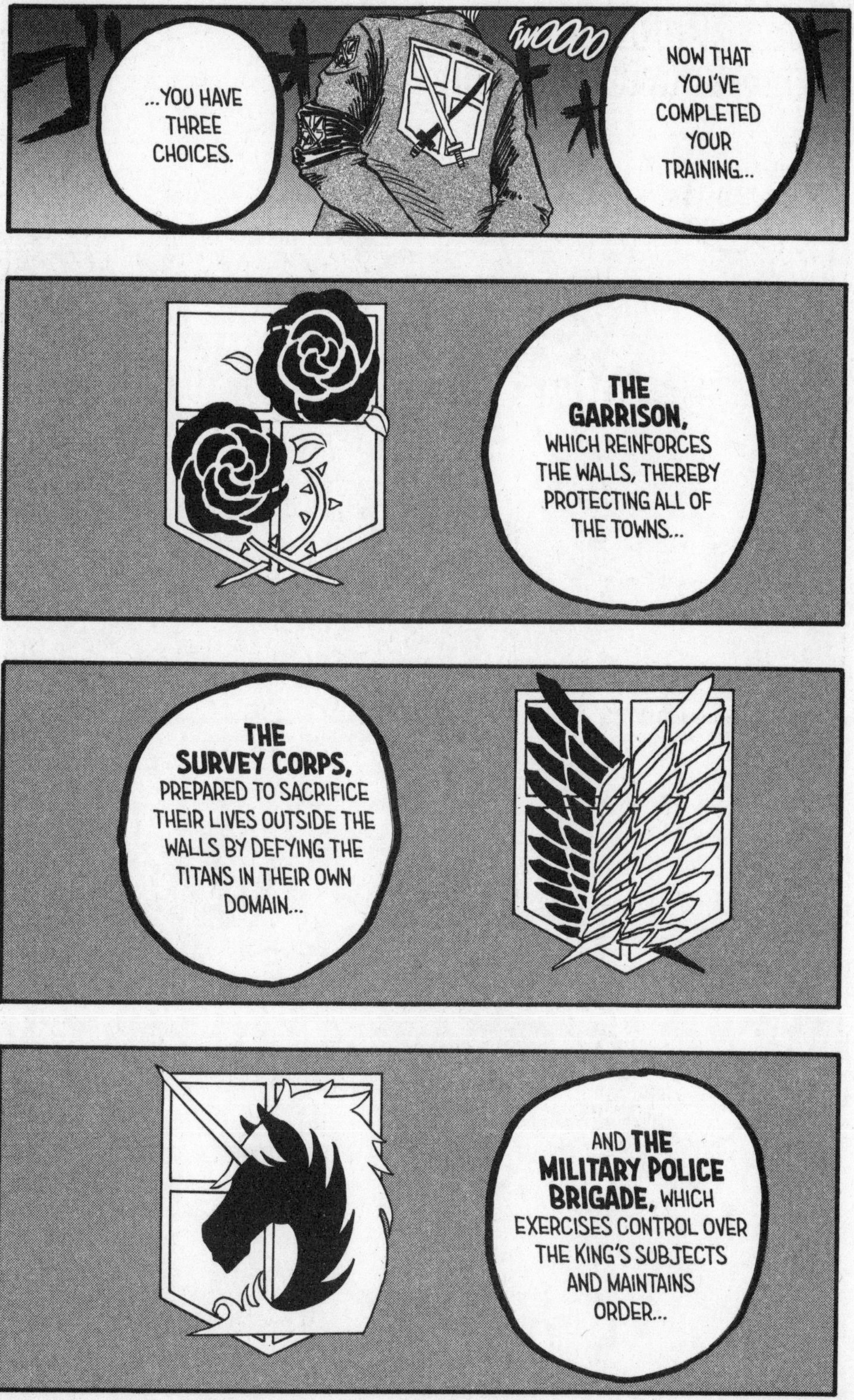
FWOOOO
NOW THAT YOU'VE COMPLETED YOUR TRAINING...
...YOU HAVE THREE CHOICES.
THE GARRISON, WHICH REINFORCES THE WALLS, THEREBY PROTECTING ALL OF THE TOWNS...
THE SURVEY CORPS, PREPARED TO SACRIFICE THEIR LIVES OUTSIDE THE WALLS BY DEFYING THE TITANS IN THEIR OWN DOMAIN...
AND THE MILITARY POLICE BRIGADE, WHICH EXERCISES CONTROL OVER THE KING'S SUBJECTS AND MAINTAINS ORDER...

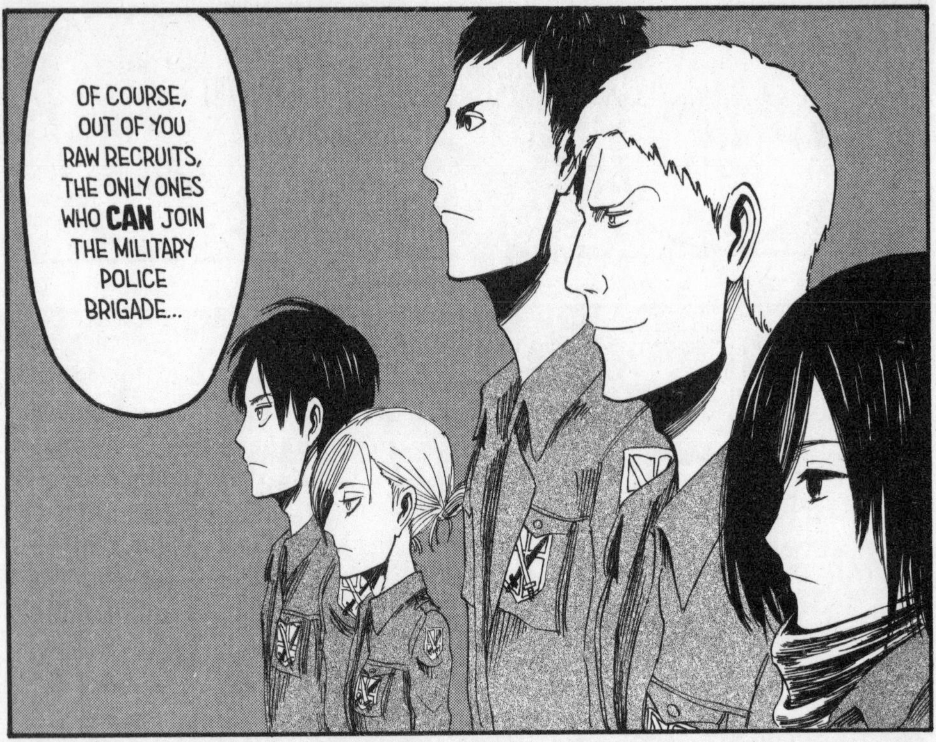
OF COURSE, OUT OF YOU RAW RECRUITS, THE ONLY ONES WHO CAN JOIN THE MILITARY POLICE BRIGADE...

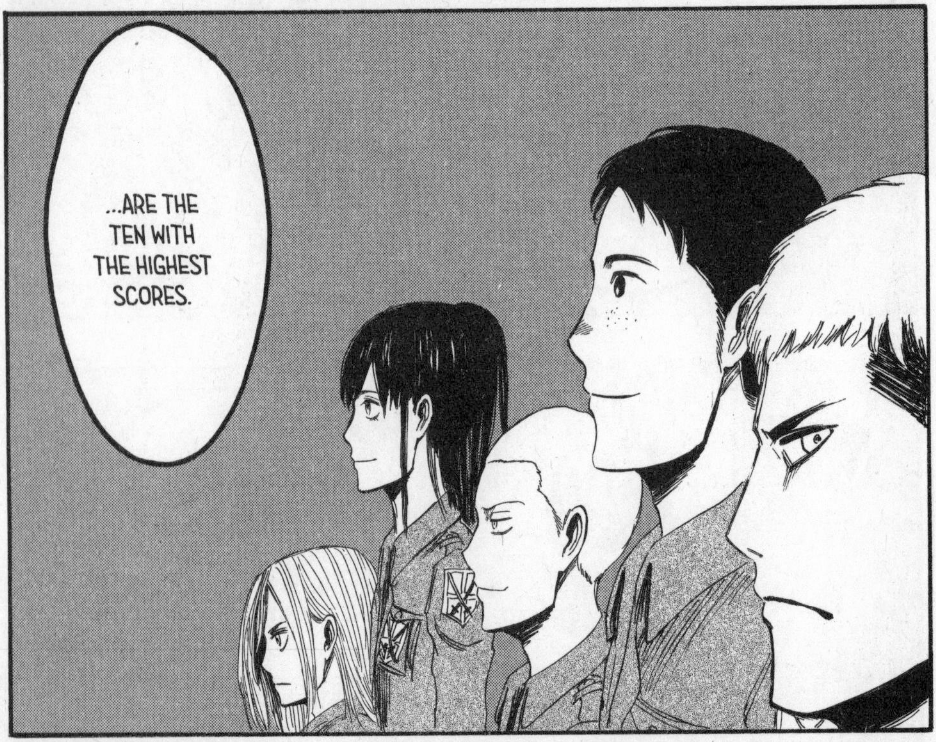
...ARE THE TEN WITH THE HIGHEST SCORES.

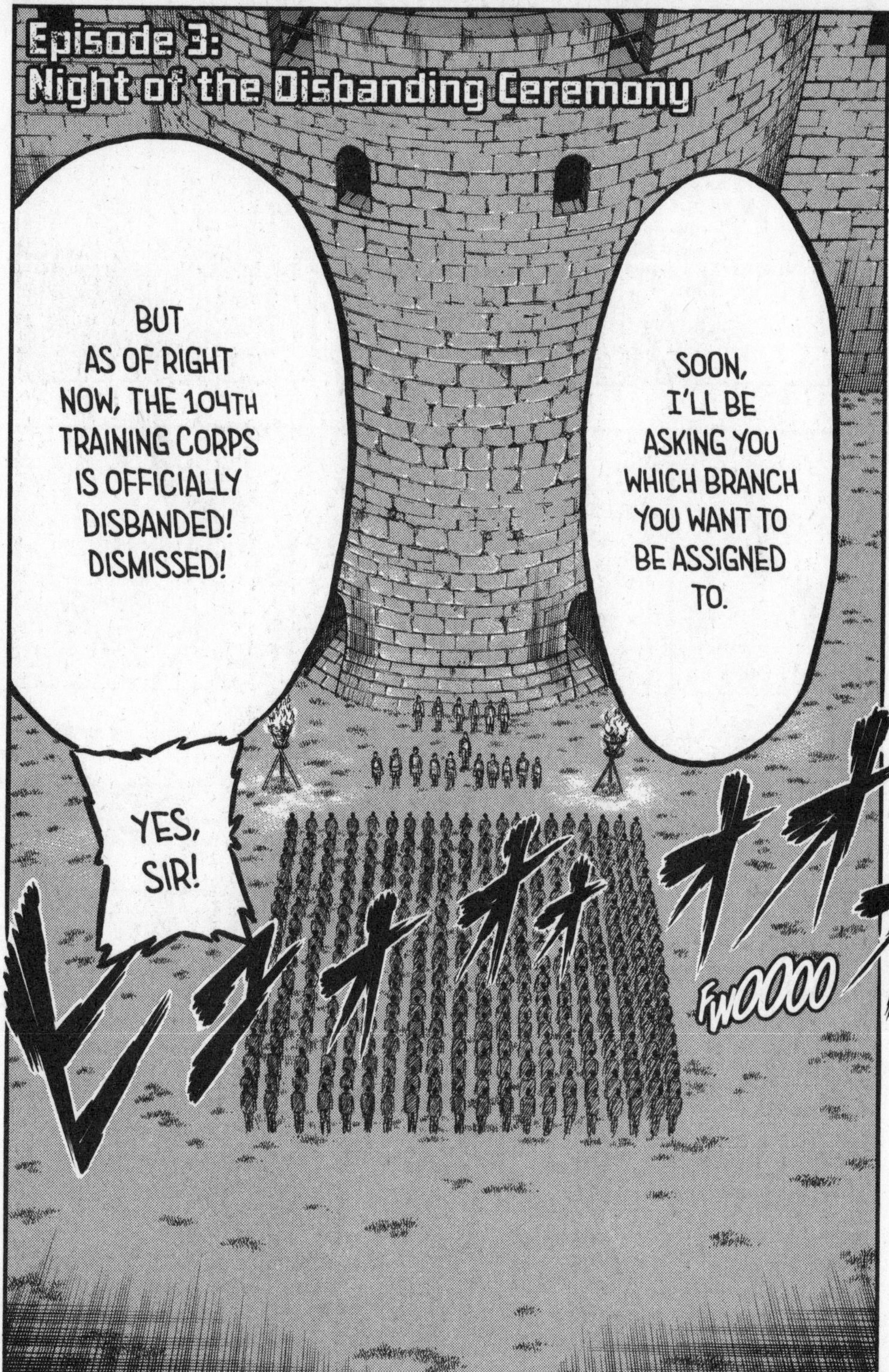
Episode 3:
Night of the Disbanding Ceremony
SOON, I'LL BE ASKING YOU WHICH BRANCH YOU WANT TO BE ASSIGNED TO.
BUT AS OF RIGHT NOW, THE 104TH TRAINING CORPS IS OFFICIALLY DISBANDED! DISMISSED!
YES, SIR!
FWOOOO

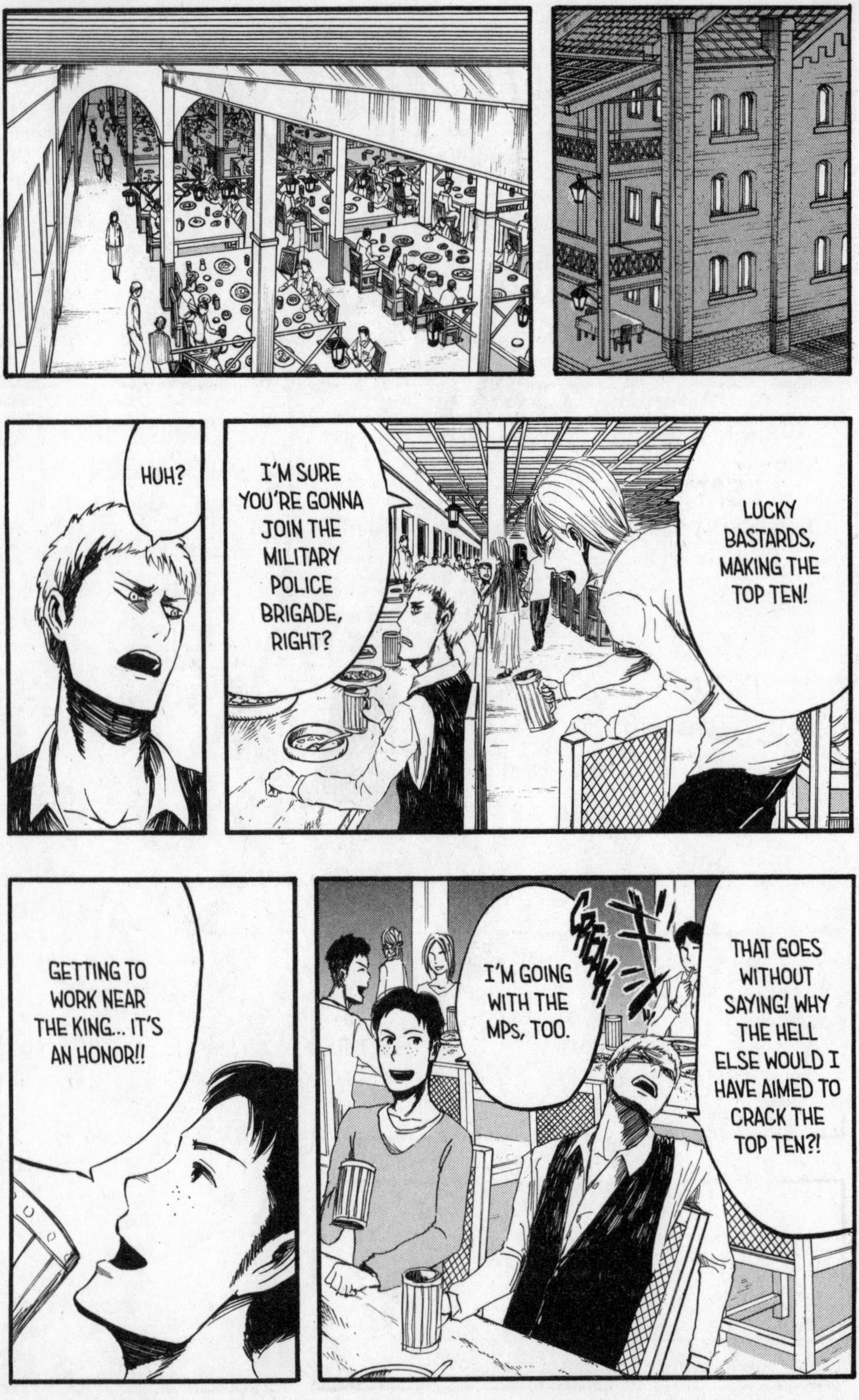
LUCKY BASTARDS, MAKING THE TOP TEN!
I'M SURE YOU'RE GONNA JOIN THE MILITARY POLICE BRIGADE, RIGHT?
HUH?
THAT GOES WITHOUT SAYING! WHY THE HELL ELSE WOULD I HAVE AIMED TO CRACK THE TOP TEN?!
CREAK
I'M GOING WITH THE MPs, TOO.
GETTING TO WORK NEAR THE KING... IT'S AN HONOR!!

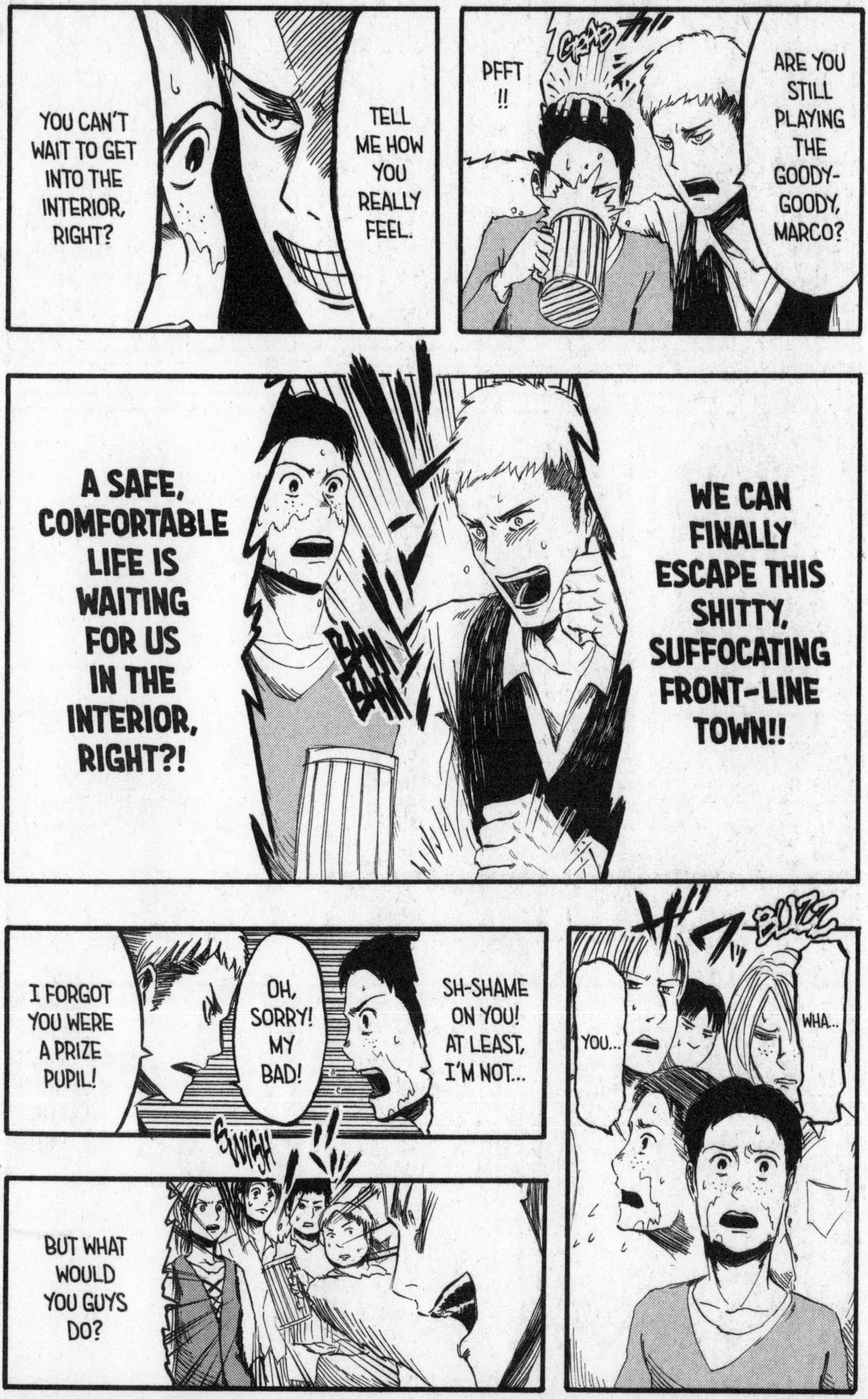
ARE YOU STILL PLAYING THE GOODY-GOODY, MARCO?
GRAB
PFFT !!
TELL ME HOW YOU REALLY FEEL.
YOU CAN'T WAIT TO GET INTO THE INTERIOR, RIGHT?
WE CAN FINALLY ESCAPE THIS SHITTY, SUFFOCATING FRONT-LINE TOWN!!
A SAFE, COMFORTABLE LIFE IS WAITING FOR US IN THE INTERIOR, RIGHT?!
BAM BAM
SH-SHAME ON YOU! AT LEAST, I'M NOT...
OH, SORRY! MY BAD!
I FORGOT YOU WERE A PRIZE PUPIL!
SWISH
BUT WHAT WOULD YOU GUYS DO?
BUZZ
WHA...
YOU...

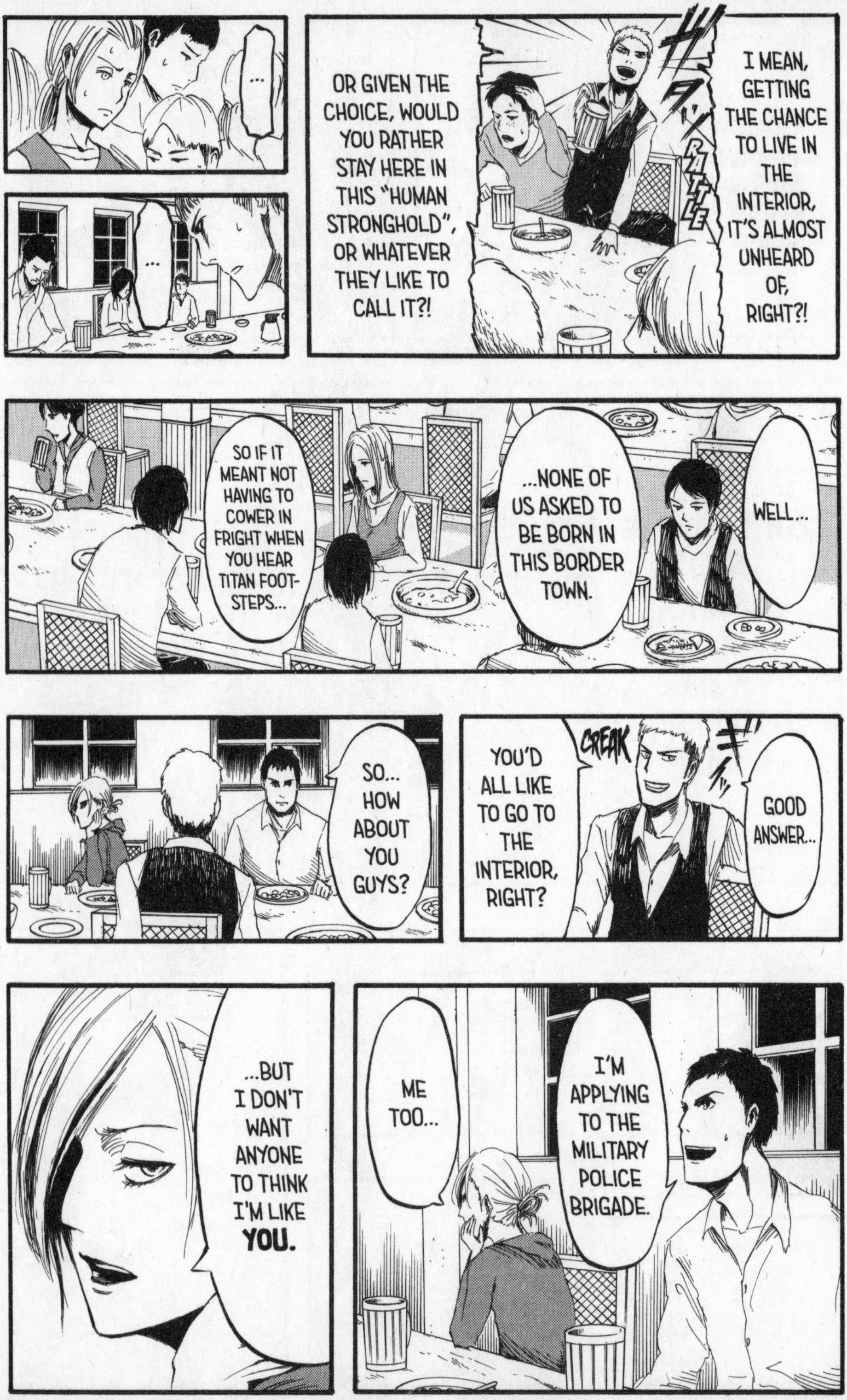
I MEAN, GETTING THE CHANCE TO LIVE IN THE INTERIOR, IT'S ALMOST UNHEARD OF, RIGHT?!
RATTLE
OR GIVEN THE CHOICE, WOULD YOU RATHER STAY HERE IN THIS "HUMAN STRONGHOLD", OR WHATEVER THEY LIKE TO CALL IT?!
...
...
WELL...
...NONE OF US ASKED TO BE BORN IN THIS BORDER TOWN.
SO IF IT MEANT NOT HAVING TO COWER IN FRIGHT WHEN YOU HEAR TITAN FOOT-STEPS...
GOOD ANSWER...
CREAK
YOU'D ALL LIKE TO GO TO THE INTERIOR, RIGHT?
SO... HOW ABOUT YOU GUYS?
I'M APPLYING TO THE MILITARY POLICE BRIGADE.
ME TOO...
...BUT I DON'T WANT ANYONE TO THINK I'M LIKE **YOU.**

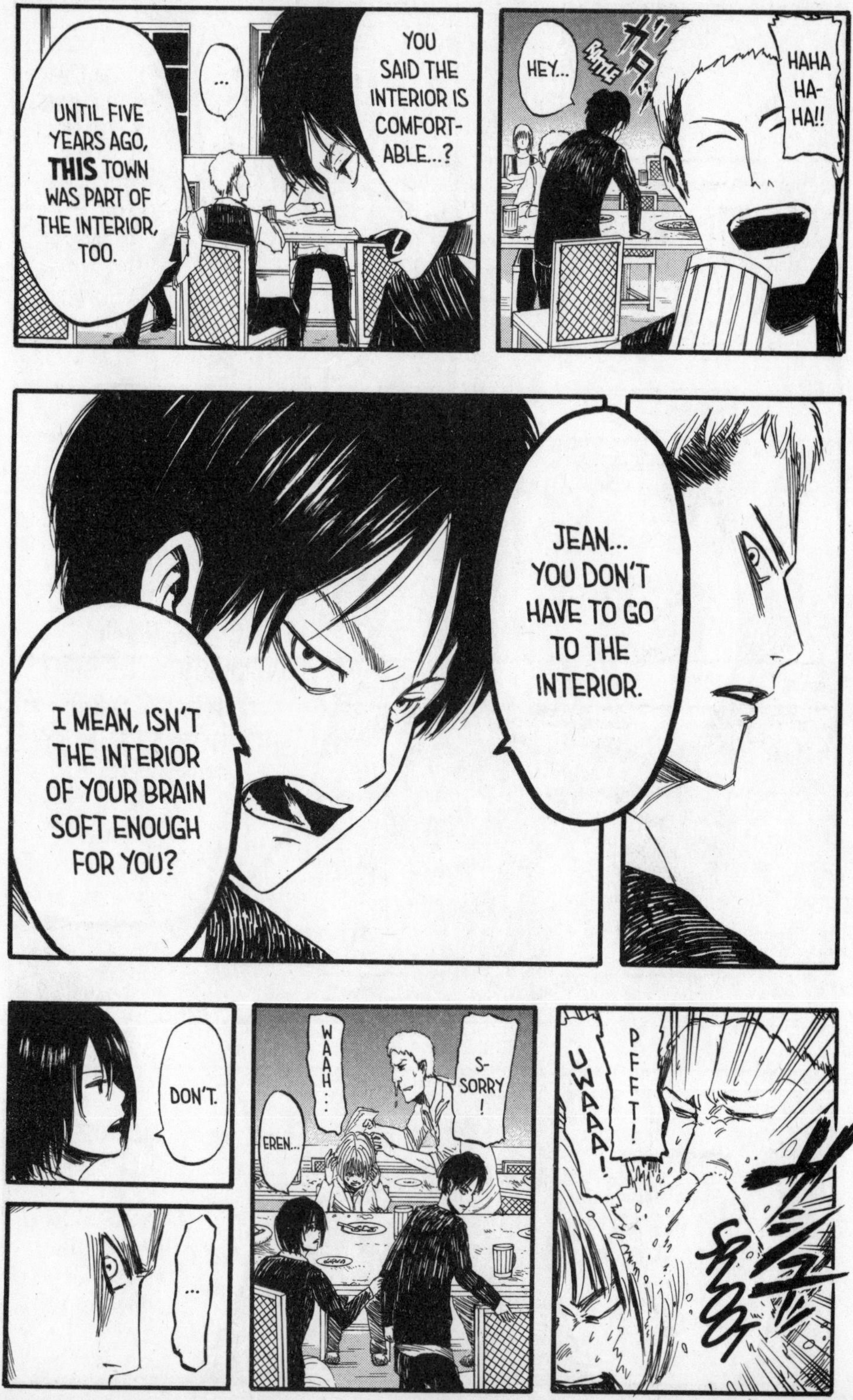
HAHA HA-HA!!
RATTLE
HEY...
YOU SAID THE INTERIOR IS COMFORT-ABLE...?
...
UNTIL FIVE YEARS AGO, THIS TOWN WAS PART OF THE INTERIOR, TOO.
JEAN... YOU DON'T HAVE TO GO TO THE INTERIOR.
I MEAN, ISN'T THE INTERIOR OF YOUR BRAIN SOFT ENOUGH FOR YOU?
PFFT!
UWAAA!
S-SORRY!
WAAH...
EREN...
DON'T.
...

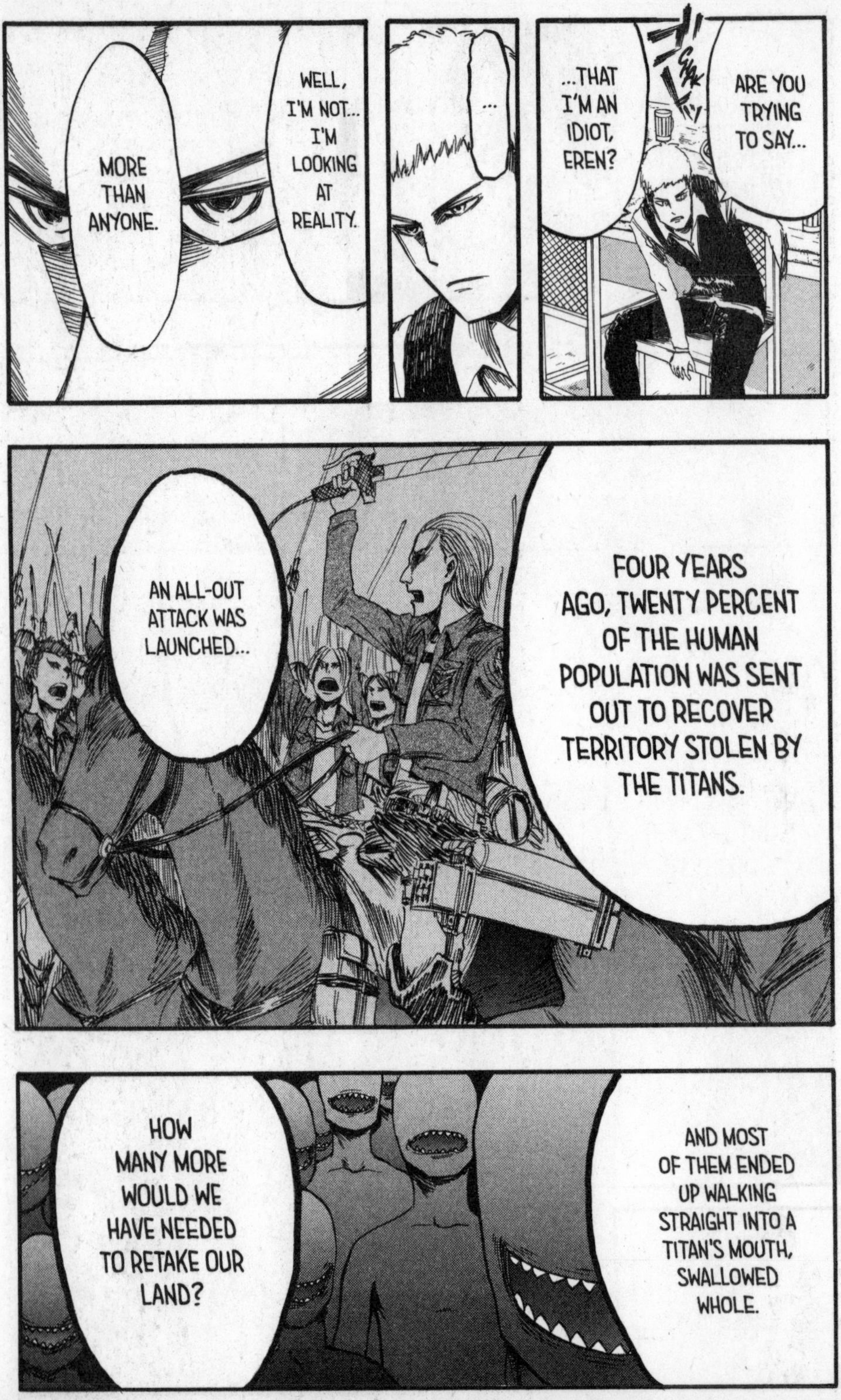
ARE YOU TRYING TO SAY...
...THAT I'M AN IDIOT, EREN?
...
WELL, I'M NOT... I'M LOOKING AT REALITY.
MORE THAN ANYONE.
FOUR YEARS AGO, TWENTY PERCENT OF THE HUMAN POPULATION WAS SENT OUT TO RECOVER TERRITORY STOLEN BY THE TITANS.
AN ALL-OUT ATTACK WAS LAUNCHED...
AND MOST OF THEM ENDED UP WALKING STRAIGHT INTO A TITAN'S MOUTH, SWALLOWED WHOLE.
HOW MANY MORE WOULD WE HAVE NEEDED TO RETAKE OUR LAND?

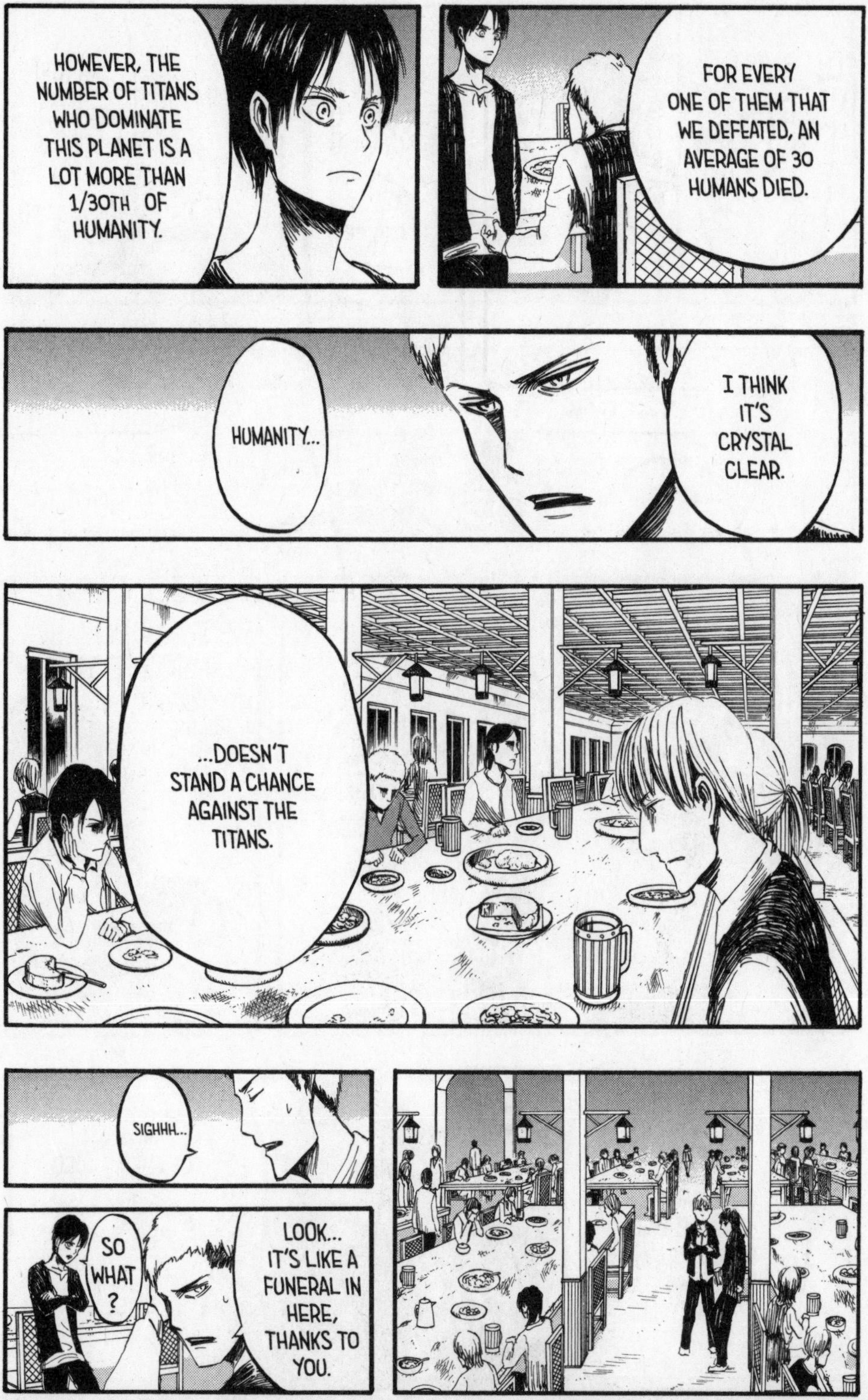
FOR EVERY ONE OF THEM THAT WE DEFEATED, AN AVERAGE OF 30 HUMANS DIED.
HOWEVER, THE NUMBER OF TITANS WHO DOMINATE THIS PLANET IS A LOT MORE THAN 1/30TH OF HUMANITY.
I THINK IT'S CRYSTAL CLEAR.
HUMANITY...
...DOESN'T STAND A CHANCE AGAINST THE TITANS.
SIGHHH...
LOOK... IT'S LIKE A FUNERAL IN HERE, THANKS TO YOU.
SO WHAT?

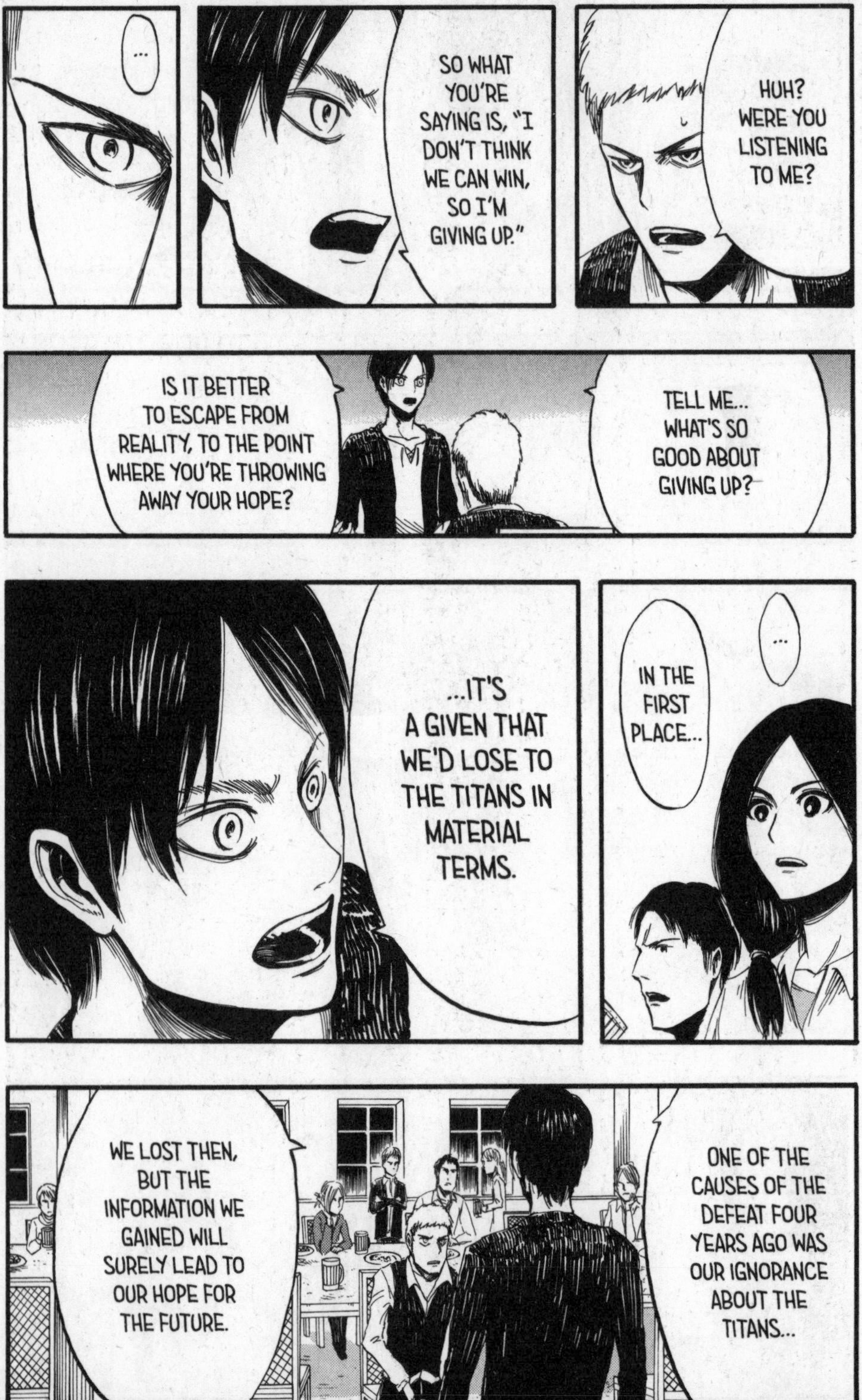
HUH? WERE YOU LISTENING TO ME?
SO WHAT YOU'RE SAYING IS, "I DON'T THINK WE CAN WIN, SO I'M GIVING UP."
...
TELL ME... WHAT'S SO GOOD ABOUT GIVING UP?
IS IT BETTER TO ESCAPE FROM REALITY, TO THE POINT WHERE YOU'RE THROWING AWAY YOUR HOPE?
...
IN THE FIRST PLACE...
...IT'S A GIVEN THAT WE'D LOSE TO THE TITANS IN MATERIAL TERMS.
ONE OF THE CAUSES OF THE DEFEAT FOUR YEARS AGO WAS OUR IGNORANCE ABOUT THE TITANS...
WE LOST THEN, BUT THE INFORMATION WE GAINED WILL SURELY LEAD TO OUR HOPE FOR THE FUTURE.

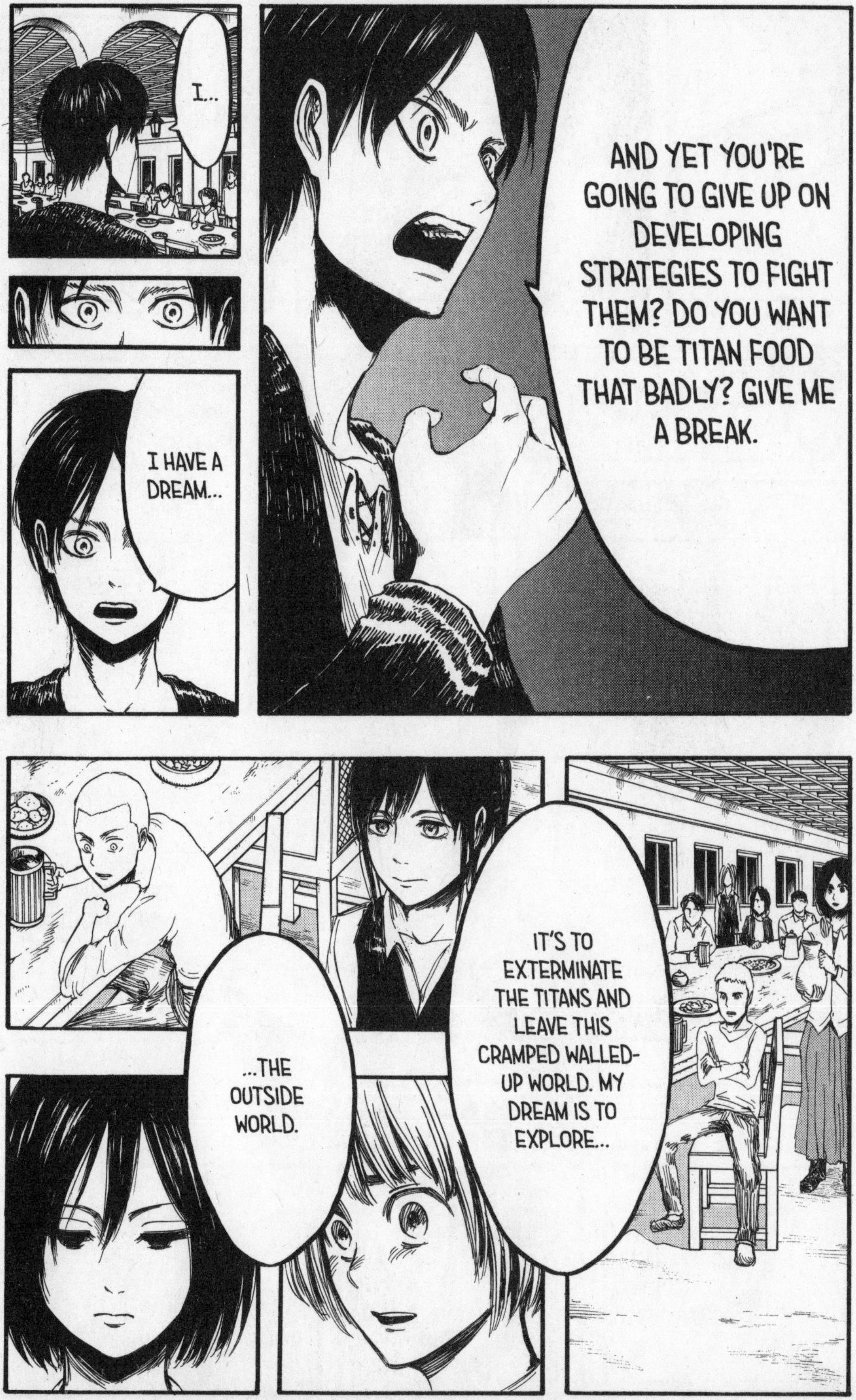
AND YET YOU'RE GOING TO GIVE UP ON DEVELOPING STRATEGIES TO FIGHT THEM? DO YOU WANT TO BE TITAN FOOD THAT BADLY? GIVE ME A BREAK.
I...
I HAVE A DREAM...
IT'S TO EXTERMINATE THE TITANS AND LEAVE THIS CRAMPED WALLED-UP WORLD. MY DREAM IS TO EXPLORE...
...THE OUTSIDE WORLD.

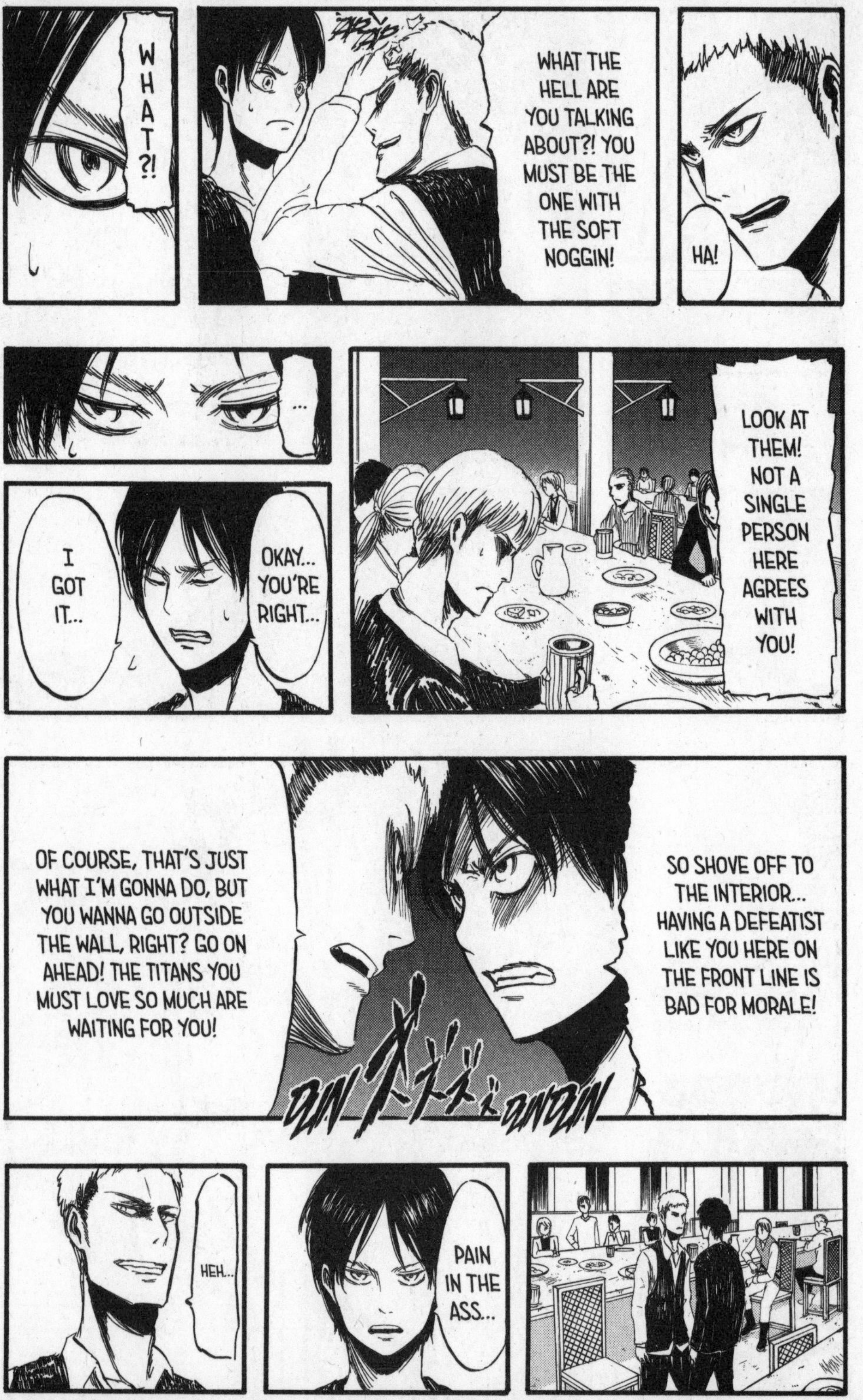
HA!
WHAT THE HELL ARE YOU TALKING ABOUT?! YOU MUST BE THE ONE WITH THE SOFT NOGGIN!
WHAT?!
LOOK AT THEM! NOT A SINGLE PERSON HERE AGREES WITH YOU!
...
OKAY... YOU'RE RIGHT...
I GOT IT...
SO SHOVE OFF TO THE INTERIOR... HAVING A DEFEATIST LIKE YOU HERE ON THE FRONT LINE IS BAD FOR MORALE!
OF COURSE, THAT'S JUST WHAT I'M GONNA DO, BUT YOU WANNA GO OUTSIDE THE WALL, RIGHT? GO ON AHEAD! THE TITANS YOU MUST LOVE SO MUCH ARE WAITING FOR YOU!
DUN DUNDUN
PAIN IN THE ASS...
HEH...

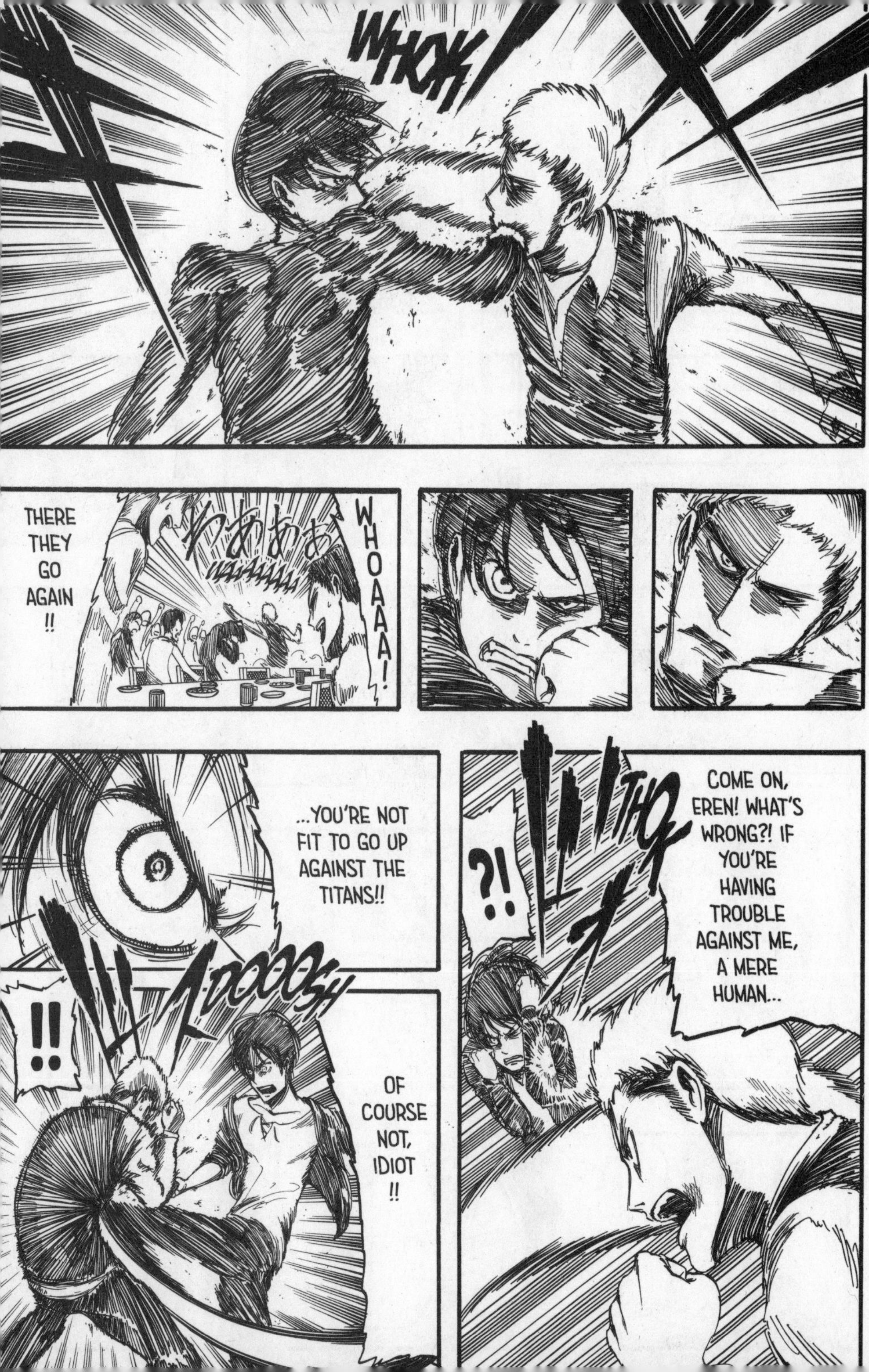

WHOK
WHOAAAA!
わあああ
THERE THEY GO AGAIN!!
COME ON, EREN! WHAT'S WRONG?! IF YOU'RE HAVING TROUBLE AGAINST ME, A MERE HUMAN...
?!
...YOU'RE NOT FIT TO GO UP AGAINST THE TITANS!!
!!
OF COURSE NOT, IDIOT!!

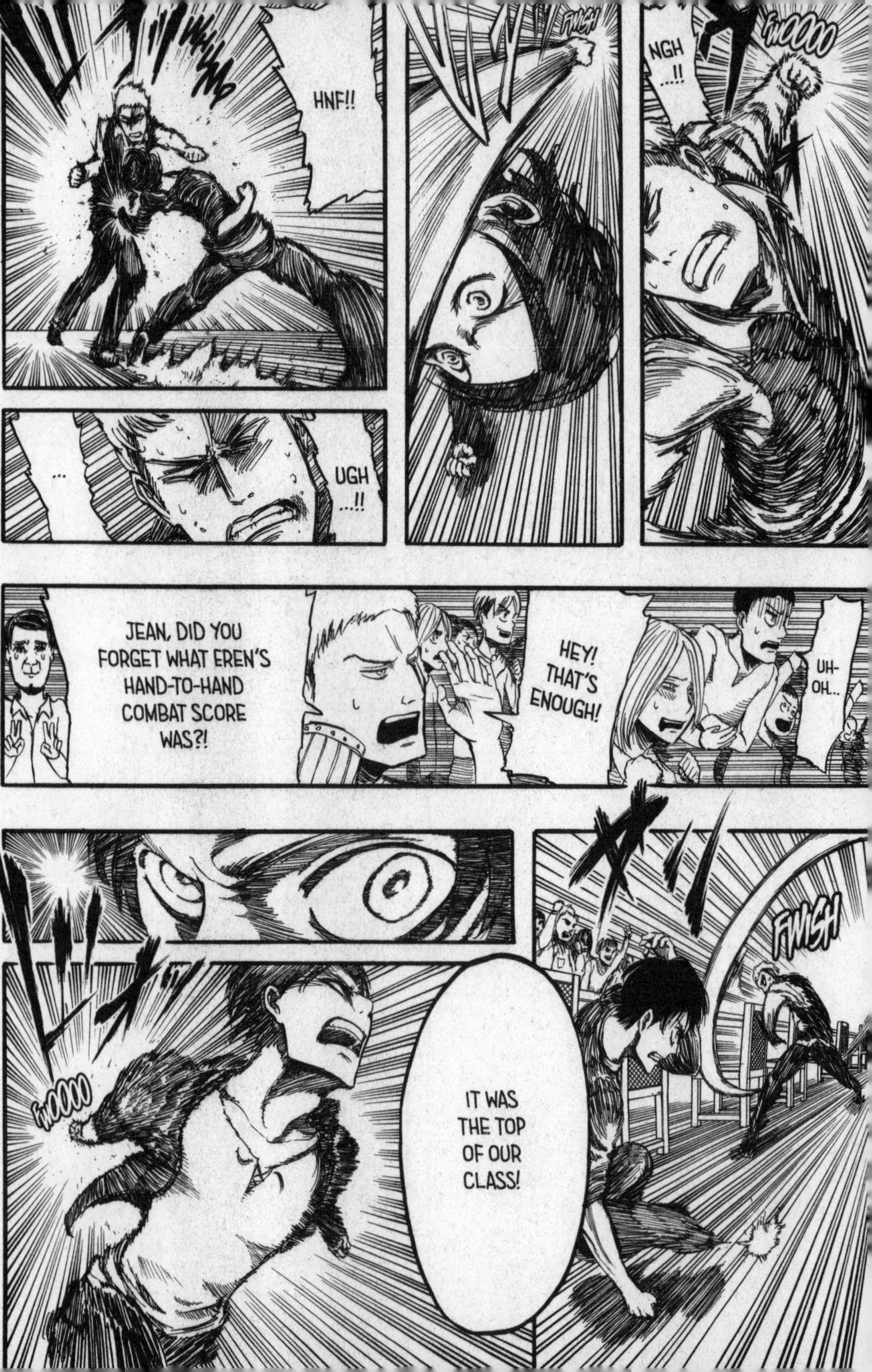
FWOOOO
NGH ...!!
FWISH
HNF!!
UGH ...!!
...
UH-OH...
HEY! THAT'S ENOUGH!
JEAN, DID YOU FORGET WHAT EREN'S HAND-TO-HAND COMBAT SCORE WAS?!
FWISH
FWOOOO
IT WAS THE TOP OF OUR CLASS!

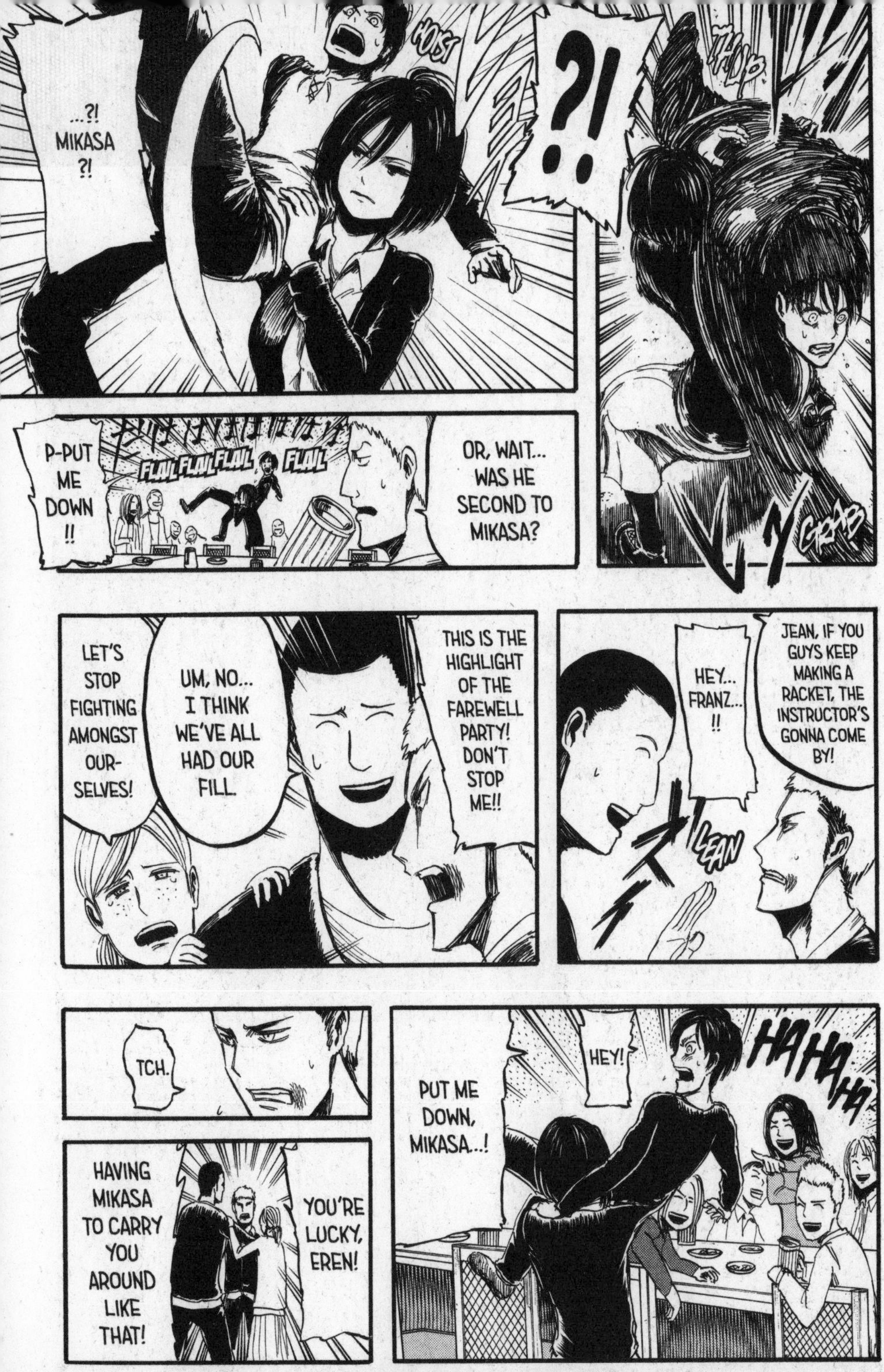
?!
THUD
GRAB
HOIST
...?! MIKASA ?!
OR, WAIT... WAS HE SECOND TO MIKASA?
FLAIL FLAIL FLAIL FLAIL
P-PUT ME DOWN !!
JEAN, IF YOU GUYS KEEP MAKING A RACKET, THE INSTRUCTOR'S GONNA COME BY!
HEY... FRANZ... !!
LEAN
THIS IS THE HIGHLIGHT OF THE FAREWELL PARTY! DON'T STOP ME!!
UM, NO... I THINK WE'VE ALL HAD OUR FILL.
LET'S STOP FIGHTING AMONGST OUR-SELVES!
HA HA HA HA
HEY!
PUT ME DOWN, MIKASA...!
TCH.
YOU'RE LUCKY, EREN!
HAVING MIKASA TO CARRY YOU AROUND LIKE THAT!

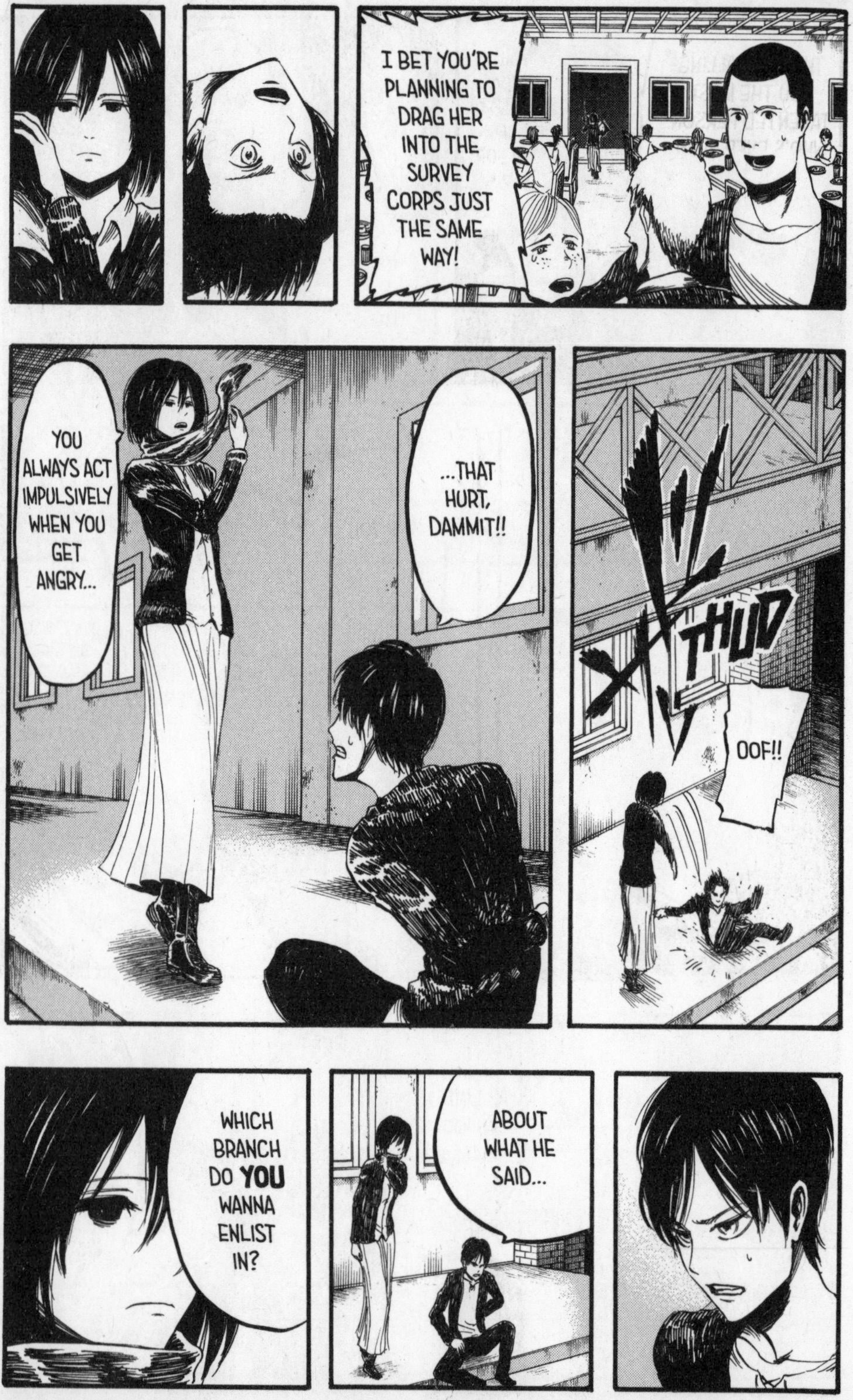
I BET YOU'RE PLANNING TO DRAG HER INTO THE SURVEY CORPS JUST THE SAME WAY!
THUD
OOF!!
...THAT HURT, DAMMIT!!
YOU ALWAYS ACT IMPULSIVELY WHEN YOU GET ANGRY...
ABOUT WHAT HE SAID...
WHICH BRANCH DO YOU WANNA ENLIST IN?

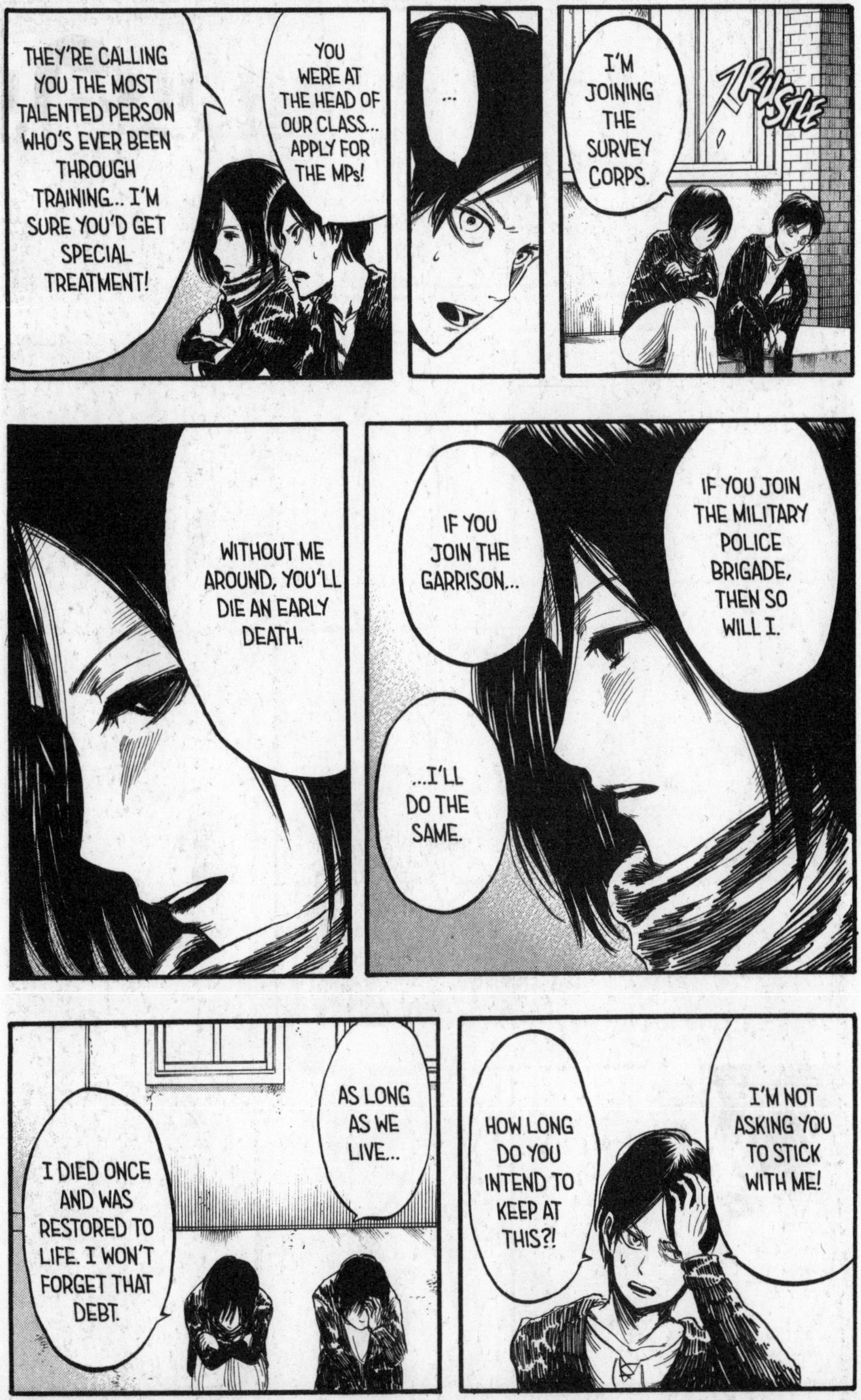
I'M JOINING THE SURVEY CORPS.
RUSTLE
...
YOU WERE AT THE HEAD OF OUR CLASS... APPLY FOR THE MPs!
THEY'RE CALLING YOU THE MOST TALENTED PERSON WHO'S EVER BEEN THROUGH TRAINING... I'M SURE YOU'D GET SPECIAL TREATMENT!
IF YOU JOIN THE MILITARY POLICE BRIGADE, THEN SO WILL I.
IF YOU JOIN THE GARRISON...
...I'LL DO THE SAME.
WITHOUT ME AROUND, YOU'LL DIE AN EARLY DEATH.
I'M NOT ASKING YOU TO STICK WITH ME!
HOW LONG DO YOU INTEND TO KEEP AT THIS?!
AS LONG AS WE LIVE...
I DIED ONCE AND WAS RESTORED TO LIFE. I WON'T FORGET THAT DEBT.

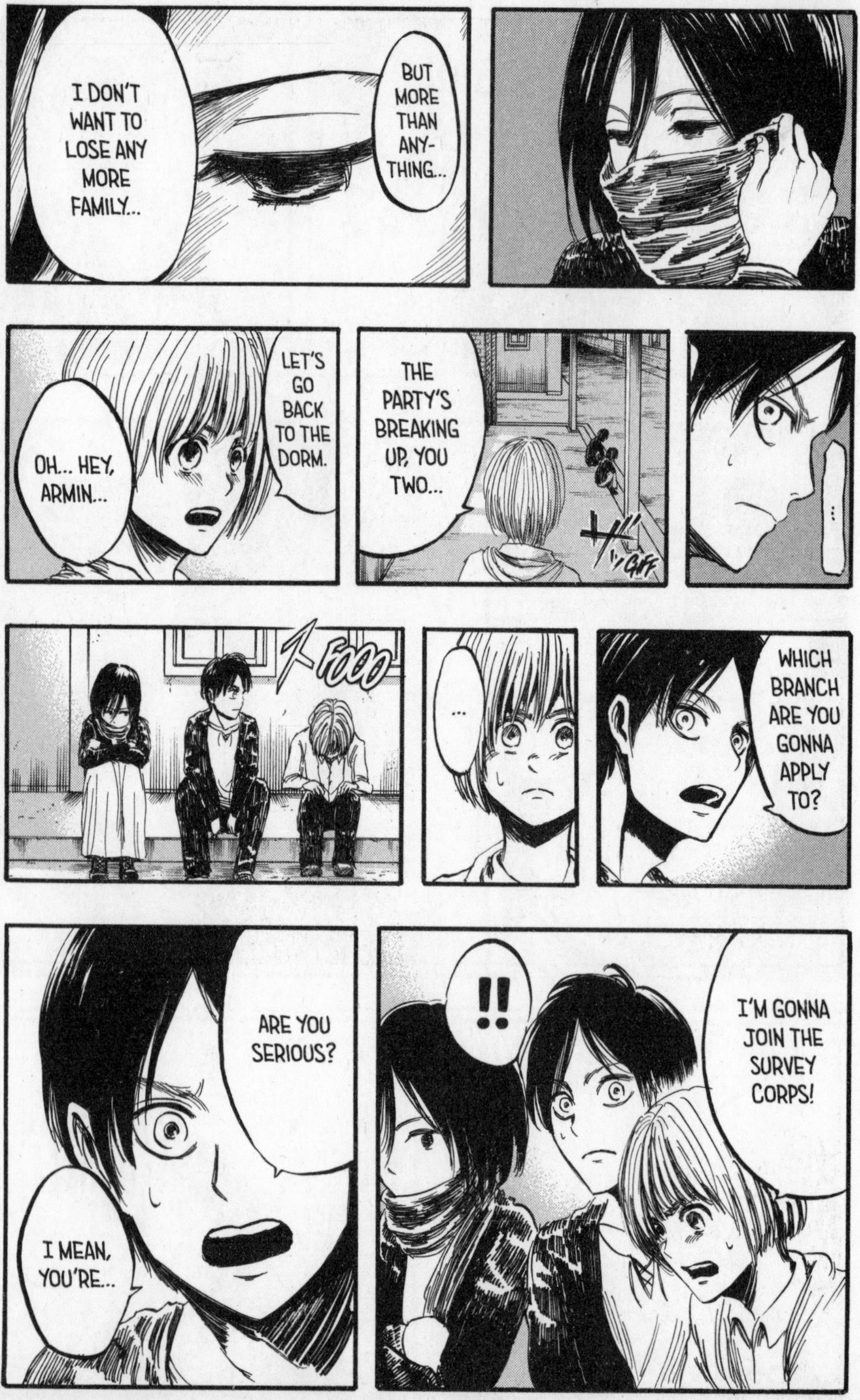
BUT MORE THAN ANY-THING...
I DON'T WANT TO LOSE ANY MORE FAMILY...
...
THE PARTY'S BREAKING UP, YOU TWO...
GIFF
LET'S GO BACK TO THE DORM.
OH... HEY, ARMIN...
WHICH BRANCH ARE YOU GONNA APPLY TO?
...
FOOO
I'M GONNA JOIN THE SURVEY CORPS!
!!
ARE YOU SERIOUS?
I MEAN, YOU'RE...

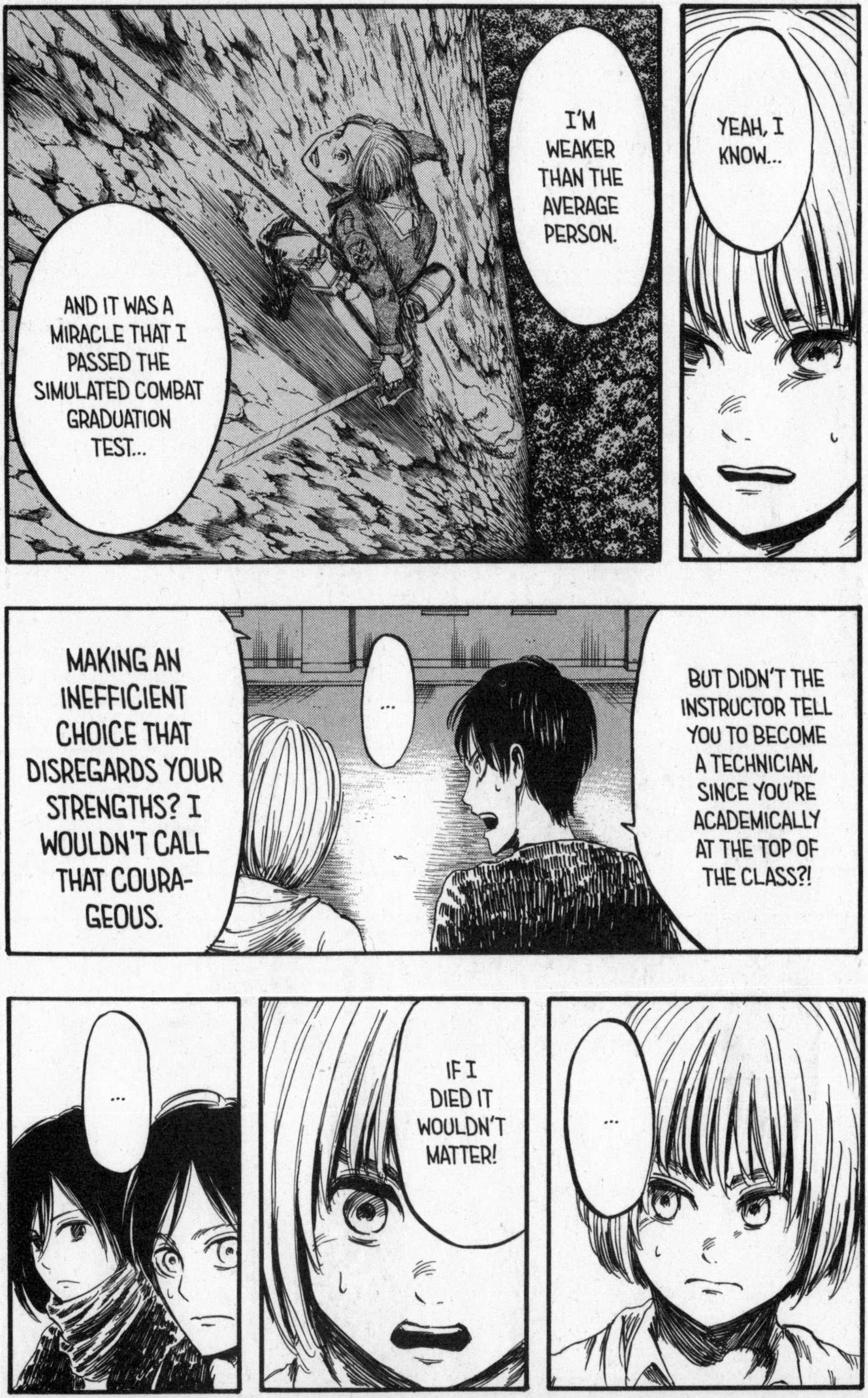
YEAH, I KNOW...
I'M WEAKER THAN THE AVERAGE PERSON.
AND IT WAS A MIRACLE THAT I PASSED THE SIMULATED COMBAT GRADUATION TEST...
BUT DIDN'T THE INSTRUCTOR TELL YOU TO BECOME A TECHNICIAN, SINCE YOU'RE ACADEMICALLY AT THE TOP OF THE CLASS?!
...
MAKING AN INEFFICIENT CHOICE THAT DISREGARDS YOUR STRENGTHS? I WOULDN'T CALL THAT COURA-GEOUS.
...
IF I DIED IT WOULDN'T MATTER!
...

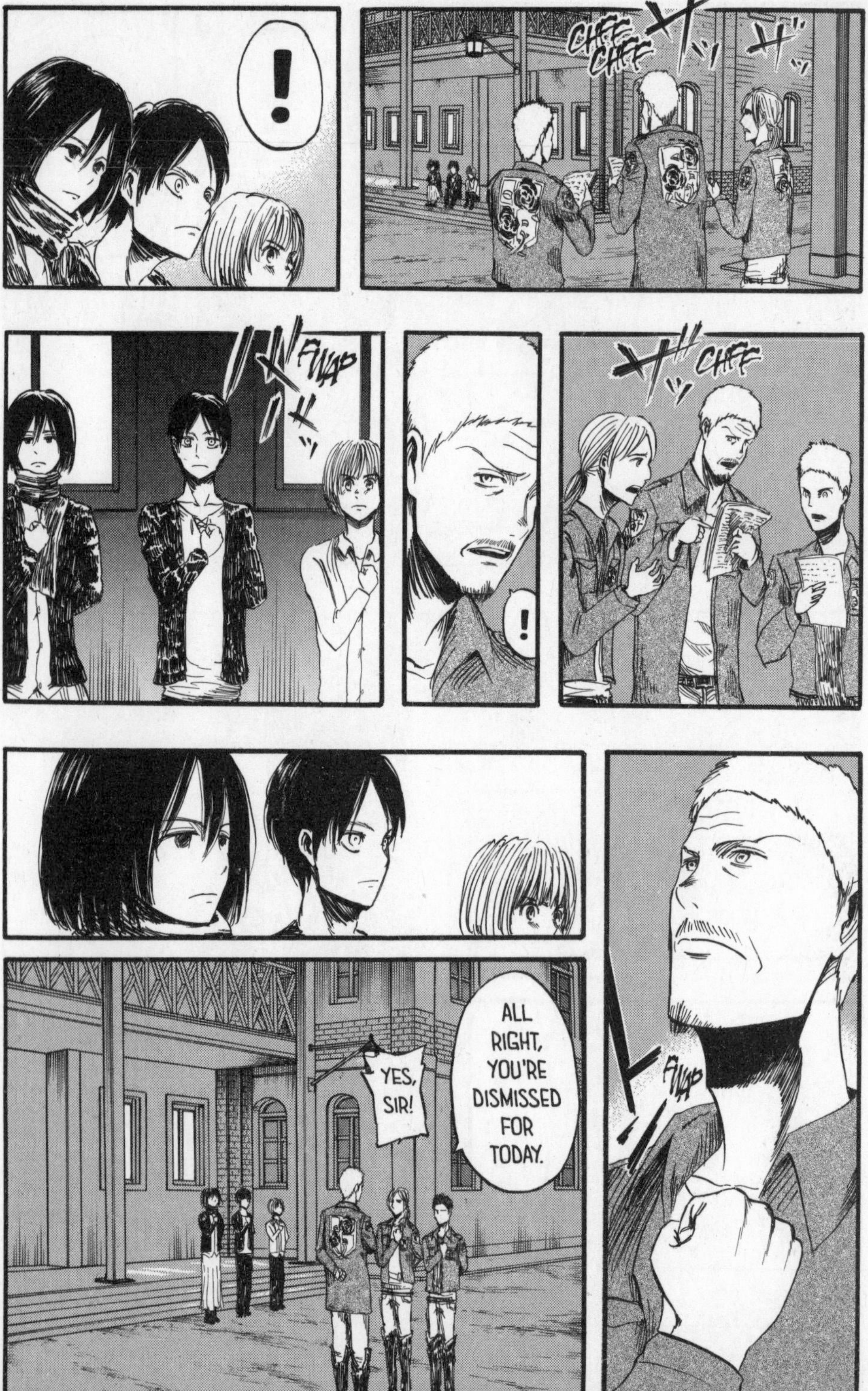

CHFF CHFF
!
CHFF
!
FWAP
FWAP
ALL RIGHT, YOU'RE DISMISSED FOR TODAY.
YES, SIR!

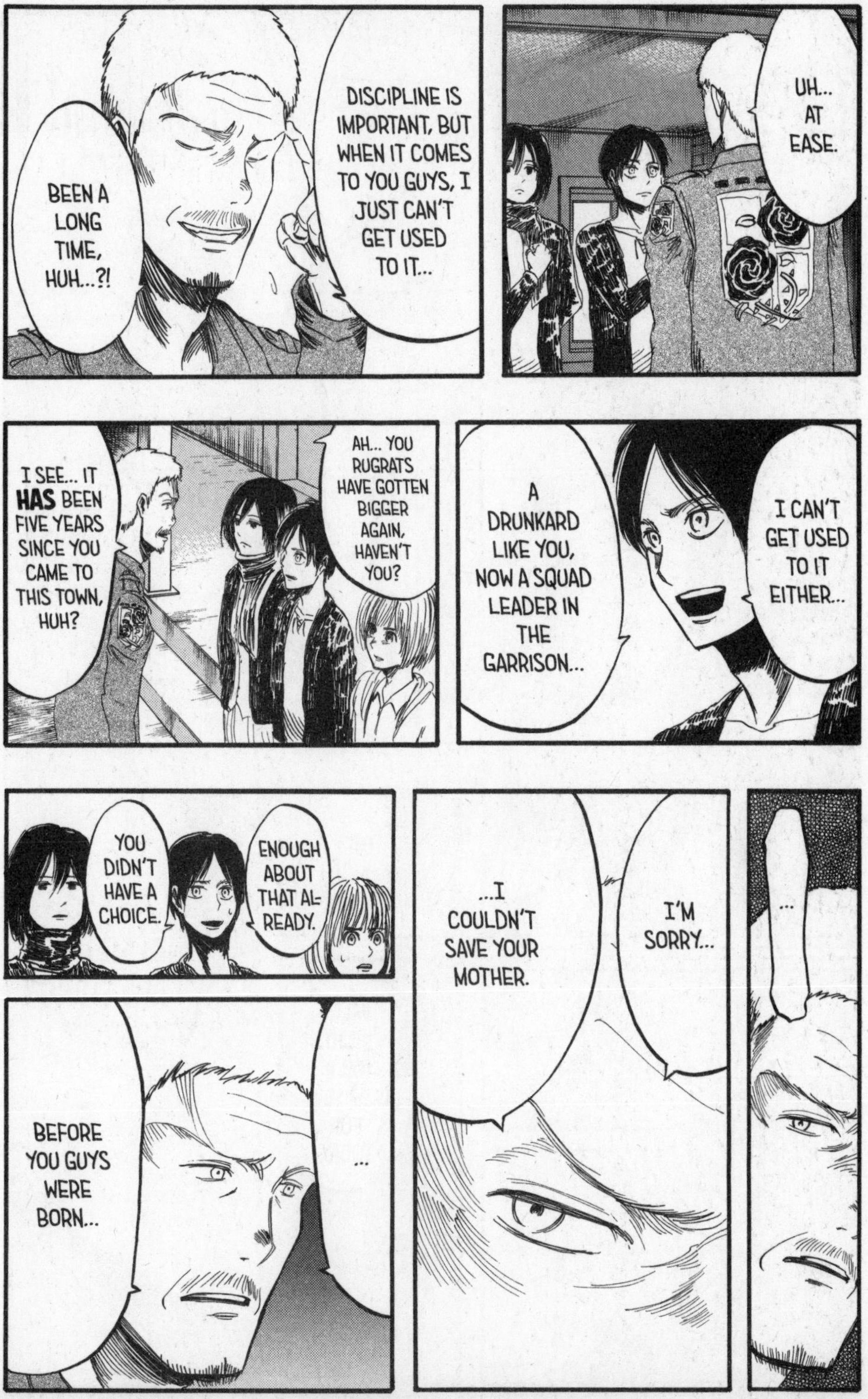
UH... AT EASE.
DISCIPLINE IS IMPORTANT, BUT WHEN IT COMES TO YOU GUYS, I JUST CAN'T GET USED TO IT...
BEEN A LONG TIME, HUH...?!
I CAN'T GET USED TO IT EITHER...
A DRUNKARD LIKE YOU, NOW A SQUAD LEADER IN THE GARRISON...
AH... YOU RUGRATS HAVE GOTTEN BIGGER AGAIN, HAVEN'T YOU?
I SEE... IT **HAS** BEEN FIVE YEARS SINCE YOU CAME TO THIS TOWN, HUH?
...
I'M SORRY...
...I COULDN'T SAVE YOUR MOTHER.
ENOUGH ABOUT THAT AL-READY.
YOU DIDN'T HAVE A CHOICE.
...
BEFORE YOU GUYS WERE BORN...

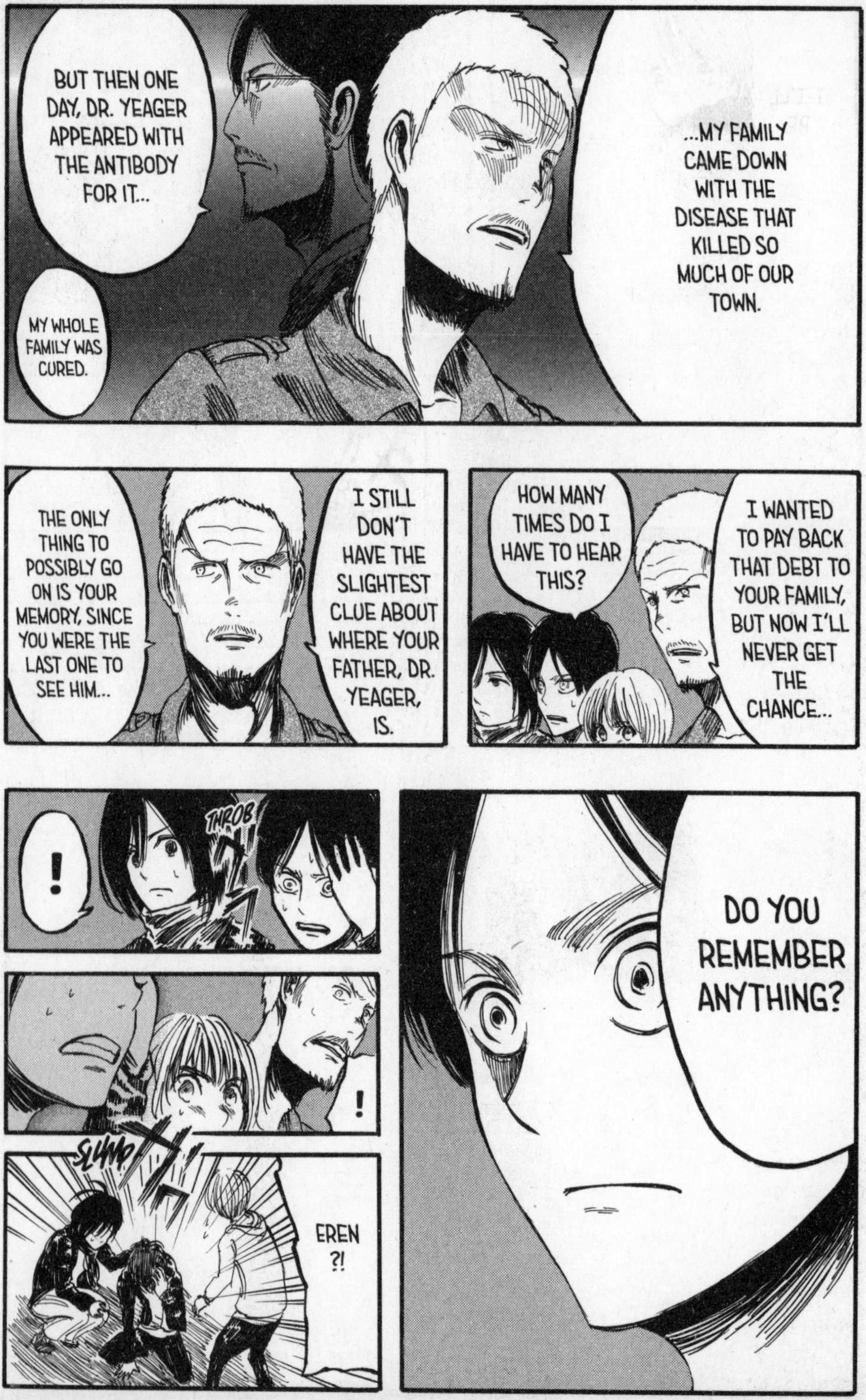
...MY FAMILY CAME DOWN WITH THE DISEASE THAT KILLED SO MUCH OF OUR TOWN.
BUT THEN ONE DAY, DR. YEAGER APPEARED WITH THE ANTIBODY FOR IT...
MY WHOLE FAMILY WAS CURED.
I WANTED TO PAY BACK THAT DEBT TO YOUR FAMILY, BUT NOW I'LL NEVER GET THE CHANCE...
HOW MANY TIMES DO I HAVE TO HEAR THIS?
I STILL DON'T HAVE THE SLIGHTEST CLUE ABOUT WHERE YOUR FATHER, DR. YEAGER, IS.
THE ONLY THING TO POSSIBLY GO ON IS YOUR MEMORY, SINCE YOU WERE THE LAST ONE TO SEE HIM...
DO YOU REMEMBER ANYTHING?
THROB
!
!
SLUMP
EREN ?!

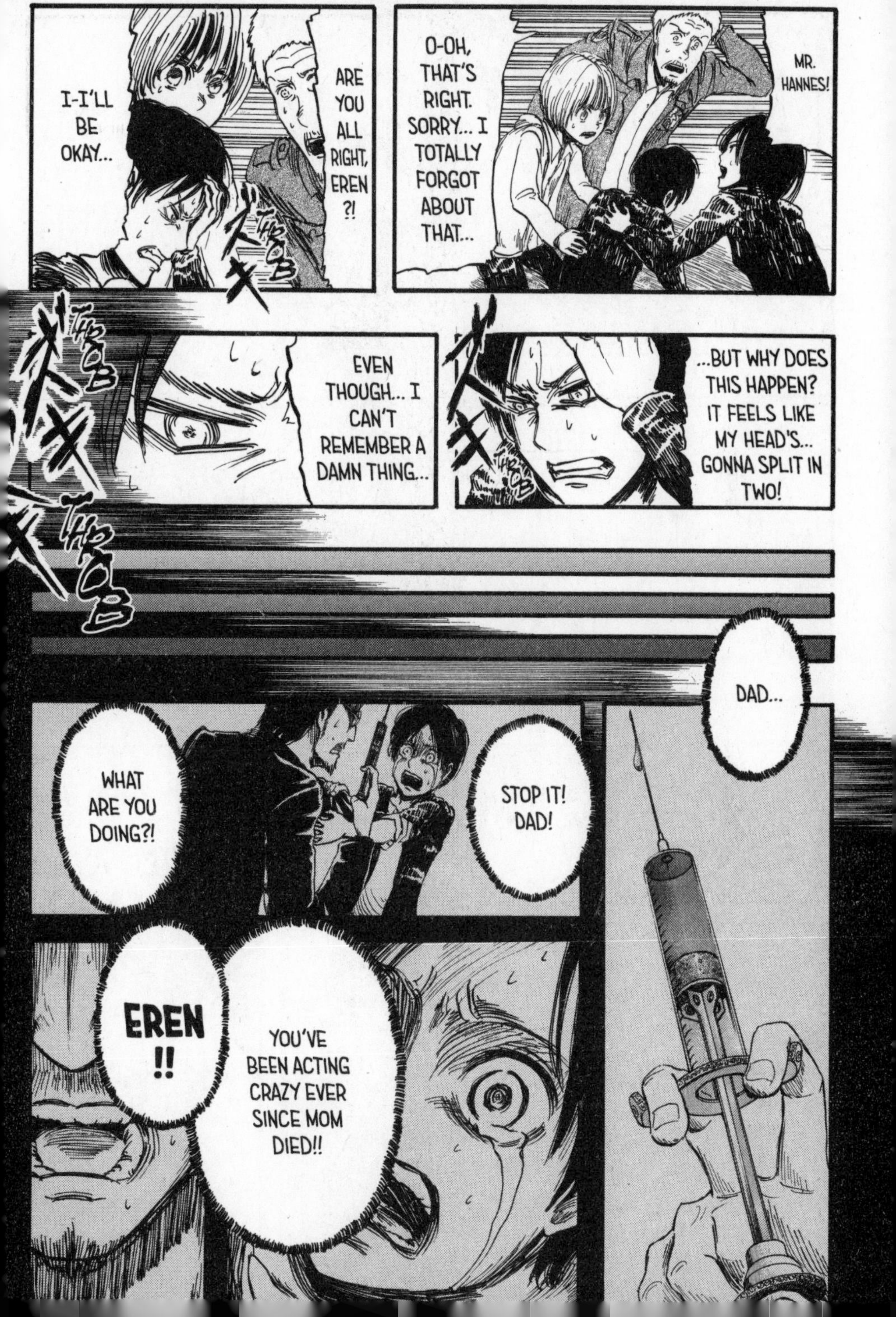
MR. HANNES!
O-OH, THAT'S RIGHT. SORRY... I TOTALLY FORGOT ABOUT THAT...
ARE YOU ALL RIGHT, EREN?!
I-I'LL BE OKAY...
THROB
...BUT WHY DOES THIS HAPPEN? IT FEELS LIKE MY HEAD'S... GONNA SPLIT IN TWO!
THROB
EVEN THOUGH... I CAN'T REMEMBER A DAMN THING...
THROB
THROB
DAD...
STOP IT! DAD!
WHAT ARE YOU DOING?!
YOU'VE BEEN ACTING CRAZY EVER SINCE MOM DIED!!
EREN!!

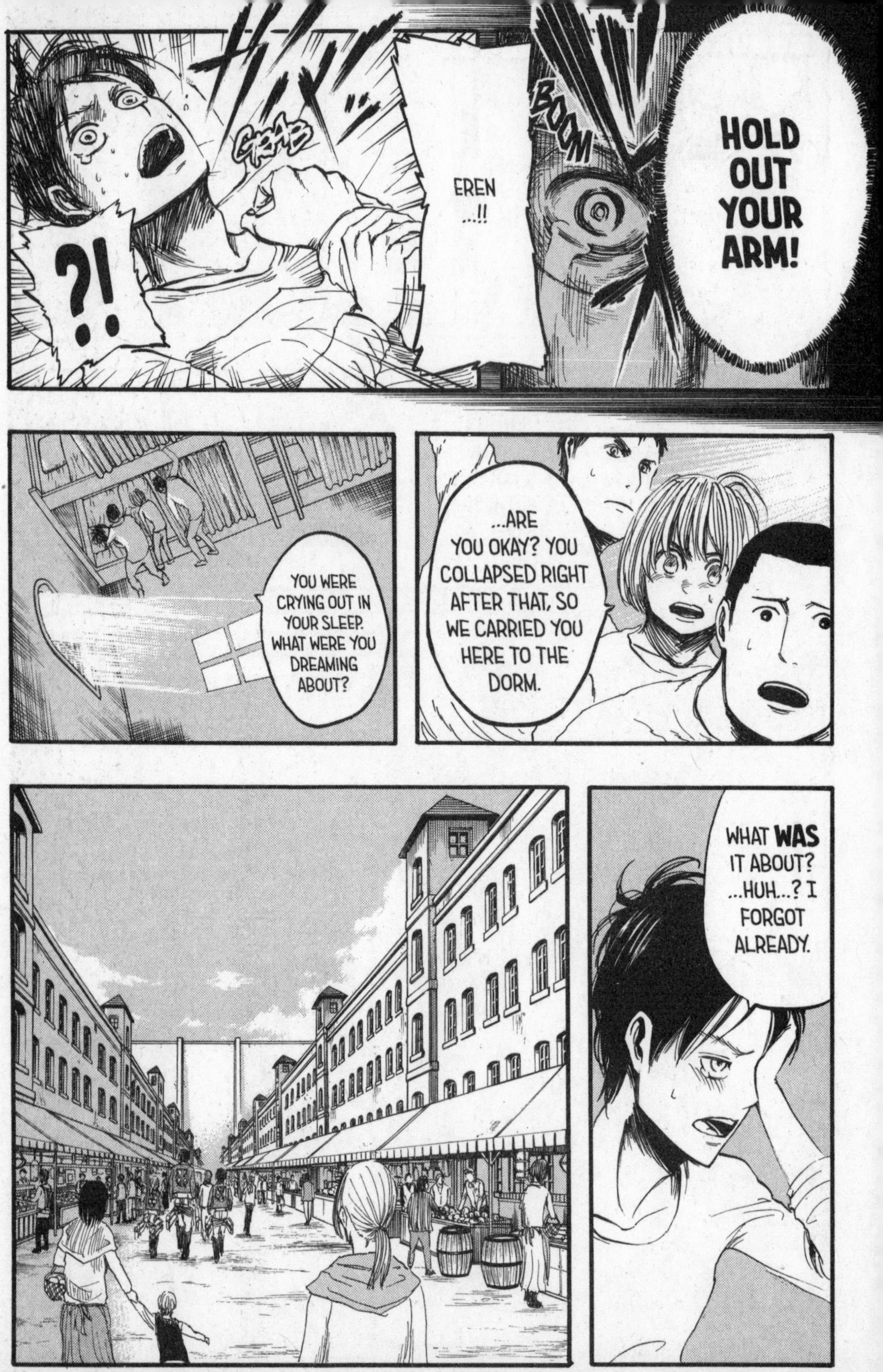
HOLD OUT YOUR ARM!
BOOM
EREN ...!!
GRAB
?!
...ARE YOU OKAY? YOU COLLAPSED RIGHT AFTER THAT, SO WE CARRIED YOU HERE TO THE DORM.
YOU WERE CRYING OUT IN YOUR SLEEP. WHAT WERE YOU DREAMING ABOUT?
WHAT WAS IT ABOUT? ...HUH...? I FORGOT ALREADY.

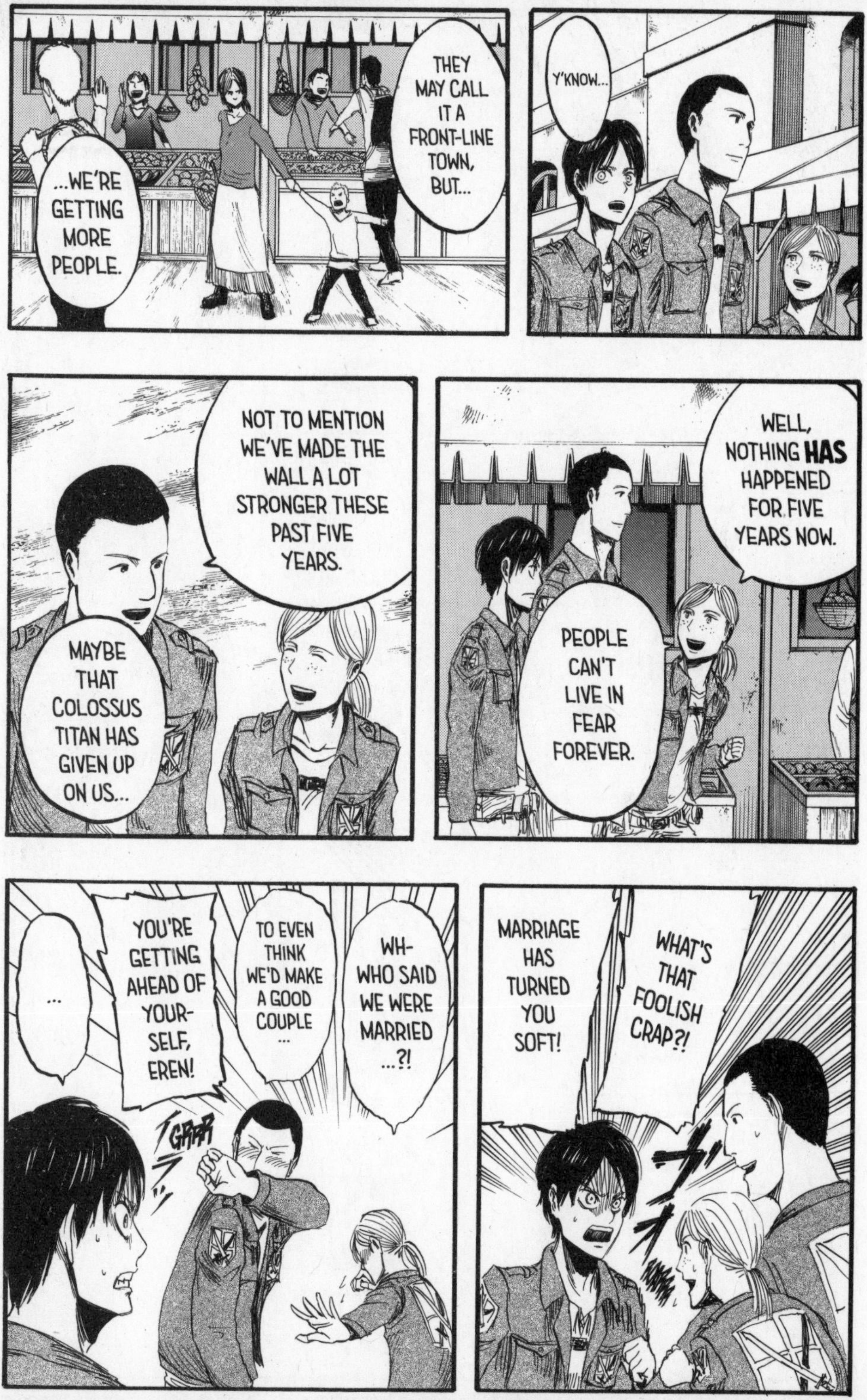
Y'KNOW...
THEY MAY CALL IT A FRONT-LINE TOWN, BUT...
...WE'RE GETTING MORE PEOPLE.
WELL, NOTHING **HAS** HAPPENED FOR FIVE YEARS NOW.
PEOPLE CAN'T LIVE IN FEAR FOREVER.
NOT TO MENTION WE'VE MADE THE WALL A LOT STRONGER THESE PAST FIVE YEARS.
MAYBE THAT COLOSSUS TITAN HAS GIVEN UP ON US...
WHAT'S THAT FOOLISH CRAP?!
MARRIAGE HAS TURNED YOU SOFT!
WH- WHO SAID WE WERE MARRIED ...?!
TO EVEN THINK WE'D MAKE A GOOD COUPLE ...
YOU'RE GETTING AHEAD OF YOUR-SELF, EREN!
...
GRRR

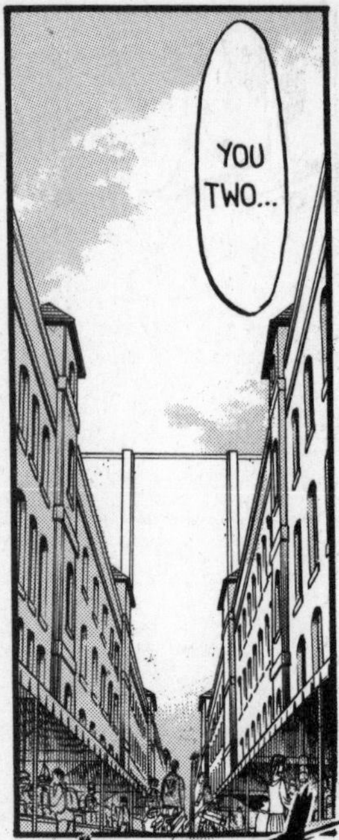
YOU TWO...
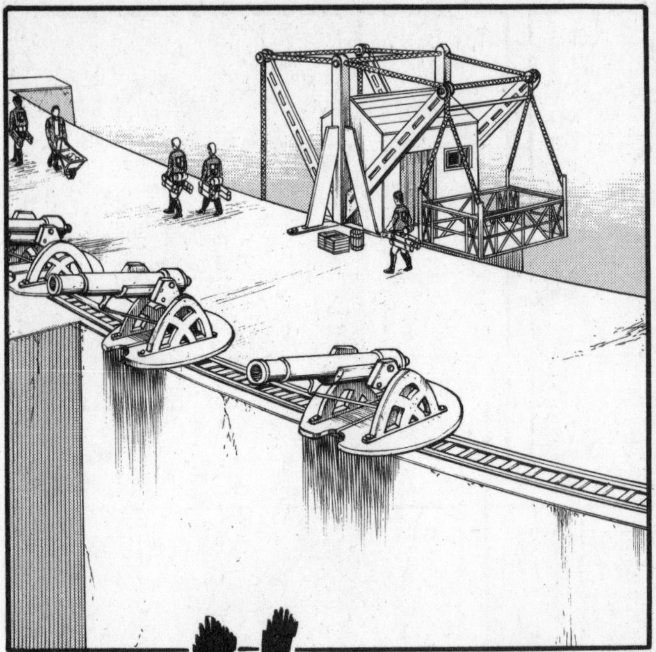
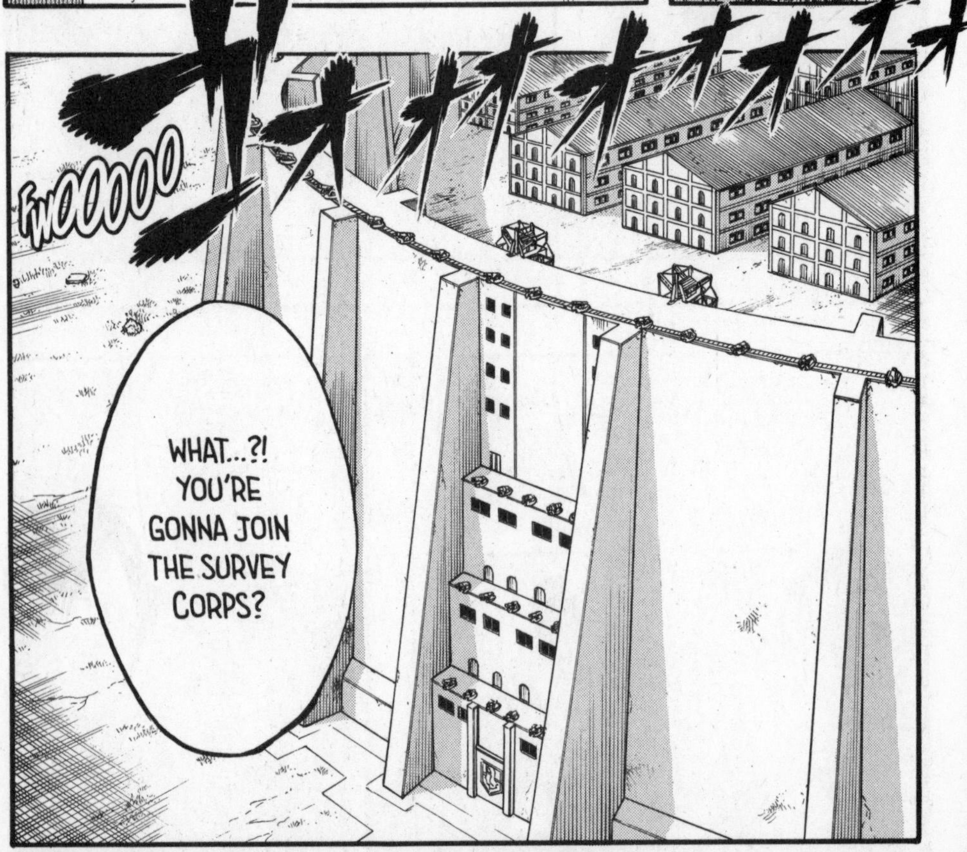
FWOOOOO
WHAT...?! YOU'RE GONNA JOIN THE SURVEY CORPS?

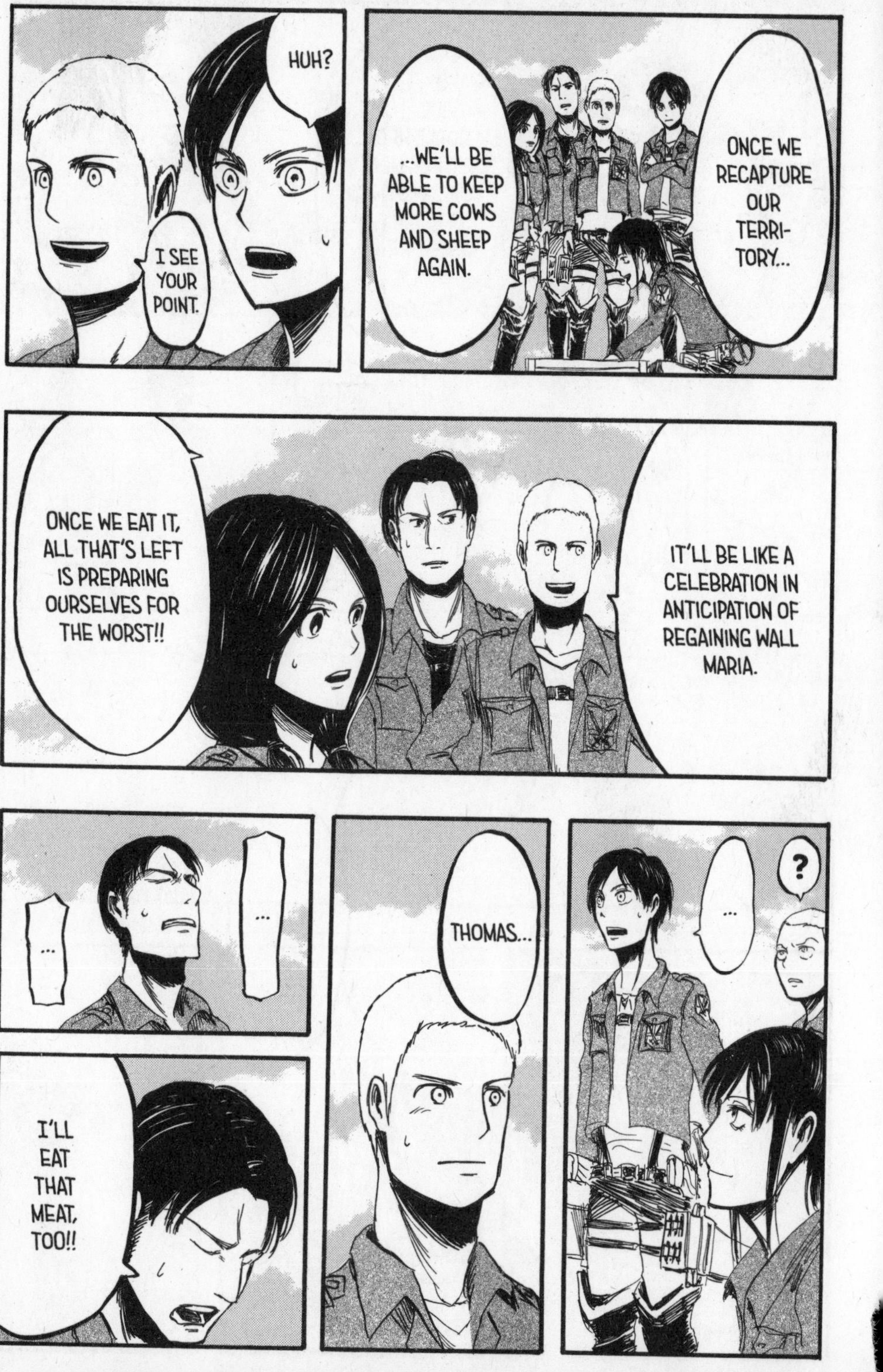
ONCE WE RECAPTURE OUR TERRITORY...
...WE'LL BE ABLE TO KEEP MORE COWS AND SHEEP AGAIN.
HUH?
I SEE YOUR POINT.
IT'LL BE LIKE A CELEBRATION IN ANTICIPATION OF REGAINING WALL MARIA.
ONCE WE EAT IT, ALL THAT'S LEFT IS PREPARING OURSELVES FOR THE WORST!!
?
...
THOMAS...
...
...
I'LL EAT THAT MEAT, TOO!!

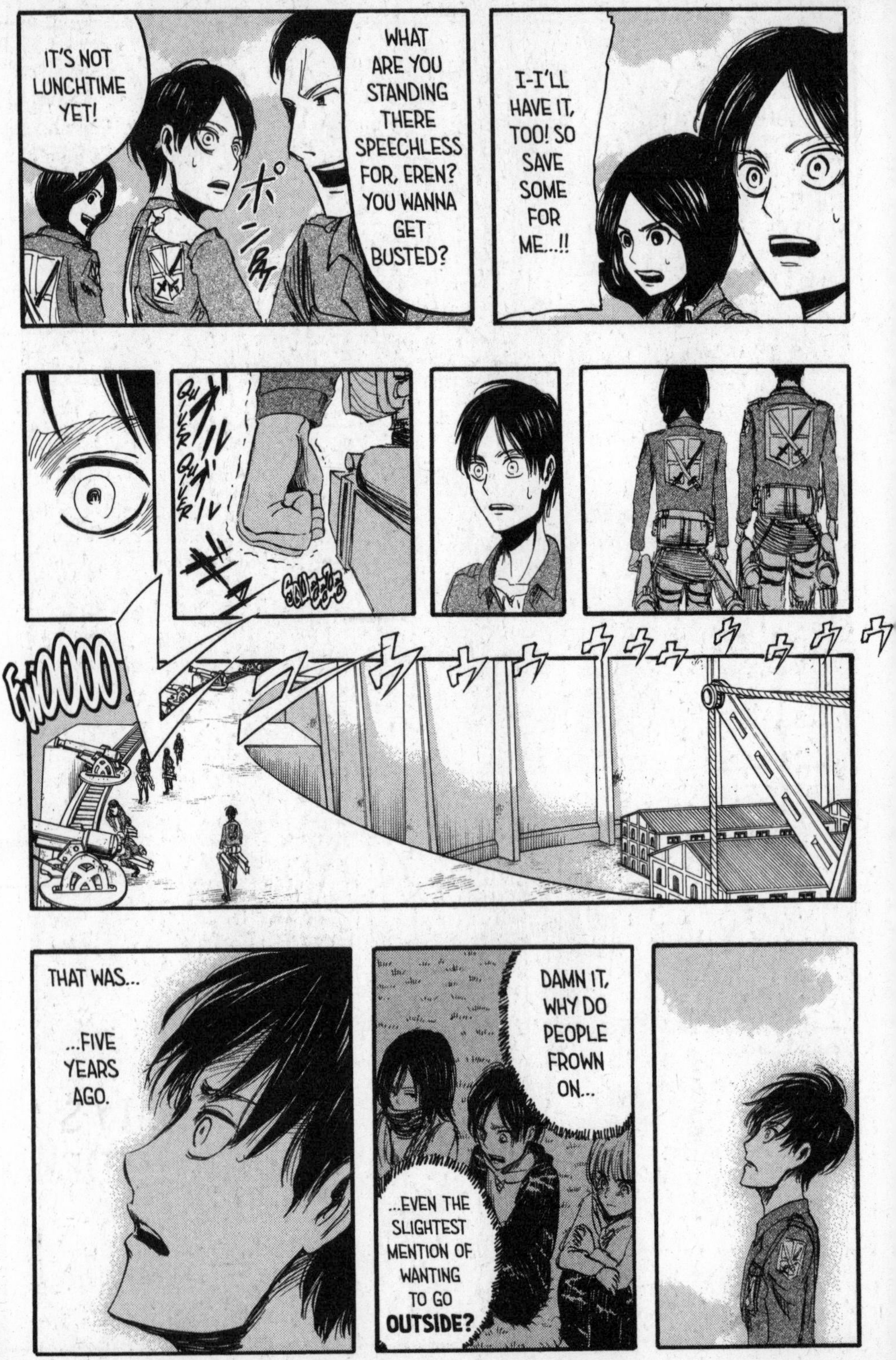
I-I'LL HAVE IT, TOO! SO SAVE SOME FOR ME...!!
WHAT ARE YOU STANDING THERE SPEECHLESS FOR, EREN? YOU WANNA GET BUSTED?
IT'S NOT LUNCHTIME YET!
QUIVER QUIVER
FWOOOO
DAMN IT, WHY DO PEOPLE FROWN ON...
...EVEN THE SLIGHTEST MENTION OF WANTING TO GO **OUTSIDE?**
THAT WAS...
...FIVE YEARS AGO.

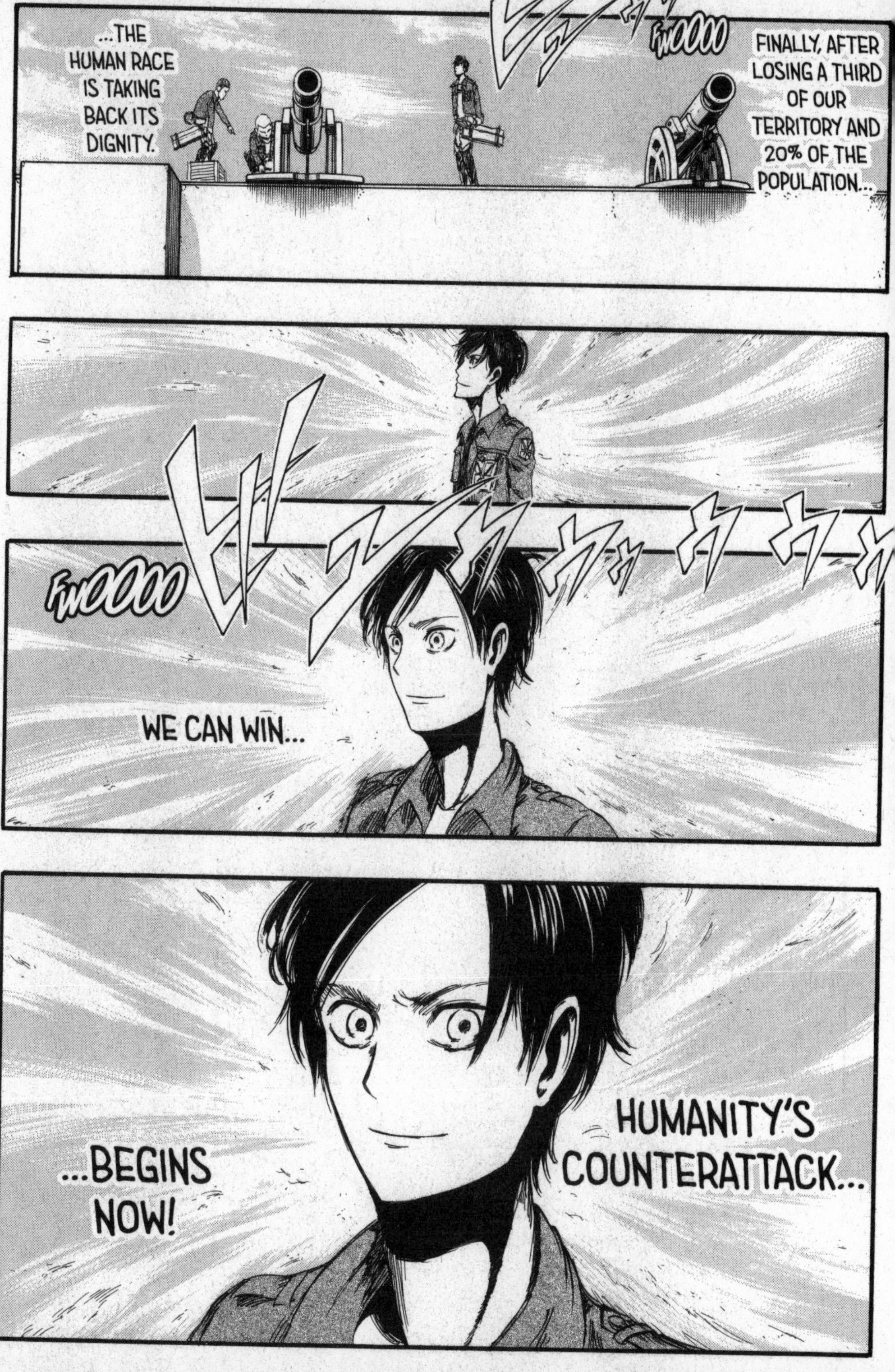
FWOOOO
FINALLY, AFTER LOSING A THIRD OF OUR TERRITORY AND 20% OF THE POPULATION...
...THE HUMAN RACE IS TAKING BACK ITS DIGNITY.
FWOOOO
WE CAN WIN...
HUMANITY'S COUNTERATTACK...
...BEGINS NOW!

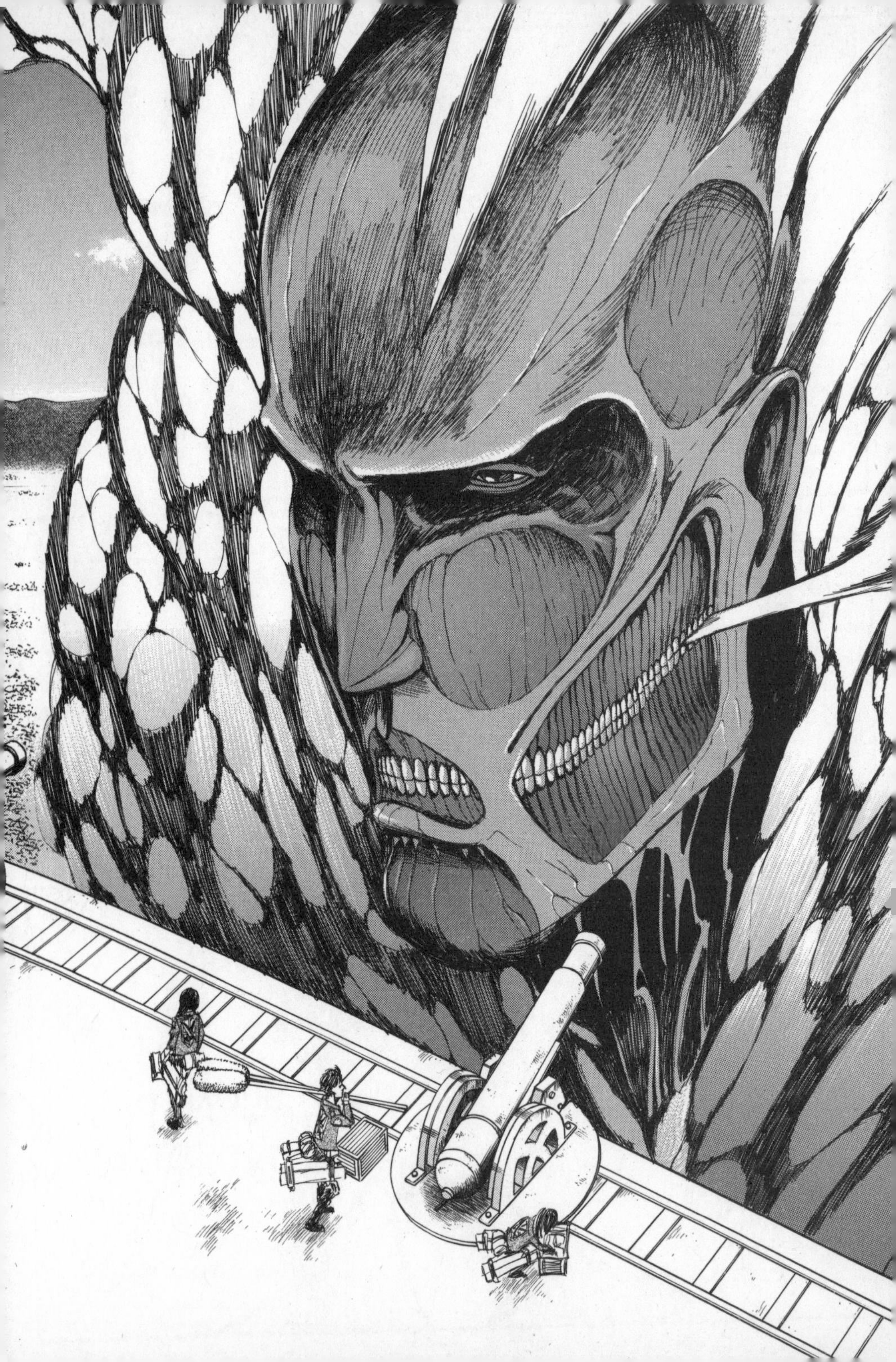

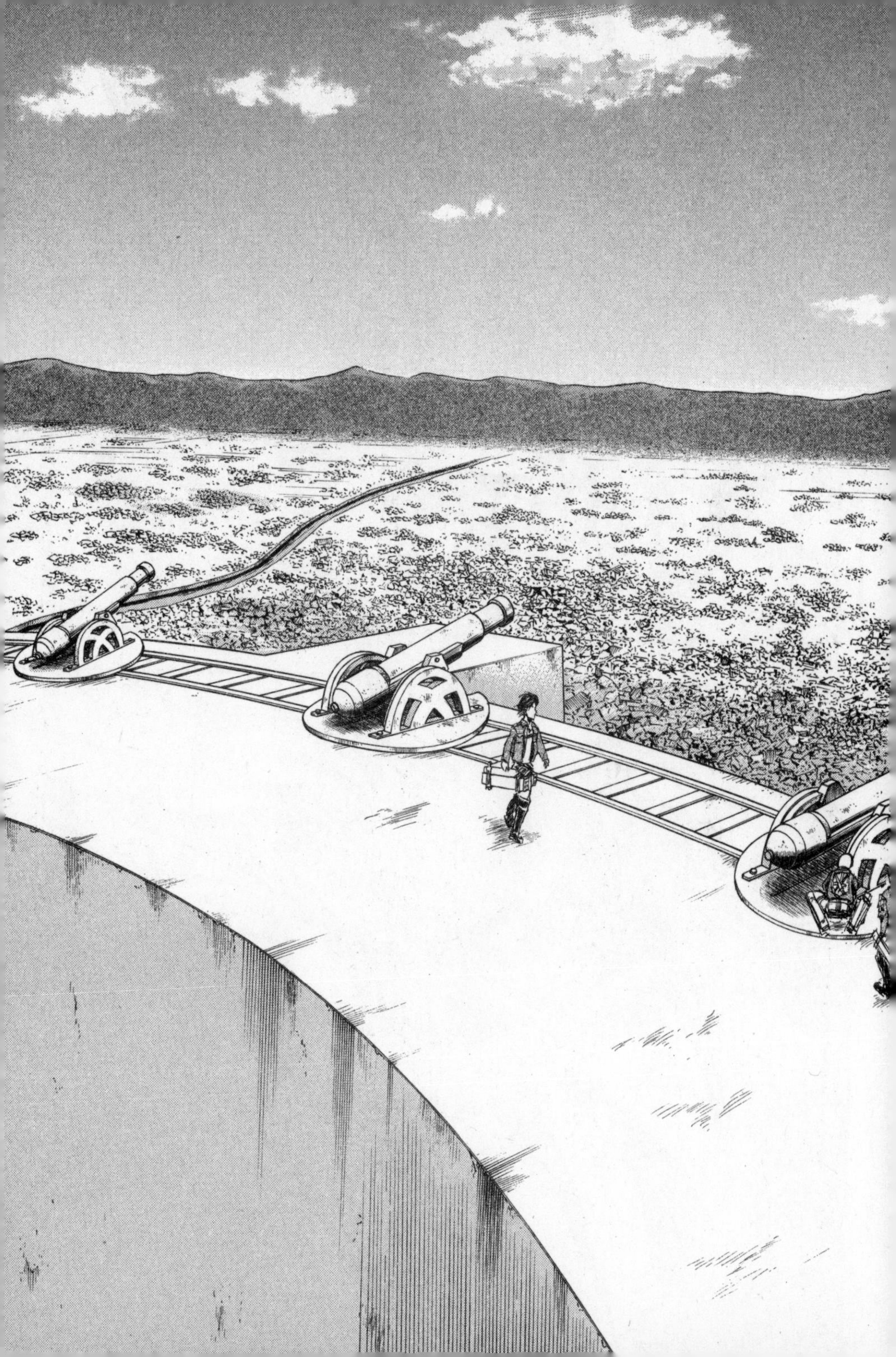

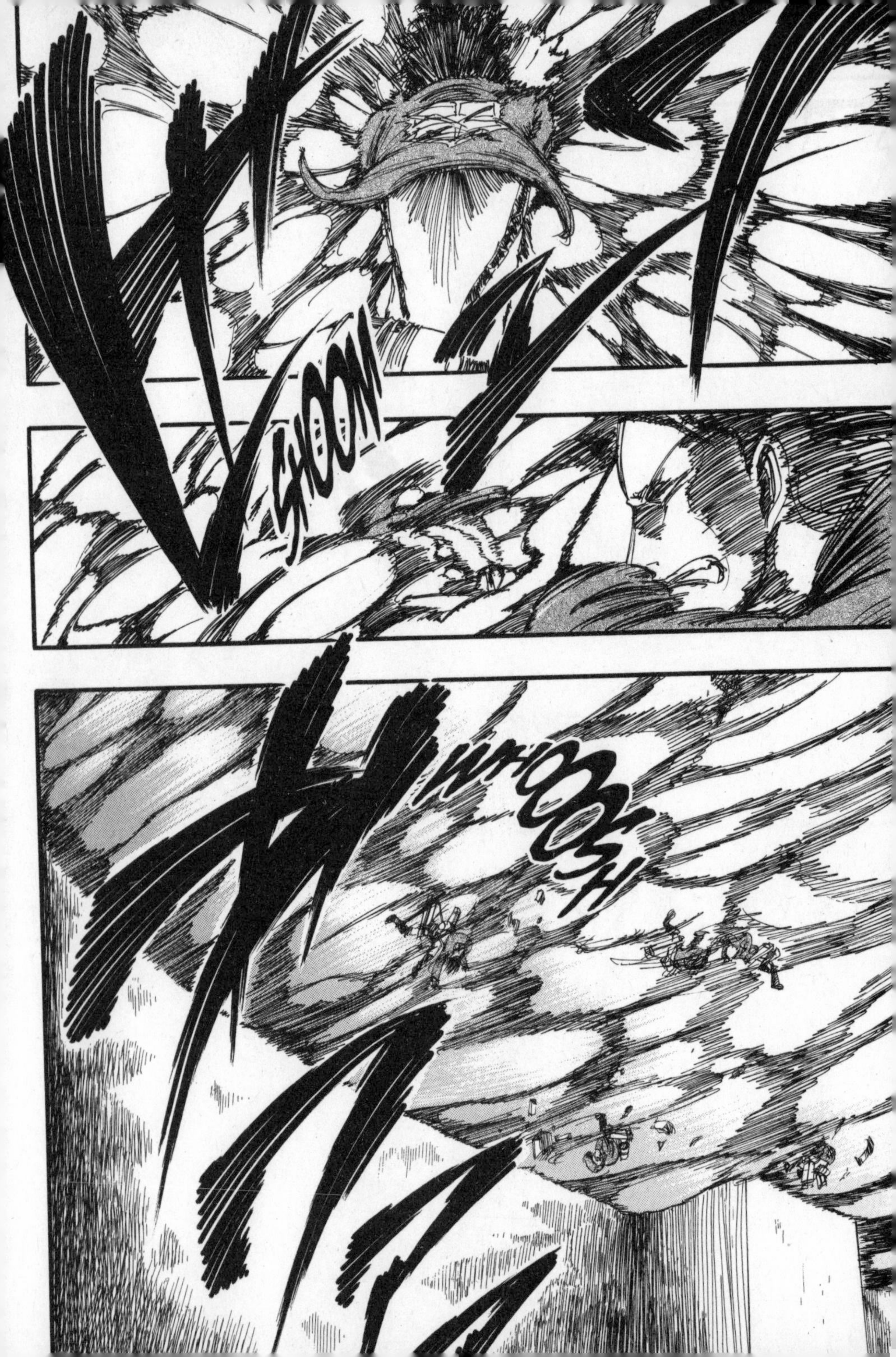
SHOOM
WHOOOSH

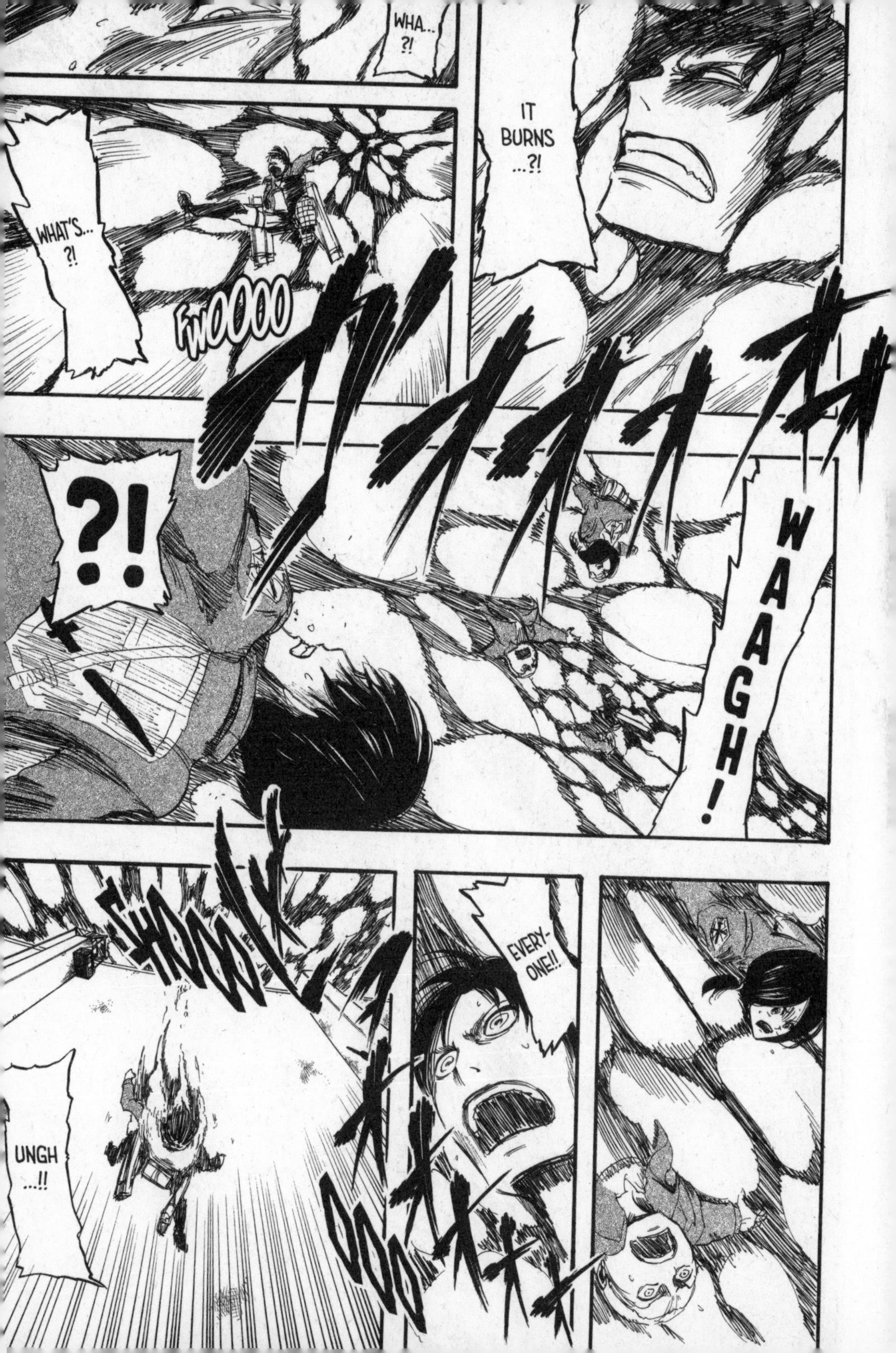
IT BURNS ...?!
WHA... ?!
WHAT'S... ?!
FWOOOO
WAAAGH!
?!
EVERY-ONE!!
UNGH ...!!

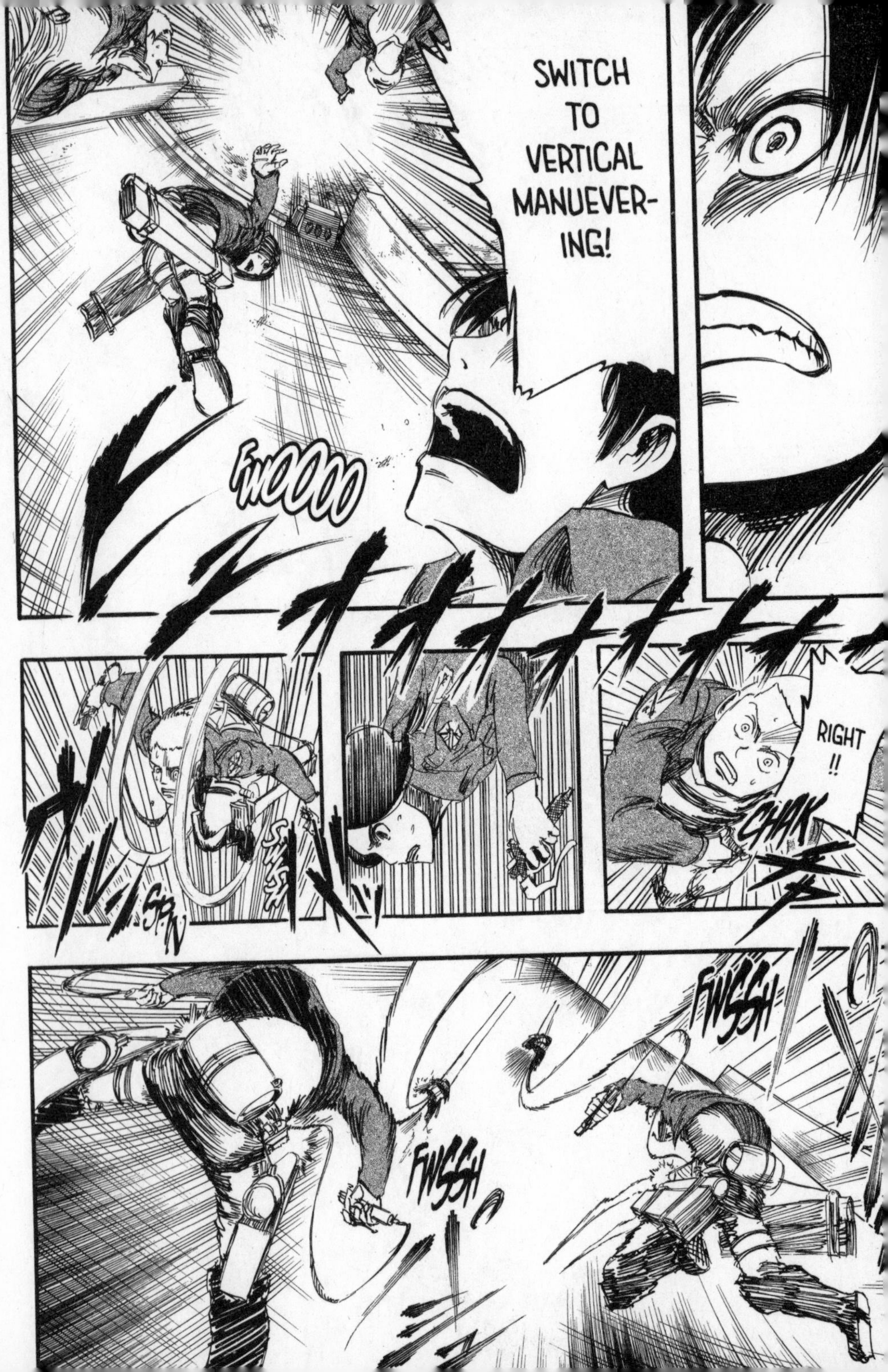
SWITCH TO VERTICAL MANUEVER-ING!
FWOOOO
RIGHT !!
CHAK
SWISH
SPIN
FWSSH
FWSSH

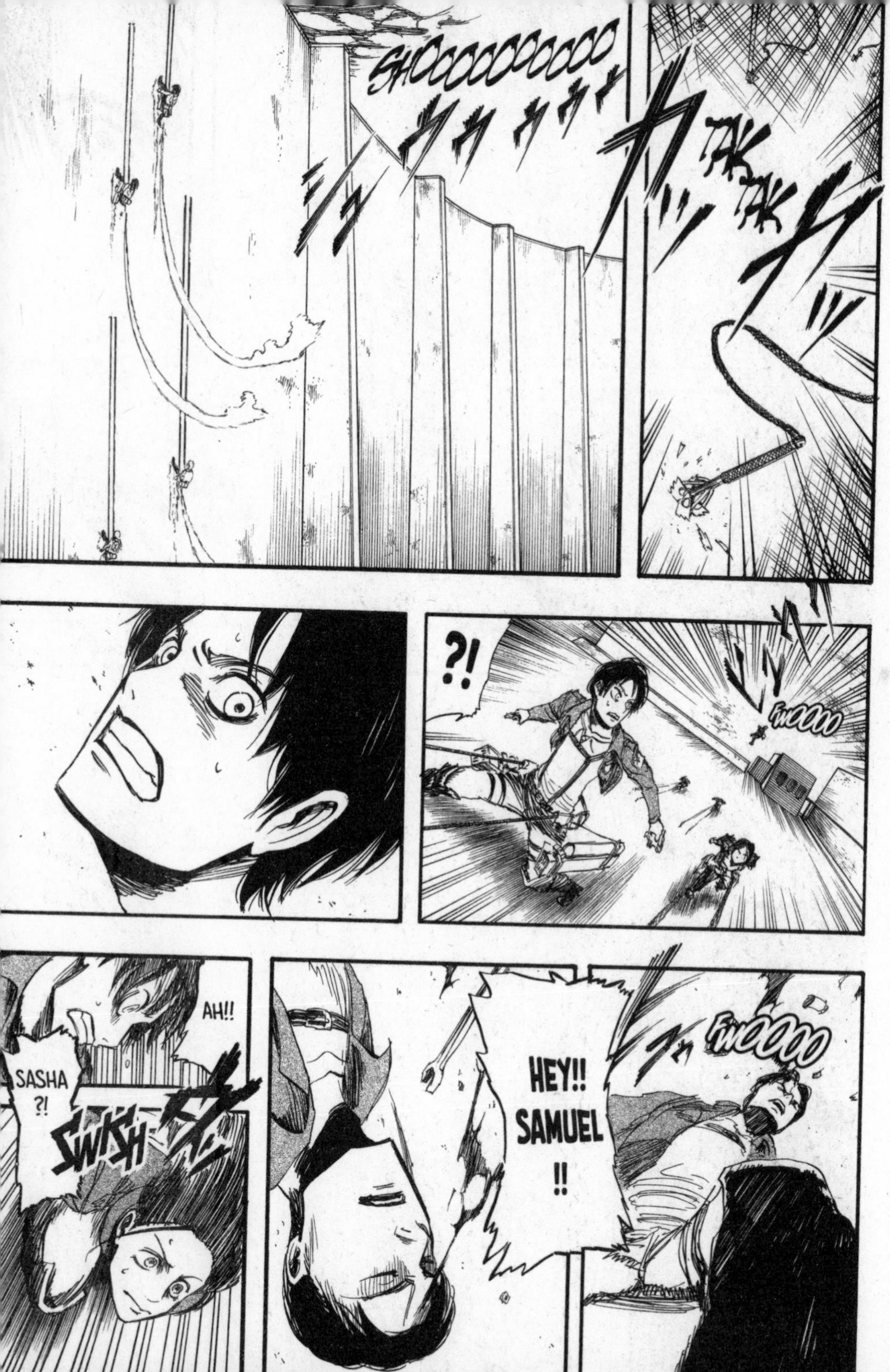
TAK TAK TAK
SHOOOOOOOOOO
?!
FWOOOO
FWOOOOO
HEY!! SAMUEL !!
AH!!
SASHA ?!
SWISH

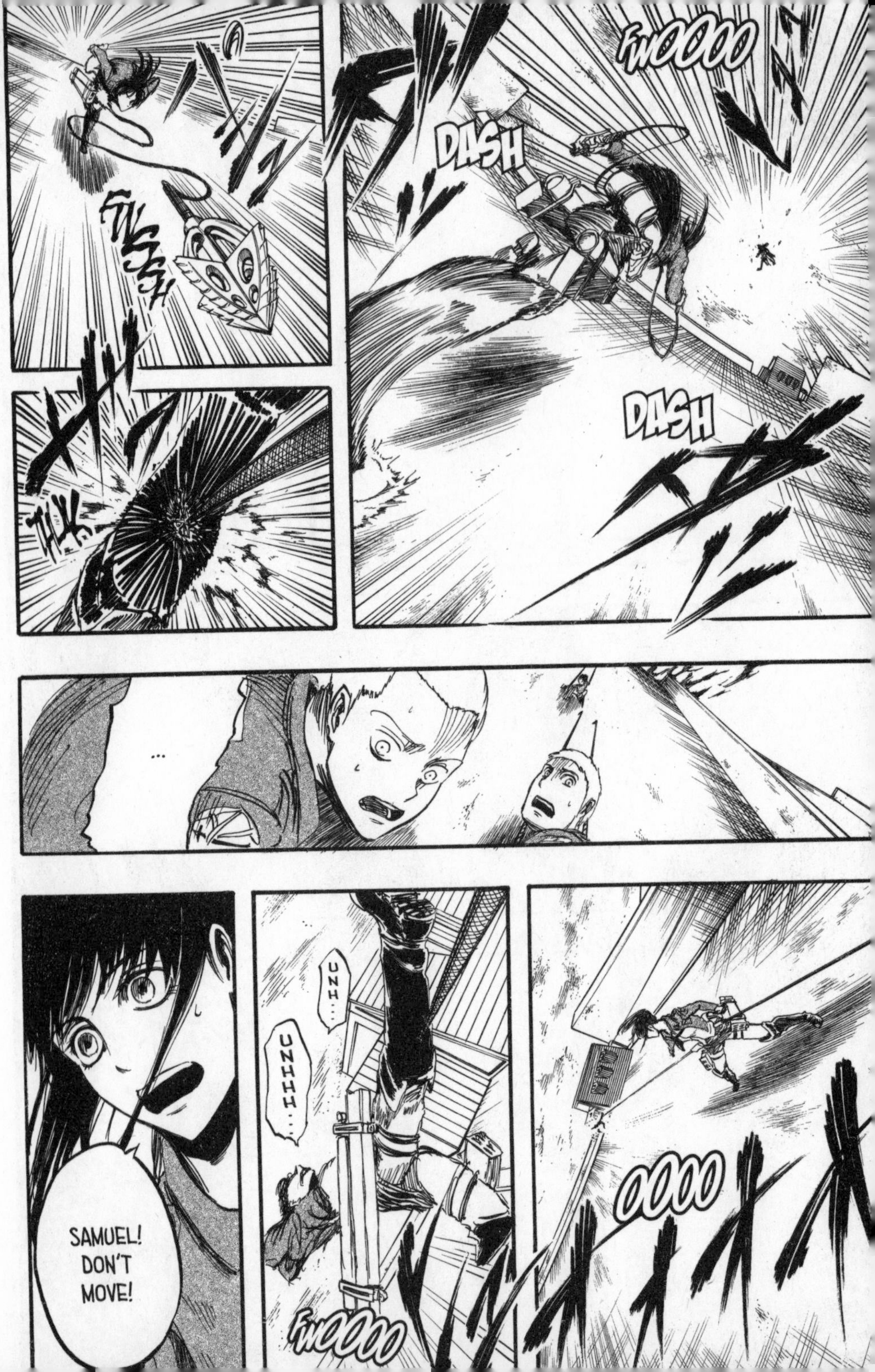
FWOOOO
DASH
DASH
FWSSSH!
...
OOOO
UNH...
UNHHH...
FWOOOO
SAMUEL! DON'T MOVE!

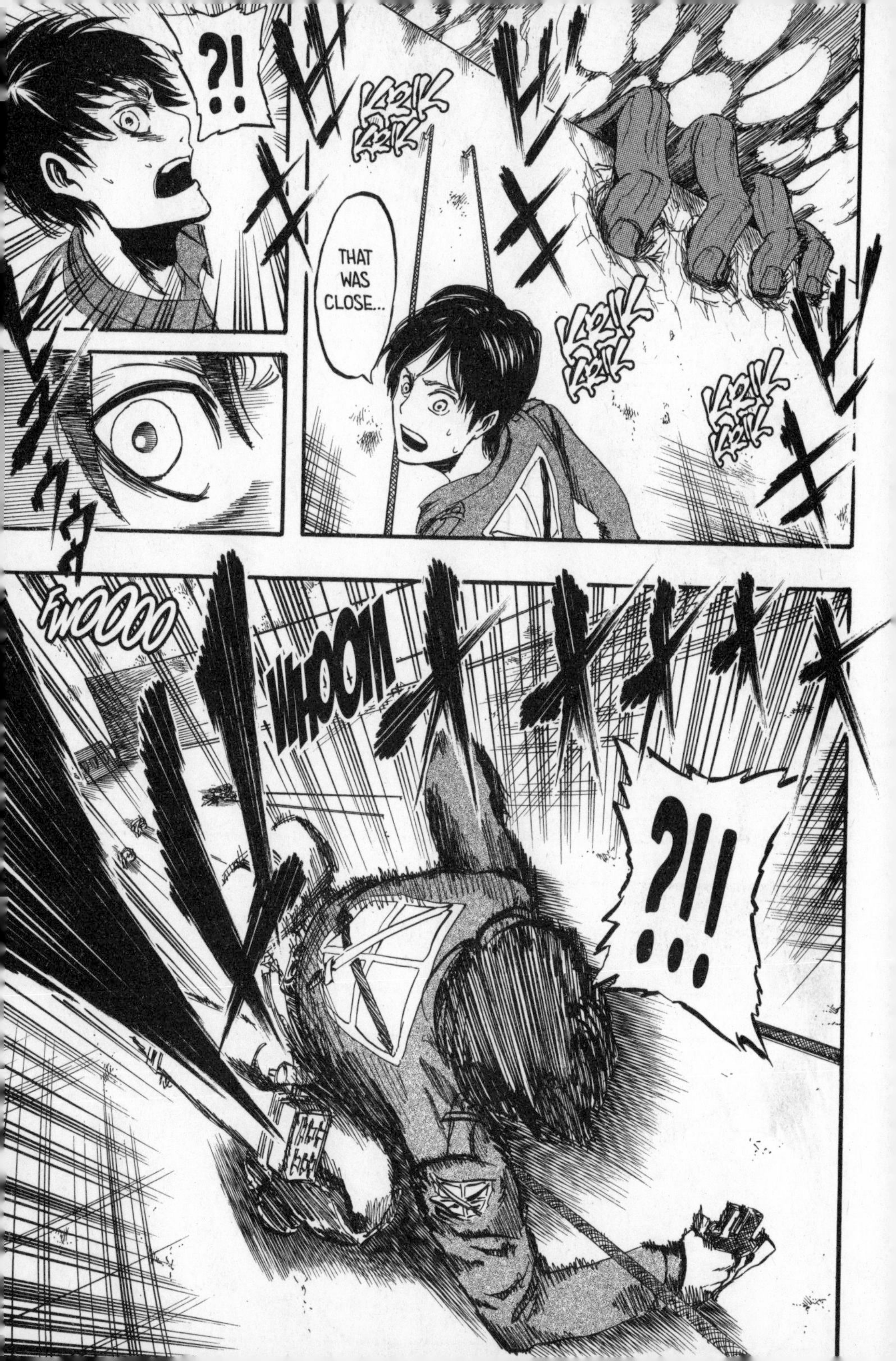
KRAK KRAK
KRAK KRAK
KRAK KRAK
THAT WAS CLOSE...
?!
FWOOOO
WHOOM
?!!

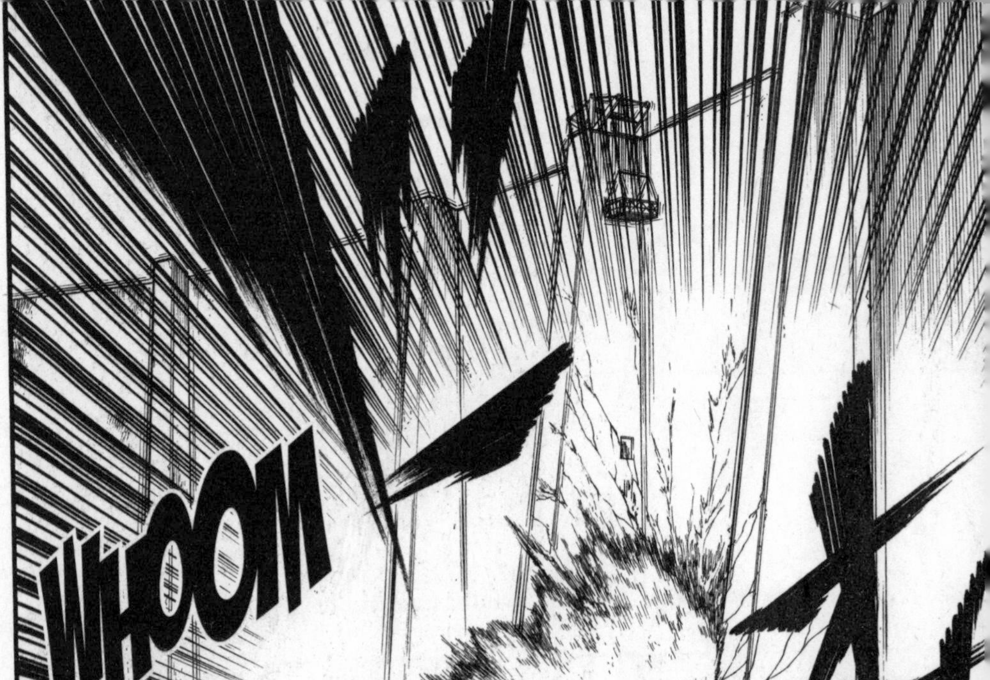
WHOOM
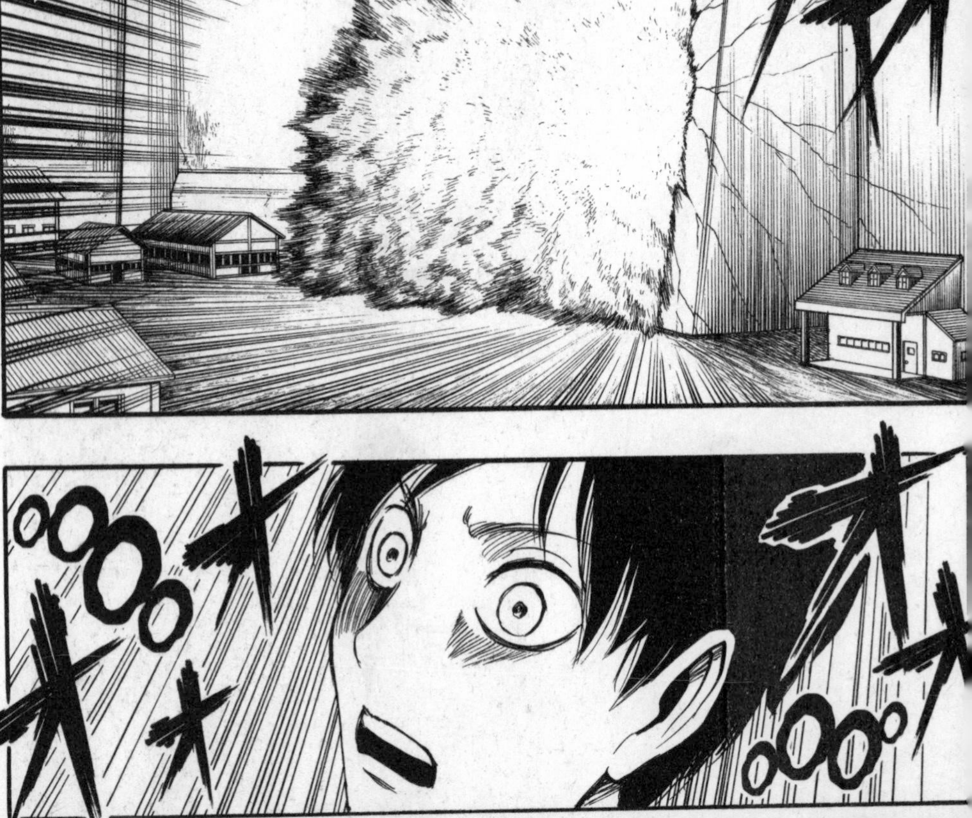

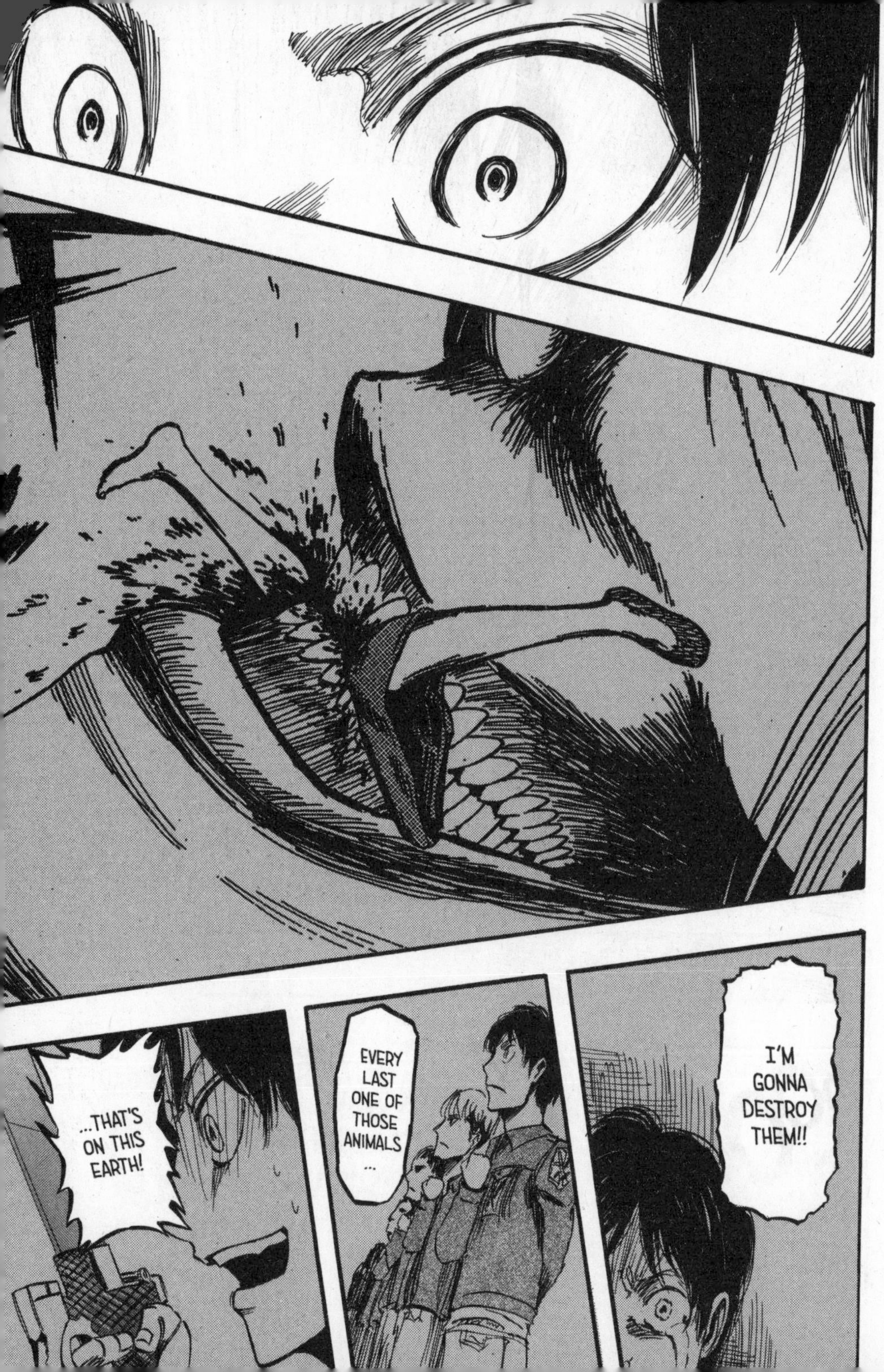
I'M GONNA DESTROY THEM!!
EVERY LAST ONE OF THOSE ANIMALS ...
...THAT'S ON THIS EARTH!

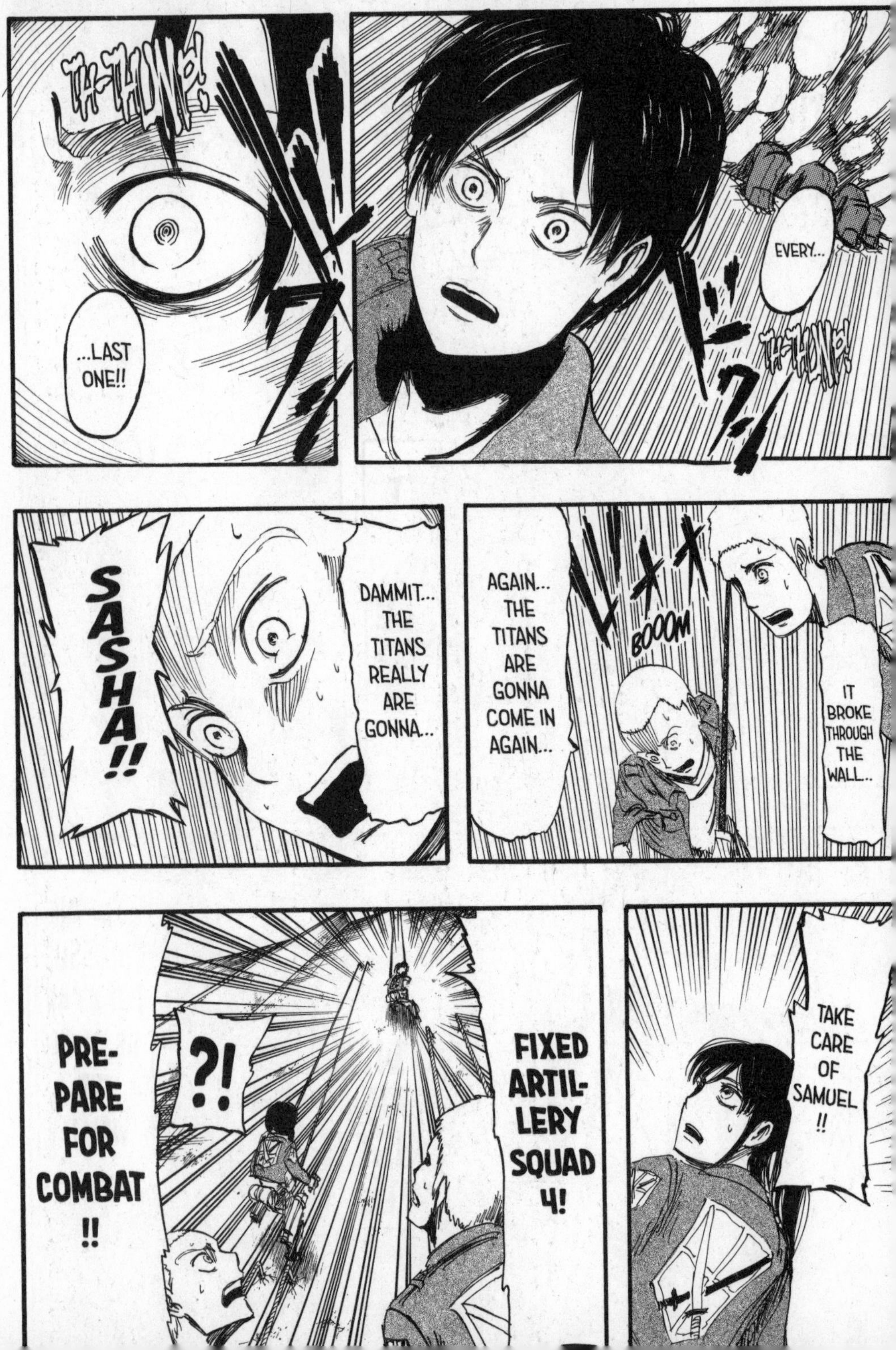
EVERY...
TA-THUNK!
TA-THUNK!
...LAST ONE!!
IT BROKE THROUGH THE WALL...
BOOOM
AGAIN... THE TITANS ARE GONNA COME IN AGAIN...
DAMMIT... THE TITANS REALLY ARE GONNA...
SASHA!!
TAKE CARE OF SAMUEL !!
FIXED ARTIL-LERY SQUAD 4!
?!
PRE-PARE FOR COMBAT !!

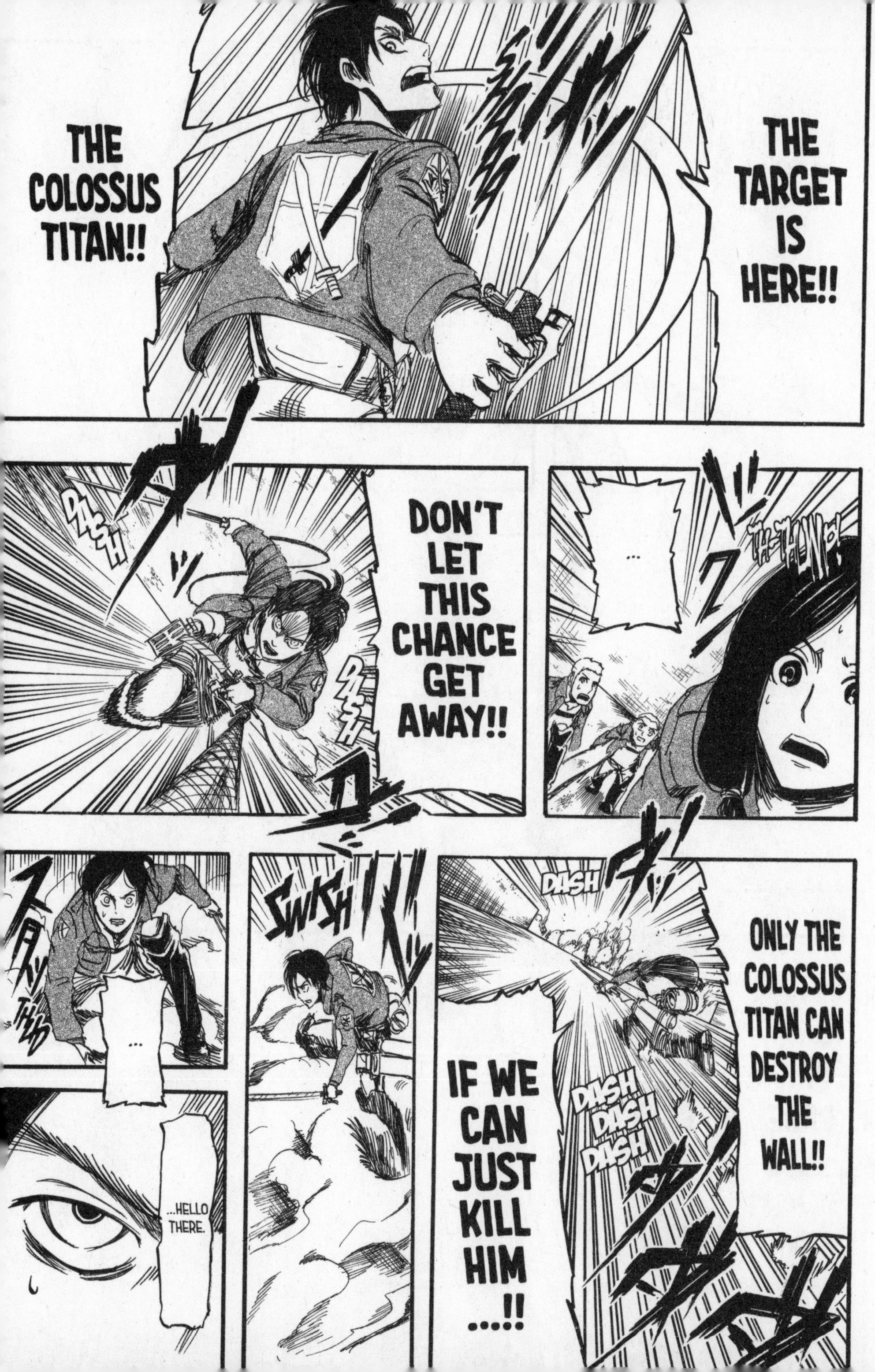
THE TARGET IS HERE!!
THE COLOSSUS TITAN!!
...
DON'T LET THIS CHANCE GET AWAY!!
DASH
DASH
DASH
ONLY THE COLOSSUS TITAN CAN DESTROY THE WALL!!
DASH DASH DASH
IF WE CAN JUST KILL HIM ....!!
SWISH
...
...HELLO THERE.

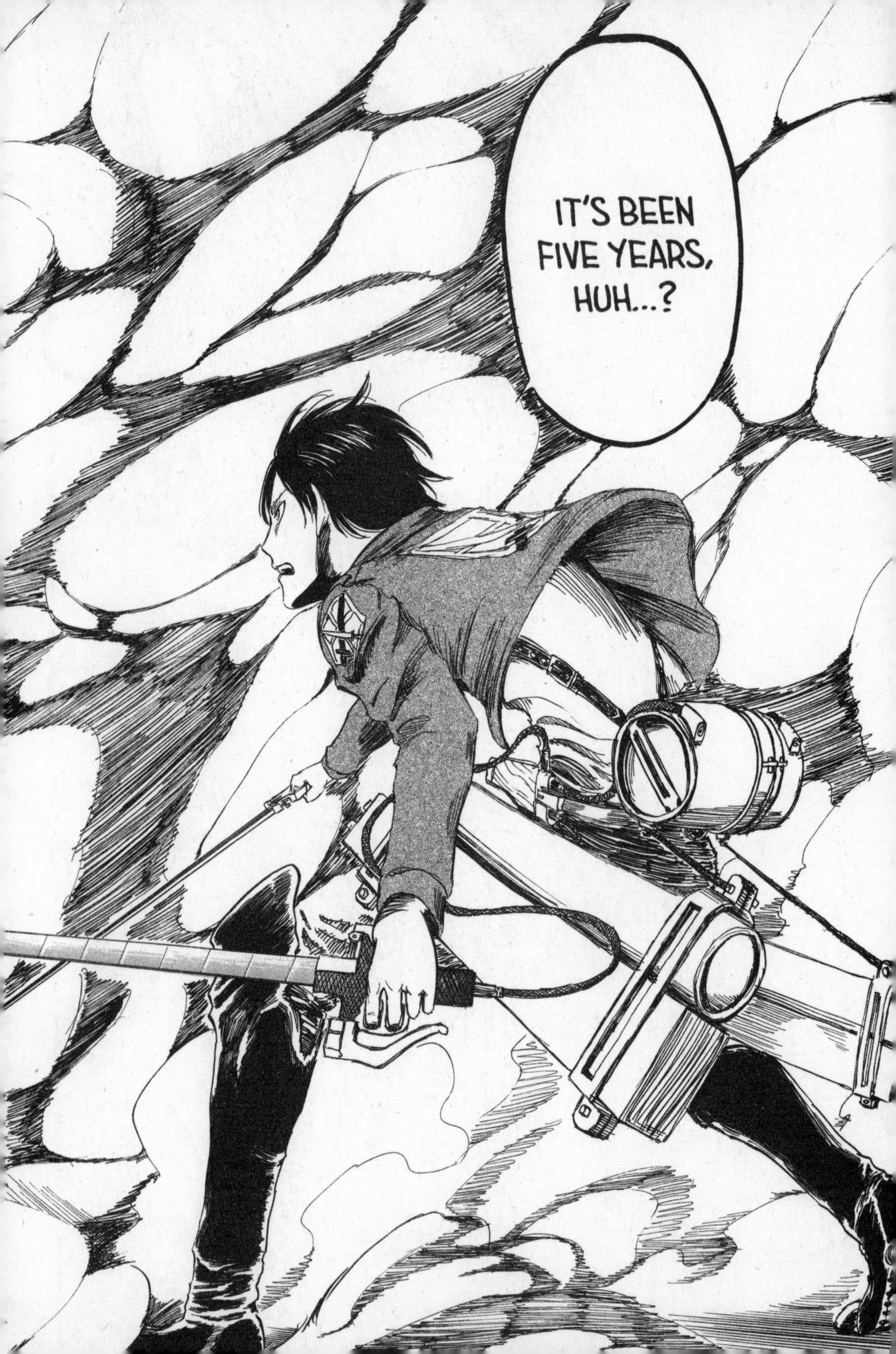
IT'S BEEN FIVE YEARS, HUH...?

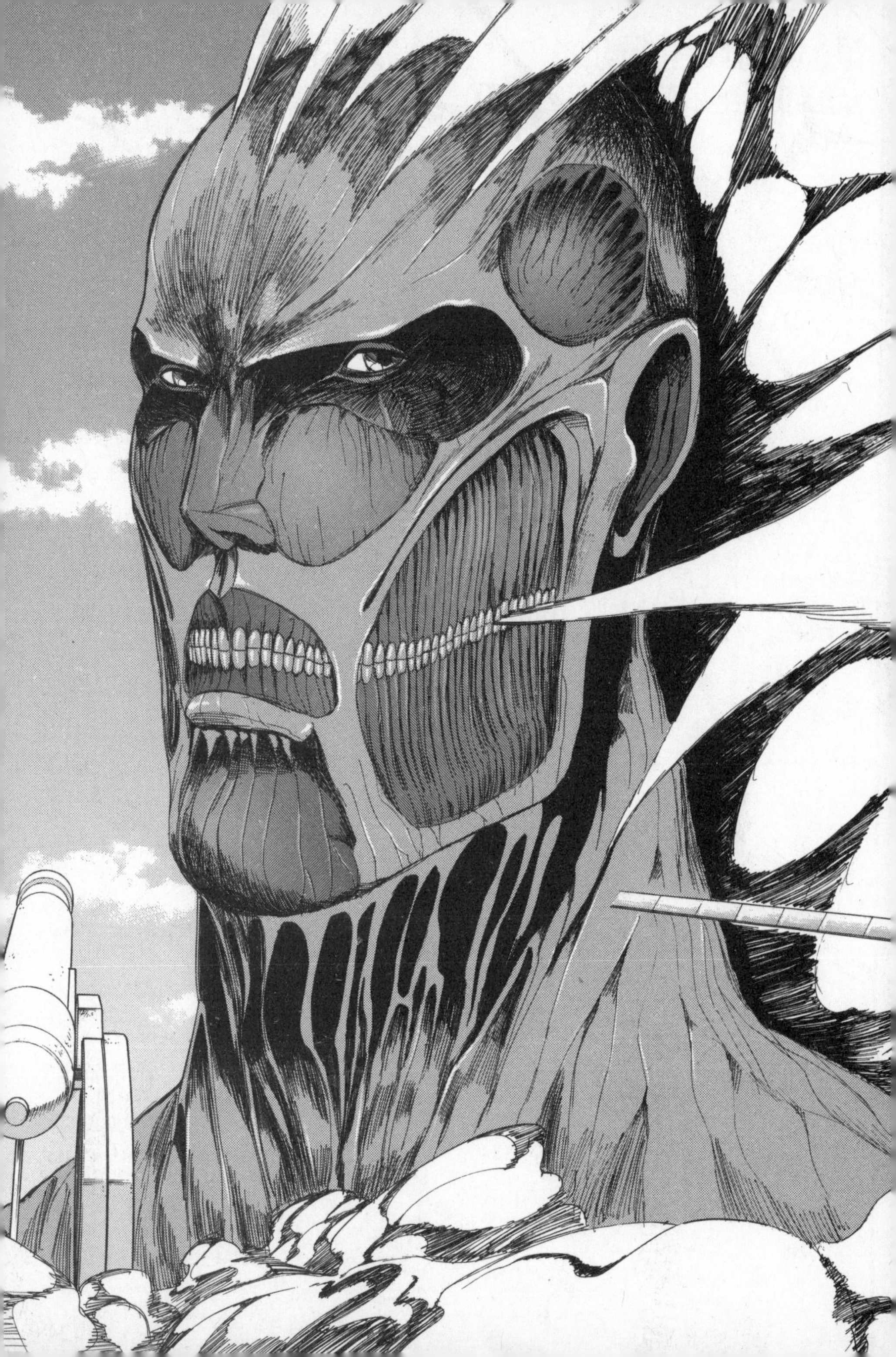

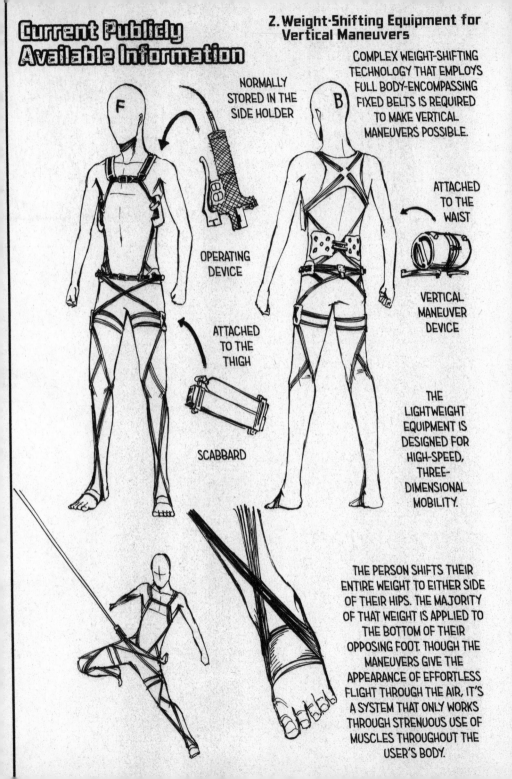

Current Publicly Available Information

2. Weight-Shifting Equipment for Vertical Maneuvers

COMPLEX WEIGHT-SHIFTING TECHNOLOGY THAT EMPLOYS FULL BODY-ENCOMPASSING FIXED BELTS IS REQUIRED TO MAKE VERTICAL MANEUVERS POSSIBLE.

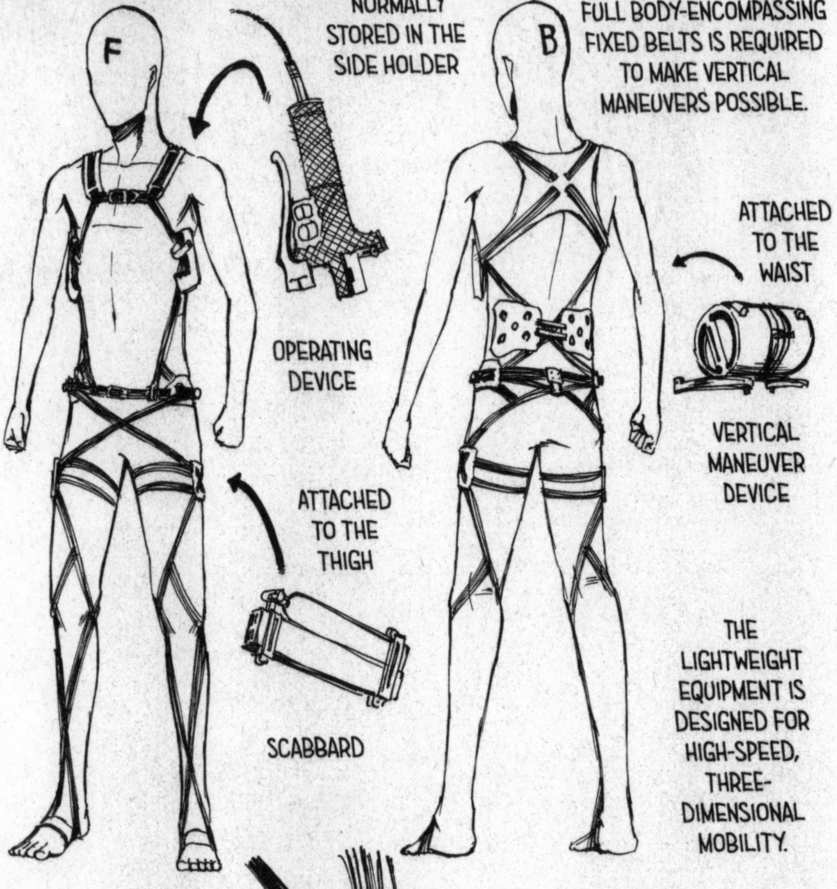

F
NORMALLY STORED IN THE SIDE HOLDER
OPERATING DEVICE
ATTACHED TO THE THIGH
SCABBARD
B
ATTACHED TO THE WAIST
VERTICAL MANEUVER DEVICE

THE LIGHTWEIGHT EQUIPMENT IS DESIGNED FOR HIGH-SPEED, THREE-DIMENSIONAL MOBILITY.

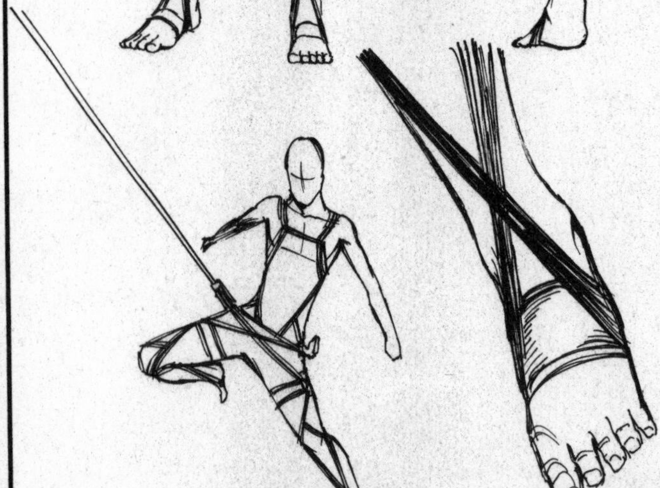

THE PERSON SHIFTS THEIR ENTIRE WEIGHT TO EITHER SIDE OF THEIR HIPS. THE MAJORITY OF THAT WEIGHT IS APPLIED TO THE BOTTOM OF THEIR OPPOSING FOOT. THOUGH THE MANEUVERS GIVE THE APPEARANCE OF EFFORTLESS FLIGHT THROUGH THE AIR, IT'S A SYSTEM THAT ONLY WORKS THROUGH STRENUOUS USE OF MUSCLES THROUGHOUT THE USER'S BODY.

Episode 4:
First Battle

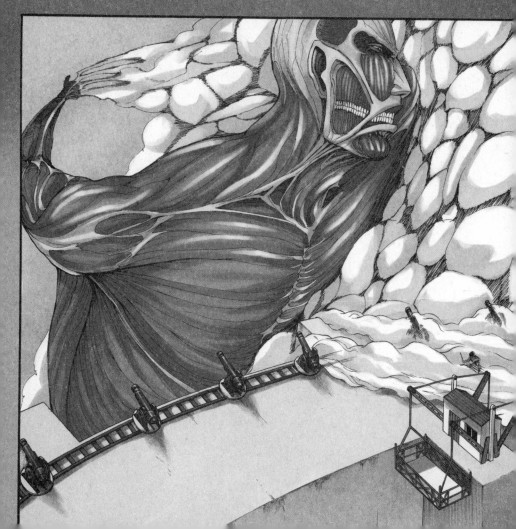

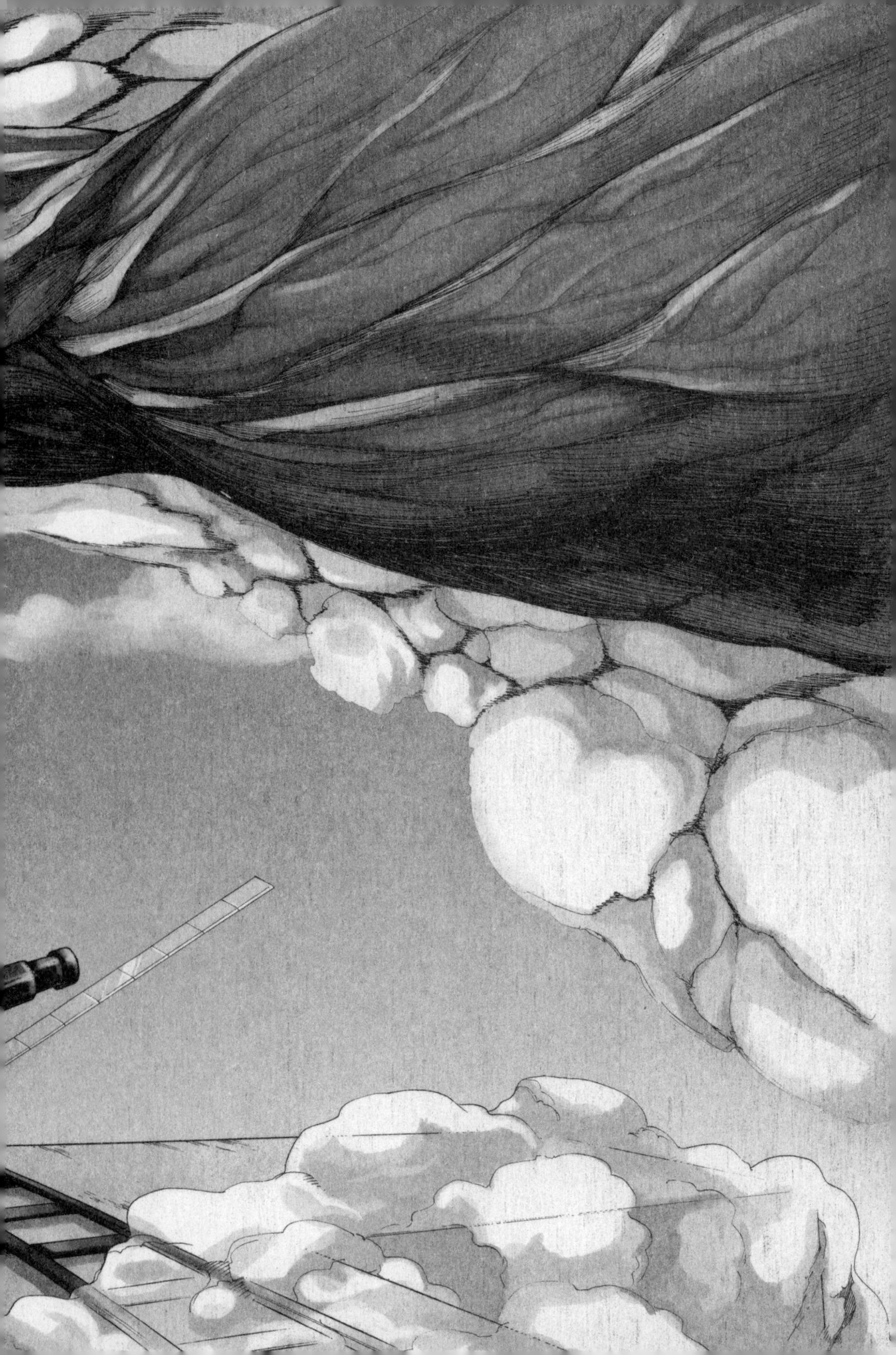

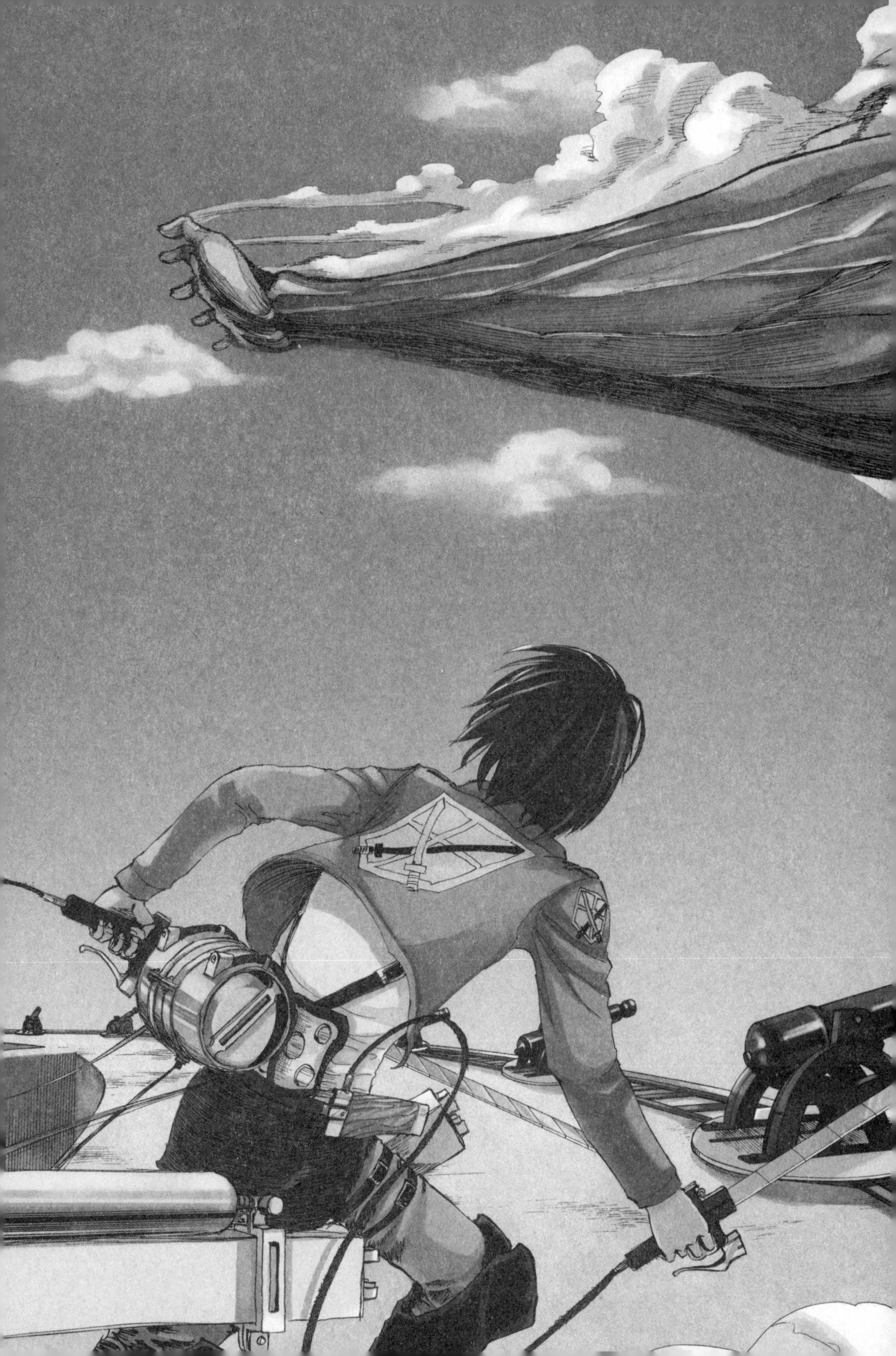

Current Publicly Available Information

3. A Basic Overview of the Vertical Maneuvering Devices

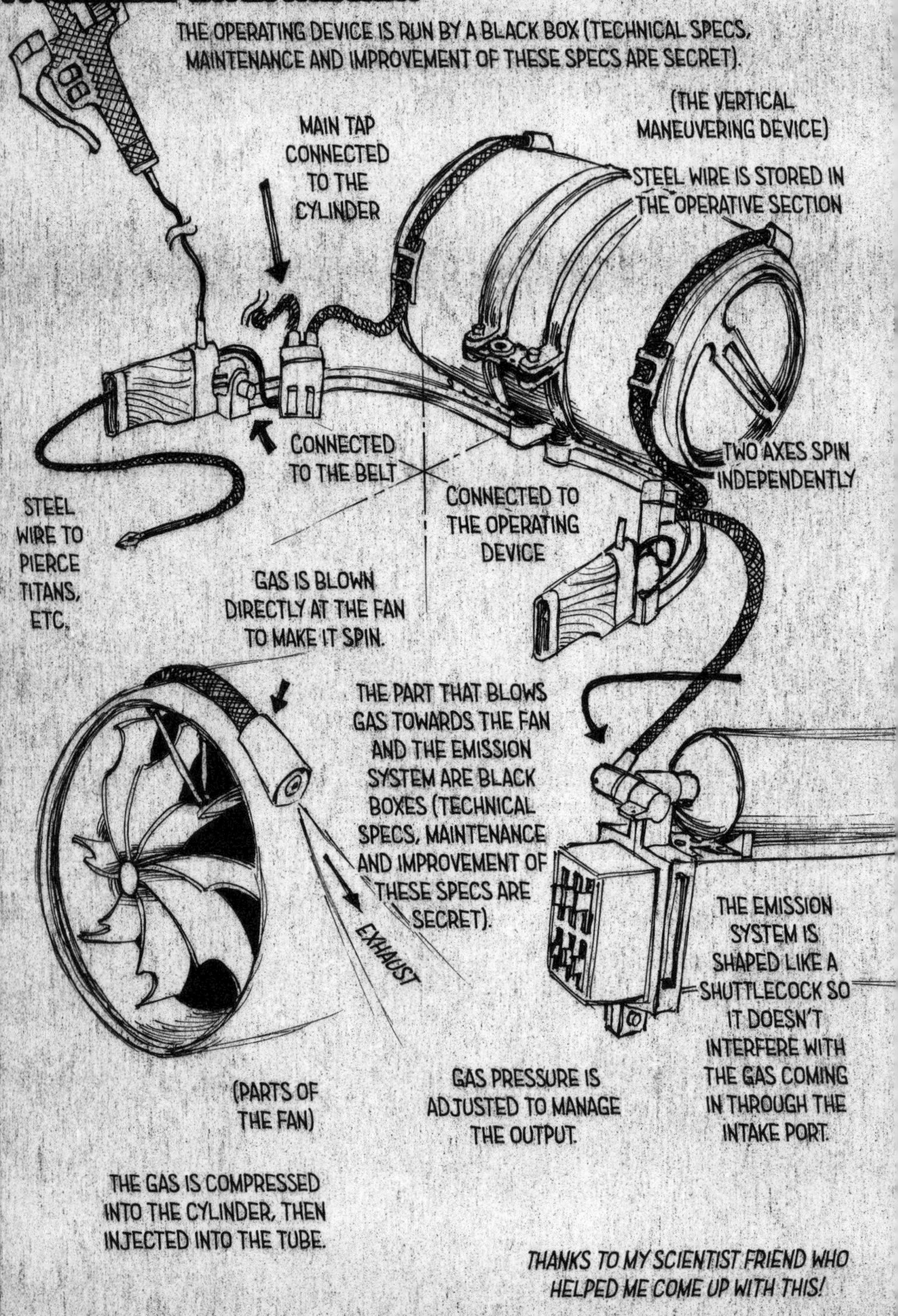
THE OPERATING DEVICE IS RUN BY A BLACK BOX (TECHNICAL SPECS, MAINTENANCE AND IMPROVEMENT OF THESE SPECS ARE SECRET).
(THE VERTICAL MANEUVERING DEVICE)
MAIN TAP CONNECTED TO THE CYLINDER
STEEL WIRE IS STORED IN THE OPERATIVE SECTION
TWO AXES SPIN INDEPENDENTLY
CONNECTED TO THE BELT
CONNECTED TO THE OPERATING DEVICE
STEEL WIRE TO PIERCE TITANS, ETC.
GAS IS BLOWN DIRECTLY AT THE FAN TO MAKE IT SPIN.
THE PART THAT BLOWS GAS TOWARDS THE FAN AND THE EMISSION SYSTEM ARE BLACK BOXES (TECHNICAL SPECS, MAINTENANCE AND IMPROVEMENT OF THESE SPECS ARE SECRET).
EXHAUST
THE EMISSION SYSTEM IS SHAPED LIKE A SHUTTLECOCK SO IT DOESN'T INTERFERE WITH THE GAS COMING IN THROUGH THE INTAKE PORT.
(PARTS OF THE FAN)
GAS PRESSURE IS ADJUSTED TO MANAGE THE OUTPUT.
THE GAS IS COMPRESSED INTO THE CYLINDER, THEN INJECTED INTO THE TUBE.
THANKS TO MY SCIENTIST FRIEND WHO HELPED ME COME UP WITH THIS!

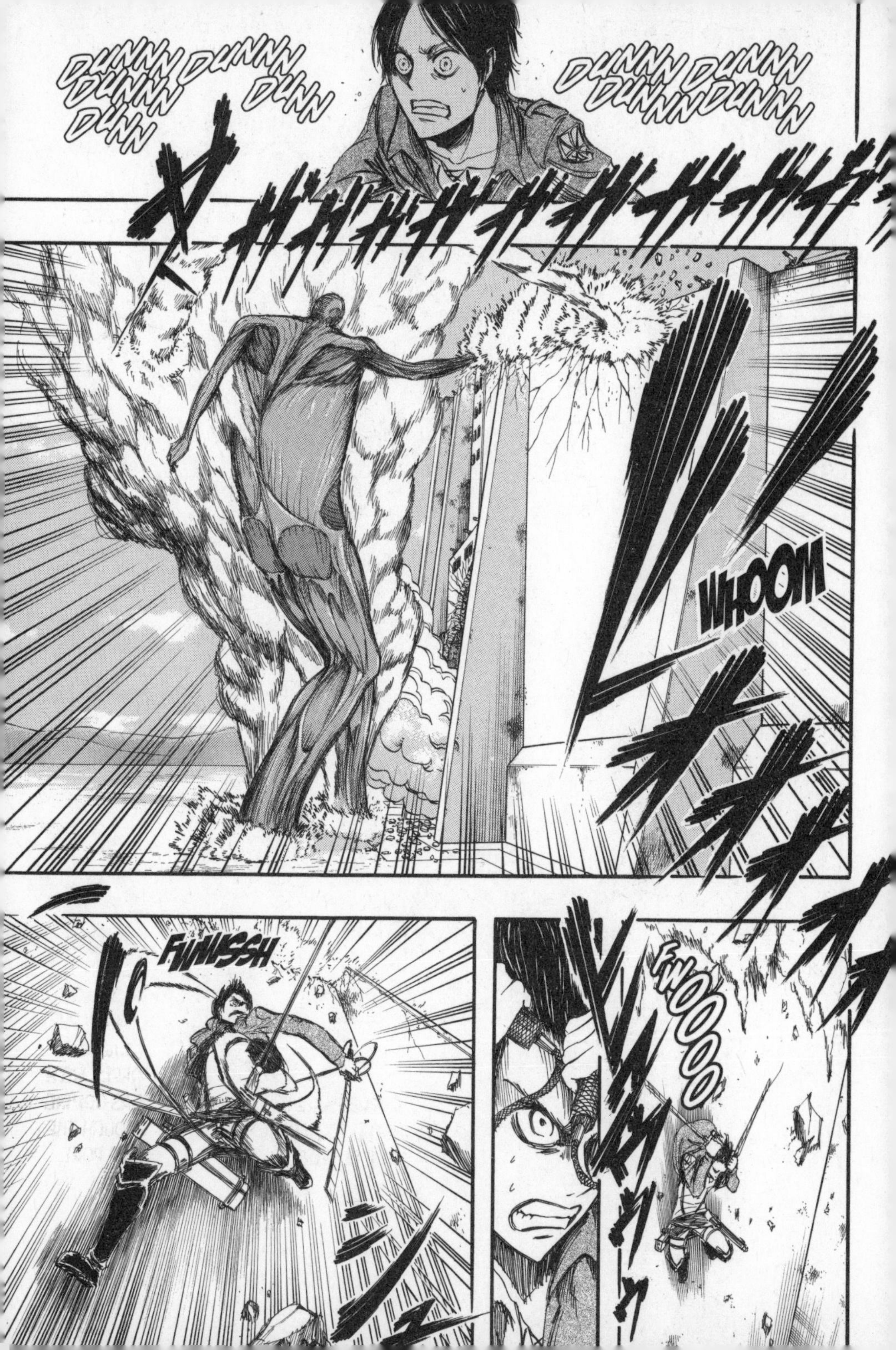
DUNNN DUNNN DUNNN DUNNN
DUNNN DUNNN DUNN DUNN
WHOOM
FWOOOO
FWUSSH

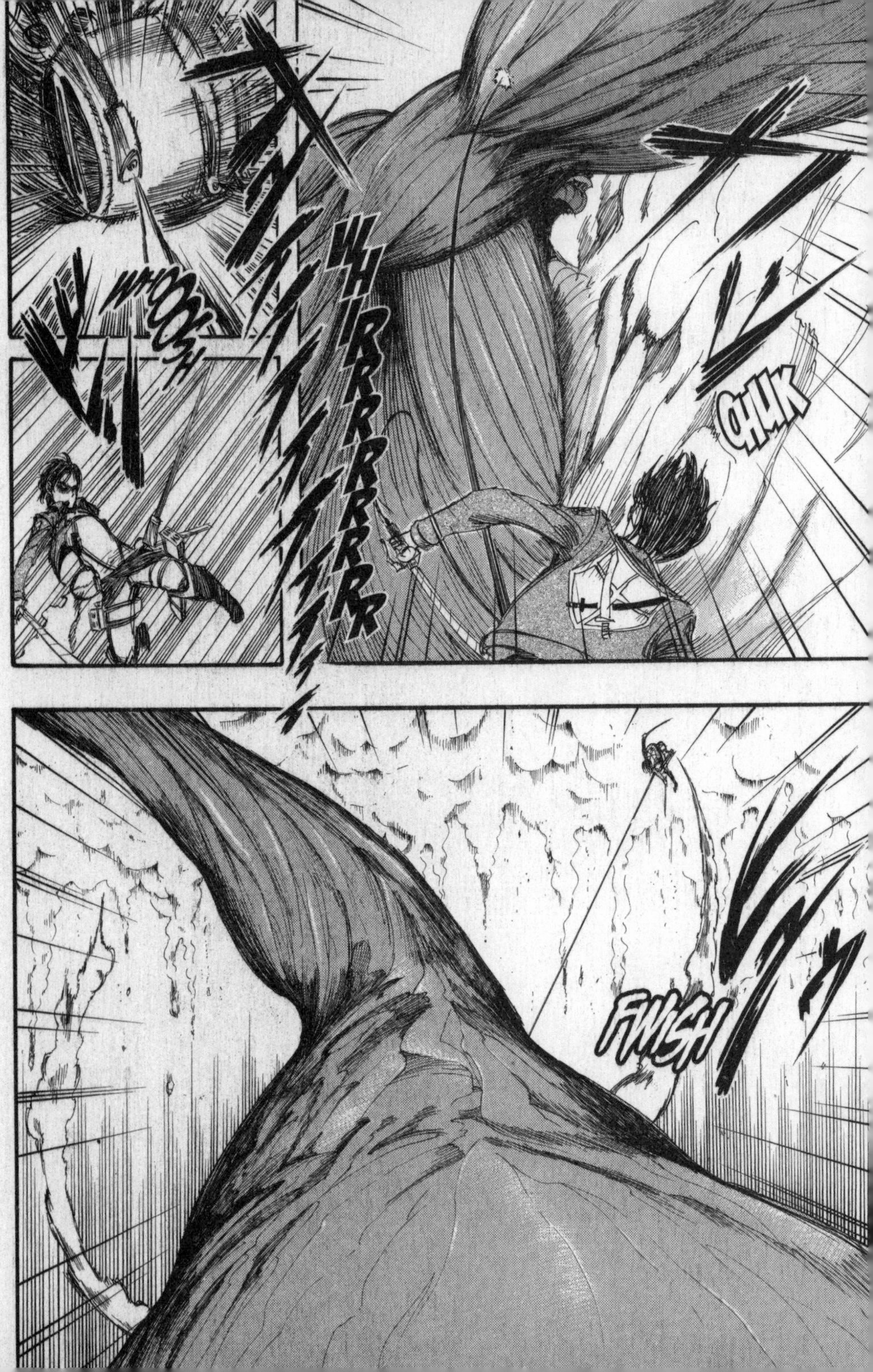
CHUK
WHIRRRRRRRRR
WHOOOSH
FWISH

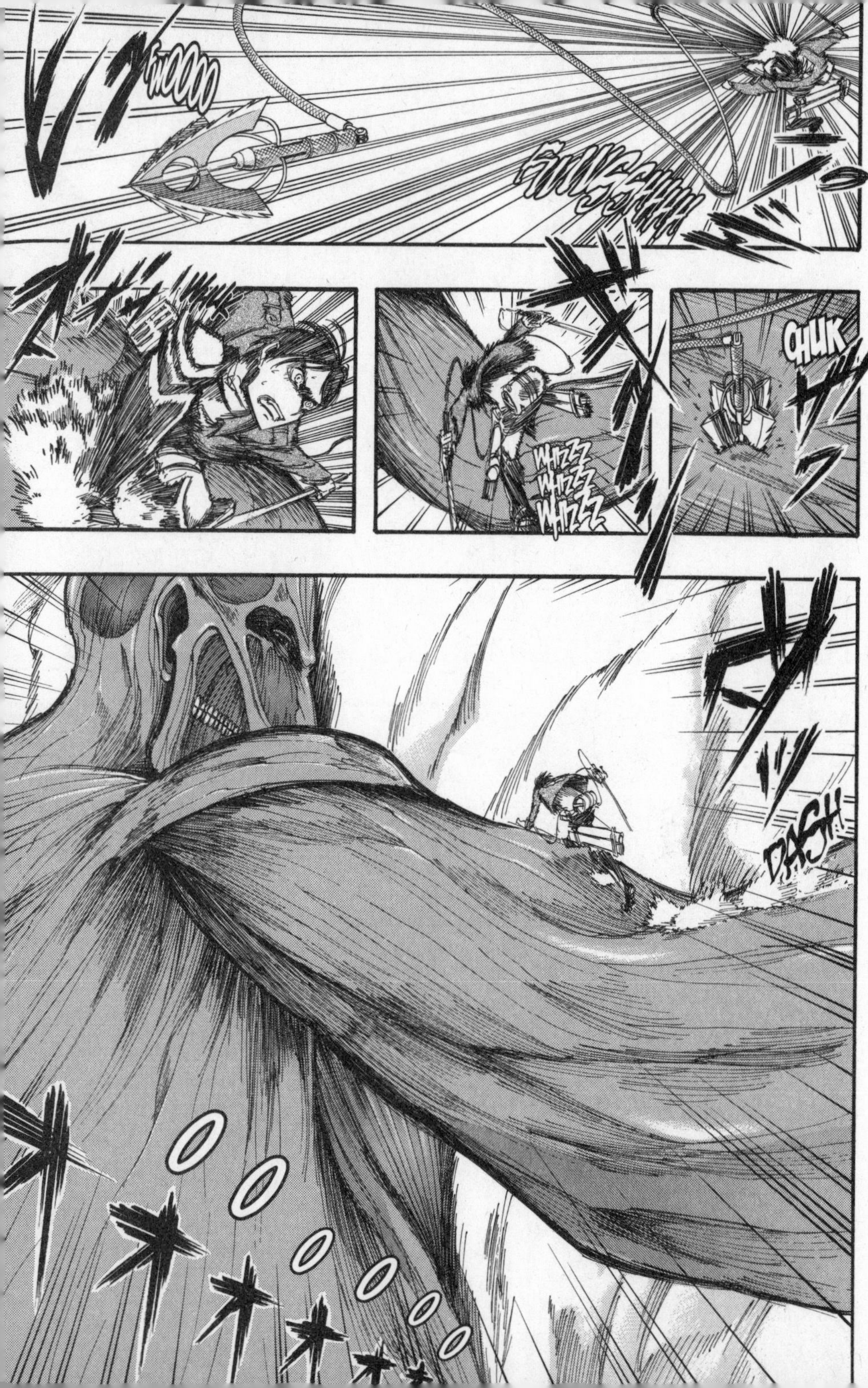
FWOOOO
FWUSHHHH!!
CHUK
WHIZZZ
WHIZZZ
WHIZZZ
DASH!

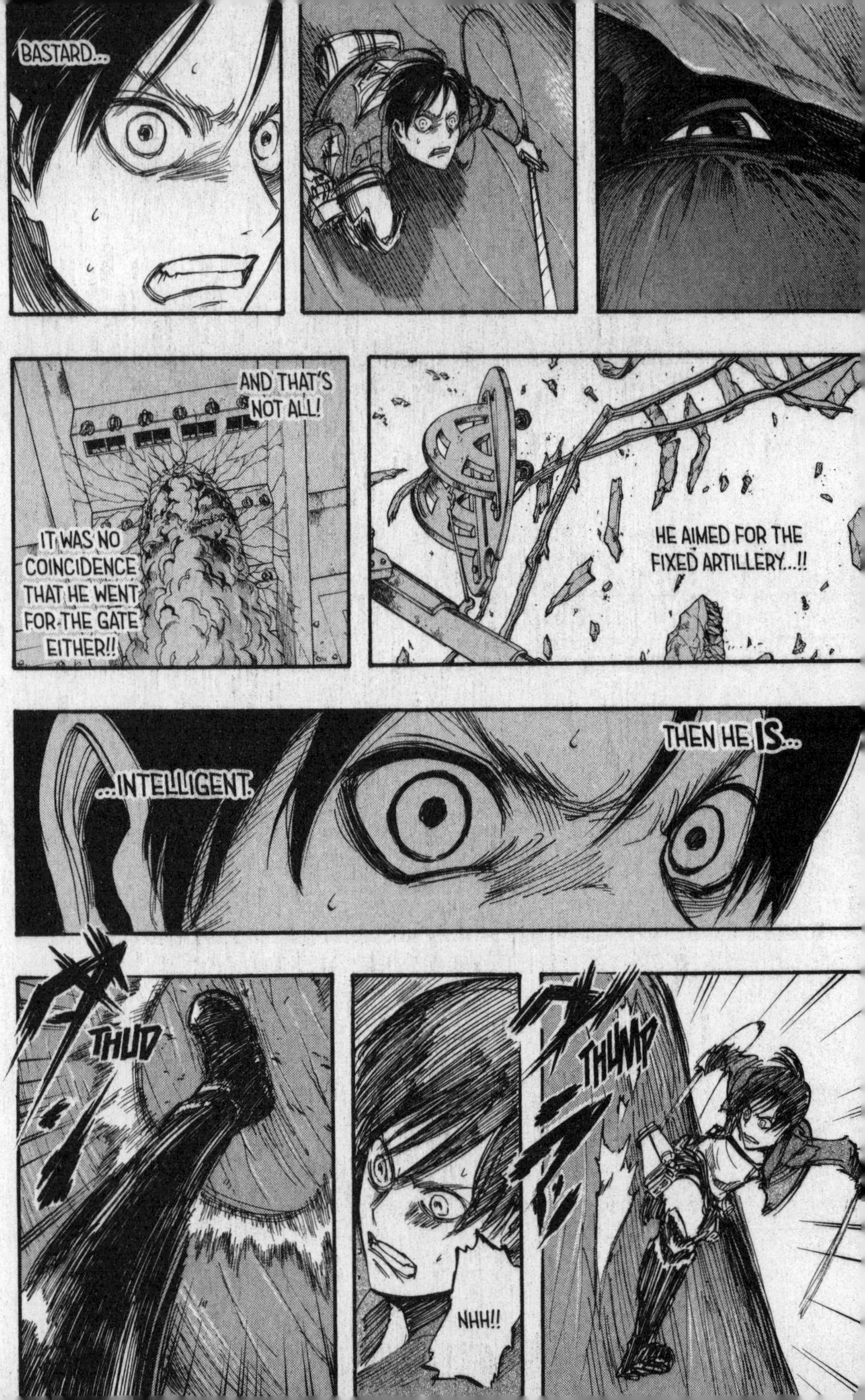
BASTARD...
HE AIMED FOR THE FIXED ARTILLERY...!!
AND THAT'S NOT ALL!
IT WAS NO COINCIDENCE THAT HE WENT FOR THE GATE EITHER!!
THEN HE IS...
...INTELLIGENT.
THUMP
NHH!!
THUD

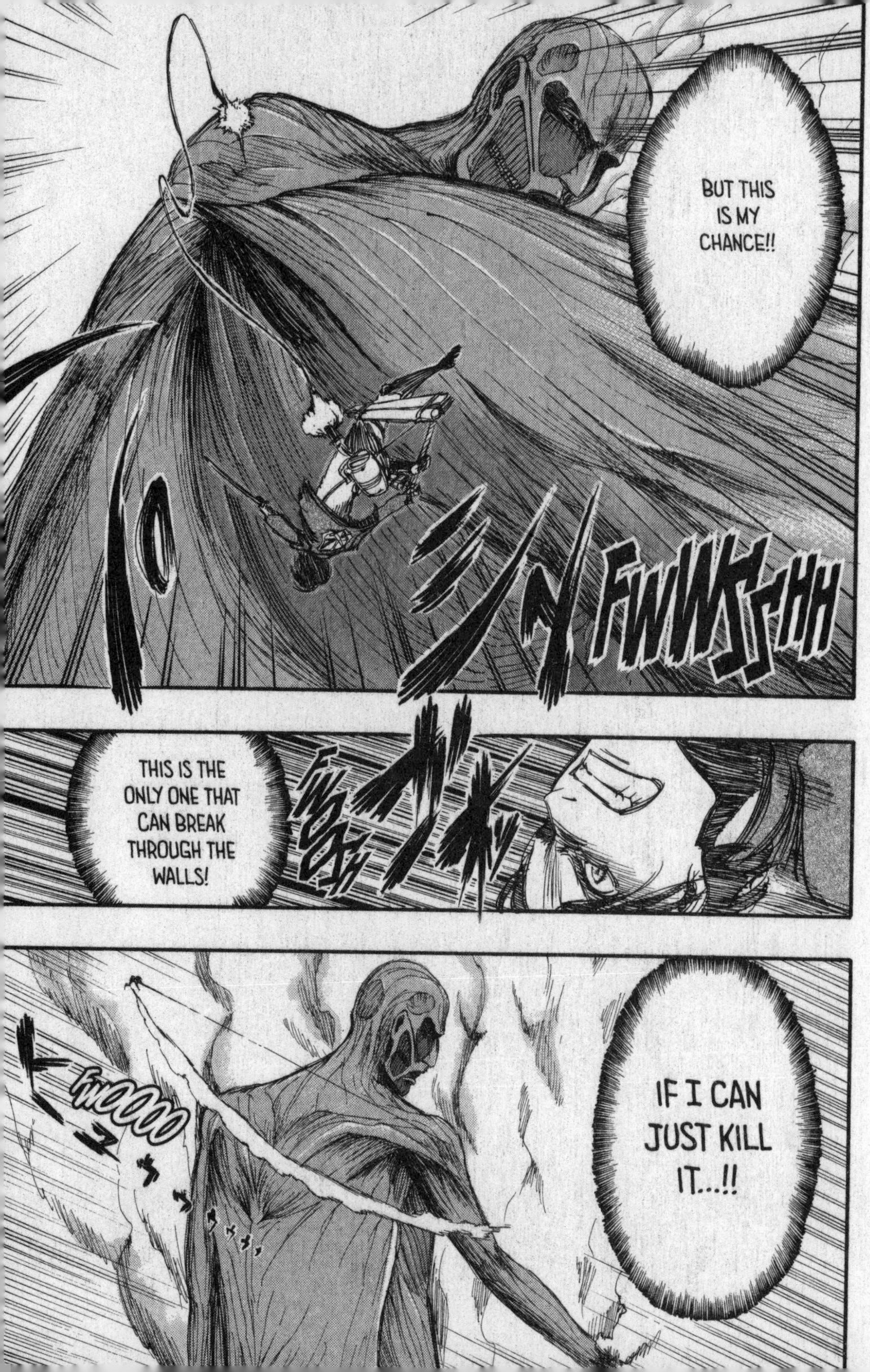
BUT THIS IS MY CHANCE!!
THIS IS THE ONLY ONE THAT CAN BREAK THROUGH THE WALLS!
IF I CAN JUST KILL IT...!!

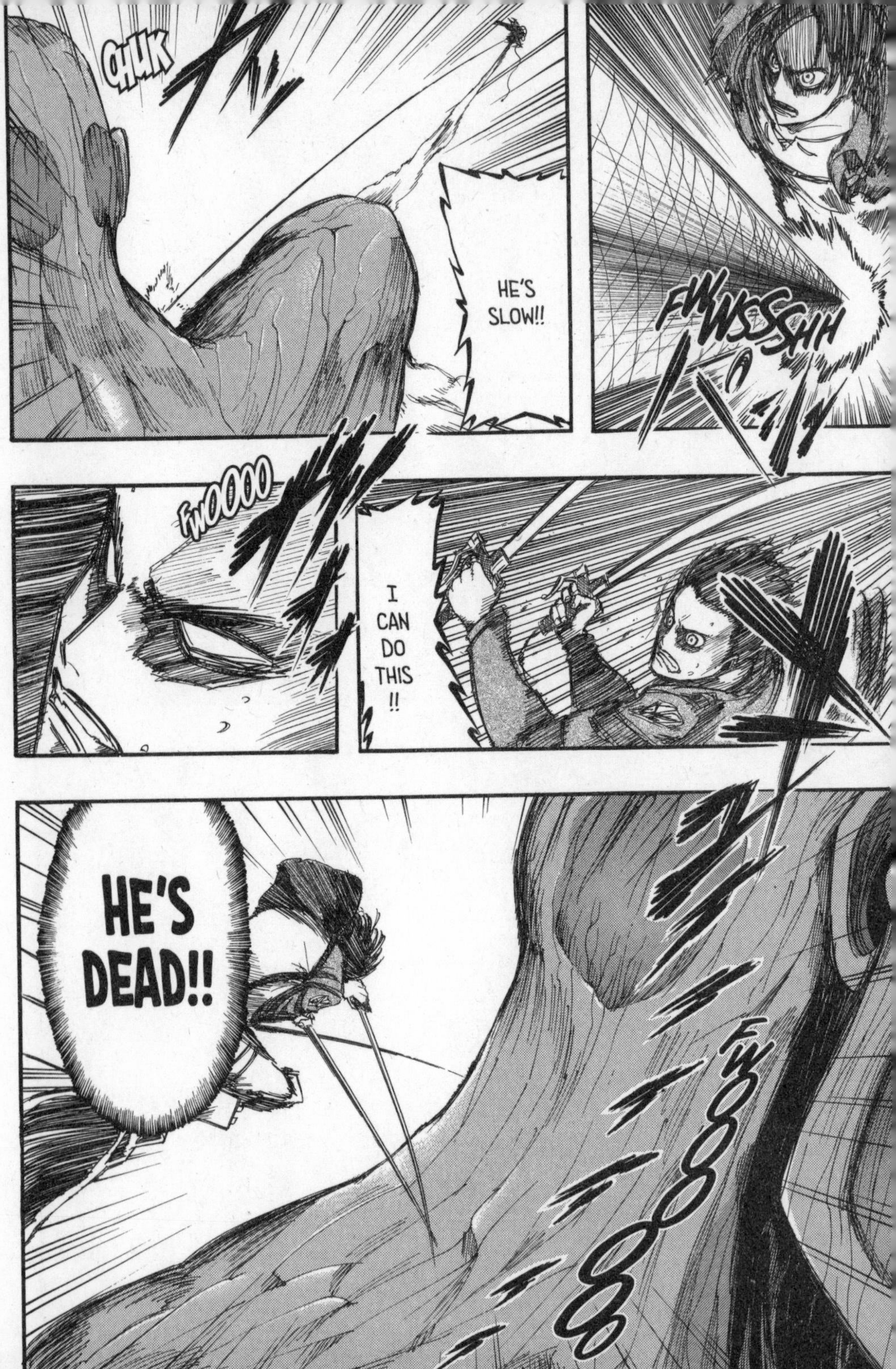
FWWSSHH
CHUK
HE'S SLOW!!
I CAN DO THIS!!
FWOOOO
HE'S DEAD!!
FWOOOOOOO

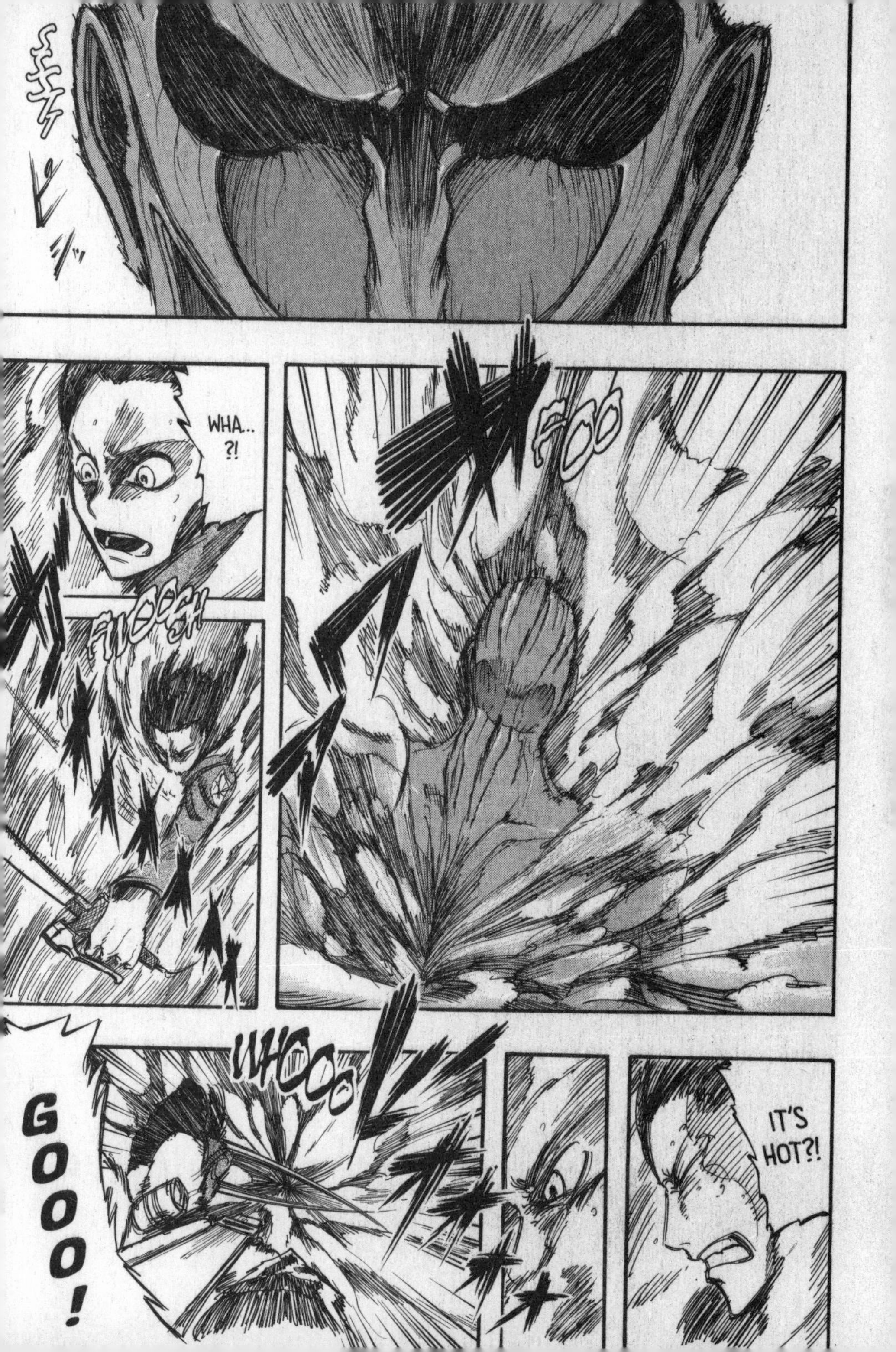
FOO
WHA... ?!
FWOOSH
IT'S HOT?!
WHOOO
GOOOO!

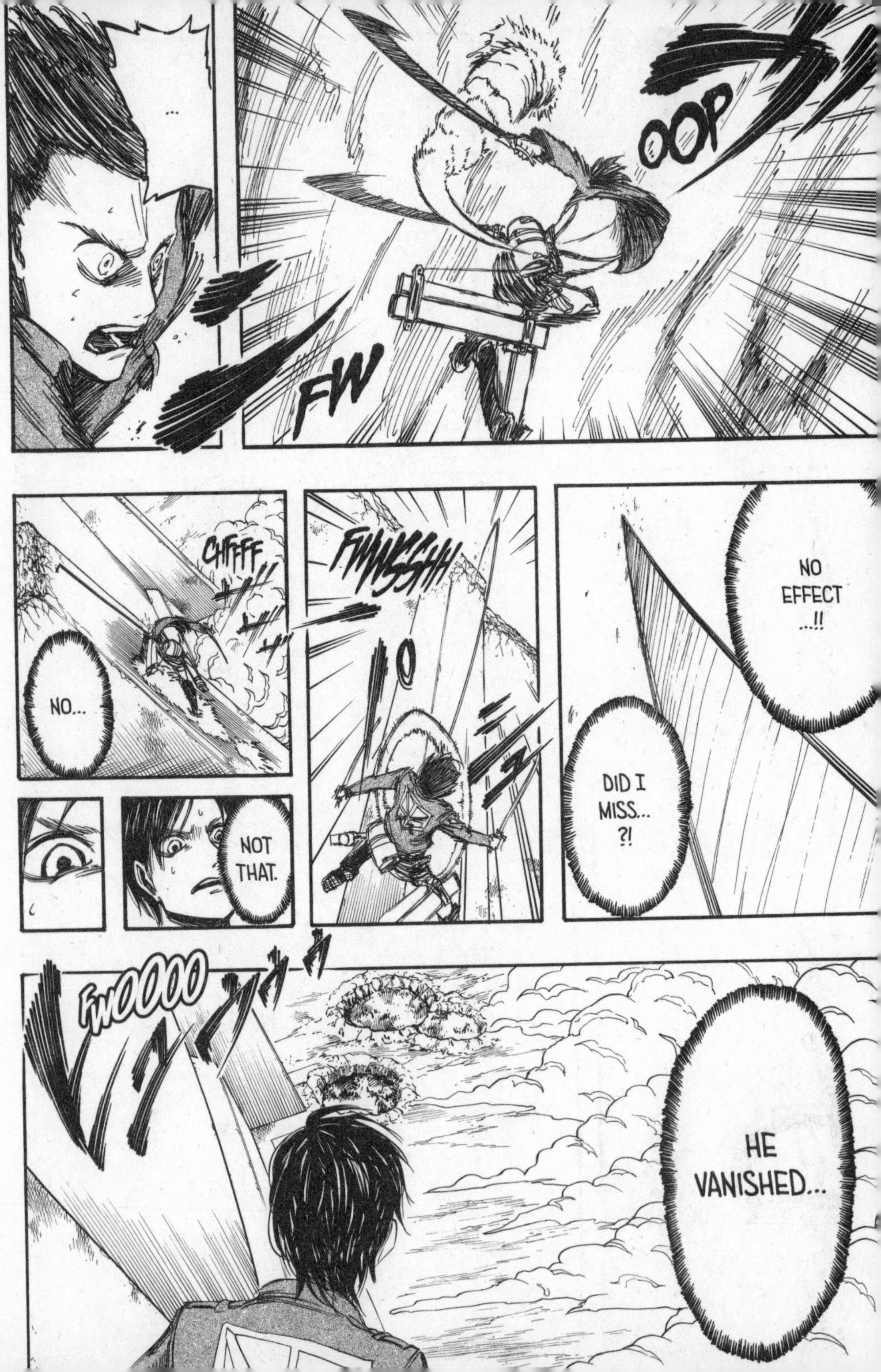
OOP
FW
...
NO EFFECT ...!!
DID I MISS... ?!
FWASSHH
CHFFFF
NO...
NOT THAT.
FWOOOO
HE VANISHED...

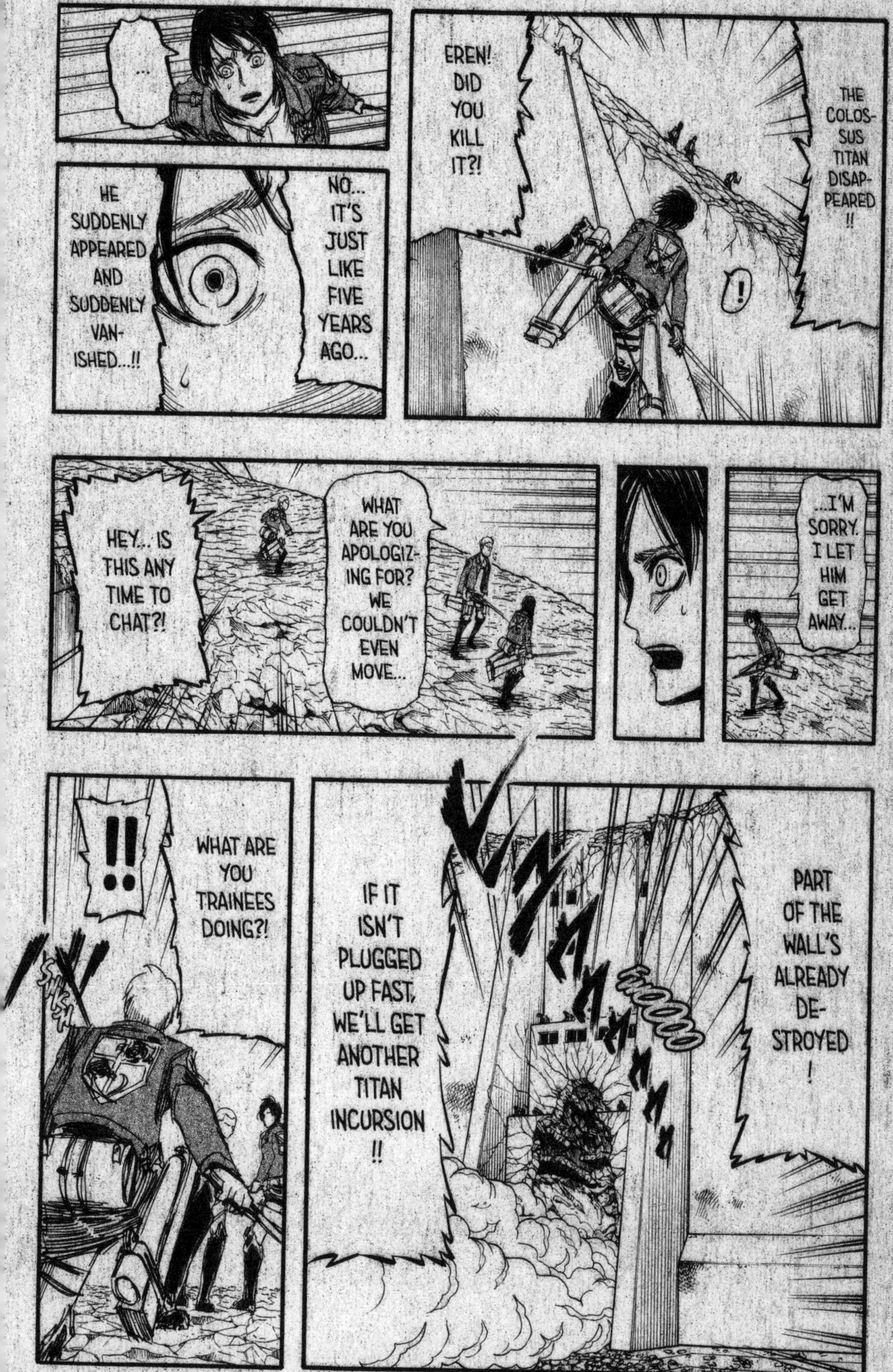

EREN! DID YOU KILL IT?!
THE COLOSSUS TITAN DISAPPEARED!!
!
...
NO... IT'S JUST LIKE FIVE YEARS AGO...
HE SUDDENLY APPEARED AND SUDDENLY VANISHED...!!
...I'M SORRY. I LET HIM GET AWAY...
WHAT ARE YOU APOLOGIZING FOR? WE COULDN'T EVEN MOVE...
HEY... IS THIS ANY TIME TO CHAT?!
PART OF THE WALL'S ALREADY DESTROYED!
IF IT ISN'T PLUGGED UP FAST, WE'LL GET ANOTHER TITAN INCURSION!!
!!
WHAT ARE YOU TRAINEES DOING?!

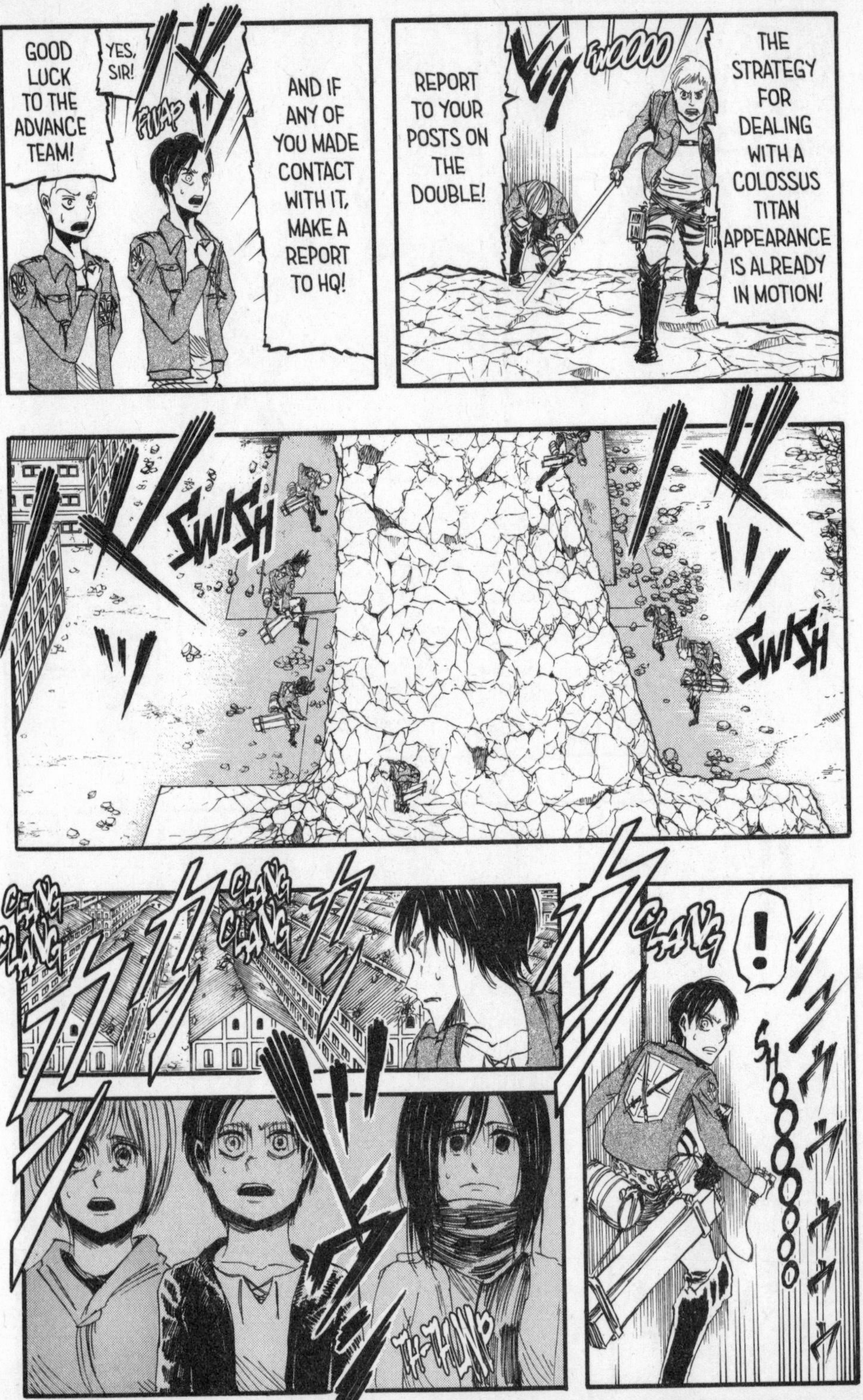
THE STRATEGY FOR DEALING WITH A COLOSSUS TITAN APPEARANCE IS ALREADY IN MOTION!
FWOOOO
REPORT TO YOUR POSTS ON THE DOUBLE!
AND IF ANY OF YOU MADE CONTACT WITH IT, MAKE A REPORT TO HQ!
FWAP
YES, SIR!
GOOD LUCK TO THE ADVANCE TEAM!
SWISH
SWISH
CLANG
!
SHOOOOOOO
CLANG CLANG
CLANG CLANG
TA-THUNK

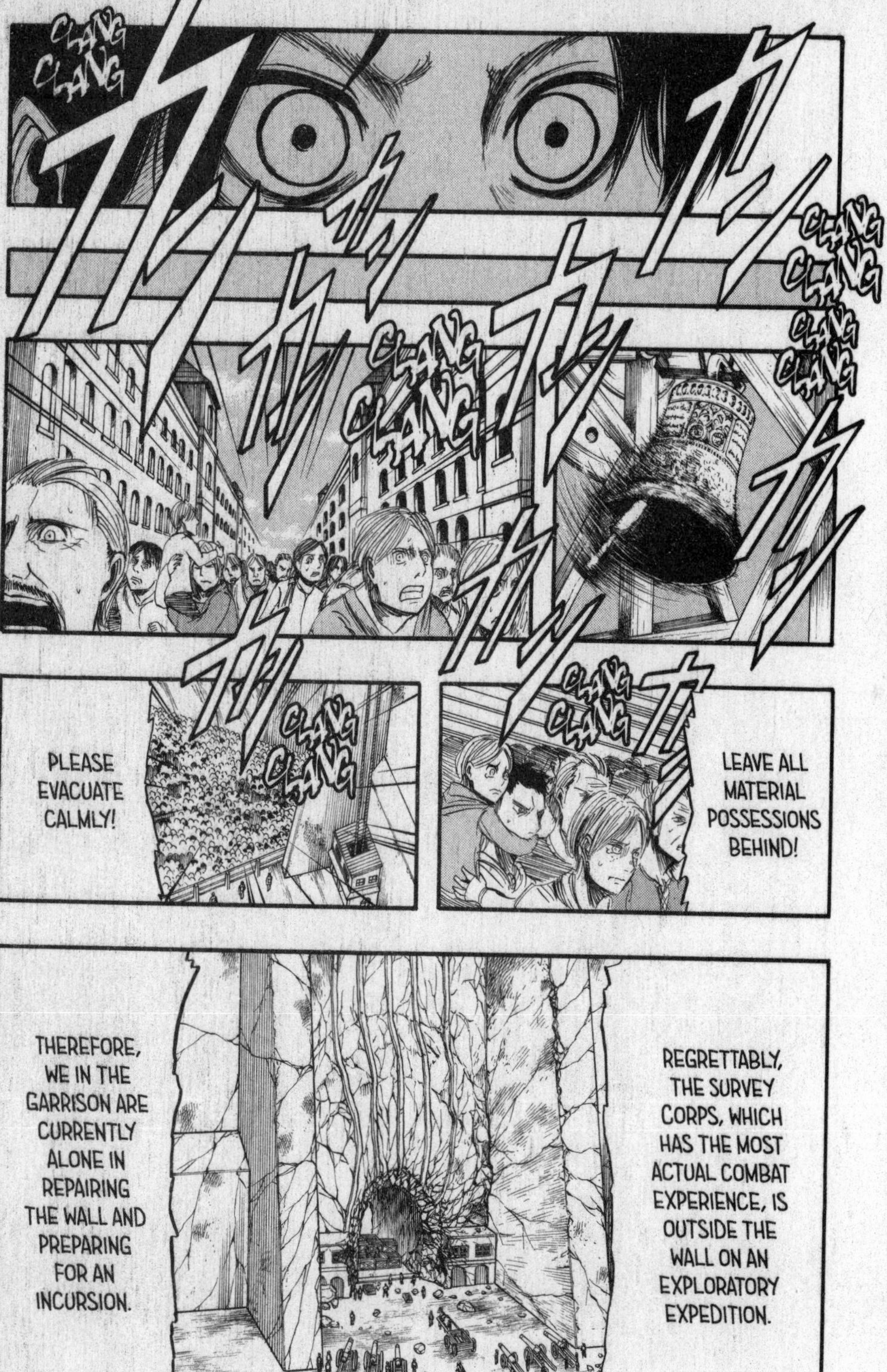
CLANG CLANG
CLANG CLANG CLANG CLANG
CLANG CLANG
CLANG CLANG
LEAVE ALL MATERIAL POSSESSIONS BEHIND!
CLANG CLANG
PLEASE EVACUATE CALMLY!
REGRETTABLY, THE SURVEY CORPS, WHICH HAS THE MOST ACTUAL COMBAT EXPERIENCE, IS OUTSIDE THE WALL ON AN EXPLORATORY EXPEDITION.
THEREFORE, WE IN THE GARRISON ARE CURRENTLY ALONE IN REPAIRING THE WALL AND PREPARING FOR AN INCURSION.

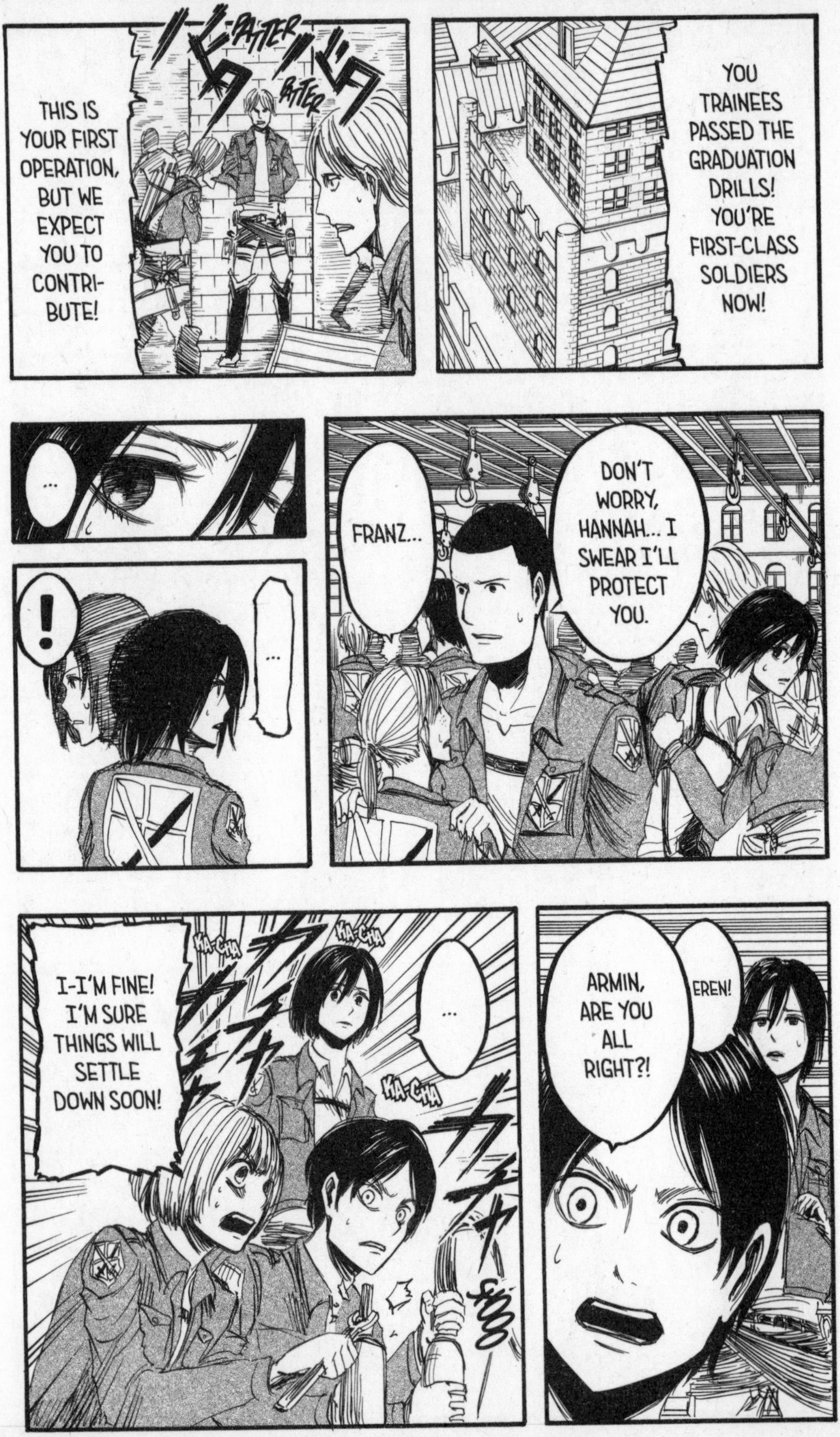
YOU TRAINEES PASSED THE GRADUATION DRILLS! YOU'RE FIRST-CLASS SOLDIERS NOW!
BATTER
BATTER
THIS IS YOUR FIRST OPERATION, BUT WE EXPECT YOU TO CONTRIBUTE!
DON'T WORRY, HANNAH... I SWEAR I'LL PROTECT YOU.
FRANZ...
...
...
!
EREN!
ARMIN, ARE YOU ALL RIGHT?!
KA-CHA
...
KA-CHA
KA-CHA
I-I'M FINE! I'M SURE THINGS WILL SETTLE DOWN SOON!

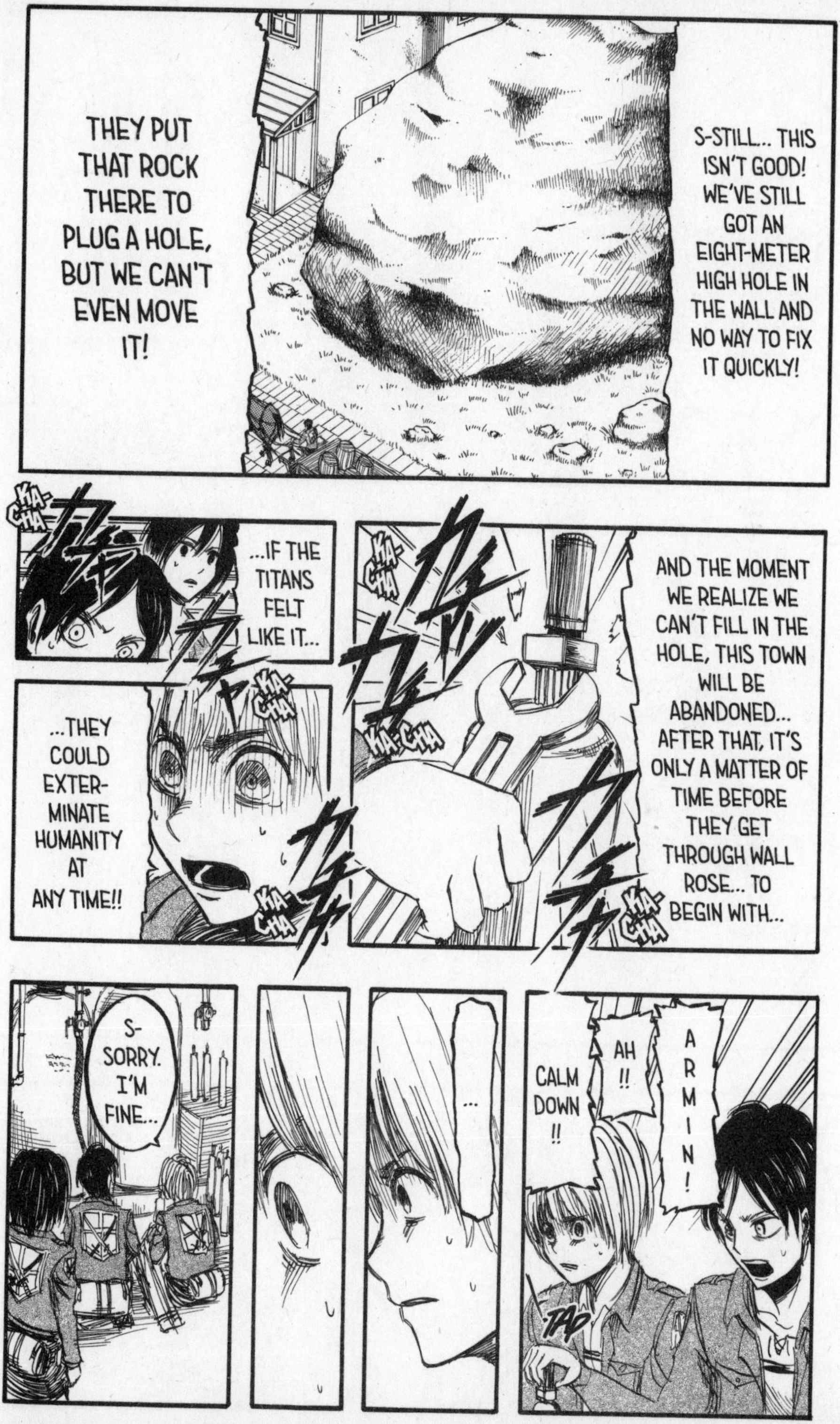
S-STILL... THIS ISN'T GOOD! WE'VE STILL GOT AN EIGHT-METER HIGH HOLE IN THE WALL AND NO WAY TO FIX IT QUICKLY!
THEY PUT THAT ROCK THERE TO PLUG A HOLE, BUT WE CAN'T EVEN MOVE IT!
KA-CHA
KA-CHA
AND THE MOMENT WE REALIZE WE CAN'T FILL IN THE HOLE, THIS TOWN WILL BE ABANDONED... AFTER THAT, IT'S ONLY A MATTER OF TIME BEFORE THEY GET THROUGH WALL ROSE... TO BEGIN WITH...
KA-CHA
KA-CHA
...IF THE TITANS FELT LIKE IT...
KA-CHA
KA-CHA
...THEY COULD EXTERMINATE HUMANITY AT ANY TIME!!
KA-CHA
ARMIN!
AH!!
CALM DOWN!!
TAP
...
S-SORRY. I'M FINE...

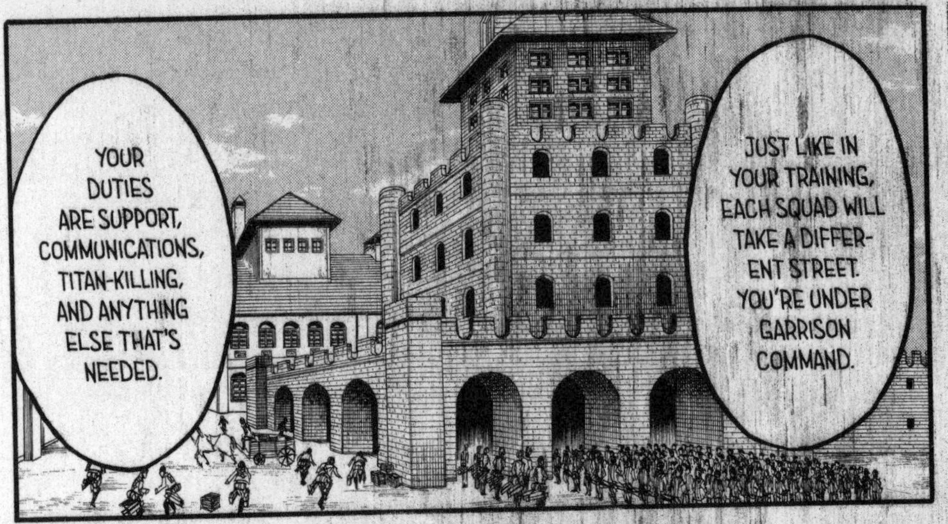
JUST LIKE IN YOUR TRAINING, EACH SQUAD WILL TAKE A DIFFER-ENT STREET. YOU'RE UNDER GARRISON COMMAND.
YOUR DUTIES ARE SUPPORT, COMMUNICATIONS, TITAN-KILLING, AND ANYTHING ELSE THAT'S NEEDED.

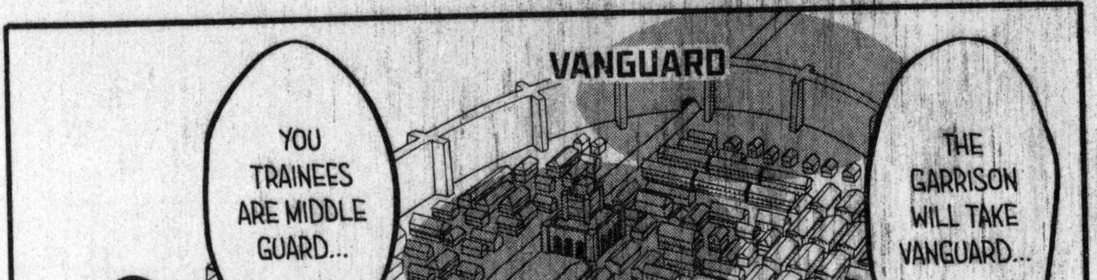
THE GARRISON WILL TAKE VANGUARD...
VANGUARD
YOU TRAINEES ARE MIDDLE GUARD...
MIDDLE GUARD
AND THE GARRISON'S ELITE UNIT WILL BE REARGUARD.
REARGUARD

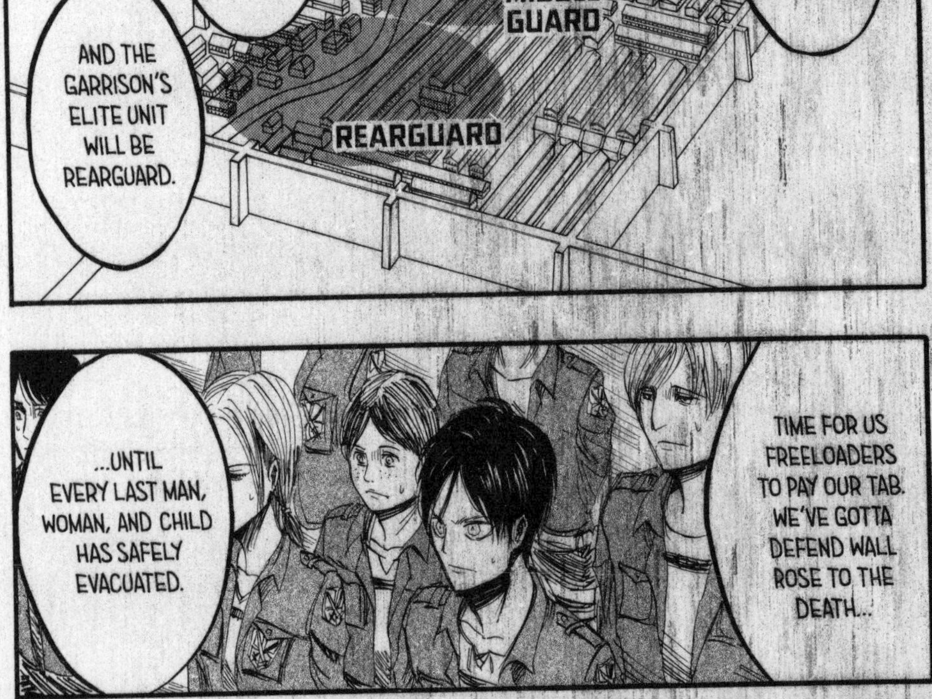
TIME FOR US FREELOADERS TO PAY OUR TAB. WE'VE GOTTA DEFEND WALL ROSE TO THE DEATH...
...UNTIL EVERY LAST MAN, WOMAN, AND CHILD HAS SAFELY EVACUATED.

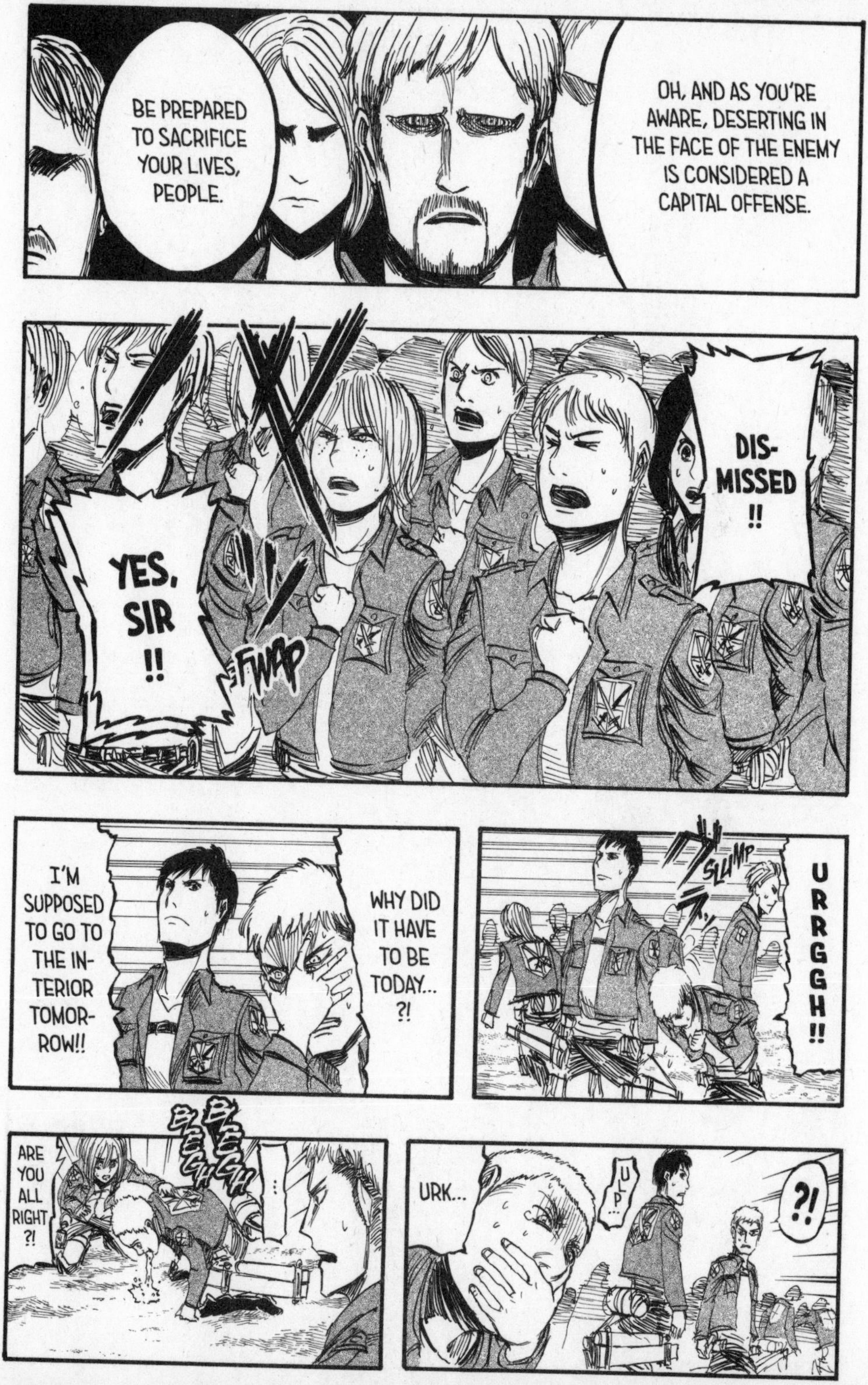
OH, AND AS YOU'RE AWARE, DESERTING IN THE FACE OF THE ENEMY IS CONSIDERED A CAPITAL OFFENSE.
BE PREPARED TO SACRIFICE YOUR LIVES, PEOPLE.
DIS-MISSED!!
YES, SIR!!
FWAP
URRGGH!!
SLUMP
WHY DID IT HAVE TO BE TODAY...?!
I'M SUPPOSED TO GO TO THE IN-TERIOR TOMOR-ROW!!
?!
ULP...
URK...
...
BLEEGH
BLEEGH
ARE YOU ALL RIGHT?!

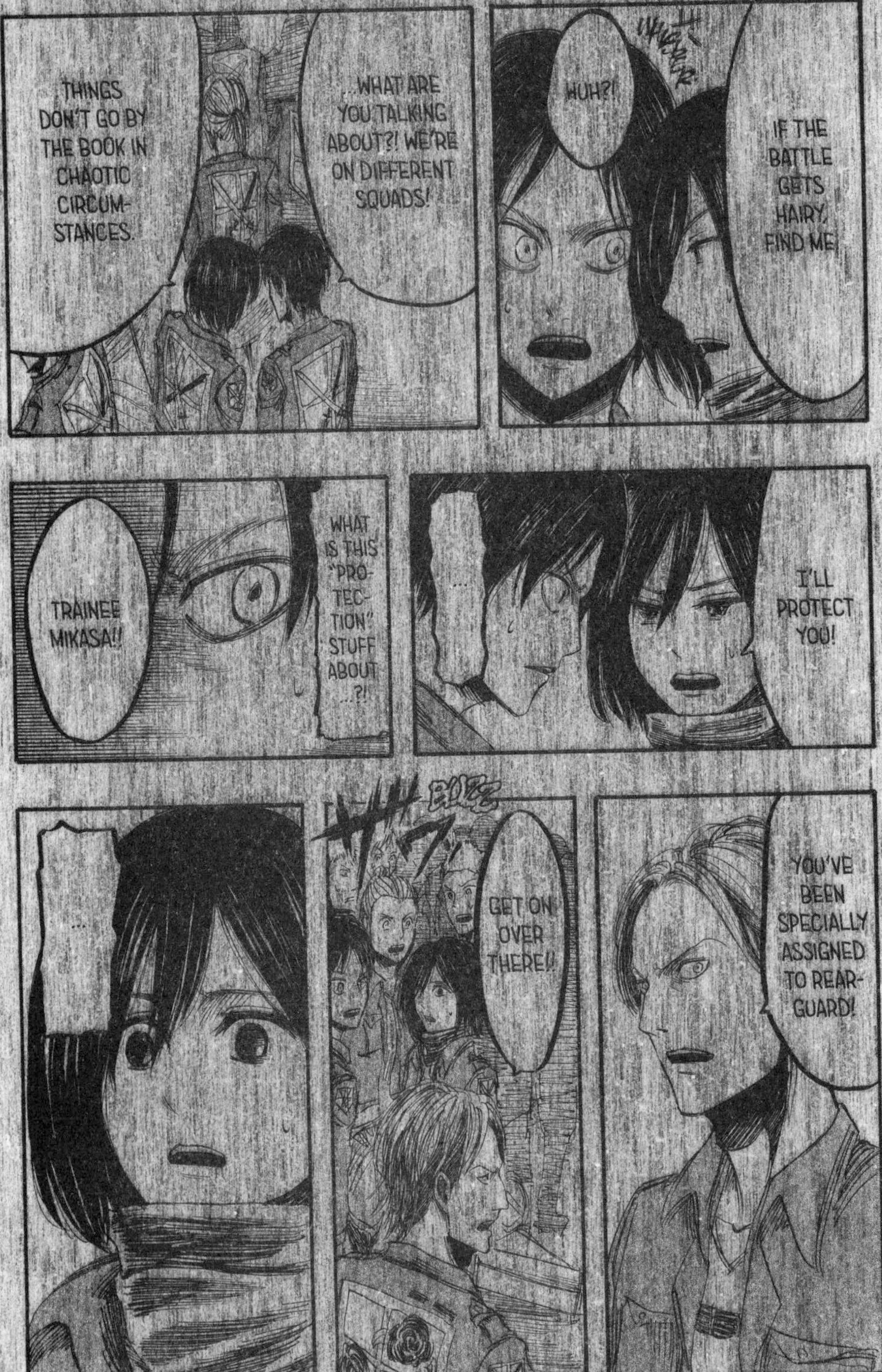
IF THE BATTLE GETS HAIRY, FIND ME.
HUH?!
...WHAT ARE YOU TALKING ABOUT?! WE'RE ON DIFFERENT SQUADS!
THINGS DON'T GO BY THE BOOK IN CHAOTIC CIRCUM-STANCES.
I'LL PROTECT YOU!
...
WHAT IS THIS "PRO-TEC-TION" STUFF ABOUT ...?!
TRAINEE MIKASA!!
YOU'VE BEEN SPECIALLY ASSIGNED TO REAR-GUARD!
GET ON OVER THERE!!
...

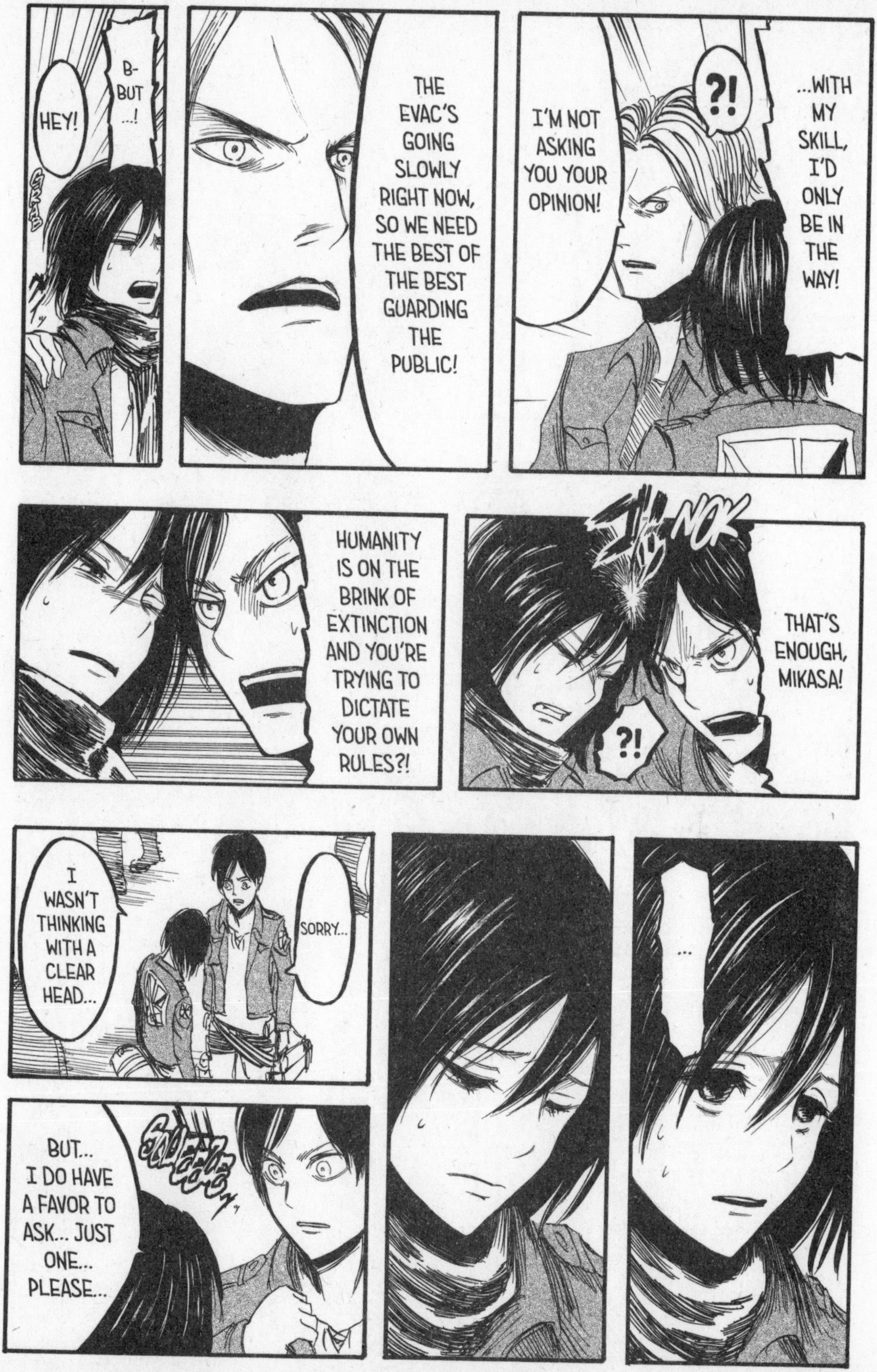
...WITH MY SKILL, I'D ONLY BE IN THE WAY!
?!
I'M NOT ASKING YOU YOUR OPINION!
THE EVAC'S GOING SLOWLY RIGHT NOW, SO WE NEED THE BEST OF THE BEST GUARDING THE PUBLIC!
B- BUT ...!
HEY!
THAT'S ENOUGH, MIKASA!
?!
HUMANITY IS ON THE BRINK OF EXTINCTION AND YOU'RE TRYING TO DICTATE YOUR OWN RULES?!
...
SORRY...
I WASN'T THINKING WITH A CLEAR HEAD...
BUT... I DO HAVE A FAVOR TO ASK... JUST ONE... PLEASE...

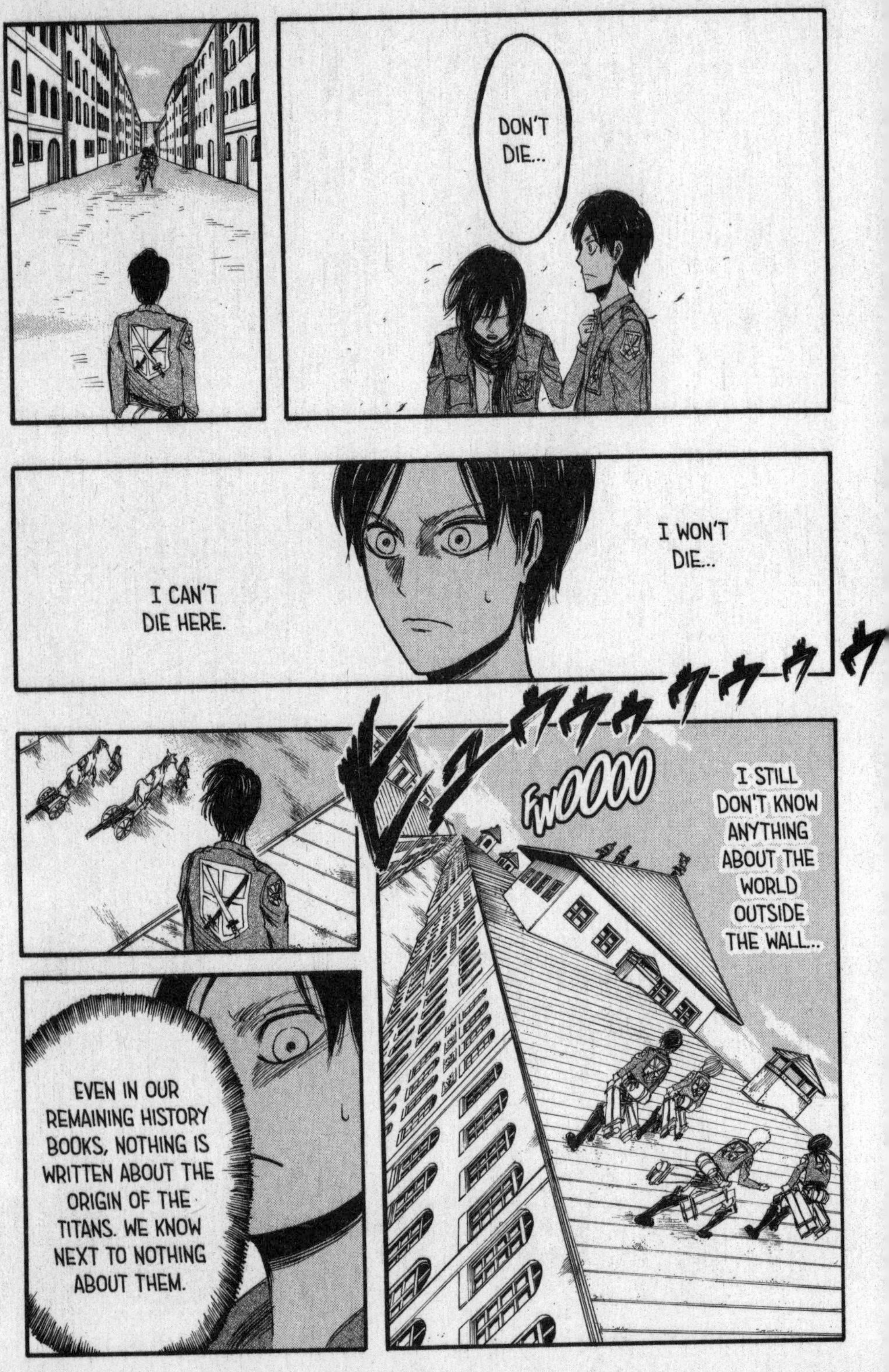
DON'T DIE...
I WON'T DIE...
I CAN'T DIE HERE.
FWOOOO
I STILL DON'T KNOW ANYTHING ABOUT THE WORLD OUTSIDE THE WALL...
EVEN IN OUR REMAINING HISTORY BOOKS, NOTHING IS WRITTEN ABOUT THE ORIGIN OF THE TITANS. WE KNOW NEXT TO NOTHING ABOUT THEM.

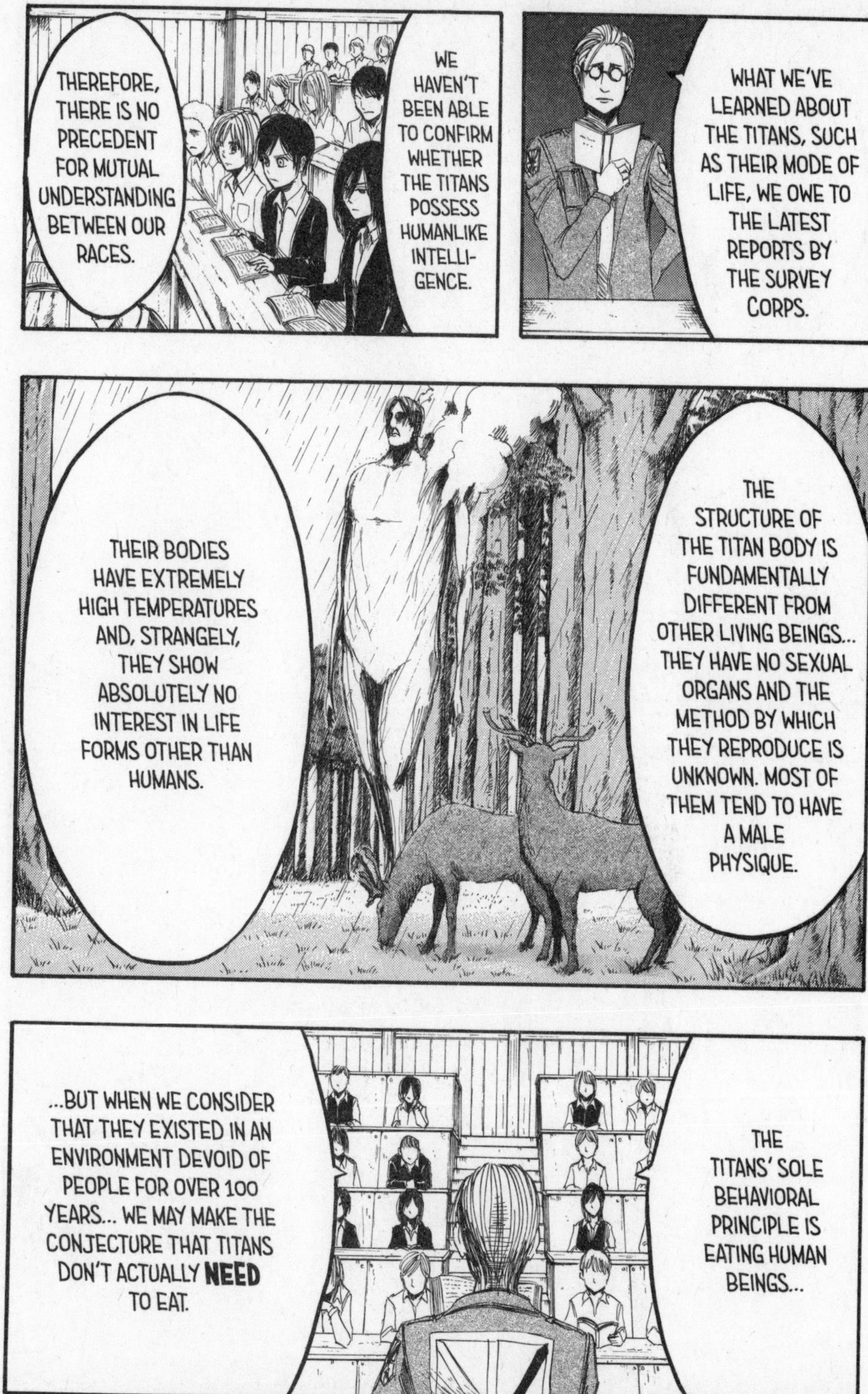
WHAT WE'VE LEARNED ABOUT THE TITANS, SUCH AS THEIR MODE OF LIFE, WE OWE TO THE LATEST REPORTS BY THE SURVEY CORPS.
WE HAVEN'T BEEN ABLE TO CONFIRM WHETHER THE TITANS POSSESS HUMANLIKE INTELLI-GENCE.
THEREFORE, THERE IS NO PRECEDENT FOR MUTUAL UNDERSTANDING BETWEEN OUR RACES.
THE STRUCTURE OF THE TITAN BODY IS FUNDAMENTALLY DIFFERENT FROM OTHER LIVING BEINGS... THEY HAVE NO SEXUAL ORGANS AND THE METHOD BY WHICH THEY REPRODUCE IS UNKNOWN. MOST OF THEM TEND TO HAVE A MALE PHYSIQUE.
THEIR BODIES HAVE EXTREMELY HIGH TEMPERATURES AND, STRANGELY, THEY SHOW ABSOLUTELY NO INTEREST IN LIFE FORMS OTHER THAN HUMANS.
THE TITANS' SOLE BEHAVIORAL PRINCIPLE IS EATING HUMAN BEINGS...
...BUT WHEN WE CONSIDER THAT THEY EXISTED IN AN ENVIRONMENT DEVOID OF PEOPLE FOR OVER 100 YEARS... WE MAY MAKE THE CONJECTURE THAT TITANS DON'T ACTUALLY **NEED** TO EAT.

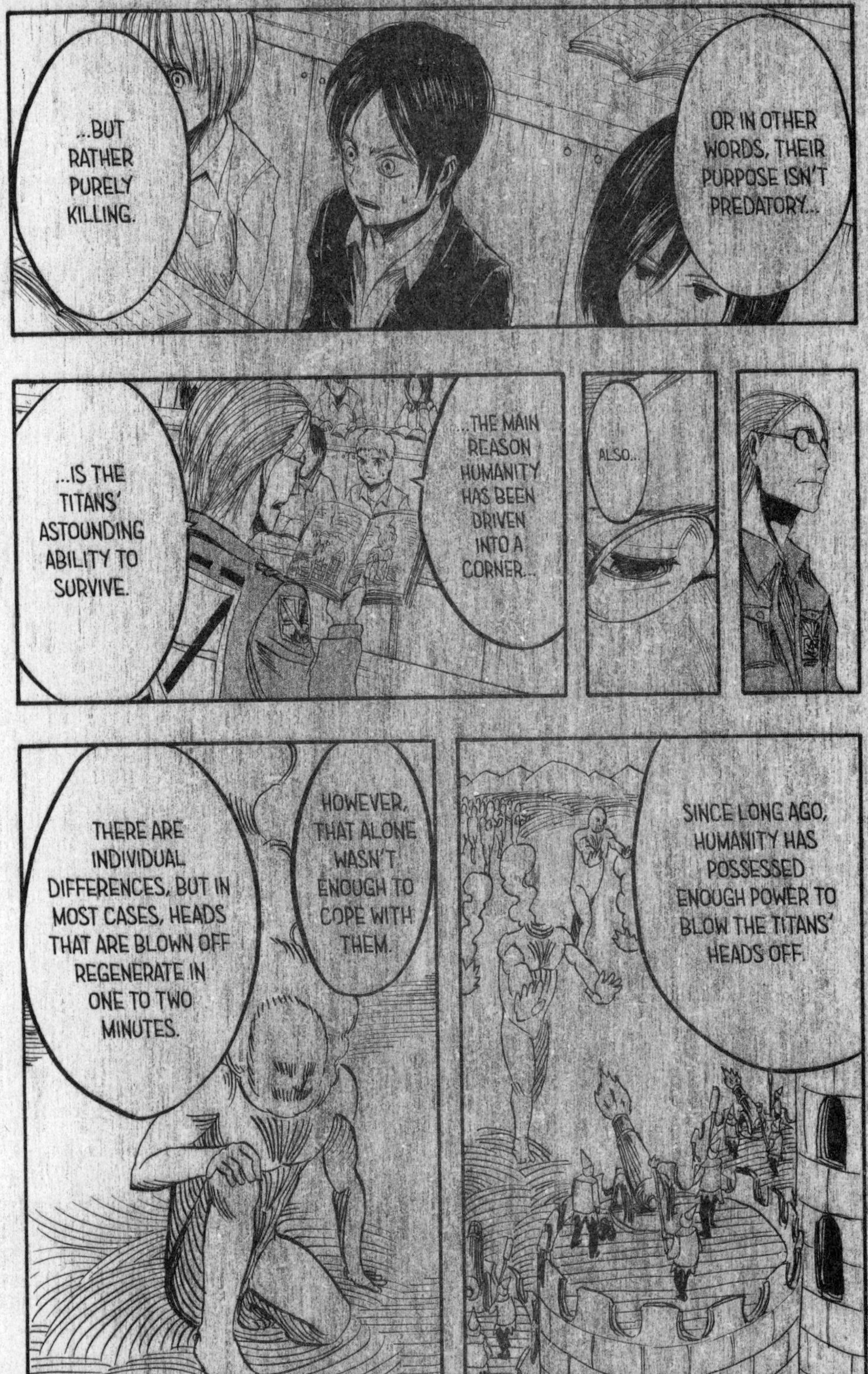
OR IN OTHER WORDS, THEIR PURPOSE ISN'T PREDATORY...
...BUT RATHER PURELY KILLING.
ALSO...
...THE MAIN REASON HUMANITY HAS BEEN DRIVEN INTO A CORNER...
...IS THE TITANS' ASTOUNDING ABILITY TO SURVIVE.
SINCE LONG AGO, HUMANITY HAS POSSESSED ENOUGH POWER TO BLOW THE TITANS' HEADS OFF.
HOWEVER, THAT ALONE WASN'T ENOUGH TO COPE WITH THEM.
THERE ARE INDIVIDUAL DIFFERENCES, BUT IN MOST CASES, HEADS THAT ARE BLOWN OFF REGENERATE IN ONE TO TWO MINUTES.

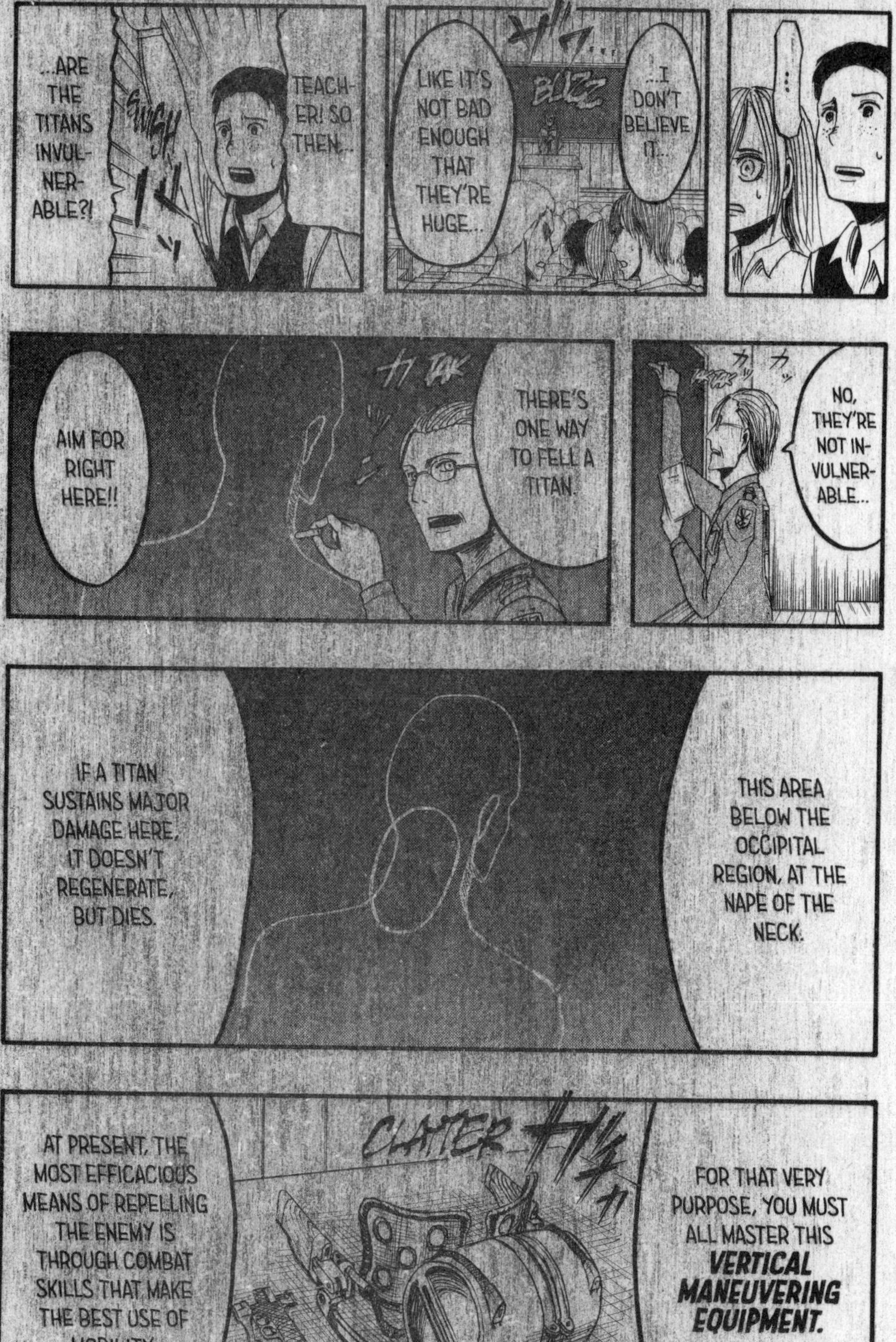
...
BUZZ
...I DON'T BELIEVE IT...
LIKE IT'S NOT BAD ENOUGH THAT THEY'RE HUGE...
TEACHER! SO THEN...
SWISH
...ARE THE TITANS INVULNERABLE?!
NO, THEY'RE NOT INVULNERABLE...
TAK
THERE'S ONE WAY TO FELL A TITAN.
TAK
AIM FOR RIGHT HERE!!
THIS AREA BELOW THE OCCIPITAL REGION, AT THE NAPE OF THE NECK.
IF A TITAN SUSTAINS MAJOR DAMAGE HERE, IT DOESN'T REGENERATE, BUT DIES.
FOR THAT VERY PURPOSE, YOU MUST ALL MASTER THIS ***VERTICAL MANEUVERING EQUIPMENT.***
CLATTER
AT PRESENT, THE MOST EFFICACIOUS MEANS OF REPELLING THE ENEMY IS THROUGH COMBAT SKILLS THAT MAKE THE BEST USE OF MOBILITY.

EACH HAND USES THE GRIP OF THIS DEVICE TO OPERATE THE SYSTEM.
THE FIRING MECHANISM AT BOTH SIDES OF THE WAIST LAUNCHES AN ANCHOR.
STEEL WIRE DISCHARGED FROM INSIDE A CYLINDER IS REELED IN THROUGH PRESSURIZED GAS.
THIS RE-PLACEABLE BLADE IS YOUR WEAPON.
IN ORDER TO CUT THROUGH A CHUNK OF TOUGH MEAT, THE BLADE IS MADE TO BE FLEXIBLE.
YOU USE THESE TWO BLADES TO SLICE THROUGH THE AREA.
IF THE ATTACK HITS THE TITAN'S VITAL SPOT, IT DIES INSTANTLY, BEFORE ITS REGENERATIVE SYSTEM CAN KICK IN.
FINALLY...
FINALLY...
...WE CAN BE USEFUL.

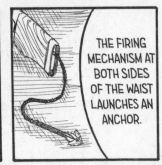

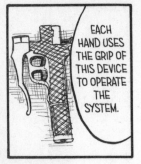

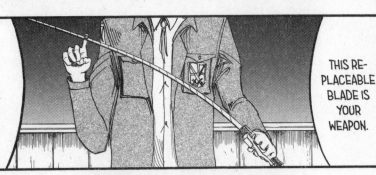

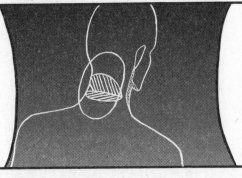

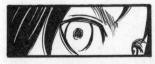

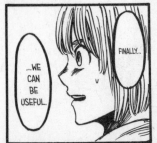

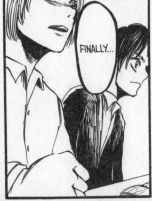

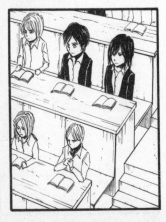

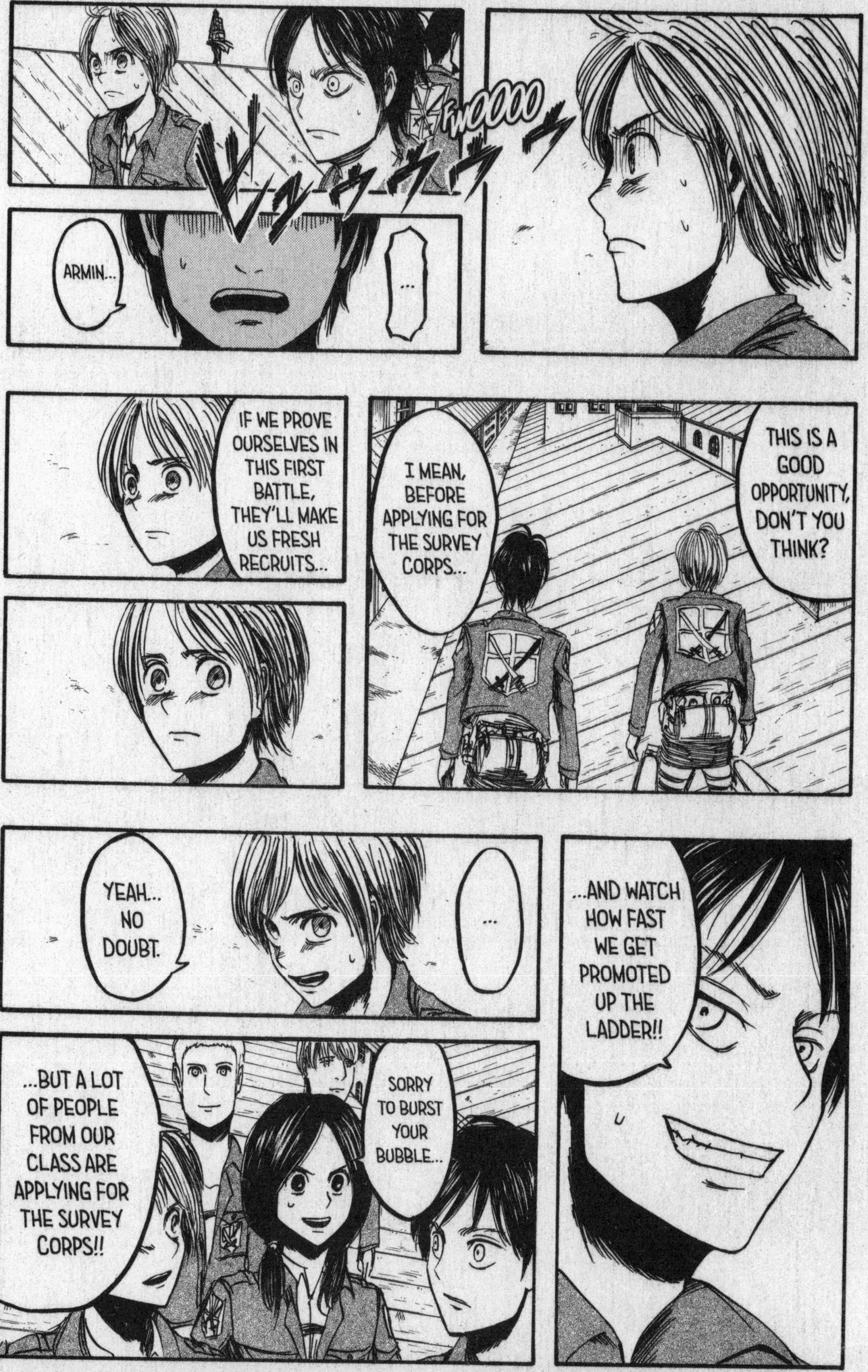
FWOOOO
...
ARMIN...
THIS IS A GOOD OPPORTUNITY, DON'T YOU THINK?
I MEAN, BEFORE APPLYING FOR THE SURVEY CORPS...
IF WE PROVE OURSELVES IN THIS FIRST BATTLE, THEY'LL MAKE US FRESH RECRUITS...
...AND WATCH HOW FAST WE GET PROMOTED UP THE LADDER!!
...
YEAH... NO DOUBT.
SORRY TO BURST YOUR BUBBLE...
...BUT A LOT OF PEOPLE FROM OUR CLASS ARE APPLYING FOR THE SURVEY CORPS!!

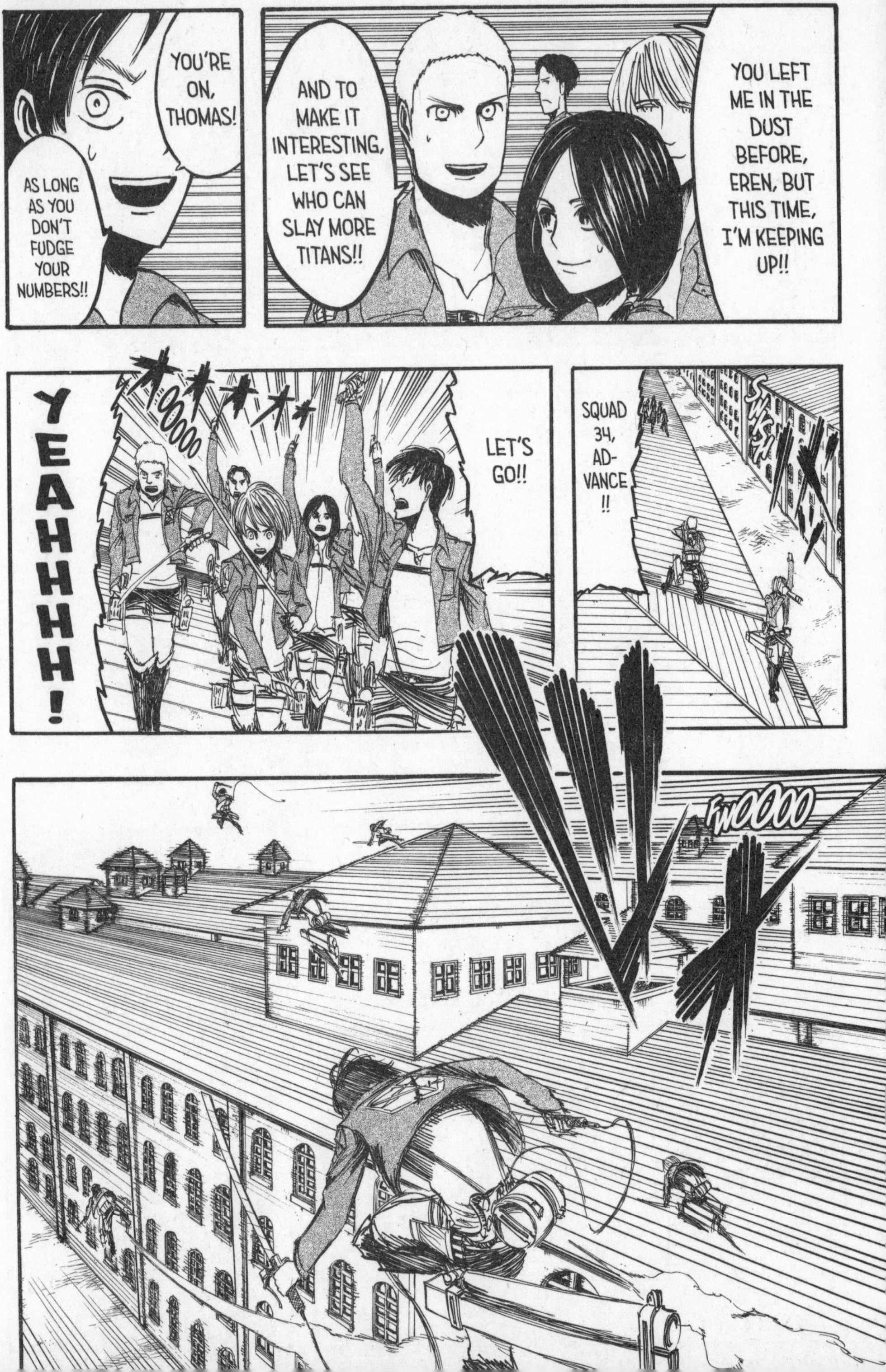
YOU LEFT ME IN THE DUST BEFORE, EREN, BUT THIS TIME, I'M KEEPING UP!!
AND TO MAKE IT INTERESTING, LET'S SEE WHO CAN SLAY MORE TITANS!!
YOU'RE ON, THOMAS!
AS LONG AS YOU DON'T FUDGE YOUR NUMBERS!!
SWSH
SQUAD 34, AD-VANCE!!
LET'S GO!!
OOOOO
YEAHHHHH!
FWOOOO

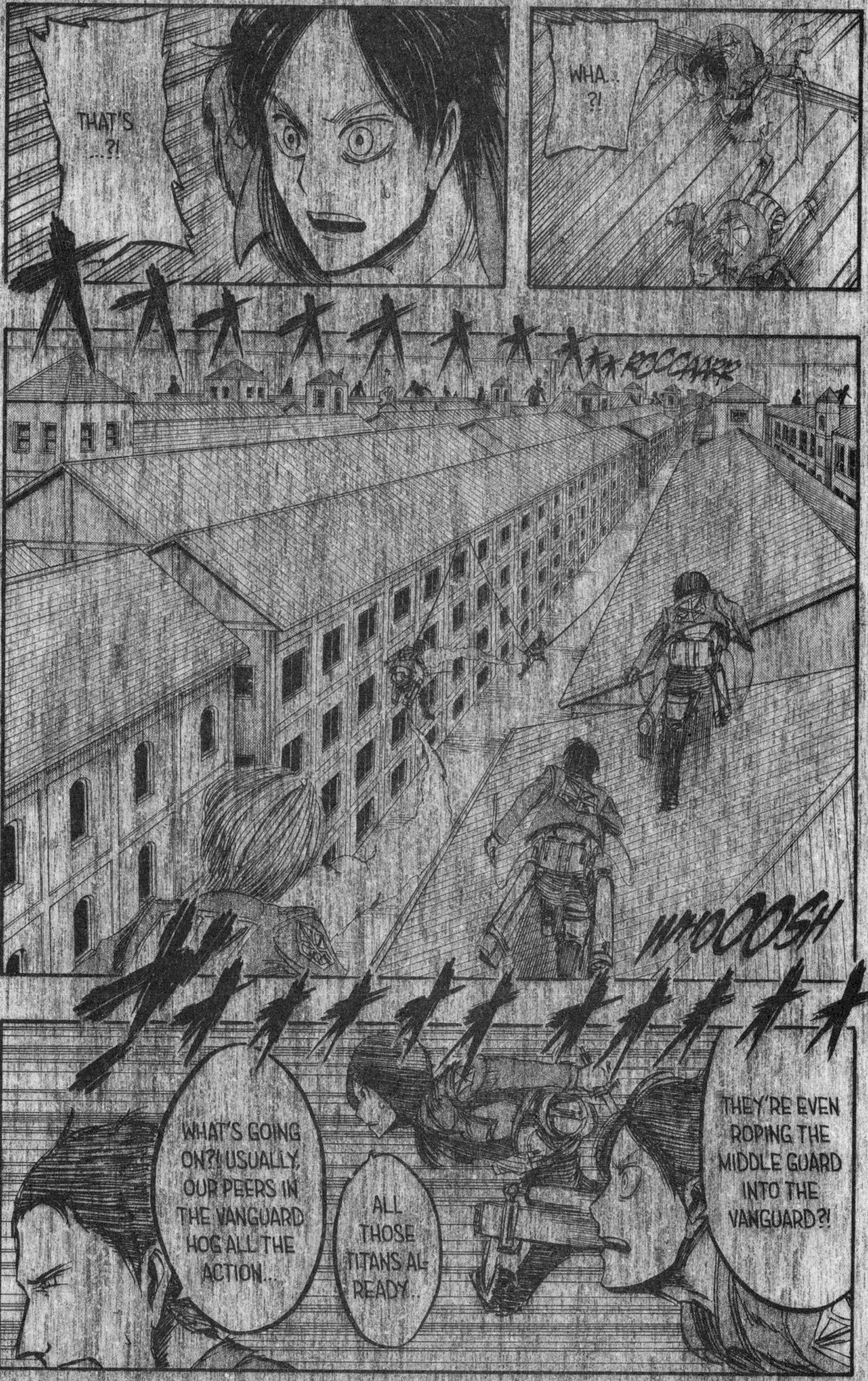
WHA... ?!
THAT'S ...?!
ROOAARR
WHOOOSH
THEY'RE EVEN ROPING THE MIDDLE GUARD INTO THE VANGUARD?!
ALL THOSE TITANS AL-READY...
WHAT'S GOING ON?! USUALLY, OUR PEERS IN THE VANGUARD HOG ALL THE ACTION...

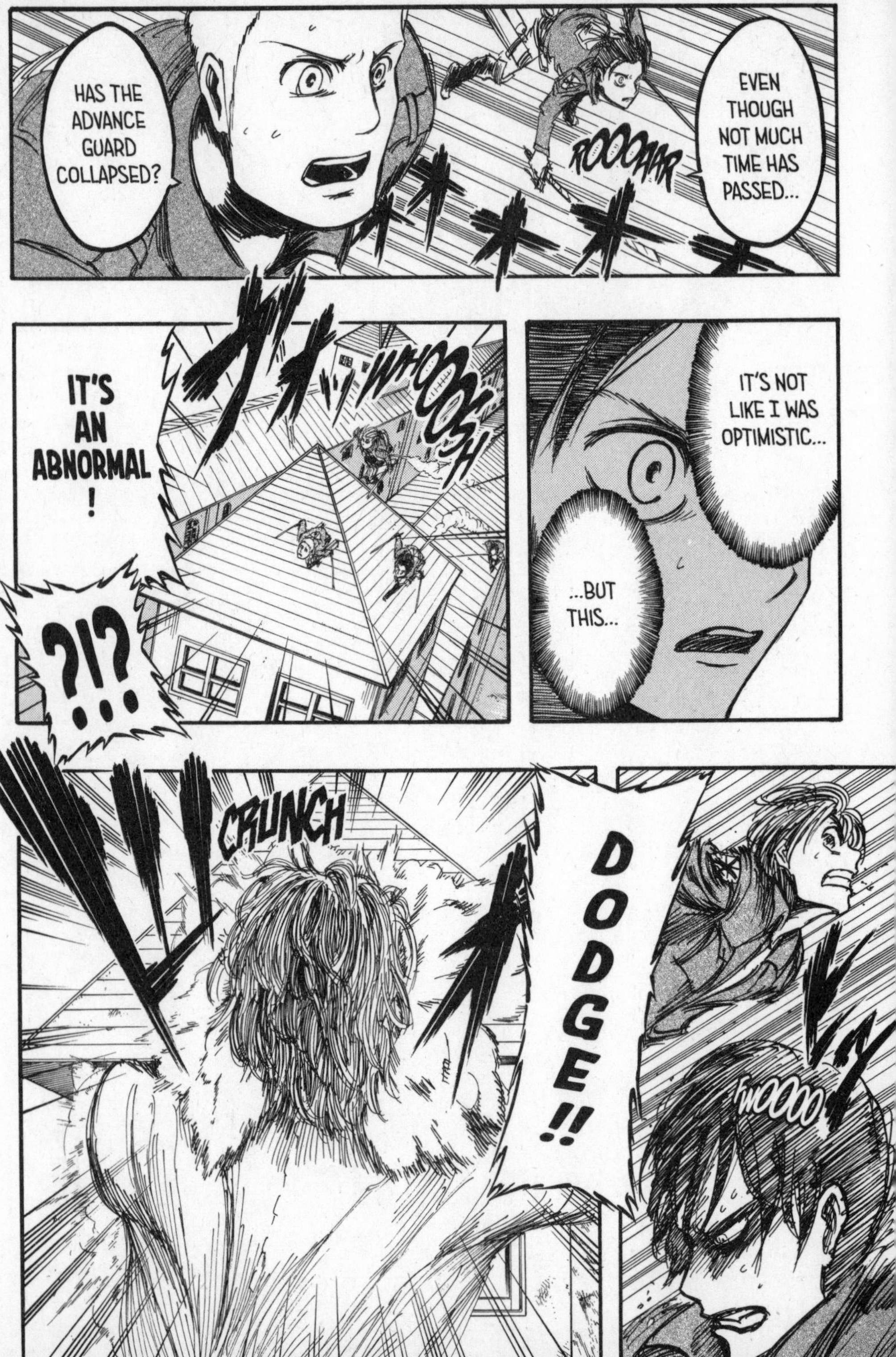
EVEN THOUGH NOT MUCH TIME HAS PASSED...
ROOOAAR
HAS THE ADVANCE GUARD COLLAPSED?
IT'S NOT LIKE I WAS OPTIMISTIC...
...BUT THIS...
WHOOOSH
IT'S AN ABNORMAL!
?!?
DODGE!!
FWOOOO
CRUNCH

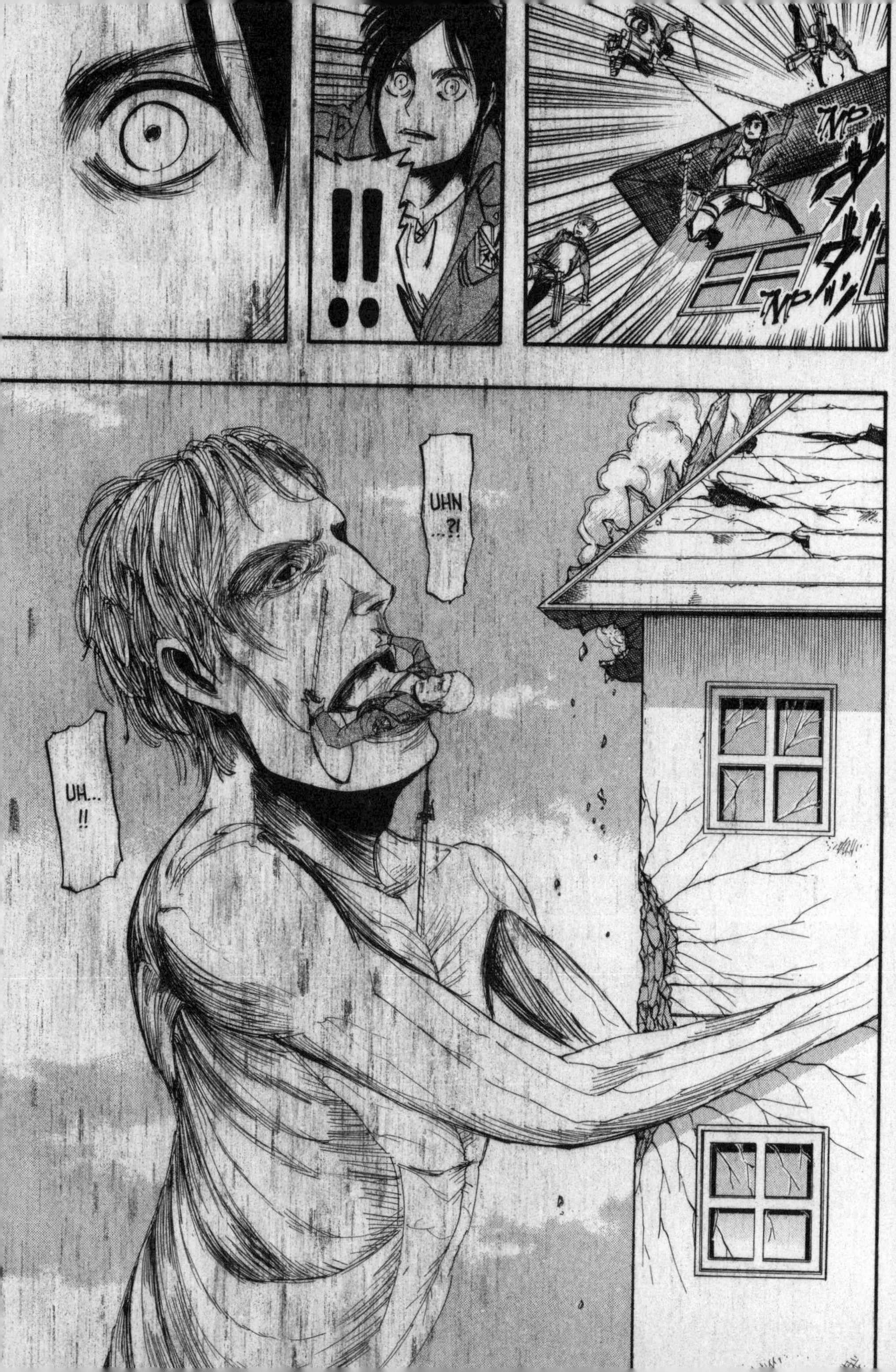
!!
UHN ...?!
UH... !!

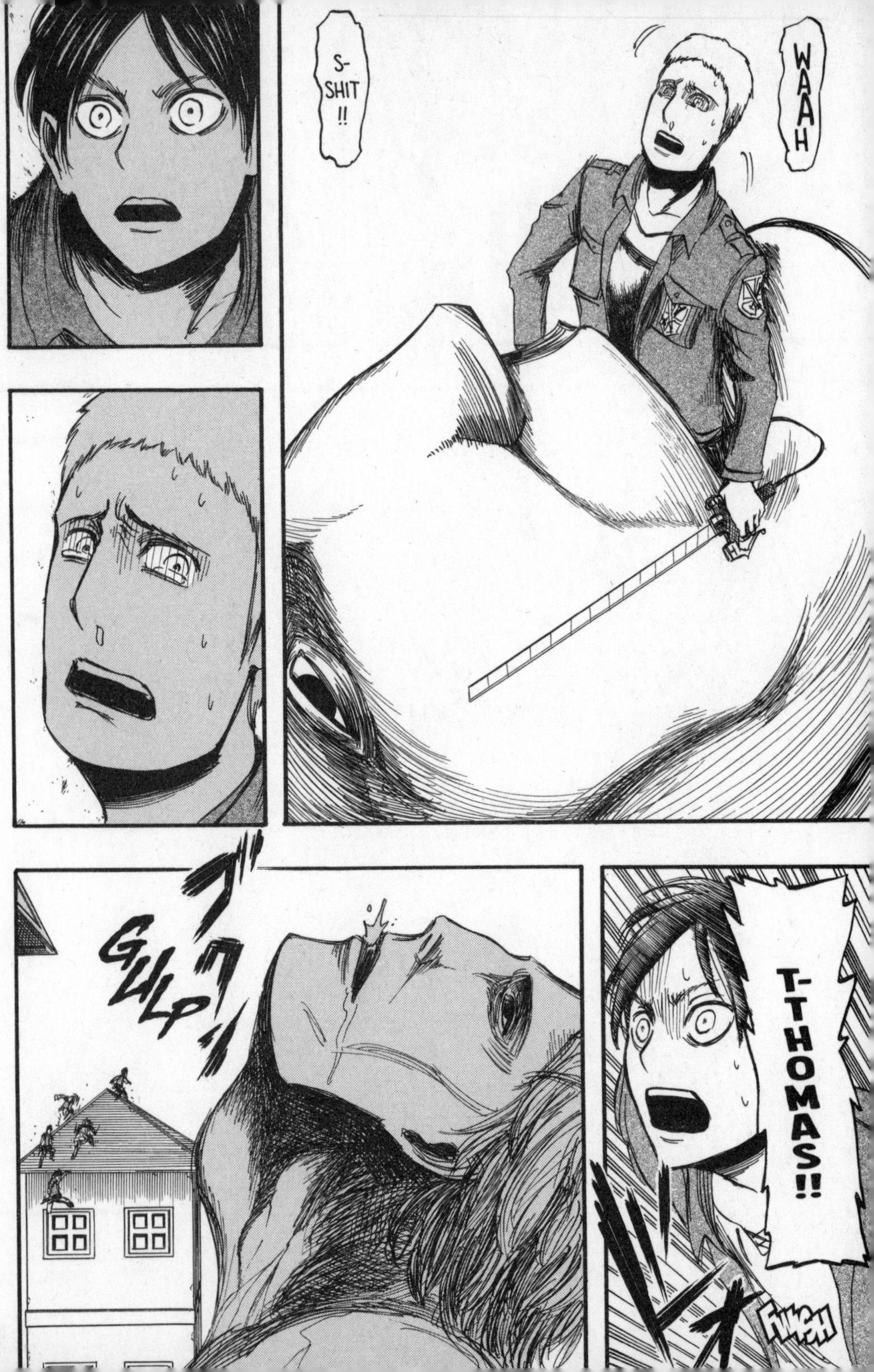
WAAAH
S-SHIT!!
T-THOMAS!!
FWISH
GULP

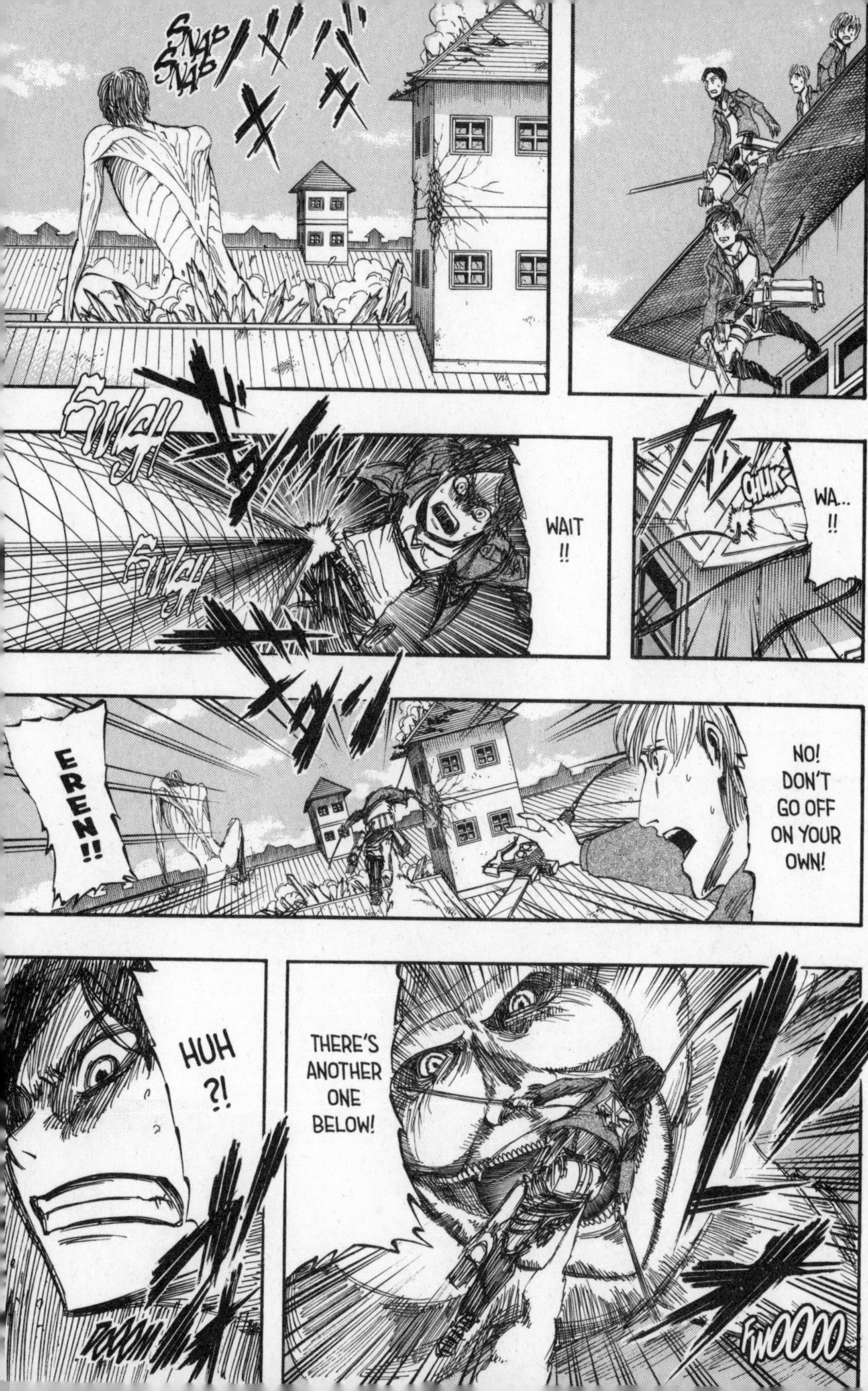
Snap Snap
Chuk
WA... !!
Swish
WAIT !!
Swish
NO! DON'T GO OFF ON YOUR OWN!
EREN!!
THERE'S ANOTHER ONE BELOW!
FWOOOO
HUH ?!

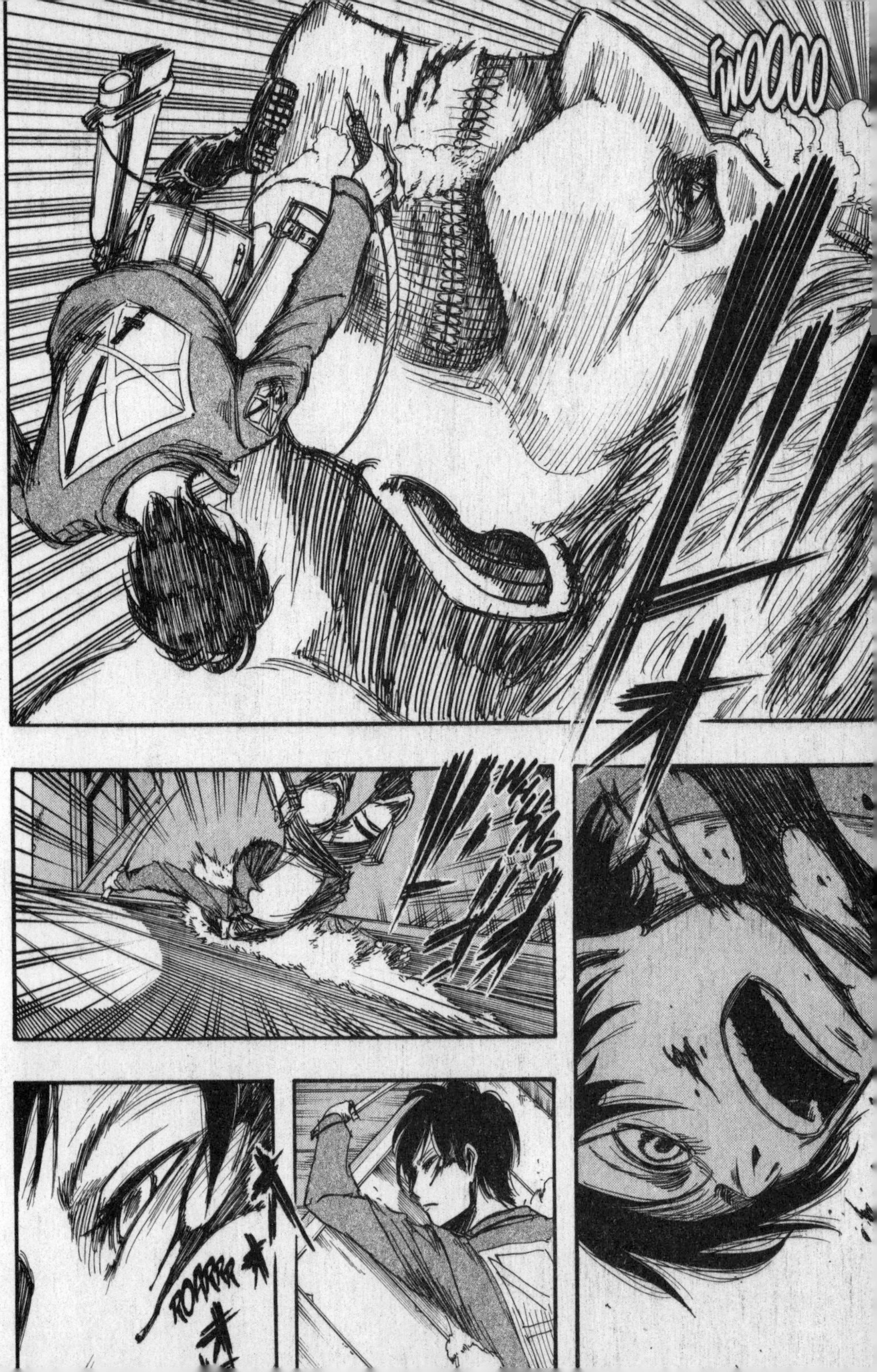
FWOOOO
WHUMP
ROARRR

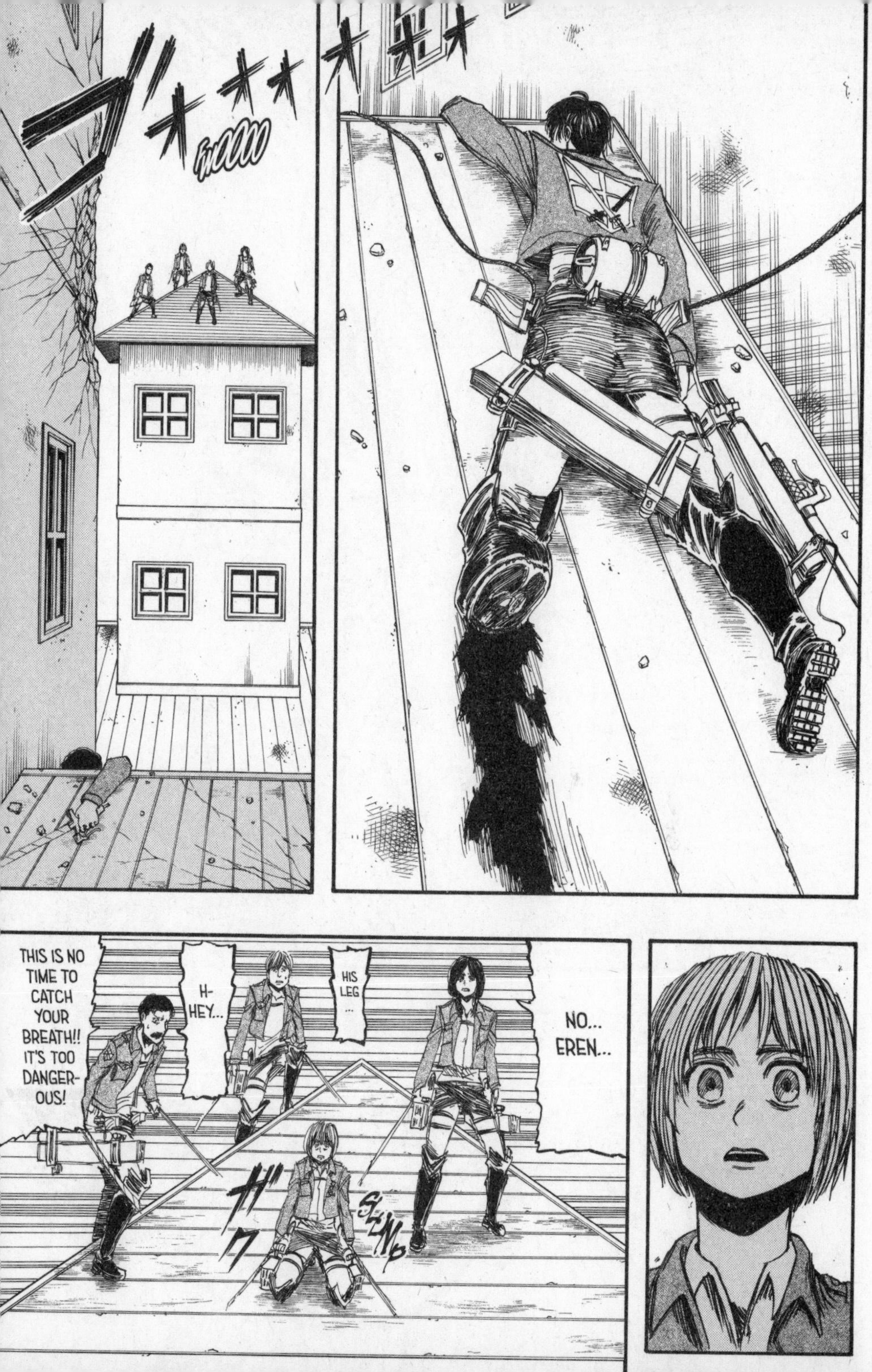
ゴオオオオ
FWOOOO
NO... EREN...
HIS LEG ...
H-HEY...
THIS IS NO TIME TO CATCH YOUR BREATH!! IT'S TOO DANGER-OUS!
ガク
SLUMP

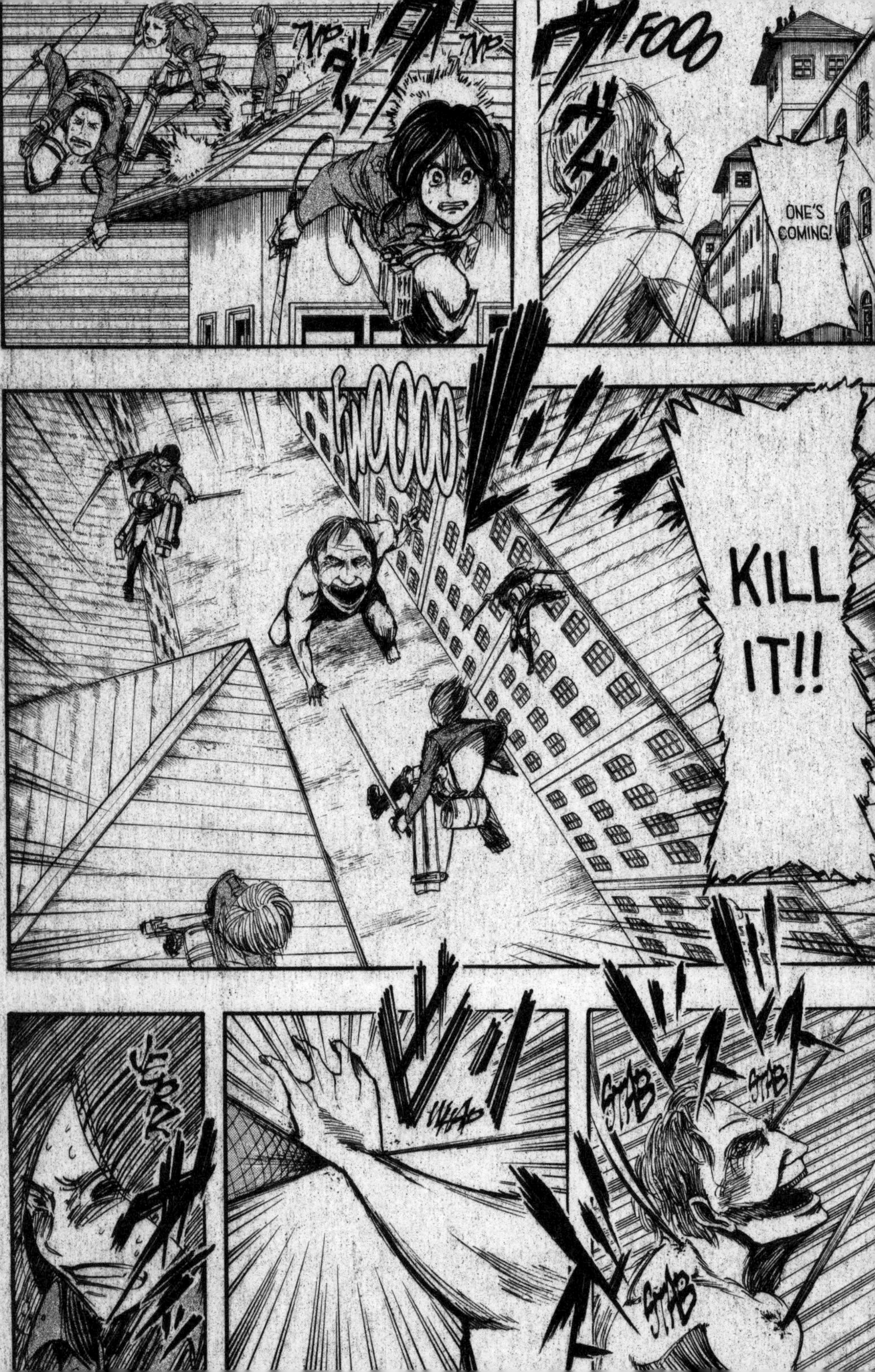
FOOO
ONE'S COMING!
TMP
TMP
FWOOOO
KILL IT!!
STAB
STAB
STAB

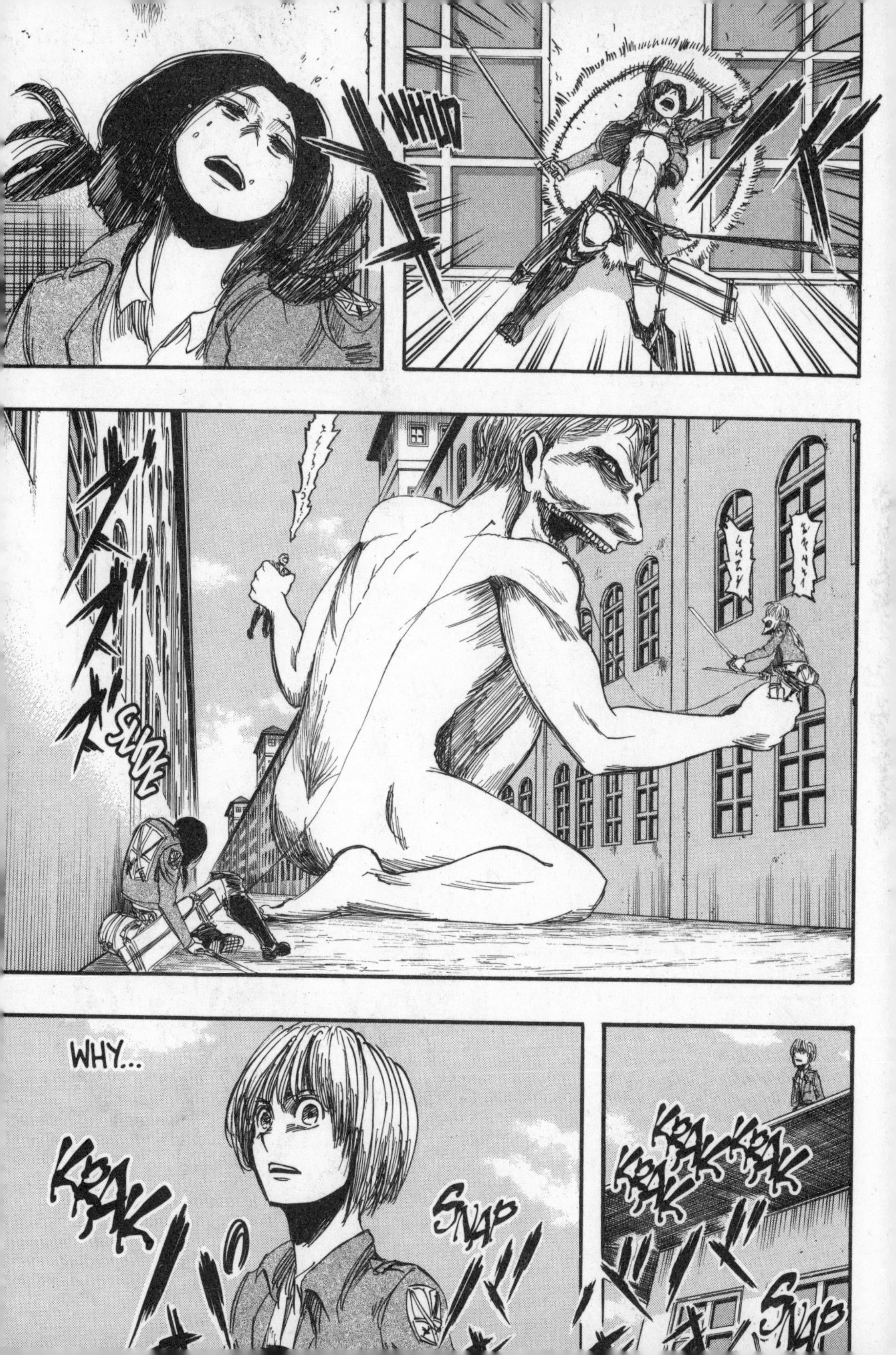
WHUD
SLIDE
KRAK KRAK KRAK KRAK
WHY...
SNAP
KRAK
SNAP

...DO I...   WHY...

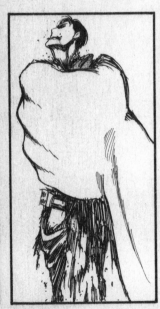

... MY COM-
RADES BEING
EATEN?

...HAVE TO
WATCH...

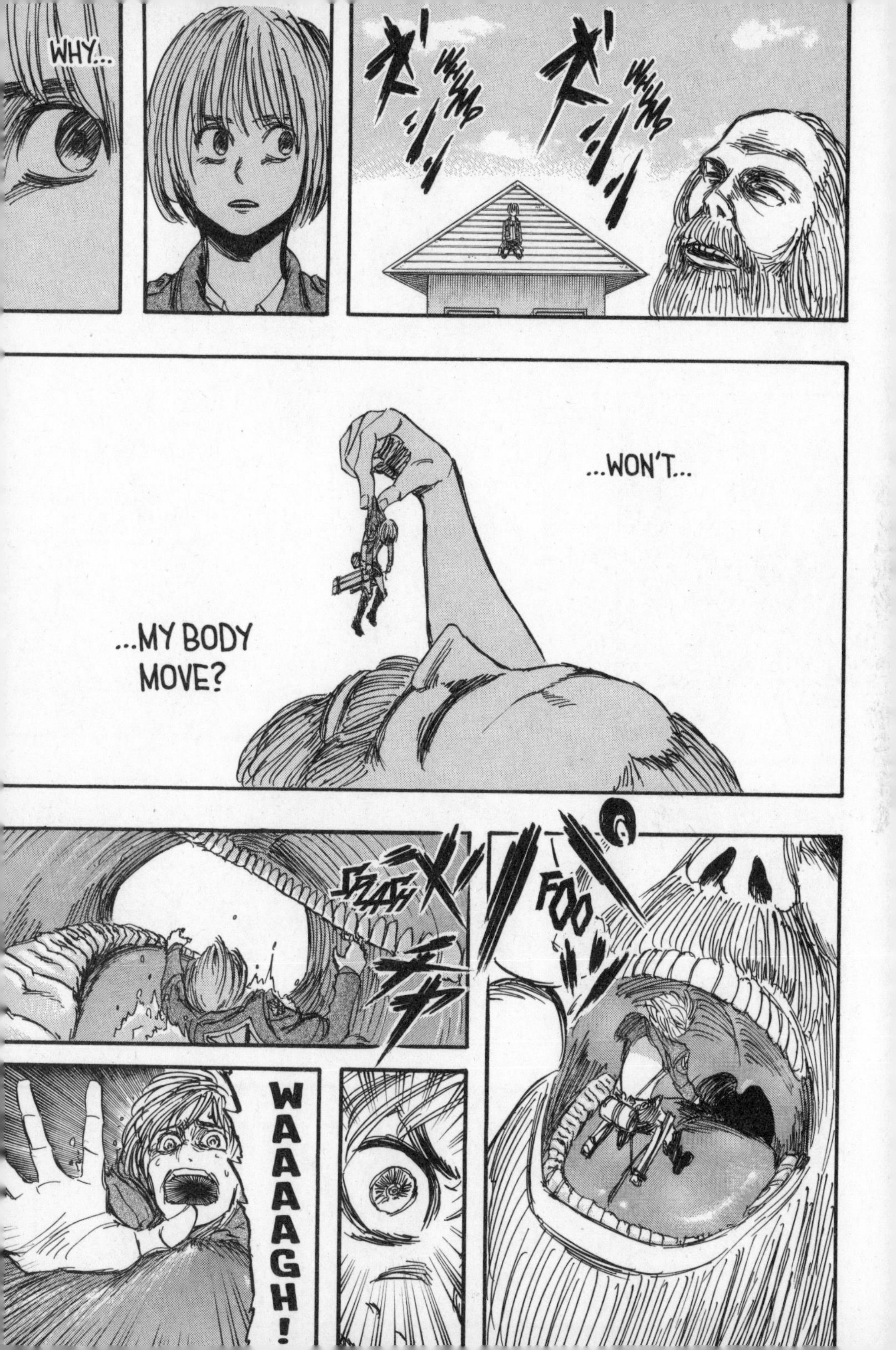

ズシン
ズシン
WHY...
...WON'T...
...MY BODY MOVE?
FOO
SPLASH
WAAAAAGH!

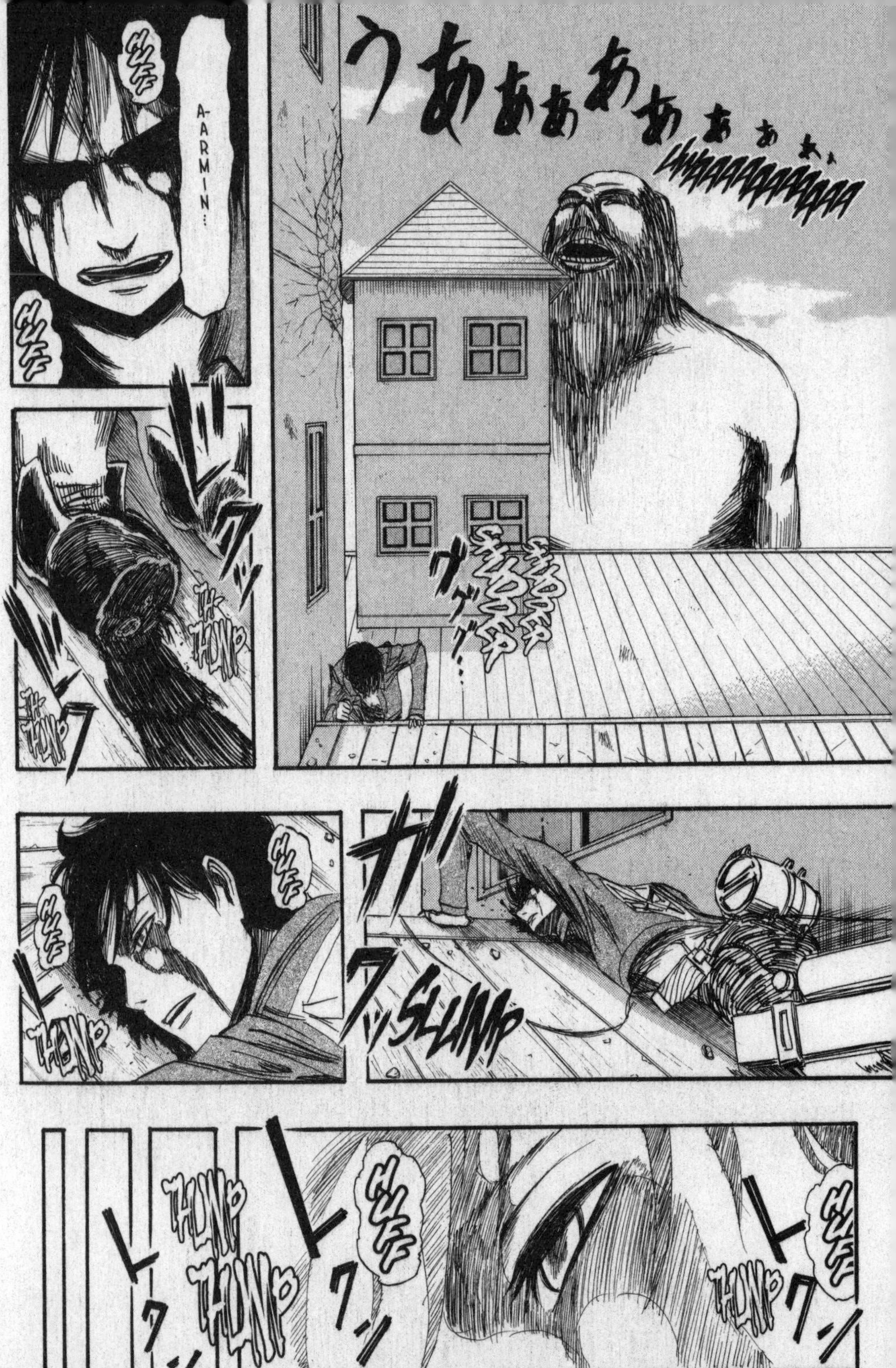
うあああああああぁぁ
UWAAAAAAAAAAAAA
SHUDDER SHUDDER
A-ARMIN...
HUFF
HUFF
THUMP
THUMP
SLUMP
HUFF
HUFF
THUMP
HUFF
THUMP
HUFF
THUMP
THUMP

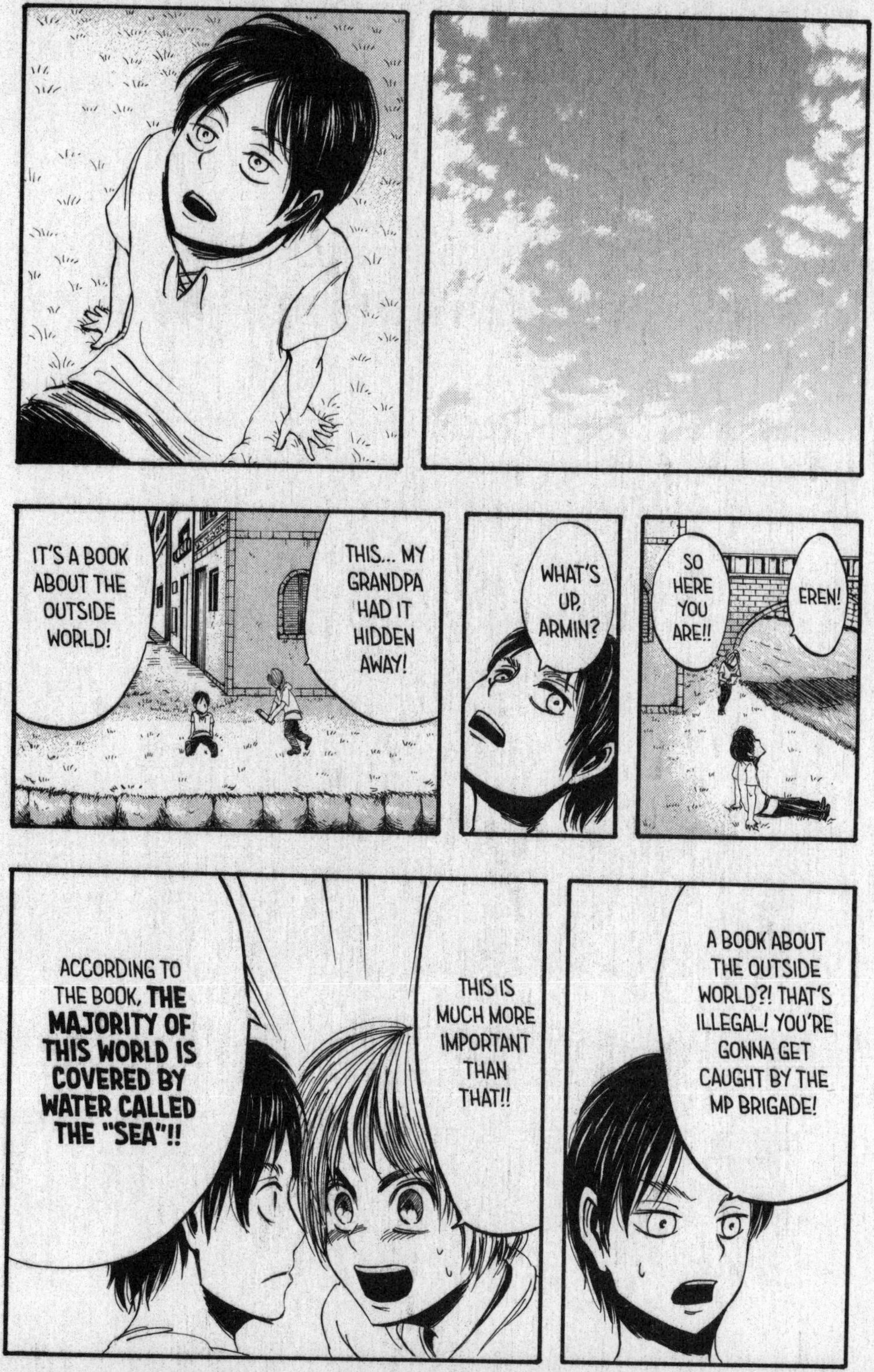
EREN!
SO HERE YOU ARE!!
WHAT'S UP, ARMIN?
THIS... MY GRANDPA HAD IT HIDDEN AWAY!
IT'S A BOOK ABOUT THE OUTSIDE WORLD!
A BOOK ABOUT THE OUTSIDE WORLD?! THAT'S ILLEGAL! YOU'RE GONNA GET CAUGHT BY THE MP BRIGADE!
THIS IS MUCH MORE IMPORTANT THAN THAT!!
ACCORDING TO THE BOOK, **THE MAJORITY OF THIS WORLD IS COVERED BY WATER CALLED THE "SEA"!!**

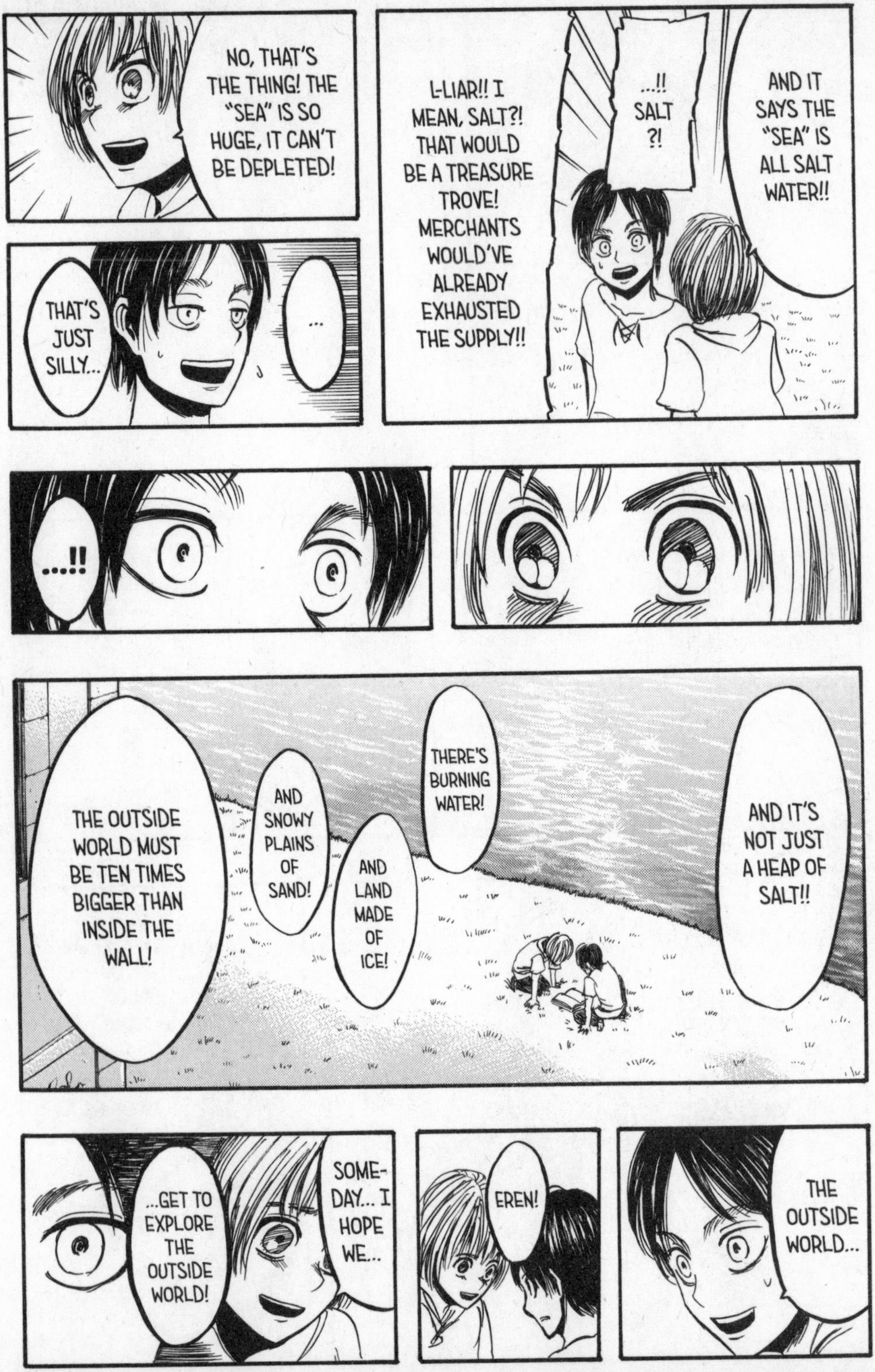
AND IT SAYS THE "SEA" IS ALL SALT WATER!!
...!! SALT ?!
L-LIAR!! I MEAN, SALT?! THAT WOULD BE A TREASURE TROVE! MERCHANTS WOULD'VE ALREADY EXHAUSTED THE SUPPLY!!
NO, THAT'S THE THING! THE "SEA" IS SO HUGE, IT CAN'T BE DEPLETED!
...
THAT'S JUST SILLY...
...!!
AND IT'S NOT JUST A HEAP OF SALT!!
THERE'S BURNING WATER!
AND LAND MADE OF ICE!
AND SNOWY PLAINS OF SAND!
THE OUTSIDE WORLD MUST BE TEN TIMES BIGGER THAN INSIDE THE WALL!
THE OUTSIDE WORLD...
EREN!
SOME-DAY... I HOPE WE...
...GET TO EXPLORE THE OUTSIDE WORLD!

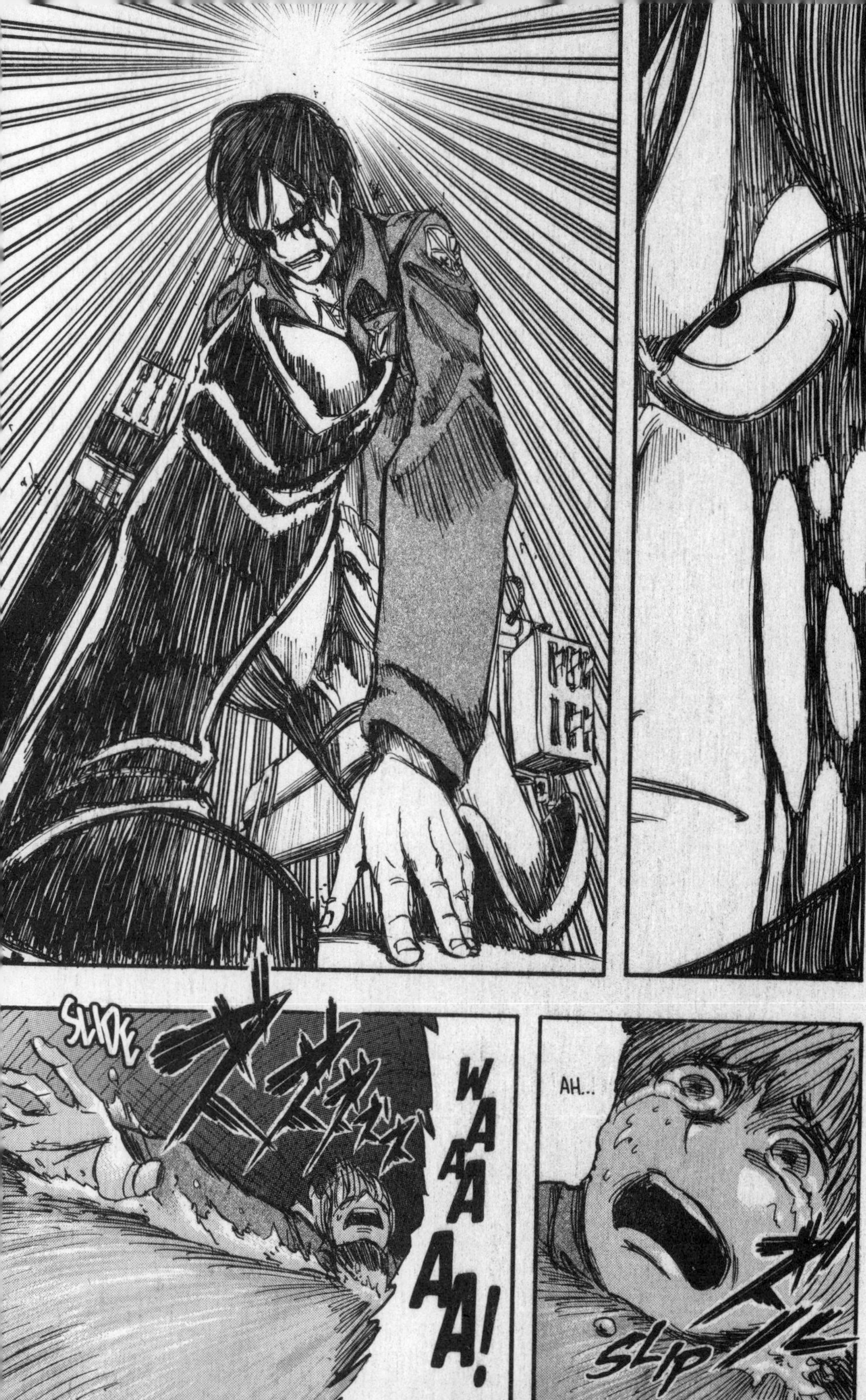
AH...
SLIP
SLIDE
WAAAAAA!

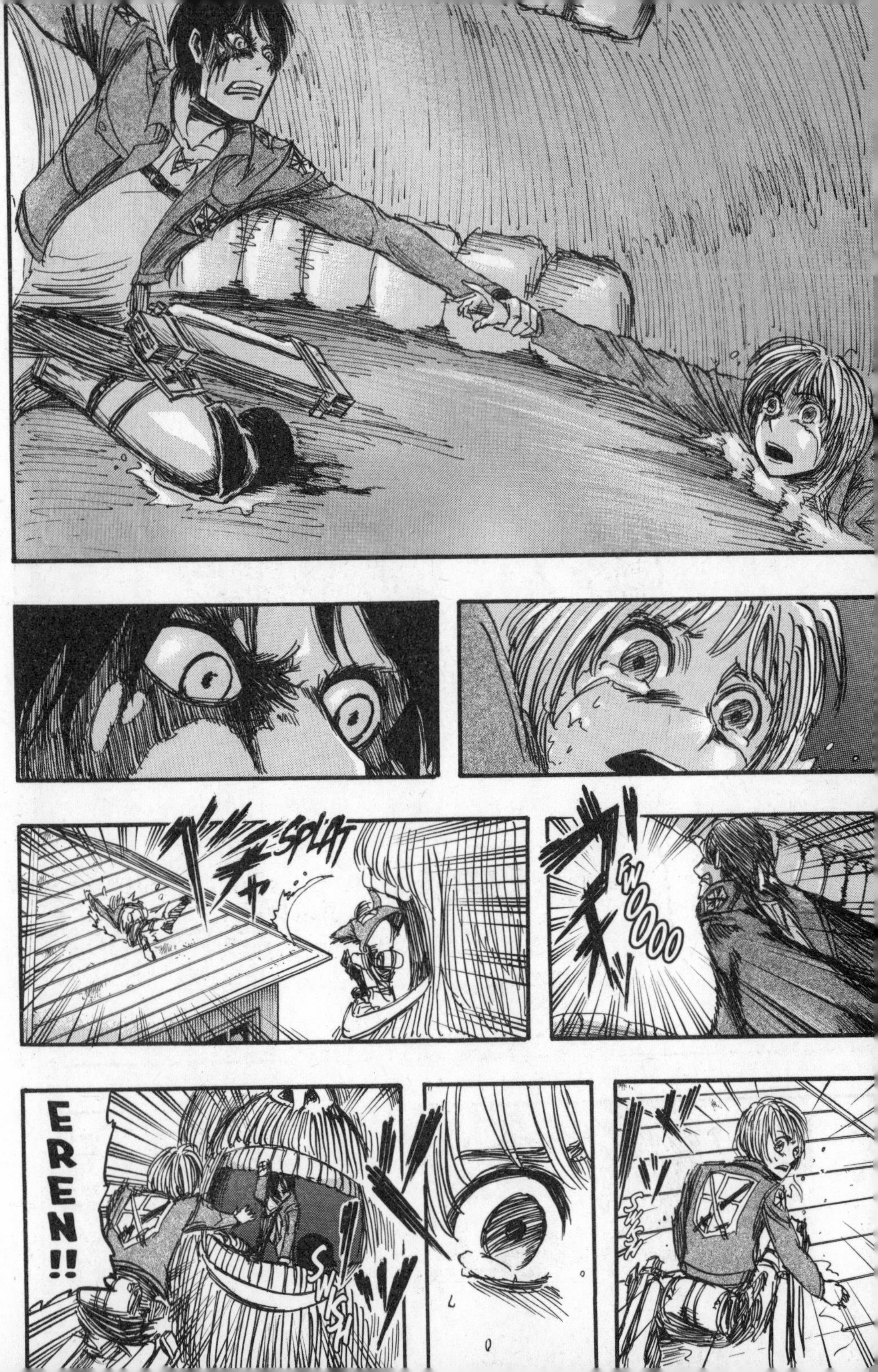
FWOOOO
SPLAT
EREN!!
SWISH

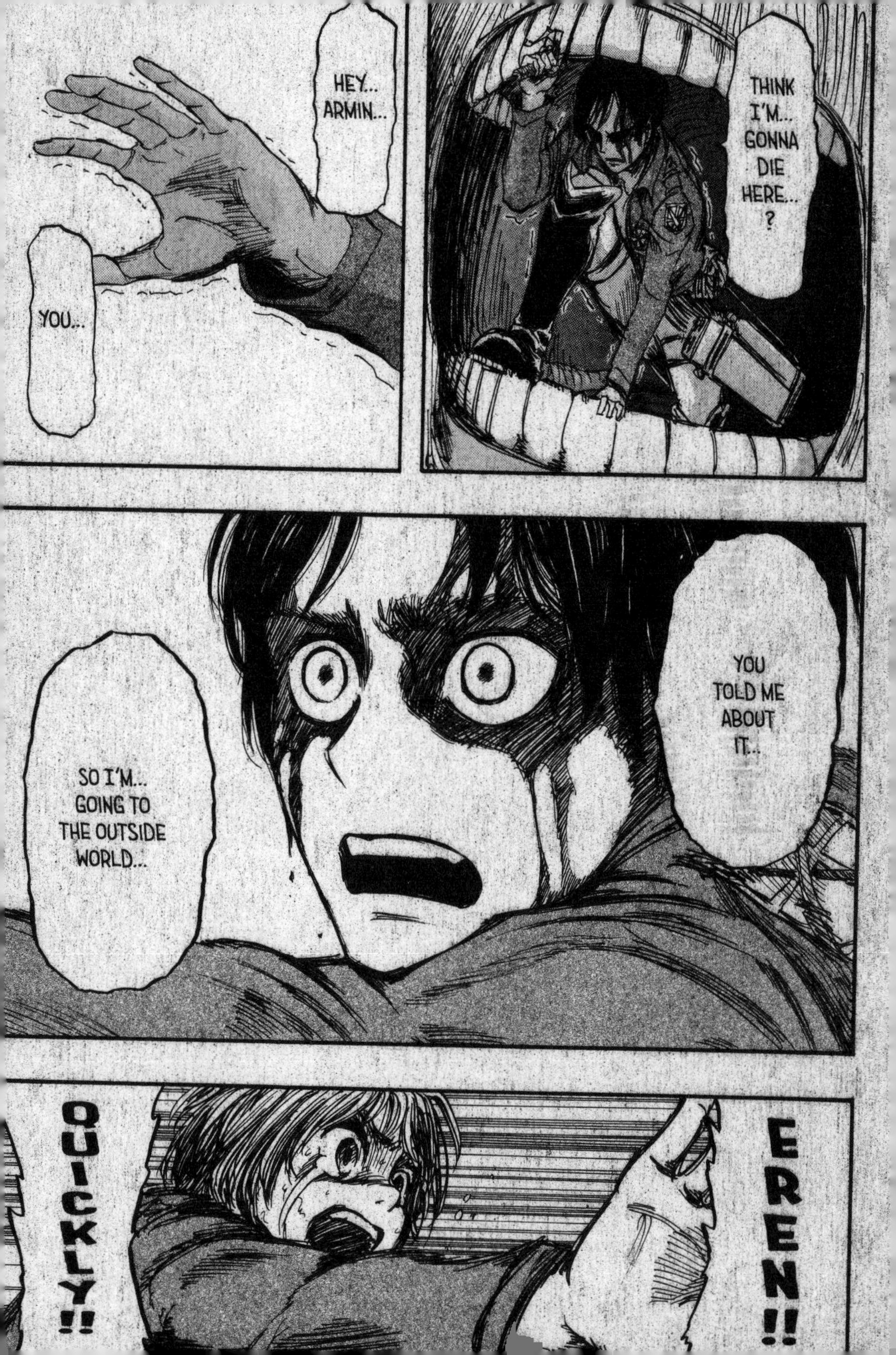
THINK I'M... GONNA DIE HERE... ?
HEY... ARMIN...
YOU...
YOU TOLD ME ABOUT IT...
SO I'M... GOING TO THE OUTSIDE WORLD...
EREN!!
QUICKLY!!

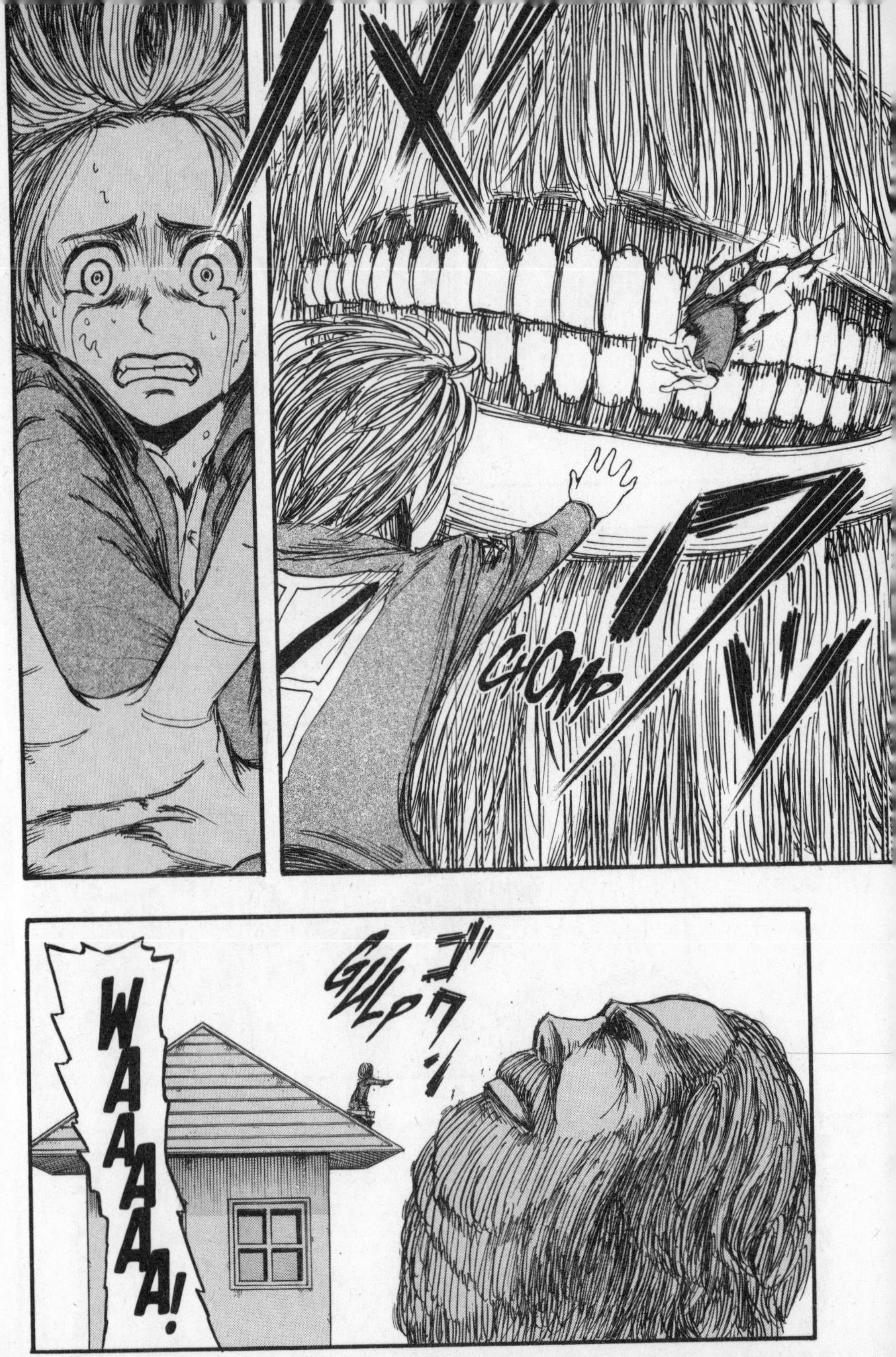
CHOMP
GULP
ゴクン
WAAAAA!

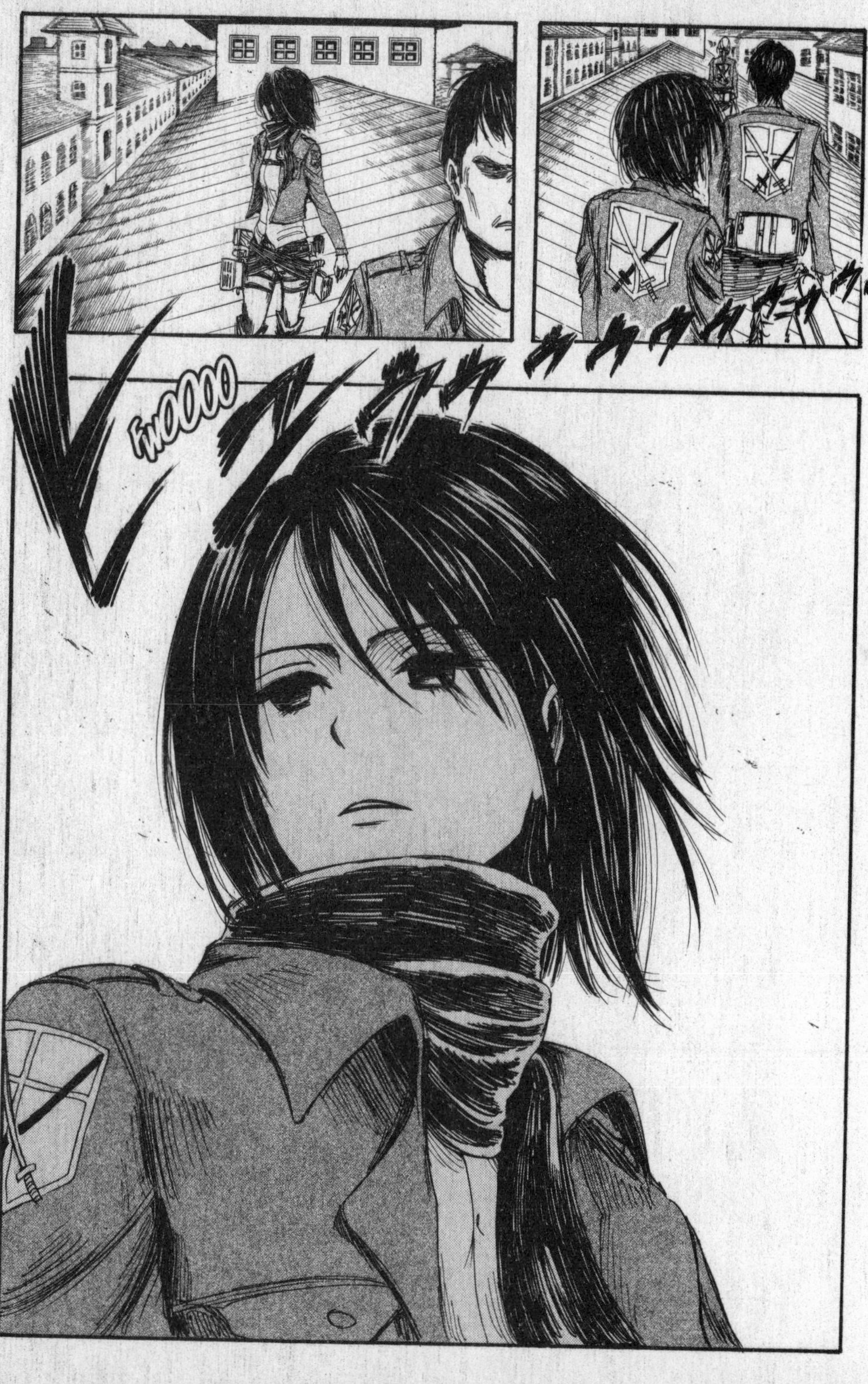
FWOOOO

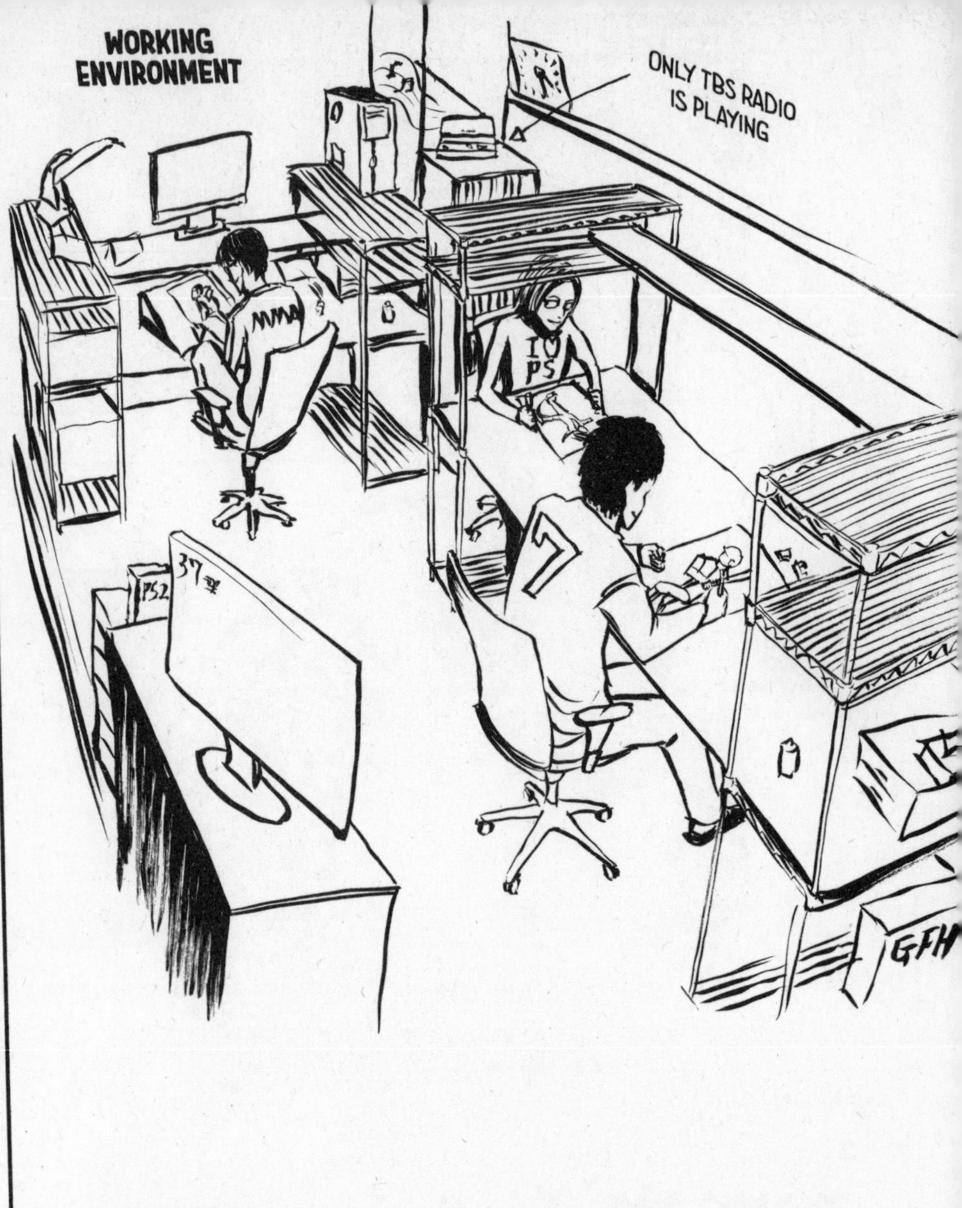
WORKING ENVIRONMENT
ONLY TBS RADIO IS PLAYING
MMA
I PS
PS2
GFH

SHINX-SAN
OUMI-SAN
SOMETIMES TAKANIWA-SAN

EVERYONE WHO READ
"ATTACK ON TITAN"

THANK YOU VERY MUCH

ULTRA-SPECIAL BONUS!!*

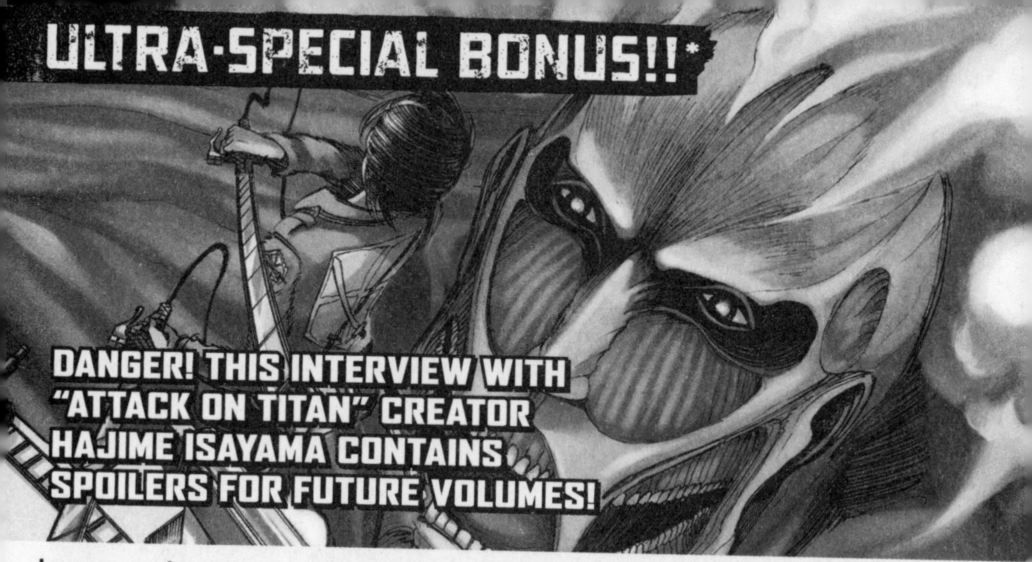

DANGER! THIS INTERVIEW WITH "ATTACK ON TITAN" CREATOR HAJIME ISAYAMA CONTAINS SPOILERS FOR FUTURE VOLUMES!

Japanese readers sent in questions to ask Mr. Isayama, and his editor asked him a few. Here we present his answers. Just be careful: Some of them contain major spoilers for later volumes! We recommend you read Vol. 2, then come back and read this interview.

EDITOR: Thank you for being here today. We've received a lot of questions from the readers. Please answer to the best of your ability.
MR. ISAYAMA: I have a feeling most of my answers will be boring, but... fire away. Nothing is taboo.

Then let's begin. "Why did you decide on giants as the theme of this work?"
ISA: Well, giants are kind of gross, aren't they? That's why.

"Has anything in your life changed since the series has become so popular?"
ISA: I got a weird phone call from my bank. They were wondering about the sudden increase of funds in my savings, so they probably thought I was running some bank transfer scam. (Laughs.)

"Do you have a way to clear out the cobwebs when you're tired or when you need to decide some important story point?"
ISA: Shadowboxing with the hanging lamp cord in my house is very soothing.

"What made you decide to become a manga artist?"
ISA: I just decided one day, is all. I had a habit of doodling and daydreaming anyway, so I was fortunate that my interests were compatible with something that's profitable.

"Mr. Isayama, what is your fetish?"
ISA: I have a body hair fetish.

"How do you get over those times when making manga gets tough?"
ISA: I don't. (Laughs.) I think it's always equal parts tough and fun.

"Where do you get your ideas for stories?"
ISA: This doesn't have to do with creating stories, but when I'm half-awake, like just before I drift off to sleep, my mind gets flooded with information I've seen or heard subconsciously. I call it "Super Enlightenment Time." And this is true, I'm not kidding.

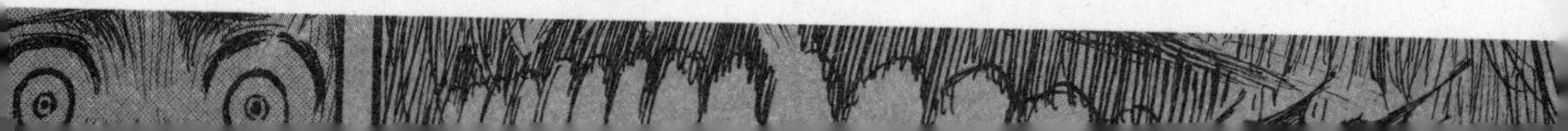

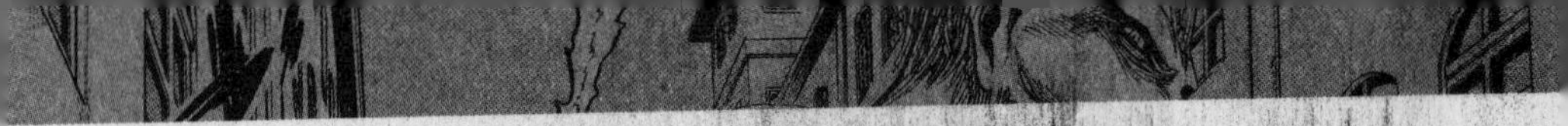

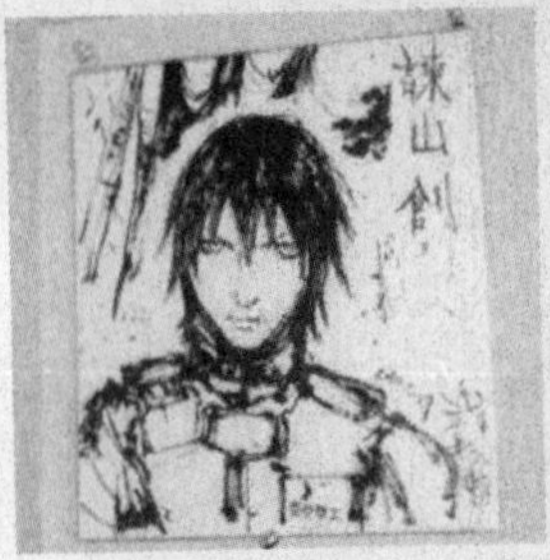
諫山創

A signed sketch by an artist Mr. Isayama respects, Mr. Nihei. It's a treasured possession that hangs on his wall.

On to the next question... "Is there a manga artist whom you respect?"
ISA: There are plenty of them. Of course, there are my fellow manga artists in Betsu Maga, but also Tsutomu Nihei, Ryoji Minagawa, Kentaro Miura, Hideki Arai, Tooru Mitsumine, and I could go on and on. I'm still a fledgling.

"Who is your favorite character in Attack on Titan?"
ISA: That would be Jean. Jean comes right out and says what he's thinking, even if it's something you normally couldn't say. That's what I like about him.

"Out of all the manga you've read, what influenced you most?"
ISA: ARMS.

"How far ahead do you have Attack on Titan plotted out?"
ISA: In broad strokes, I've got it pretty well thought out to way, way down the line. And I've got outlines that say like, such-and-such a truth will be revealed in volume 5 and around volume 10, this situation is going to happen. See, if I didn't decide these things before it sees publication, I wouldn't even be able to come up with ideas. Although I don't flesh it out until I'm actually working on it...

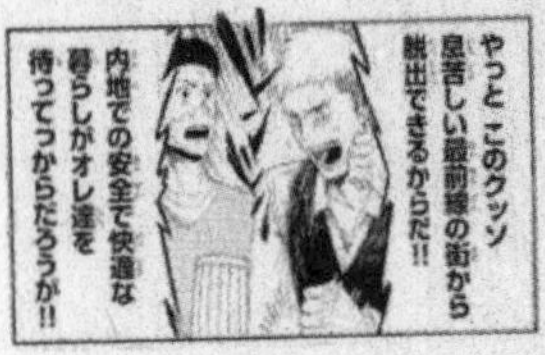
やっと このクソン
息苦しい最前線の街から
脱出できるからだ!!
内地での安全で快適な
暮らしがオレ達を
待ってっからだろうが!!

Jean Kirstein. I like the name, too.

"What do you think of Miyajima (Masanori Miyajima)?"
ISA: He's got a permanent crease on his nose from his glasses.

"Aren't you going to have female Titans?"
ISA: I wonder if I should say this... They're rare.

"I always forget how the kanji for 'Isa' in your last name goes. Is there a good way to remember how to write it?"
ISA: You can write it however. I'll answer either way.

"Mr. Isayama, I want to see where you work!"
ISA: That's the one thing I hope you'll cut me some slack on! I really don't want to show you, since it's a mess...

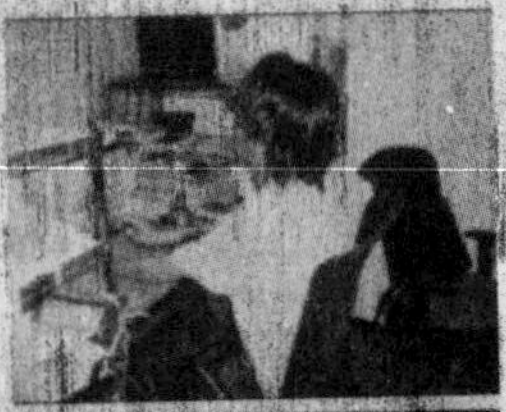

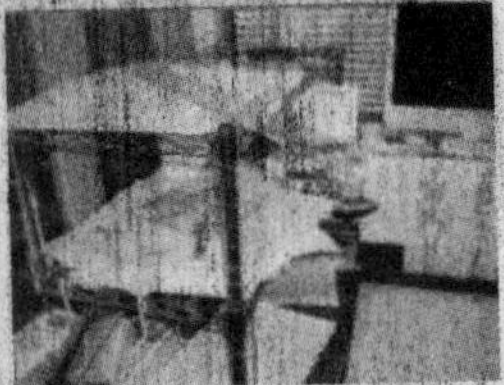

We went ahead and took photos of Mr. Isayama's studio.

"If you were on a desert island and could only have three things, what would you choose besides me and a guitar?"
ISA: Other than you and a guitar, I guess I would bring a U.S. military fleet.

"Mr. Isayama, what were you like as a child?"
ISA: I don't really want to recall my childhood...

"Do you use a model for the Titans?"
ISA: For the Titan version of Eren, I use martial artist Yuushin Okami's body as a model. My ideal is the physique of a middleweight mixed martial artist. I only use the shape of the body as a model.

"I'm guessing that drawing Titans after a long time would do things to your mind. Do you have nightmares about them?"
ISA: I don't think giants are really scary in the first place, so no, never.

"What's the scariest thing in the world?"
ISA: A bunch of middle school girls looking at me and going, "Eww" while laughing.

"Please tell me your basic one-month schedule."
ISA: I take a week to storyboard and three weeks to draw.

"Mikasa is always wearing the scarf she got from Eren. Doesn't she get hot?"
ISA: She doesn't wear it when it's hot outside.

"Mr. Isayama, at what age did you start drawing?"
ISA: I have a memory of being praised for a drawing I did of a dragon when I was in kindergarten.

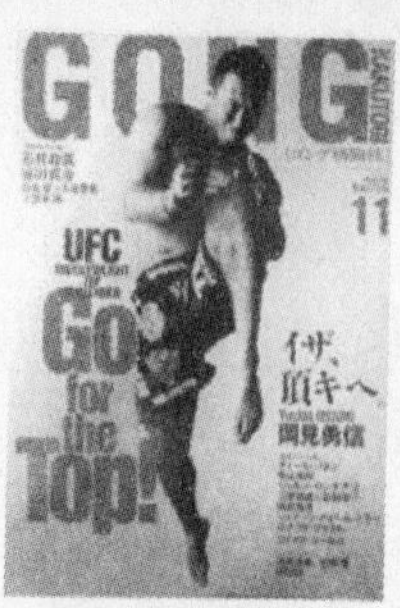
GONG
11
UFC
Go for the Top!

Yūshin Okami, whom Mr. Isayama uses as a model.

"Are you ever mistaken for the artist who does (soccer series) Giant Killing?"
ISA: Just recently, my own editor made that mistake.

"What manga do you recommend right now?"
ISA: All-Rounder Meguru and Iron Wind!!

"Mr. Isayama, which Attack on Titan character most resembles you?"
ISA: Hmm... Mr. Hannes and the Garrison soldiers in volume 1 who sit around drinking booze.

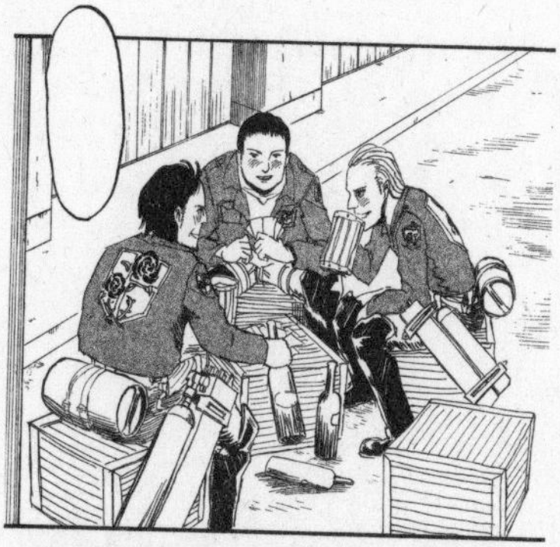

These Garrison soldiers drink alcohol in the middle of the afternoon. Surely Mr. Isayama doesn't do *that* at work?!

"Is there a story that you want to do after finishing Attack on Titan?"
ISA: There's a story I've had in my mind since high school. If I get lucky enough for it to be published someday, I hope everyone reads it!

"Do you have a favorite scene in Attack on Titan?"
ISA: The scene where the TV studio gets taken over and rock music plays. Sorry...

"What's your favorite food?"
ISA: I'm not really into food.**

"How do you spend your free time?"
ISA: Drooling as I surf the net.

"What would you look like if you were a Titan, Mr. Isayama?"
ISA: I'm sure I'd look something like this. (Laughs.)

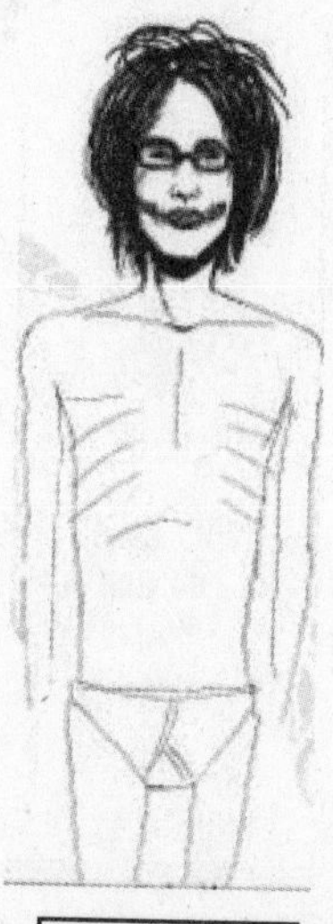

Scary in a way...

Thank you very much! One last question. "From what page does the story really get going?"
ISA: Just wait for the 420th page and up! Please keep reading!

* This interview originally appeared in Bessatsu Shonen Magazine December 2010 issue.
**Apparently, if he's not careful, he'll drop to 40 kilos [88 lbs] without realizing it...

ATTACK on TITAN

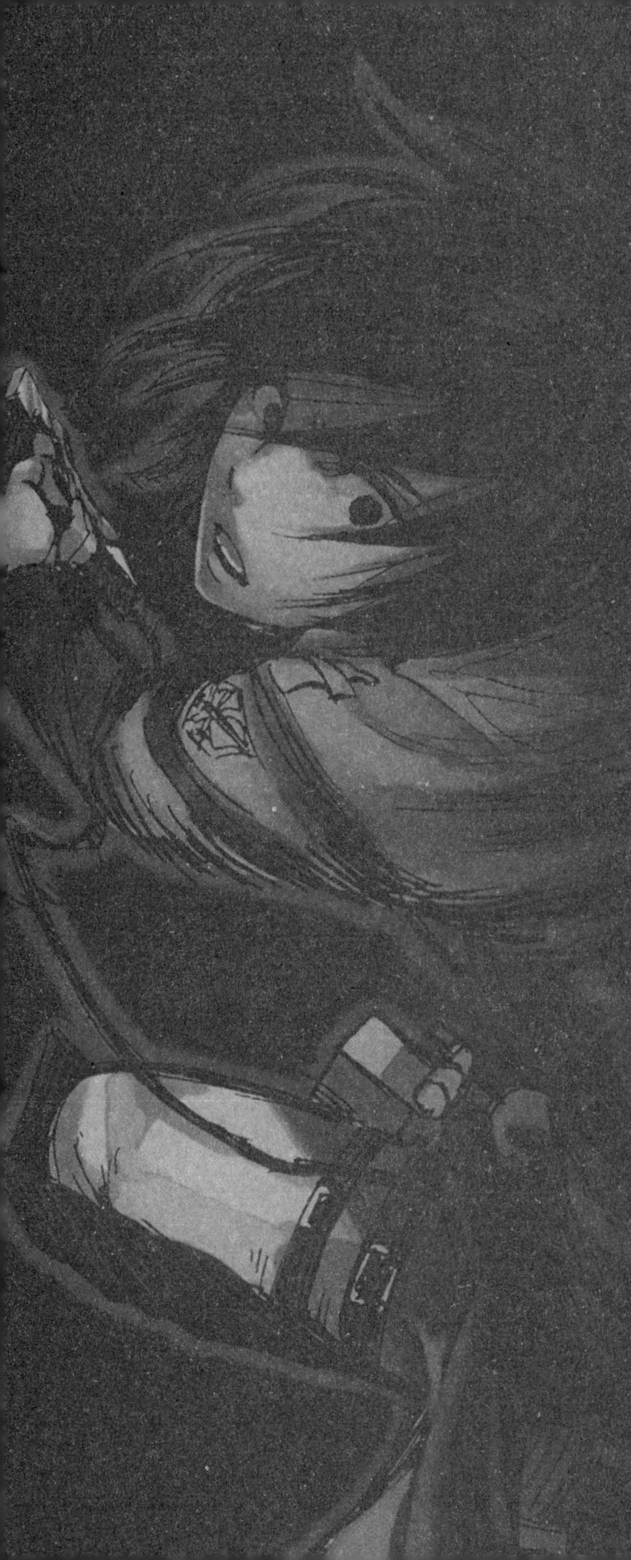

ATTACK ON TITAN 2

HAJIME ISAYAMA

The World of "Attack on Titan"

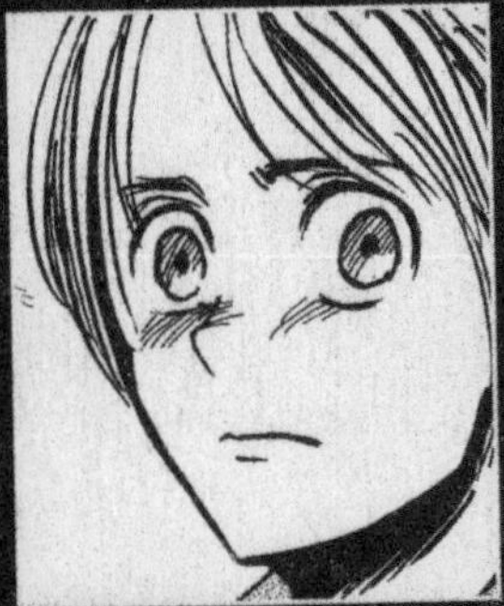

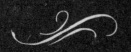

Armin Arlert
Eren and Mikasa's childhood friend. Armin excels academically, but barely passed the training corps because of his poor physical skills. He lost Eren right in front of his eyes.

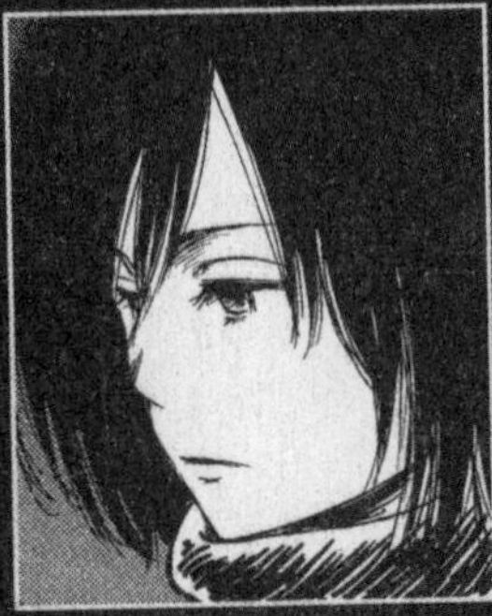

Mikasa Ackerman
Mikasa graduated at the top of her training corps. Raised alongside Eren, she tenaciously tried to protect him, but is currently unaware that he was eaten by a Titan.

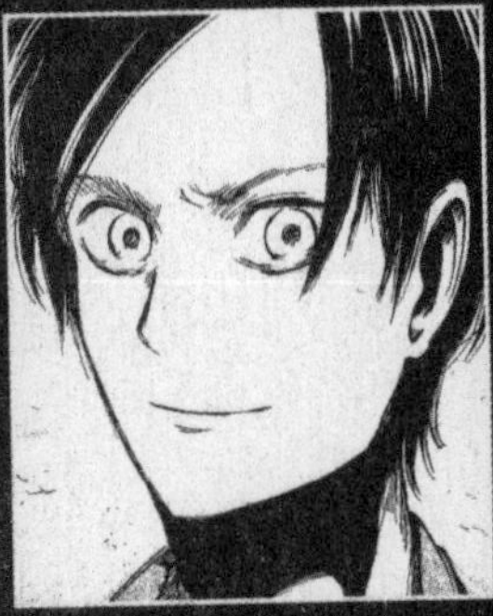

Eren Yeager
Longing for the world outside the wall, Eren aimed to join the Survey Corps. He graduated fifth in his training corps, but was swallowed by a Titan.

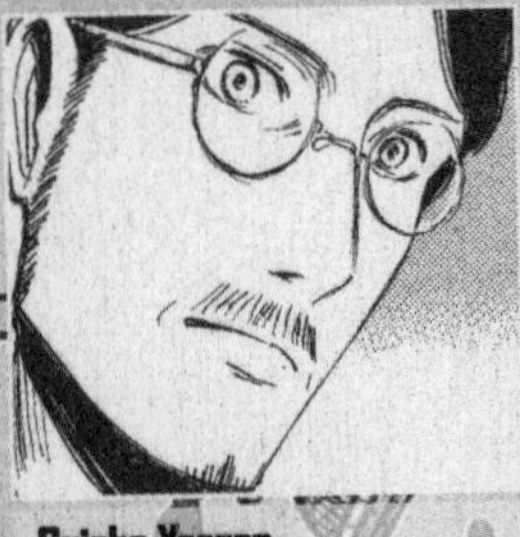

Grisha Yeager
A doctor and Eren's father. He went missing after the Titan attack five years ago.

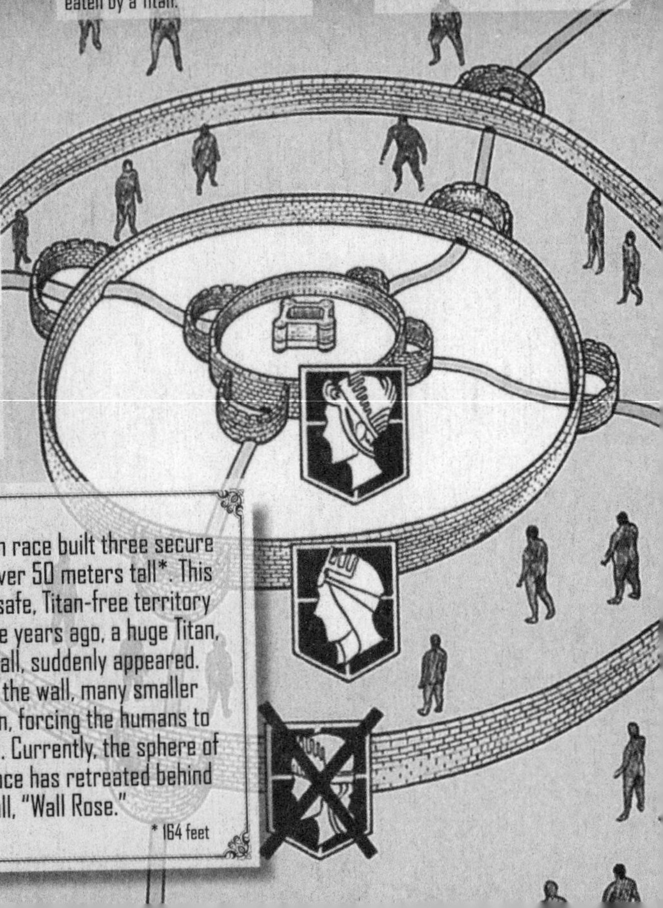

100 years ago, the human race built three secure concentric walls, each over 50 meters tall*. This successfully secured a safe, Titan-free territory for humans. However, five years ago, a huge Titan, taller than the outer wall, suddenly appeared. After it broke through the wall, many smaller Titans found their way in, forcing the humans to abandon their outer wall. Currently, the sphere of activity of the human race has retreated behind its second wall, "Wall Rose."

* 164 feet

TITANS

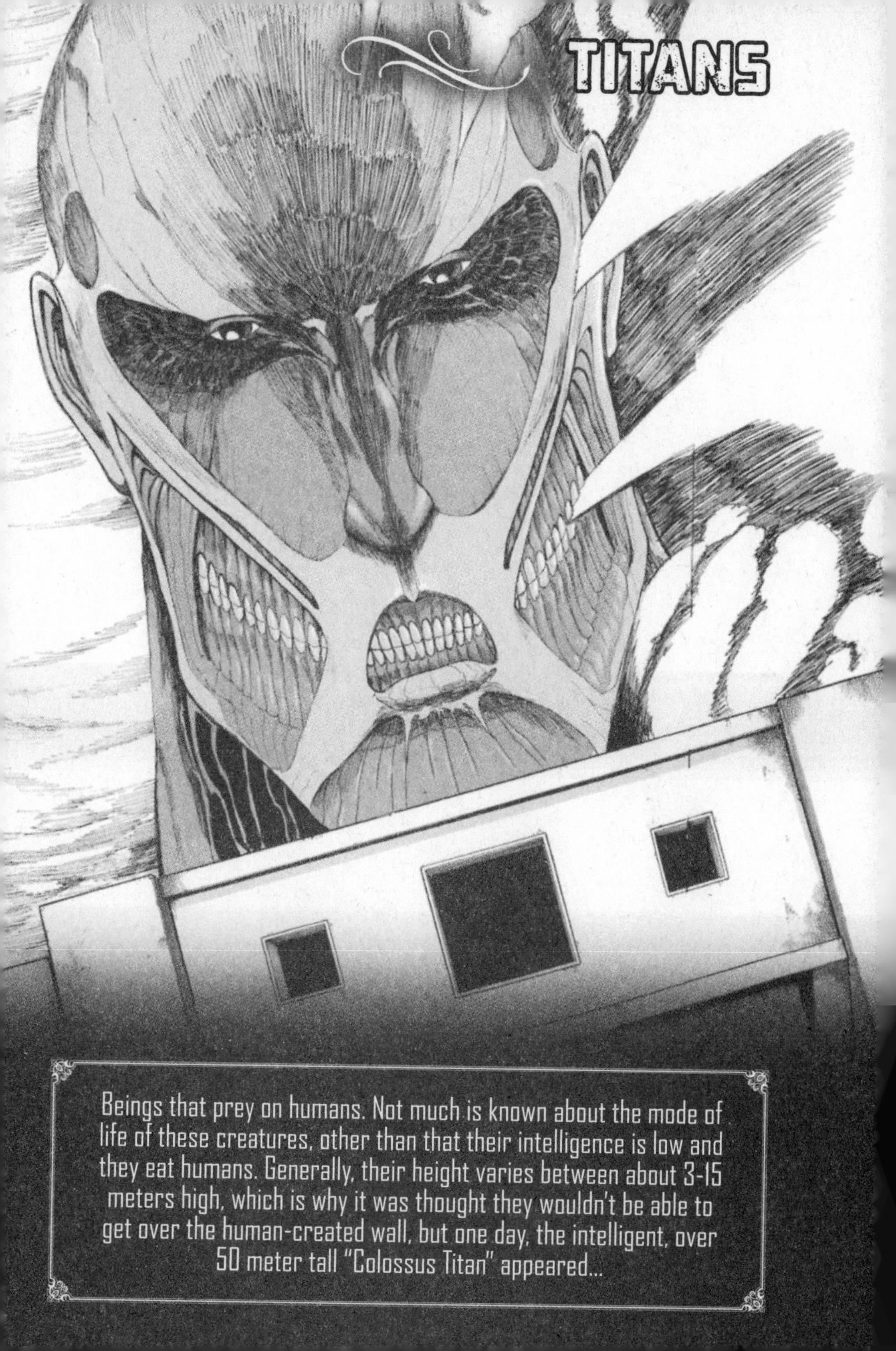

Beings that prey on humans. Not much is known about the mode of life of these creatures, other than that their intelligence is low and they eat humans. Generally, their height varies between about 3-15 meters high, which is why it was thought they wouldn't be able to get over the human-created wall, but one day, the intelligent, over 50 meter tall "Colossus Titan" appeared...

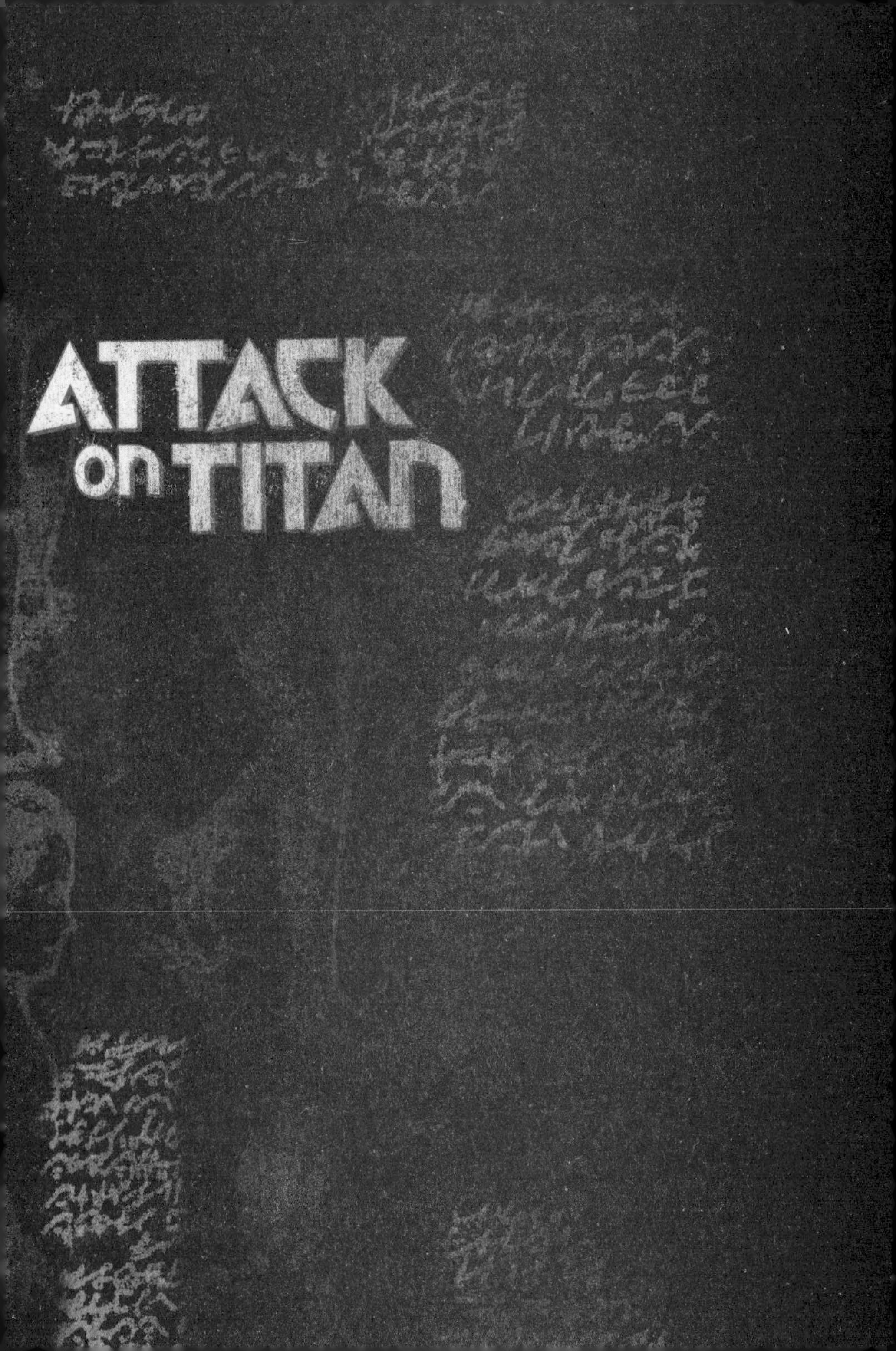
ATTACK on TITAN

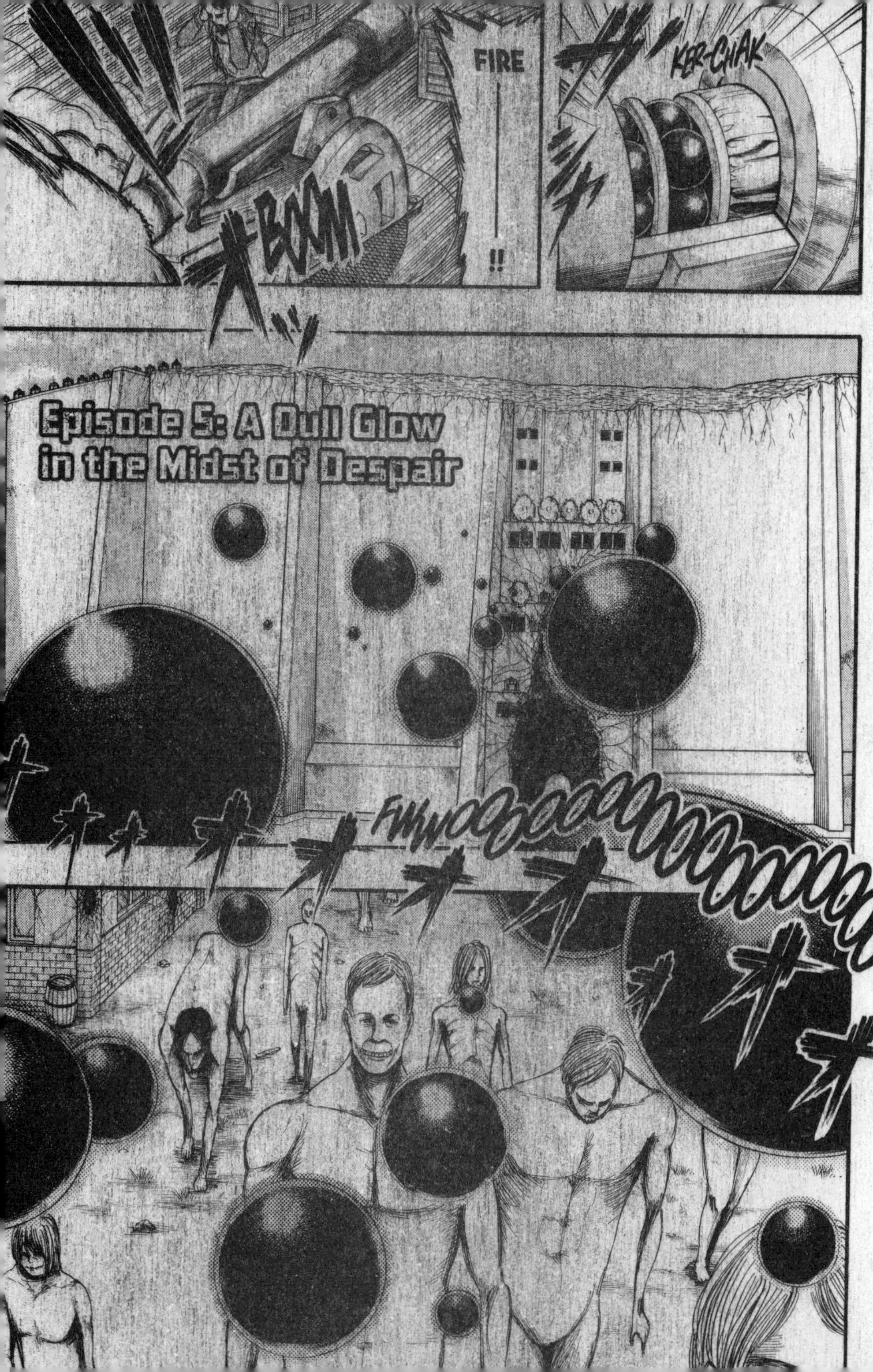
KER-CHAK
FIRE
!!
BOOM
Episode 5: A Dull Glow in the Midst of Despair
FWWOOOOOOOOOOOOOOOOOO

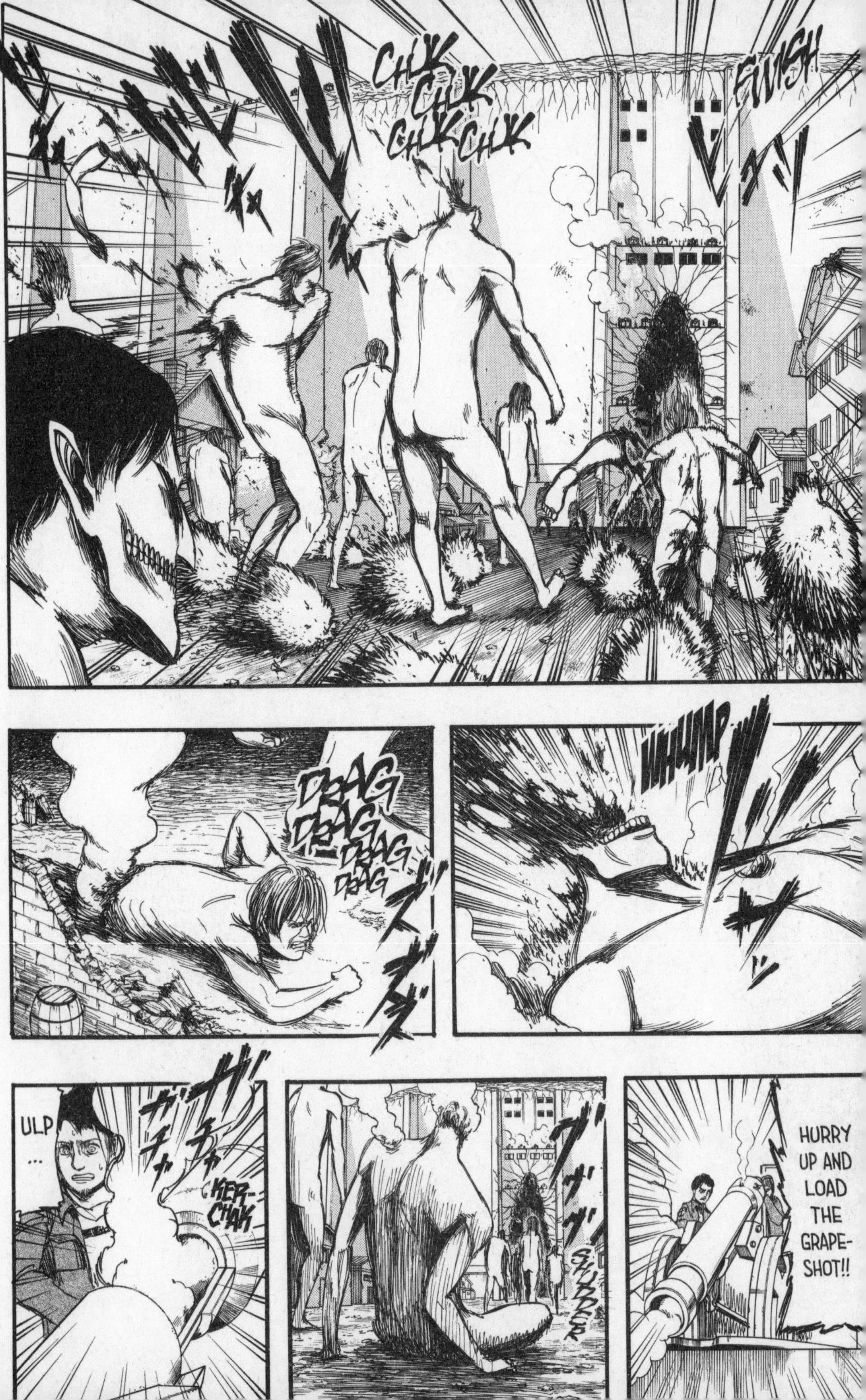
FWISH
CHK CHK CHK CHK CHK
WHUMP
DRAG DRAG DRAG DRAG DRAG
HURRY UP AND LOAD THE GRAPE-SHOT!!
SHUDDER
ULP ...
KER-CHAK

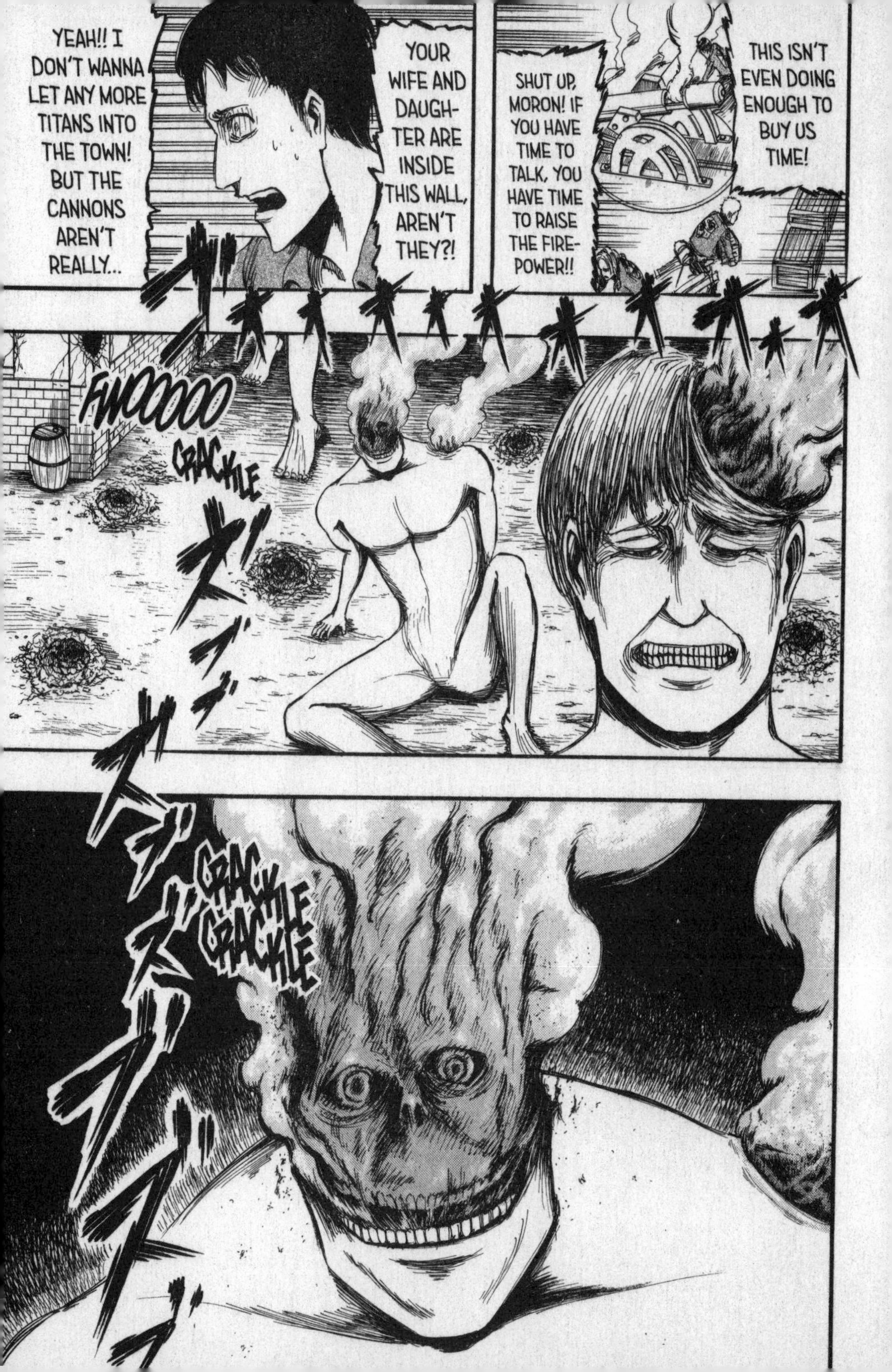
THIS ISN'T EVEN DOING ENOUGH TO BUY US TIME!
SHUT UP, MORON! IF YOU HAVE TIME TO TALK, YOU HAVE TIME TO RAISE THE FIRE-POWER!!
YOUR WIFE AND DAUGH-TER ARE INSIDE THIS WALL, AREN'T THEY?!
YEAH!! I DON'T WANNA LET ANY MORE TITANS INTO THE TOWN! BUT THE CANNONS AREN'T REALLY...
FWOOOOOO
CRACKLE
CRACKLE CRACKLE

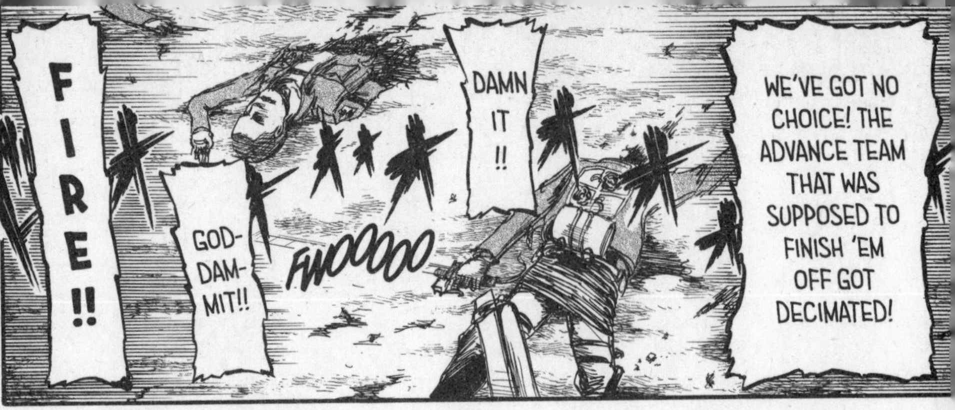
WE'VE GOT NO CHOICE! THE ADVANCE TEAM THAT WAS SUPPOSED TO FINISH 'EM OFF GOT DECIMATED!
DAMN IT!!
FWOOOOO
GOD-DAMMIT!!
FIRE!!
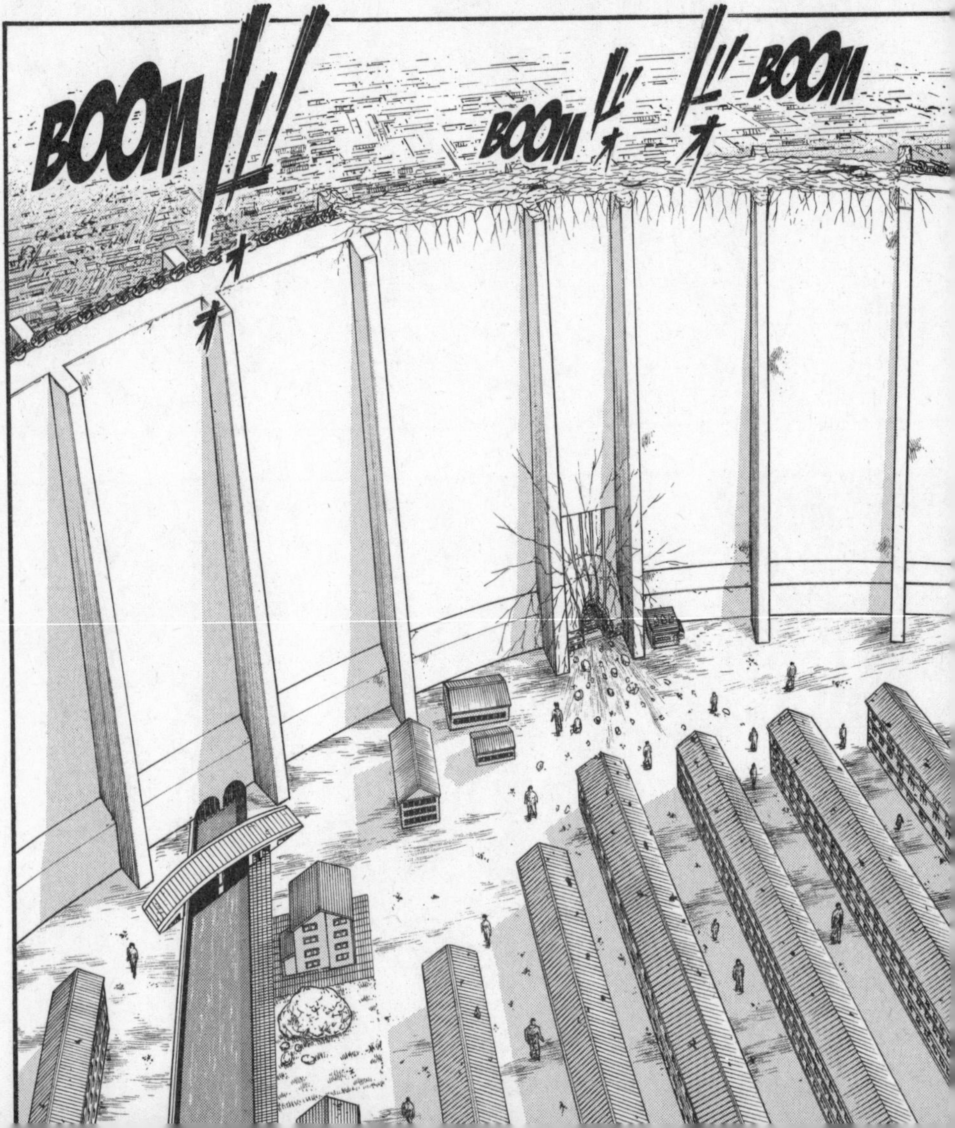
BOOM
BOOM
BOOM

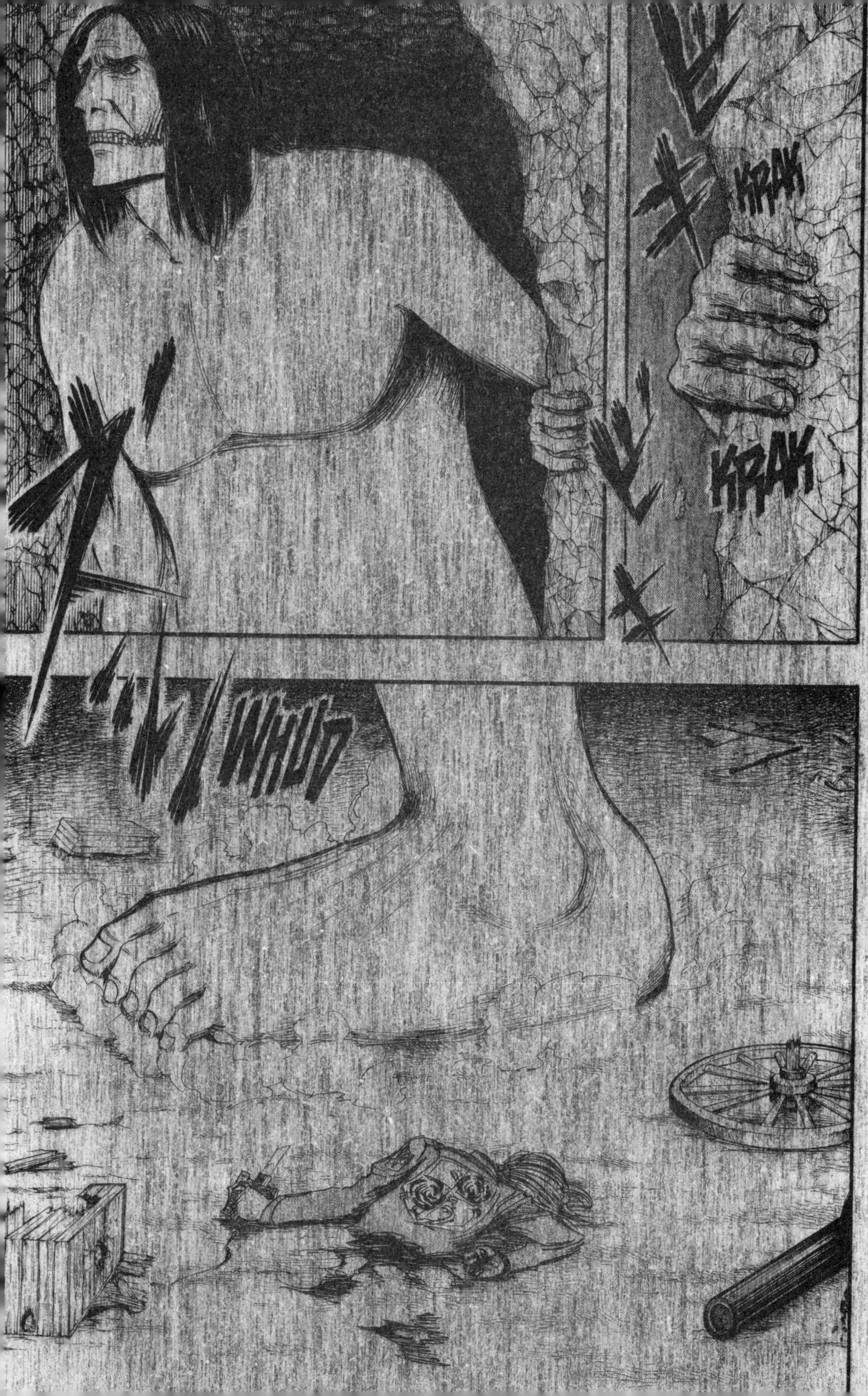
KRAK
KRAK
WHUD

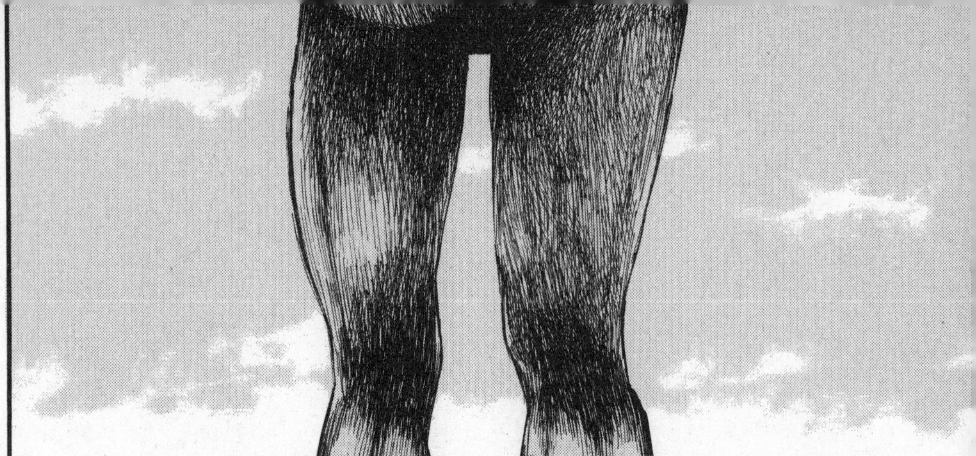
WHUD
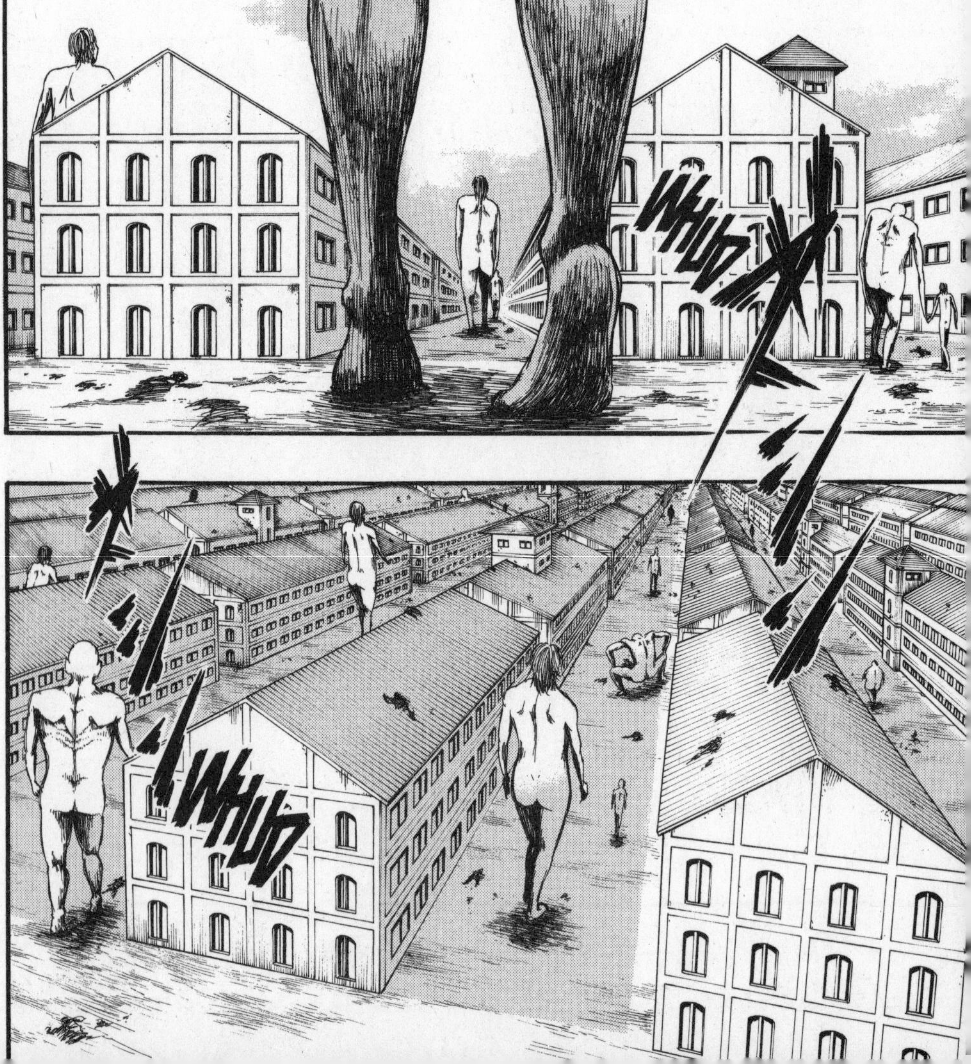
WHUD

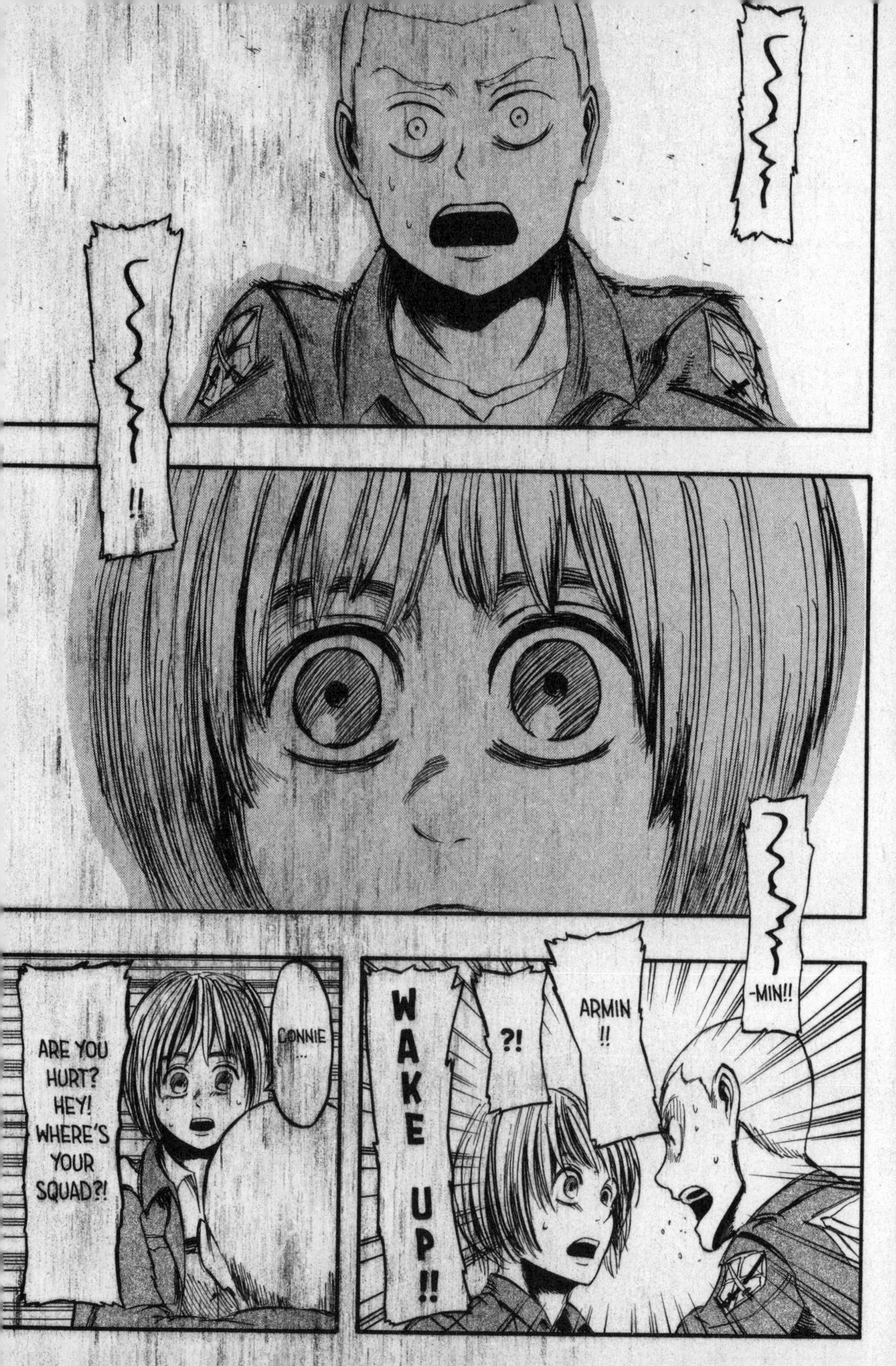
!!
-MIN!!
ARMIN !!
?!
WAKE UP!!
CONNIE ...
ARE YOU HURT? HEY! WHERE'S YOUR SQUAD?!

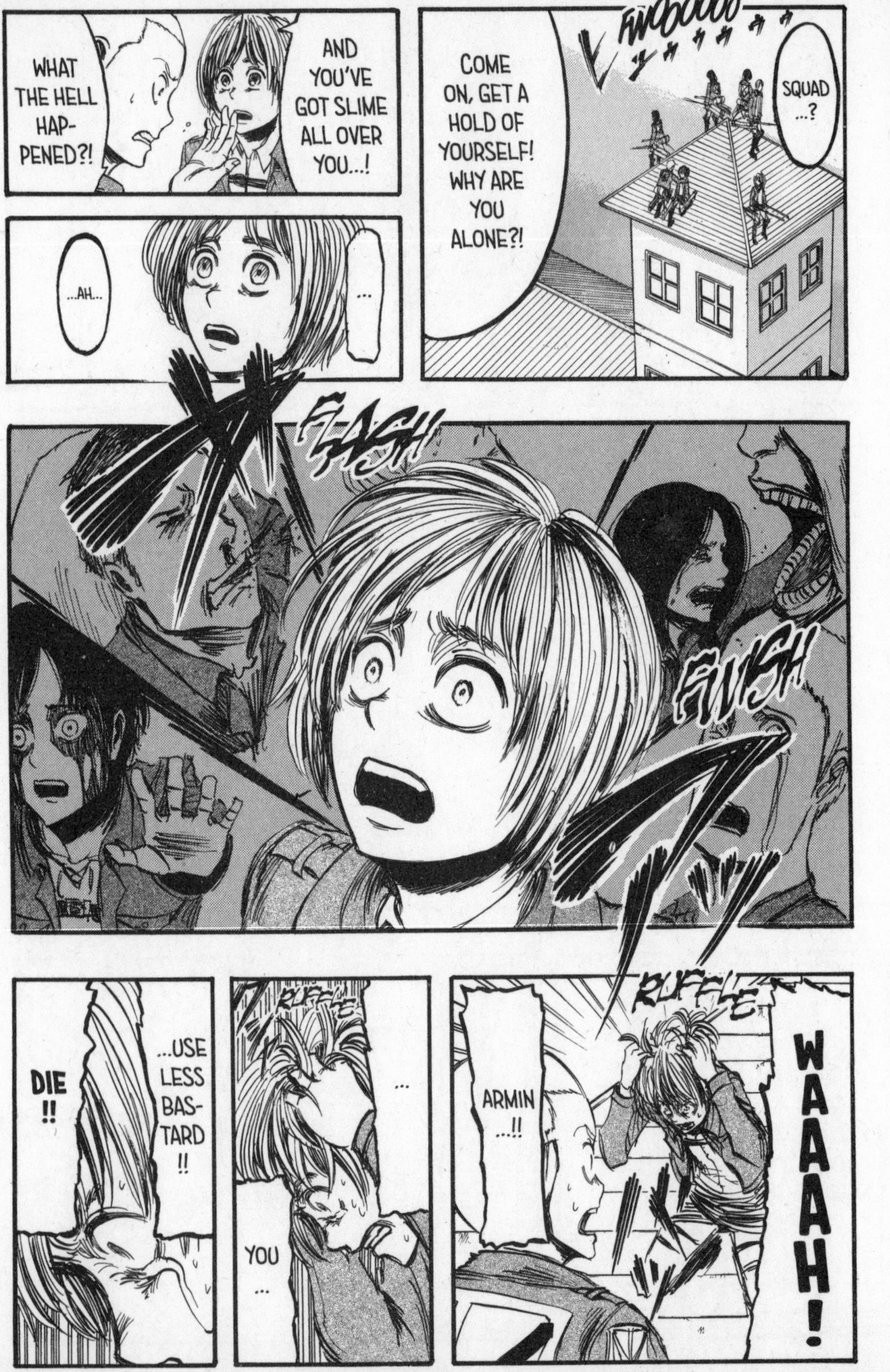
FWOOOOOO
SQUAD ...?
COME ON, GET A HOLD OF YOURSELF! WHY ARE YOU ALONE?!
AND YOU'VE GOT SLIME ALL OVER YOU...!
WHAT THE HELL HAP-PENED?!
...
...AH...
FLASH
FWISH
WAAAH!
RUFFLE
ARMIN ...!!
RUFFLE
...
YOU ...
...USE LESS BAS-TARD !!
DIE !!

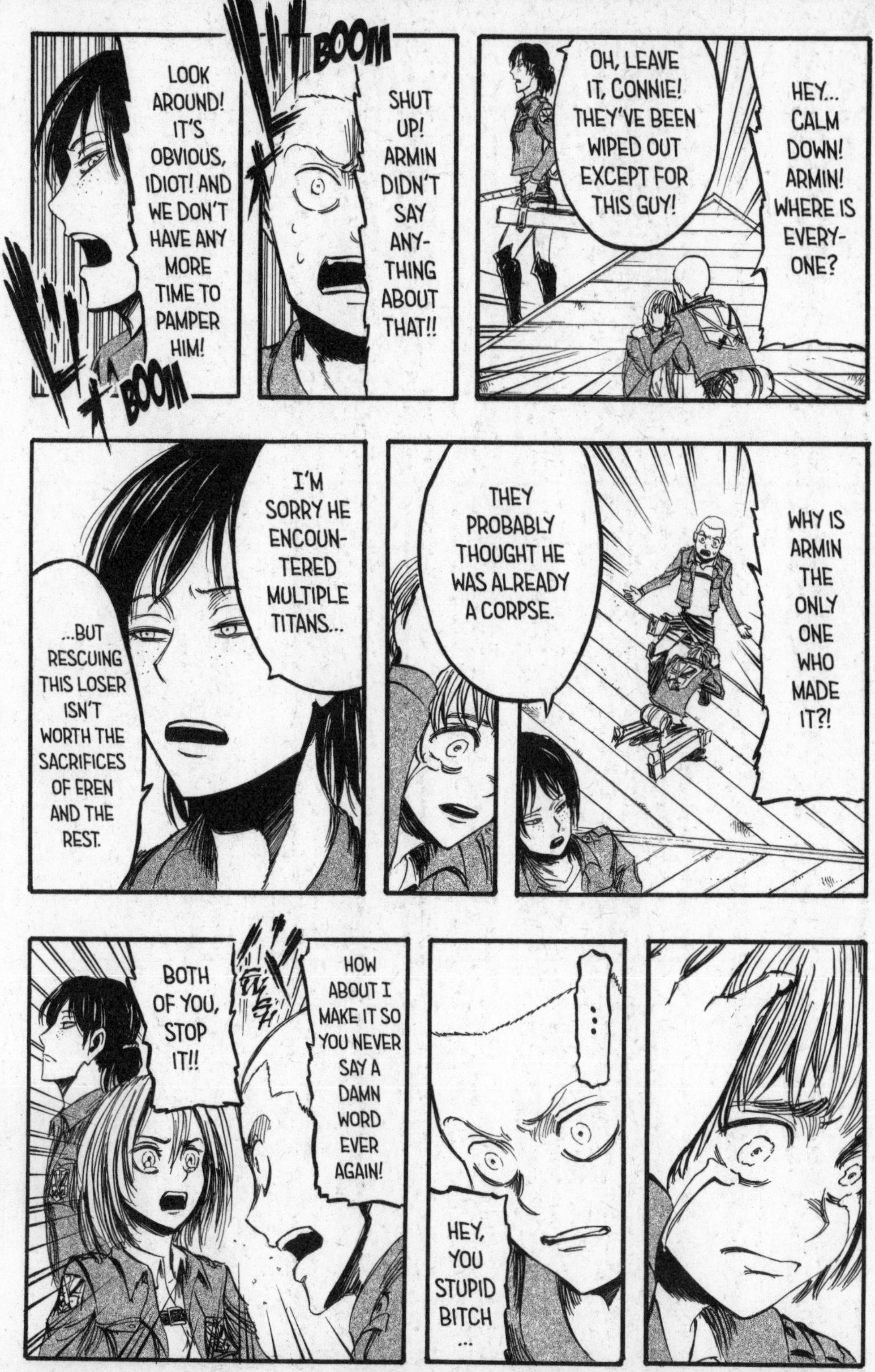
HEY... CALM DOWN! ARMIN! WHERE IS EVERYONE?
OH, LEAVE IT, CONNIE! THEY'VE BEEN WIPED OUT EXCEPT FOR THIS GUY!
BOOM
SHUT UP! ARMIN DIDN'T SAY ANY-THING ABOUT THAT!!
LOOK AROUND! IT'S OBVIOUS, IDIOT! AND WE DON'T HAVE ANY MORE TIME TO PAMPER HIM!
BOOM
WHY IS ARMIN THE ONLY ONE WHO MADE IT?!
THEY PROBABLY THOUGHT HE WAS ALREADY A CORPSE.
I'M SORRY HE ENCOUN-TERED MULTIPLE TITANS...
...BUT RESCUING THIS LOSER ISN'T WORTH THE SACRIFICES OF EREN AND THE REST.
...
HEY, YOU STUPID BITCH...
HOW ABOUT I MAKE IT SO YOU NEVER SAY A DAMN WORD EVER AGAIN!
BOTH OF YOU, STOP IT!!

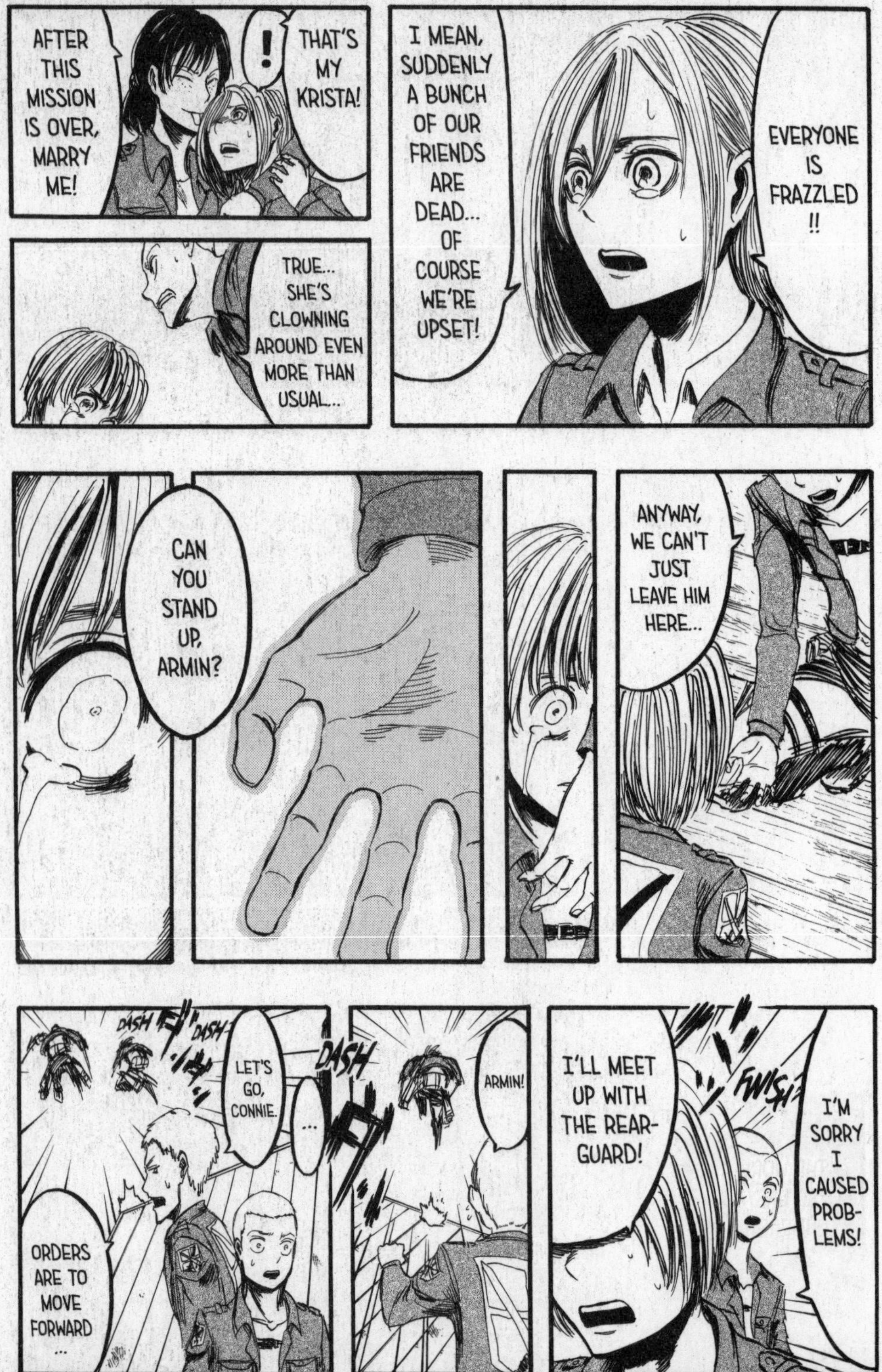
EVERYONE IS FRAZZLED!!
I MEAN, SUDDENLY A BUNCH OF OUR FRIENDS ARE DEAD... OF COURSE WE'RE UPSET!
!
THAT'S MY KRISTA!
AFTER THIS MISSION IS OVER, MARRY ME!
TRUE... SHE'S CLOWNING AROUND EVEN MORE THAN USUAL...
ANYWAY, WE CAN'T JUST LEAVE HIM HERE...
CAN YOU STAND UP, ARMIN?
FWISH
I'M SORRY I CAUSED PROBLEMS!
I'LL MEET UP WITH THE REAR-GUARD!
ARMIN!
DASH
LET'S GO, CONNIE.
...
DASH
DASH
ORDERS ARE TO MOVE FORWARD ...

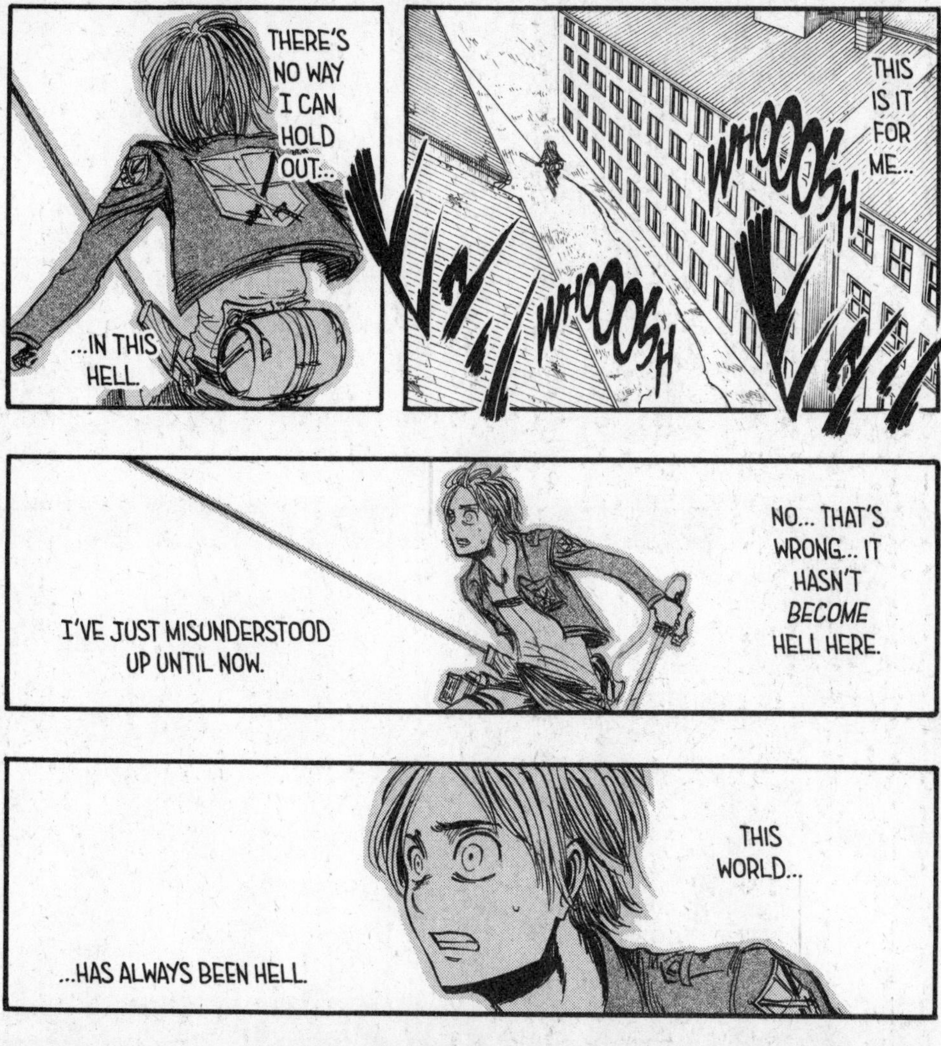
THIS IS IT FOR ME...
WHOOOSH
WHOOOSH
THERE'S NO WAY I CAN HOLD OUT...
...IN THIS HELL.
NO... THAT'S WRONG... IT HASN'T *BECOME* HELL HERE.
I'VE JUST MISUNDERSTOOD UP UNTIL NOW.
THIS WORLD...
...HAS ALWAYS BEEN HELL.
THE STRONG EAT THE WEAK.
THE WORLD'S SO EASY TO UNDERSTAND, IT'S ALMOST OBLIGING...

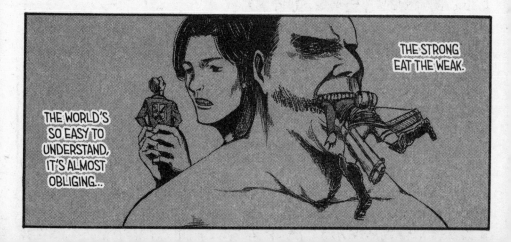

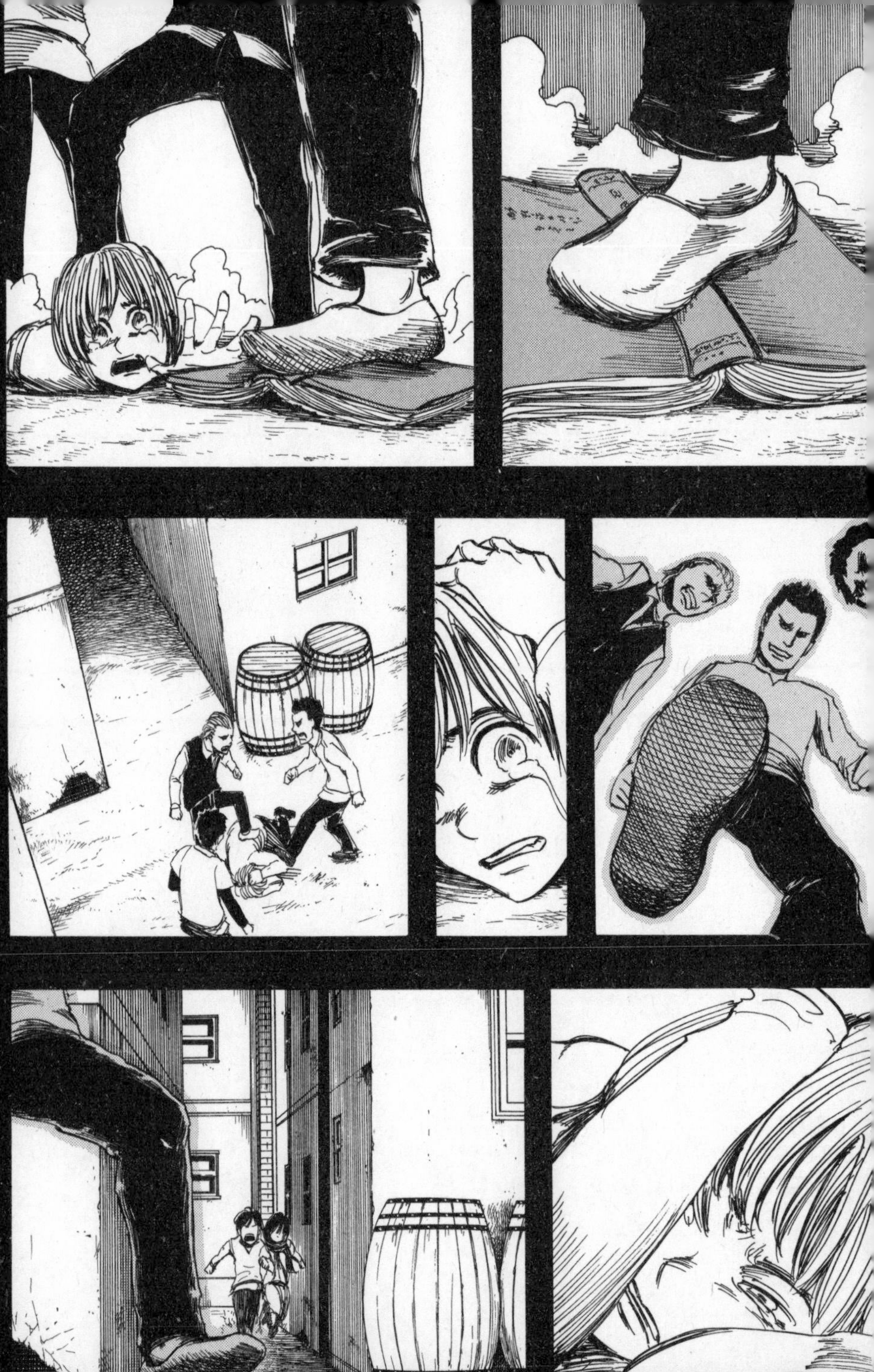

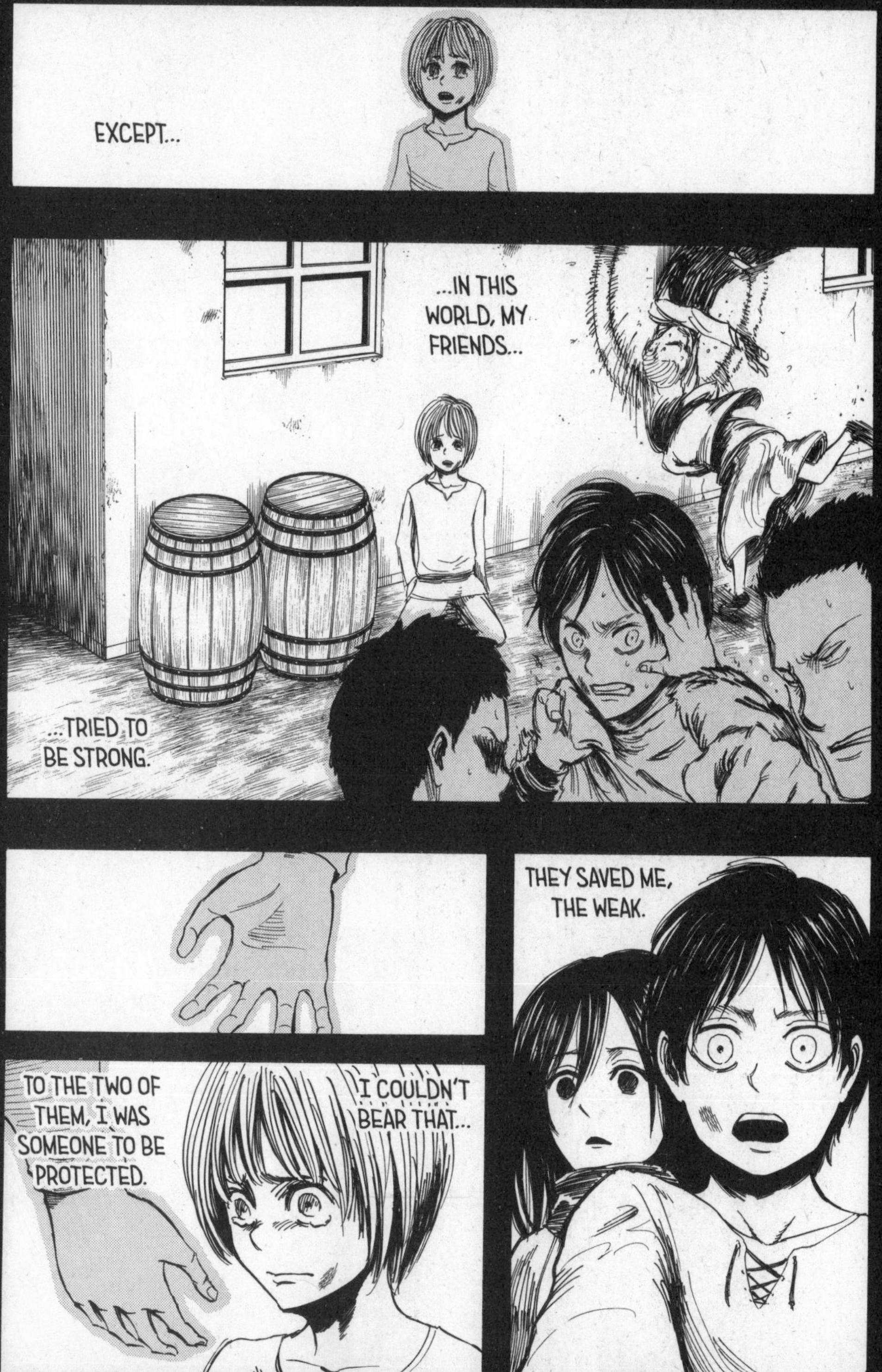
EXCEPT...
...IN THIS WORLD, MY FRIENDS...
...TRIED TO BE STRONG.
THEY SAVED ME, THE WEAK.
TO THE TWO OF THEM, I WAS SOMEONE TO BE PROTECTED.
I COULDN'T BEAR THAT...

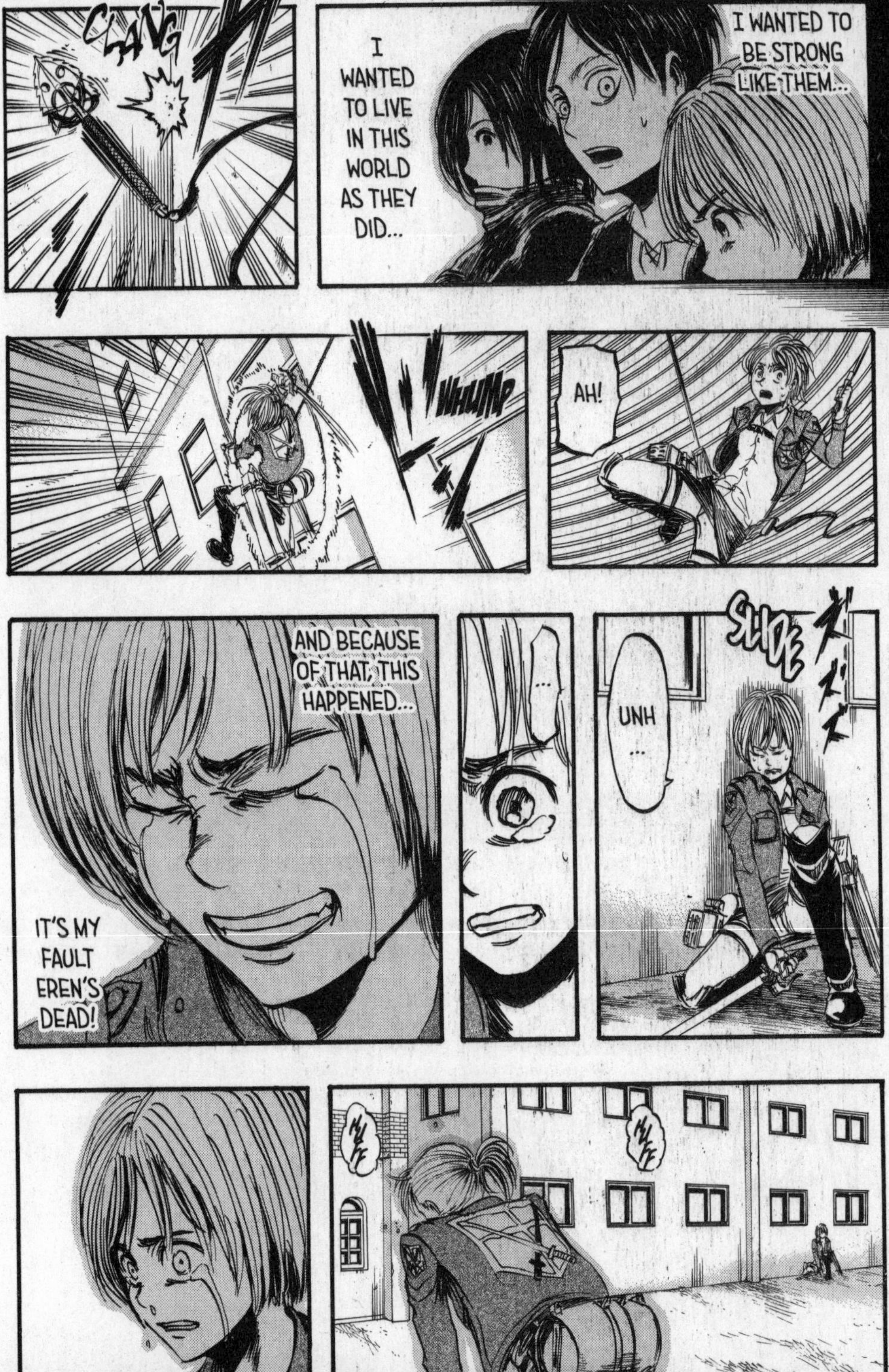
I WANTED TO BE STRONG LIKE THEM...
I WANTED TO LIVE IN THIS WORLD AS THEY DID...
CLANG
AH!
WHUMP
SLIDE
UNH ...
...
AND BECAUSE OF THAT, THIS HAPPENED...
IT'S MY FAULT EREN'S DEAD!
HUFF
HUFF

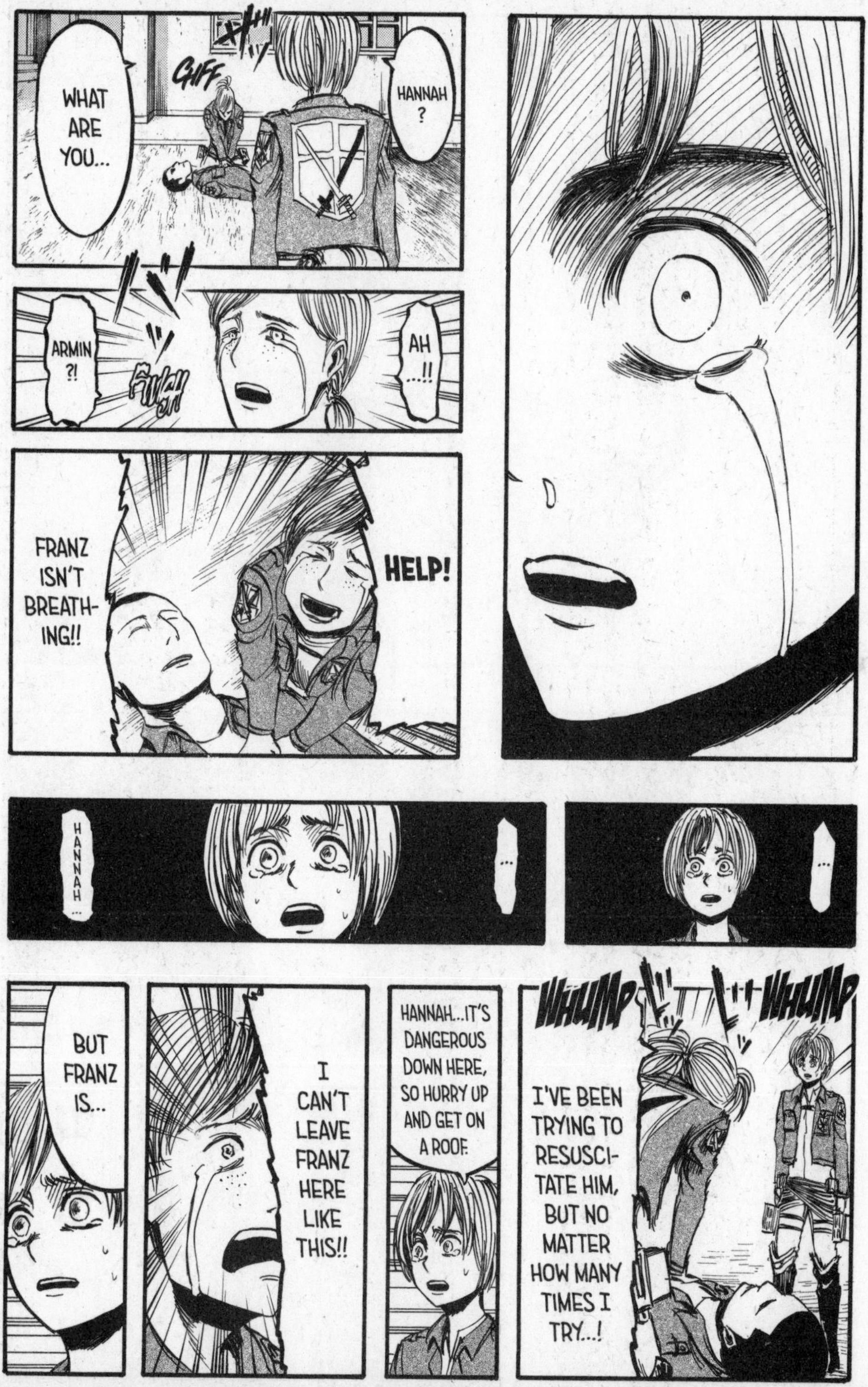
HANNAH ?
WHAT ARE YOU...
AH ...!!
ARMIN ?!
HELP!
FRANZ ISN'T BREATHING!!
...
...
HANNAH...
WHUMP WHUMP
I'VE BEEN TRYING TO RESUSCITATE HIM, BUT NO MATTER HOW MANY TIMES I TRY...!
HANNAH...IT'S DANGEROUS DOWN HERE, SO HURRY UP AND GET ON A ROOF.
I CAN'T LEAVE FRANZ HERE LIKE THIS!!
BUT FRANZ IS...

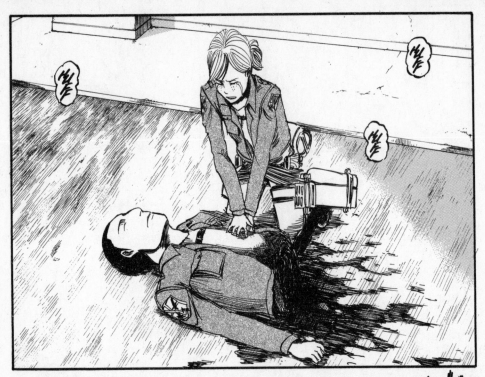

ENOUGH ...STOP IT...

...

NO GOOD AT ALL...

IT WON'T DO ANY GOOD...

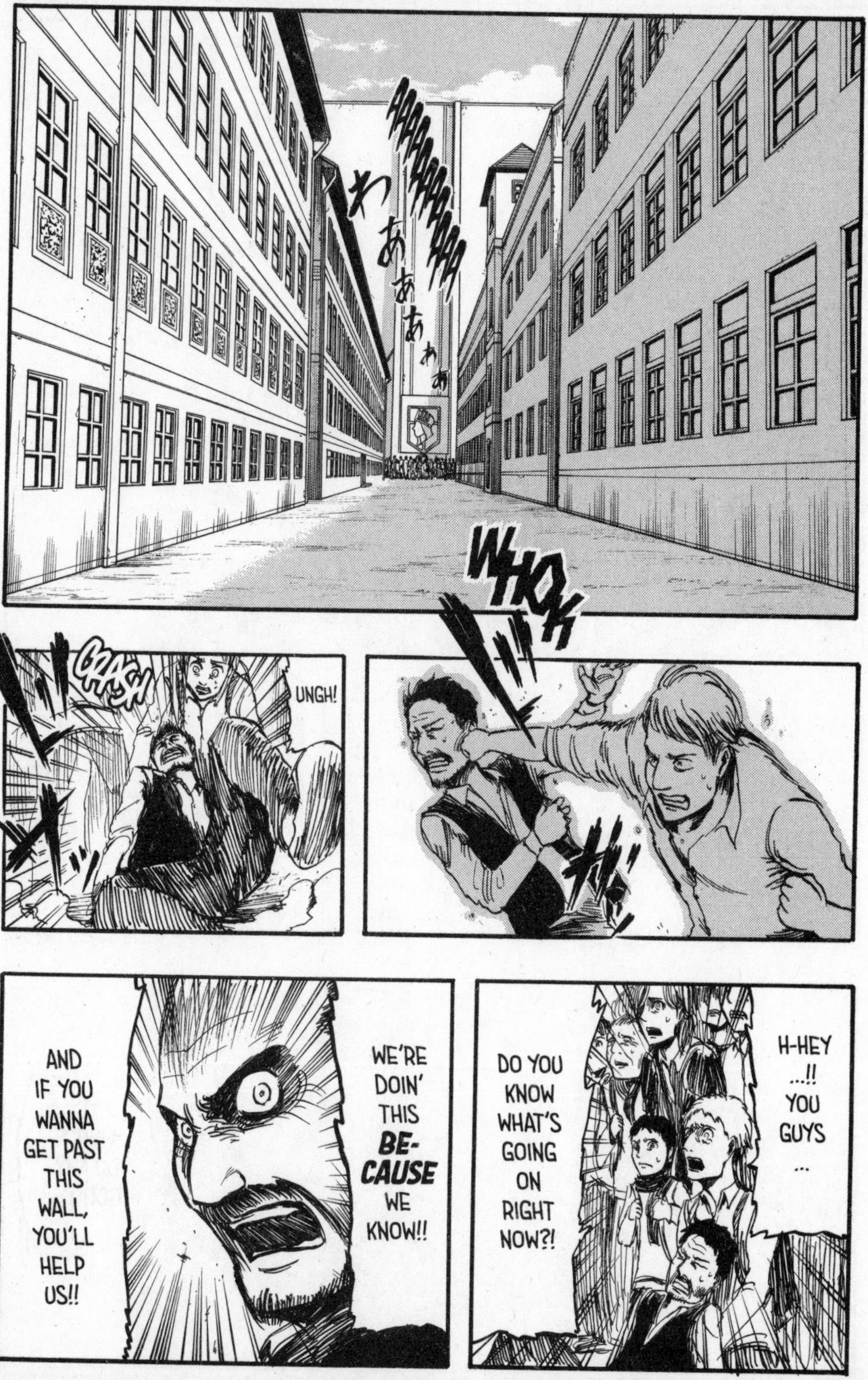
AAAAAAAAAAAAA
わあああああ
WHOK
CRASH
UNGH!
H-HEY ...!! YOU GUYS ...
DO YOU KNOW WHAT'S GOING ON RIGHT NOW?!
WE'RE DOIN' THIS BE-CAUSE WE KNOW!!
AND IF YOU WANNA GET PAST THIS WALL, YOU'LL HELP US!!

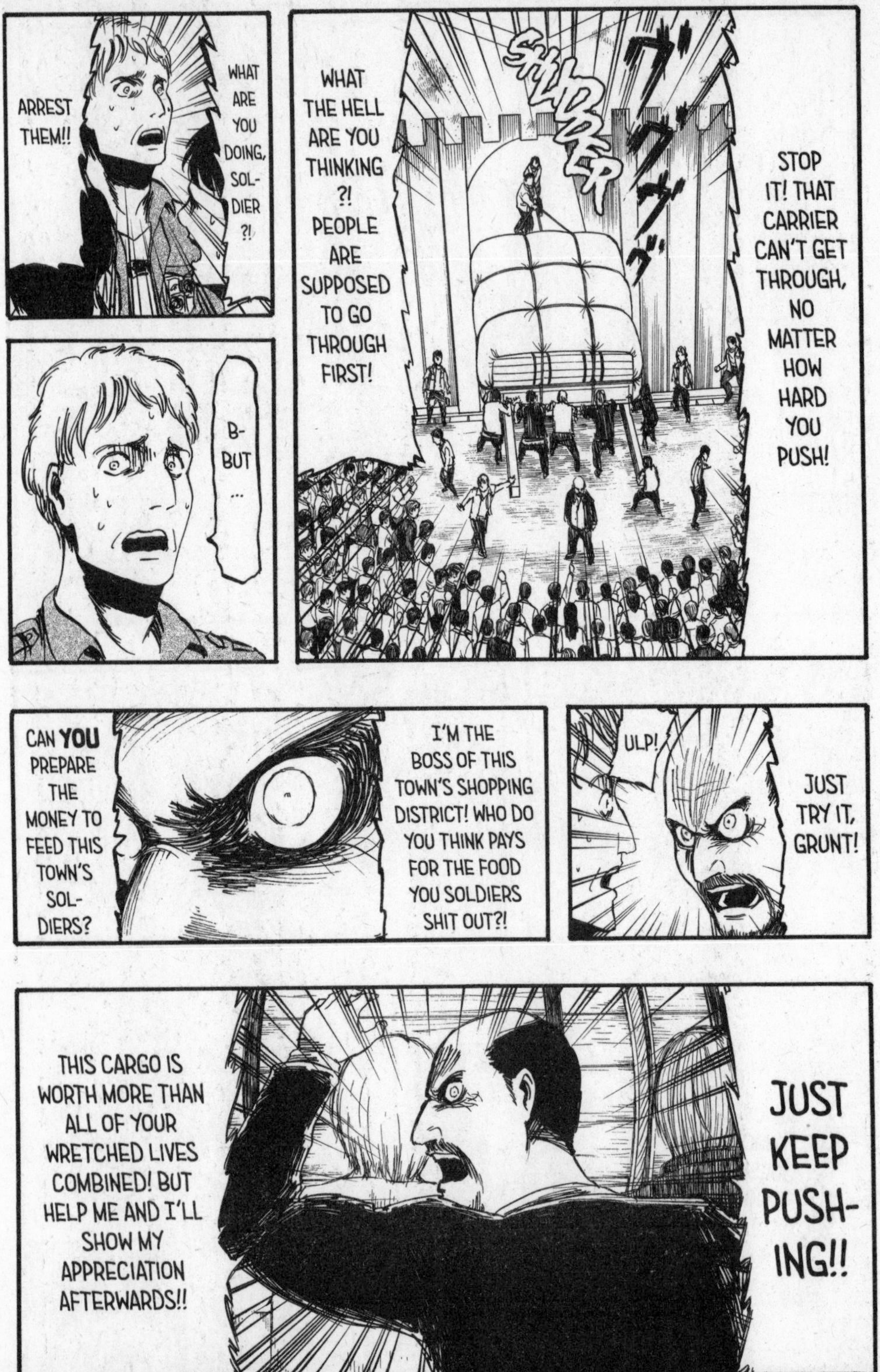
SHUDDER
STOP IT! THAT CARRIER CAN'T GET THROUGH, NO MATTER HOW HARD YOU PUSH!
WHAT THE HELL ARE YOU THINKING?! PEOPLE ARE SUPPOSED TO GO THROUGH FIRST!
WHAT ARE YOU DOING, SOL-DIER?!
ARREST THEM!!
B-BUT...
ULP!
JUST TRY IT, GRUNT!
I'M THE BOSS OF THIS TOWN'S SHOPPING DISTRICT! WHO DO YOU THINK PAYS FOR THE FOOD YOU SOLDIERS SHIT OUT?!
CAN **YOU** PREPARE THE MONEY TO FEED THIS TOWN'S SOL-DIERS?
JUST KEEP PUSH-ING!!
THIS CARGO IS WORTH MORE THAN ALL OF YOUR WRETCHED LIVES COMBINED! BUT HELP ME AND I'LL SHOW MY APPRECIATION AFTERWARDS!!

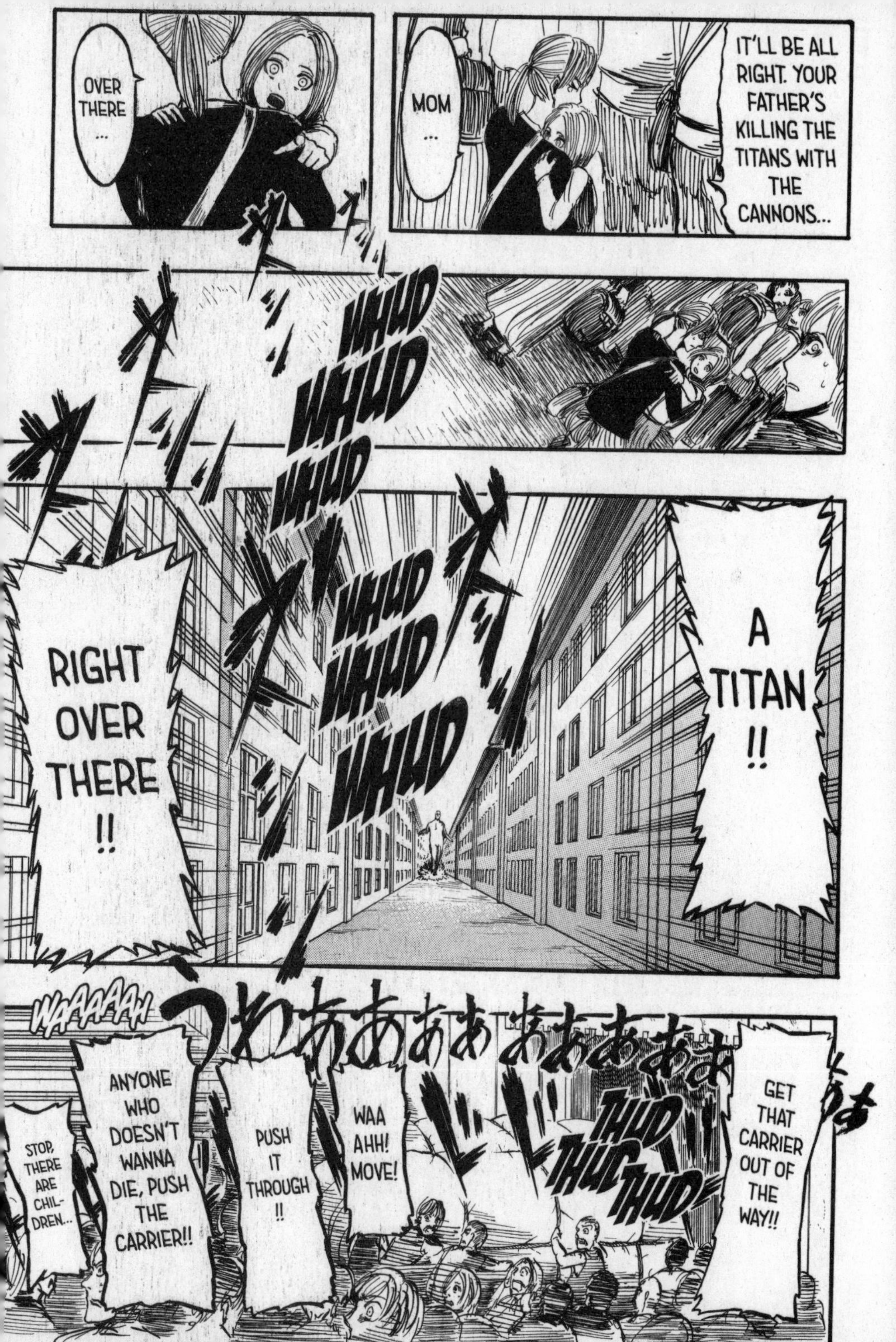
IT'LL BE ALL RIGHT. YOUR FATHER'S KILLING THE TITANS WITH THE CANNONS...
MOM ...
OVER THERE ...
WHUD WHUD WHUD WHUD
A TITAN !!
WHUD WHUD WHUD
RIGHT OVER THERE !!
WAAAAAH
GET THAT CARRIER OUT OF THE WAY!!
THUD THUD THUD
WAA AHH! MOVE!
PUSH IT THROUGH !!
ANYONE WHO DOESN'T WANNA DIE, PUSH THE CARRIER!!
STOP, THERE ARE CHIL-DREN...

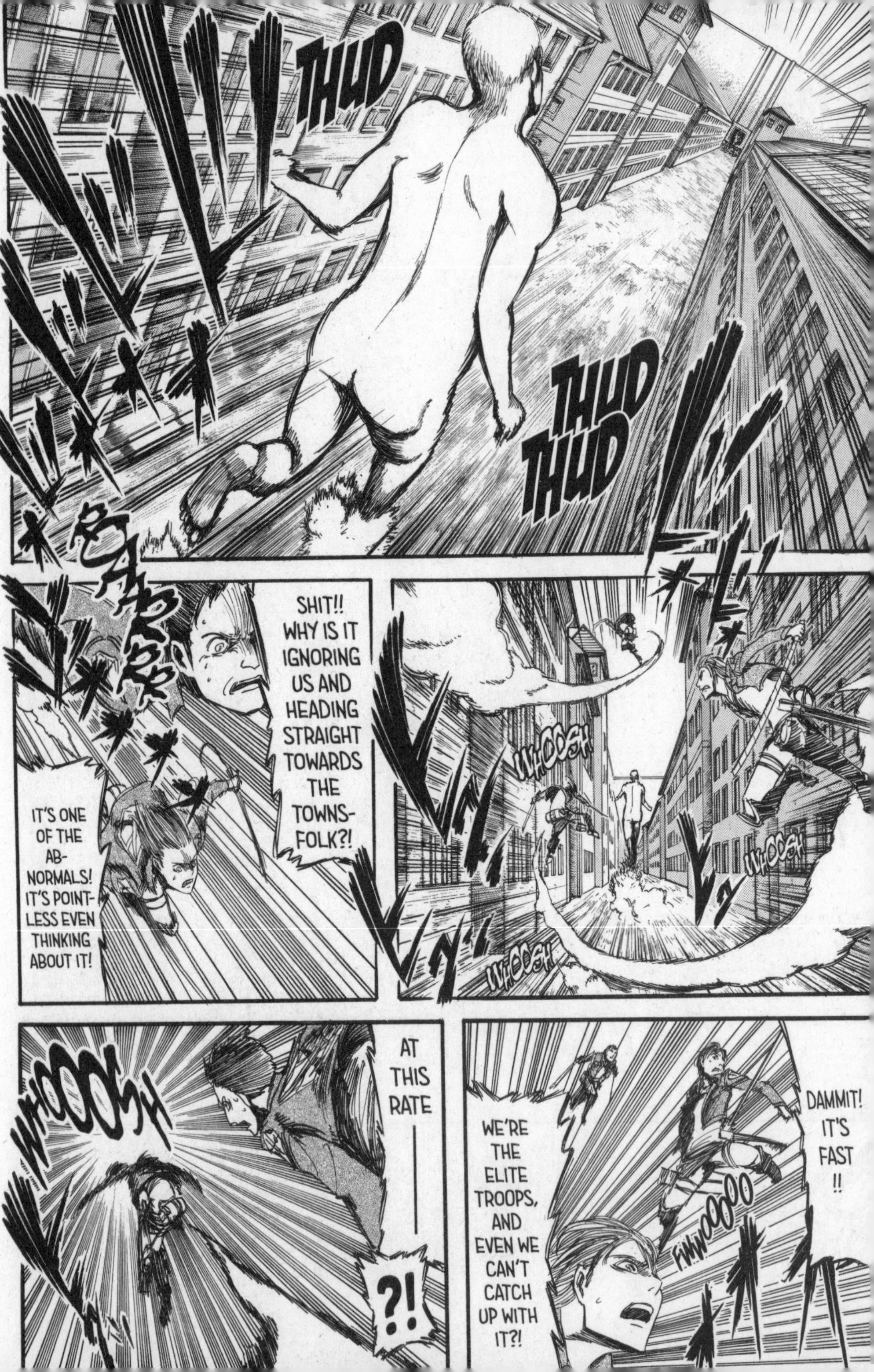
THUD
THUD THUD
WHOOSH
WHOOSH
WHOOSH
SHIT!! WHY IS IT IGNORING US AND HEADING STRAIGHT TOWARDS THE TOWNSFOLK?!
IT'S ONE OF THE ABNORMALS! IT'S POINTLESS EVEN THINKING ABOUT IT!
DAMMIT! IT'S FAST!!
FWWOOOOO
WE'RE THE ELITE TROOPS, AND EVEN WE CAN'T CATCH UP WITH IT?!
AT THIS RATE—
WHOOOSH
?!

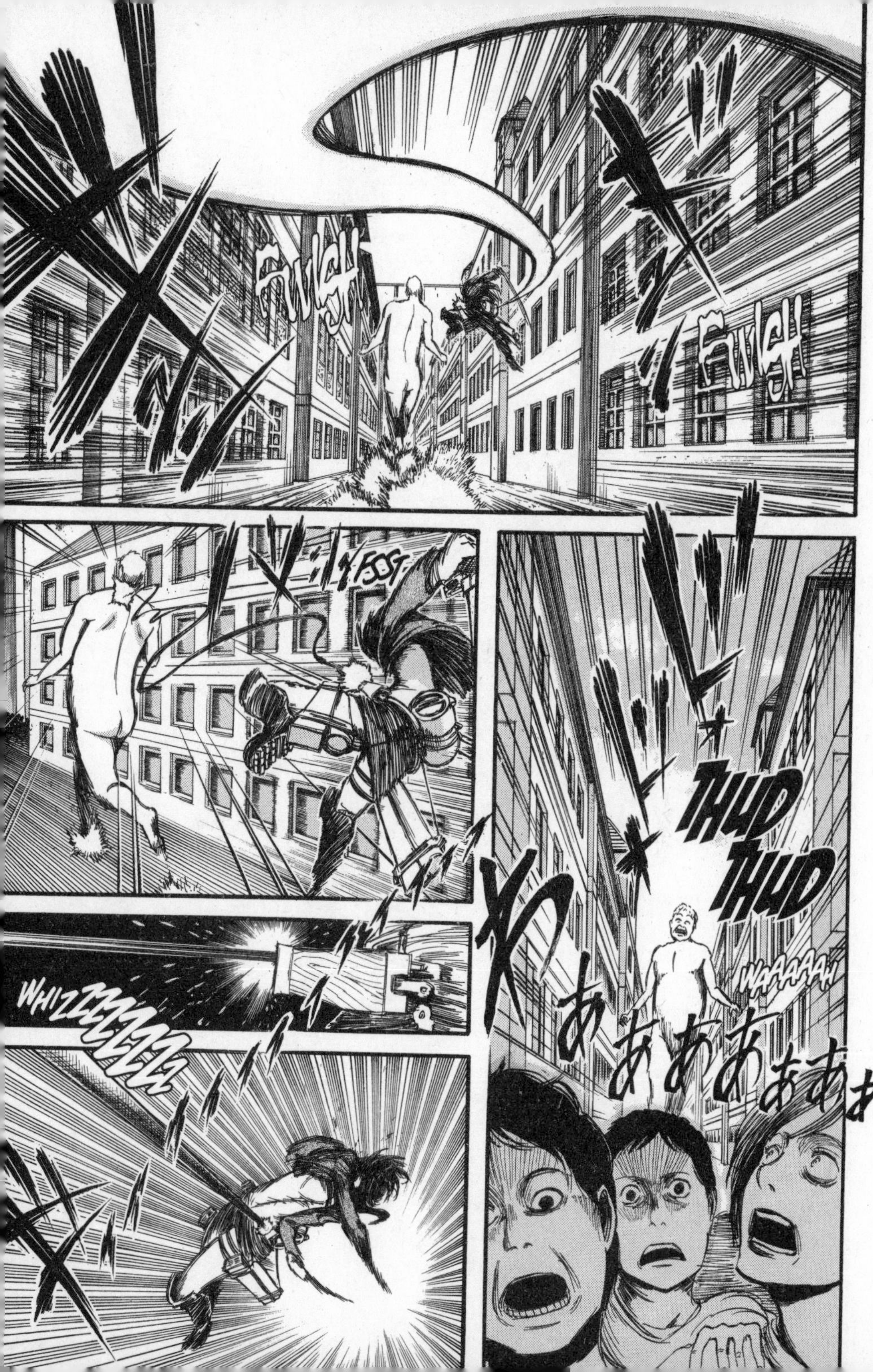
SWISH
SWISH
FSST
THUD THUD
WAAAAAH
WHIZZZZZZ

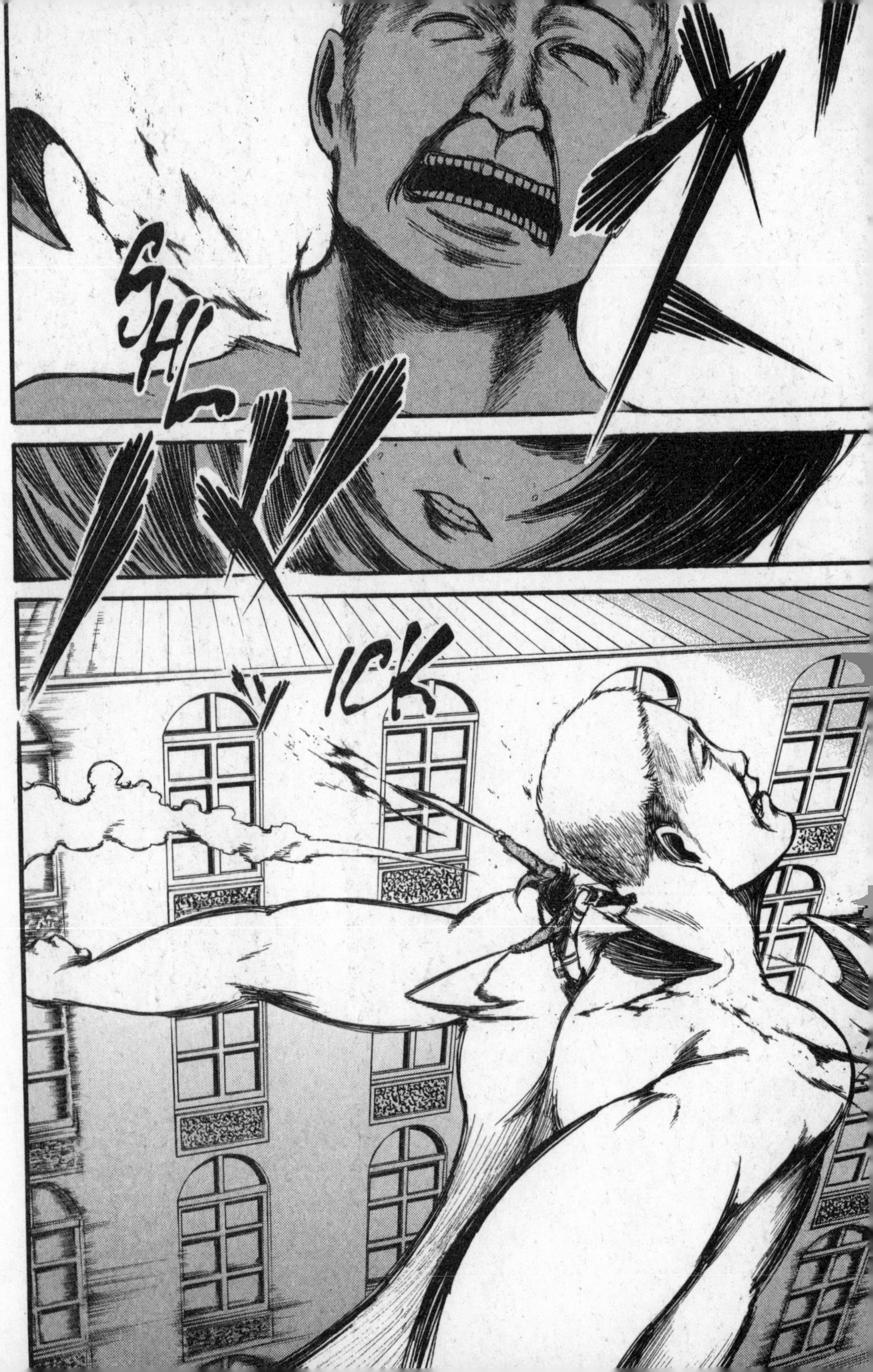
SHLK
ICK

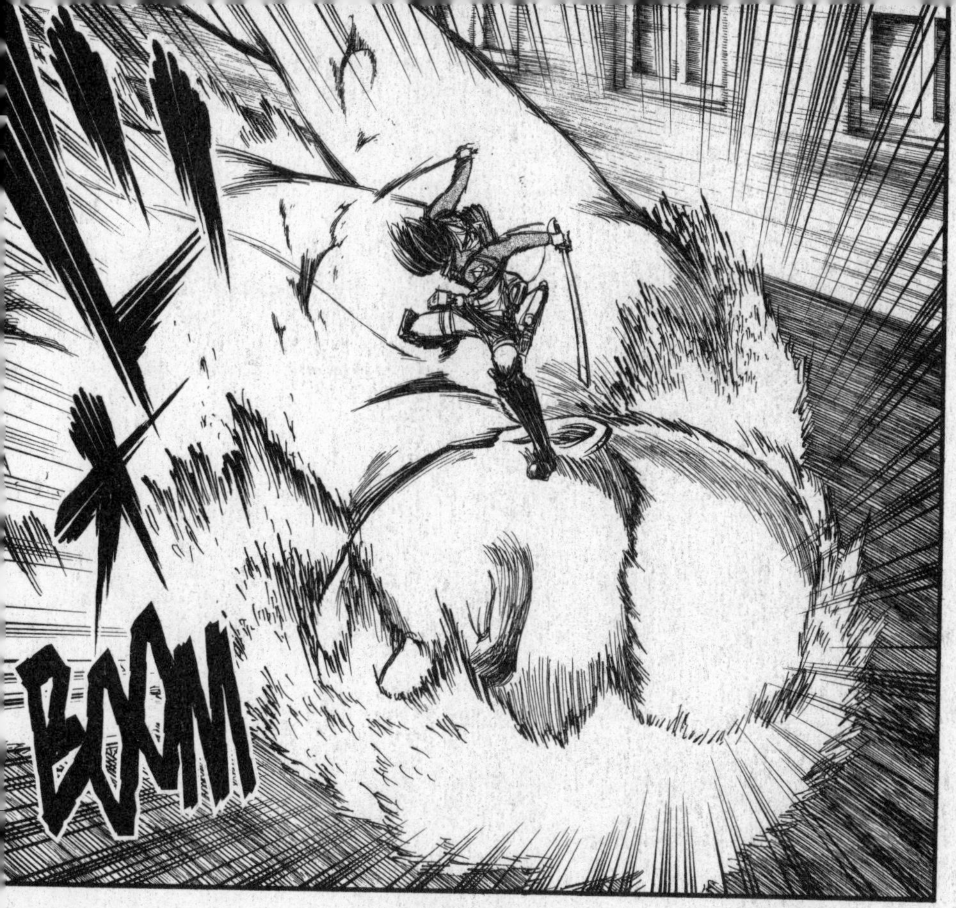
BOOM
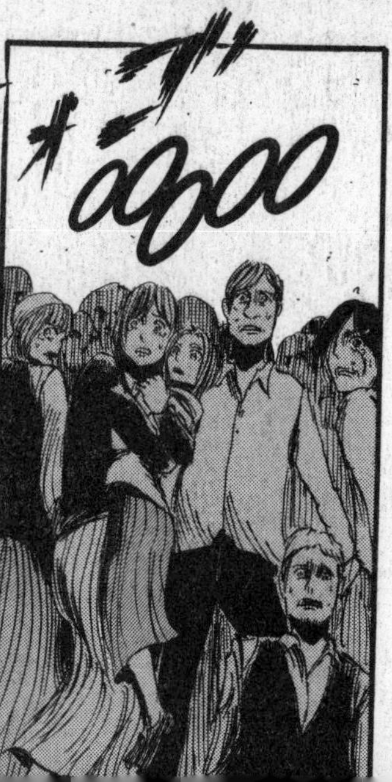
OOOOO
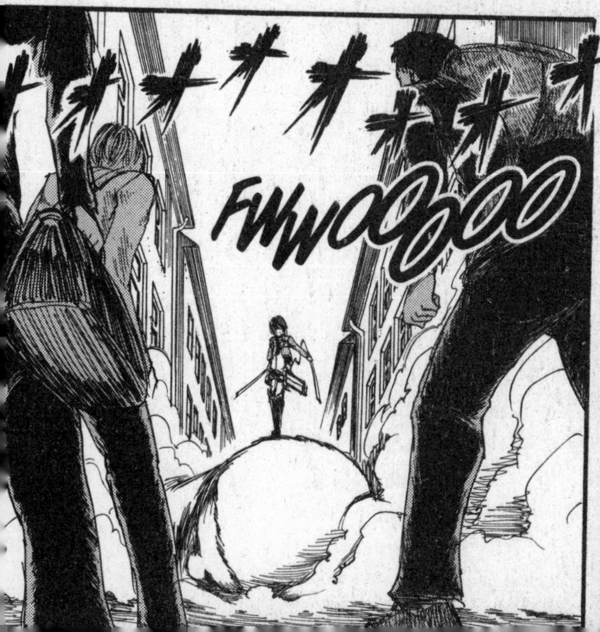
FWWOOOOOO

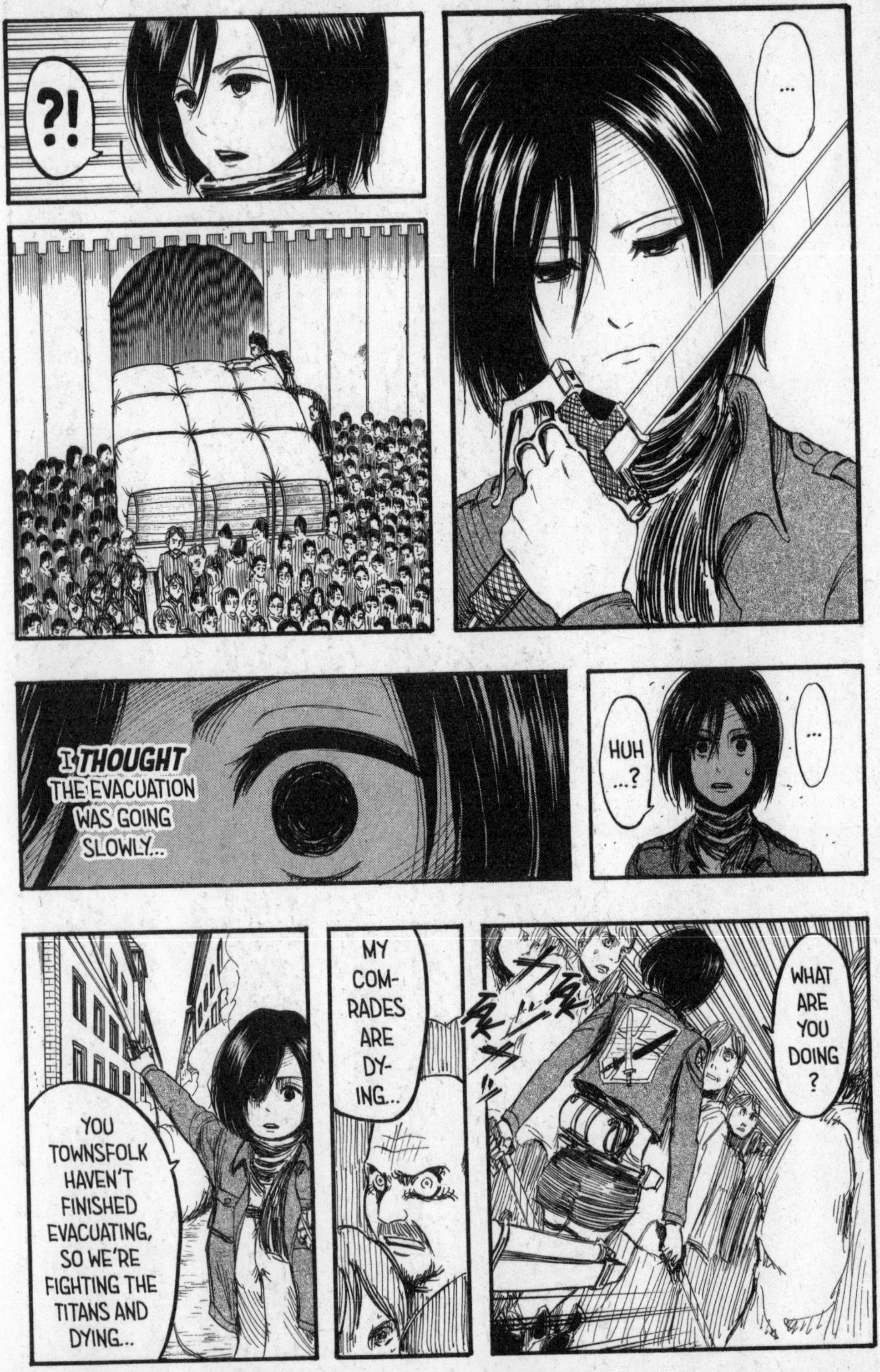
...
?!
...
HUH ...?
I THOUGHT THE EVACUATION WAS GOING SLOWLY...
WHAT ARE YOU DOING?
MY COMRADES ARE DYING...
YOU TOWNSFOLK HAVEN'T FINISHED EVACUATING, SO WE'RE FIGHTING THE TITANS AND DYING...

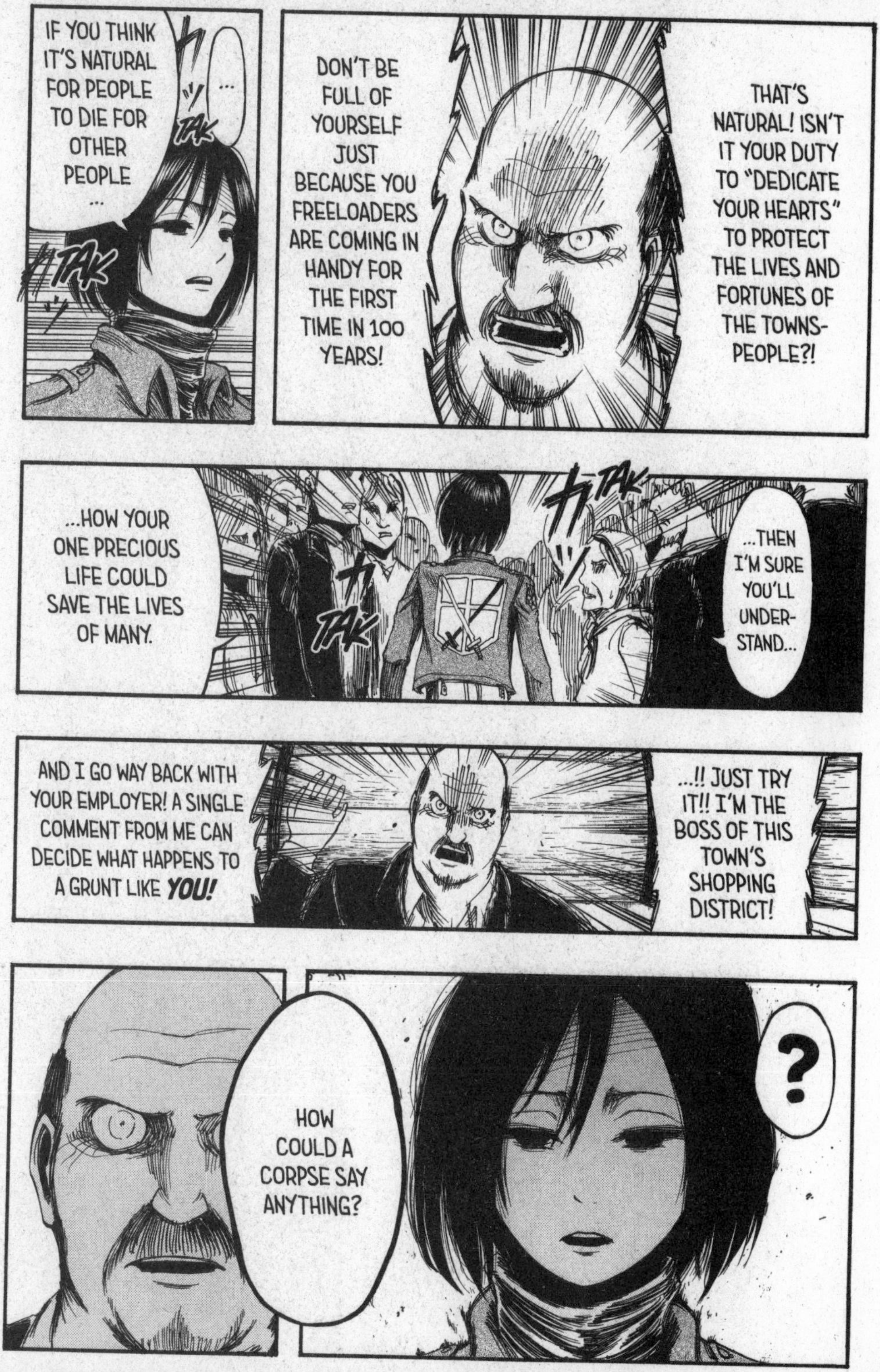
DON'T BE FULL OF YOURSELF JUST BECAUSE YOU FREELOADERS ARE COMING IN HANDY FOR THE FIRST TIME IN 100 YEARS!
THAT'S NATURAL! ISN'T IT YOUR DUTY TO "DEDICATE YOUR HEARTS" TO PROTECT THE LIVES AND FORTUNES OF THE TOWNS-PEOPLE?!
TAK
...
TAK
IF YOU THINK IT'S NATURAL FOR PEOPLE TO DIE FOR OTHER PEOPLE ...
TAK
...THEN I'M SURE YOU'LL UNDER-STAND...
TAK
...HOW YOUR ONE PRECIOUS LIFE COULD SAVE THE LIVES OF MANY.
...!! JUST TRY IT!! I'M THE BOSS OF THIS TOWN'S SHOPPING DISTRICT!
AND I GO WAY BACK WITH YOUR EMPLOYER! A SINGLE COMMENT FROM ME CAN DECIDE WHAT HAPPENS TO A GRUNT LIKE YOU!
?
HOW COULD A CORPSE SAY ANYTHING?

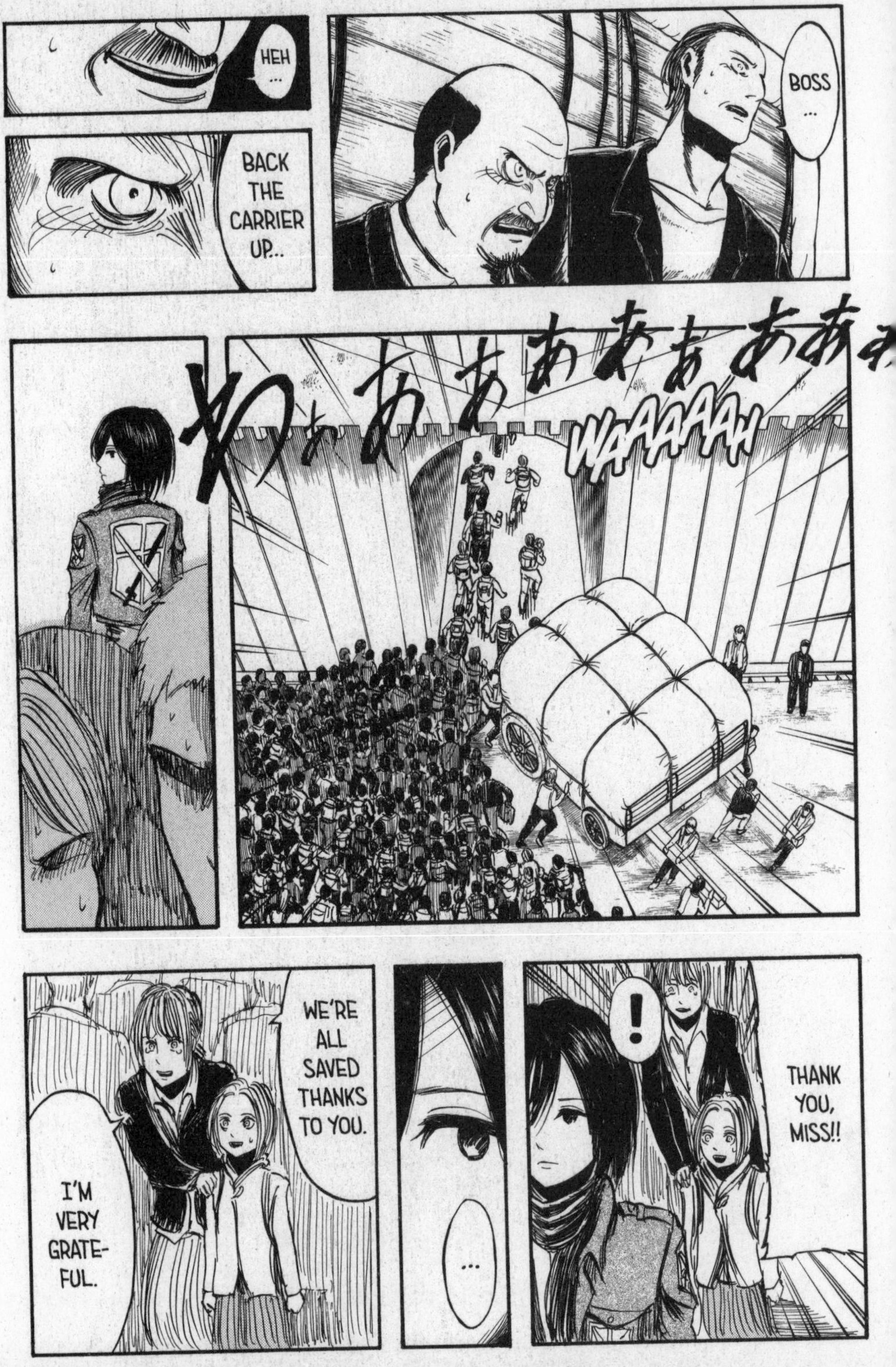
BOSS ...
HEH ...
BACK THE CARRIER UP...
WAAAAAH
!
THANK YOU, MISS!!
...
WE'RE ALL SAVED THANKS TO YOU.
I'M VERY GRATE-FUL.

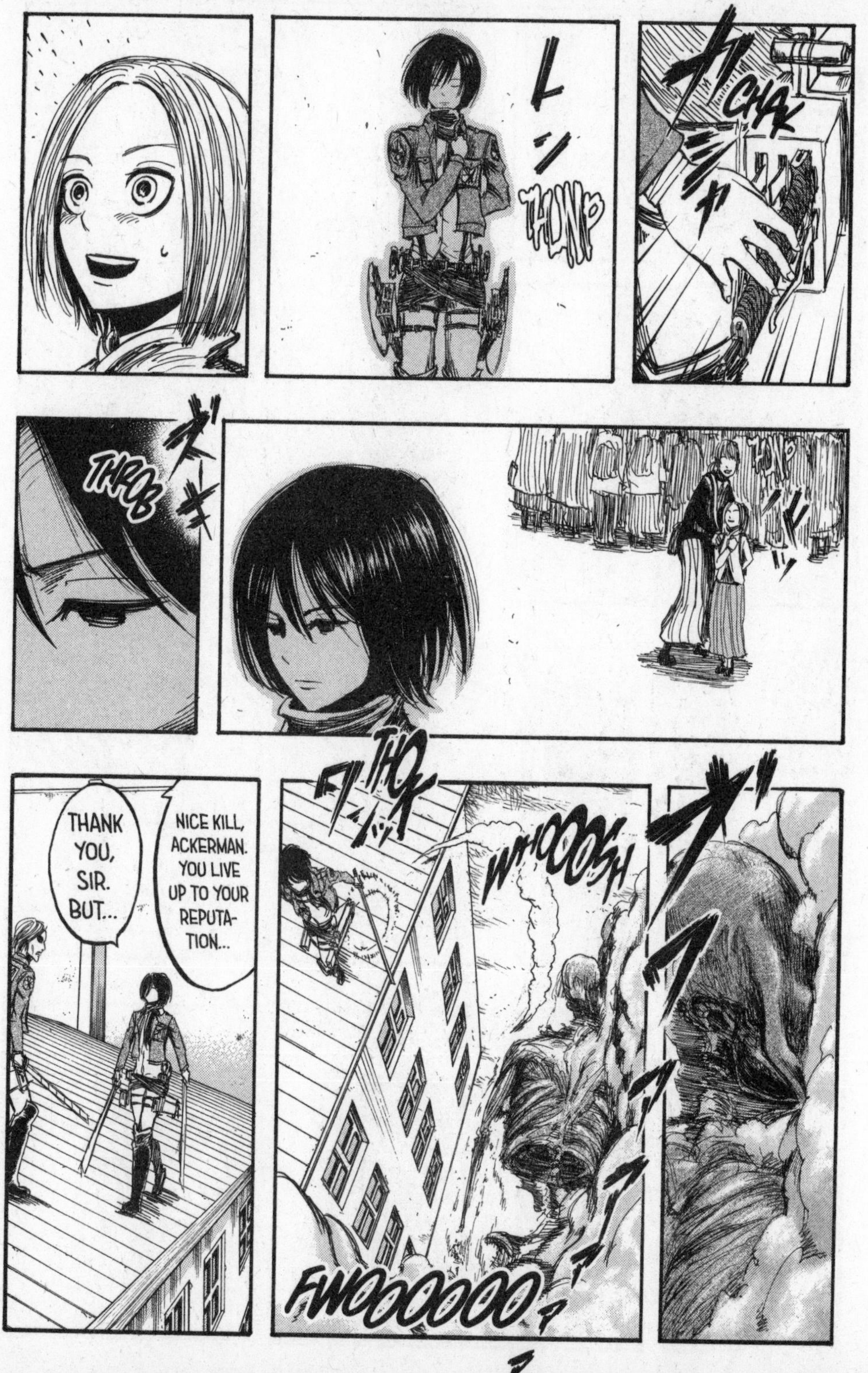
CHAK
THUMP
THUMP
THROB
THOK
WHOOOSH
FWOOOOOOO
NICE KILL, ACKERMAN. YOU LIVE UP TO YOUR REPUTATION...
THANK YOU, SIR. BUT...

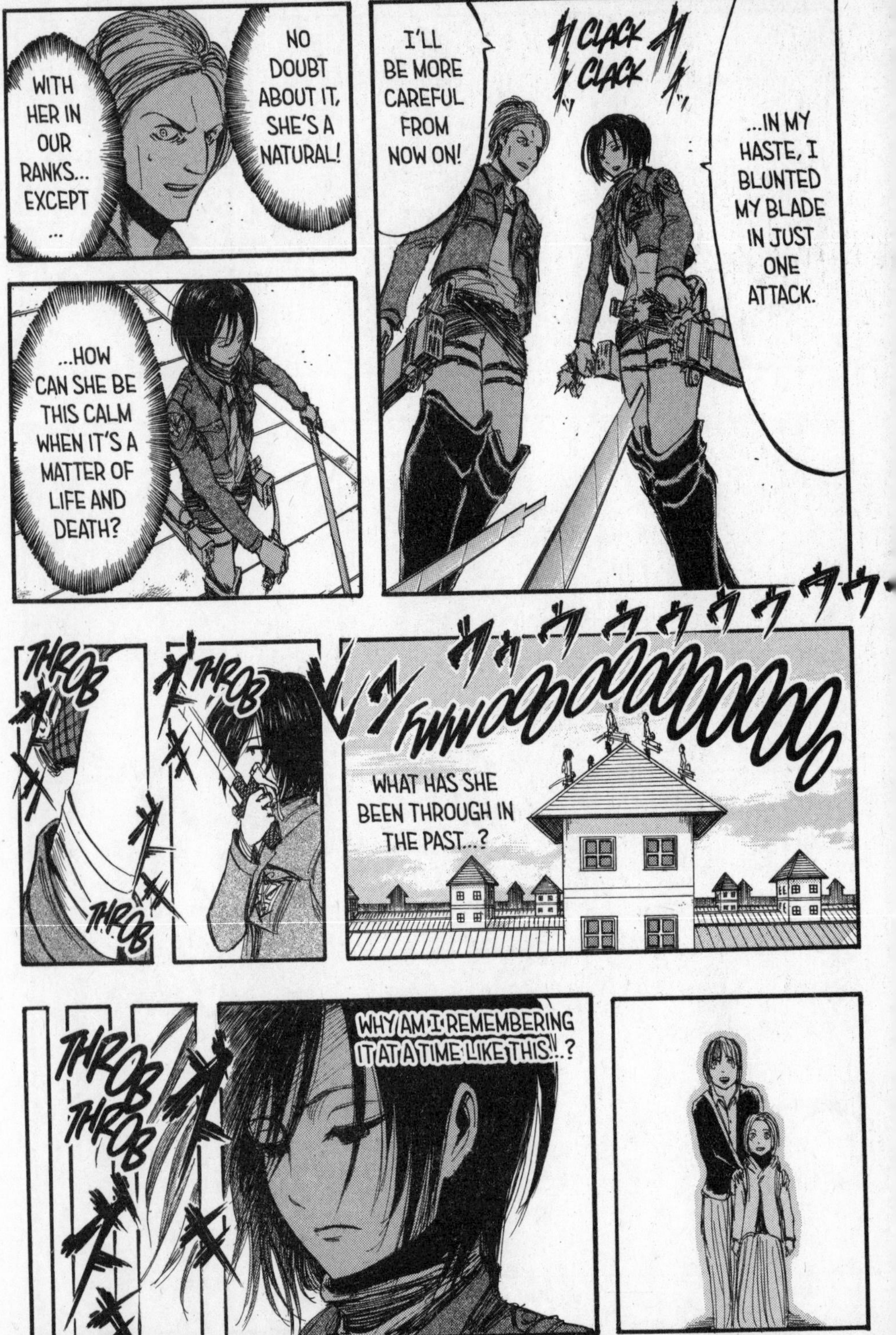
CLACK CLACK
...IN MY HASTE, I BLUNTED MY BLADE IN JUST ONE ATTACK.
I'LL BE MORE CAREFUL FROM NOW ON!
NO DOUBT ABOUT IT, SHE'S A NATURAL!
WITH HER IN OUR RANKS... EXCEPT ...
...HOW CAN SHE BE THIS CALM WHEN IT'S A MATTER OF LIFE AND DEATH?
FWWOOOOOOOOOOOO
WHAT HAS SHE BEEN THROUGH IN THE PAST...?
THROB
THROB
THROB
WHY AM I REMEMBERING IT AT A TIME LIKE THIS...?
THROB THROB

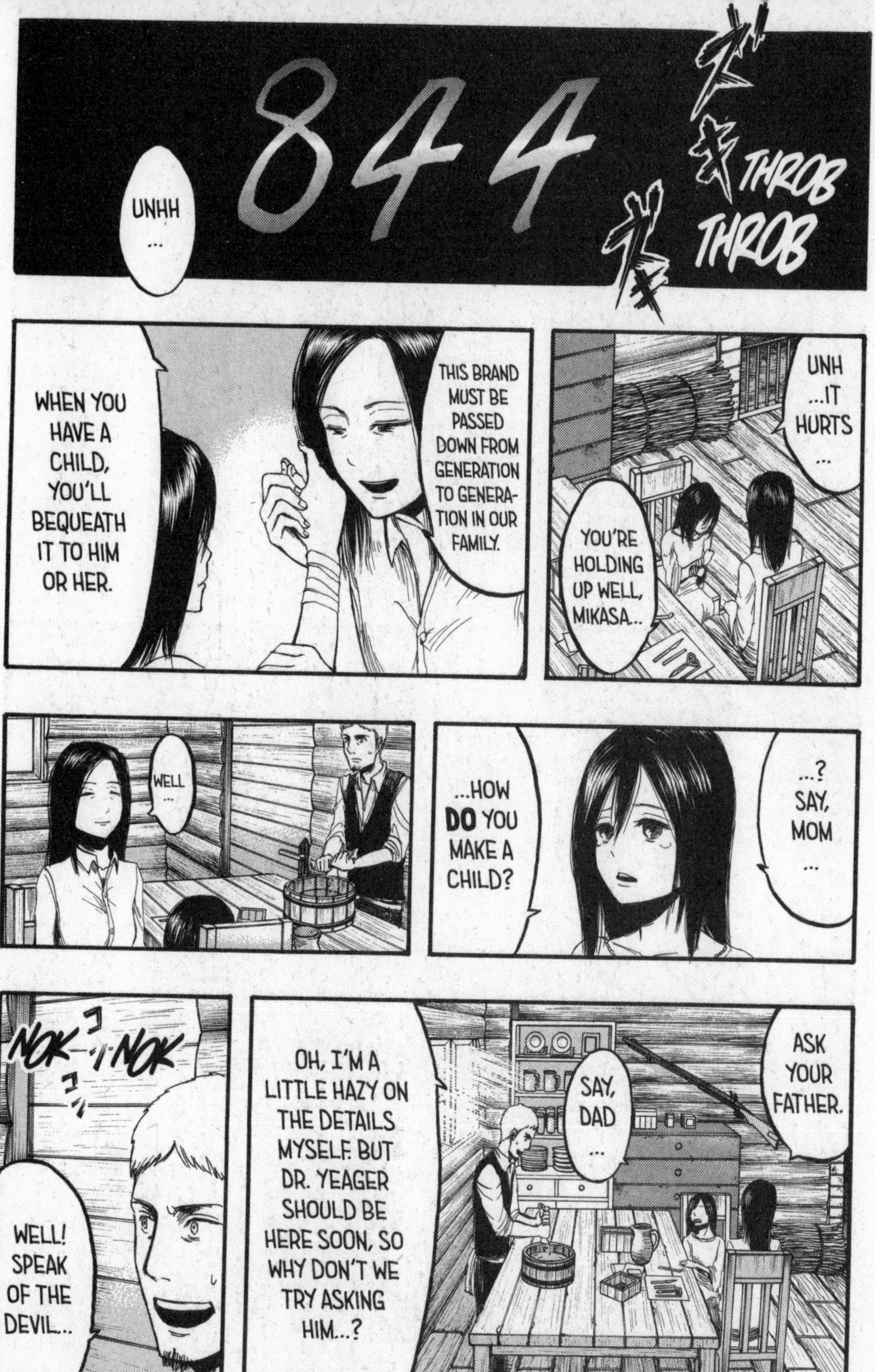
THROB THROB
844
UNHH ...
UNH ...IT HURTS ...
YOU'RE HOLDING UP WELL, MIKASA...
THIS BRAND MUST BE PASSED DOWN FROM GENERATION TO GENERA-TION IN OUR FAMILY.
WHEN YOU HAVE A CHILD, YOU'LL BEQUEATH IT TO HIM OR HER.
...? SAY, MOM ...
...HOW DO YOU MAKE A CHILD?
WELL ...
ASK YOUR FATHER.
SAY, DAD ...
OH, I'M A LITTLE HAZY ON THE DETAILS MYSELF. BUT DR. YEAGER SHOULD BE HERE SOON, SO WHY DON'T WE TRY ASKING HIM...?
NOK NOK
WELL! SPEAK OF THE DEVIL...

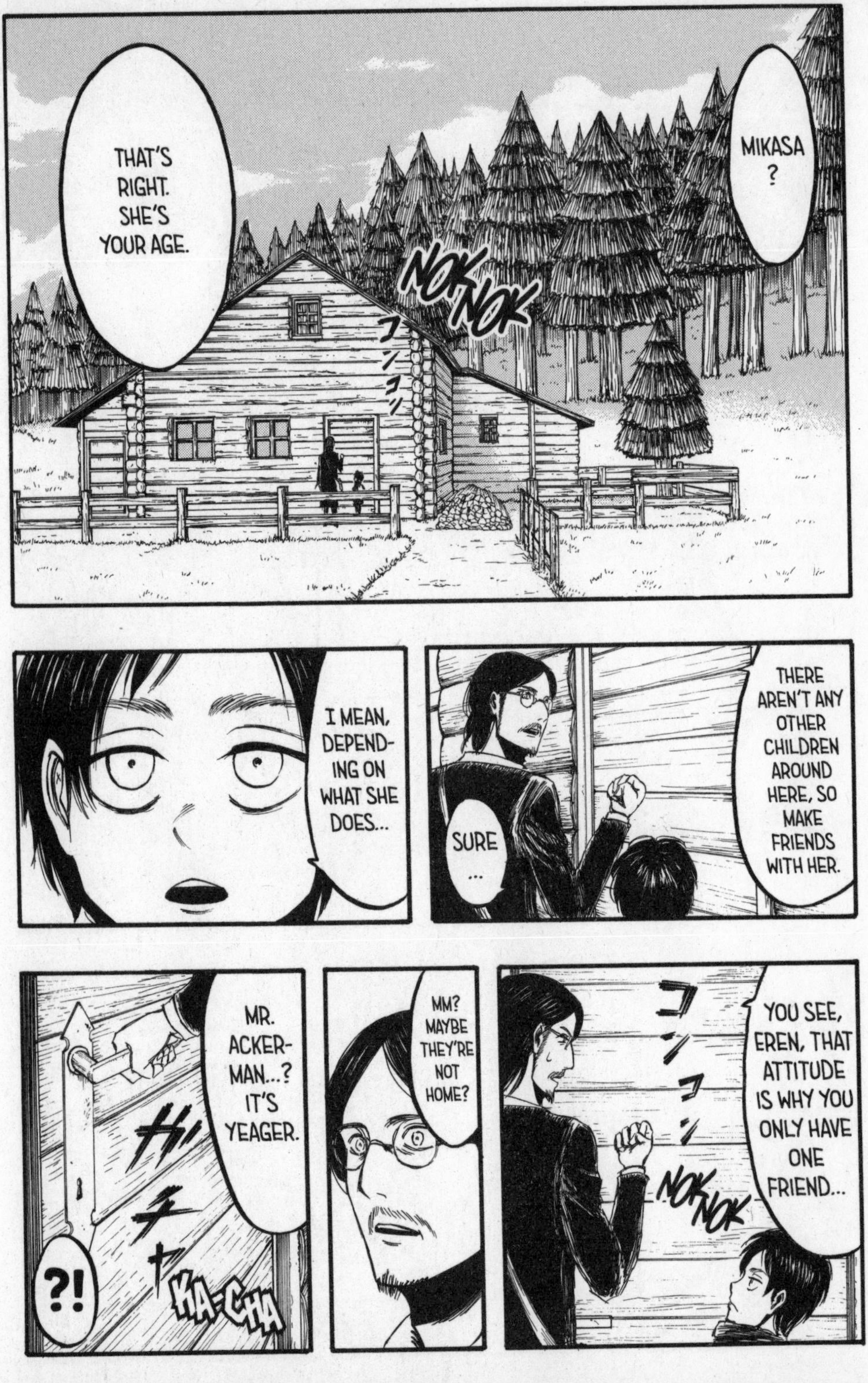
MIKASA ?
NOK NOK
コンコン
THAT'S RIGHT. SHE'S YOUR AGE.
THERE AREN'T ANY OTHER CHILDREN AROUND HERE, SO MAKE FRIENDS WITH HER.
SURE ...
I MEAN, DEPENDING ON WHAT SHE DOES...
YOU SEE, EREN, THAT ATTITUDE IS WHY YOU ONLY HAVE ONE FRIEND...
コンコン
NOK NOK
MM? MAYBE THEY'RE NOT HOME?
MR. ACKER-MAN...? IT'S YEAGER.
ガチャ
KA-CHA
?!

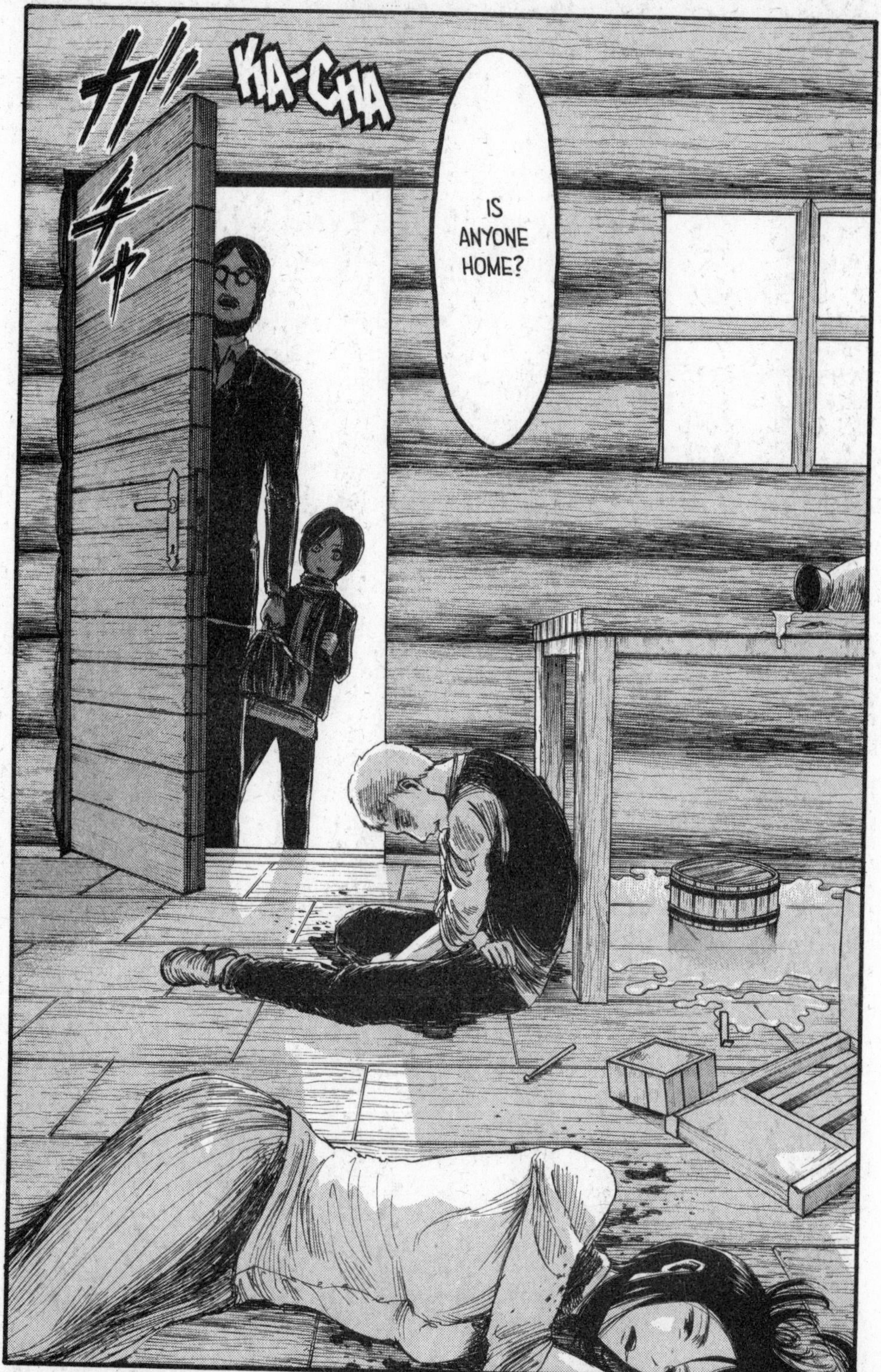
KA-CHA
IS ANYONE HOME?

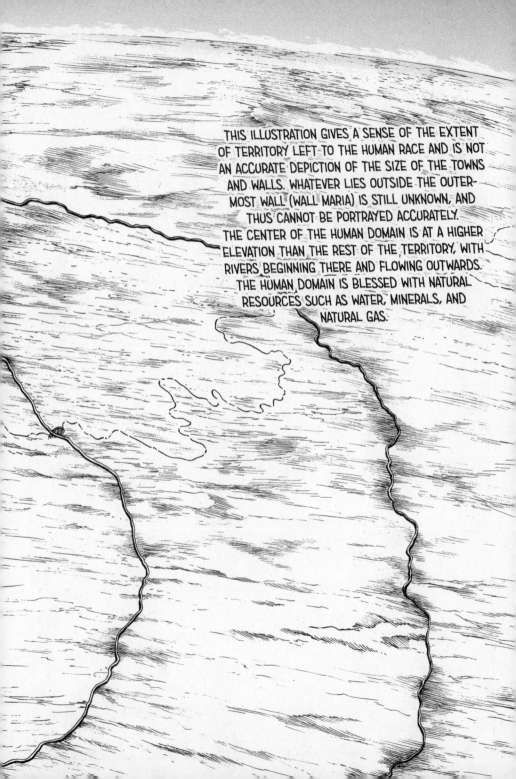

THIS ILLUSTRATION GIVES A SENSE OF THE EXTENT OF TERRITORY LEFT TO THE HUMAN RACE AND IS NOT AN ACCURATE DEPICTION OF THE SIZE OF THE TOWNS AND WALLS. WHATEVER LIES OUTSIDE THE OUTER-MOST WALL (WALL MARIA) IS STILL UNKNOWN, AND THUS CANNOT BE PORTRAYED ACCURATELY. THE CENTER OF THE HUMAN DOMAIN IS AT A HIGHER ELEVATION THAN THE REST OF THE TERRITORY, WITH RIVERS BEGINNING THERE AND FLOWING OUTWARDS. THE HUMAN DOMAIN IS BLESSED WITH NATURAL RESOURCES SUCH AS WATER, MINERALS, AND NATURAL GAS.

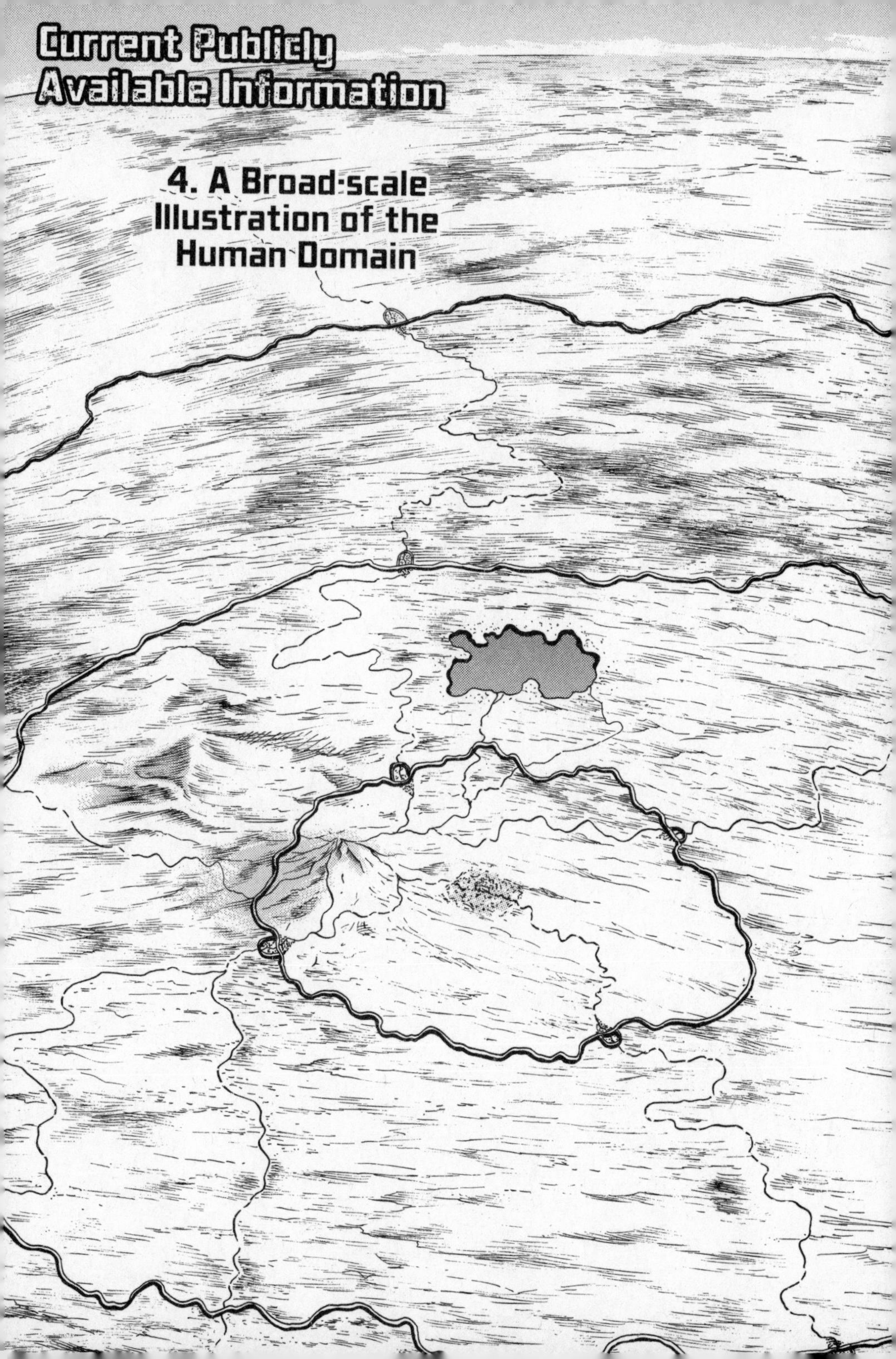
Current Publicly Available Information
4. A Broad-scale Illustration of the Human Domain

ATTACK on TITAN

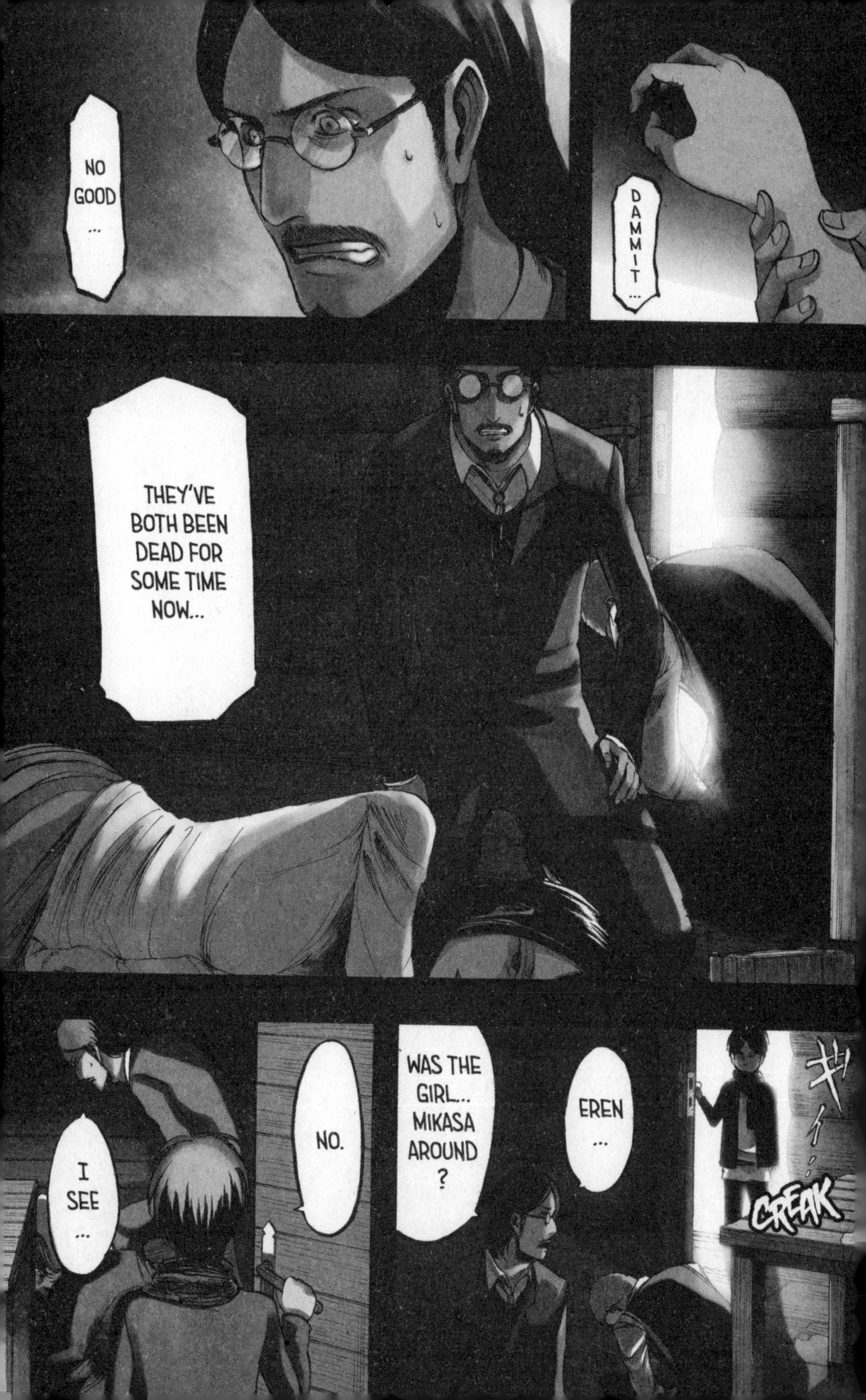
DAMMIT...
NO GOOD...
THEY'VE BOTH BEEN DEAD FOR SOME TIME NOW...
CREAK
EREN...
WAS THE GIRL... MIKASA AROUND?
NO.
I SEE...

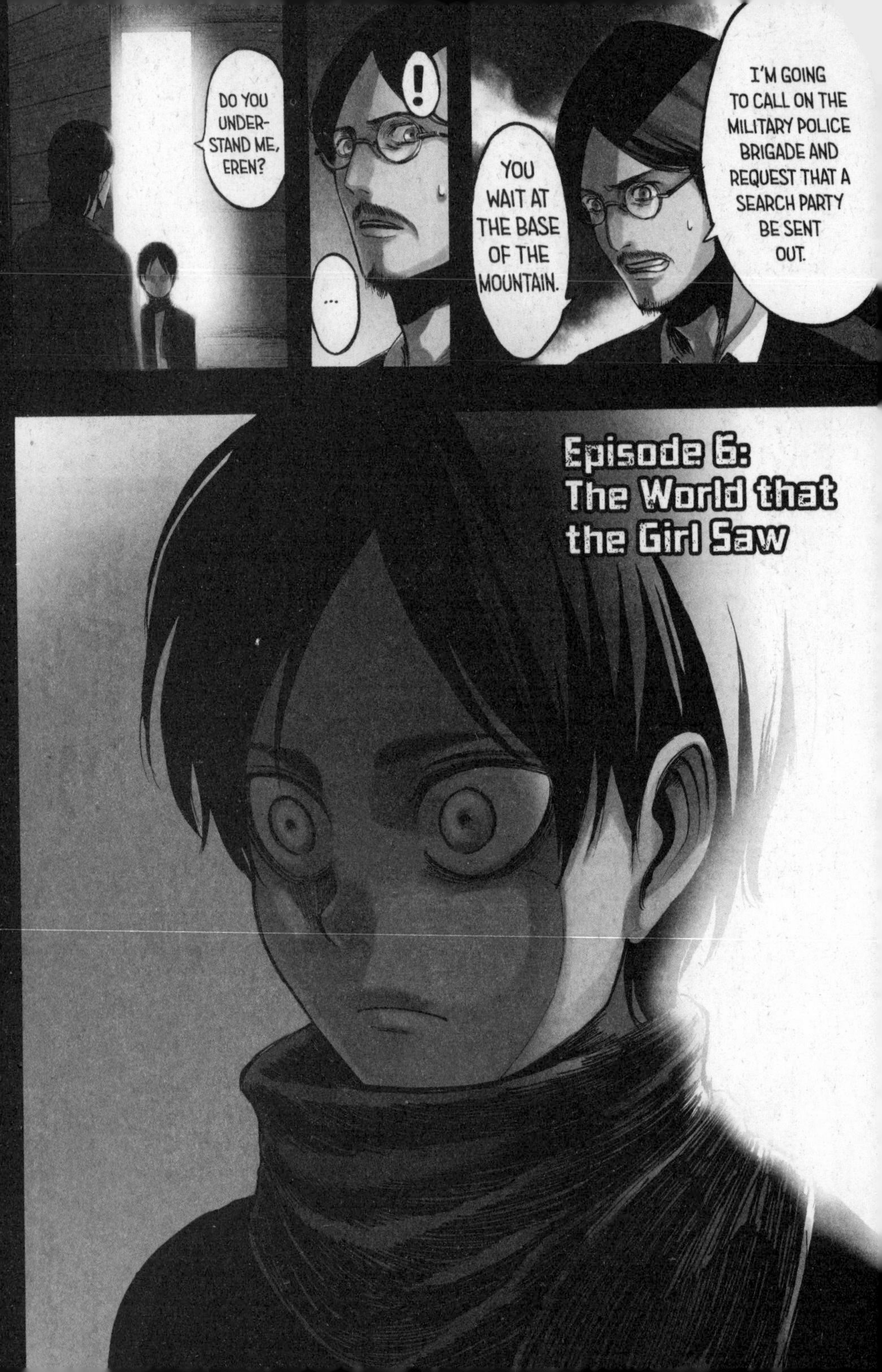
I'M GOING TO CALL ON THE MILITARY POLICE BRIGADE AND REQUEST THAT A SEARCH PARTY BE SENT OUT.
!
YOU WAIT AT THE BASE OF THE MOUNTAIN.
...
DO YOU UNDER-STAND ME, EREN?
Episode 6: The World that the Girl Saw

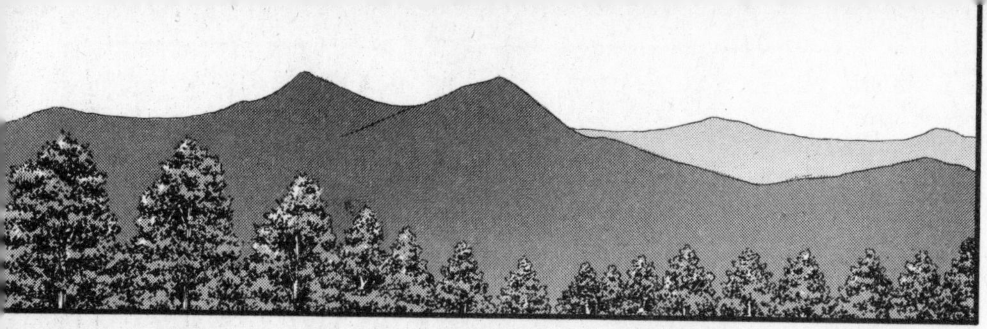

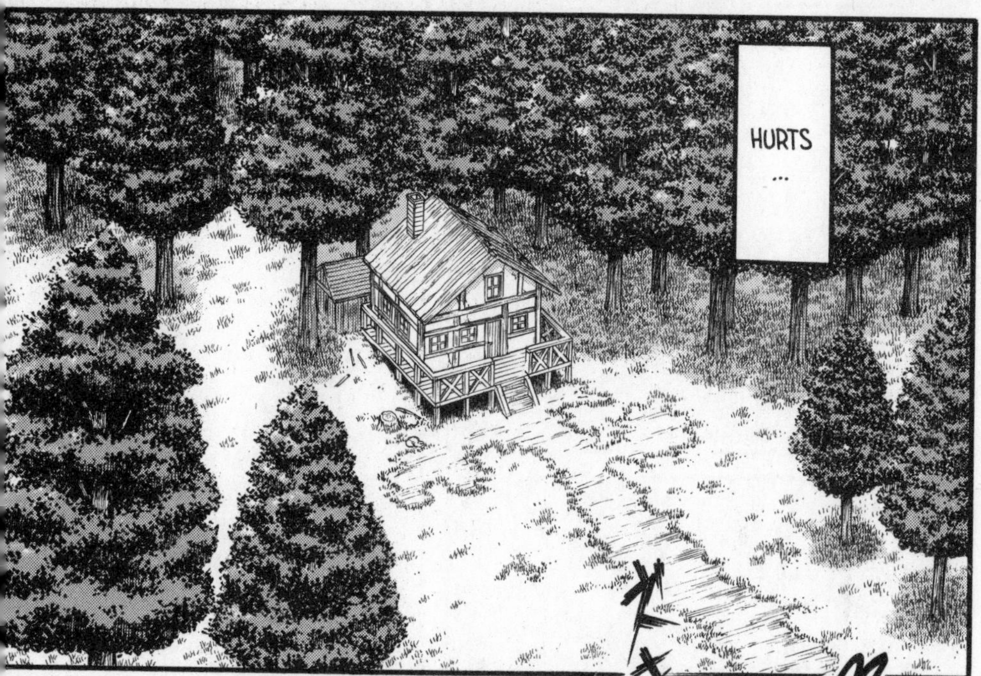
HURTS
...

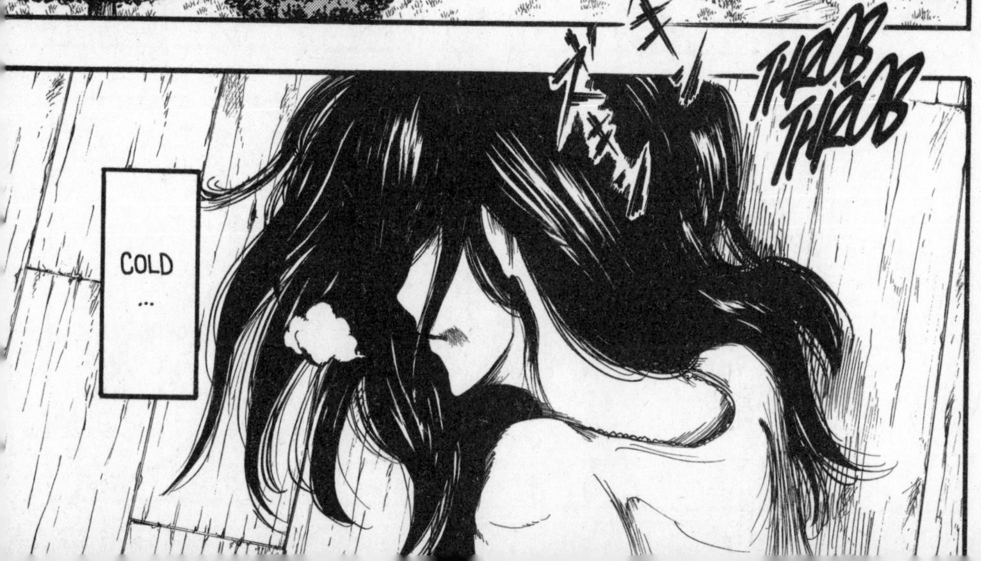
THROB THROB
COLD
...

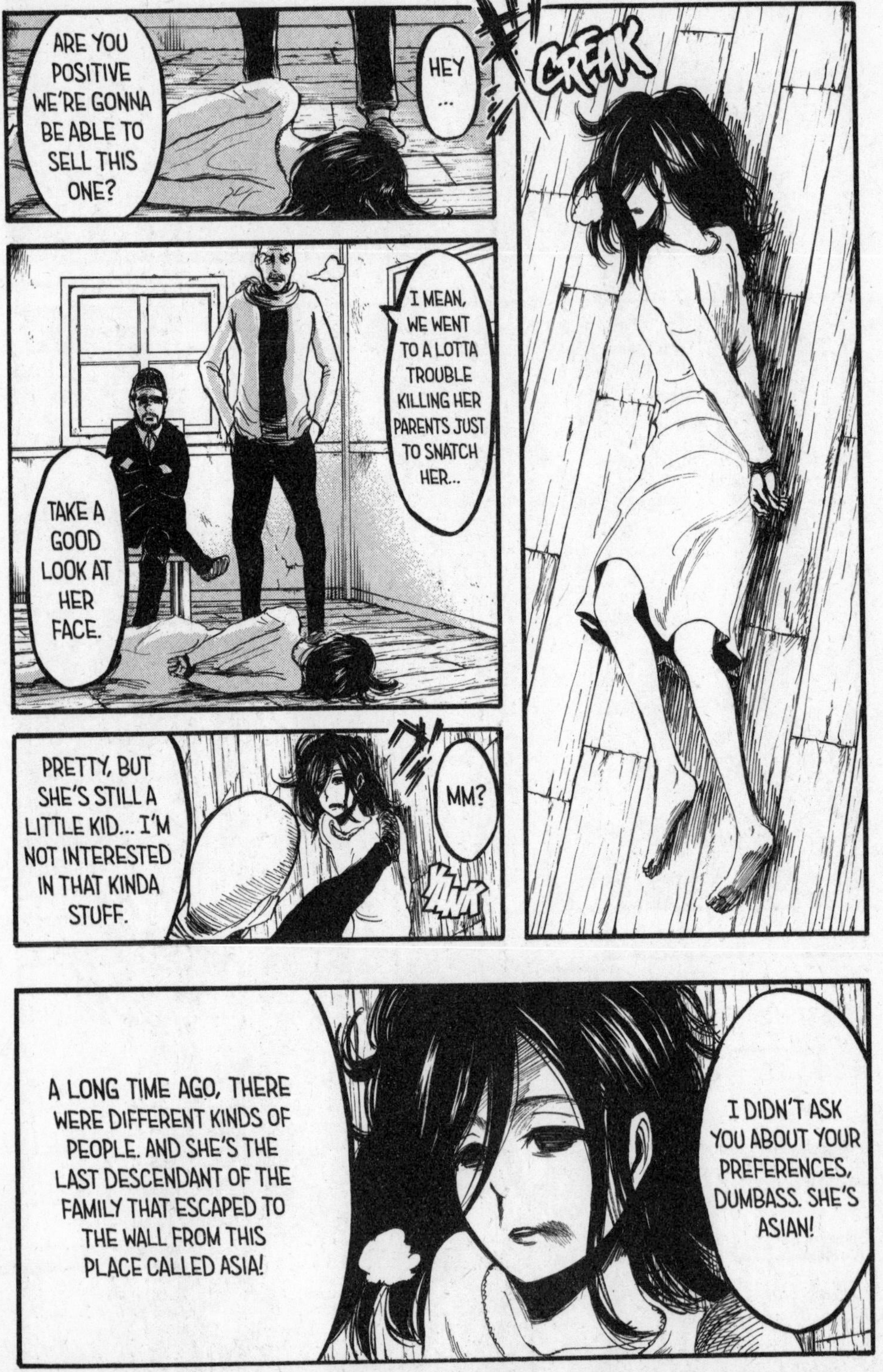
CREAK
HEY ...
ARE YOU POSITIVE WE'RE GONNA BE ABLE TO SELL THIS ONE?
I MEAN, WE WENT TO A LOTTA TROUBLE KILLING HER PARENTS JUST TO SNATCH HER...
TAKE A GOOD LOOK AT HER FACE.
MM?
YANK
PRETTY, BUT SHE'S STILL A LITTLE KID... I'M NOT INTERESTED IN THAT KINDA STUFF.
I DIDN'T ASK YOU ABOUT YOUR PREFERENCES, DUMBASS. SHE'S ASIAN!
A LONG TIME AGO, THERE WERE DIFFERENT KINDS OF PEOPLE. AND SHE'S THE LAST DESCENDANT OF THE FAMILY THAT ESCAPED TO THE WALL FROM THIS PLACE CALLED ASIA!

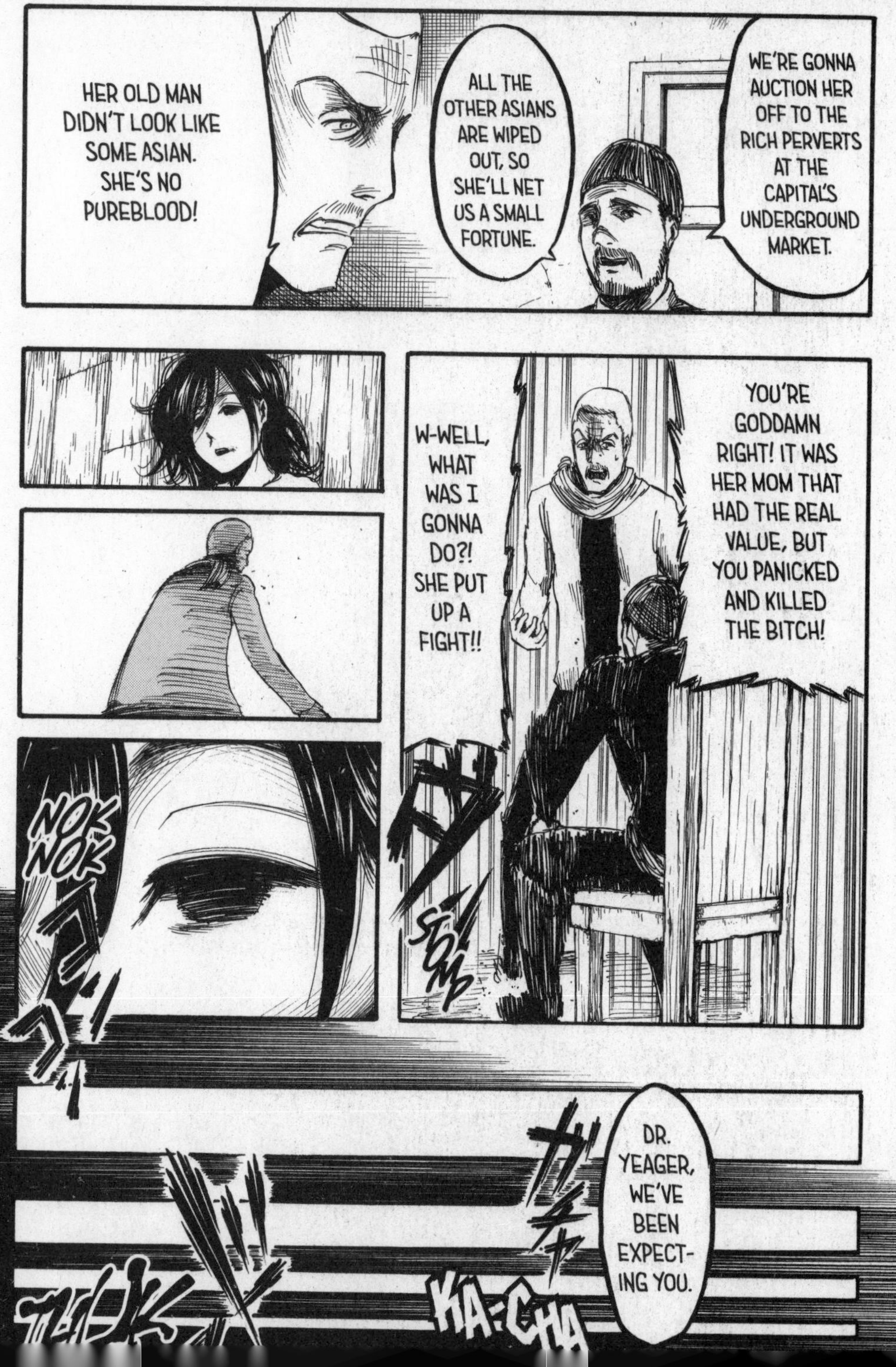
WE'RE GONNA AUCTION HER OFF TO THE RICH PERVERTS AT THE CAPITAL'S UNDERGROUND MARKET.
ALL THE OTHER ASIANS ARE WIPED OUT, SO SHE'LL NET US A SMALL FORTUNE.
HER OLD MAN DIDN'T LOOK LIKE SOME ASIAN. SHE'S NO PUREBLOOD!
YOU'RE GODDAMN RIGHT! IT WAS HER MOM THAT HAD THE REAL VALUE, BUT YOU PANICKED AND KILLED THE BITCH!
W-WELL, WHAT WAS I GONNA DO?! SHE PUT UP A FIGHT!!
STOMP
NOK NOK
DR. YEAGER, WE'VE BEEN EXPECTING YOU.
KA-CHA

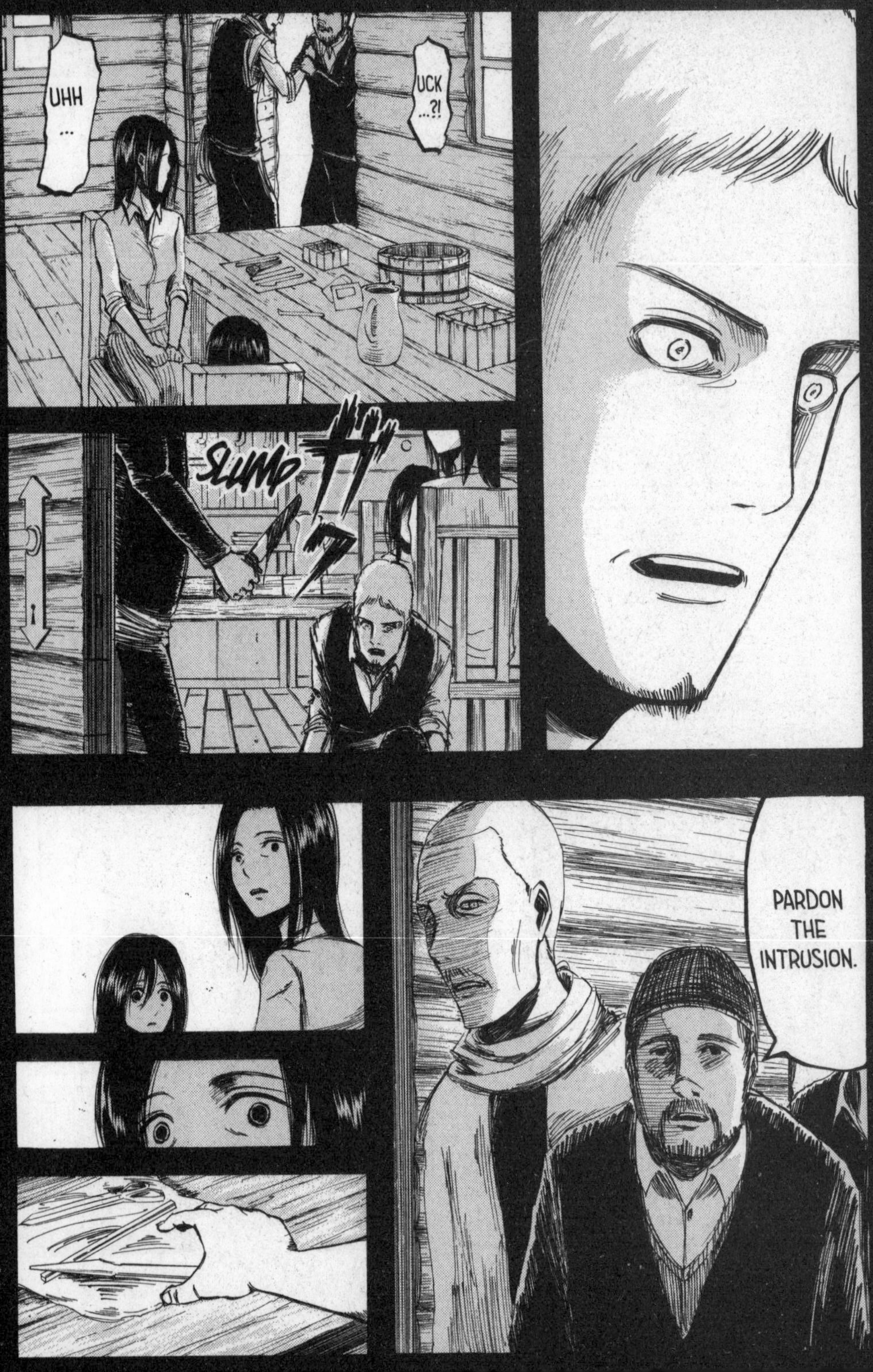
UCK ...?!
UHH ...
SLUMP
PARDON THE INTRUSION.

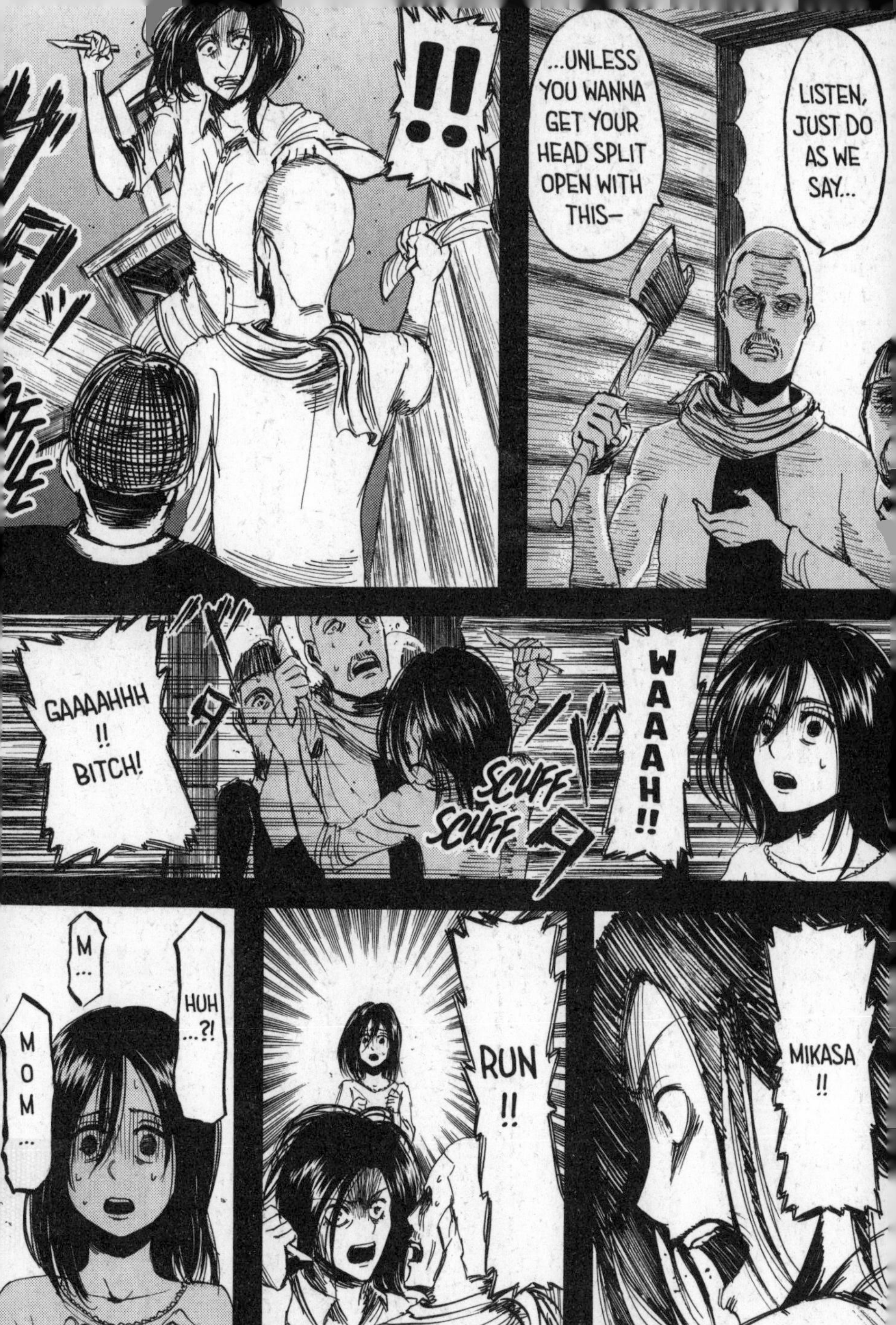
LISTEN, JUST DO AS WE SAY...
...UNLESS YOU WANNA GET YOUR HEAD SPLIT OPEN WITH THIS—
!!
WAAAH!!
SCUFF SCUFF
GAAAAHHH!! BITCH!
MIKASA!!
RUN!!
HUH...?!
M...
MOM...

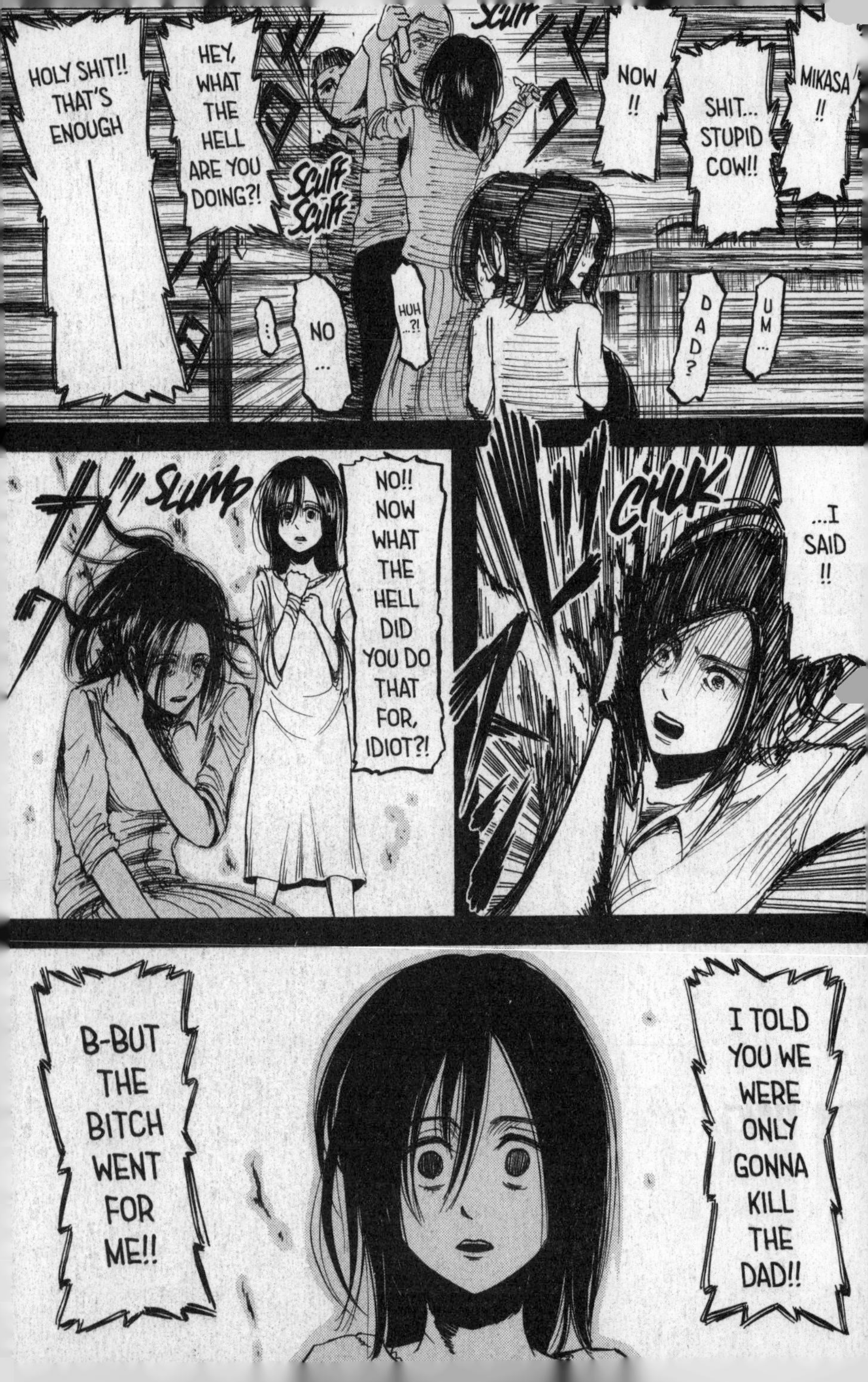
MIKASA !!
SHIT... STUPID COW!!
NOW !!
SCUFF
HEY, WHAT THE HELL ARE YOU DOING?!
HOLY SHIT!! THAT'S ENOUGH
SCUFF SCUFF
UM ...
DAD?
HUH ...?!
NO ...
...
...I SAID !!
CHUK
NO!! NOW WHAT THE HELL DID YOU DO THAT FOR, IDIOT?!
SLUMP
I TOLD YOU WE WERE ONLY GONNA KILL THE DAD!!
B-BUT THE BITCH WENT FOR ME!!

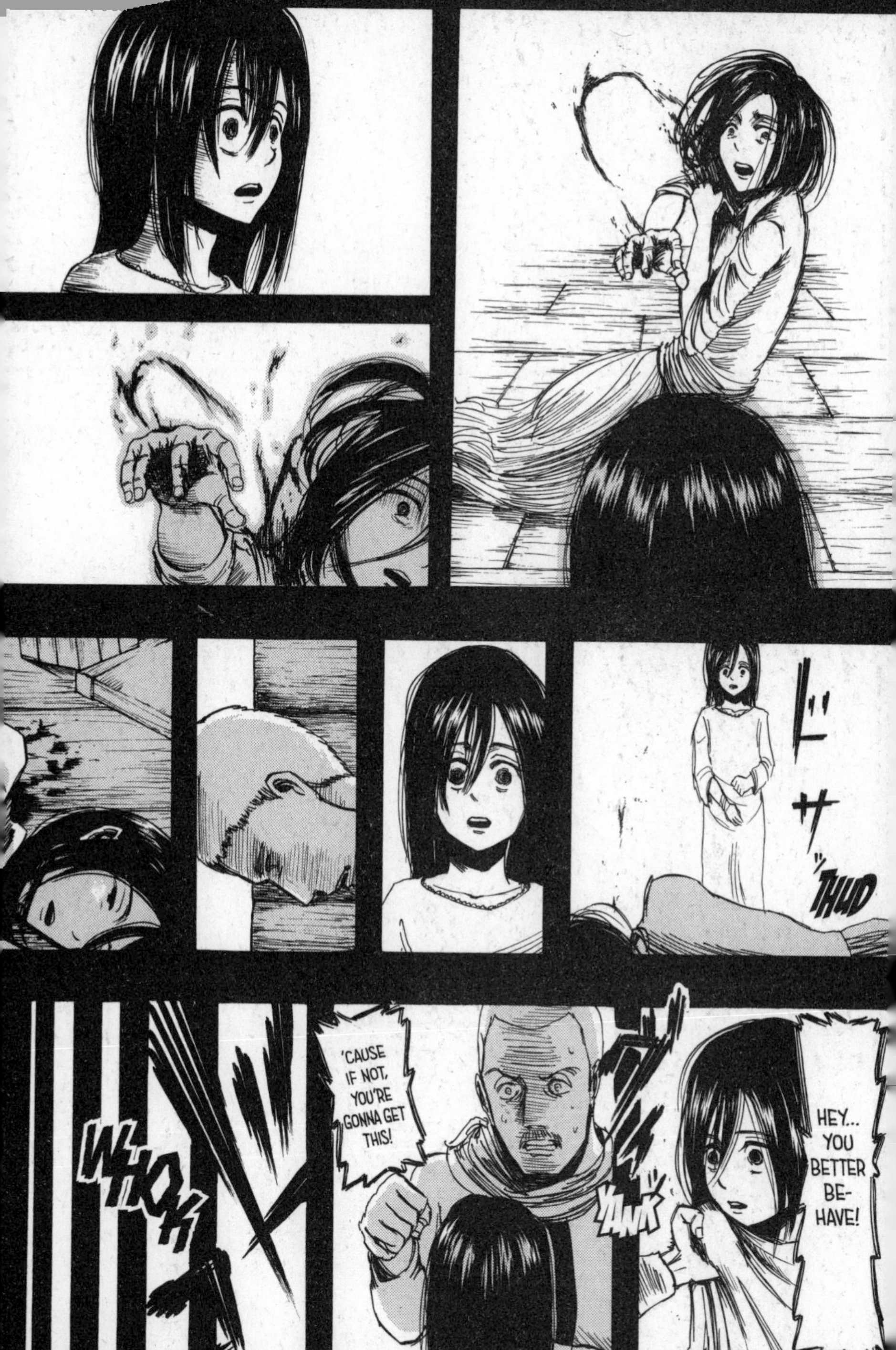
ドサ
THUD
HEY... YOU BETTER BE-HAVE!
YANK
'CAUSE IF NOT, YOU'RE GONNA GET THIS!
WHOK

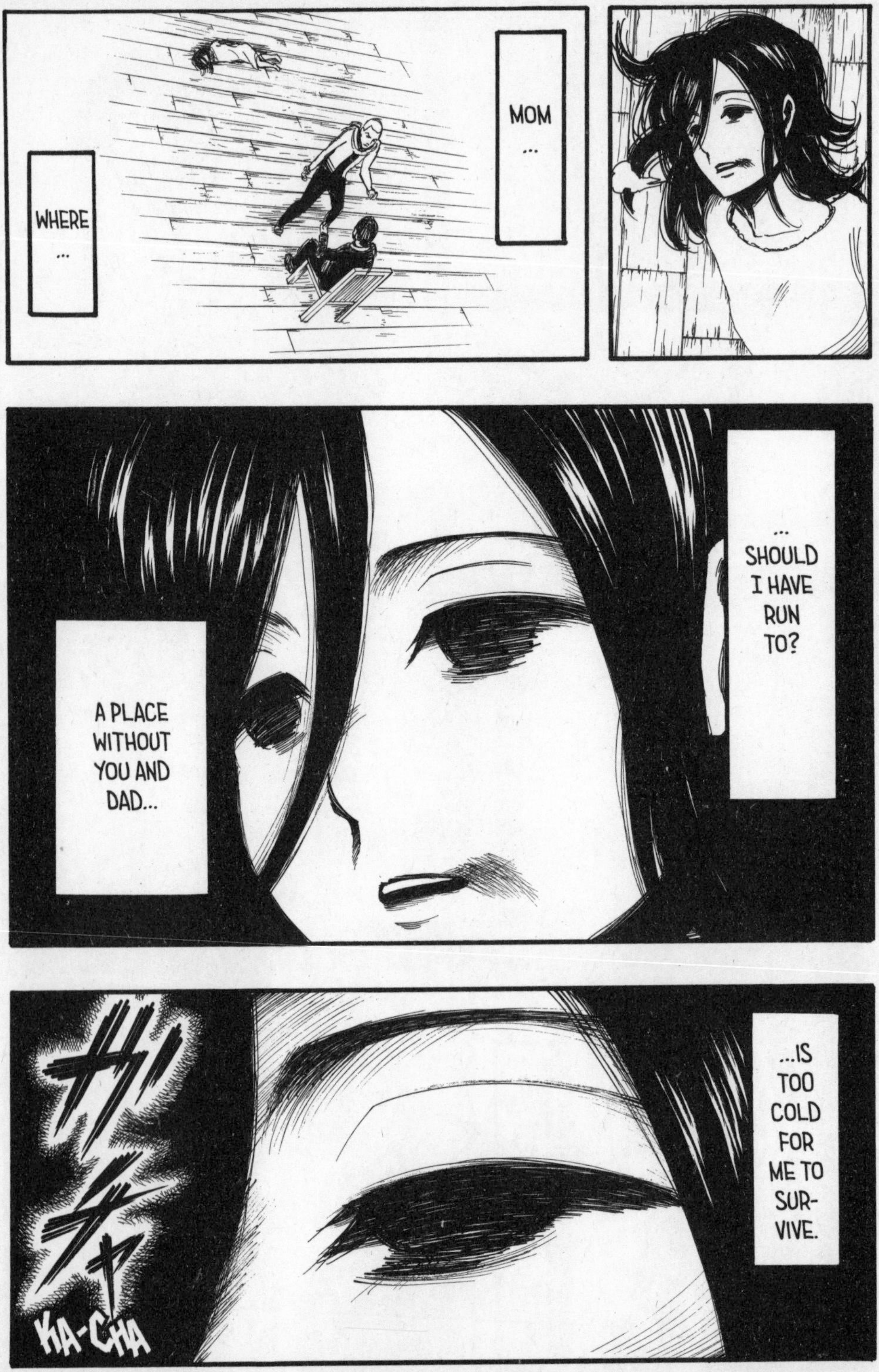
MOM ...
WHERE ...
... SHOULD I HAVE RUN TO?
A PLACE WITHOUT YOU AND DAD...
...IS TOO COLD FOR ME TO SUR-VIVE.
KA-CHA

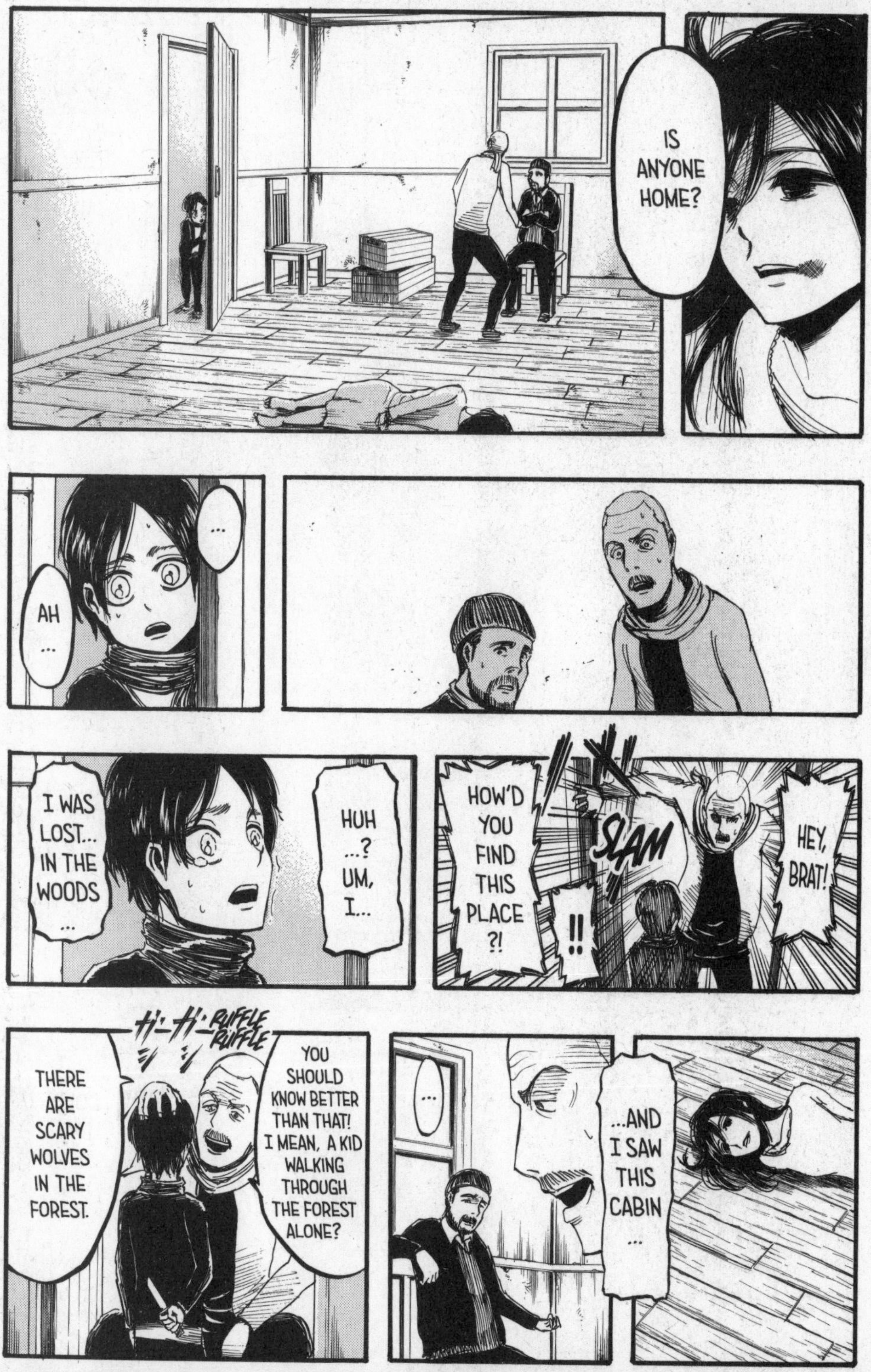
IS ANYONE HOME?
...
AH ...
HEY, BRAT!
SLAM
HOW'D YOU FIND THIS PLACE?!
!!
HUH ...? UM, I...
I WAS LOST... IN THE WOODS ...
...AND I SAW THIS CABIN ...
...
RUFFLE RUFFLE
YOU SHOULD KNOW BETTER THAN THAT! I MEAN, A KID WALKING THROUGH THE FOREST ALONE?
THERE ARE SCARY WOLVES IN THE FOREST.

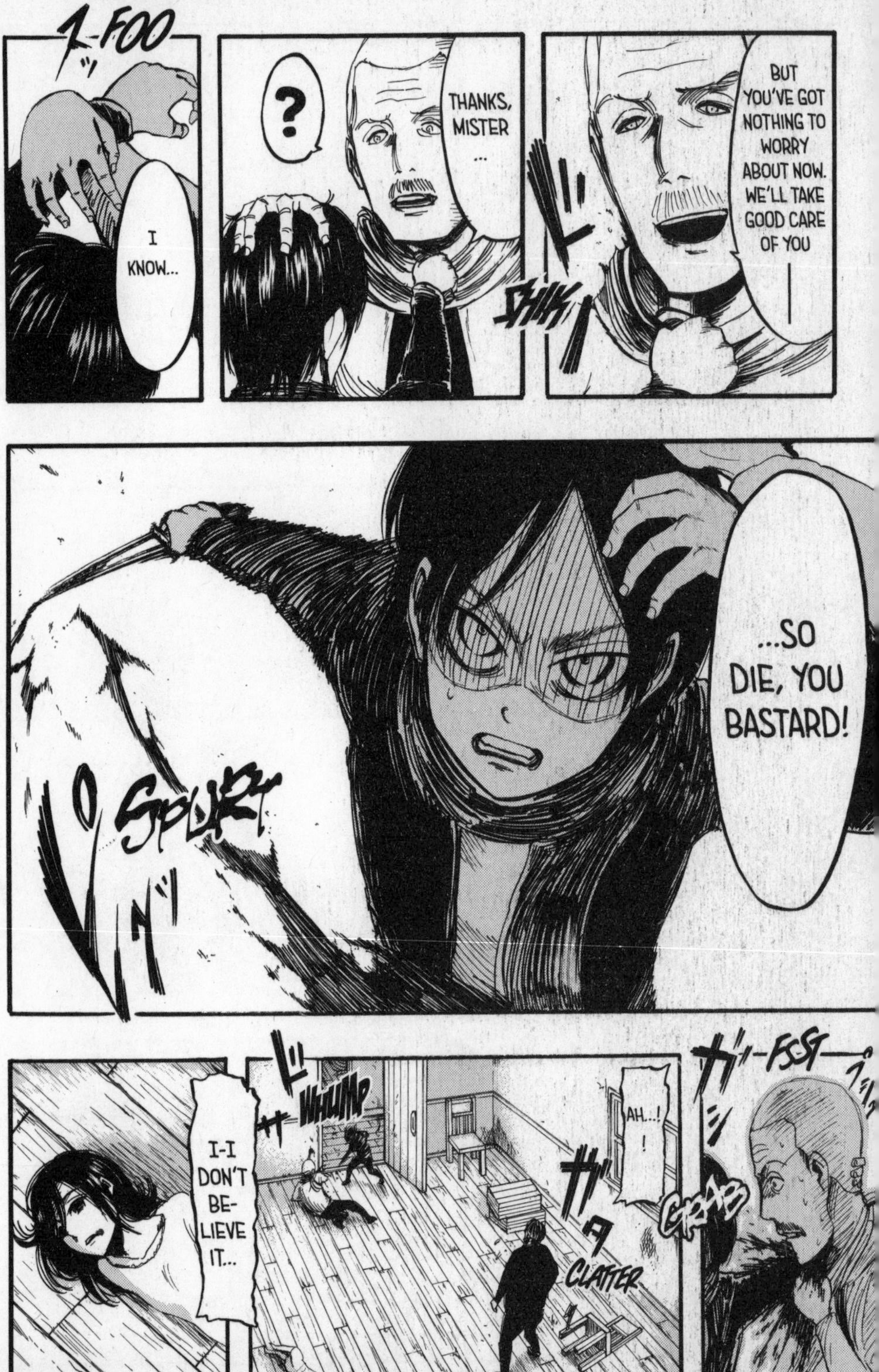

BUT YOU'VE GOT NOTHING TO WORRY ABOUT NOW. WE'LL TAKE GOOD CARE OF YOU —
SHIK
?
THANKS, MISTER ...
F-FOO
I KNOW...
...SO DIE, YOU BASTARD!
SPLURT
FS-ST
GRAB
AH...!!
WHUMP
CLATTER
I-I DON'T BE-LIEVE IT...

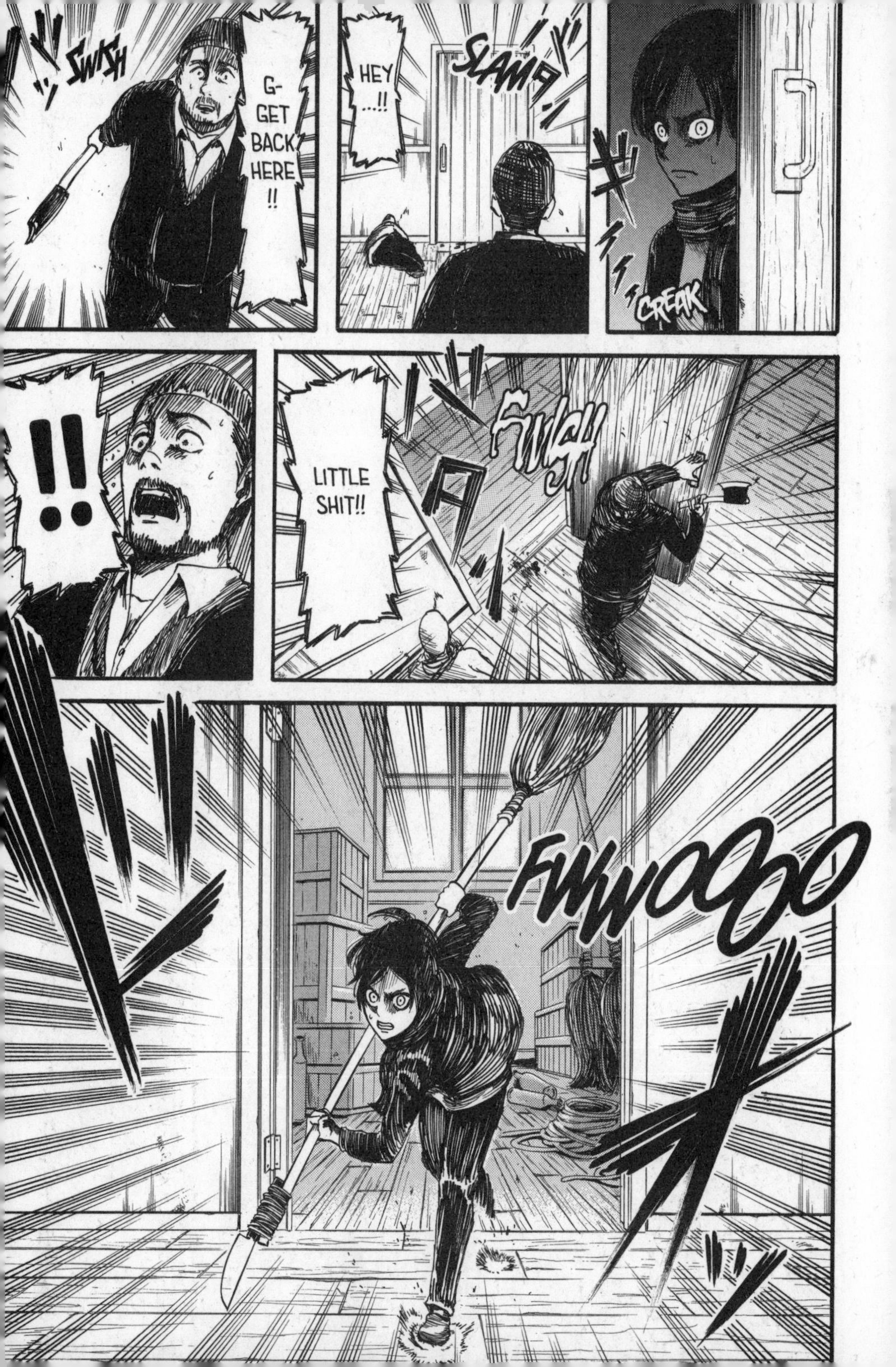
CREAK
SLAM
HEY ...!!
SWISH
G-GET BACK HERE!!
FWISH
LITTLE SHIT!!
!!
FWOOOO

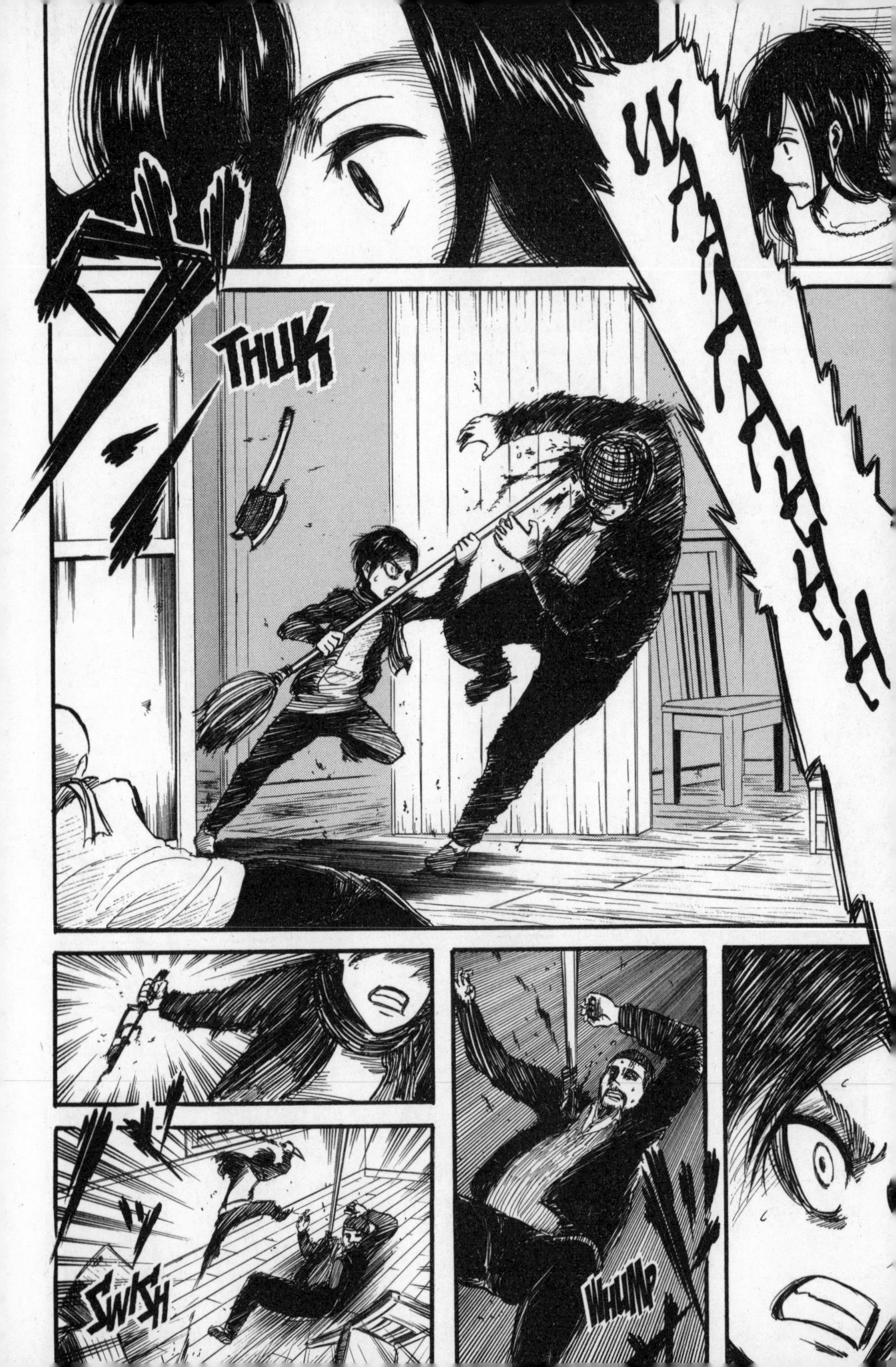
WAAAAAHHHH
THUK
SWISH
WHUMP

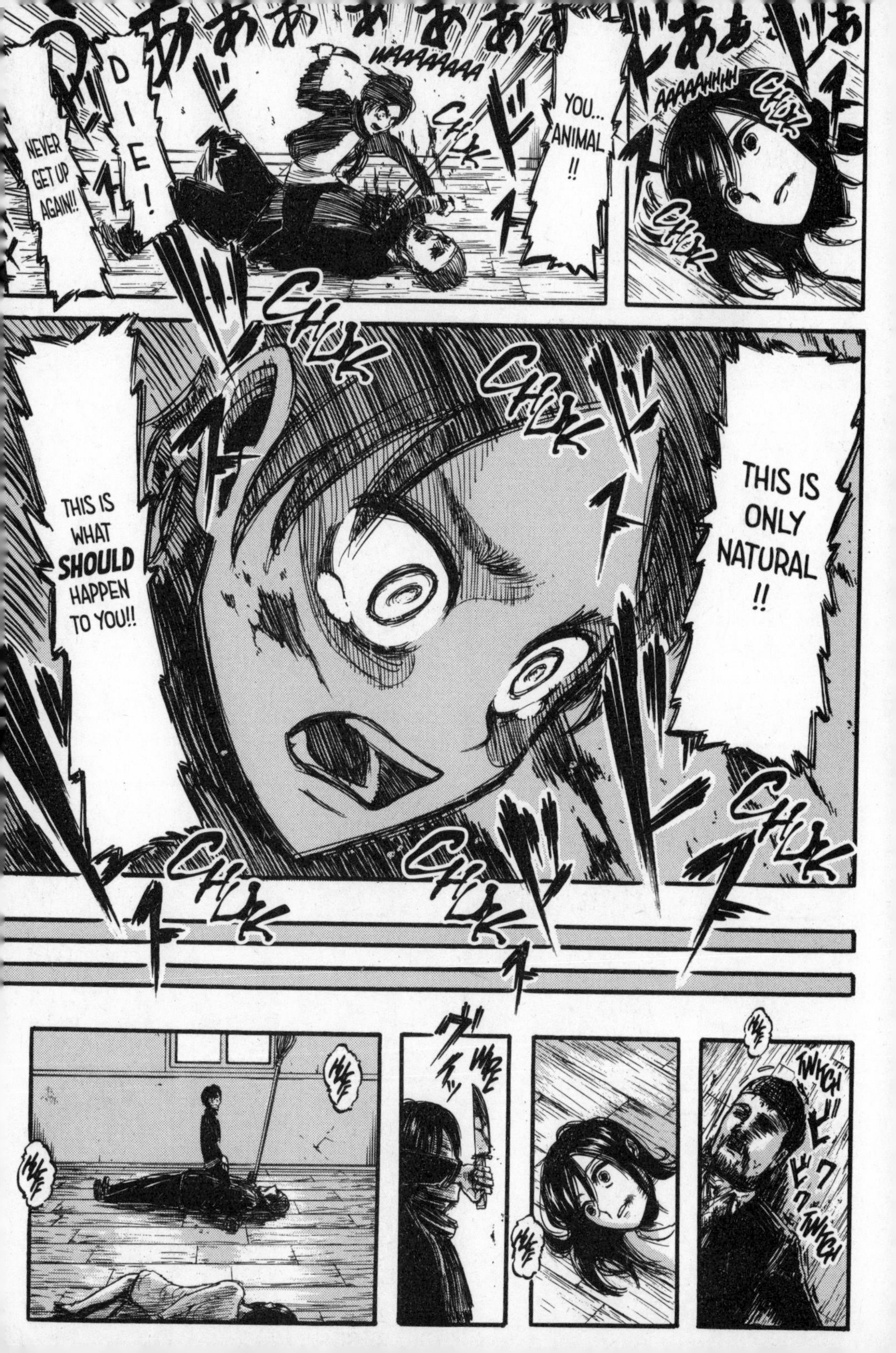
AAAAAHHHH
CHUK
CHUK
YOU... ANIMAL!!
CHUK
WAAAAAAAAA
DIE!
NEVER GET UP AGAIN!!
THIS IS ONLY NATURAL!!
CHUK
CHUK
THIS IS WHAT **SHOULD** HAPPEN TO YOU!!
CHUK
CHUK
CHUK
TWKCH
TWKCH

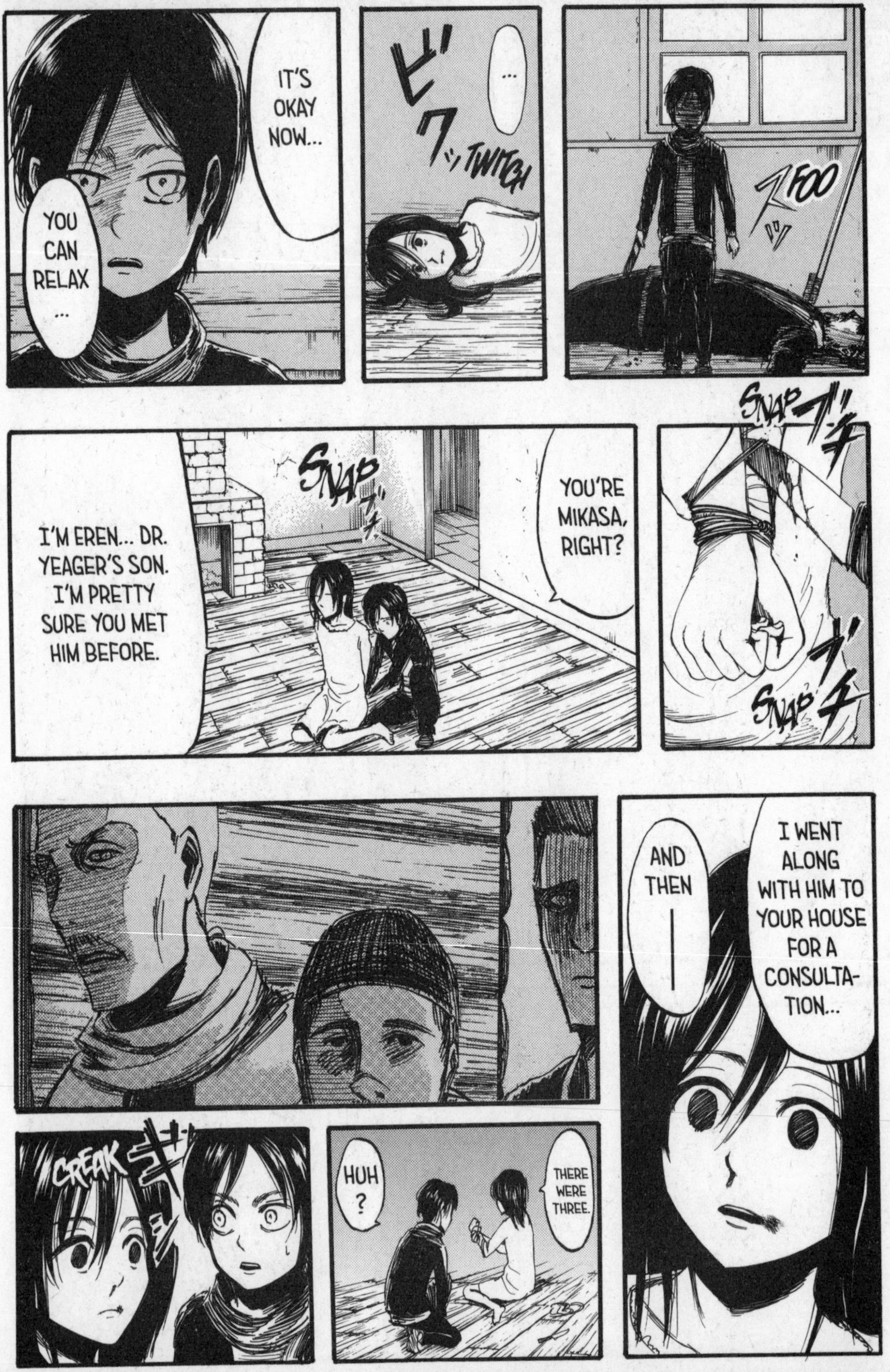
FOO
...
TWITCH
IT'S OKAY NOW...
YOU CAN RELAX ...
SNAP
SNAP
YOU'RE MIKASA, RIGHT?
SNAP
I'M EREN... DR. YEAGER'S SON. I'M PRETTY SURE YOU MET HIM BEFORE.
I WENT ALONG WITH HIM TO YOUR HOUSE FOR A CONSULTA-TION...
AND THEN —
THERE WERE THREE.
HUH ?
CREAK

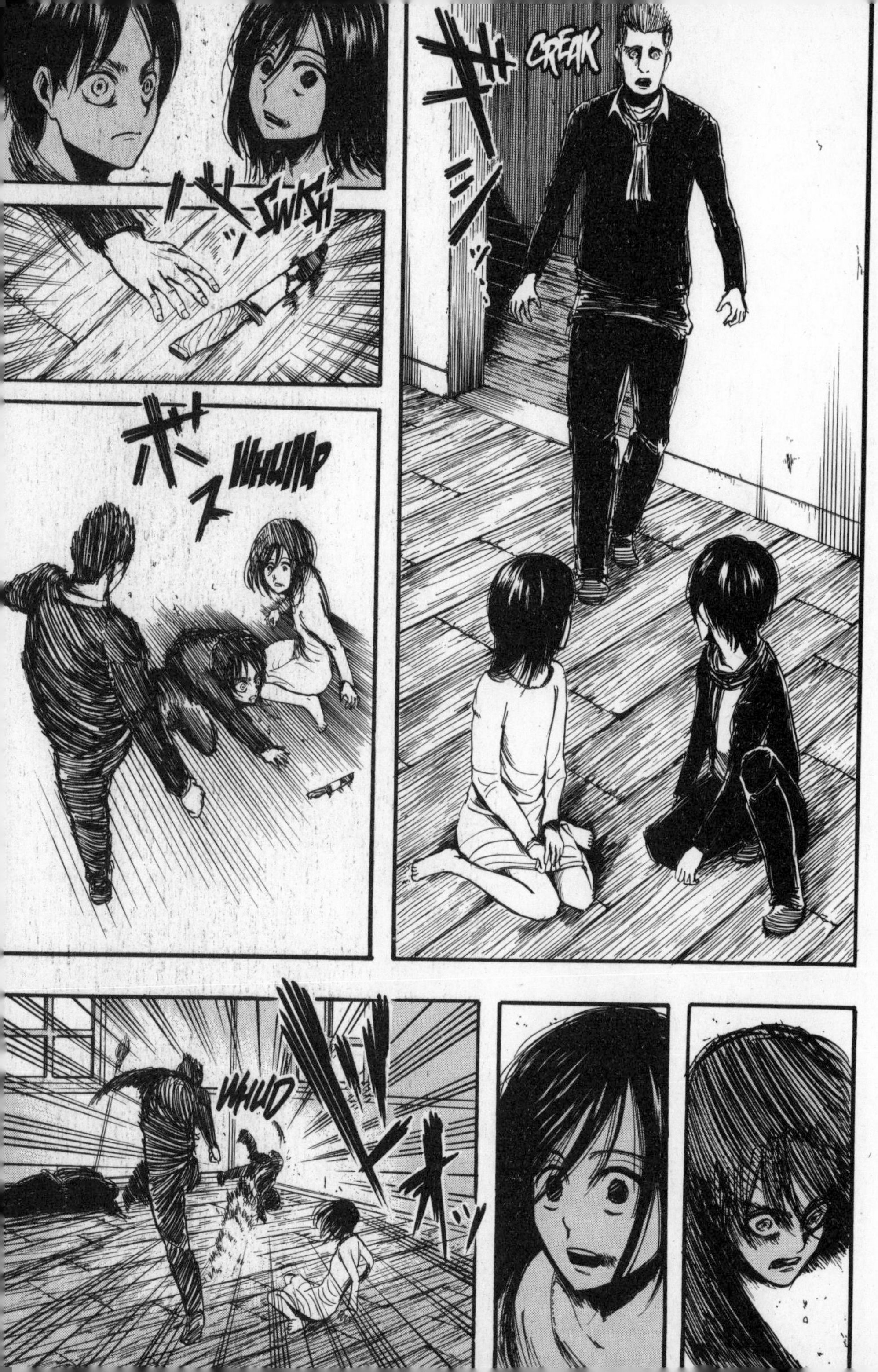
CREAK
SWISH
WHUMP
WHUD

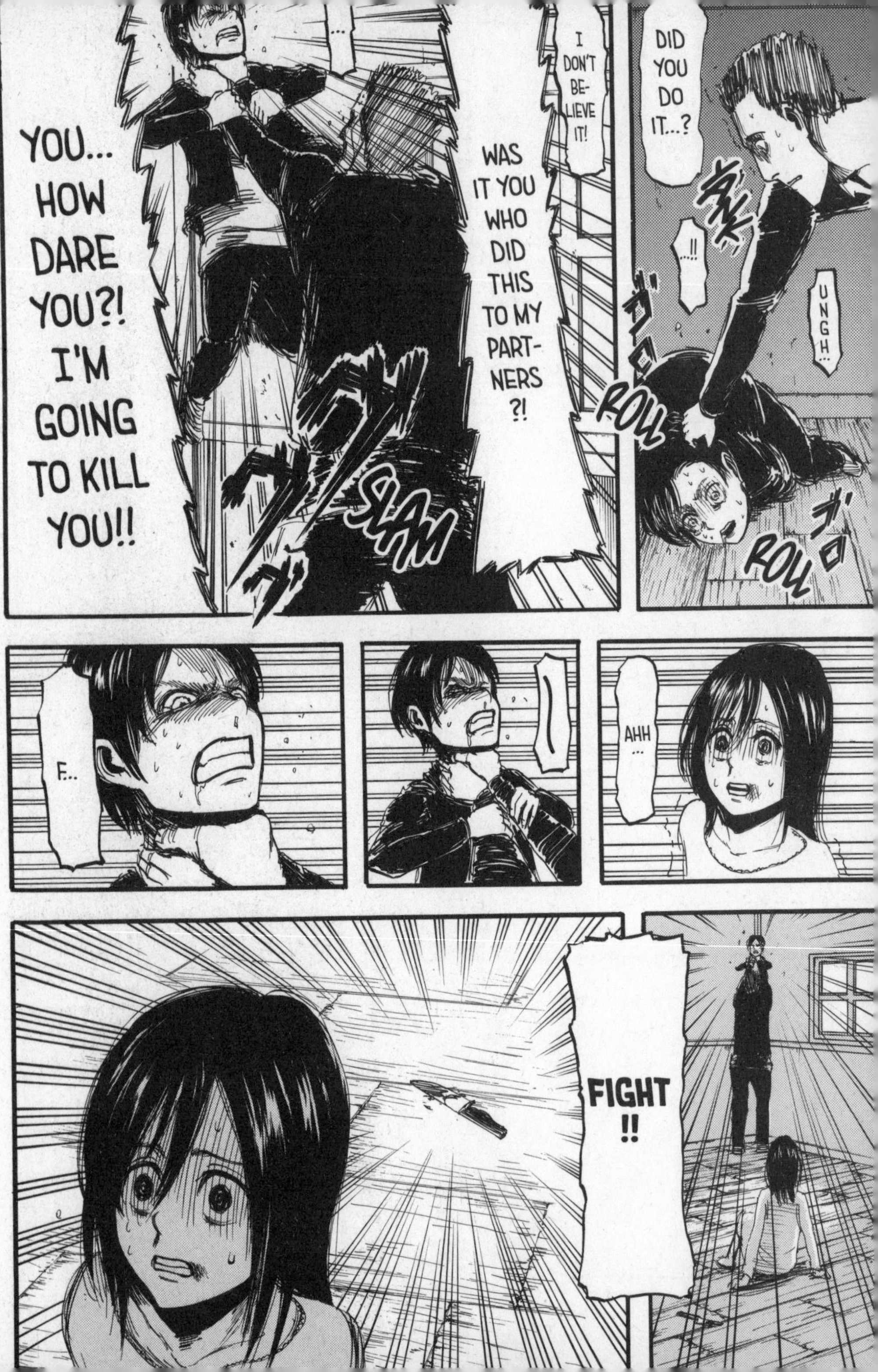
DID YOU DO IT...?
YANK
...!!
UNGH...
ROLL
ROLL
I DON'T BE-LIEVE IT!
WAS IT YOU WHO DID THIS TO MY PART-NERS?!
...
SLAM
YOU... HOW DARE YOU?! I'M GOING TO KILL YOU!!
AHH...
!
F...
FIGHT!!

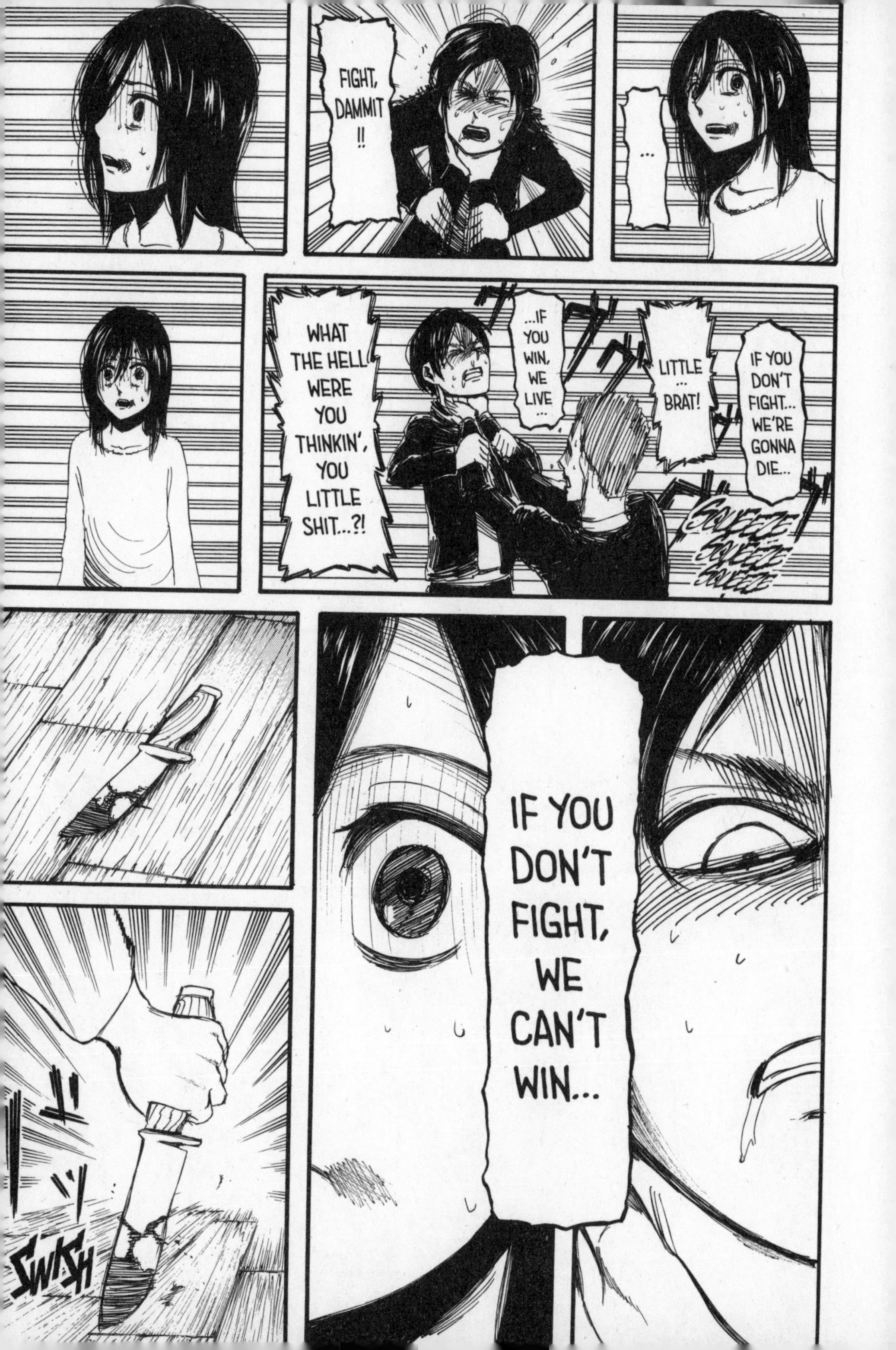
...
FIGHT, DAMMIT!!
IF YOU DON'T FIGHT... WE'RE GONNA DIE...
LITTLE... BRAT!
...IF YOU WIN, WE LIVE...
WHAT THE HELL WERE YOU THINKIN', YOU LITTLE SHIT...?!
SQUEEZE SQUEEZE SQUEEZE
IF YOU DON'T FIGHT, WE CAN'T WIN...
SWISH

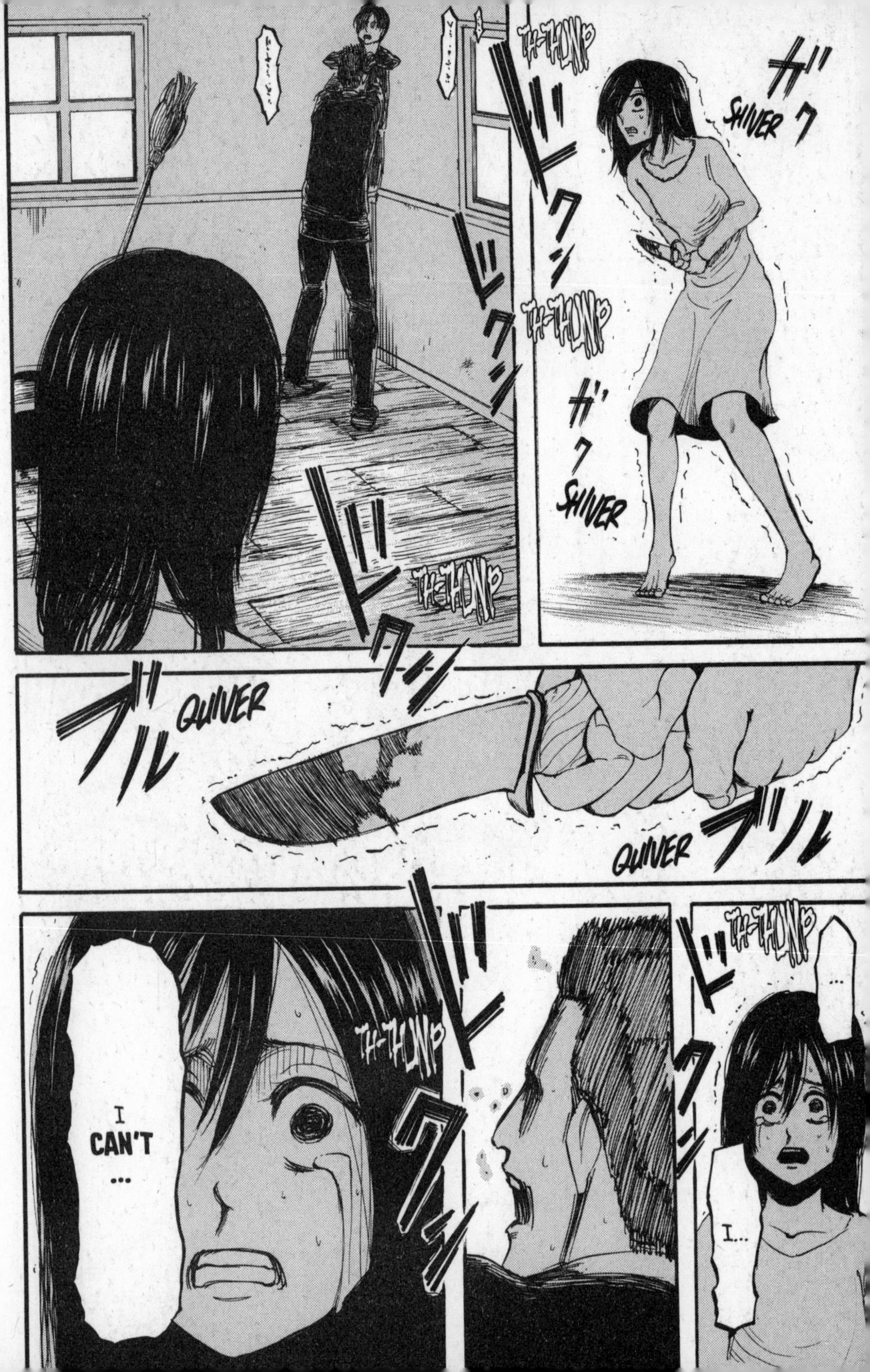
TH-THUMP
SHIVER
TH-THUMP
SHIVER
TH-THUMP
QUIVER
QUIVER
TH-THUMP
...
I...
TH-THUMP
I CAN'T ...

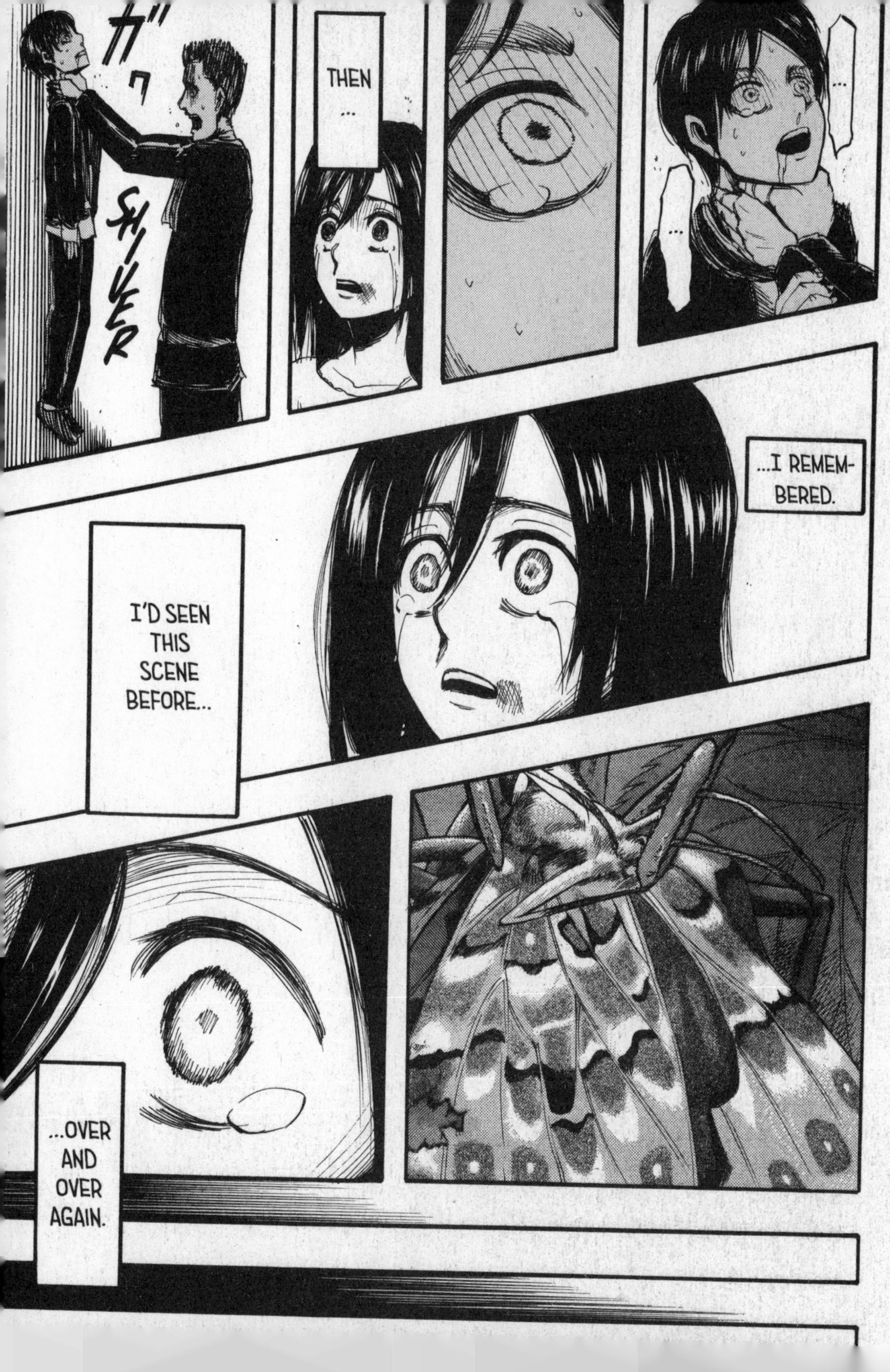
...
...
THEN ...
SHIVER
...I REMEMBERED.
I'D SEEN THIS SCENE BEFORE...
...OVER AND OVER AGAIN.

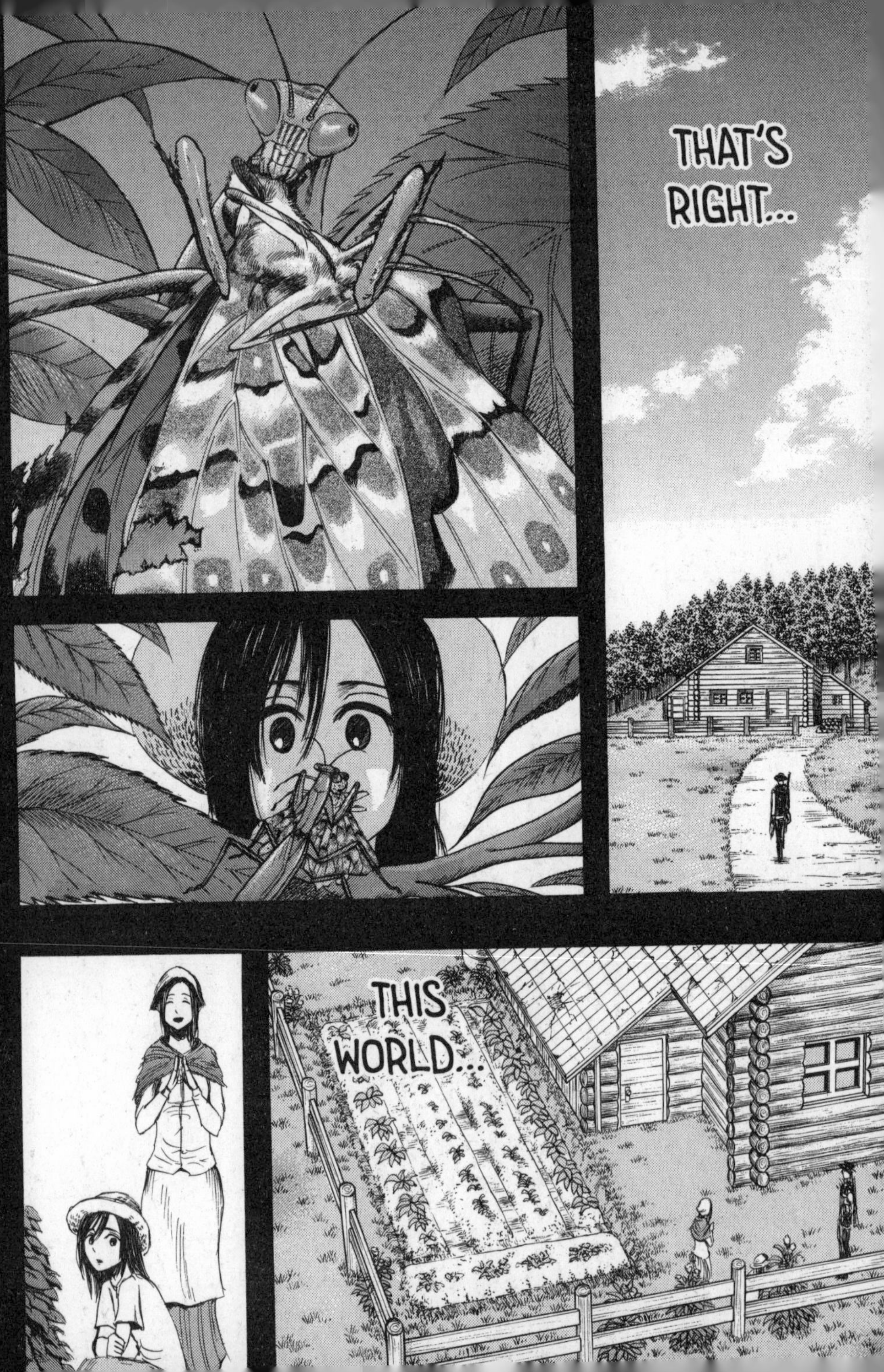
THAT'S RIGHT...
THIS WORLD...

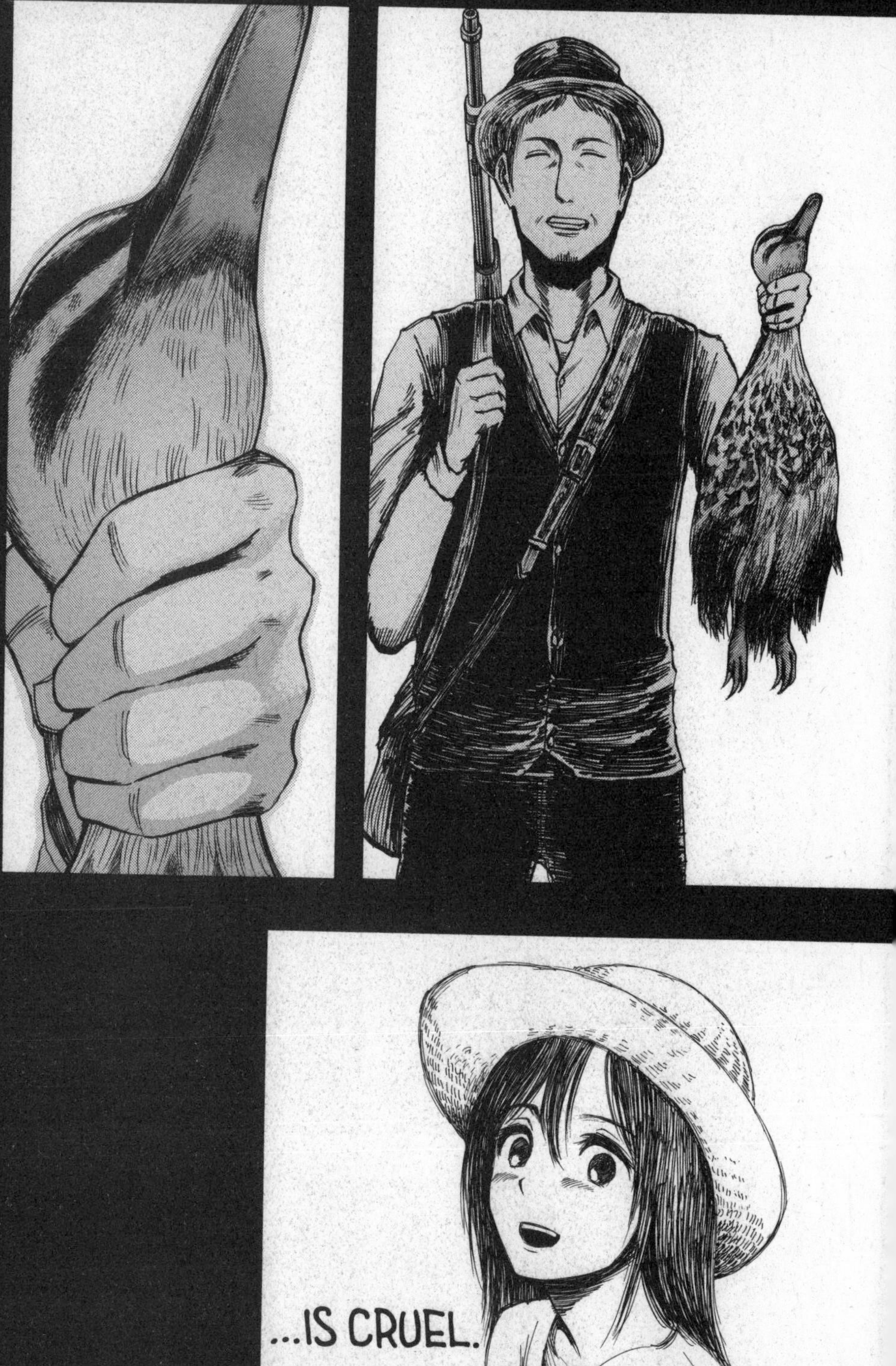
...IS CRUEL.

IT HIT ME THAT LIVING WAS LIKE A MIRACLE. AND IN THAT INSTANT...

...MY BODY STOPPED TREMBLING.

FIGHT...

FROM THAT MOMENT, I WAS ABLE TO PERFECTLY...

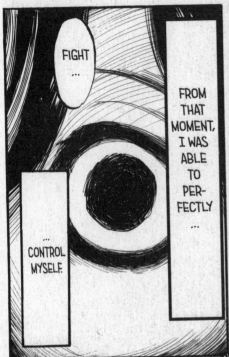

...CONTROL MYSELF.

CREAK CREAK CREAK

TH-THUMP

KR

FIGHT!

TH-THUMP

FIGHT!!

AK

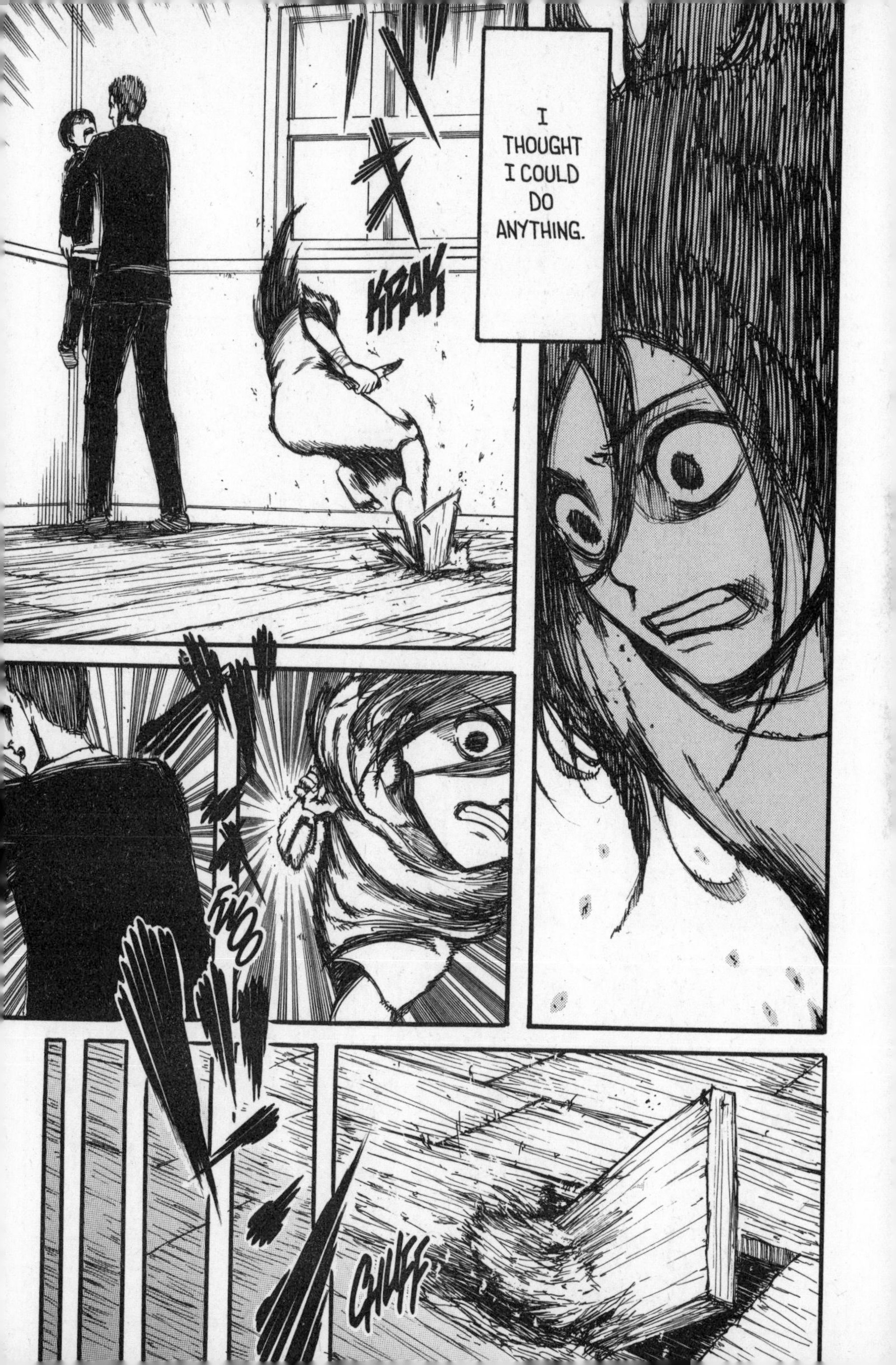
I THOUGHT I COULD DO ANYTHING.
KRAK
FWOO
GUK

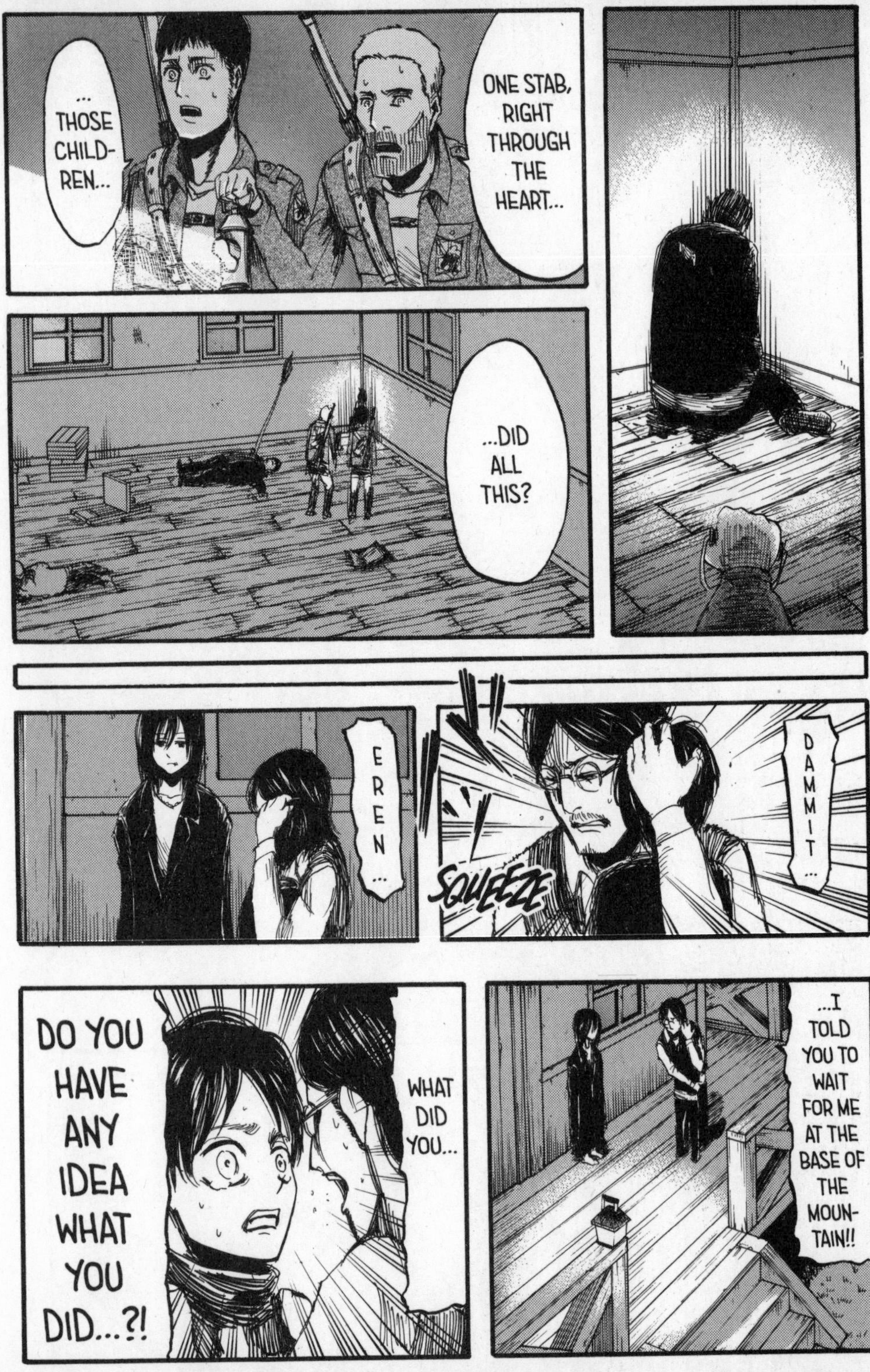
ONE STAB, RIGHT THROUGH THE HEART...
... THOSE CHILD-REN...
...DID ALL THIS?
DAMMIT...
SQUEEZE
EREN...
...I TOLD YOU TO WAIT FOR ME AT THE BASE OF THE MOUN-TAIN!!
WHAT DID YOU...
DO YOU HAVE ANY IDEA WHAT YOU DID...?!

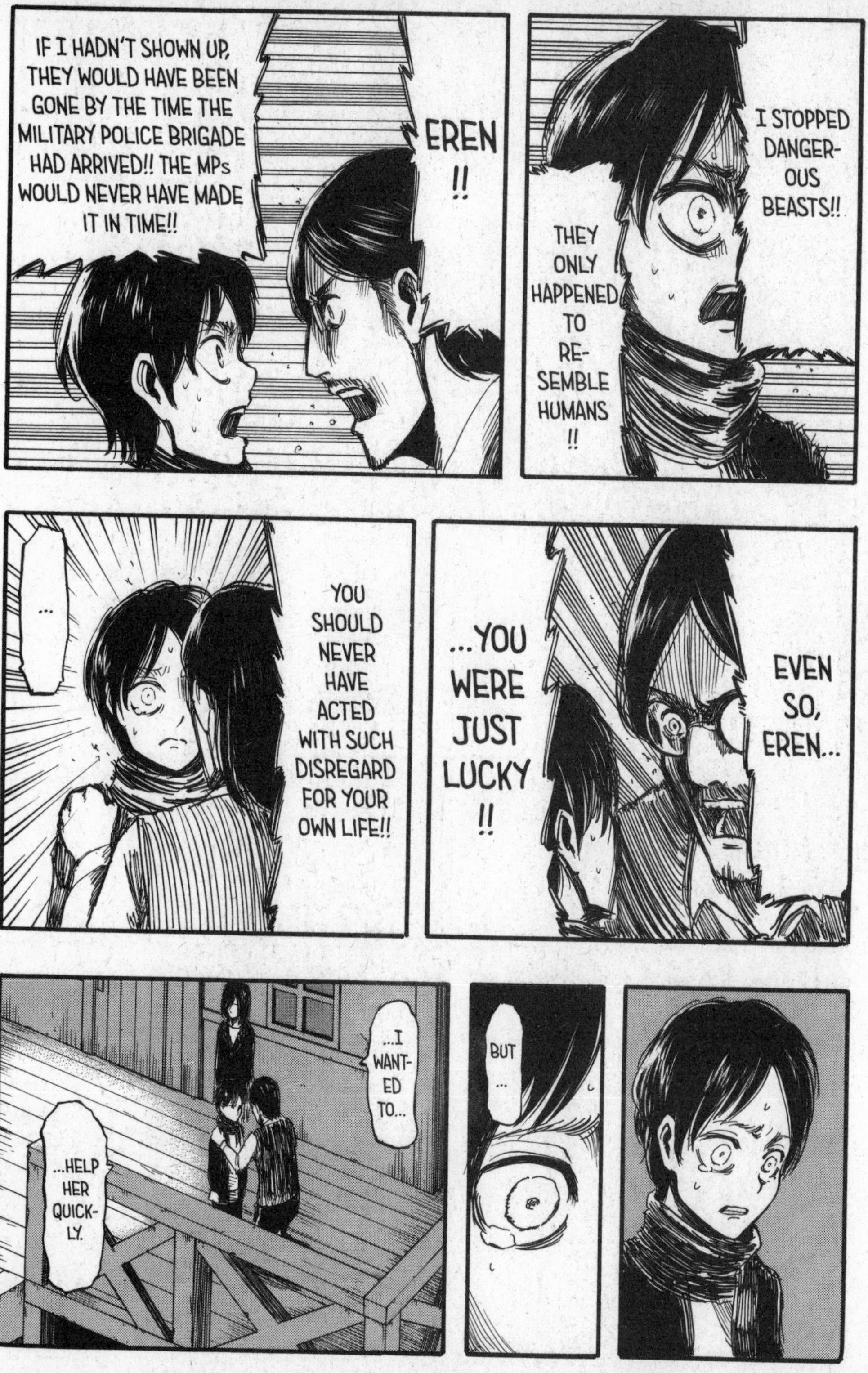
I STOPPED DANGER-OUS BEASTS!!
THEY ONLY HAPPENED TO RE-SEMBLE HUMANS !!
EREN !!
IF I HADN'T SHOWN UP, THEY WOULD HAVE BEEN GONE BY THE TIME THE MILITARY POLICE BRIGADE HAD ARRIVED!! THE MPs WOULD NEVER HAVE MADE IT IN TIME!!
EVEN SO, EREN...
...YOU WERE JUST LUCKY !!
YOU SHOULD NEVER HAVE ACTED WITH SUCH DISREGARD FOR YOUR OWN LIFE!!
...
BUT ...
...I WANT-ED TO...
...HELP HER QUICK-LY.

MIKASA
...

...

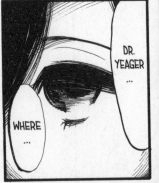

DR. YEAGER
...

WHERE
...

DO YOU REMEMBER ME? I MET YOU SEVERAL TIMES WHEN YOU WERE STILL LITTLE, BUT...

...SHOULD I GO...

...FROM HERE?

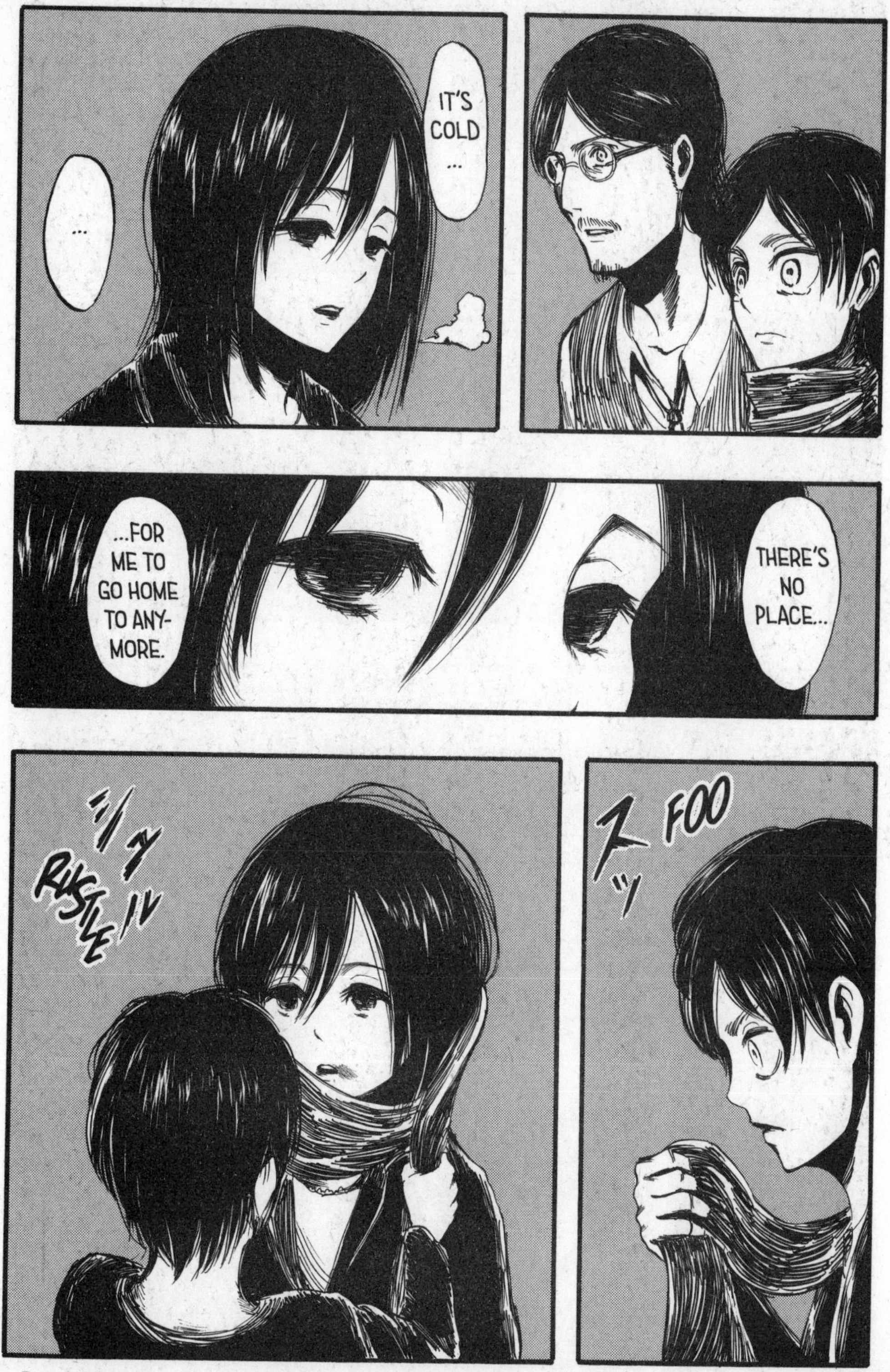
IT'S COLD ...
...
THERE'S NO PLACE...
...FOR ME TO GO HOME TO ANY-MORE.
スッ
FOO
シュル
RUSTLE

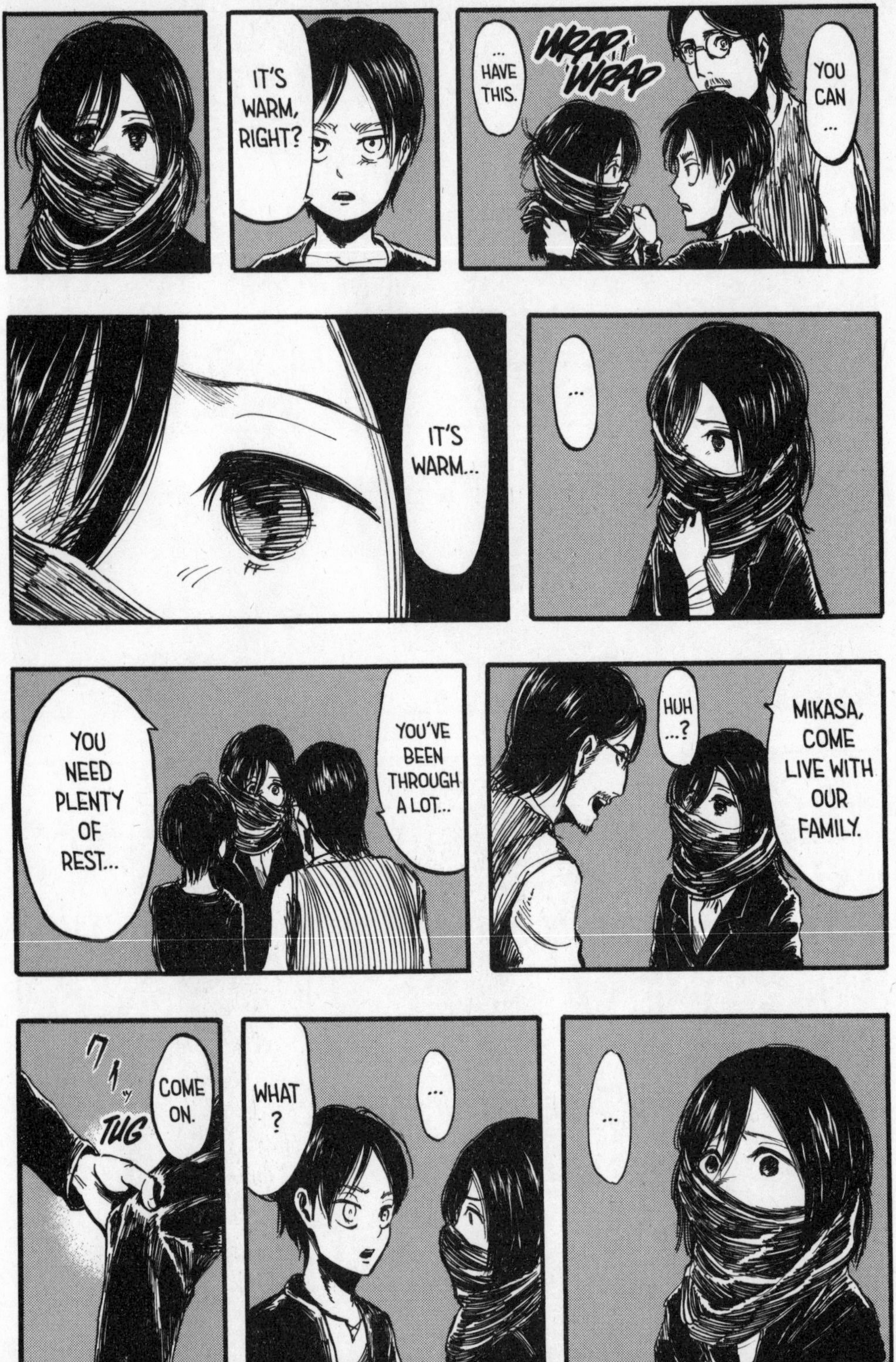
YOU CAN ...
WRAP WRAP
... HAVE THIS.
IT'S WARM, RIGHT?
...
IT'S WARM...
MIKASA, COME LIVE WITH OUR FAMILY.
HUH ...?
YOU'VE BEEN THROUGH A LOT...
YOU NEED PLENTY OF REST...
...
...
WHAT ?
COME ON.
クイッ
TUG

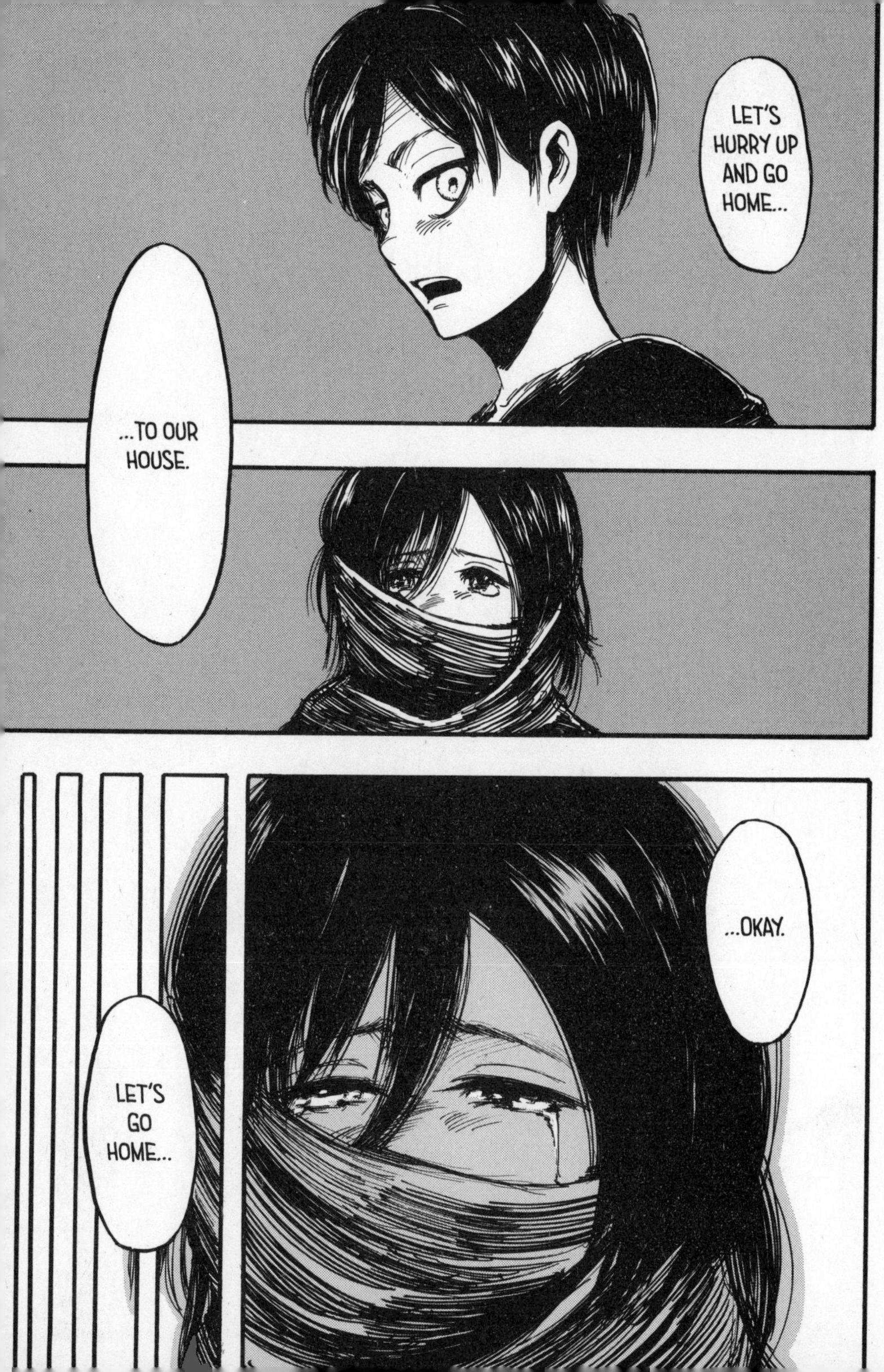
LET'S HURRY UP AND GO HOME...
...TO OUR HOUSE.
...OKAY.
LET'S GO HOME...

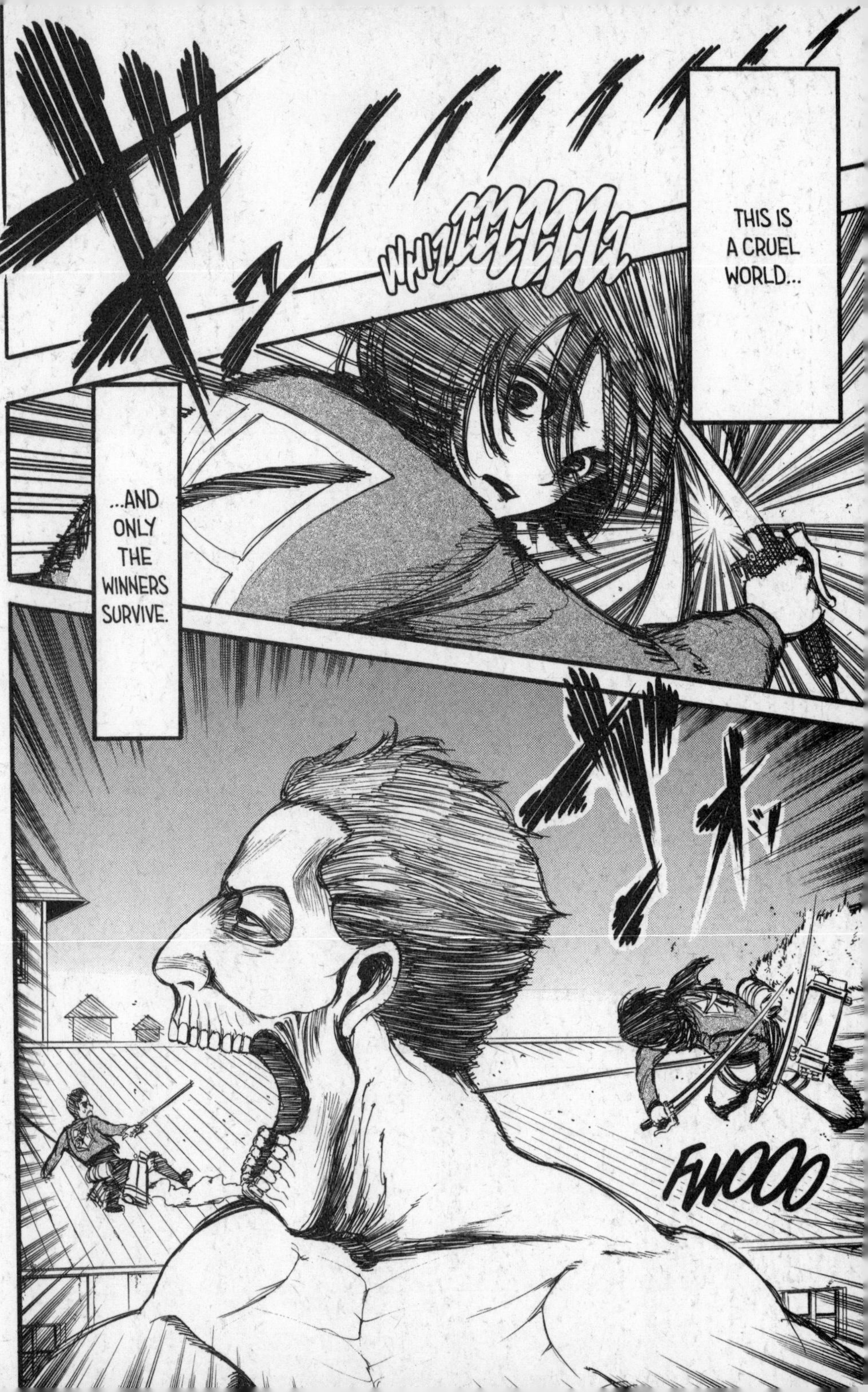
THIS IS A CRUEL WORLD...
WHIZZZZZZZZZZ
...AND ONLY THE WINNERS SURVIVE.
FWOOO

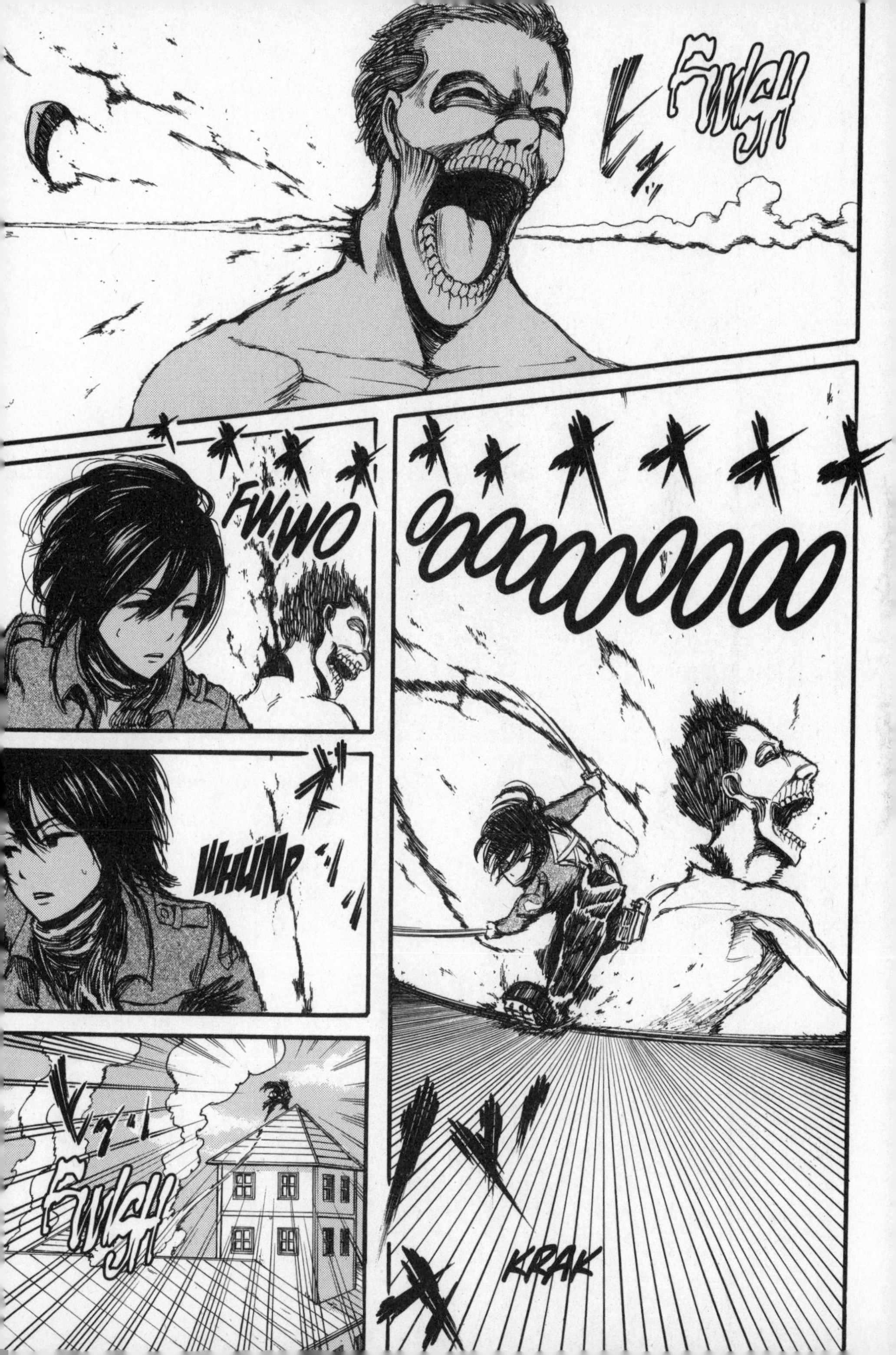
Fwagh
OOOOOOOOOO
KRAK
FWWO
WHUMP
Fwagh

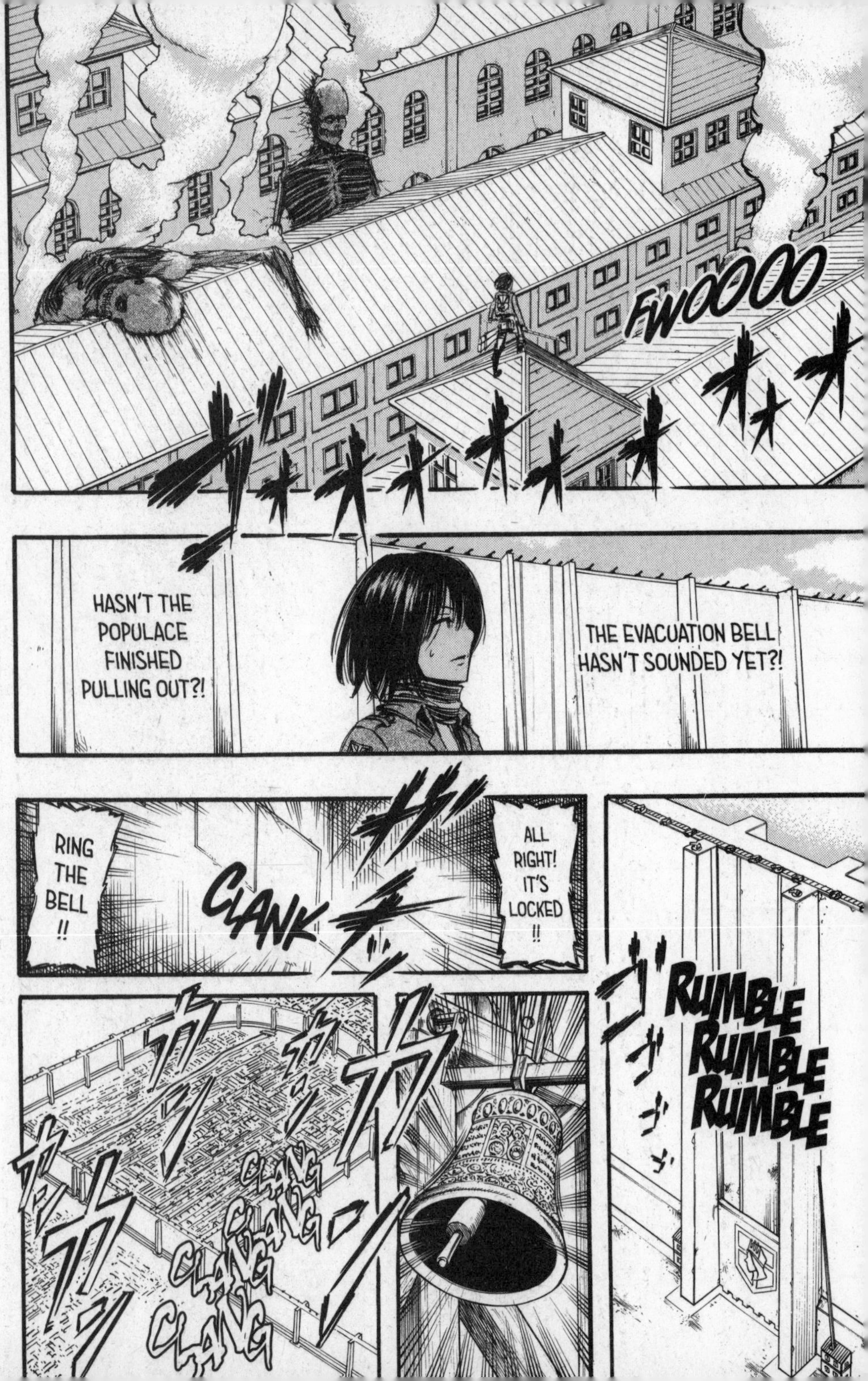
FWOOOO
THE EVACUATION BELL HASN'T SOUNDED YET?!
HASN'T THE POPULACE FINISHED PULLING OUT?!
ALL RIGHT! IT'S LOCKED!!
CLANK
RING THE BELL!!
CLANG CLANG
CLANG CLANG
RUMBLE RUMBLE RUMBLE

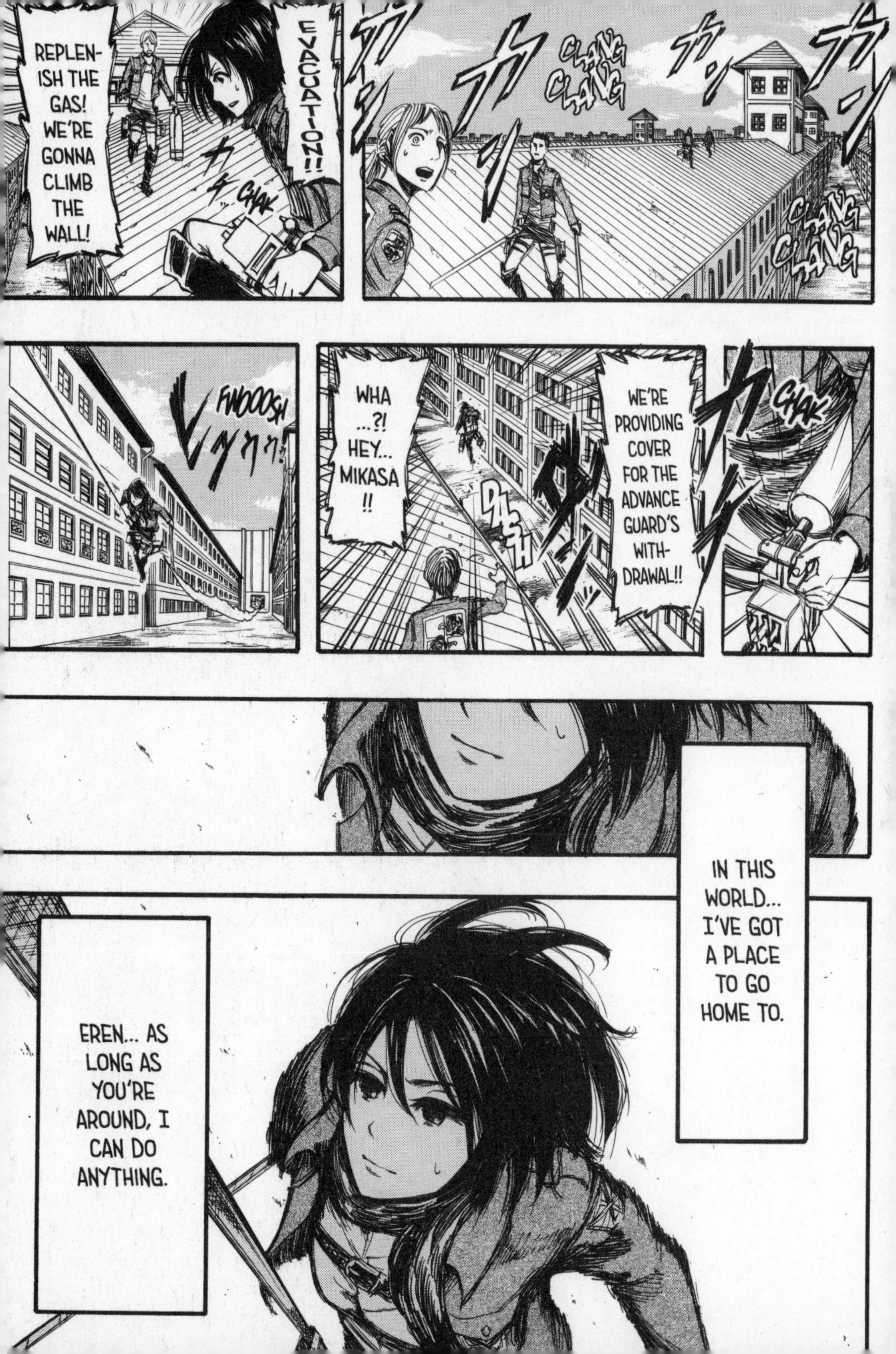
CLANG CLANG
CLANG CLANG
EVACUATION!!
REPLEN-ISH THE GAS! WE'RE GONNA CLIMB THE WALL!
CHAK
CHAK
WE'RE PROVIDING COVER FOR THE ADVANCE GUARD'S WITH-DRAWAL!!
DASH
WHA ...?! HEY... MIKASA!!
FWOOOSH
IN THIS WORLD... I'VE GOT A PLACE TO GO HOME TO.
EREN... AS LONG AS YOU'RE AROUND, I CAN DO ANYTHING.

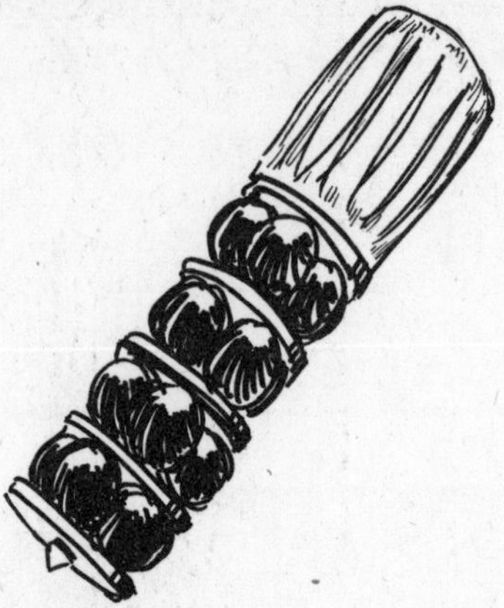

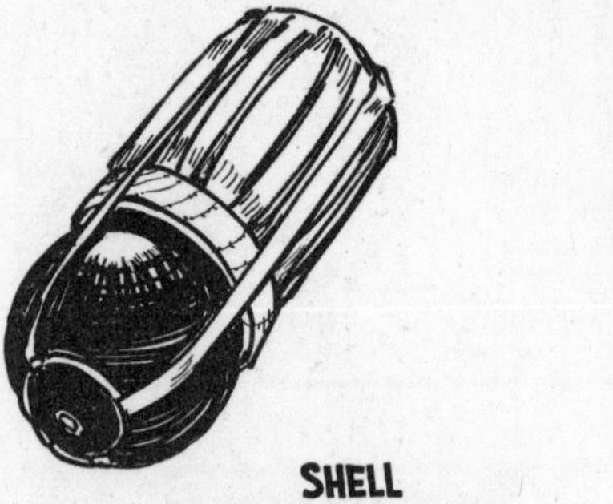

SHELL
THE GOAL IS TO KILL THE TITANS WITH THESE. IF THE TITANS' WEAK POINT CAN BE HIT, IT'S POSSIBLE TO BRING THEM DOWN WITH ONE SHOT. HOWEVER, WHEN FIRING AT A MOVING TARGET WITH AN UNRIFLED CANNON, ACCURACY IS LOW, SO AIMING AND HITTING THE CREATURES AT A PRECISE SPOT IS VERY DIFFICULT. THE OUTCOME IS USUALLY UNSUCCESSFUL.

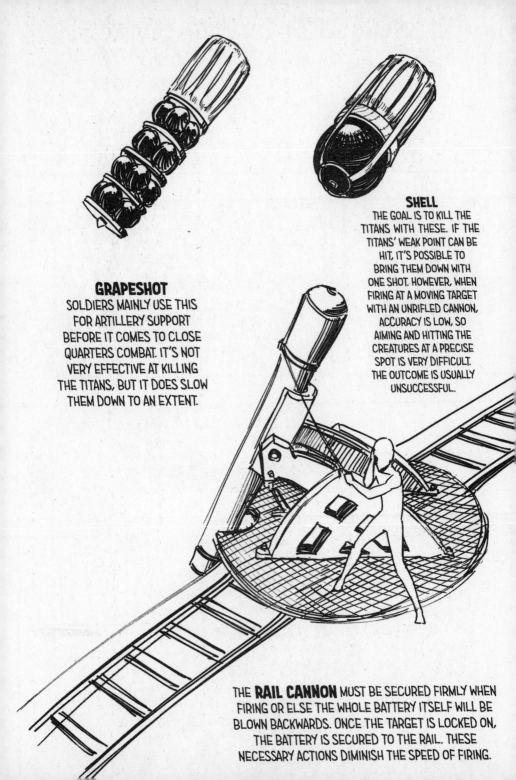

GRAPESHOT
SOLDIERS MAINLY USE THIS FOR ARTILLERY SUPPORT BEFORE IT COMES TO CLOSE QUARTERS COMBAT. IT'S NOT VERY EFFECTIVE AT KILLING THE TITANS, BUT IT DOES SLOW THEM DOWN TO AN EXTENT.

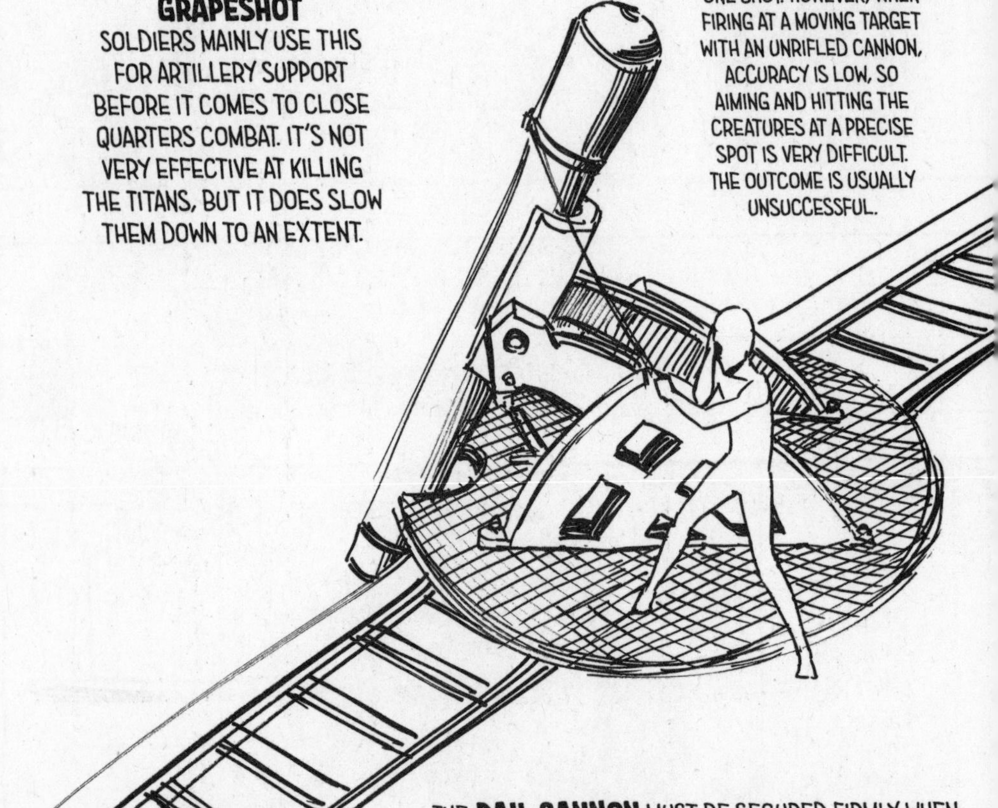

THE **RAIL CANNON** MUST BE SECURED FIRMLY WHEN FIRING OR ELSE THE WHOLE BATTERY ITSELF WILL BE BLOWN BACKWARDS. ONCE THE TARGET IS LOCKED ON, THE BATTERY IS SECURED TO THE RAIL. THESE NECESSARY ACTIONS DIMINISH THE SPEED OF FIRING.

Current Publicly Available Information

5. Wall-mounted Artillery

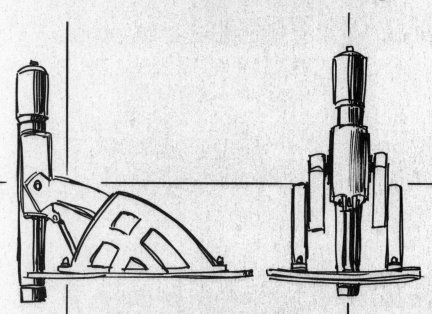

BEFORE THE ERA OF VERTICAL MANEUVERING GEAR, CANNONS WERE THE MAIN ANTI-TITAN WEAPON, BUT THEY LACKED MOBILITY AND WERE EXTREMELY DIFFICULT TO USE IN A GROUND WAR. ON THE OTHER HAND, THE WALL'S DEFENSE HAS BEEN IMPROVED THROUGH THE INSTALLATION OF MOUNTED CANNONS.

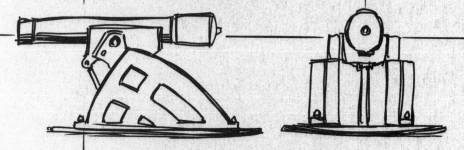

THE DIFFERENCE BETWEEN THESE AND TRADITIONAL MOBILE CANNONS IS THAT THE MOUNTED MODEL HAS THE ABILITY TO FIRE VERTICALLY DOWNWARD. THEIR STRUCTURE ALSO MITIGATES RECOIL.

ATTACK on TITAN

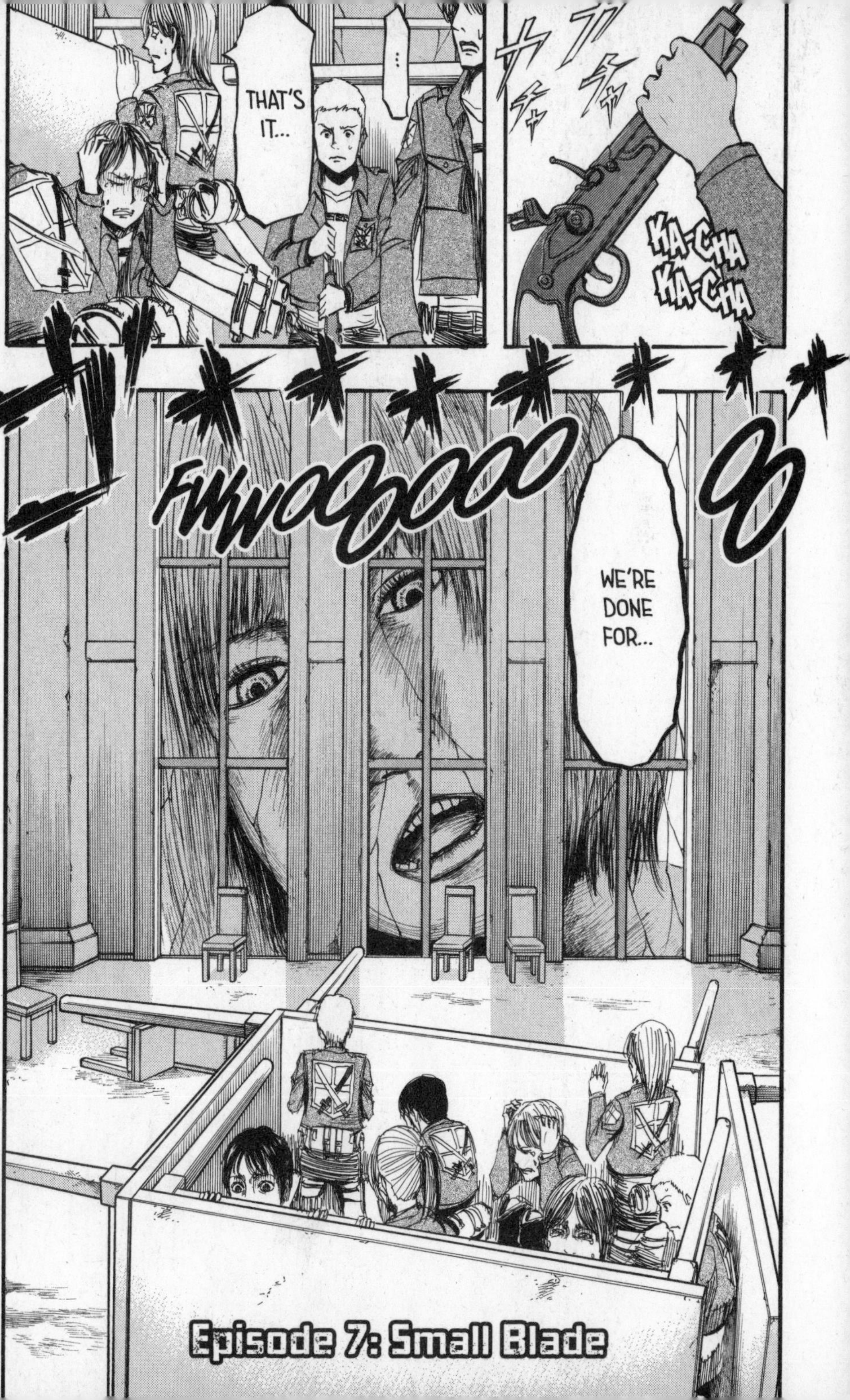
KA-CHA KA-CHA
...
THAT'S IT...
FWWOOOOOOO
WE'RE DONE FOR...

Episode 7: Small Blade

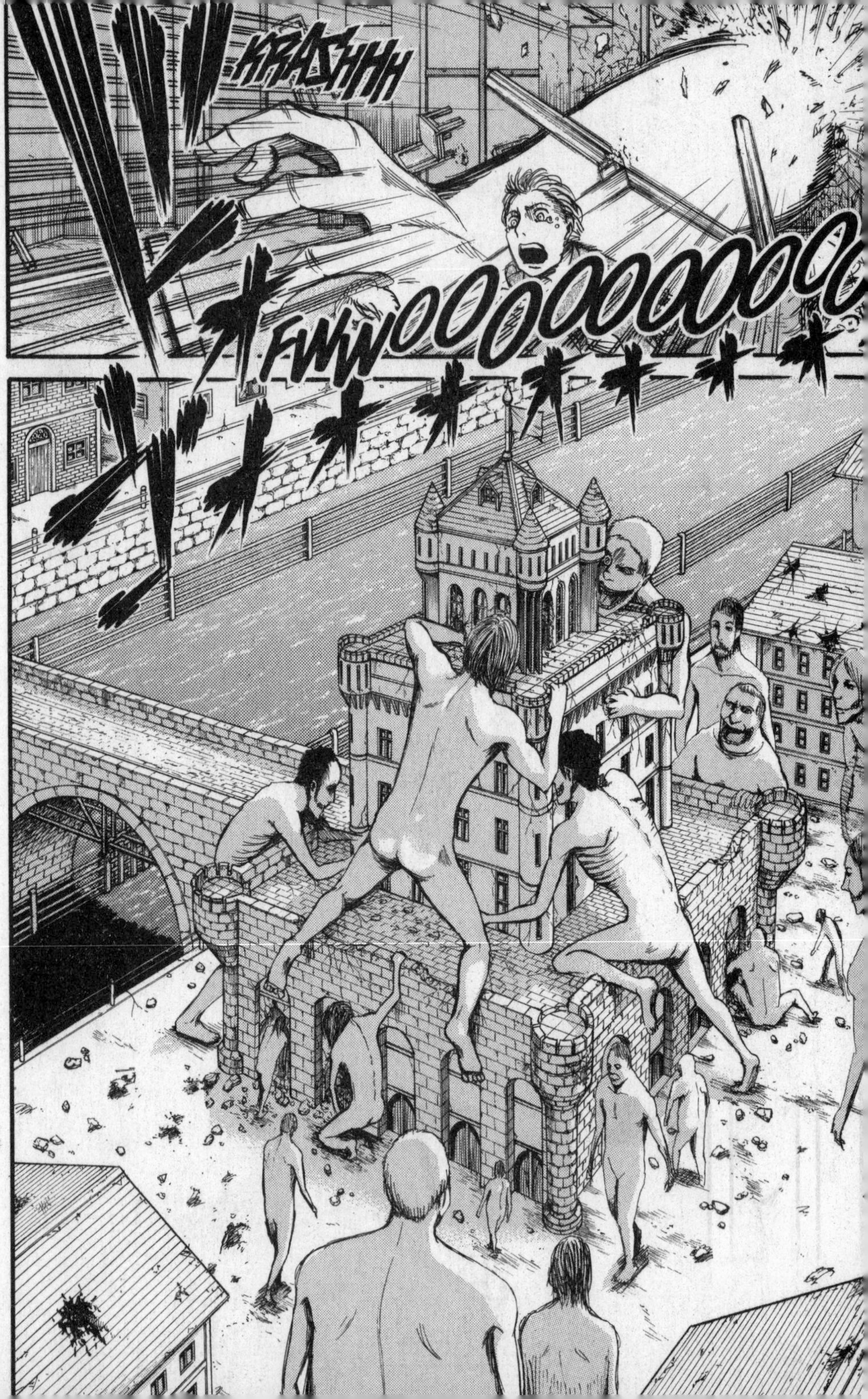
KRASHHH
FWWOOOOOOOOOO

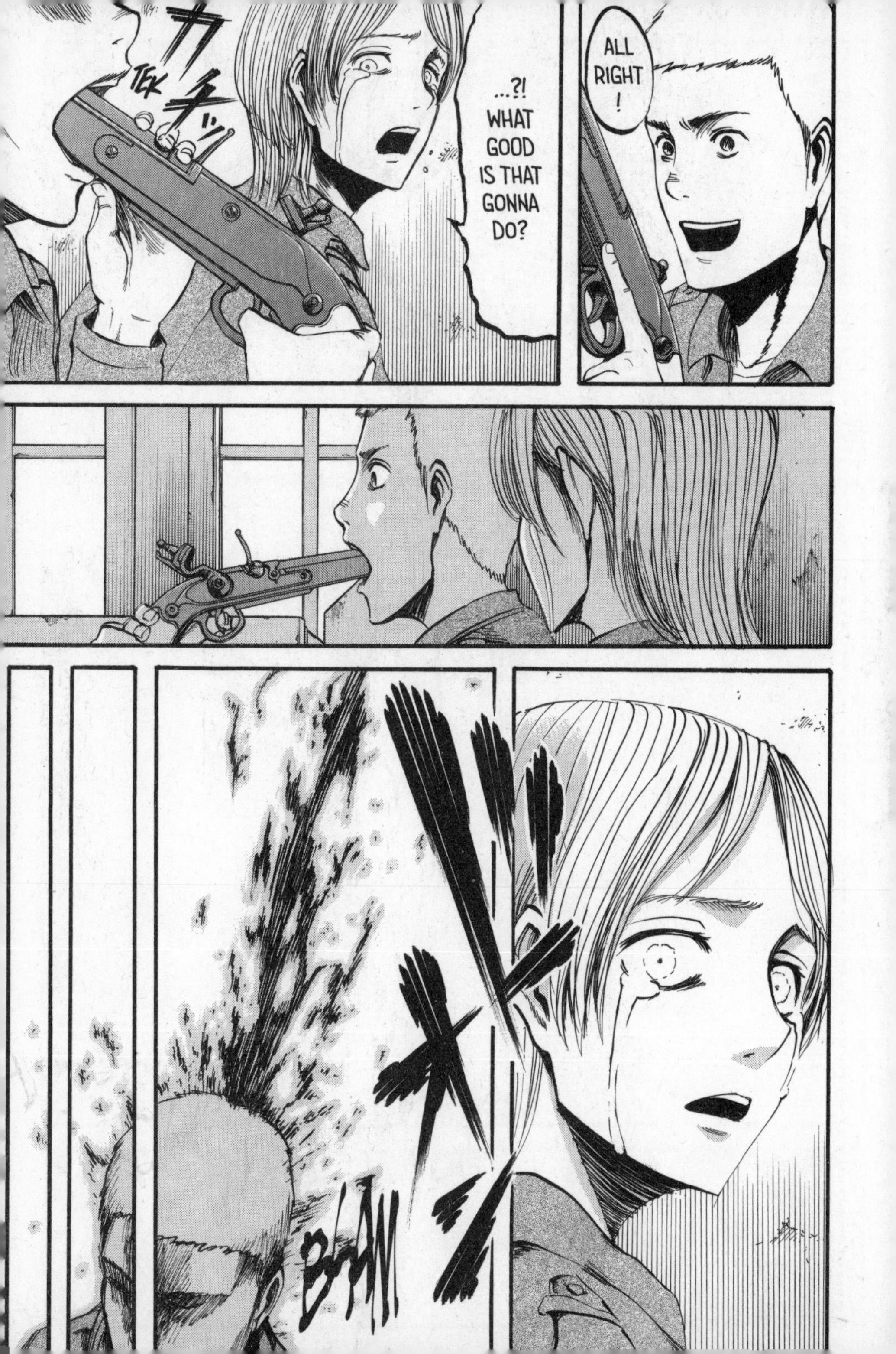
ALL RIGHT!
TEK
...?! WHAT GOOD IS THAT GONNA DO?
BLAM

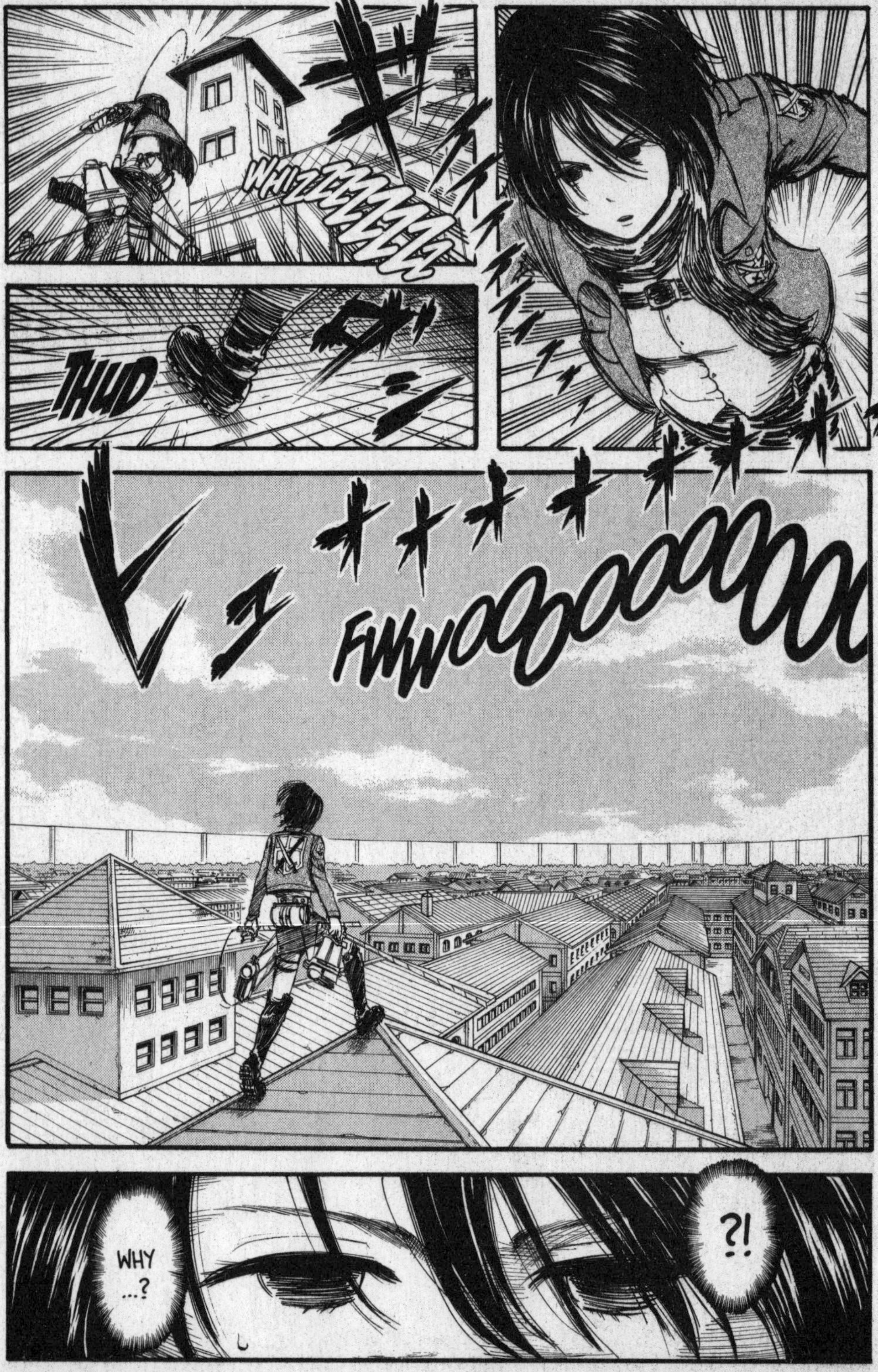
WHIZZZMMMMM
THUD
FWWOOOOOOOO
?!
WHY ...?

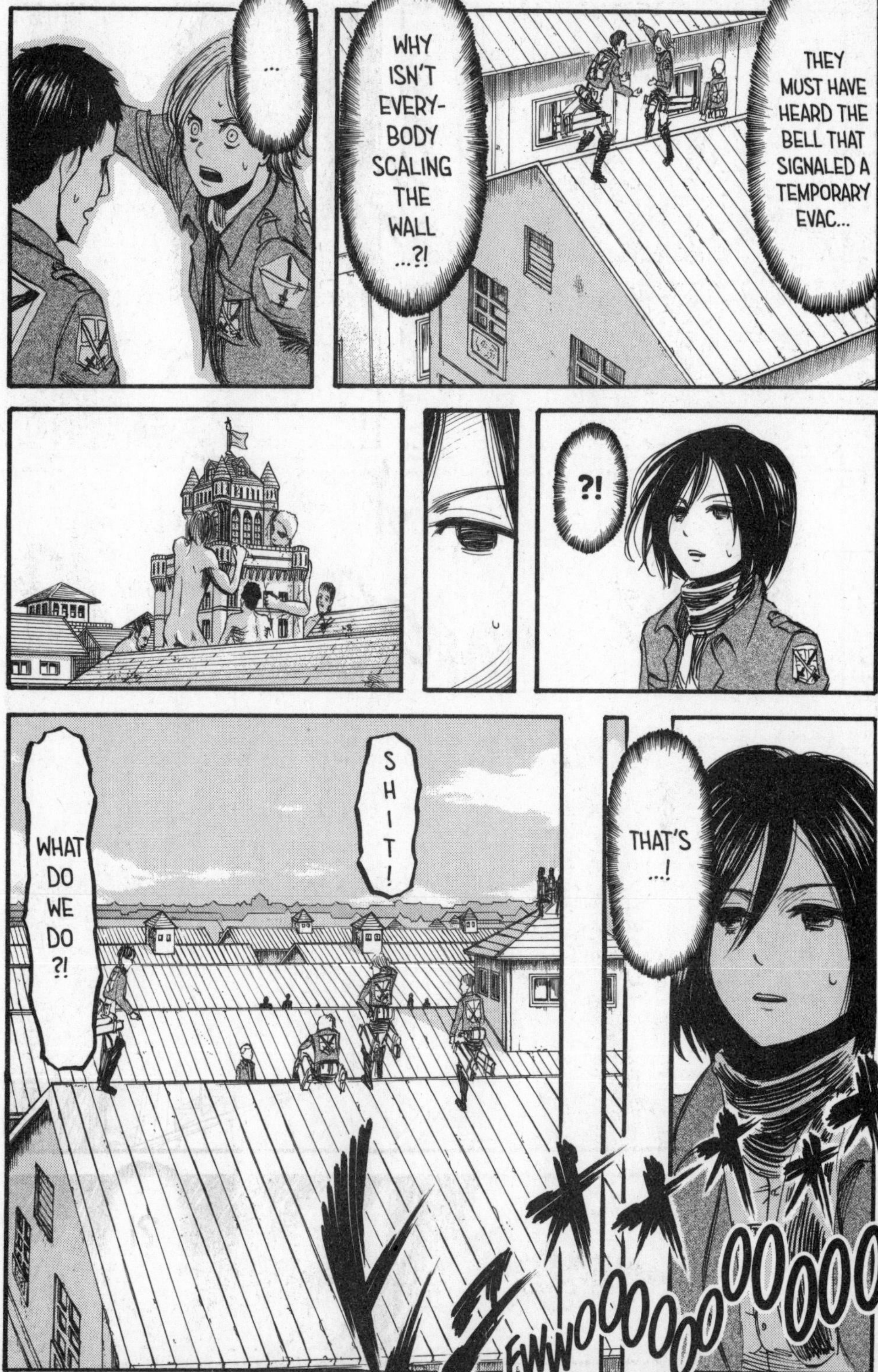
THEY MUST HAVE HEARD THE BELL THAT SIGNALED A TEMPORARY EVAC...
WHY ISN'T EVERY-BODY SCALING THE WALL ...?!
...
?!
THAT'S ...!
FWWOOOOOOOOOOOO
SHIT!
WHAT DO WE DO ?!

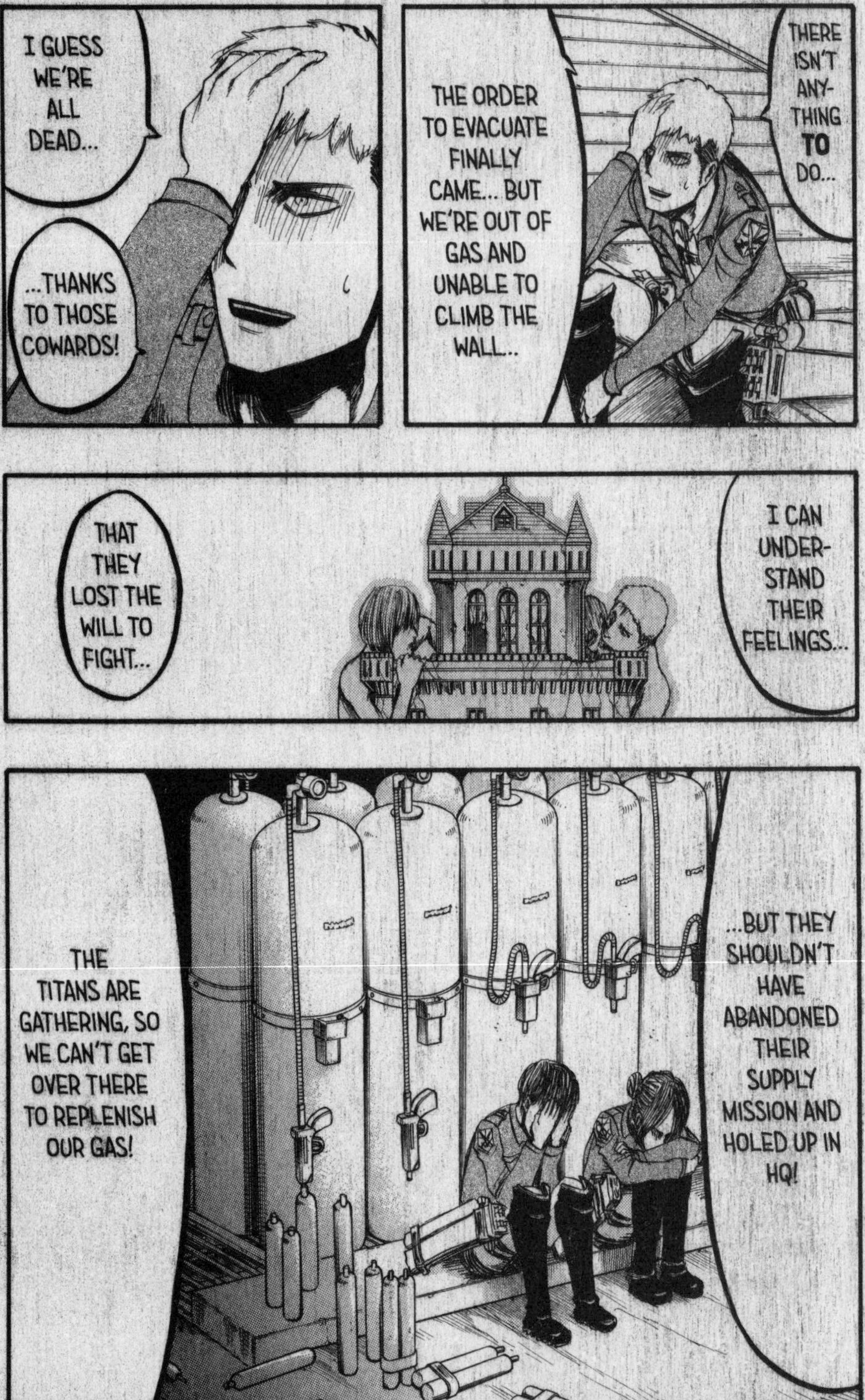
THERE ISN'T ANYTHING TO DO...
THE ORDER TO EVACUATE FINALLY CAME... BUT WE'RE OUT OF GAS AND UNABLE TO CLIMB THE WALL...
I GUESS WE'RE ALL DEAD...
...THANKS TO THOSE COWARDS!
I CAN UNDERSTAND THEIR FEELINGS...
THAT THEY LOST THE WILL TO FIGHT...
...BUT THEY SHOULDN'T HAVE ABANDONED THEIR SUPPLY MISSION AND HOLED UP IN HQ!
THE TITANS ARE GATHERING, SO WE CAN'T GET OVER THERE TO REPLENISH OUR GAS!

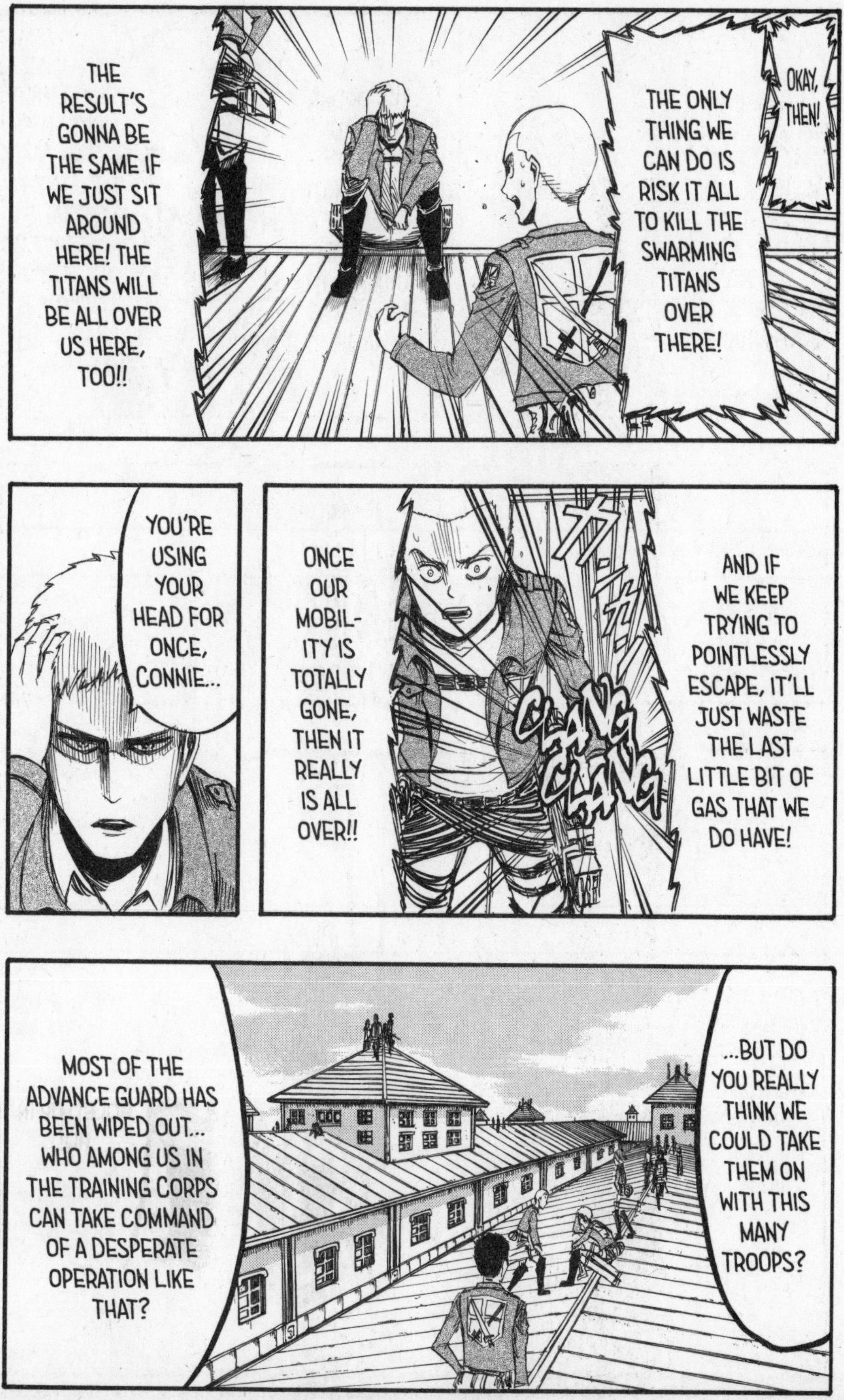
OKAY, THEN!
THE ONLY THING WE CAN DO IS RISK IT ALL TO KILL THE SWARMING TITANS OVER THERE!
THE RESULT'S GONNA BE THE SAME IF WE JUST SIT AROUND HERE! THE TITANS WILL BE ALL OVER US HERE, TOO!!
AND IF WE KEEP TRYING TO POINTLESSLY ESCAPE, IT'LL JUST WASTE THE LAST LITTLE BIT OF GAS THAT WE DO HAVE!
CLANG CLANG
ONCE OUR MOBIL-ITY IS TOTALLY GONE, THEN IT REALLY IS ALL OVER!!
YOU'RE USING YOUR HEAD FOR ONCE, CONNIE...
...BUT DO YOU REALLY THINK WE COULD TAKE THEM ON WITH THIS MANY TROOPS?
MOST OF THE ADVANCE GUARD HAS BEEN WIPED OUT... WHO AMONG US IN THE TRAINING CORPS CAN TAKE COMMAND OF A DESPERATE OPERATION LIKE THAT?

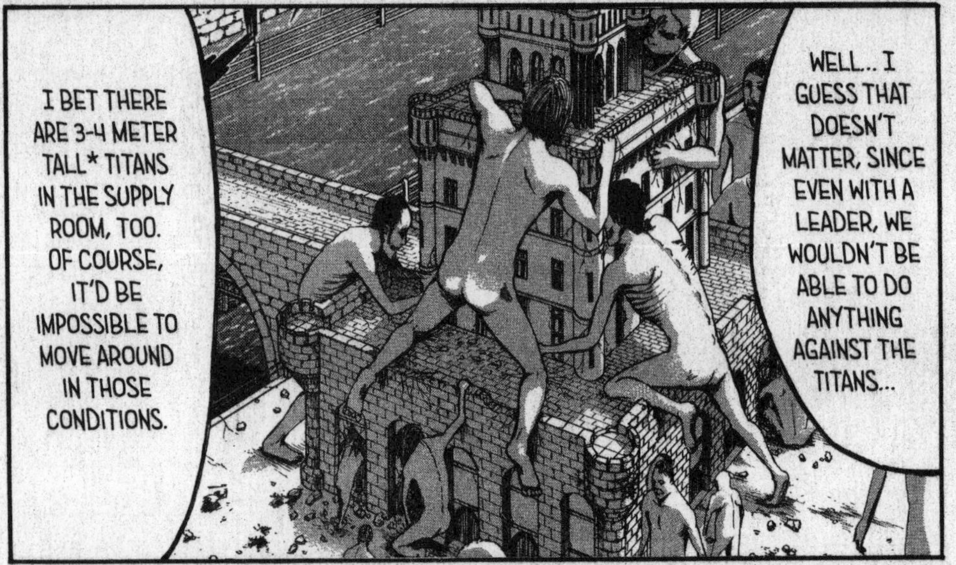
WELL.. I GUESS THAT DOESN'T MATTER, SINCE EVEN WITH A LEADER, WE WOULDN'T BE ABLE TO DO ANYTHING AGAINST THE TITANS...
I BET THERE ARE 3-4 METER TALL* TITANS IN THE SUPPLY ROOM, TOO. OF COURSE, IT'D BE IMPOSSIBLE TO MOVE AROUND IN THOSE CONDITIONS.

* approx. 10-13 feet tall

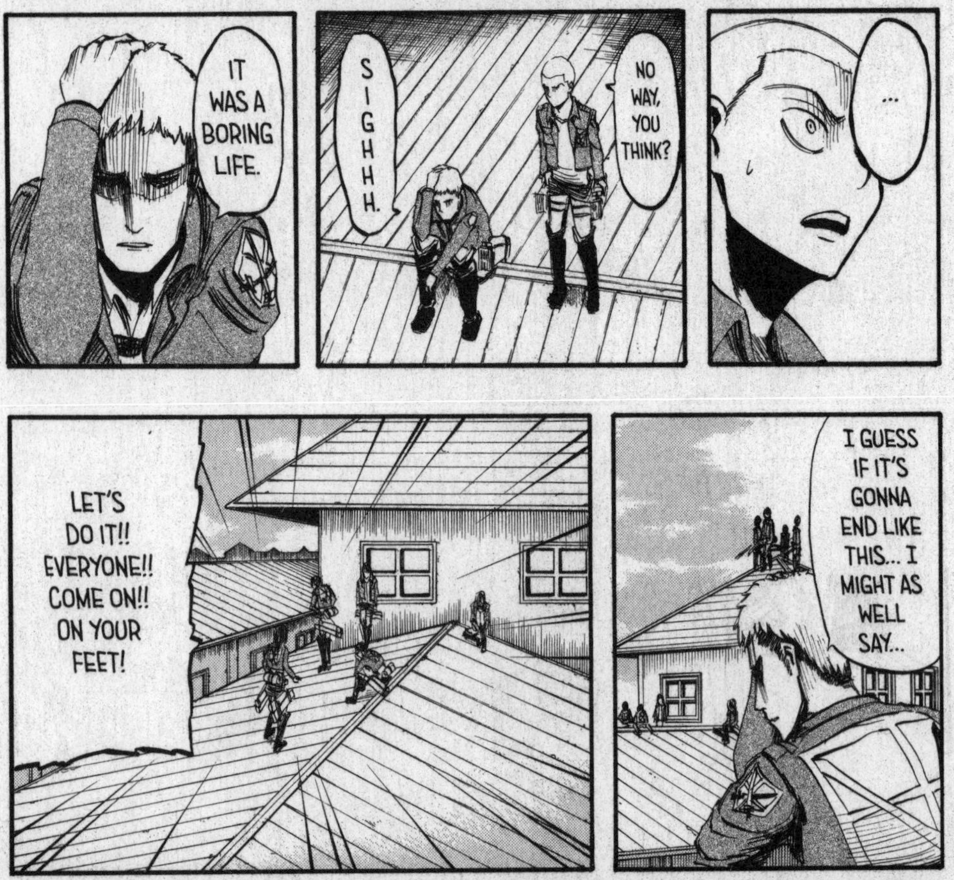
...
NO WAY, YOU THINK?
SIGHHH.
IT WAS A BORING LIFE.
I GUESS IF IT'S GONNA END LIKE THIS... I MIGHT AS WELL SAY...
LET'S DO IT!! EVERYONE!! COME ON!! ON YOUR FEET!

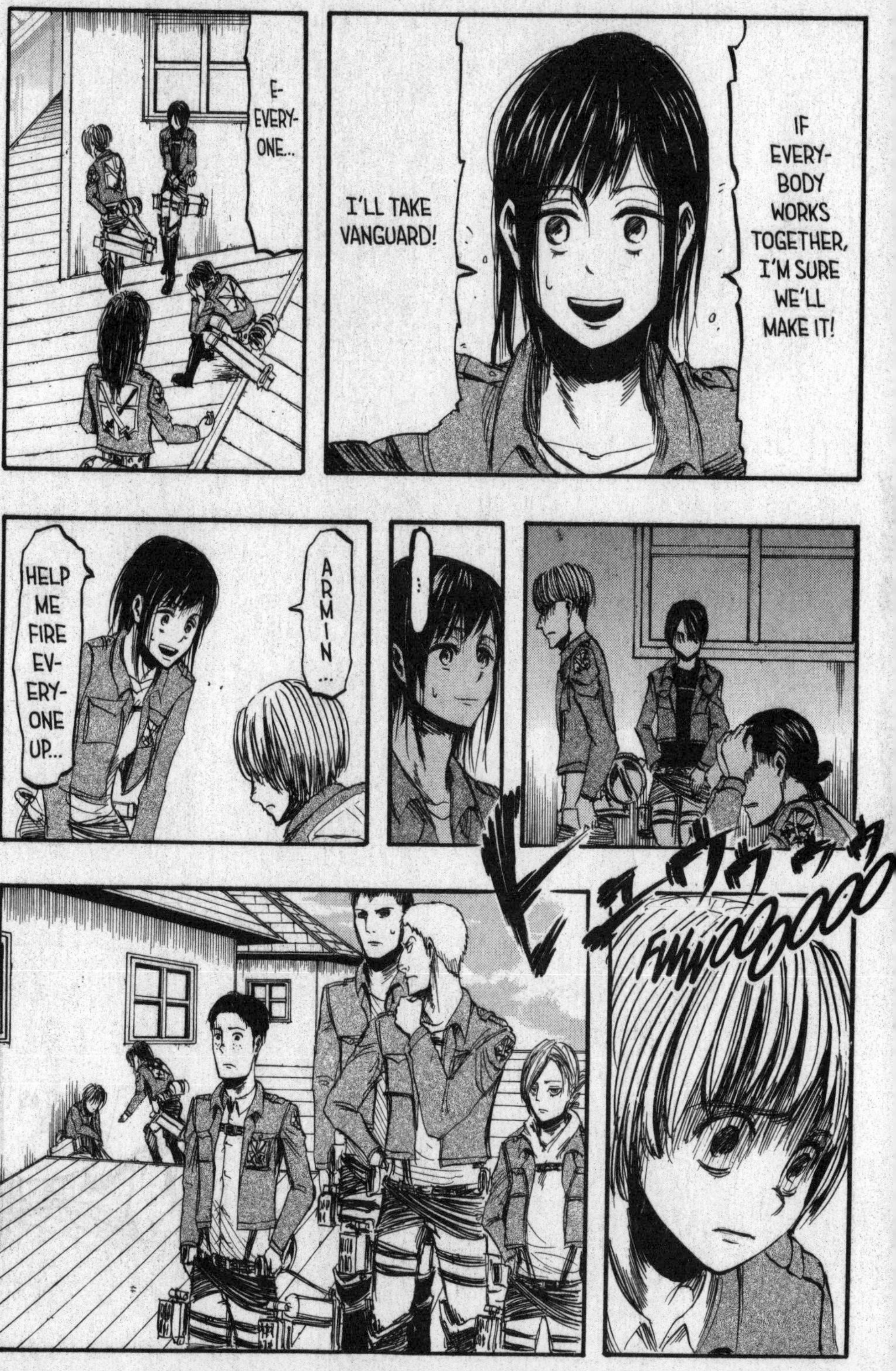
IF EVERYBODY WORKS TOGETHER, I'M SURE WE'LL MAKE IT!
I'LL TAKE VANGUARD!
E- EVERYONE...
...
ARMIN...
HELP ME FIRE EVERYONE UP...
FWWOOOOO

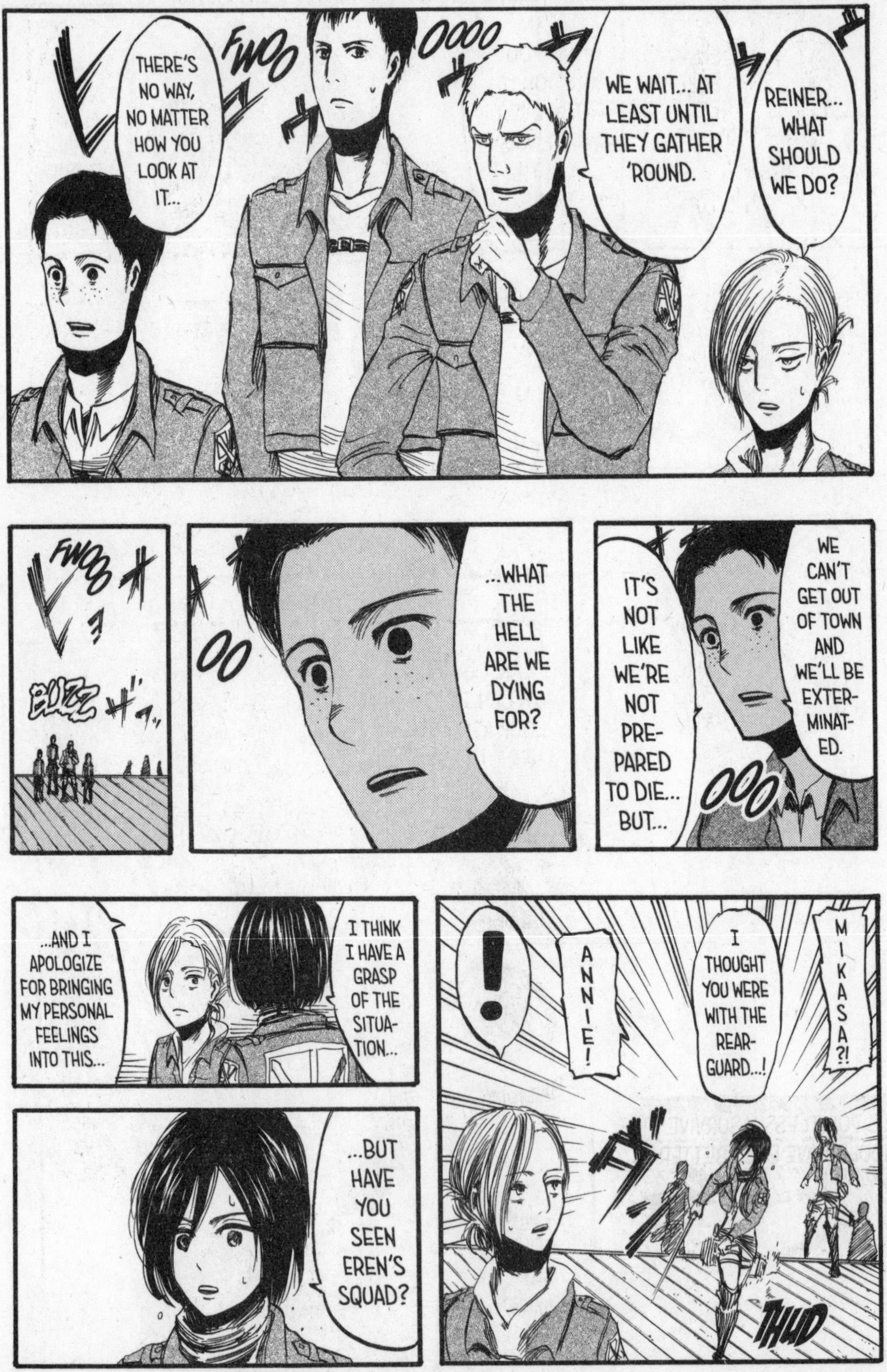
REINER... WHAT SHOULD WE DO?
WE WAIT... AT LEAST UNTIL THEY GATHER 'ROUND.
FWOOOOOOO
THERE'S NO WAY, NO MATTER HOW YOU LOOK AT IT...
WE CAN'T GET OUT OF TOWN AND WE'LL BE EXTERMINATED.
IT'S NOT LIKE WE'RE NOT PREPARED TO DIE... BUT...
OOO
...WHAT THE HELL ARE WE DYING FOR?
OO
FWOOO
BUZZ
MIKASA?!
I THOUGHT YOU WERE WITH THE REARGUARD...!
ANNIE!
!
THUD
I THINK I HAVE A GRASP OF THE SITUATION...
...AND I APOLOGIZE FOR BRINGING MY PERSONAL FEELINGS INTO THIS...
...BUT HAVE YOU SEEN EREN'S SQUAD?

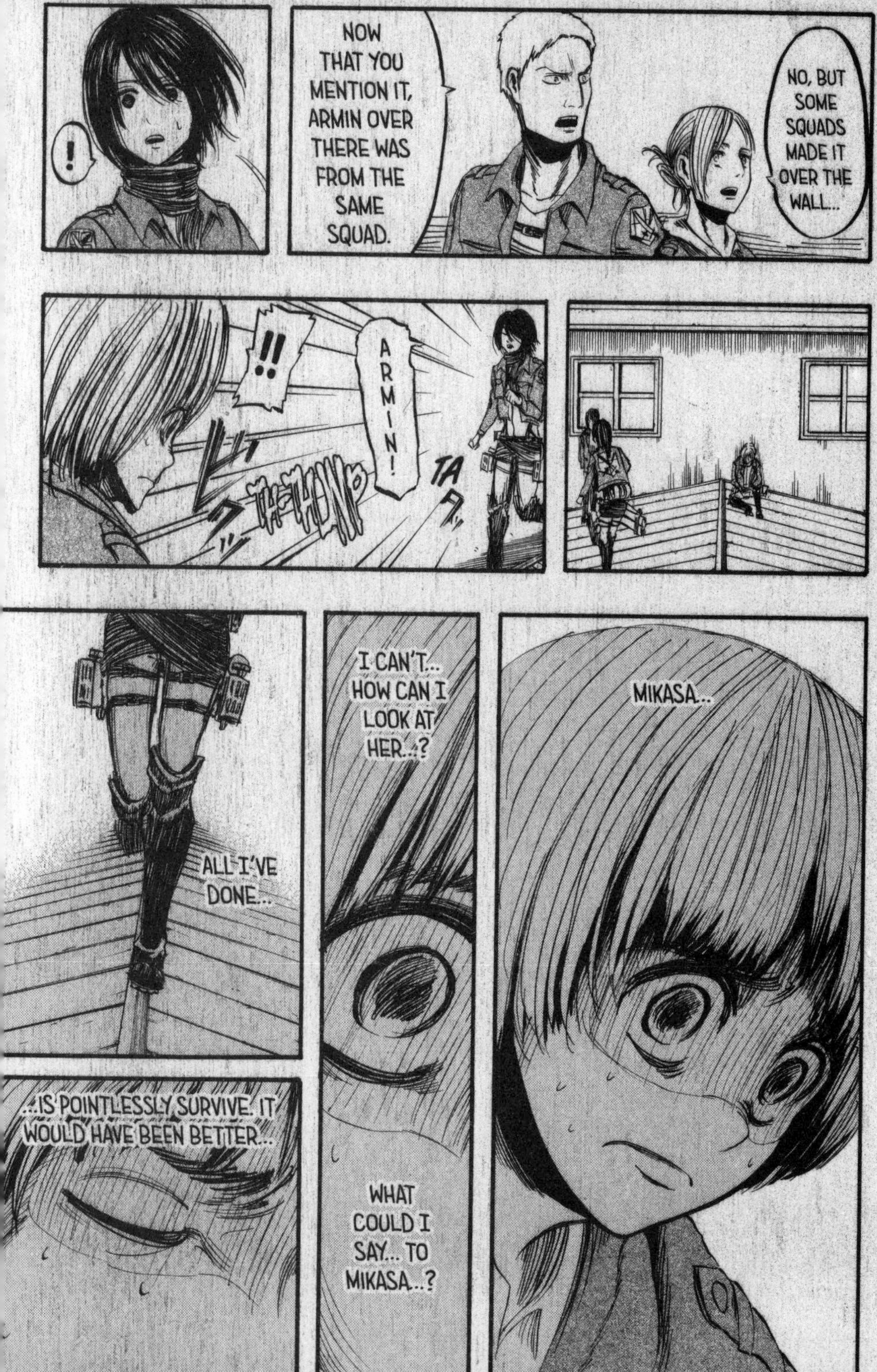
NO, BUT SOME SQUADS MADE IT OVER THE WALL...
NOW THAT YOU MENTION IT, ARMIN OVER THERE WAS FROM THE SAME SQUAD.
!
ARMIN!
TA TA
!!
MIKASA...
I CAN'T... HOW CAN I LOOK AT HER...?
WHAT COULD I SAY... TO MIKASA...?
ALL I'VE DONE...
...IS POINTLESSLY SURVIVE. IT WOULD HAVE BEEN BETTER...

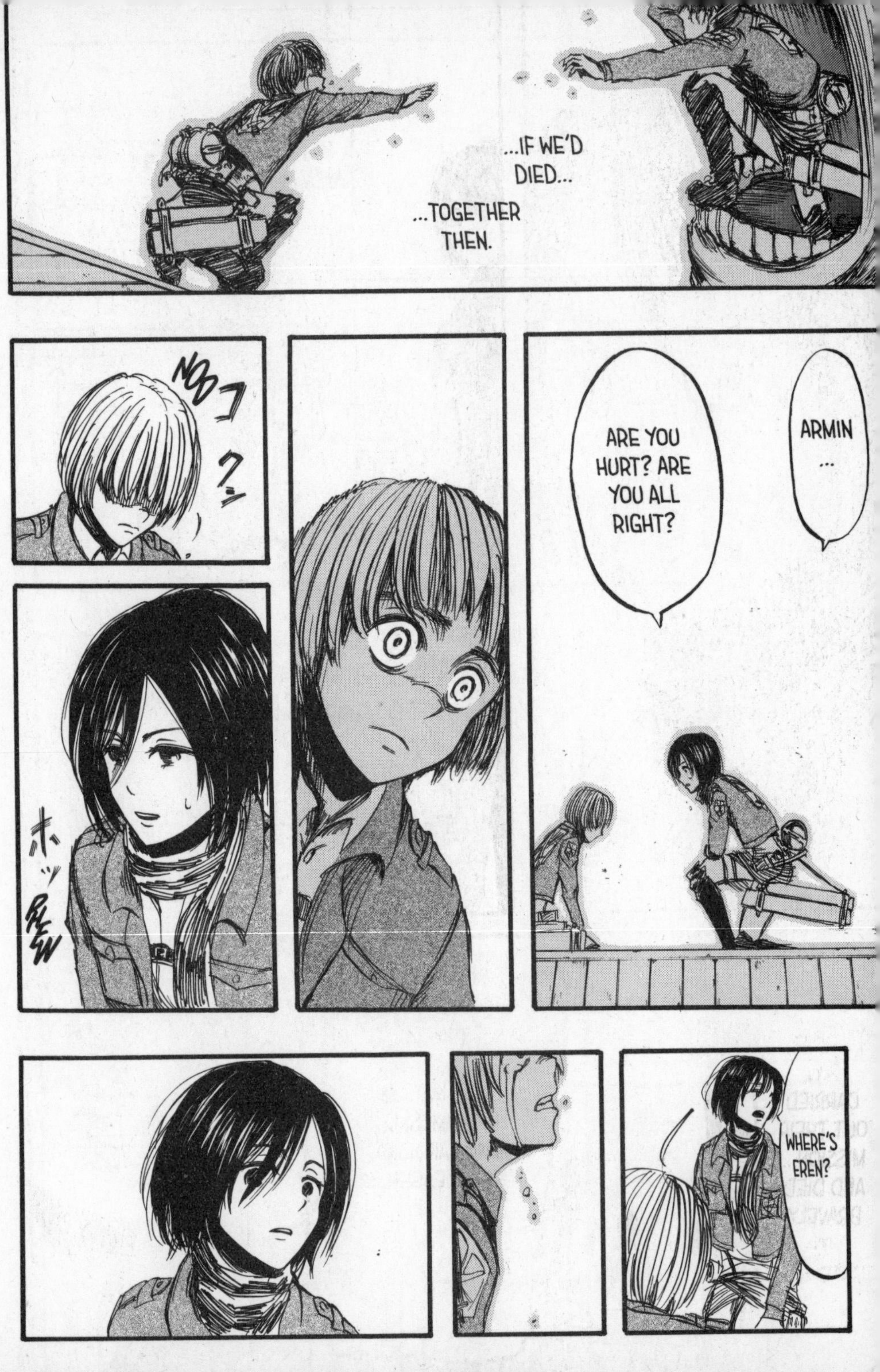
...IF WE'D DIED...
...TOGETHER THEN.
ARMIN ...
ARE YOU HURT? ARE YOU ALL RIGHT?
NOD
PHEW
WHERE'S EREN?

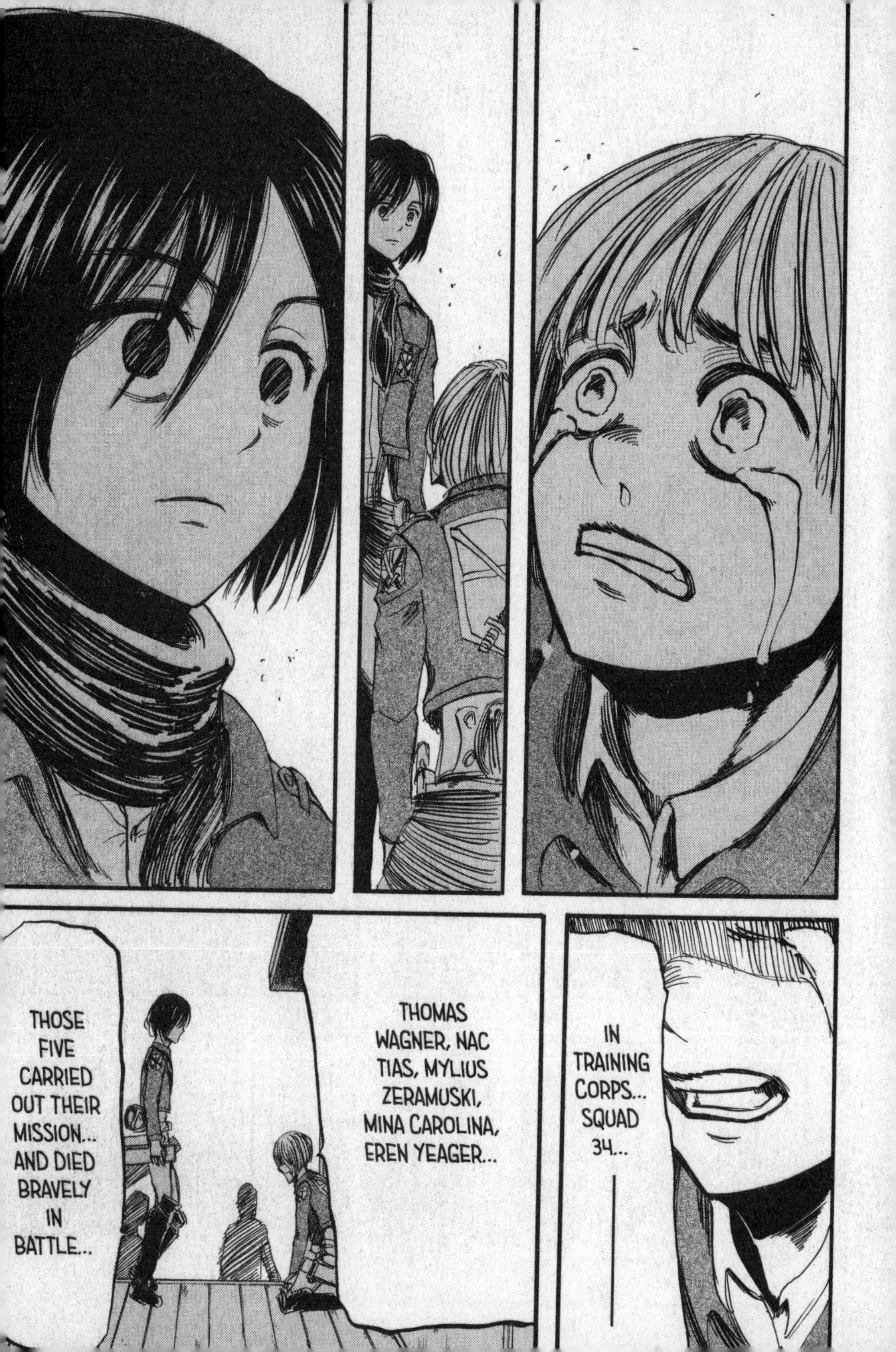
IN TRAINING CORPS... SQUAD 34...
THOMAS WAGNER, NAC TIAS, MYLIUS ZERAMUSKI, MINA CAROLINA, EREN YEAGER...
THOSE FIVE CARRIED OUT THEIR MISSION... AND DIED BRAVELY IN BATTLE...

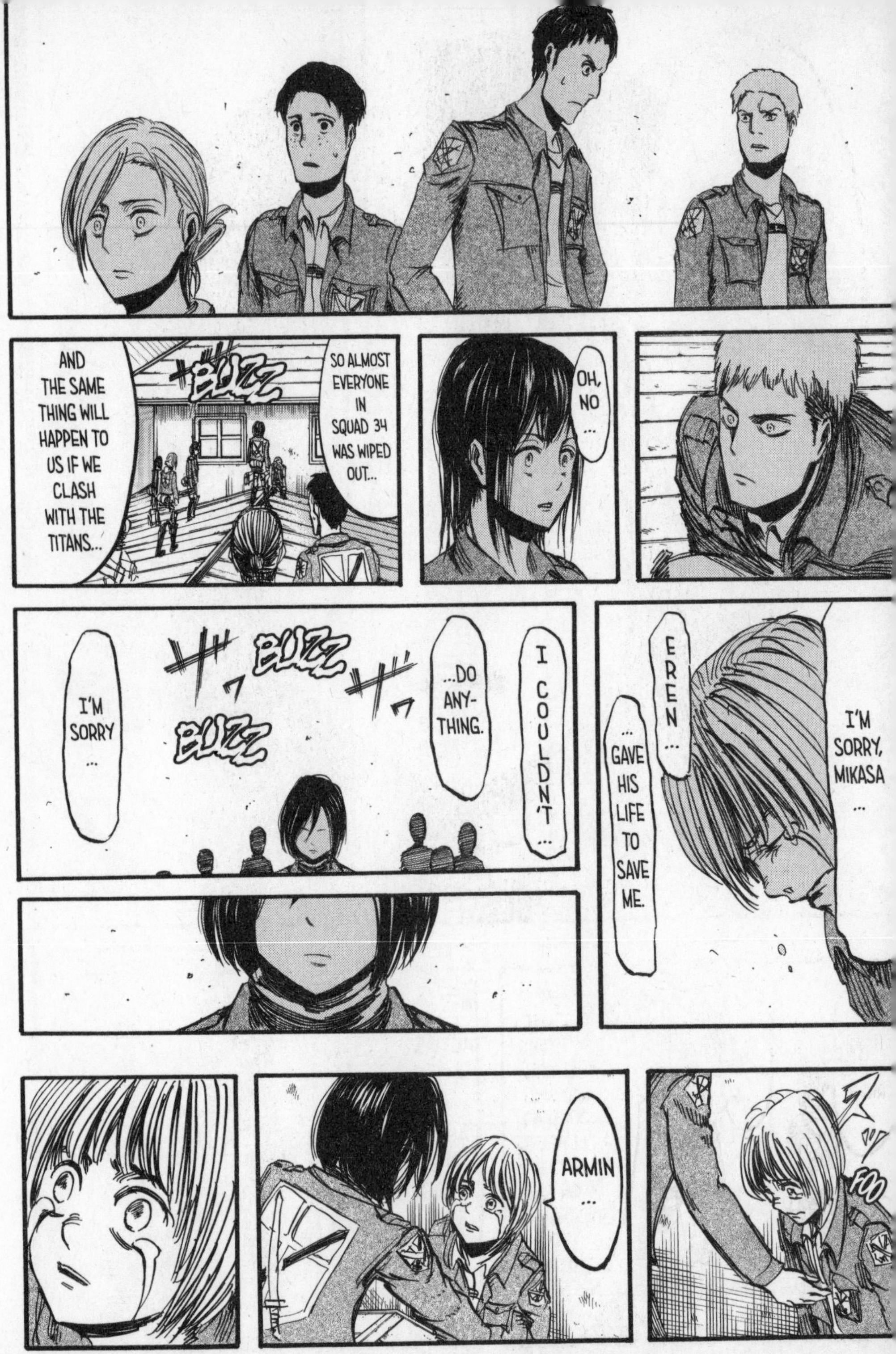
OH, NO ...
SO ALMOST EVERYONE IN SQUAD 34 WAS WIPED OUT...
BUZZ
AND THE SAME THING WILL HAPPEN TO US IF WE CLASH WITH THE TITANS...
I'M SORRY, MIKASA ...
EREN ...
... GAVE HIS LIFE TO SAVE ME.
I COULDN'T ...
...DO ANYTHING.
BUZZ
BUZZ
I'M SORRY ...
FOO
ARMIN ...

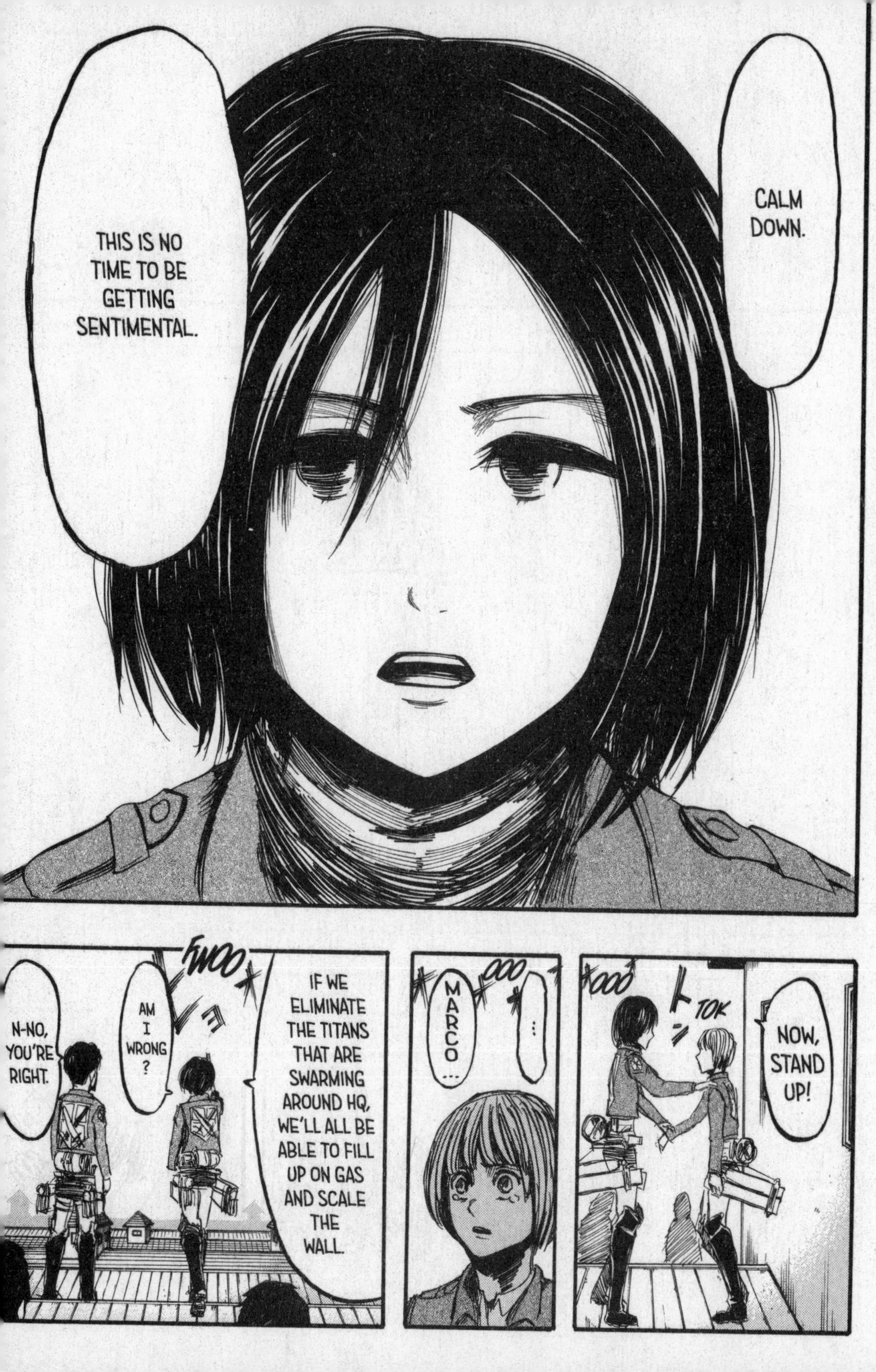
CALM DOWN.
THIS IS NO TIME TO BE GETTING SENTIMENTAL.
FWOOO
TOK
NOW, STAND UP!
OOO
...
MARCO...
FWOO
IF WE ELIMINATE THE TITANS THAT ARE SWARMING AROUND HQ, WE'LL ALL BE ABLE TO FILL UP ON GAS AND SCALE THE WALL.
AM I WRONG?
N-NO, YOU'RE RIGHT.

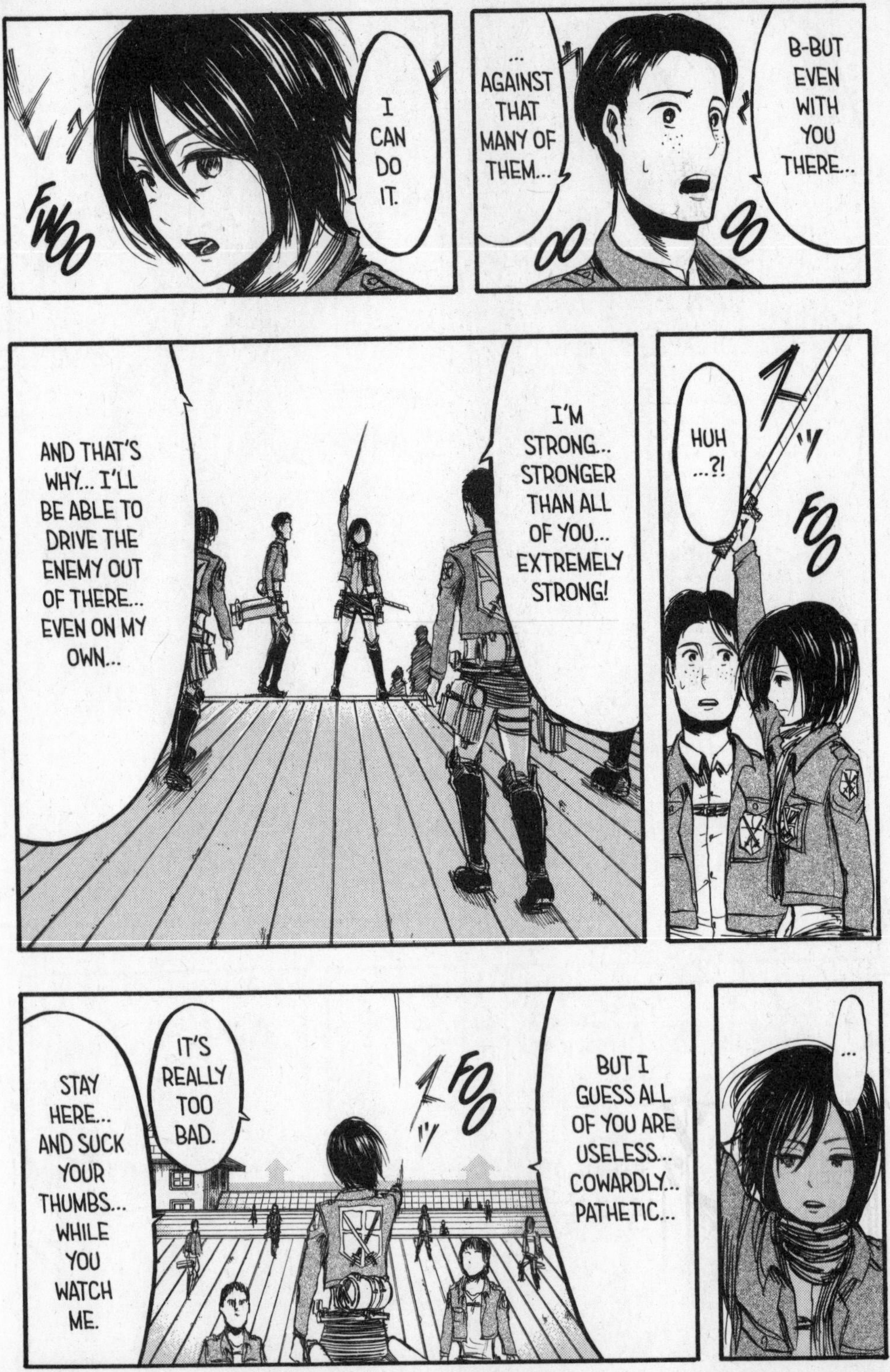
B-BUT EVEN WITH YOU THERE...
OO
... AGAINST THAT MANY OF THEM...
OO
I CAN DO IT.
FWOO
HUH ...?!
FOO
I'M STRONG... STRONGER THAN ALL OF YOU... EXTREMELY STRONG!
AND THAT'S WHY... I'LL BE ABLE TO DRIVE THE ENEMY OUT OF THERE... EVEN ON MY OWN...
...
BUT I GUESS ALL OF YOU ARE USELESS... COWARDLY... PATHETIC...
FOO
IT'S REALLY TOO BAD.
STAY HERE... AND SUCK YOUR THUMBS... WHILE YOU WATCH ME.

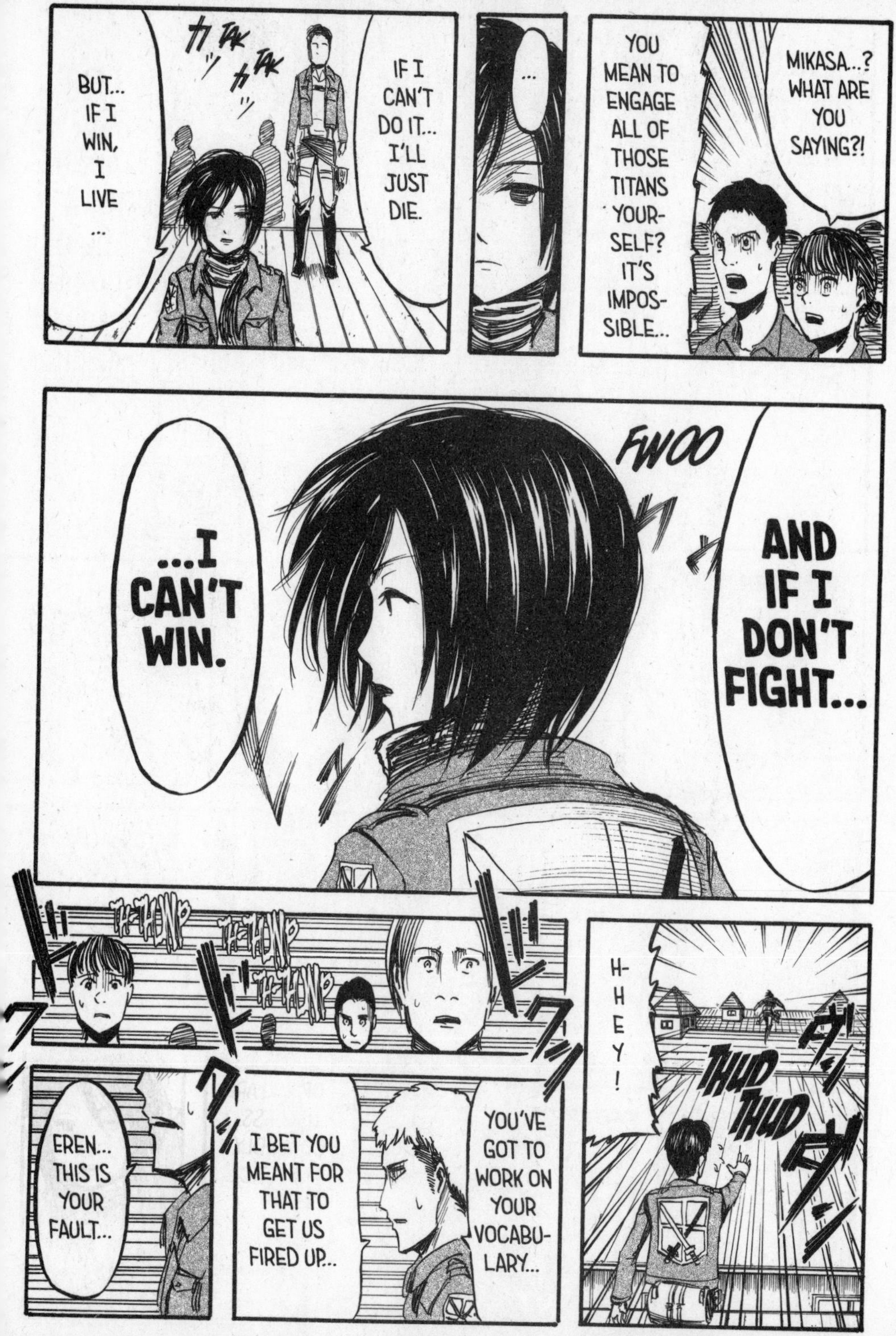
MIKASA...? WHAT ARE YOU SAYING?!
YOU MEAN TO ENGAGE ALL OF THOSE TITANS YOURSELF? IT'S IMPOSSIBLE...
...
IF I CAN'T DO IT... I'LL JUST DIE.
TAK
TAK
BUT... IF I WIN, I LIVE ...
FWOO
AND IF I DON'T FIGHT...
...I CAN'T WIN.
H-HEY!
THUD
THUD
THA-THUMP
THA-THUMP
THA-THUMP
YOU'VE GOT TO WORK ON YOUR VOCABULARY...
I BET YOU MEANT FOR THAT TO GET US FIRED UP...
EREN... THIS IS YOUR FAULT...

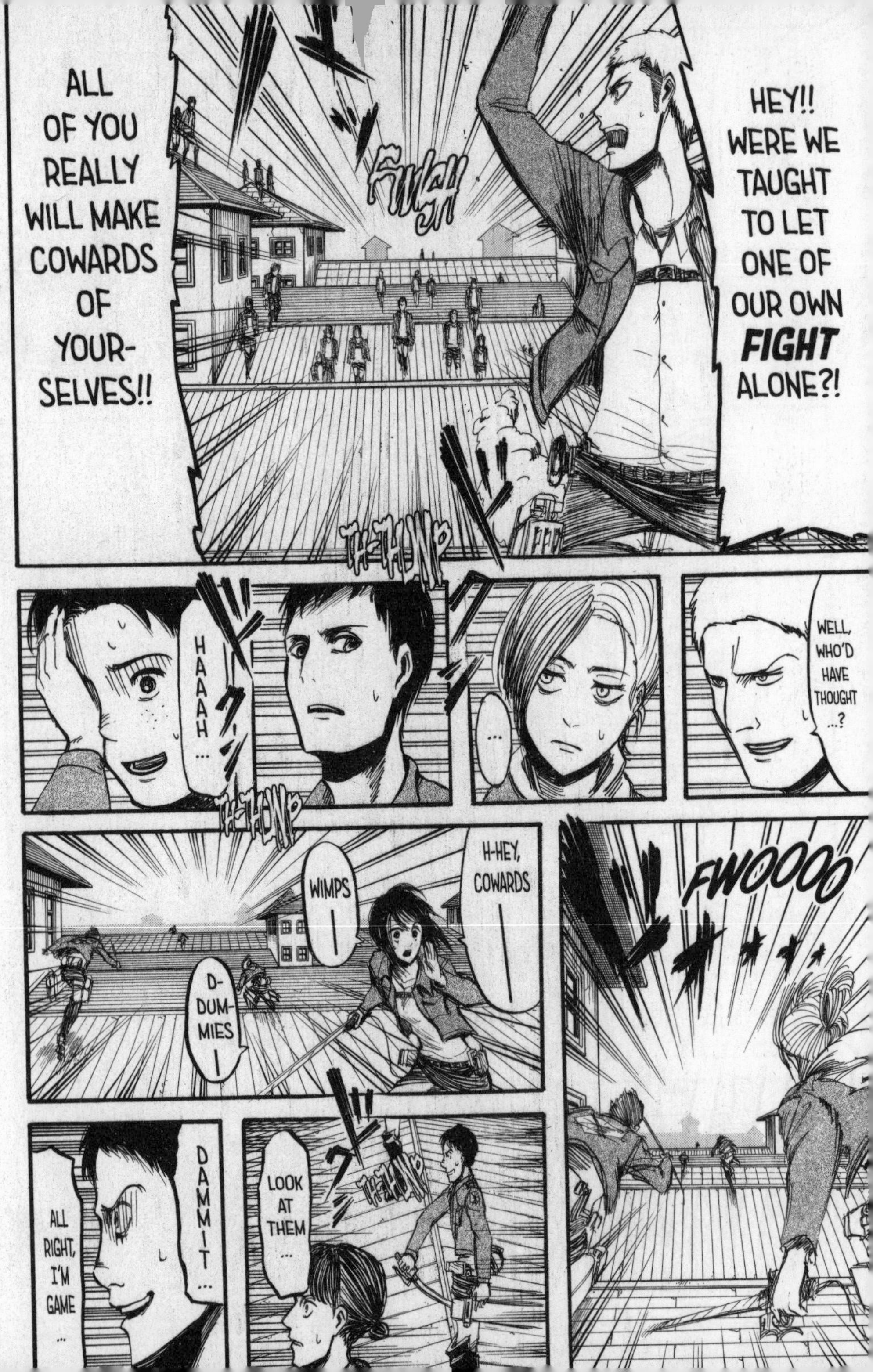
HEY!! WERE WE TAUGHT TO LET ONE OF OUR OWN **FIGHT** ALONE?!
ALL OF YOU REALLY WILL MAKE COWARDS OF YOUR-SELVES!!
WELL, WHO'D HAVE THOUGHT ...?
...
HAAAAH ...
FWOOOO
H-HEY, COWARDS —
WIMPS —
D-DUMMIES —
LOOK AT THEM ...
DAMMIT ...
ALL RIGHT, I'M GAME ...

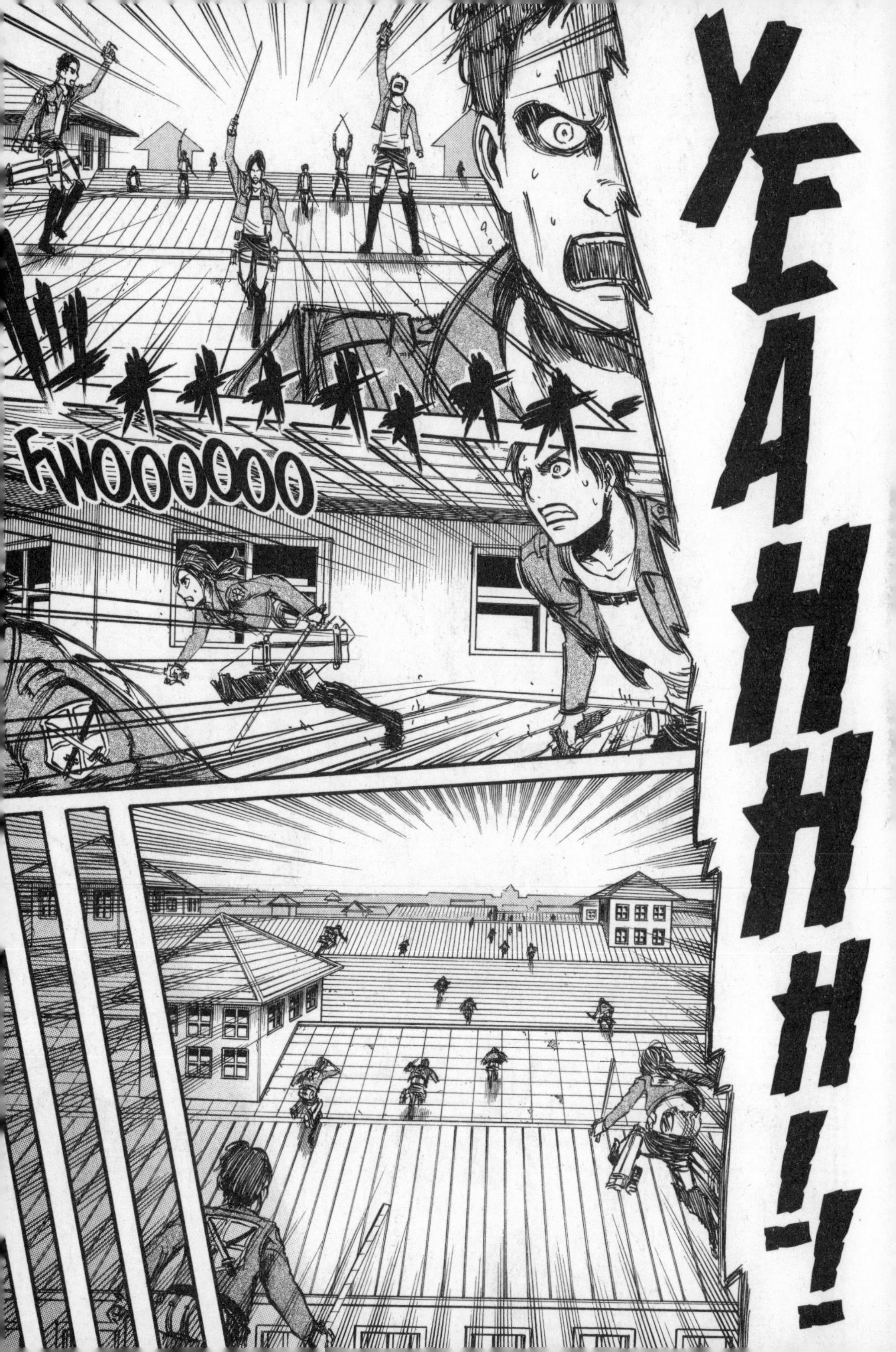

YEAHHHH!!!
FWOOOOOO

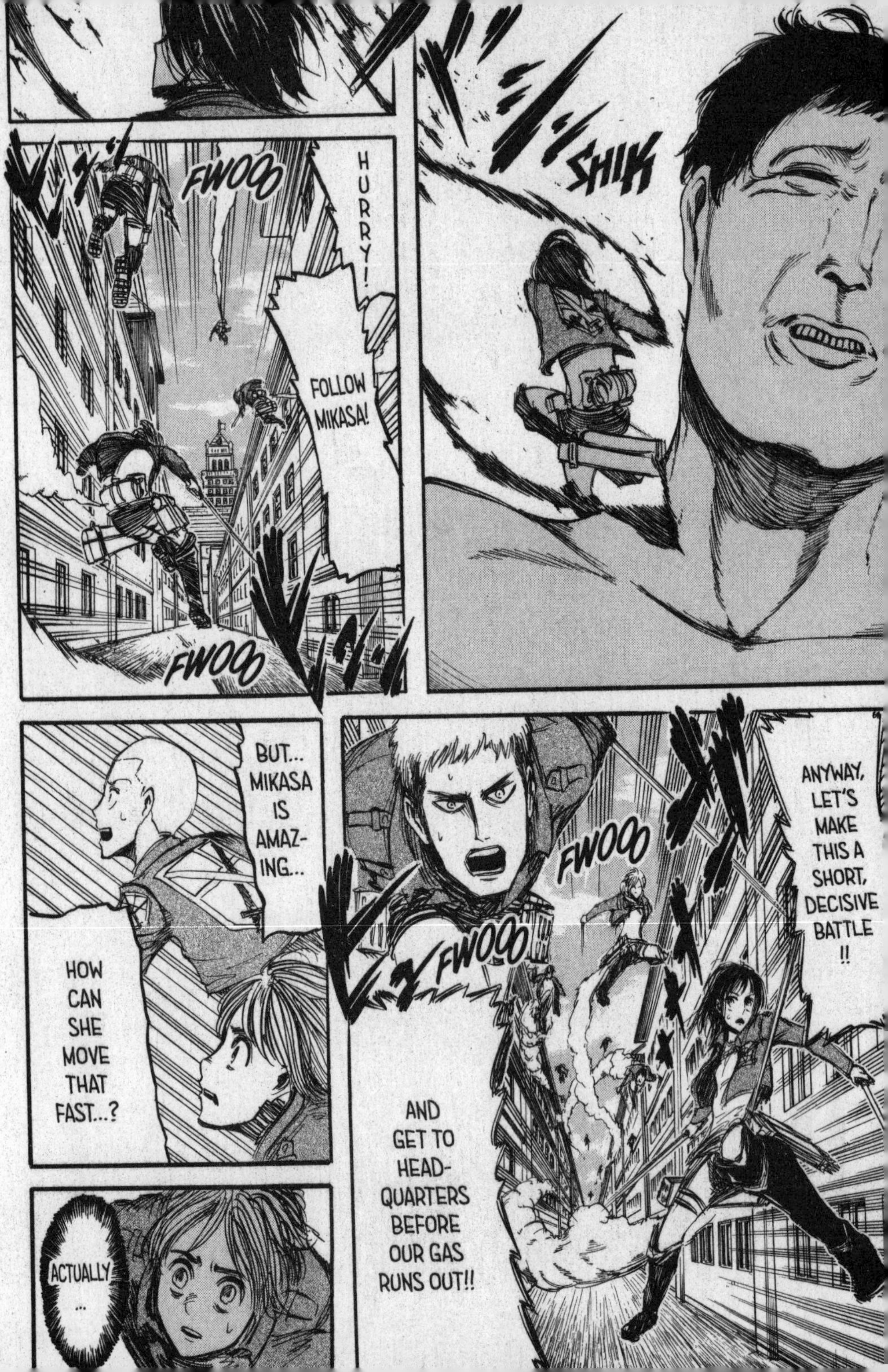
SHIK
FWOOO
HURRY!
FOLLOW MIKASA!
FWOOO
ANYWAY, LET'S MAKE THIS A SHORT, DECISIVE BATTLE!!
FWOOO
FWOOO
AND GET TO HEAD-QUARTERS BEFORE OUR GAS RUNS OUT!!
BUT... MIKASA IS AMAZ-ING...
HOW CAN SHE MOVE THAT FAST...?
ACTUALLY...

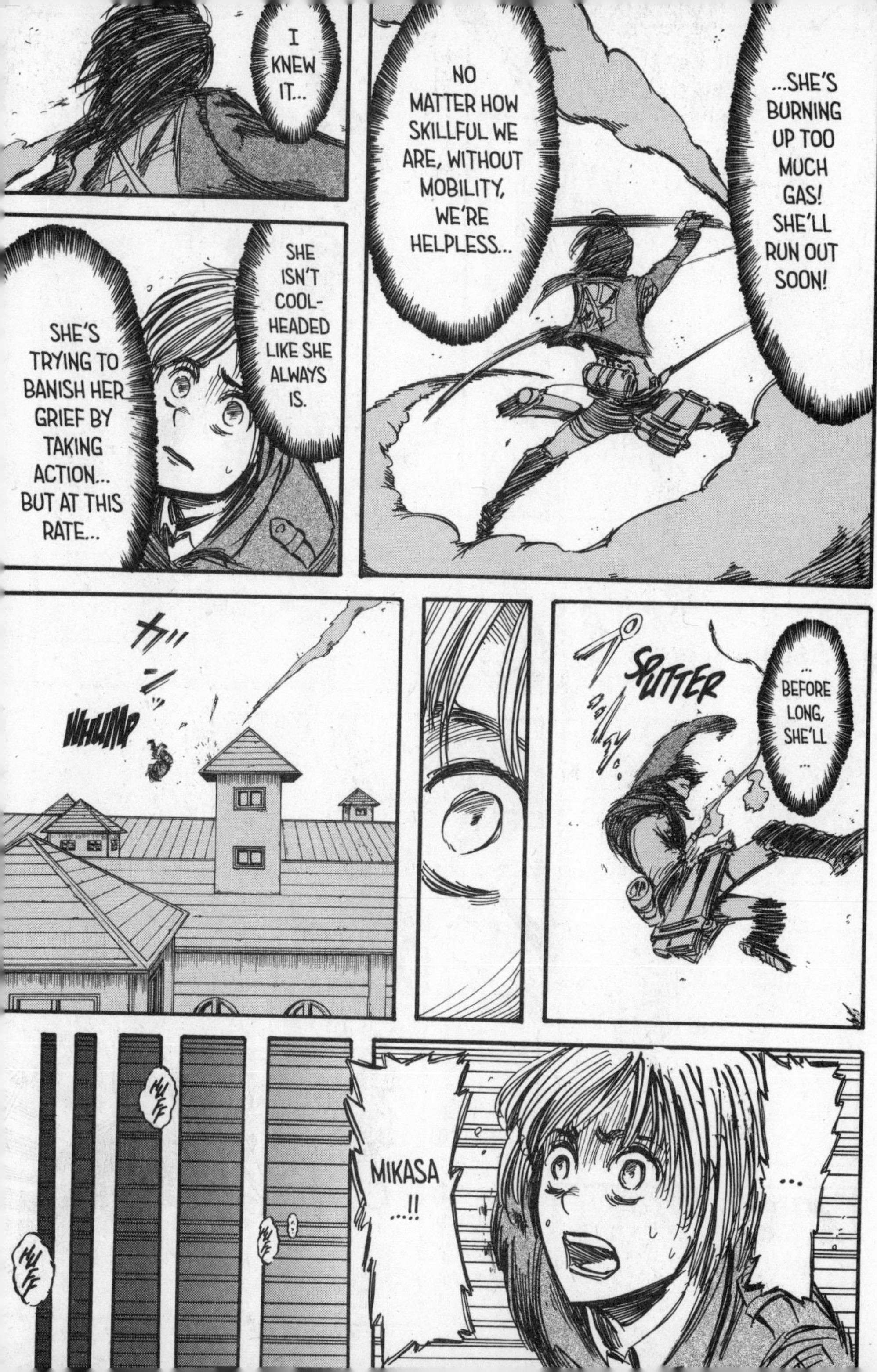
...SHE'S BURNING UP TOO MUCH GAS! SHE'LL RUN OUT SOON!
NO MATTER HOW SKILLFUL WE ARE, WITHOUT MOBILITY, WE'RE HELPLESS...
I KNEW IT...
SHE ISN'T COOL-HEADED LIKE SHE ALWAYS IS.
SHE'S TRYING TO BANISH HER GRIEF BY TAKING ACTION... BUT AT THIS RATE...
... BEFORE LONG, SHE'LL ...
SPUTTER
WHUMP
...
MIKASA ...!!
HUFF
HUFF
HUFF

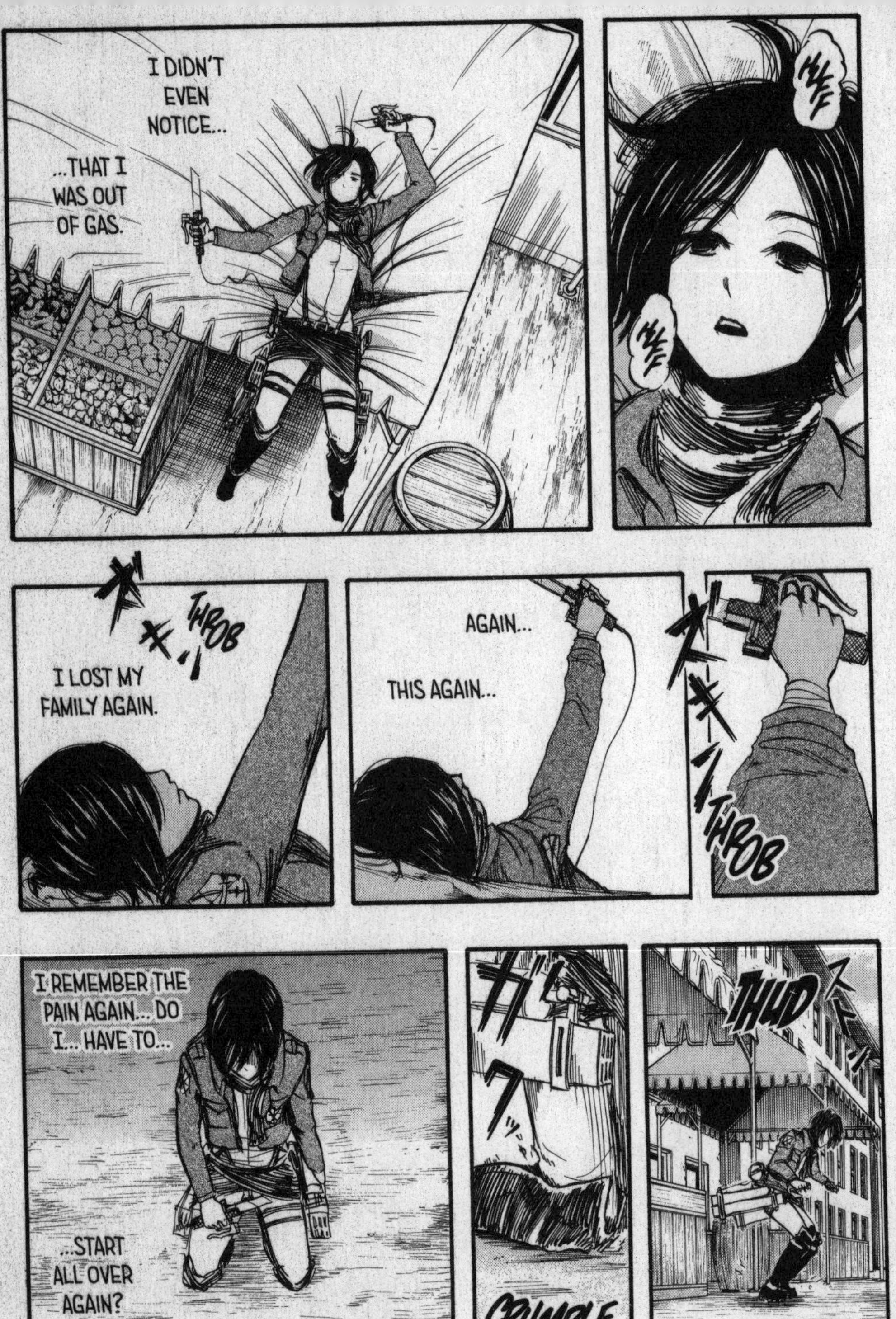
I DIDN'T EVEN NOTICE...
...THAT I WAS OUT OF GAS.
THROB
AGAIN...
THIS AGAIN...
THROB
I LOST MY FAMILY AGAIN.
THUD
CRUMPLE
I REMEMBER THE PAIN AGAIN... DO I... HAVE TO...
...START ALL OVER AGAIN?

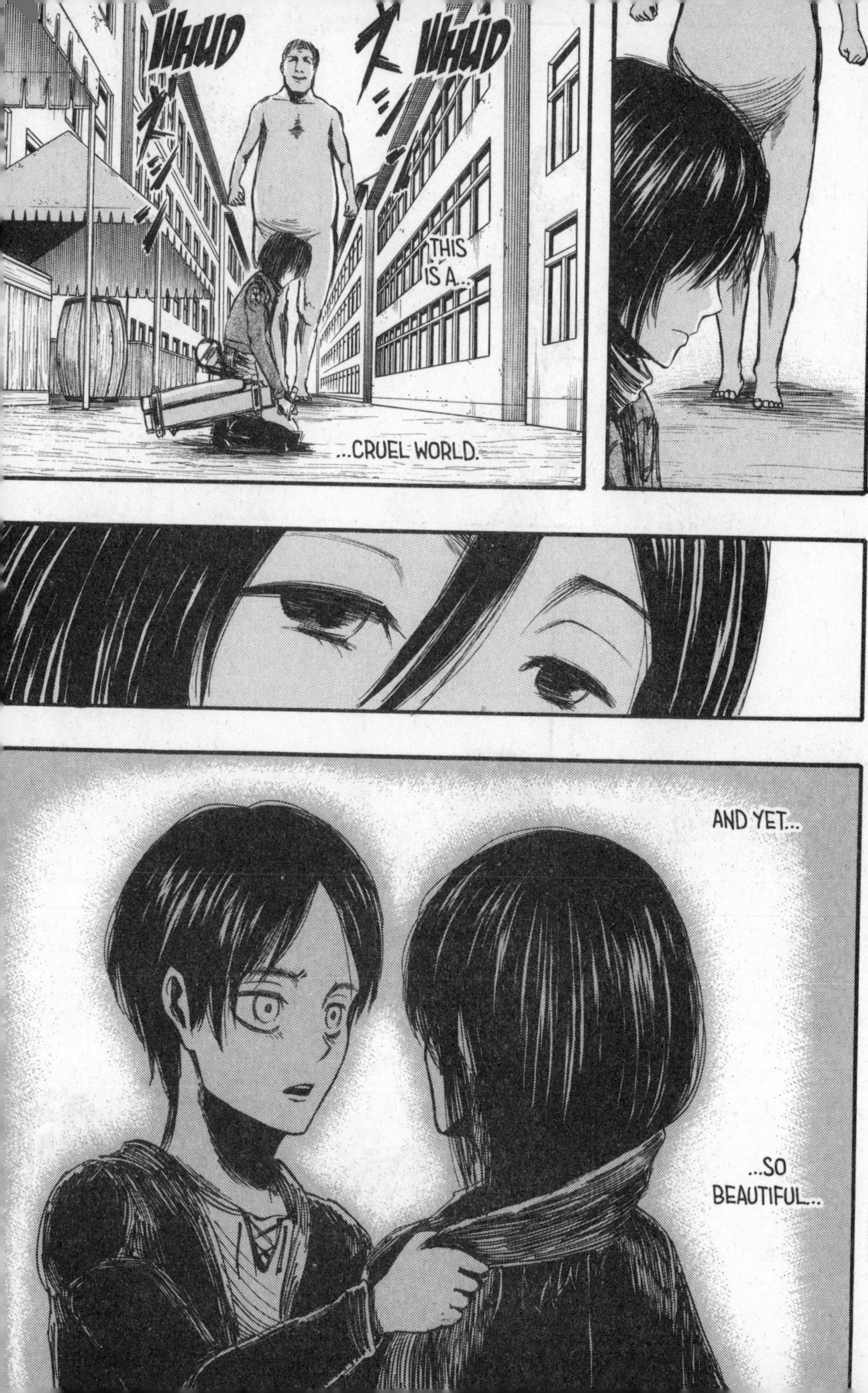
WHUD
WHUD
THIS IS A...
...CRUEL WORLD.
AND YET...
...SO BEAUTIFUL...

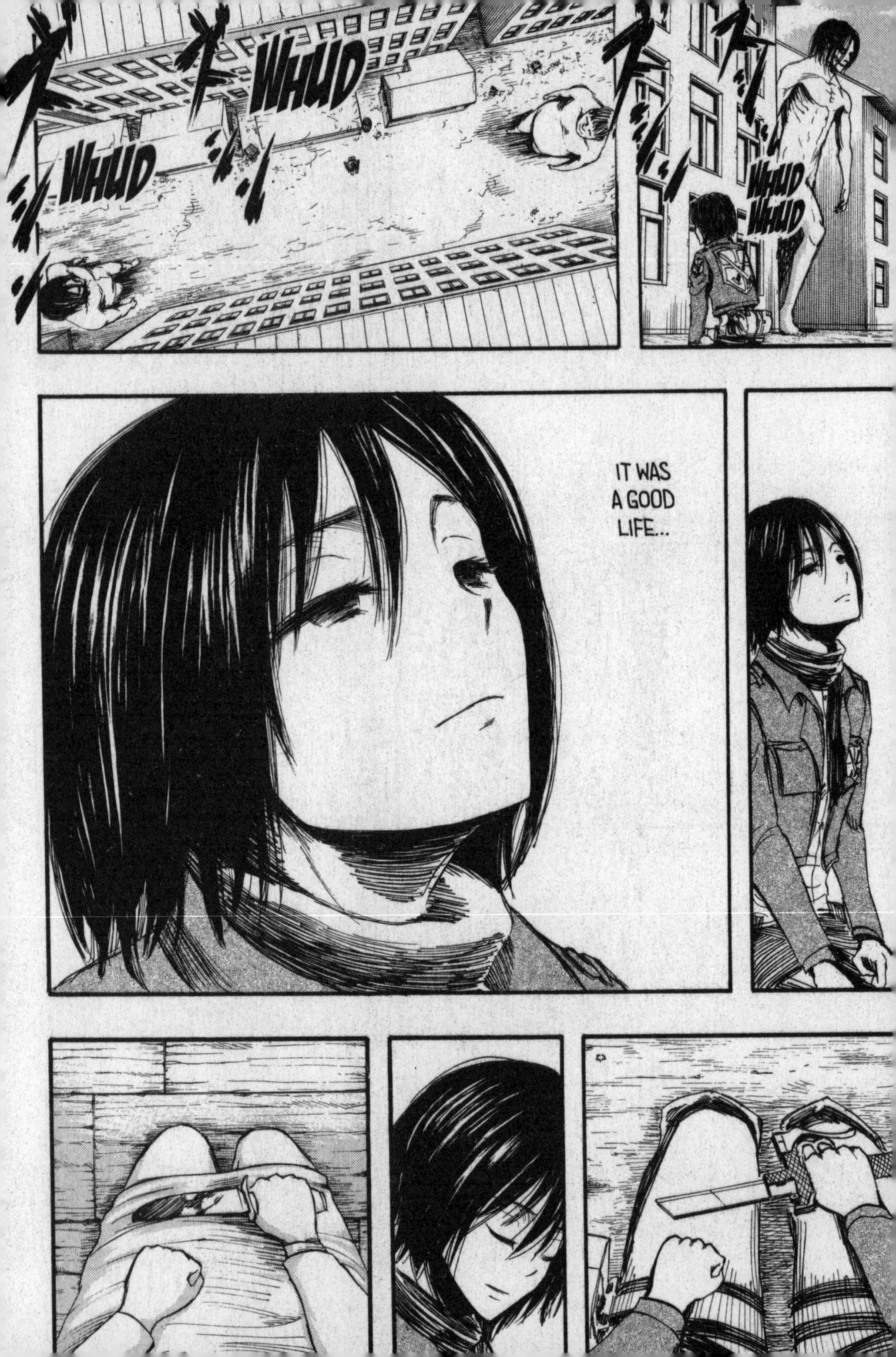
WHUD
WHUD
WHUD
WHUD
IT WAS
A GOOD
LIFE...

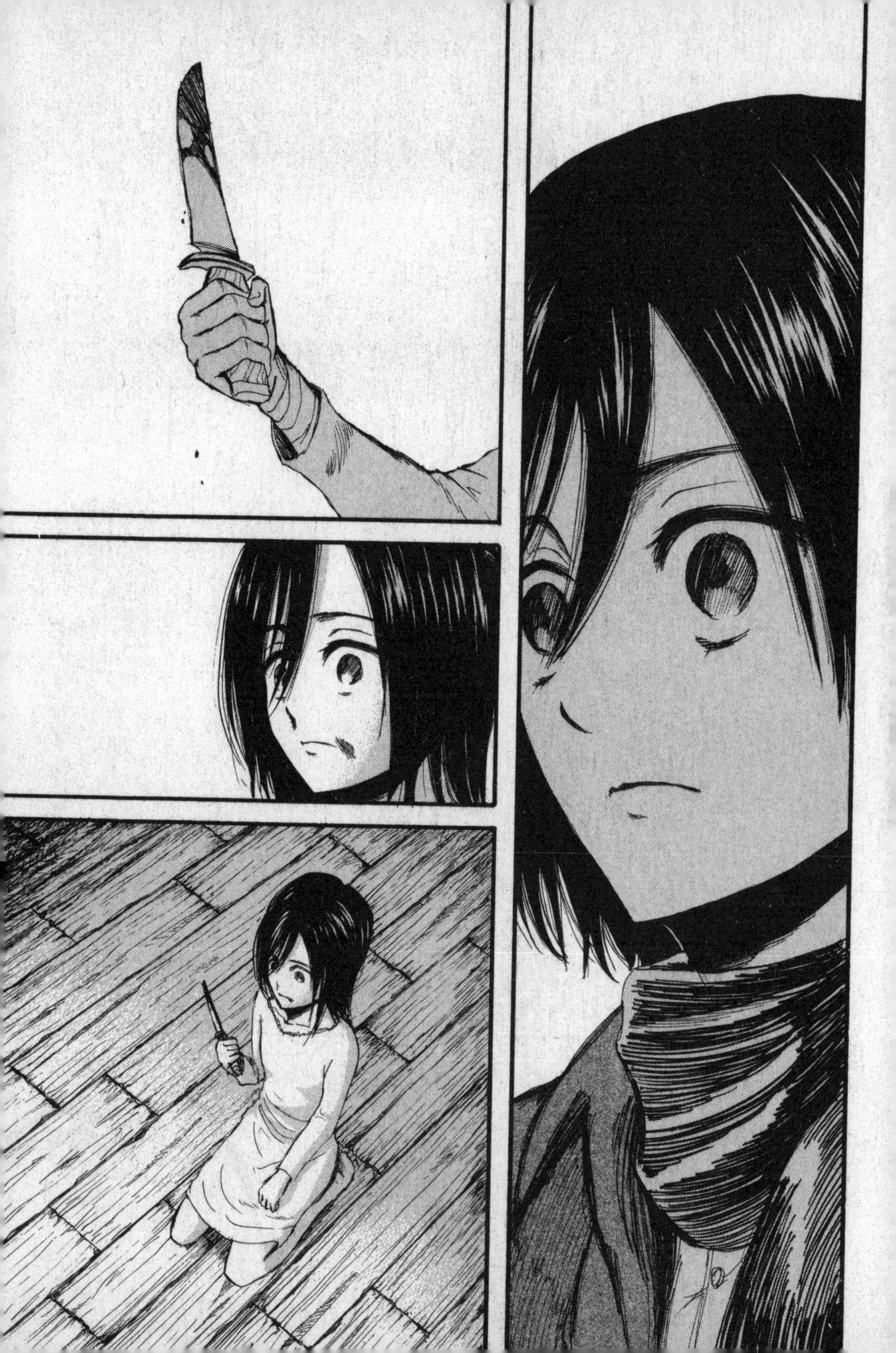

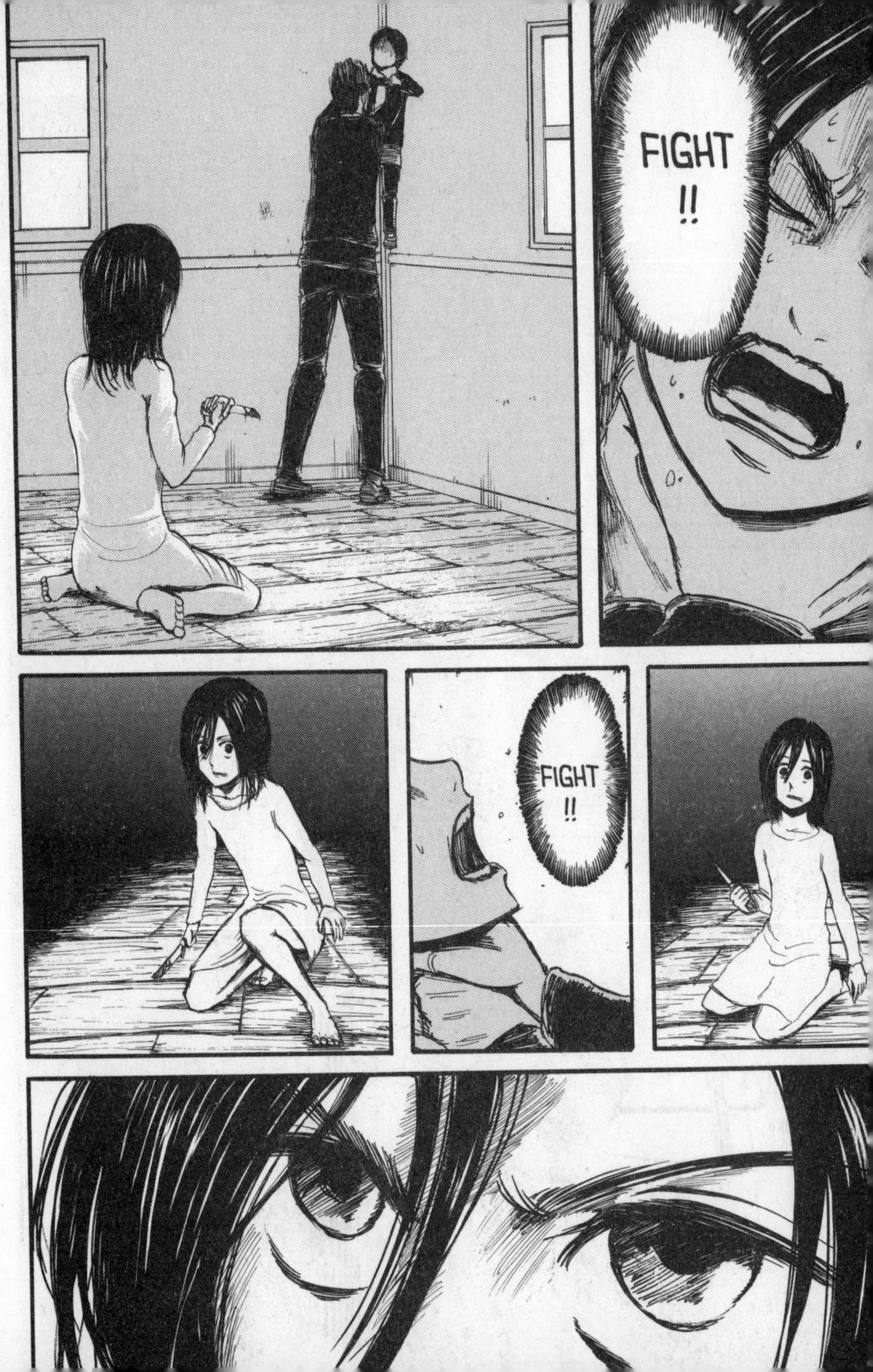
FIGHT !!
FIGHT !!

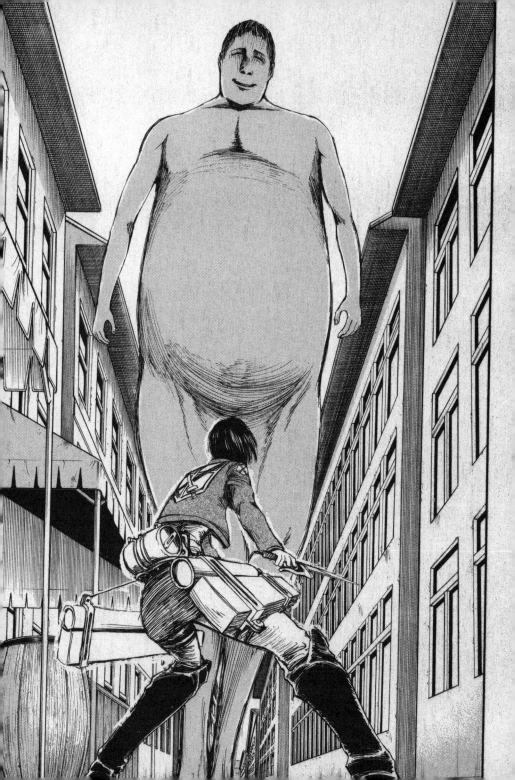

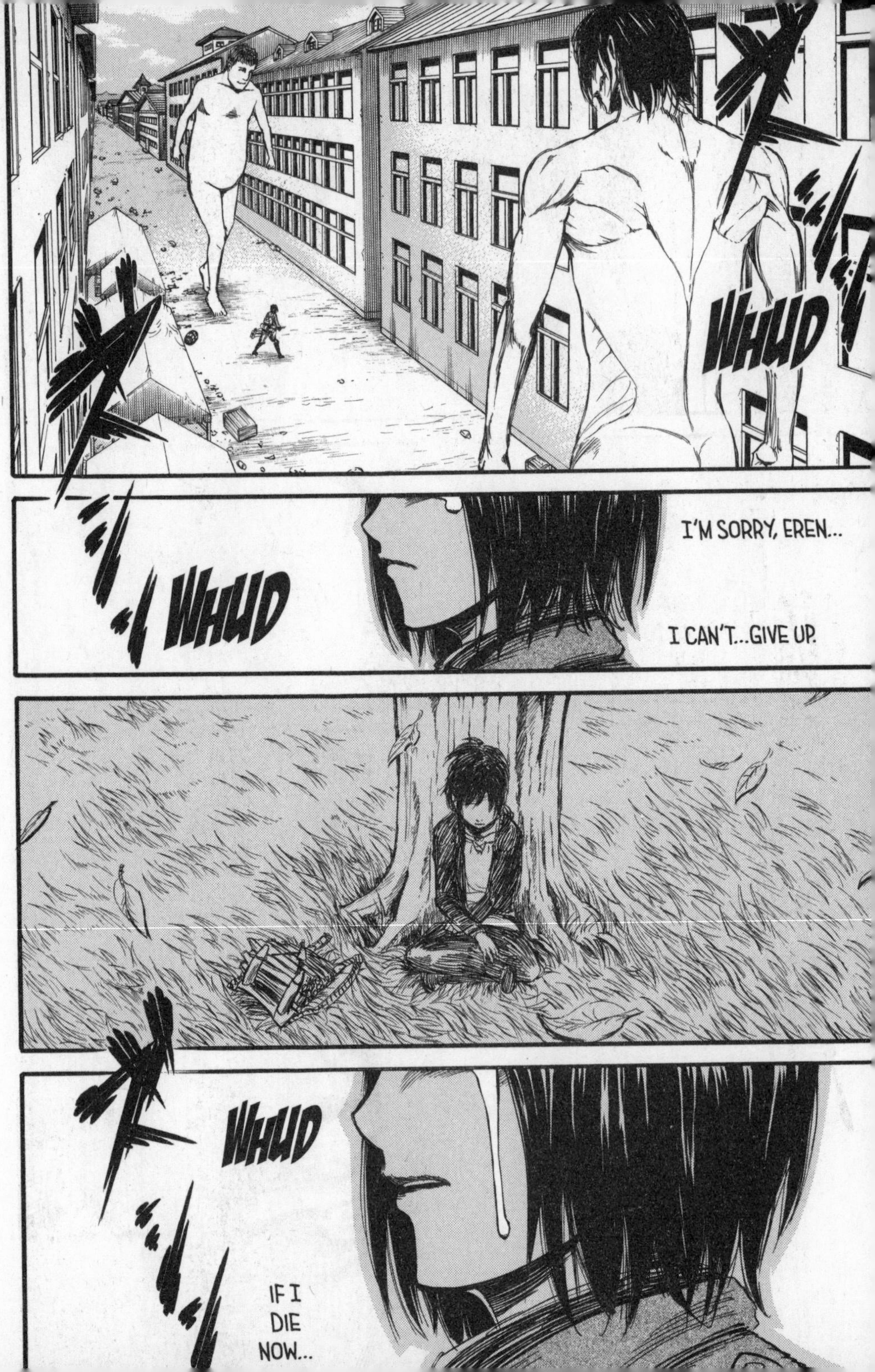
WHUD
I'M SORRY, EREN...
I CAN'T...GIVE UP.
WHUD
WHUD
IF I DIE NOW...

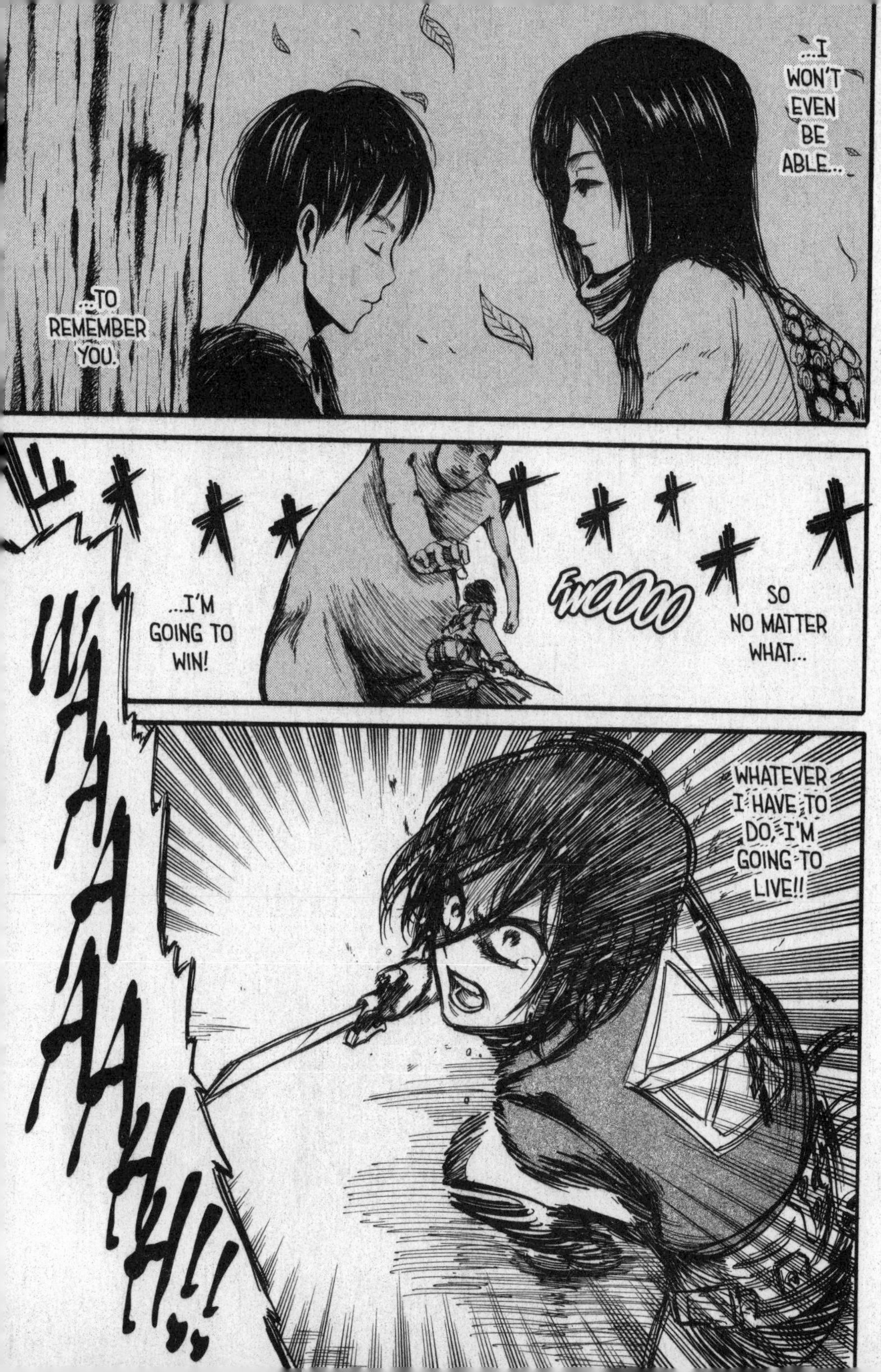
...I WON'T EVEN BE ABLE...
...TO REMEMBER YOU.
SO NO MATTER WHAT...
FWOOOO
...I'M GOING TO WIN!
WHATEVER I HAVE TO DO, I'M GOING TO LIVE!!
WAAAAAHH!!

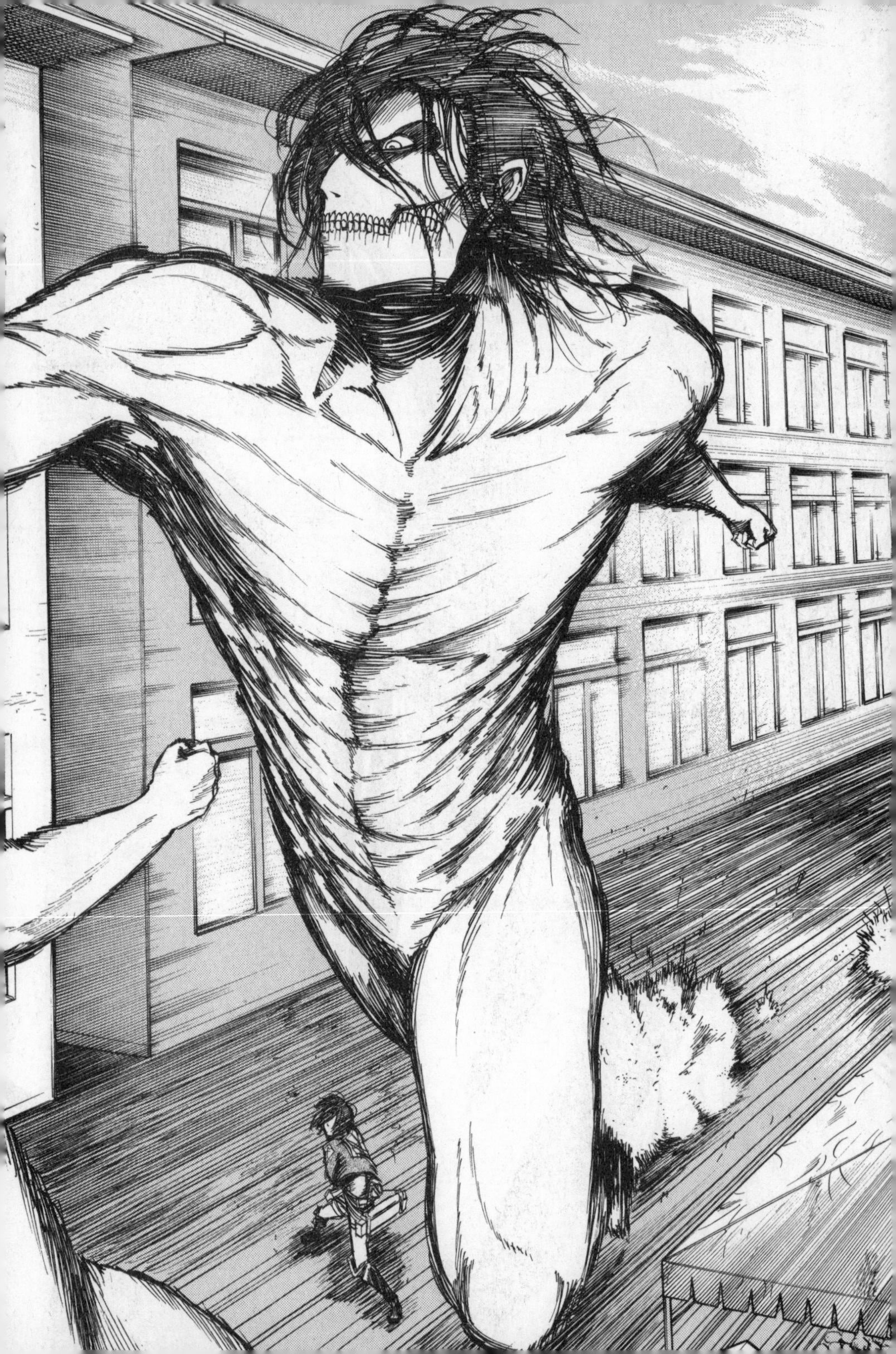

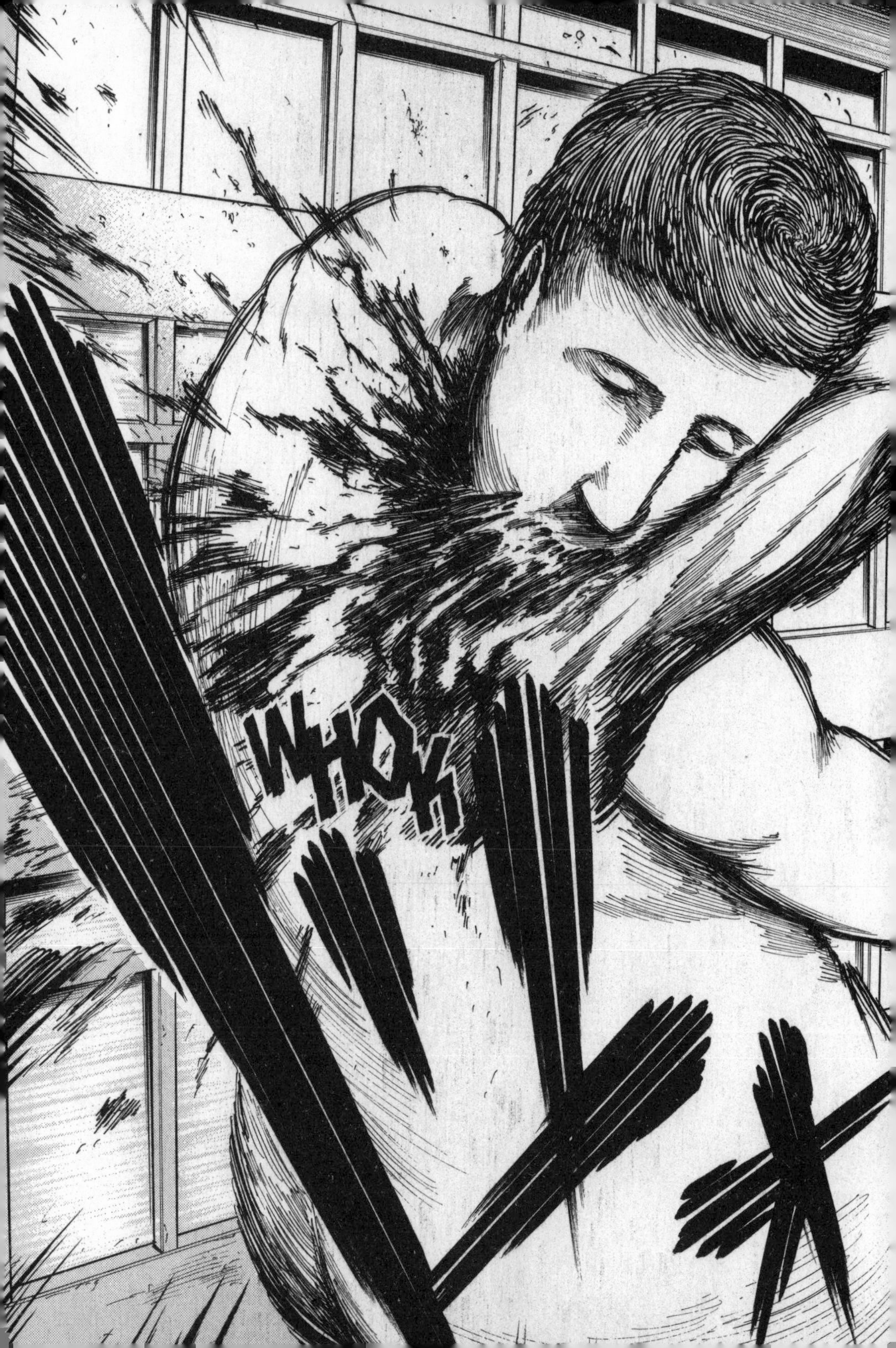
WHOK

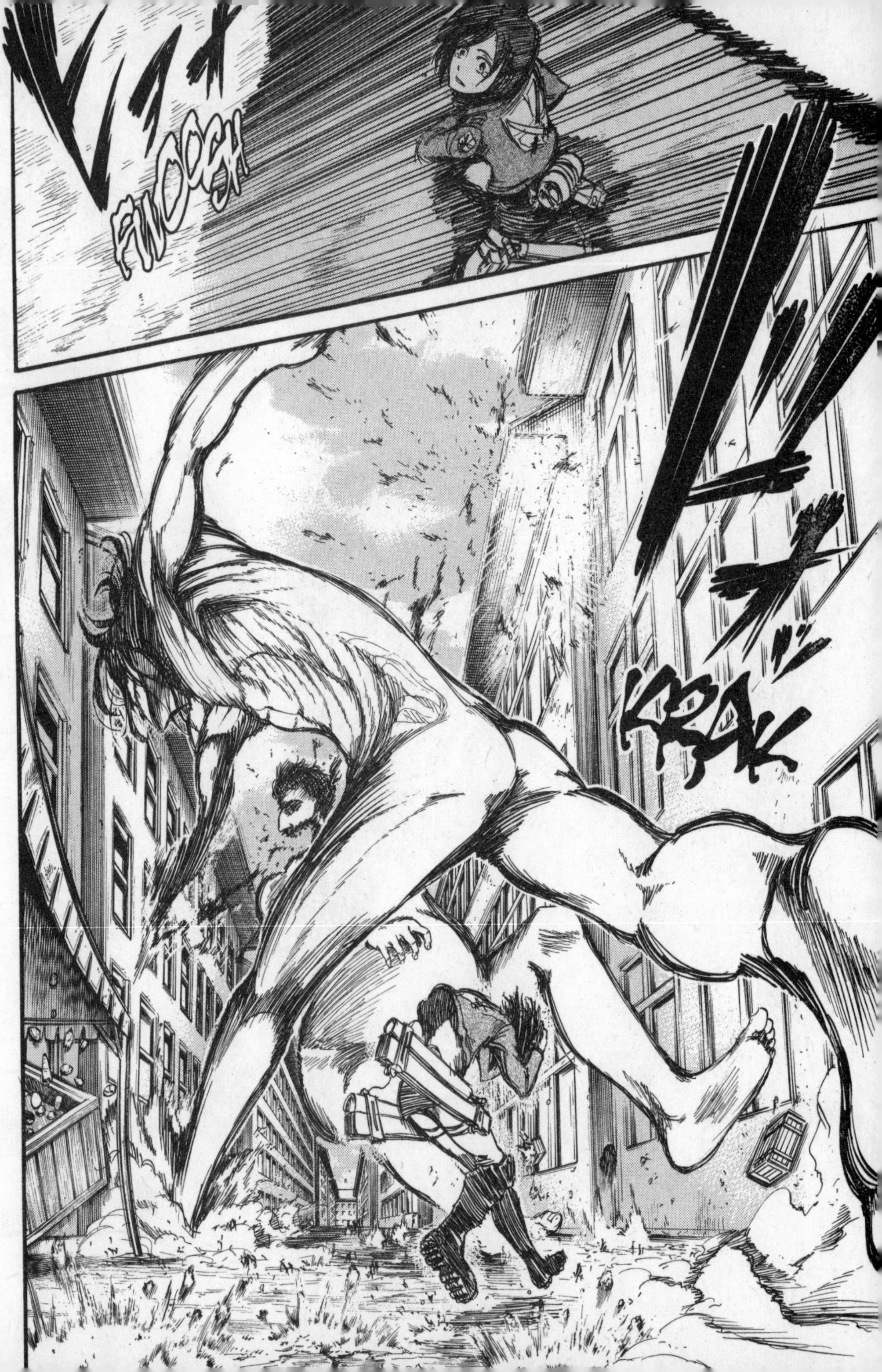
FWOOSH
KRAK

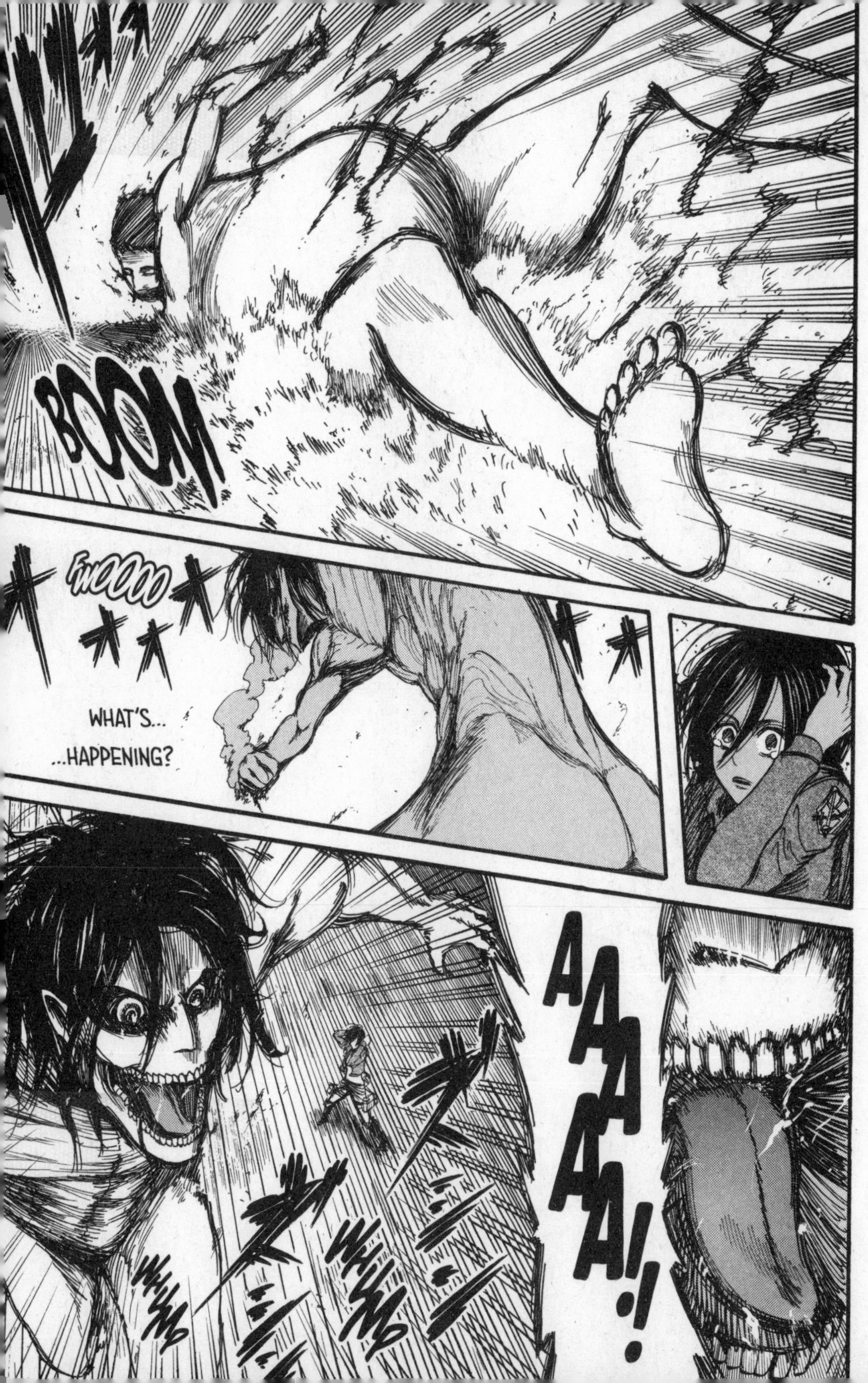
BOOM
FWOOOO
WHAT'S...
...HAPPENING?
AAAAA!!

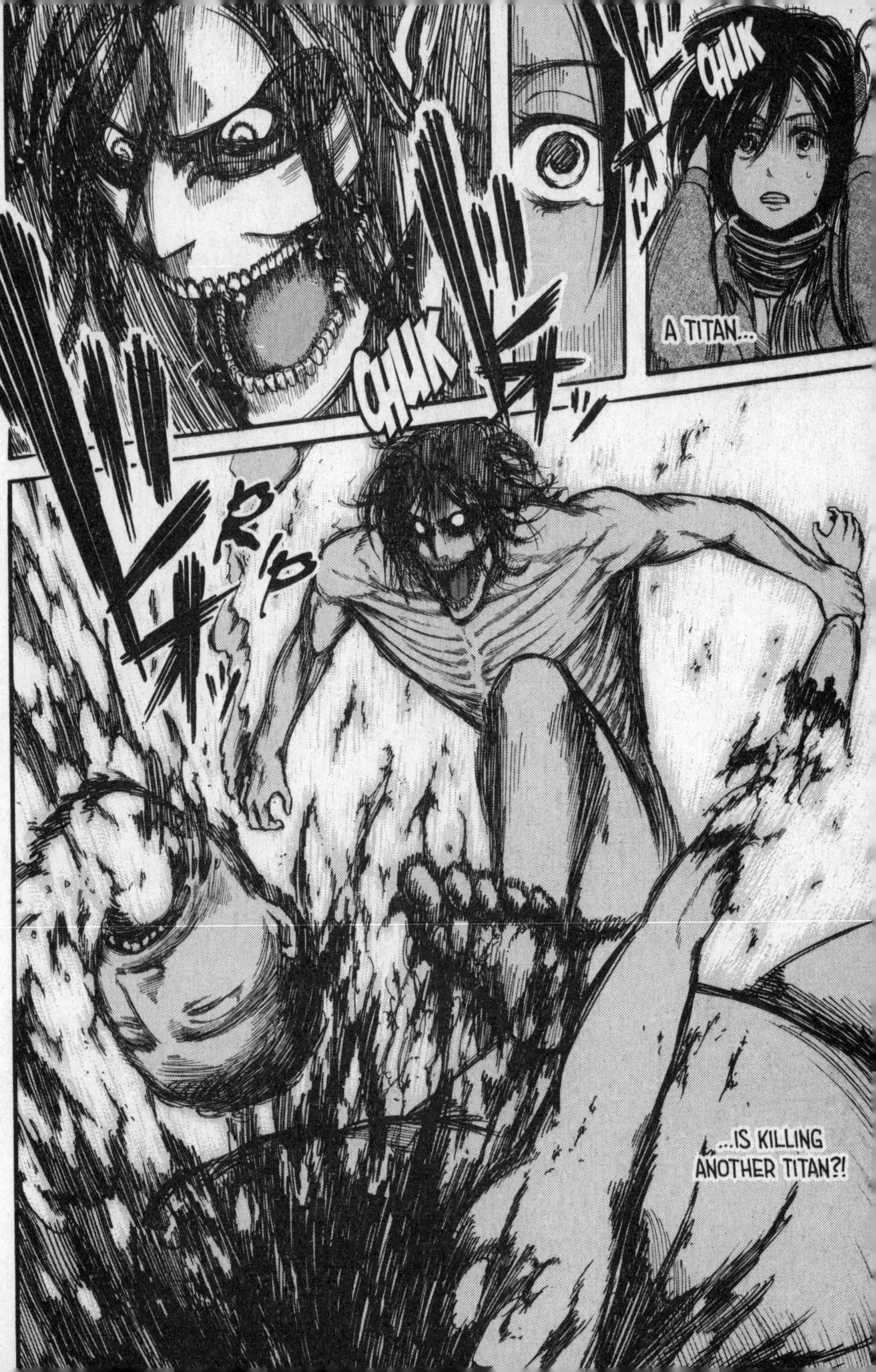
CHUK
A TITAN...
CHUK
RIP
...IS KILLING
ANOTHER TITAN?!

没表紙案

Rejected Cover Proposal

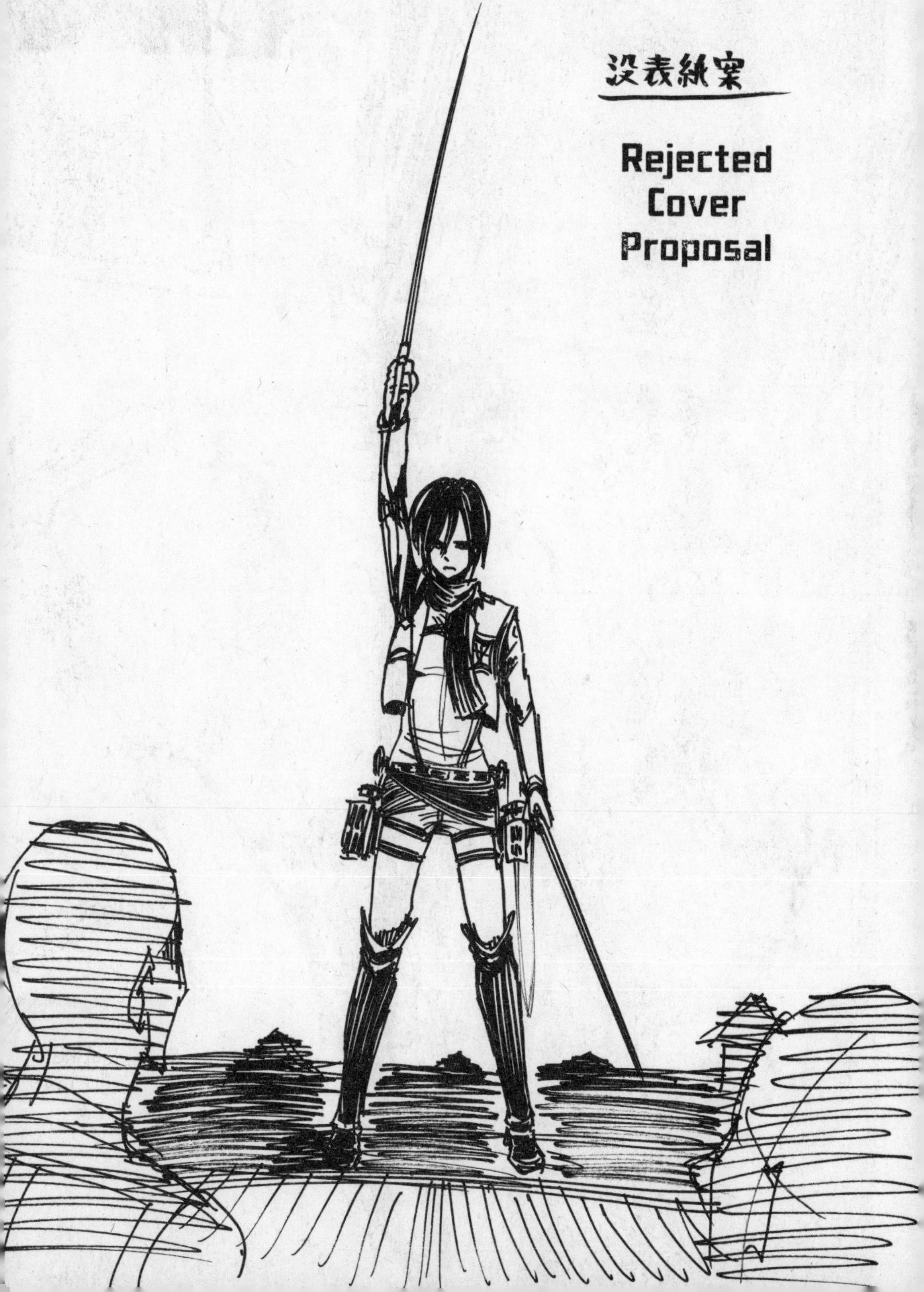

ATTACK on TITAN

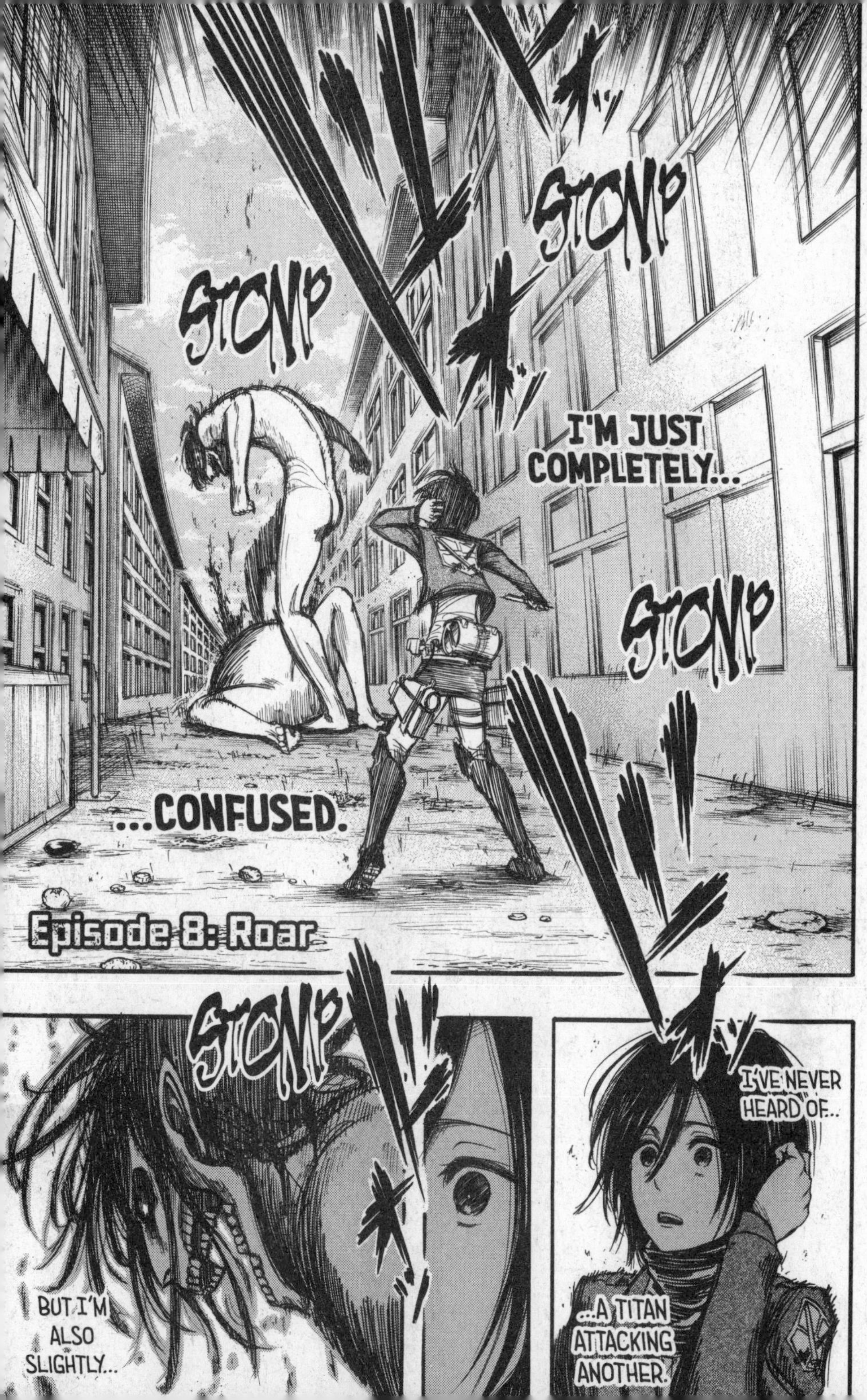
STOMP
STOMP
I'M JUST COMPLETELY...
STOMP
...CONFUSED.
Episode 8: Roar
STOMP
I'VE NEVER HEARD OF...
...A TITAN ATTACKING ANOTHER.
BUT I'M ALSO SLIGHTLY...

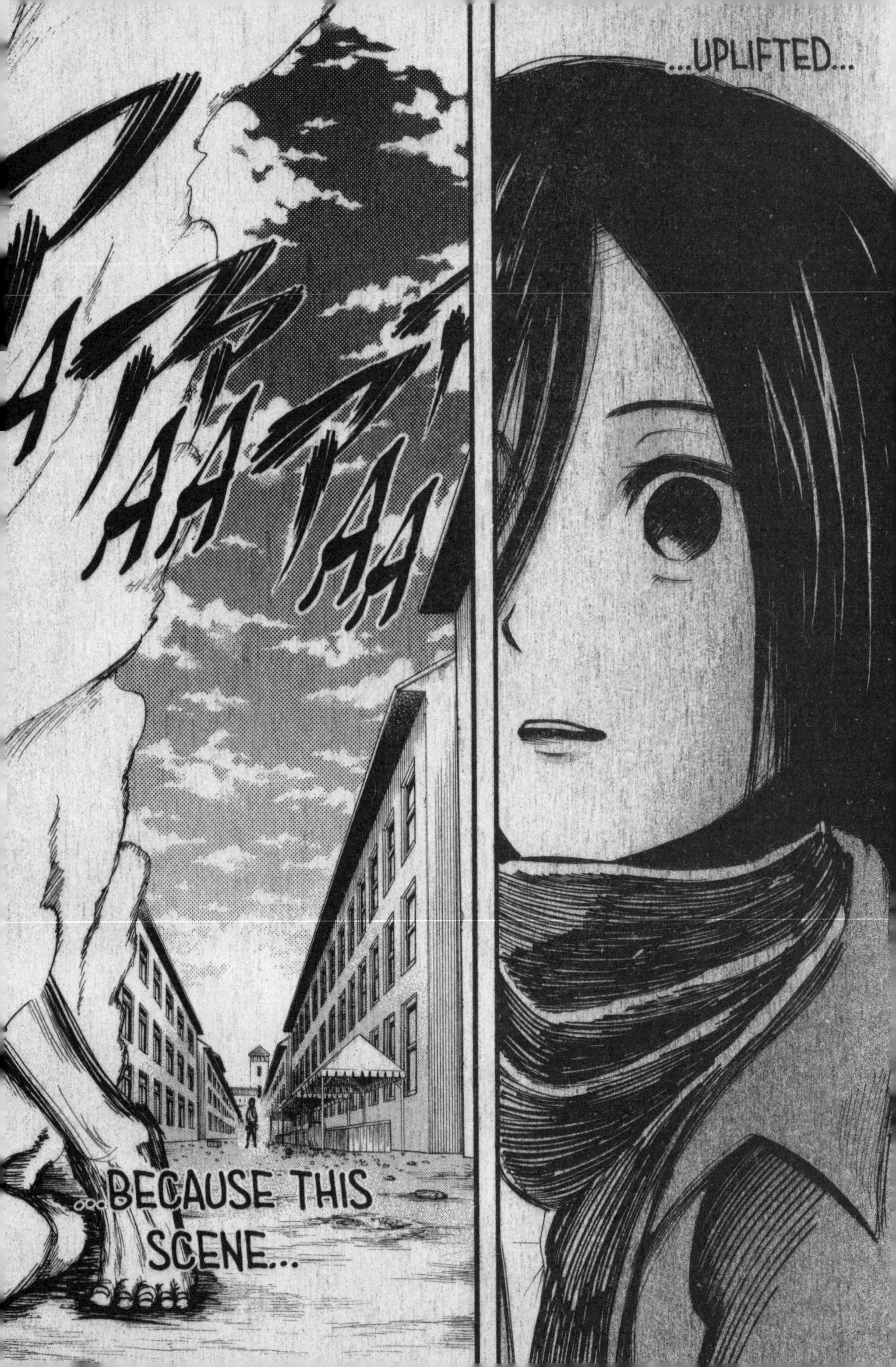

...UPLIFTED...
AAAAAA
...BECAUSE THIS SCENE...

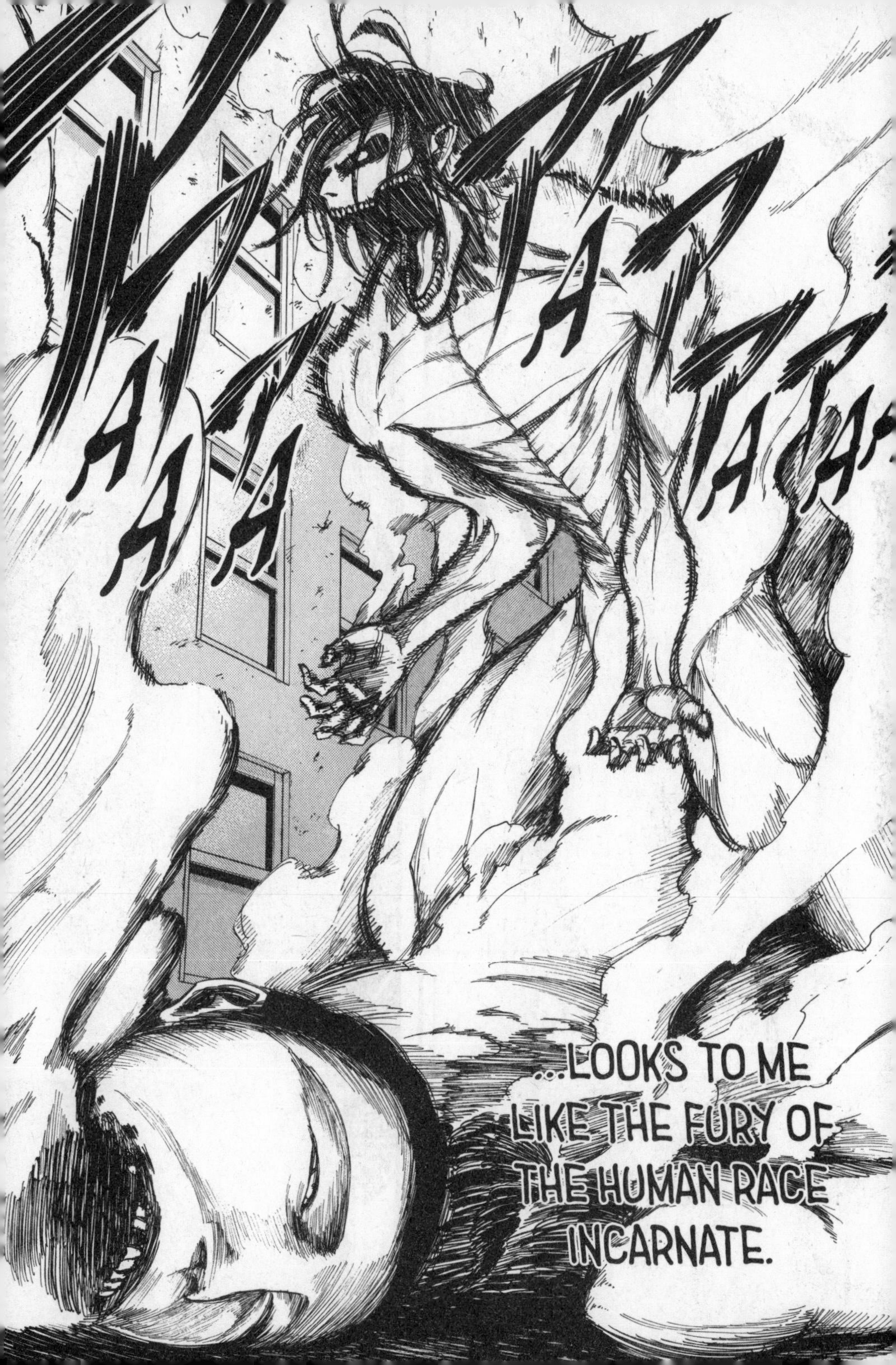
…LOOKS TO ME LIKE THE FURY OF THE HUMAN RACE INCARNATE.

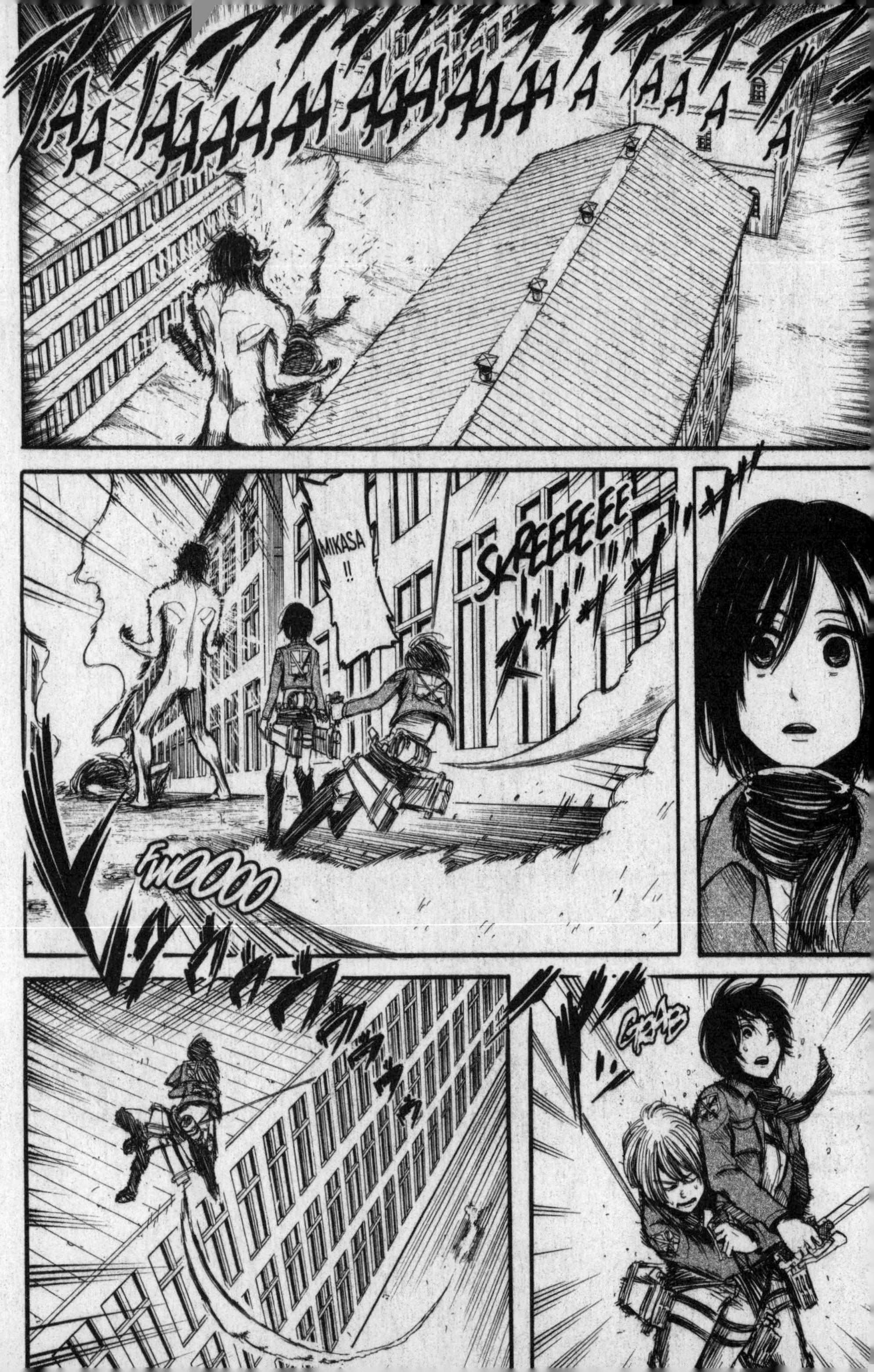
AAAAAAAAAAAAAAAAAA
MIKASA !!
SKREEEEEE
FWOOOOO
GRAB

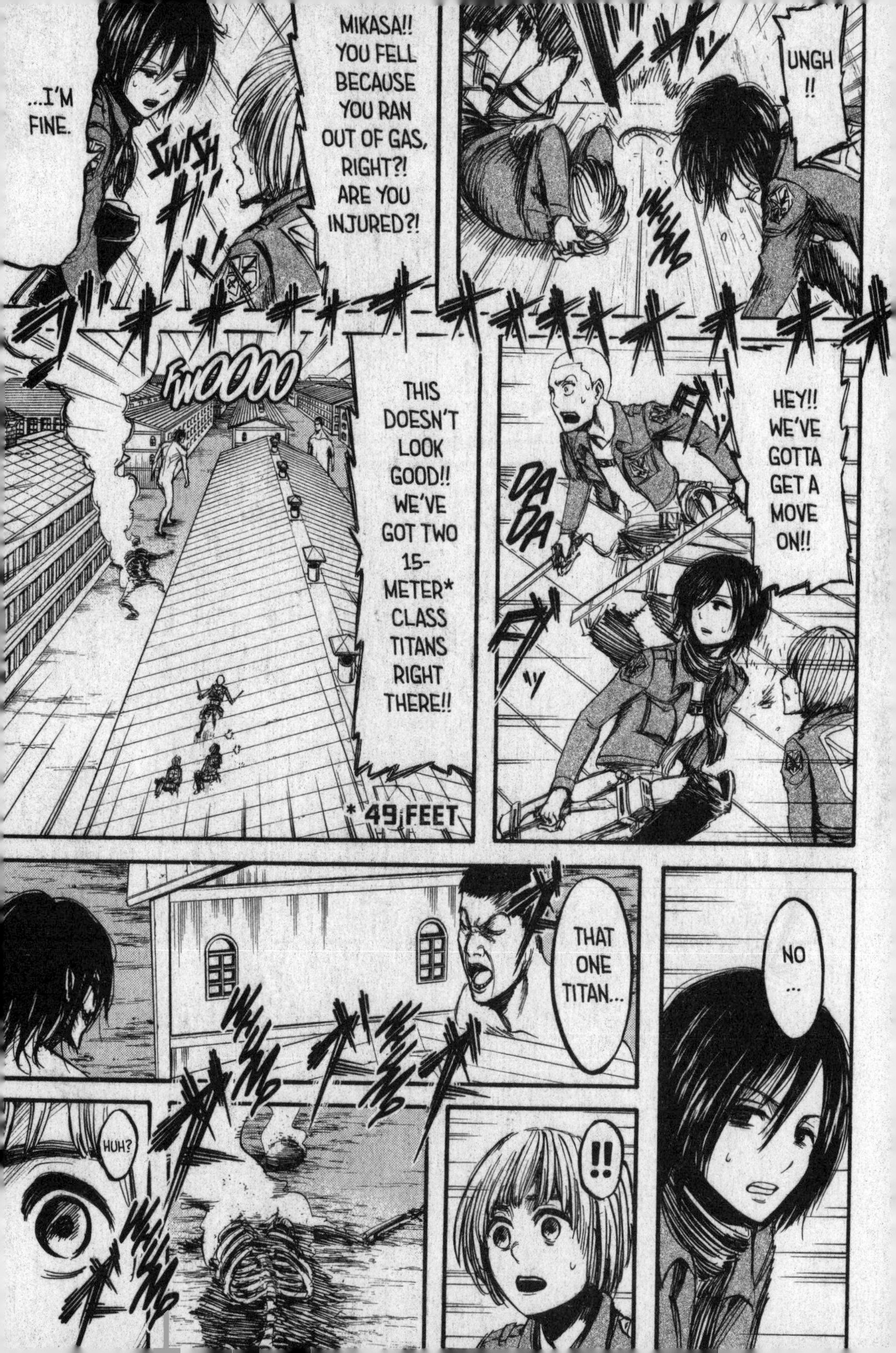
UNGH !!
MIKASA!! YOU FELL BECAUSE YOU RAN OUT OF GAS, RIGHT?! ARE YOU INJURED?!
SWISH
...I'M FINE.
HEY!! WE'VE GOTTA GET A MOVE ON!!
DA DA
FWOOOO
THIS DOESN'T LOOK GOOD!! WE'VE GOT TWO 15-METER* CLASS TITANS RIGHT THERE!!
* 49 FEET
NO ...
THAT ONE TITAN...
!!
HUH?

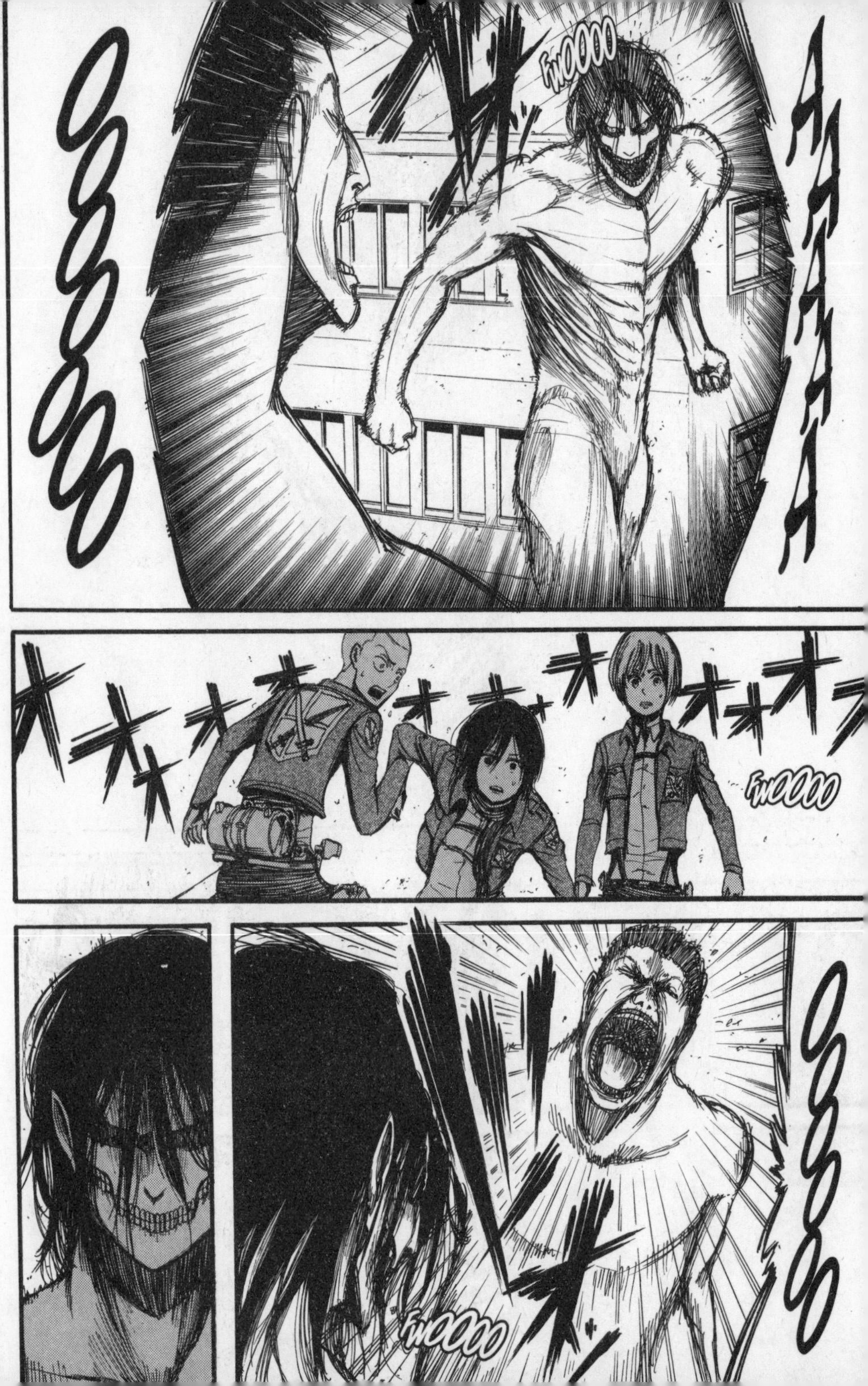
FWOOOO
FWOOOO
FWOOOO

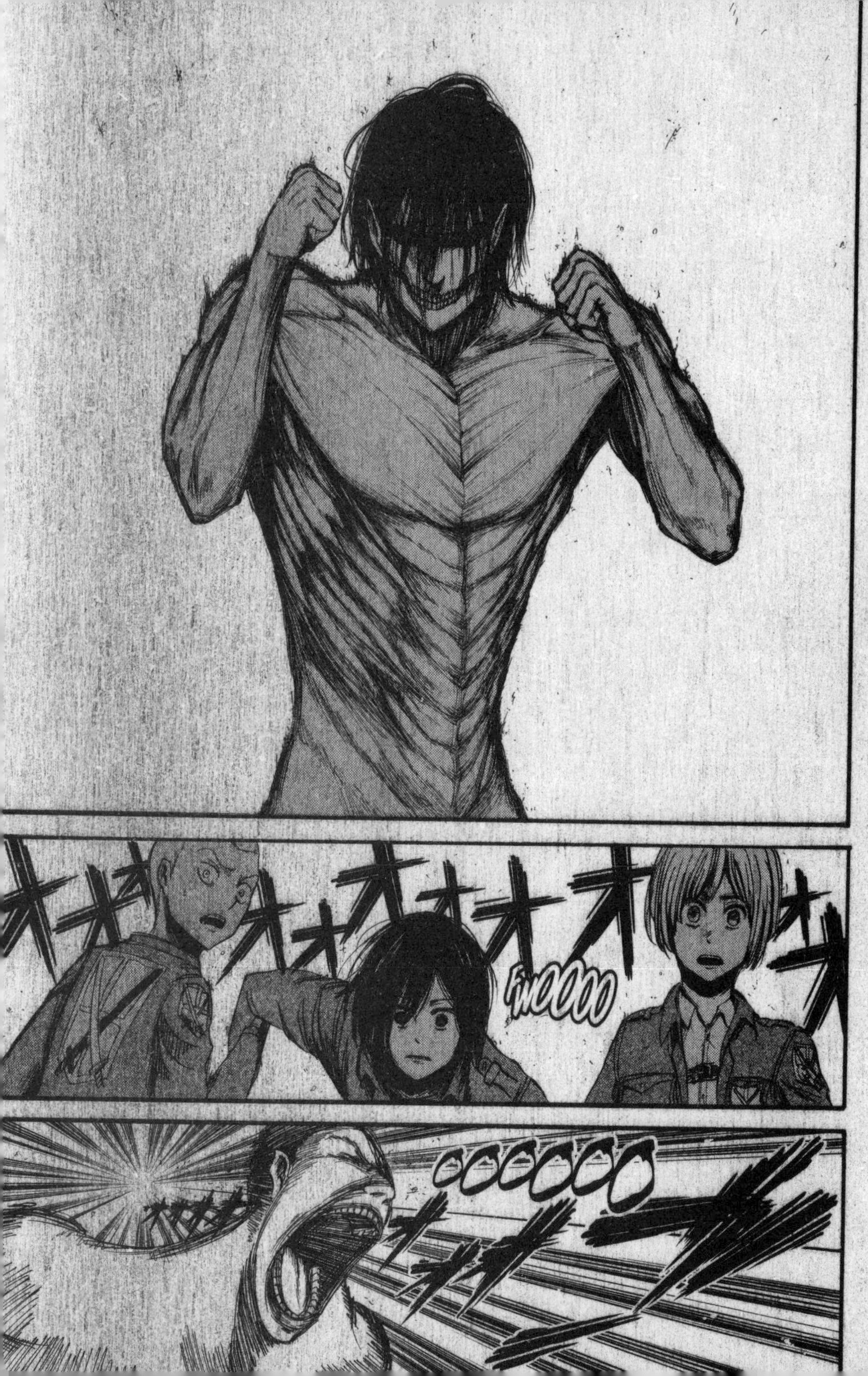
FWOOOO
OOOOOO

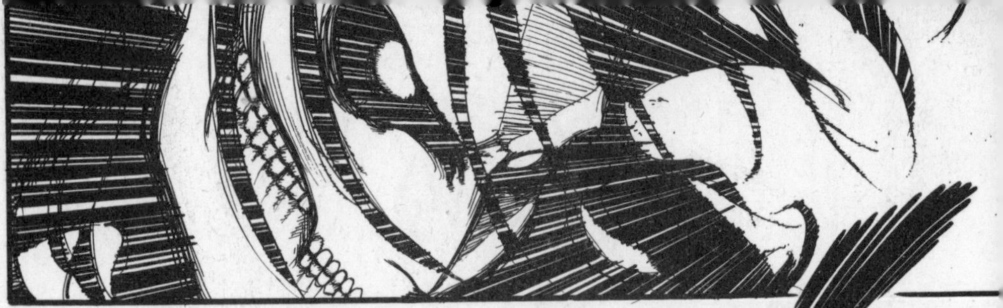

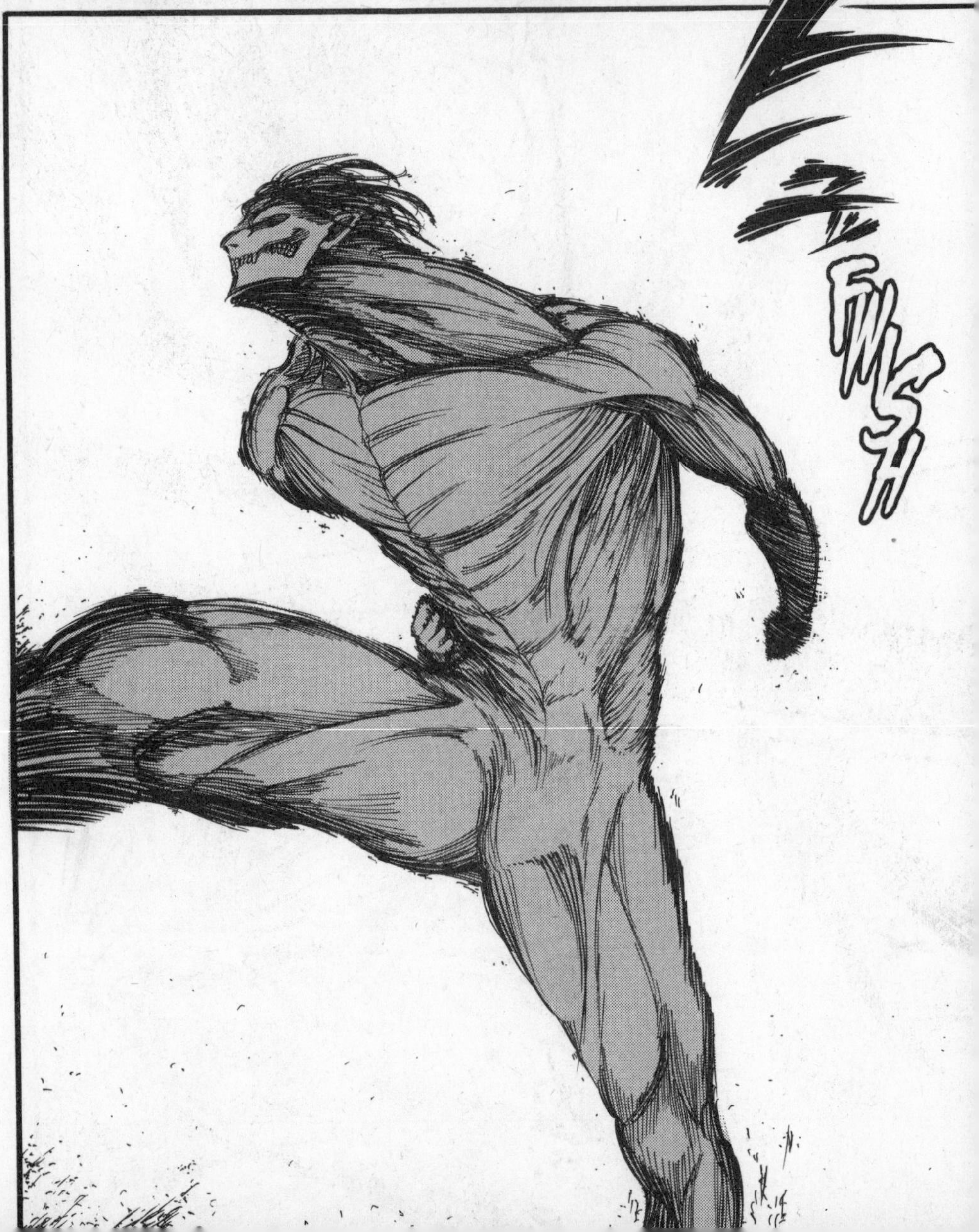
FWISH

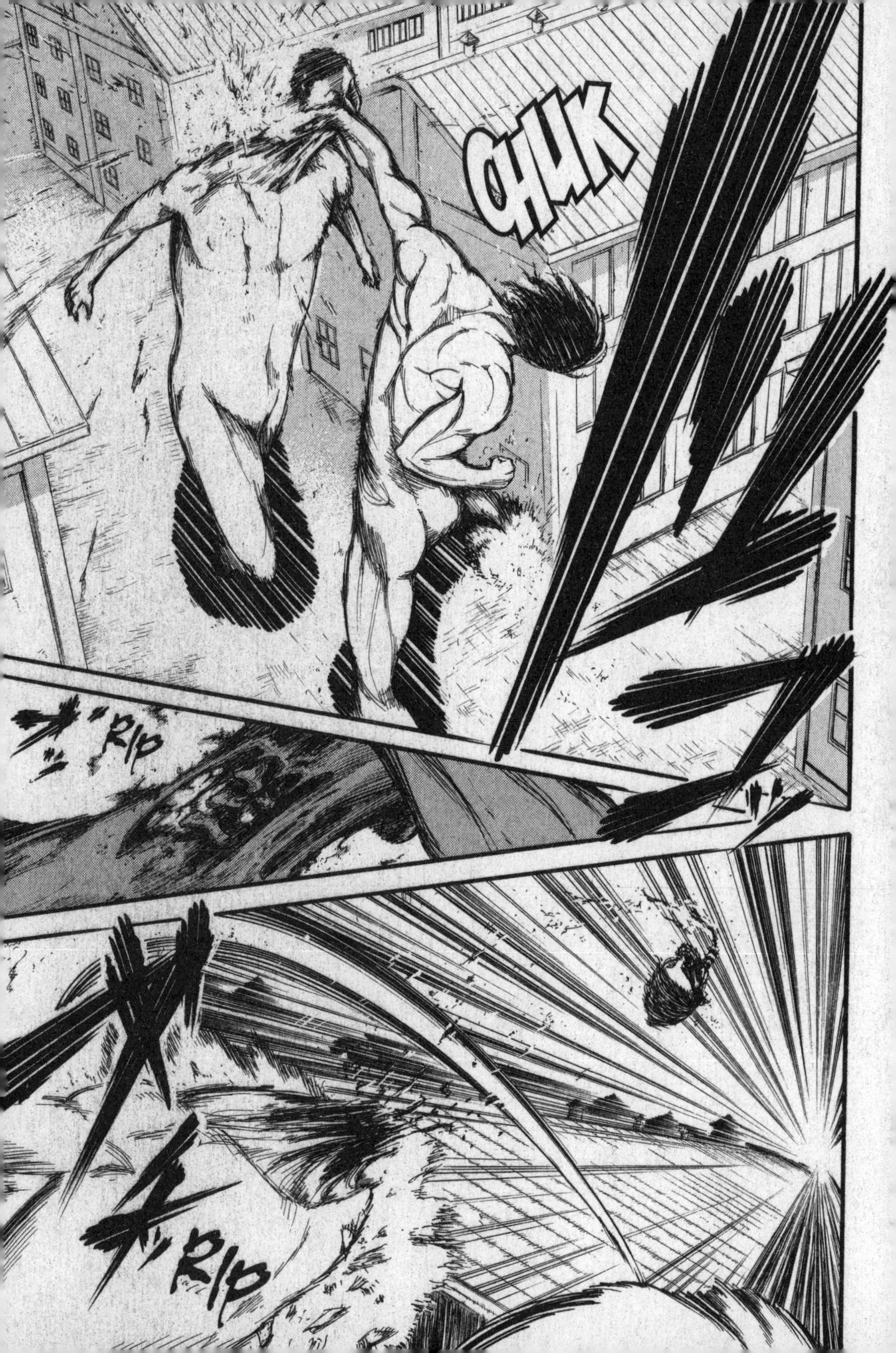
CHUK
RIP
RIP

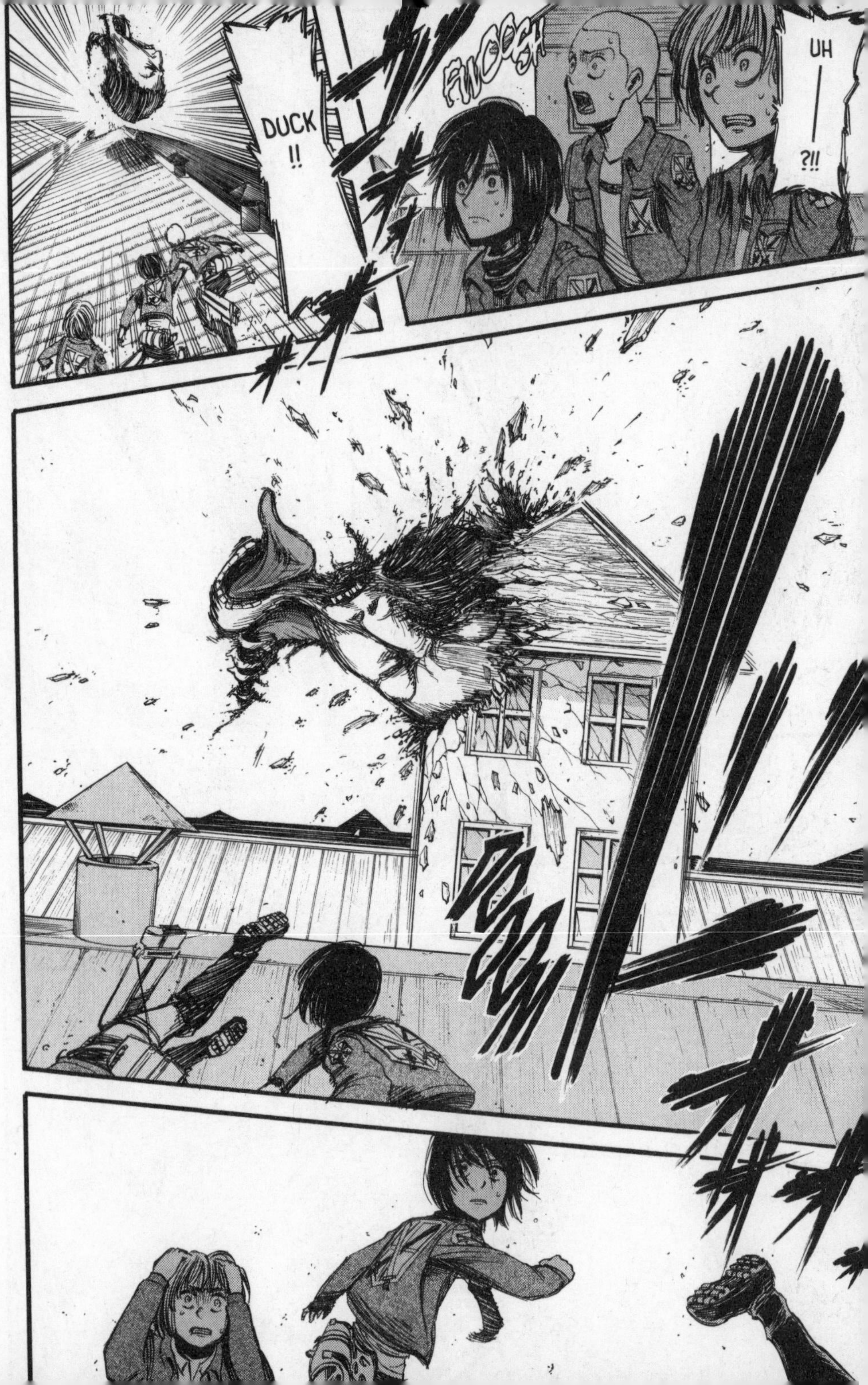
UH
?!!
FWOOSH
DUCK
!!
DOOM

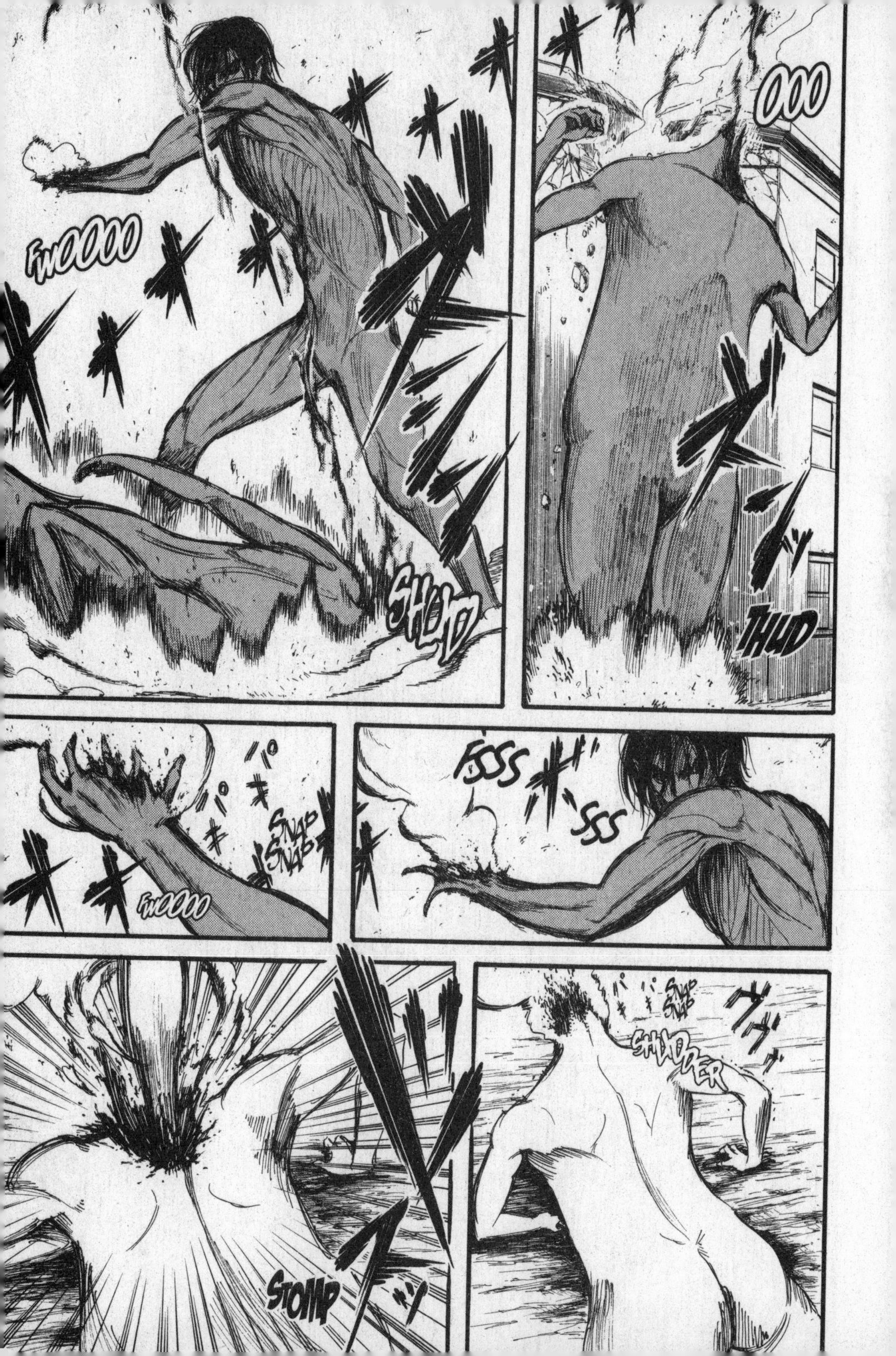
OOO
THUD
FWOOOO
SHLUD
FSSS
SSS
SNAP
SNAP
FWOOOO
SNAP
SNAP
SHUDDER
STOMP

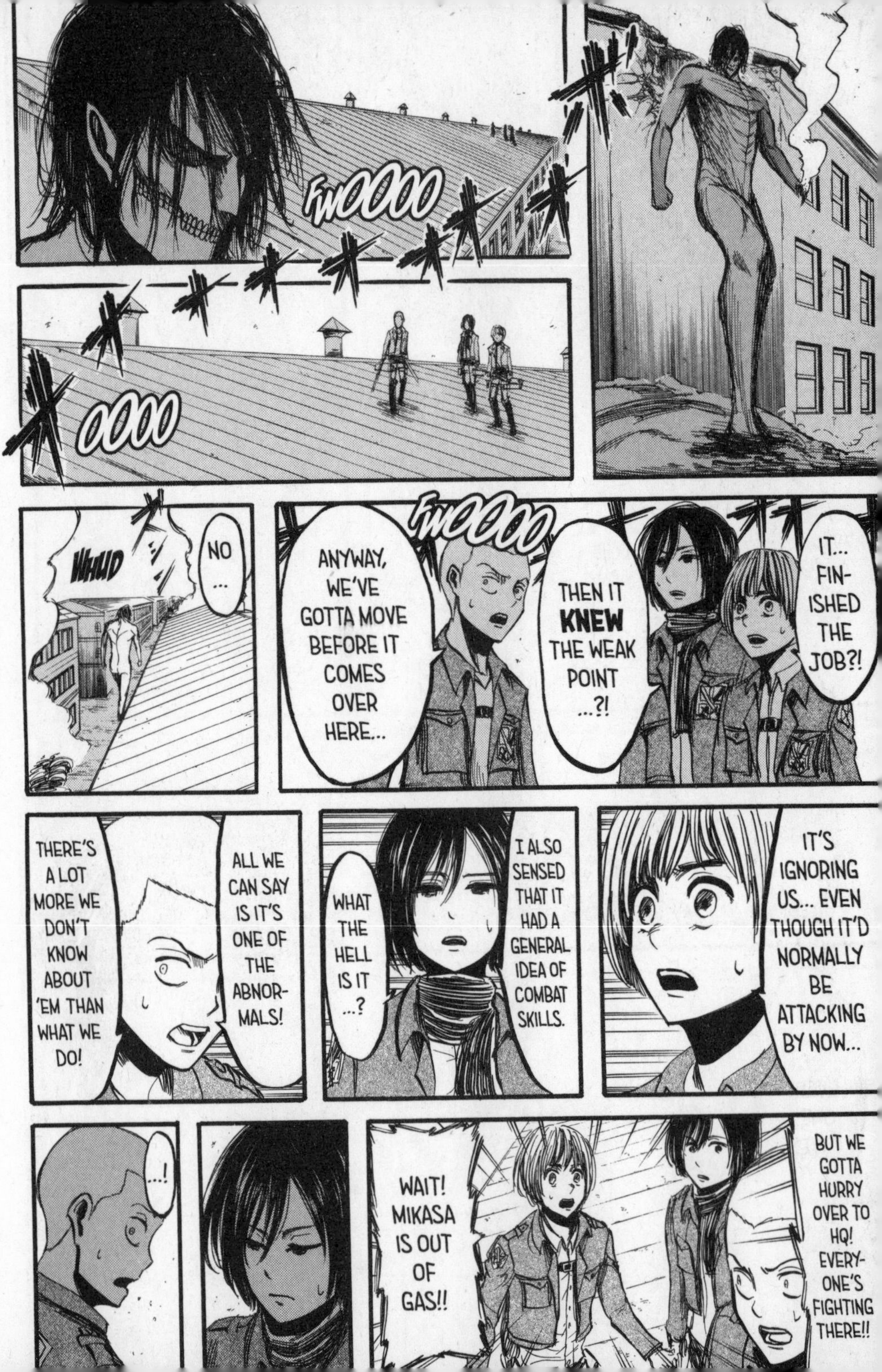
FWOOOO
OOOO
IT... FIN-ISHED THE JOB?!
THEN IT KNEW THE WEAK POINT ...?!
FWOOOO
ANYWAY, WE'VE GOTTA MOVE BEFORE IT COMES OVER HERE...
NO ...
WHUD
IT'S IGNORING US... EVEN THOUGH IT'D NORMALLY BE ATTACKING BY NOW...
I ALSO SENSED THAT IT HAD A GENERAL IDEA OF COMBAT SKILLS.
WHAT THE HELL IS IT ...?
ALL WE CAN SAY IS IT'S ONE OF THE ABNORMALS!
THERE'S A LOT MORE WE DON'T KNOW ABOUT 'EM THAN WHAT WE DO!
BUT WE GOTTA HURRY OVER TO HQ! EVERY-ONE'S FIGHTING THERE!!
WAIT! MIKASA IS OUT OF GAS!!
...!

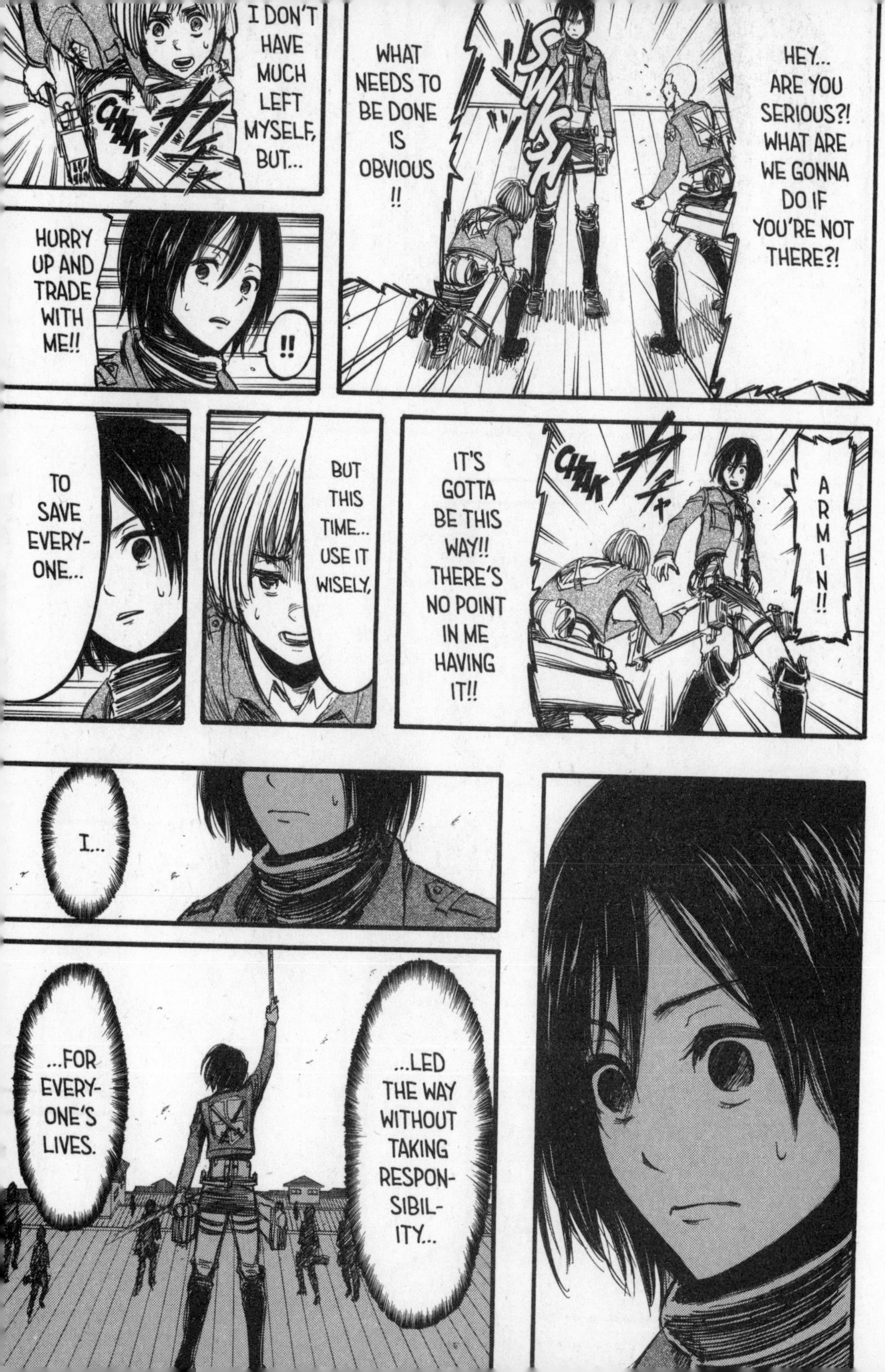
HEY... ARE YOU SERIOUS?! WHAT ARE WE GONNA DO IF YOU'RE NOT THERE?!
SWISH
WHAT NEEDS TO BE DONE IS OBVIOUS!!
I DON'T HAVE MUCH LEFT MYSELF, BUT...
CHAK
HURRY UP AND TRADE WITH ME!!
!!
ARMIN!!
CHAK
IT'S GOTTA BE THIS WAY!! THERE'S NO POINT IN ME HAVING IT!!
BUT THIS TIME... USE IT WISELY,
TO SAVE EVERY-ONE...
I...
...LED THE WAY WITHOUT TAKING RESPON-SIBIL-ITY...
...FOR EVERY-ONE'S LIVES.

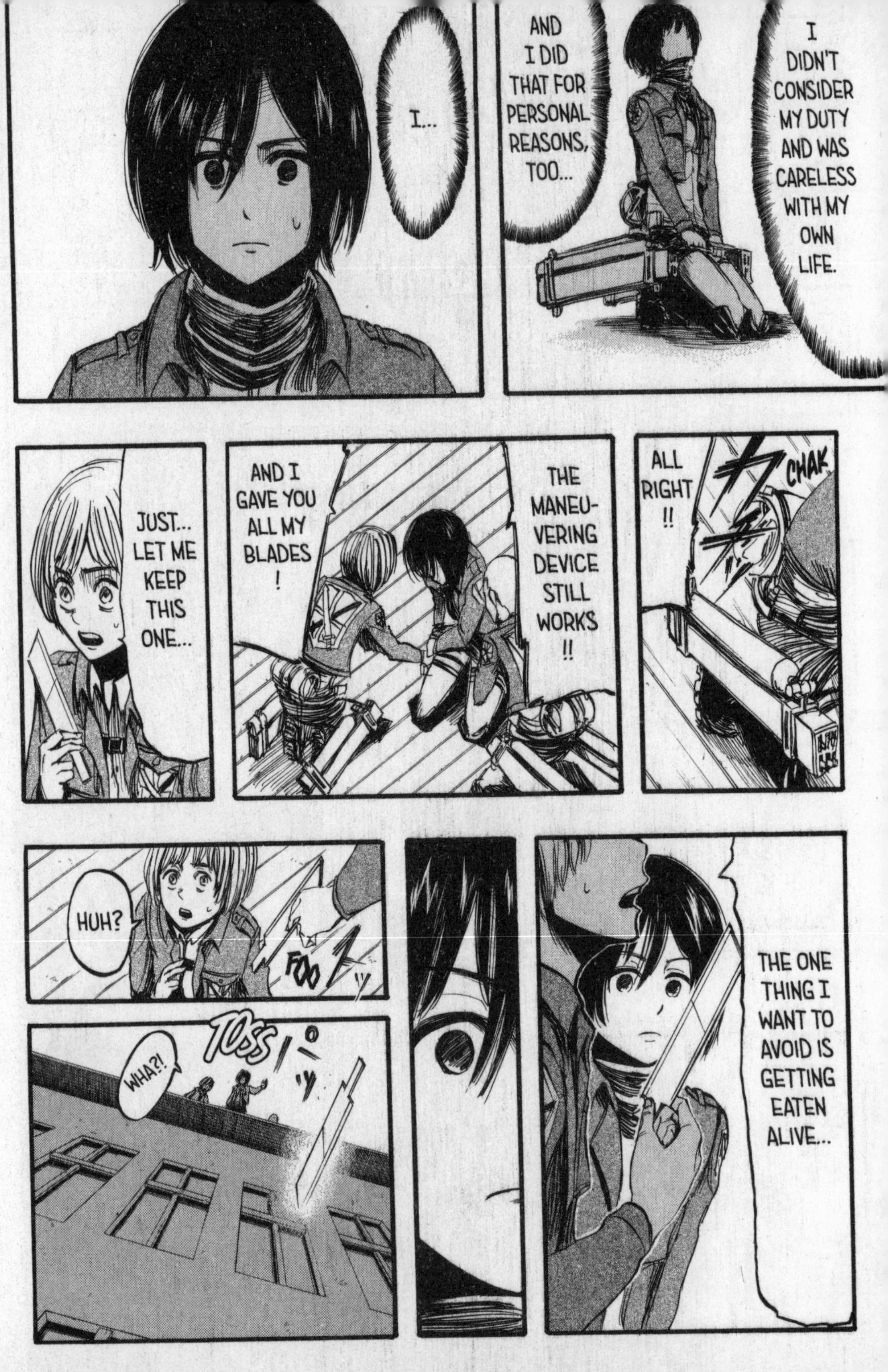
I DIDN'T CONSIDER MY DUTY AND WAS CARELESS WITH MY OWN LIFE.
AND I DID THAT FOR PERSONAL REASONS, TOO...
I...
ALL RIGHT!!
CHAK
THE MANEU-VERING DEVICE STILL WORKS!!
AND I GAVE YOU ALL MY BLADES!
JUST... LET ME KEEP THIS ONE...
THE ONE THING I WANT TO AVOID IS GETTING EATEN ALIVE...
HUH?
FOO
WHA?!
TOSS

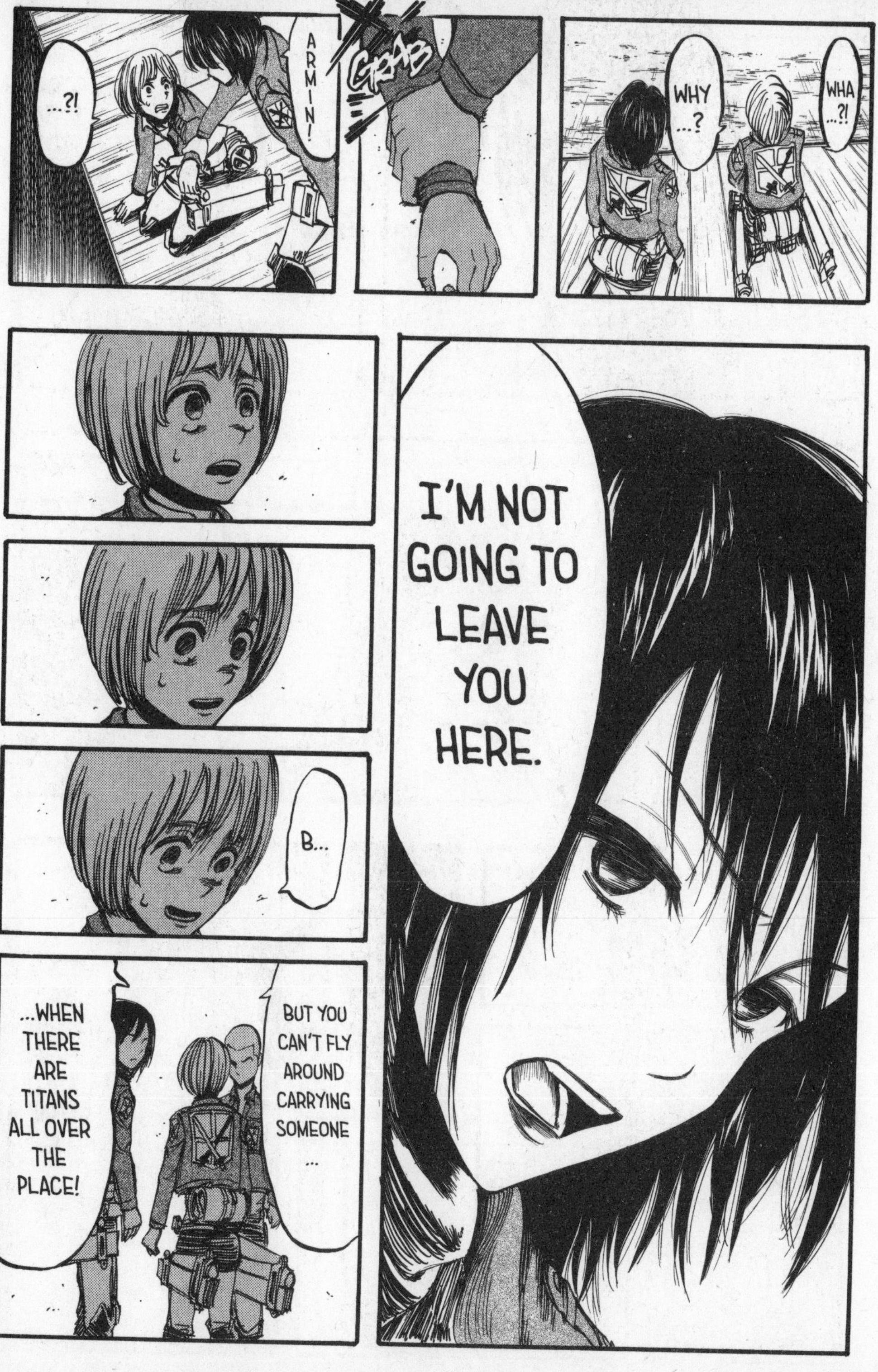
WHA ...?!
WHY ...?
GRAB
ARMIN!
...?!
I'M NOT GOING TO LEAVE YOU HERE.
B...
BUT YOU CAN'T FLY AROUND CARRYING SOMEONE ...
...WHEN THERE ARE TITANS ALL OVER THE PLACE!

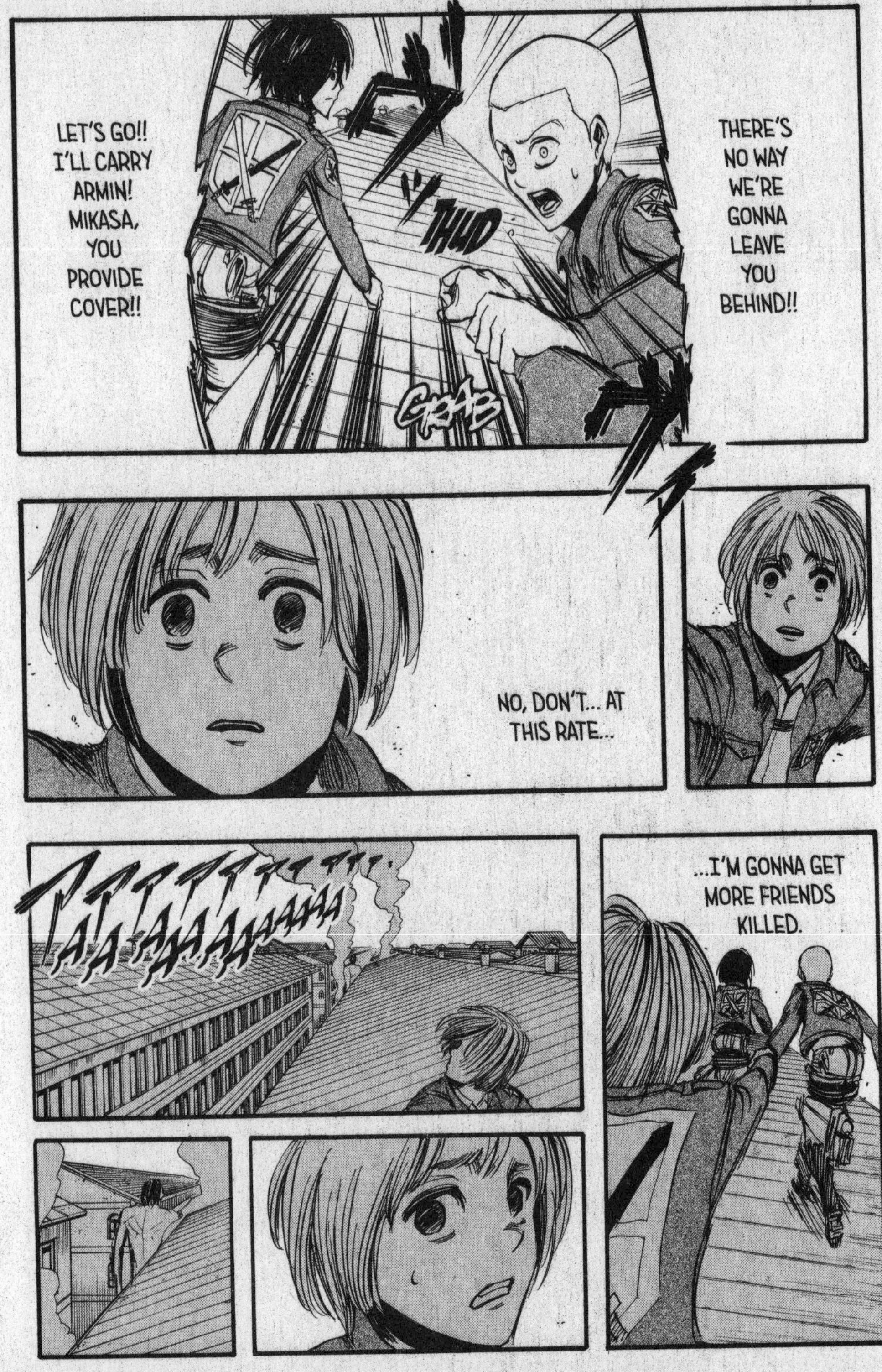
THERE'S NO WAY WE'RE GONNA LEAVE YOU BEHIND!!
LET'S GO!! I'LL CARRY ARMIN! MIKASA, YOU PROVIDE COVER!!
THUD
GRAB
NO, DON'T... AT THIS RATE...
...I'M GONNA GET MORE FRIENDS KILLED.

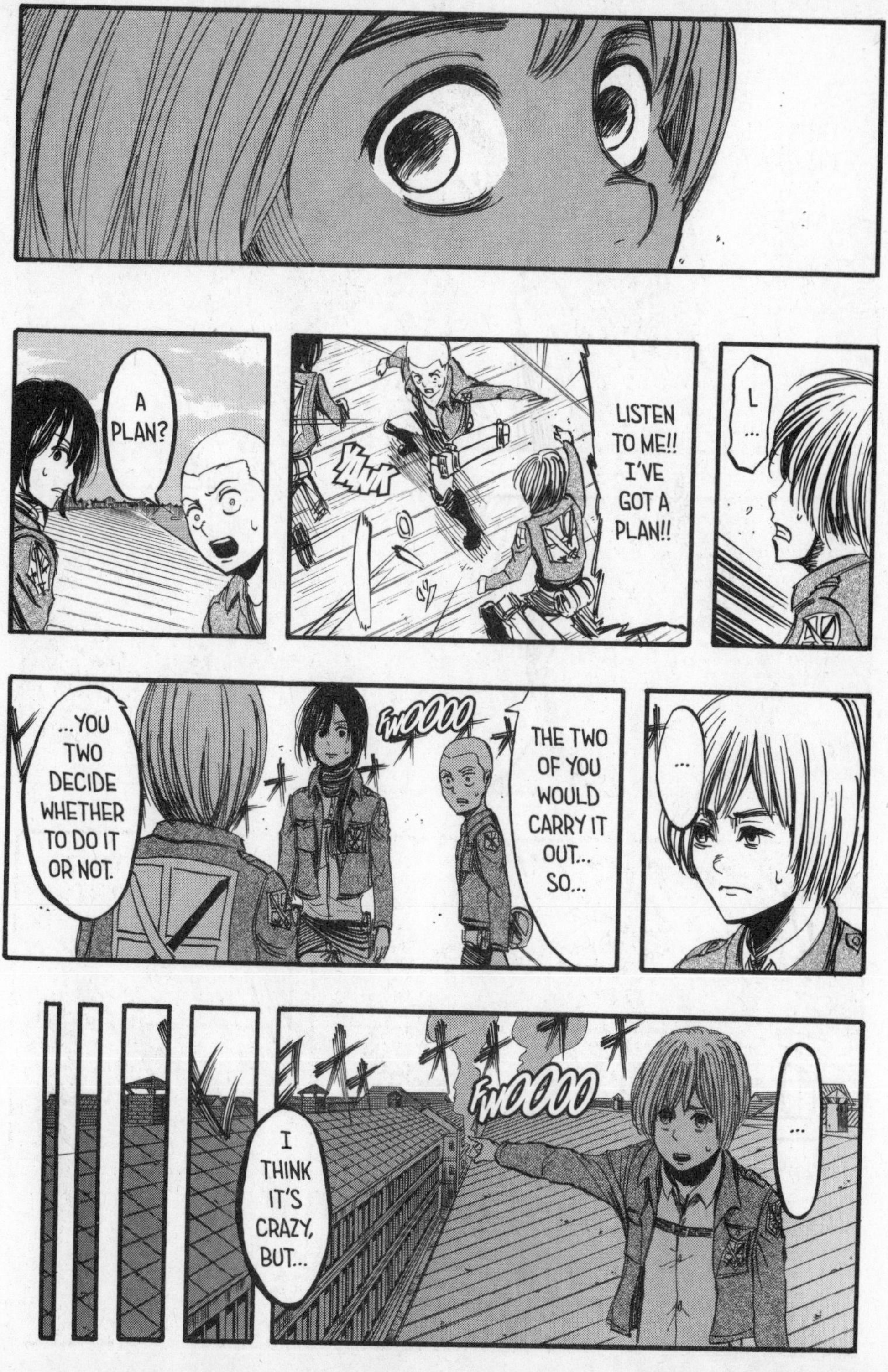
L ...
LISTEN TO ME!! I'VE GOT A PLAN!!
YANK
A PLAN?
...
THE TWO OF YOU WOULD CARRY IT OUT... SO...
FWOOOO
...YOU TWO DECIDE WHETHER TO DO IT OR NOT.
...
FWOOOO
I THINK IT'S CRAZY, BUT...

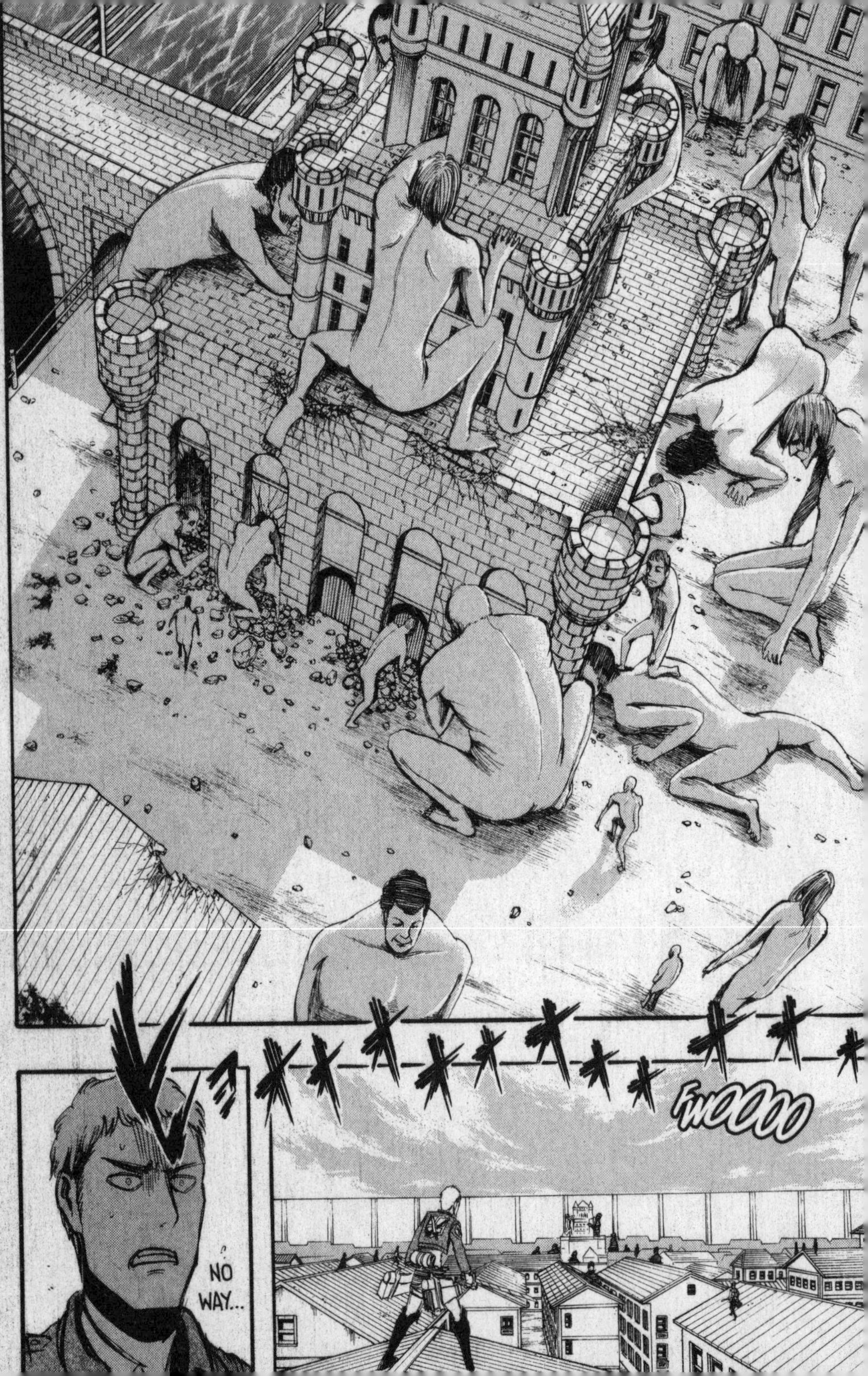
FWOOOO
NO WAY...

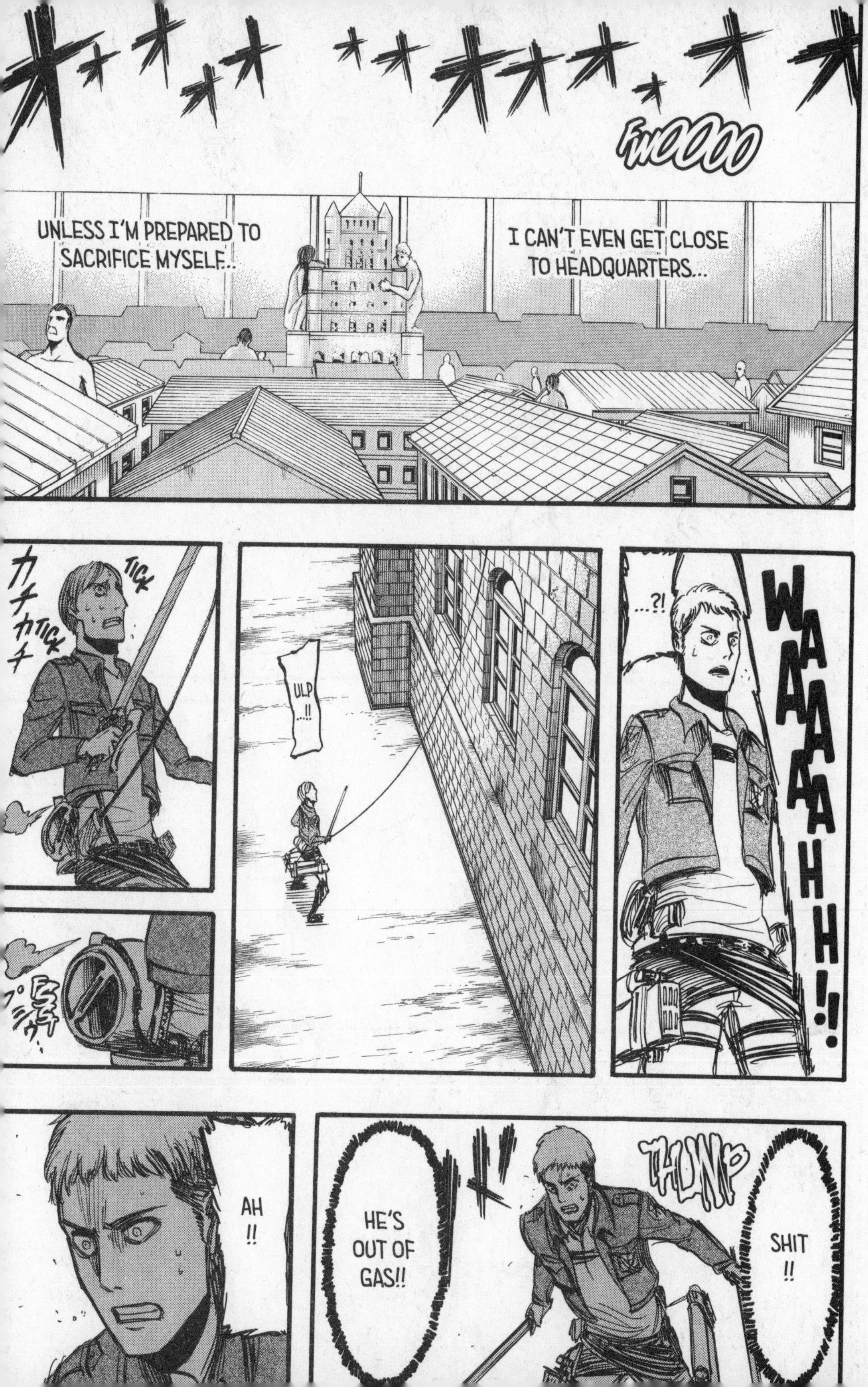

オォォォ オォ オォォォ ォォォォ
FWOOOOO
I CAN'T EVEN GET CLOSE TO HEADQUARTERS...
UNLESS I'M PREPARED TO SACRIFICE MYSELF...
...?!
WAAAAAH!!!
ULP ...!!
カチカチ
TICK TICK
THUMP
SHIT !!
HE'S OUT OF GAS!!
AH !!

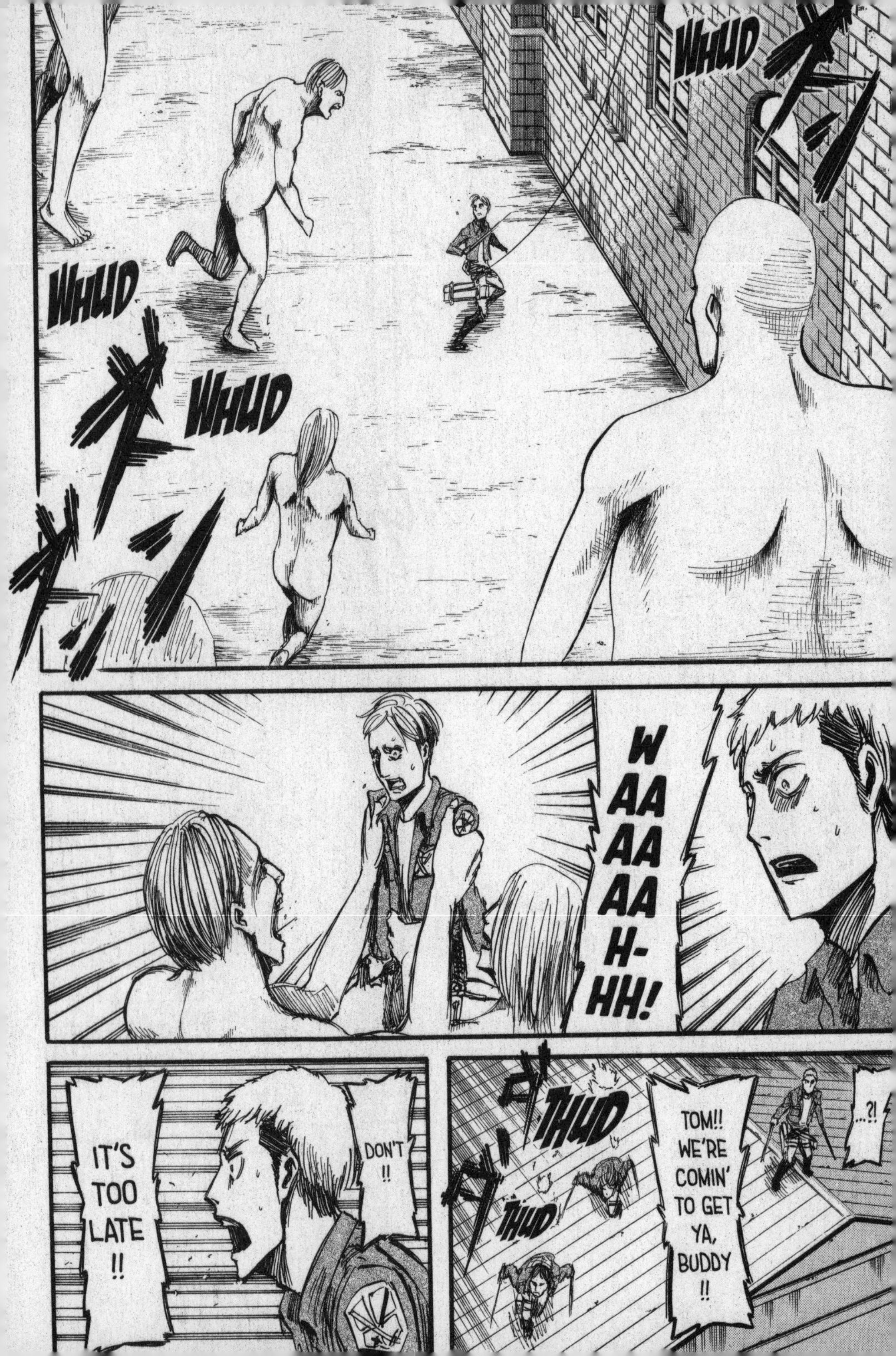
WHUD
WHUD
WHUD
WAAAAAAAAAH-HH!
...?!
TOM!! WE'RE COMIN' TO GET YA, BUDDY !!
THUD
THUD
DON'T !!
IT'S TOO LATE !!

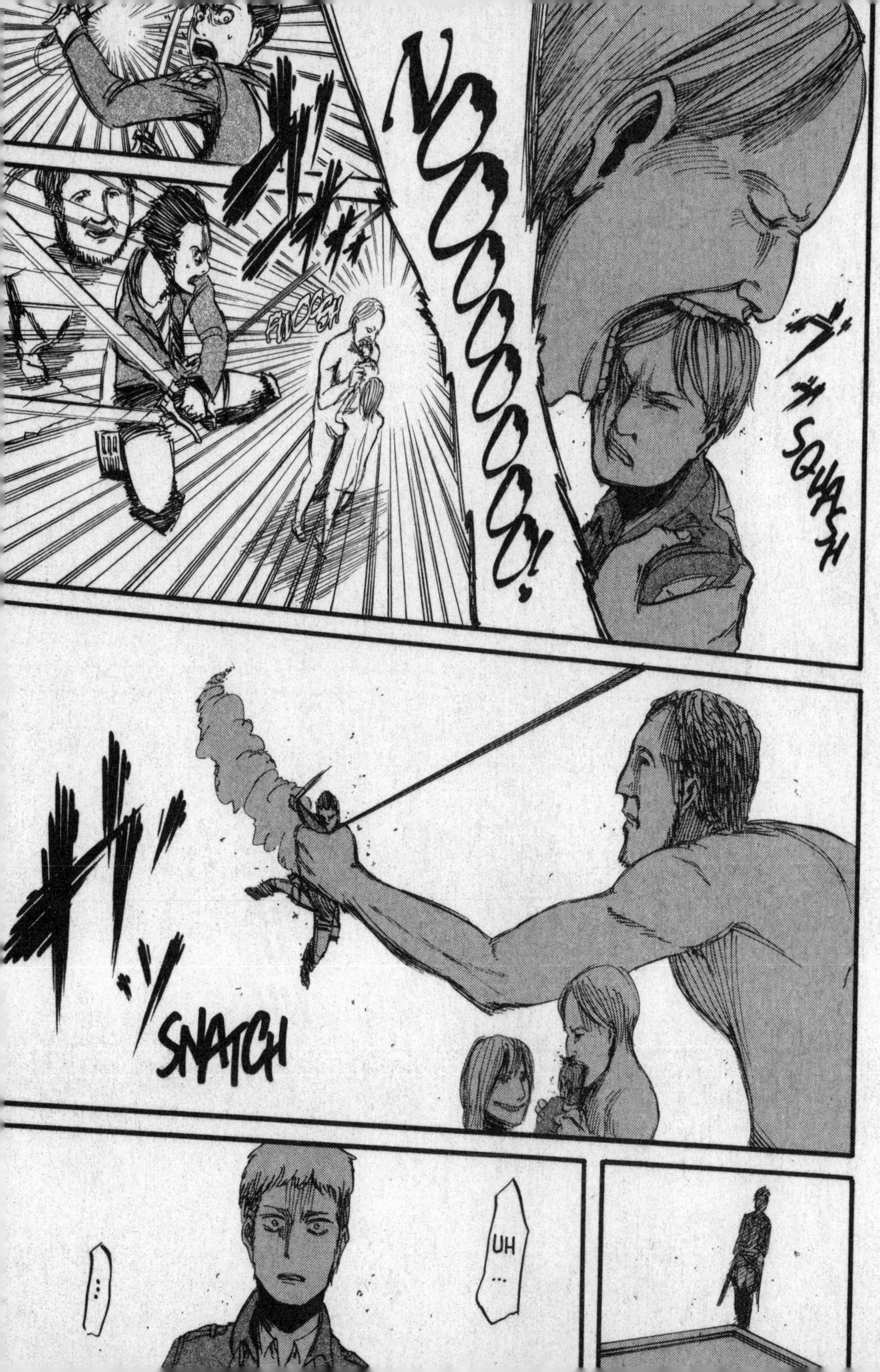
SQUASH
NOOOOOOOOO!
FWOOSH
SNATCH
UH ...
...

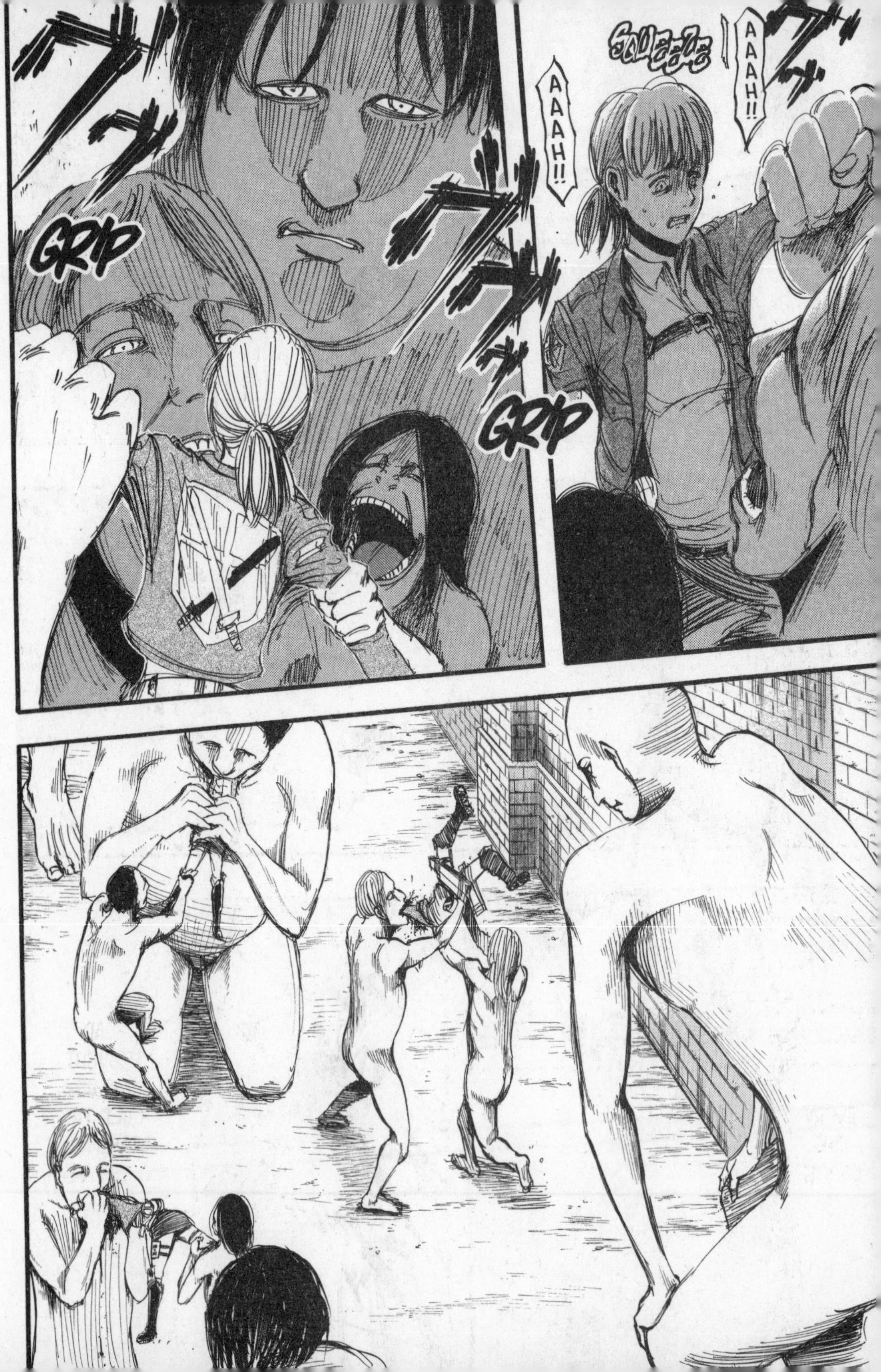
SQUEEEZE
AAAAH!!
AAAAH!!
GRIP
GRIP

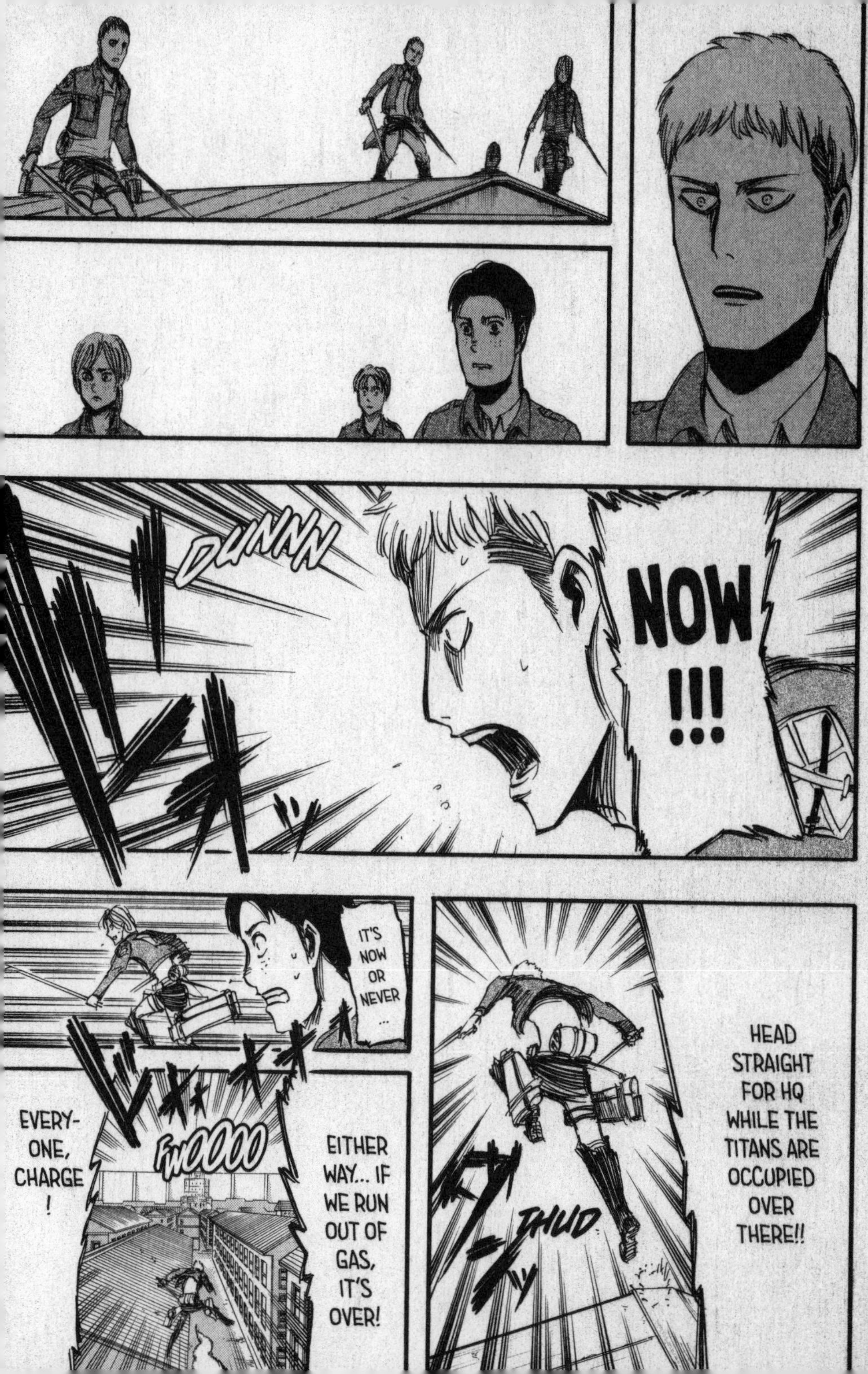
DUNNN
NOW!!!
HEAD STRAIGHT FOR HQ WHILE THE TITANS ARE OCCUPIED OVER THERE!!
THUD
IT'S NOW OR NEVER...
EITHER WAY... IF WE RUN OUT OF GAS, IT'S OVER!
EVERY-ONE, CHARGE!
FWOOOO

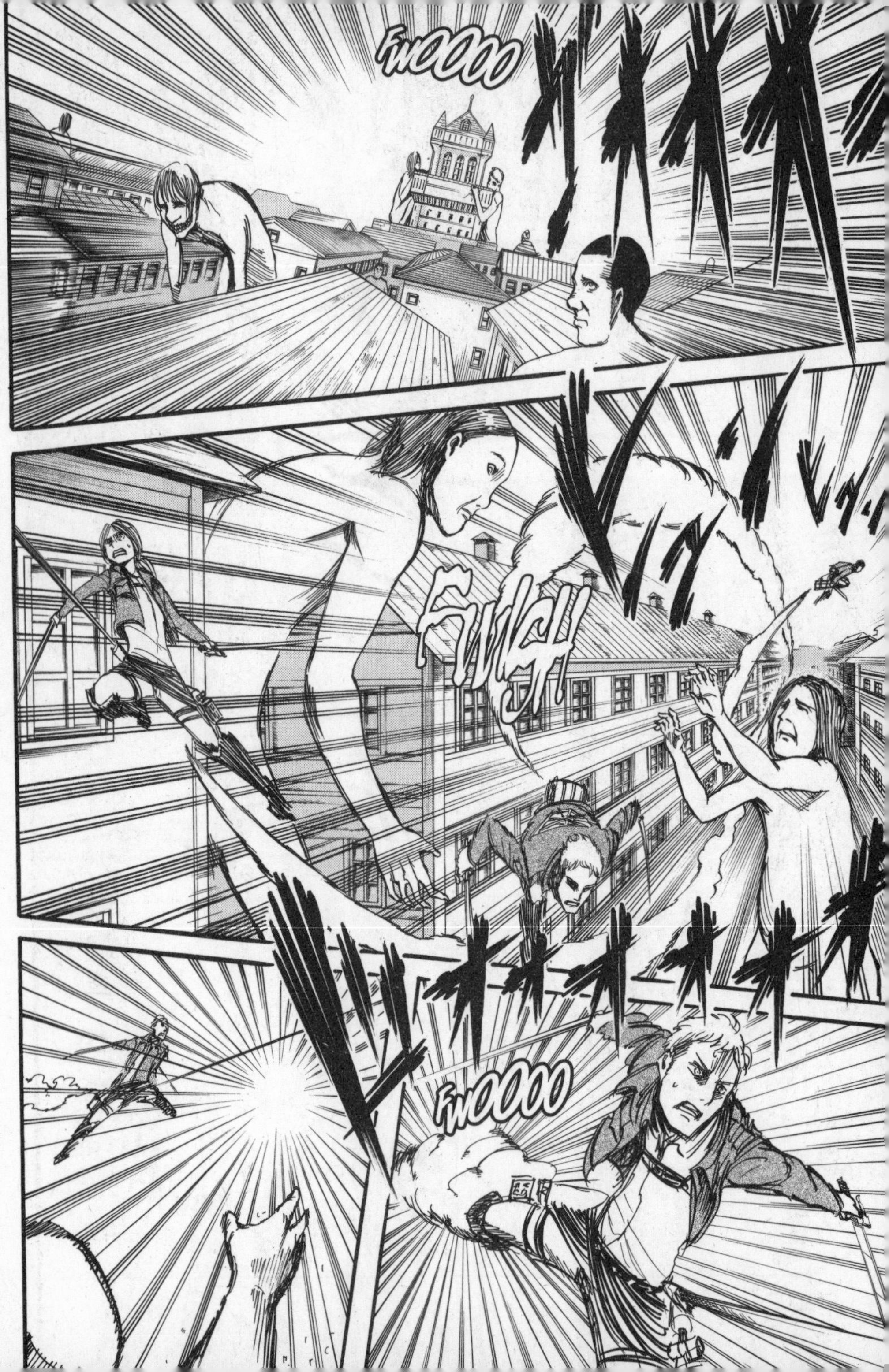
FWOOOO
FWIGH
FWOOOO

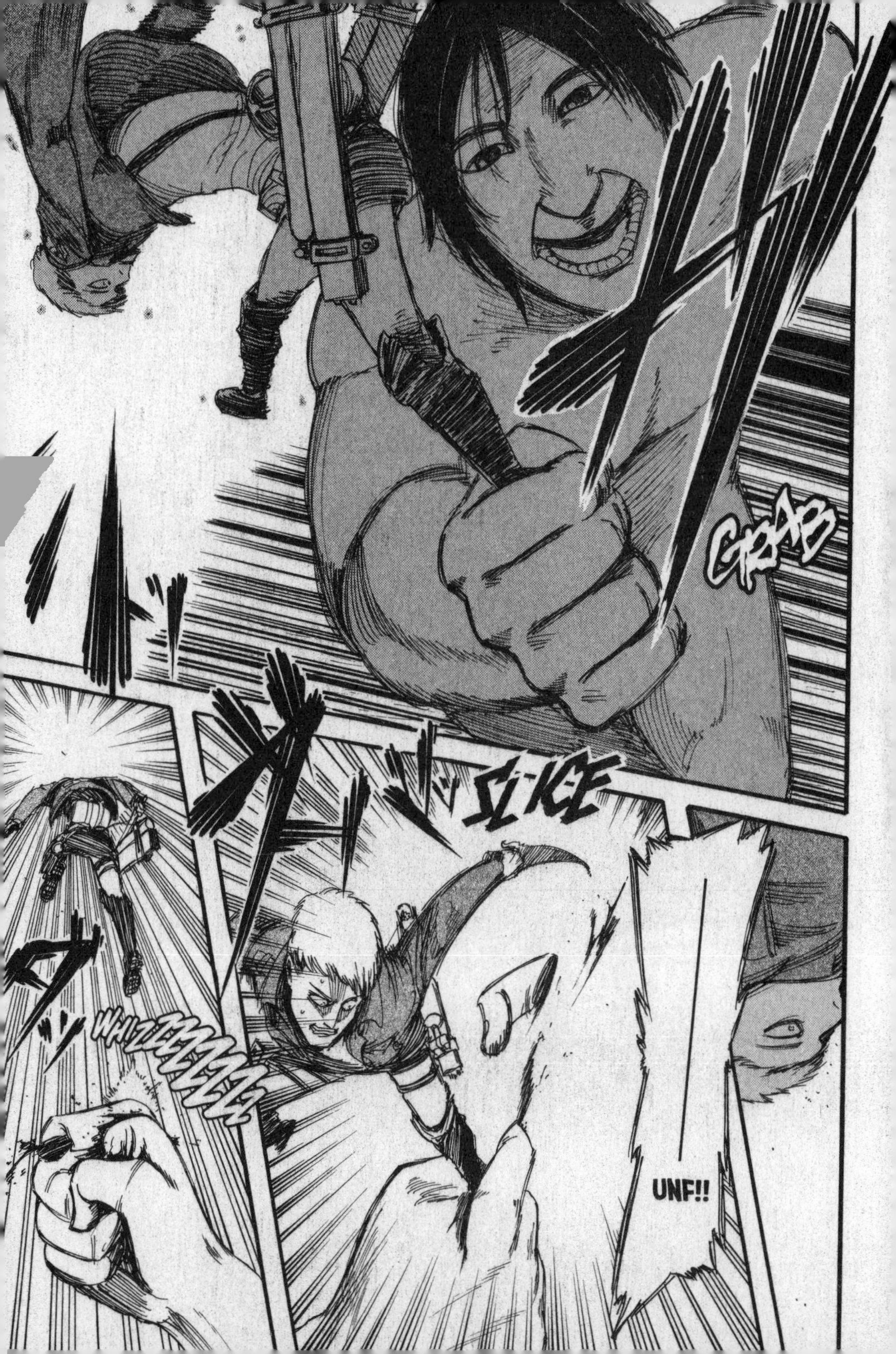
GRAB
SLICE
UNF!!

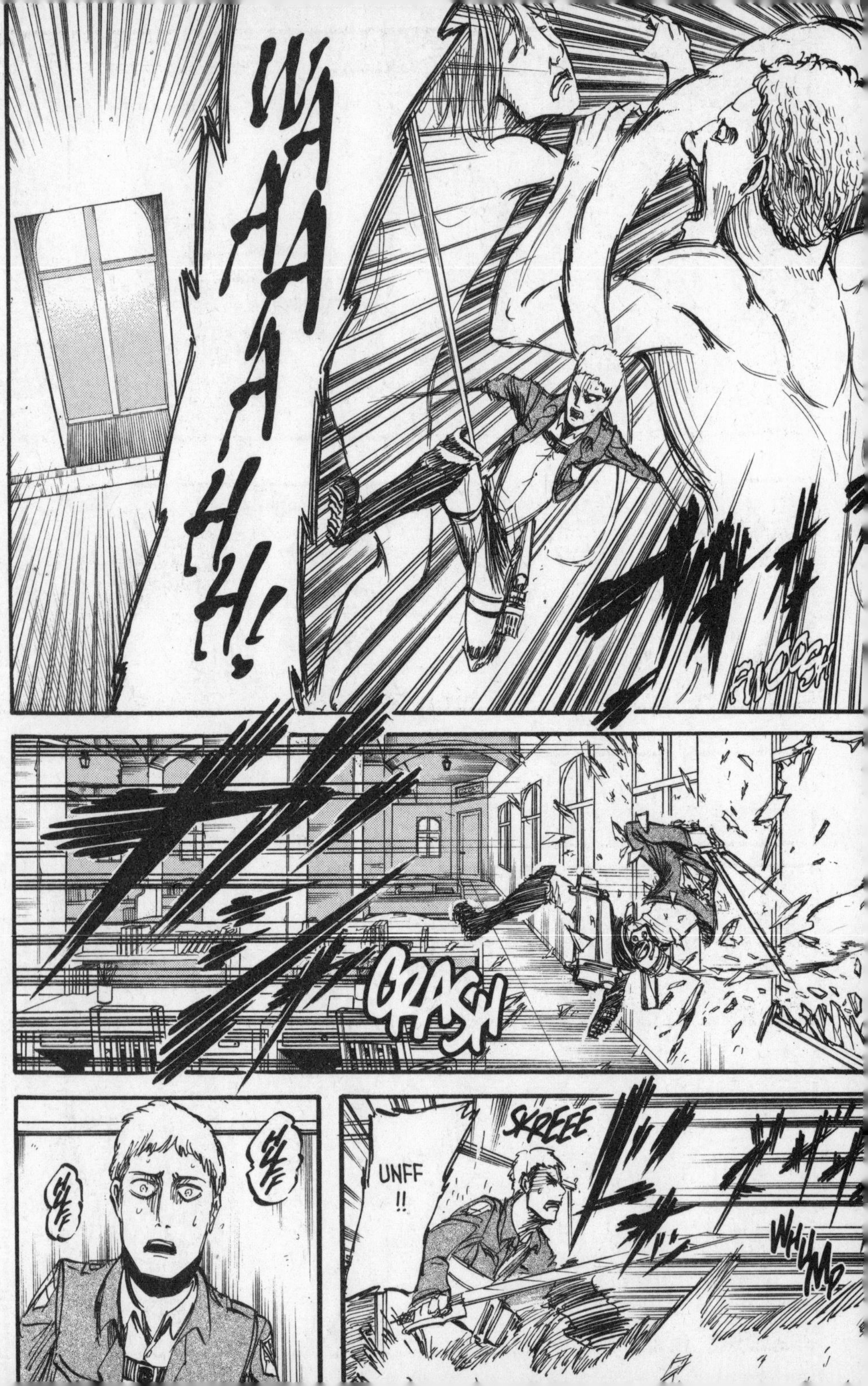
WAAAAHHHH!!
FWOOSH
CRASH
UNFF !!
SKREEE
WHUMP

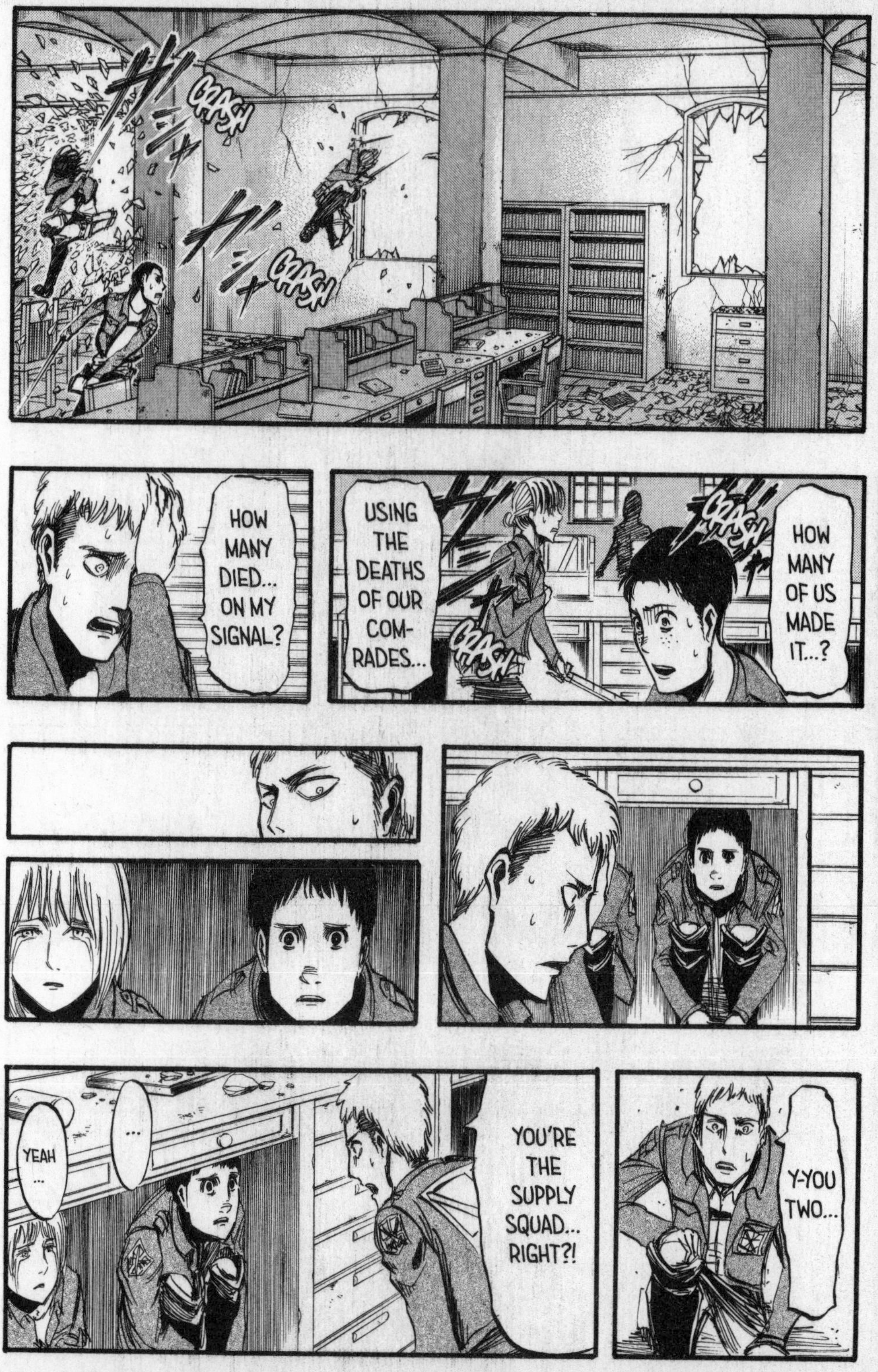
CRASH
CRASH
HOW MANY OF US MADE IT...?
CRASH
USING THE DEATHS OF OUR COM-RADES...
CRASH
HOW MANY DIED... ON MY SIGNAL?
Y-YOU TWO...
YOU'RE THE SUPPLY SQUAD... RIGHT?!
...
YEAH ...

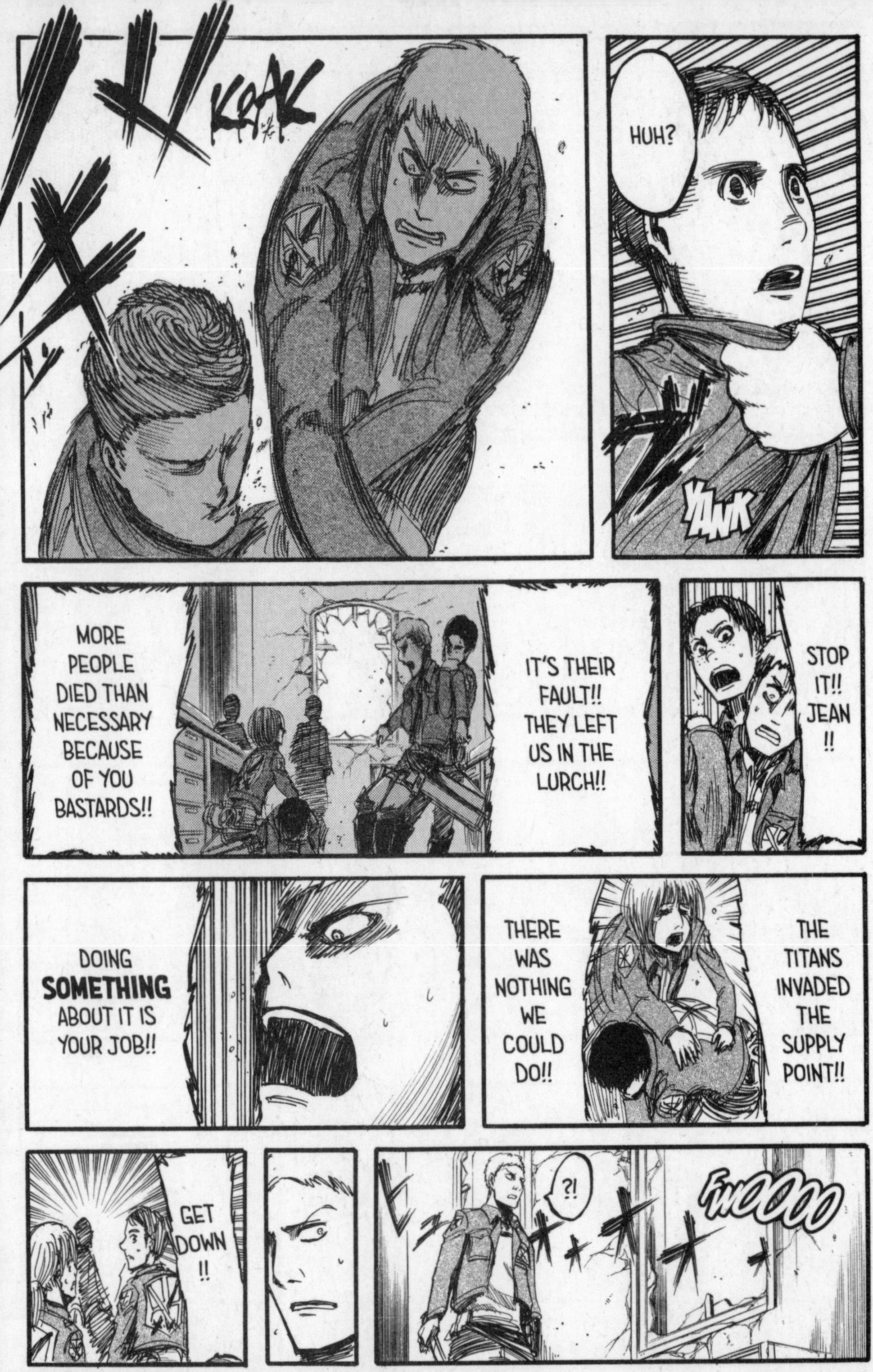
HUH?
YANK
KRAK
STOP IT!! JEAN !!
IT'S THEIR FAULT!! THEY LEFT US IN THE LURCH!!
MORE PEOPLE DIED THAN NECESSARY BECAUSE OF YOU BASTARDS!!
THE TITANS INVADED THE SUPPLY POINT!!
THERE WAS NOTHING WE COULD DO!!
DOING SOMETHING ABOUT IT IS YOUR JOB!!
FWOOOOO
?!
GET DOWN !!

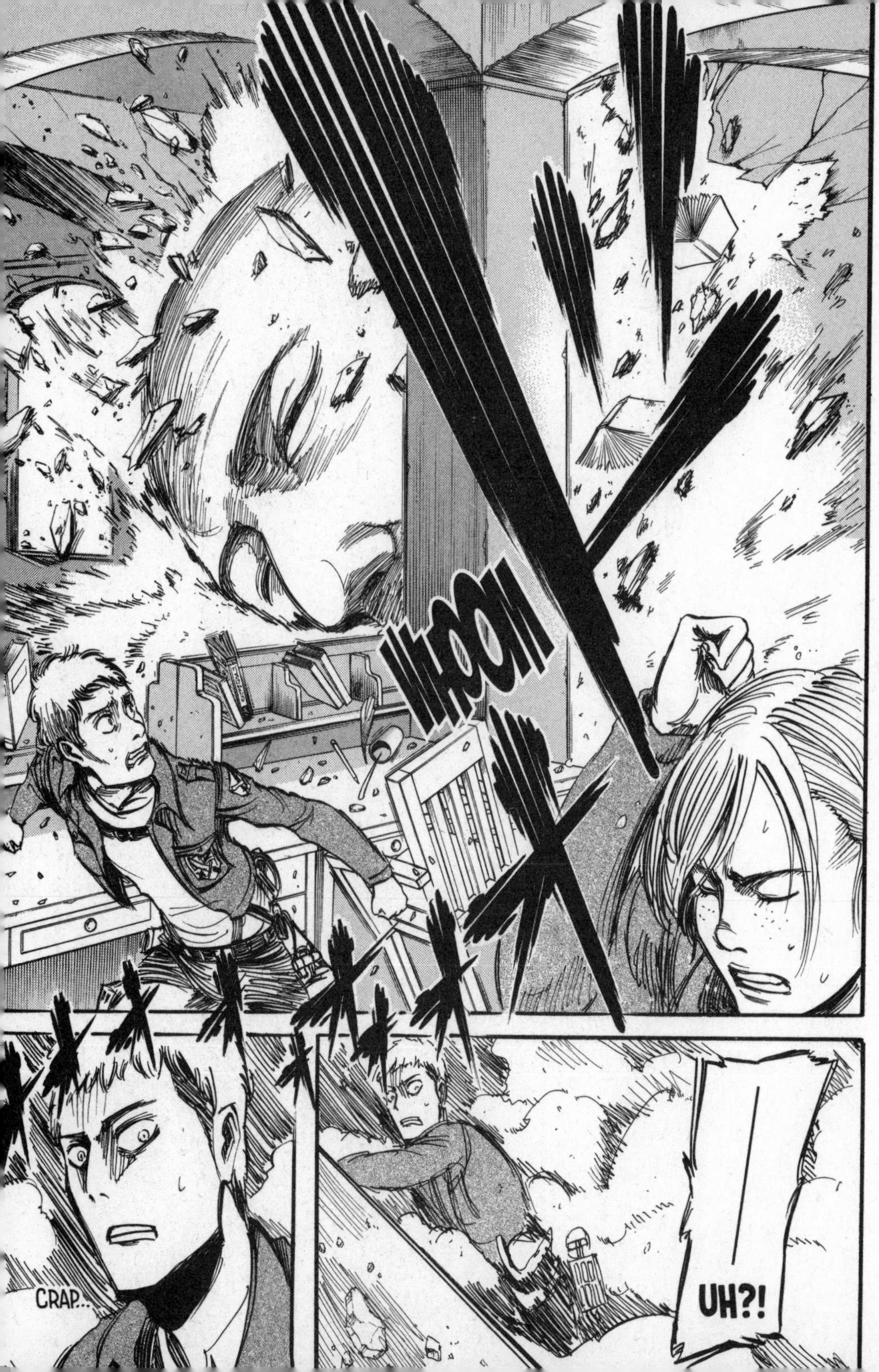
WHOOM
UH?!
CRAP...

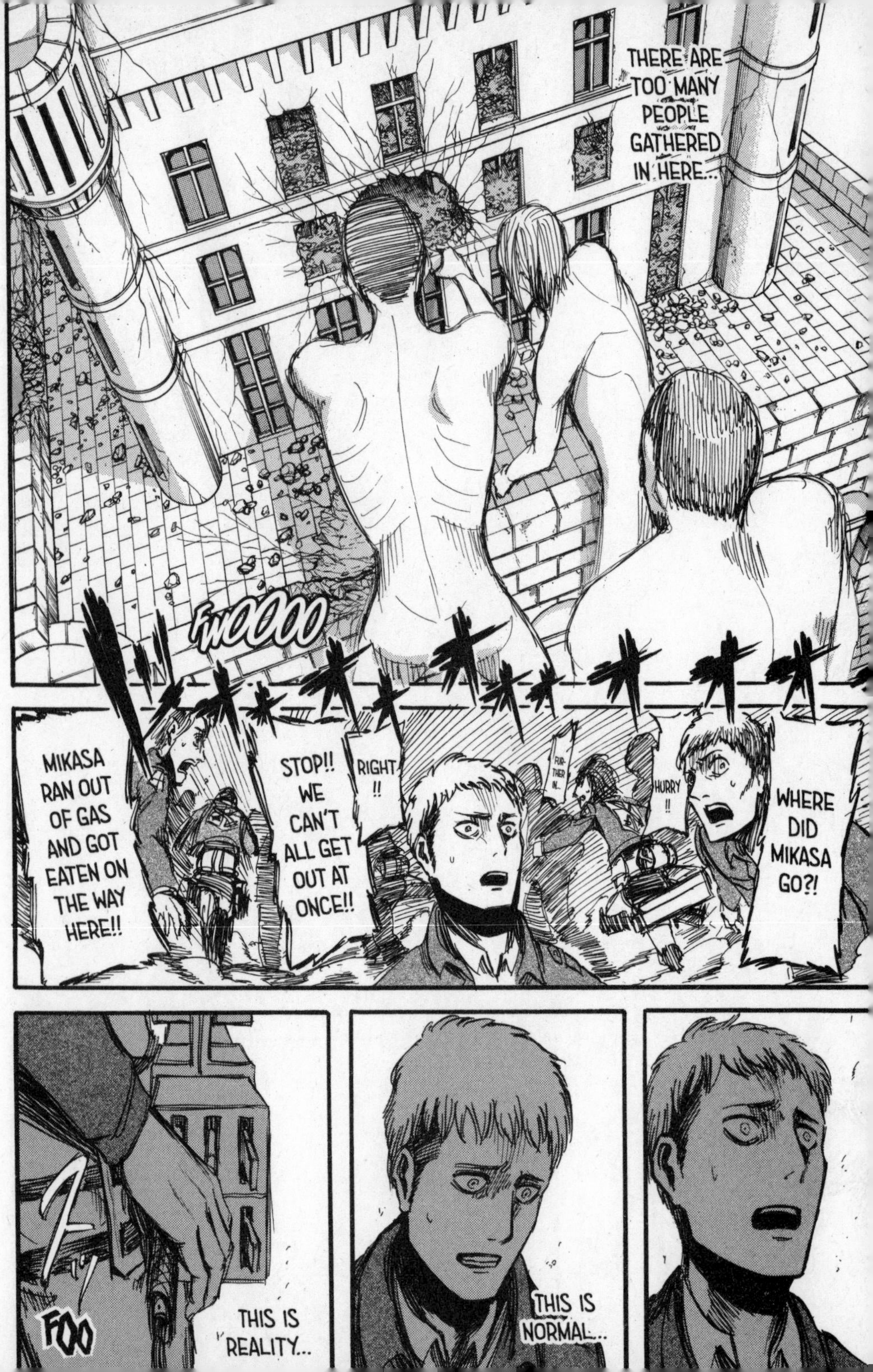
THERE ARE TOO MANY PEOPLE GATHERED IN HERE...
FWOOOO
WHERE DID MIKASA GO?!
HURRY !!
FURTHER IN...
RIGHT !!
STOP!! WE CAN'T ALL GET OUT AT ONCE!!
MIKASA RAN OUT OF GAS AND GOT EATEN ON THE WAY HERE!!
THIS IS NORMAL...
THIS IS REALITY...
FOO

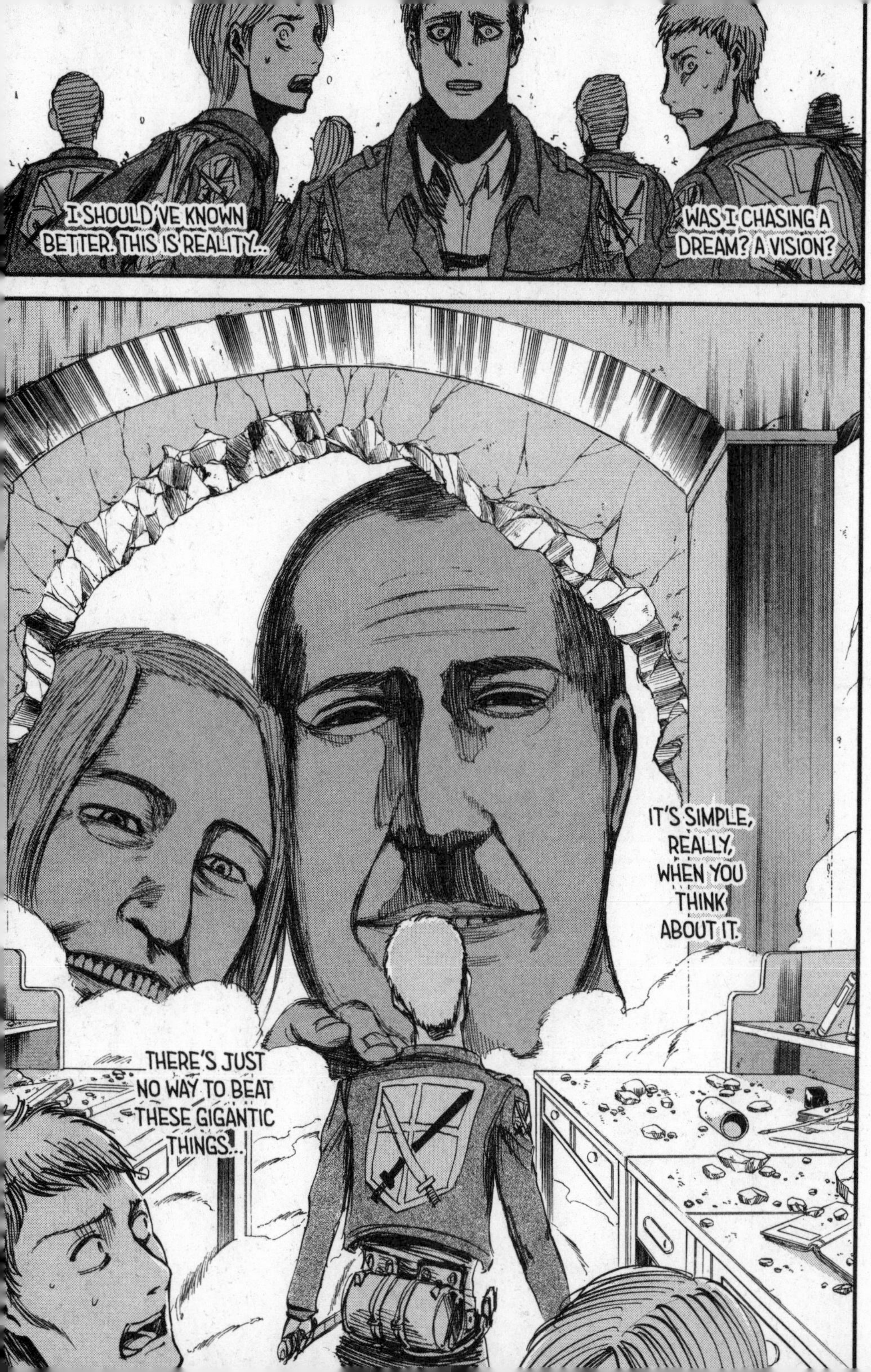
WAS I CHASING A DREAM? A VISION?
I SHOULD'VE KNOWN BETTER. THIS IS REALITY...
IT'S SIMPLE, REALLY, WHEN YOU THINK ABOUT IT.
THERE'S JUST NO WAY TO BEAT THESE GIGANTIC THINGS...

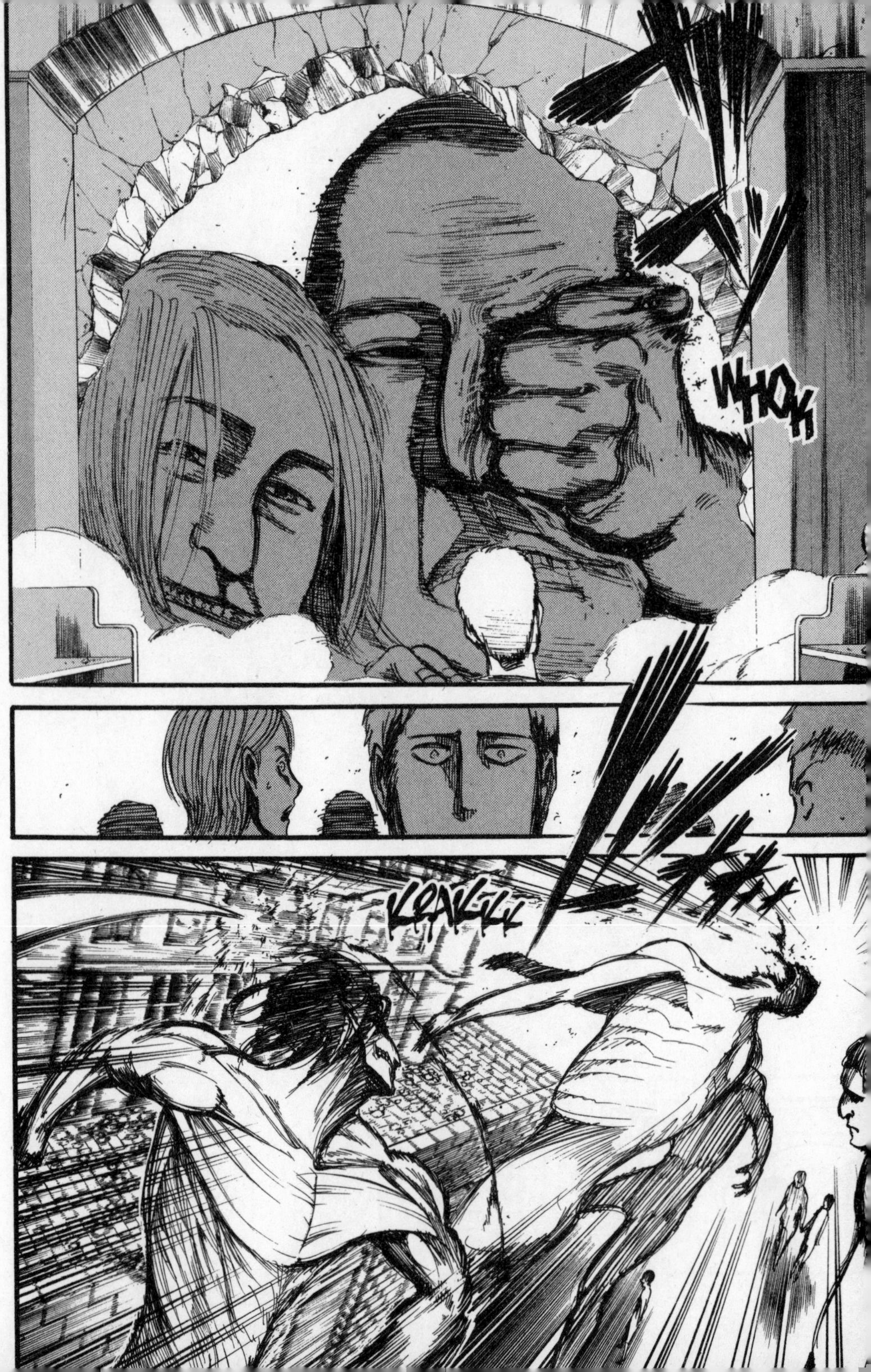
WHOK
KRAKH

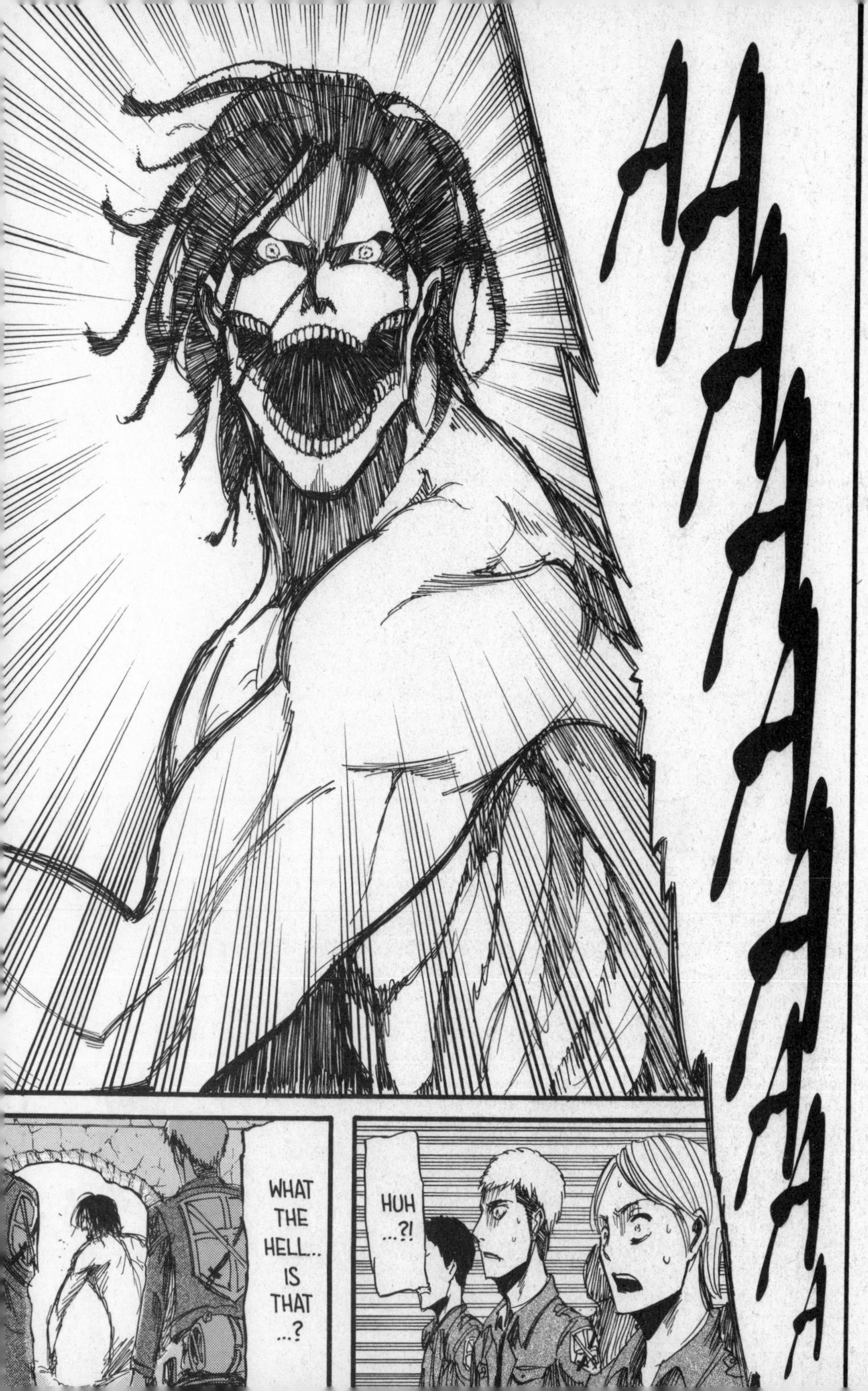
HUH ...?!
WHAT THE HELL... IS THAT ...?

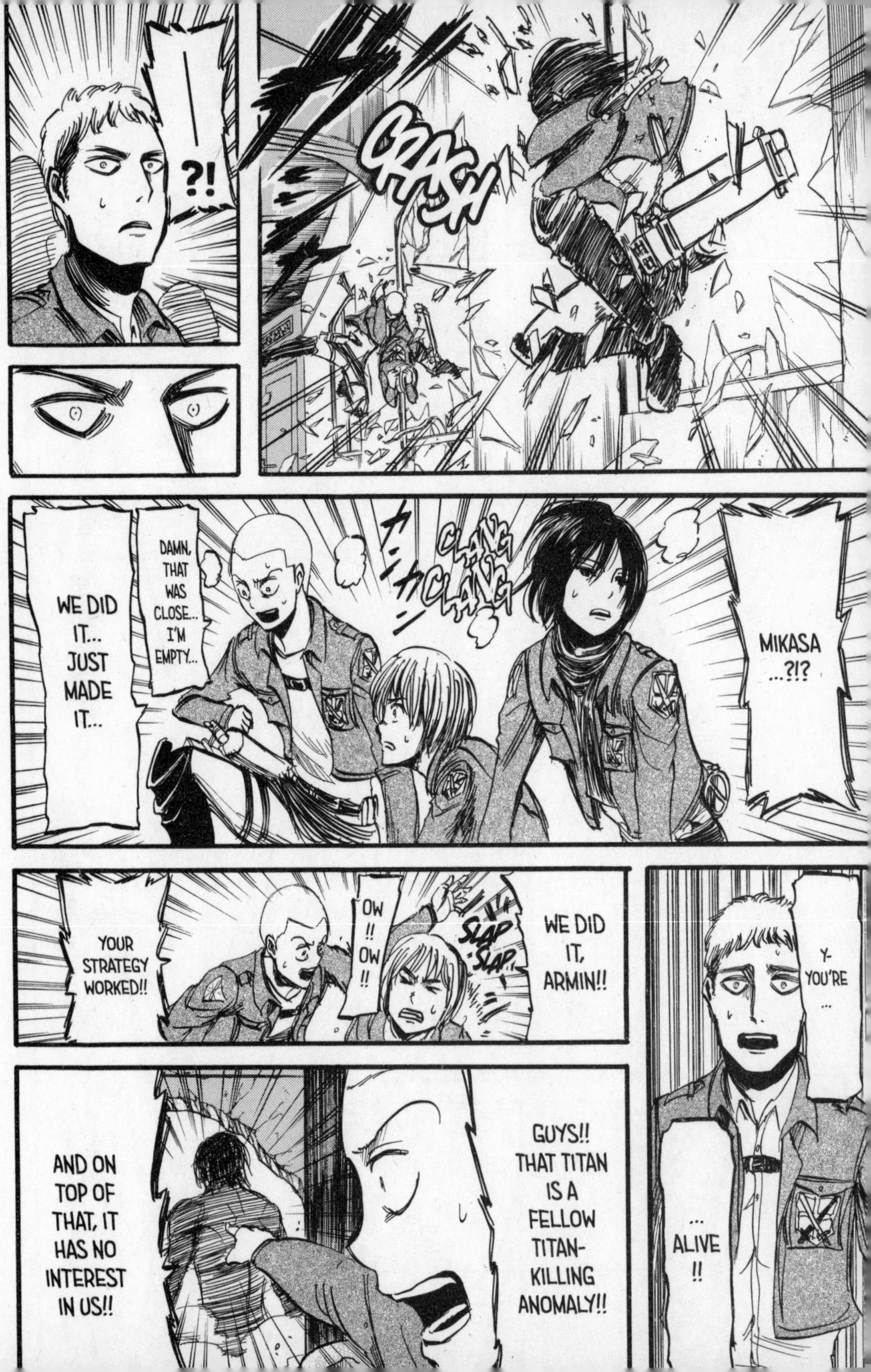
CRASH
?!
MIKASA ...?!?
CLANG CLANG
DAMN, THAT WAS CLOSE... I'M EMPTY...
WE DID IT... JUST MADE IT...
Y-YOU'RE ...
... ALIVE !!
WE DID IT, ARMIN!!
SLAP SLAP
OW!! OW!!
YOUR STRATEGY WORKED!!
GUYS!! THAT TITAN IS A FELLOW TITAN-KILLING ANOMALY!!
AND ON TOP OF THAT, IT HAS NO INTEREST IN US!!

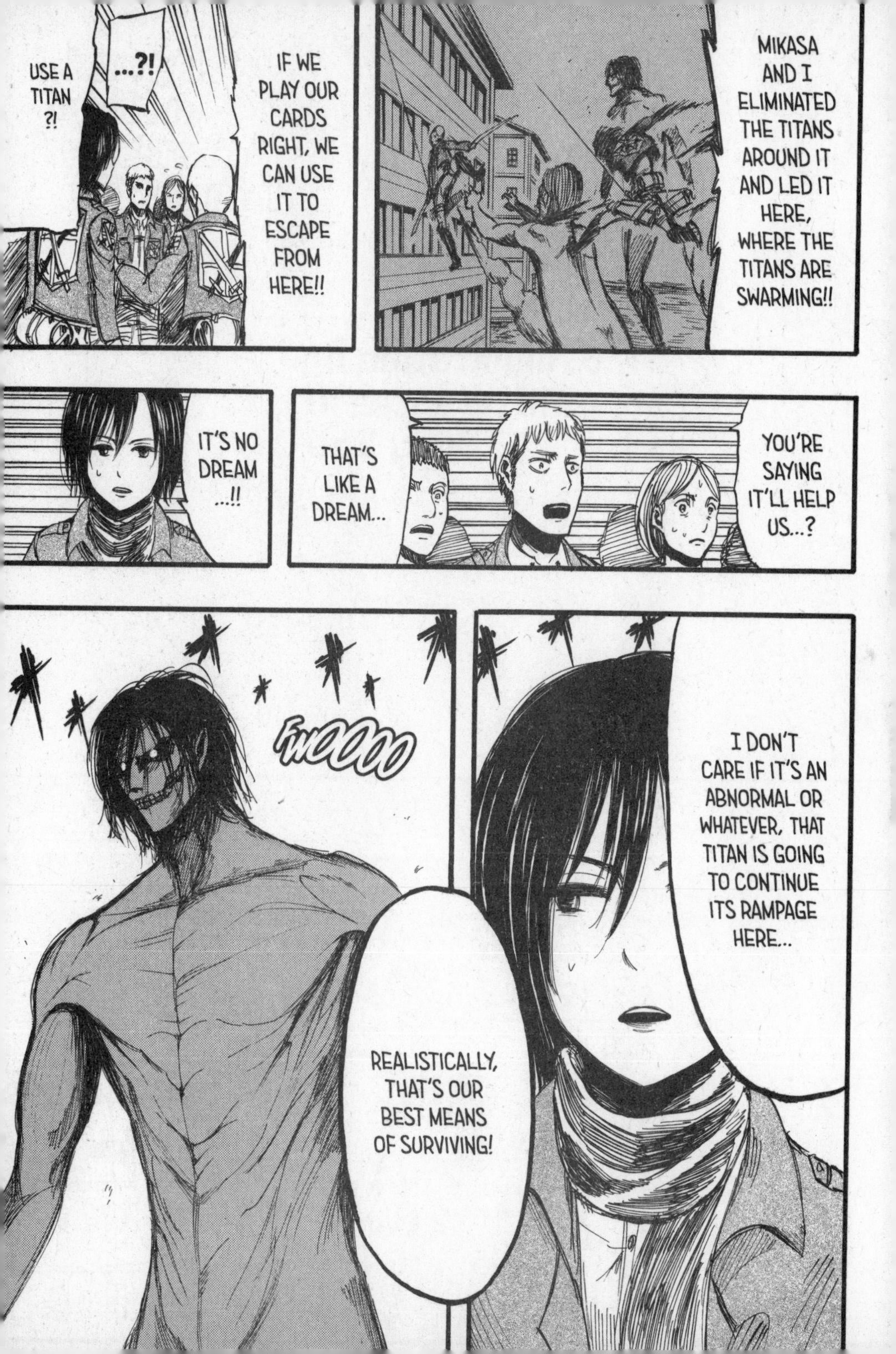
MIKASA AND I ELIMINATED THE TITANS AROUND IT AND LED IT HERE, WHERE THE TITANS ARE SWARMING!!
IF WE PLAY OUR CARDS RIGHT, WE CAN USE IT TO ESCAPE FROM HERE!!
...?!
USE A TITAN ?!
YOU'RE SAYING IT'LL HELP US...?
THAT'S LIKE A DREAM...
IT'S NO DREAM ...!!
I DON'T CARE IF IT'S AN ABNORMAL OR WHATEVER, THAT TITAN IS GOING TO CONTINUE ITS RAMPAGE HERE...
REALISTICALLY, THAT'S OUR BEST MEANS OF SURVIVING!
FWOOOOO

6. Illustration of Differences in Body Size

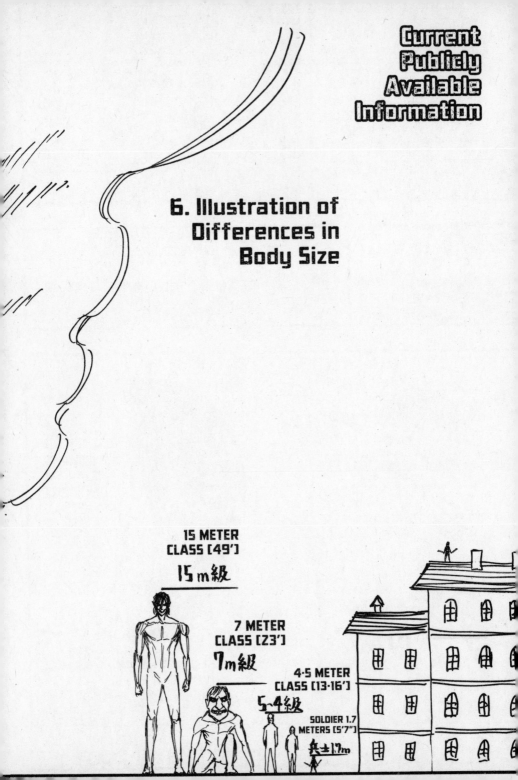

15 METER
CLASS [49']

15m級

7 METER
CLASS [23']

7m級

4·5 METER
CLASS [13·16']

5~4級

SOLDIER 1.7
METERS [5'7"]

兵士1.7m

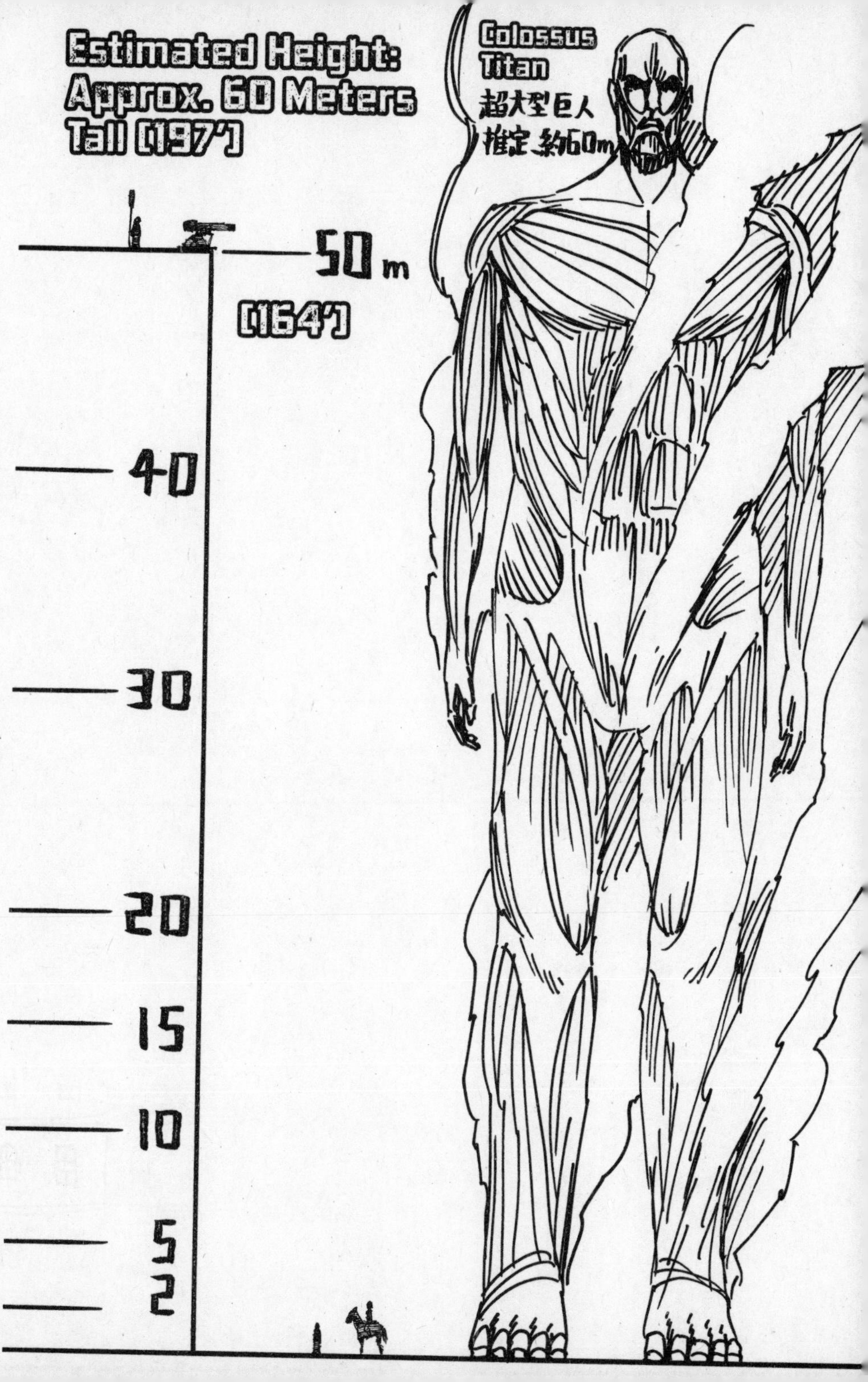
Estimated Height: Approx. 60 Meters Tall [197']
Colossus Titan
超大型巨人
推定 約60m
50 m
[164']
40
30
20
15
10
5
2

ATTACK on TITAN

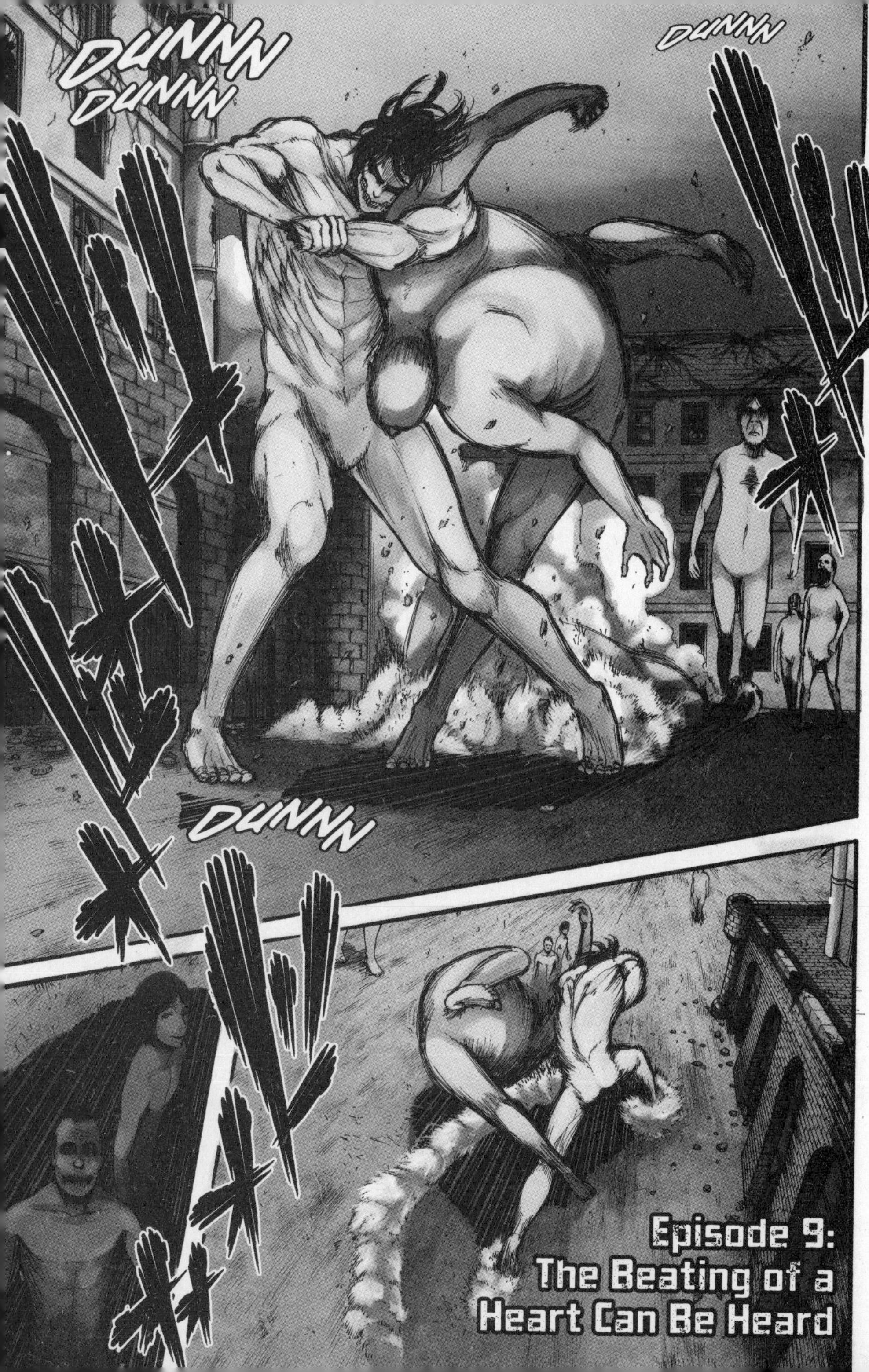
DUNNN
DUNNN
DUNNN
DUNNN
Episode 9:
The Beating of a
Heart Can Be Heard

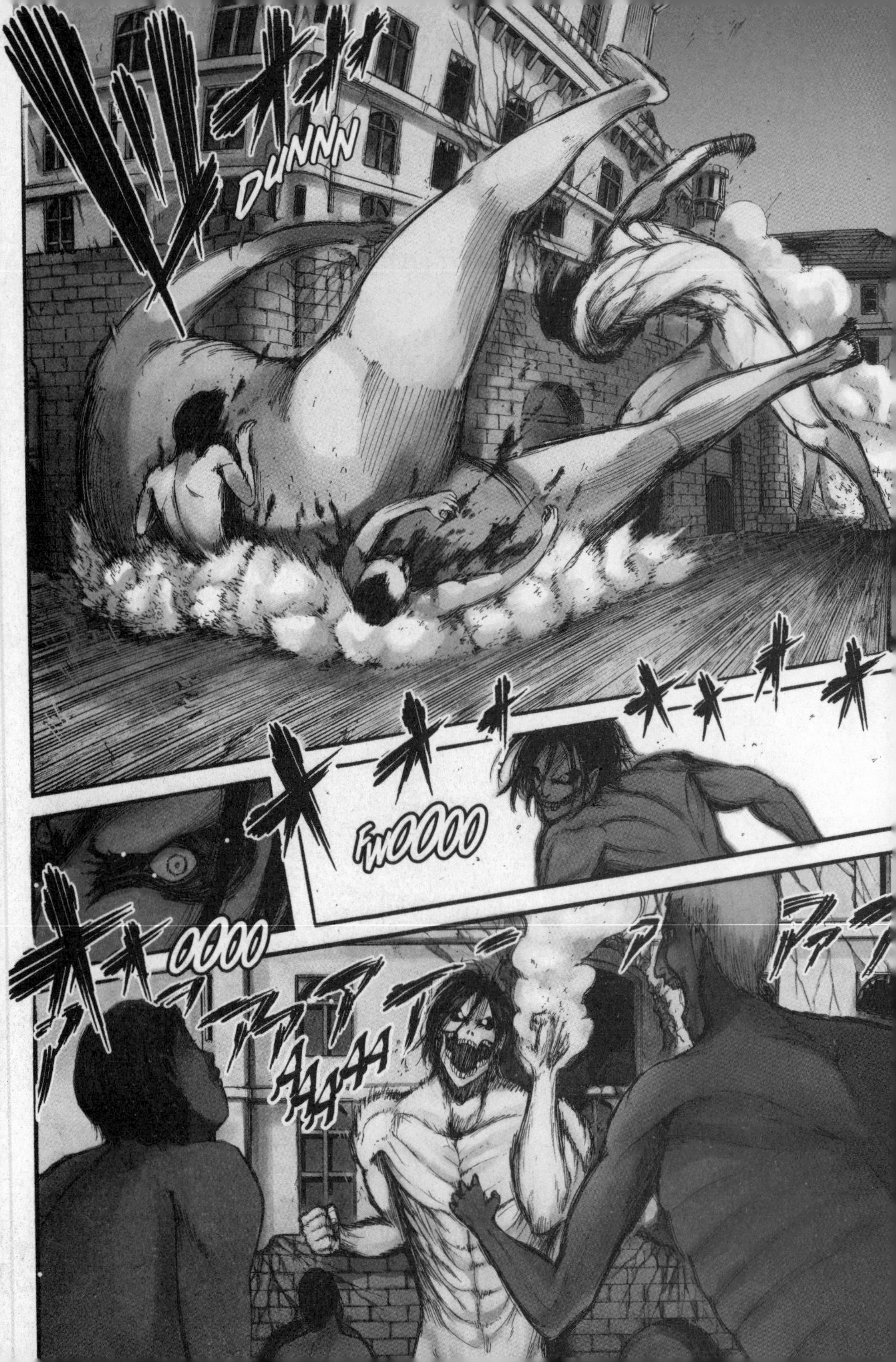
DUNNN
FWOOOO
OOOO
AAAA

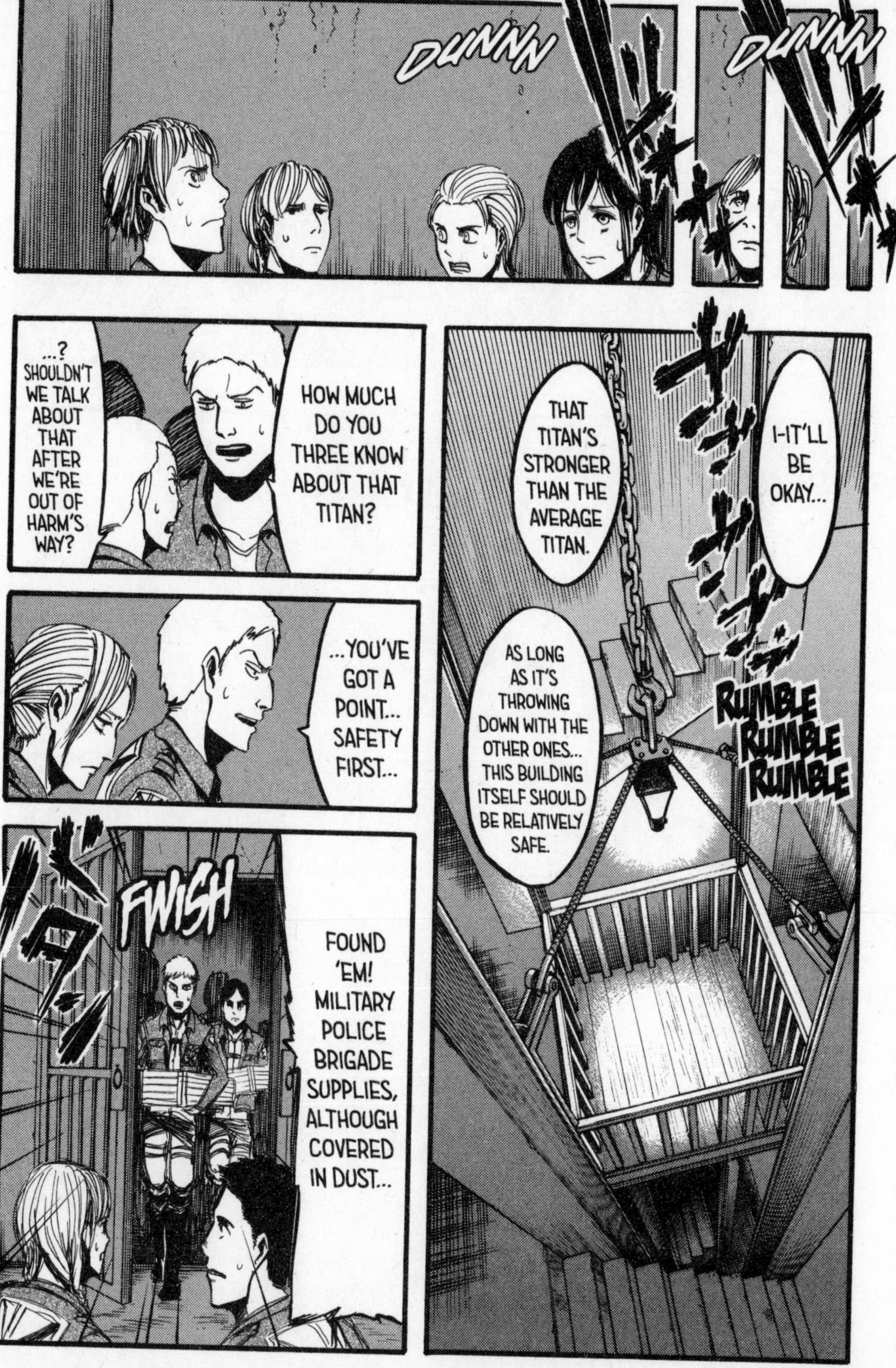
DUNNN
DUNNN
I-IT'LL BE OKAY...
THAT TITAN'S STRONGER THAN THE AVERAGE TITAN.
AS LONG AS IT'S THROWING DOWN WITH THE OTHER ONES... THIS BUILDING ITSELF SHOULD BE RELATIVELY SAFE.
RUMBLE RUMBLE RUMBLE
HOW MUCH DO YOU THREE KNOW ABOUT THAT TITAN?
...? SHOULDN'T WE TALK ABOUT THAT AFTER WE'RE OUT OF HARM'S WAY?
...YOU'VE GOT A POINT... SAFETY FIRST...
FOUND 'EM! MILITARY POLICE BRIGADE SUPPLIES, ALTHOUGH COVERED IN DUST...
FWISH

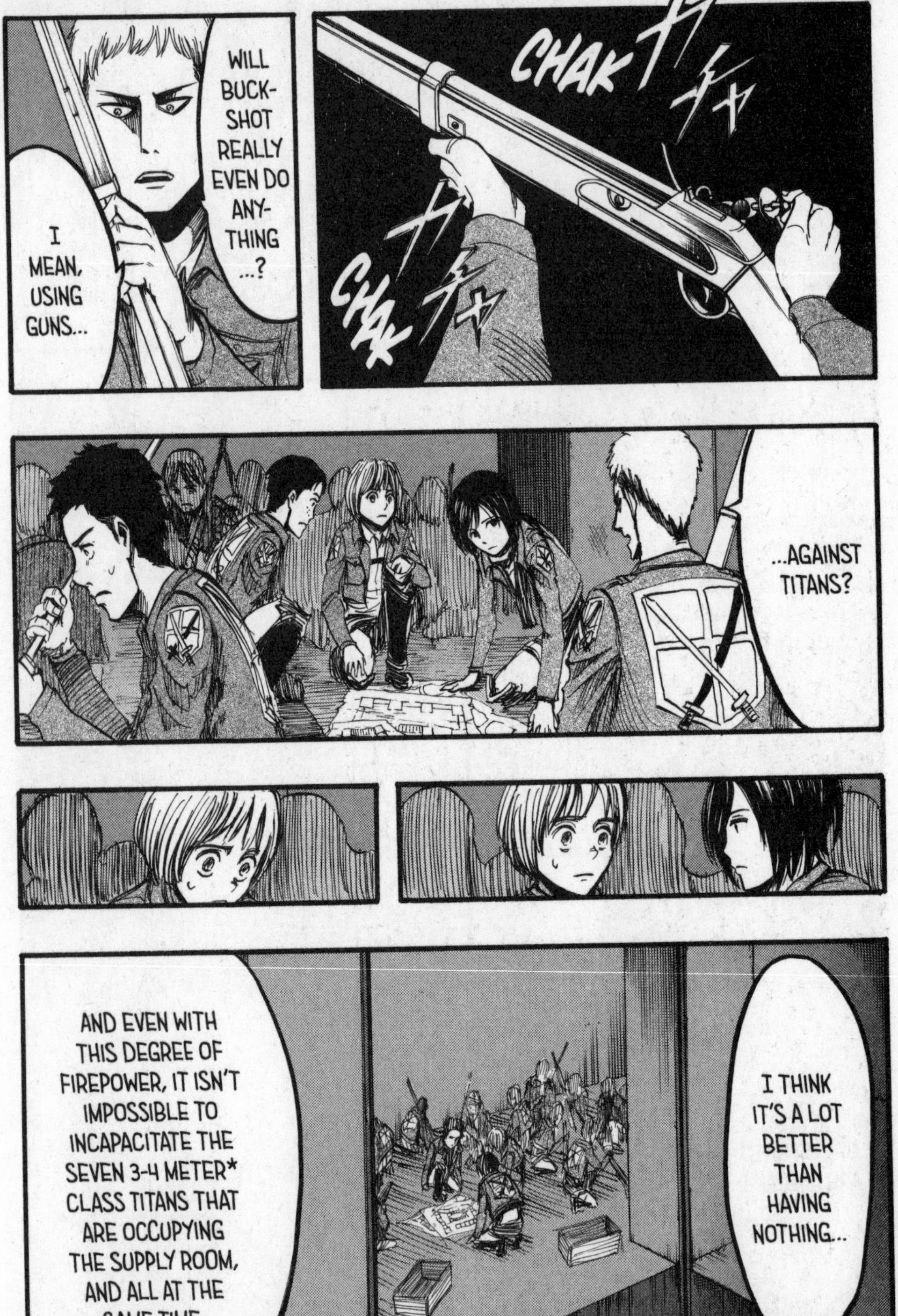
CHAK
カチャ
CHAK
カチャ
WILL BUCK-SHOT REALLY EVEN DO ANY-THING ...?
I MEAN, USING GUNS...
...AGAINST TITANS?
I THINK IT'S A LOT BETTER THAN HAVING NOTHING...
AND EVEN WITH THIS DEGREE OF FIREPOWER, IT ISN'T IMPOSSIBLE TO INCAPACITATE THE SEVEN 3-4 METER* CLASS TITANS THAT ARE OCCUPYING THE SUPPLY ROOM, AND ALL AT THE SAME TIME.

* APPROX. 10-13'

FIRST... WE USE THE LIFT TO LOWER MOST OF US FROM THE CENTER OF THE CEILING. IF THOSE SEVEN TITANS ARE "NORMALS", A LARGE NUMBER OF PEOPLE SHOULD BE ENOUGH TO DRAW THEM TO THE CENTER OF THE ROOM.

NEXT, THE PEOPLE IN THE LIFT WILL FIRE AT THE SEVEN TITANS' FACES SIMULTANE-OUSLY... THUS ROBBING THEM OF THEIR VISION.

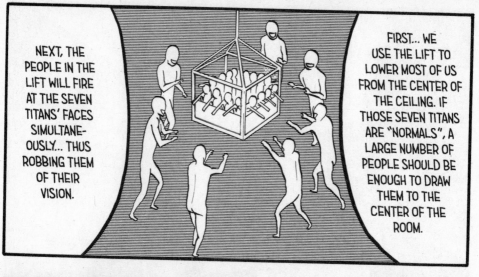

...THE NEXT INSTANT WILL DECIDE EVERY-THING.

AND THEN...

SEVEN PEOPLE HIDING NEAR THE CEILING WILL SWOOP DOWN IN TIME WITH THE FIRING AND SLASH THE TITANS' VITAL SPOT. IN OTHER WORDS...

...EVERYTHING RIDES ON THIS ONE ATTACK. ALL OF OUR LIVES ARE AT STAKE.

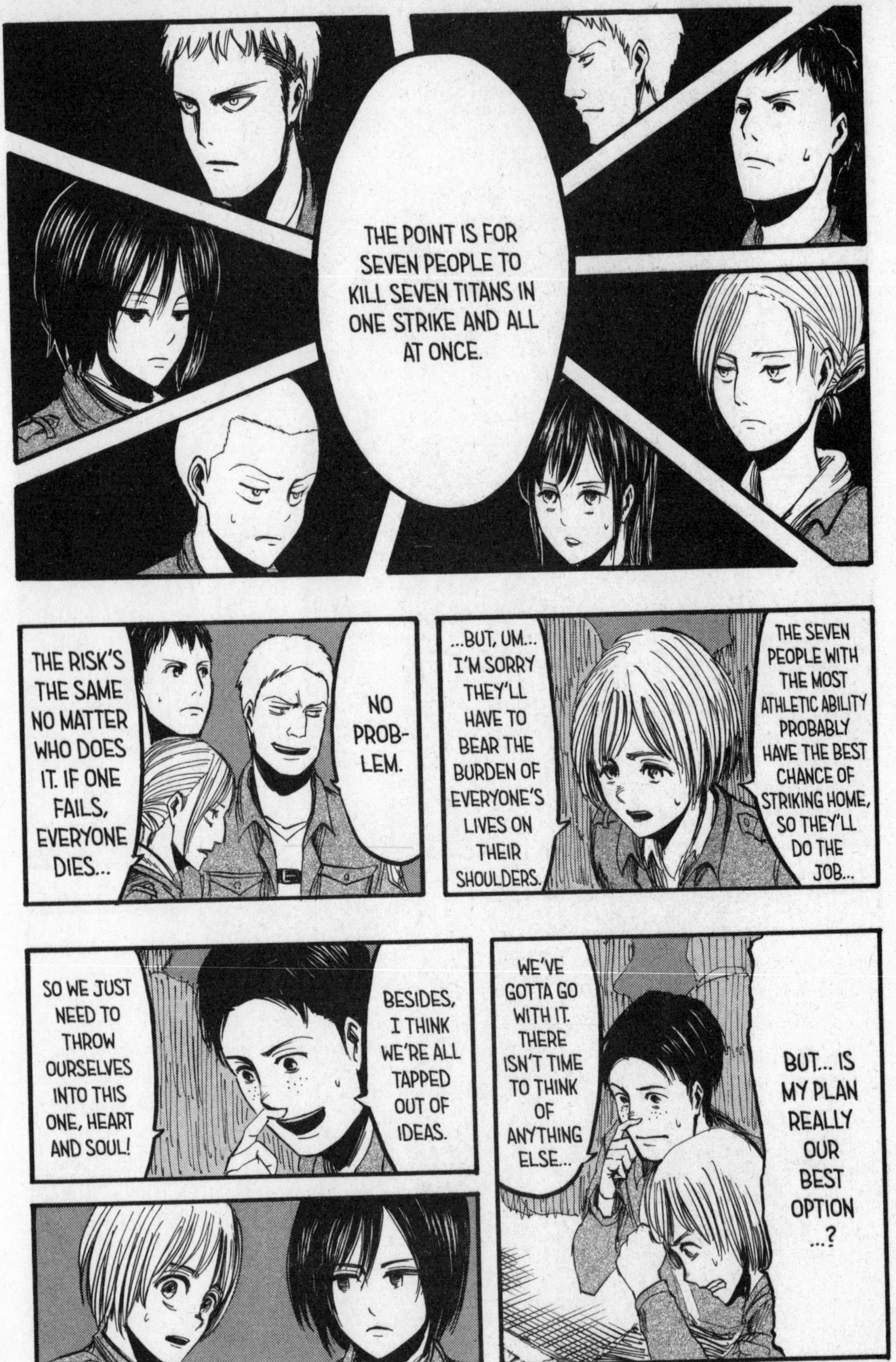
THE POINT IS FOR SEVEN PEOPLE TO KILL SEVEN TITANS IN ONE STRIKE AND ALL AT ONCE.
THE SEVEN PEOPLE WITH THE MOST ATHLETIC ABILITY PROBABLY HAVE THE BEST CHANCE OF STRIKING HOME, SO THEY'LL DO THE JOB...
...BUT, UM... I'M SORRY THEY'LL HAVE TO BEAR THE BURDEN OF EVERYONE'S LIVES ON THEIR SHOULDERS.
NO PROB-LEM.
THE RISK'S THE SAME NO MATTER WHO DOES IT. IF ONE FAILS, EVERYONE DIES...
WE'VE GOTTA GO WITH IT. THERE ISN'T TIME TO THINK OF ANYTHING ELSE...
BUT... IS MY PLAN REALLY OUR BEST OPTION ...?
BESIDES, I THINK WE'RE ALL TAPPED OUT OF IDEAS.
SO WE JUST NEED TO THROW OURSELVES INTO THIS ONE, HEART AND SOUL!

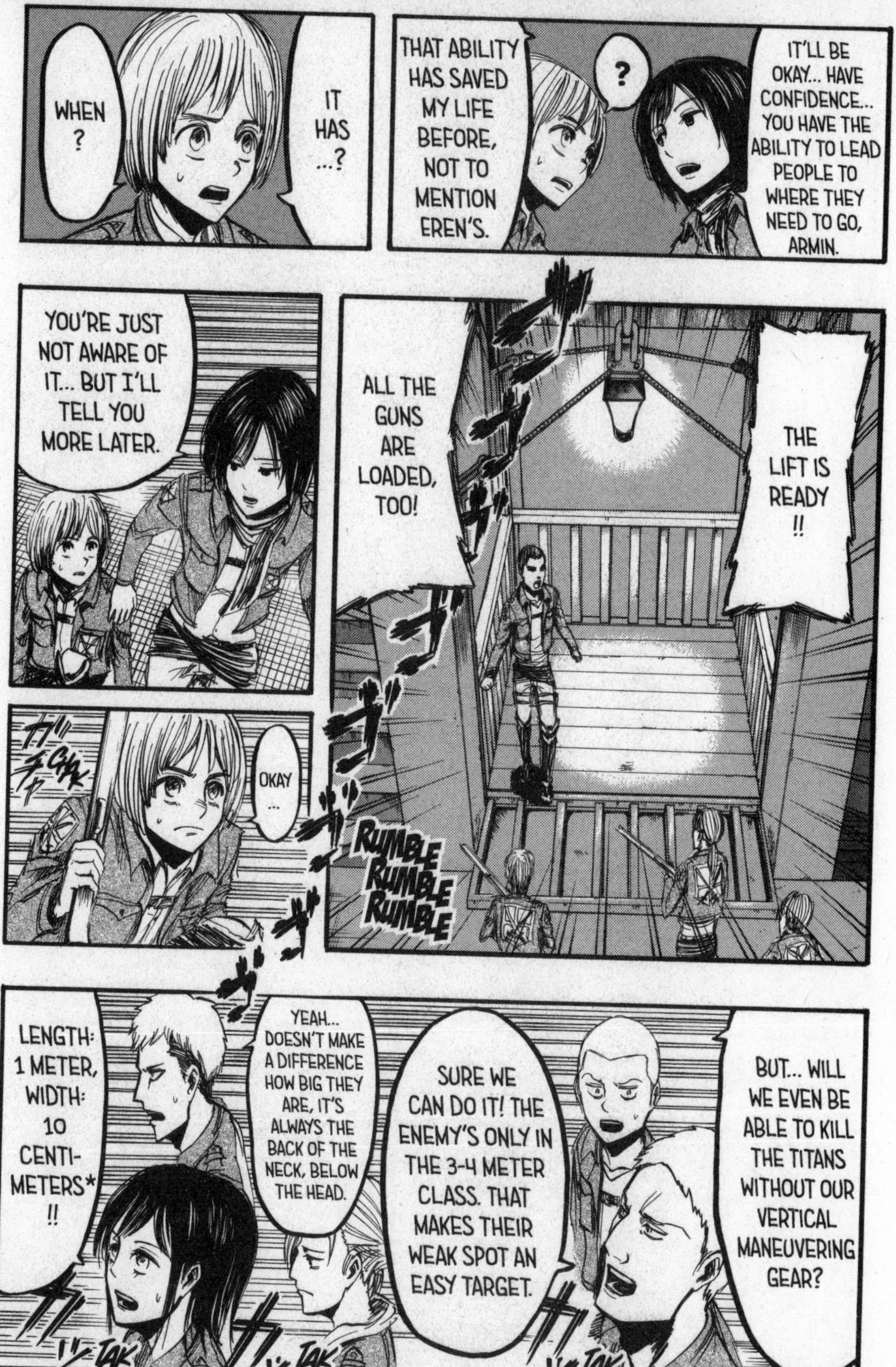
IT'LL BE OKAY... HAVE CONFIDENCE... YOU HAVE THE ABILITY TO LEAD PEOPLE TO WHERE THEY NEED TO GO, ARMIN.
?
THAT ABILITY HAS SAVED MY LIFE BEFORE, NOT TO MENTION EREN'S.
IT HAS ...?
WHEN ?
THE LIFT IS READY !!
ALL THE GUNS ARE LOADED, TOO!
RUMBLE RUMBLE RUMBLE
YOU'RE JUST NOT AWARE OF IT... BUT I'LL TELL YOU MORE LATER.
OKAY ...
GCHAK
BUT... WILL WE EVEN BE ABLE TO KILL THE TITANS WITHOUT OUR VERTICAL MANEUVERING GEAR?
SURE WE CAN DO IT! THE ENEMY'S ONLY IN THE 3-4 METER CLASS. THAT MAKES THEIR WEAK SPOT AN EASY TARGET.
TAK
YEAH... DOESN'T MAKE A DIFFERENCE HOW BIG THEY ARE, IT'S ALWAYS THE BACK OF THE NECK, BELOW THE HEAD.
TAK
LENGTH: 1 METER, WIDTH: 10 CENTI-METERS* !!
TAK

LENGTH: APPROX. 3', WIDTH: APPROX. 4"

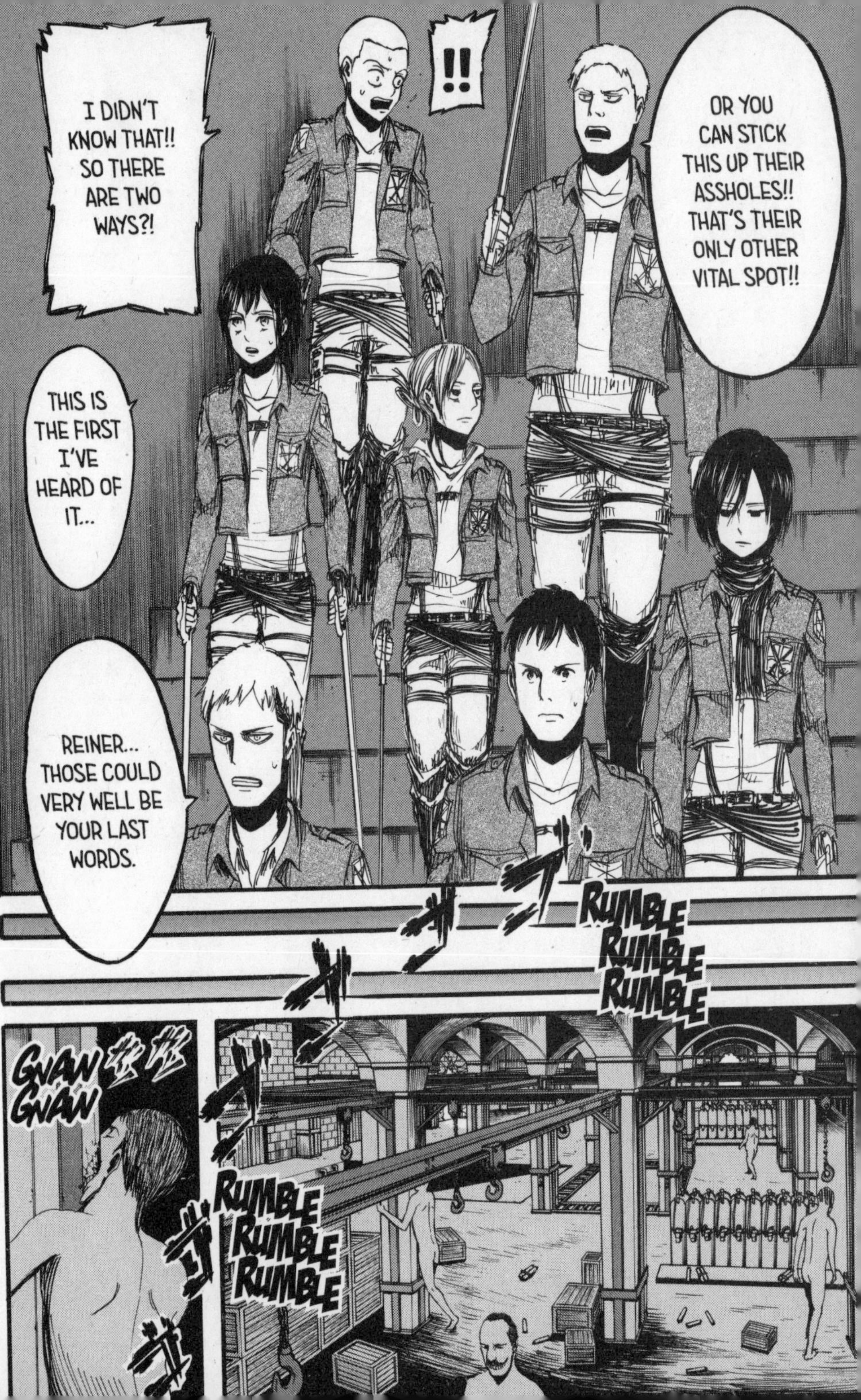
OR YOU CAN STICK THIS UP THEIR ASSHOLES!! THAT'S THEIR ONLY OTHER VITAL SPOT!!
!!
I DIDN'T KNOW THAT!! SO THERE ARE TWO WAYS?!
THIS IS THE FIRST I'VE HEARD OF IT...
REINER... THOSE COULD VERY WELL BE YOUR LAST WORDS.
RUMBLE RUMBLE RUMBLE
RUMBLE RUMBLE RUMBLE
GNAW GNAW

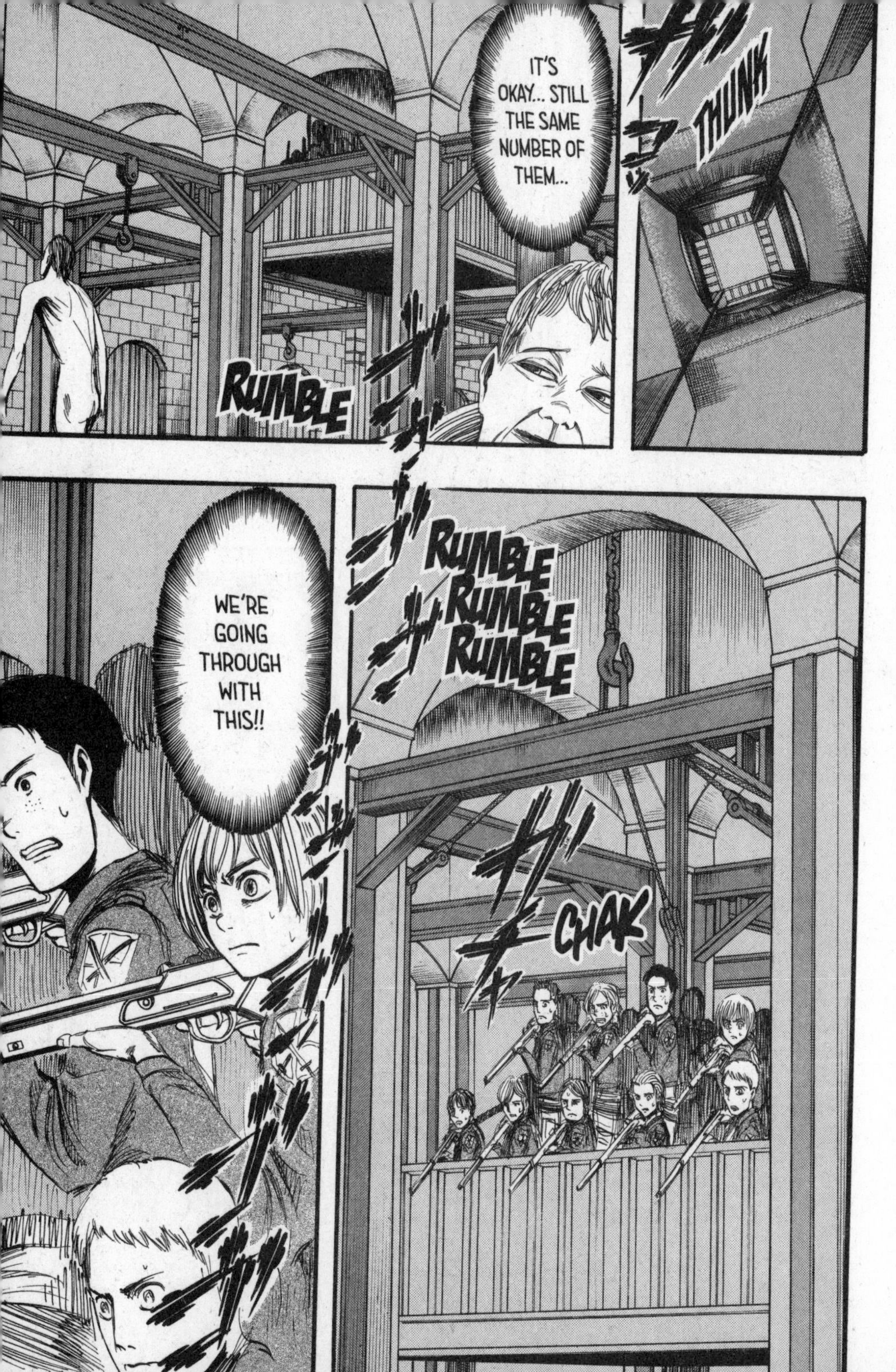
THUNK
IT'S OKAY... STILL THE SAME NUMBER OF THEM...
RUMBLE
RUMBLE RUMBLE RUMBLE
CHAK
WE'RE GOING THROUGH WITH THIS!!

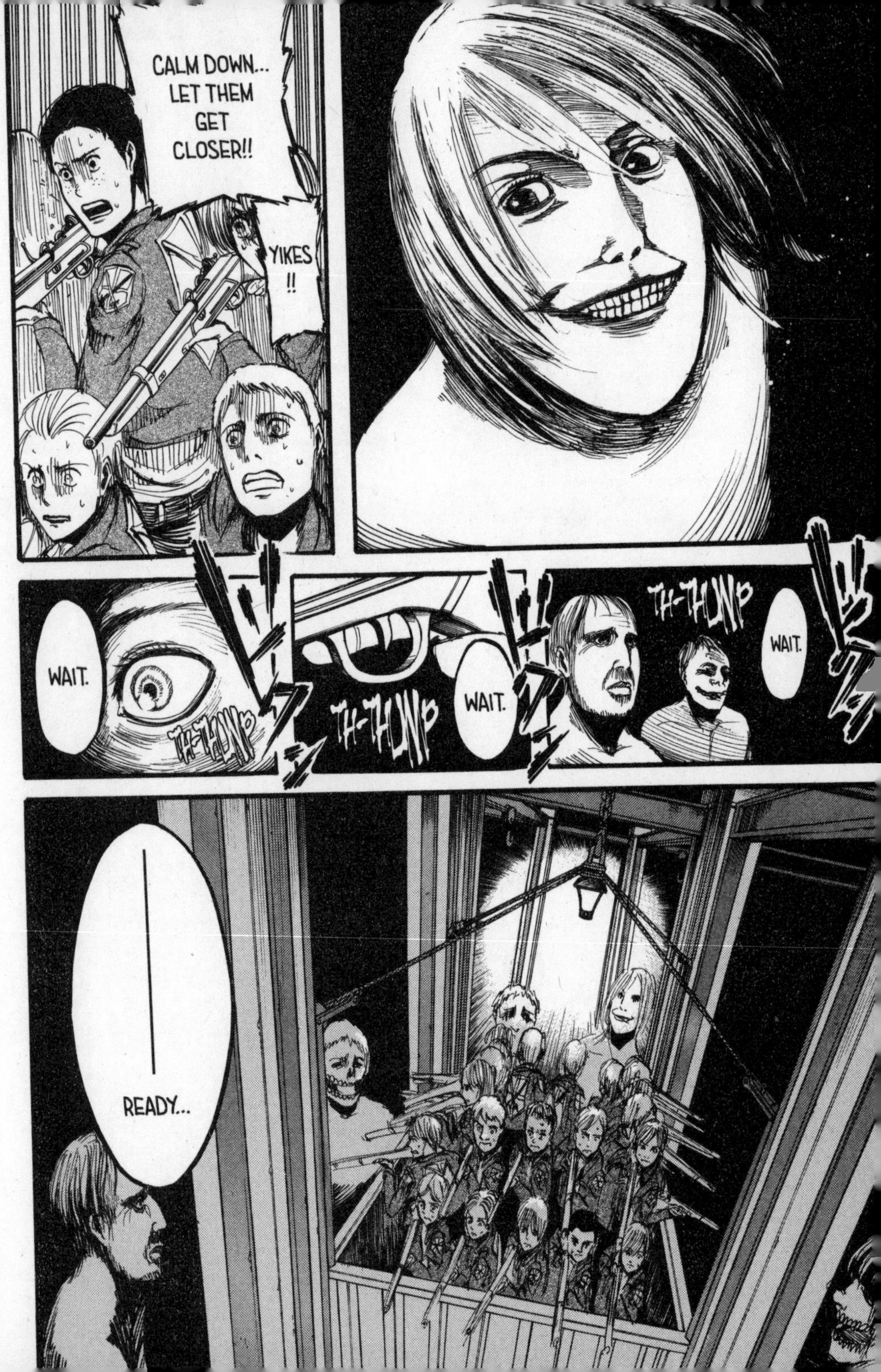
CALM DOWN... LET THEM GET CLOSER!!
YIKES !!
WAIT.
TH-THUMP
WAIT.
TH-THUMP
WAIT.
TH-THUMP
READY...

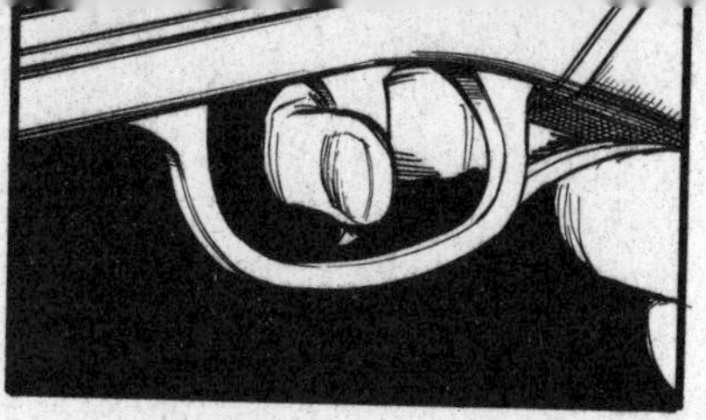
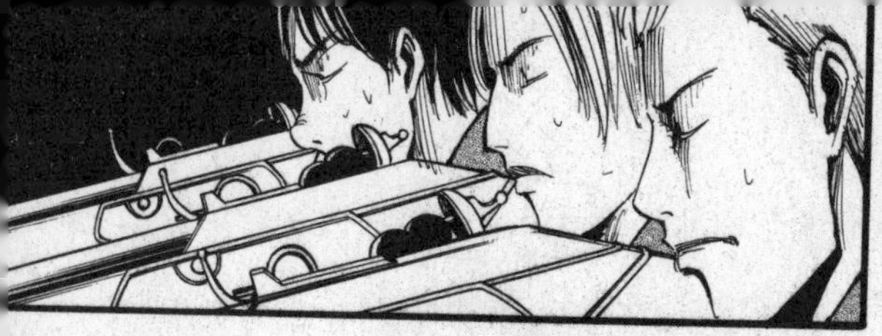
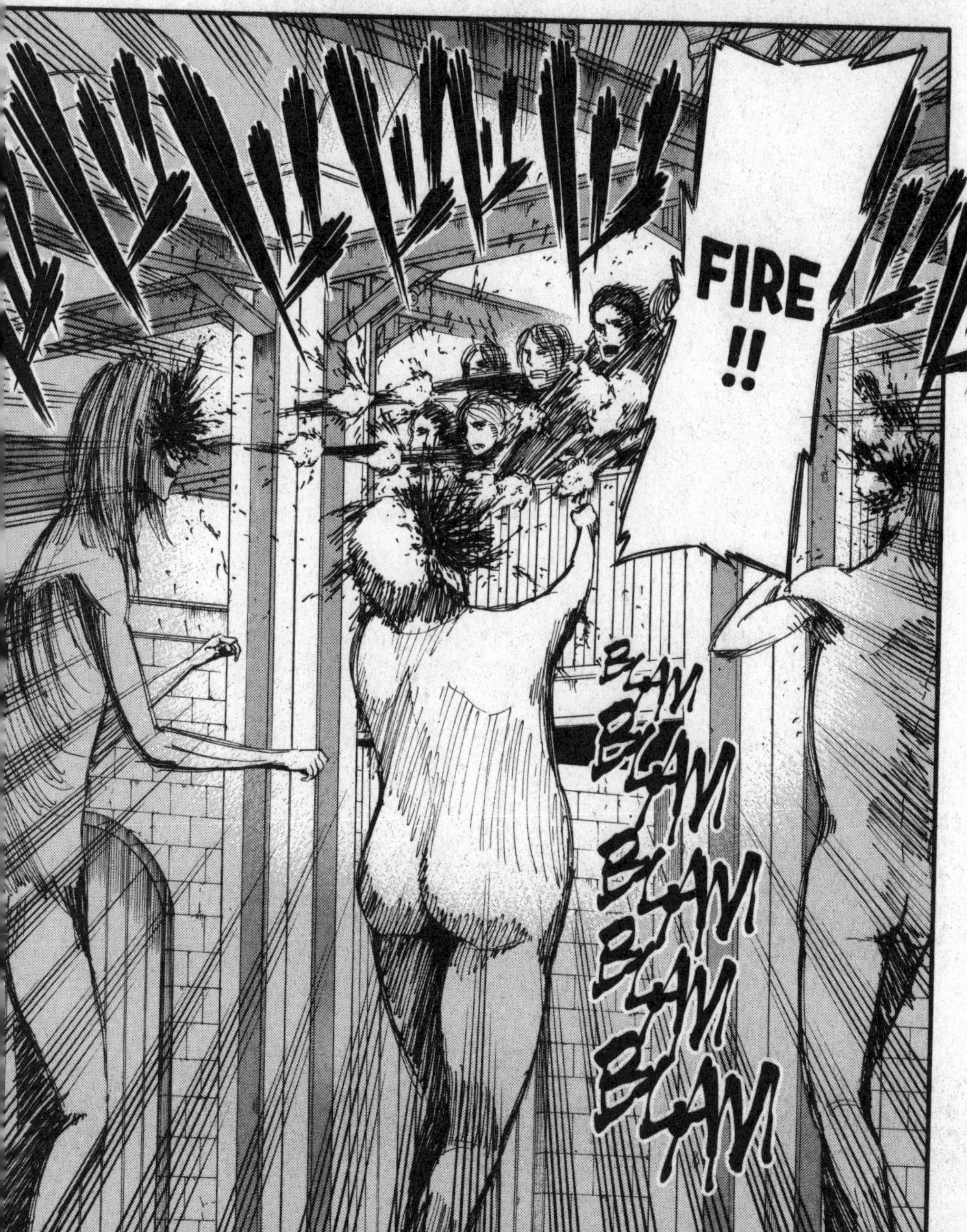
FIRE !!
BLAM
BLAM
BLAM
BLAM
BLAM
BLAM

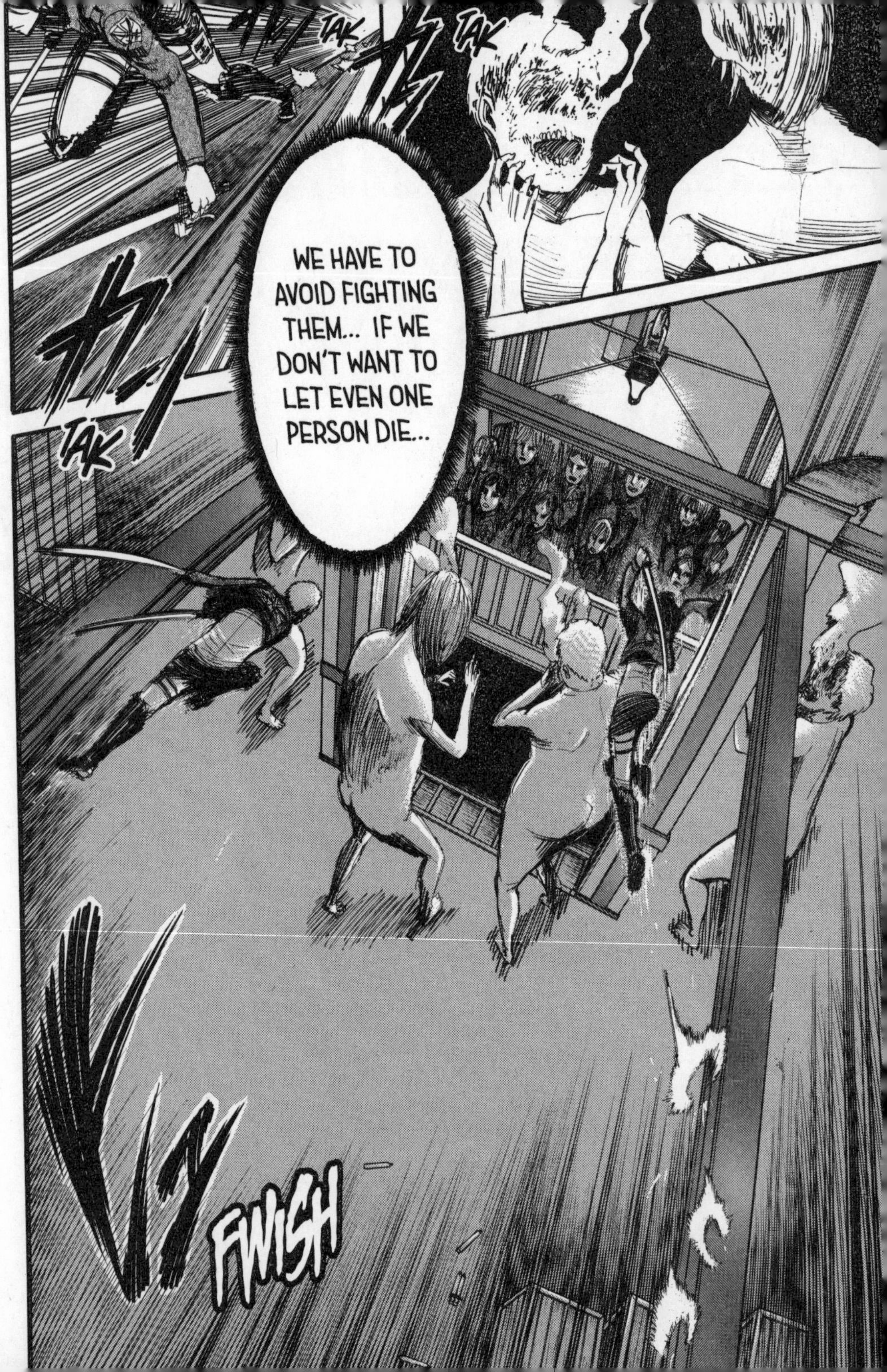
TAK
TAK
WE HAVE TO AVOID FIGHTING THEM... IF WE DON'T WANT TO LET EVEN ONE PERSON DIE...
TAK
FWISH

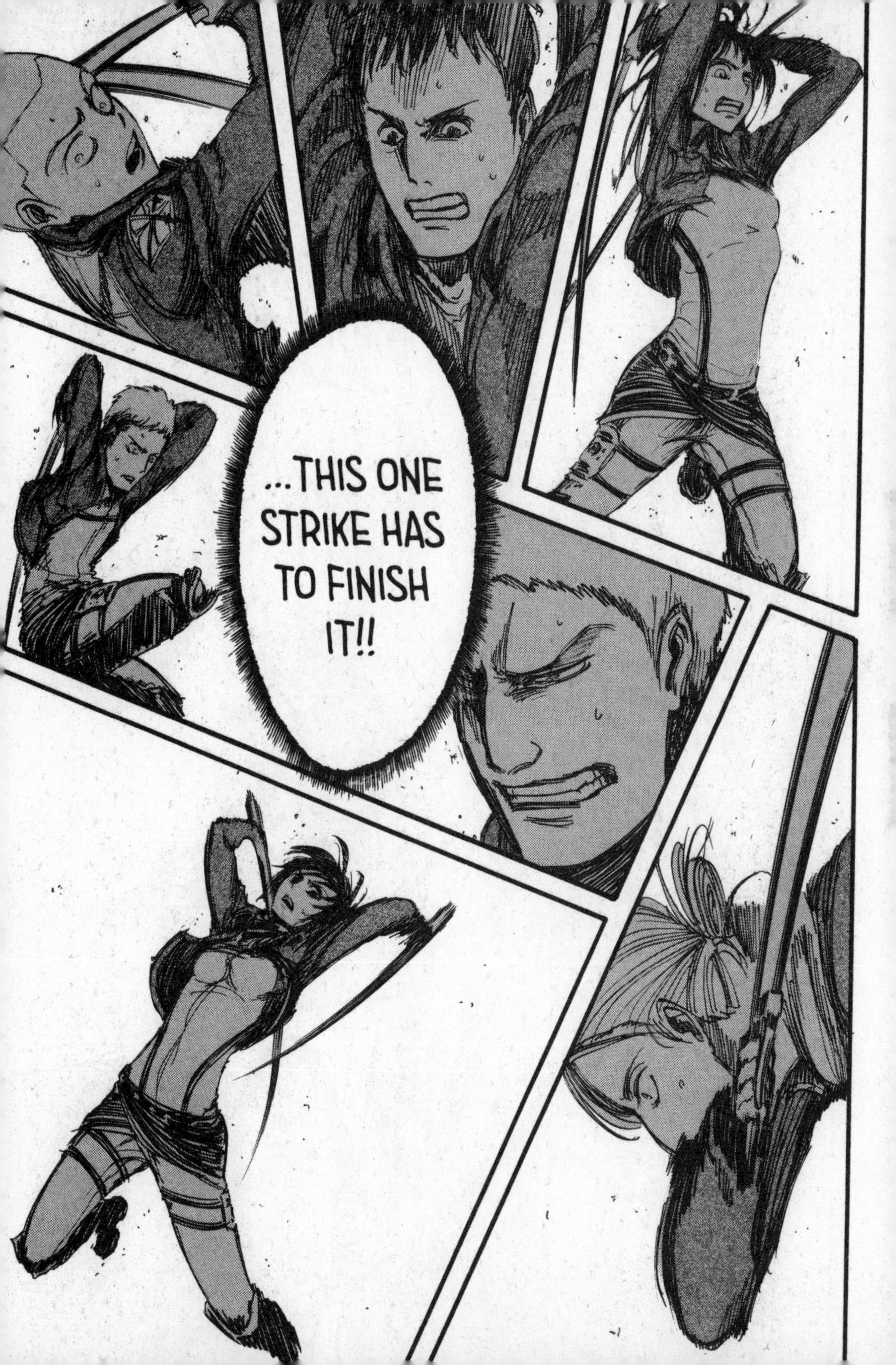
...THIS ONE STRIKE HAS TO FINISH IT!!

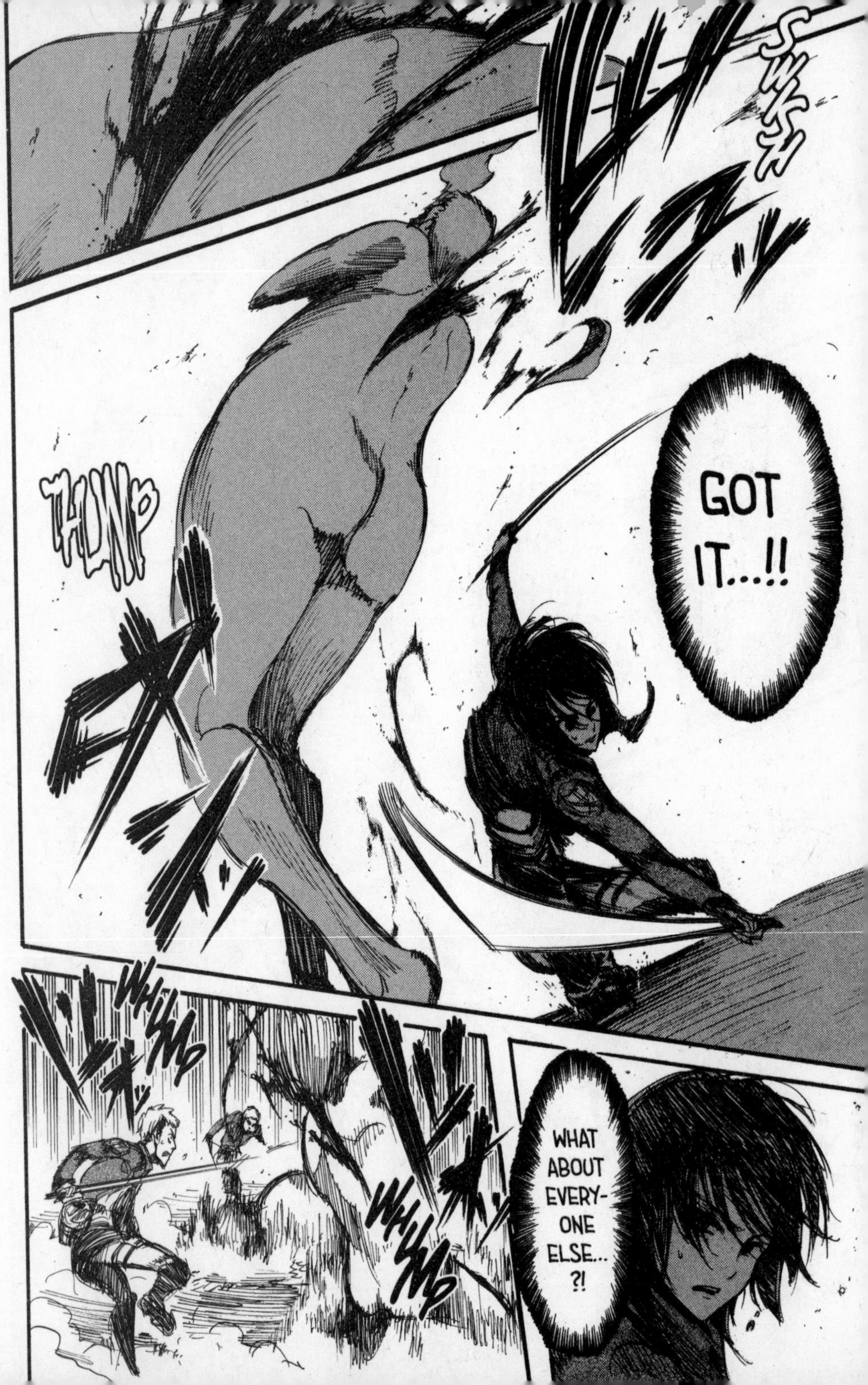
SWISH
THUNP
GOT IT...!!
WHUMP
WHUMP
WHAT ABOUT EVERY-ONE ELSE...?!

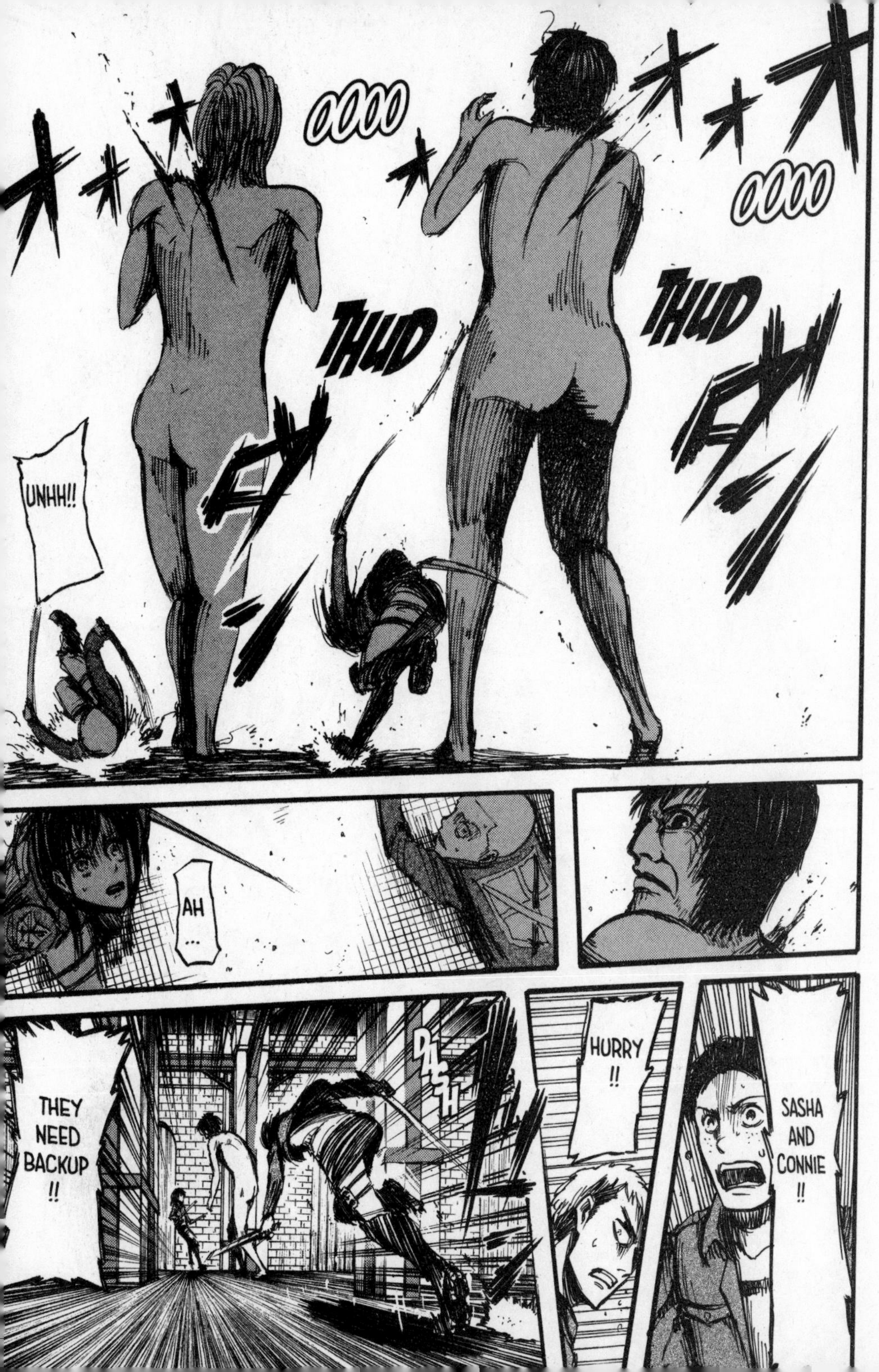
OOOO
OOOO
THUD
THUD
UNHH!!
AH ...
SASHA AND CONNIE !!
HURRY !!
DASH
THEY NEED BACKUP !!

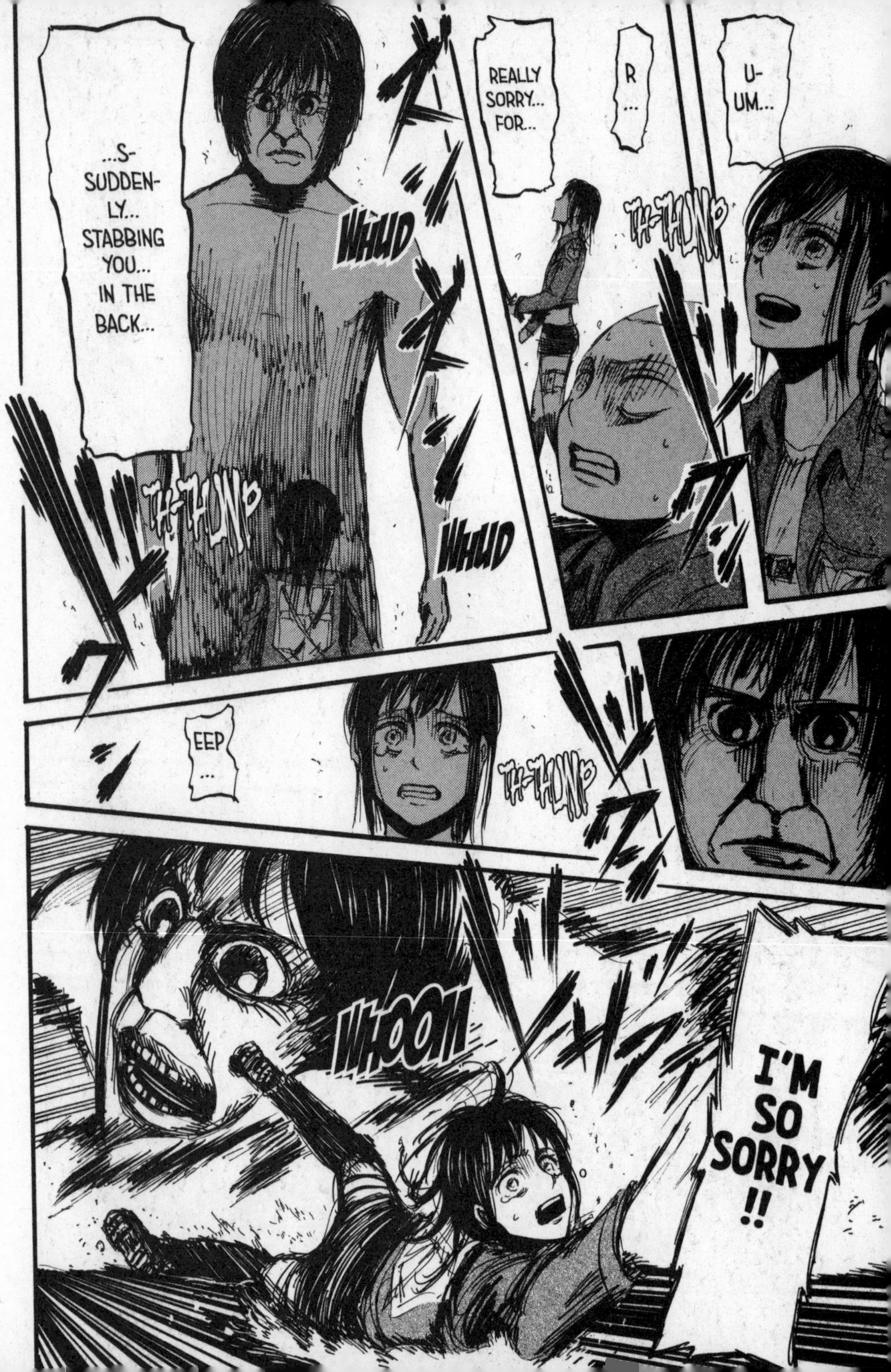
U-UM...
TH-THUMP
R...
REALLY SORRY... FOR...
WHUD
...S-SUDDENLY... STABBING YOU... IN THE BACK...
WHUD
TH-THUMP
TH-THUMP
EEP...
WHOOM
I'M SO SORRY!!

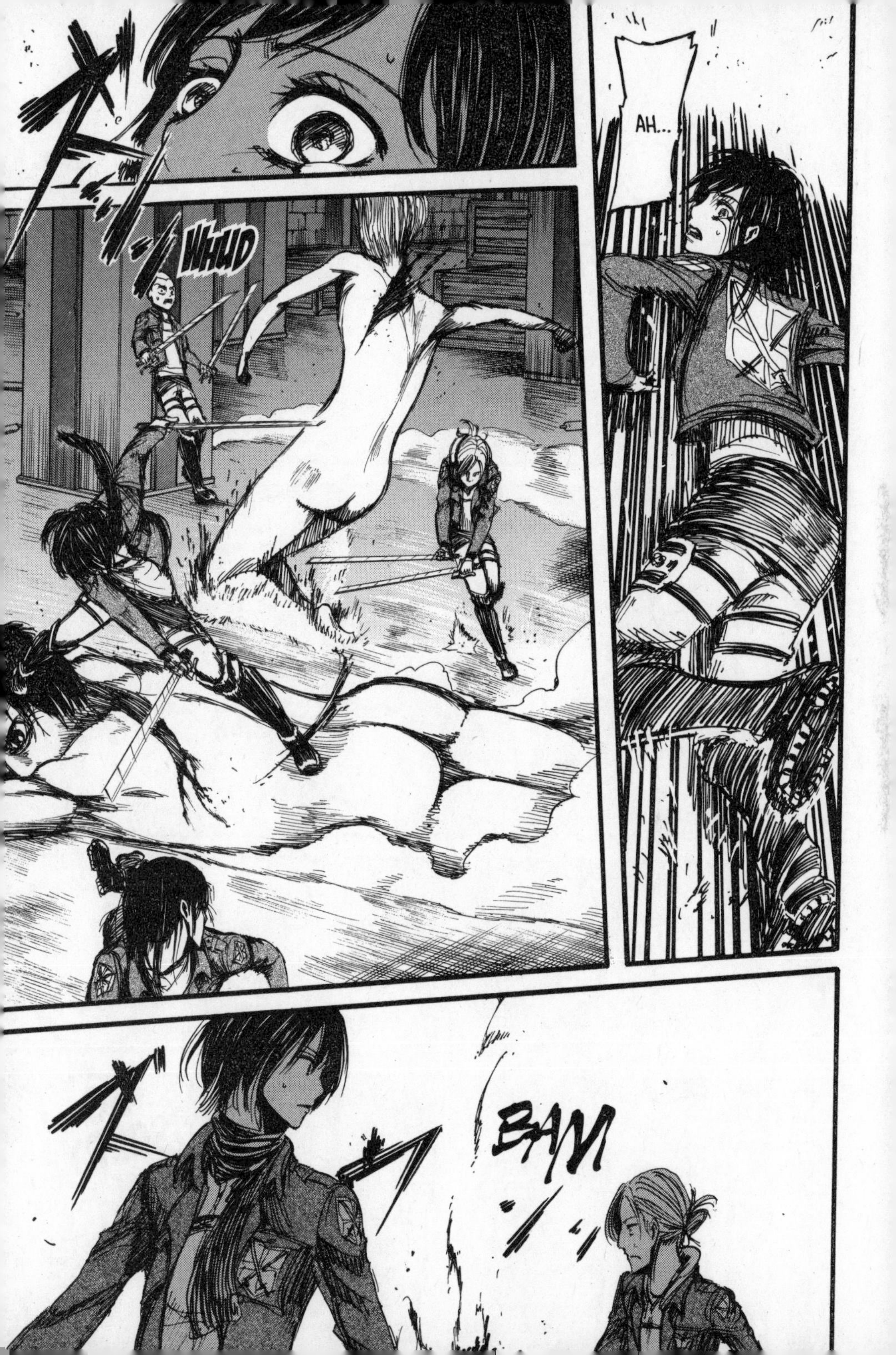
AH...
WHUD
BAM

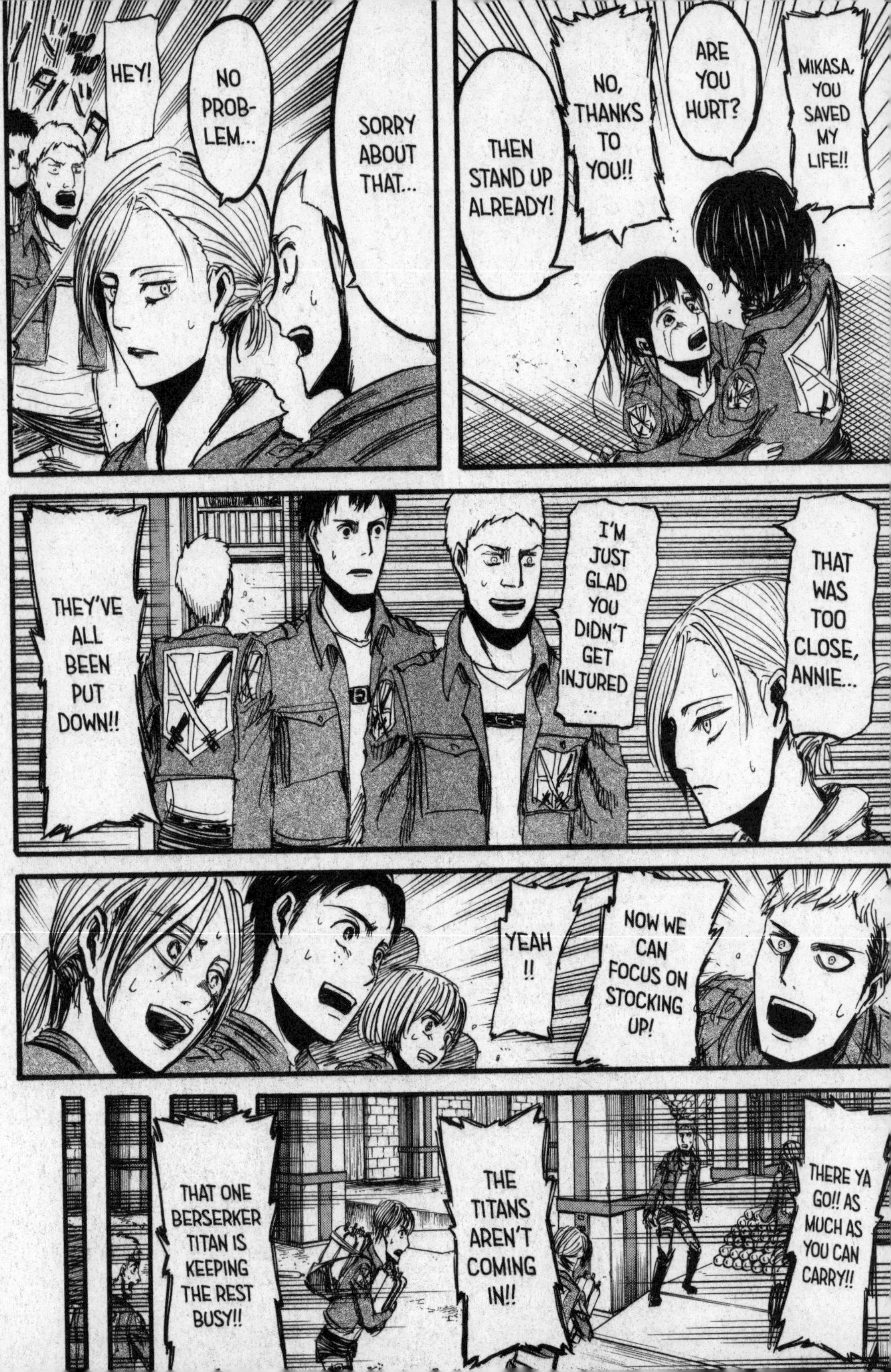
MIKASA, YOU SAVED MY LIFE!!
ARE YOU HURT?
NO, THANKS TO YOU!!
THEN STAND UP ALREADY!
SORRY ABOUT THAT...
NO PROBLEM...
HEY!
THUD THUD
THAT WAS TOO CLOSE, ANNIE...
I'M JUST GLAD YOU DIDN'T GET INJURED...
THEY'VE ALL BEEN PUT DOWN!!
NOW WE CAN FOCUS ON STOCKING UP!
YEAH!!
THERE YA GO!! AS MUCH AS YOU CAN CARRY!!
THE TITANS AREN'T COMING IN!!
THAT ONE BERSERKER TITAN IS KEEPING THE REST BUSY!!

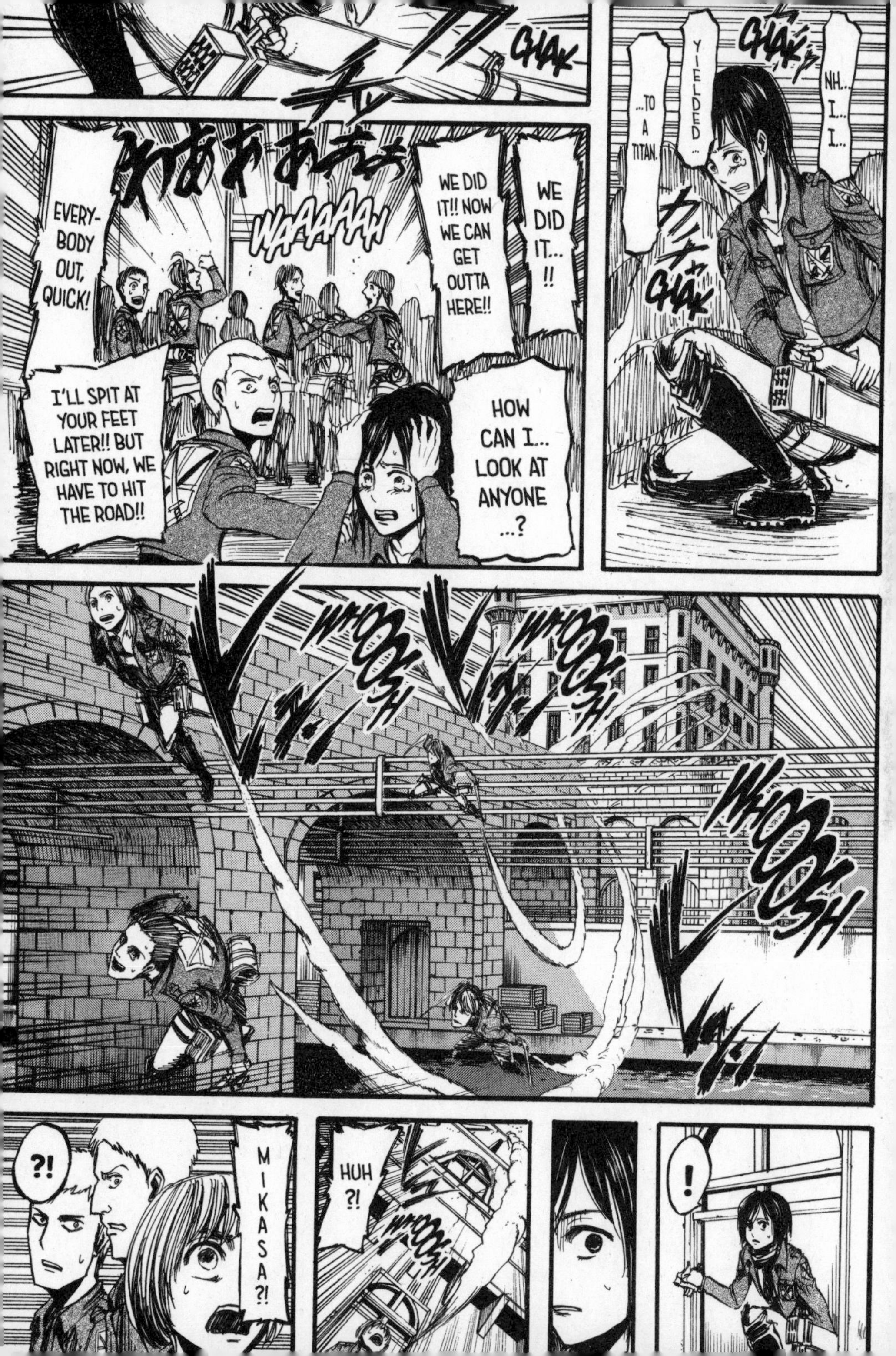
CHAK
NH... I... I...
YIELDED...
...TO A TITAN.
CHAK
CHAK
WE DID IT...!!
WE DID IT!! NOW WE CAN GET OUTTA HERE!!
WAAAAAH
EVERY-BODY OUT, QUICK!
HOW CAN I... LOOK AT ANYONE...?
I'LL SPIT AT YOUR FEET LATER!! BUT RIGHT NOW, WE HAVE TO HIT THE ROAD!!
WHOOOSH
WHOOOSH
WHOOOSH
!
HUH?!
WHOOSH
MIKASA?!
?!

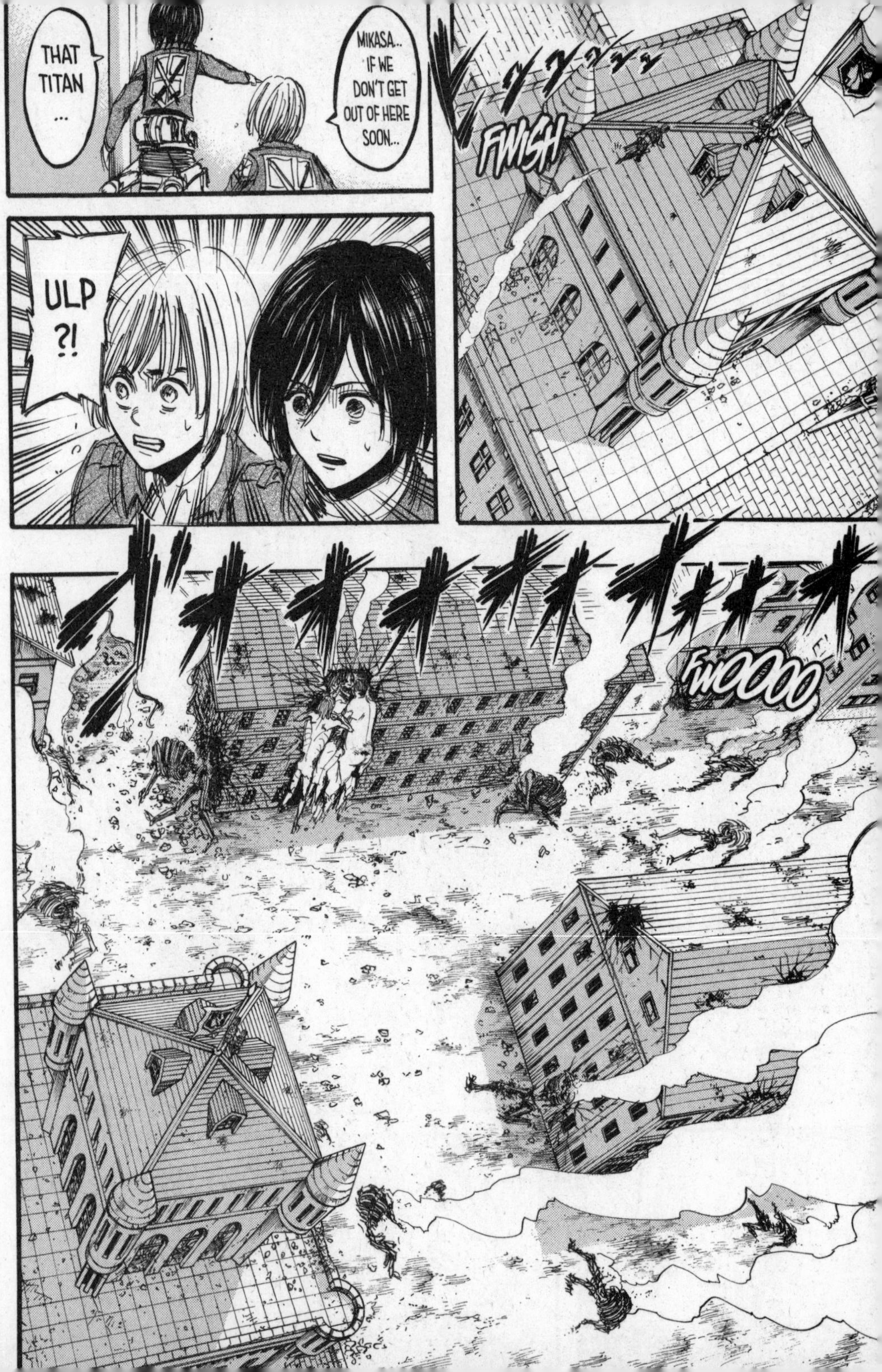
FWISH
MIKASA.. IF WE DON'T GET OUT OF HERE SOON...
THAT TITAN ...
ULP ?!
FWOOOO

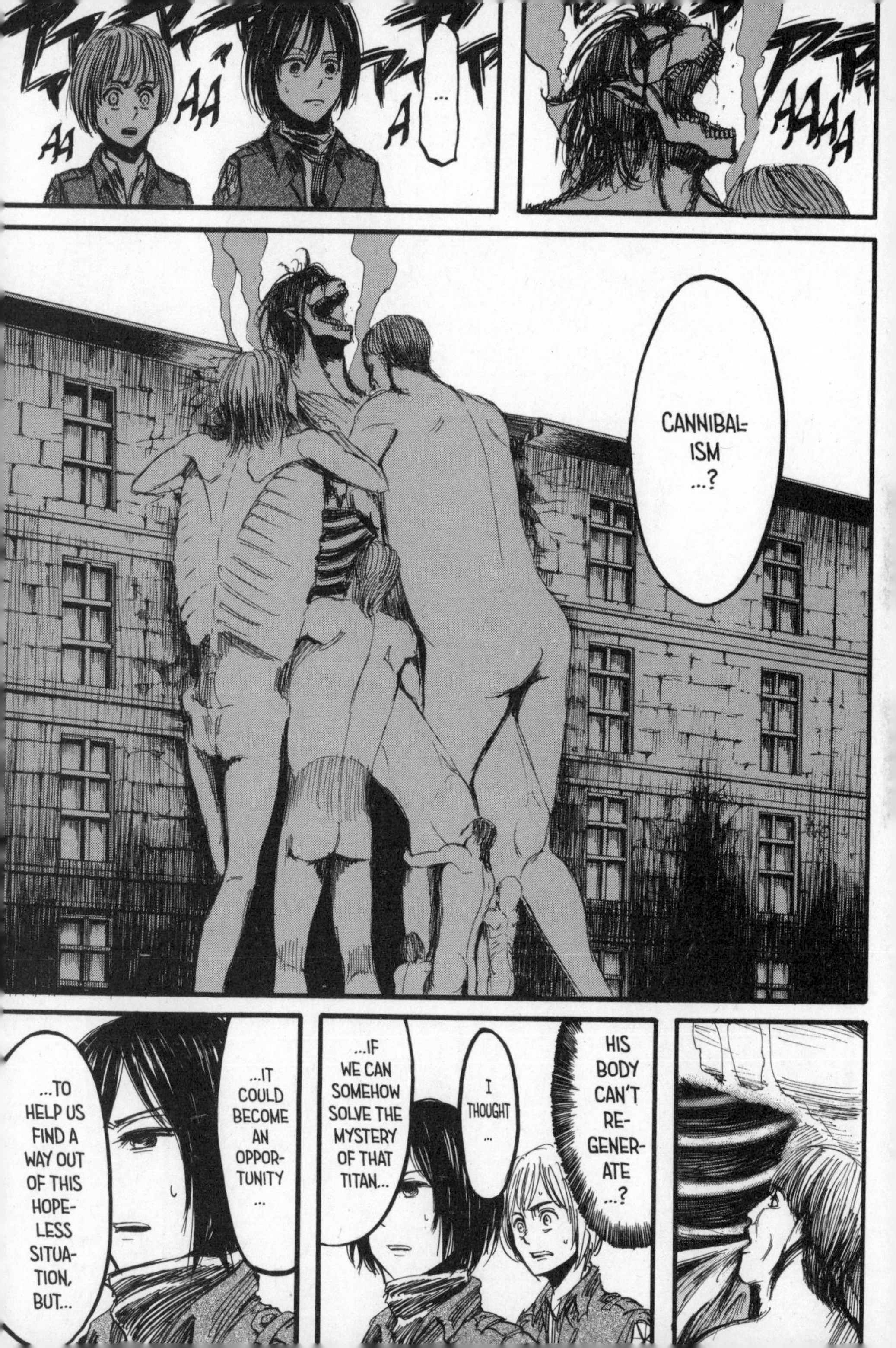
AAAA
...
CANNIBALISM ...?
HIS BODY CAN'T REGENERATE ...?
I THOUGHT ...
...IF WE CAN SOMEHOW SOLVE THE MYSTERY OF THAT TITAN...
...IT COULD BECOME AN OPPORTUNITY ...
...TO HELP US FIND A WAY OUT OF THIS HOPELESS SITUATION, BUT...

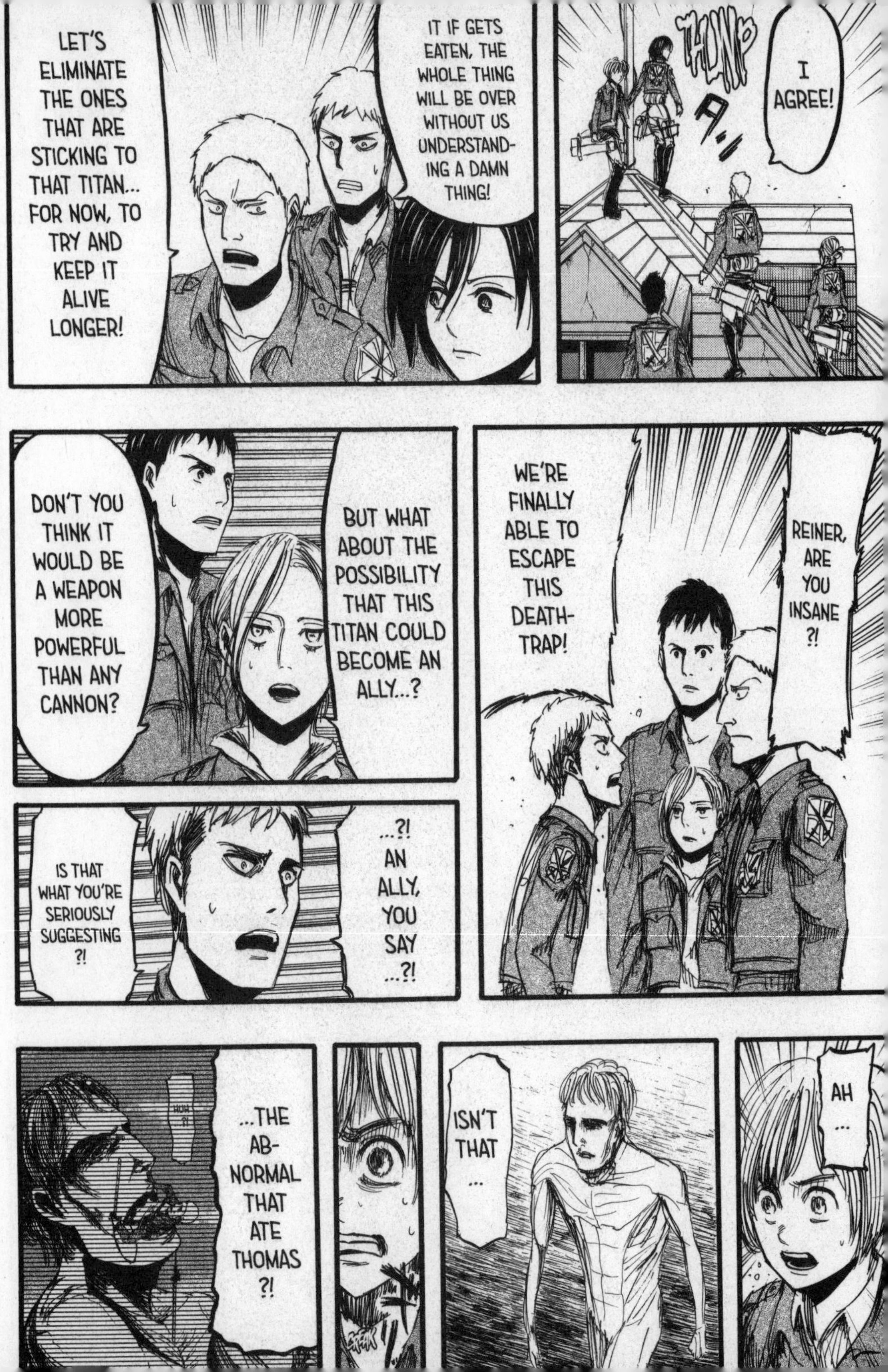
I AGREE!
THUMP
IT IF GETS EATEN, THE WHOLE THING WILL BE OVER WITHOUT US UNDERSTAND-ING A DAMN THING!
LET'S ELIMINATE THE ONES THAT ARE STICKING TO THAT TITAN... FOR NOW, TO TRY AND KEEP IT ALIVE LONGER!
REINER, ARE YOU INSANE ?!
WE'RE FINALLY ABLE TO ESCAPE THIS DEATH-TRAP!
BUT WHAT ABOUT THE POSSIBILITY THAT THIS TITAN COULD BECOME AN ALLY...?
DON'T YOU THINK IT WOULD BE A WEAPON MORE POWERFUL THAN ANY CANNON?
...?! AN ALLY, YOU SAY ...?!
IS THAT WHAT YOU'RE SERIOUSLY SUGGESTING ?!
AH ...
ISN'T THAT ...
...THE AB-NORMAL THAT ATE THOMAS ?!
HUH ?!

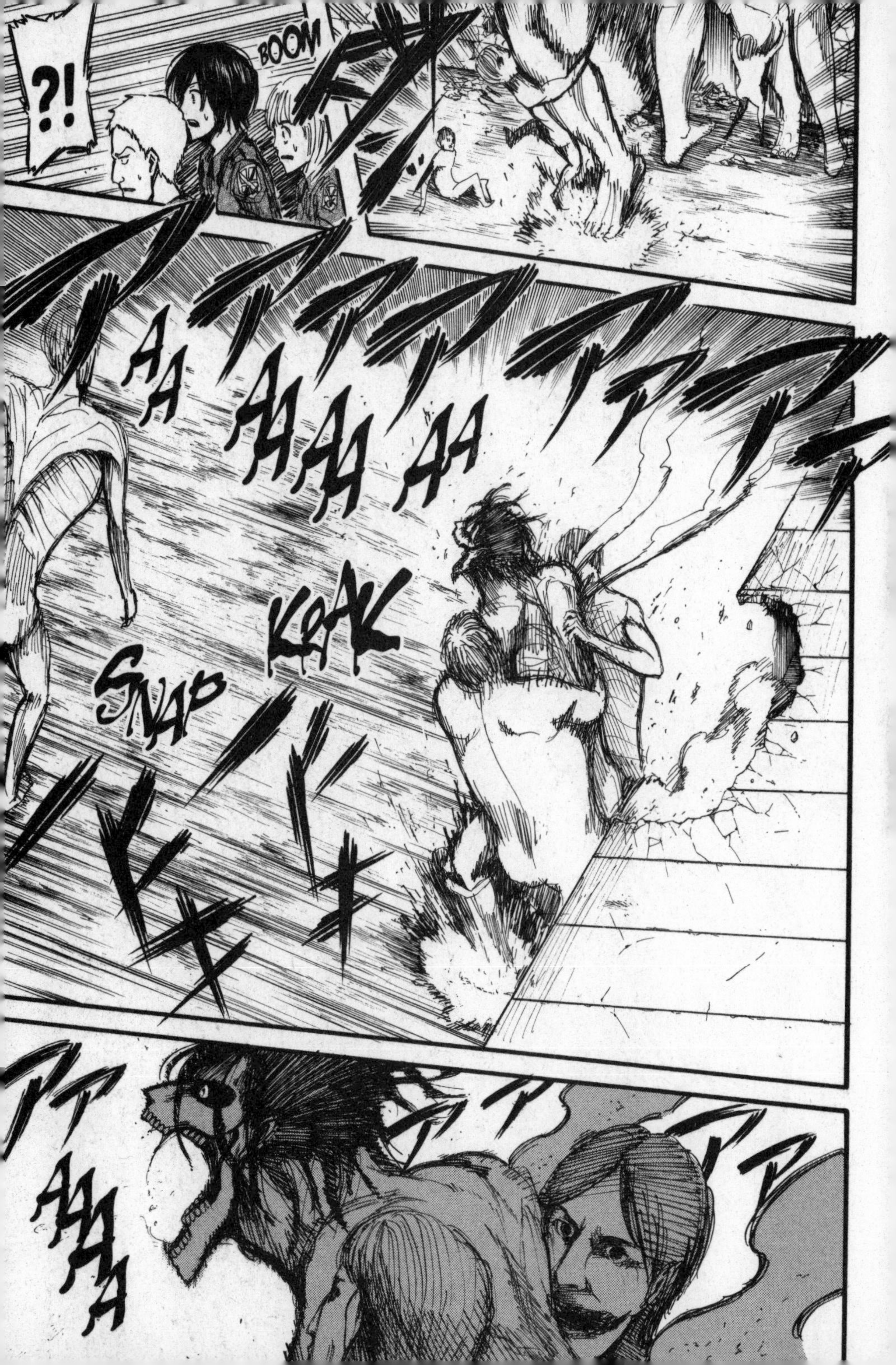
BOOM
?!
AAAAAAAAA
KRAK
SNAP
AAAAA

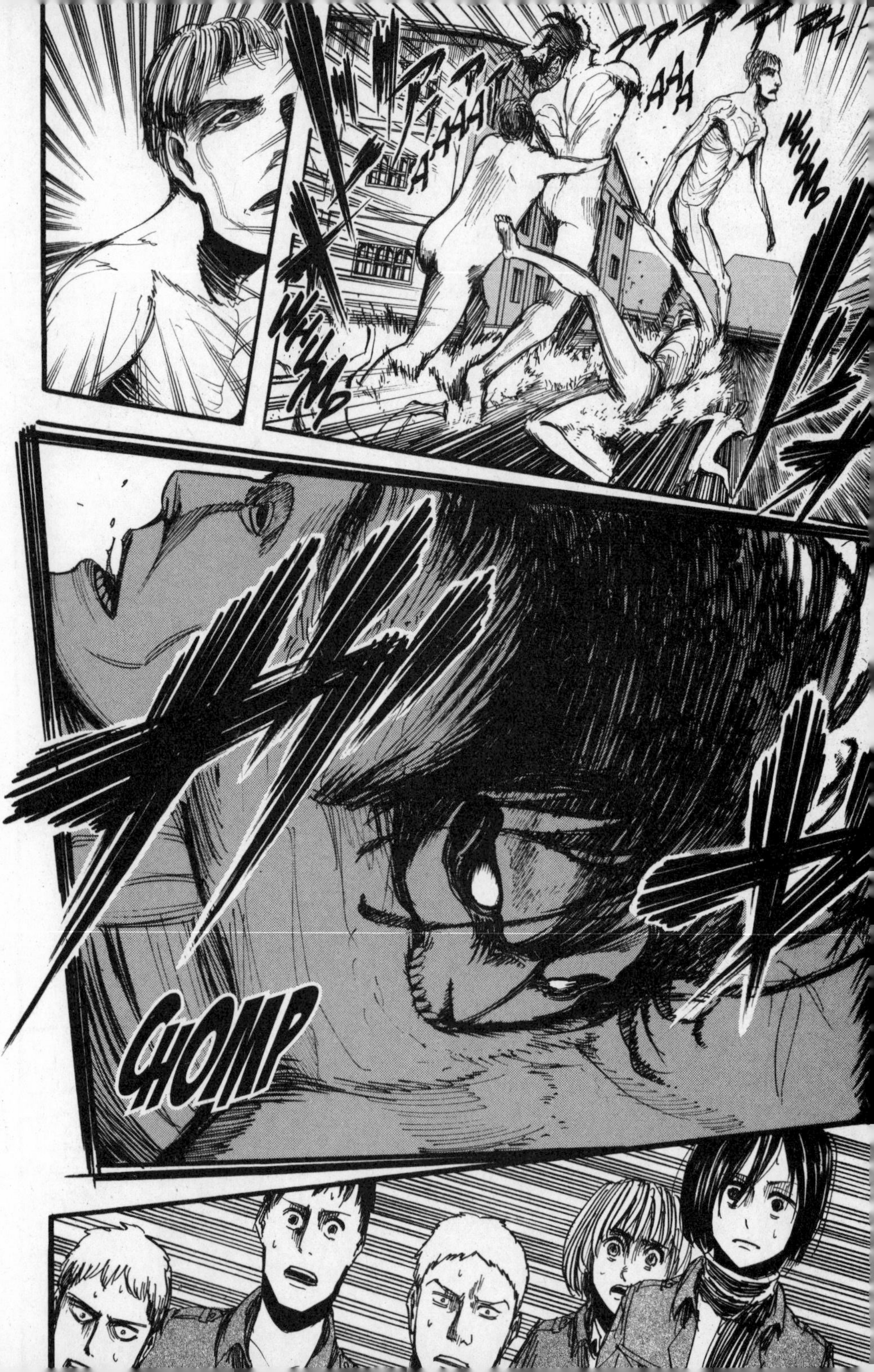
AAAA
AAAAA
WHUMP
WHUMP
CHOMP

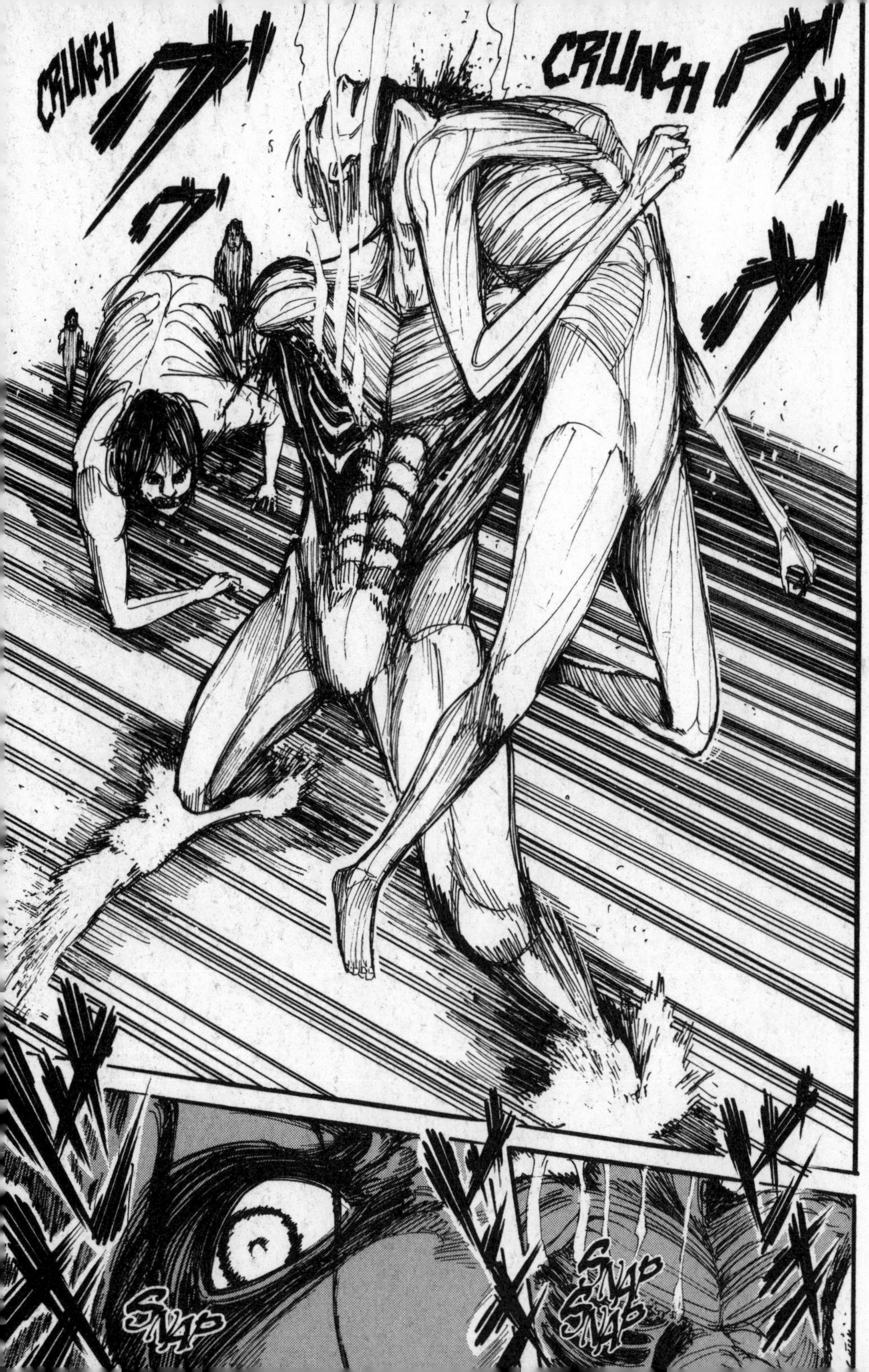
CRUNCH
CRUNCH
SNAP SNAP
SNAP

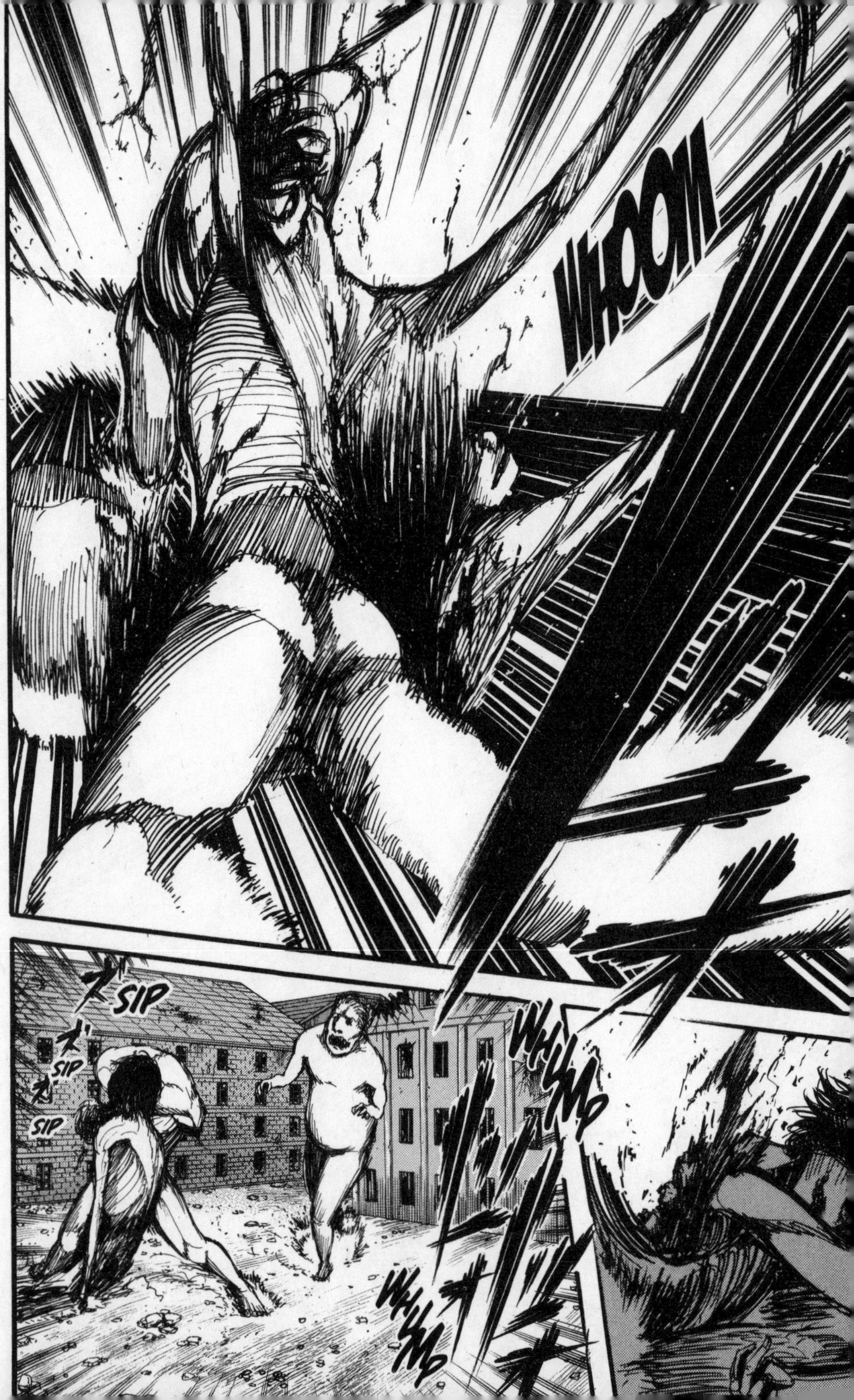
WHOOM
WHUMP
WHUMP
SIP
SIP
SIP

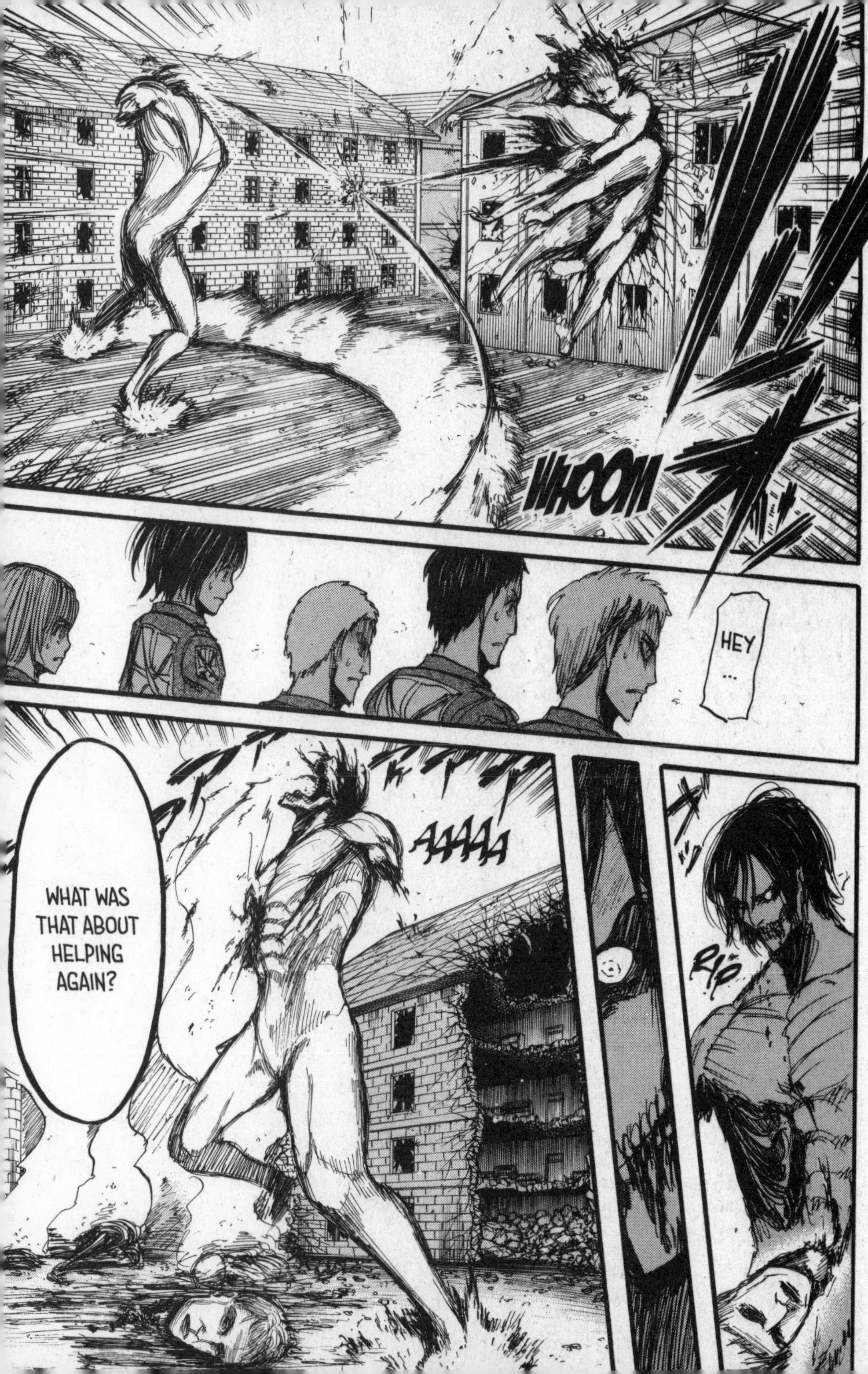
WHOOM
HEY ...
RIP
WHAT WAS THAT ABOUT HELPING AGAIN?

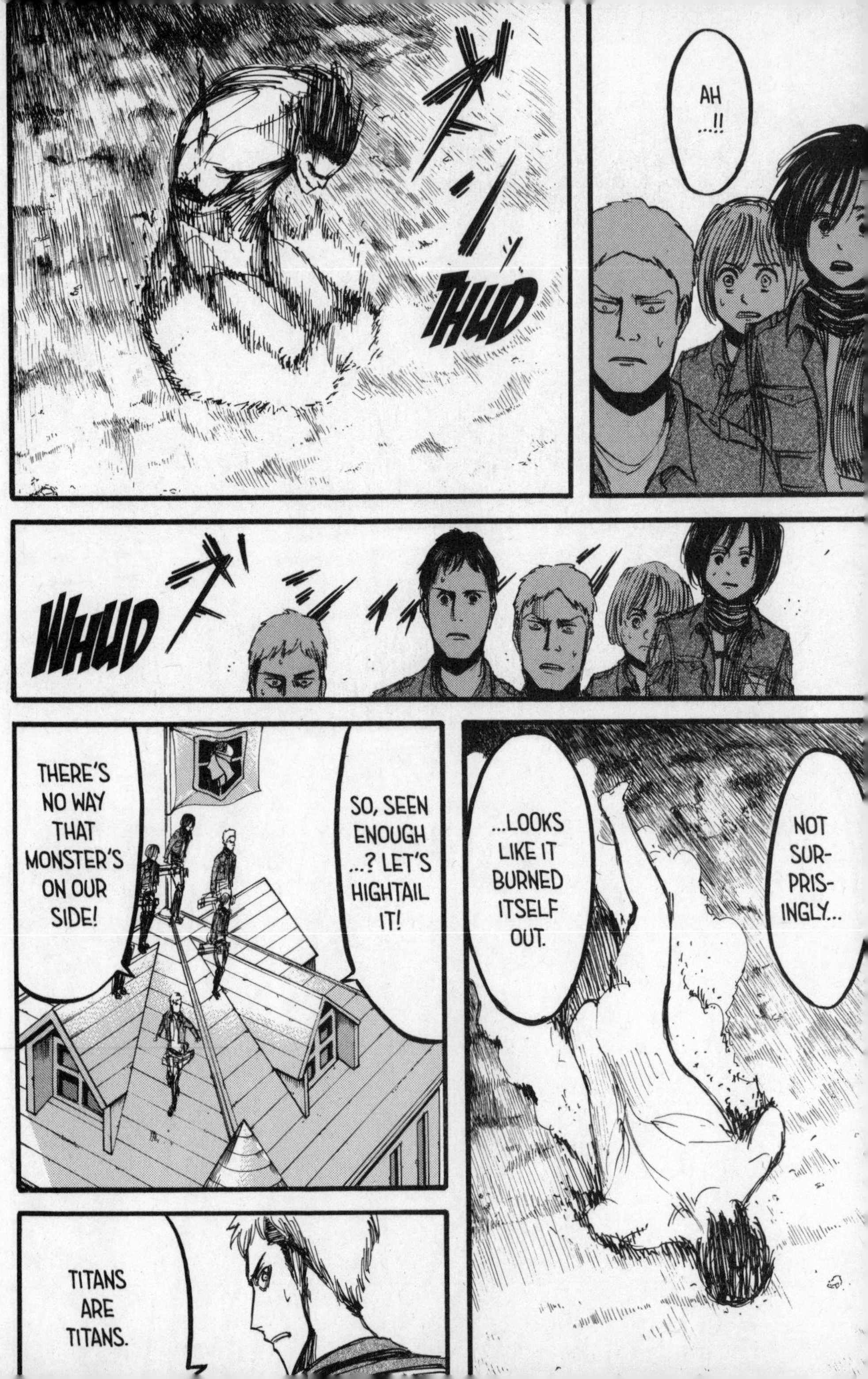
AH ...!!
THUD
WHUD
NOT SURPRISINGLY...
...LOOKS LIKE IT BURNED ITSELF OUT.
SO, SEEN ENOUGH ...? LET'S HIGHTAIL IT!
THERE'S NO WAY THAT MONSTER'S ON OUR SIDE!
TITANS ARE TITANS.

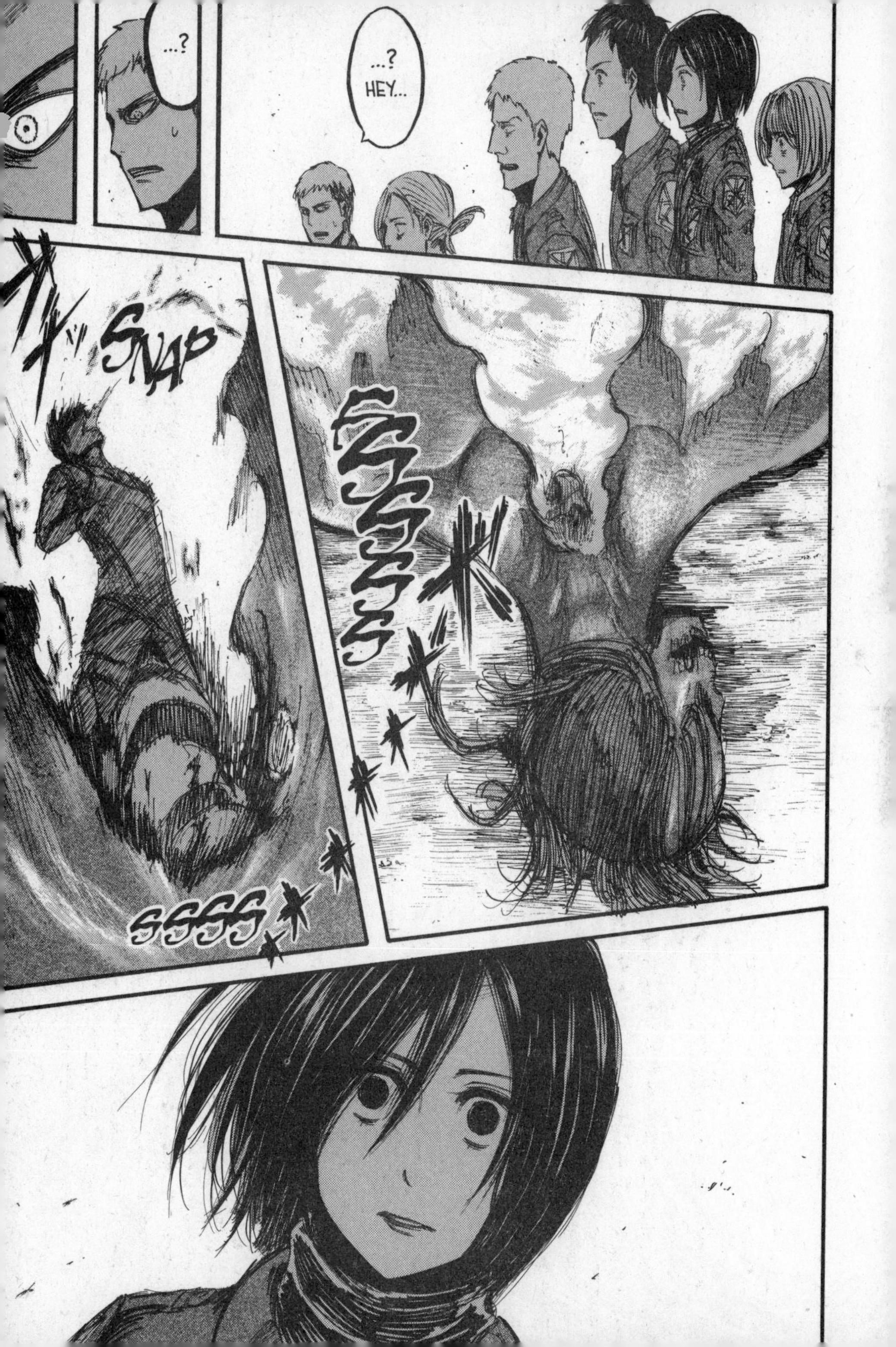
...? HEY...
...?
SSSSS
SNAP
SSSS

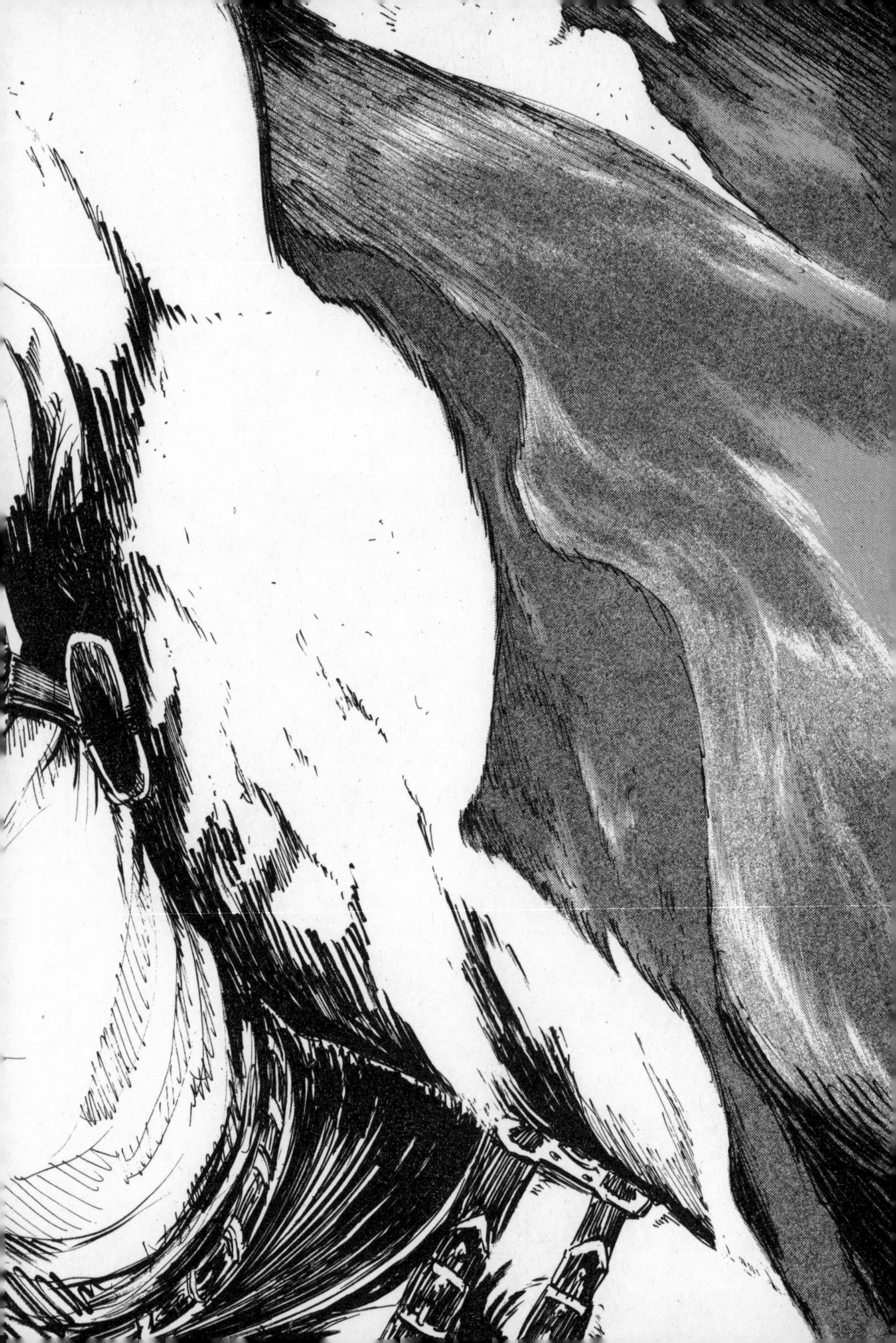

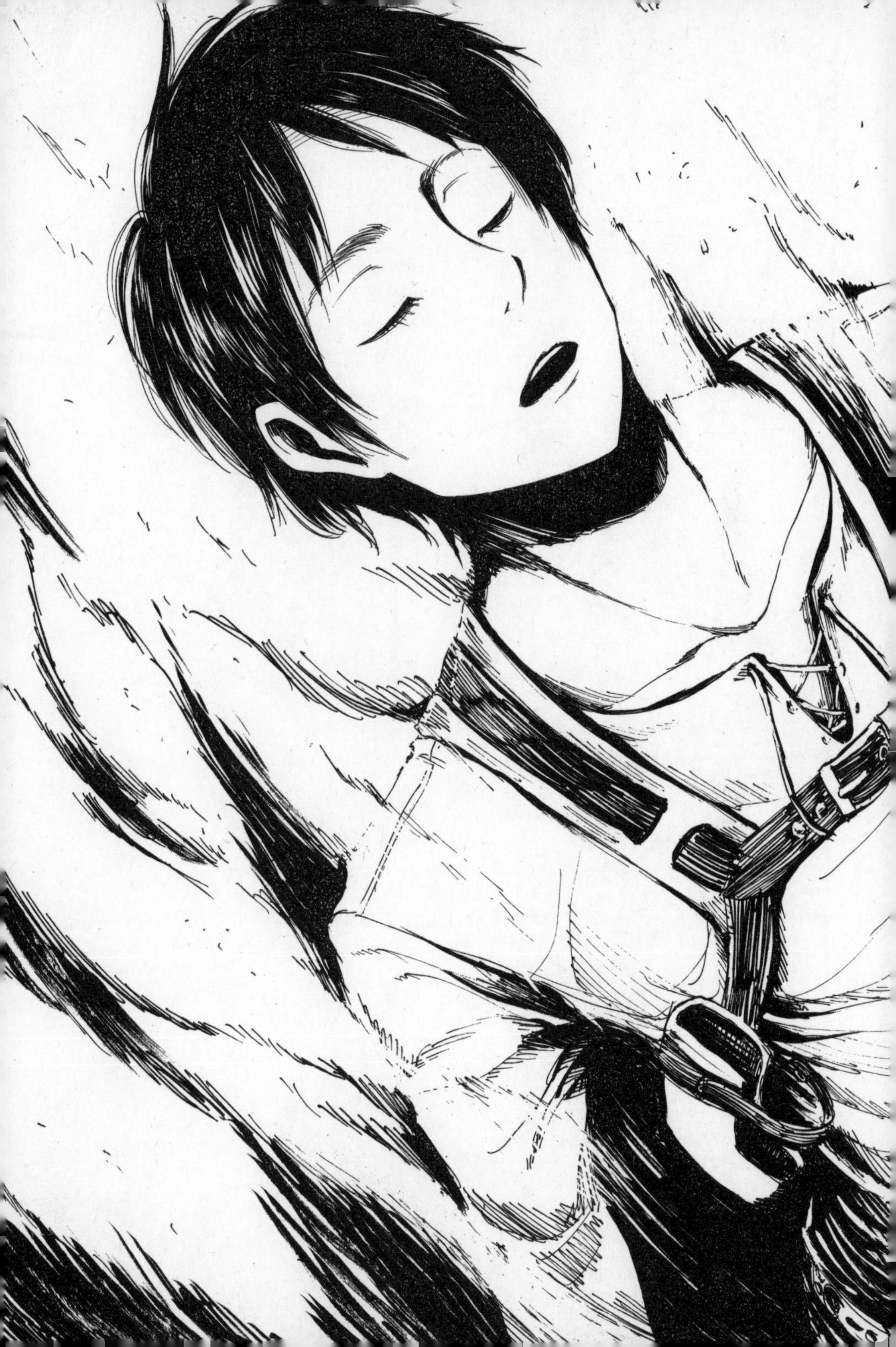

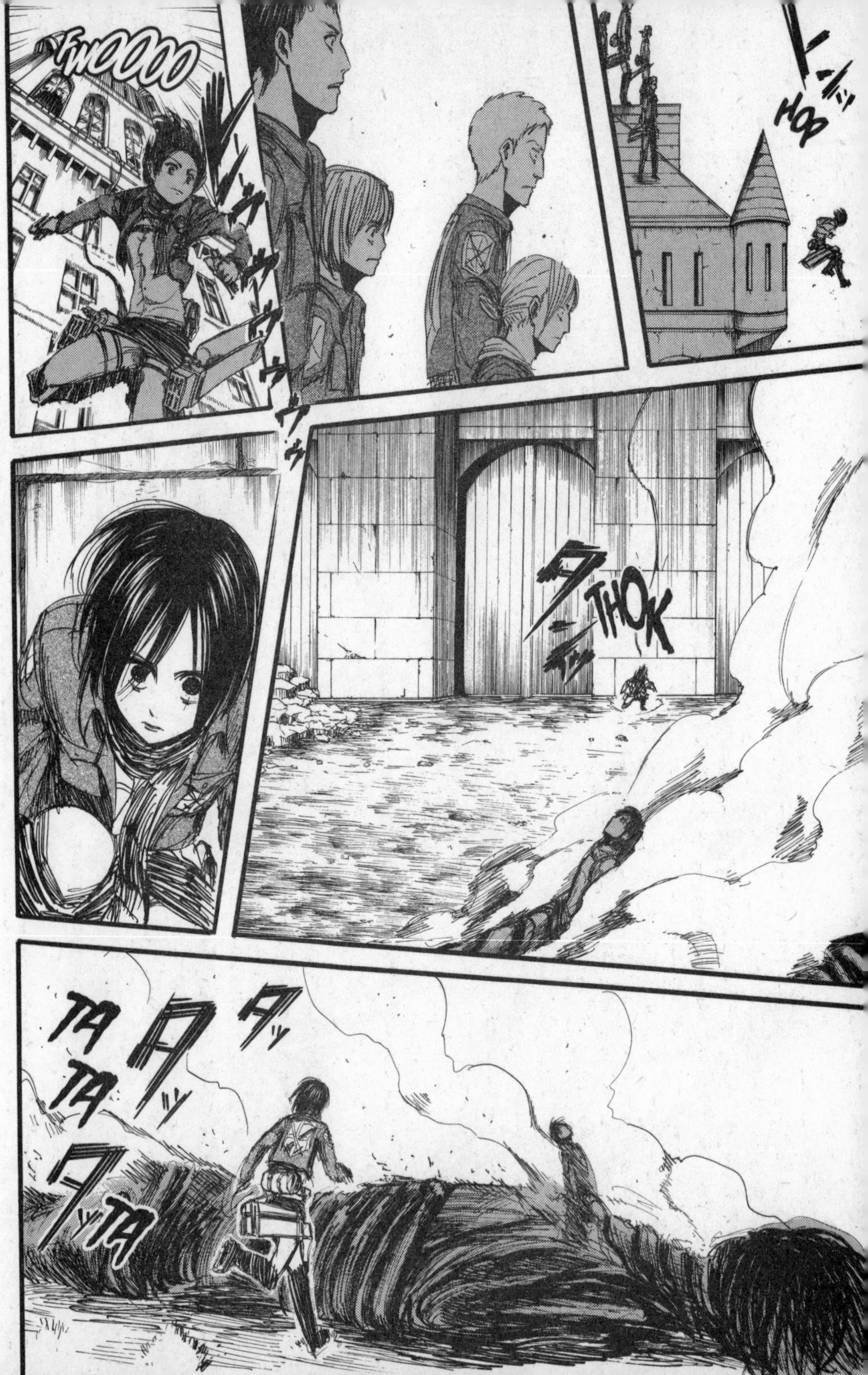
HOP
FWOOOO
THOK
TA TA TA TA

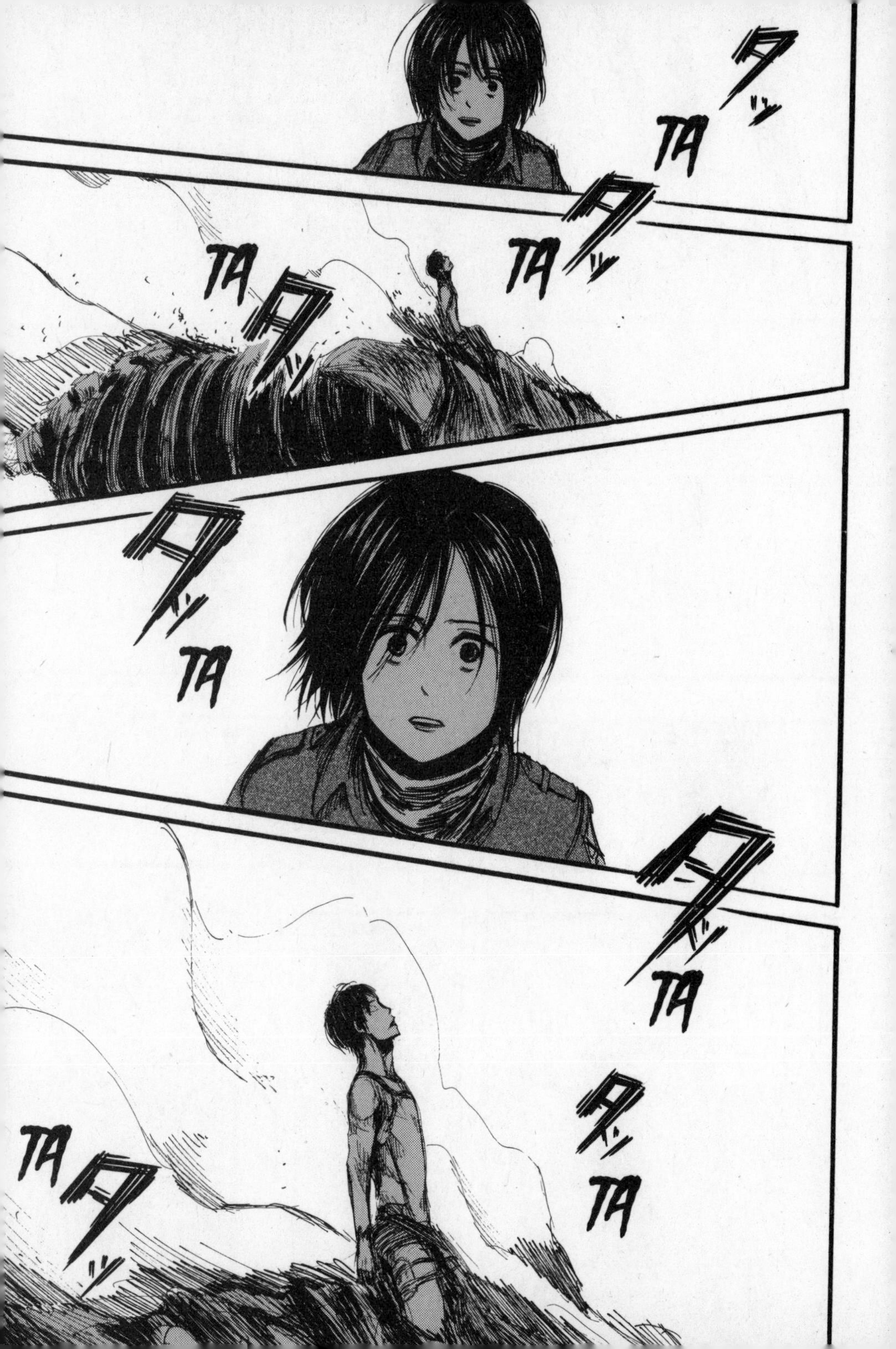
タッ
TA
タッ
TA
TA
タッ
タッ
TA
タッ
TA
タッ
TA
TA
タッ

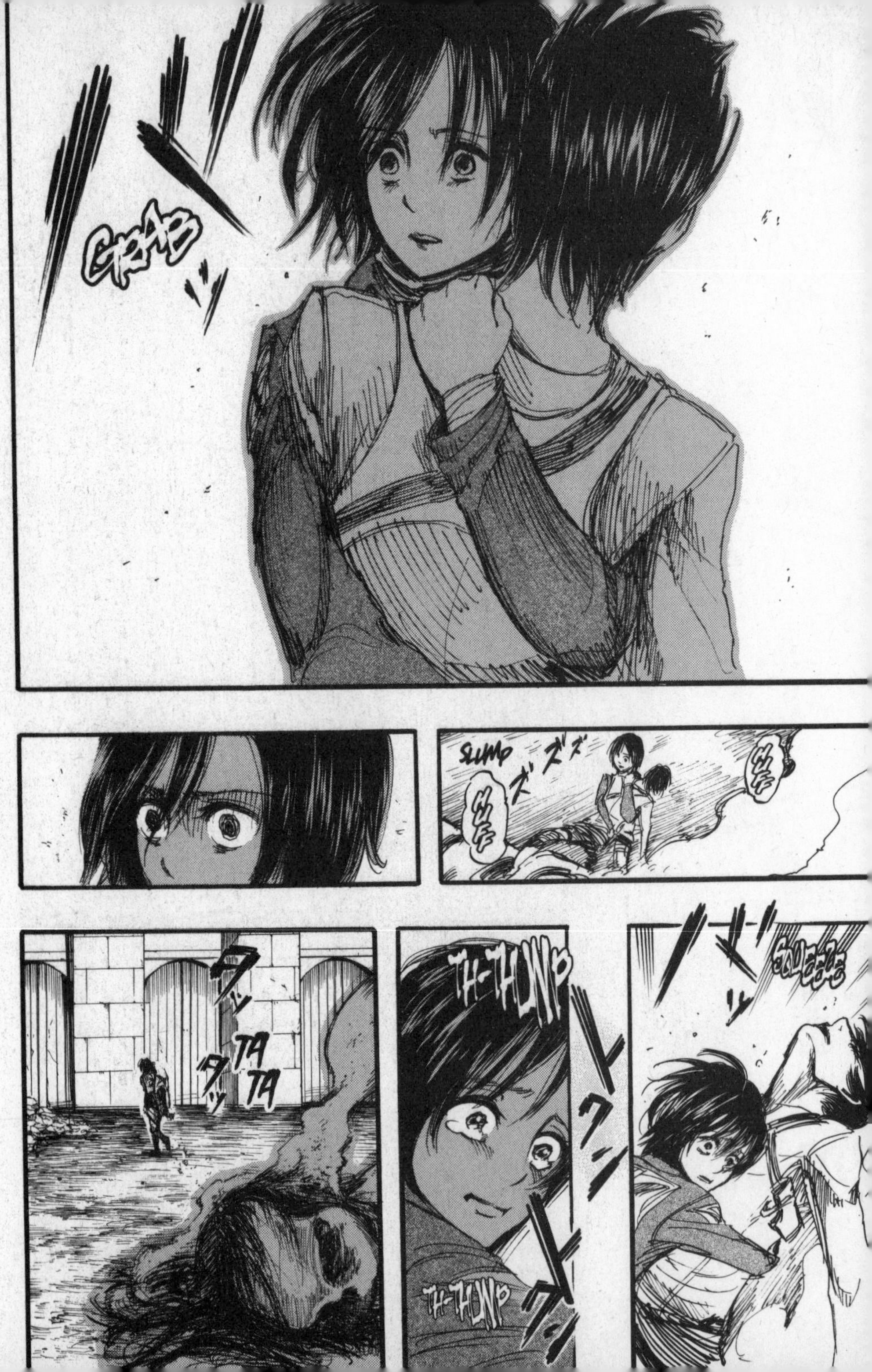
GRAB
HUFF
SLUMP
HUFF
SQUEEZE
TH-THUMP
TH-THUMP
TA TA

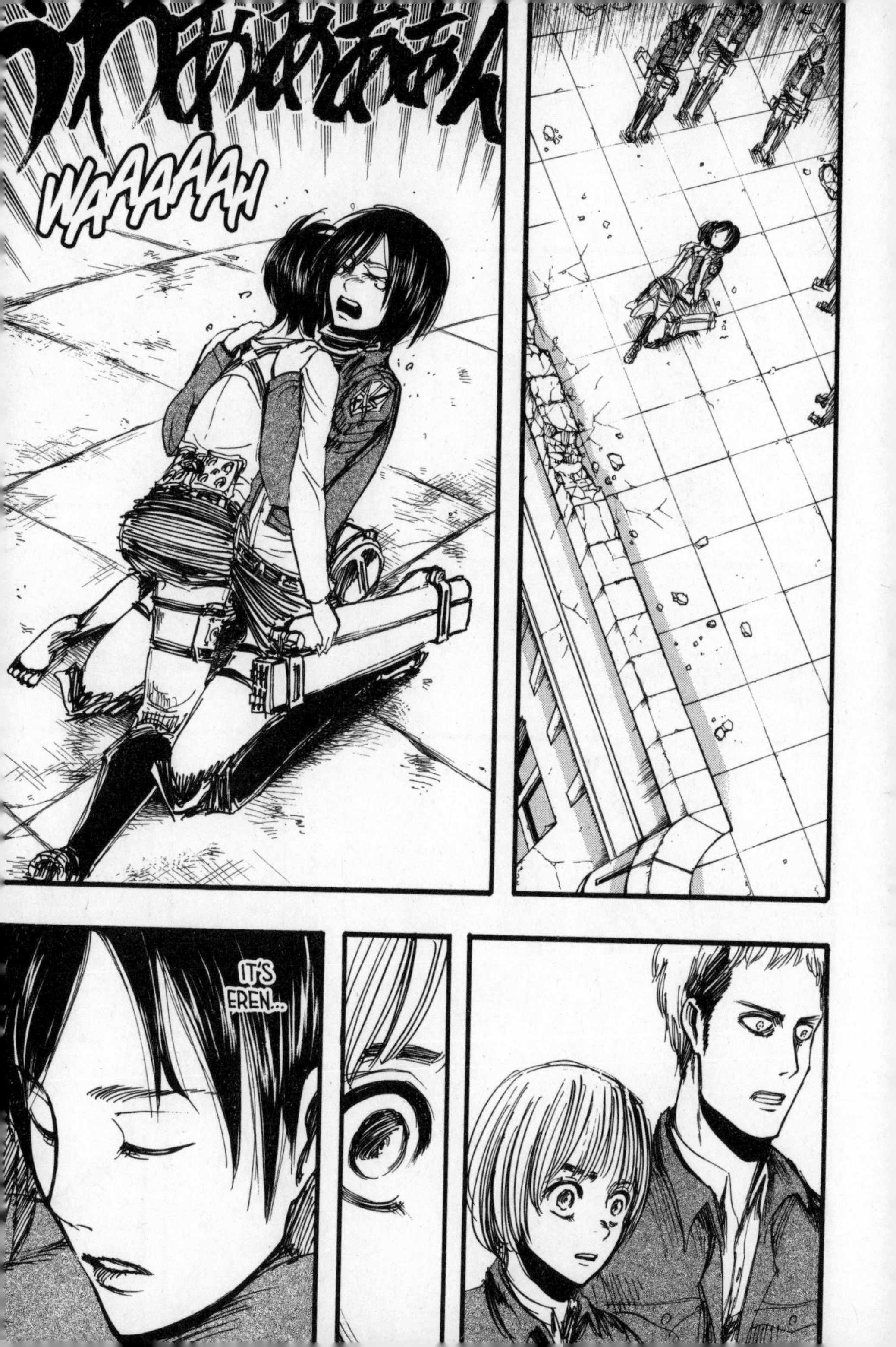

うわぁあああん
WAAAAAH
IT'S EREN...

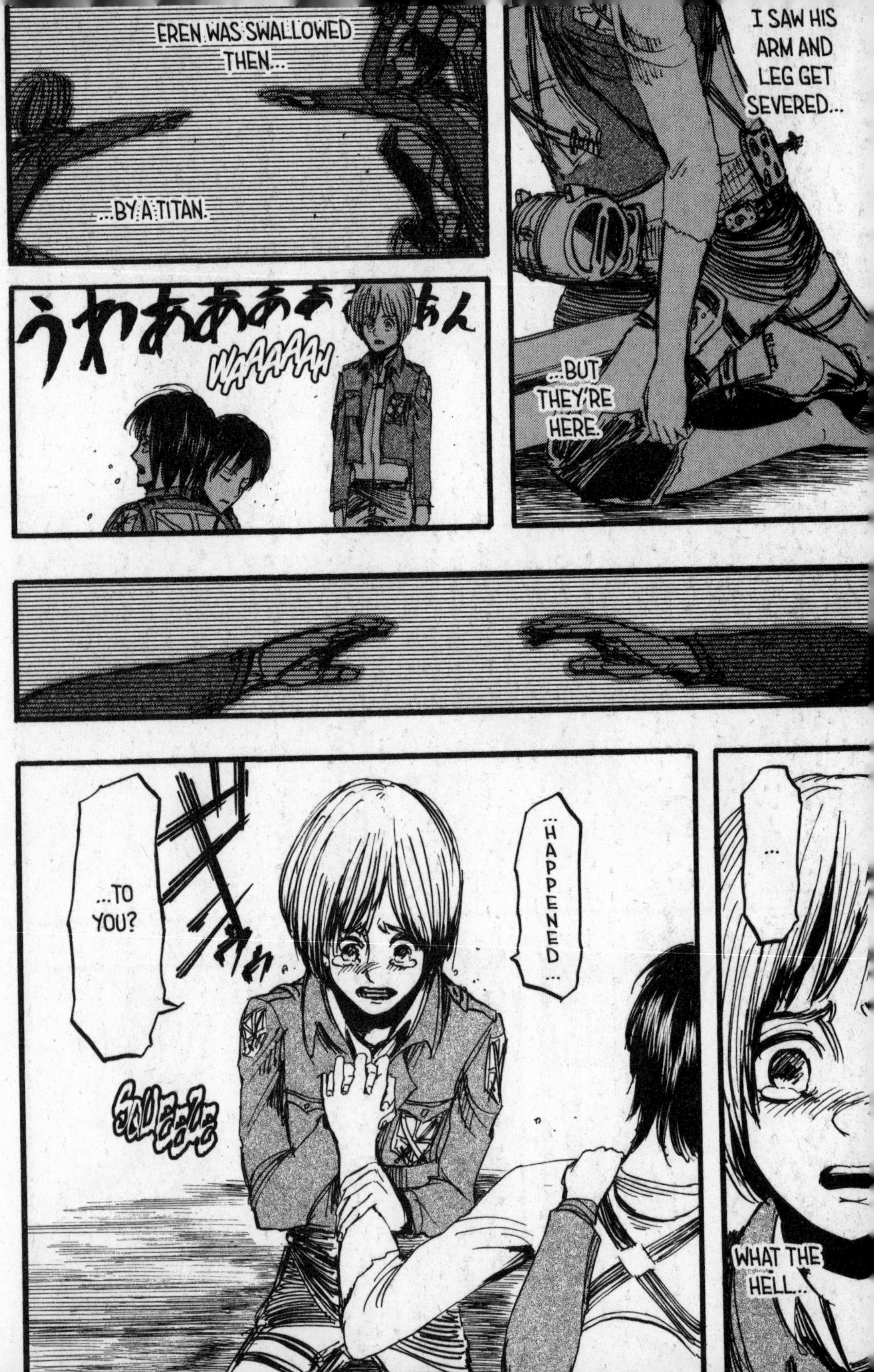
I SAW HIS ARM AND LEG GET SEVERED...
...BUT THEY'RE HERE.
EREN WAS SWALLOWED THEN...
...BY A TITAN.
うわああああああん
WAAAAAH
...
WHAT THE HELL...
...HAPPENED...
...TO YOU?
SQUEEZE

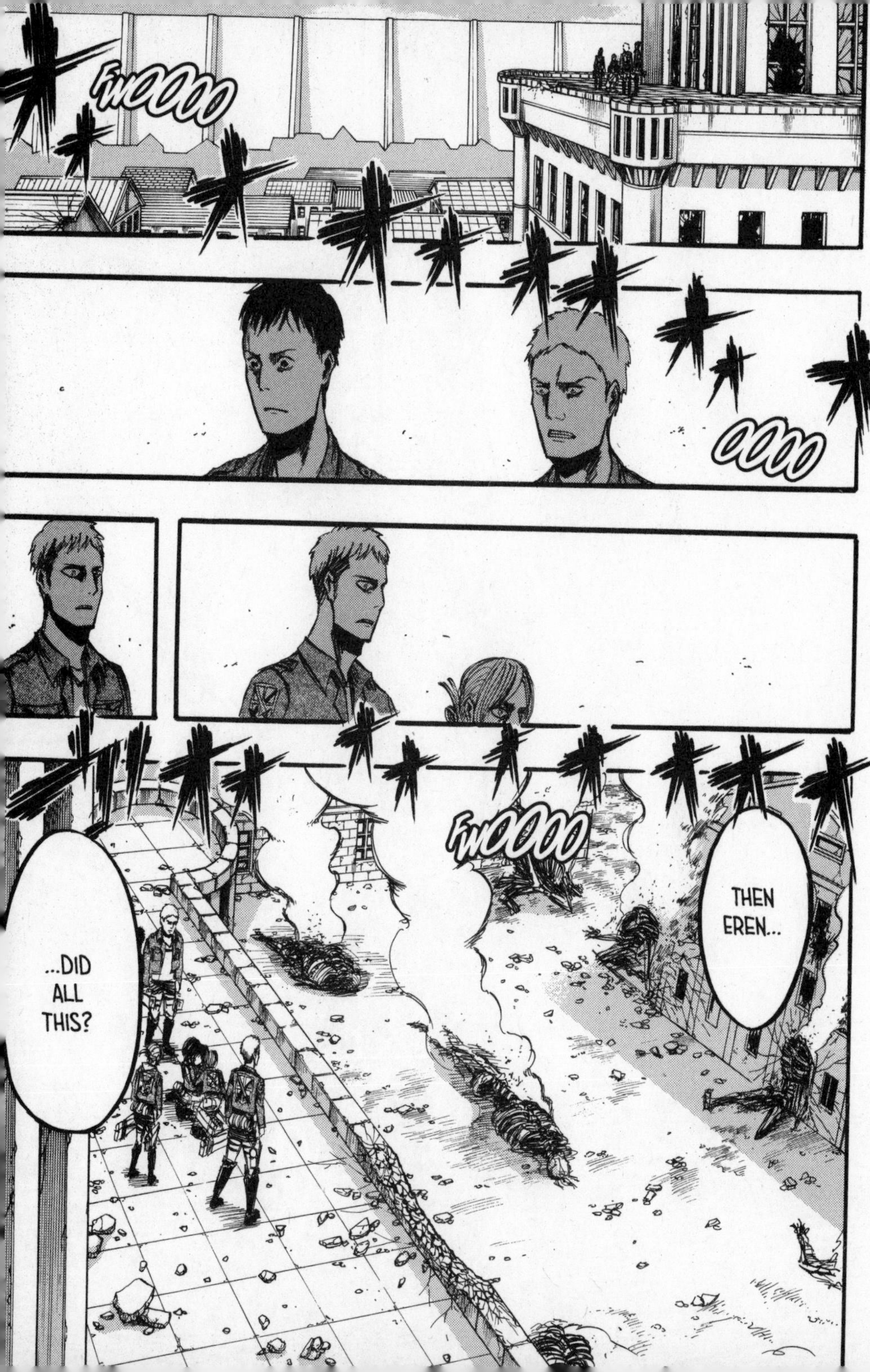
FWOOOO
OOOO
FWOOOO
THEN EREN...
...DID ALL THIS?

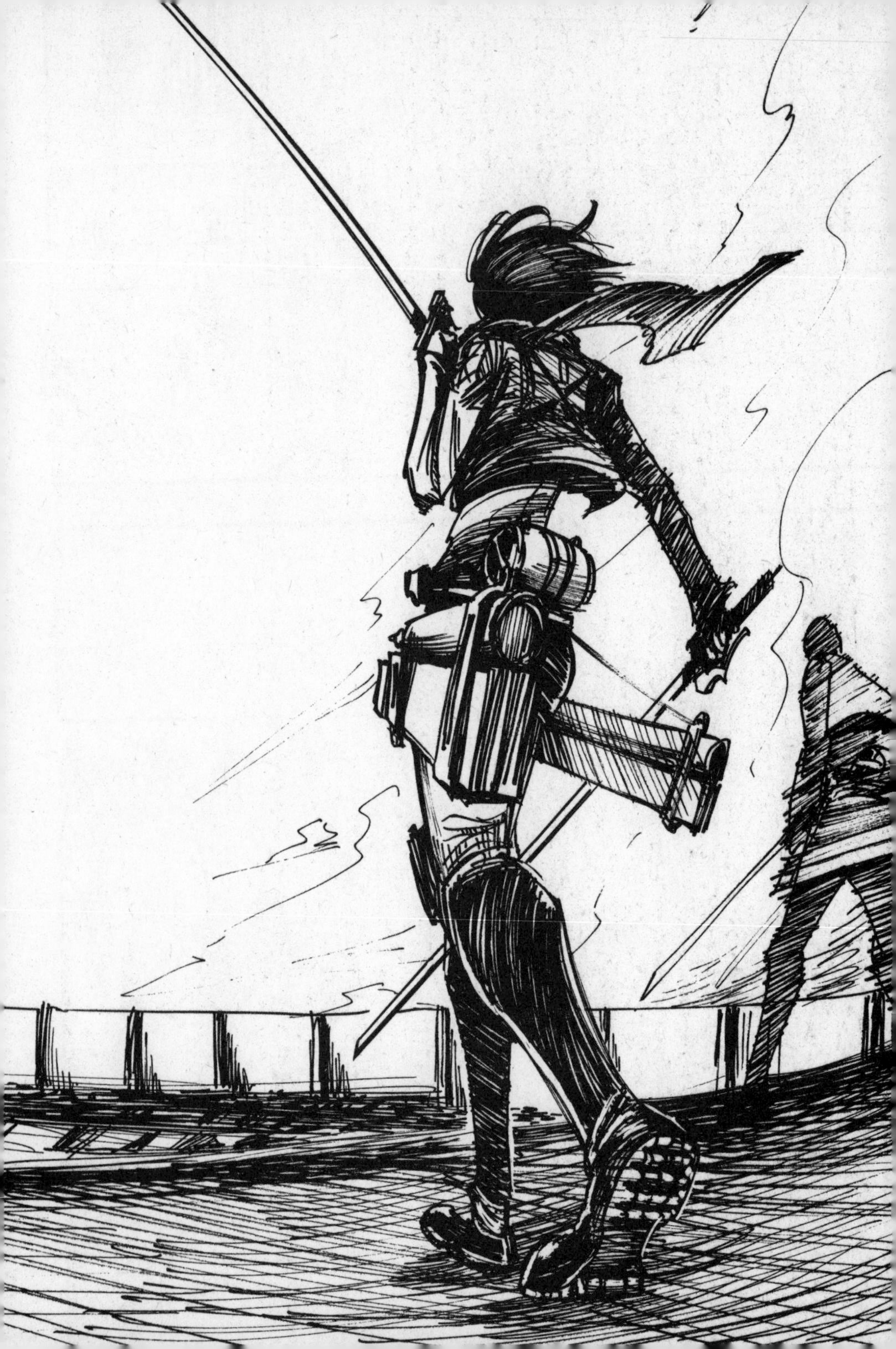

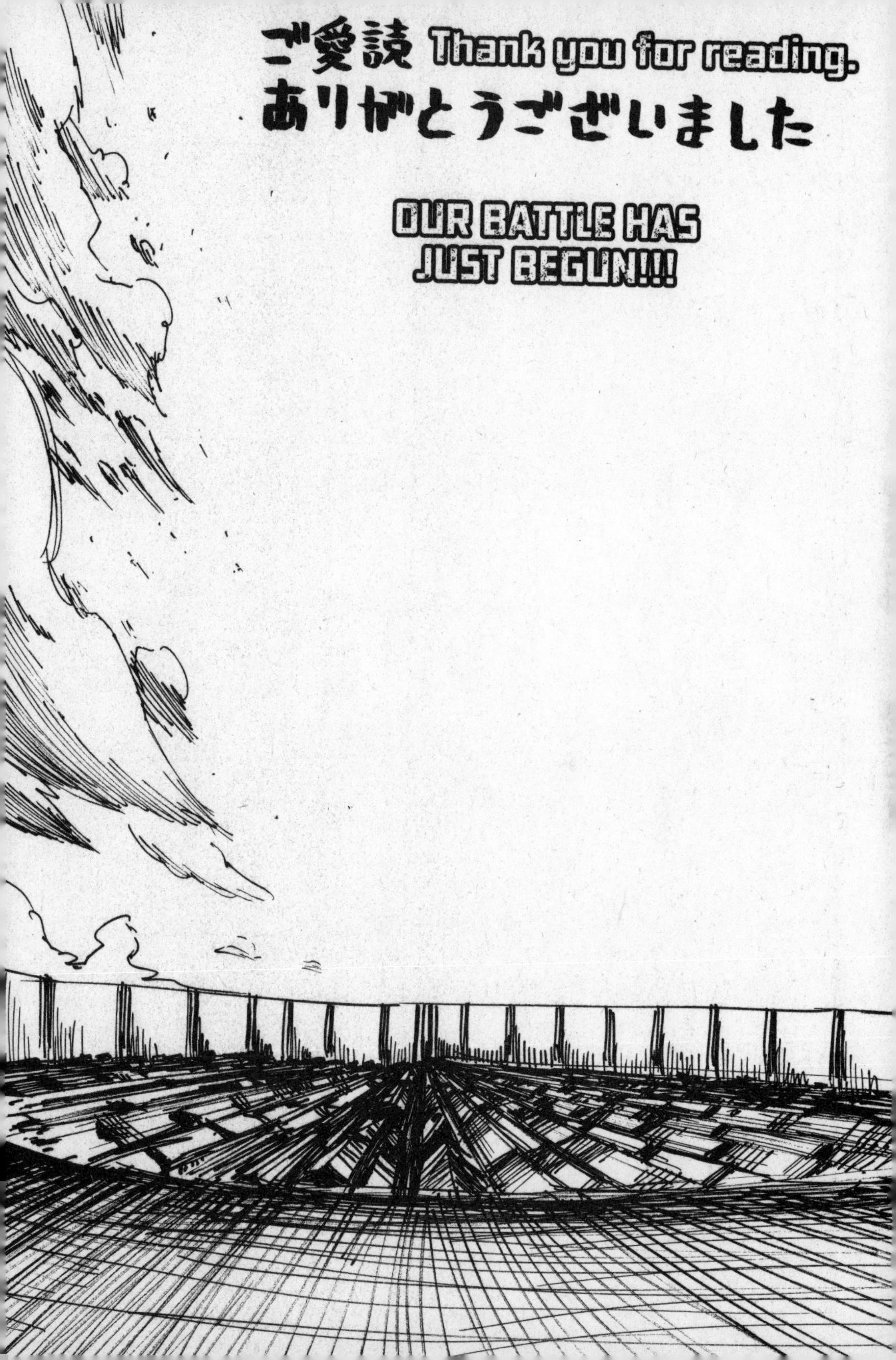
ご愛読 Thank you for reading.
ありがとうございました
OUR BATTLE HAS JUST BEGUN!!!!

ATTACK on TITAN

ATTACK ON TITAN
3
HAJIME ISAYAMA

The World of "Attack on Titan"

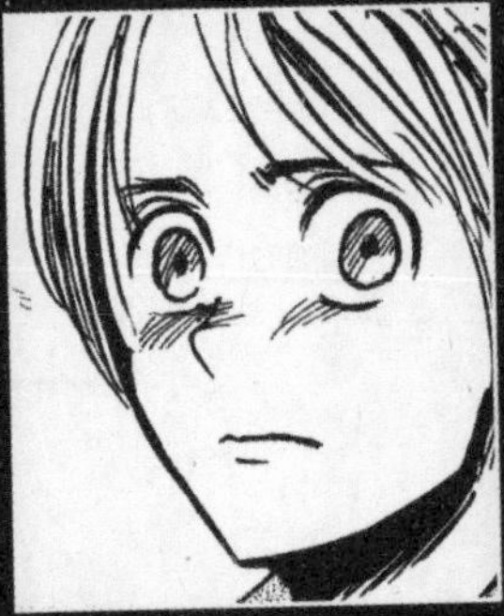

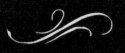

Armin Arlert
Eren and Mikasa's childhood friend, he is physically weak and feels that he has gone through life with them protecting him.

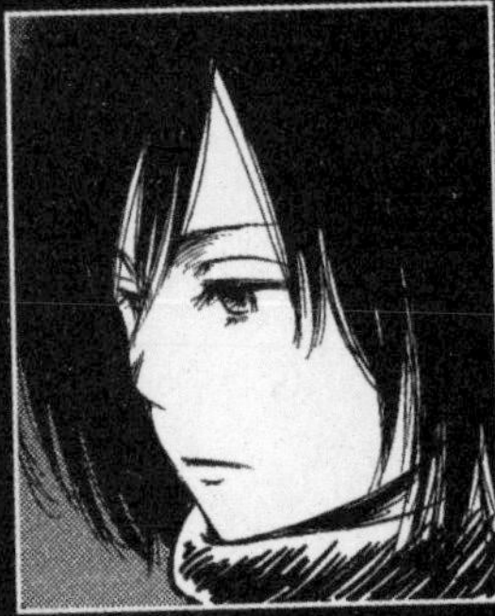

Mikasa Ackerman
Mikasa graduated at the top of her training corps. She lost her parents before her eyes. Afterward she becomes committed to protecting Eren, who was raised alongside her.

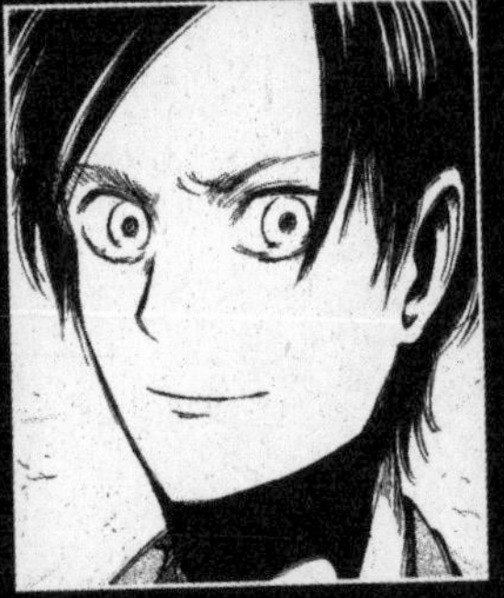

Eren Yeager
Longing for the world outside the wall, Eren aimed to join the Survey Corps. He was swallowed by a Titan, but was later discovered inside a Titan.

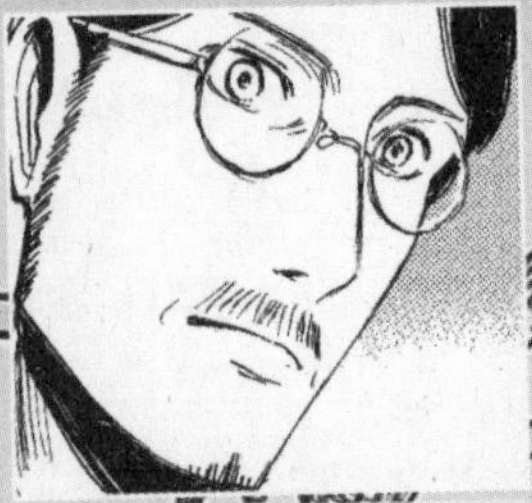

Grisha Yeager
A doctor and Eren's father. He went missing after the Titan attack five years ago.

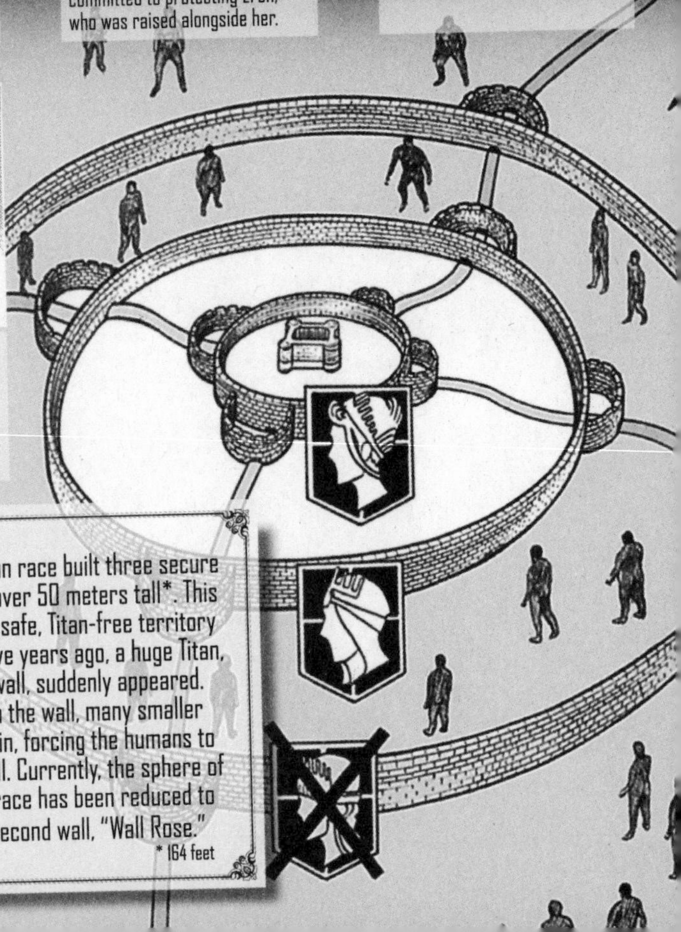

100 years ago, the human race built three secure concentric walls, each over 50 meters tall*. This successfully secured a safe, Titan-free territory for humans. However, five years ago, a huge Titan, taller than the outer wall, suddenly appeared. After it broke through the wall, many smaller Titans found their way in, forcing the humans to abandon their outer wall. Currently, the sphere of activity of the human race has been reduced to the area behind the second wall, "Wall Rose."

* 164 feet

TITANS

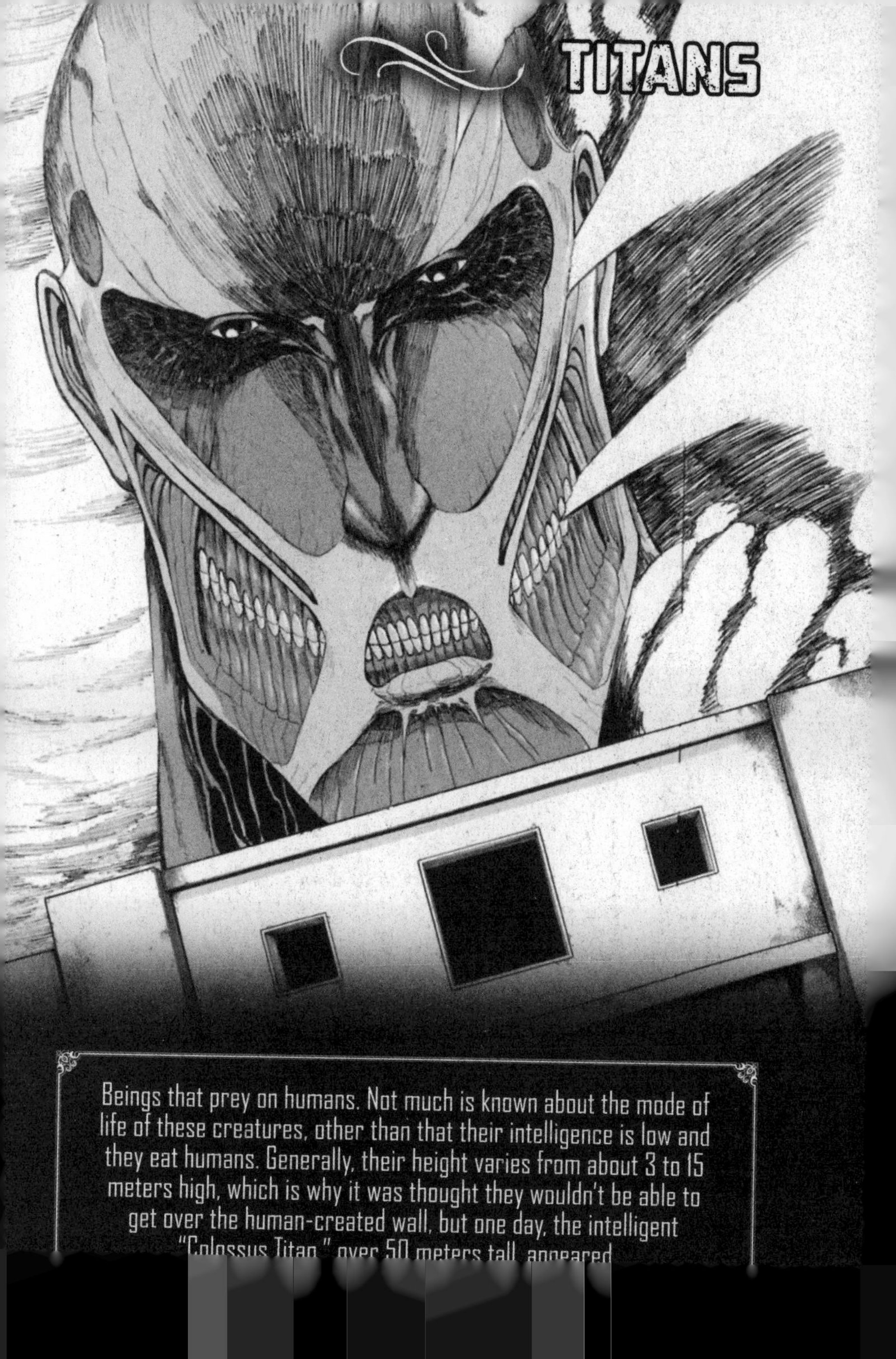

Beings that prey on humans. Not much is known about the mode of life of these creatures, other than that their intelligence is low and they eat humans. Generally, their height varies from about 3 to 15 meters high, which is why it was thought they wouldn't be able to get over the human-created wall, but one day, the intelligent "Colossus Titan," over 50 meters tall, appeared.

ATTACK on TITAN

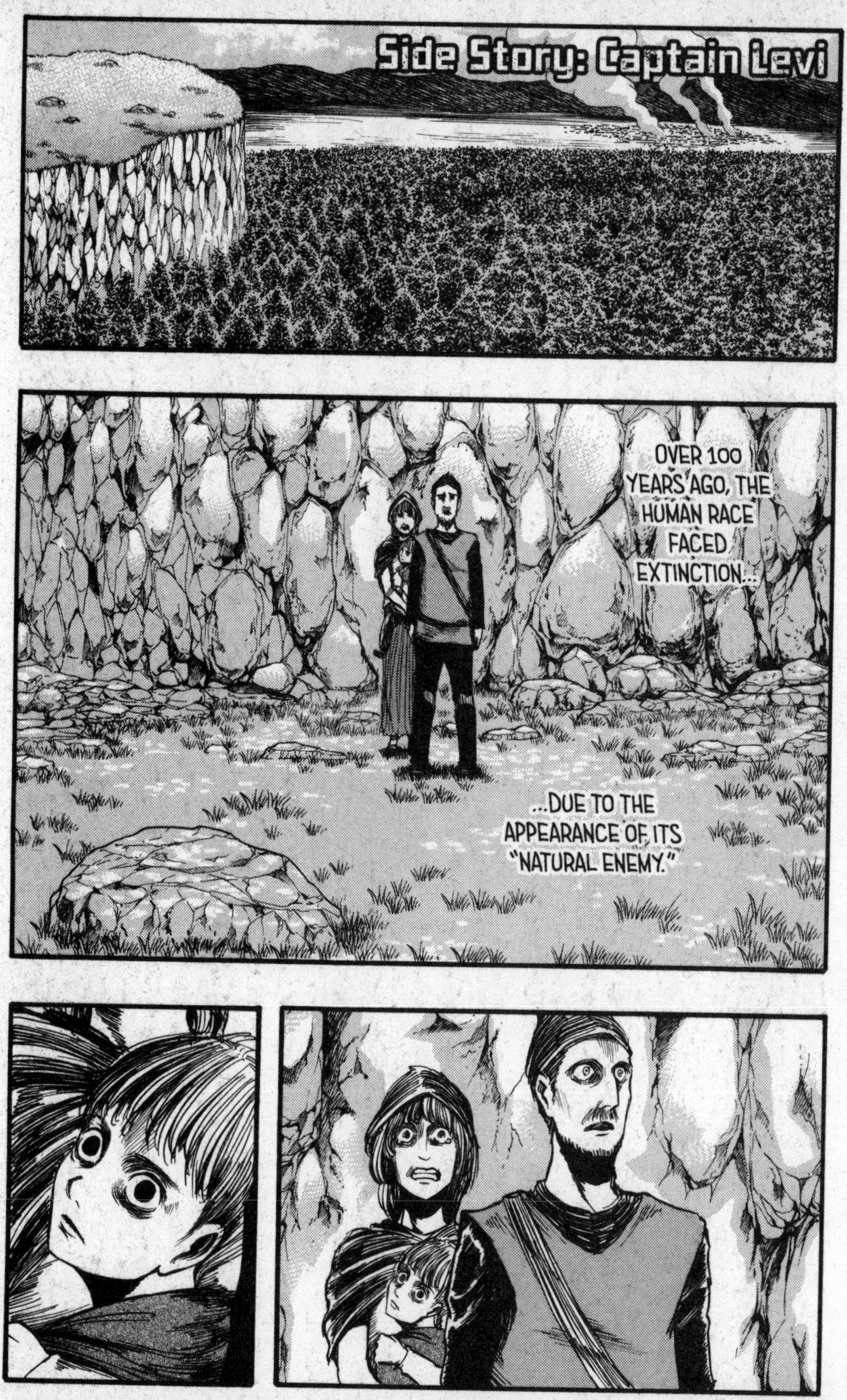
Side Story: Captain Levi
OVER 100 YEARS AGO, THE HUMAN RACE FACED EXTINCTION...
...DUE TO THE APPEARANCE OF ITS "NATURAL ENEMY."

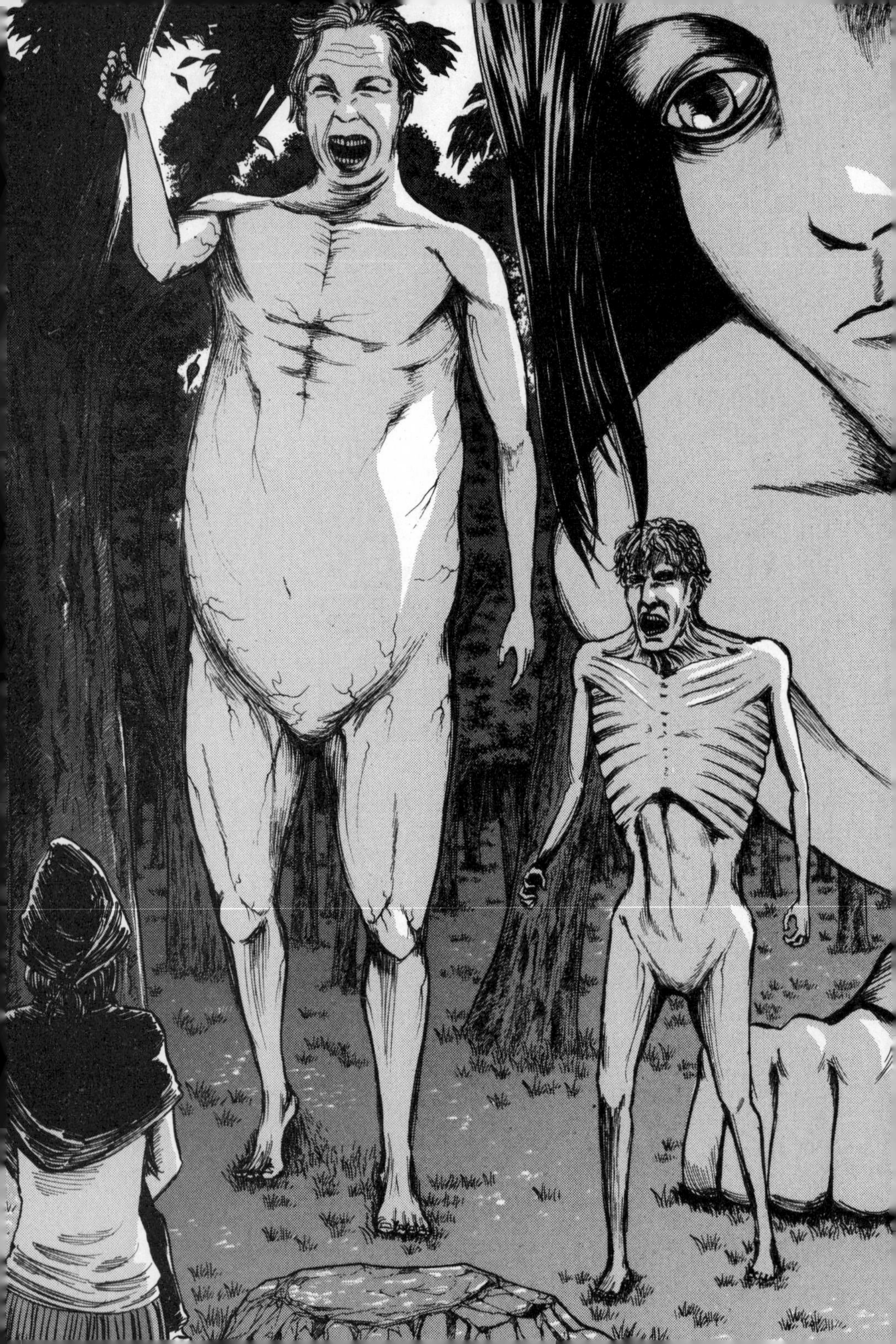

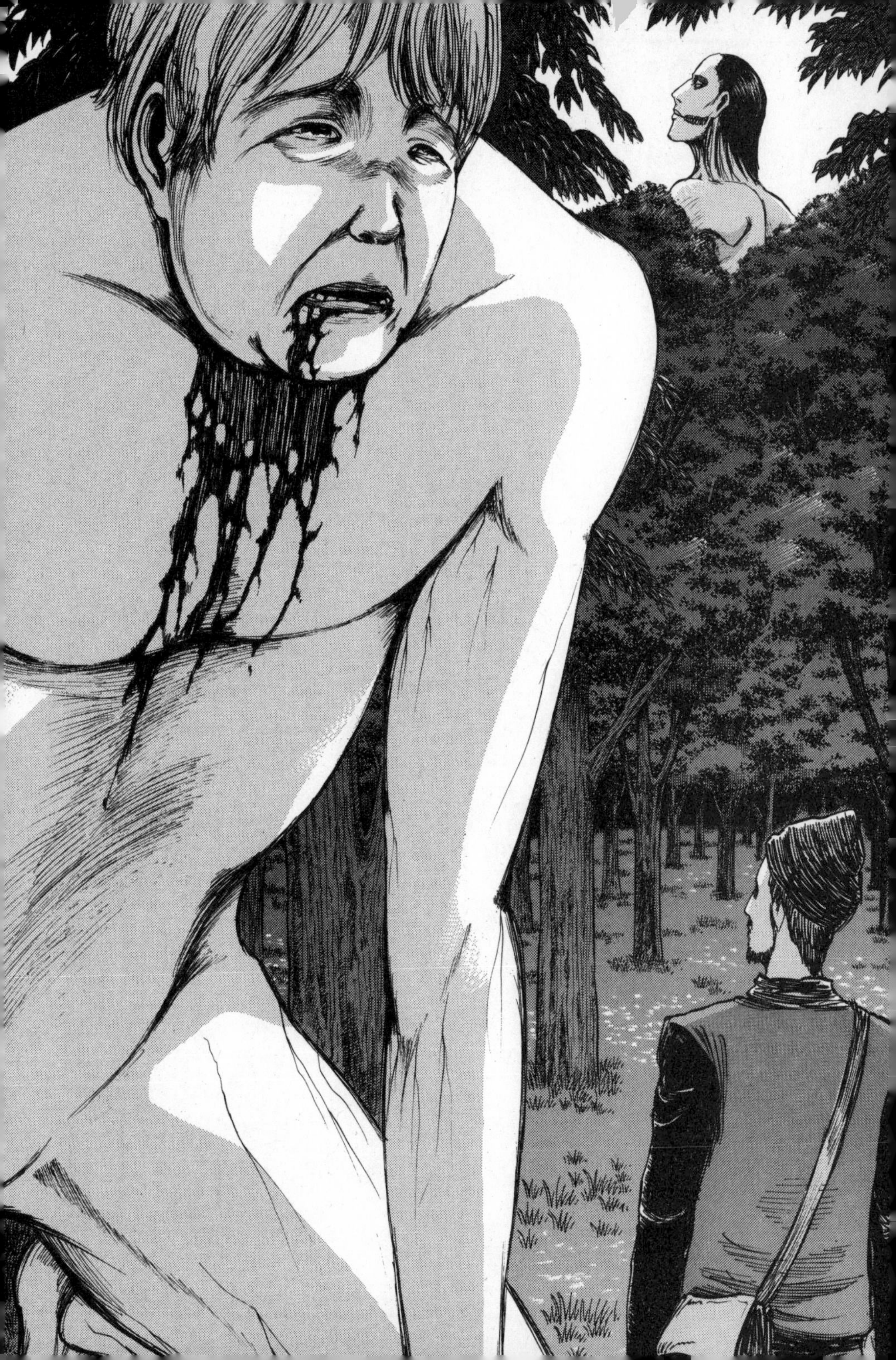

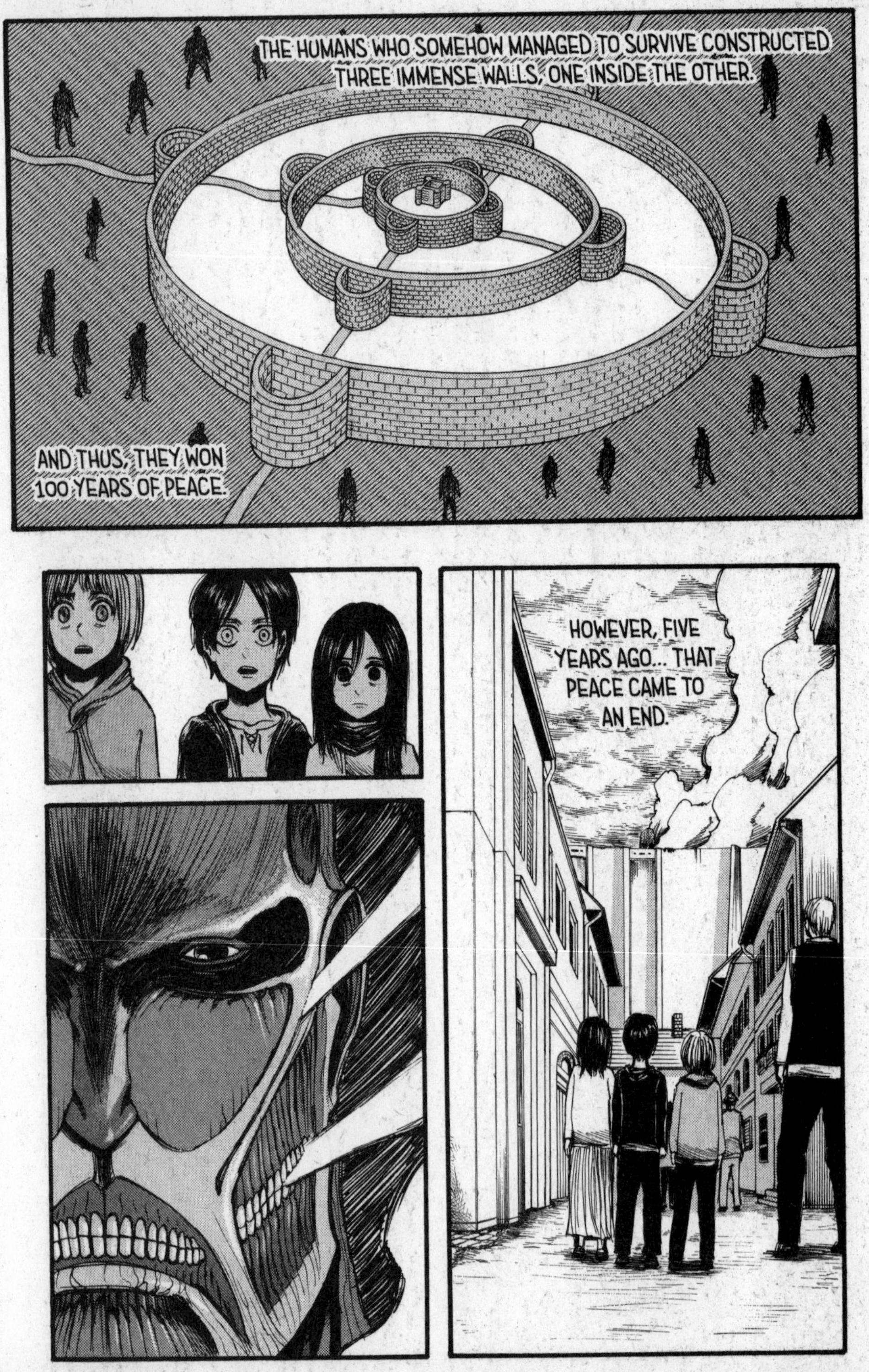
THE HUMANS WHO SOMEHOW MANAGED TO SURVIVE CONSTRUCTED THREE IMMENSE WALLS, ONE INSIDE THE OTHER.
AND THUS, THEY WON 100 YEARS OF PEACE.
HOWEVER, FIVE YEARS AGO... THAT PEACE CAME TO AN END.

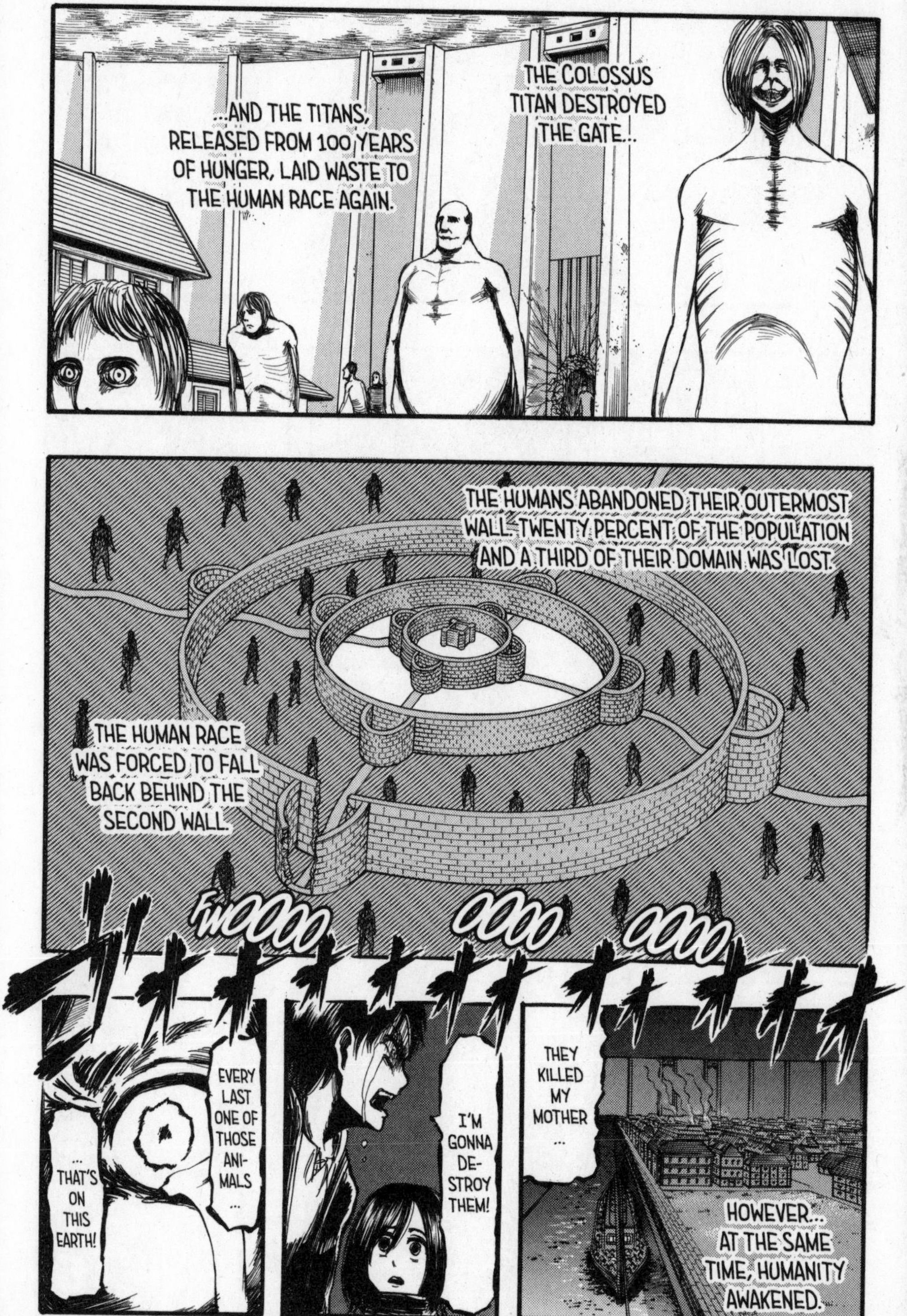
THE COLOSSUS TITAN DESTROYED THE GATE...
...AND THE TITANS, RELEASED FROM 100 YEARS OF HUNGER, LAID WASTE TO THE HUMAN RACE AGAIN.
THE HUMANS ABANDONED THEIR OUTERMOST WALL. TWENTY PERCENT OF THE POPULATION AND A THIRD OF THEIR DOMAIN WAS LOST.
THE HUMAN RACE WAS FORCED TO FALL BACK BEHIND THE SECOND WALL.
FWOOOO OOOO OOOO
THEY KILLED MY MOTHER ...
HOWEVER... AT THE SAME TIME, HUMANITY AWAKENED.
I'M GONNA DE-STROY THEM!
EVERY LAST ONE OF THOSE ANI-MALS ...
... THAT'S ON THIS EARTH!

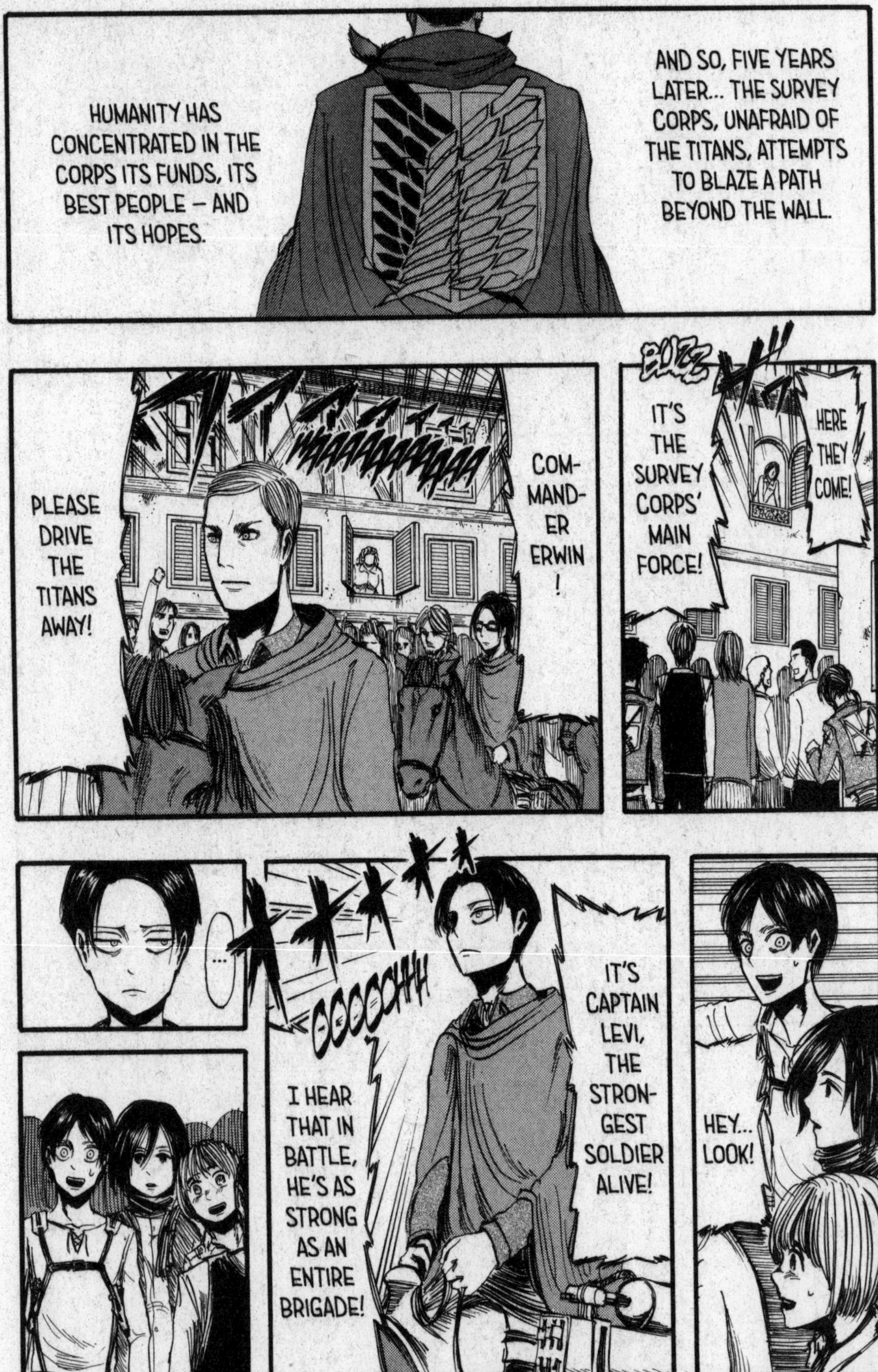
AND SO, FIVE YEARS LATER... THE SURVEY CORPS, UNAFRAID OF THE TITANS, ATTEMPTS TO BLAZE A PATH BEYOND THE WALL.
HUMANITY HAS CONCENTRATED IN THE CORPS ITS FUNDS, ITS BEST PEOPLE — AND ITS HOPES.
BUZZ
HERE THEY COME!
IT'S THE SURVEY CORPS' MAIN FORCE!
WAAAAAAAAAAAA
COM-MAND-ER ERWIN!
PLEASE DRIVE THE TITANS AWAY!
HEY... LOOK!
IT'S CAPTAIN LEVI, THE STRON-GEST SOLDIER ALIVE!
OOOOOHHH
I HEAR THAT IN BATTLE, HE'S AS STRONG AS AN ENTIRE BRIGADE!
...

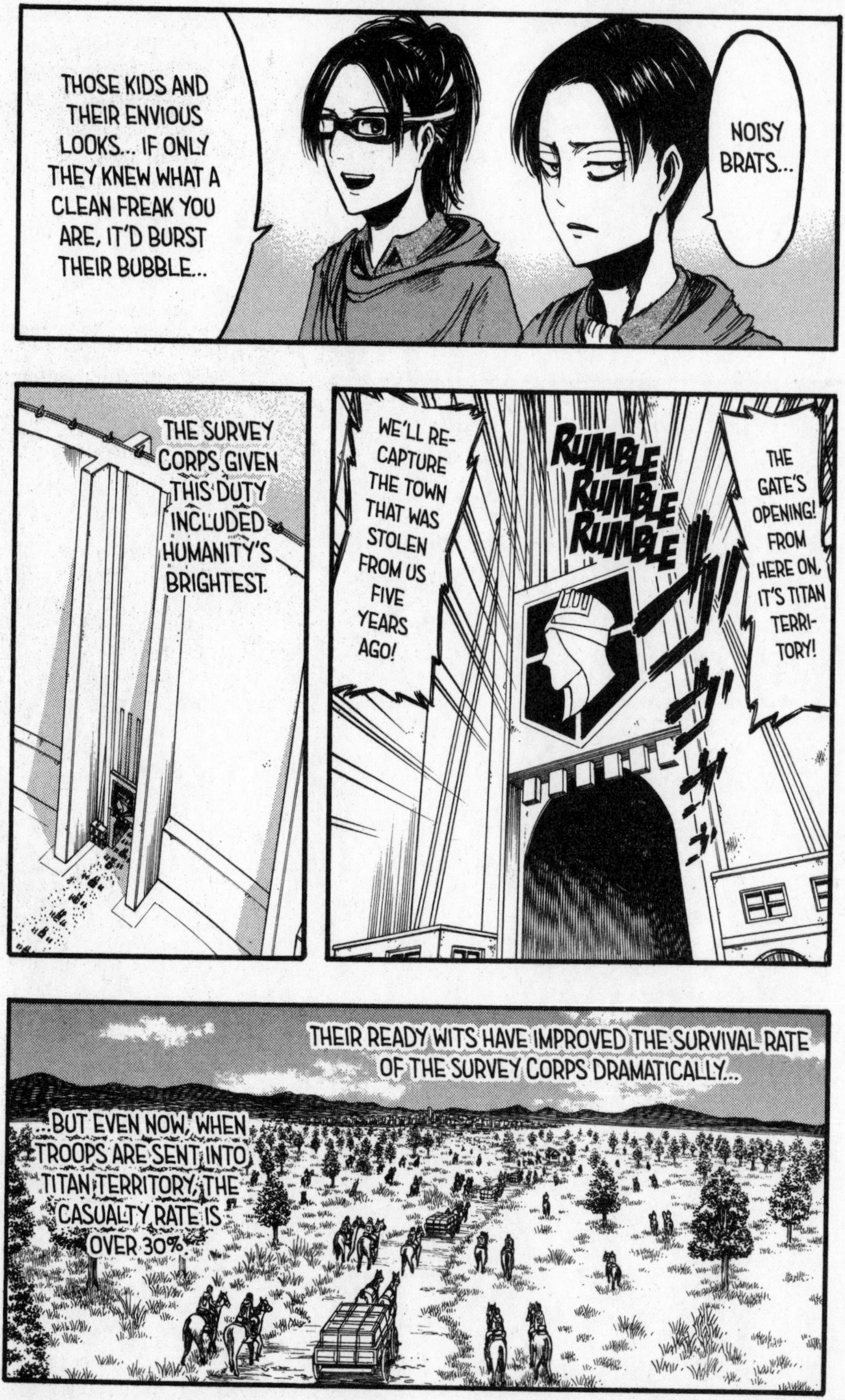
NOISY BRATS...
THOSE KIDS AND THEIR ENVIOUS LOOKS... IF ONLY THEY KNEW WHAT A CLEAN FREAK YOU ARE, IT'D BURST THEIR BUBBLE...
THE GATE'S OPENING! FROM HERE ON, IT'S TITAN TERRITORY!
RUMBLE RUMBLE RUMBLE
WE'LL RE-CAPTURE THE TOWN THAT WAS STOLEN FROM US FIVE YEARS AGO!
THE SURVEY CORPS GIVEN THIS DUTY INCLUDED HUMANITY'S BRIGHTEST.
THEIR READY WITS HAVE IMPROVED THE SURVIVAL RATE OF THE SURVEY CORPS DRAMATICALLY...
...BUT EVEN NOW, WHEN TROOPS ARE SENT INTO TITAN TERRITORY, THE CASUALTY RATE IS OVER 30%.

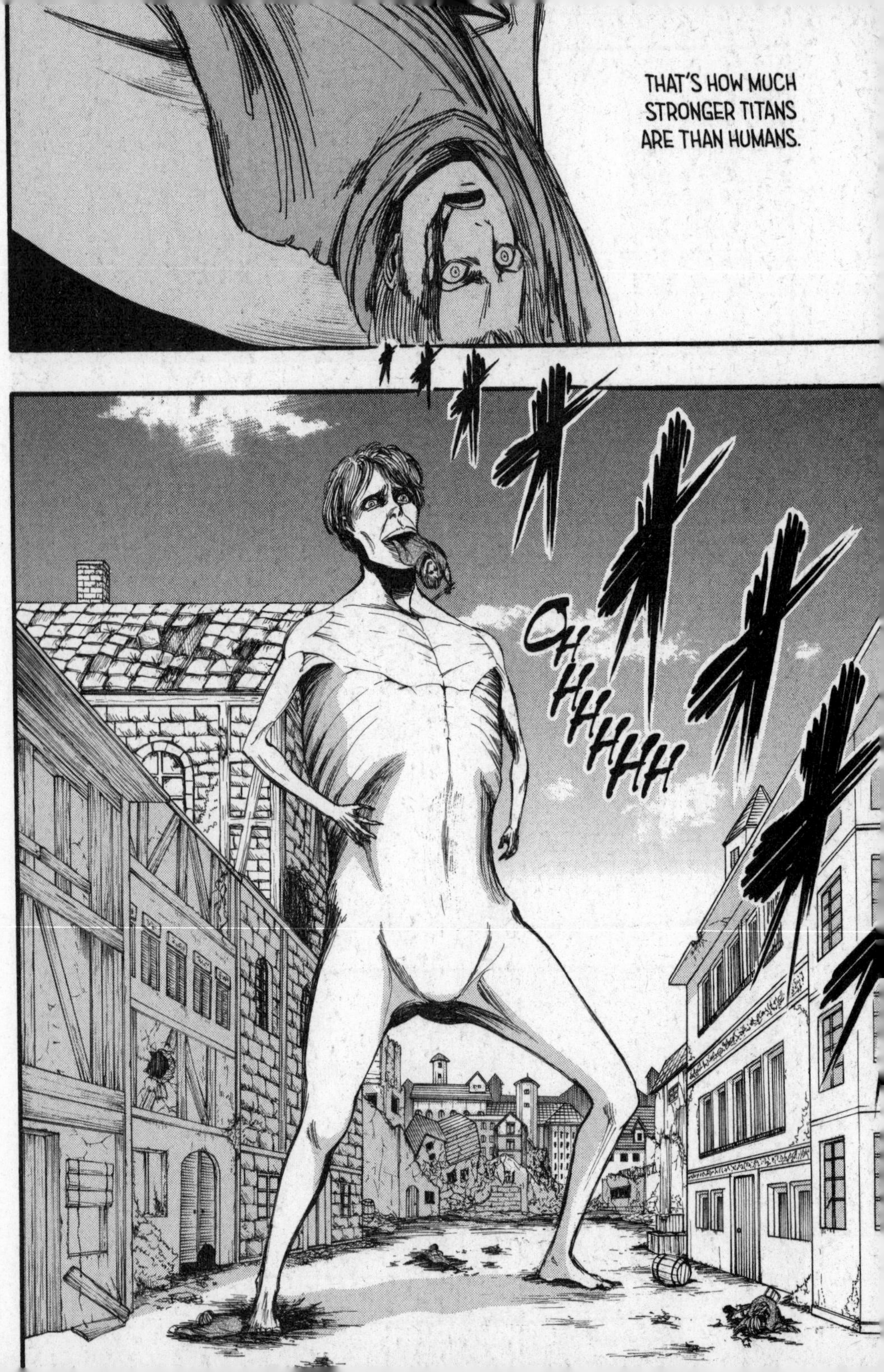
THAT'S HOW MUCH STRONGER TITANS ARE THAN HUMANS.
OHHHHHHH

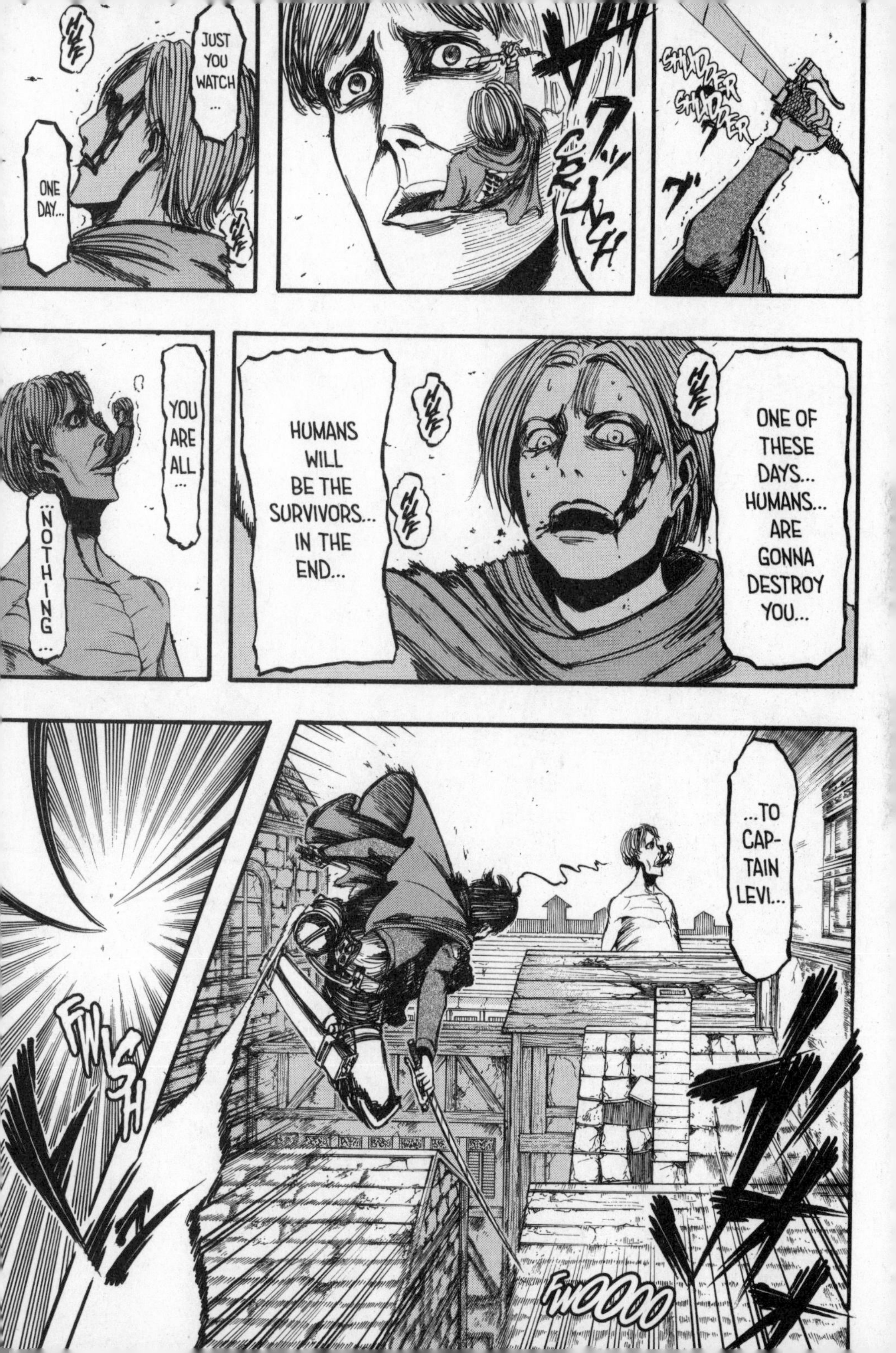
SHUDDER SHUDDER
CRUNCH
JUST YOU WATCH ...
ONE DAY...
ONE OF THESE DAYS... HUMANS... ARE GONNA DESTROY YOU...
HUMANS WILL BE THE SURVIVORS... IN THE END...
YOU ARE ALL ...
...NOTHING ...
...TO CAPTAIN LEVI...
FWOOOO
FWISH

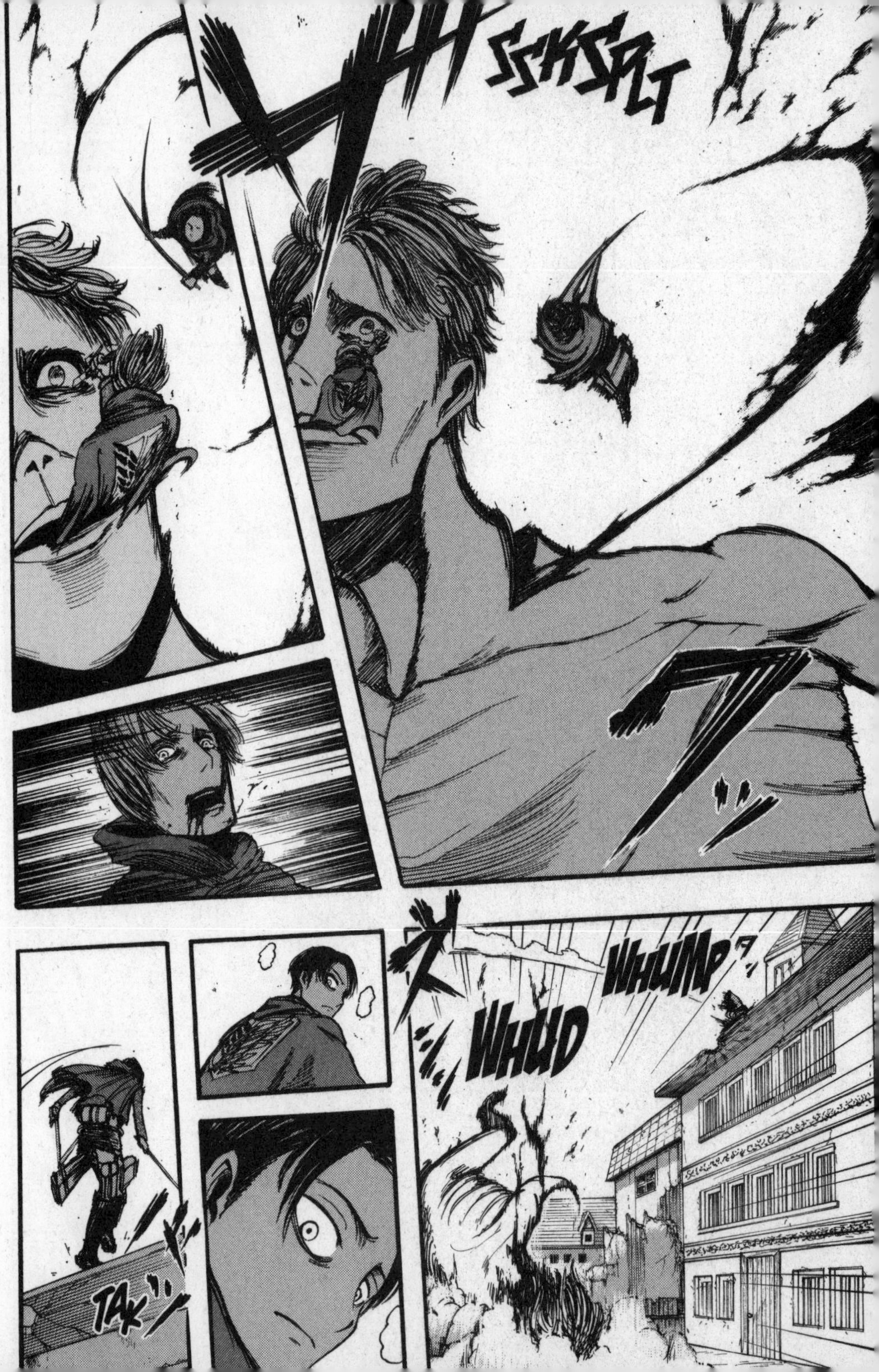
SSKSPLT
WHUMP
WHUD
TAK

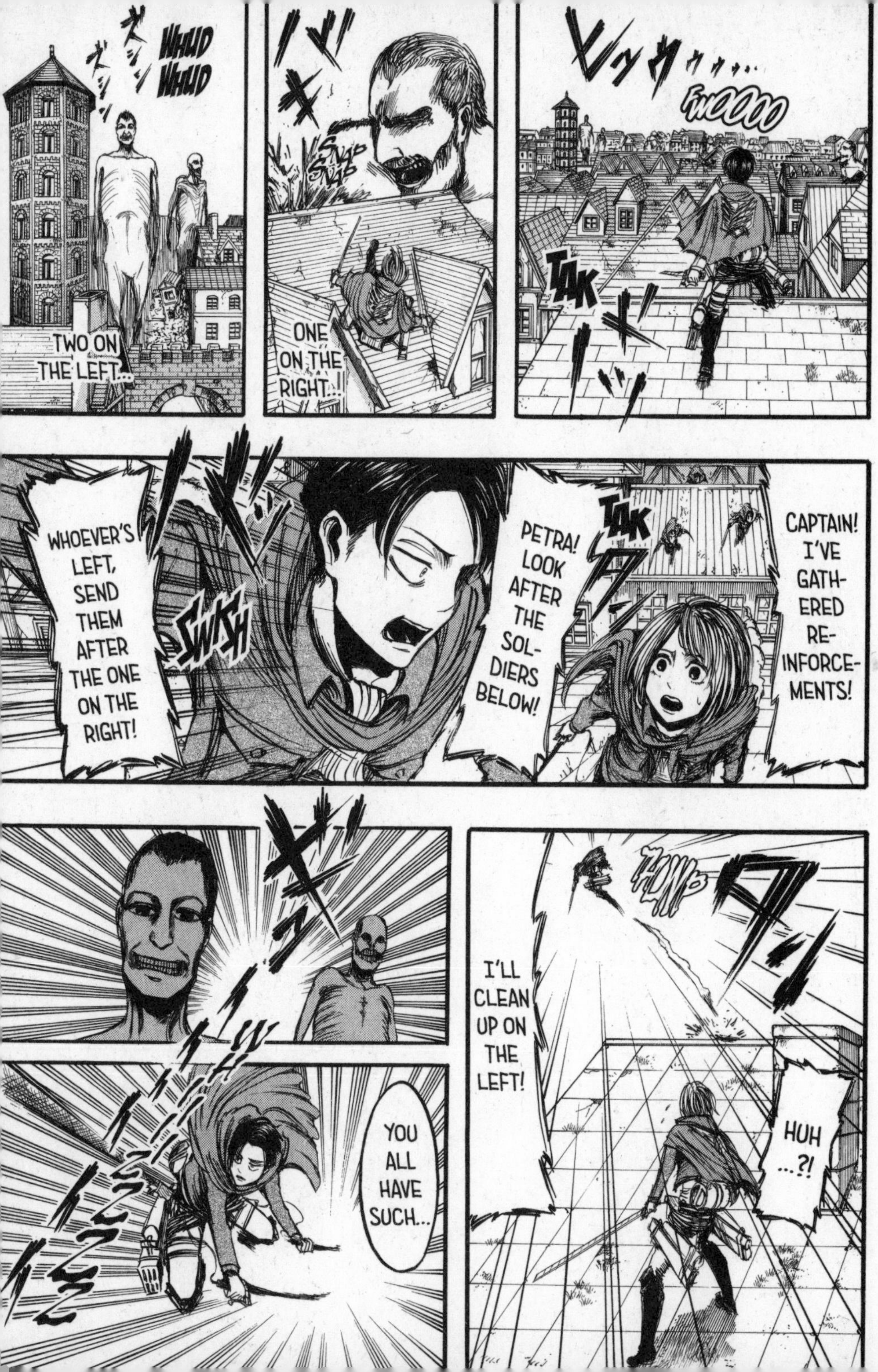
FWOOOO
TAK
SNAP SNAP
ONE ON THE RIGHT...!
WHUD WHUD
TWO ON THE LEFT...
CAPTAIN! I'VE GATHERED REINFORCEMENTS!
TAK
PETRA! LOOK AFTER THE SOLDIERS BELOW!
SWISH
WHOEVER'S LEFT, SEND THEM AFTER THE ONE ON THE RIGHT!
I'LL CLEAN UP ON THE LEFT!
HUH ...?!
YOU ALL HAVE SUCH...

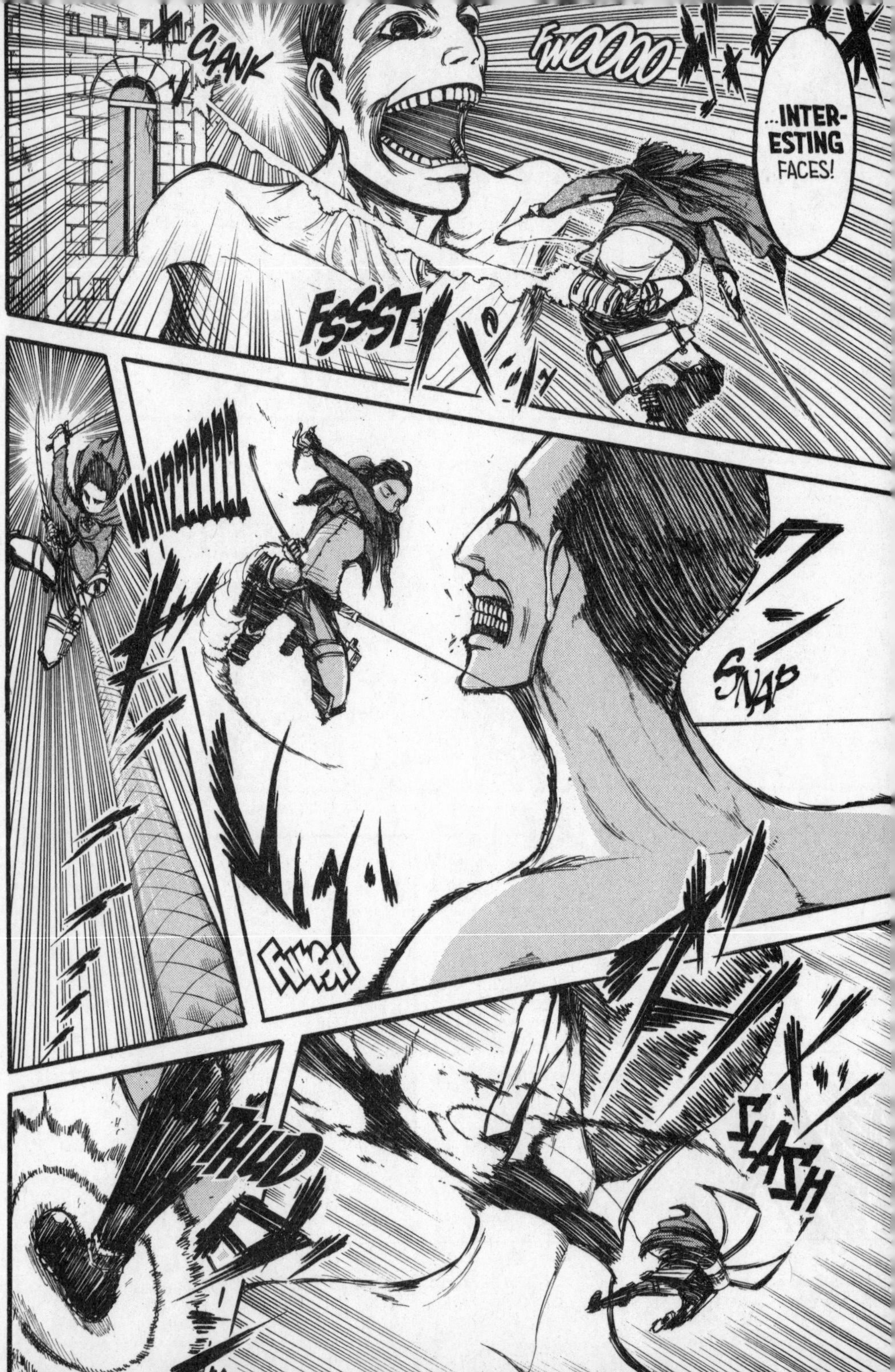

...INTER-ESTING FACES!
FWOOOOO
CLANK
FSSST
SNAP
FWISH
WHIZZZZZZ
SLASH
THUD

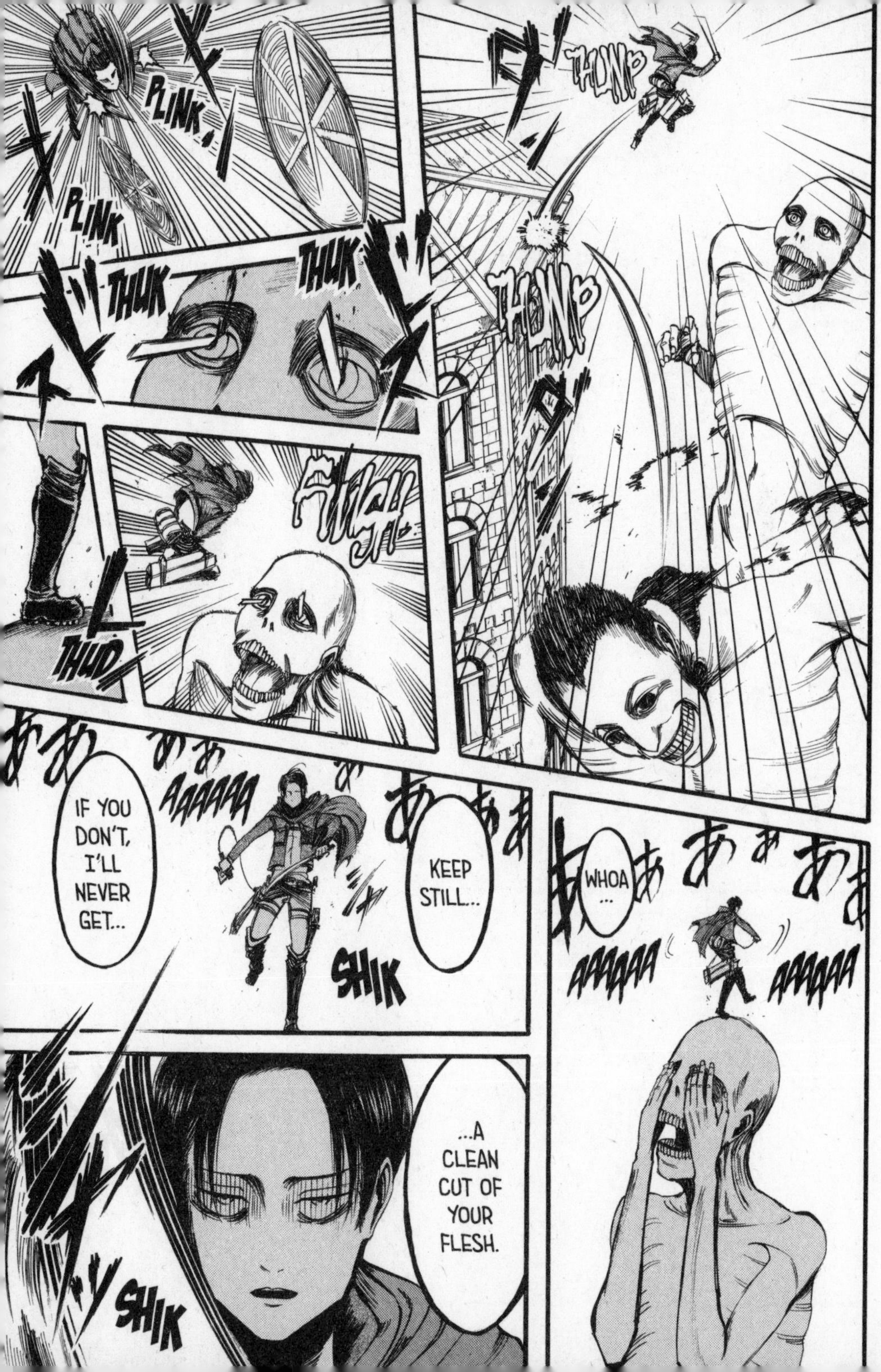
THUNP
THUNP
PLINK
PLINK
THUK
THUK
FWISH
THUD
WHOA...
AAAAAA
AAAAAA
KEEP STILL...
AAAAAA
IF YOU DON'T, I'LL NEVER GET...
SHIK
...A CLEAN CUT OF YOUR FLESH.
SHIK

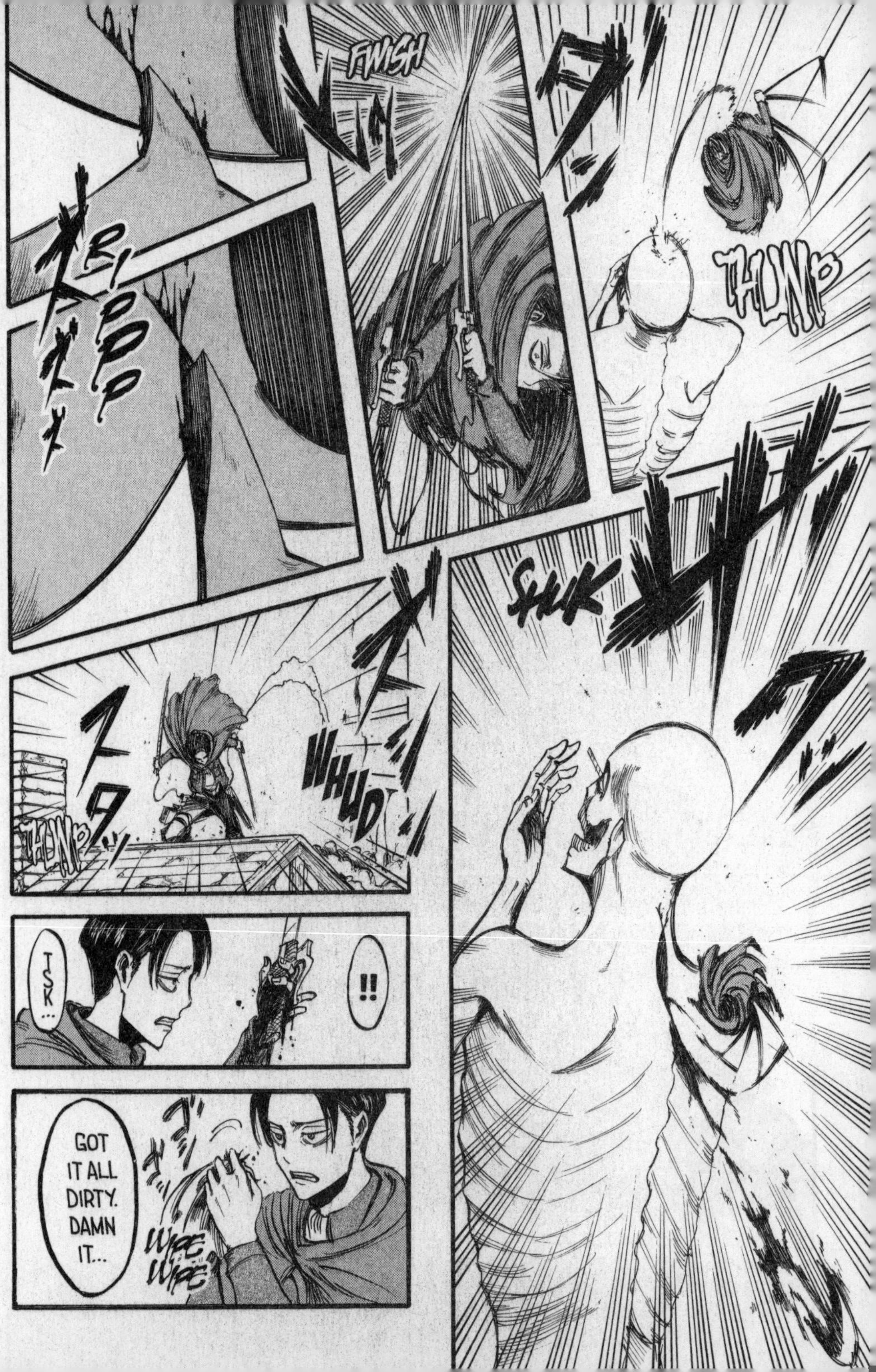
THUMP
FWISH
RIPPPP
SHUK
WHUD
THUMP
!!
TSK...
GOT IT ALL DIRTY. DAMN IT...
WIPE WIPE

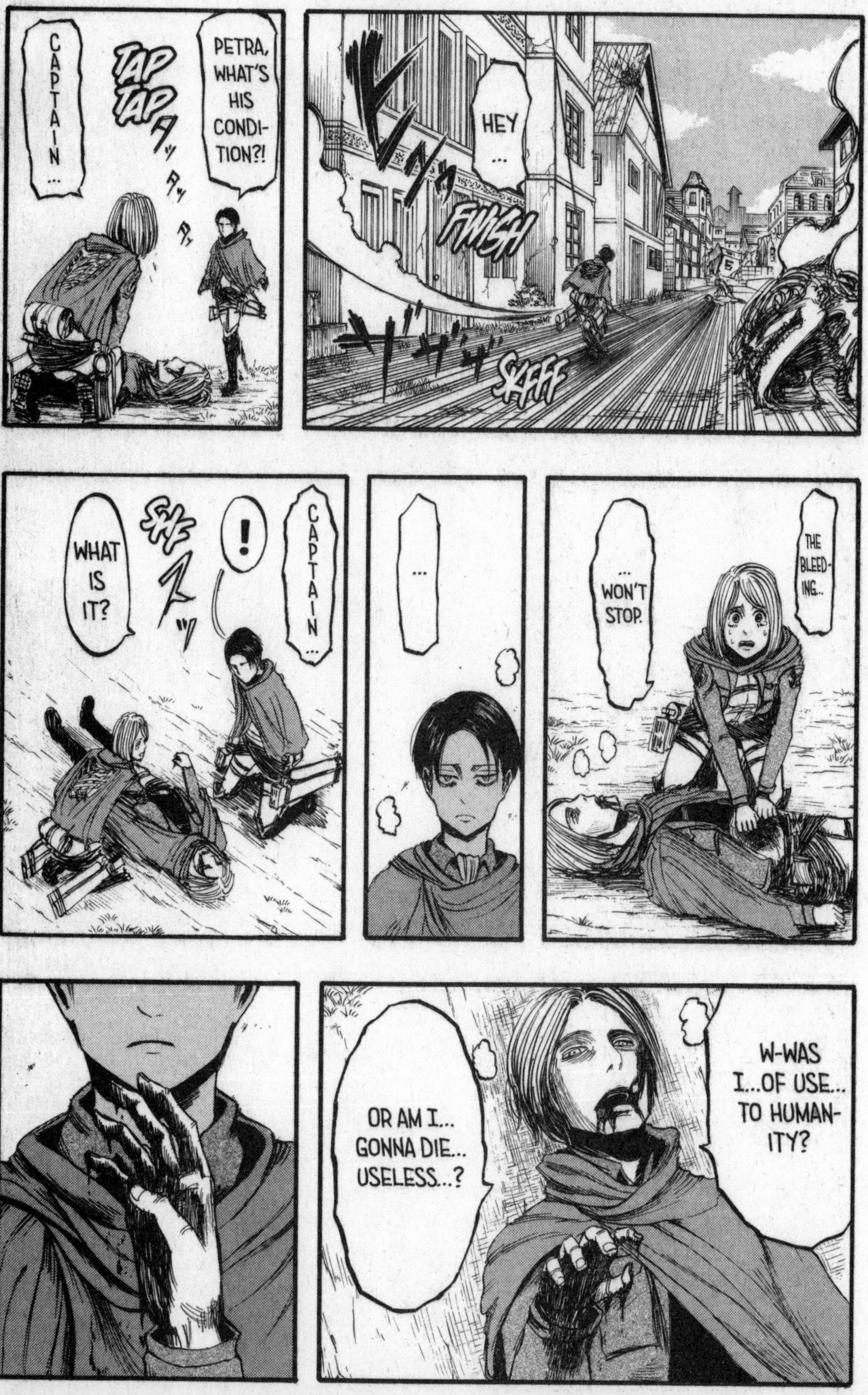

HEY ...
FWISH
SKFFF
PETRA, WHAT'S HIS CONDITION?!
TAP TAP
CAPTAIN ...
THE BLEED-ING...
... WON'T STOP.
...
CAPTAIN ...
!
SKF
WHAT IS IT?
W-WAS I...OF USE... TO HUMAN-ITY?
OR AM I... GONNA DIE... USELESS...?

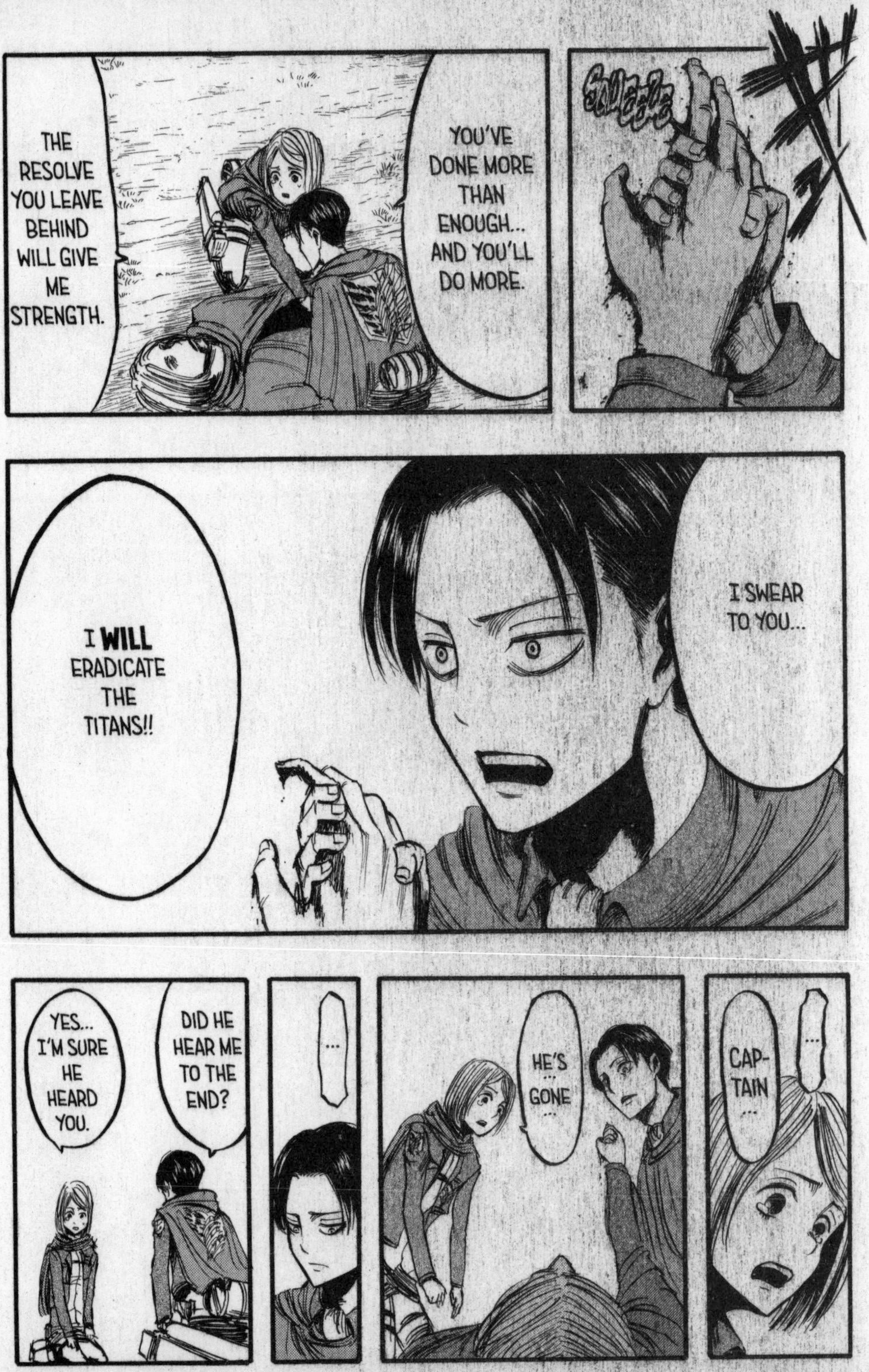

YOU'VE DONE MORE THAN ENOUGH... AND YOU'LL DO MORE.
THE RESOLVE YOU LEAVE BEHIND WILL GIVE ME STRENGTH.
I SWEAR TO YOU...
I **WILL** ERADICATE THE TITANS!!
...
CAP-TAIN...
HE'S... GONE...
...
DID HE HEAR ME TO THE END?
YES... I'M SURE HE HEARD YOU.

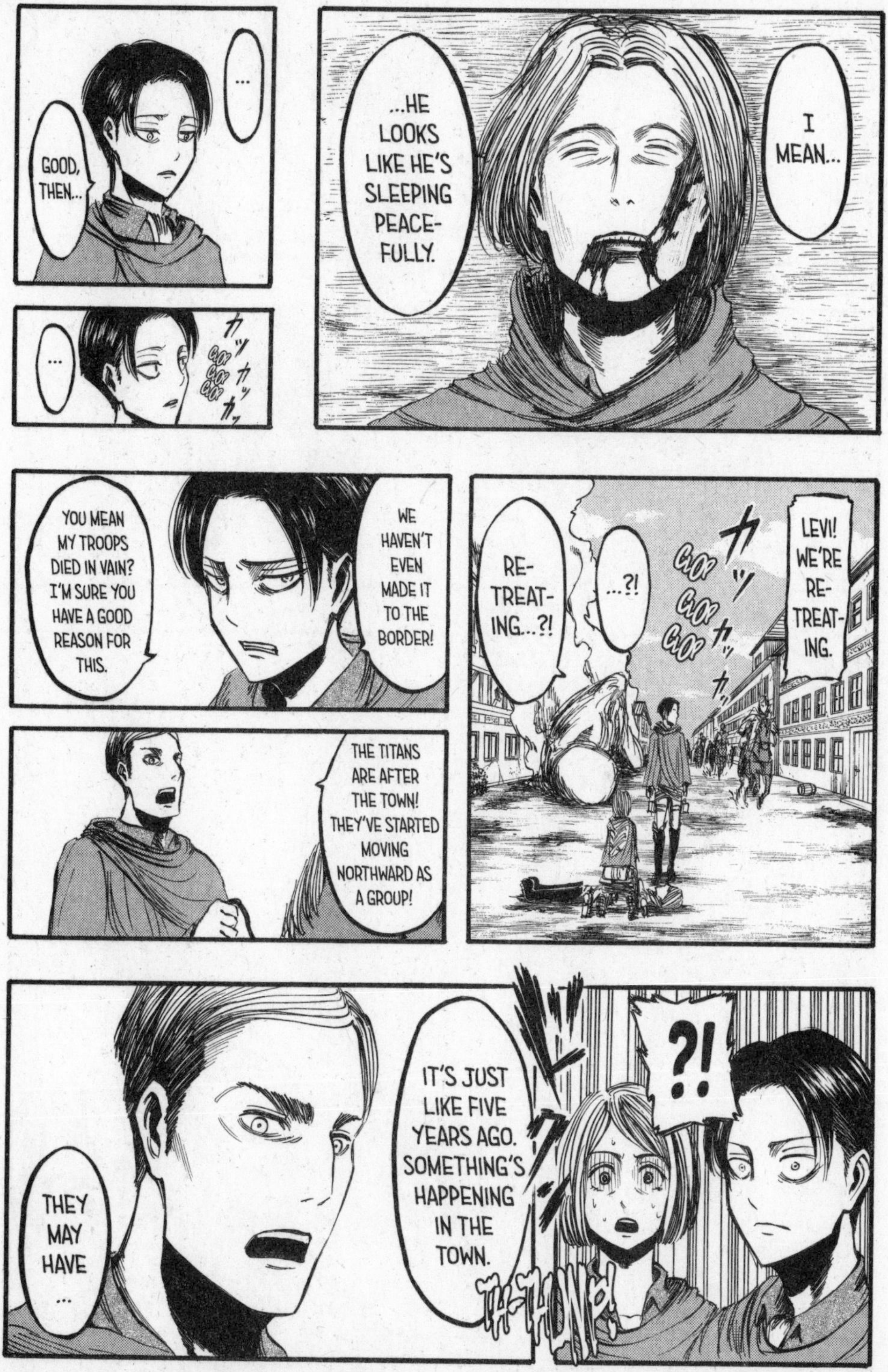
I MEAN...
...HE LOOKS LIKE HE'S SLEEPING PEACE-FULLY.
...
GOOD, THEN...
...
CLOP CLOP CLOP
LEVI! WE'RE RE-TREAT-ING.
CLOP CLOP CLOP
...?!
RE-TREAT-ING...?!
WE HAVEN'T EVEN MADE IT TO THE BORDER!
YOU MEAN MY TROOPS DIED IN VAIN? I'M SURE YOU HAVE A GOOD REASON FOR THIS.
THE TITANS ARE AFTER THE TOWN! THEY'VE STARTED MOVING NORTHWARD AS A GROUP!
?!
IT'S JUST LIKE FIVE YEARS AGO. SOMETHING'S HAPPENING IN THE TOWN.
TH-THOMP!
THEY MAY HAVE ...

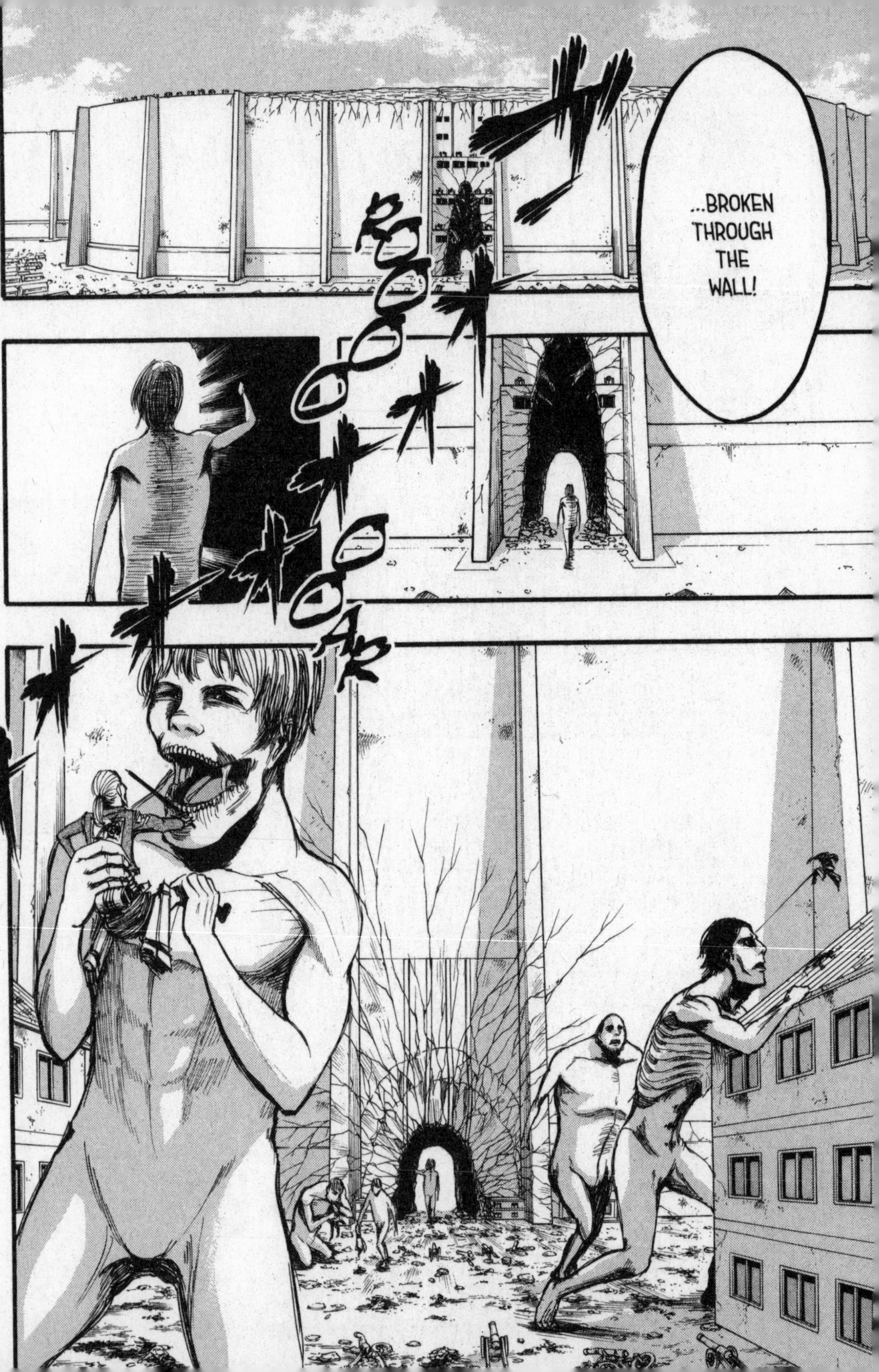
...BROKEN THROUGH THE WALL!
ROOOOOOAR

Current Publicly Available Information

7. The Current State of the Survey Corps

THE CHIEF PURPOSE OF THE SURVEY CORPS WAS TO EXPLORE THE LAND OUTSIDE THE WALL, BUT THE ACTUAL ACTIVITIES OF THE CORPS CHANGED AFTER THE FALL OF WALL MARIA.

SINCE THE FALL, THE CORPS HAS BEEN LAYING THE GROUNDWORK FOR THE SECOND WALL MARIA RECAPTURE OPERATION. BRAVING SHIGANSHINA DISTRICT, WHERE THE WALL WAS DESTROYED, A LARGE FORCE HAS BEEN POSITIONING SUPPLIES IN THE ABANDONED TOWNS AND VILLAGES SCATTERED ALONG THEIR ROUTE, ESTABLISHING A SUPPLY LINE FOR THE CORPS.

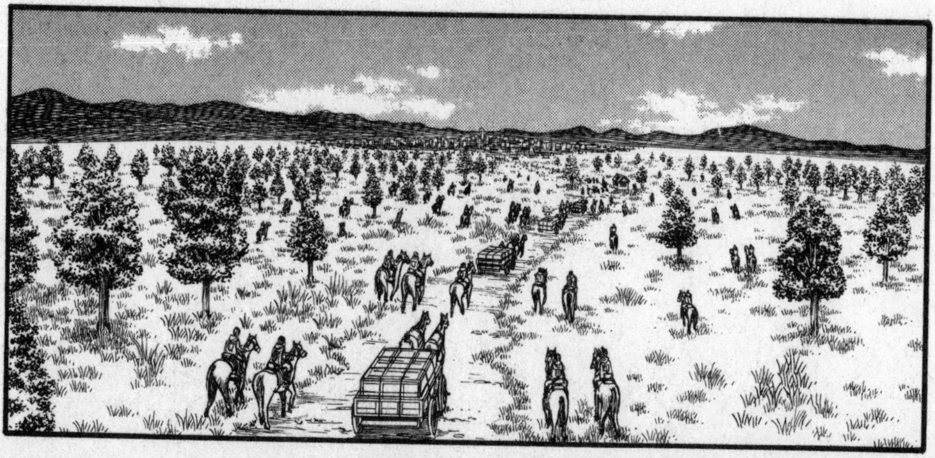

ATTACK on TITAN

Episode 10: Where's the Left Arm?

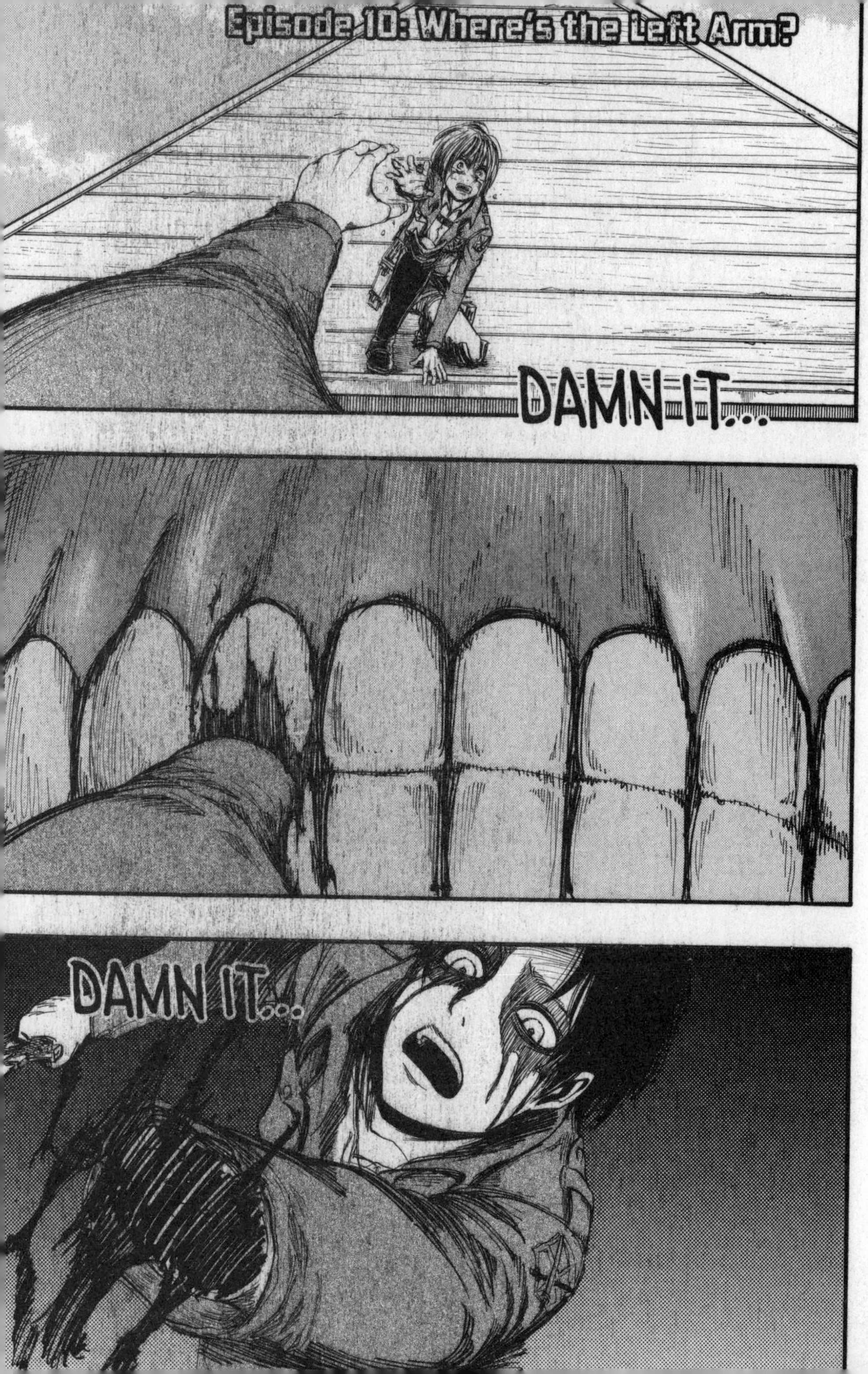
DAMN IT...
DAMN IT...

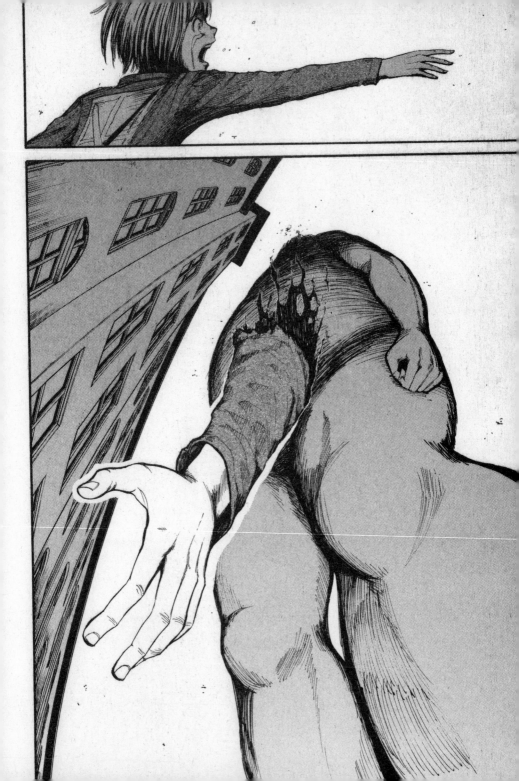

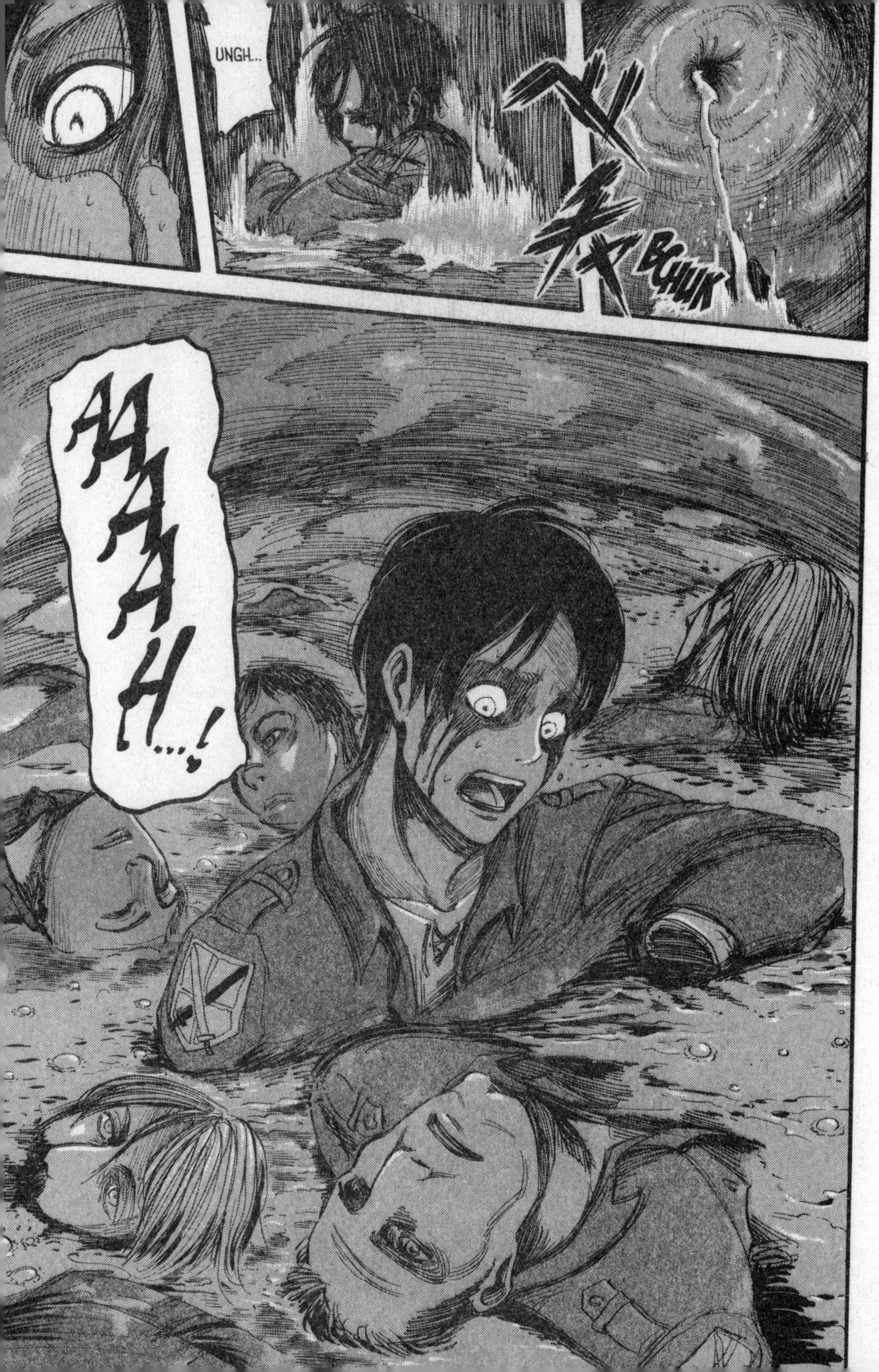

BCHUK
UNGH...
AAAAH...!

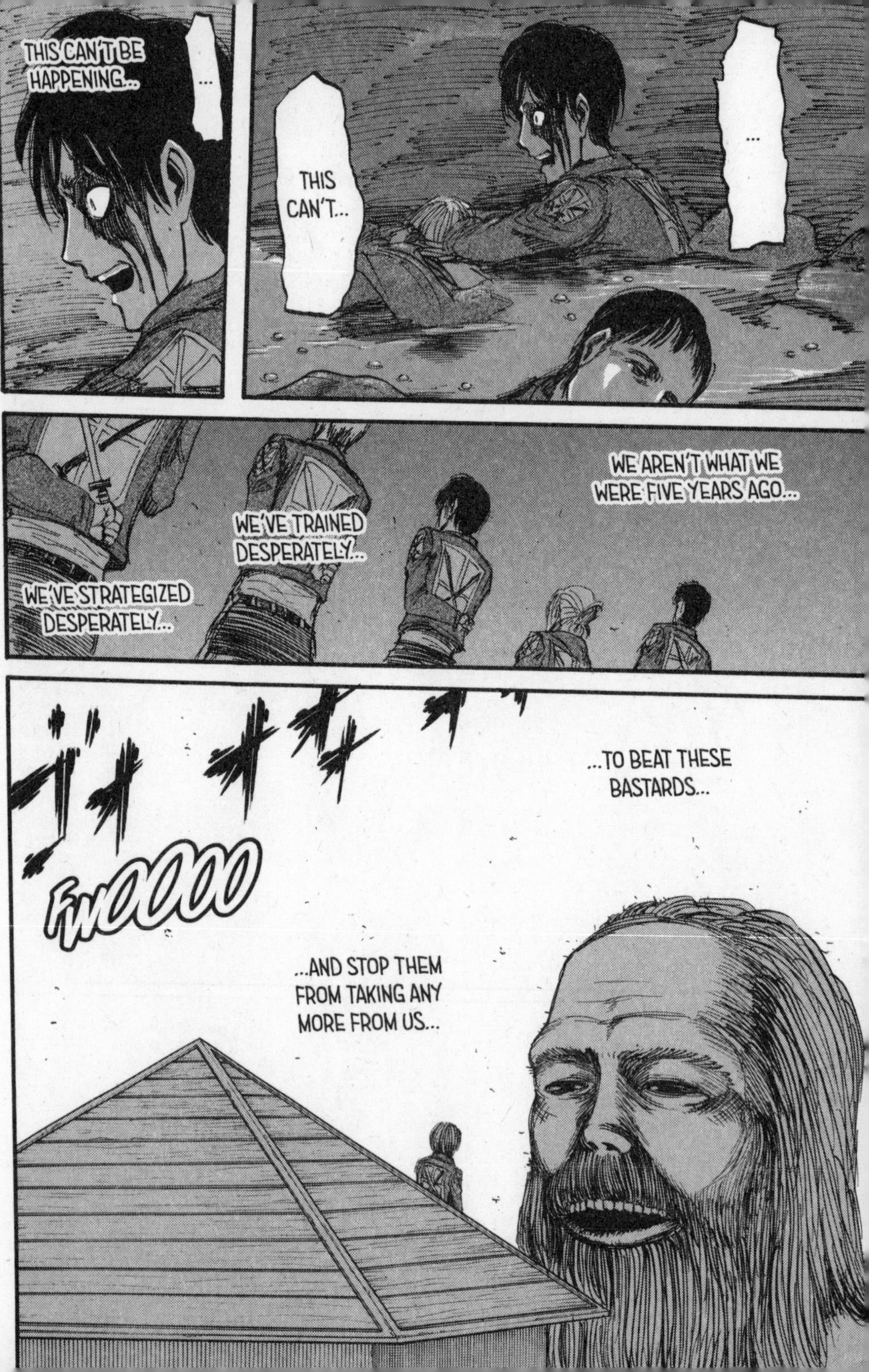
...
THIS CAN'T...
...
THIS CAN'T BE HAPPENING...
WE AREN'T WHAT WE WERE FIVE YEARS AGO...
WE'VE TRAINED DESPERATELY...
WE'VE STRATEGIZED DESPERATELY...
...TO BEAT THESE BASTARDS...
FWOOOO
...AND STOP THEM FROM TAKING ANY MORE FROM US...

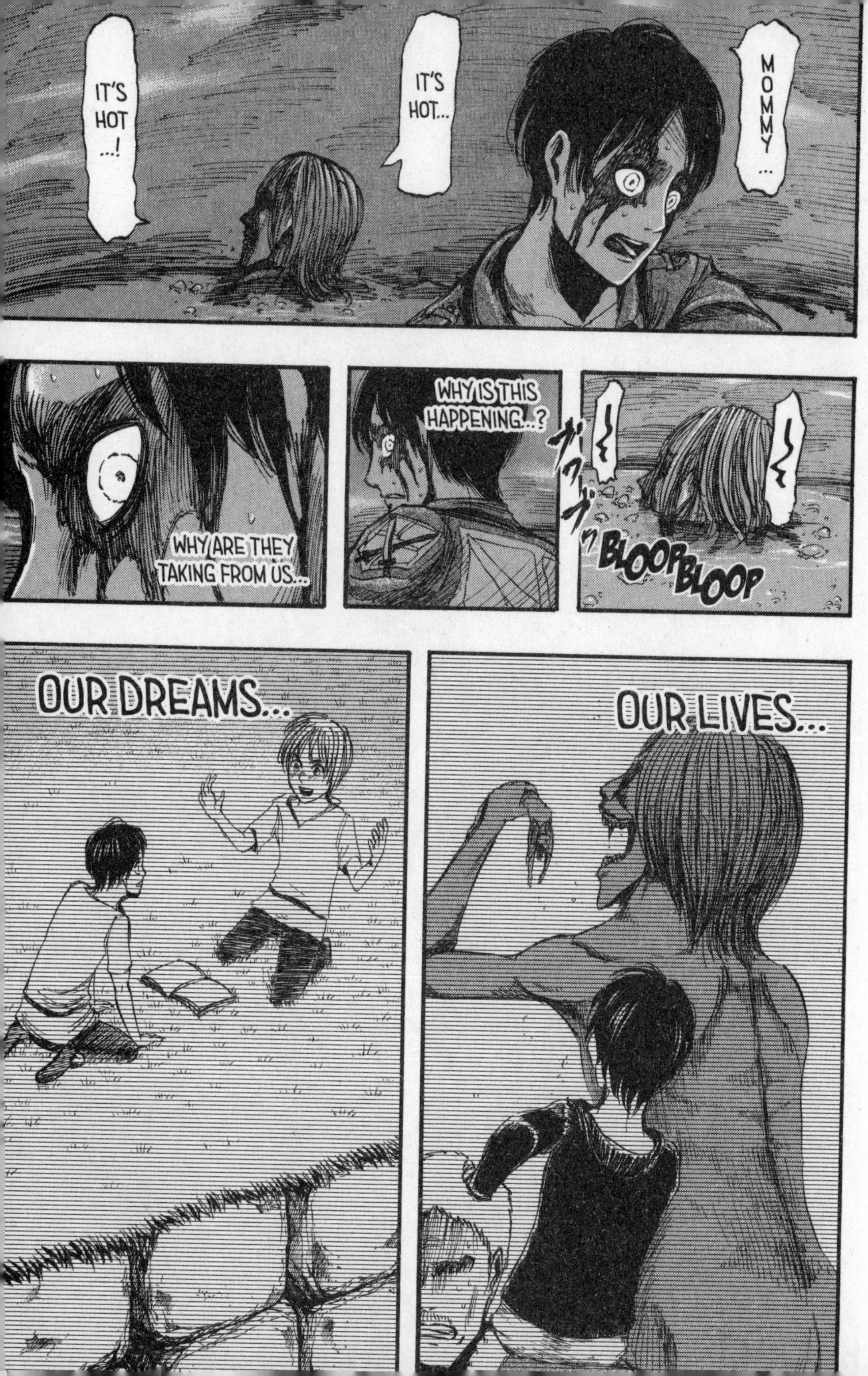
MOMMY...
IT'S HOT...
IT'S HOT...!
ブクブク
BLOOP BLOOP
WHY IS THIS HAPPENING...?
WHY ARE THEY TAKING FROM US...
OUR LIVES...
OUR DREAMS...

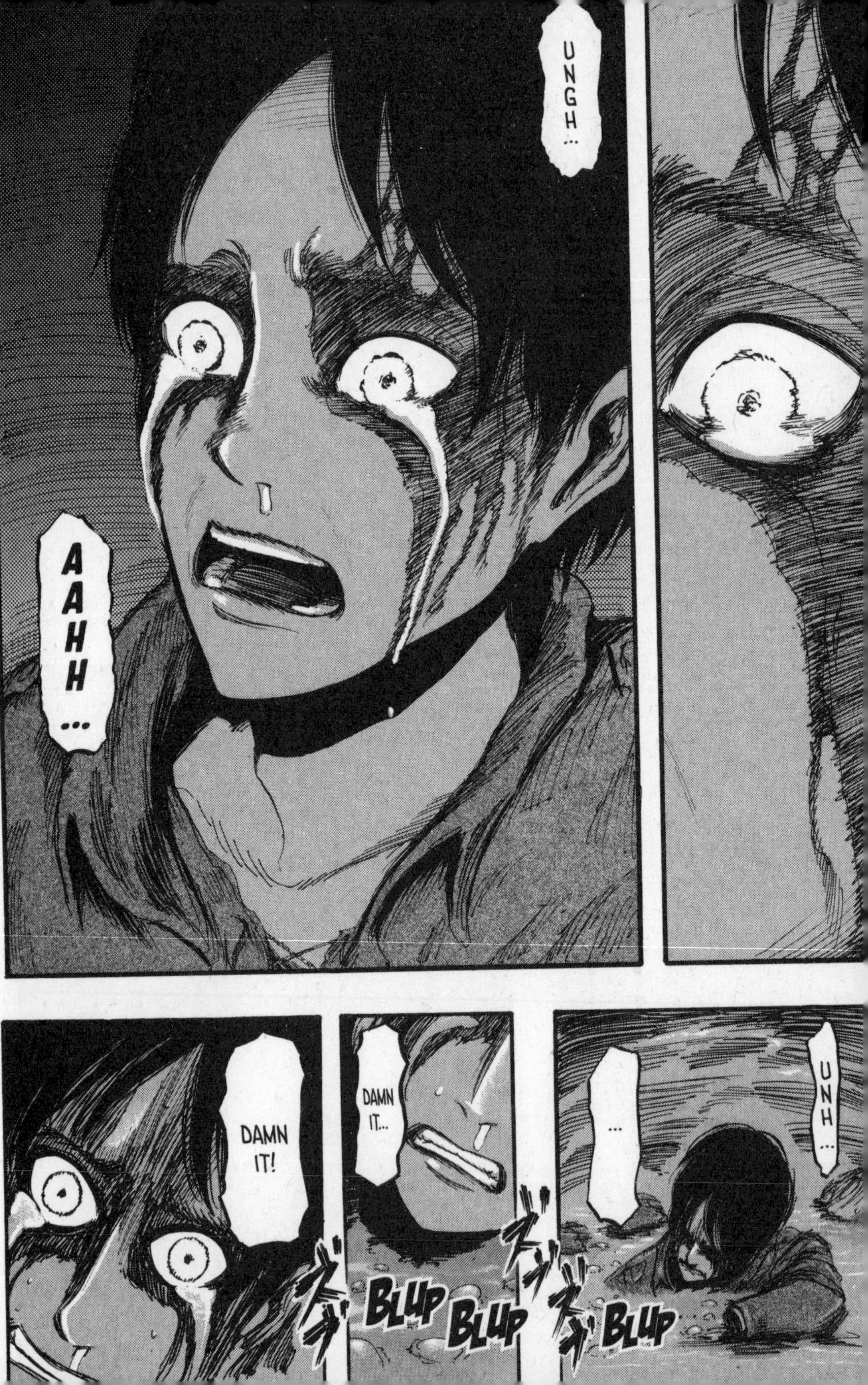
UNGH...
AAHH...
UNH...
...
BLUP
DAMN IT...
BLUP
DAMN IT!
BLUP

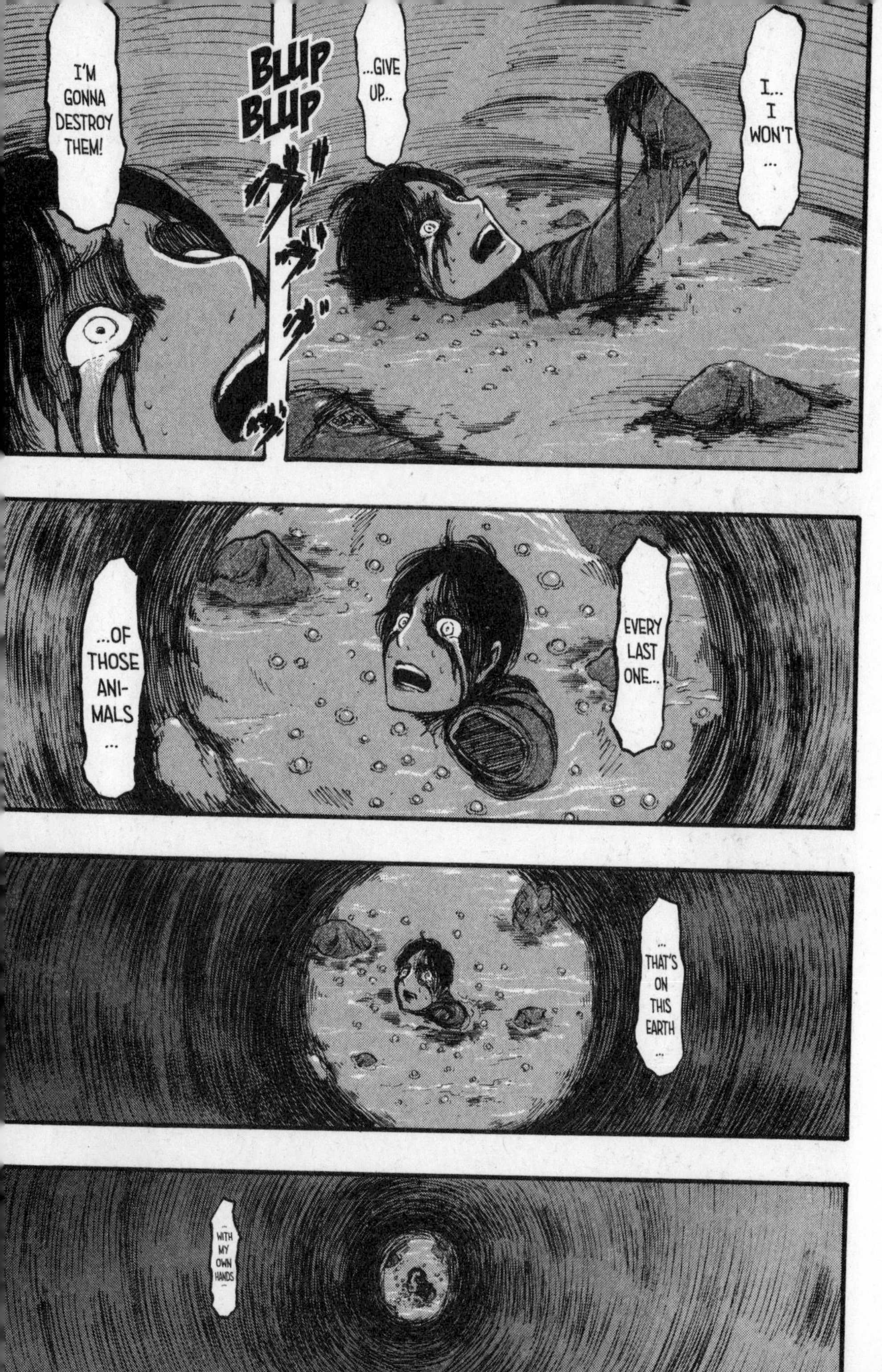
I... I WON'T ...
...GIVE UP...
BLUP BLUP
I'M GONNA DESTROY THEM!
EVERY LAST ONE...
...OF THOSE ANI-MALS ...
... THAT'S ON THIS EARTH ...
... WITH MY OWN HANDS ...

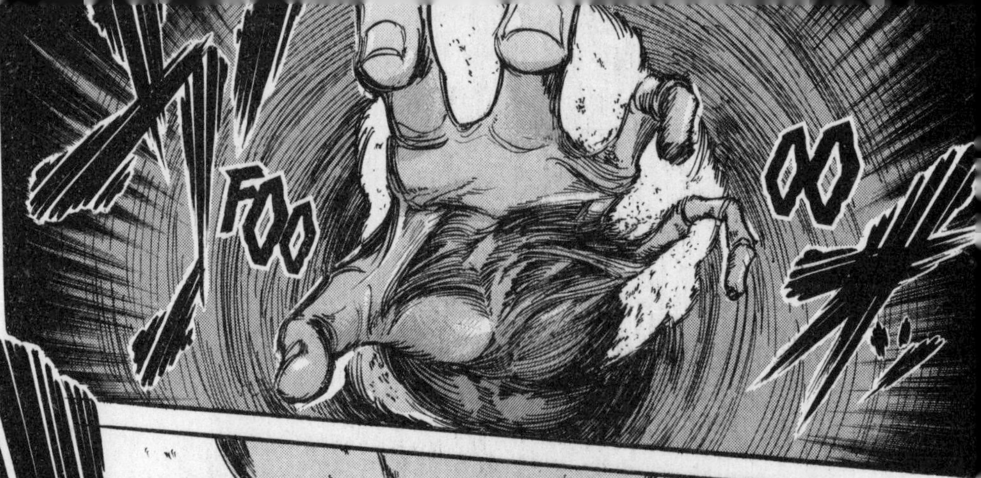
FOO
OO
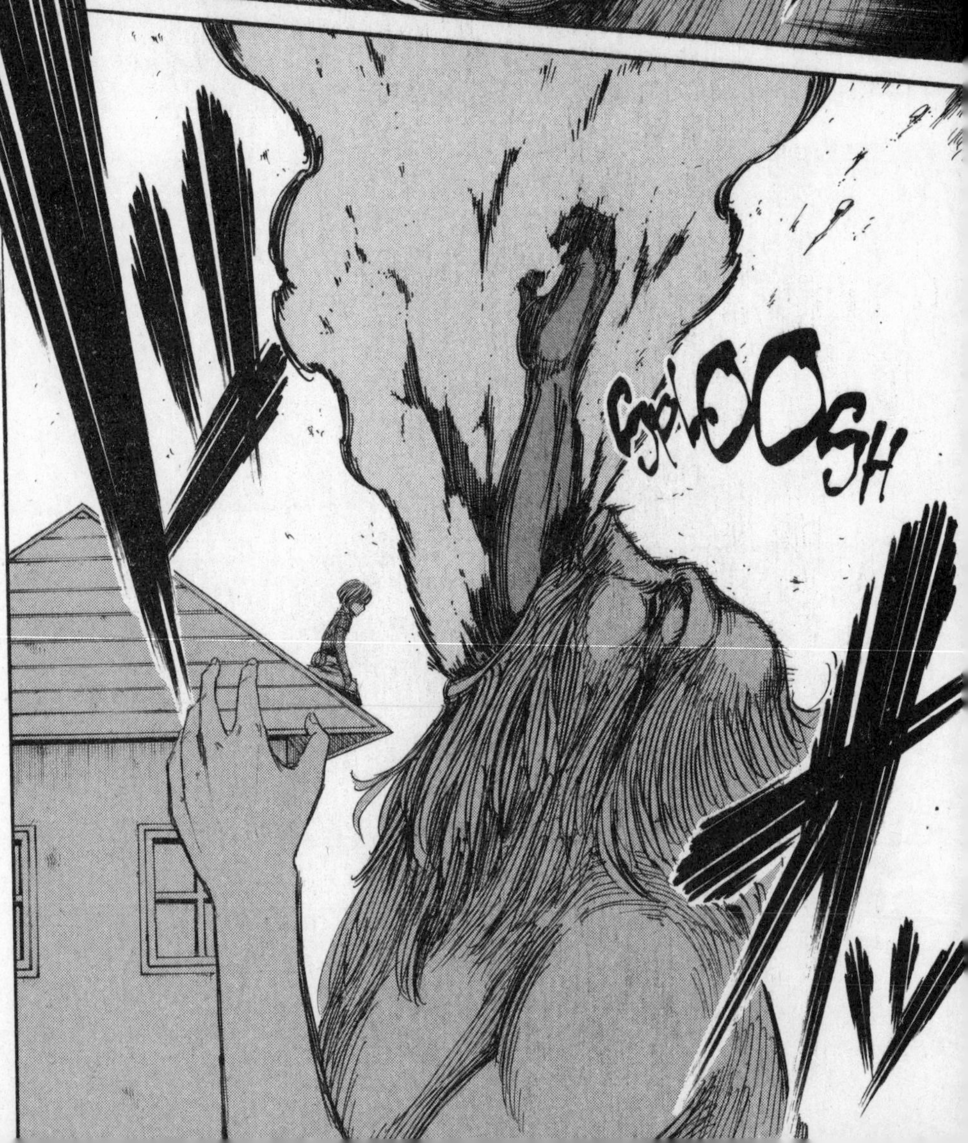
SPLOOSH

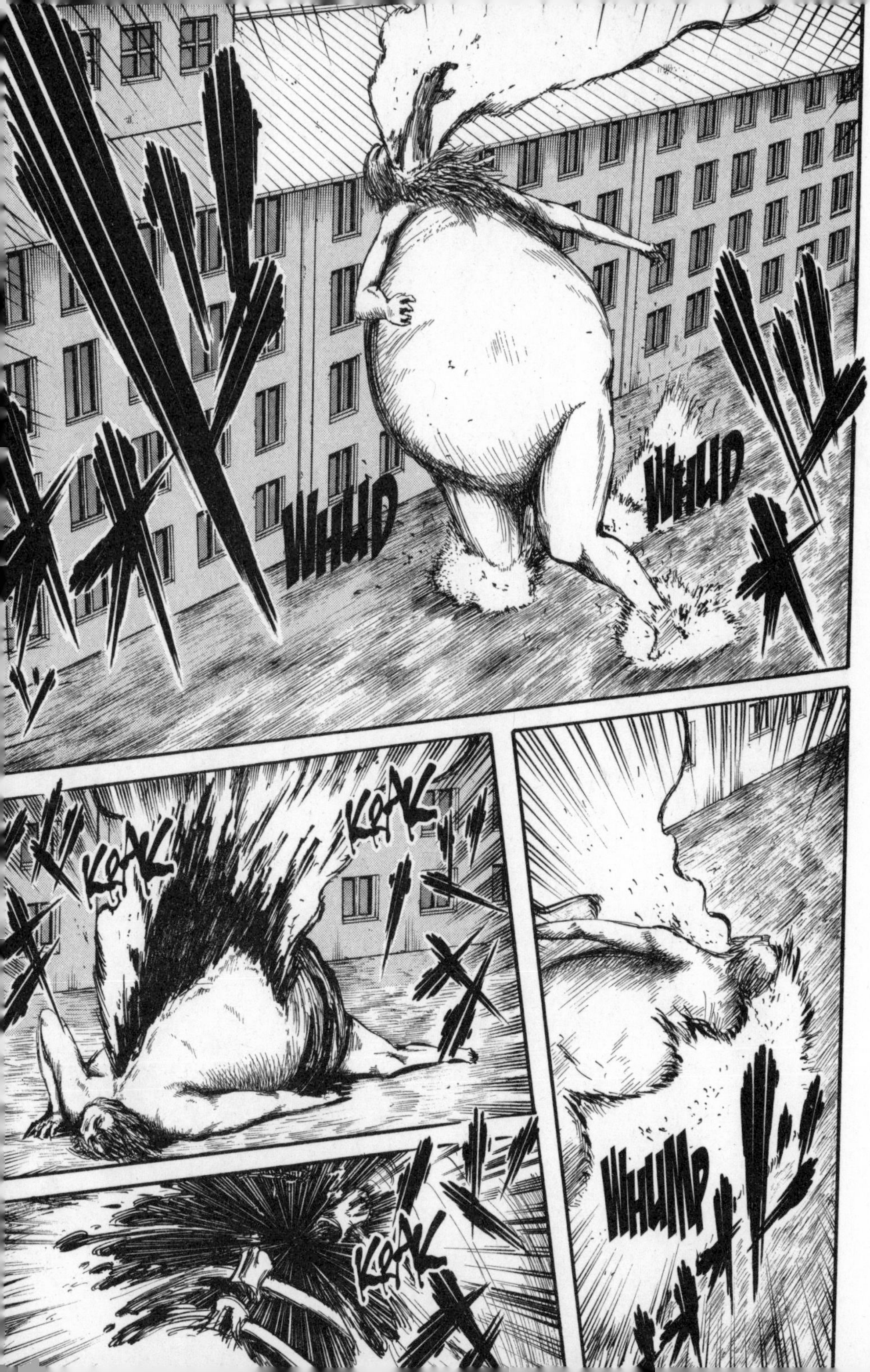
WHUD
WHUD
WHUMP
KRAK
KRAK
KRAK

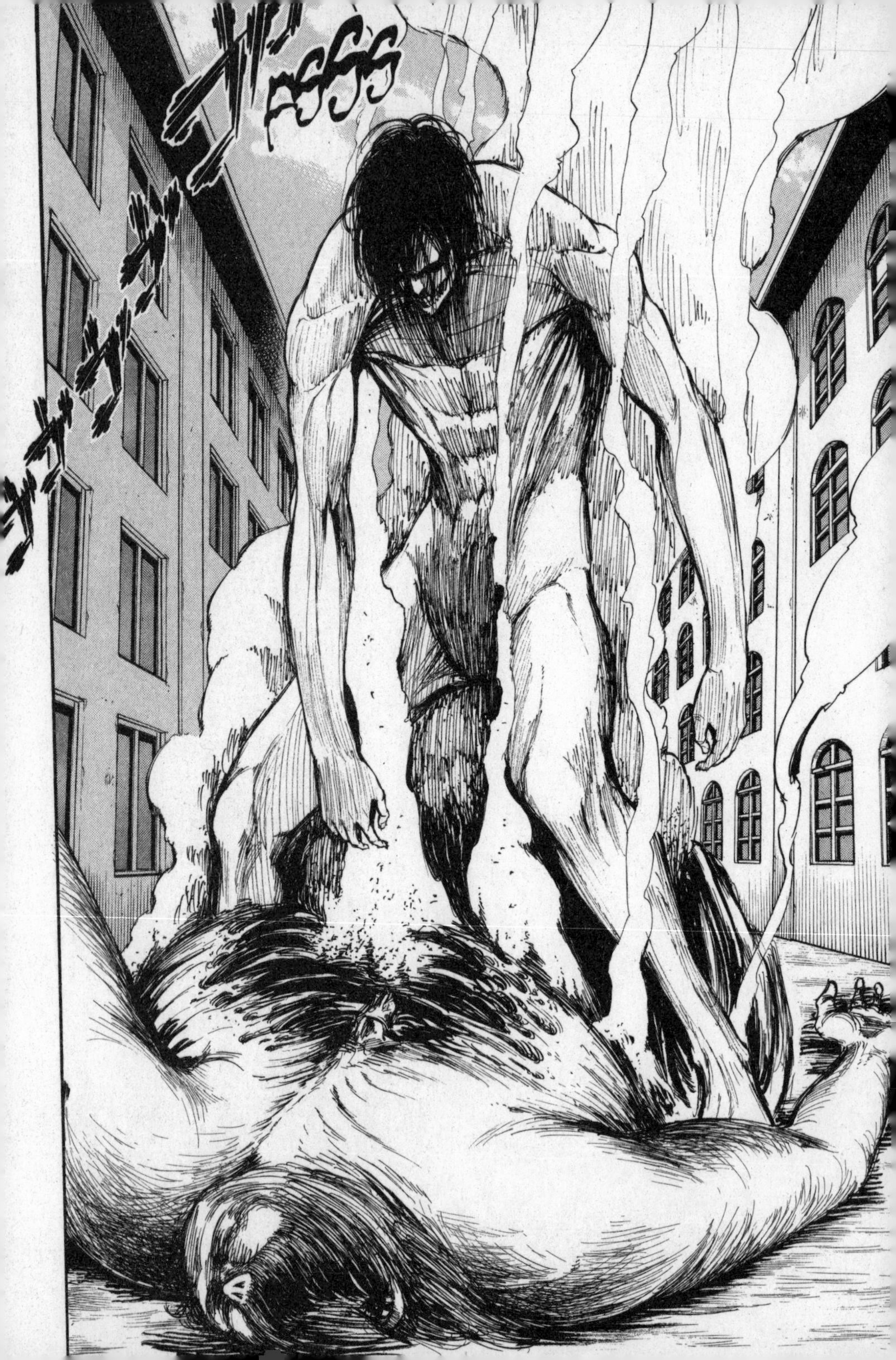
FSSS

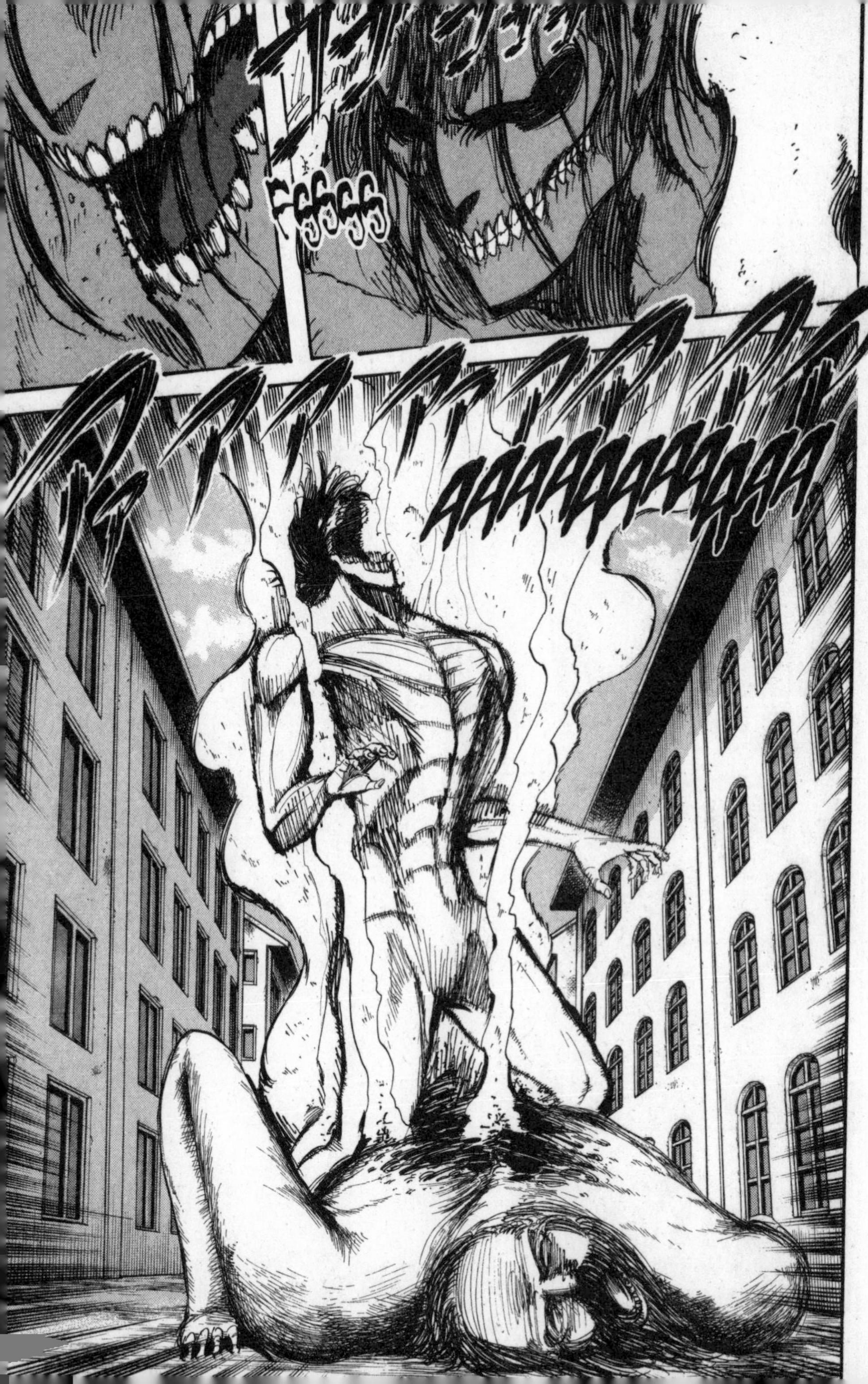
Fssss

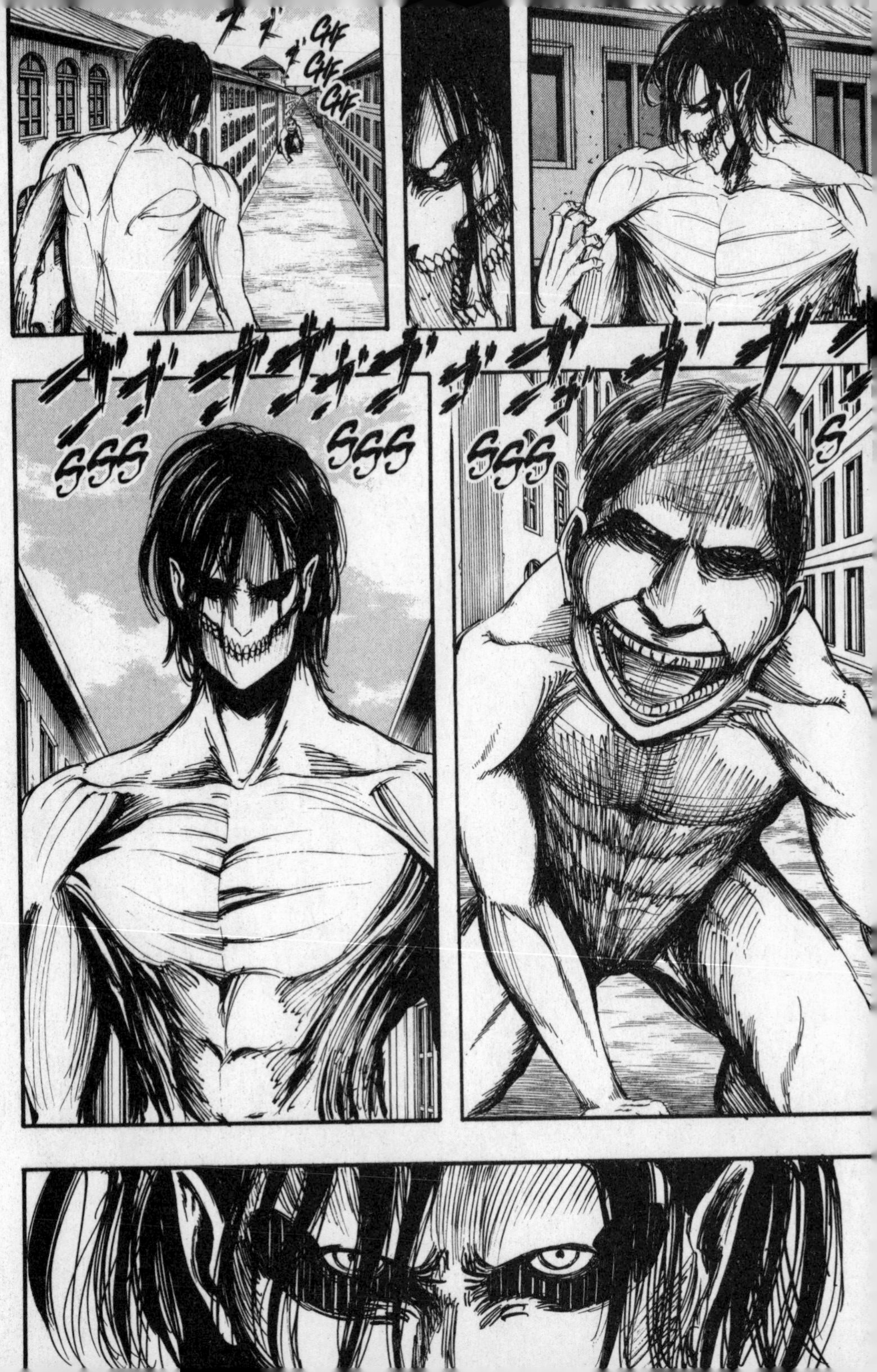
CHF
CHF
CHF
SSS
SSS
SSS
S

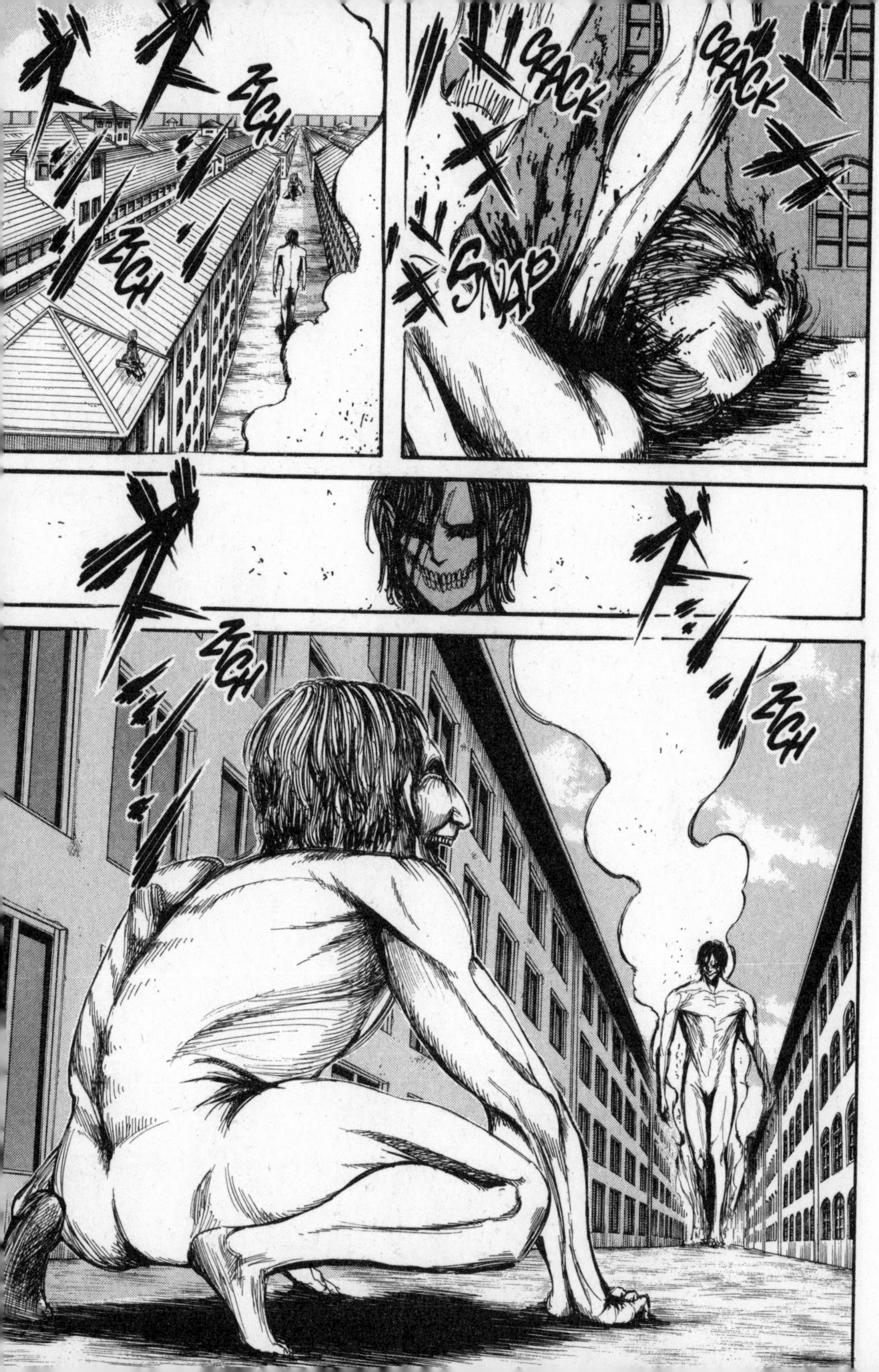
CRACK
CRACK
SNAP
ZCH
ZCH
ZCH
ZCH

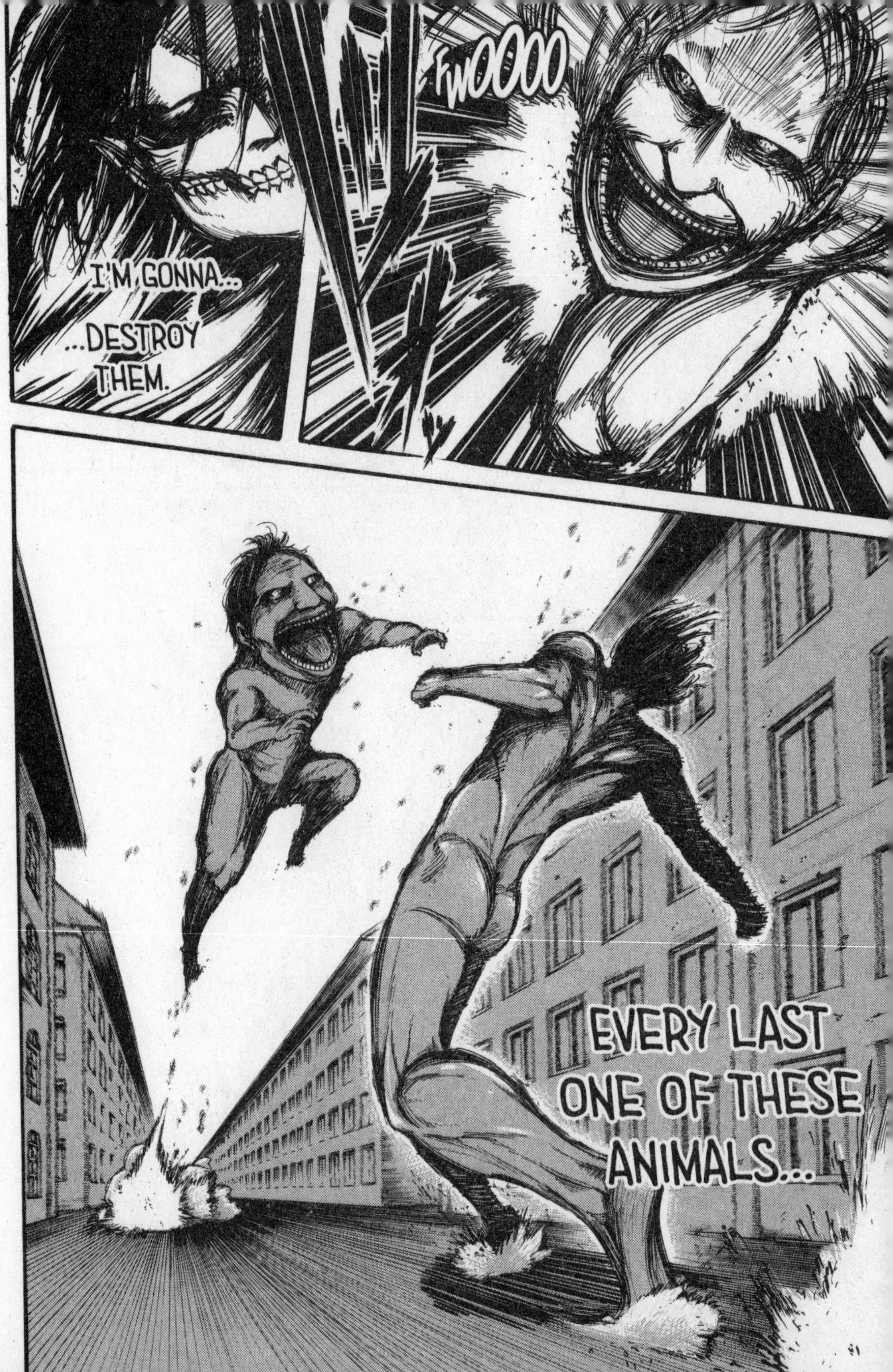
FWOOOO
I'M GONNA...
...DESTROY THEM.
EVERY LAST ONE OF THESE ANIMALS...

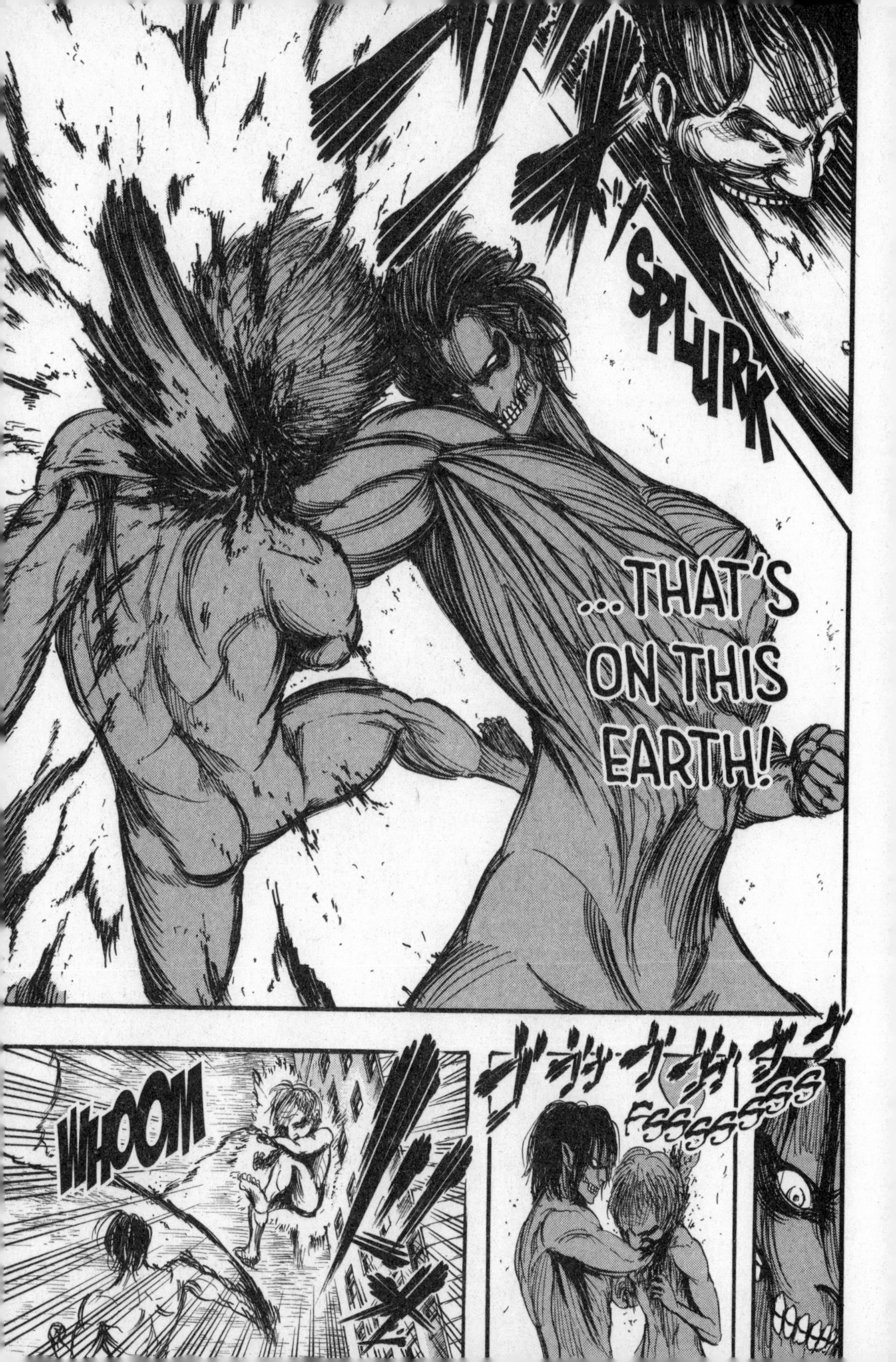
SPLURK
...THAT'S ON THIS EARTH!
FSSSSSSSS
WHOOM

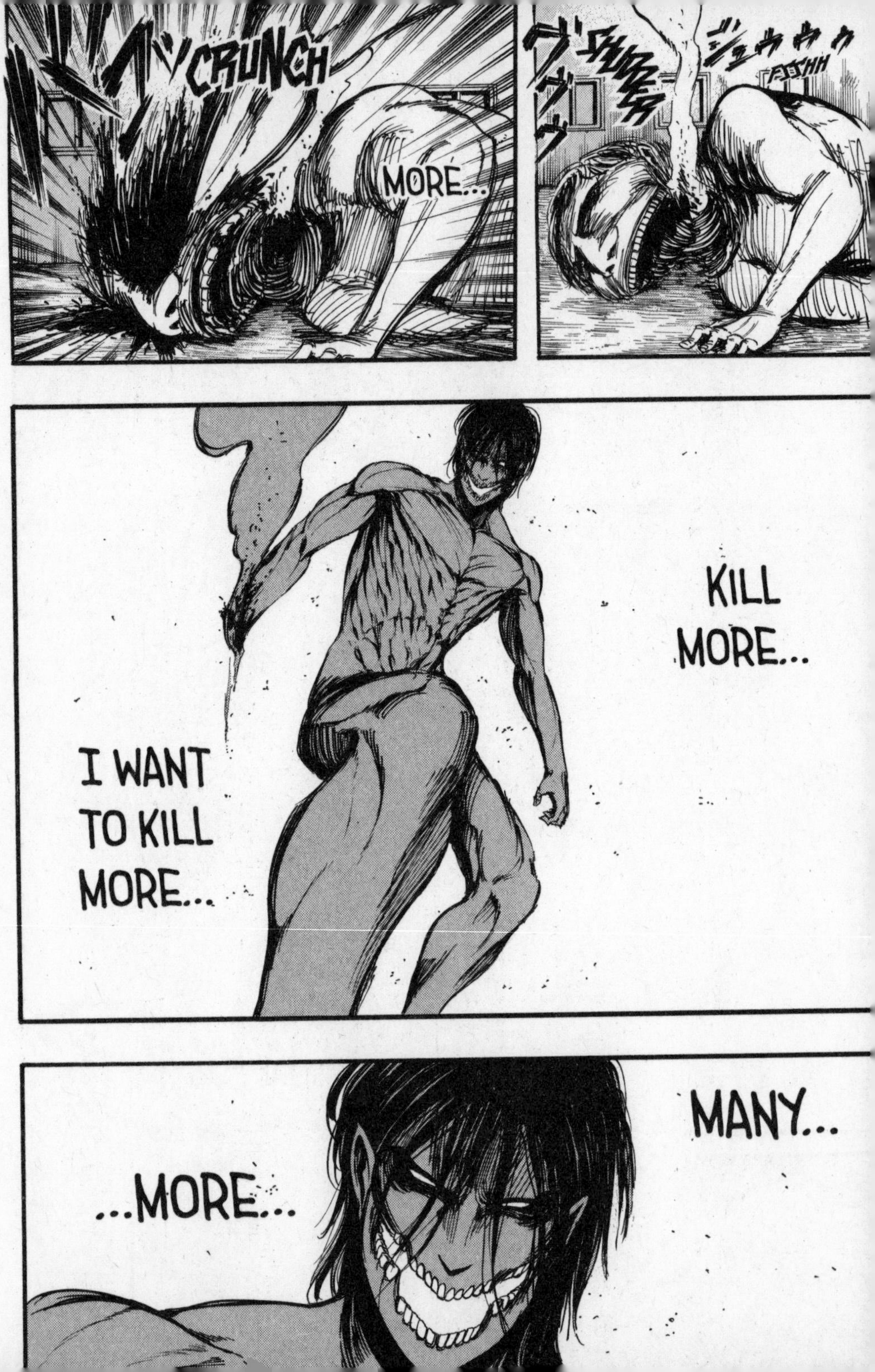
ジュウウウ
FSSHH
CRUNCH
MORE...
KILL MORE...
I WANT TO KILL MORE...
MANY...
...MORE...

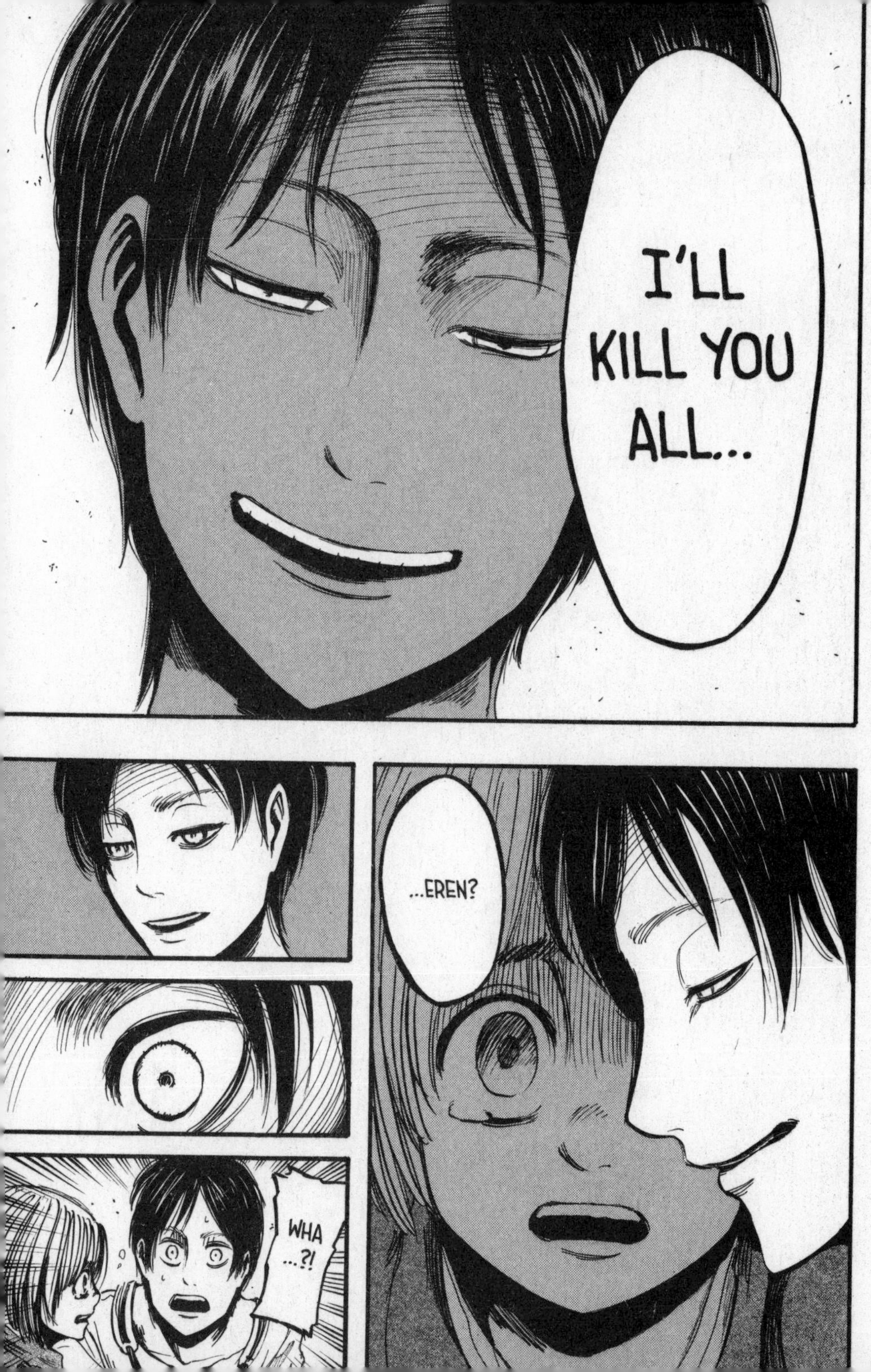
I'LL KILL YOU ALL...
...EREN?
WHA ...?!

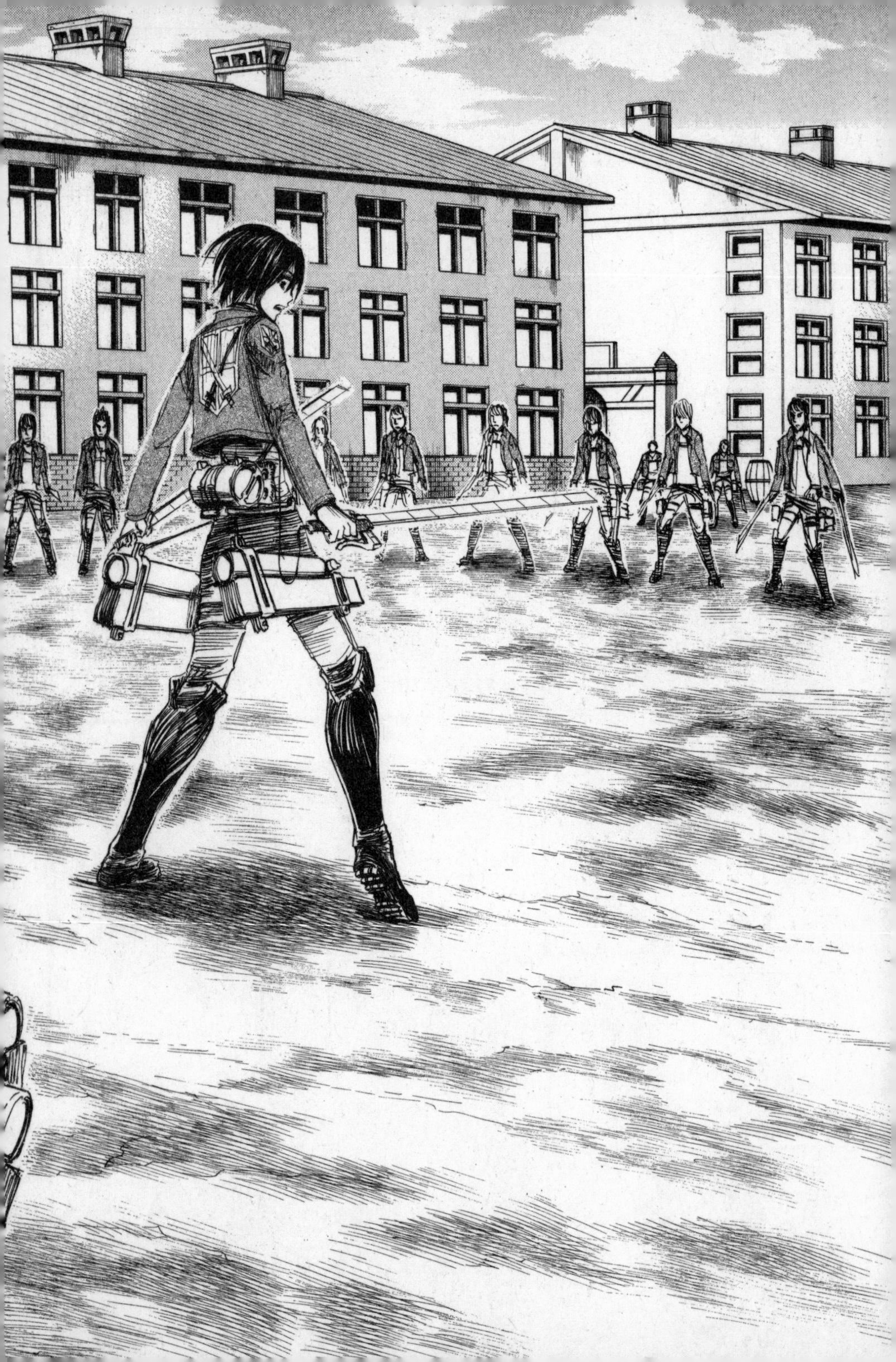

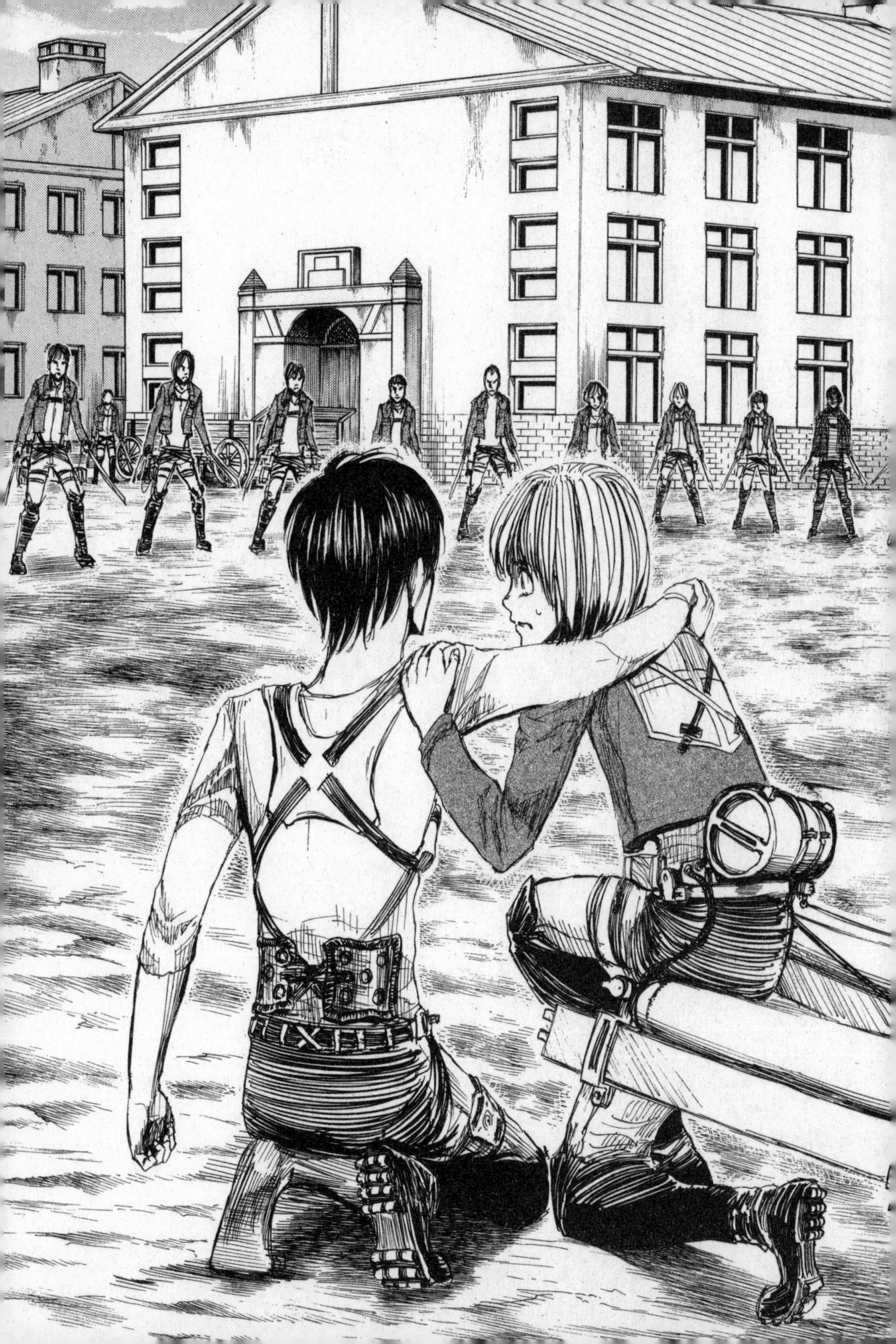

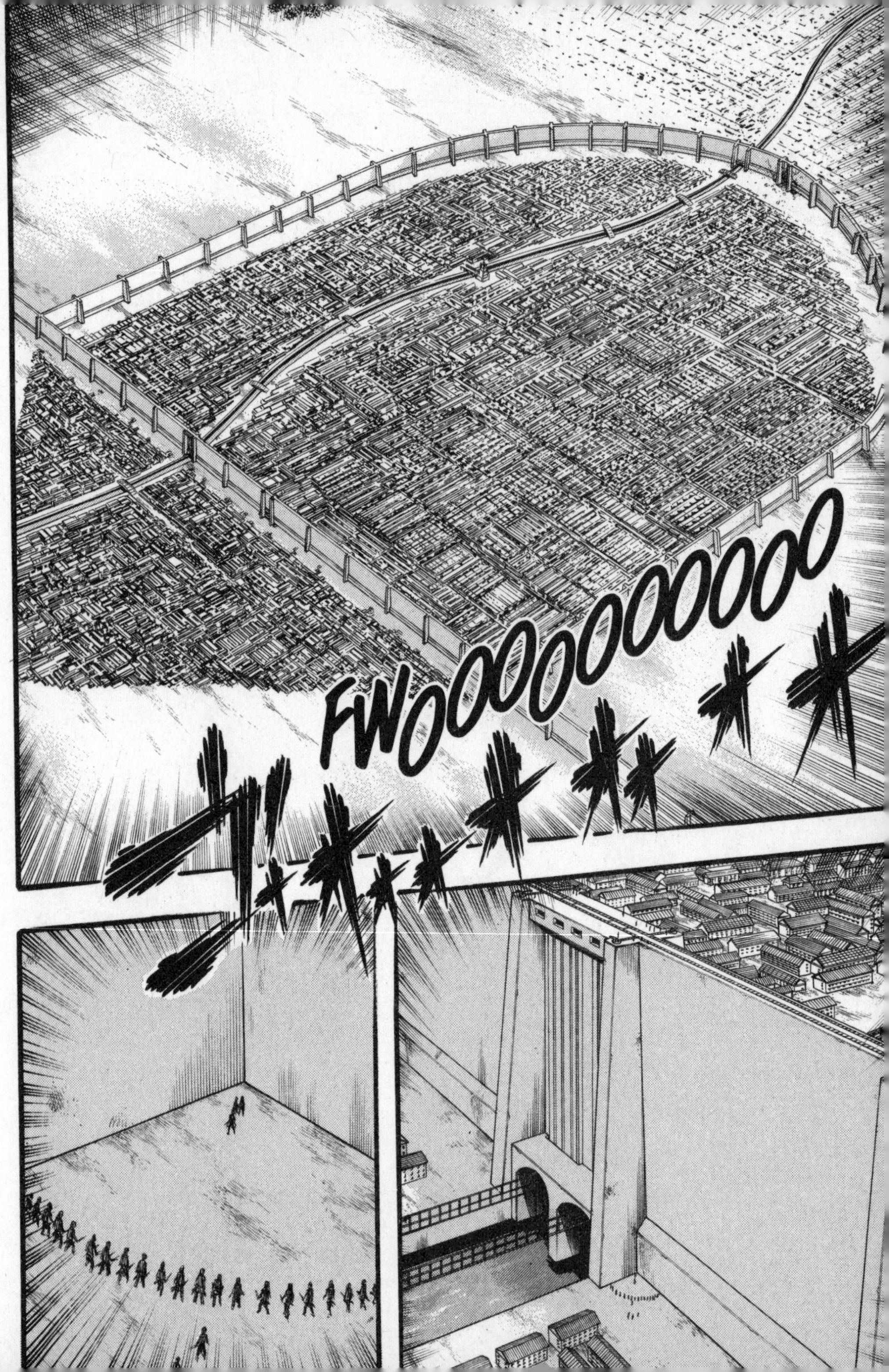
FWOOOOOOOOOOO

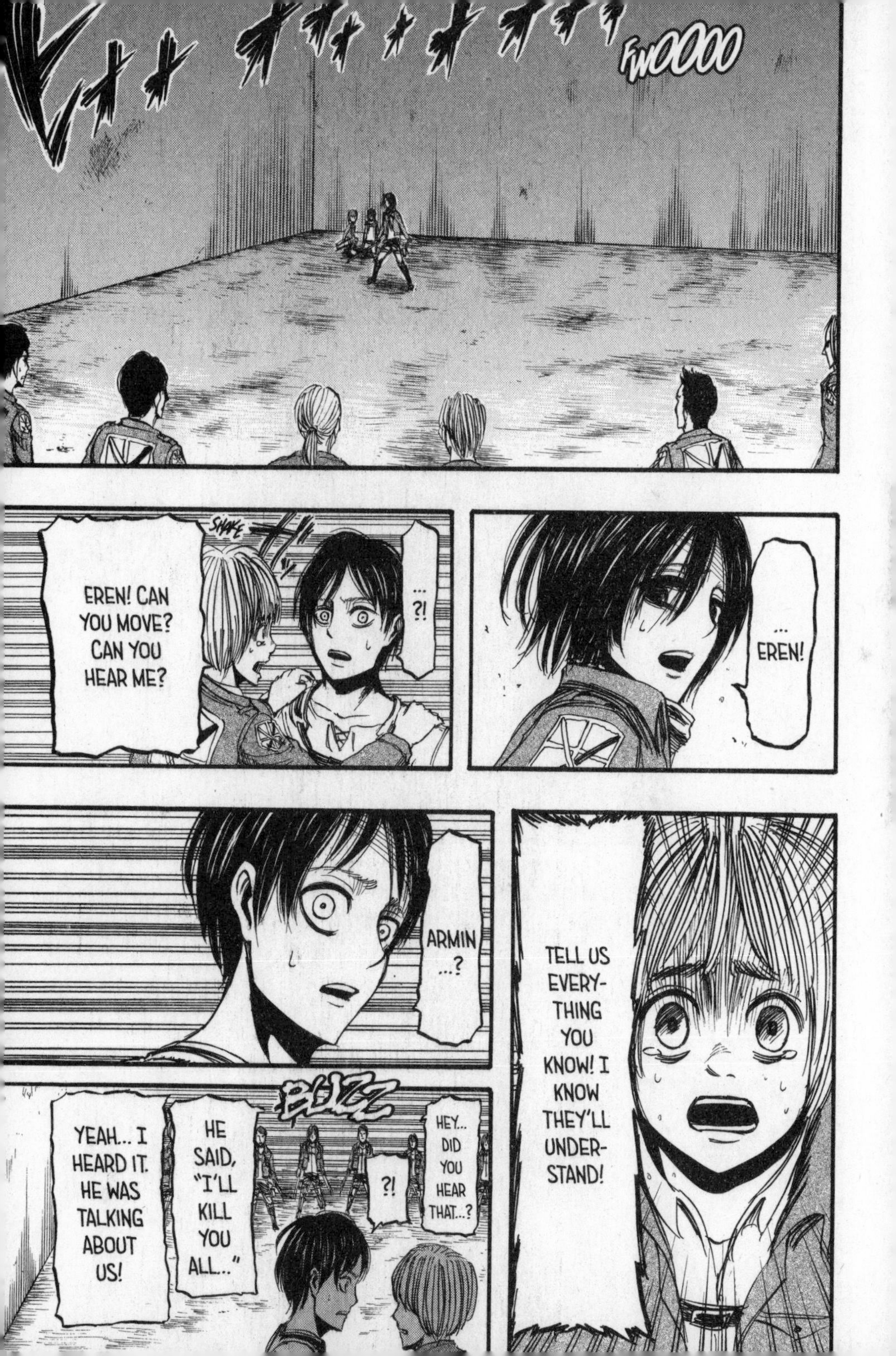
FWOOOO
... EREN!
SHAKE
...?!
EREN! CAN YOU MOVE? CAN YOU HEAR ME?
ARMIN ...?
TELL US EVERYTHING YOU KNOW! I KNOW THEY'LL UNDERSTAND!
BUZZ
HEY... DID YOU HEAR THAT...?
?!
HE SAID, "I'LL KILL YOU ALL..."
YEAH... I HEARD IT. HE WAS TALKING ABOUT US!

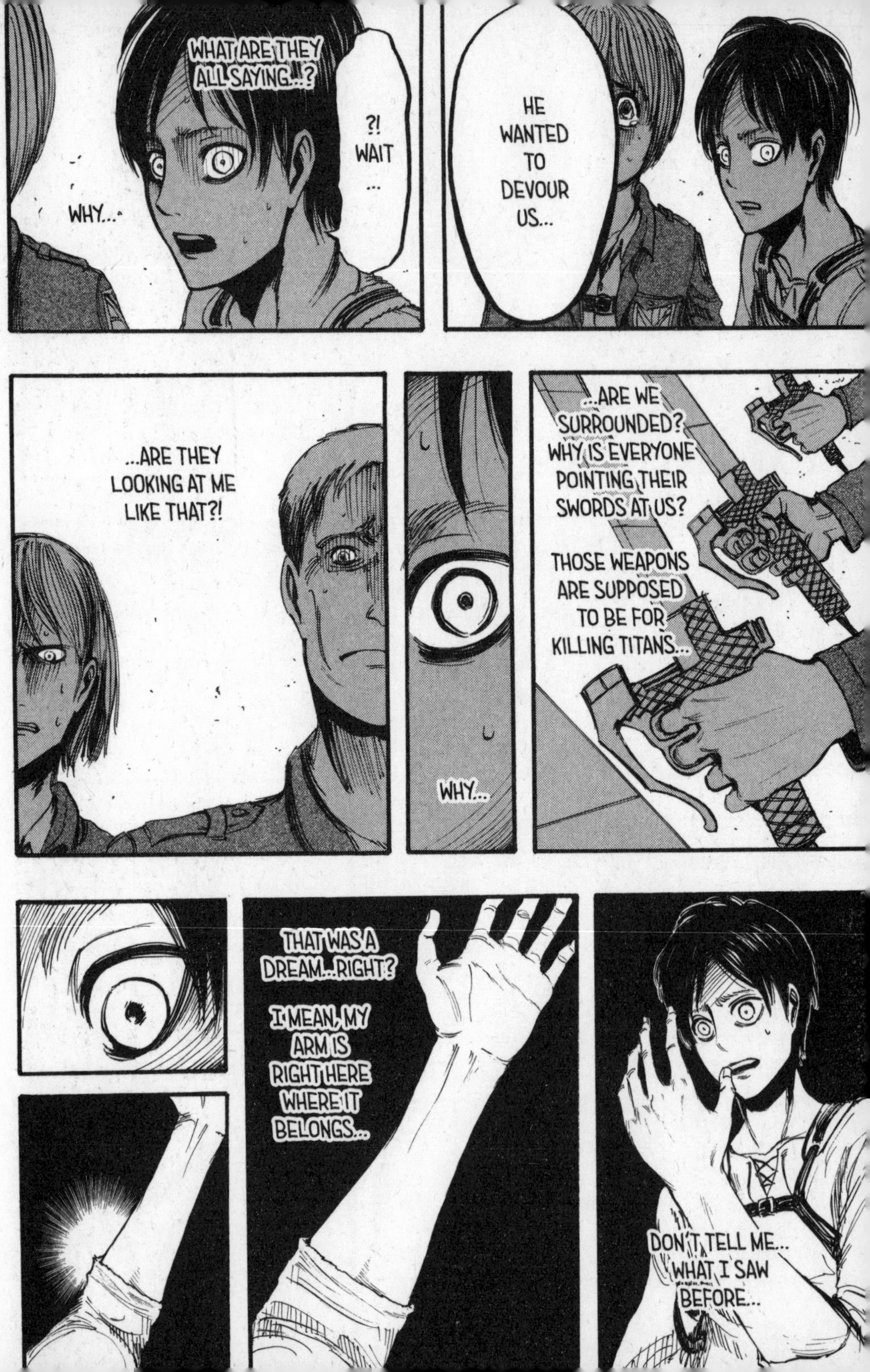
HE WANTED TO DEVOUR US...
?! WAIT ...
WHAT ARE THEY ALL SAYING...?
WHY...
...ARE WE SURROUNDED? WHY IS EVERYONE POINTING THEIR SWORDS AT US?
THOSE WEAPONS ARE SUPPOSED TO BE FOR KILLING TITANS...
WHY...
...ARE THEY LOOKING AT ME LIKE THAT?!
DON'T TELL ME... WHAT I SAW BEFORE...
THAT WAS A DREAM...RIGHT?
I MEAN, MY ARM IS RIGHT HERE WHERE IT BELONGS...

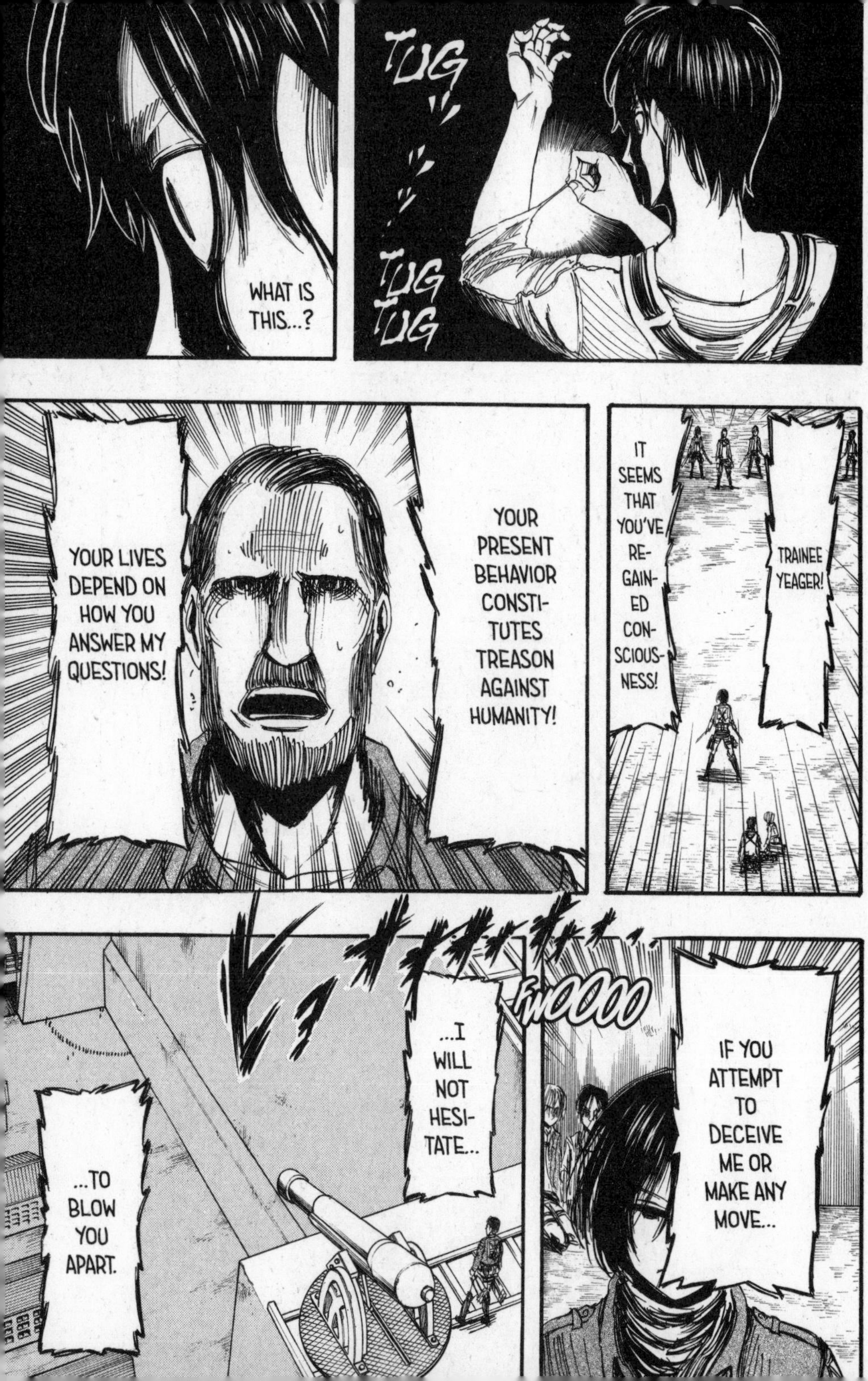
TUG
TUG TUG
WHAT IS THIS...?
TRAINEE YEAGER!
IT SEEMS THAT YOU'VE REGAINED CONSCIOUSNESS!
YOUR PRESENT BEHAVIOR CONSTITUTES TREASON AGAINST HUMANITY!
YOUR LIVES DEPEND ON HOW YOU ANSWER MY QUESTIONS!
FWOOOO
IF YOU ATTEMPT TO DECEIVE ME OR MAKE ANY MOVE...
...I WILL NOT HESITATE...
...TO BLOW YOU APART.

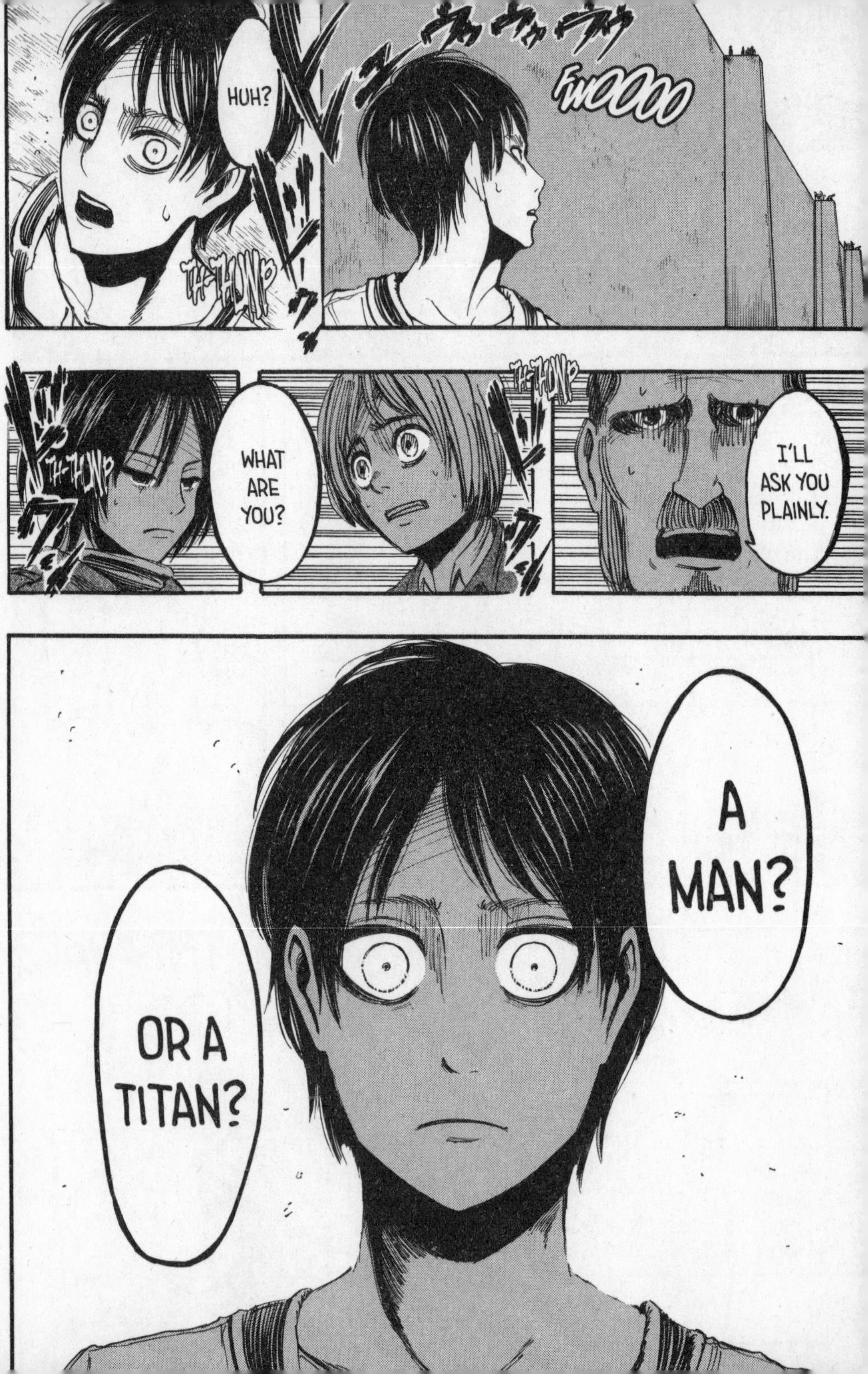
FWOOOOO
HUH?
TH-THUMP
I'LL ASK YOU PLAINLY.
TH-THUMP
WHAT ARE YOU?
TH-THUMP
A MAN?
OR A TITAN?

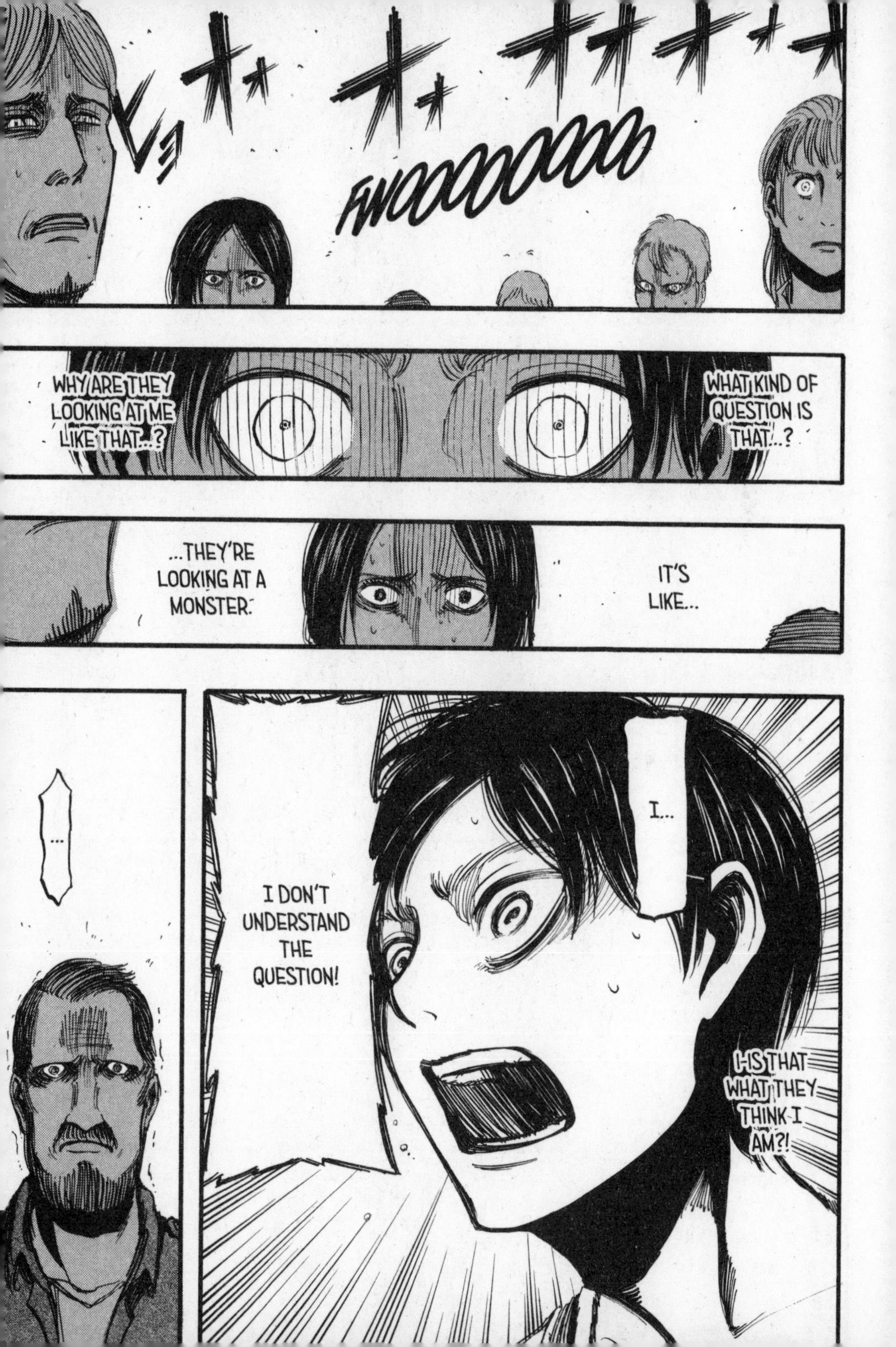
FWOOOOOOOO
WHAT KIND OF QUESTION IS THAT...?
WHY ARE THEY LOOKING AT ME LIKE THAT...?
IT'S LIKE...
...THEY'RE LOOKING AT A MONSTER.
I...
I DON'T UNDERSTAND THE QUESTION!
I-IS THAT WHAT THEY THINK I AM?!
...

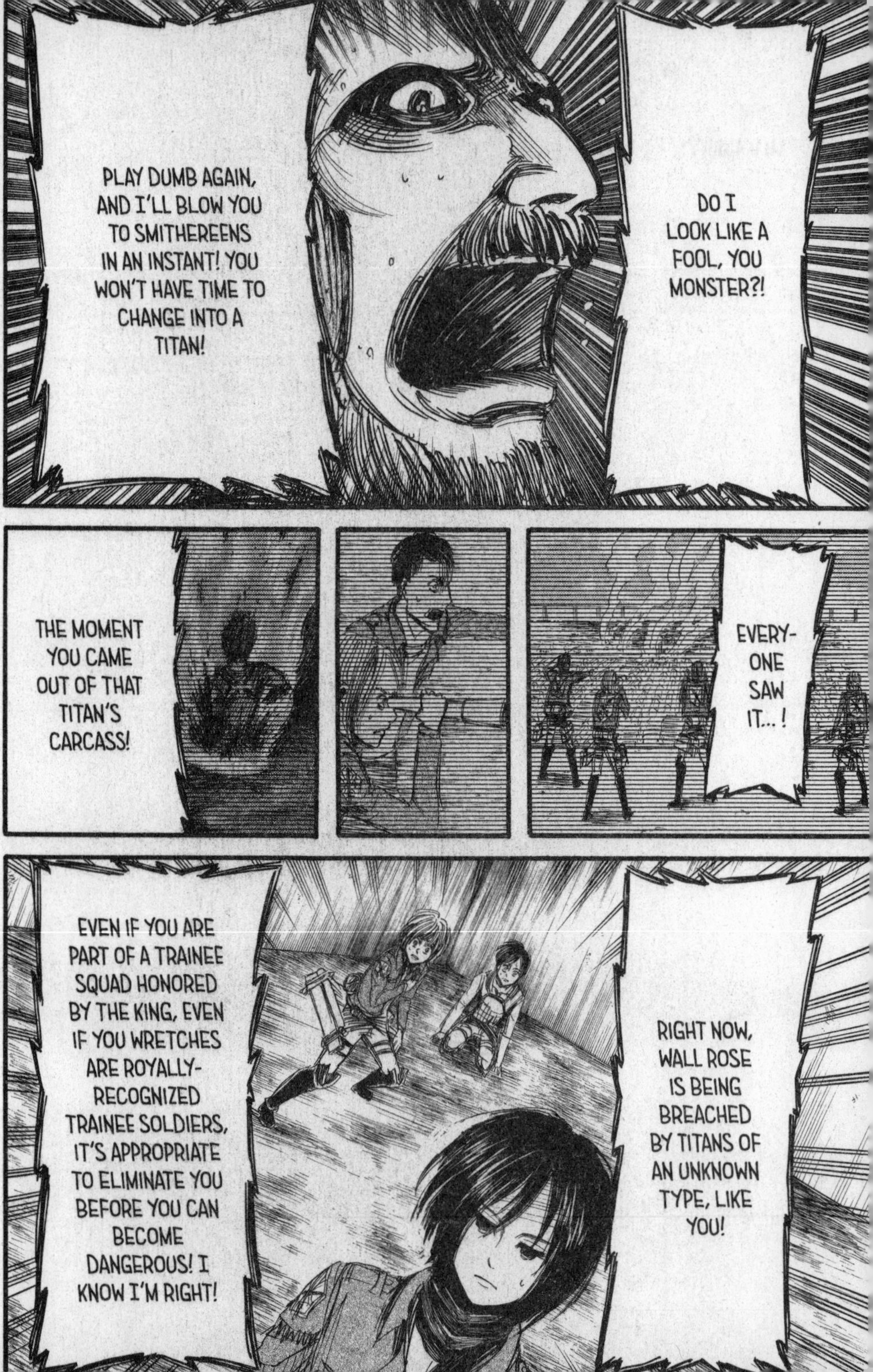
DO I LOOK LIKE A FOOL, YOU MONSTER?!
PLAY DUMB AGAIN, AND I'LL BLOW YOU TO SMITHEREENS IN AN INSTANT! YOU WON'T HAVE TIME TO CHANGE INTO A TITAN!
EVERY-ONE SAW IT... !
THE MOMENT YOU CAME OUT OF THAT TITAN'S CARCASS!
RIGHT NOW, WALL ROSE IS BEING BREACHED BY TITANS OF AN UNKNOWN TYPE, LIKE YOU!
EVEN IF YOU ARE PART OF A TRAINEE SQUAD HONORED BY THE KING, EVEN IF YOU WRETCHES ARE ROYALLY-RECOGNIZED TRAINEE SOLDIERS, IT'S APPROPRIATE TO ELIMINATE YOU BEFORE YOU CAN BECOME DANGEROUS! I KNOW I'M RIGHT!

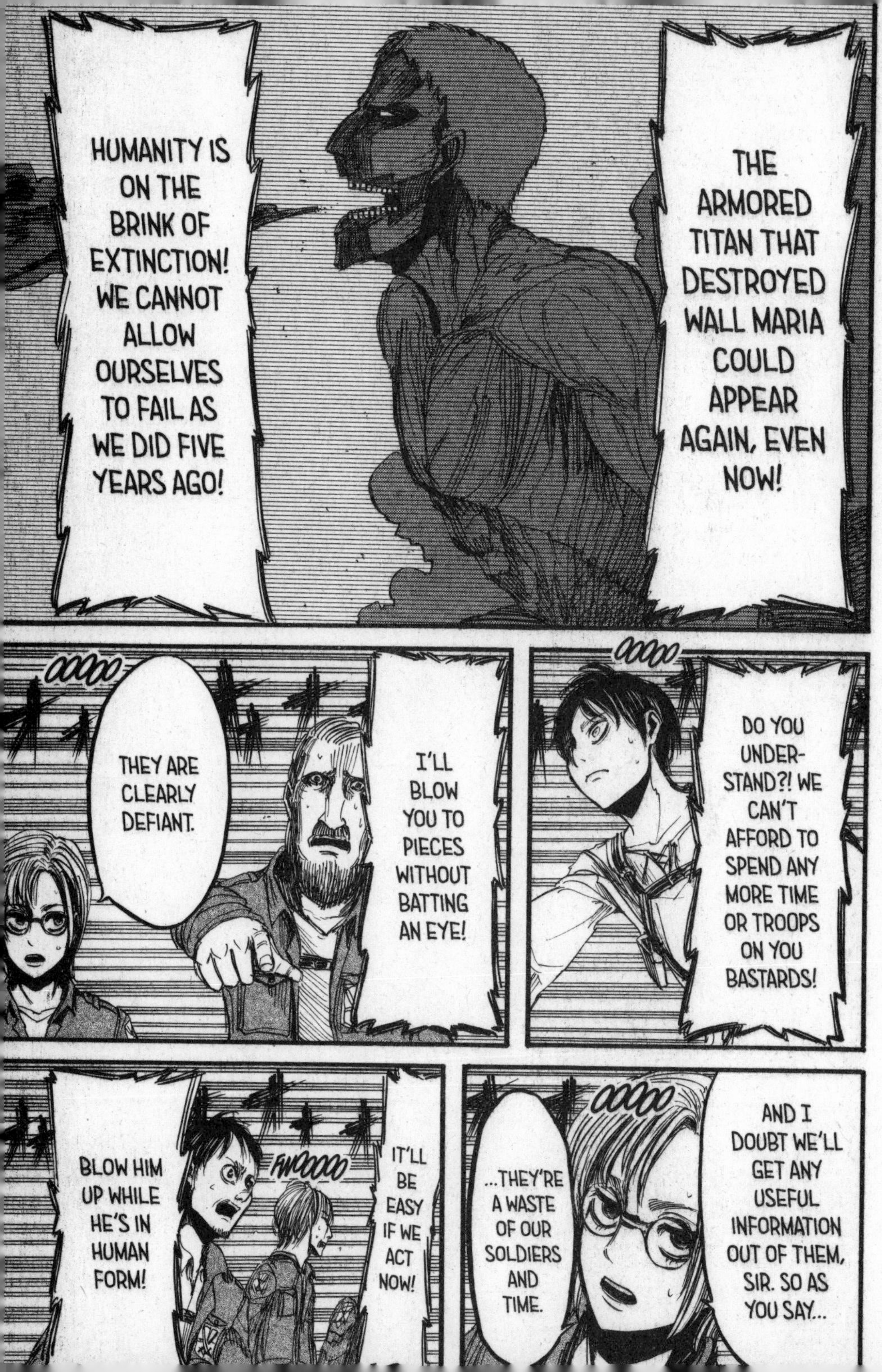
THE ARMORED TITAN THAT DESTROYED WALL MARIA COULD APPEAR AGAIN, EVEN NOW!
HUMANITY IS ON THE BRINK OF EXTINCTION! WE CANNOT ALLOW OURSELVES TO FAIL AS WE DID FIVE YEARS AGO!
OOOOO
DO YOU UNDER-STAND?! WE CAN'T AFFORD TO SPEND ANY MORE TIME OR TROOPS ON YOU BASTARDS!
I'LL BLOW YOU TO PIECES WITHOUT BATTING AN EYE!
THEY ARE CLEARLY DEFIANT.
OOOOO
AND I DOUBT WE'LL GET ANY USEFUL INFORMATION OUT OF THEM, SIR. SO AS YOU SAY...
OOOOO
...THEY'RE A WASTE OF OUR SOLDIERS AND TIME.
IT'LL BE EASY IF WE ACT NOW!
FWOOOOO
BLOW HIM UP WHILE HE'S IN HUMAN FORM!

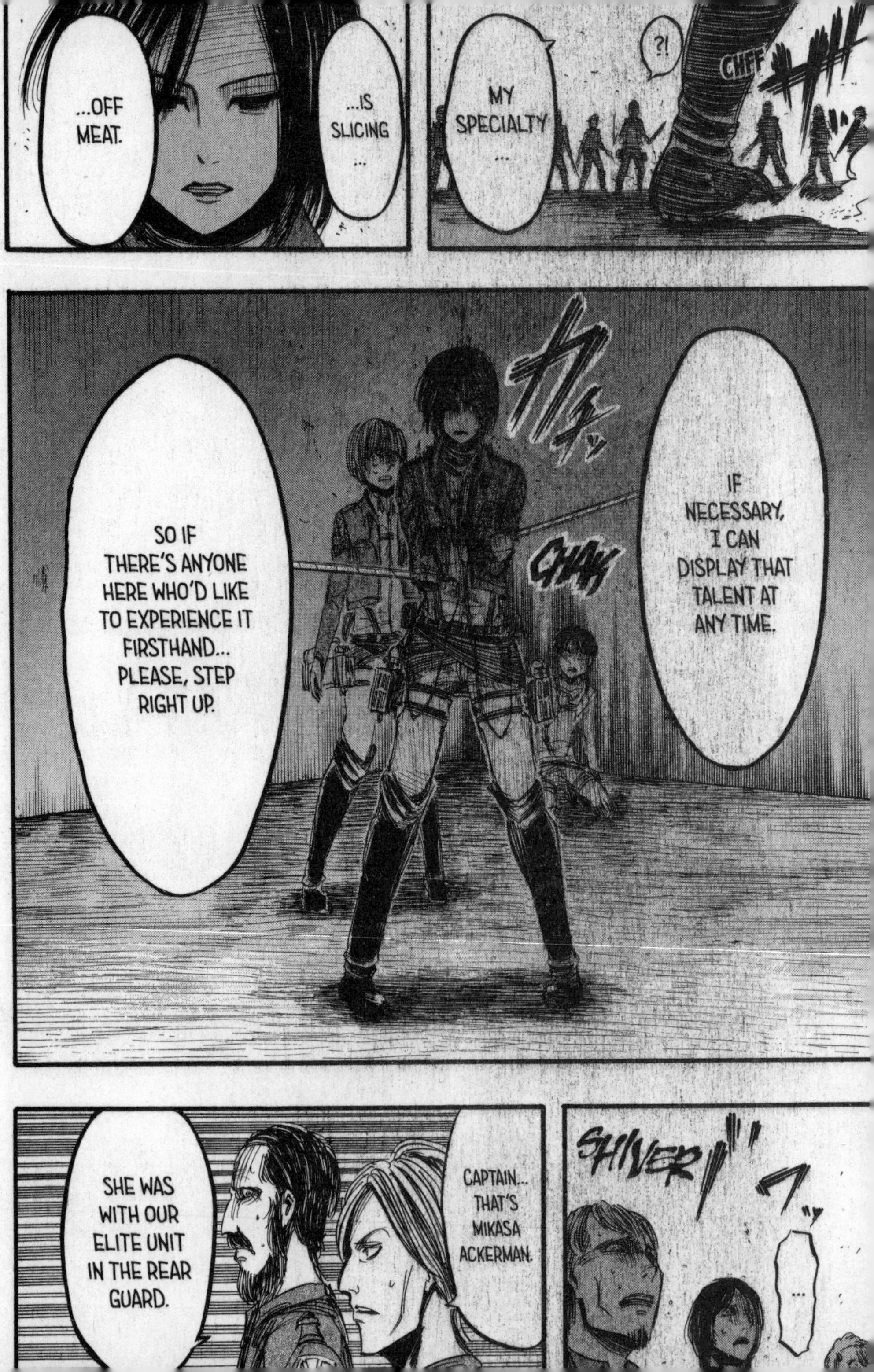
?!
CHFF
MY SPECIALTY ...
...IS SLICING ...
...OFF MEAT.
IF NECESSARY, I CAN DISPLAY THAT TALENT AT ANY TIME.
CHAK
SO IF THERE'S ANYONE HERE WHO'D LIKE TO EXPERIENCE IT FIRSTHAND... PLEASE, STEP RIGHT UP.
SHIVER
...
CAPTAIN... THAT'S MIKASA ACKERMAN.
SHE WAS WITH OUR ELITE UNIT IN THE REAR GUARD.

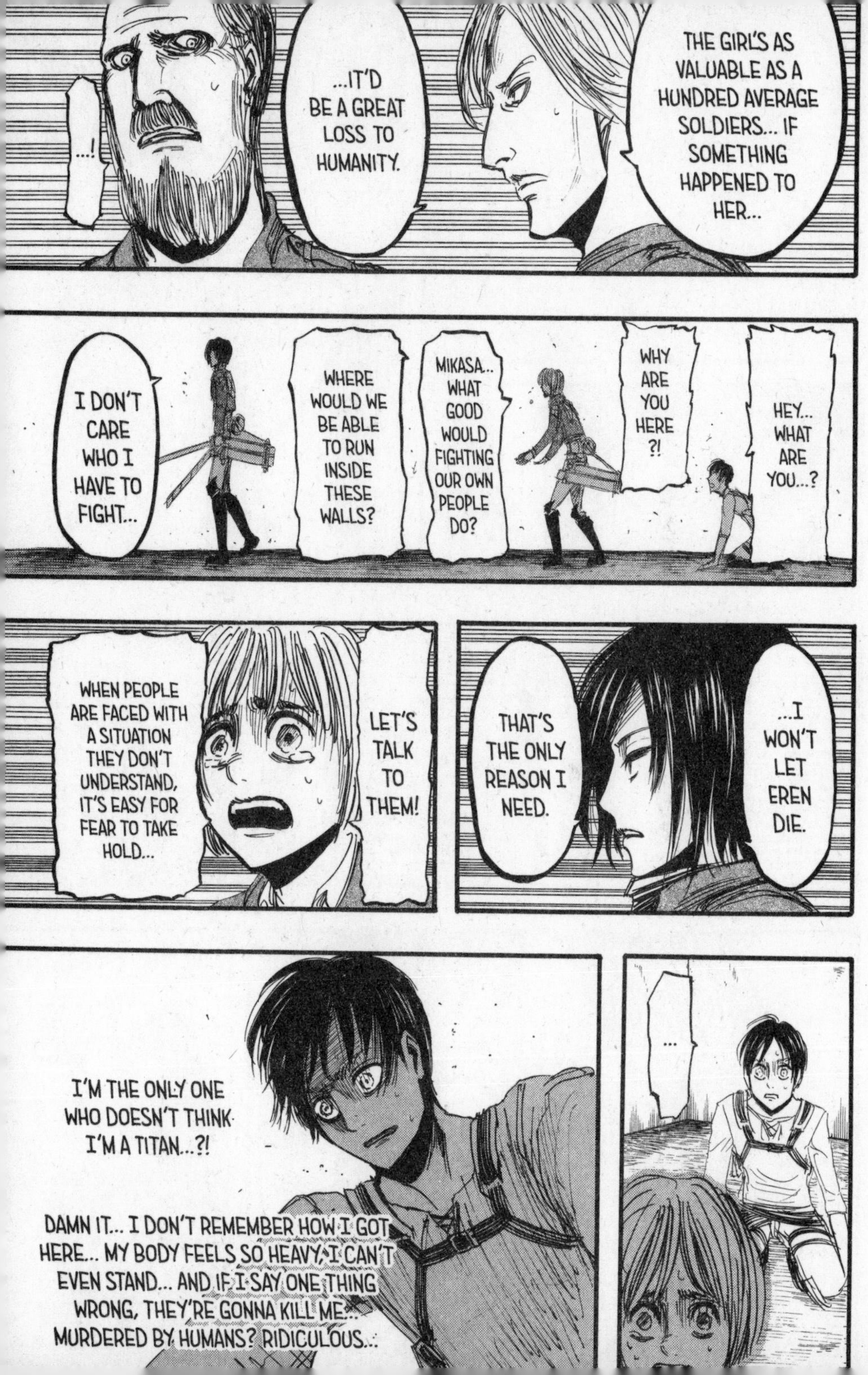
THE GIRL'S AS VALUABLE AS A HUNDRED AVERAGE SOLDIERS... IF SOMETHING HAPPENED TO HER...
...IT'D BE A GREAT LOSS TO HUMANITY.
...!
HEY... WHAT ARE YOU...?
WHY ARE YOU HERE?!
MIKASA... WHAT GOOD WOULD FIGHTING OUR OWN PEOPLE DO?
WHERE WOULD WE BE ABLE TO RUN INSIDE THESE WALLS?
I DON'T CARE WHO I HAVE TO FIGHT...
...I WON'T LET EREN DIE.
THAT'S THE ONLY REASON I NEED.
LET'S TALK TO THEM!
WHEN PEOPLE ARE FACED WITH A SITUATION THEY DON'T UNDERSTAND, IT'S EASY FOR FEAR TO TAKE HOLD...
...
I'M THE ONLY ONE WHO DOESN'T THINK I'M A TITAN...?!
DAMN IT... I DON'T REMEMBER HOW I GOT HERE... MY BODY FEELS SO HEAVY, I CAN'T EVEN STAND... AND IF I SAY ONE THING WRONG, THEY'RE GONNA KILL ME... MURDERED BY HUMANS? RIDICULOUS...

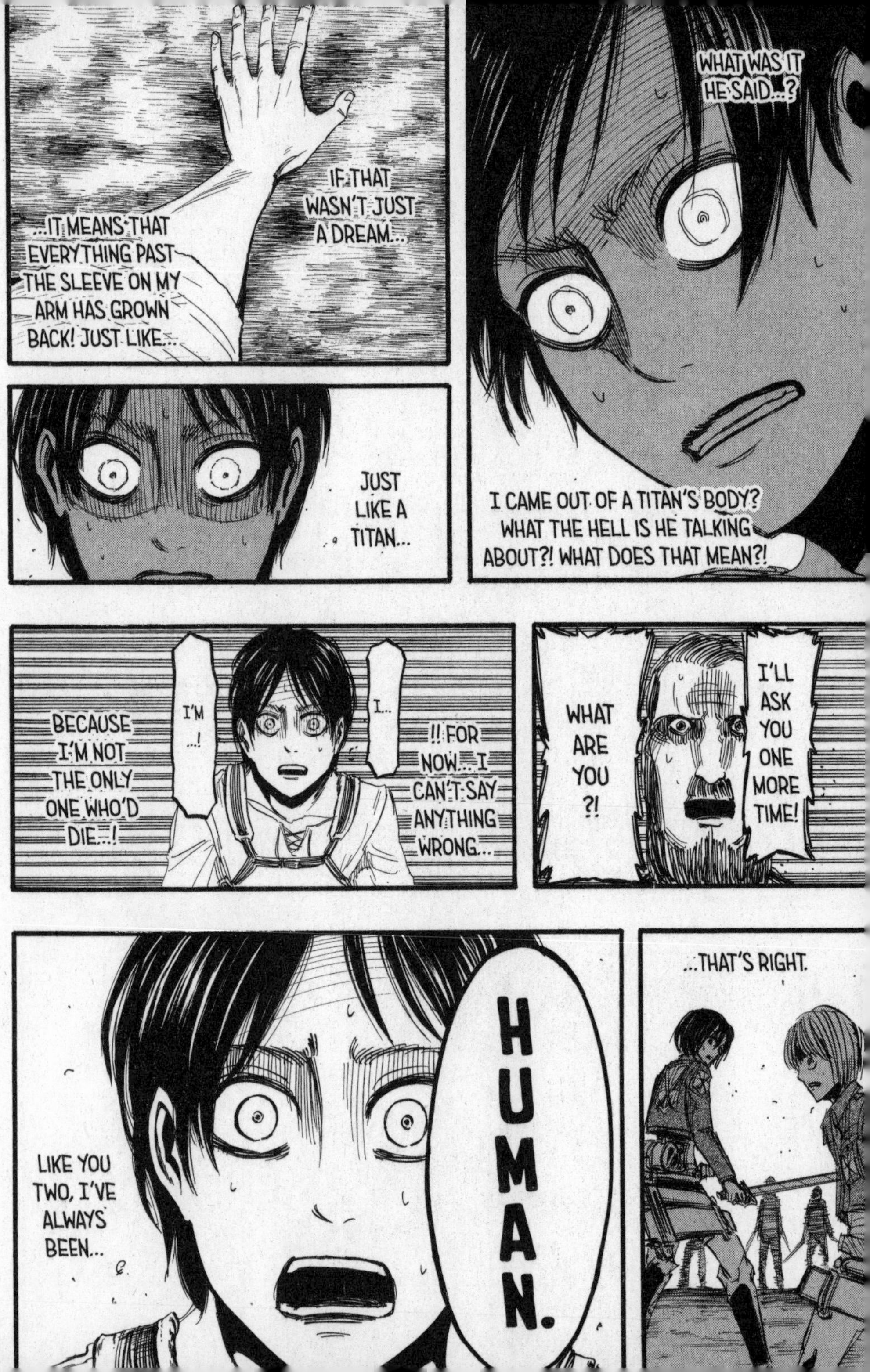
WHAT WAS IT HE SAID...?
I CAME OUT OF A TITAN'S BODY? WHAT THE HELL IS HE TALKING ABOUT?! WHAT DOES THAT MEAN?!
IF THAT WASN'T JUST A DREAM...
...IT MEANS THAT EVERYTHING PAST THE SLEEVE ON MY ARM HAS GROWN BACK! JUST LIKE...
JUST LIKE A TITAN...
I'LL ASK YOU ONE MORE TIME!
WHAT ARE YOU ?!
I...
!! FOR NOW... I CAN'T SAY ANYTHING WRONG...
I'M ...!
BECAUSE I'M NOT THE ONLY ONE WHO'D DIE...!
...THAT'S RIGHT.
LIKE YOU TWO, I'VE ALWAYS BEEN...
HUMAN.

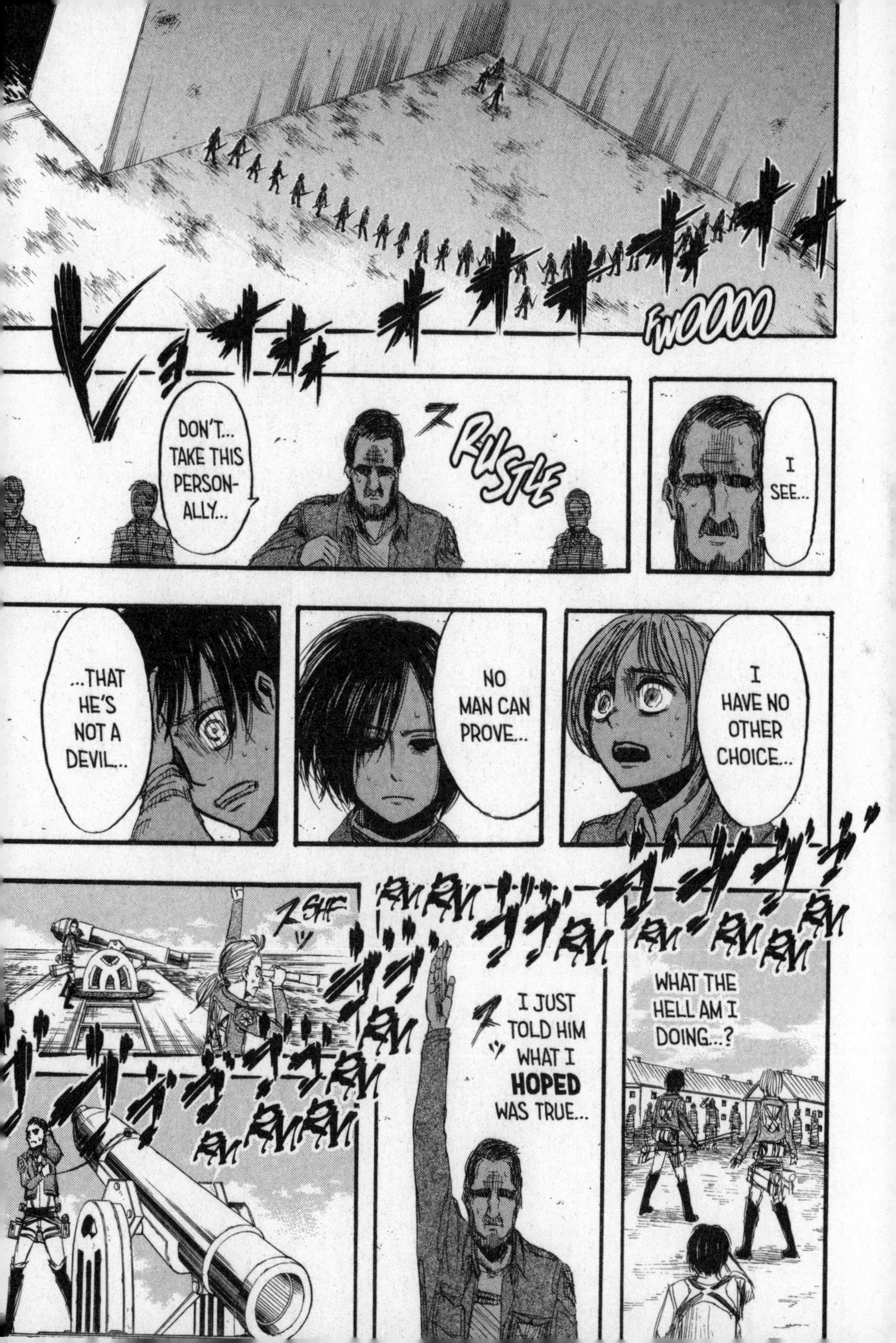
FWOOOO
I SEE...
DON'T... TAKE THIS PERSON-ALLY...
RUSTLE
I HAVE NO OTHER CHOICE...
NO MAN CAN PROVE...
...THAT HE'S NOT A DEVIL...
RM RM RM RM RM RM
WHAT THE HELL AM I DOING...?
I JUST TOLD HIM WHAT I **HOPED** WAS TRUE...
SHF
RM RM RM RM RM

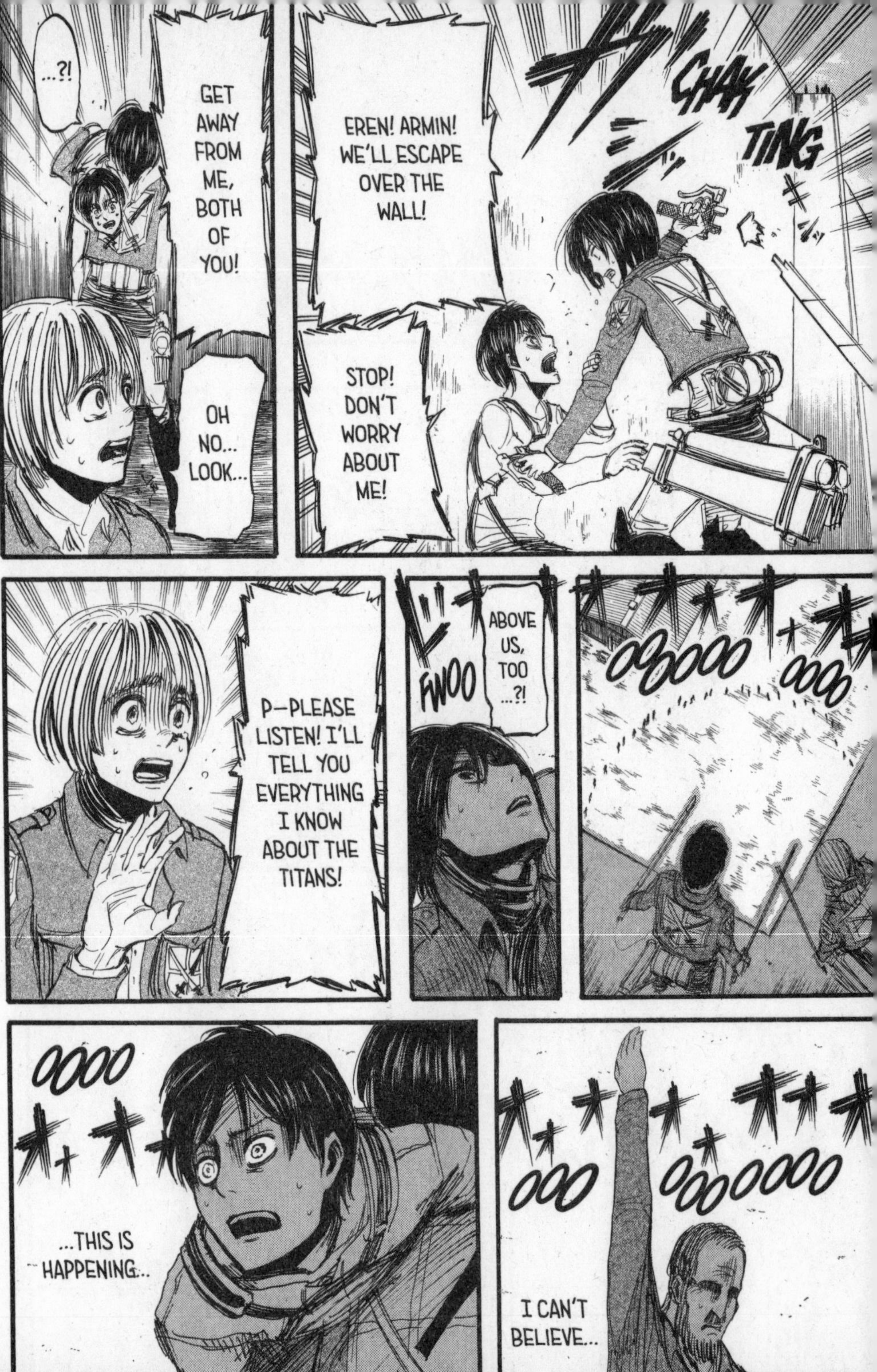
CHAK
TING
EREN! ARMIN! WE'LL ESCAPE OVER THE WALL!
STOP! DON'T WORRY ABOUT ME!
...?!
GET AWAY FROM ME, BOTH OF YOU!
OH NO... LOOK...
OOOOOO
OOOO
FWOO
ABOVE US, TOO ...?!
P—PLEASE LISTEN! I'LL TELL YOU EVERYTHING I KNOW ABOUT THE TITANS!
OOO
OOOOOOOO
I CAN'T BELIEVE...
OOOO
...THIS IS HAPPENING...

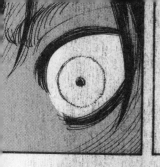

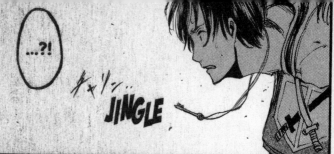

...?!
キャリン…
JINGLE
EREN...
WHEN I GET HOME... I'LL SHOW YOU WHAT'S IN THE BASEMENT...
...THAT I'VE BEEN KEEPING SECRET ALL THIS TIME.

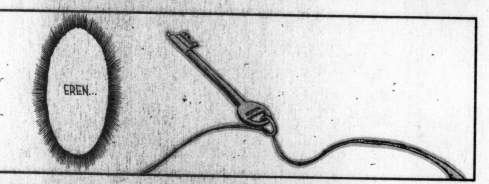

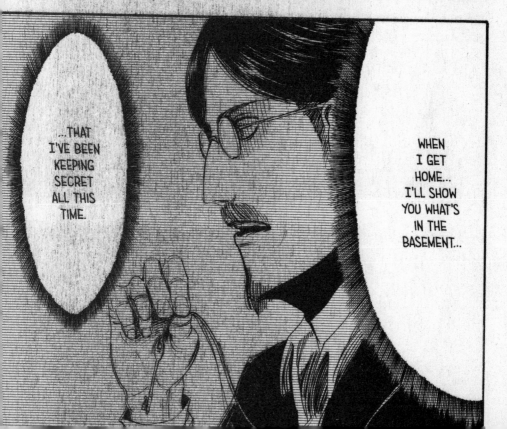

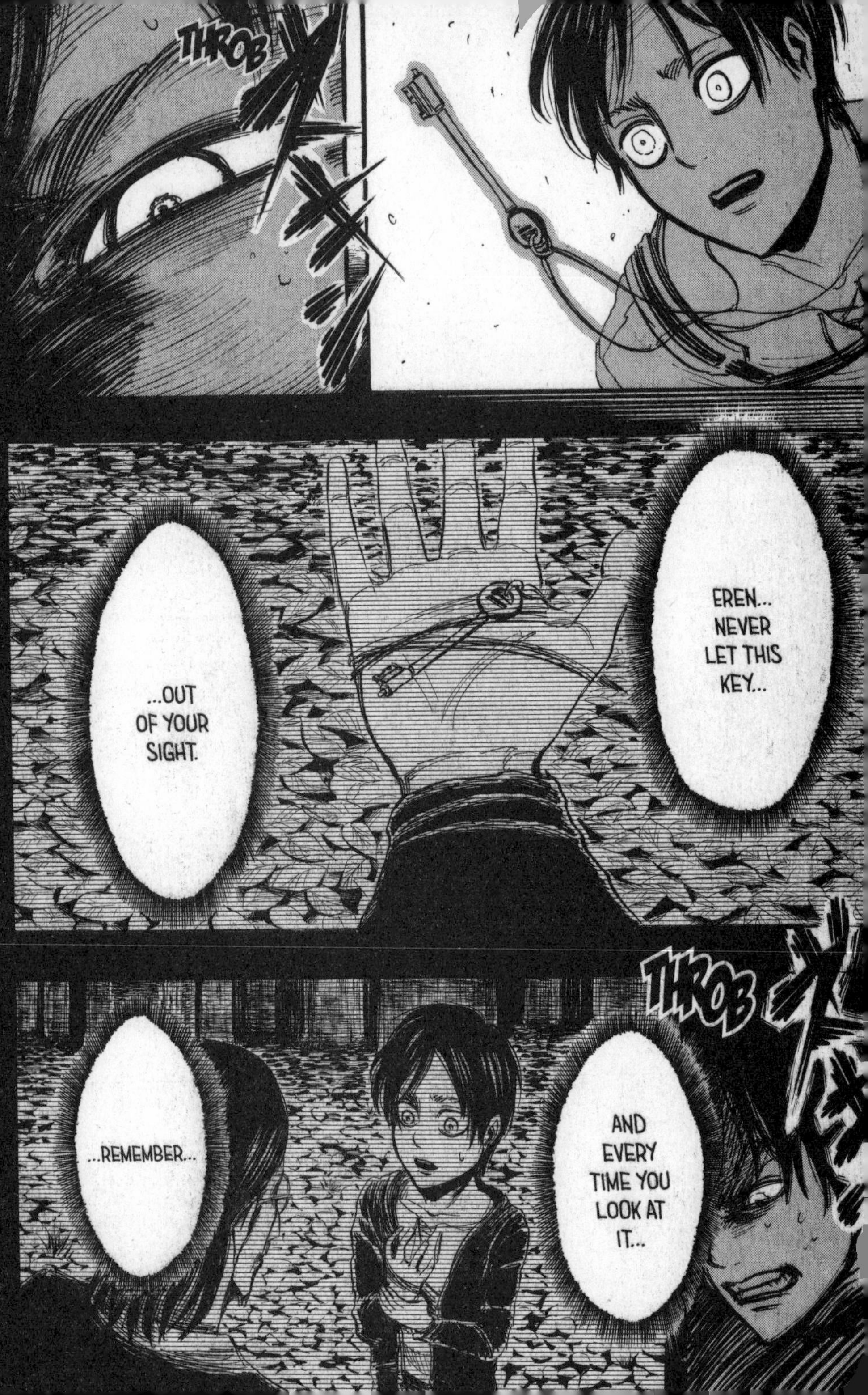
THROB
EREN... NEVER LET THIS KEY...
...OUT OF YOUR SIGHT.
THROB
AND EVERY TIME YOU LOOK AT IT...
...REMEMBER...

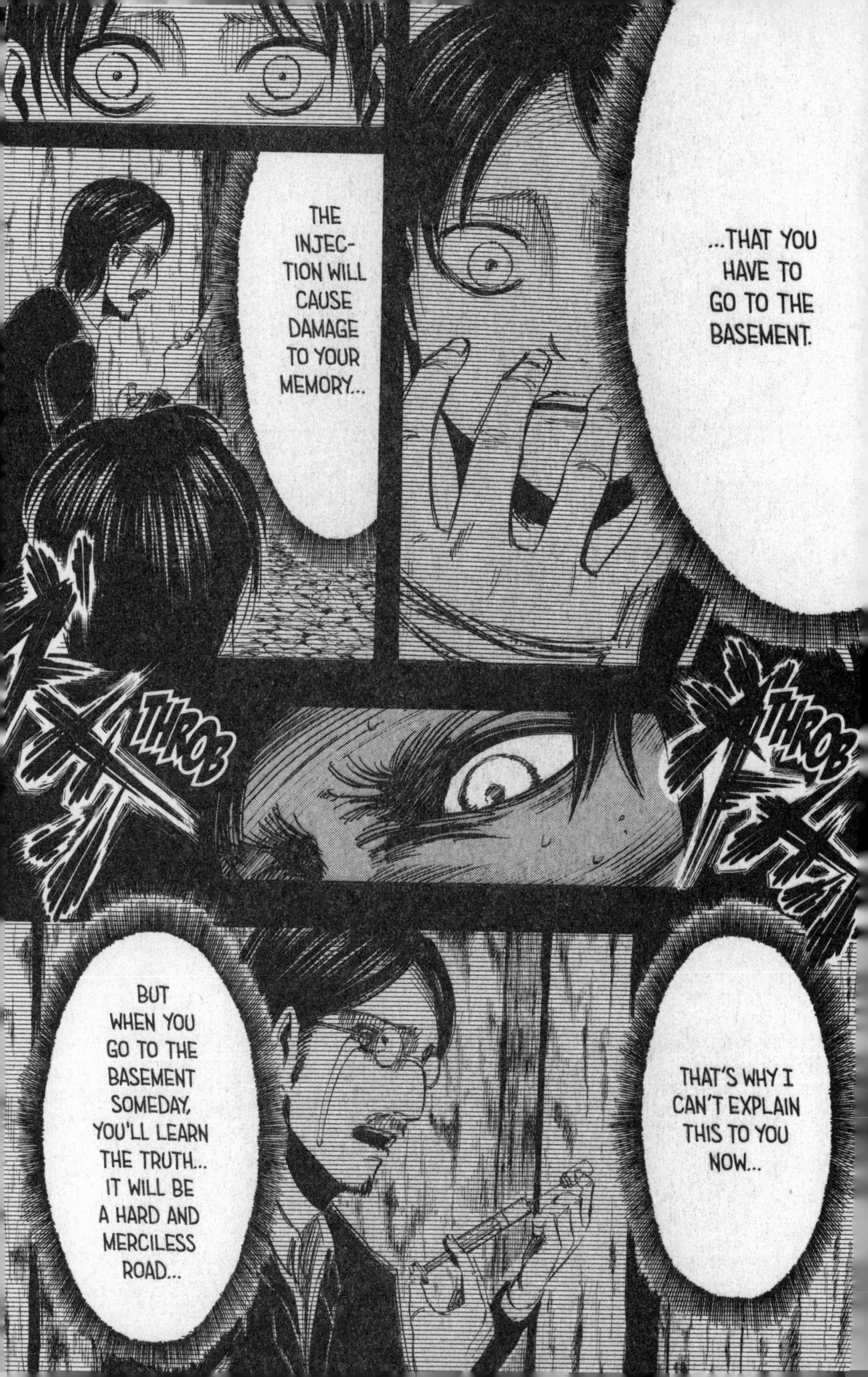
...THAT YOU HAVE TO GO TO THE BASEMENT.
THE INJECTION WILL CAUSE DAMAGE TO YOUR MEMORY...
THROB
THROB
THAT'S WHY I CAN'T EXPLAIN THIS TO YOU NOW...
BUT WHEN YOU GO TO THE BASEMENT SOMEDAY, YOU'LL LEARN THE TRUTH... IT WILL BE A HARD AND MERCILESS ROAD...

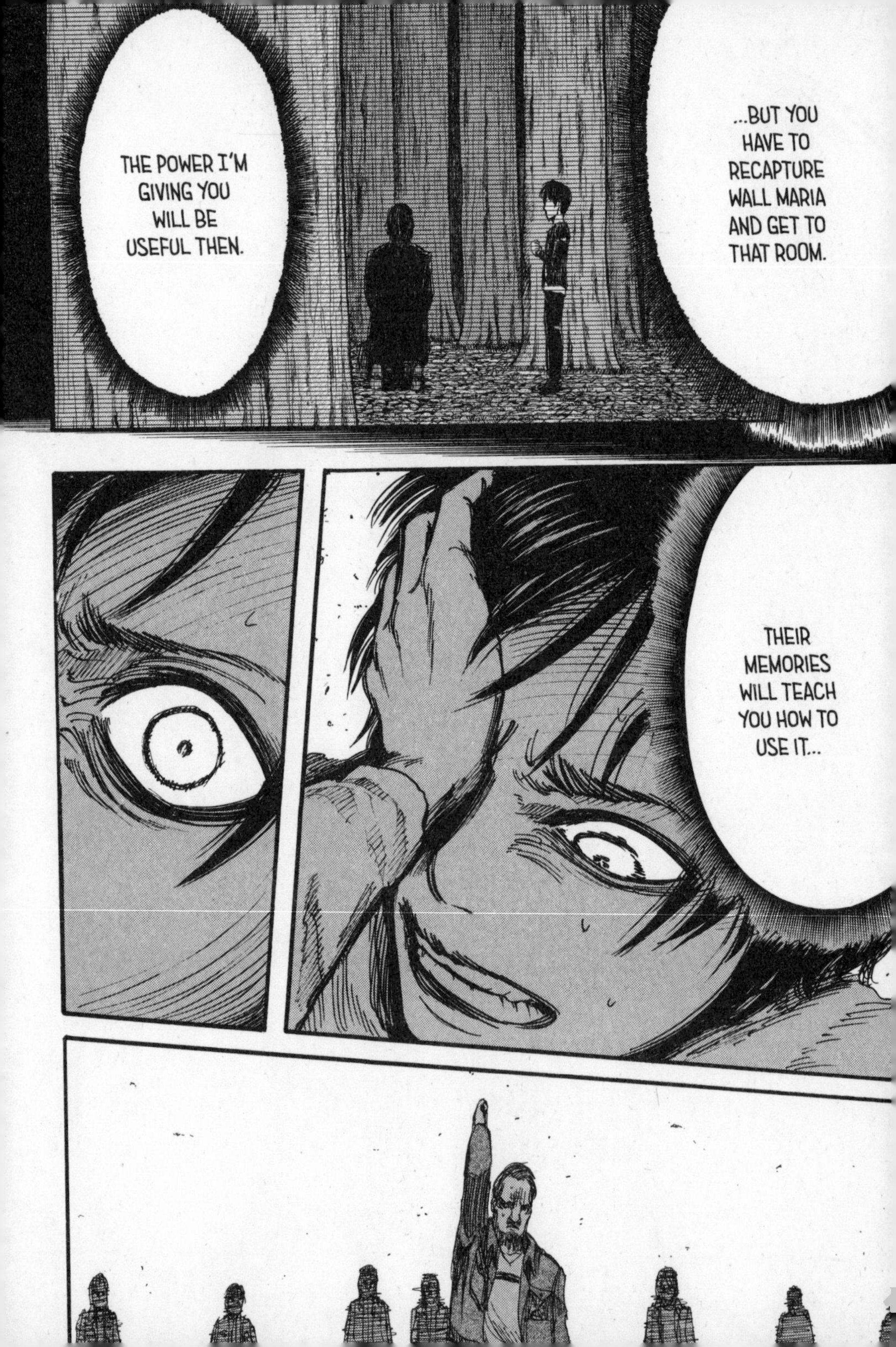
...BUT YOU HAVE TO RECAPTURE WALL MARIA AND GET TO THAT ROOM.
THE POWER I'M GIVING YOU WILL BE USEFUL THEN.
THEIR MEMORIES WILL TEACH YOU HOW TO USE IT...

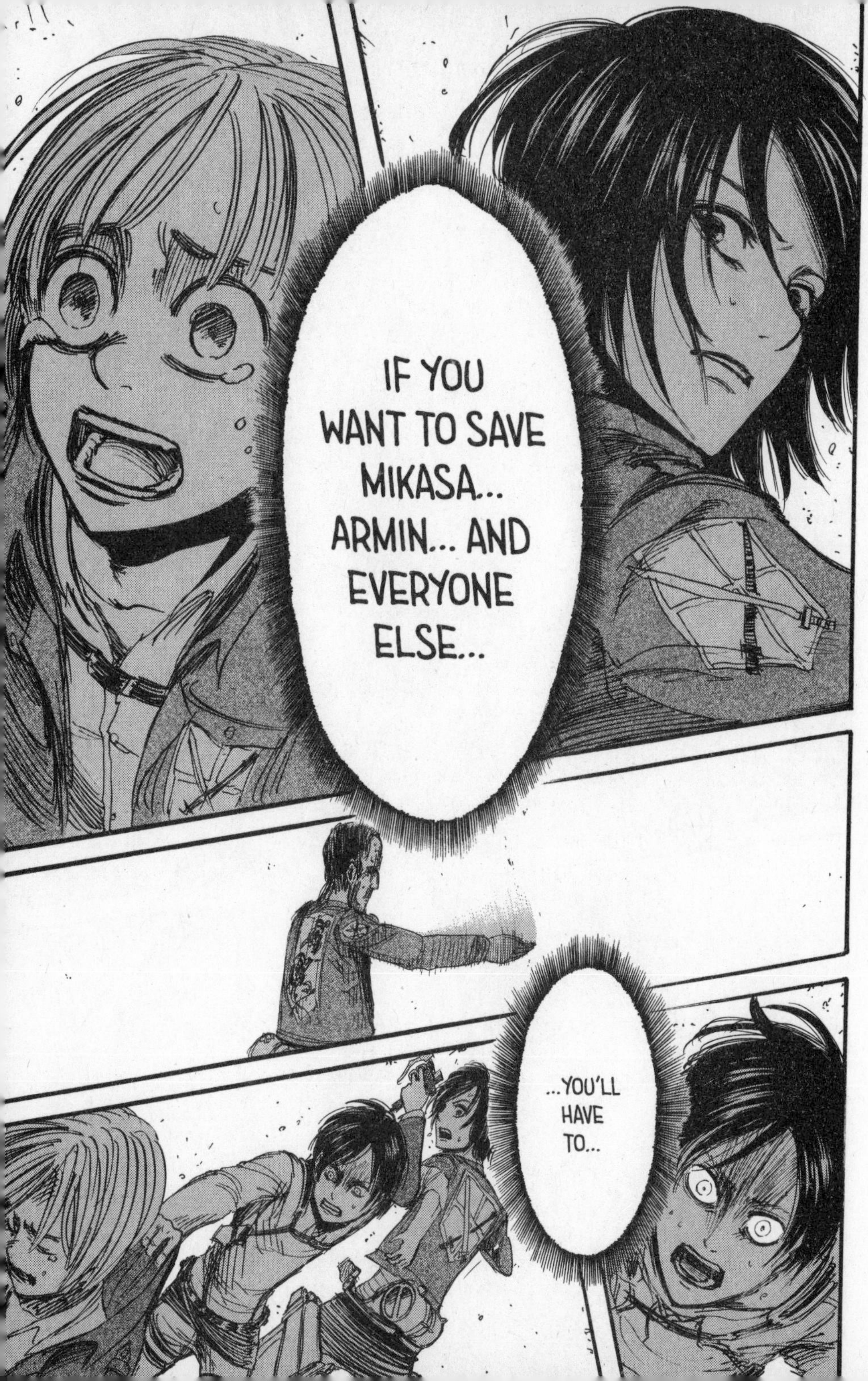
IF YOU WANT TO SAVE MIKASA... ARMIN... AND EVERYONE ELSE...
...YOU'LL HAVE TO...

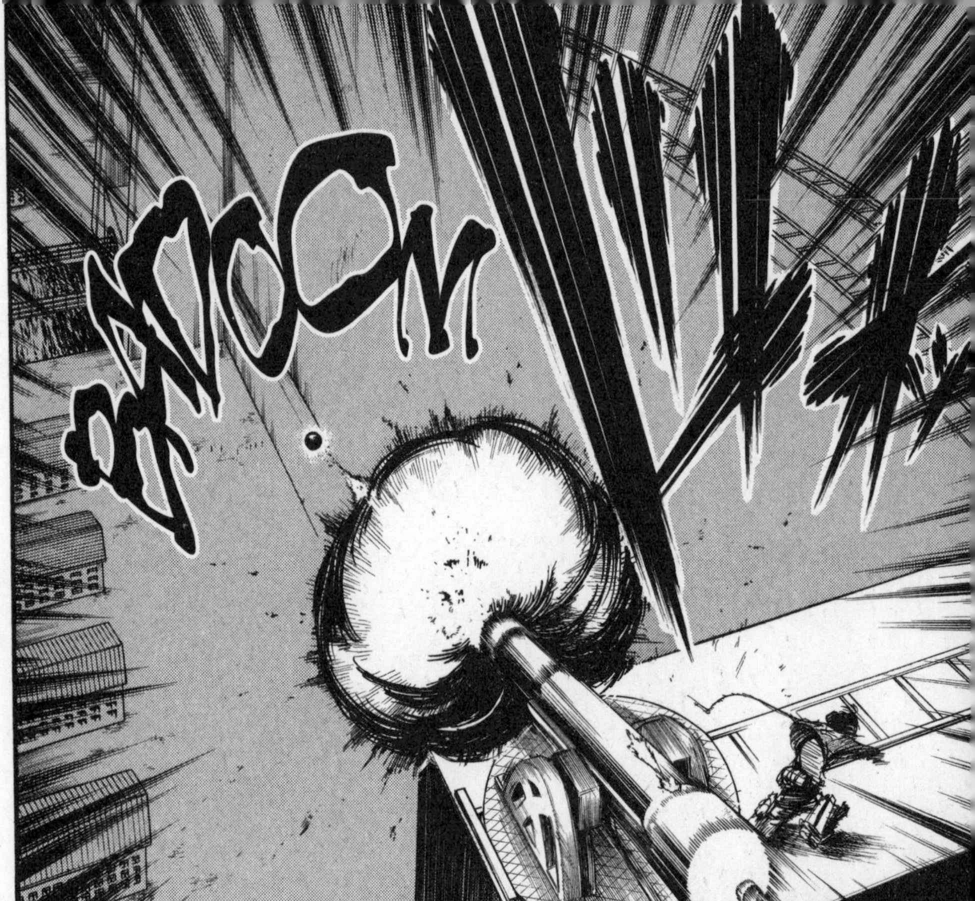
BOOOM
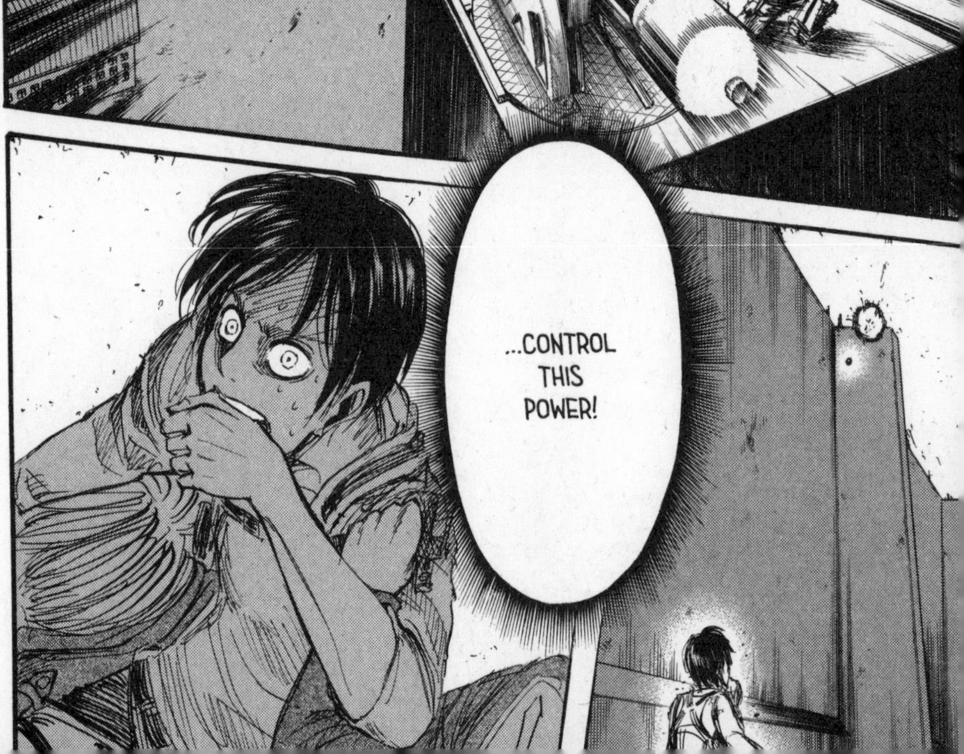
...CONTROL THIS POWER!

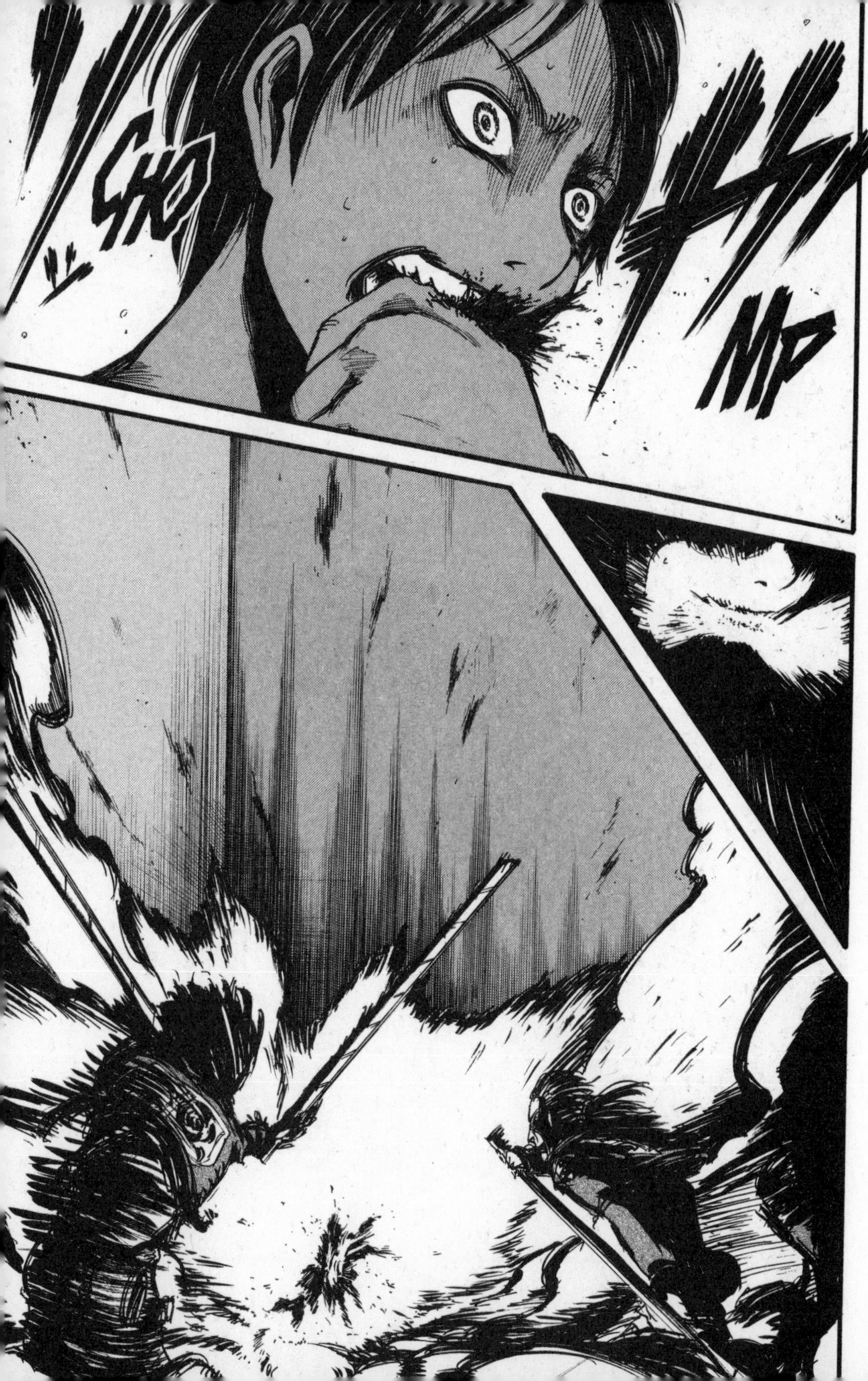
CHO
MP

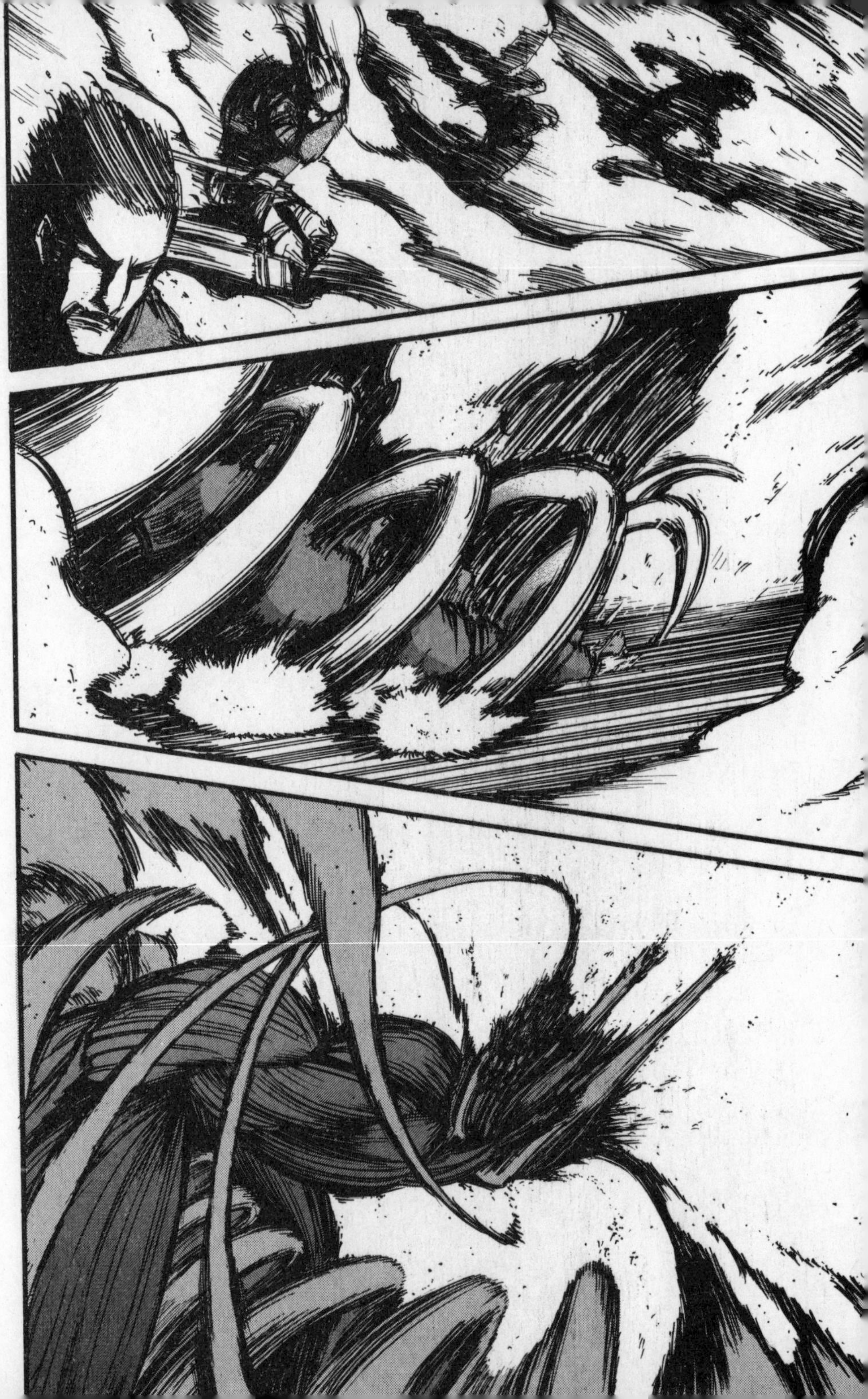

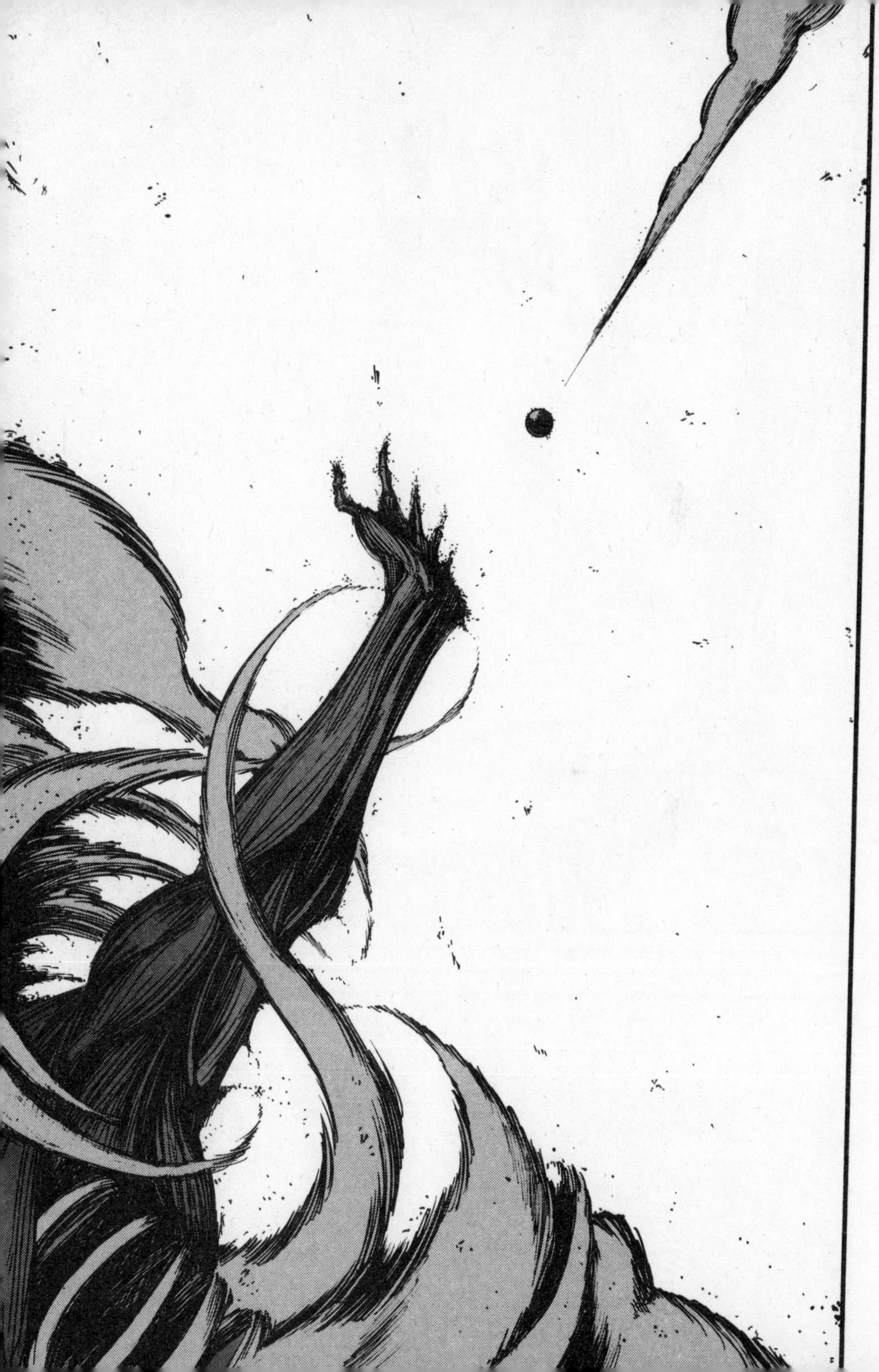

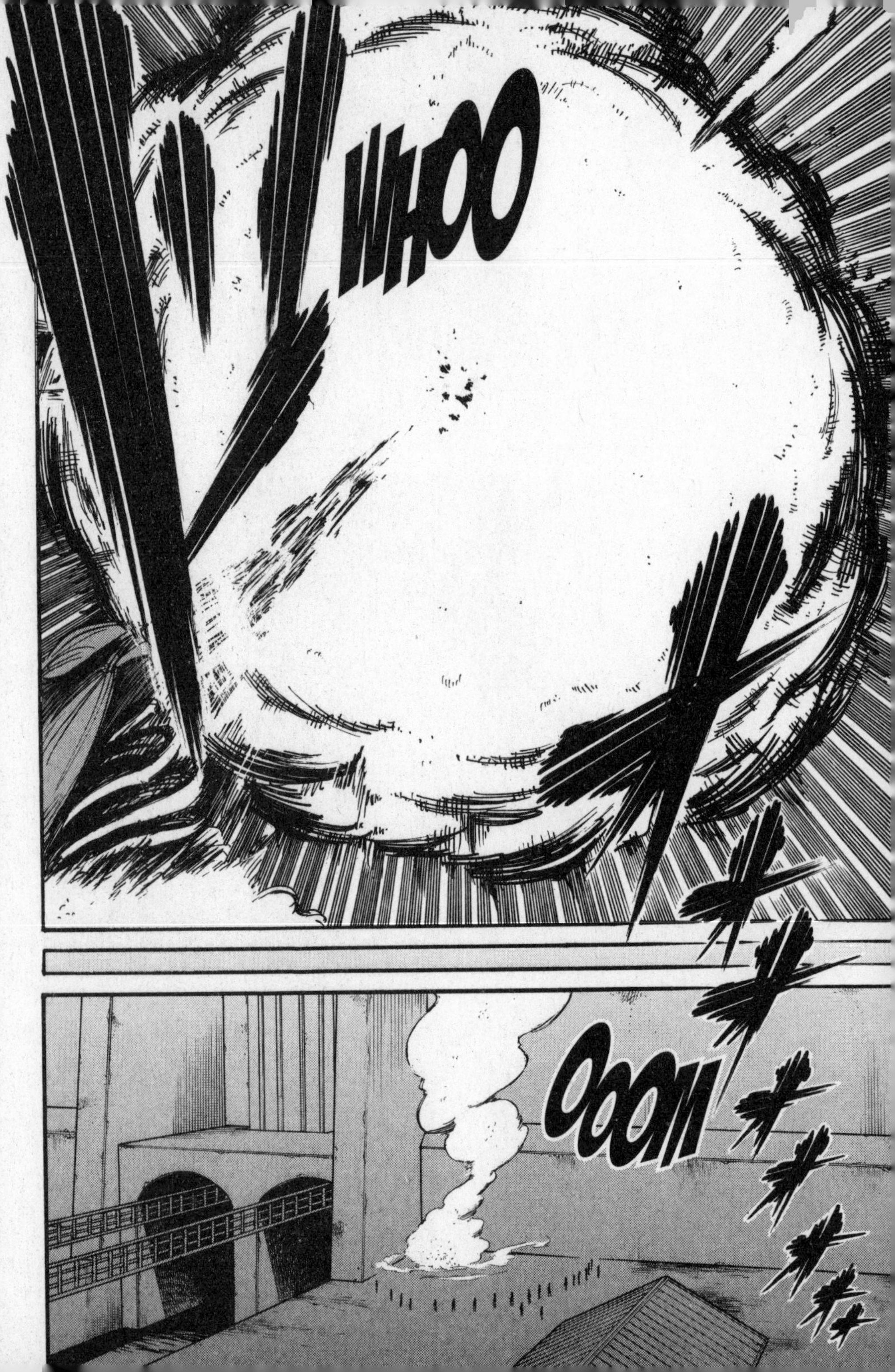
WHOO
OOOM

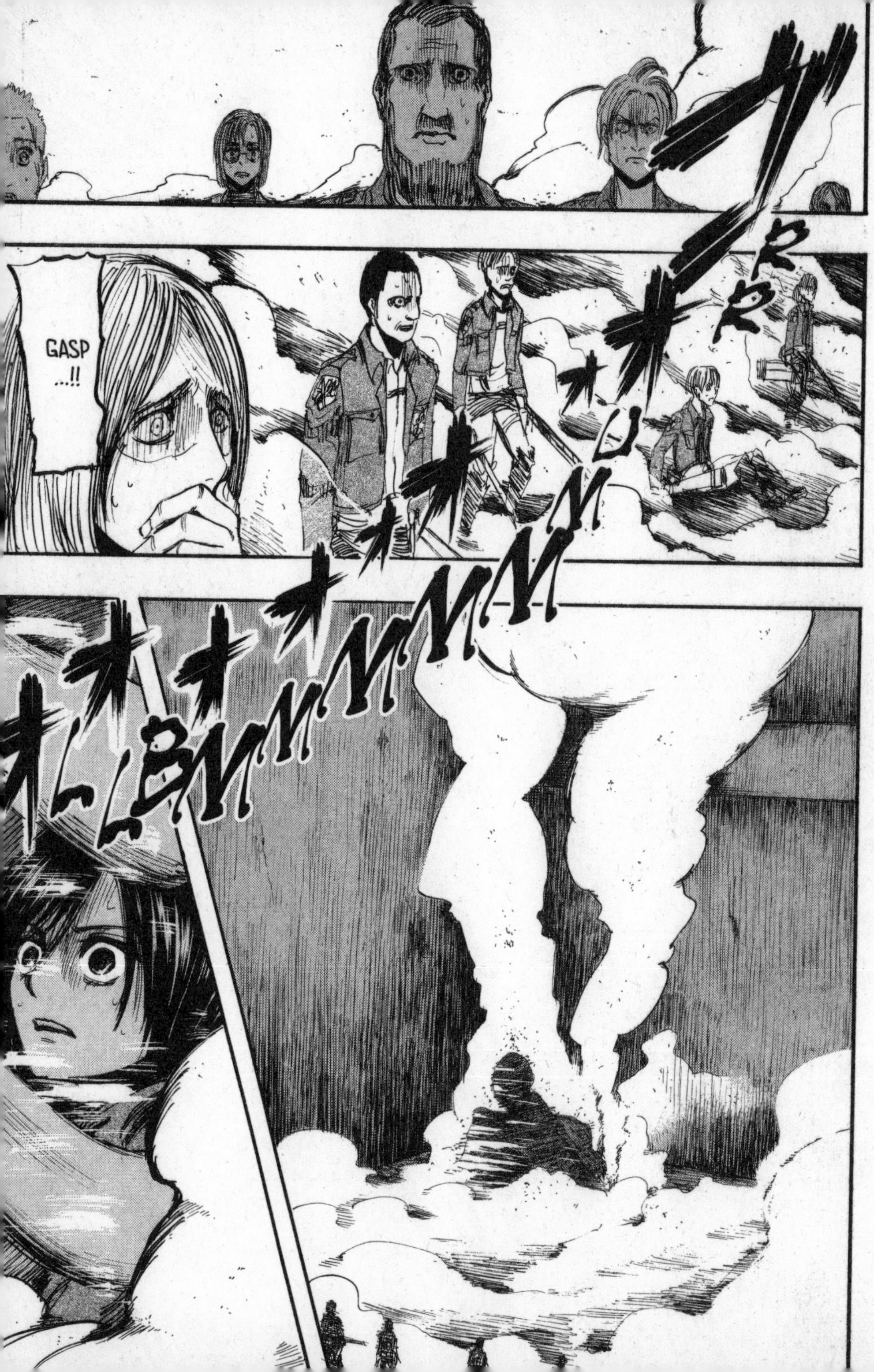
RRUM
GASP ...!!
BMMMMMMM

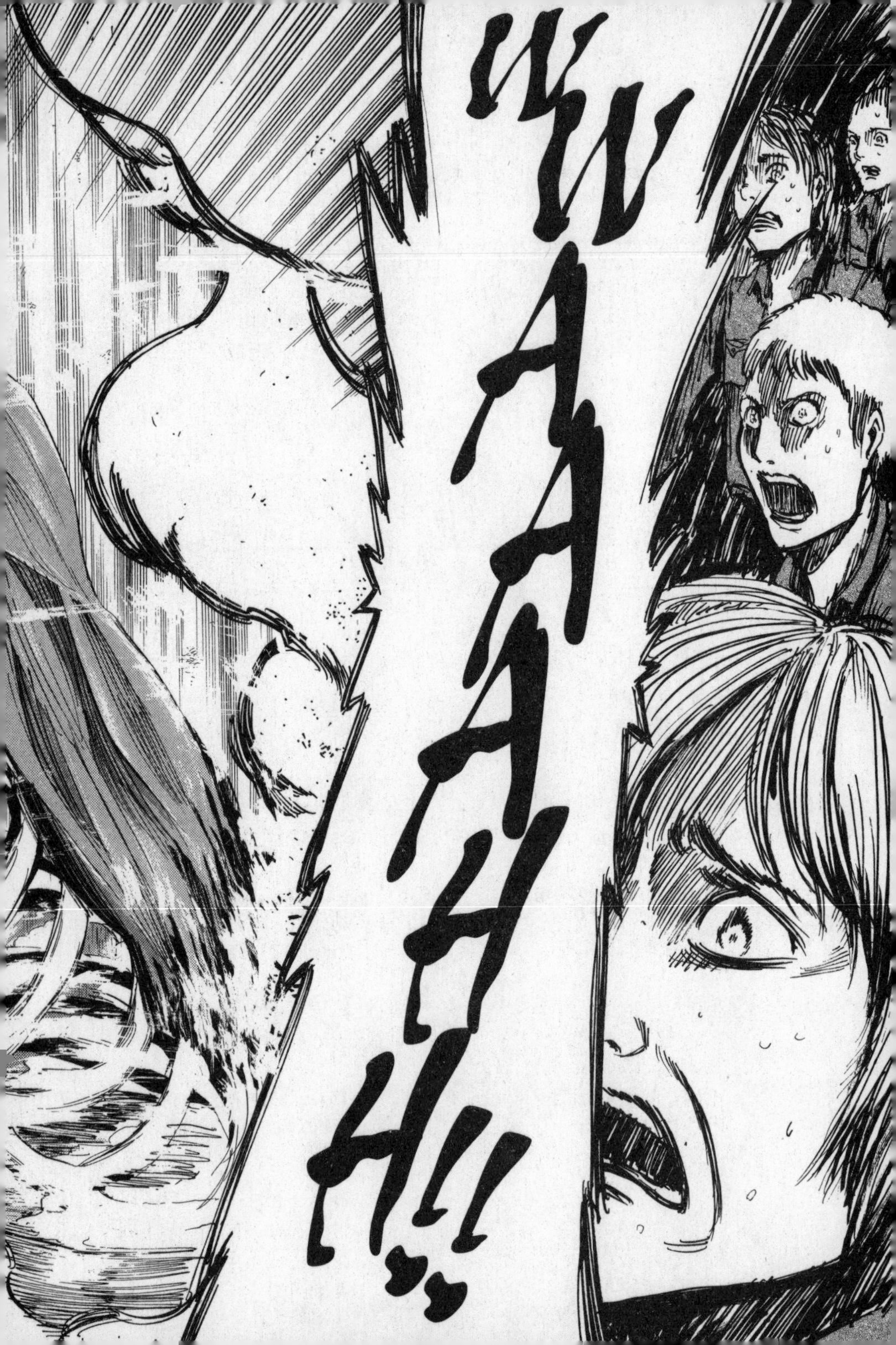
WAAAAAAH!!

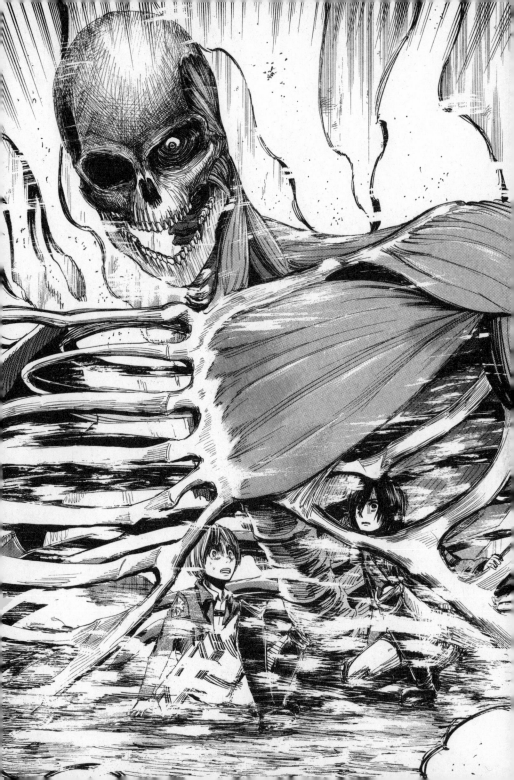

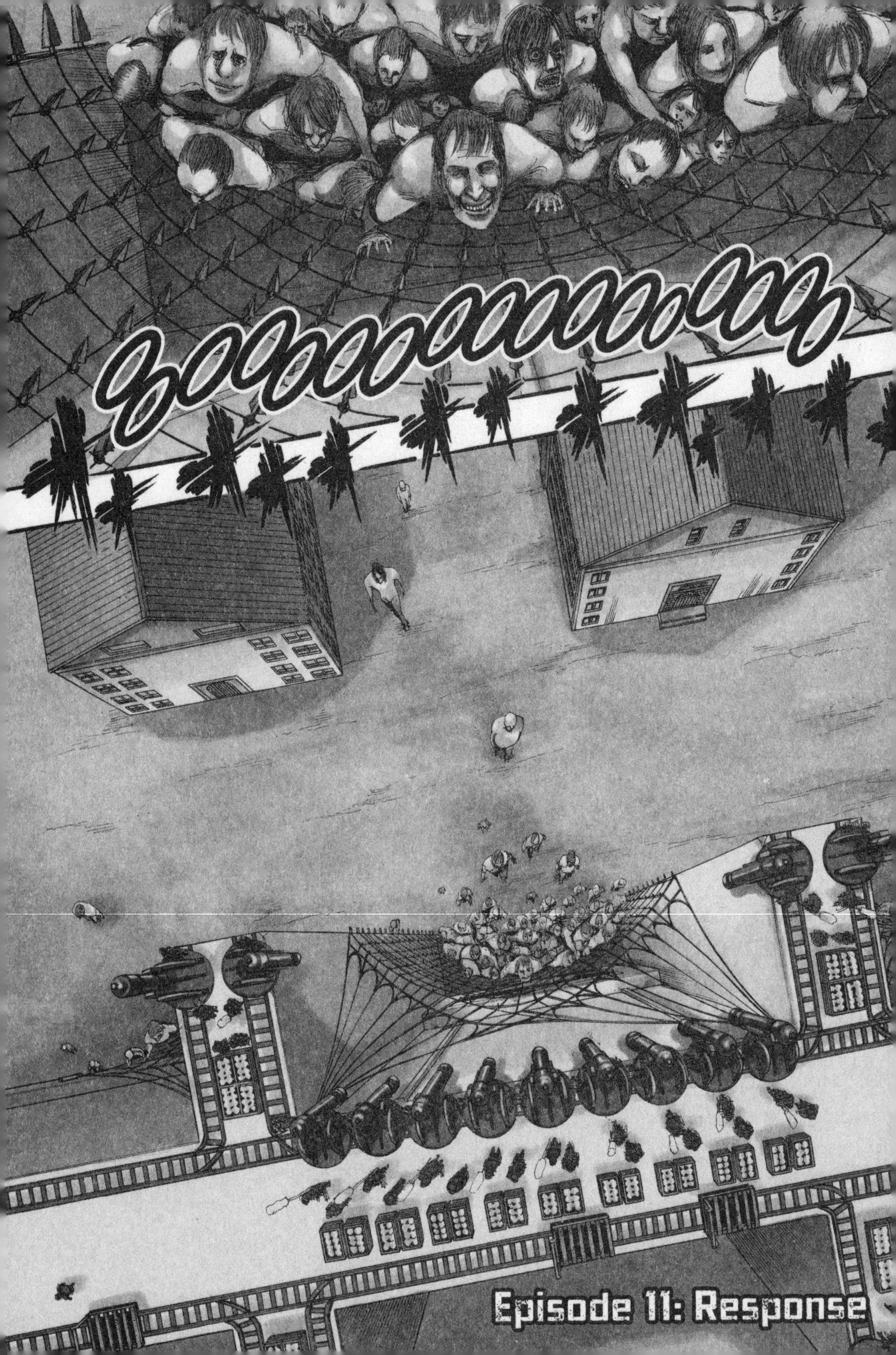
ZOOOOOOOOOM
Episode 11: Response

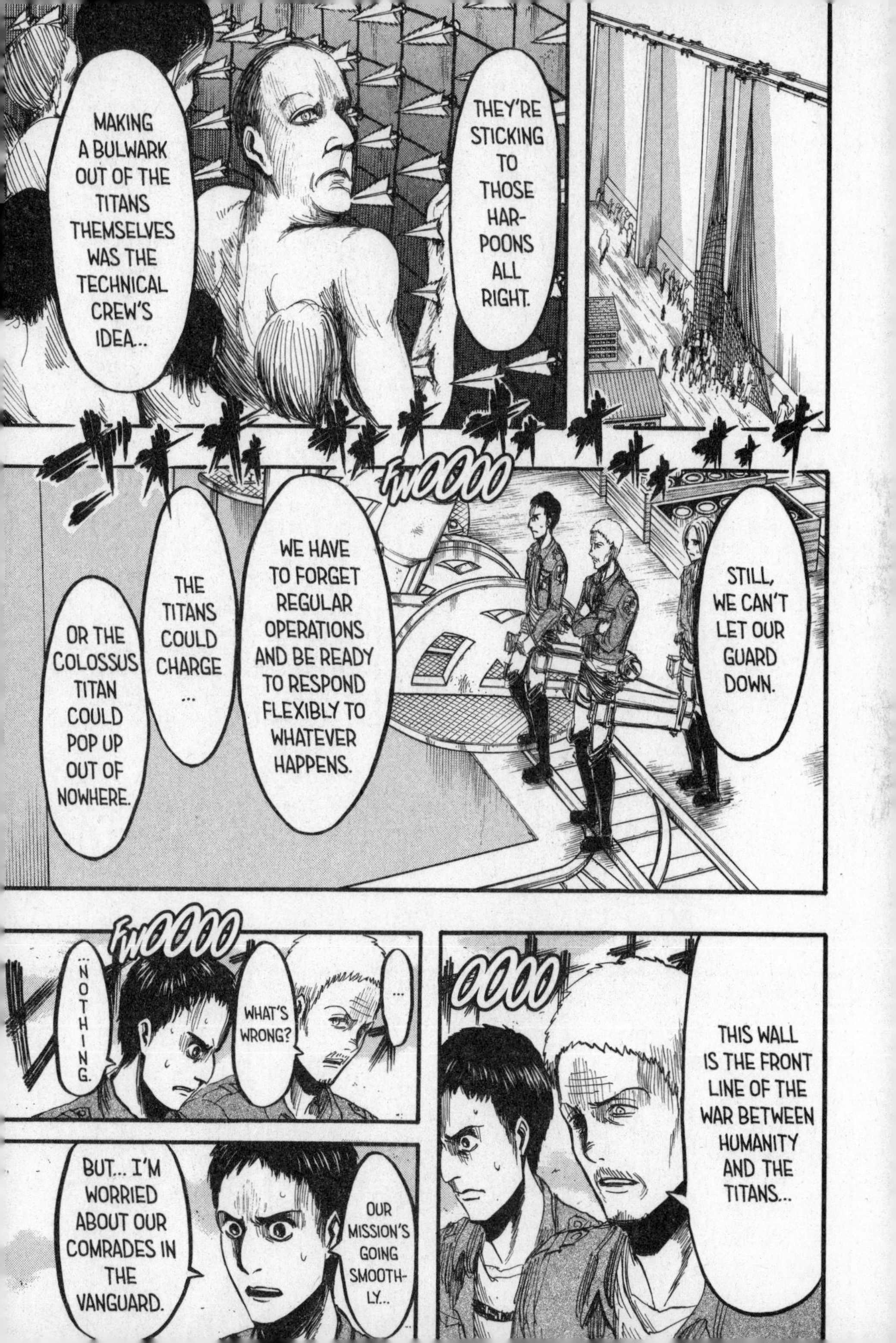
THEY'RE STICKING TO THOSE HAR-POONS ALL RIGHT.
MAKING A BULWARK OUT OF THE TITANS THEMSELVES WAS THE TECHNICAL CREW'S IDEA...
FWOOOO
STILL, WE CAN'T LET OUR GUARD DOWN.
WE HAVE TO FORGET REGULAR OPERATIONS AND BE READY TO RESPOND FLEXIBLY TO WHATEVER HAPPENS.
THE TITANS COULD CHARGE...
OR THE COLOSSUS TITAN COULD POP UP OUT OF NOWHERE.
OOOO
THIS WALL IS THE FRONT LINE OF THE WAR BETWEEN HUMANITY AND THE TITANS...
FWOOOO
...
WHAT'S WRONG?
...NOTHING.
OUR MISSION'S GOING SMOOTH-LY...
BUT... I'M WORRIED ABOUT OUR COMRADES IN THE VANGUARD.

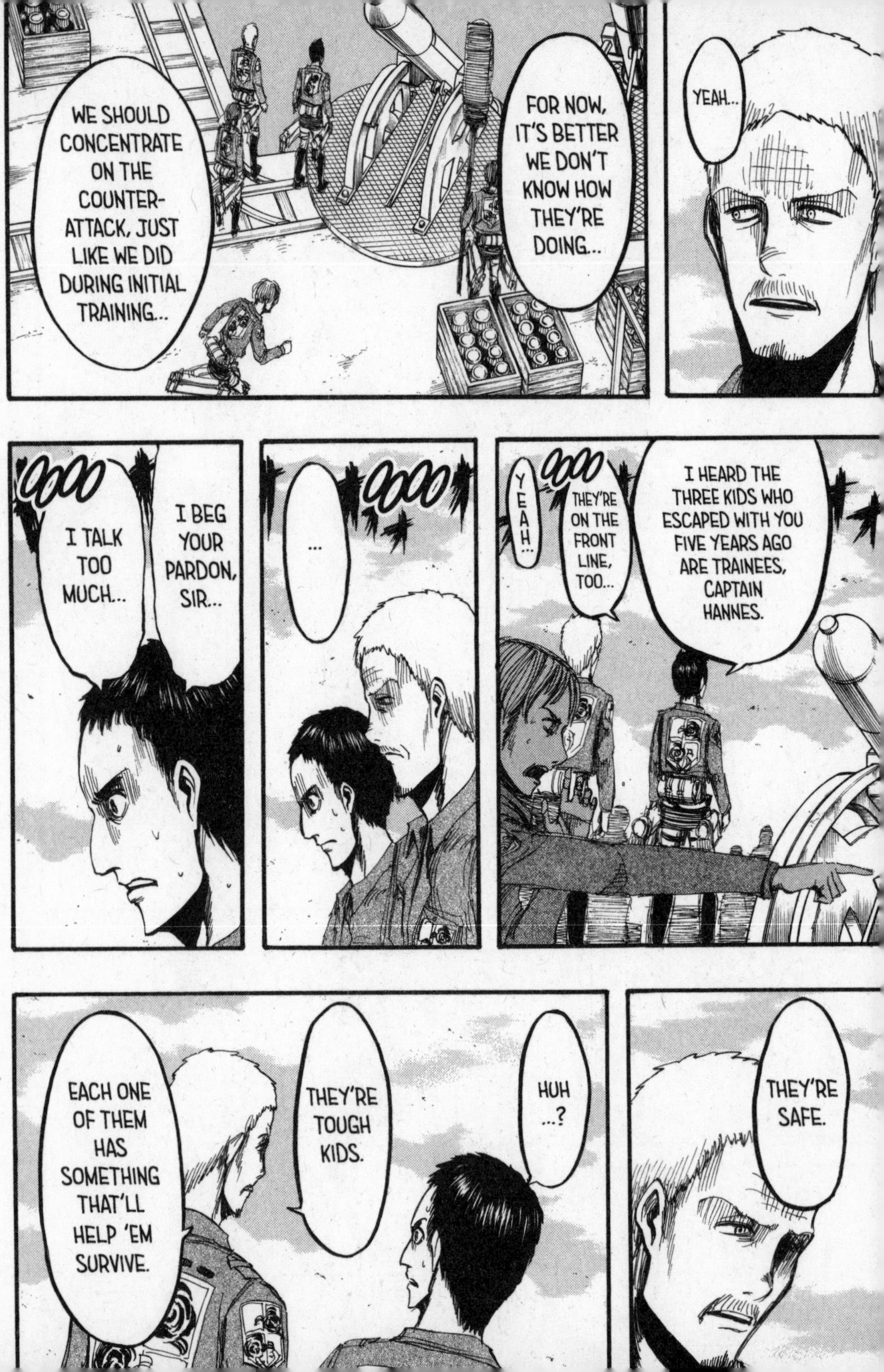
YEAH...
FOR NOW, IT'S BETTER WE DON'T KNOW HOW THEY'RE DOING...
WE SHOULD CONCENTRATE ON THE COUNTER-ATTACK, JUST LIKE WE DID DURING INITIAL TRAINING...
I HEARD THE THREE KIDS WHO ESCAPED WITH YOU FIVE YEARS AGO ARE TRAINEES, CAPTAIN HANNES.
YEAH...
THEY'RE ON THE FRONT LINE, TOO...
...
I BEG YOUR PARDON, SIR...
I TALK TOO MUCH...
THEY'RE SAFE.
HUH ...?
THEY'RE TOUGH KIDS.
EACH ONE OF THEM HAS SOMETHING THAT'LL HELP 'EM SURVIVE.

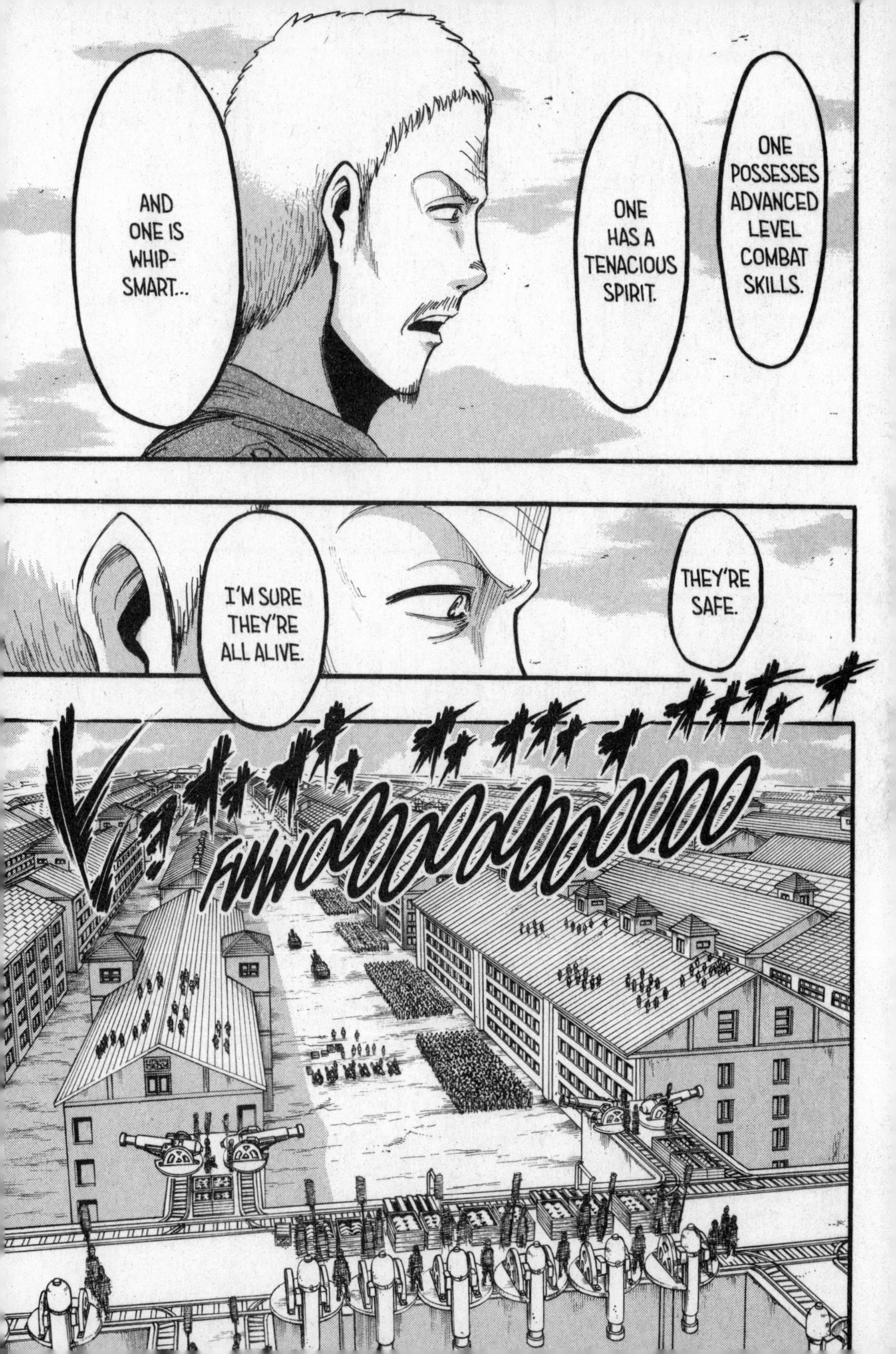
ONE POSSESSES ADVANCED LEVEL COMBAT SKILLS.
ONE HAS A TENACIOUS SPIRIT.
AND ONE IS WHIP-SMART...
THEY'RE SAFE.
I'M SURE THEY'RE ALL ALIVE.
FWWOOOOOOOOOOO

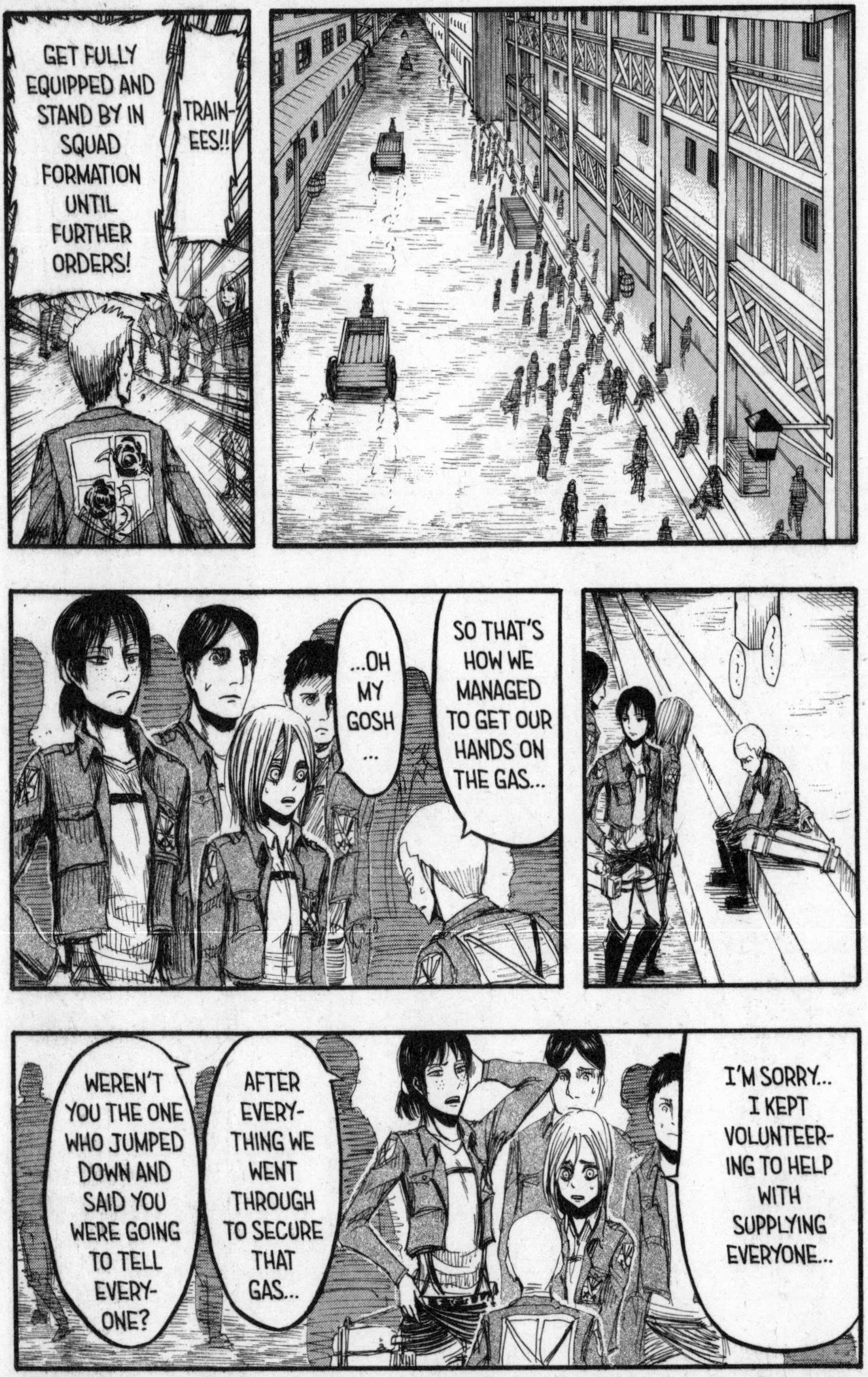
TRAIN-EES!!
GET FULLY EQUIPPED AND STAND BY IN SQUAD FORMATION UNTIL FURTHER ORDERS!
SO THAT'S HOW WE MANAGED TO GET OUR HANDS ON THE GAS...
...OH MY GOSH ...
I'M SORRY... I KEPT VOLUNTEER-ING TO HELP WITH SUPPLYING EVERYONE...
AFTER EVERY-THING WE WENT THROUGH TO SECURE THAT GAS...
WEREN'T YOU THE ONE WHO JUMPED DOWN AND SAID YOU WERE GOING TO TELL EVERY-ONE?

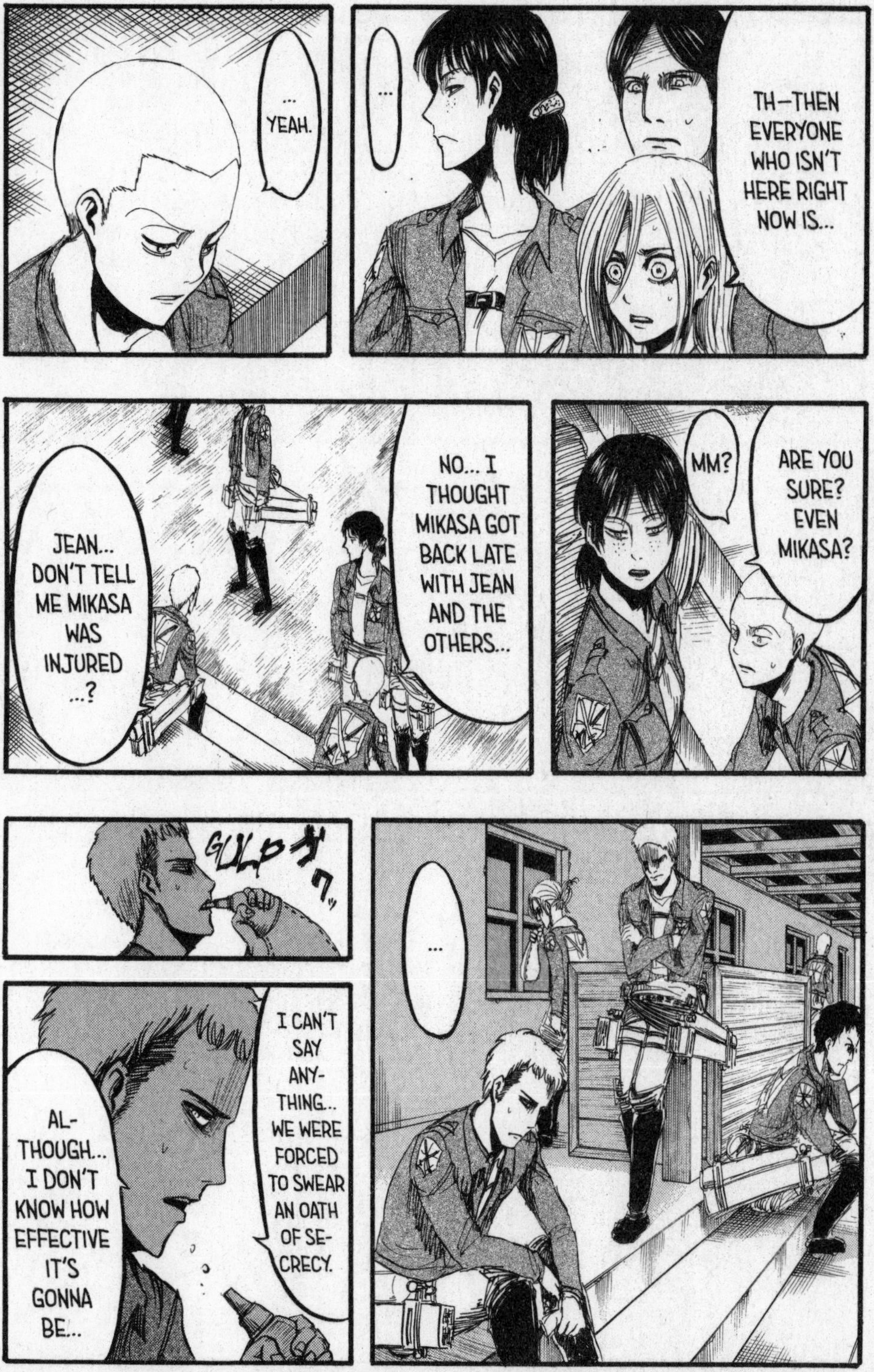
TH—THEN EVERYONE WHO ISN'T HERE RIGHT NOW IS...
...
... YEAH.
ARE YOU SURE? EVEN MIKASA?
MM?
NO... I THOUGHT MIKASA GOT BACK LATE WITH JEAN AND THE OTHERS...
JEAN... DON'T TELL ME MIKASA WAS INJURED ...?
...
GULP
I CAN'T SAY ANYTHING... WE WERE FORCED TO SWEAR AN OATH OF SECRECY.
ALTHOUGH... I DON'T KNOW HOW EFFECTIVE IT'S GONNA BE...

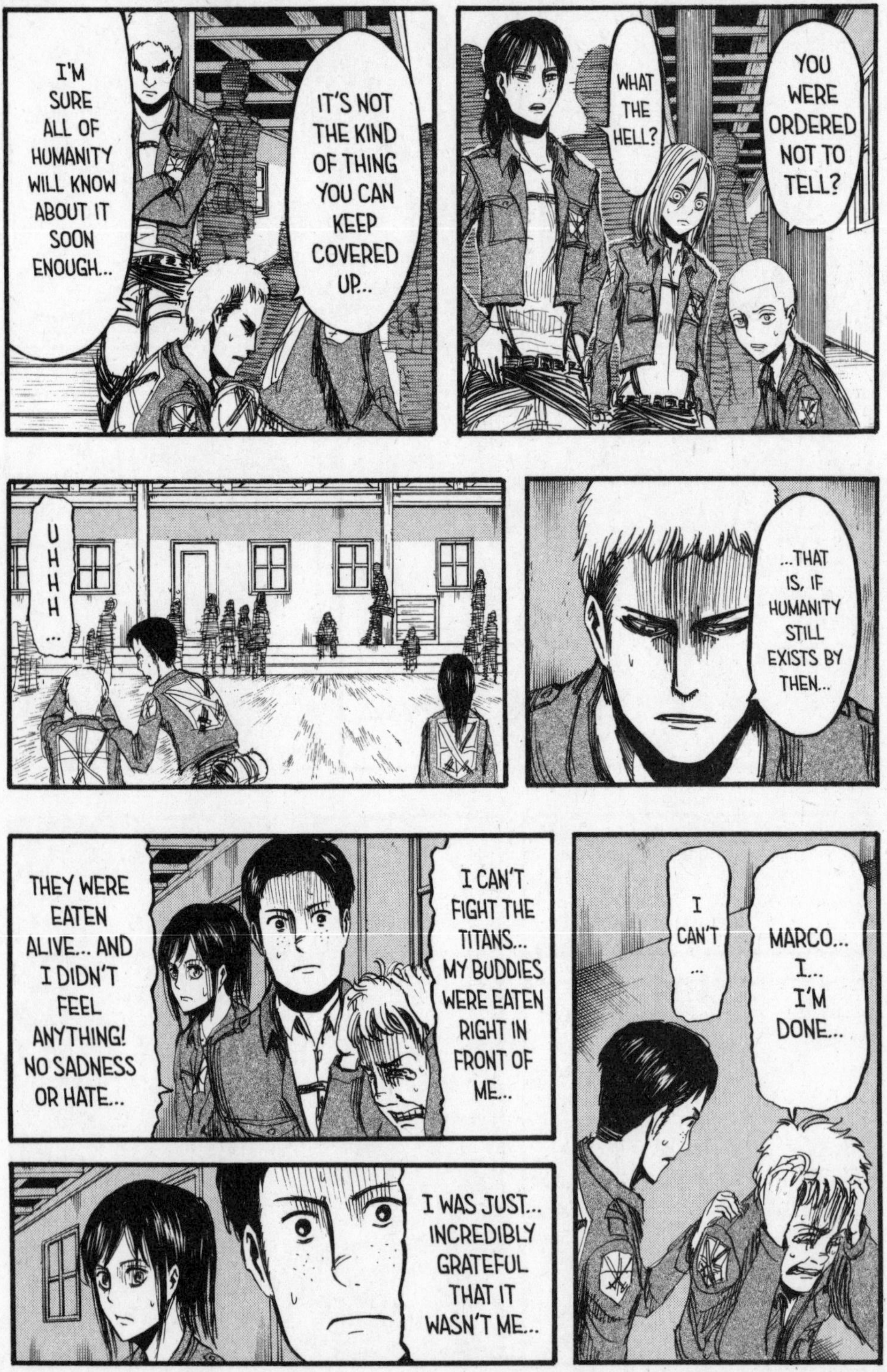
YOU WERE ORDERED NOT TO TELL?
WHAT THE HELL?
IT'S NOT THE KIND OF THING YOU CAN KEEP COVERED UP...
I'M SURE ALL OF HUMANITY WILL KNOW ABOUT IT SOON ENOUGH...
...THAT IS, IF HUMANITY STILL EXISTS BY THEN...
UHHH...
MARCO... I... I'M DONE...
I CAN'T...
I CAN'T FIGHT THE TITANS... MY BUDDIES WERE EATEN RIGHT IN FRONT OF ME...
THEY WERE EATEN ALIVE... AND I DIDN'T FEEL ANYTHING! NO SADNESS OR HATE...
I WAS JUST... INCREDIBLY GRATEFUL THAT IT WASN'T ME...

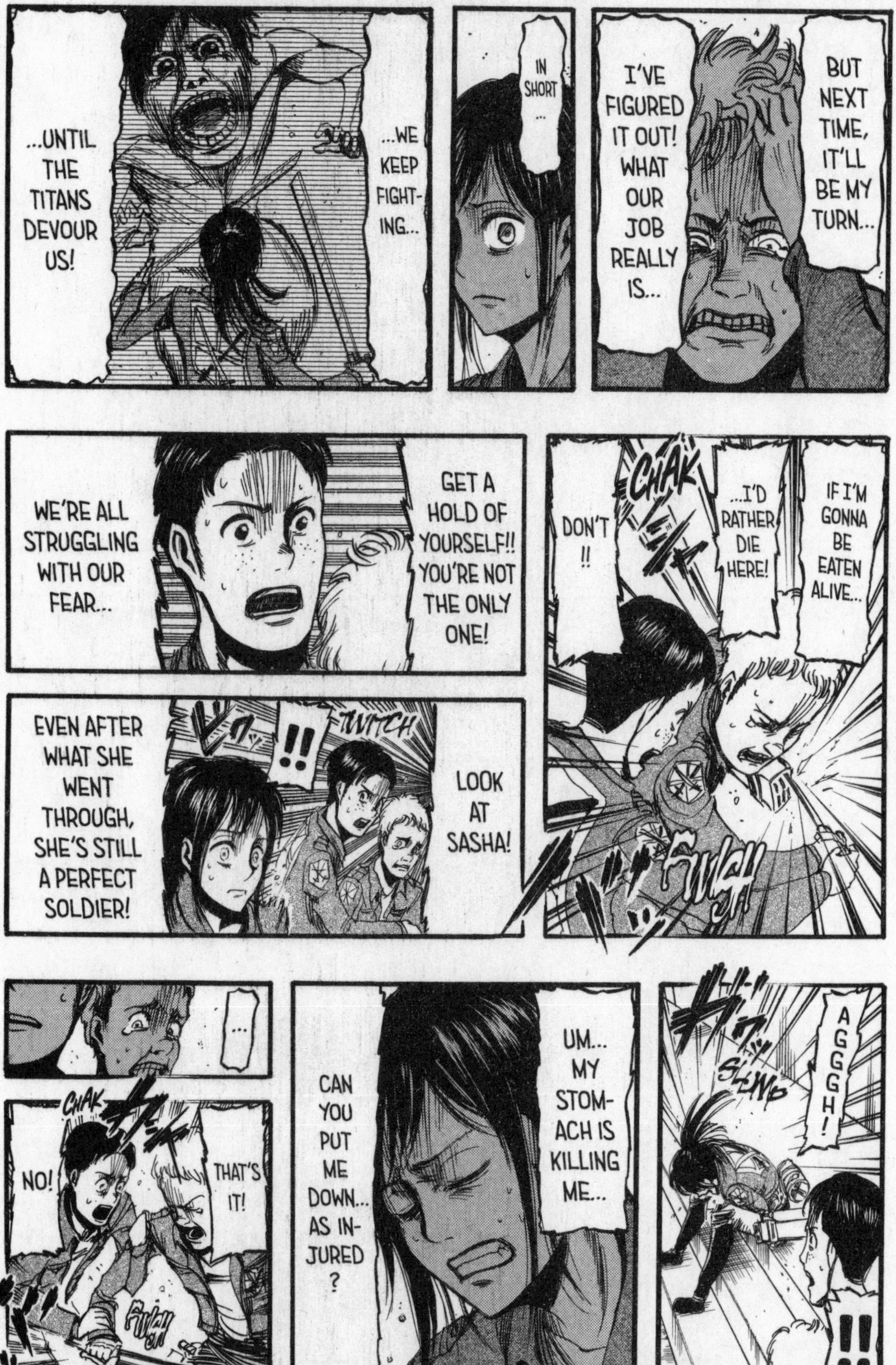
BUT NEXT TIME, IT'LL BE MY TURN...
I'VE FIGURED IT OUT! WHAT OUR JOB REALLY IS...
IN SHORT ...
...WE KEEP FIGHTING...
...UNTIL THE TITANS DEVOUR US!
IF I'M GONNA BE EATEN ALIVE...
...I'D RATHER DIE HERE!
CHAK
DON'T !!
FWISH
GET A HOLD OF YOURSELF!! YOU'RE NOT THE ONLY ONE!
WE'RE ALL STRUGGLING WITH OUR FEAR...
TWITCH
!!
LOOK AT SASHA!
EVEN AFTER WHAT SHE WENT THROUGH, SHE'S STILL A PERFECT SOLDIER!
AGGGH!
SLUMP
!!
UM... MY STOMACH IS KILLING ME...
CAN YOU PUT ME DOWN... AS INJURED?
...
CHAK
THAT'S IT!
NO!
FWISH

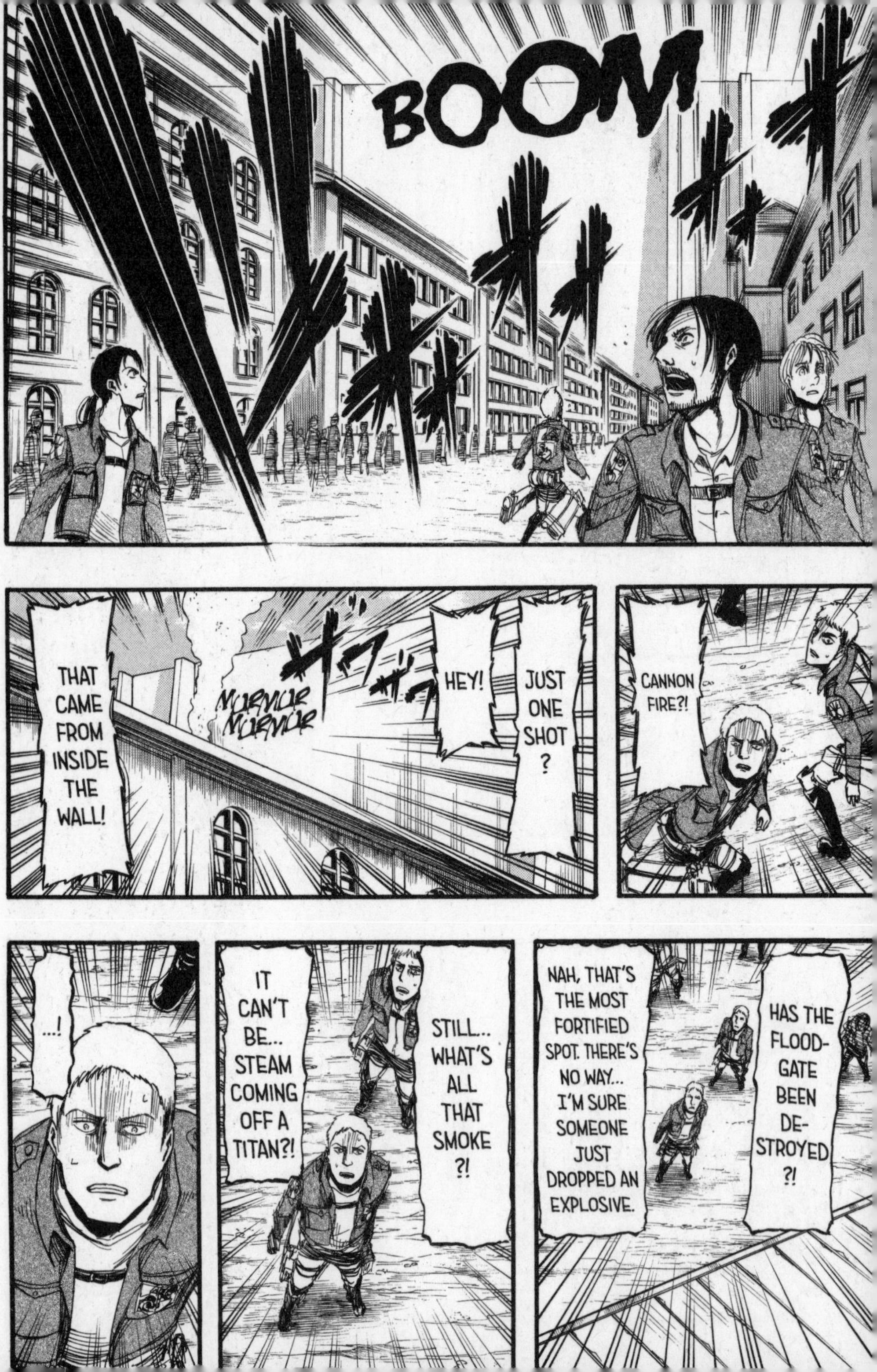
BOOM
CANNON FIRE?!
JUST ONE SHOT ?
HEY!
MURMUR MURMUR
THAT CAME FROM INSIDE THE WALL!
HAS THE FLOOD-GATE BEEN DE-STROYED ?!
NAH, THAT'S THE MOST FORTIFIED SPOT. THERE'S NO WAY... I'M SURE SOMEONE JUST DROPPED AN EXPLOSIVE.
STILL... WHAT'S ALL THAT SMOKE ?!
IT CAN'T BE... STEAM COMING OFF A TITAN?!
...!

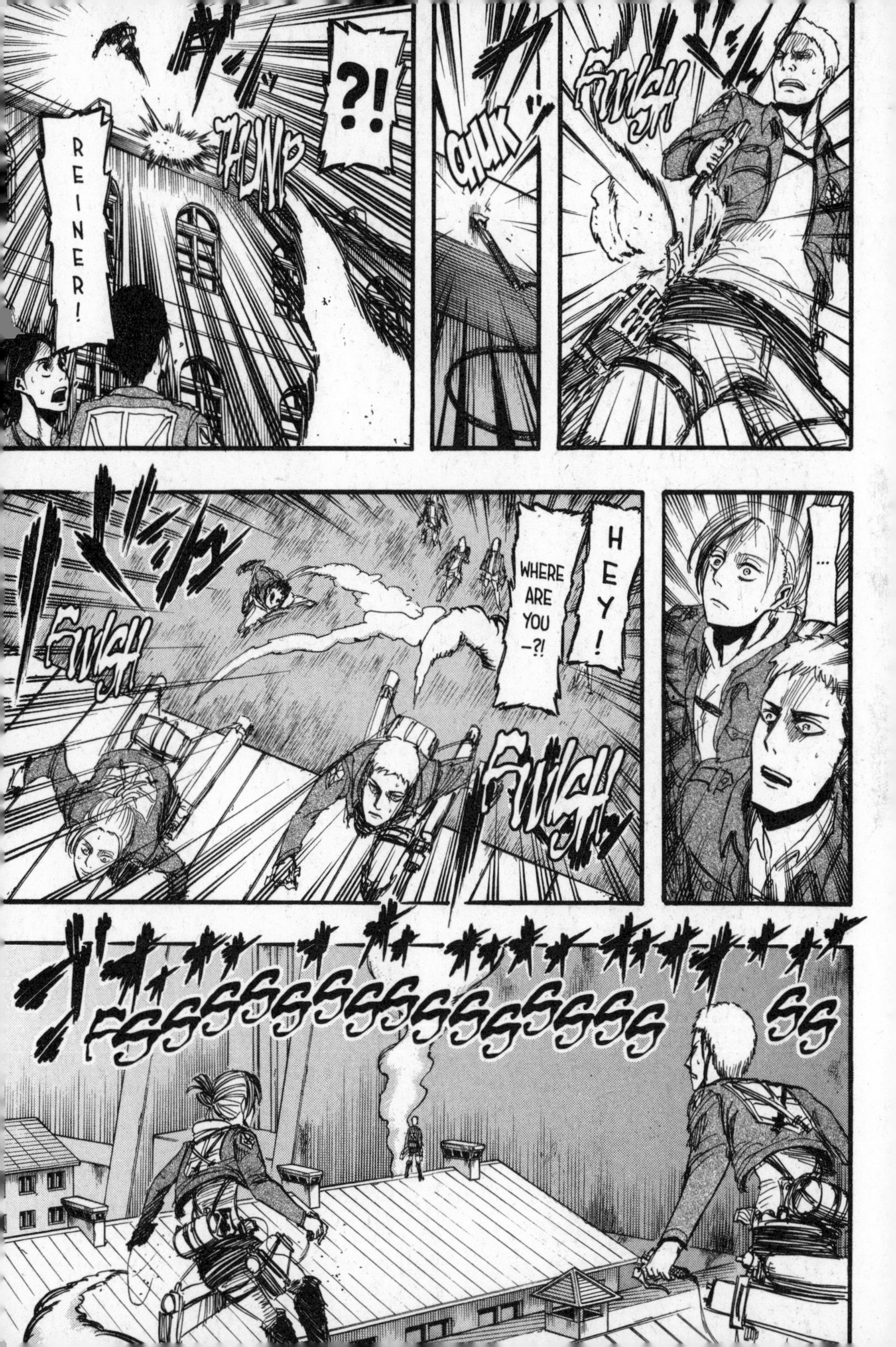

FWISH
CHUK
?!
THWP
REINER!
...
HEY!
WHERE ARE YOU—?!
FWISH
FWISH
FSSSSSSSSSSSSSSS SS

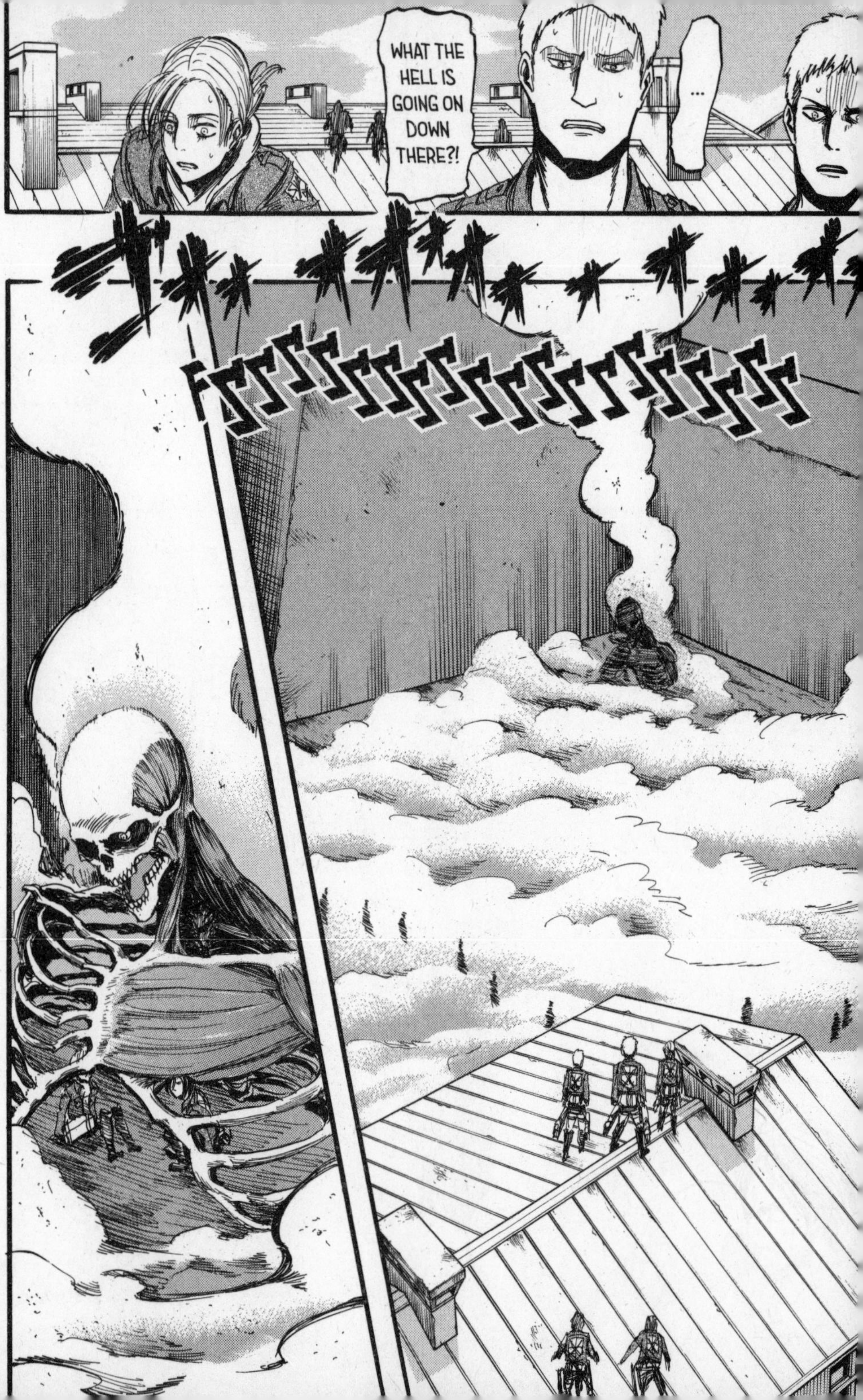
...
WHAT THE HELL IS GOING ON DOWN THERE?!
FSSSSSSSSSSSSSSSSSS

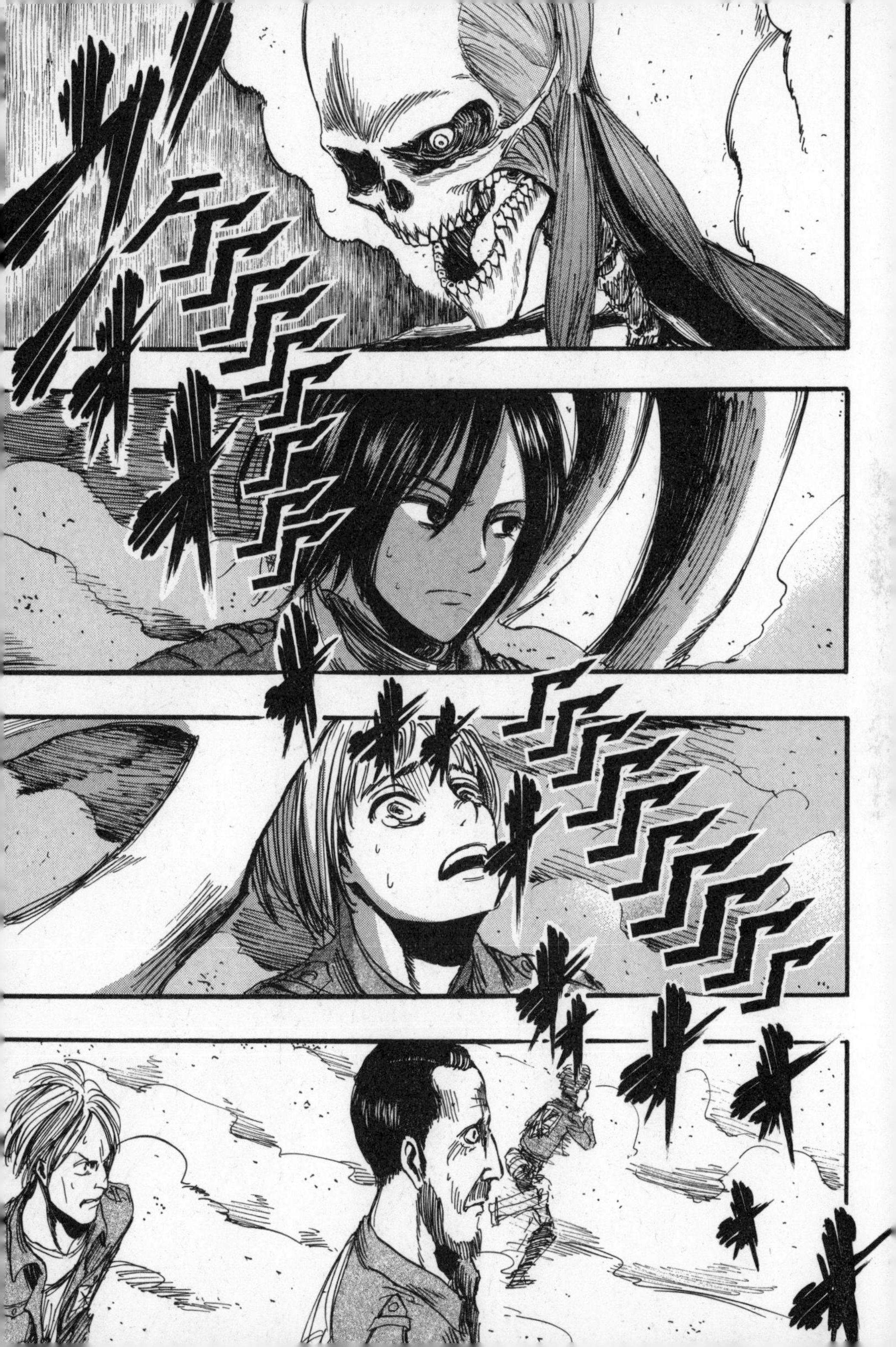

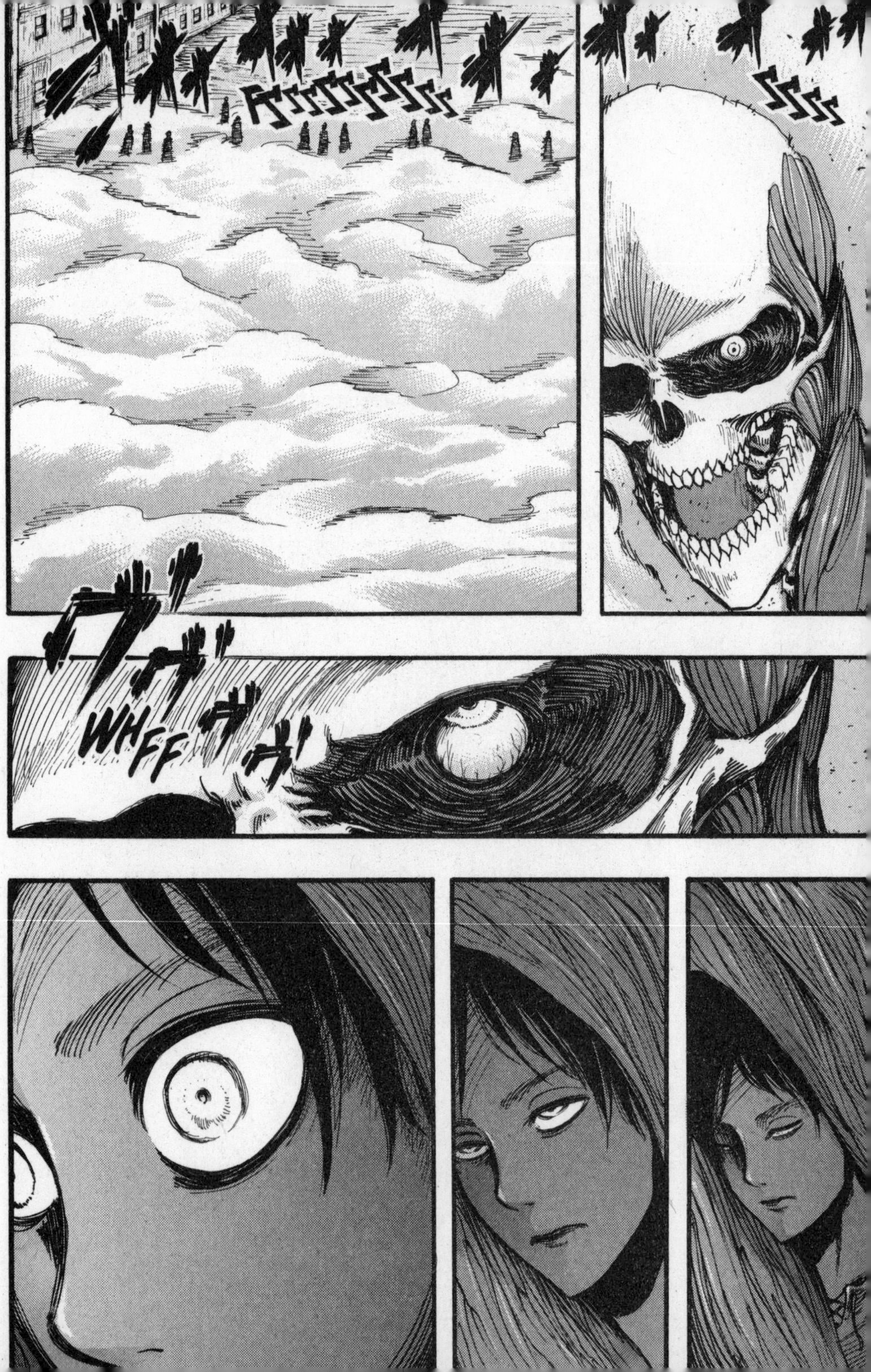
SSSS
FSSSSSSSSS
WHFF

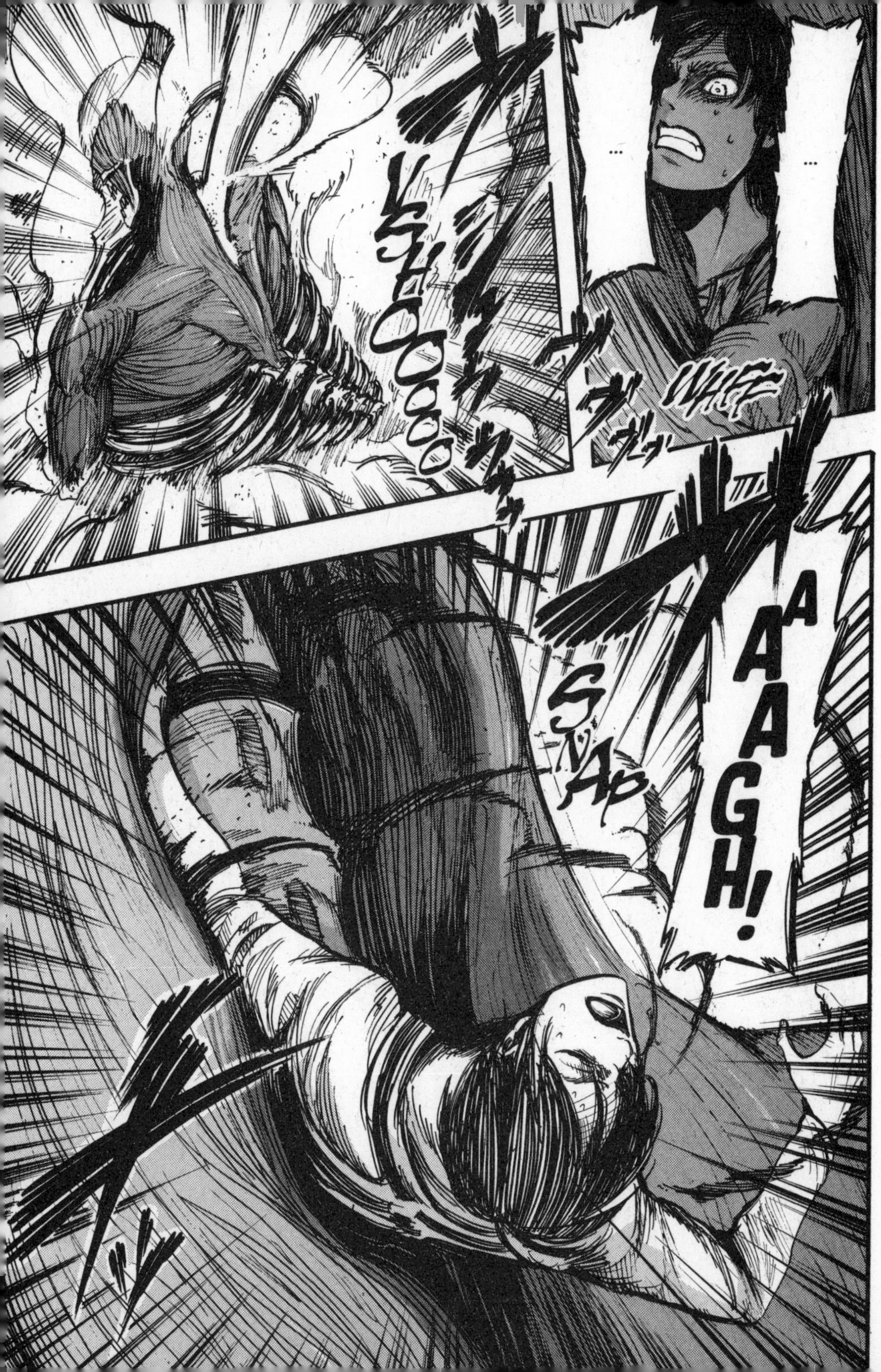

...
...
WHIFF
KSHOOOOOO
AAAAGH!
SNAP

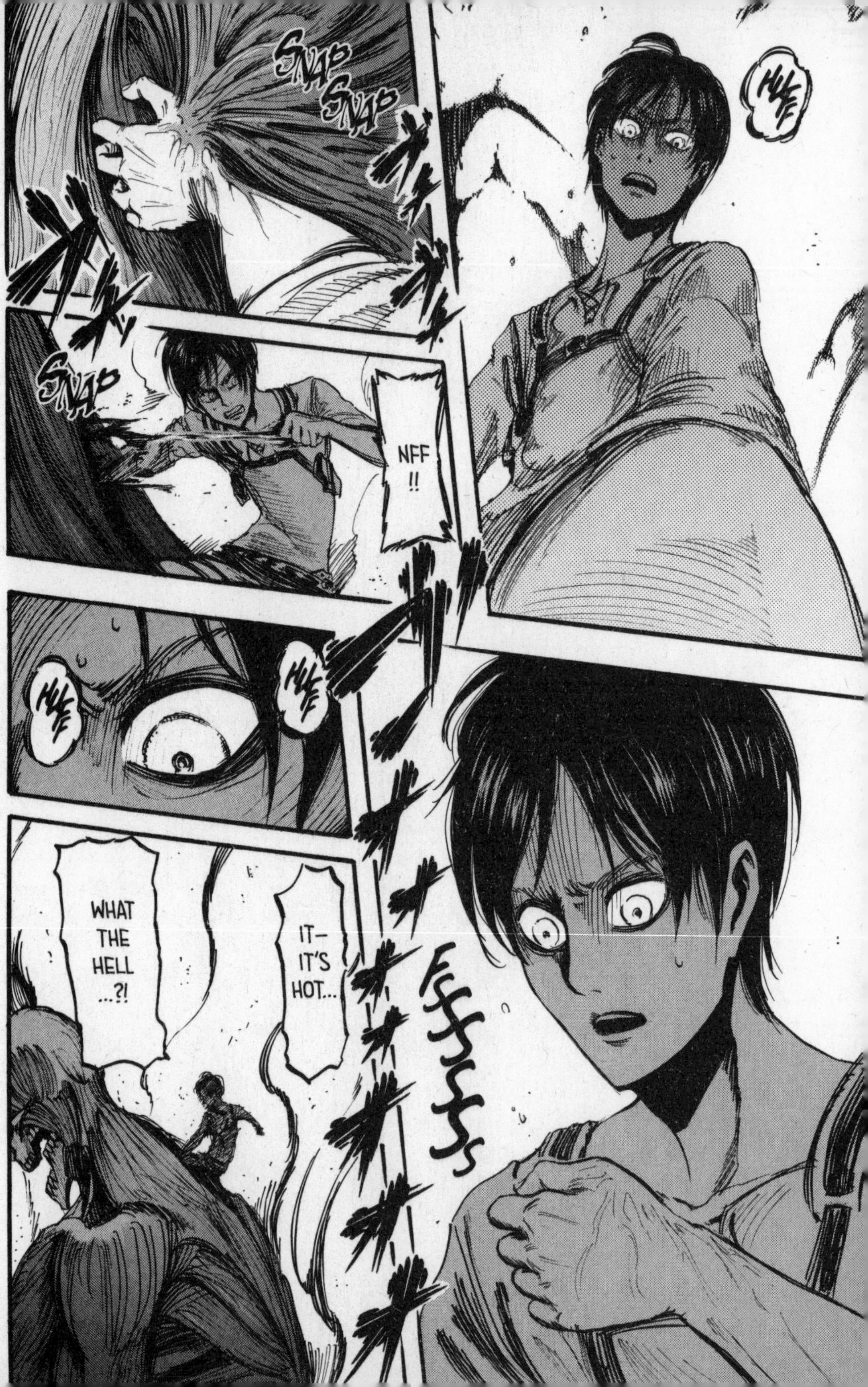
SNAP SNAP
SNAP
NFF !!
IT— IT'S HOT...
WHAT THE HELL ...?!

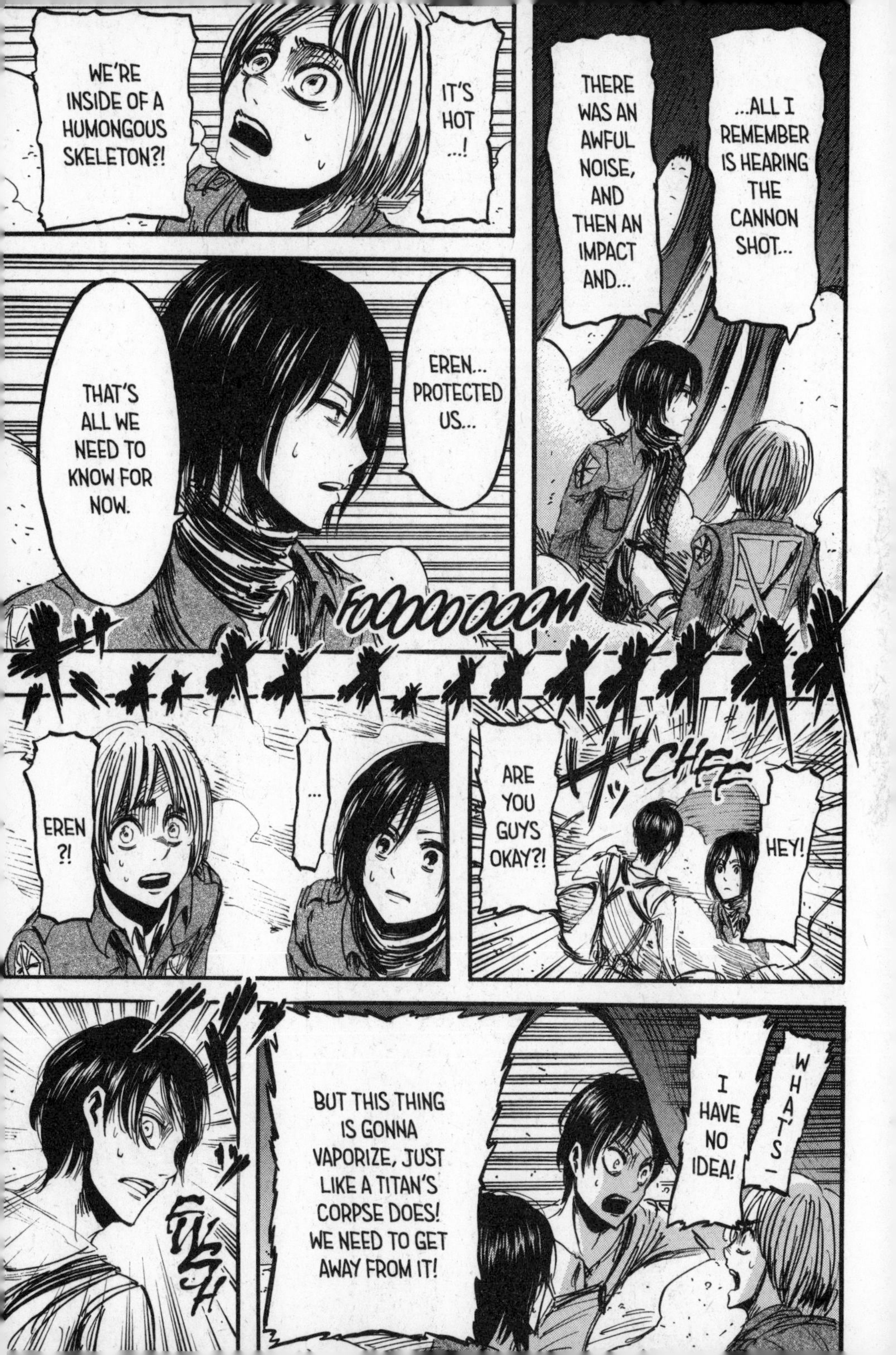
...ALL I REMEMBER IS HEARING THE CANNON SHOT...
THERE WAS AN AWFUL NOISE, AND THEN AN IMPACT AND...
IT'S HOT ...!
WE'RE INSIDE OF A HUMONGOUS SKELETON?!
EREN... PROTECTED US...
THAT'S ALL WE NEED TO KNOW FOR NOW.
FOOOOOOOOM
HEY!
CHFF
ARE YOU GUYS OKAY?!
...
EREN ?!
WHAT'S—
I HAVE NO IDEA!
BUT THIS THING IS GONNA VAPORIZE, JUST LIKE A TITAN'S CORPSE DOES! WE NEED TO GET AWAY FROM IT!
FWSH

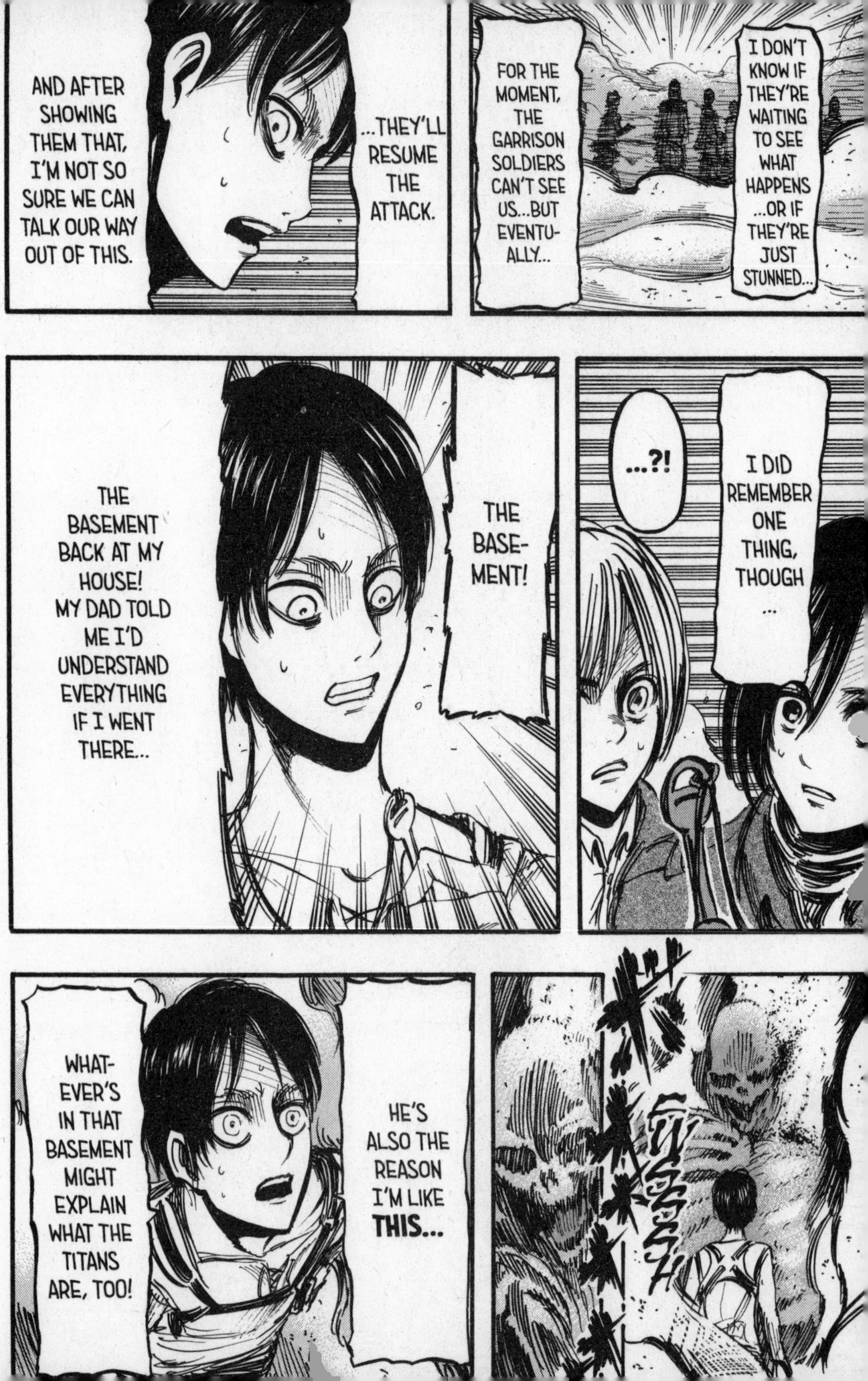
I DON'T KNOW IF THEY'RE WAITING TO SEE WHAT HAPPENS ...OR IF THEY'RE JUST STUNNED...
FOR THE MOMENT, THE GARRISON SOLDIERS CAN'T SEE US...BUT EVENTUALLY...
...THEY'LL RESUME THE ATTACK.
AND AFTER SHOWING THEM THAT, I'M NOT SO SURE WE CAN TALK OUR WAY OUT OF THIS.
I DID REMEMBER ONE THING, THOUGH ...
...?!
THE BASEMENT!
THE BASEMENT BACK AT MY HOUSE! MY DAD TOLD ME I'D UNDERSTAND EVERYTHING IF I WENT THERE...
HE'S ALSO THE REASON I'M LIKE **THIS...**
WHATEVER'S IN THAT BASEMENT MIGHT EXPLAIN WHAT THE TITANS ARE, TOO!

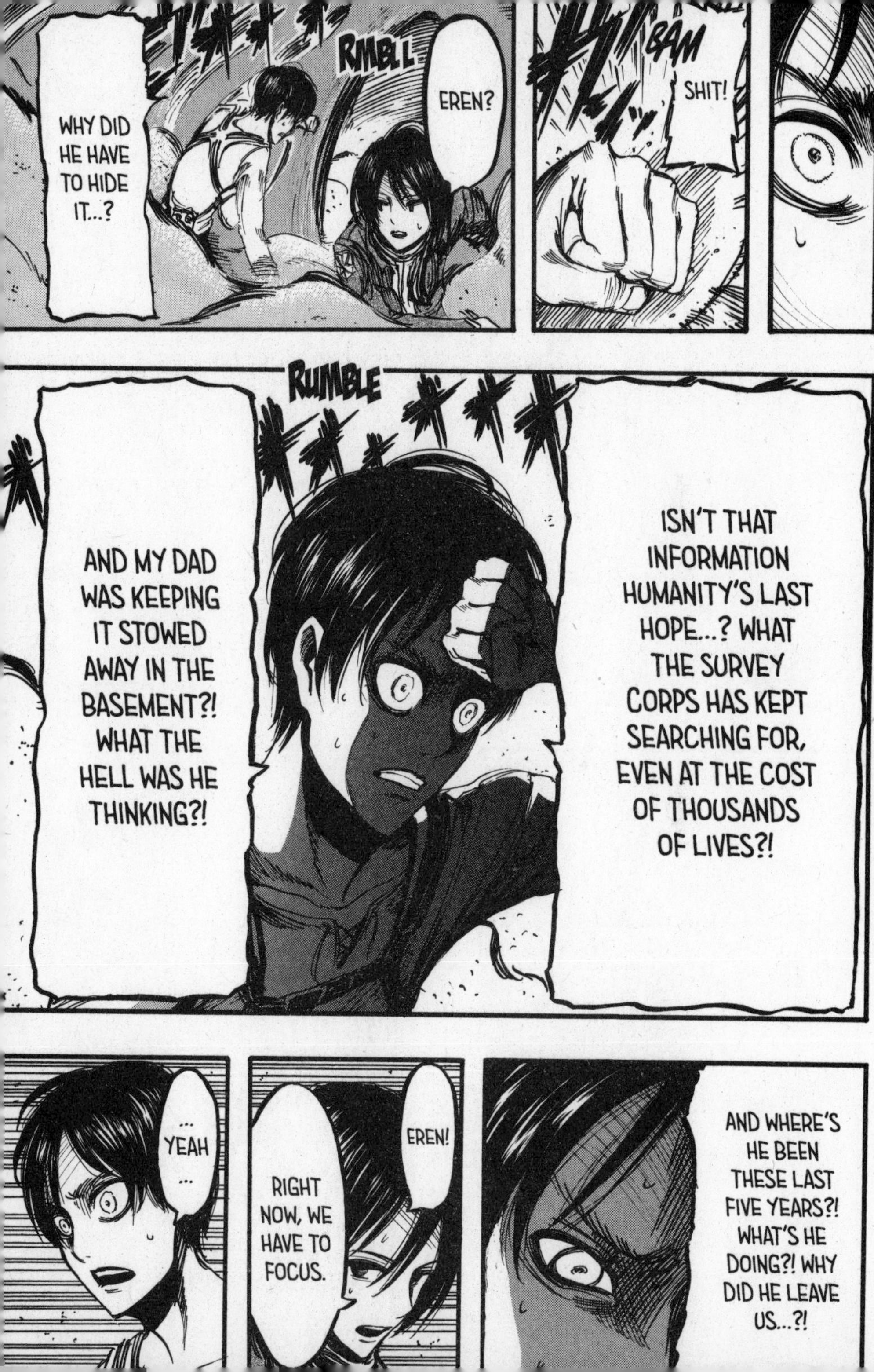
BAM
SHIT!
RMBLL
EREN?
WHY DID HE HAVE TO HIDE IT...?
RUMBLE
ISN'T THAT INFORMATION HUMANITY'S LAST HOPE...? WHAT THE SURVEY CORPS HAS KEPT SEARCHING FOR, EVEN AT THE COST OF THOUSANDS OF LIVES?!
AND MY DAD WAS KEEPING IT STOWED AWAY IN THE BASEMENT?! WHAT THE HELL WAS HE THINKING?!
AND WHERE'S HE BEEN THESE LAST FIVE YEARS?! WHAT'S HE DOING?! WHY DID HE LEAVE US...?!
EREN!
RIGHT NOW, WE HAVE TO FOCUS.
... YEAH ...

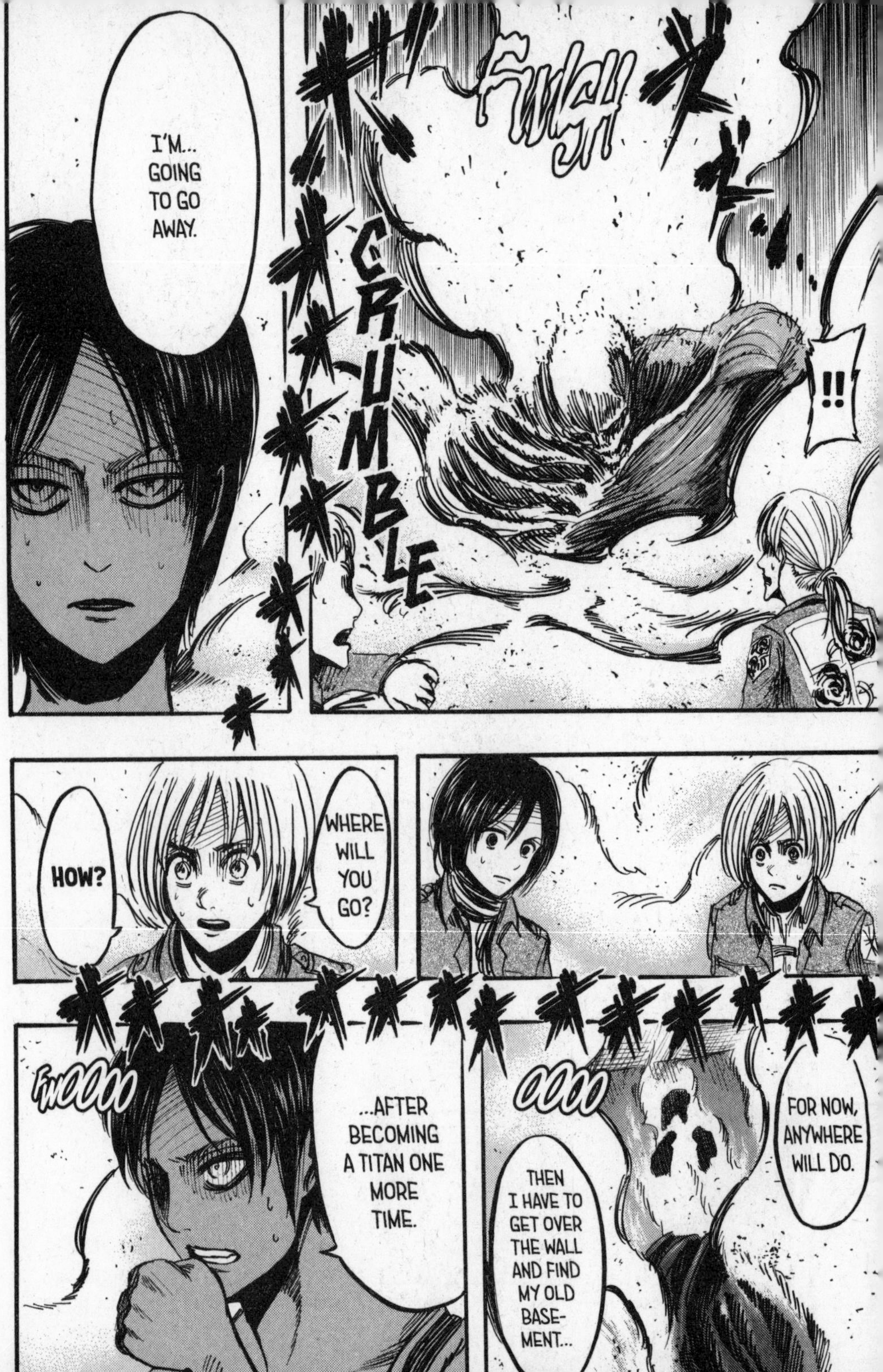
CRUMBLE
!!
I'M... GOING TO GO AWAY.
WHERE WILL YOU GO?
HOW?
FOR NOW, ANYWHERE WILL DO.
THEN I HAVE TO GET OVER THE WALL AND FIND MY OLD BASEMENT...
OOOO
FWOOOO
...AFTER BECOMING A TITAN ONE MORE TIME.

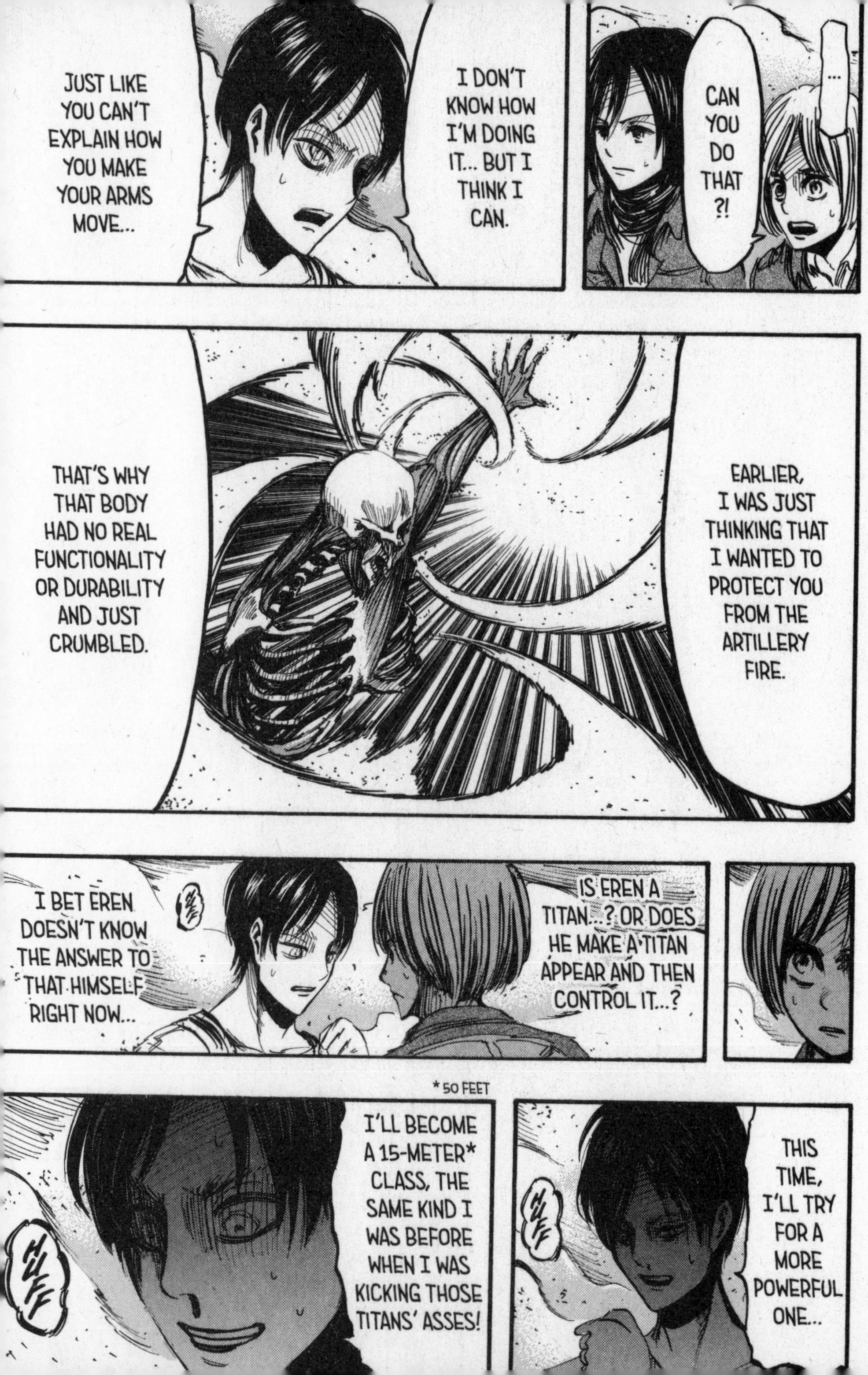
...
CAN YOU DO THAT?!
I DON'T KNOW HOW I'M DOING IT... BUT I THINK I CAN.
JUST LIKE YOU CAN'T EXPLAIN HOW YOU MAKE YOUR ARMS MOVE...
EARLIER, I WAS JUST THINKING THAT I WANTED TO PROTECT YOU FROM THE ARTILLERY FIRE.
THAT'S WHY THAT BODY HAD NO REAL FUNCTIONALITY OR DURABILITY AND JUST CRUMBLED.
IS EREN A TITAN...? OR DOES HE MAKE A TITAN APPEAR AND THEN CONTROL IT...?
I BET EREN DOESN'T KNOW THE ANSWER TO THAT HIMSELF RIGHT NOW...
HUFF
THIS TIME, I'LL TRY FOR A MORE POWERFUL ONE...
I'LL BECOME A 15-METER* CLASS, THE SAME KIND I WAS BEFORE WHEN I WAS KICKING THOSE TITANS' ASSES!
HUFF
* 50 FEET

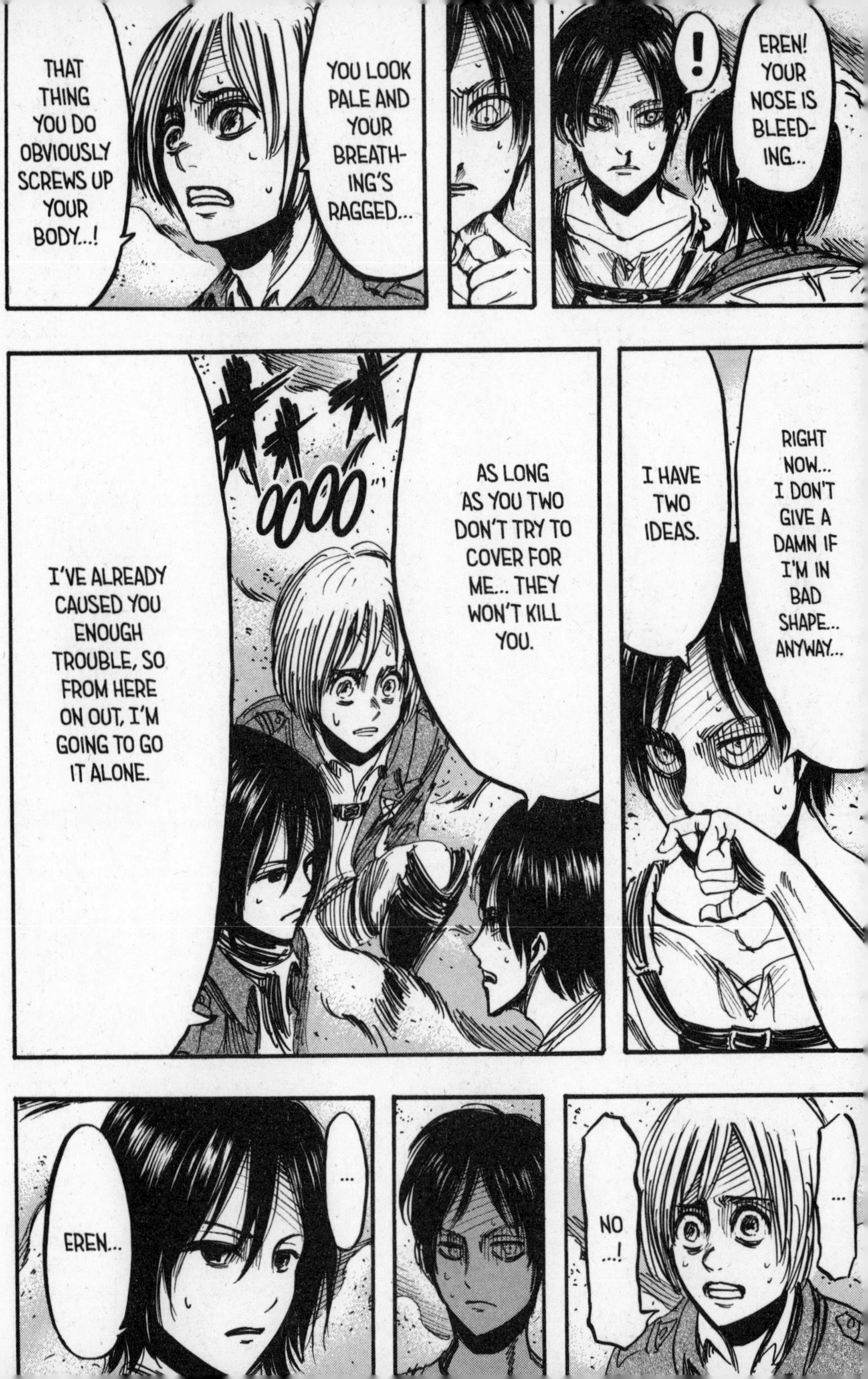
!
EREN! YOUR NOSE IS BLEEDING...
YOU LOOK PALE AND YOUR BREATHING'S RAGGED...
THAT THING YOU DO OBVIOUSLY SCREWS UP YOUR BODY...!
RIGHT NOW... I DON'T GIVE A DAMN IF I'M IN BAD SHAPE... ANYWAY...
I HAVE TWO IDEAS.
AS LONG AS YOU TWO DON'T TRY TO COVER FOR ME... THEY WON'T KILL YOU.
I'VE ALREADY CAUSED YOU ENOUGH TROUBLE, SO FROM HERE ON OUT, I'M GOING TO GO IT ALONE.
...
NO ...!
...
EREN...

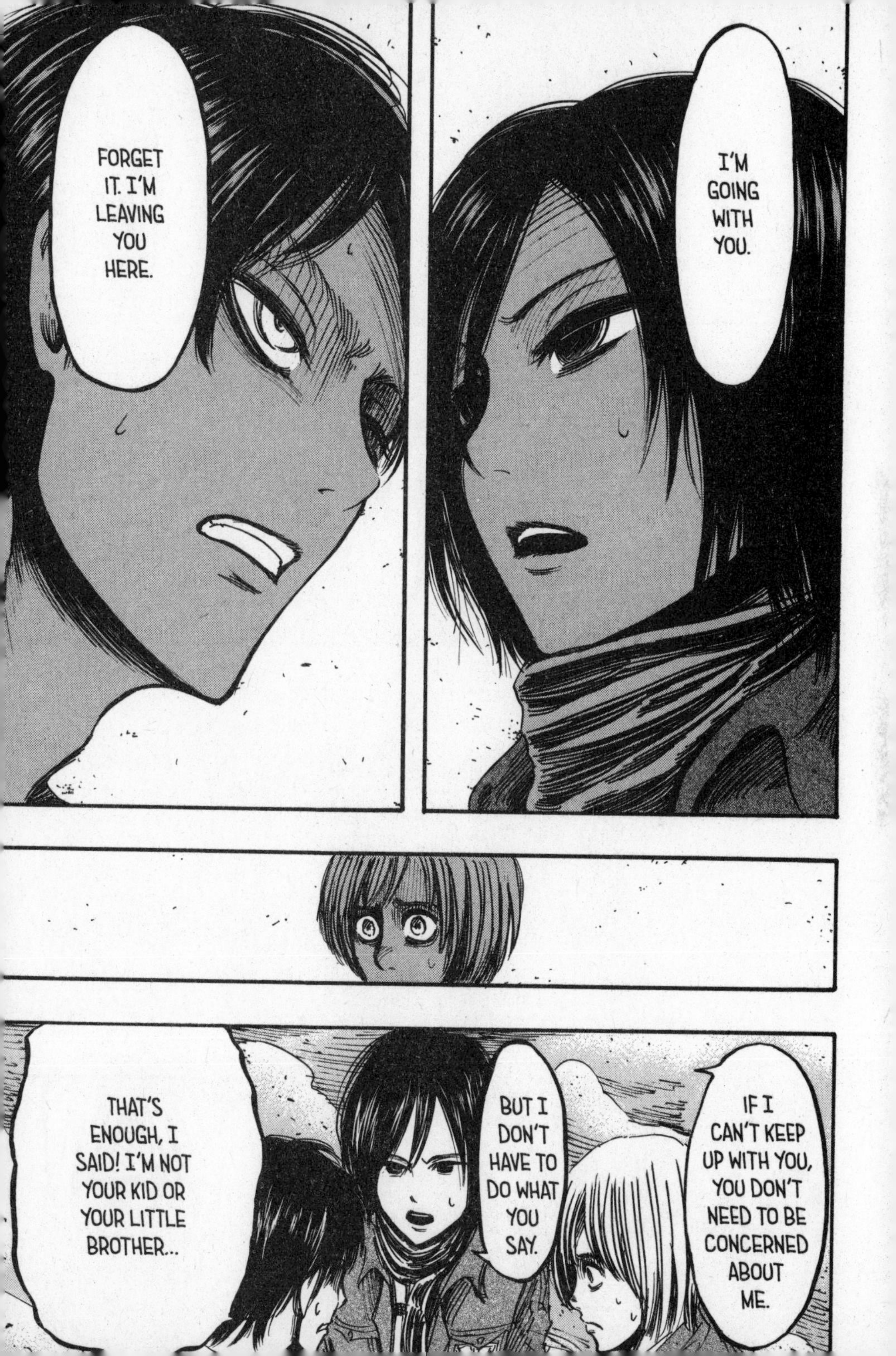
I'M GOING WITH YOU.
FORGET IT. I'M LEAVING YOU HERE.
IF I CAN'T KEEP UP WITH YOU, YOU DON'T NEED TO BE CONCERNED ABOUT ME.
BUT I DON'T HAVE TO DO WHAT YOU SAY.
THAT'S ENOUGH, I SAID! I'M NOT YOUR KID OR YOUR LITTLE BROTHER...

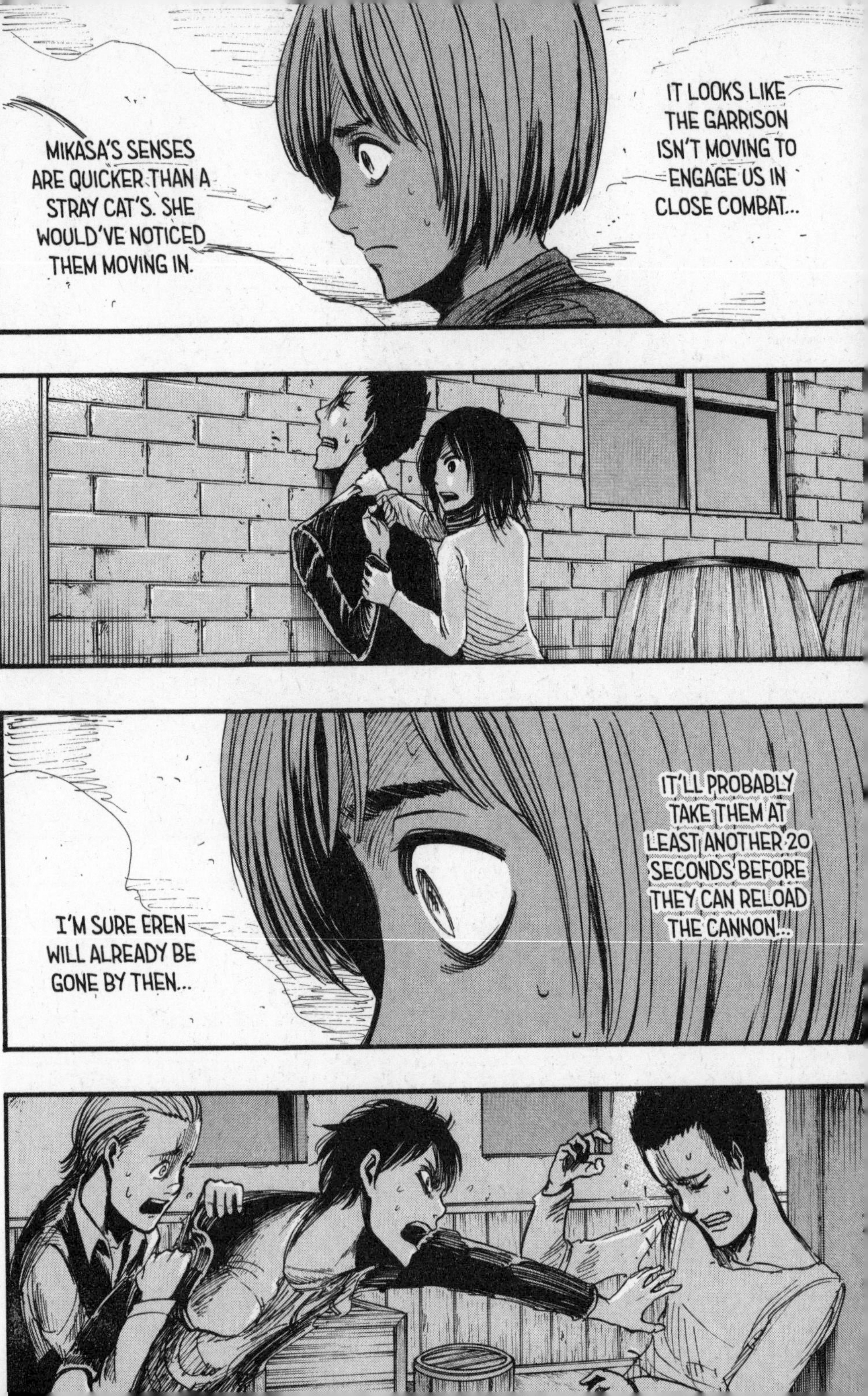
IT LOOKS LIKE THE GARRISON ISN'T MOVING TO ENGAGE US IN CLOSE COMBAT...
MIKASA'S SENSES ARE QUICKER THAN A STRAY CAT'S. SHE WOULD'VE NOTICED THEM MOVING IN.
IT'LL PROBABLY TAKE THEM AT LEAST ANOTHER 20 SECONDS BEFORE THEY CAN RELOAD THE CANNON...
I'M SURE EREN WILL ALREADY BE GONE BY THEN...

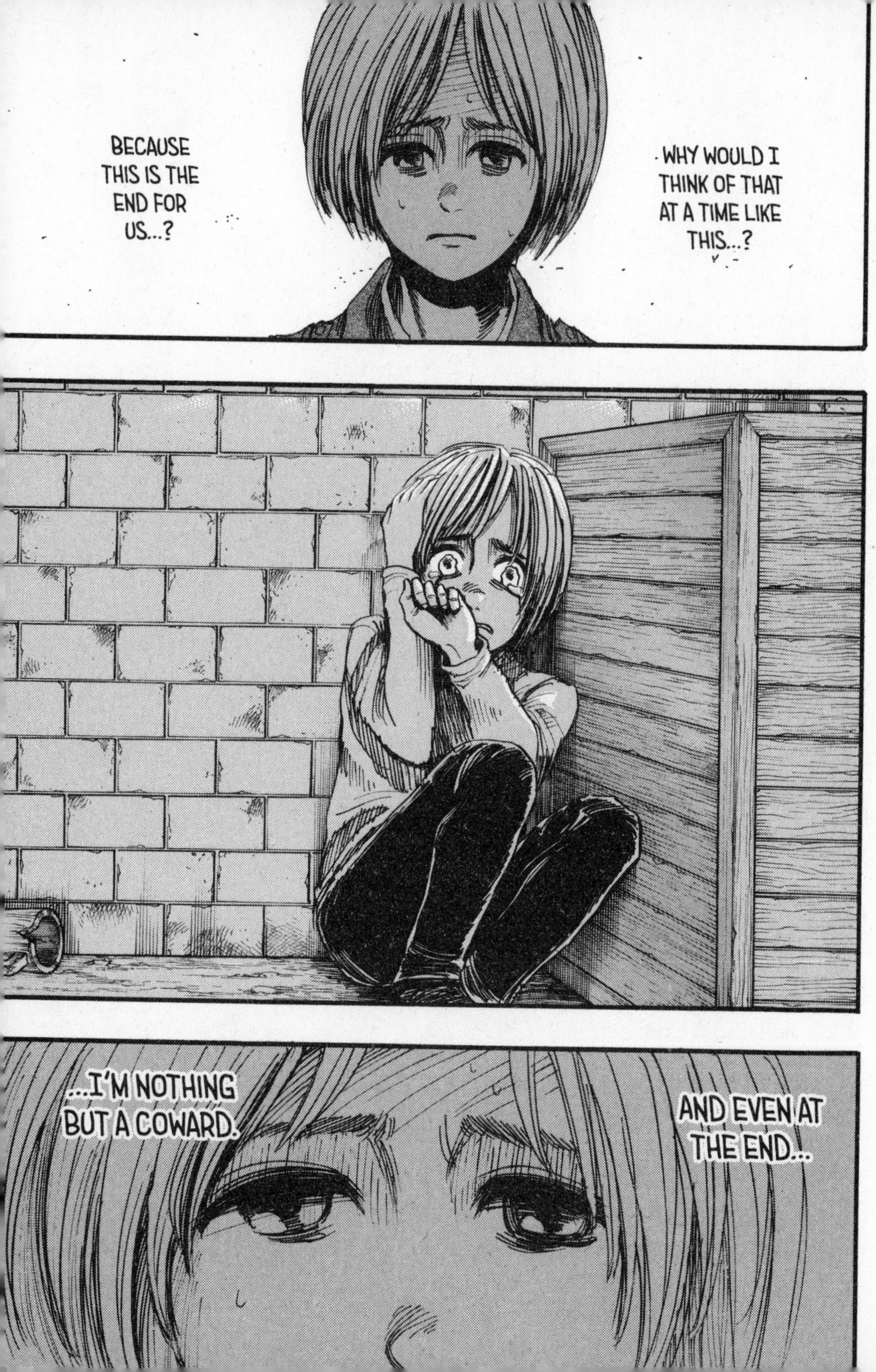
WHY WOULD I THINK OF THAT AT A TIME LIKE THIS...?
BECAUSE THIS IS THE END FOR US...?
AND EVEN AT THE END...
...I'M NOTHING BUT A COWARD.

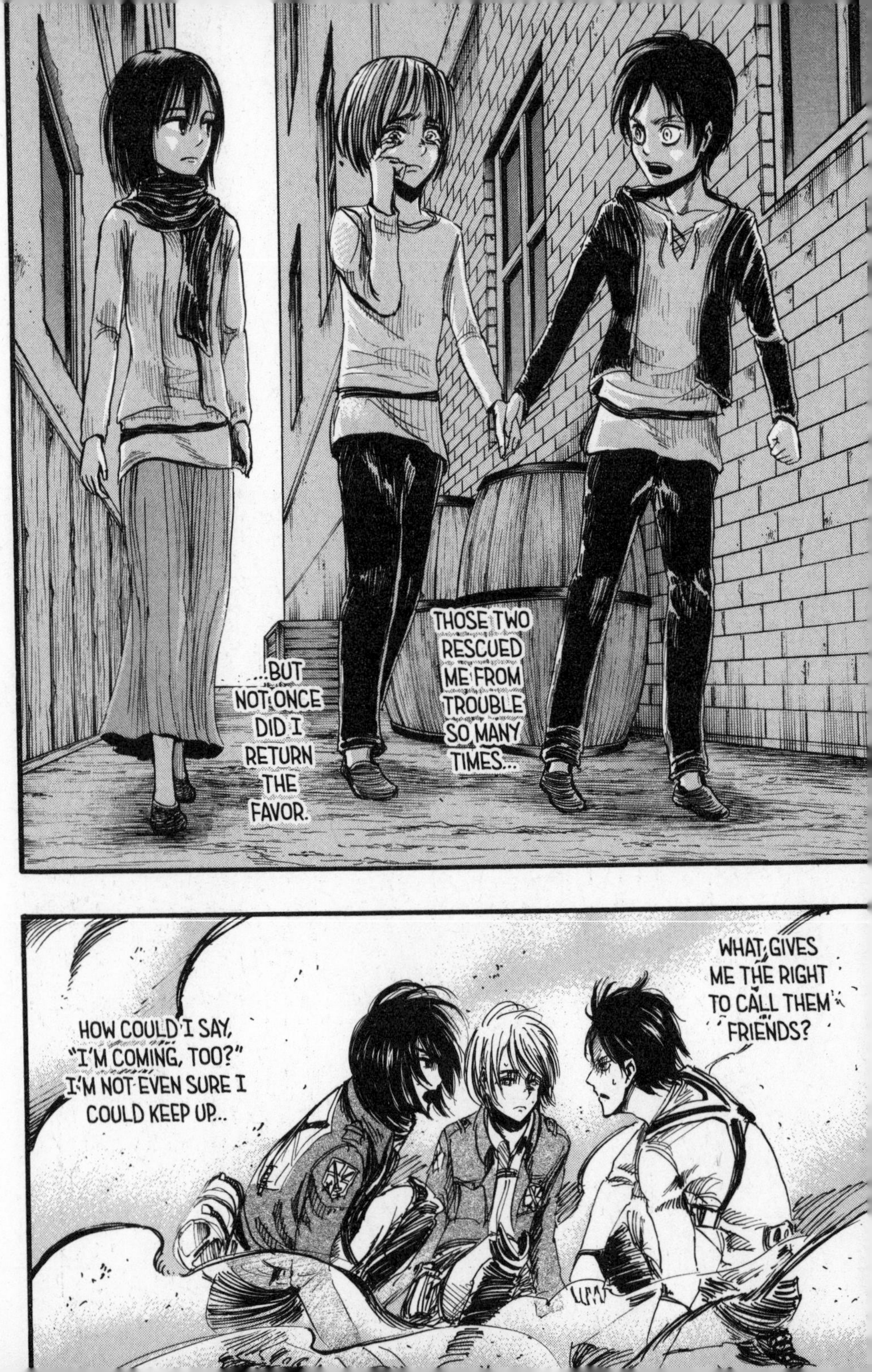
THOSE TWO RESCUED ME FROM TROUBLE SO MANY TIMES...
...BUT NOT ONCE DID I RETURN THE FAVOR.
WHAT GIVES ME THE RIGHT TO CALL THEM FRIENDS?
HOW COULD I SAY, "I'M COMING, TOO?" I'M NOT EVEN SURE I COULD KEEP UP...

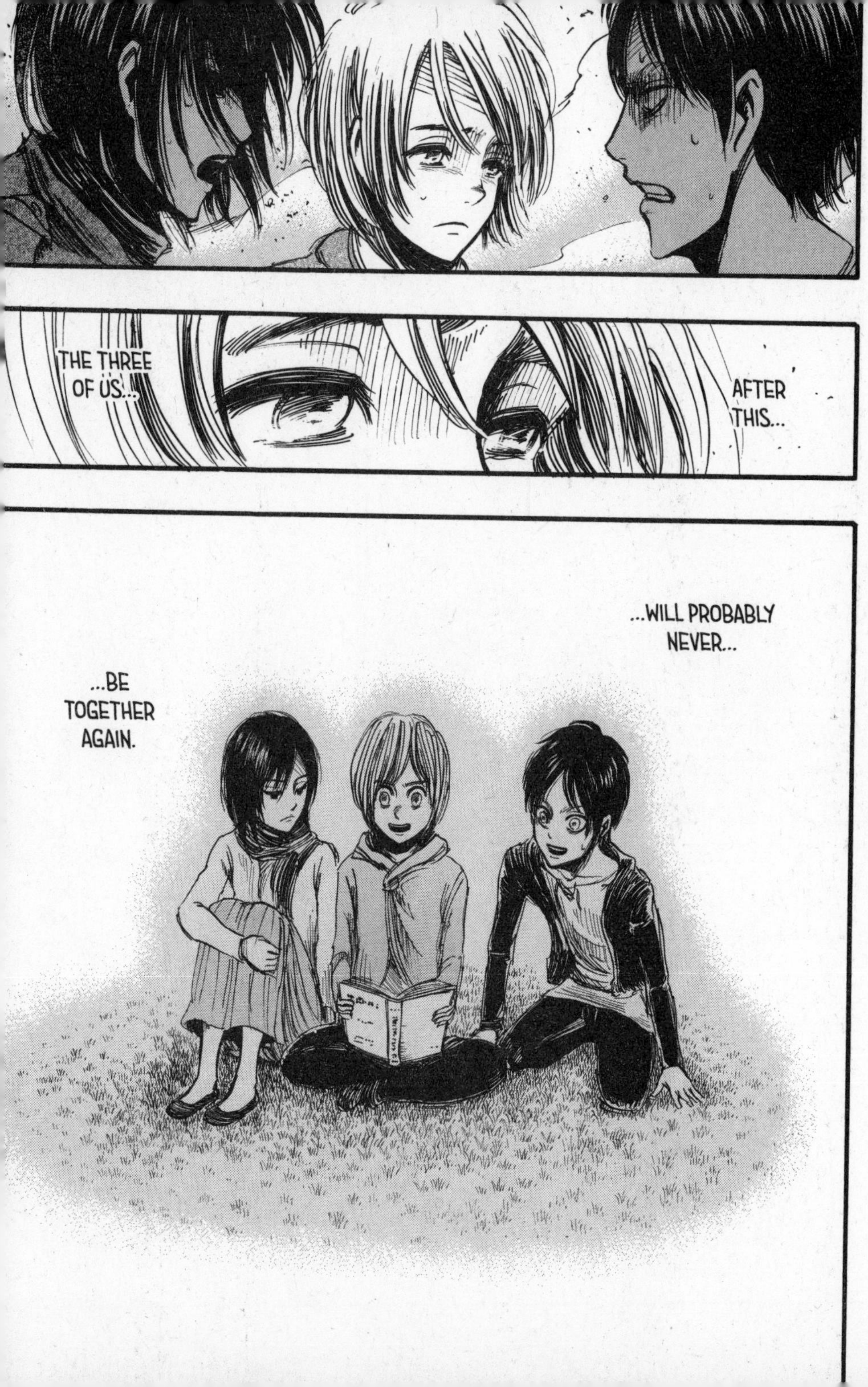
AFTER THIS...
THE THREE OF US...
...WILL PROBABLY NEVER...
...BE TOGETHER AGAIN.

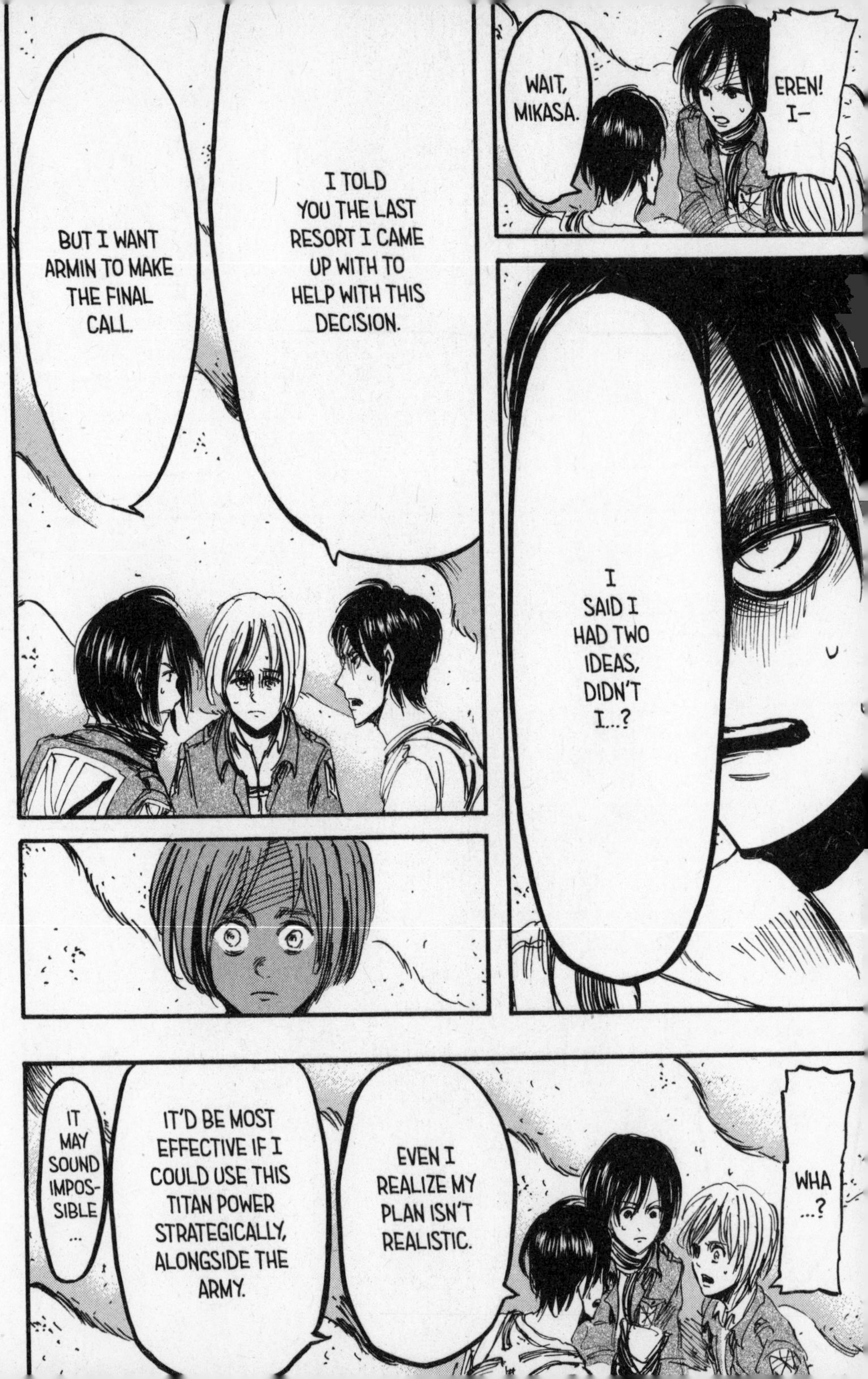
EREN! I—
WAIT, MIKASA.
I SAID I HAD TWO IDEAS, DIDN'T I...?
I TOLD YOU THE LAST RESORT I CAME UP WITH TO HELP WITH THIS DECISION.
BUT I WANT ARMIN TO MAKE THE FINAL CALL.
WHA ...?
EVEN I REALIZE MY PLAN ISN'T REALISTIC.
IT'D BE MOST EFFECTIVE IF I COULD USE THIS TITAN POWER STRATEGICALLY, ALONGSIDE THE ARMY.
IT MAY SOUND IMPOS-SIBLE ...

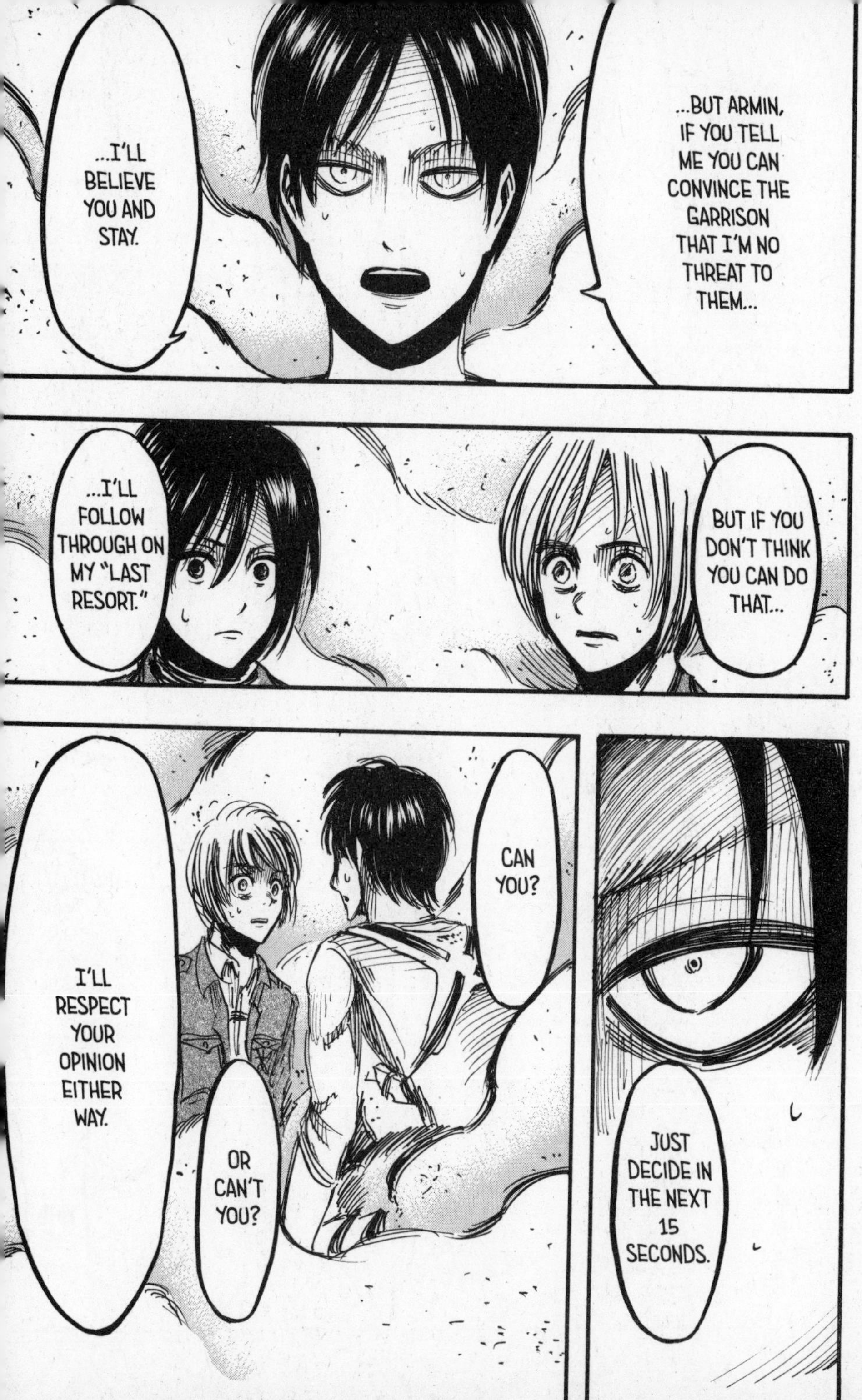
...BUT ARMIN, IF YOU TELL ME YOU CAN CONVINCE THE GARRISON THAT I'M NO THREAT TO THEM...
...I'LL BELIEVE YOU AND STAY.
BUT IF YOU DON'T THINK YOU CAN DO THAT...
...I'LL FOLLOW THROUGH ON MY "LAST RESORT."
JUST DECIDE IN THE NEXT 15 SECONDS.
CAN YOU?
OR CAN'T YOU?
I'LL RESPECT YOUR OPINION EITHER WAY.

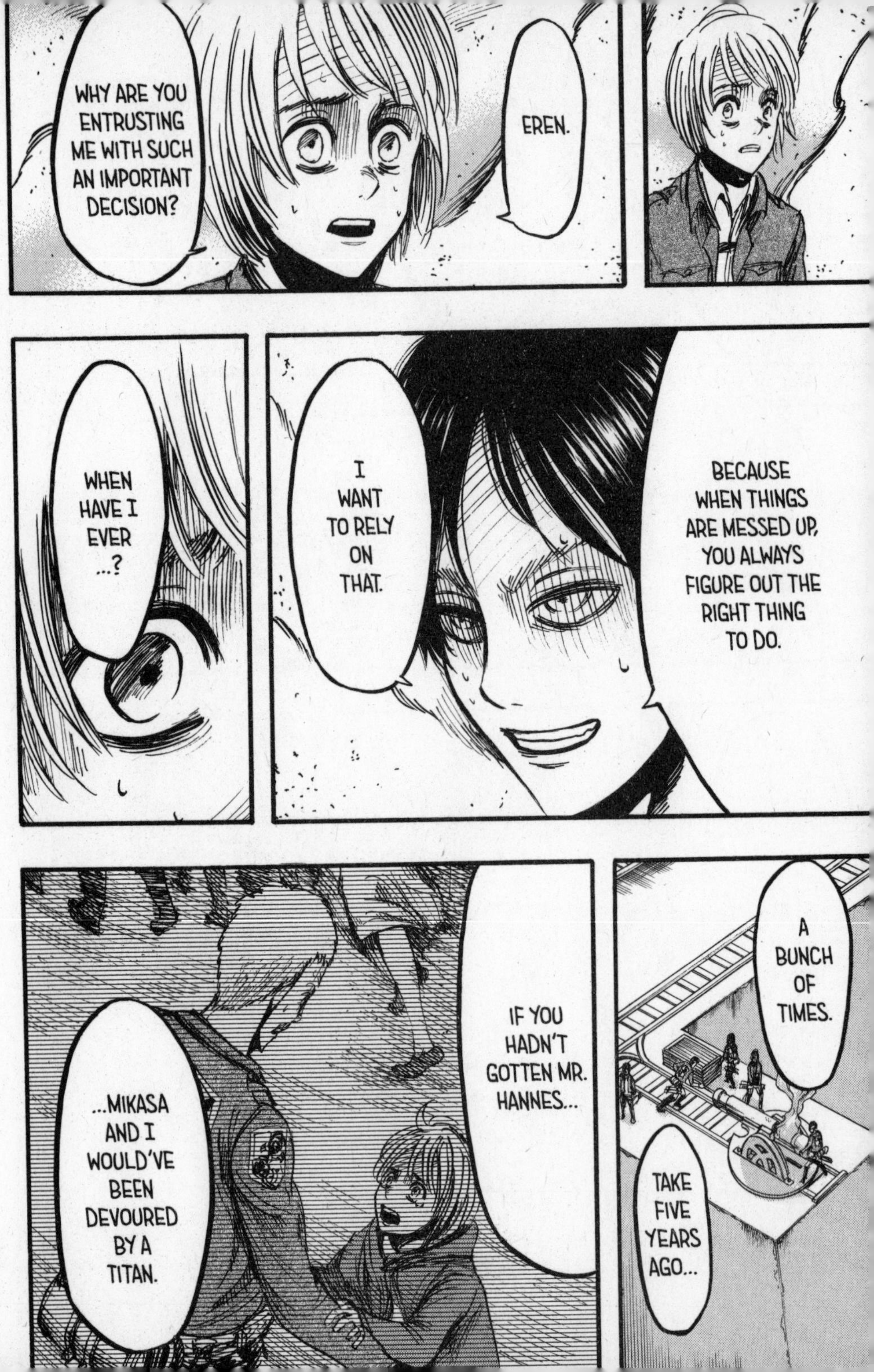
EREN.
WHY ARE YOU ENTRUSTING ME WITH SUCH AN IMPORTANT DECISION?
BECAUSE WHEN THINGS ARE MESSED UP, YOU ALWAYS FIGURE OUT THE RIGHT THING TO DO.
I WANT TO RELY ON THAT.
WHEN HAVE I EVER ...?
A BUNCH OF TIMES.
TAKE FIVE YEARS AGO...
IF YOU HADN'T GOTTEN MR. HANNES...
...MIKASA AND I WOULD'VE BEEN DEVOURED BY A TITAN.

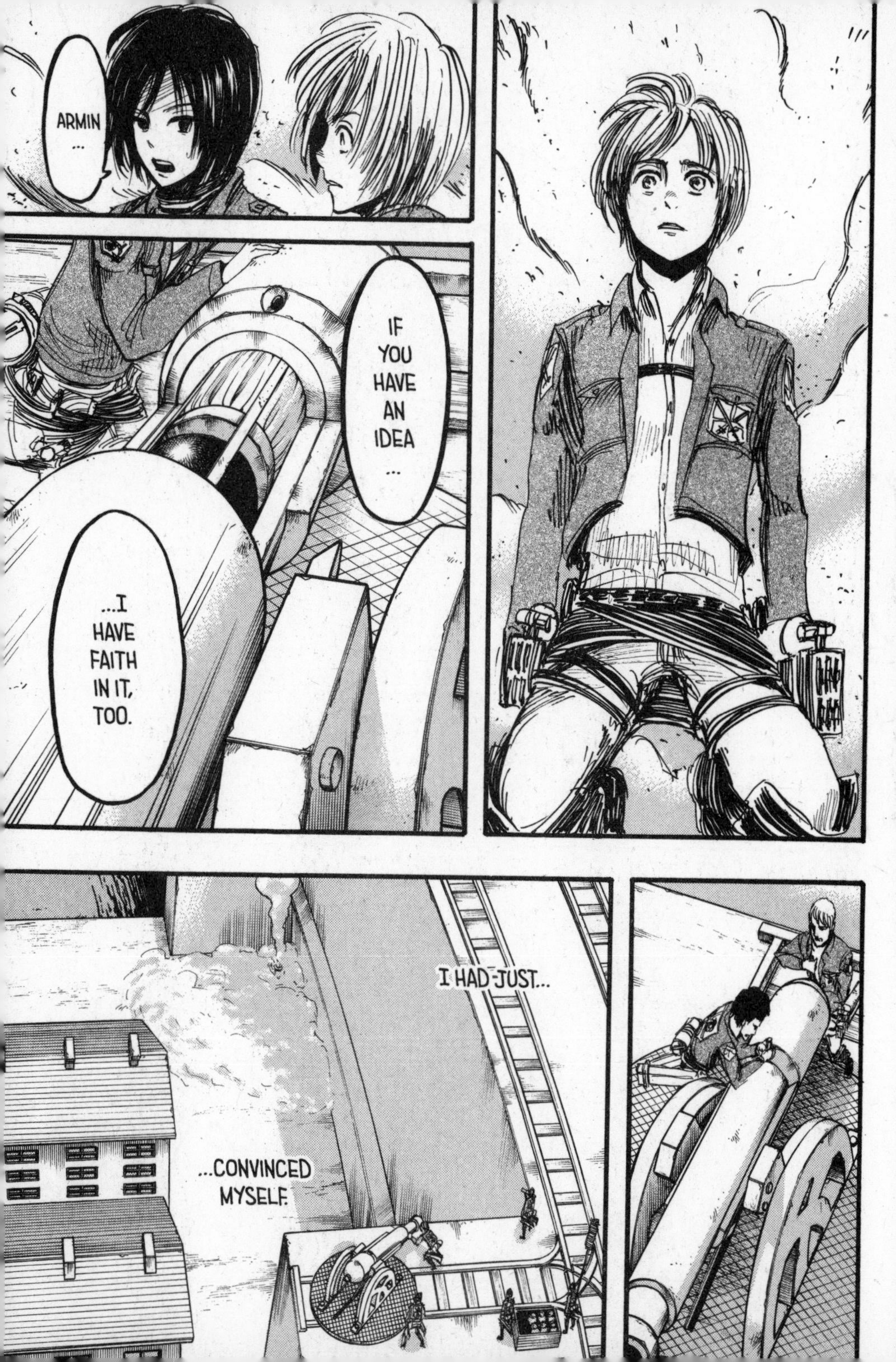
ARMIN ...
IF YOU HAVE AN IDEA ...
...I HAVE FAITH IN IT, TOO.
I HAD JUST...
...CONVINCED MYSELF.

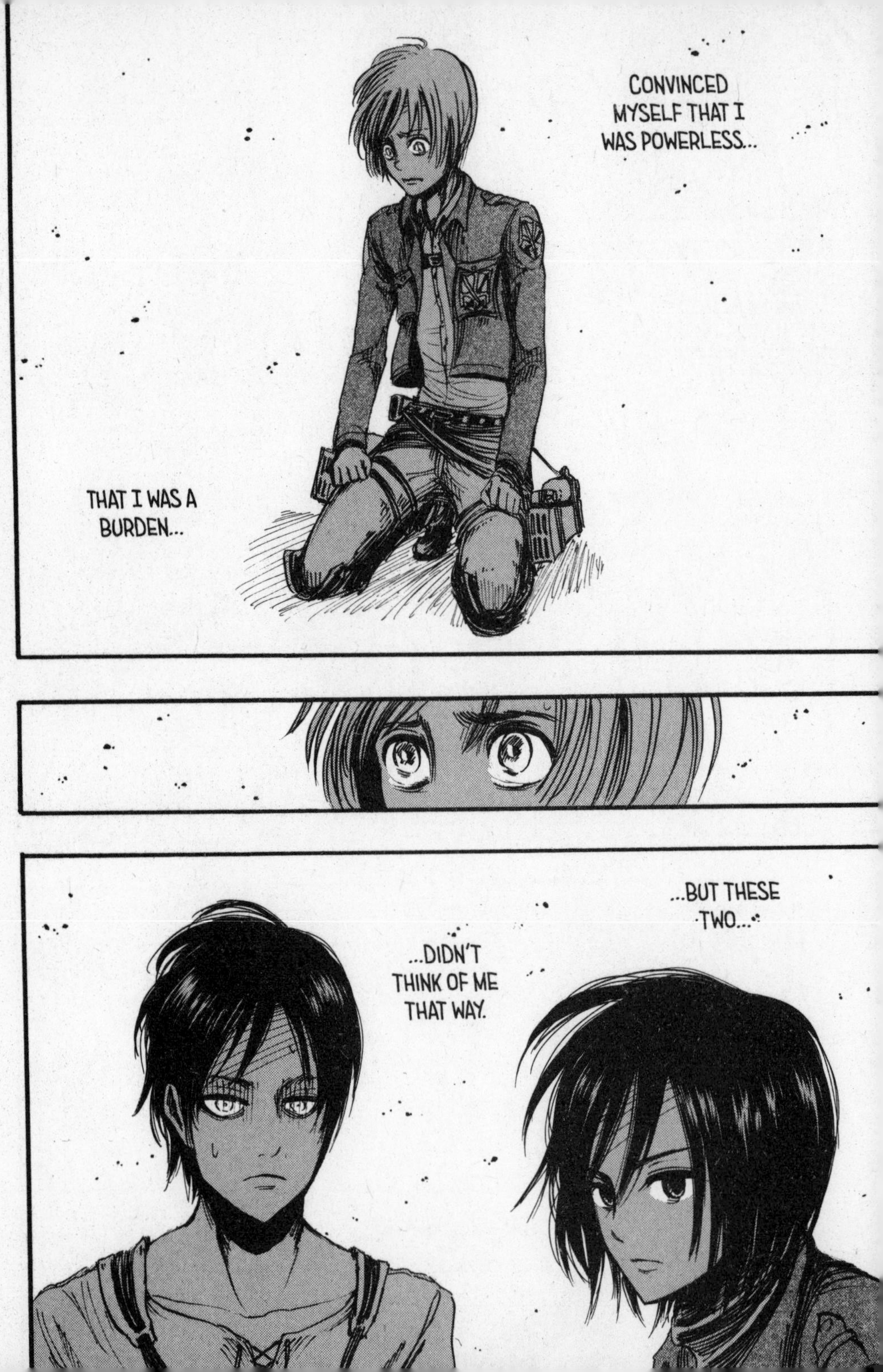
CONVINCED MYSELF THAT I WAS POWERLESS...
THAT I WAS A BURDEN...
...BUT THESE TWO...
...DIDN'T THINK OF ME THAT WAY.

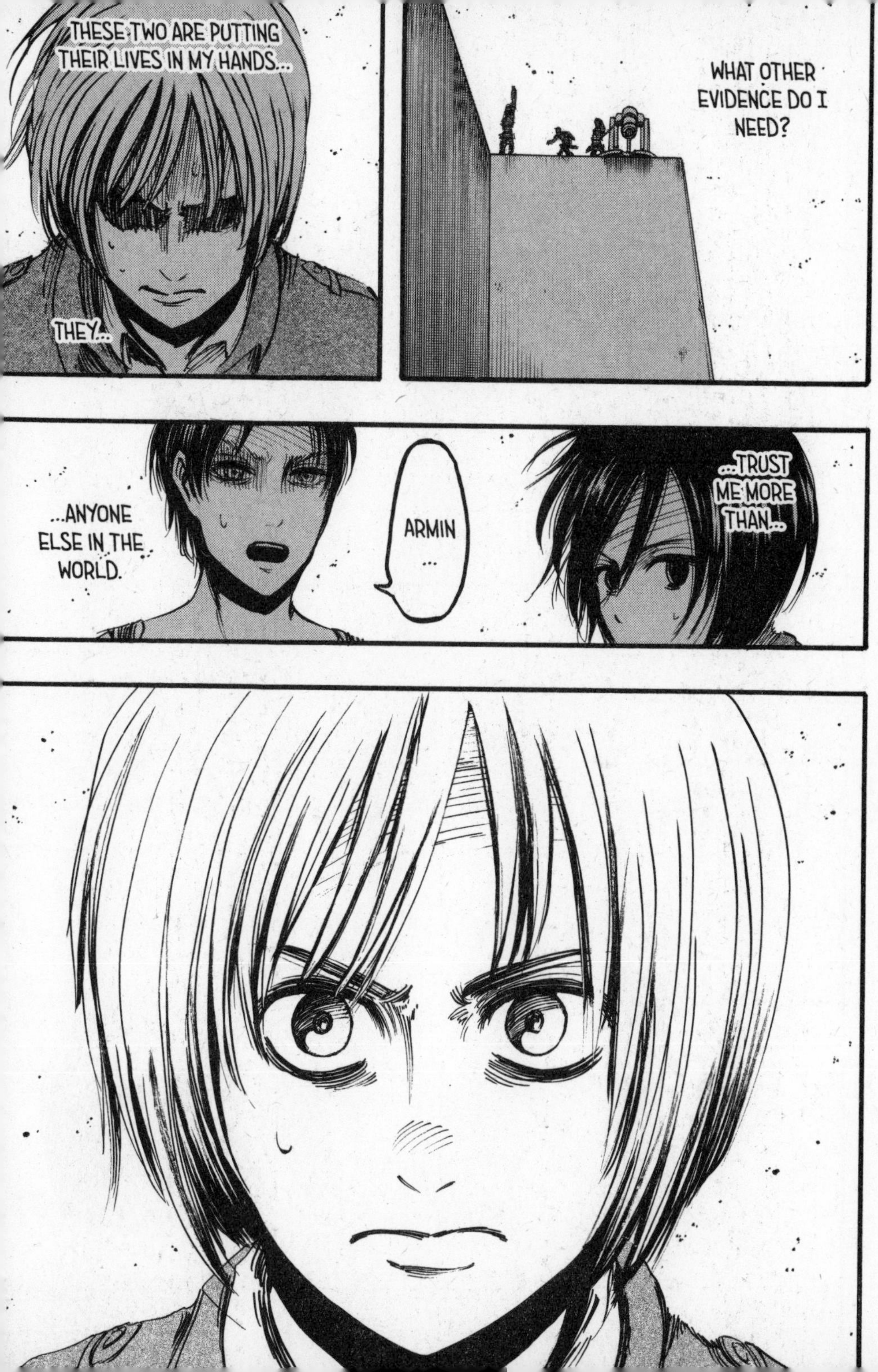
WHAT OTHER EVIDENCE DO I NEED?
THESE TWO ARE PUTTING THEIR LIVES IN MY HANDS...
THEY...
...TRUST ME MORE THAN...
ARMIN ...
...ANYONE ELSE IN THE WORLD.

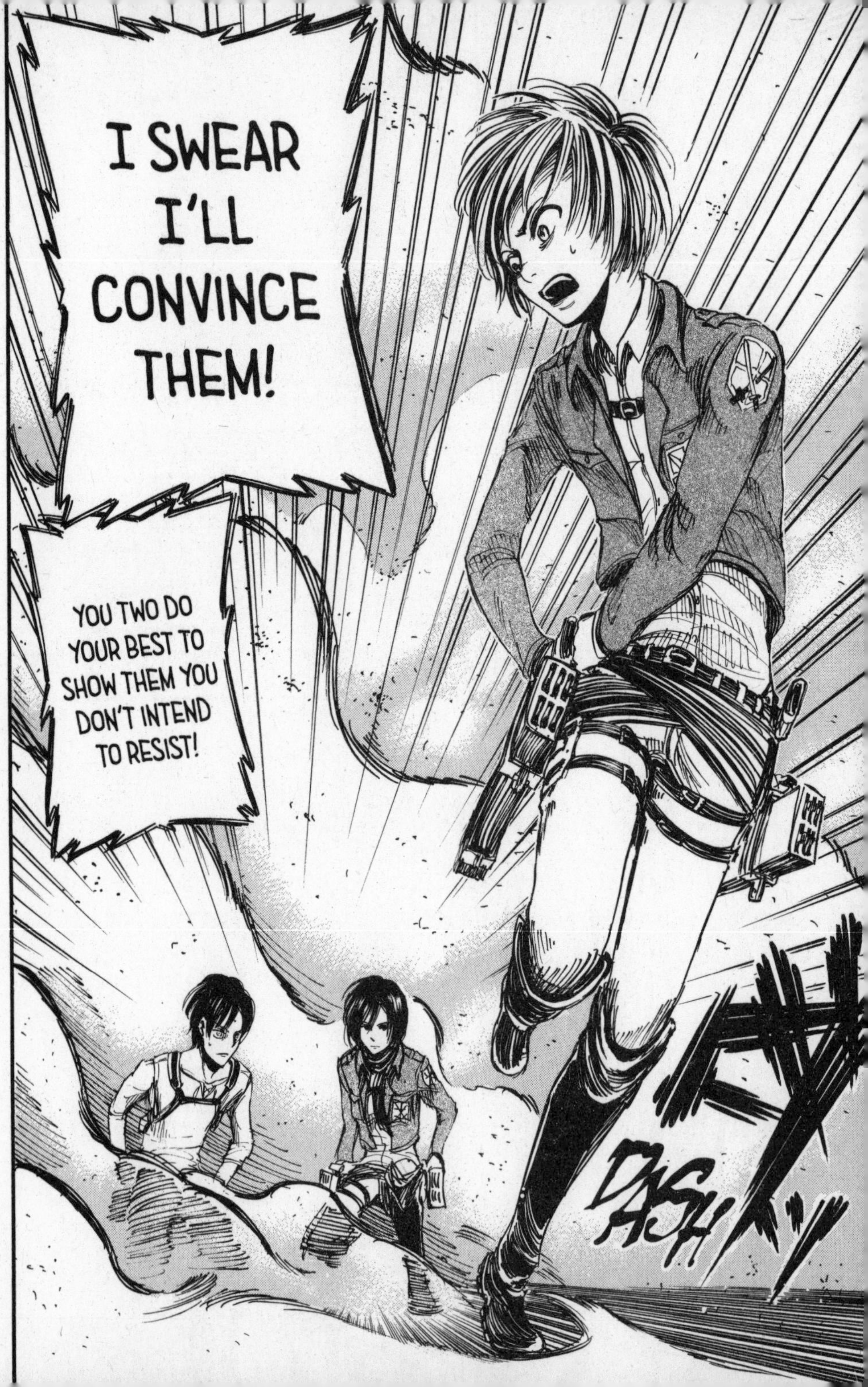
I SWEAR I'LL CONVINCE THEM!
YOU TWO DO YOUR BEST TO SHOW THEM YOU DON'T INTEND TO RESIST!
ダッ
DASH

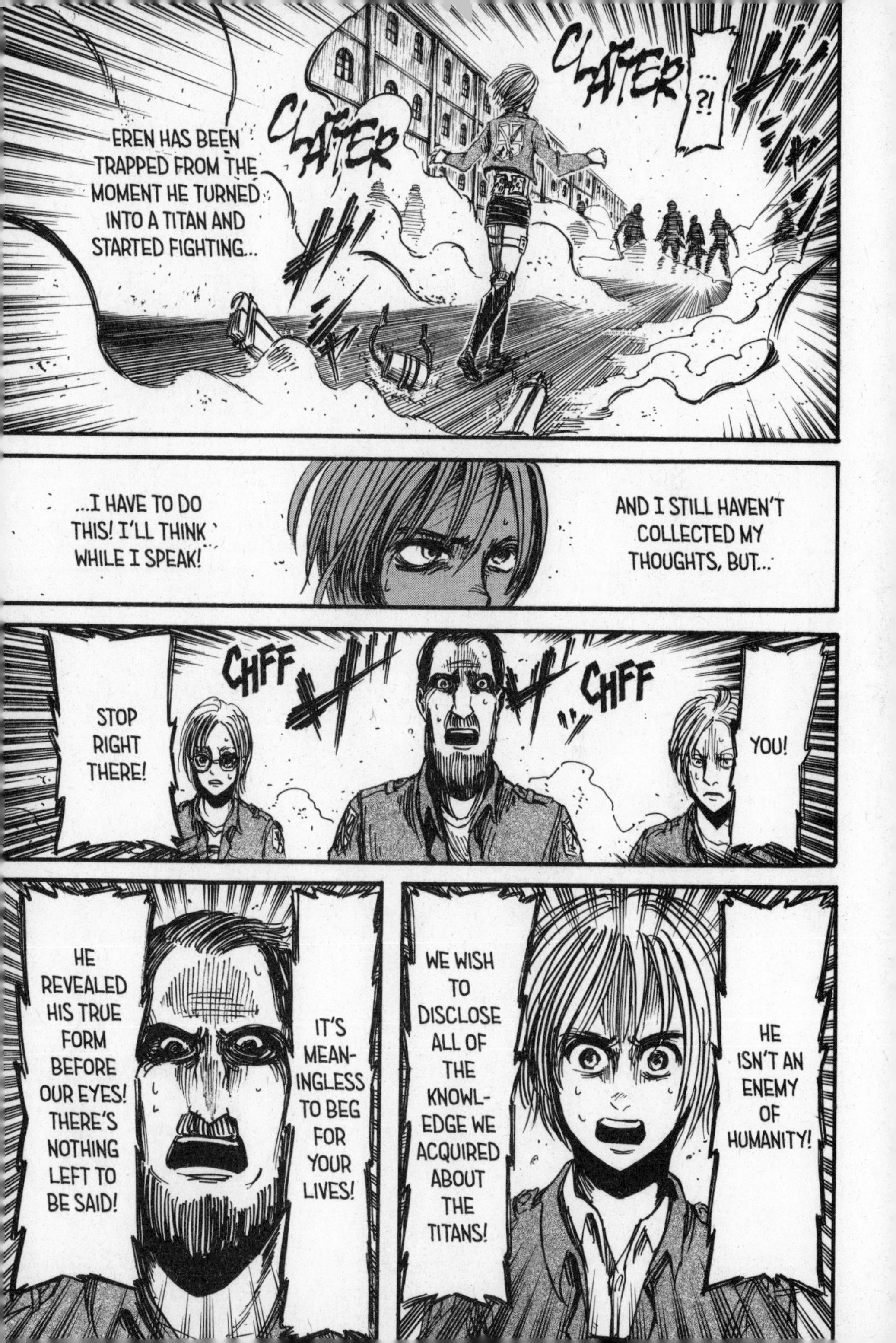
CHATTER
...?!
CHATTER
EREN HAS BEEN TRAPPED FROM THE MOMENT HE TURNED INTO A TITAN AND STARTED FIGHTING...
AND I STILL HAVEN'T COLLECTED MY THOUGHTS, BUT...
...I HAVE TO DO THIS! I'LL THINK WHILE I SPEAK!
YOU!
CHFF
CHFF
STOP RIGHT THERE!
HE ISN'T AN ENEMY OF HUMANITY!
WE WISH TO DISCLOSE ALL OF THE KNOWL-EDGE WE ACQUIRED ABOUT THE TITANS!
IT'S MEAN-INGLESS TO BEG FOR YOUR LIVES!
HE REVEALED HIS TRUE FORM BEFORE OUR EYES! THERE'S NOTHING LEFT TO BE SAID!

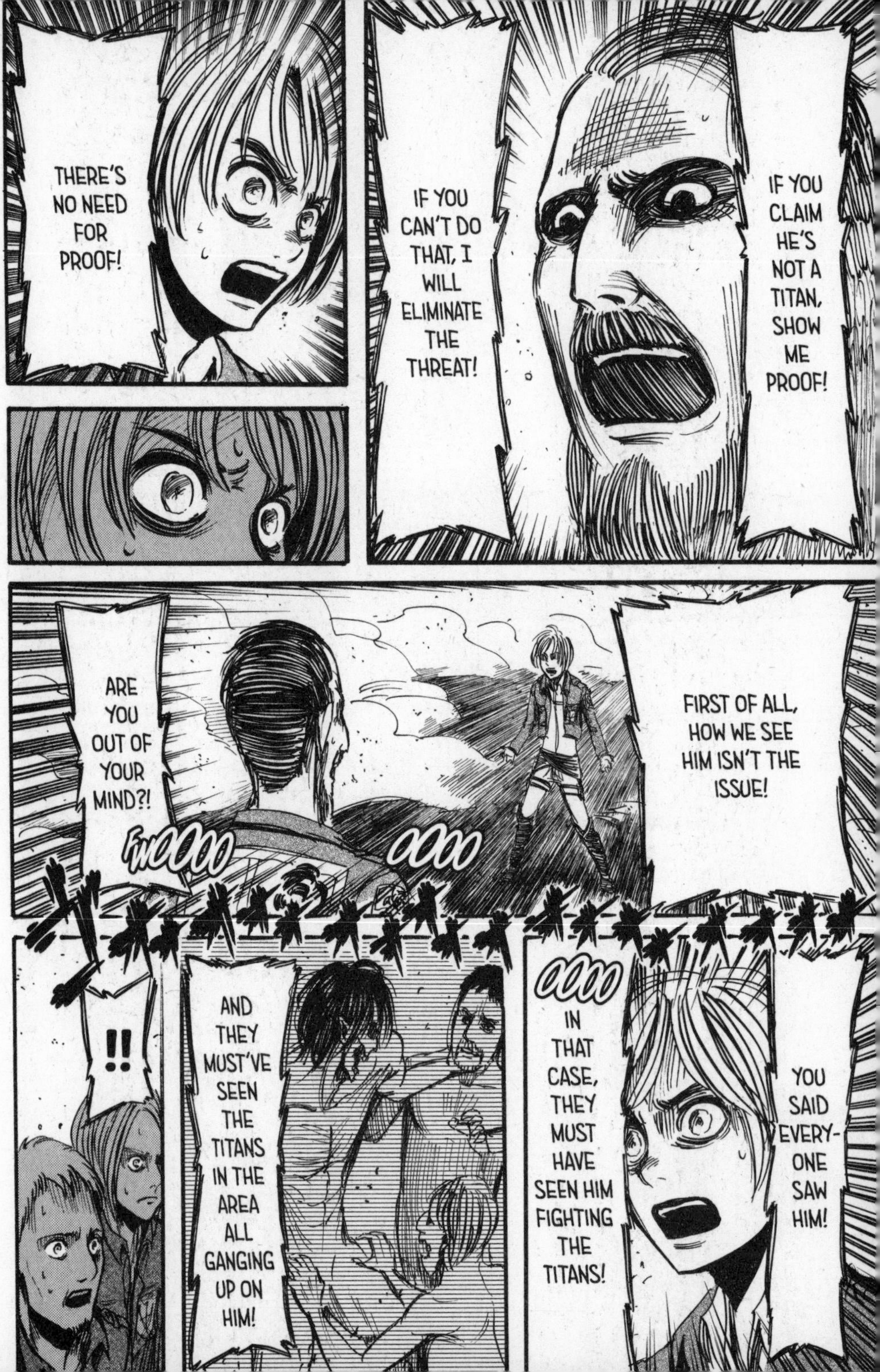
IF YOU CLAIM HE'S NOT A TITAN, SHOW ME PROOF!
IF YOU CAN'T DO THAT, I WILL ELIMINATE THE THREAT!
THERE'S NO NEED FOR PROOF!
FIRST OF ALL, HOW WE SEE HIM ISN'T THE ISSUE!
ARE YOU OUT OF YOUR MIND?!
FWOOOO
OOOO
YOU SAID EVERY-ONE SAW HIM!
OOOO
IN THAT CASE, THEY MUST HAVE SEEN HIM FIGHTING THE TITANS!
AND THEY MUST'VE SEEN THE TITANS IN THE AREA ALL GANGING UP ON HIM!
!!

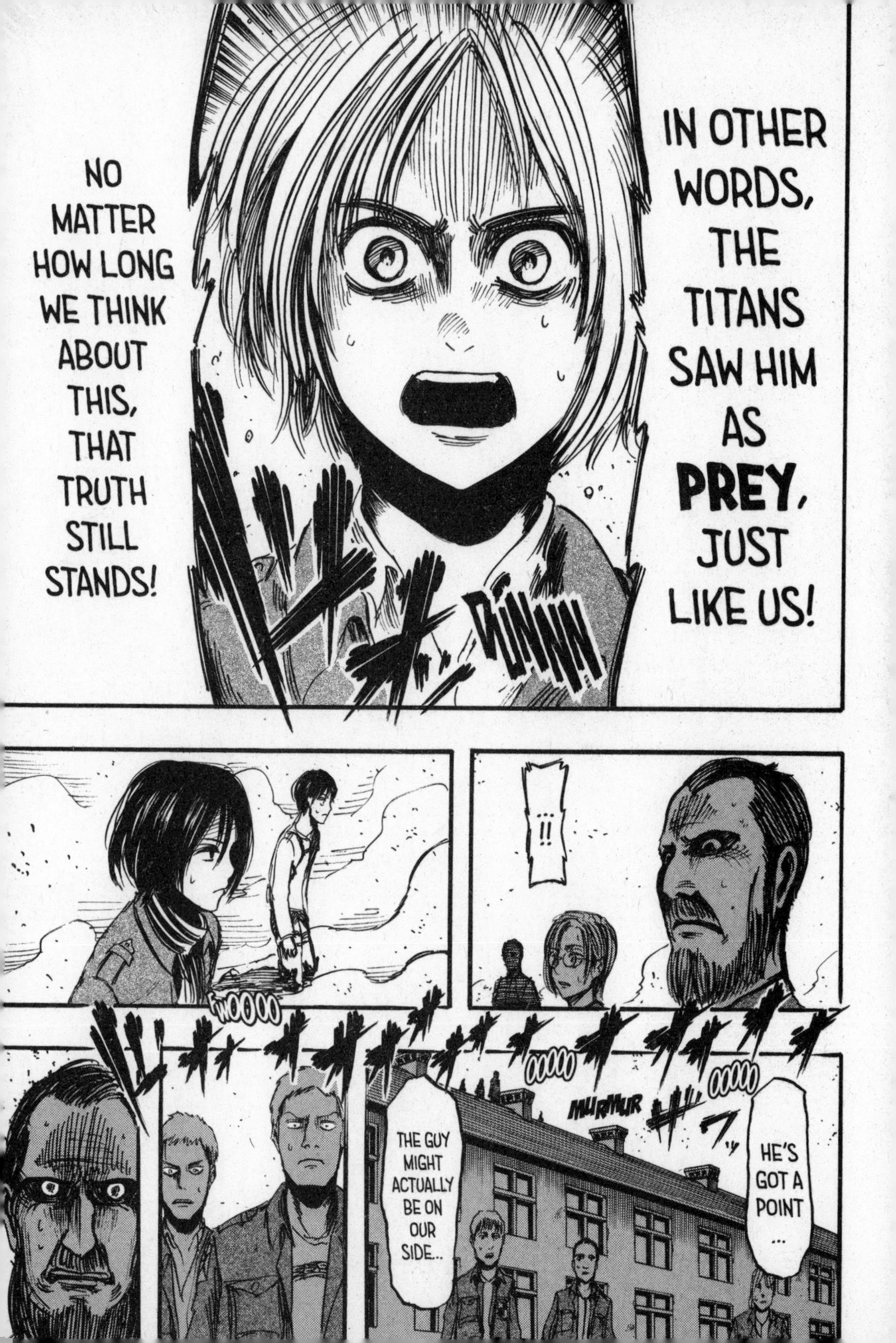
IN OTHER WORDS, THE TITANS SAW HIM AS PREY, JUST LIKE US!
NO MATTER HOW LONG WE THINK ABOUT THIS, THAT TRUTH STILL STANDS!
DÚNNN
...!!
FWOOOO
OOOOO
OOOOO
MURMUR
HE'S GOT A POINT ...
THE GUY MIGHT ACTUALLY BE ON OUR SIDE...

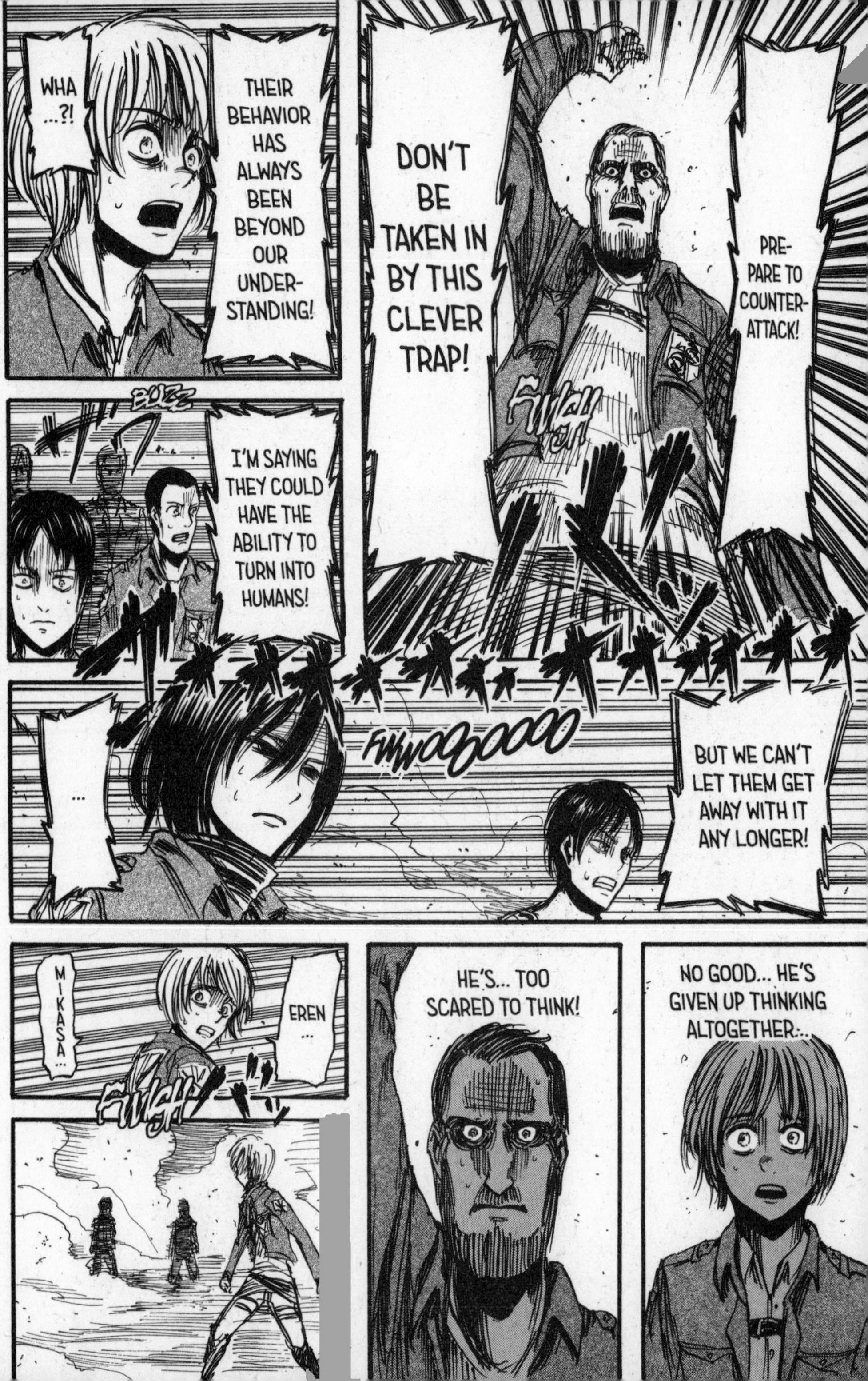
DON'T BE TAKEN IN BY THIS CLEVER TRAP!
PRE-PARE TO COUNTER-ATTACK!
FWISH
THEIR BEHAVIOR HAS ALWAYS BEEN BEYOND OUR UNDER-STANDING!
WHA ...?!
BUZZ
I'M SAYING THEY COULD HAVE THE ABILITY TO TURN INTO HUMANS!
BUT WE CAN'T LET THEM GET AWAY WITH IT ANY LONGER!
FWOOOOOOO
...
NO GOOD... HE'S GIVEN UP THINKING ALTOGETHER...
HE'S... TOO SCARED TO THINK!
EREN ...
MIKASA ...
FWISH

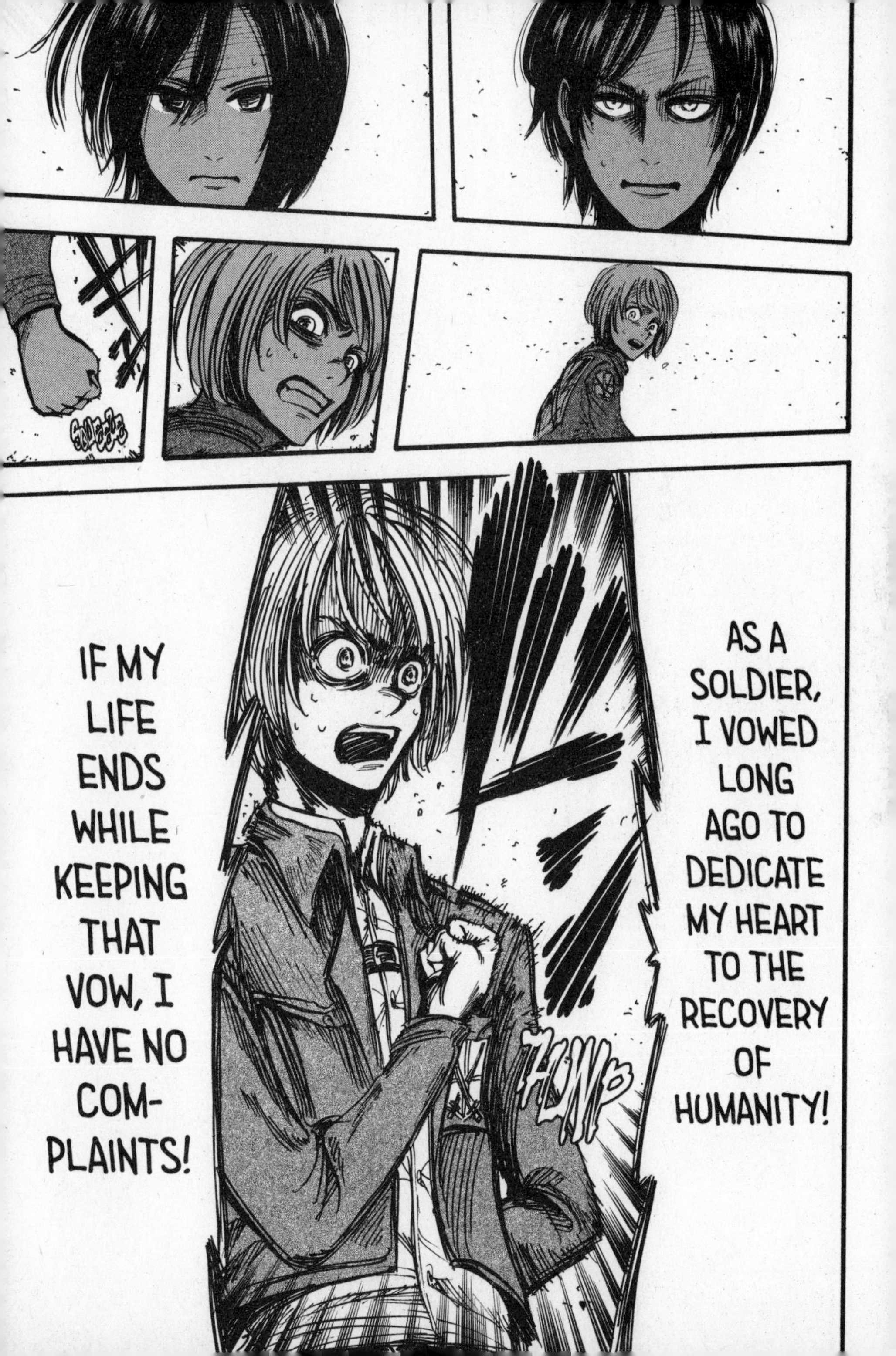
AS A SOLDIER, I VOWED LONG AGO TO DEDICATE MY HEART TO THE RECOVERY OF HUMANITY!
THUMP
IF MY LIFE ENDS WHILE KEEPING THAT VOW, I HAVE NO COM- PLAINTS!

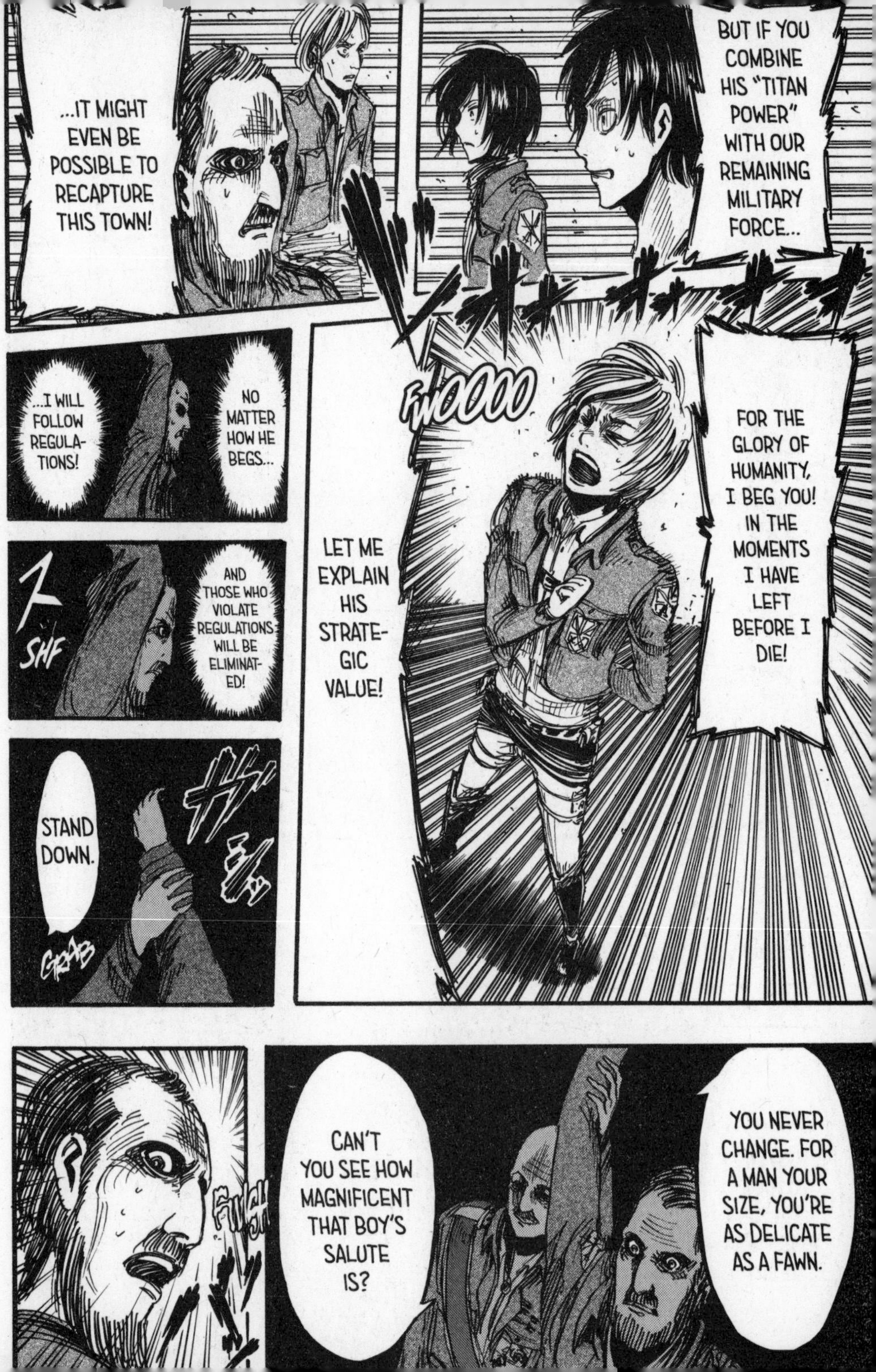
BUT IF YOU COMBINE HIS "TITAN POWER" WITH OUR REMAINING MILITARY FORCE...
...IT MIGHT EVEN BE POSSIBLE TO RECAPTURE THIS TOWN!
FOR THE GLORY OF HUMANITY, I BEG YOU! IN THE MOMENTS I HAVE LEFT BEFORE I DIE!
FWOOOO
LET ME EXPLAIN HIS STRATEGIC VALUE!
NO MATTER HOW HE BEGS...
...I WILL FOLLOW REGULATIONS!
AND THOSE WHO VIOLATE REGULATIONS WILL BE ELIMINATED!
SHF
STAND DOWN.
GRAB
YOU NEVER CHANGE. FOR A MAN YOUR SIZE, YOU'RE AS DELICATE AS A FAWN.
CAN'T YOU SEE HOW MAGNIFICENT THAT BOY'S SALUTE IS?
FWISH

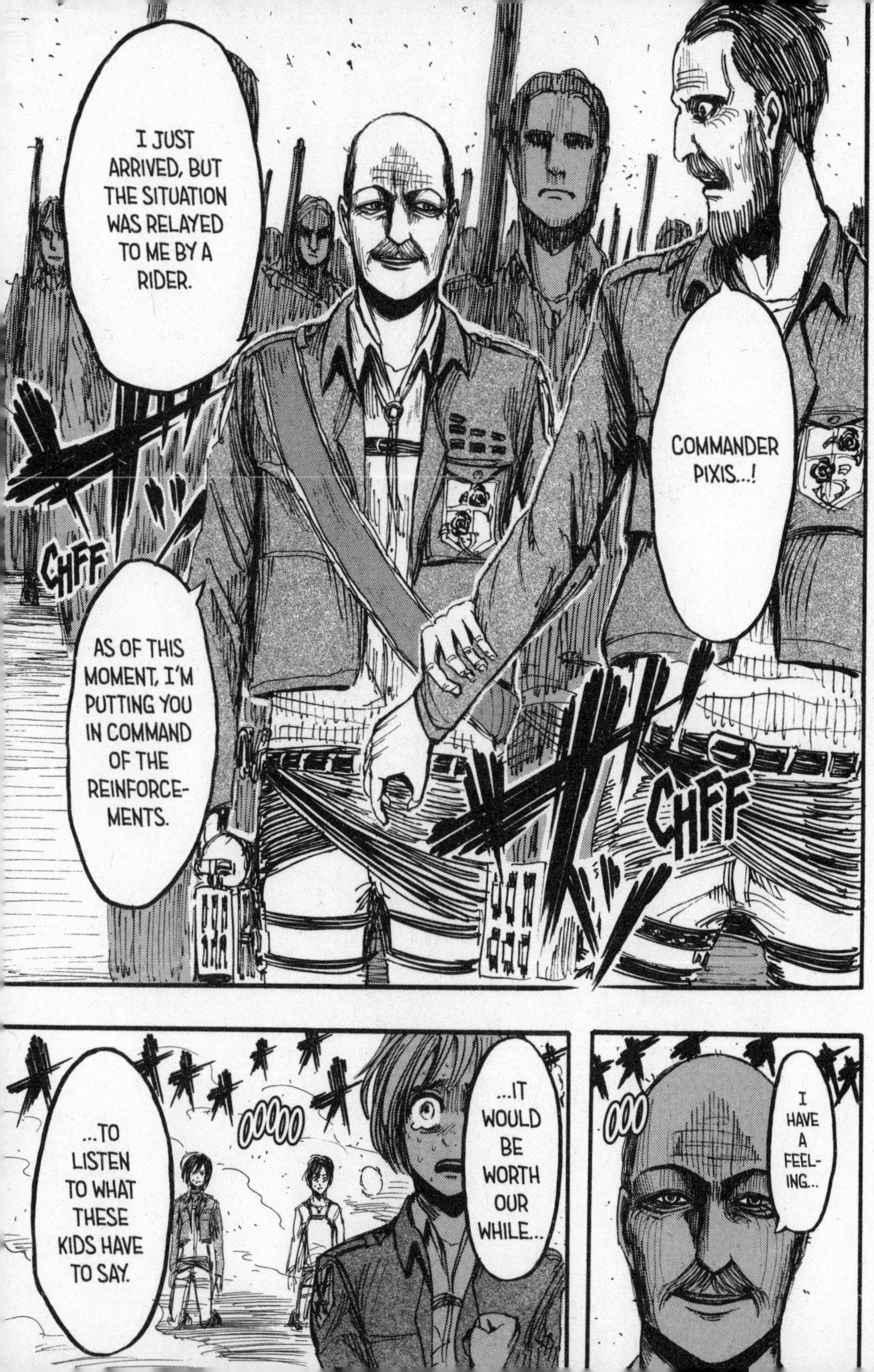
COMMANDER PIXIS...!
I JUST ARRIVED, BUT THE SITUATION WAS RELAYED TO ME BY A RIDER.
CHFF
CHFF
AS OF THIS MOMENT, I'M PUTTING YOU IN COMMAND OF THE REINFORCE-MENTS.
I HAVE A FEEL-ING...
...IT WOULD BE WORTH OUR WHILE...
...TO LISTEN TO WHAT THESE KIDS HAVE TO SAY.

ATTACK on TITAN

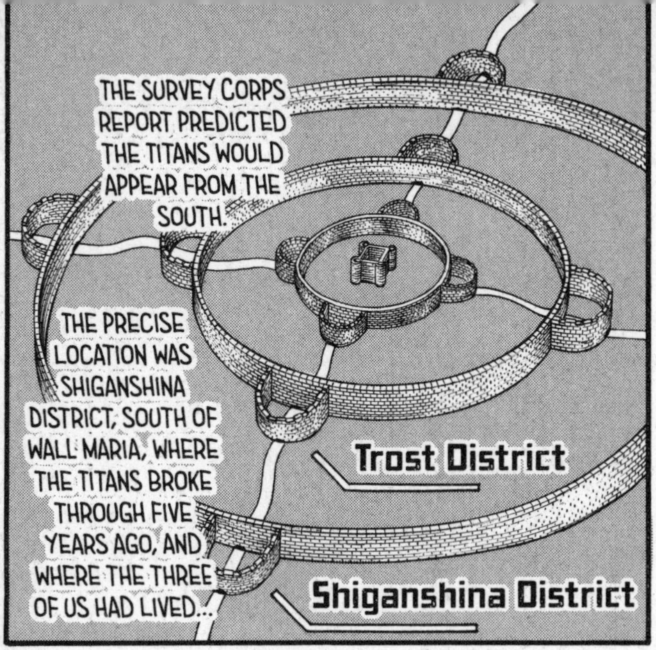
THE SURVEY CORPS REPORT PREDICTED THE TITANS WOULD APPEAR FROM THE SOUTH.
THE PRECISE LOCATION WAS SHIGANSHINA DISTRICT, SOUTH OF WALL MARIA, WHERE THE TITANS BROKE THROUGH FIVE YEARS AGO, AND WHERE THE THREE OF US HAD LIVED...
Trost District
Shiganshina District
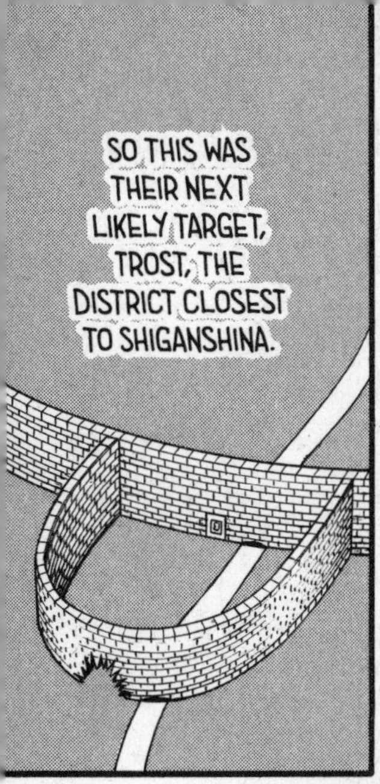
SO THIS WAS THEIR NEXT LIKELY TARGET, TROST, THE DISTRICT CLOSEST TO SHIGANSHINA.
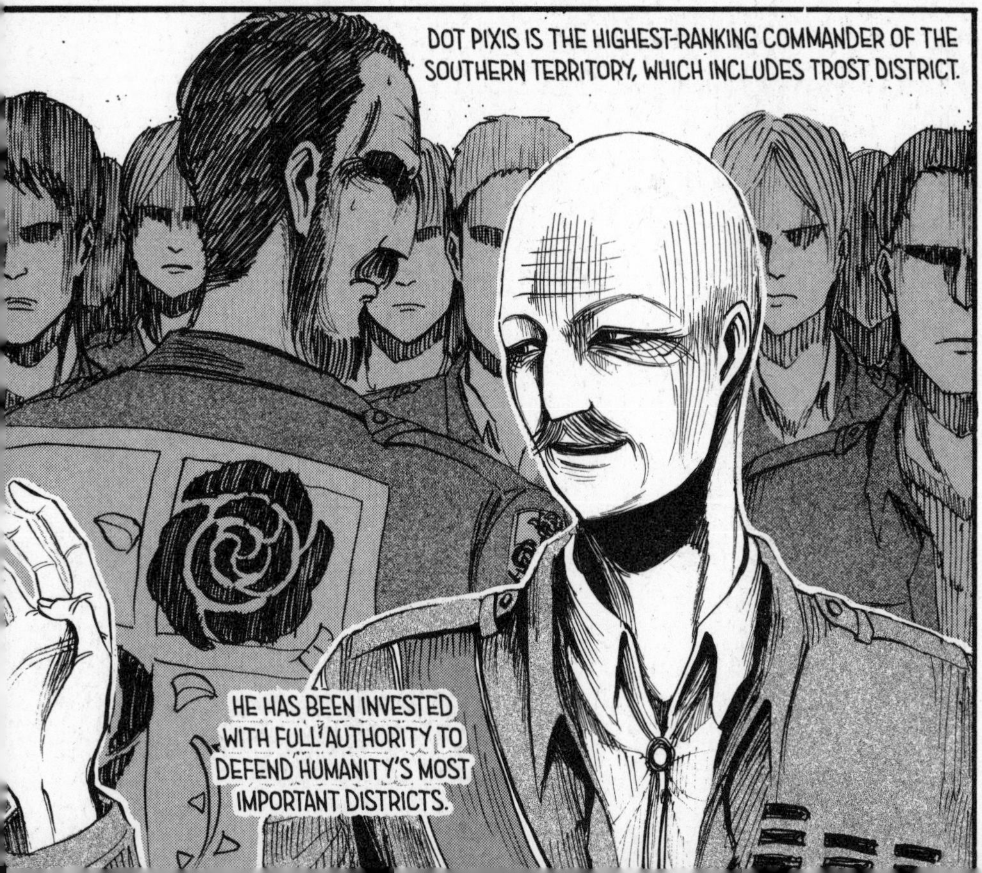
DOT PIXIS IS THE HIGHEST-RANKING COMMANDER OF THE SOUTHERN TERRITORY, WHICH INCLUDES TROST DISTRICT.
HE HAS BEEN INVESTED WITH FULL AUTHORITY TO DEFEND HUMANITY'S MOST IMPORTANT DISTRICTS.

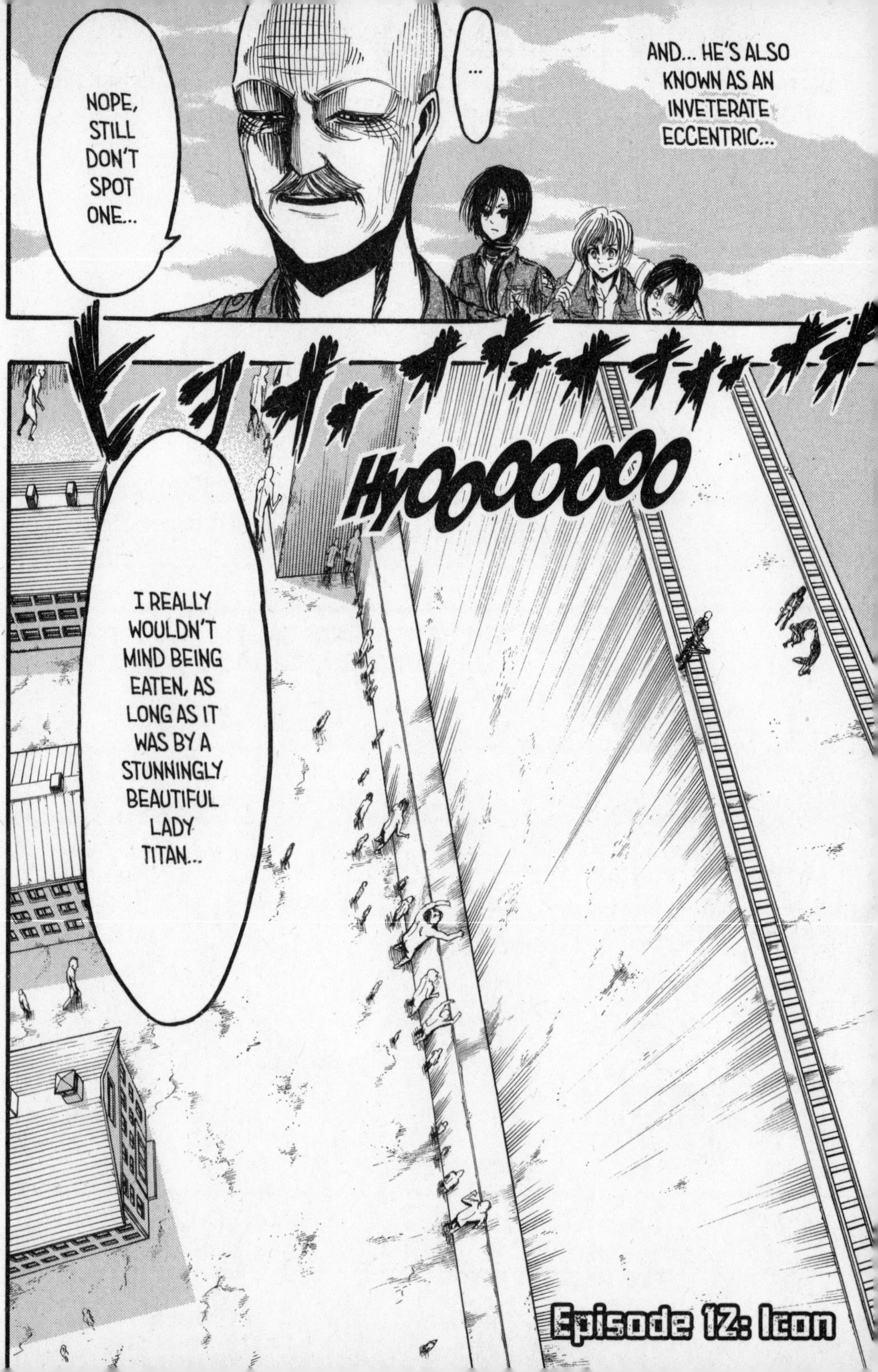
AND... HE'S ALSO KNOWN AS AN INVETERATE ECCENTRIC...
...
NOPE, STILL DON'T SPOT ONE...
HYOOOOOOO
I REALLY WOULDN'T MIND BEING EATEN, AS LONG AS IT WAS BY A STUNNINGLY BEAUTIFUL LADY TITAN...
Episode 12: Icon

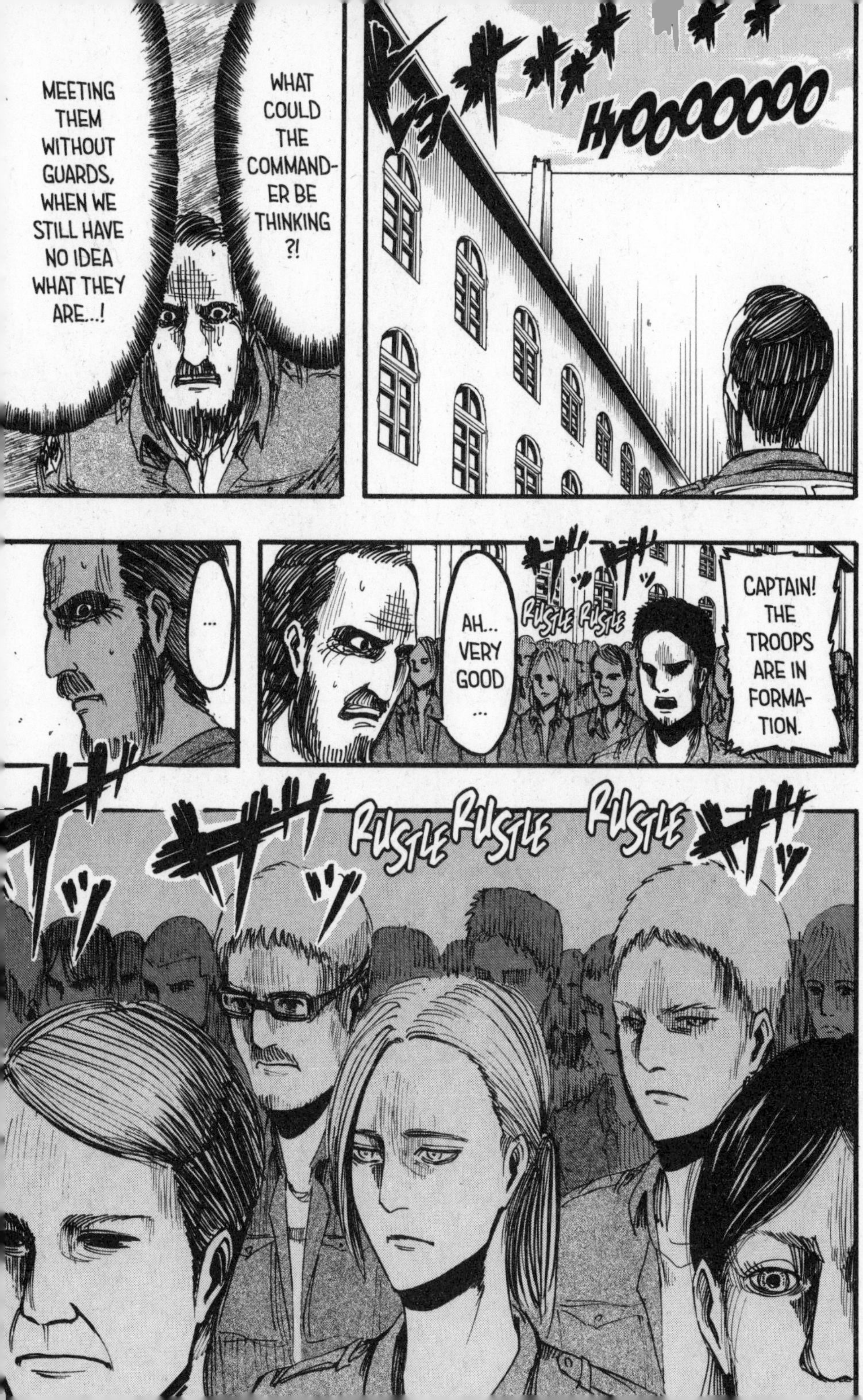
HYOOOOOOO
WHAT COULD THE COMMANDER BE THINKING?!
MEETING THEM WITHOUT GUARDS, WHEN WE STILL HAVE NO IDEA WHAT THEY ARE...!
CAPTAIN! THE TROOPS ARE IN FORMATION.
RUSTLE RUSTLE
AH... VERY GOOD ...
...
RUSTLE RUSTLE
RUSTLE

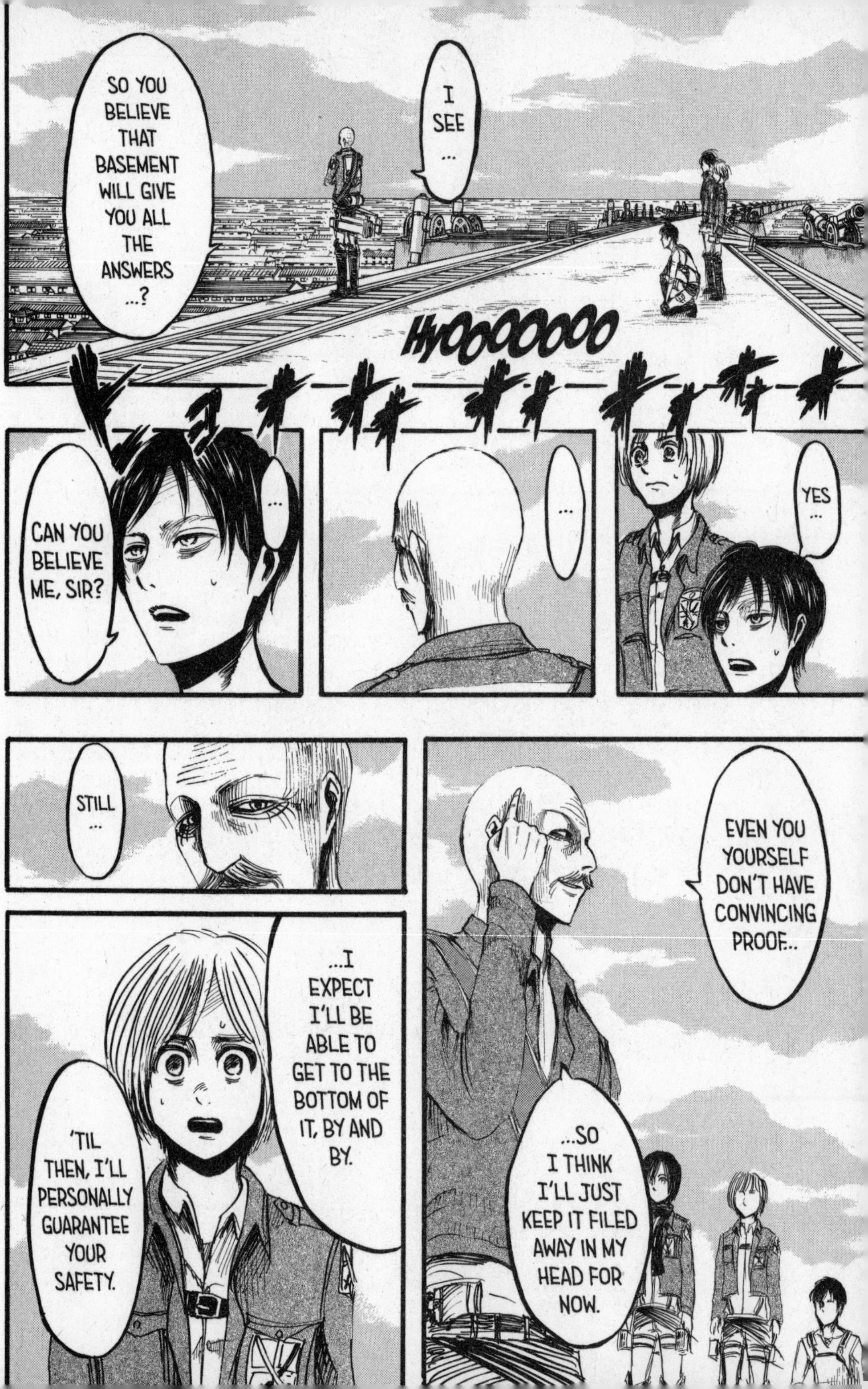
I SEE ...
SO YOU BELIEVE THAT BASEMENT WILL GIVE YOU ALL THE ANSWERS ...?
HYOOOOOOO
YES ...
...
...
CAN YOU BELIEVE ME, SIR?
EVEN YOU YOURSELF DON'T HAVE CONVINCING PROOF..
...SO I THINK I'LL JUST KEEP IT FILED AWAY IN MY HEAD FOR NOW.
STILL ...
...I EXPECT I'LL BE ABLE TO GET TO THE BOTTOM OF IT, BY AND BY.
'TIL THEN, I'LL PERSONALLY GUARANTEE YOUR SAFETY.

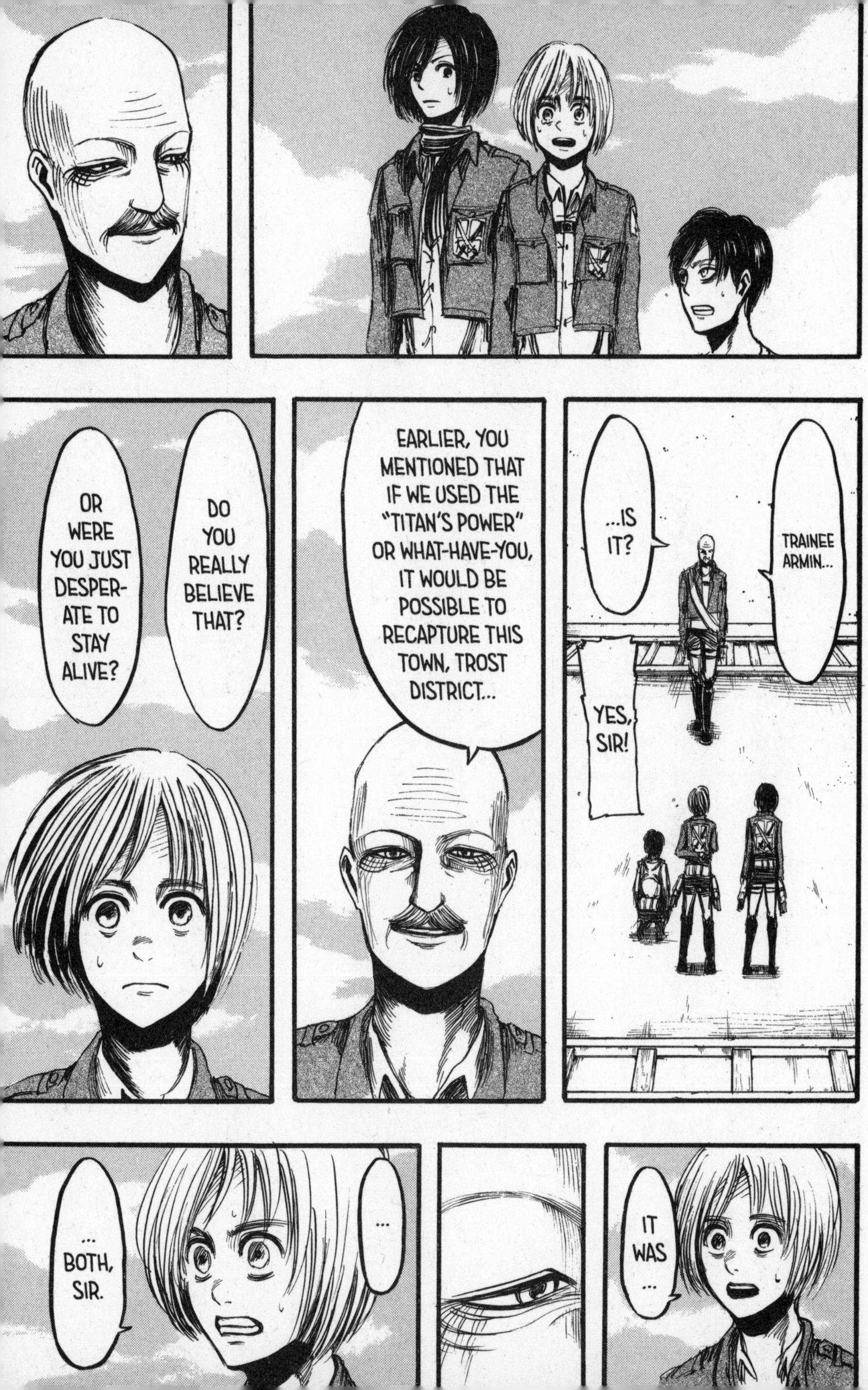
TRAINEE ARMIN...
...IS IT?
YES, SIR!
EARLIER, YOU MENTIONED THAT IF WE USED THE "TITAN'S POWER" OR WHAT-HAVE-YOU, IT WOULD BE POSSIBLE TO RECAPTURE THIS TOWN, TROST DISTRICT...
DO YOU REALLY BELIEVE THAT?
OR WERE YOU JUST DESPERATE TO STAY ALIVE?
IT WAS ...
...
... BOTH, SIR.

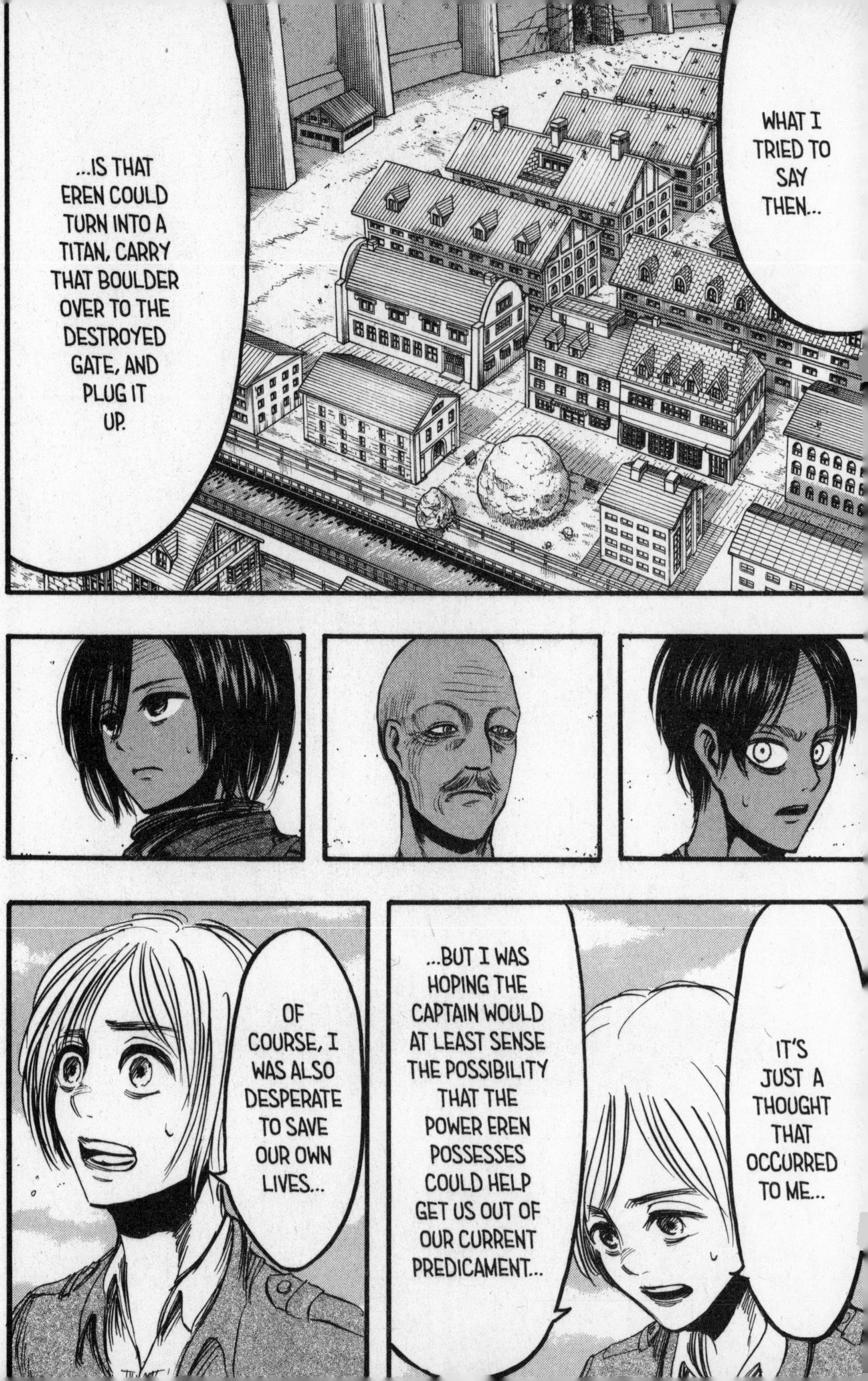
WHAT I TRIED TO SAY THEN...
...IS THAT EREN COULD TURN INTO A TITAN, CARRY THAT BOULDER OVER TO THE DESTROYED GATE, AND PLUG IT UP.
IT'S JUST A THOUGHT THAT OCCURRED TO ME...
...BUT I WAS HOPING THE CAPTAIN WOULD AT LEAST SENSE THE POSSIBILITY THAT THE POWER EREN POSSESSES COULD HELP GET US OUT OF OUR CURRENT PREDICAMENT...
OF COURSE, I WAS ALSO DESPERATE TO SAVE OUR OWN LIVES...

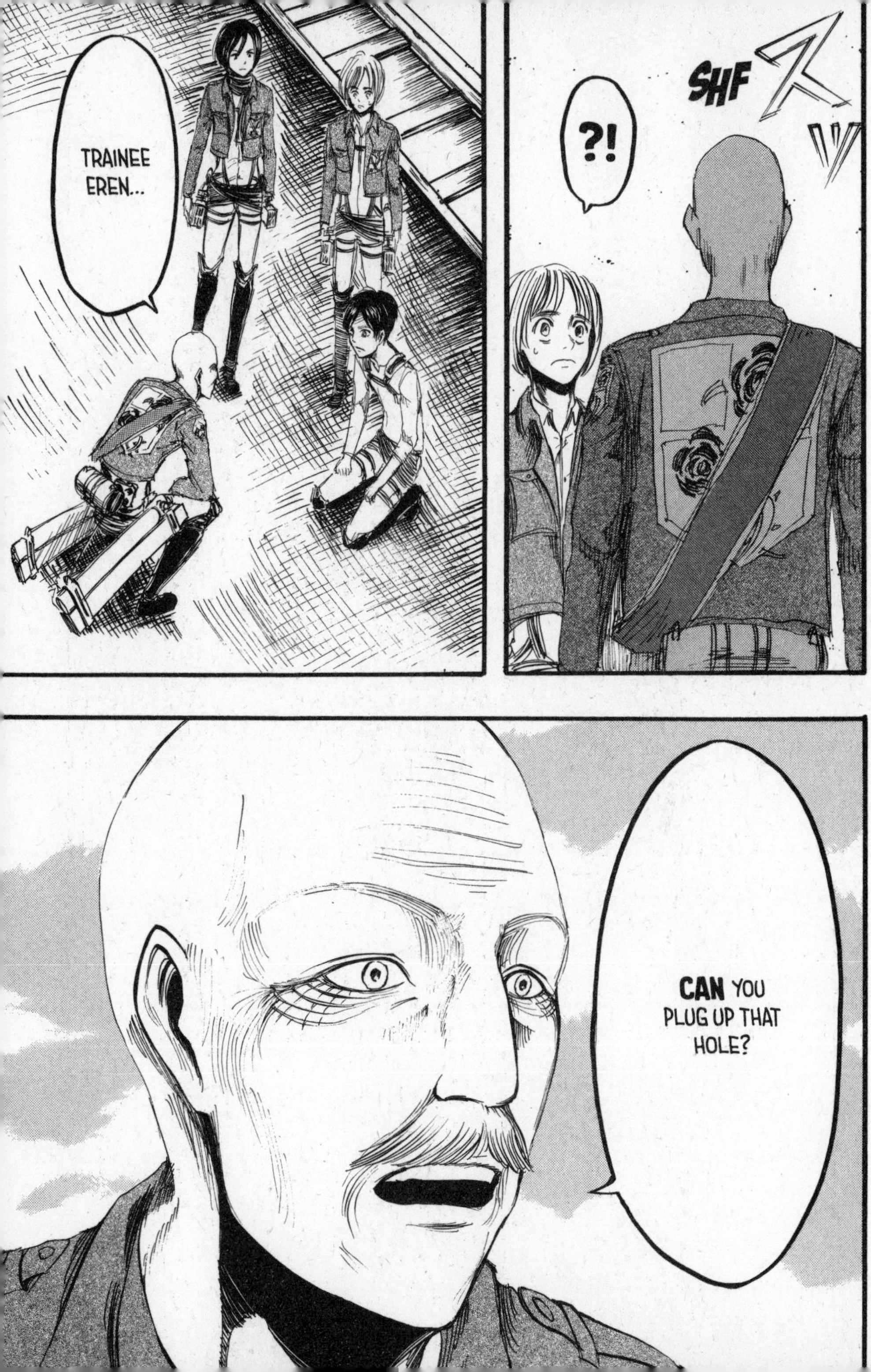
SHF
?!
TRAINEE EREN...
CAN YOU PLUG UP THAT HOLE?

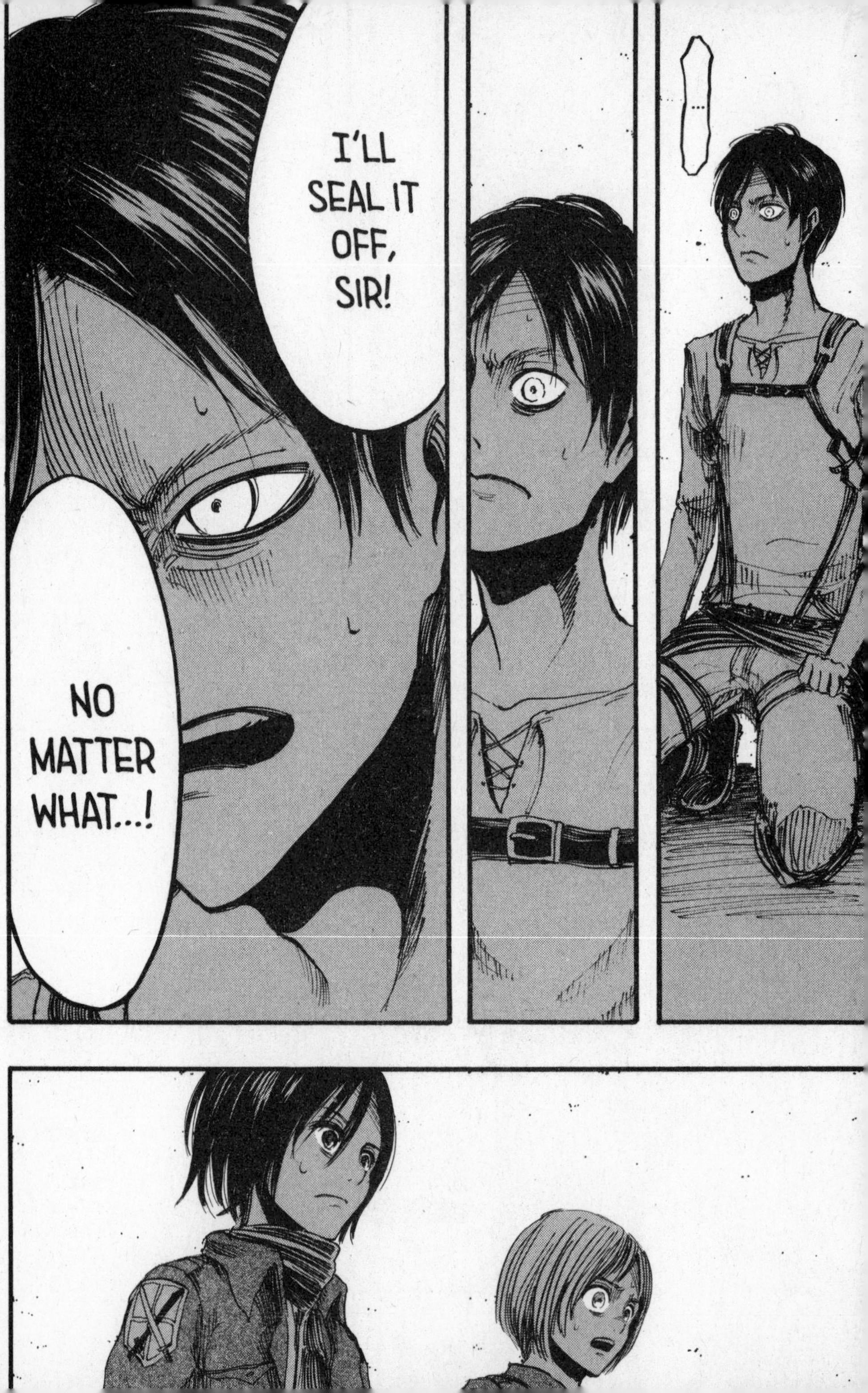
...!
I'LL SEAL IT OFF, SIR!
NO MATTER WHAT...!

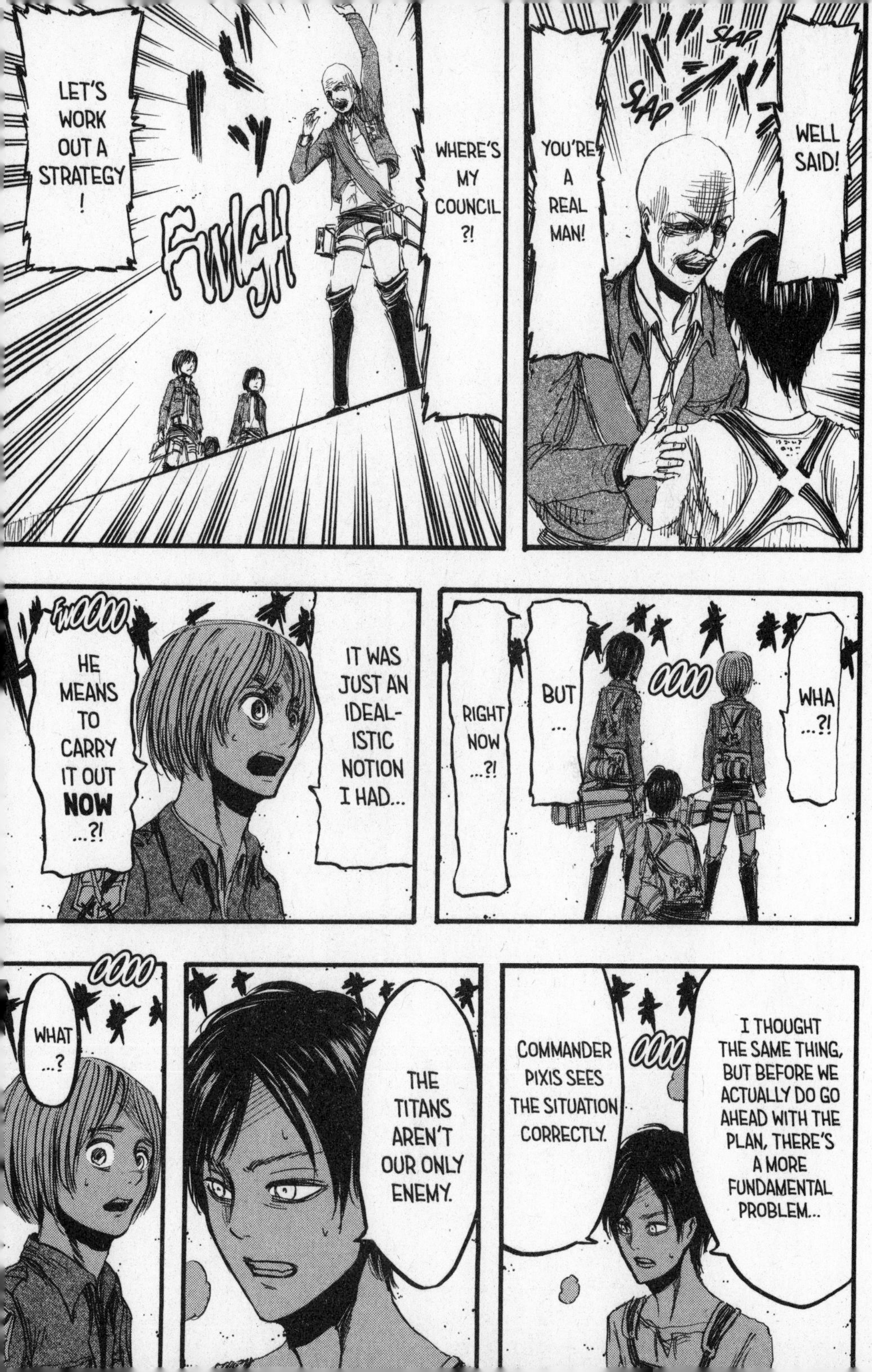
SLAP
SLAP
WELL SAID!
YOU'RE A REAL MAN!
WHERE'S MY COUNCIL ?!
LET'S WORK OUT A STRATEGY !
WHA ...?!
OOOO
BUT ...
RIGHT NOW ...?!
IT WAS JUST AN IDEAL-ISTIC NOTION I HAD...
FWOOOO
HE MEANS TO CARRY IT OUT **NOW** ...?!
I THOUGHT THE SAME THING, BUT BEFORE WE ACTUALLY DO GO AHEAD WITH THE PLAN, THERE'S A MORE FUNDAMENTAL PROBLEM...
OOOO
COMMANDER PIXIS SEES THE SITUATION CORRECTLY.
THE TITANS AREN'T OUR ONLY ENEMY.
OOOO
WHAT ...?

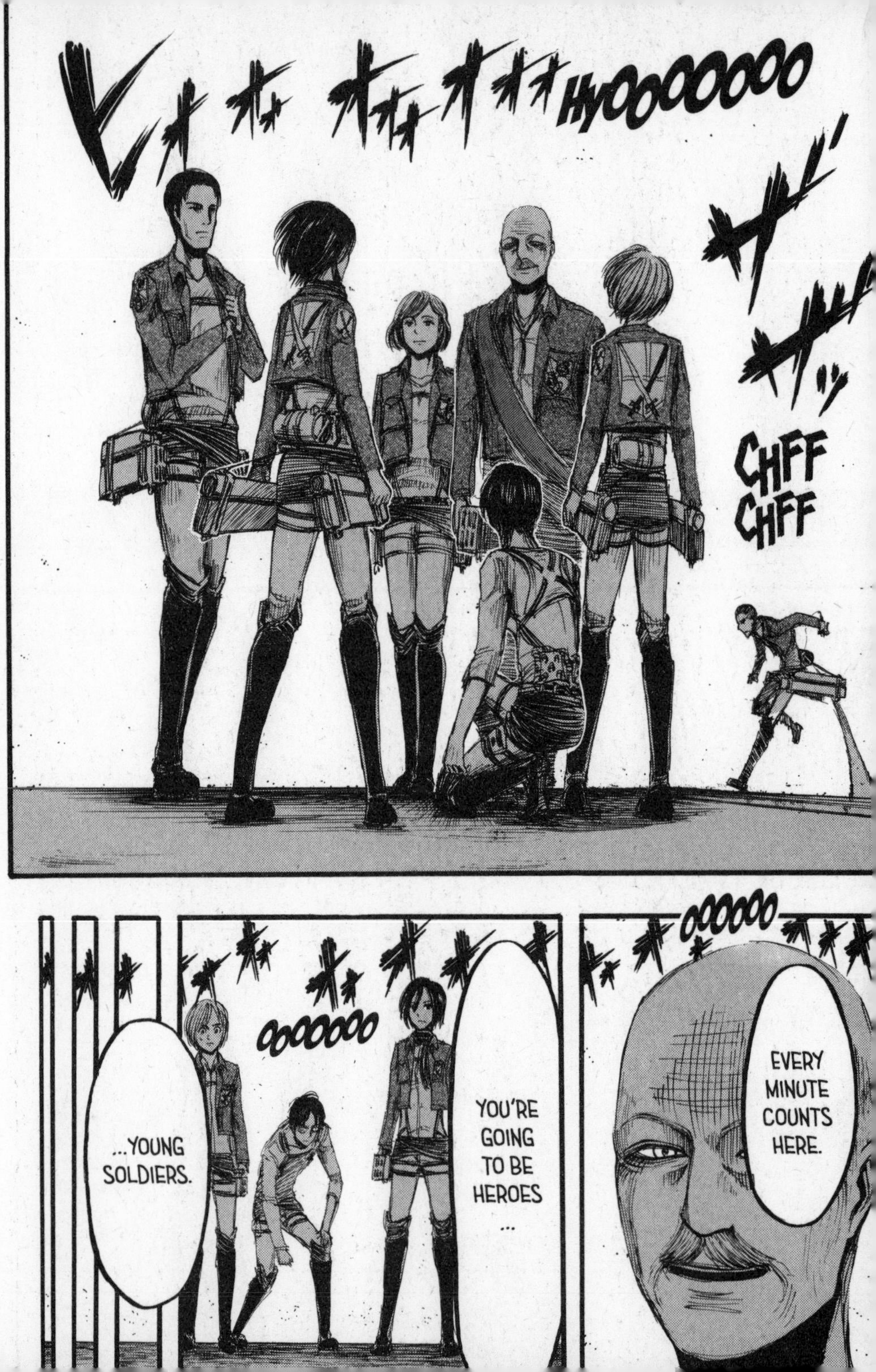
HYOOOOOOO
CHFF CHFF
OOOOOO
EVERY MINUTE COUNTS HERE.
OOOOOO
YOU'RE GOING TO BE HEROES ...
...YOUNG SOLDIERS.

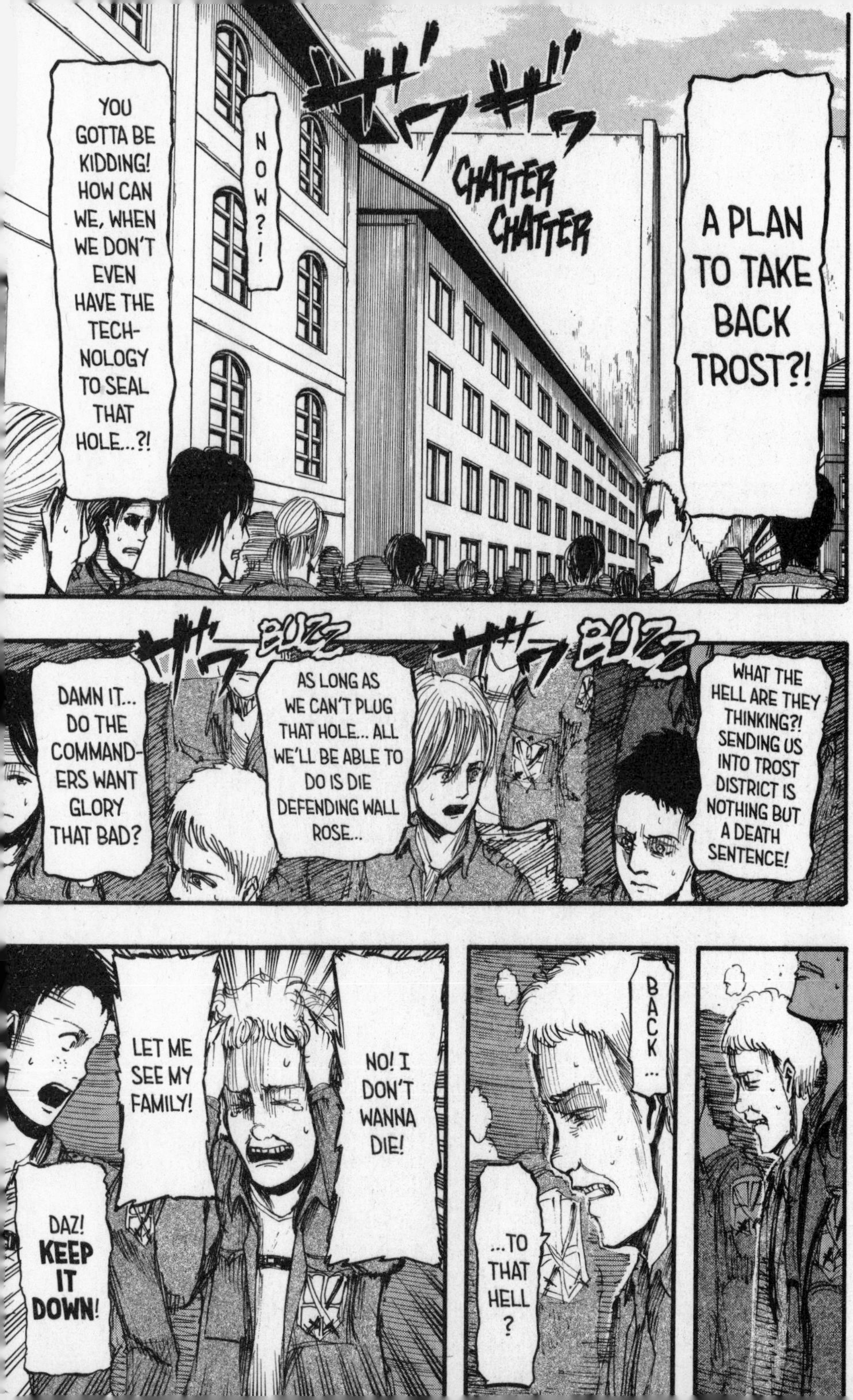
A PLAN TO TAKE BACK TROST?!
CHATTER CHATTER
NOW?!
YOU GOTTA BE KIDDING! HOW CAN WE, WHEN WE DON'T EVEN HAVE THE TECHNOLOGY TO SEAL THAT HOLE...?!
BUZZ
BUZZ
WHAT THE HELL ARE THEY THINKING?! SENDING US INTO TROST DISTRICT IS NOTHING BUT A DEATH SENTENCE!
AS LONG AS WE CAN'T PLUG THAT HOLE... ALL WE'LL BE ABLE TO DO IS DIE DEFENDING WALL ROSE...
DAMN IT... DO THE COMMANDERS WANT GLORY THAT BAD?
BACK...
...TO THAT HELL?
NO! I DON'T WANNA DIE!
LET ME SEE MY FAMILY!
DAZ! **KEEP IT DOWN!**

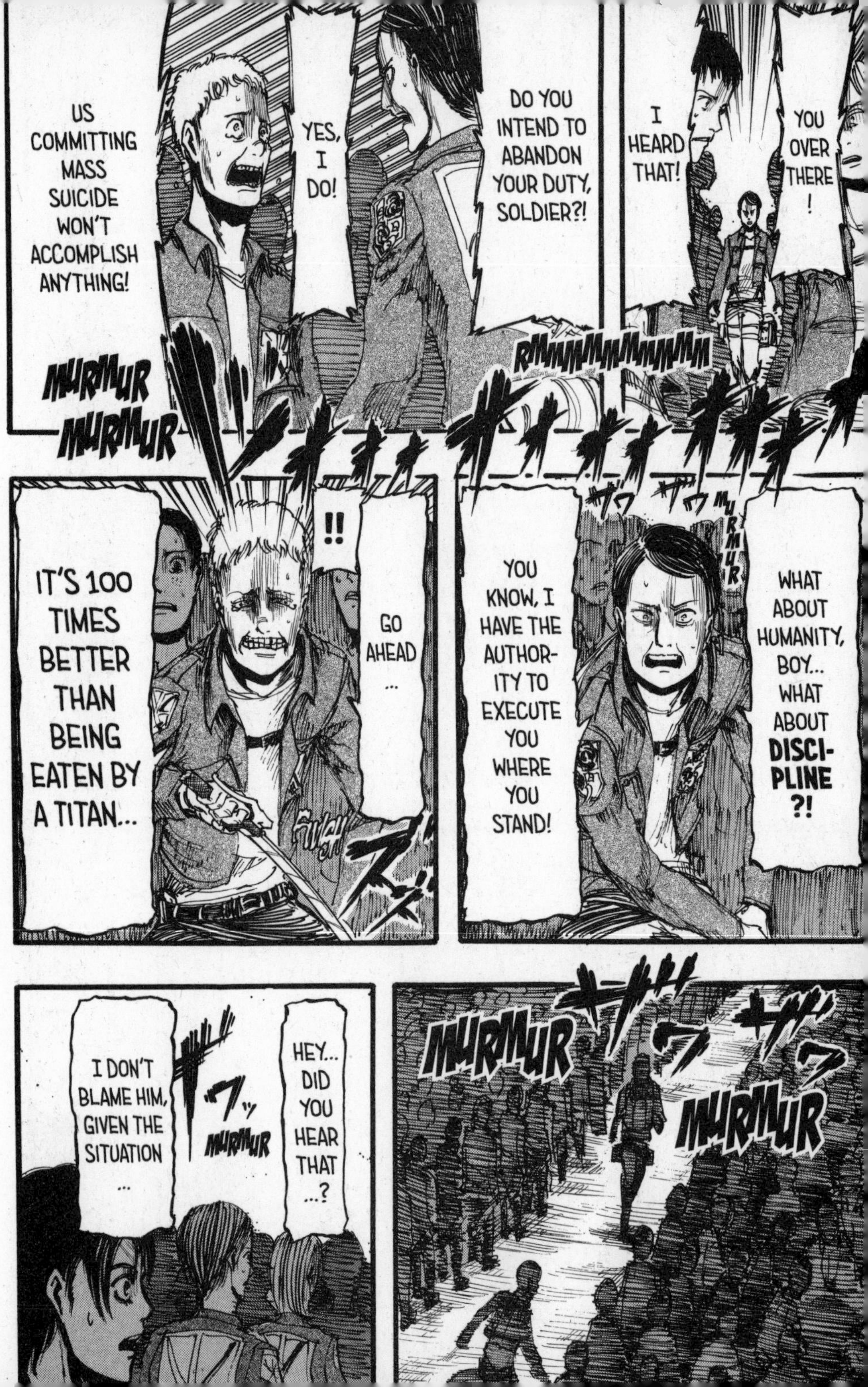
YOU OVER THERE!
I HEARD THAT!
DO YOU INTEND TO ABANDON YOUR DUTY, SOLDIER?!
YES, I DO!
US COMMITTING MASS SUICIDE WON'T ACCOMPLISH ANYTHING!
MURMUR MURMUR
WHAT ABOUT HUMANITY, BOY... WHAT ABOUT DISCIPLINE?!
MURMUR
YOU KNOW, I HAVE THE AUTHORITY TO EXECUTE YOU WHERE YOU STAND!
GO AHEAD...
!!
IT'S 100 TIMES BETTER THAN BEING EATEN BY A TITAN...
MURMUR
MURMUR
HEY... DID YOU HEAR THAT...?
MURMUR
I DON'T BLAME HIM, GIVEN THE SITUATION...

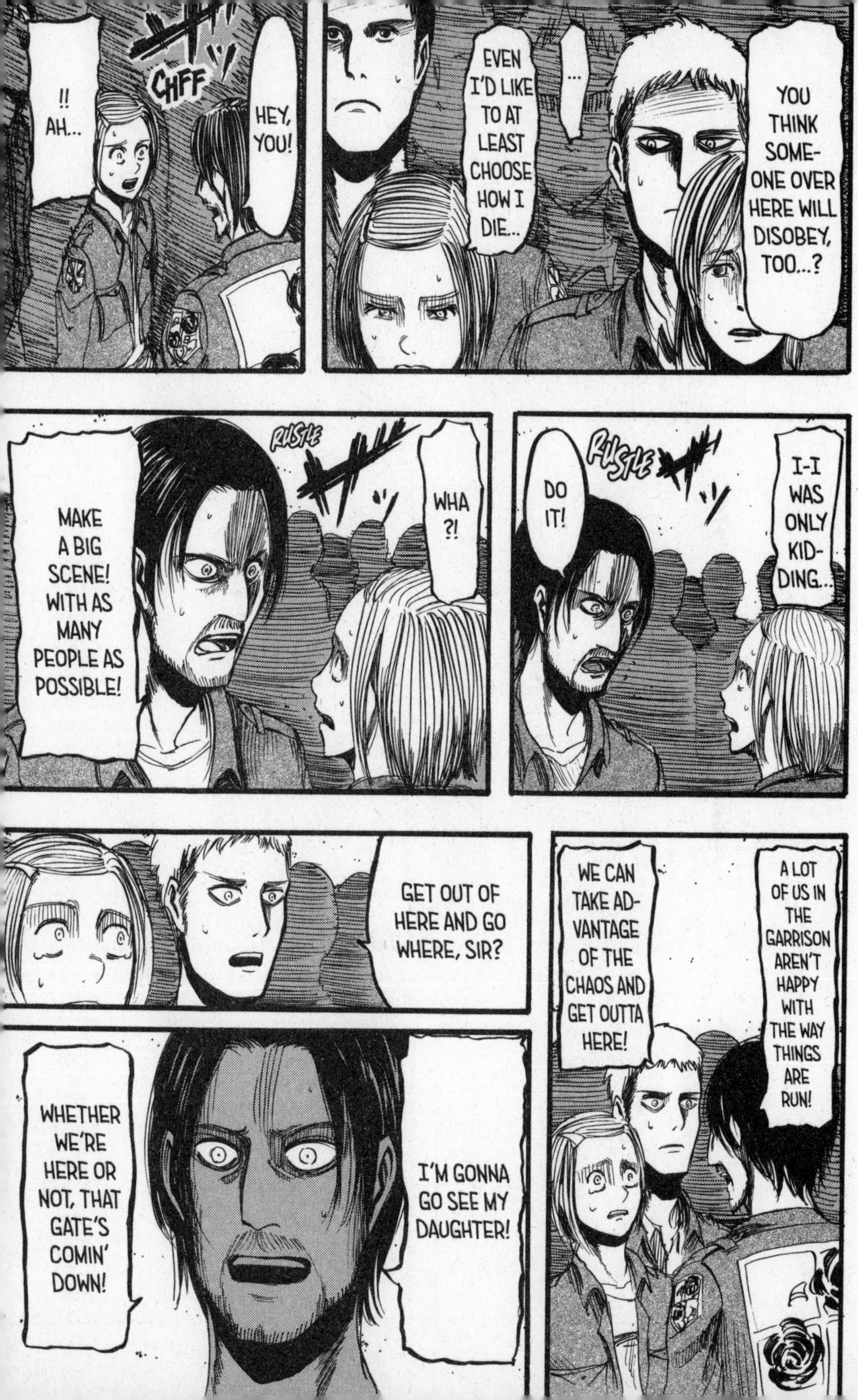
YOU THINK SOME-ONE OVER HERE WILL DISOBEY, TOO...?
...
EVEN I'D LIKE TO AT LEAST CHOOSE HOW I DIE...
HEY, YOU!
CHFF
!! AH...
I-I WAS ONLY KID-DING...
RUSTLE
DO IT!
WHA ?!
RUSTLE
MAKE A BIG SCENE! WITH AS MANY PEOPLE AS POSSIBLE!
A LOT OF US IN THE GARRISON AREN'T HAPPY WITH THE WAY THINGS ARE RUN!
WE CAN TAKE AD-VANTAGE OF THE CHAOS AND GET OUTTA HERE!
GET OUT OF HERE AND GO WHERE, SIR?
I'M GONNA GO SEE MY DAUGHTER!
WHETHER WE'RE HERE OR NOT, THAT GATE'S COMIN' DOWN!

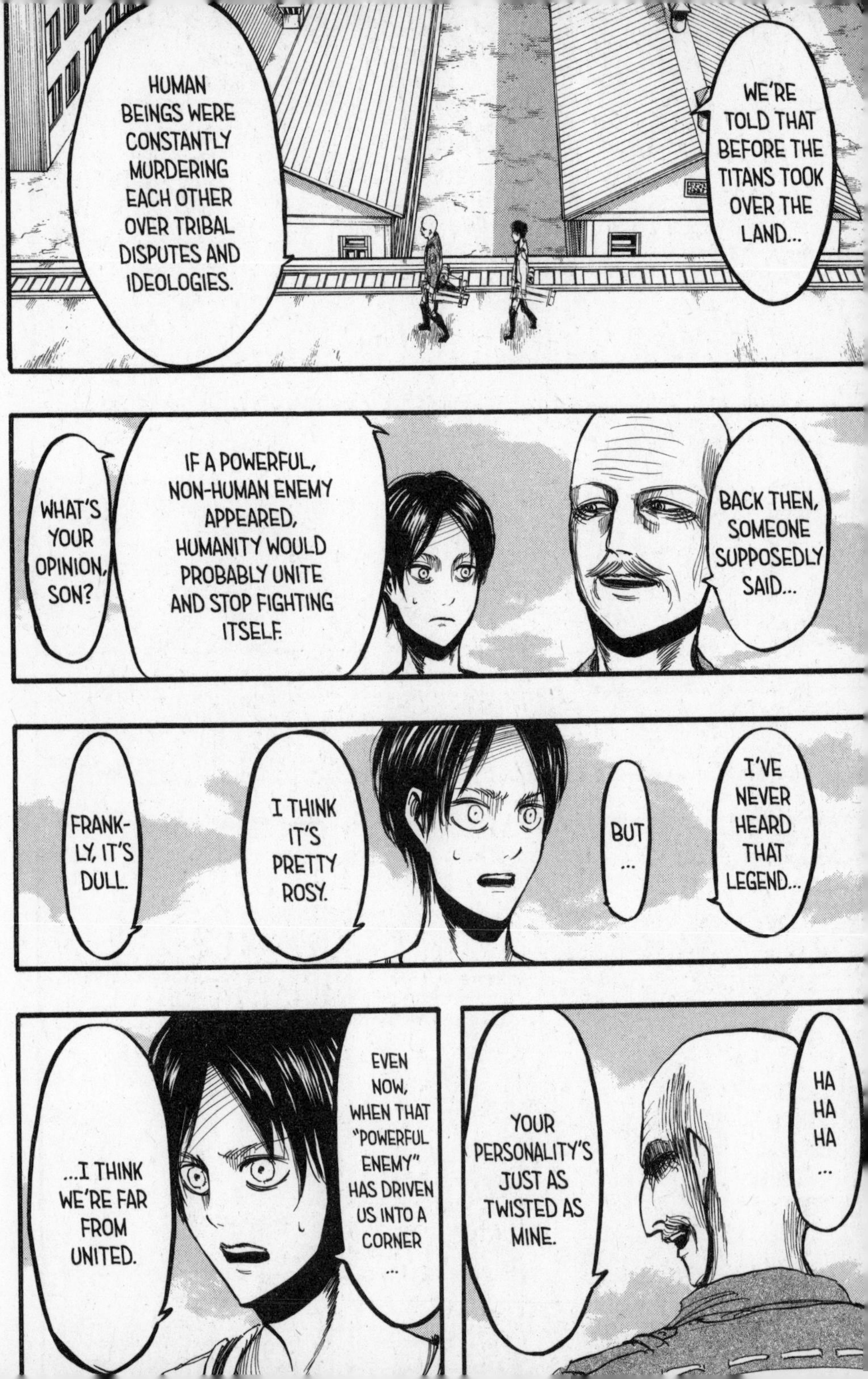

WE'RE TOLD THAT BEFORE THE TITANS TOOK OVER THE LAND...
HUMAN BEINGS WERE CONSTANTLY MURDERING EACH OTHER OVER TRIBAL DISPUTES AND IDEOLOGIES.
BACK THEN, SOMEONE SUPPOSEDLY SAID...
IF A POWERFUL, NON-HUMAN ENEMY APPEARED, HUMANITY WOULD PROBABLY UNITE AND STOP FIGHTING ITSELF.
WHAT'S YOUR OPINION, SON?
I'VE NEVER HEARD THAT LEGEND...
BUT ...
I THINK IT'S PRETTY ROSY.
FRANK-LY, IT'S DULL.
HA HA HA ...
YOUR PERSONALITY'S JUST AS TWISTED AS MINE.
EVEN NOW, WHEN THAT "POWERFUL ENEMY" HAS DRIVEN US INTO A CORNER ...
...I THINK WE'RE FAR FROM UNITED.

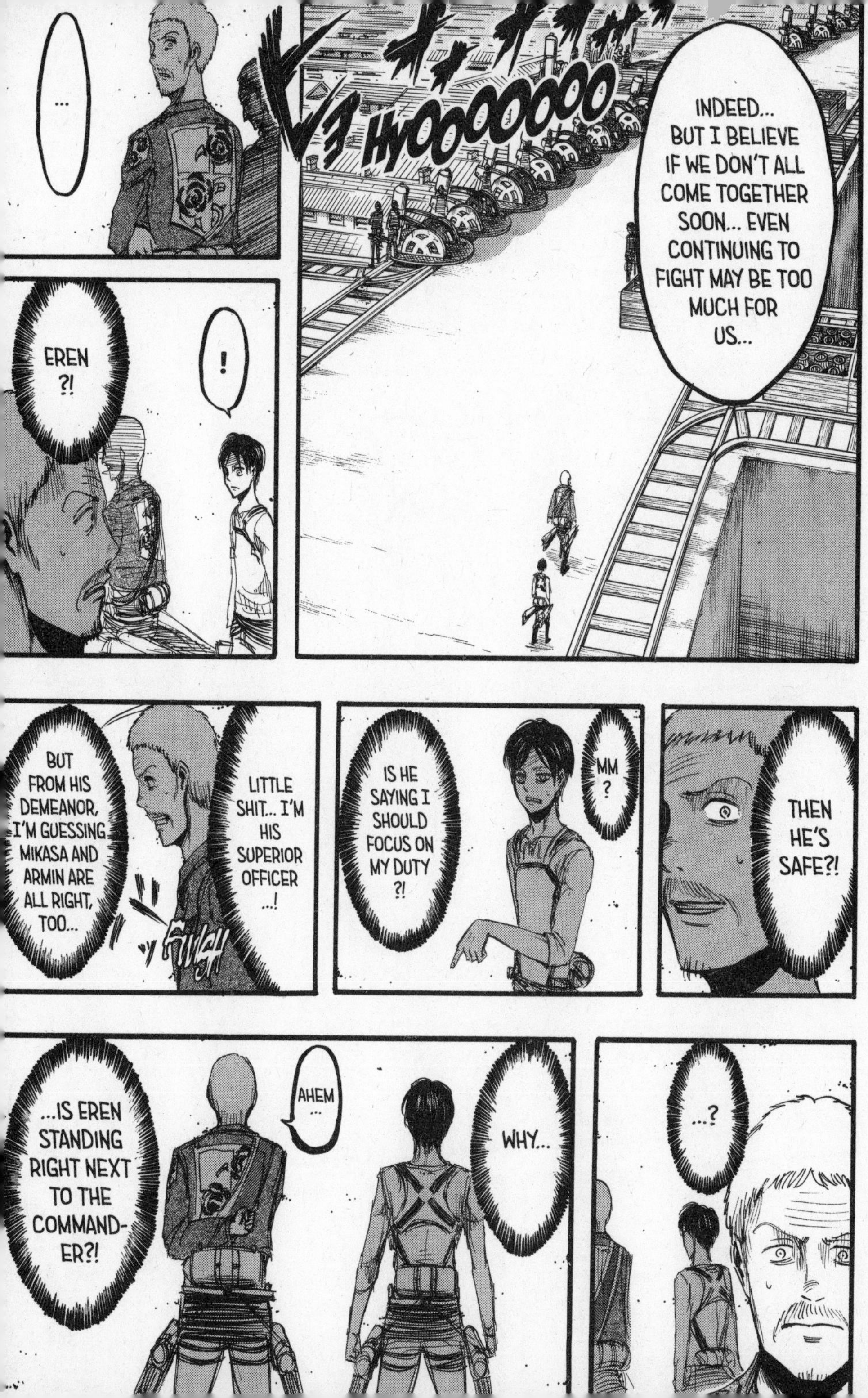
HYOOOOOOO
INDEED... BUT I BELIEVE IF WE DON'T ALL COME TOGETHER SOON... EVEN CONTINUING TO FIGHT MAY BE TOO MUCH FOR US...
...
!
EREN ?!
THEN HE'S SAFE?!
MM ?
IS HE SAYING I SHOULD FOCUS ON MY DUTY ?!
LITTLE SHIT... I'M HIS SUPERIOR OFFICER ...!
FWISH
BUT FROM HIS DEMEANOR, I'M GUESSING MIKASA AND ARMIN ARE ALL RIGHT, TOO...
...?
WHY...
AHEM ...
...IS EREN STANDING RIGHT NEXT TO THE COMMANDER?!

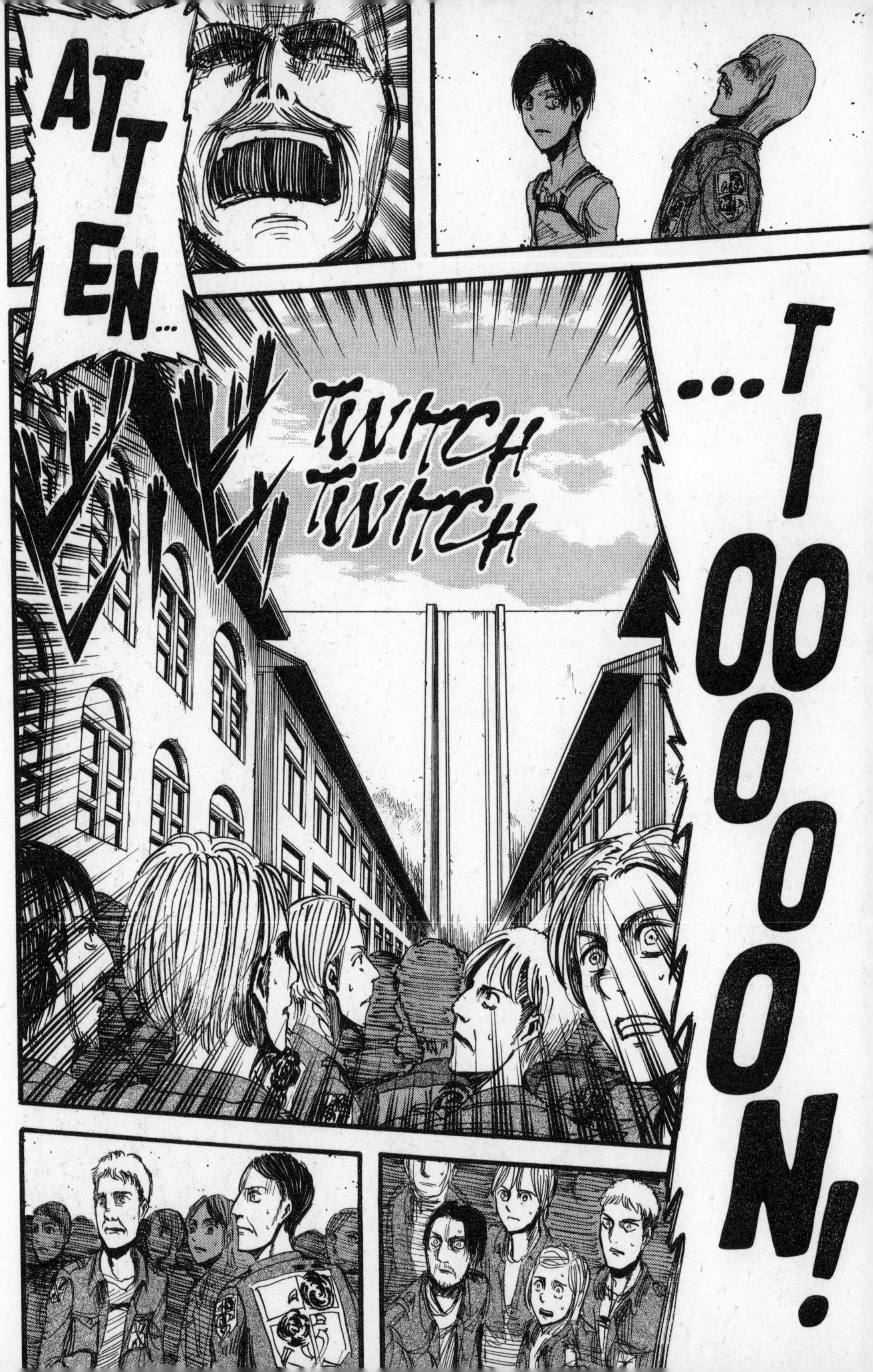
ATTEN...
...TIOOOOOON!
TWITCH TWITCH

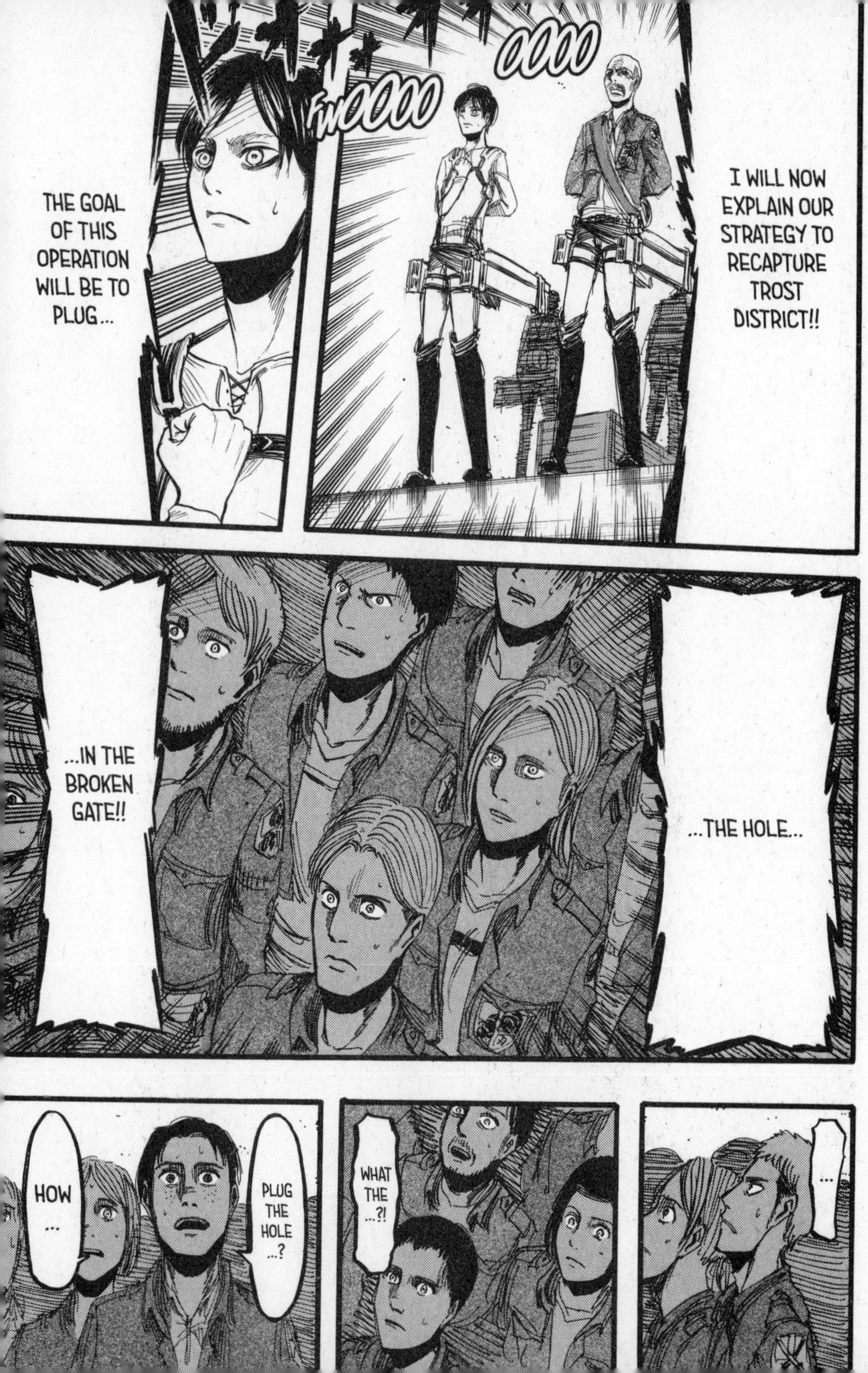
I WILL NOW EXPLAIN OUR STRATEGY TO RECAPTURE TROST DISTRICT!!
FWOOOO
OOOO
THE GOAL OF THIS OPERATION WILL BE TO PLUG...
...THE HOLE...
...IN THE BROKEN GATE!!
...
WHAT THE ...?!
PLUG THE HOLE ...?
HOW ...

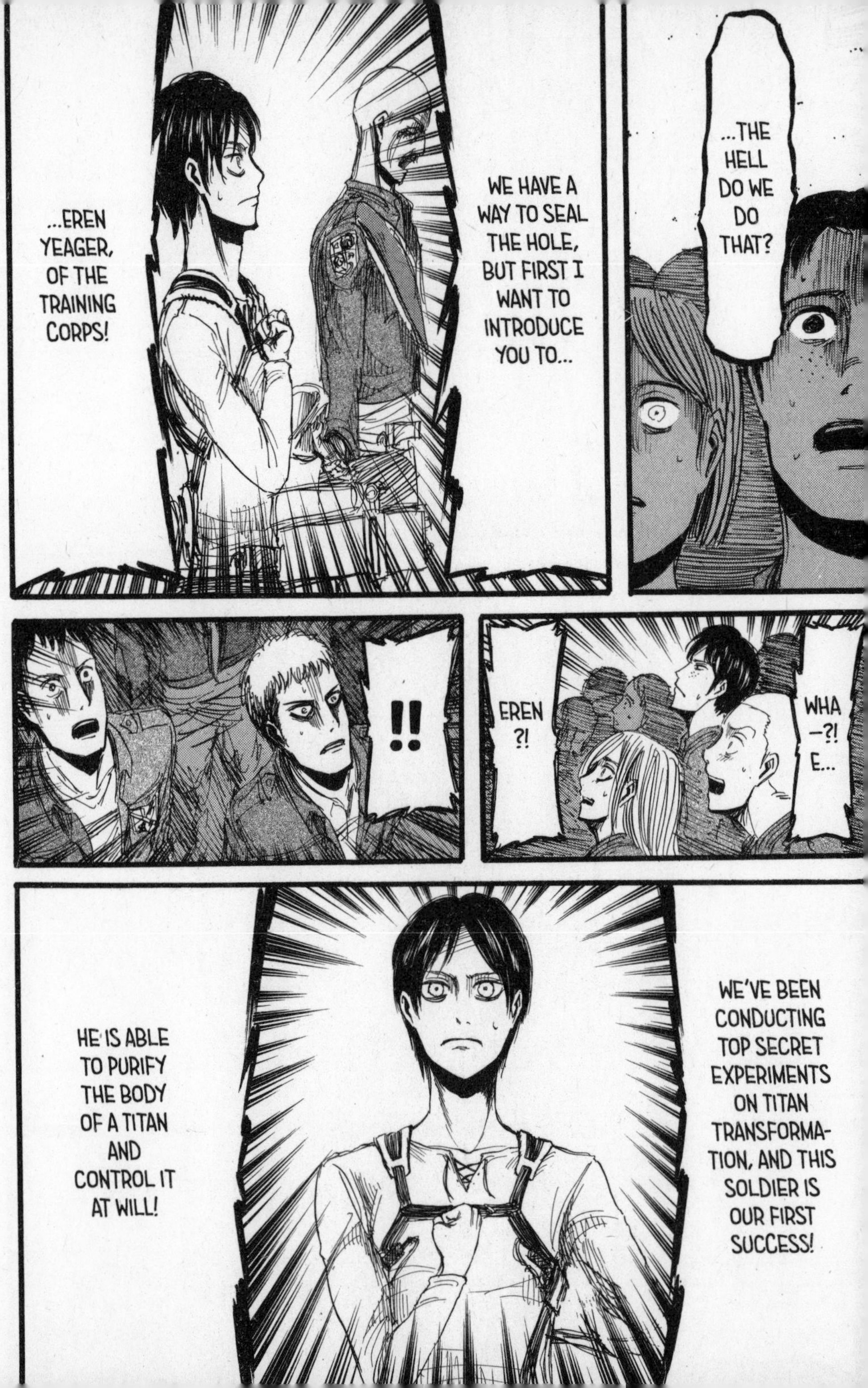
...THE HELL DO WE DO THAT?
WE HAVE A WAY TO SEAL THE HOLE, BUT FIRST I WANT TO INTRODUCE YOU TO...
...EREN YEAGER, OF THE TRAINING CORPS!
WHA—?! E...
EREN?!
!!
WE'VE BEEN CONDUCTING TOP SECRET EXPERIMENTS ON TITAN TRANSFORMA-TION, AND THIS SOLDIER IS OUR FIRST SUCCESS!
HE IS ABLE TO PURIFY THE BODY OF A TITAN AND CONTROL IT AT WILL!

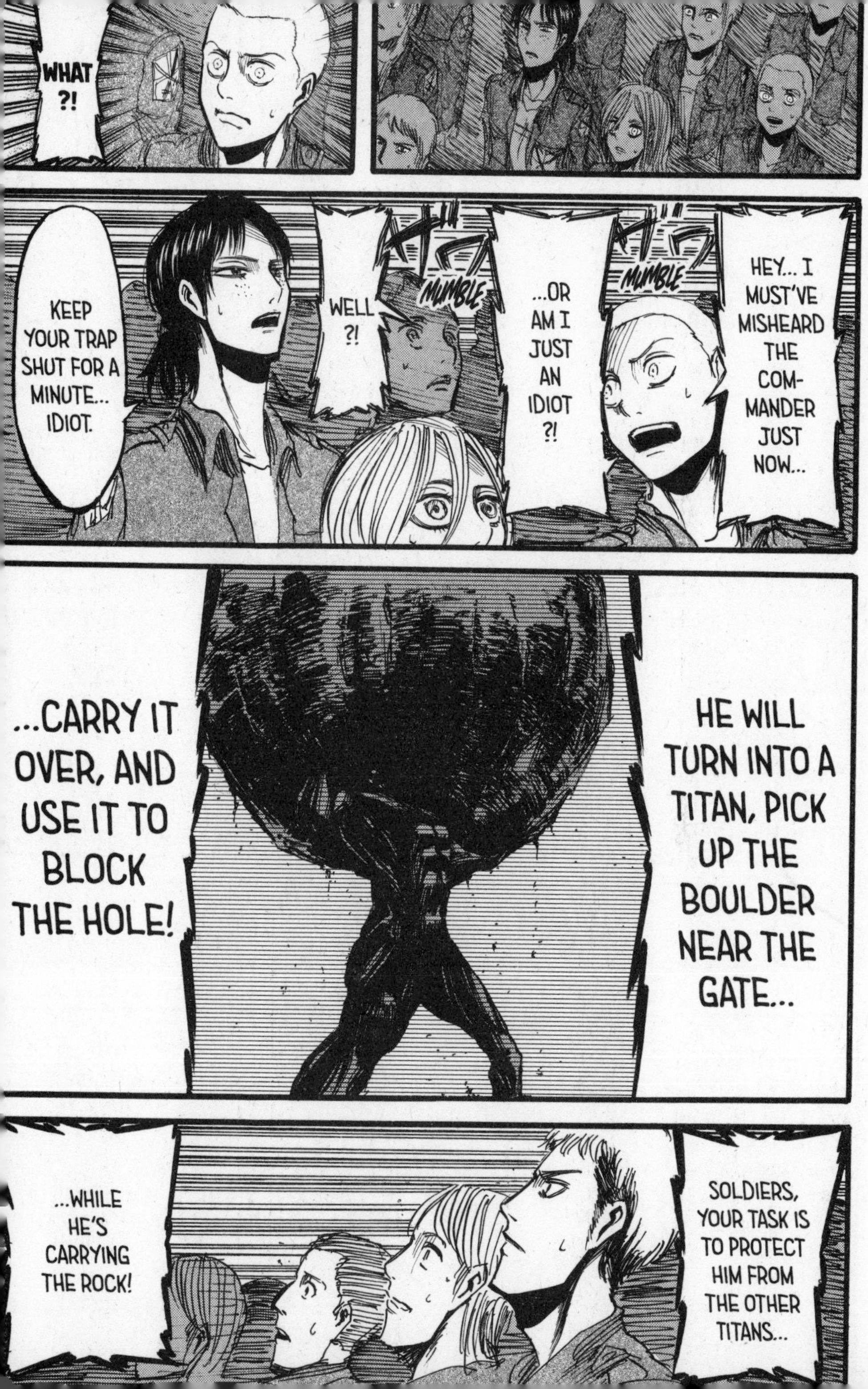
WHAT ?!
HEY... I MUST'VE MISHEARD THE COMMANDER JUST NOW...
MUMBLE
...OR AM I JUST AN IDIOT ?!
MUMBLE
WELL ?!
KEEP YOUR TRAP SHUT FOR A MINUTE... IDIOT.
HE WILL TURN INTO A TITAN, PICK UP THE BOULDER NEAR THE GATE...
...CARRY IT OVER, AND USE IT TO BLOCK THE HOLE!
SOLDIERS, YOUR TASK IS TO PROTECT HIM FROM THE OTHER TITANS...
...WHILE HE'S CARRYING THE ROCK!

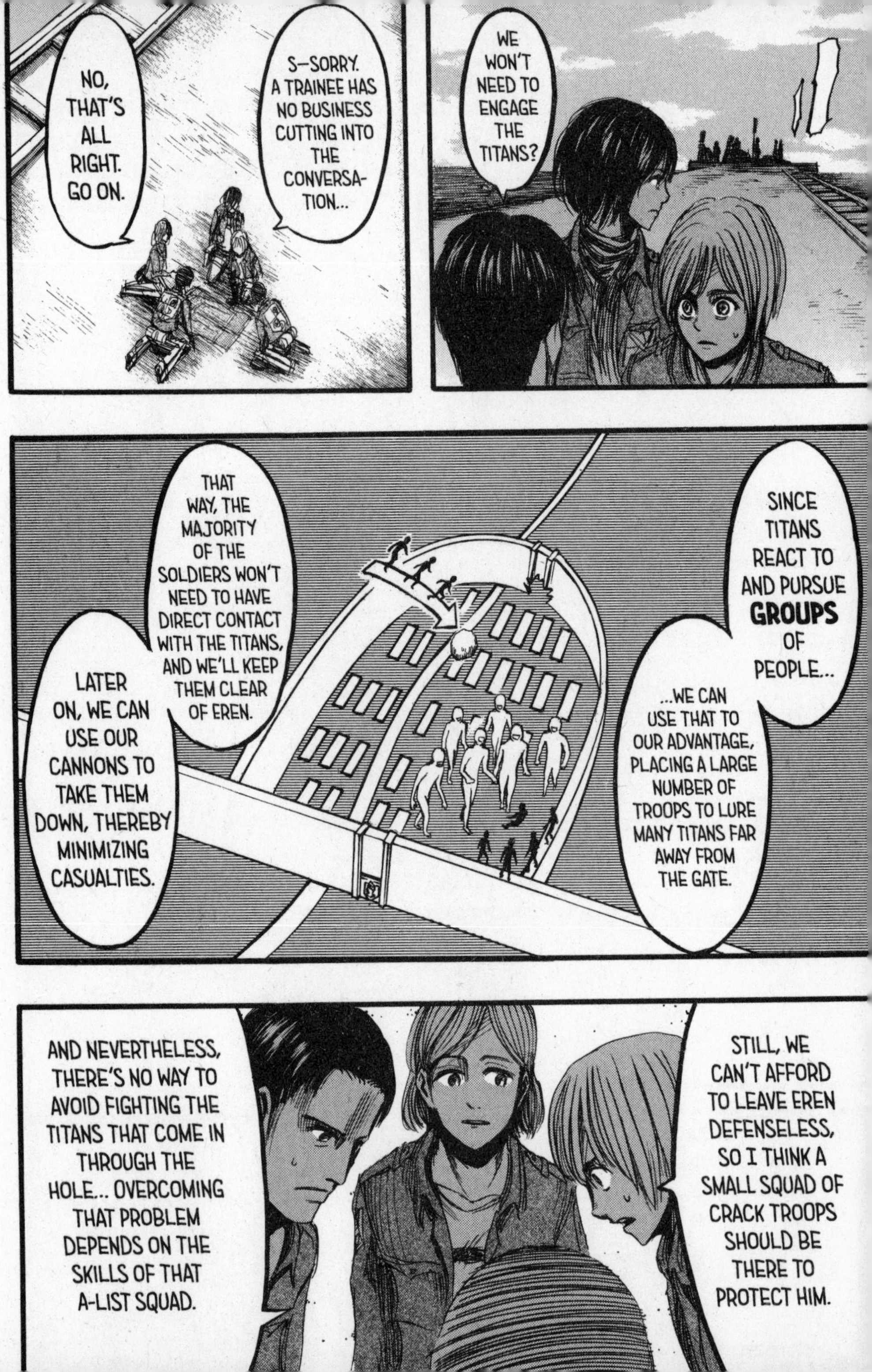
WE WON'T NEED TO ENGAGE THE TITANS?
S-SORRY. A TRAINEE HAS NO BUSINESS CUTTING INTO THE CONVERSA-TION...
NO, THAT'S ALL RIGHT. GO ON.
SINCE TITANS REACT TO AND PURSUE **GROUPS** OF PEOPLE...
...WE CAN USE THAT TO OUR ADVANTAGE, PLACING A LARGE NUMBER OF TROOPS TO LURE MANY TITANS FAR AWAY FROM THE GATE.
THAT WAY, THE MAJORITY OF THE SOLDIERS WON'T NEED TO HAVE DIRECT CONTACT WITH THE TITANS, AND WE'LL KEEP THEM CLEAR OF EREN.
LATER ON, WE CAN USE OUR CANNONS TO TAKE THEM DOWN, THEREBY MINIMIZING CASUALTIES.
STILL, WE CAN'T AFFORD TO LEAVE EREN DEFENSELESS, SO I THINK A SMALL SQUAD OF CRACK TROOPS SHOULD BE THERE TO PROTECT HIM.
AND NEVERTHELESS, THERE'S NO WAY TO AVOID FIGHTING THE TITANS THAT COME IN THROUGH THE HOLE... OVERCOMING THAT PROBLEM DEPENDS ON THE SKILLS OF THAT A-LIST SQUAD.

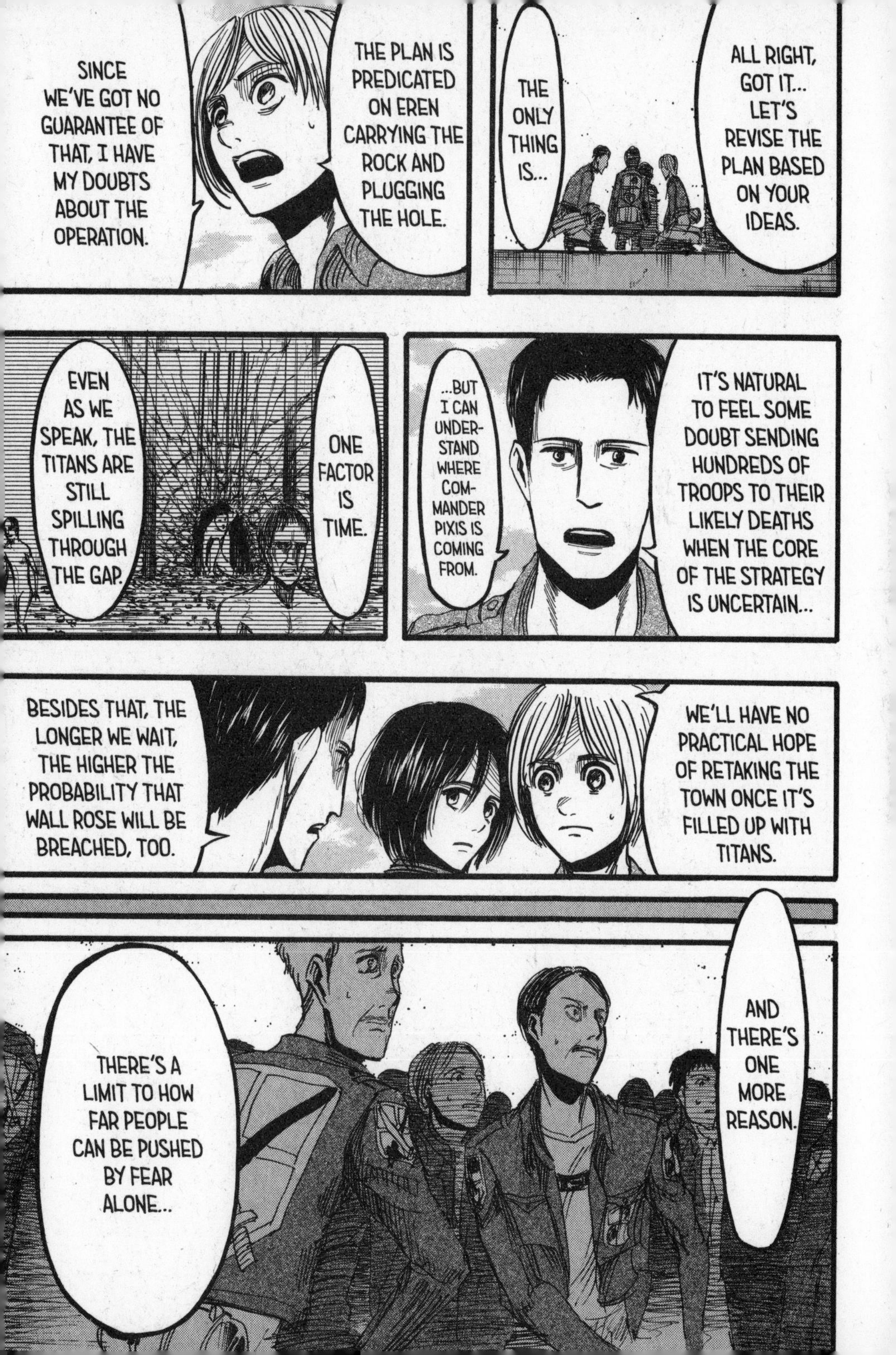
ALL RIGHT, GOT IT... LET'S REVISE THE PLAN BASED ON YOUR IDEAS.
THE ONLY THING IS...
THE PLAN IS PREDICATED ON EREN CARRYING THE ROCK AND PLUGGING THE HOLE.
SINCE WE'VE GOT NO GUARANTEE OF THAT, I HAVE MY DOUBTS ABOUT THE OPERATION.
IT'S NATURAL TO FEEL SOME DOUBT SENDING HUNDREDS OF TROOPS TO THEIR LIKELY DEATHS WHEN THE CORE OF THE STRATEGY IS UNCERTAIN...
...BUT I CAN UNDER-STAND WHERE COM-MANDER PIXIS IS COMING FROM.
ONE FACTOR IS TIME.
EVEN AS WE SPEAK, THE TITANS ARE STILL SPILLING THROUGH THE GAP.
WE'LL HAVE NO PRACTICAL HOPE OF RETAKING THE TOWN ONCE IT'S FILLED UP WITH TITANS.
BESIDES THAT, THE LONGER WE WAIT, THE HIGHER THE PROBABILITY THAT WALL ROSE WILL BE BREACHED, TOO.
AND THERE'S ONE MORE REASON.
THERE'S A LIMIT TO HOW FAR PEOPLE CAN BE PUSHED BY FEAR ALONE...

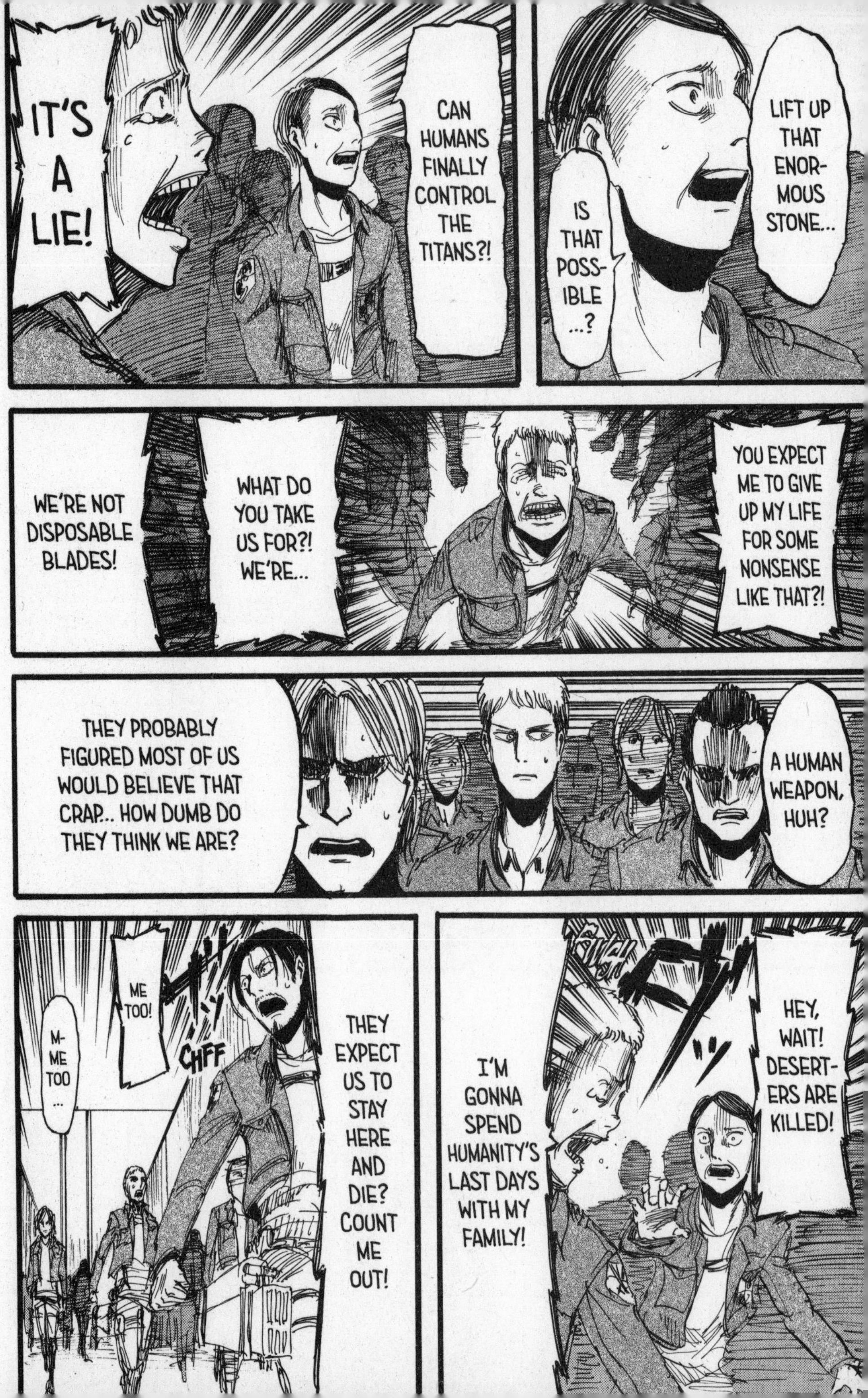
LIFT UP THAT ENOR-MOUS STONE...
IS THAT POSS-IBLE ...?
CAN HUMANS FINALLY CONTROL THE TITANS?!
IT'S A LIE!
YOU EXPECT ME TO GIVE UP MY LIFE FOR SOME NONSENSE LIKE THAT?!
WHAT DO YOU TAKE US FOR?! WE'RE...
WE'RE NOT DISPOSABLE BLADES!
A HUMAN WEAPON, HUH?
THEY PROBABLY FIGURED MOST OF US WOULD BELIEVE THAT CRAP... HOW DUMB DO THEY THINK WE ARE?
HEY, WAIT! DESERT-ERS ARE KILLED!
I'M GONNA SPEND HUMANITY'S LAST DAYS WITH MY FAMILY!
THEY EXPECT US TO STAY HERE AND DIE? COUNT ME OUT!
CHFF
ME TOO!
M-ME TOO ...

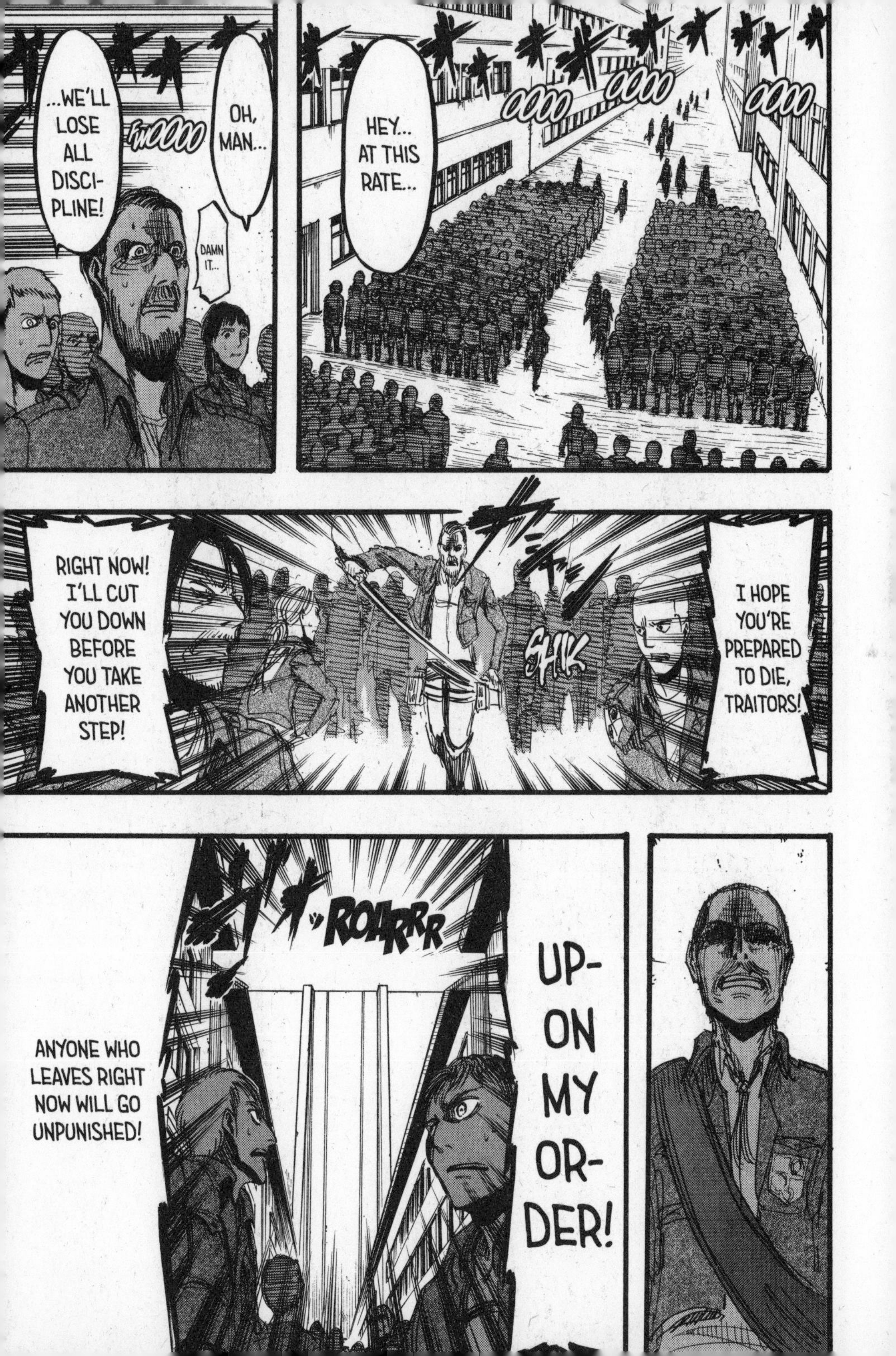
OOOO
OOOO
OOOO
HEY... AT THIS RATE...
OH, MAN...
DAMN IT...
FWOOOO
...WE'LL LOSE ALL DISCIPLINE!
I HOPE YOU'RE PREPARED TO DIE, TRAITORS!
SHIK
RIGHT NOW! I'LL CUT YOU DOWN BEFORE YOU TAKE ANOTHER STEP!
UPON MY ORDER!
ROARRR
ANYONE WHO LEAVES RIGHT NOW WILL GO UNPUNISHED!

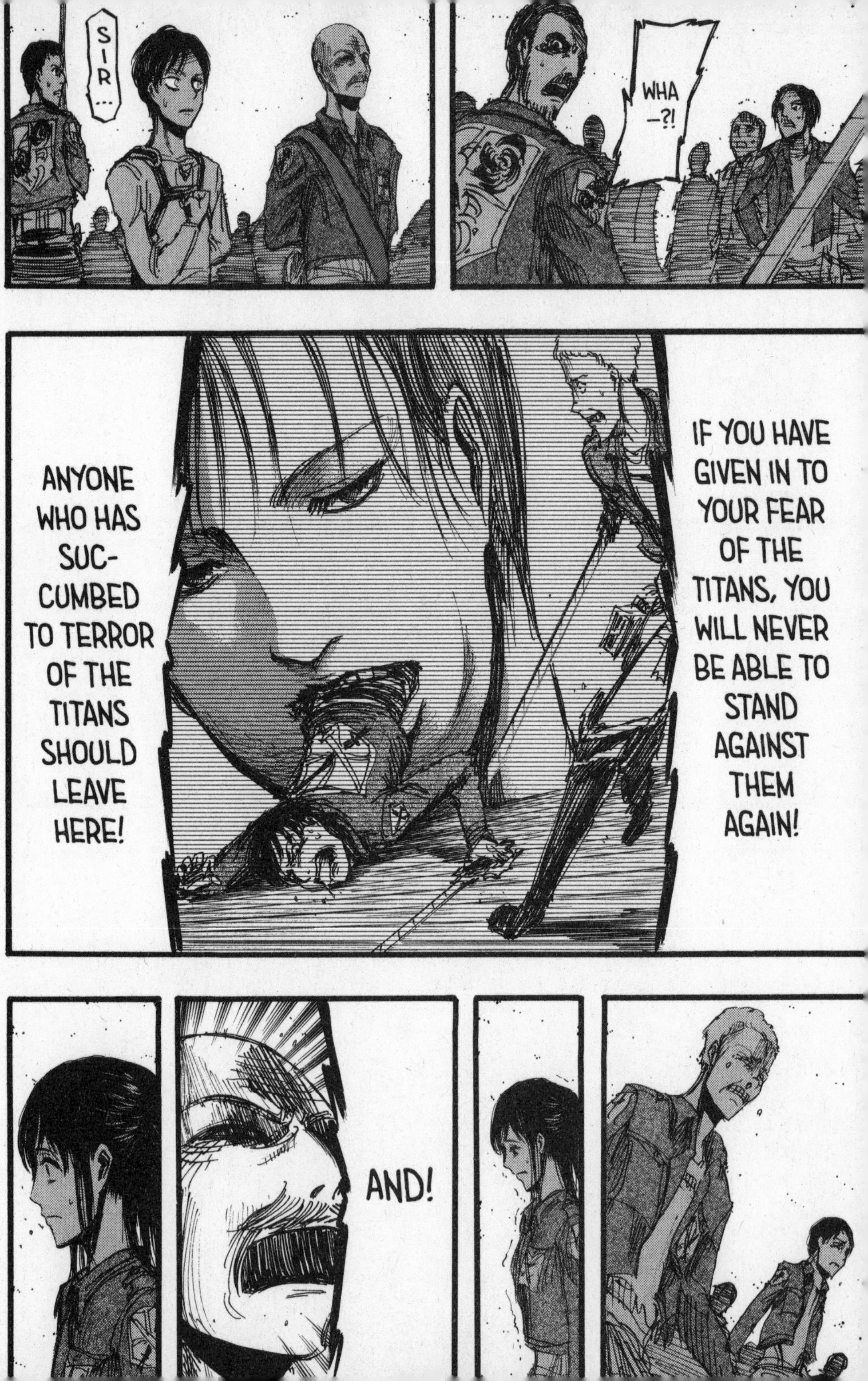
WHA —?!
SIR ...
IF YOU HAVE GIVEN IN TO YOUR FEAR OF THE TITANS, YOU WILL NEVER BE ABLE TO STAND AGAINST THEM AGAIN!
ANYONE WHO HAS SUC-CUMBED TO TERROR OF THE TITANS SHOULD LEAVE HERE!
AND!

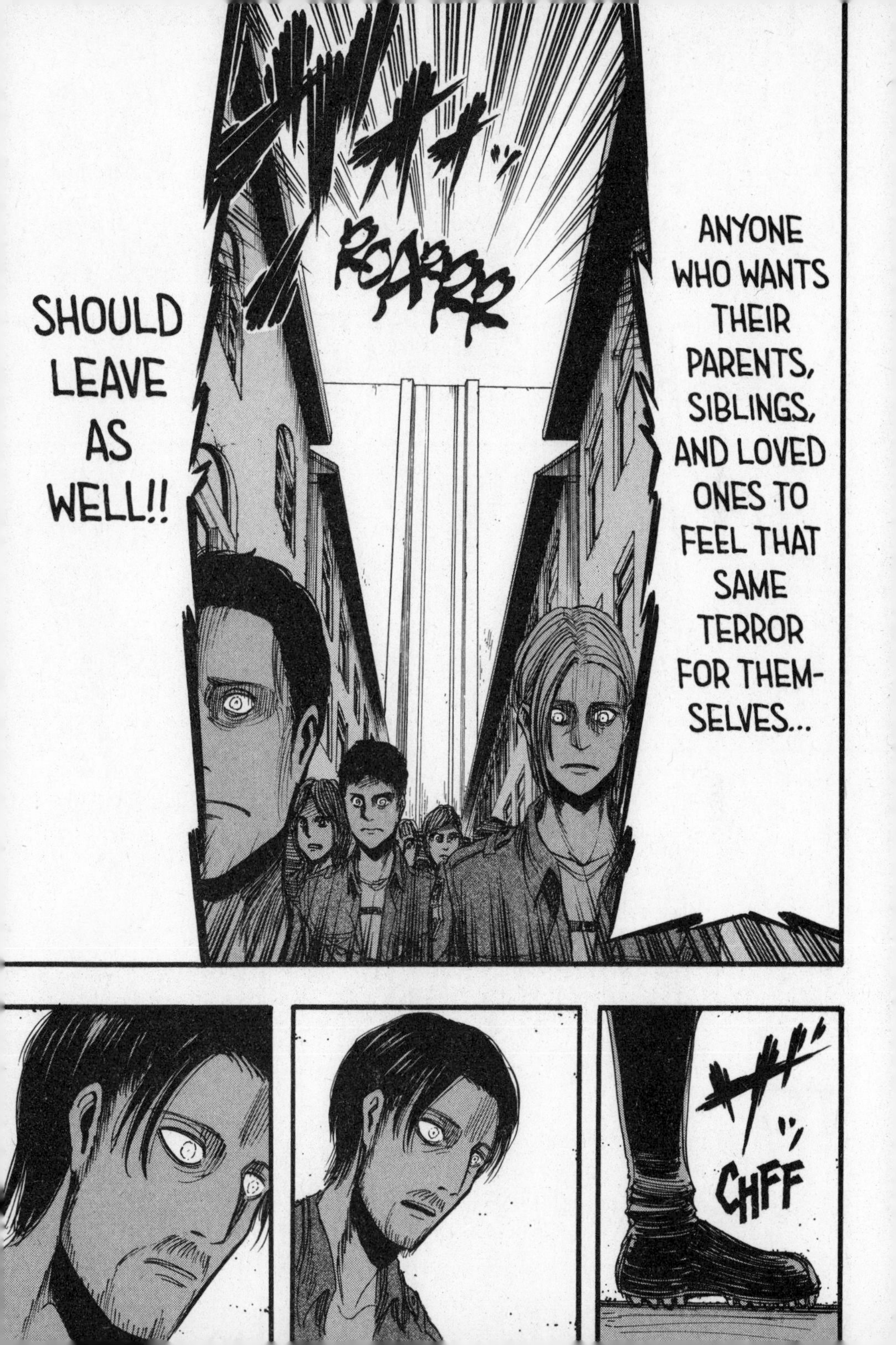
ANYONE WHO WANTS THEIR PARENTS, SIBLINGS, AND LOVED ONES TO FEEL THAT SAME TERROR FOR THEMSELVES...
ROARRR
SHOULD LEAVE AS WELL!!
CHFF

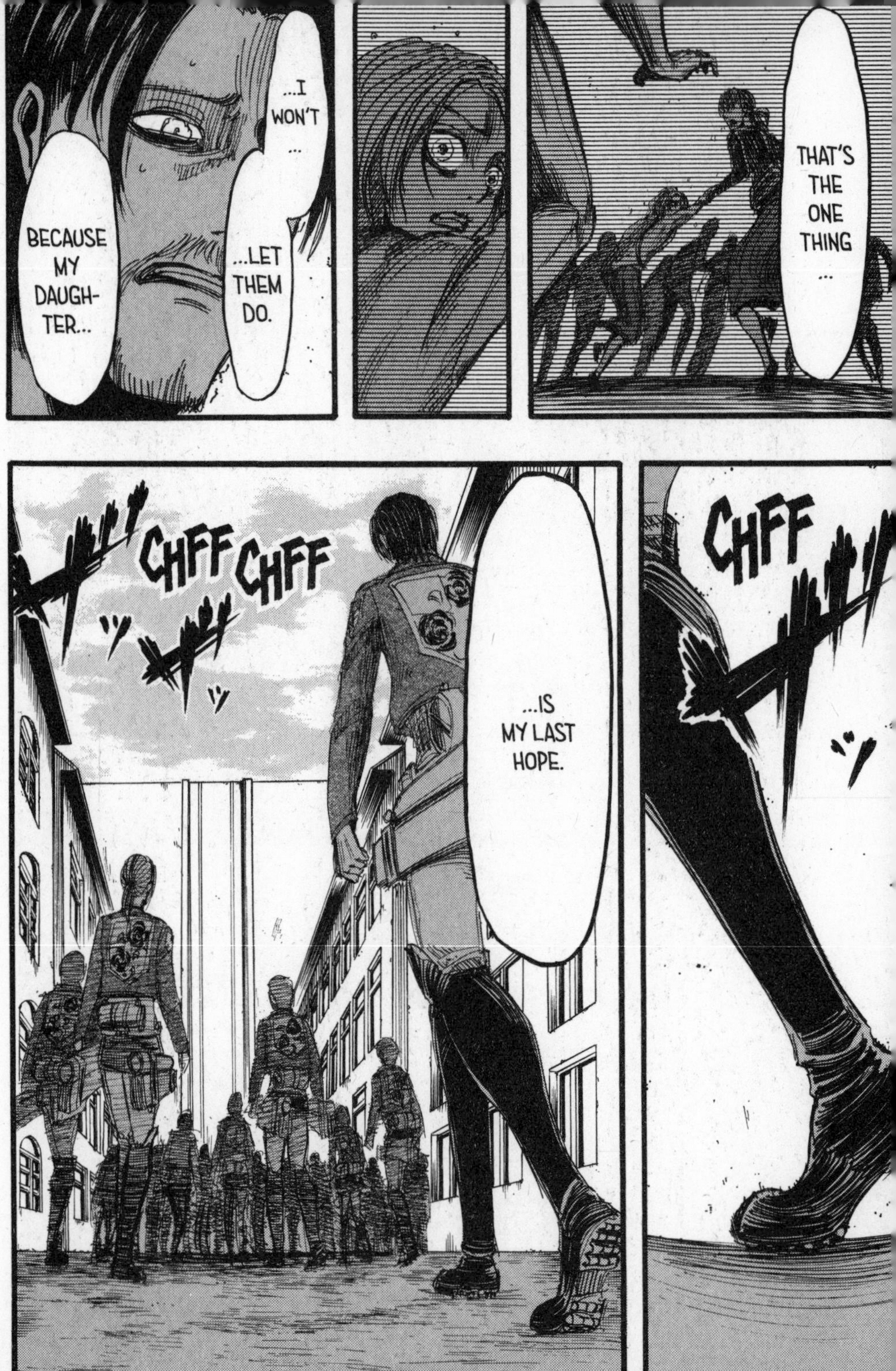
THAT'S THE ONE THING ...
...I WON'T ...
...LET THEM DO.
BECAUSE MY DAUGH-TER...
CHFF
CHFF CHFF
...IS MY LAST HOPE.

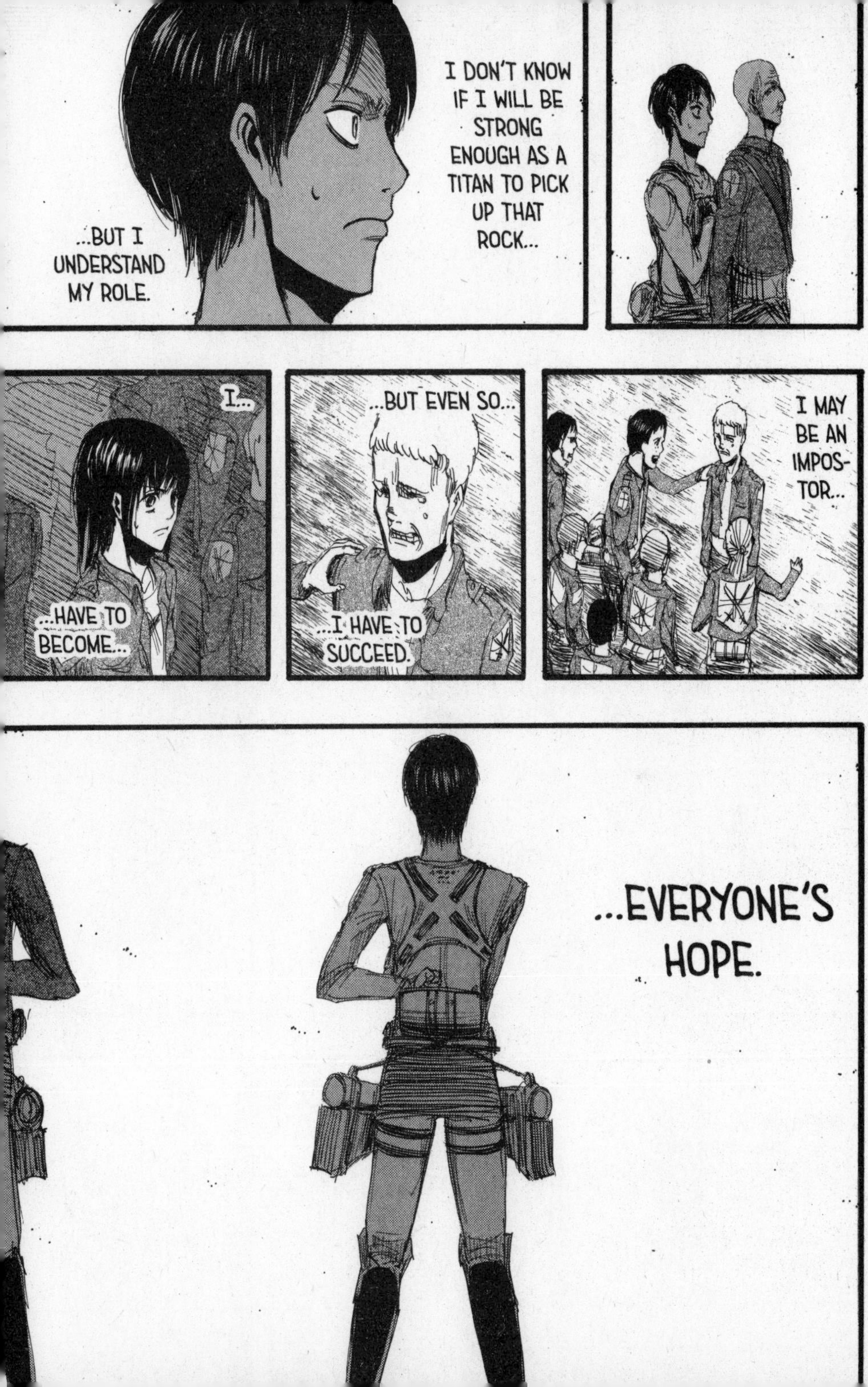
I DON'T KNOW IF I WILL BE STRONG ENOUGH AS A TITAN TO PICK UP THAT ROCK...
...BUT I UNDERSTAND MY ROLE.
I MAY BE AN IMPOS-TOR...
...BUT EVEN SO...
...I HAVE TO SUCCEED.
I...
...HAVE TO BECOME...
...EVERYONE'S HOPE.

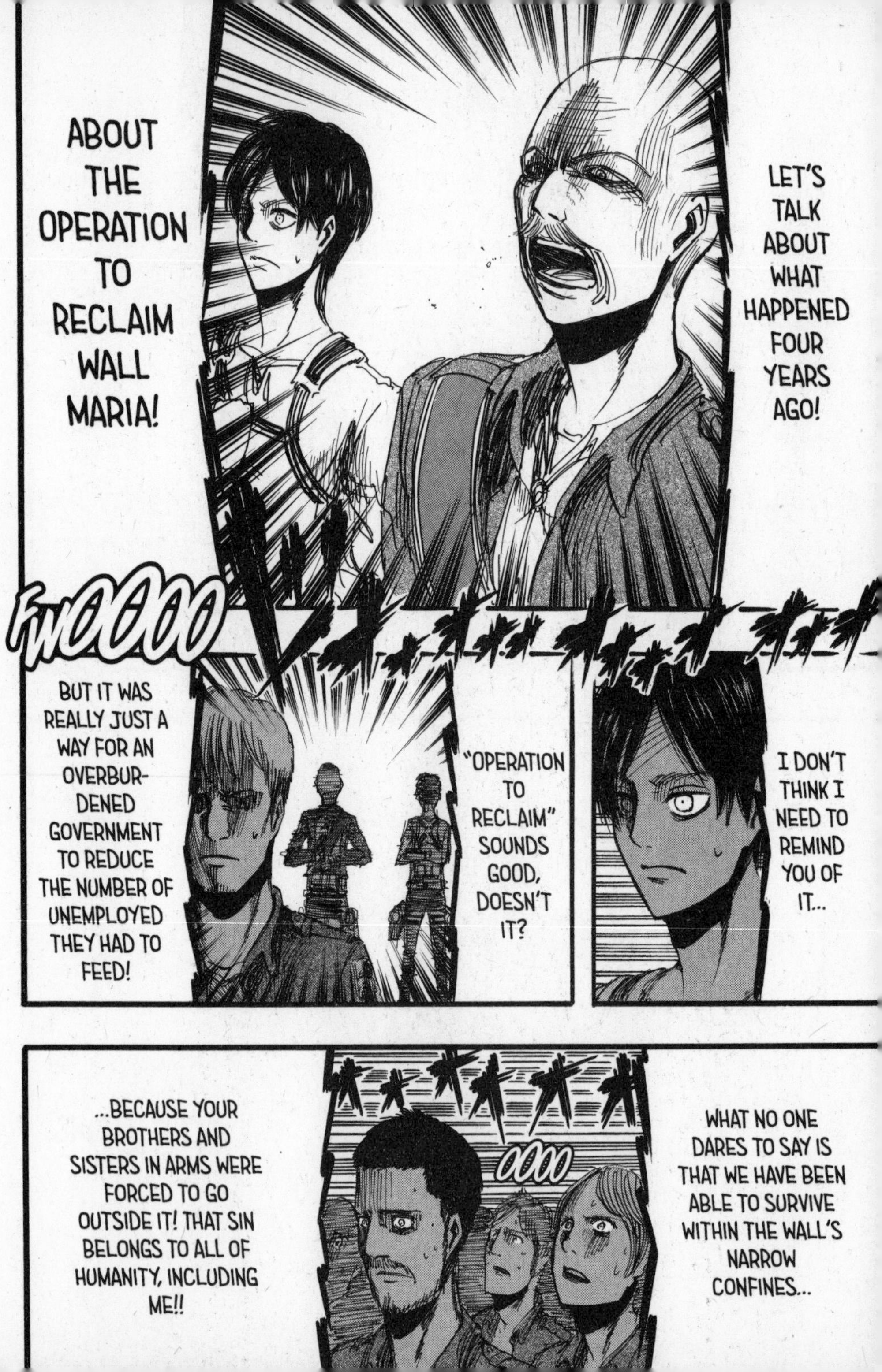
LET'S TALK ABOUT WHAT HAPPENED FOUR YEARS AGO!
ABOUT THE OPERATION TO RECLAIM WALL MARIA!
FWOOOO
I DON'T THINK I NEED TO REMIND YOU OF IT...
"OPERATION TO RECLAIM" SOUNDS GOOD, DOESN'T IT?
BUT IT WAS REALLY JUST A WAY FOR AN OVERBUR-DENED GOVERNMENT TO REDUCE THE NUMBER OF UNEMPLOYED THEY HAD TO FEED!
WHAT NO ONE DARES TO SAY IS THAT WE HAVE BEEN ABLE TO SURVIVE WITHIN THE WALL'S NARROW CONFINES...
OOOO
...BECAUSE YOUR BROTHERS AND SISTERS IN ARMS WERE FORCED TO GO OUTSIDE IT! THAT SIN BELONGS TO ALL OF HUMANITY, INCLUDING ME!!

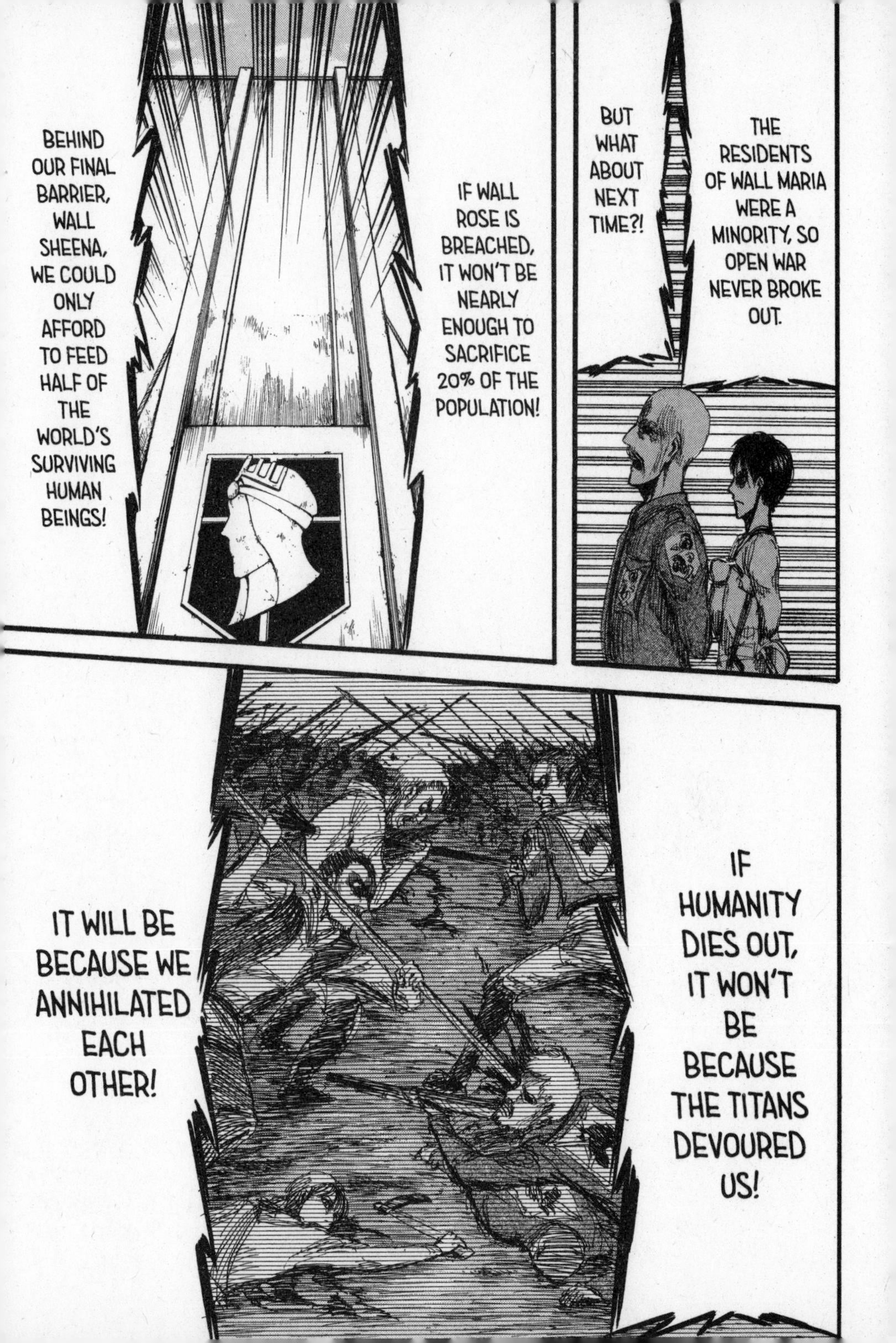
THE RESIDENTS OF WALL MARIA WERE A MINORITY, SO OPEN WAR NEVER BROKE OUT.
BUT WHAT ABOUT NEXT TIME?!
IF WALL ROSE IS BREACHED, IT WON'T BE NEARLY ENOUGH TO SACRIFICE 20% OF THE POPULATION!
BEHIND OUR FINAL BARRIER, WALL SHEENA, WE COULD ONLY AFFORD TO FEED HALF OF THE WORLD'S SURVIVING HUMAN BEINGS!
IF HUMANITY DIES OUT, IT WON'T BE BECAUSE THE TITANS DEVOURED US!
IT WILL BE BECAUSE WE ANNIHILATED EACH OTHER!

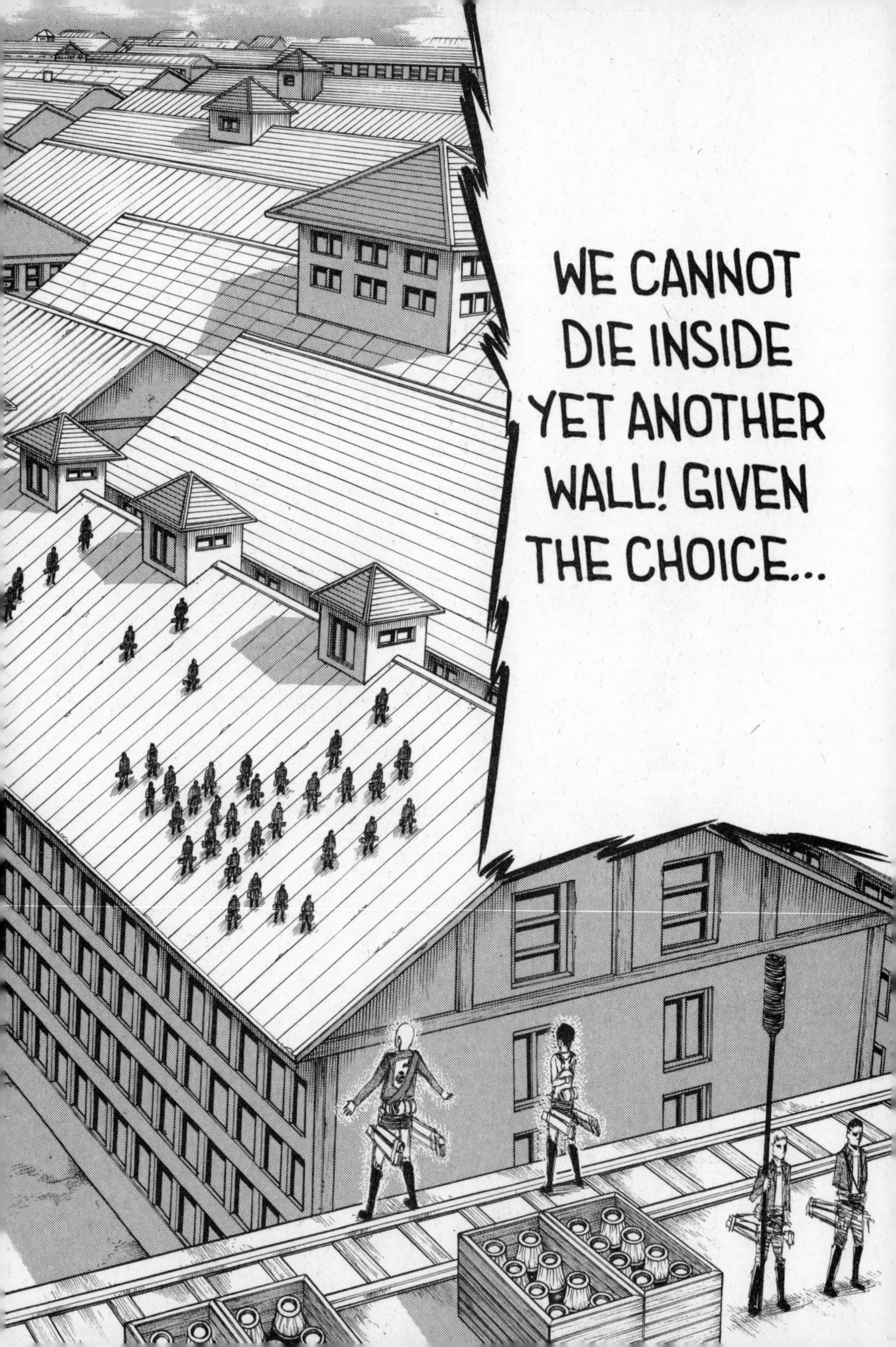
WE CANNOT DIE INSIDE YET ANOTHER WALL! GIVEN THE CHOICE...

DIE HERE!

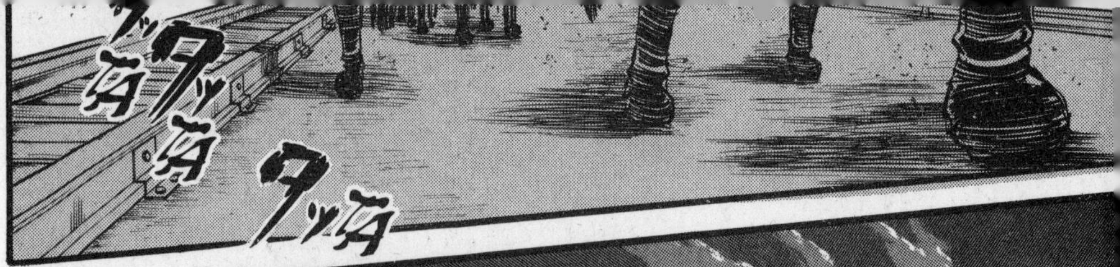

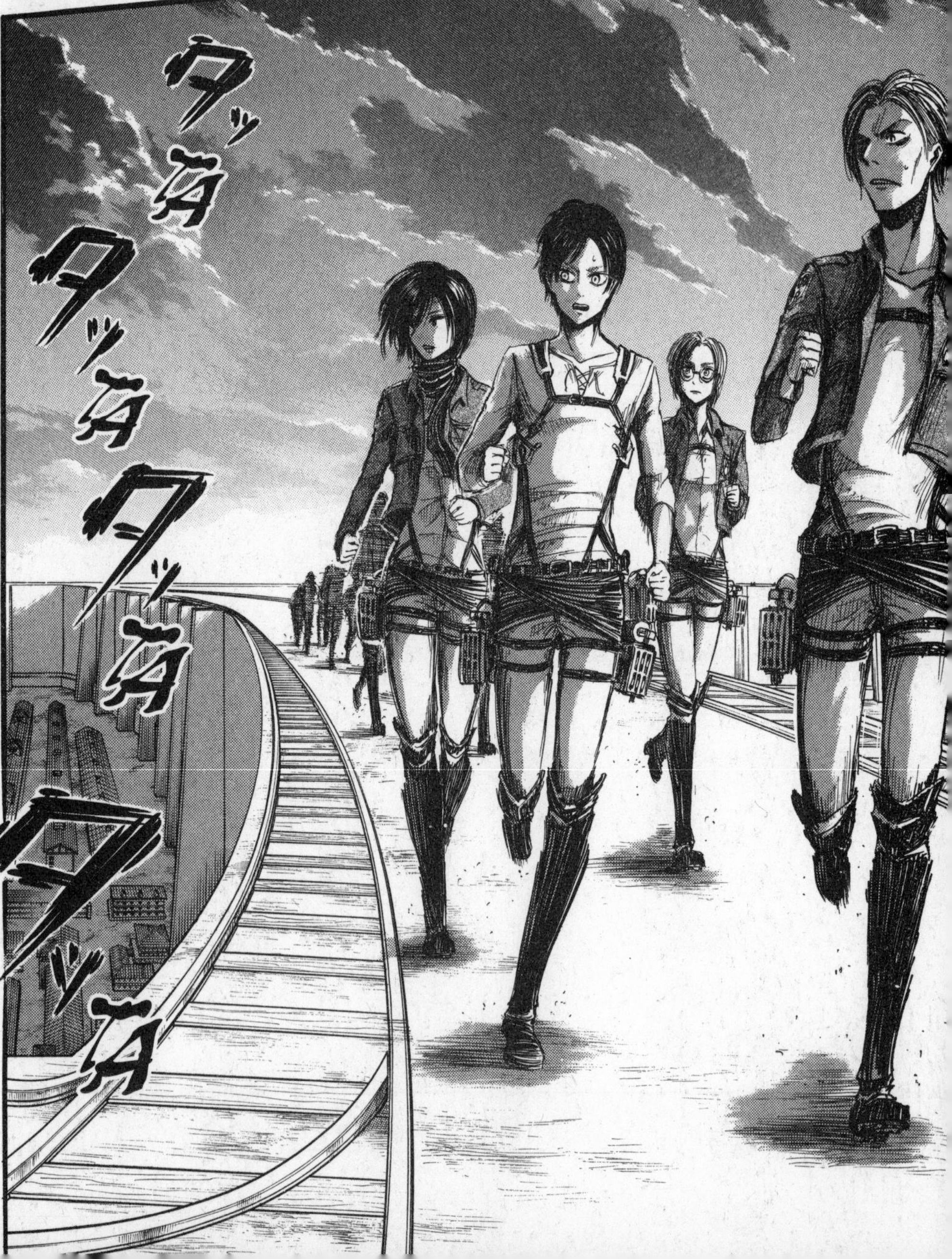

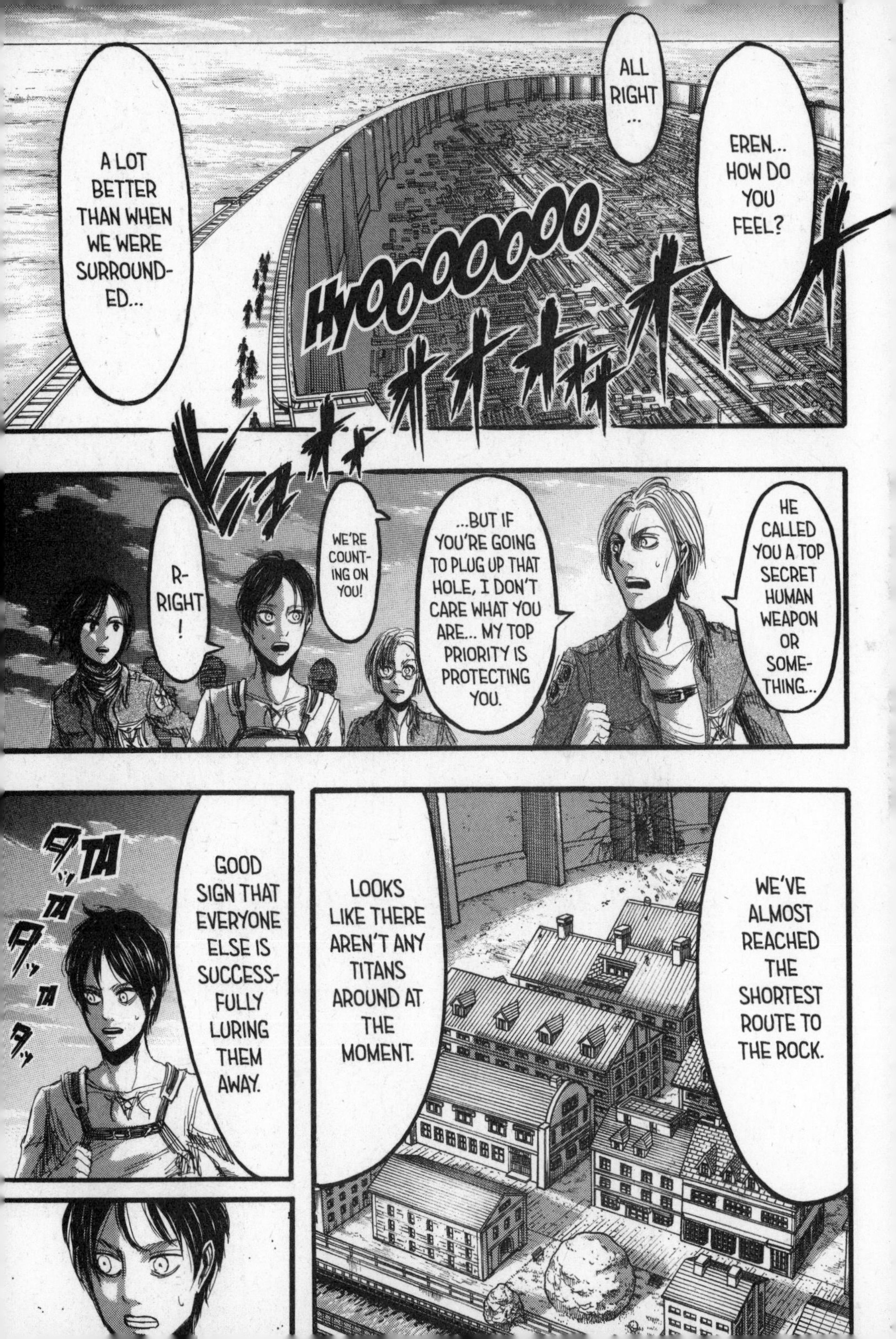
EREN... HOW DO YOU FEEL?
ALL RIGHT ...
HYOOOOOOO
A LOT BETTER THAN WHEN WE WERE SURROUND-ED...
HE CALLED YOU A TOP SECRET HUMAN WEAPON OR SOME-THING...
...BUT IF YOU'RE GOING TO PLUG UP THAT HOLE, I DON'T CARE WHAT YOU ARE... MY TOP PRIORITY IS PROTECTING YOU.
WE'RE COUNT-ING ON YOU!
R-RIGHT!
WE'VE ALMOST REACHED THE SHORTEST ROUTE TO THE ROCK.
LOOKS LIKE THERE AREN'T ANY TITANS AROUND AT THE MOMENT.
TA
TA
TA
GOOD SIGN THAT EVERYONE ELSE IS SUCCESS-FULLY LURING THEM AWAY.

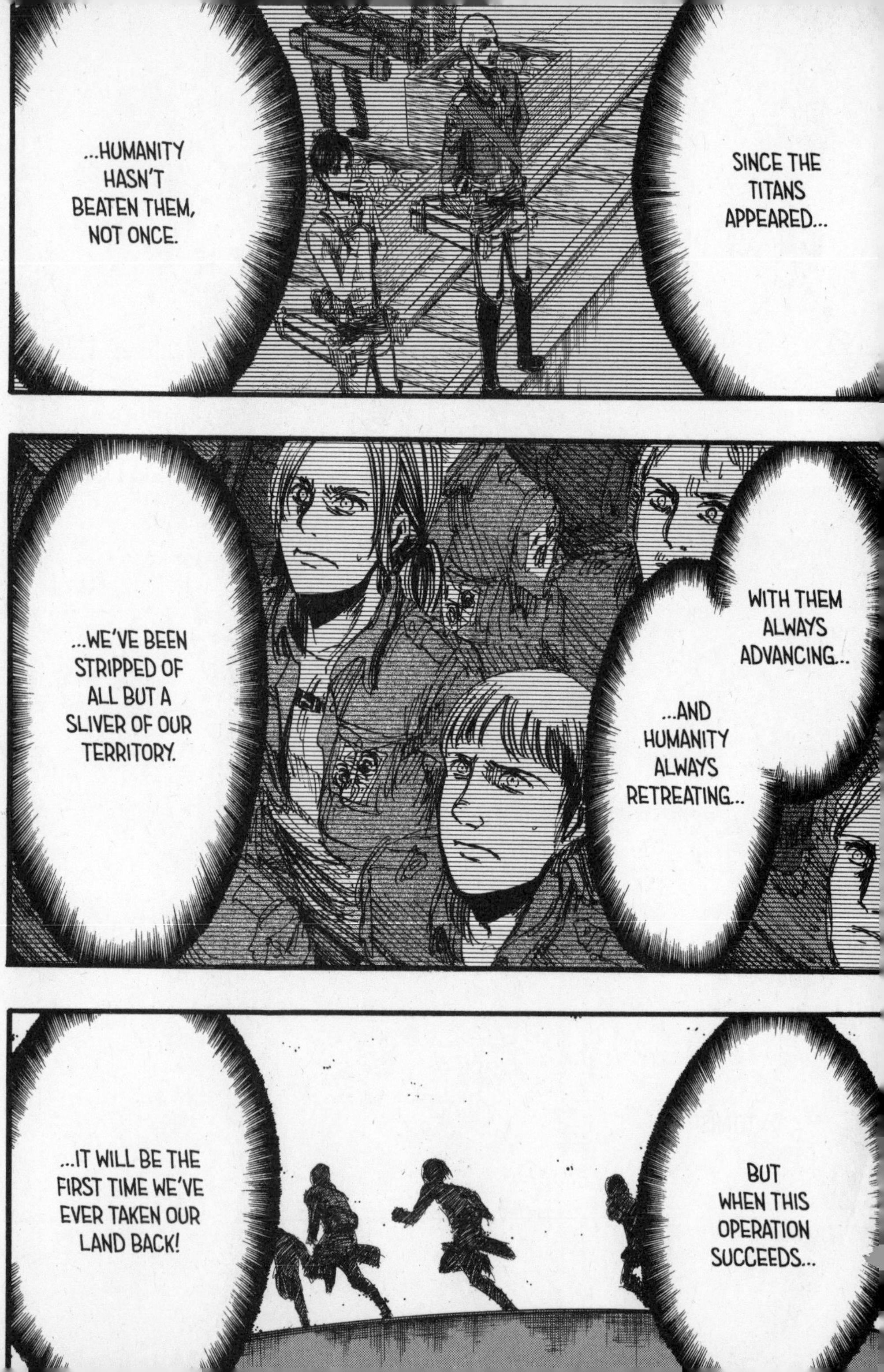
SINCE THE TITANS APPEARED...
...HUMANITY HASN'T BEATEN THEM, NOT ONCE.
WITH THEM ALWAYS ADVANCING...
...AND HUMANITY ALWAYS RETREATING...
...WE'VE BEEN STRIPPED OF ALL BUT A SLIVER OF OUR TERRITORY.
BUT WHEN THIS OPERATION SUCCEEDS...
...IT WILL BE THE FIRST TIME WE'VE EVER TAKEN OUR LAND BACK!

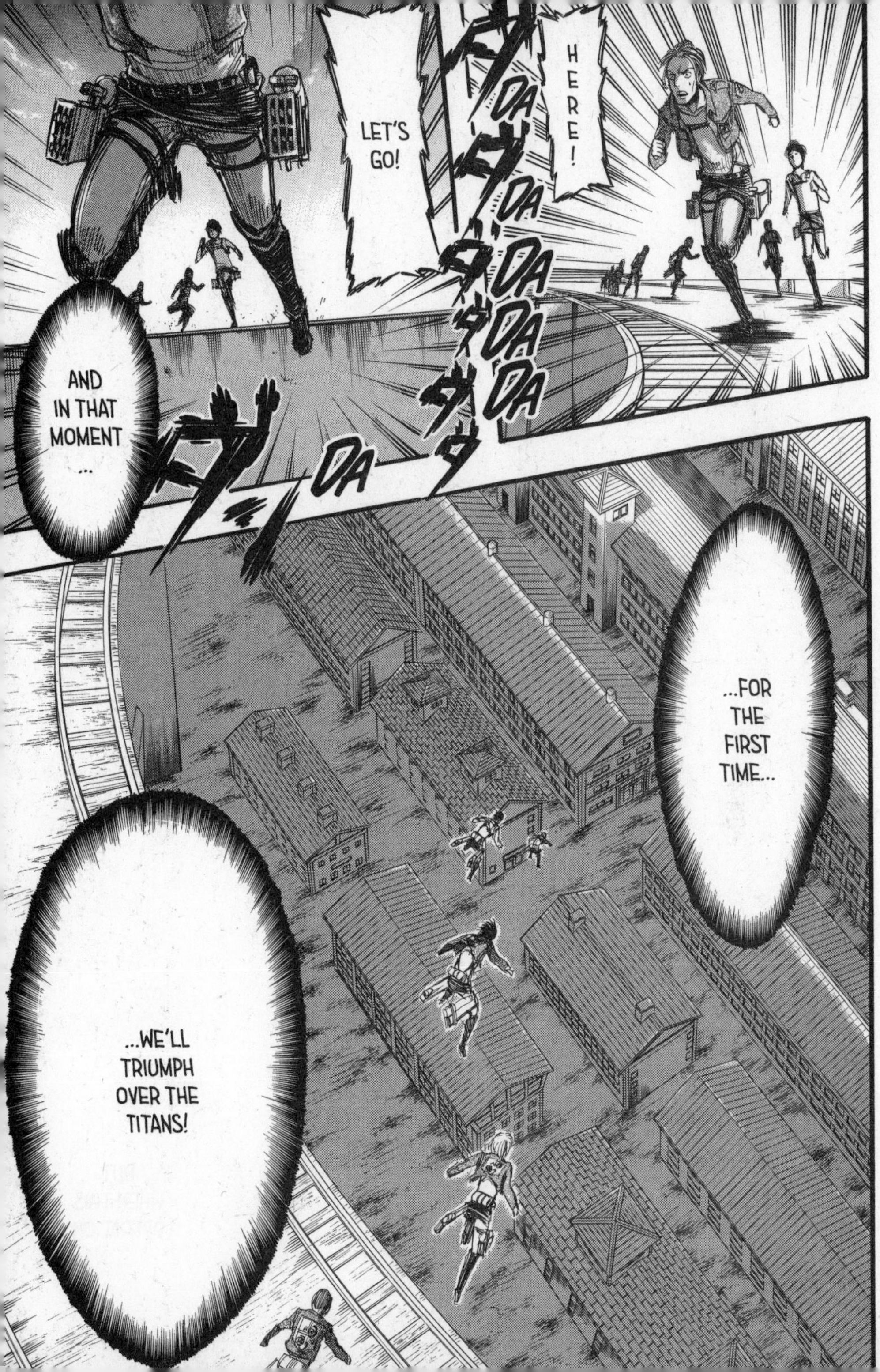
HERE!
LET'S GO!
DA DA DA DA DA DA DA
DA
AND IN THAT MOMENT ...
...FOR THE FIRST TIME...
...WE'LL TRIUMPH OVER THE TITANS!

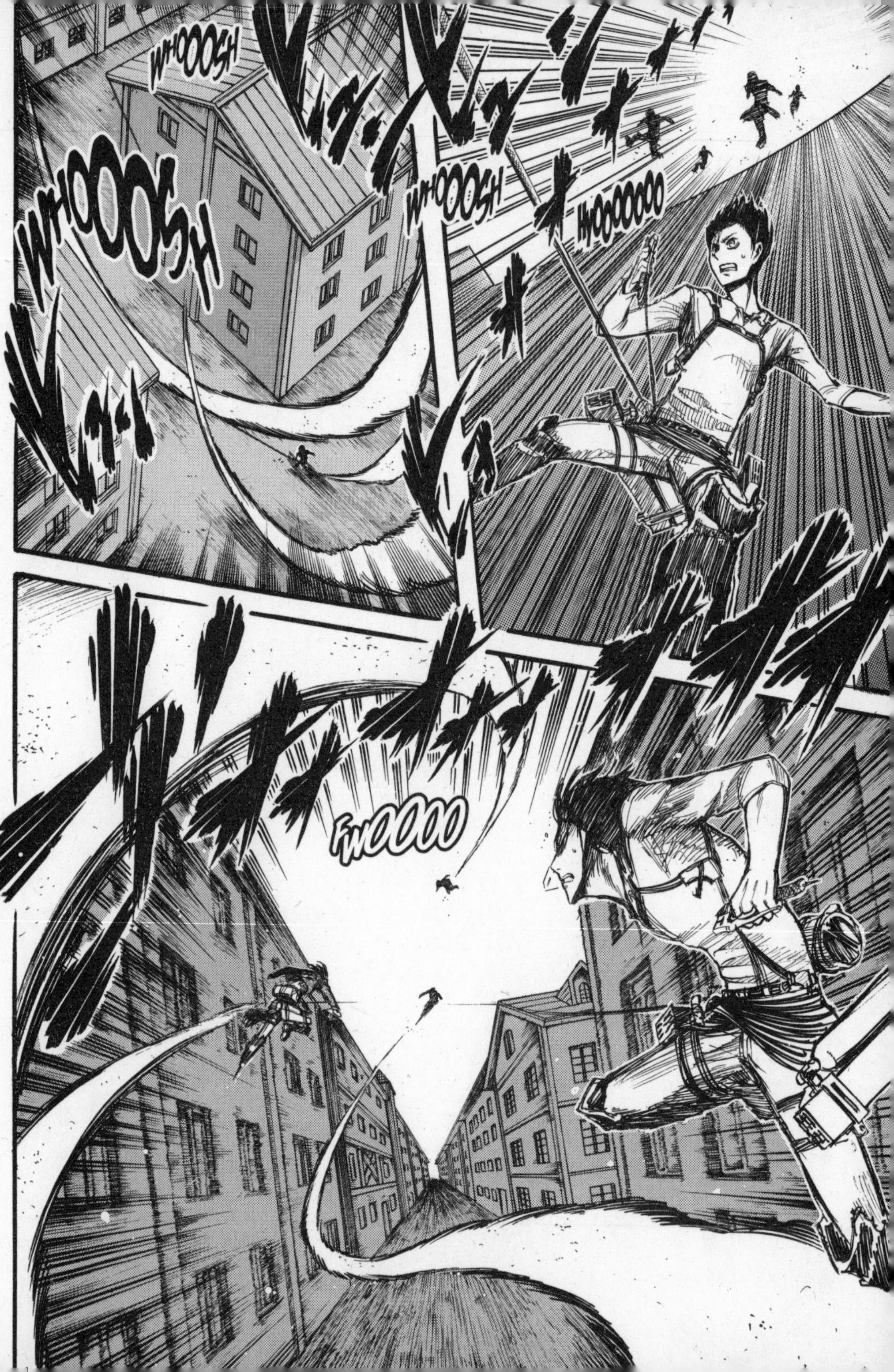
WHOOOOOOO
WHOOOSH
WHOOOSH
WHOOOSH
FWOOOO

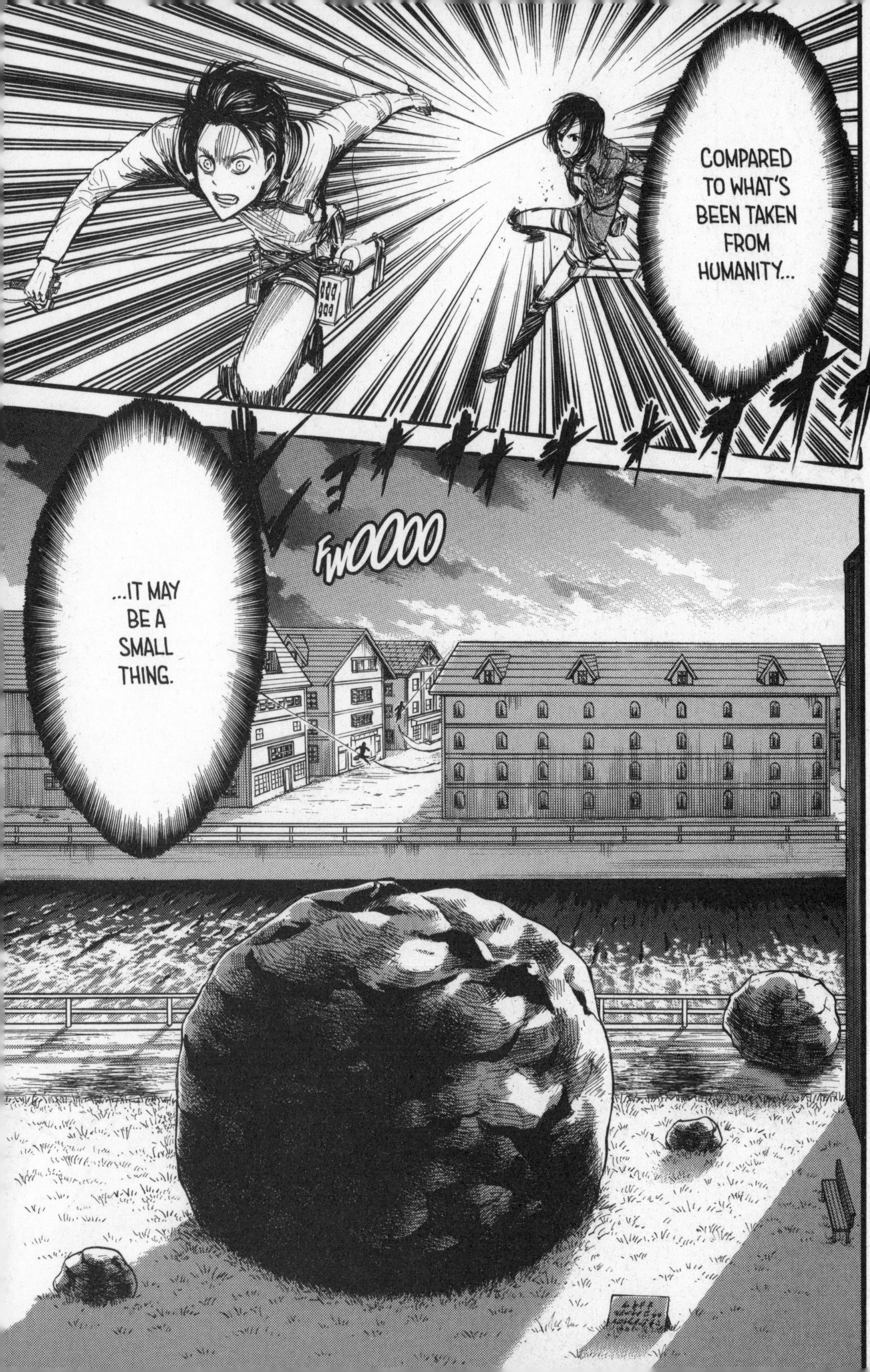
COMPARED TO WHAT'S BEEN TAKEN FROM HUMANITY...
FWOOOO
...IT MAY BE A SMALL THING.

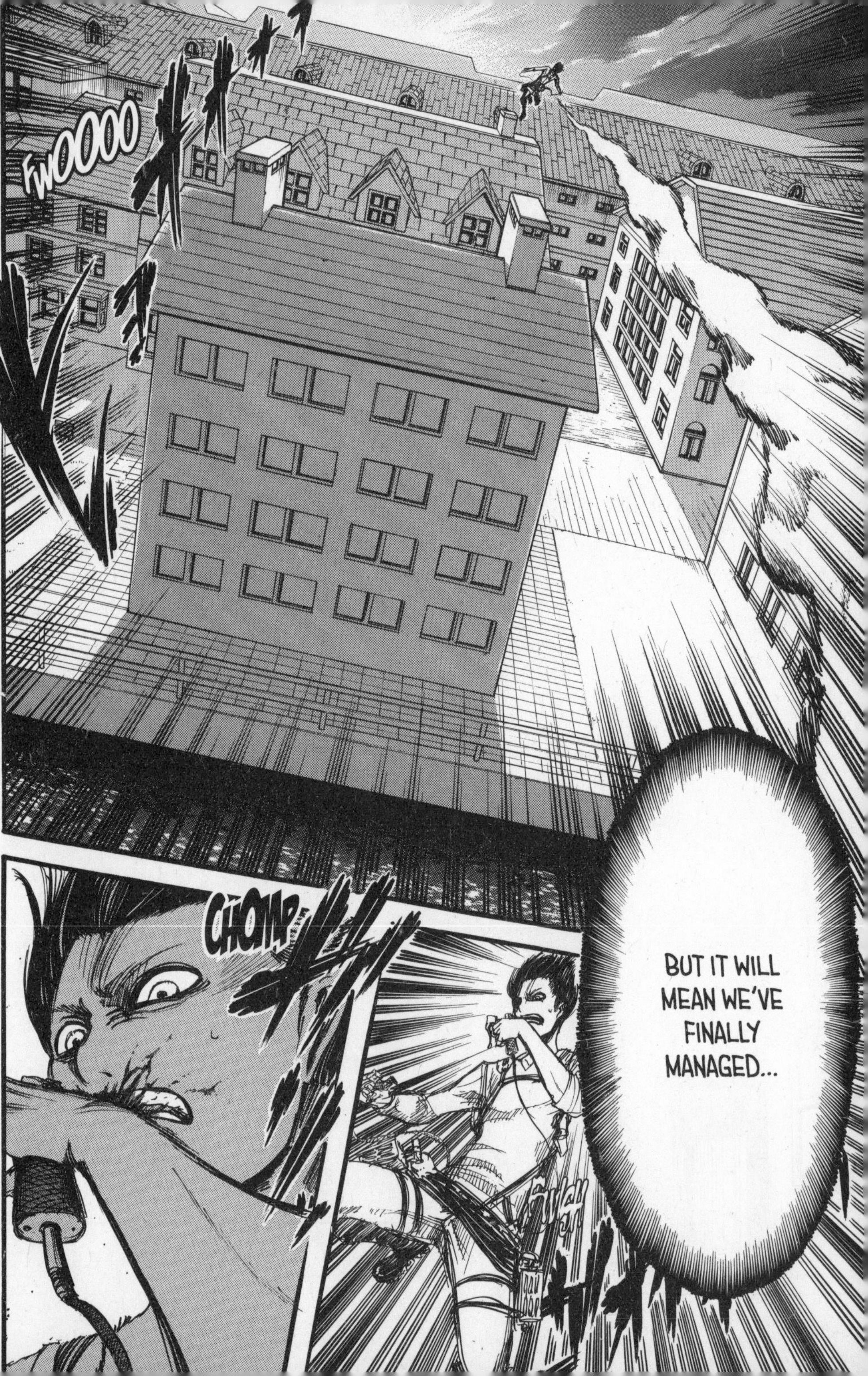
FWOOOO
BUT IT WILL MEAN WE'VE FINALLY MANAGED...
CHOMP

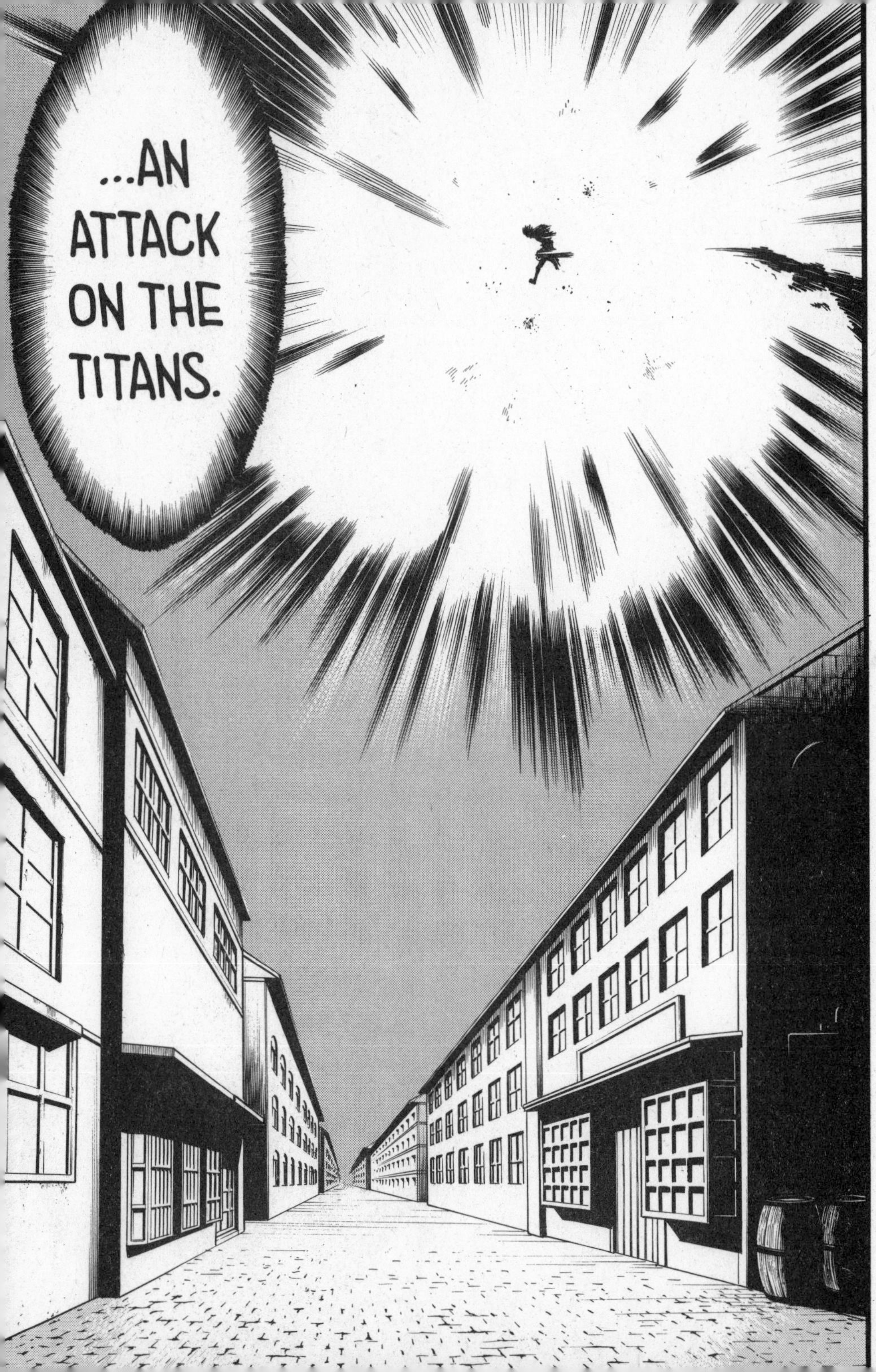
...AN ATTACK ON THE TITANS.

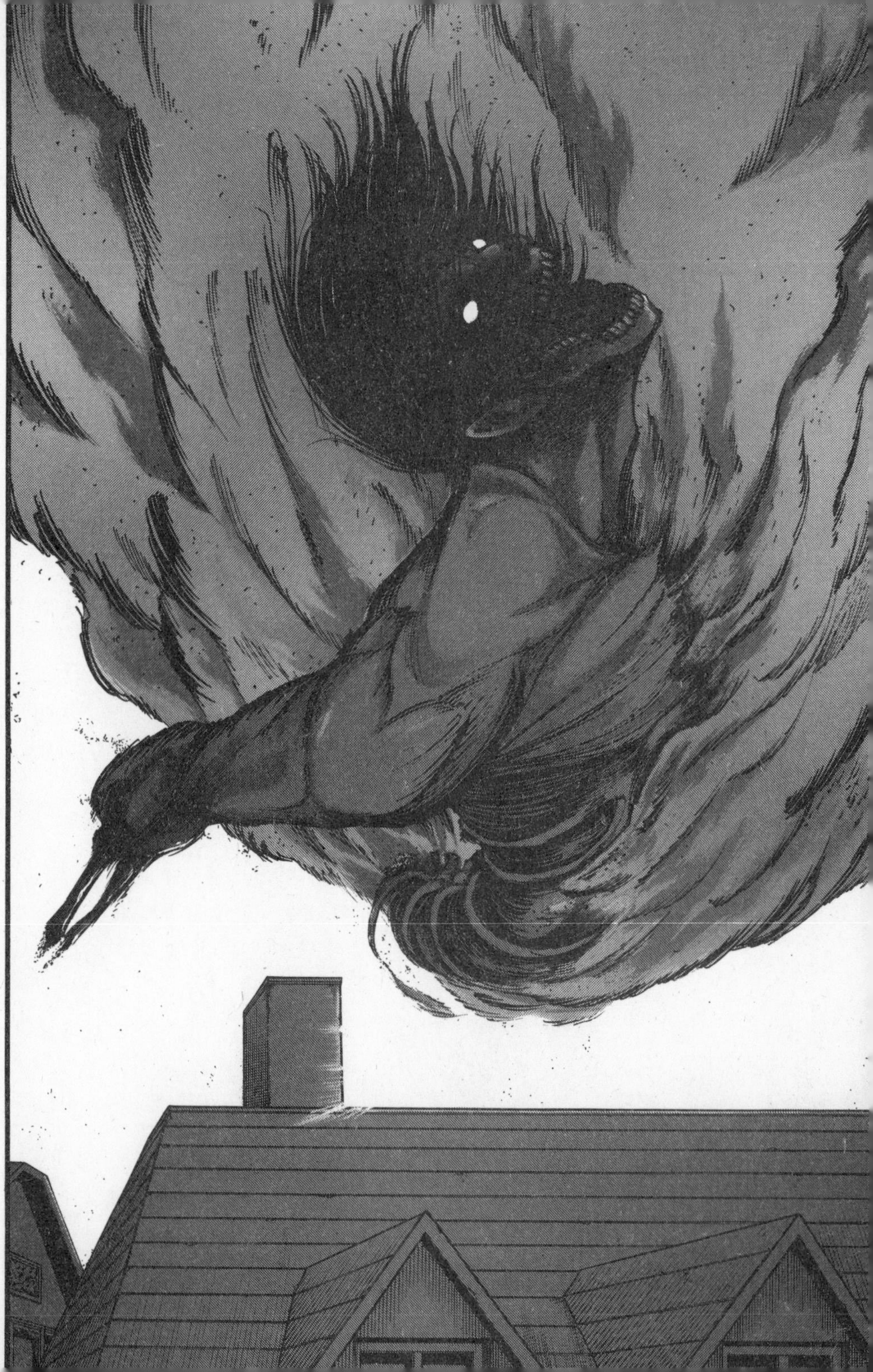

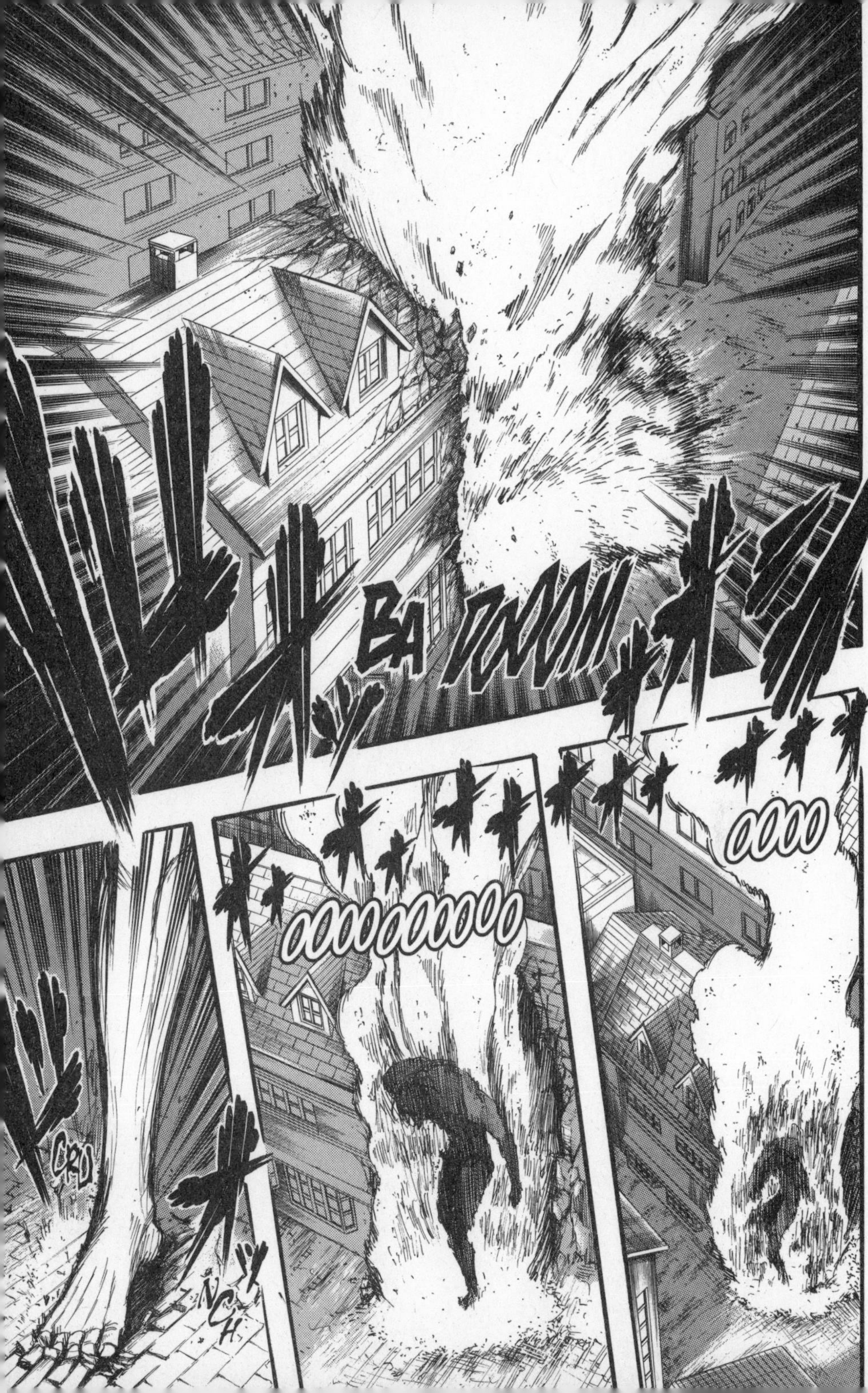
BA DOOOM
OOOO
OOOOOOOOOO
CRU
NCH

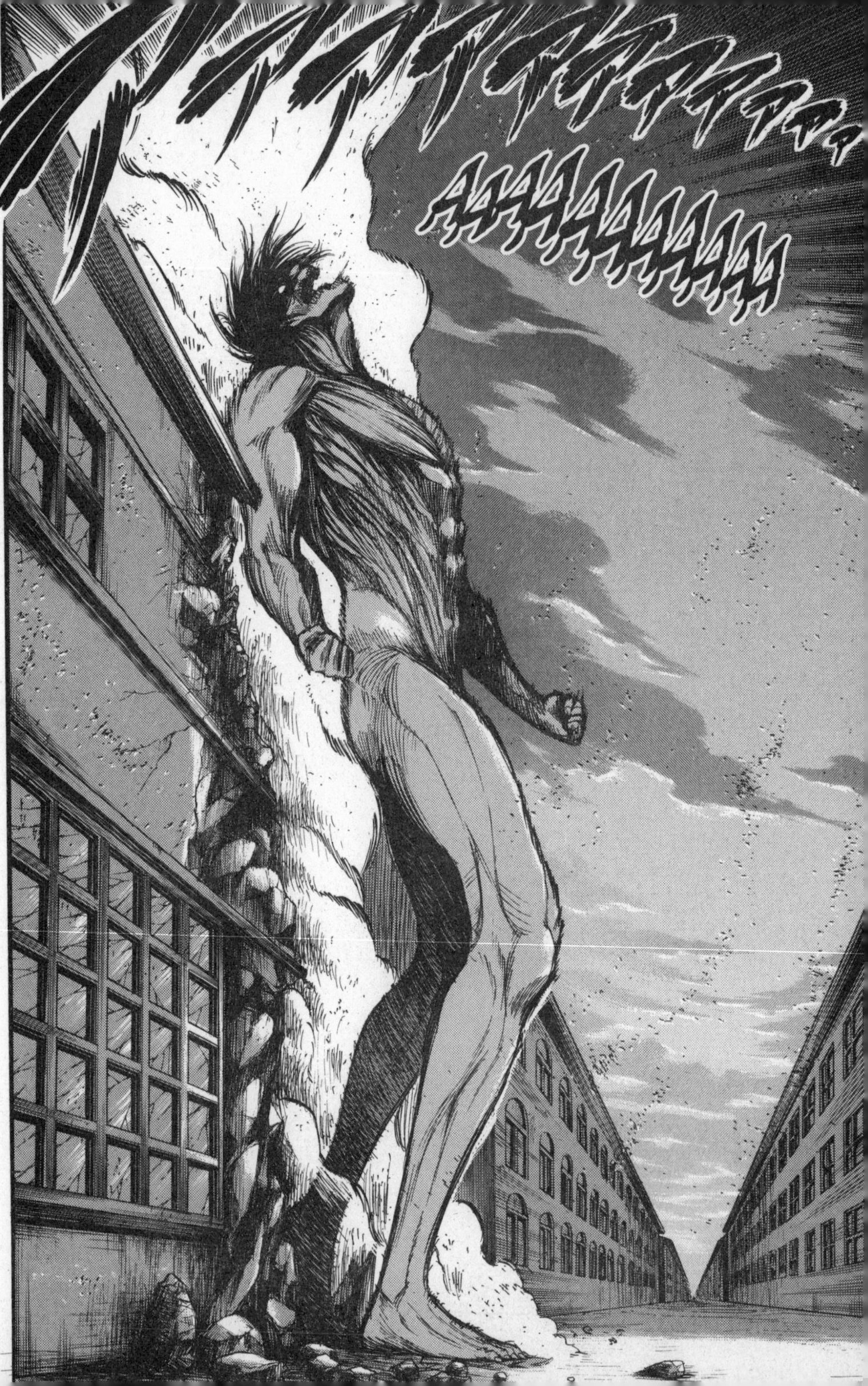
AAAAAAAAAA

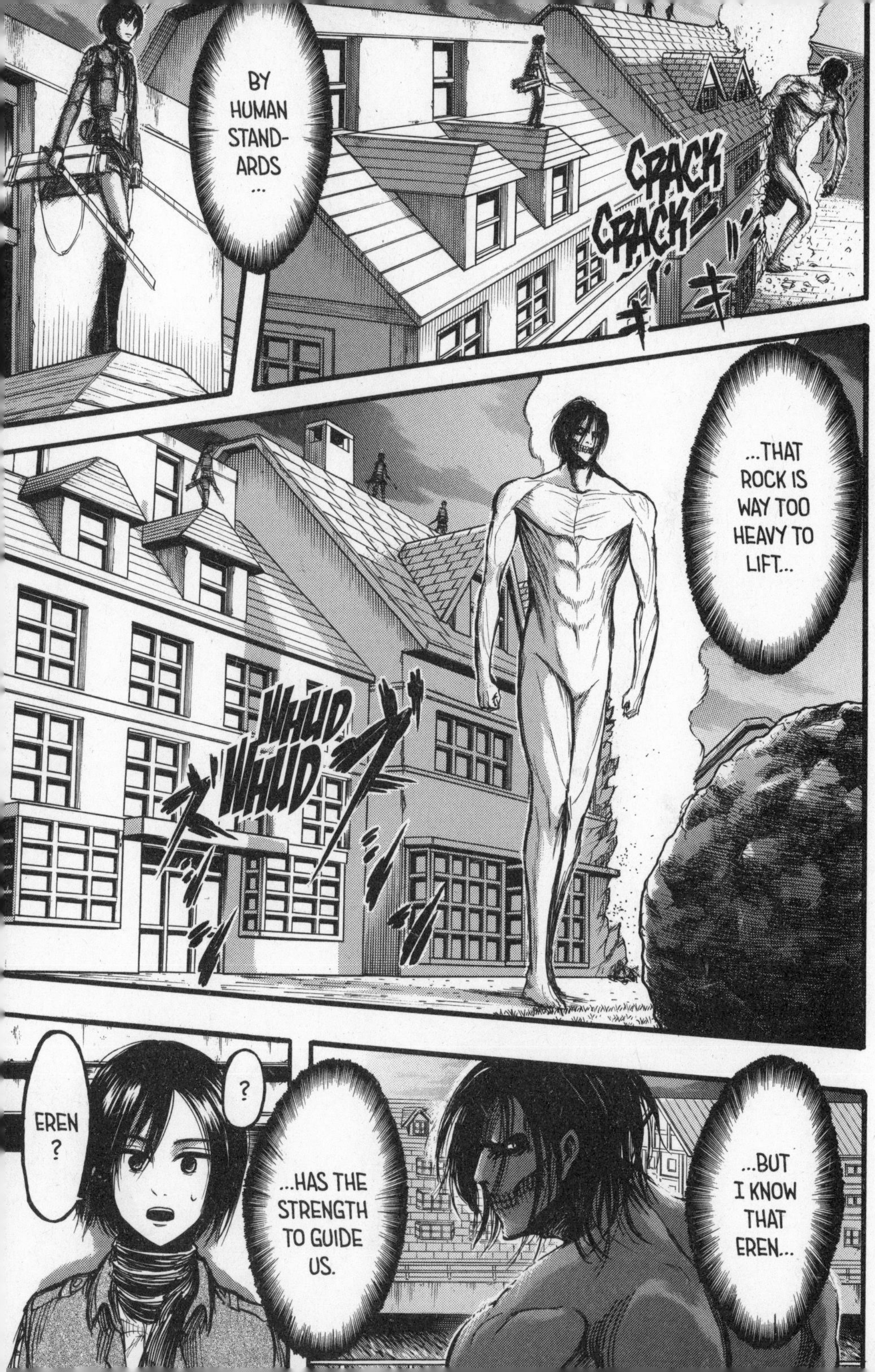
CRACK CRACK
BY HUMAN STANDARDS...
...THAT ROCK IS WAY TOO HEAVY TO LIFT...
WHUD WHUD
...BUT I KNOW THAT EREN...
...HAS THE STRENGTH TO GUIDE US.
?
EREN?

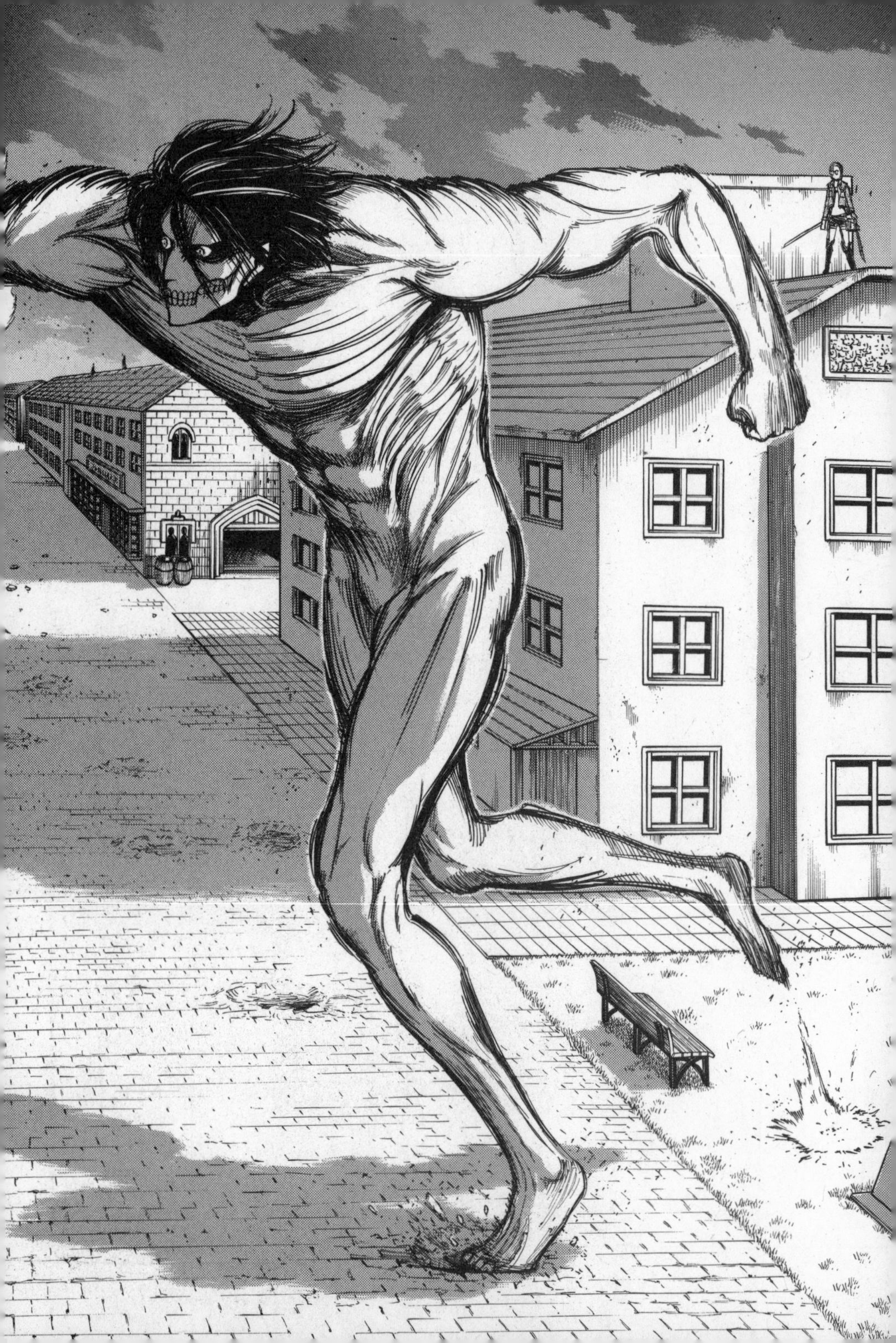

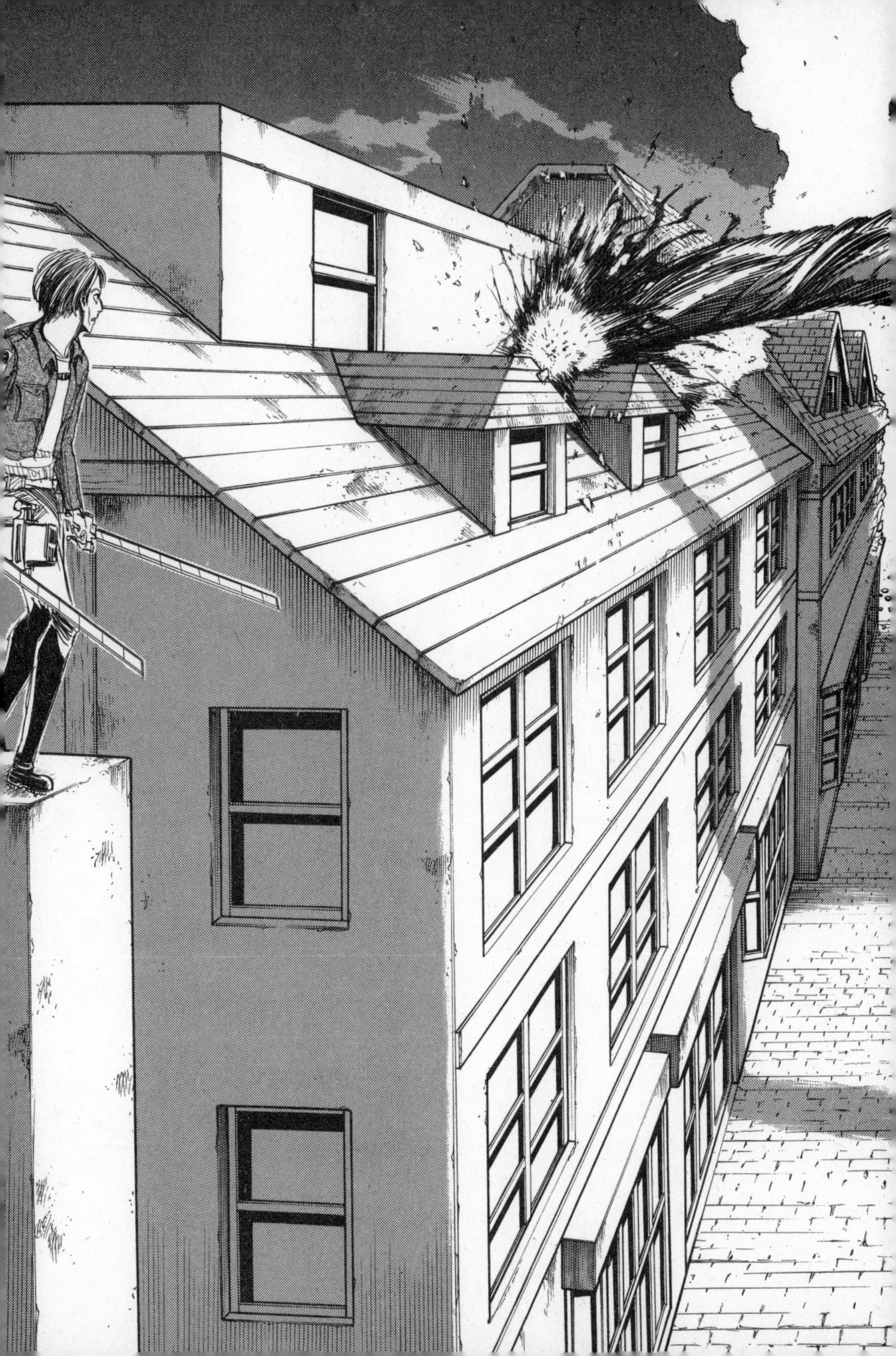

ATTACK on TITAN

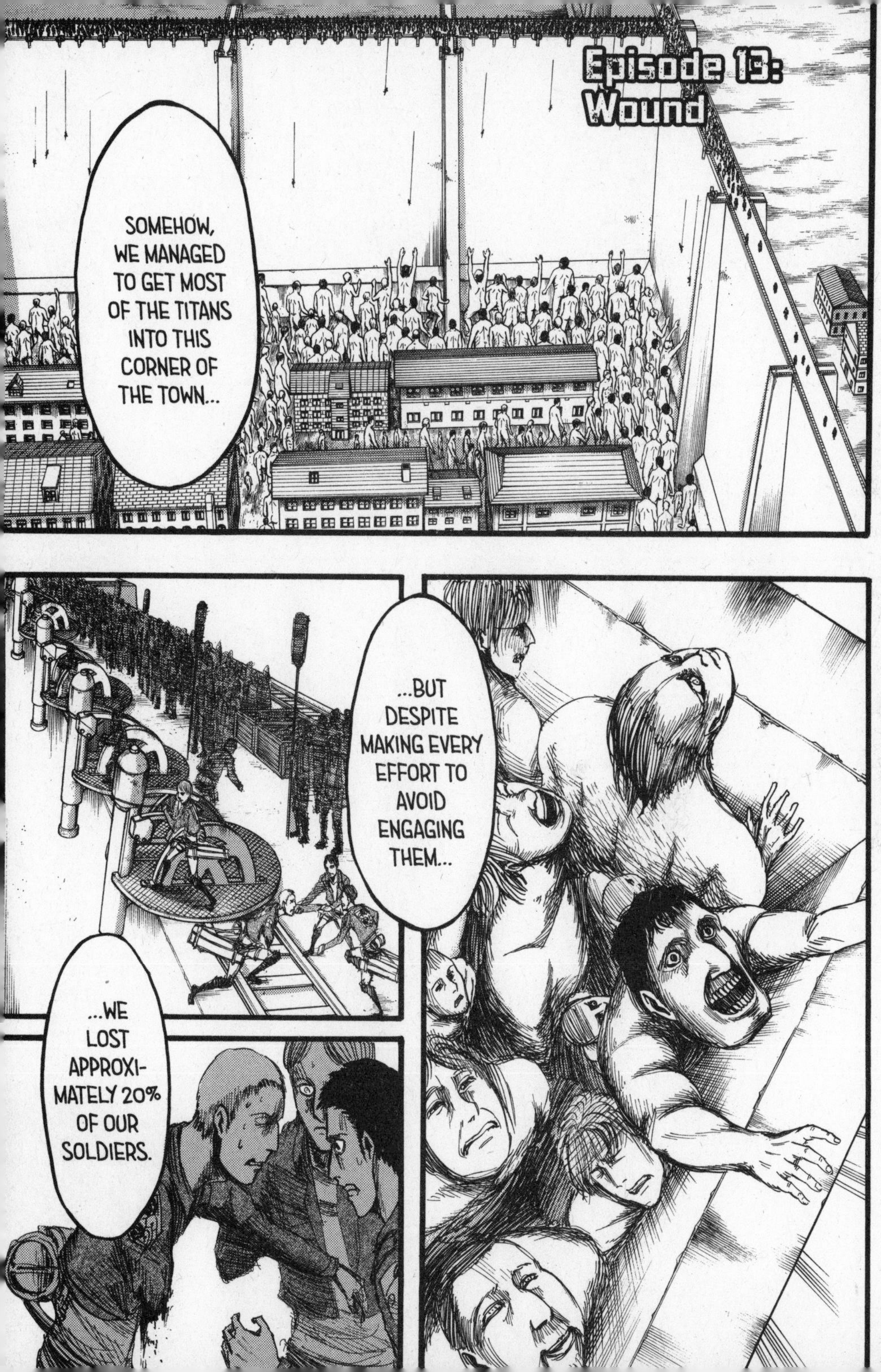
Episode 13: Wound
SOMEHOW, WE MANAGED TO GET MOST OF THE TITANS INTO THIS CORNER OF THE TOWN...
...BUT DESPITE MAKING EVERY EFFORT TO AVOID ENGAGING THEM...
...WE LOST APPROXI-MATELY 20% OF OUR SOLDIERS.

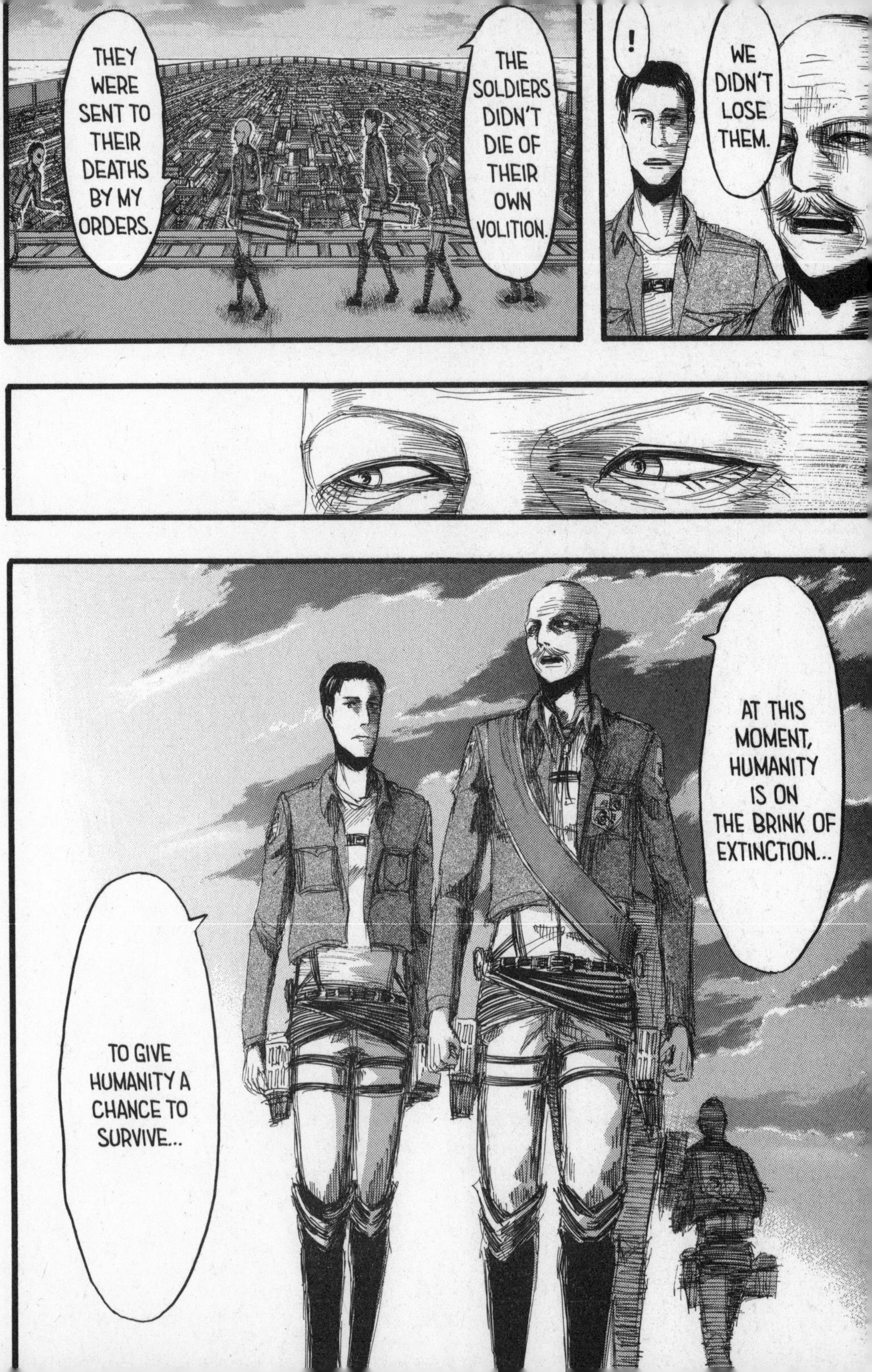
WE DIDN'T LOSE THEM.
!
THE SOLDIERS DIDN'T DIE OF THEIR OWN VOLITION.
THEY WERE SENT TO THEIR DEATHS BY MY ORDERS.
AT THIS MOMENT, HUMANITY IS ON THE BRINK OF EXTINCTION...
TO GIVE HUMANITY A CHANCE TO SURVIVE...

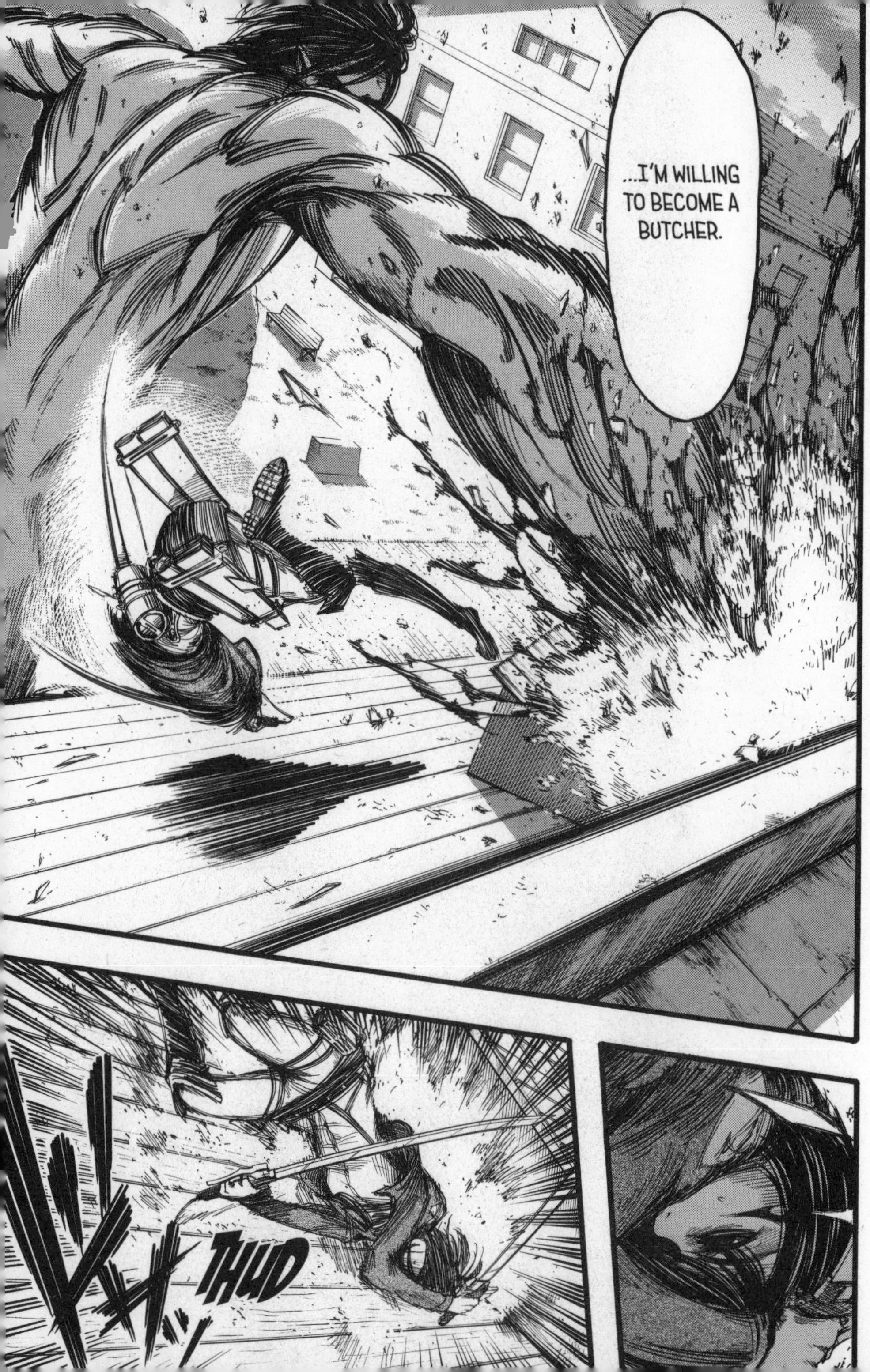
...I'M WILLING TO BECOME A BUTCHER.
THUD

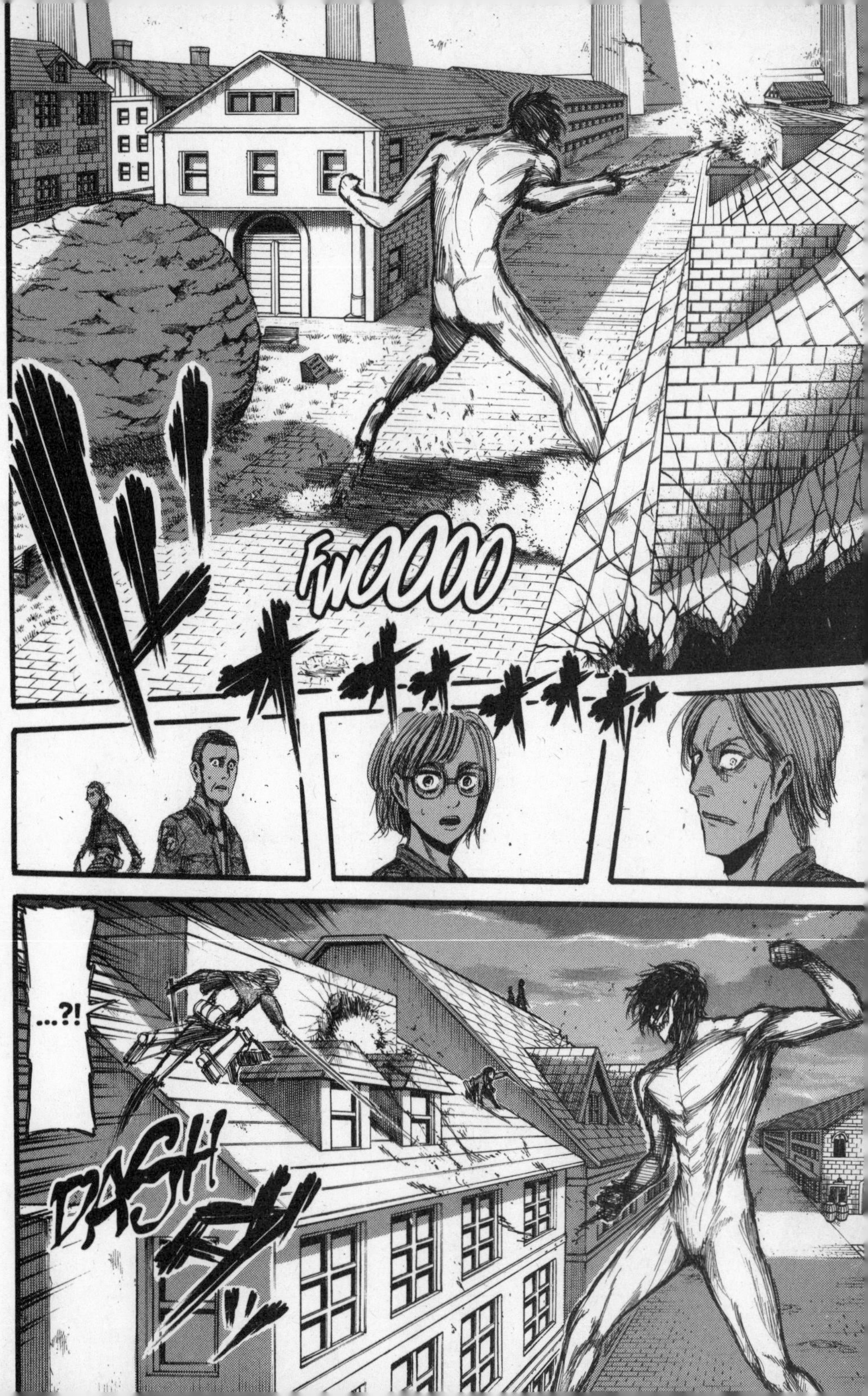
FWOOOO
...?!
DASH

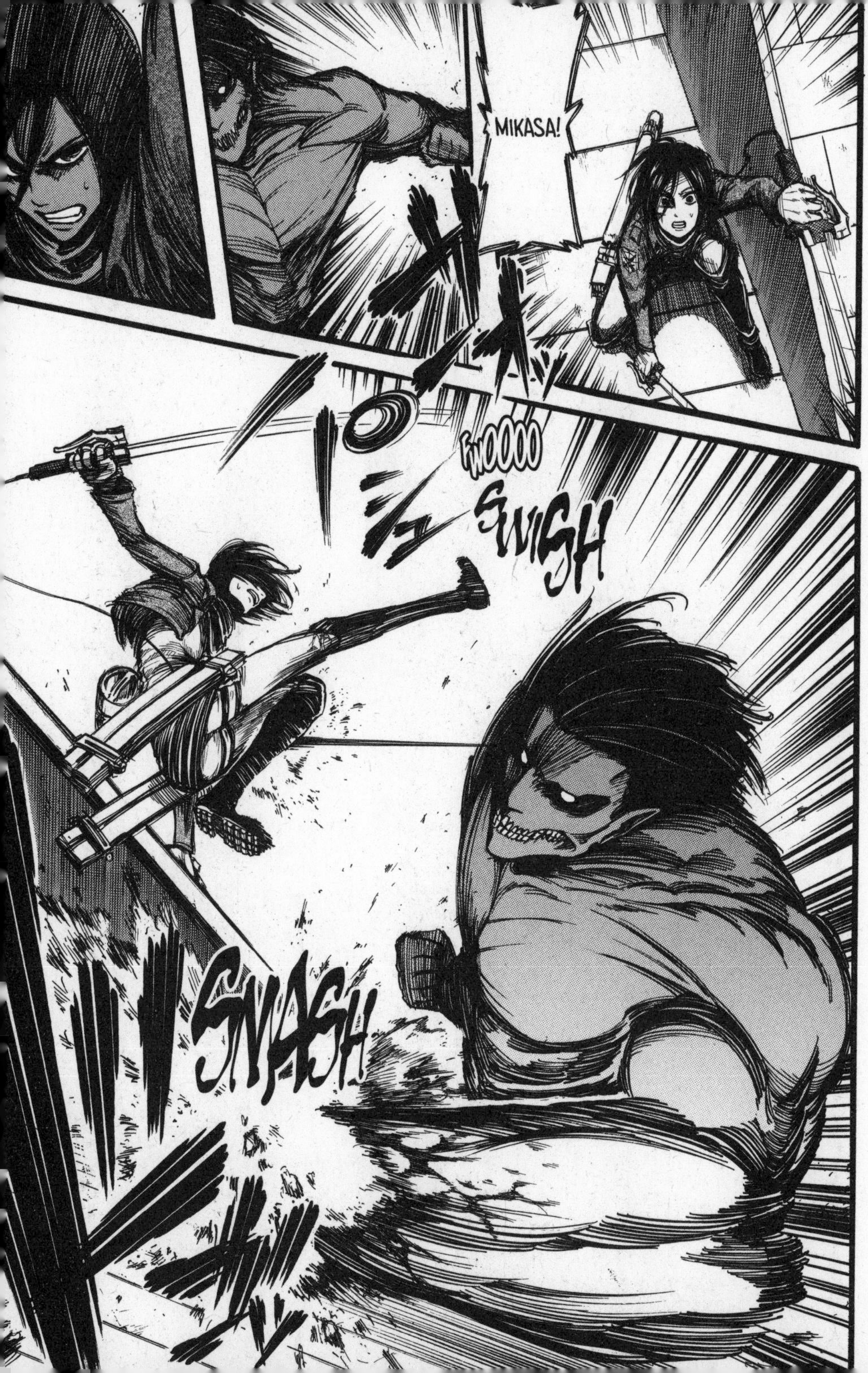
MIKASA!
FWOOOO
SWISH
SMASH!

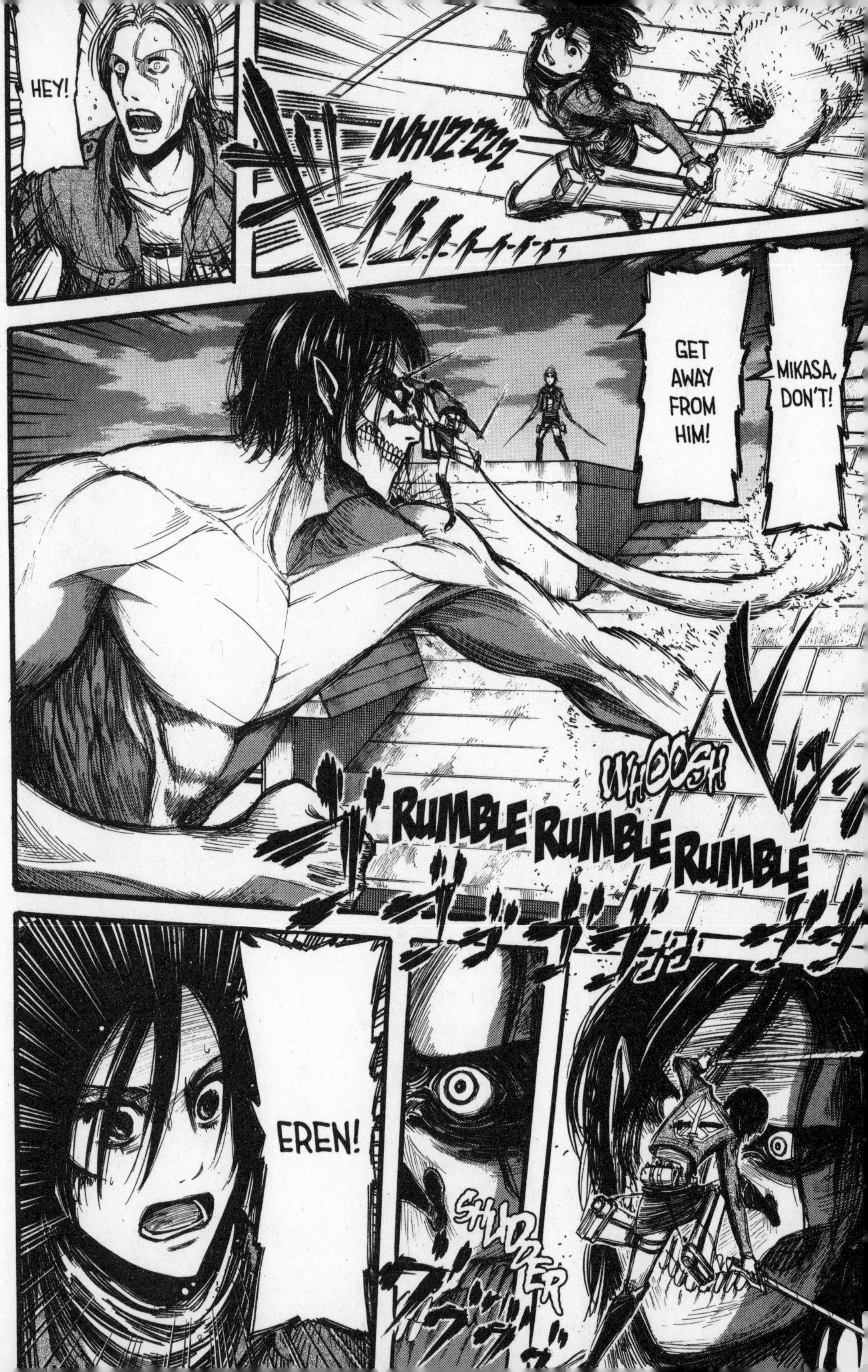
WHIZZZZ
HEY!
MIKASA, DON'T!
GET AWAY FROM HIM!
WHOOSH!
RUMBLE RUMBLE RUMBLE
SHUDDER
EREN!

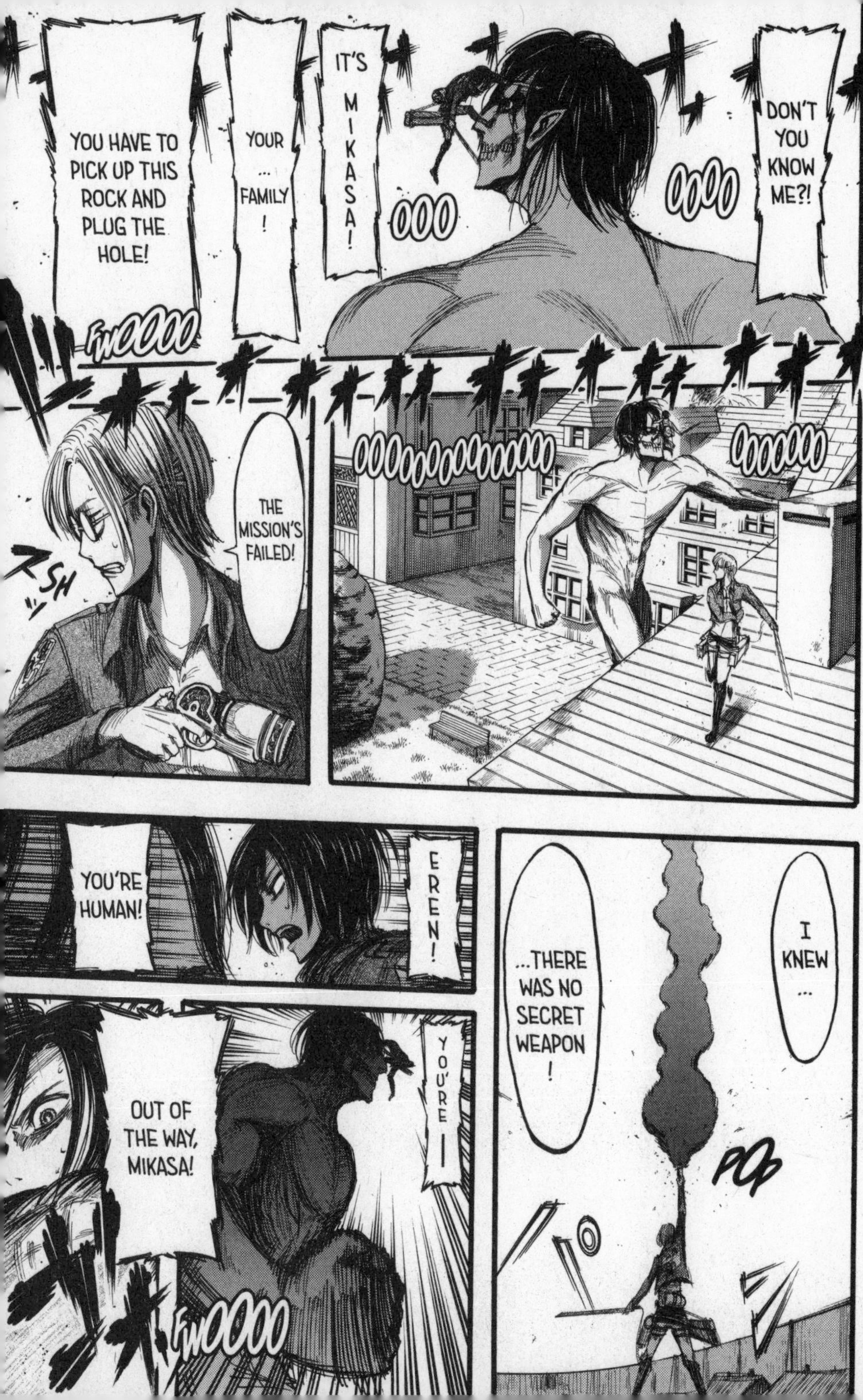
DON'T YOU KNOW ME?!
OOOO
OOO
IT'S MIKASA!
YOUR ... FAMILY!
YOU HAVE TO PICK UP THIS ROCK AND PLUG THE HOLE!
FWOOOO
OOOOOOO
OOOOOOOOOOOOOOOO
THE MISSION'S FAILED!
RSH
I KNEW ...
...THERE WAS NO SECRET WEAPON!
POP
EREN!
YOU'RE HUMAN!
YOU'RE
OUT OF THE WAY, MIKASA!
FWOOOO

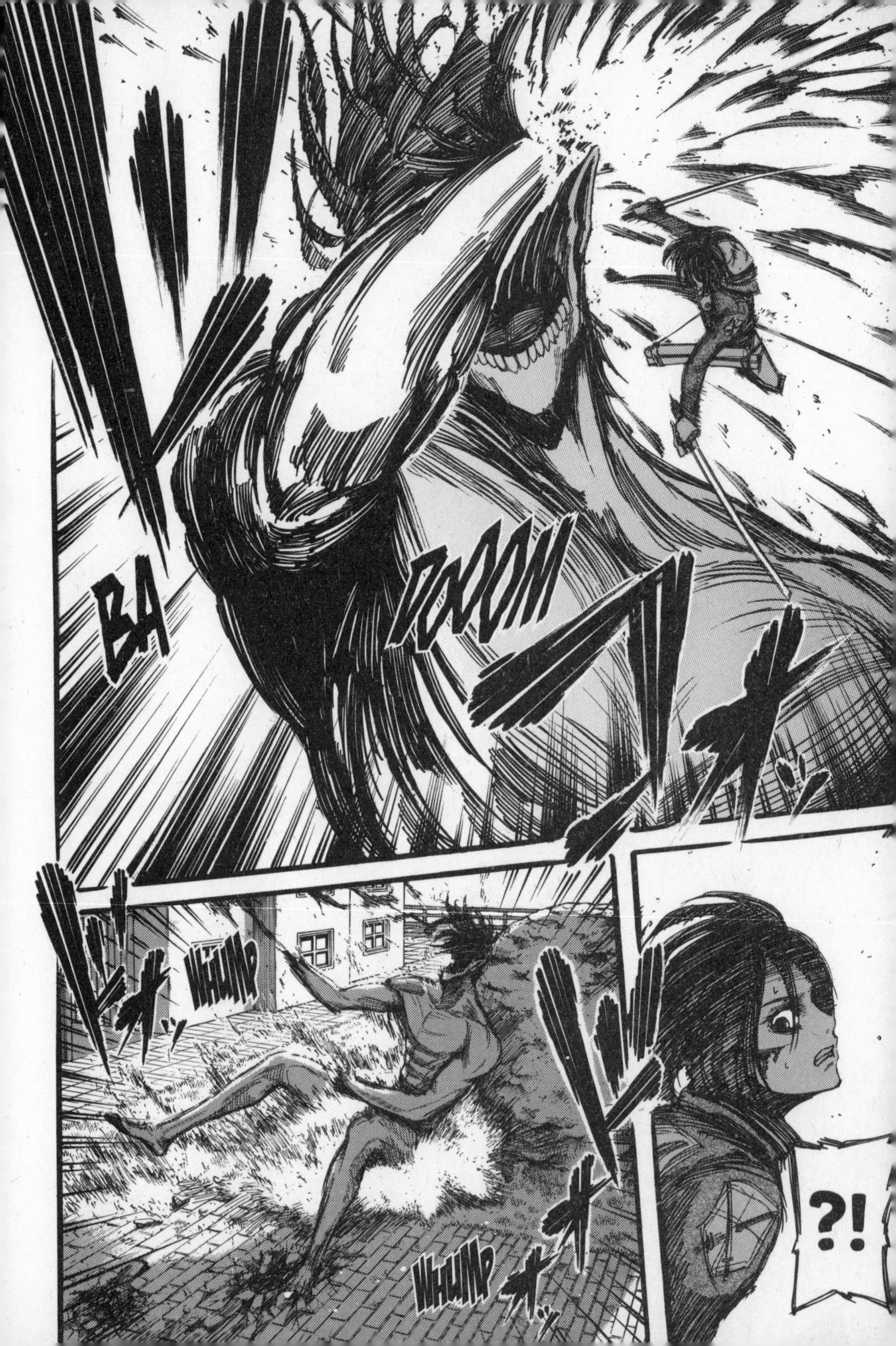
BA
DOOM
?!
WHUMP
WHUMP

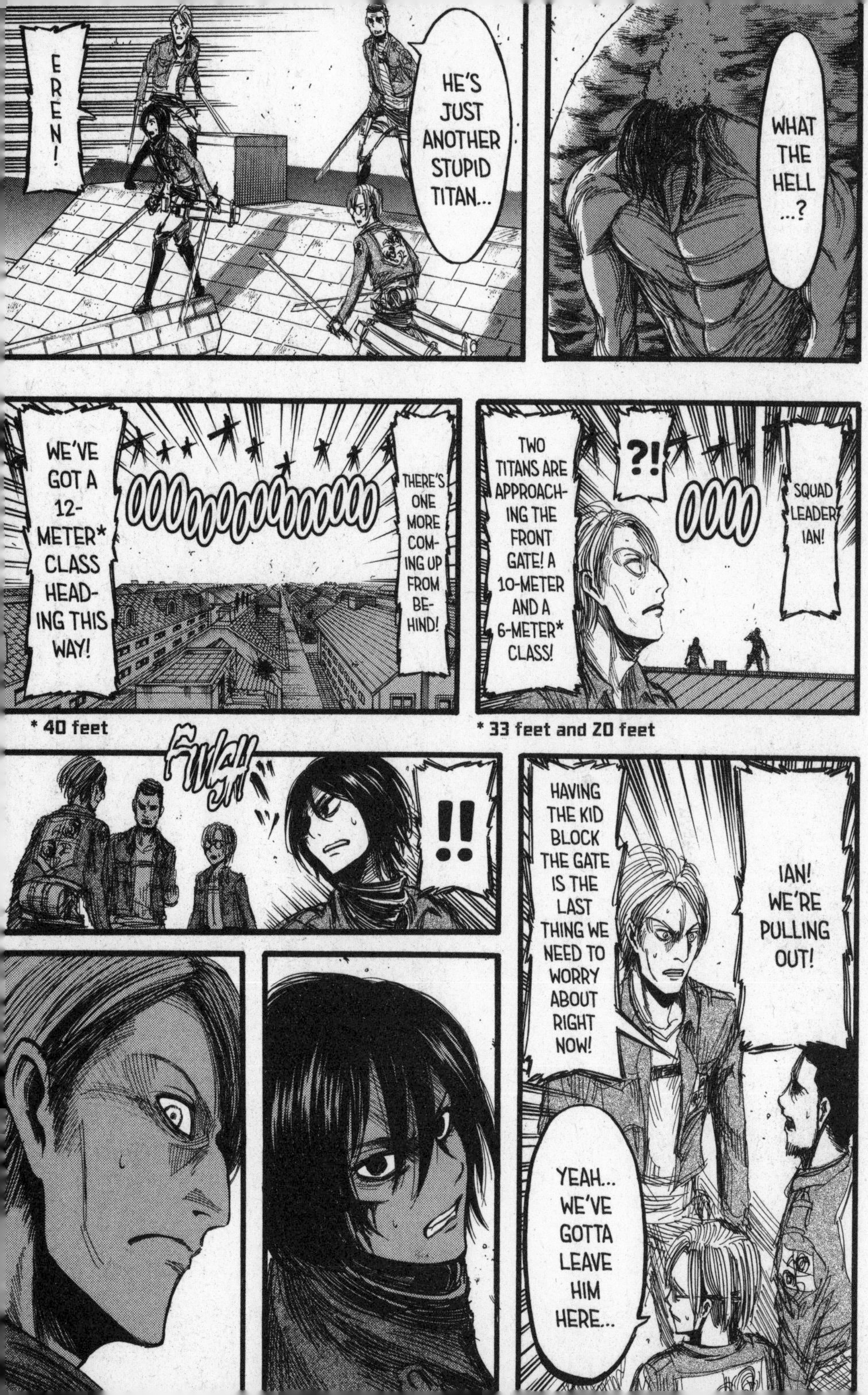
WHAT THE HELL ...?
HE'S JUST ANOTHER STUPID TITAN...
EREN!
SQUAD LEADER IAN!
OOOO
?!
TWO TITANS ARE APPROACHING THE FRONT GATE! A 10-METER AND A 6-METER* CLASS!
THERE'S ONE MORE COMING UP FROM BEHIND!
OOOOoOoOOoOOOOOO
WE'VE GOT A 12-METER* CLASS HEADING THIS WAY!
IAN! WE'RE PULLING OUT!
HAVING THE KID BLOCK THE GATE IS THE LAST THING WE NEED TO WORRY ABOUT RIGHT NOW!
YEAH... WE'VE GOTTA LEAVE HIM HERE...
!!
FWSH

* 40 feet

* 33 feet and 20 feet

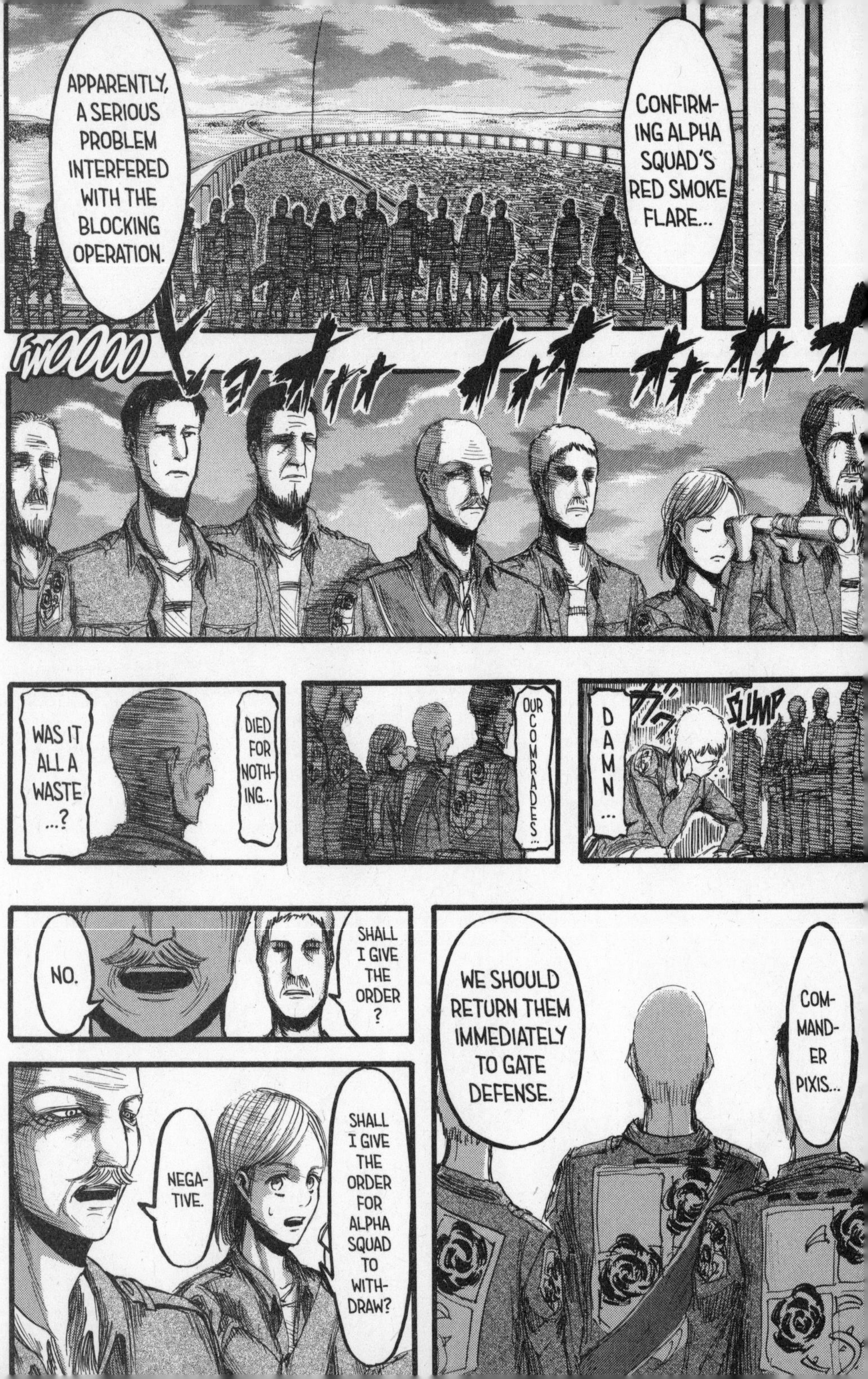
CONFIRMING ALPHA SQUAD'S RED SMOKE FLARE...
APPARENTLY, A SERIOUS PROBLEM INTERFERED WITH THE BLOCKING OPERATION.
FWOOOO
SLUMP
DAMN...
OUR COMRADES...
DIED FOR NOTHING...
WAS IT ALL A WASTE...?
COMMANDER PIXIS...
WE SHOULD RETURN THEM IMMEDIATELY TO GATE DEFENSE.
SHALL I GIVE THE ORDER?
NO.
SHALL I GIVE THE ORDER FOR ALPHA SQUAD TO WITHDRAW?
NEGATIVE.

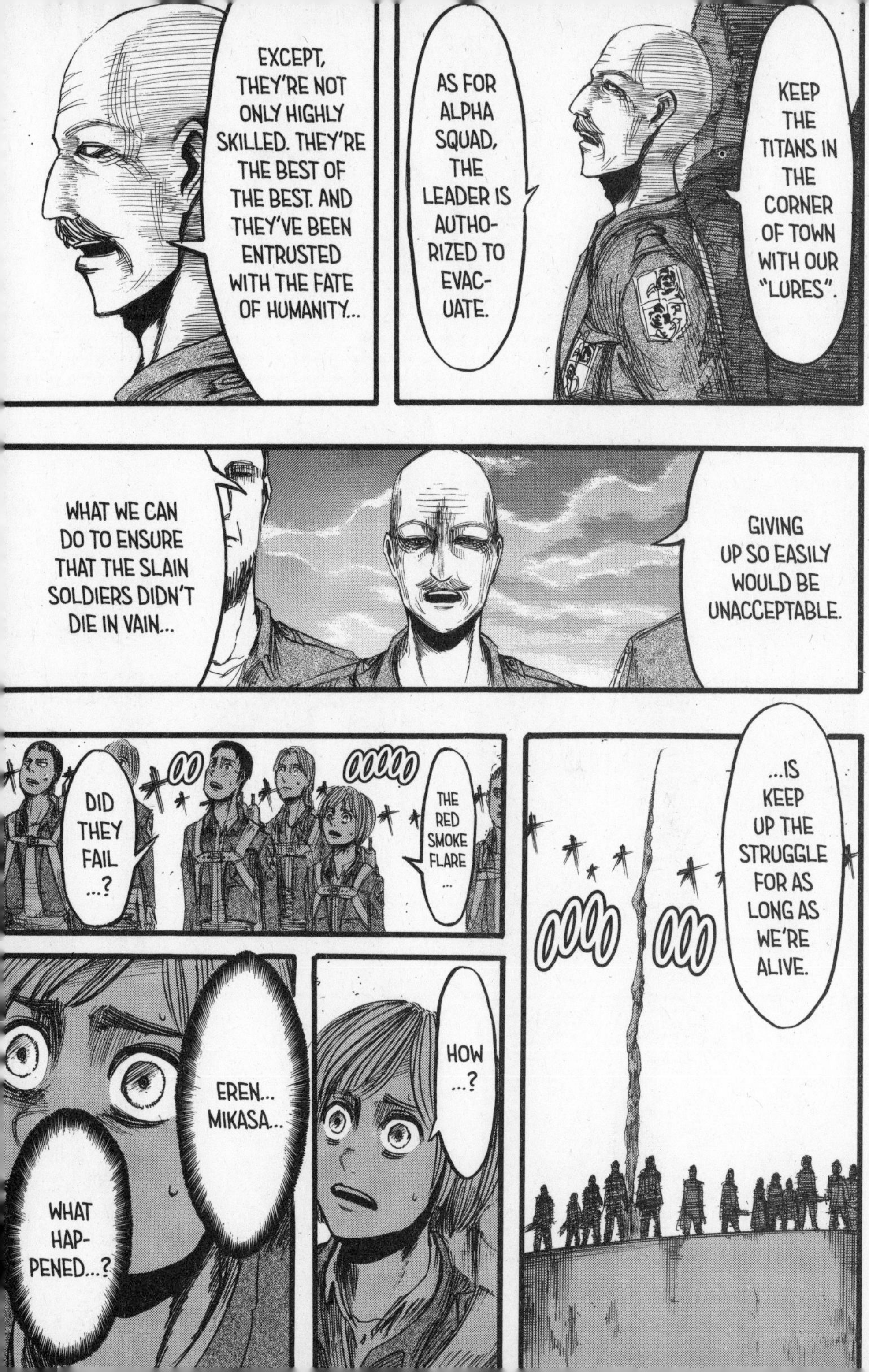
KEEP THE TITANS IN THE CORNER OF TOWN WITH OUR "LURES".
AS FOR ALPHA SQUAD, THE LEADER IS AUTHORIZED TO EVACUATE.
EXCEPT, THEY'RE NOT ONLY HIGHLY SKILLED. THEY'RE THE BEST OF THE BEST. AND THEY'VE BEEN ENTRUSTED WITH THE FATE OF HUMANITY...
GIVING UP SO EASILY WOULD BE UNACCEPTABLE.
WHAT WE CAN DO TO ENSURE THAT THE SLAIN SOLDIERS DIDN'T DIE IN VAIN...
...IS KEEP UP THE STRUGGLE FOR AS LONG AS WE'RE ALIVE.
THE RED SMOKE FLARE...
DID THEY FAIL...?
HOW...?
EREN... MIKASA...
WHAT HAPPENED...?

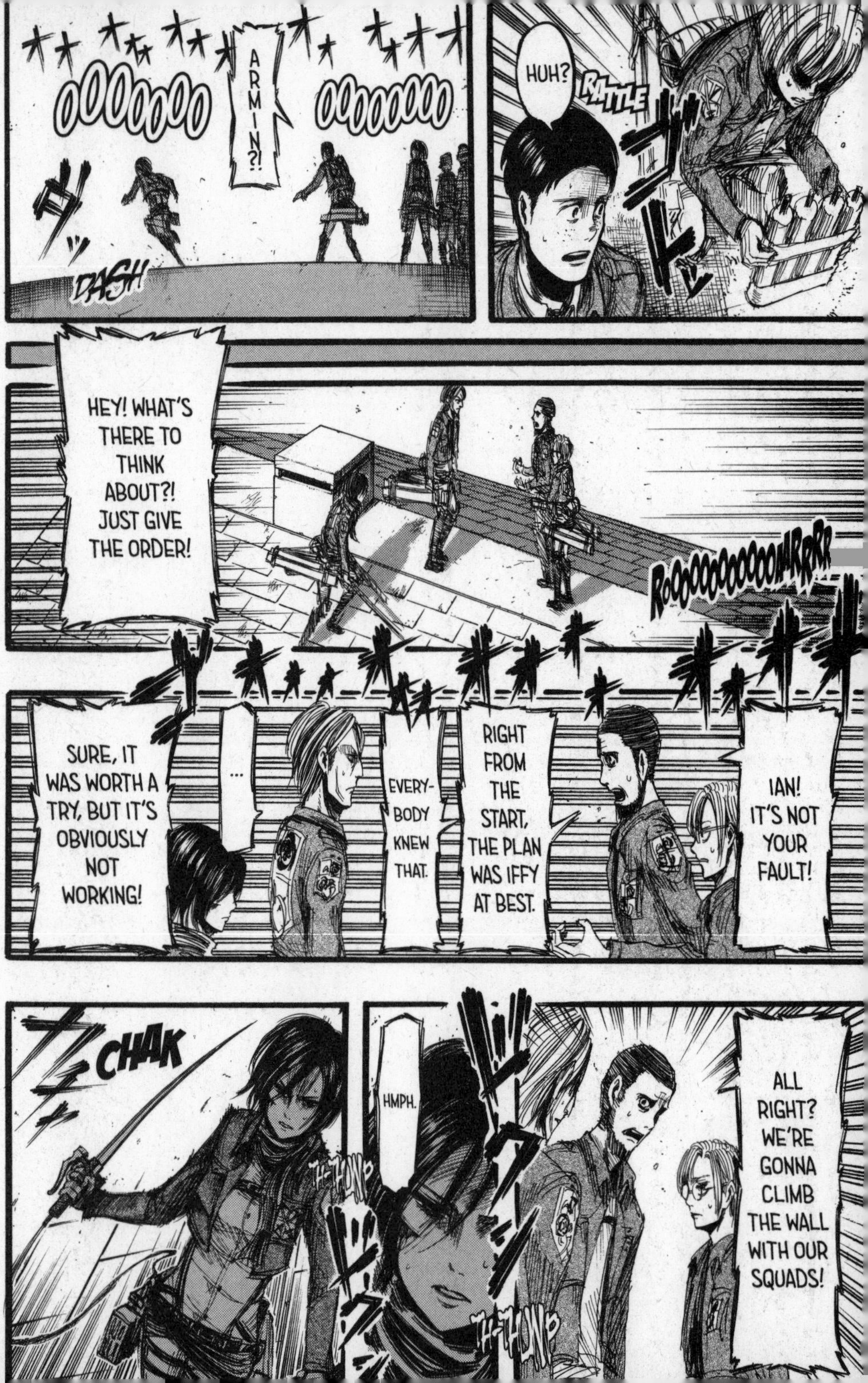
HUH?
RATTLE
OOOOOOOO
ARMIN?!
OOOOOOO
DASH
ROOOOOOOOOOOMRRRR
HEY! WHAT'S THERE TO THINK ABOUT?! JUST GIVE THE ORDER!
IAN! IT'S NOT YOUR FAULT!
RIGHT FROM THE START, THE PLAN WAS IFFY AT BEST.
EVERY-BODY KNEW THAT.
...
SURE, IT WAS WORTH A TRY, BUT IT'S OBVIOUSLY NOT WORKING!
ALL RIGHT? WE'RE GONNA CLIMB THE WALL WITH OUR SQUADS!
TH-THUMP
HMPH.
TH-THUMP
CHAK

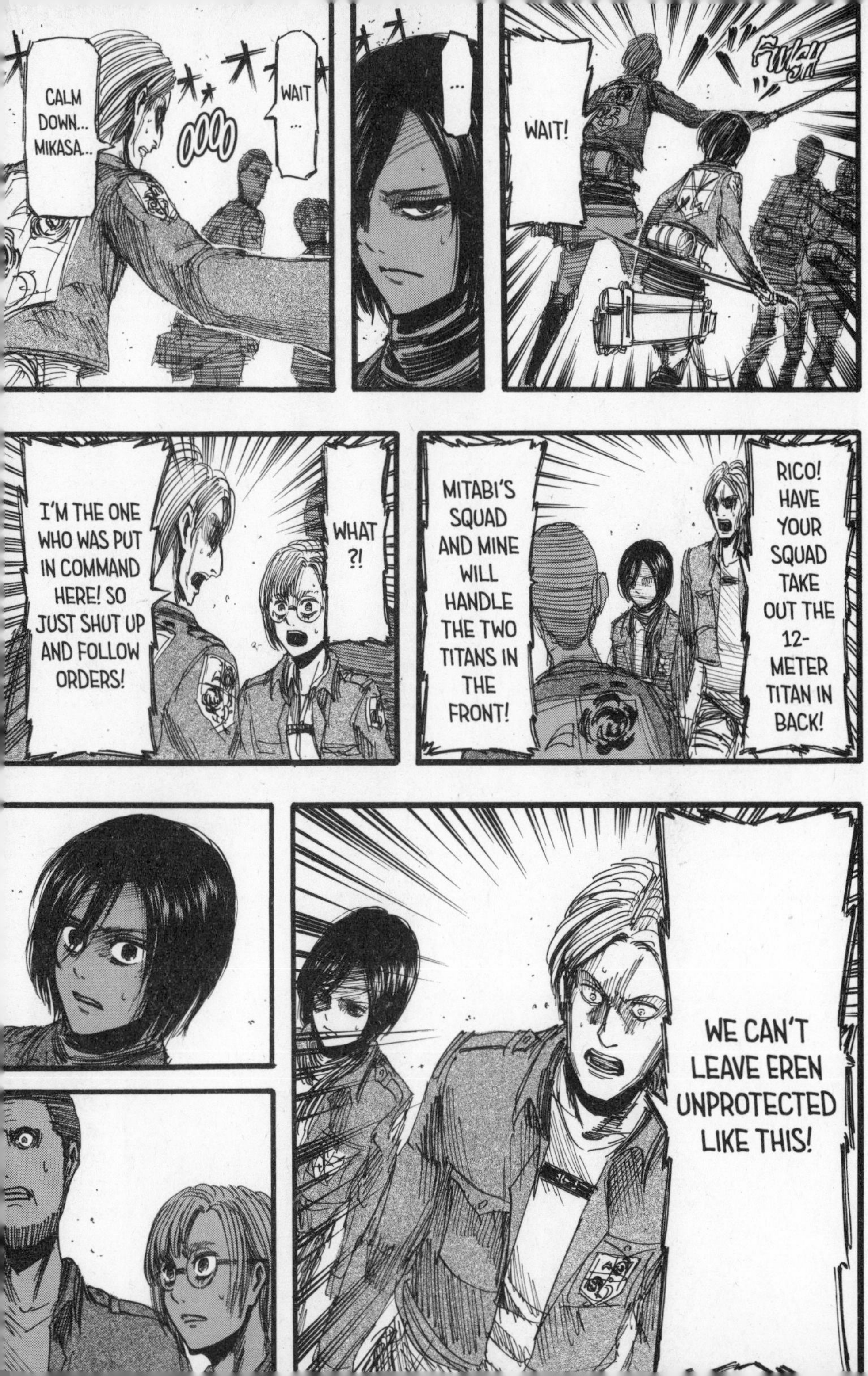
FWSH
WAIT!
...
WAIT ...
CALM DOWN... MIKASA...
RICO! HAVE YOUR SQUAD TAKE OUT THE 12-METER TITAN IN BACK!
MITABI'S SQUAD AND MINE WILL HANDLE THE TWO TITANS IN THE FRONT!
WHAT ?!
I'M THE ONE WHO WAS PUT IN COMMAND HERE! SO JUST SHUT UP AND FOLLOW ORDERS!
WE CAN'T LEAVE EREN UNPROTECTED LIKE THIS!

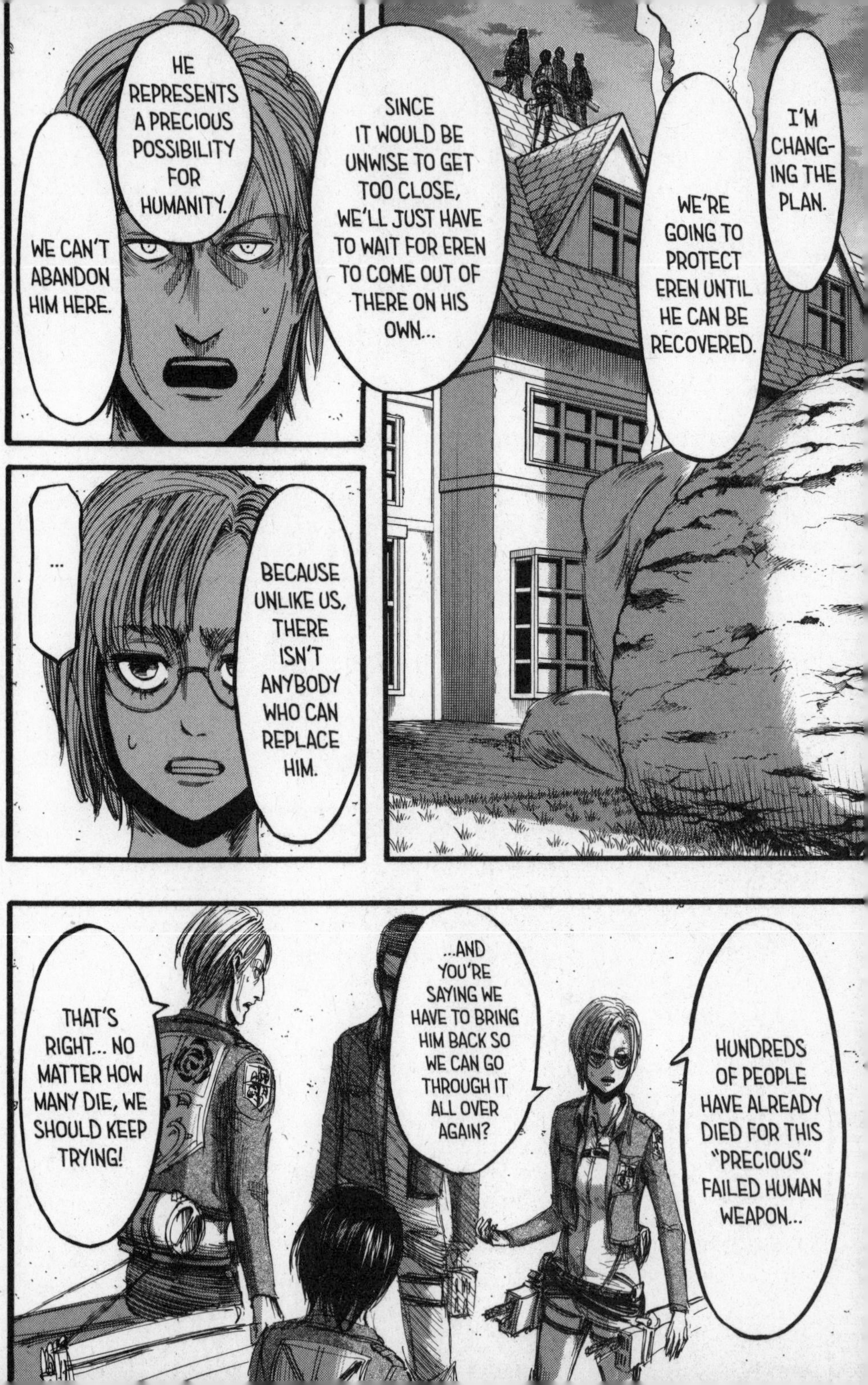
I'M CHANGING THE PLAN.
WE'RE GOING TO PROTECT EREN UNTIL HE CAN BE RECOVERED.
SINCE IT WOULD BE UNWISE TO GET TOO CLOSE, WE'LL JUST HAVE TO WAIT FOR EREN TO COME OUT OF THERE ON HIS OWN...
HE REPRESENTS A PRECIOUS POSSIBILITY FOR HUMANITY.
WE CAN'T ABANDON HIM HERE.
BECAUSE UNLIKE US, THERE ISN'T ANYBODY WHO CAN REPLACE HIM.
...
HUNDREDS OF PEOPLE HAVE ALREADY DIED FOR THIS "PRECIOUS" FAILED HUMAN WEAPON...
...AND YOU'RE SAYING WE HAVE TO BRING HIM BACK SO WE CAN GO THROUGH IT ALL OVER AGAIN?
THAT'S RIGHT... NO MATTER HOW MANY DIE, WE SHOULD KEEP TRYING!

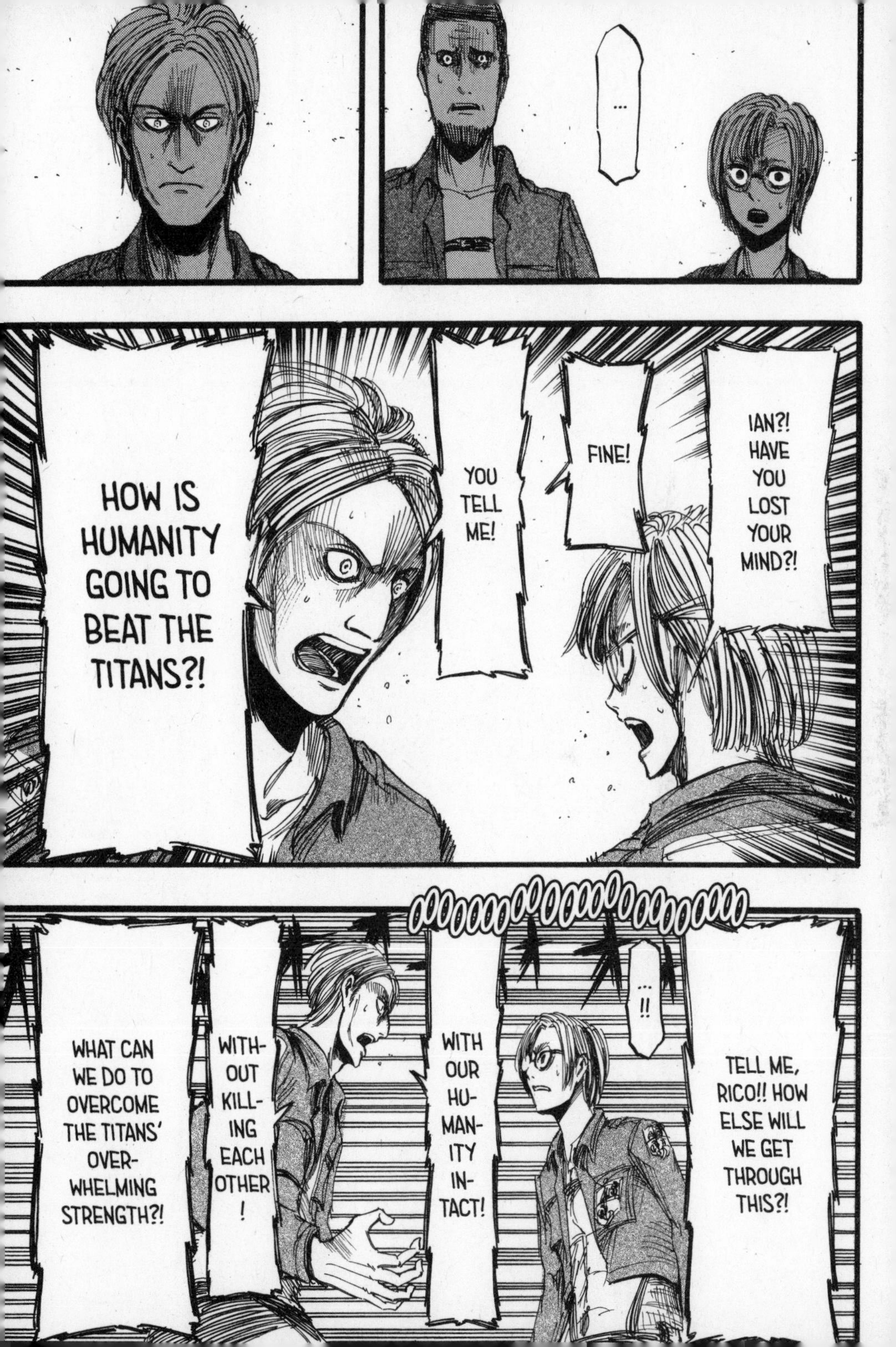
…
IAN?! HAVE YOU LOST YOUR MIND?!
FINE!
YOU TELL ME!
HOW IS HUMANITY GOING TO BEAT THE TITANS?!
OOOOOOOOOOOOOOOOOOOOOOOOO
…!!
TELL ME, RICO!! HOW ELSE WILL WE GET THROUGH THIS?!
WITH OUR HU-MAN-ITY IN-TACT!
WITH-OUT KILL-ING EACH OTHER!
WHAT CAN WE DO TO OVERCOME THE TITANS' OVER-WHELMING STRENGTH?!

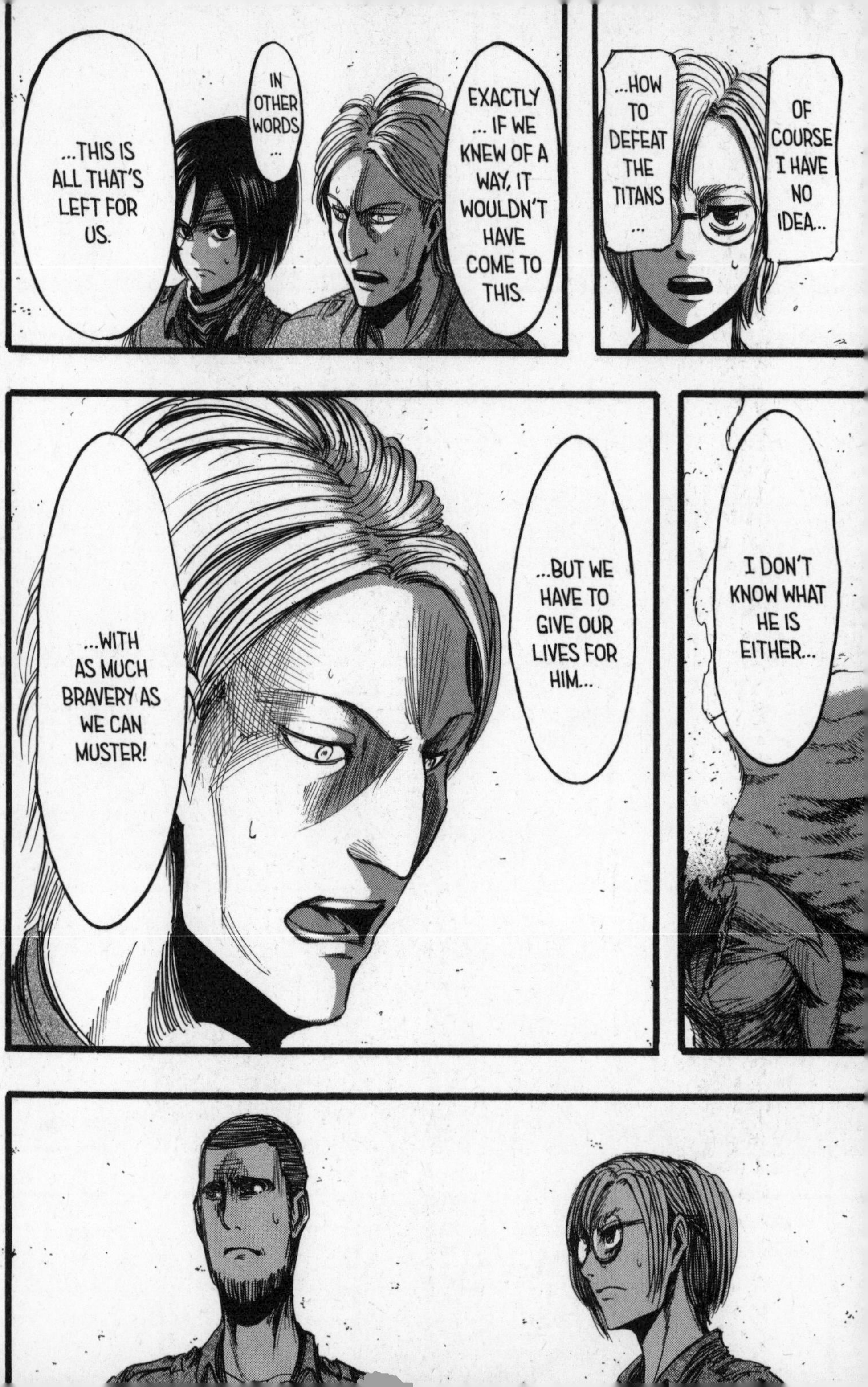
OF COURSE I HAVE NO IDEA...
...HOW TO DEFEAT THE TITANS ...
EXACTLY ... IF WE KNEW OF A WAY, IT WOULDN'T HAVE COME TO THIS.
IN OTHER WORDS ...
...THIS IS ALL THAT'S LEFT FOR US.
I DON'T KNOW WHAT HE IS EITHER...
...BUT WE HAVE TO GIVE OUR LIVES FOR HIM...
...WITH AS MUCH BRAVERY AS WE CAN MUSTER!

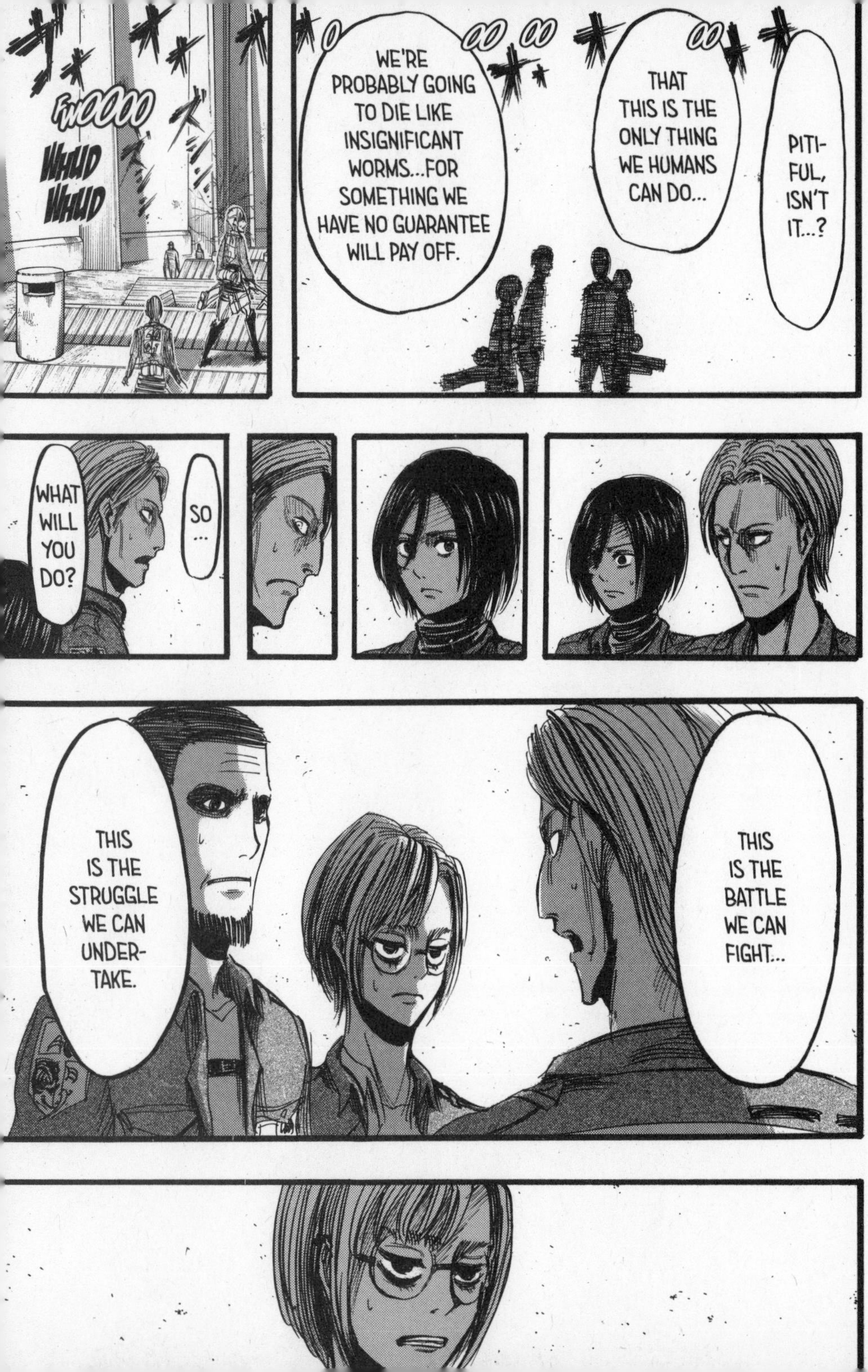
PITIFUL, ISN'T IT...?
THAT THIS IS THE ONLY THING WE HUMANS CAN DO...
WE'RE PROBABLY GOING TO DIE LIKE INSIGNIFICANT WORMS...FOR SOMETHING WE HAVE NO GUARANTEE WILL PAY OFF.
FWOOOO
WHUD
WHUD
SO...
WHAT WILL YOU DO?
THIS IS THE BATTLE WE CAN FIGHT...
THIS IS THE STRUGGLE WE CAN UNDERTAKE.

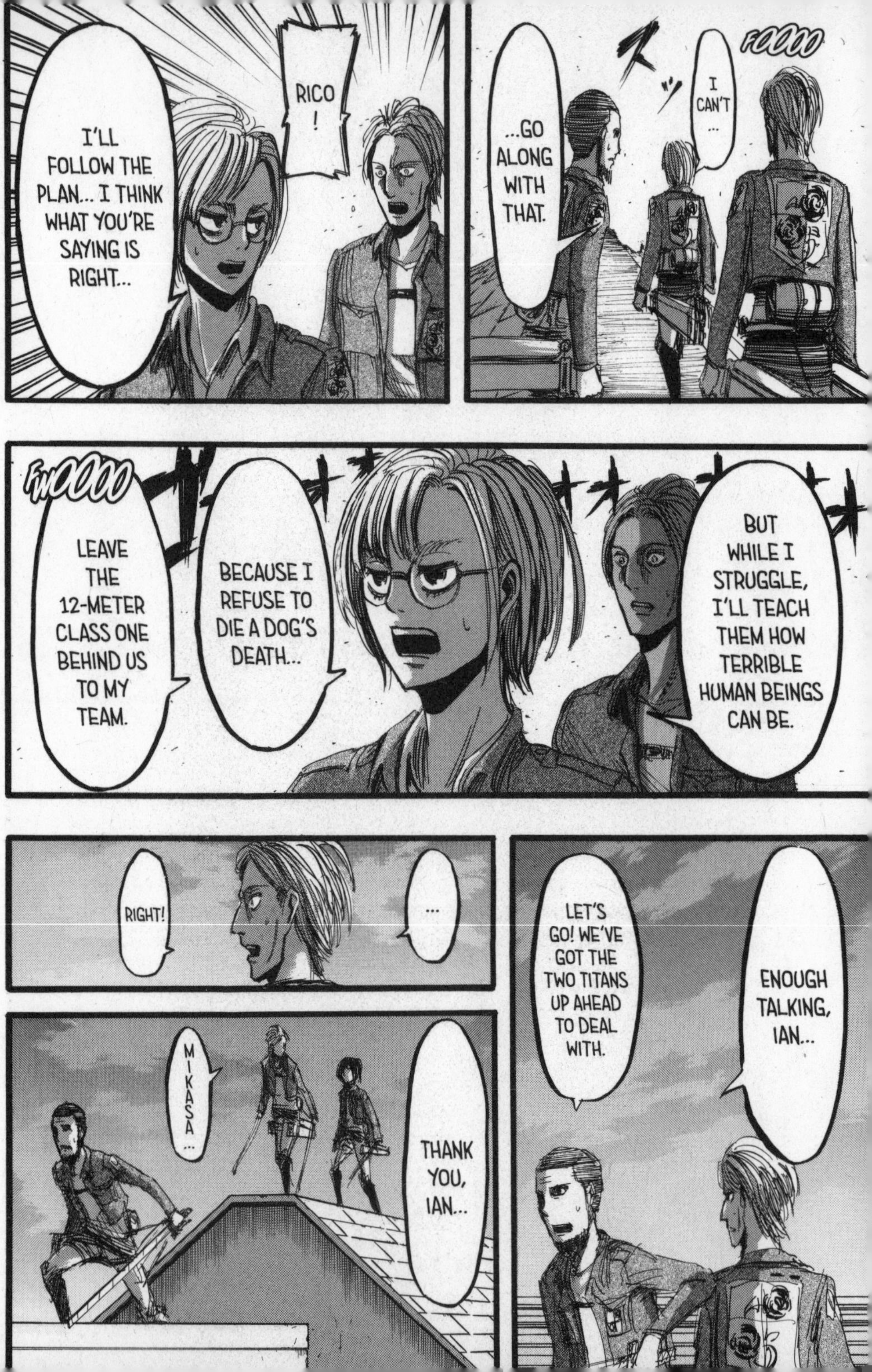
FOOOO
I CAN'T ...
...GO ALONG WITH THAT.
RICO !
I'LL FOLLOW THE PLAN... I THINK WHAT YOU'RE SAYING IS RIGHT...
BUT WHILE I STRUGGLE, I'LL TEACH THEM HOW TERRIBLE HUMAN BEINGS CAN BE.
BECAUSE I REFUSE TO DIE A DOG'S DEATH...
LEAVE THE 12-METER CLASS ONE BEHIND US TO MY TEAM.
FWOOOO
ENOUGH TALKING, IAN...
LET'S GO! WE'VE GOT THE TWO TITANS UP AHEAD TO DEAL WITH.
...
RIGHT!
THANK YOU, IAN...
MIKASA...

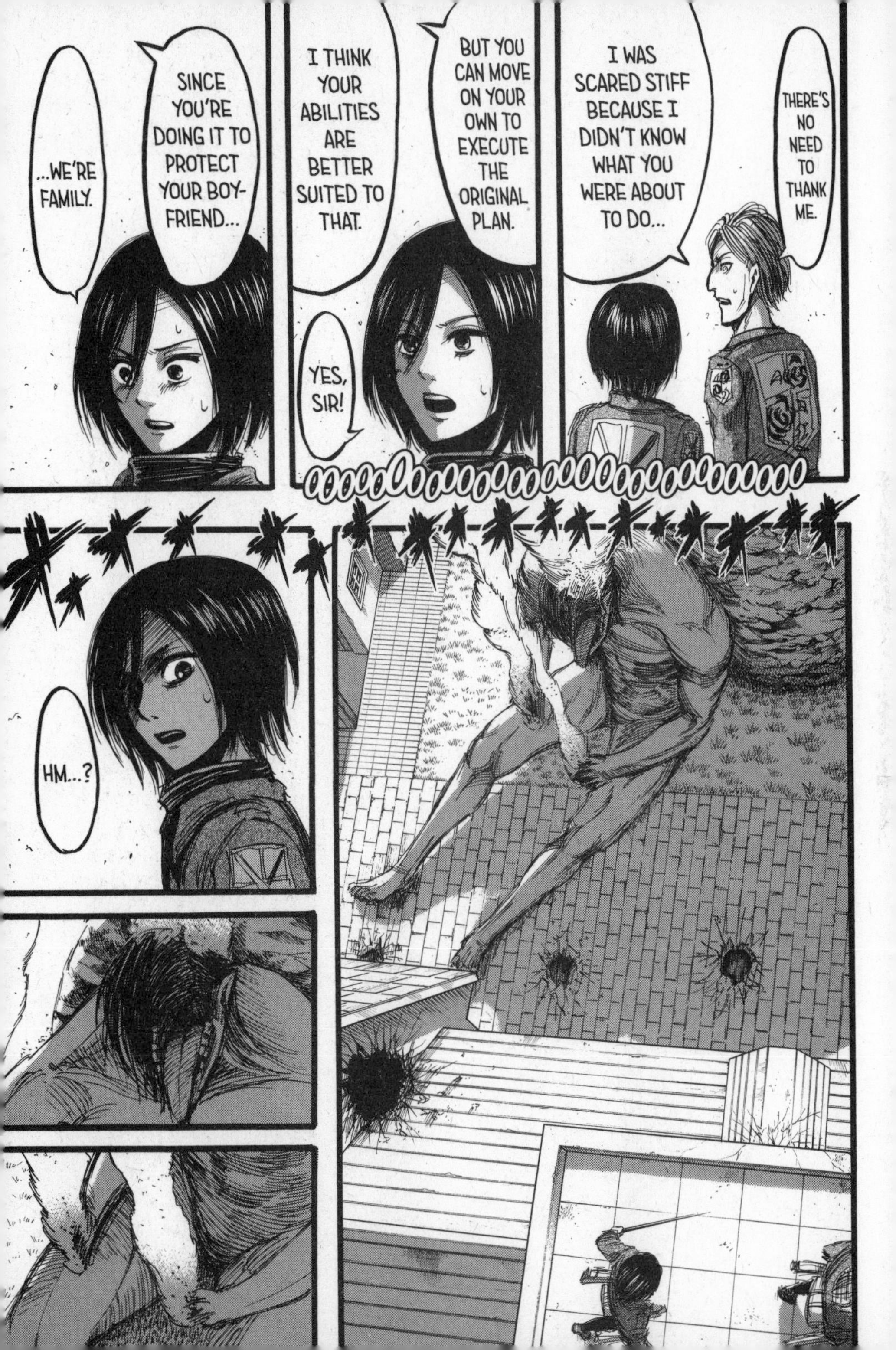
THERE'S NO NEED TO THANK ME.
I WAS SCARED STIFF BECAUSE I DIDN'T KNOW WHAT YOU WERE ABOUT TO DO...
BUT YOU CAN MOVE ON YOUR OWN TO EXECUTE THE ORIGINAL PLAN.
I THINK YOUR ABILITIES ARE BETTER SUITED TO THAT.
YES, SIR!
SINCE YOU'RE DOING IT TO PROTECT YOUR BOY-FRIEND...
...WE'RE FAMILY.
OOOOOOOOOOOOOOOOOOOOOOOOOOOOOOOOO
HM...?

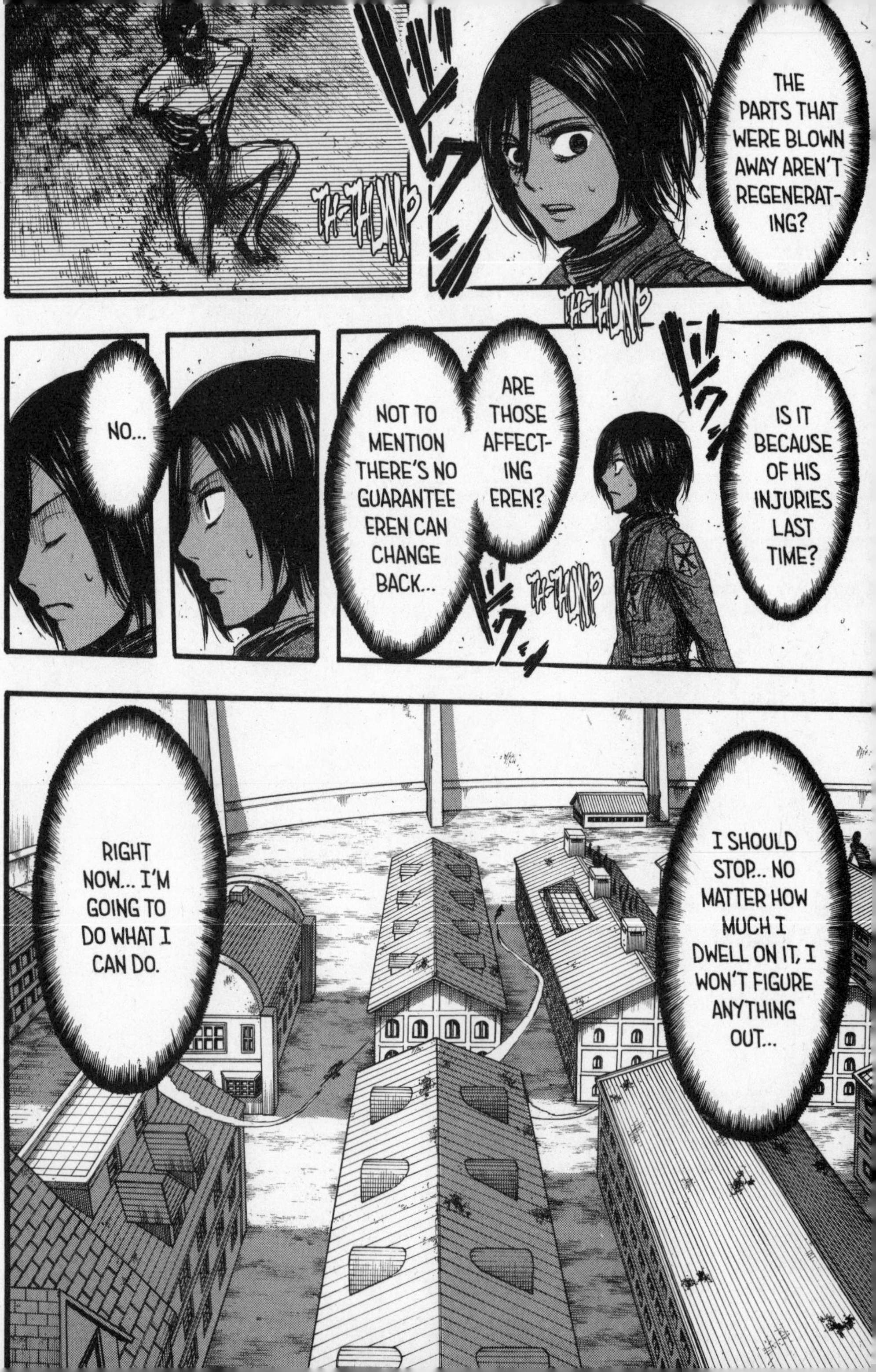
THE PARTS THAT WERE BLOWN AWAY AREN'T REGENERAT-ING?
TH-THOMP
TH-THOMP
IS IT BECAUSE OF HIS INJURIES LAST TIME?
ARE THOSE AFFECT-ING EREN?
NOT TO MENTION THERE'S NO GUARANTEE EREN CAN CHANGE BACK...
TH-THOMP
NO...
I SHOULD STOP... NO MATTER HOW MUCH I DWELL ON IT, I WON'T FIGURE ANYTHING OUT...
RIGHT NOW... I'M GOING TO DO WHAT I CAN DO.

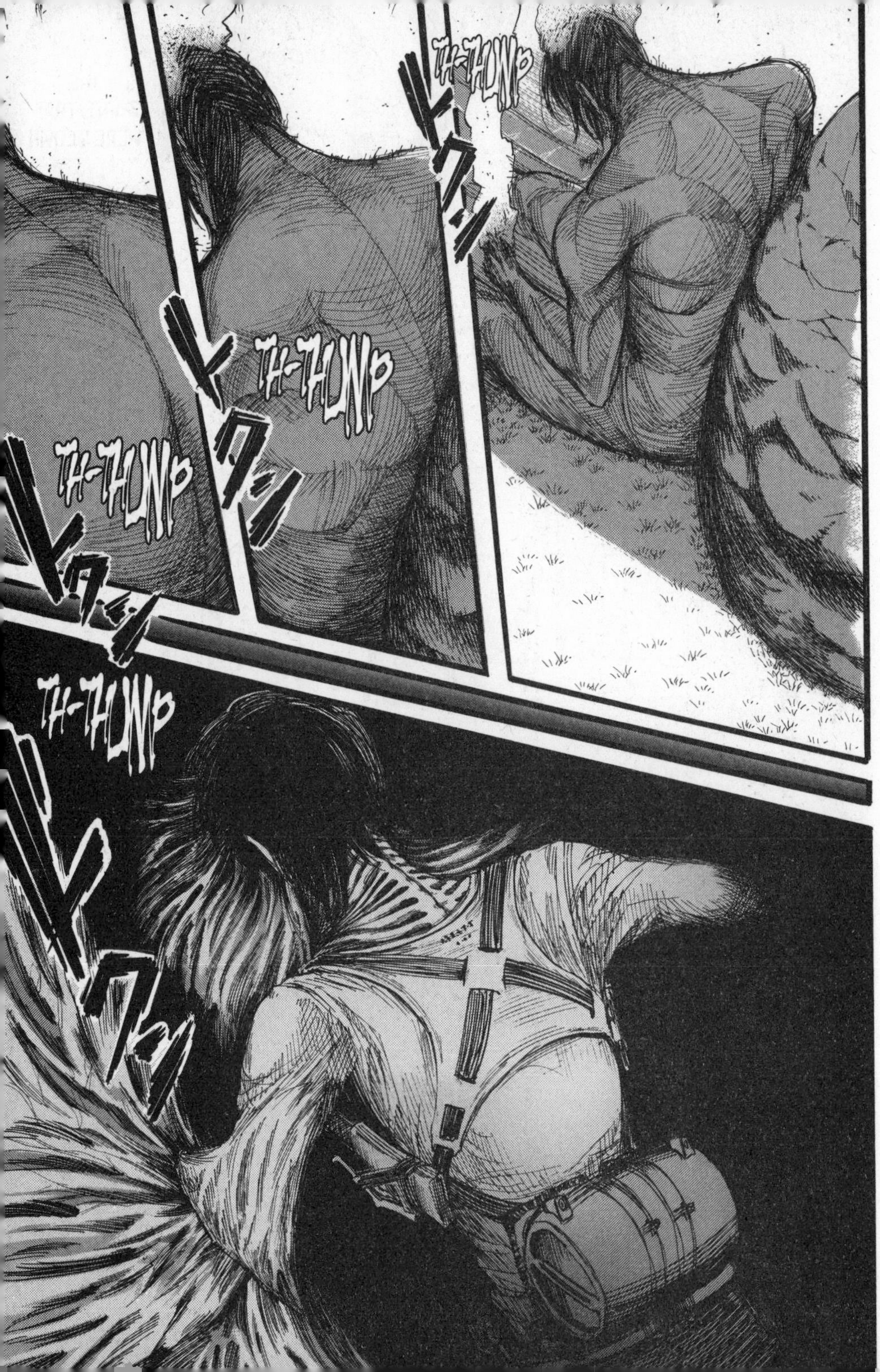
TH-THUMP
ドクン
TH-THUMP
ドクン
TH-THUMP
ドクン
TH-THUMP
ドクン

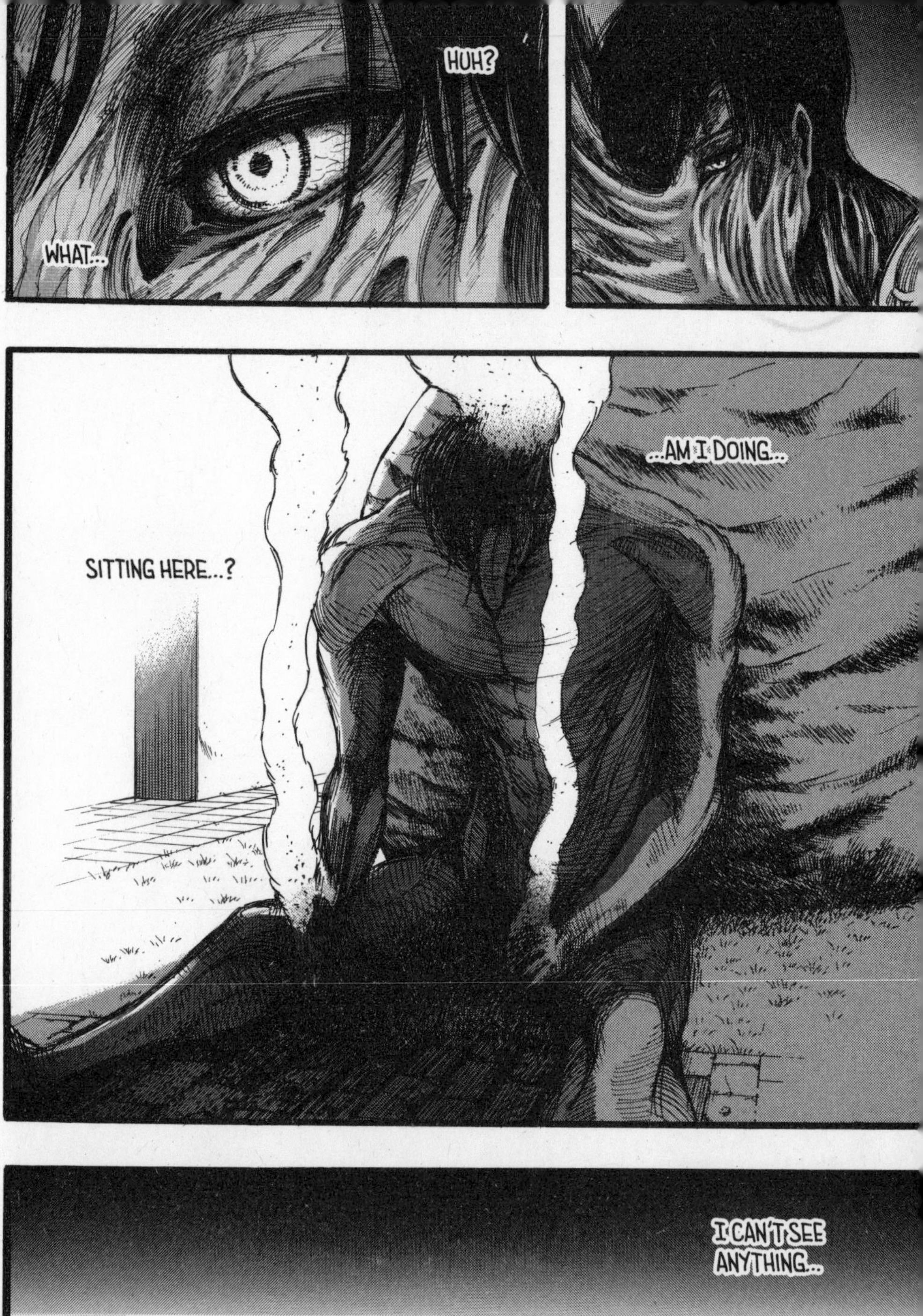
HUH?
WHAT...
...AM I DOING...
SITTING HERE...?
I CAN'T SEE ANYTHING...

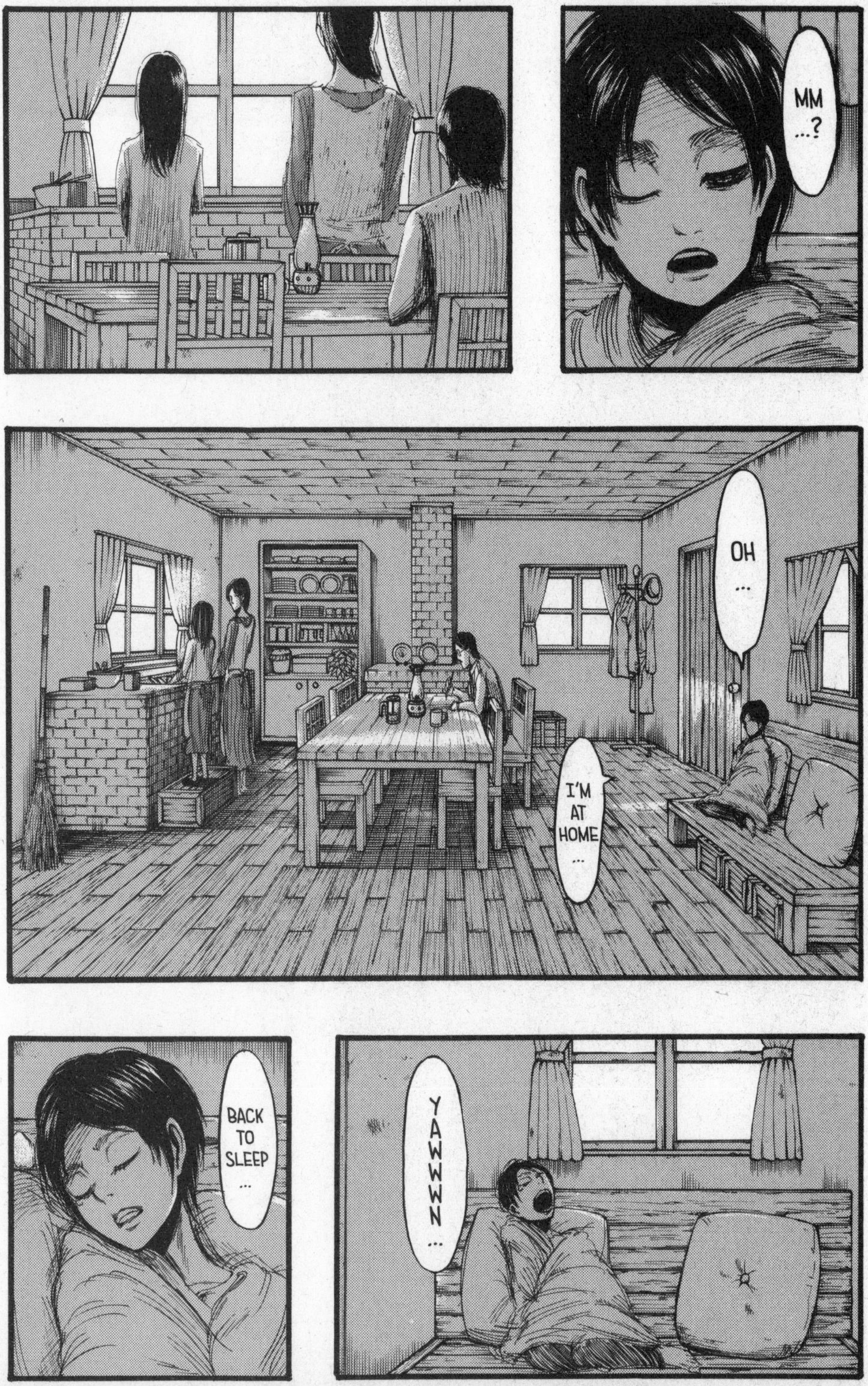
MM ...?
OH ...
I'M AT HOME ...
YAWWWN ...
BACK TO SLEEP ...

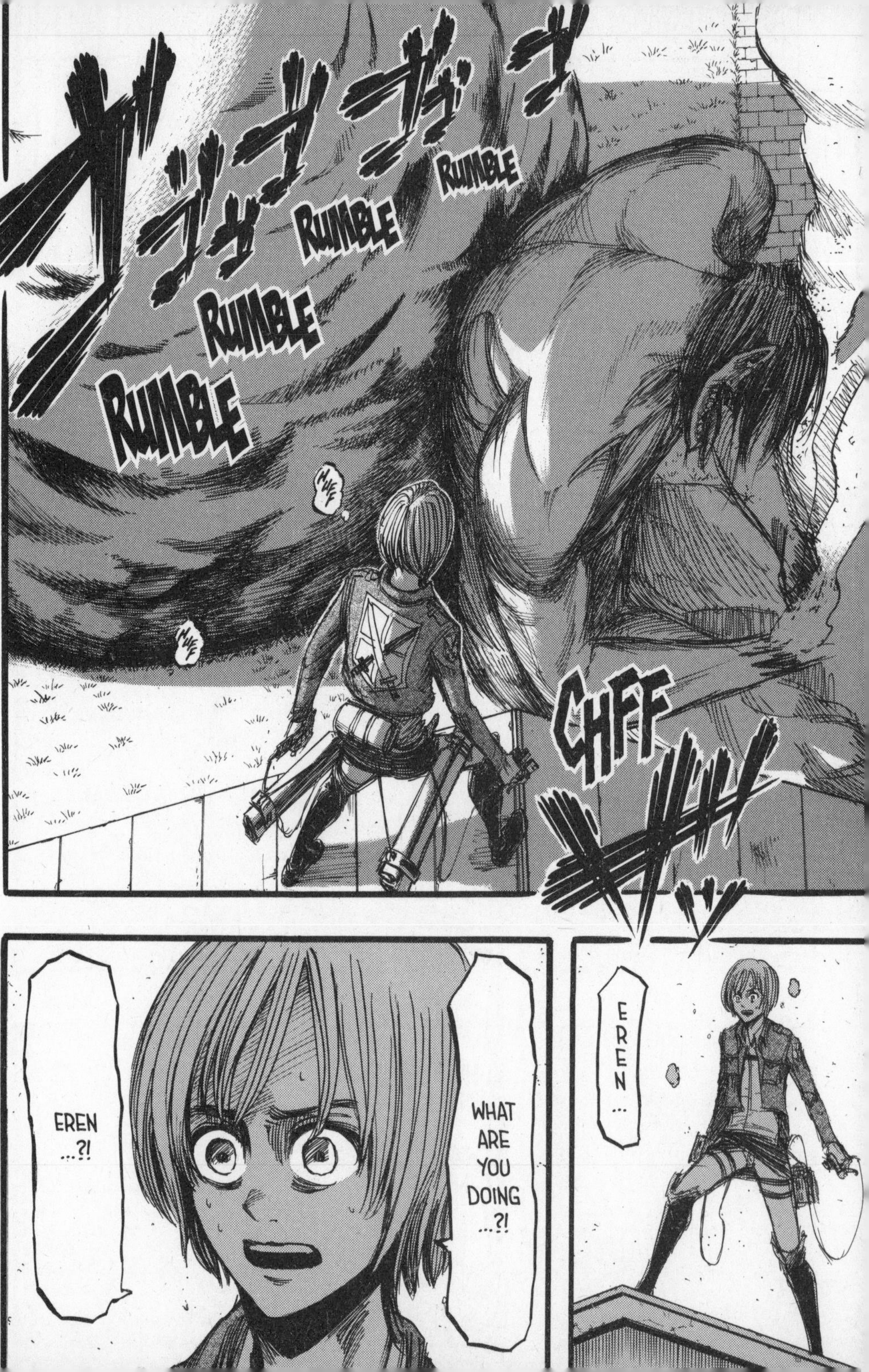
RUMBLE
RUMBLE
RUMBLE
RUMBLE
HUFF
HUFF
CHFF
EREN ...
WHAT ARE YOU DOING ...?!
EREN ...?!

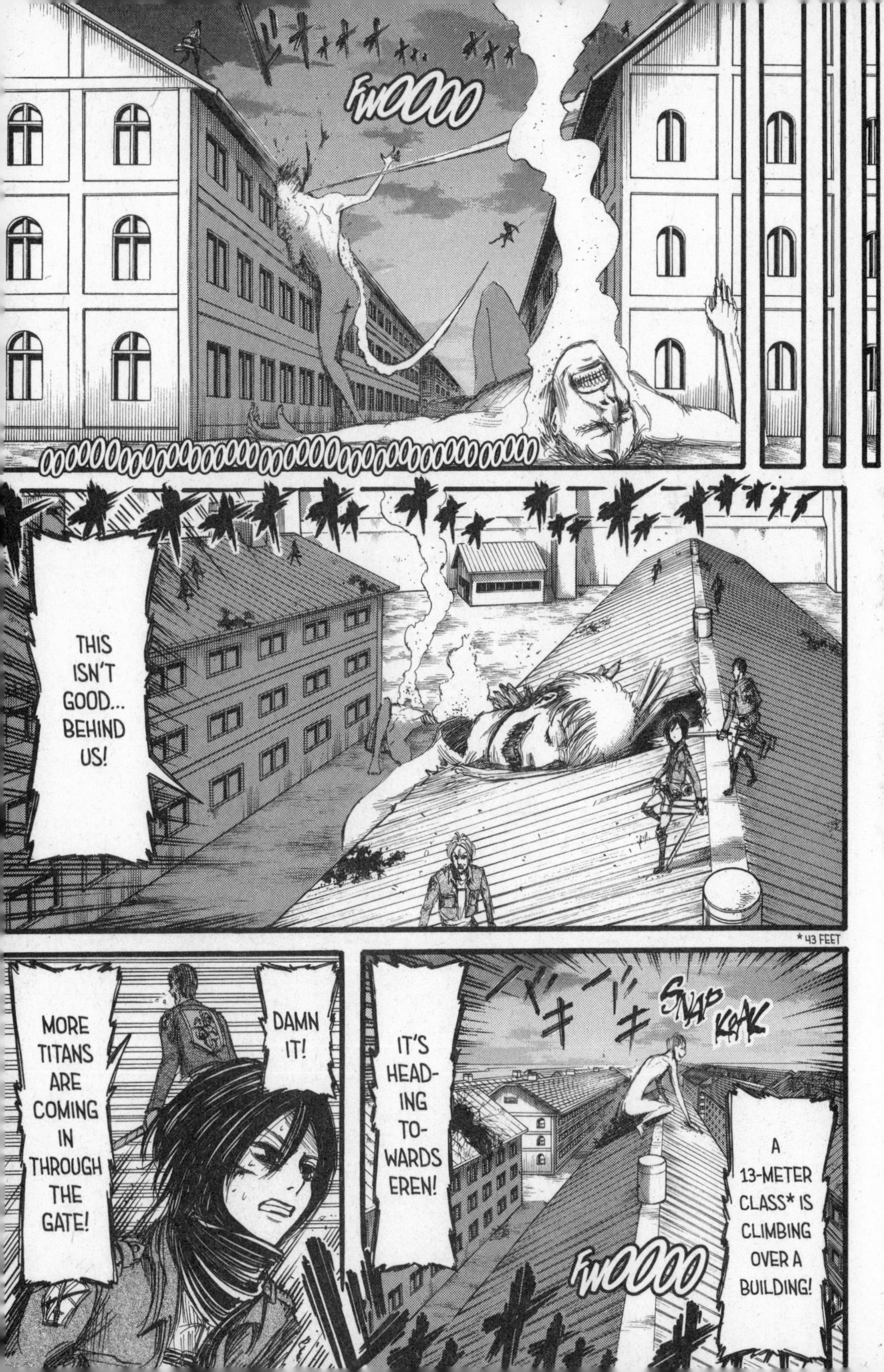
FWOOOO
OOOOOOOOOOOOOOOOOOOOOOOOOOOOOOOOOOOOOOOOOOOO
THIS ISN'T GOOD... BEHIND US!
SNAP KRAK
A 13-METER CLASS* IS CLIMBING OVER A BUILDING!
FWOOOO
IT'S HEADING TOWARDS EREN!
DAMN IT!
MORE TITANS ARE COMING IN THROUGH THE GATE!

* 43 FEET

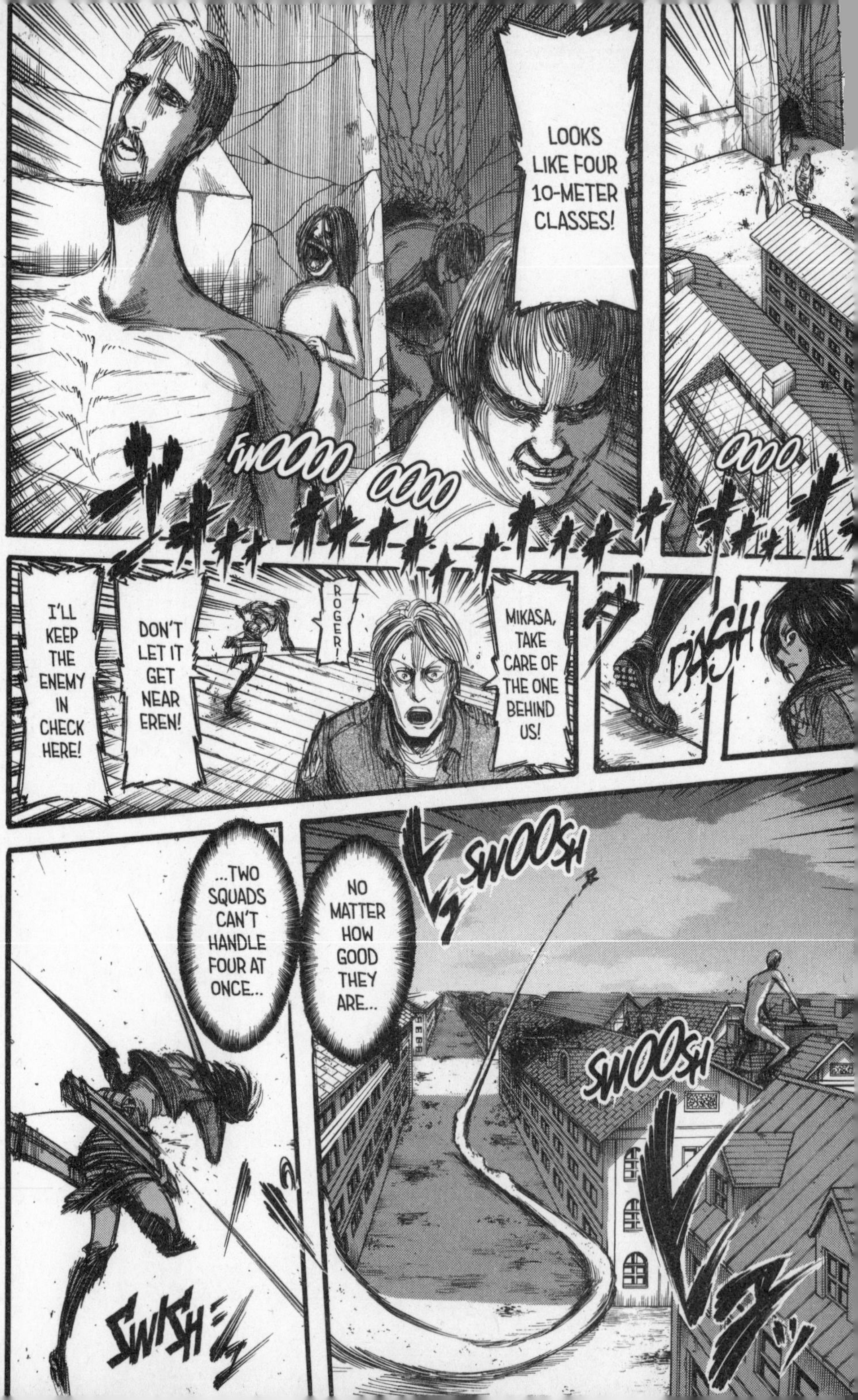
LOOKS LIKE FOUR 10-METER CLASSES!
FWOOOO OOOO OOOO
DASH
MIKASA, TAKE CARE OF THE ONE BEHIND US!
ROGER!
DON'T LET IT GET NEAR EREN!
I'LL KEEP THE ENEMY IN CHECK HERE!
SWOOSH
SWOOSH
NO MATTER HOW GOOD THEY ARE...
...TWO SQUADS CAN'T HANDLE FOUR AT ONCE...
SWISH

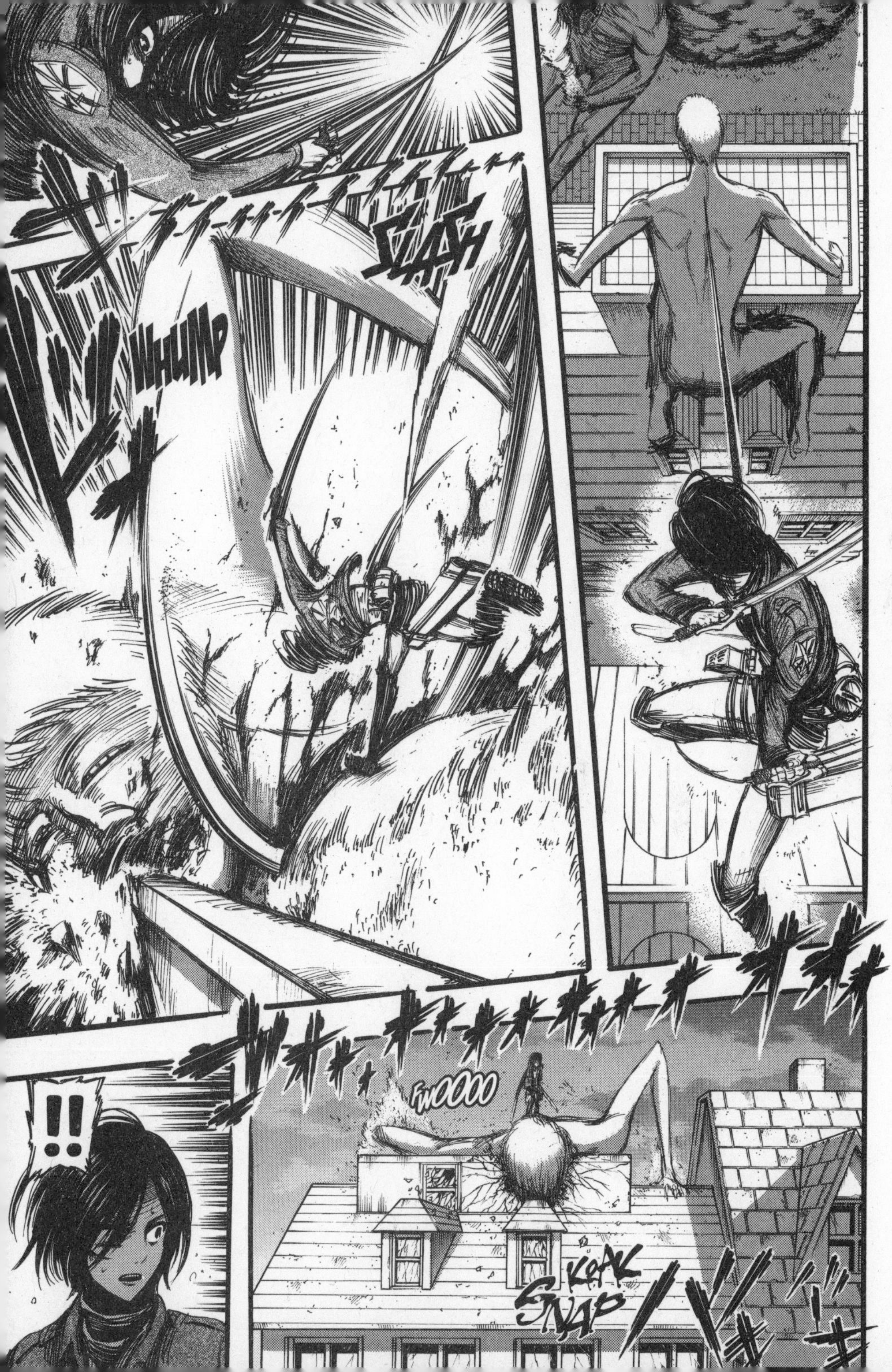
SLASH
WHUMP
FWOOOO
!!
KRAK
SNAP

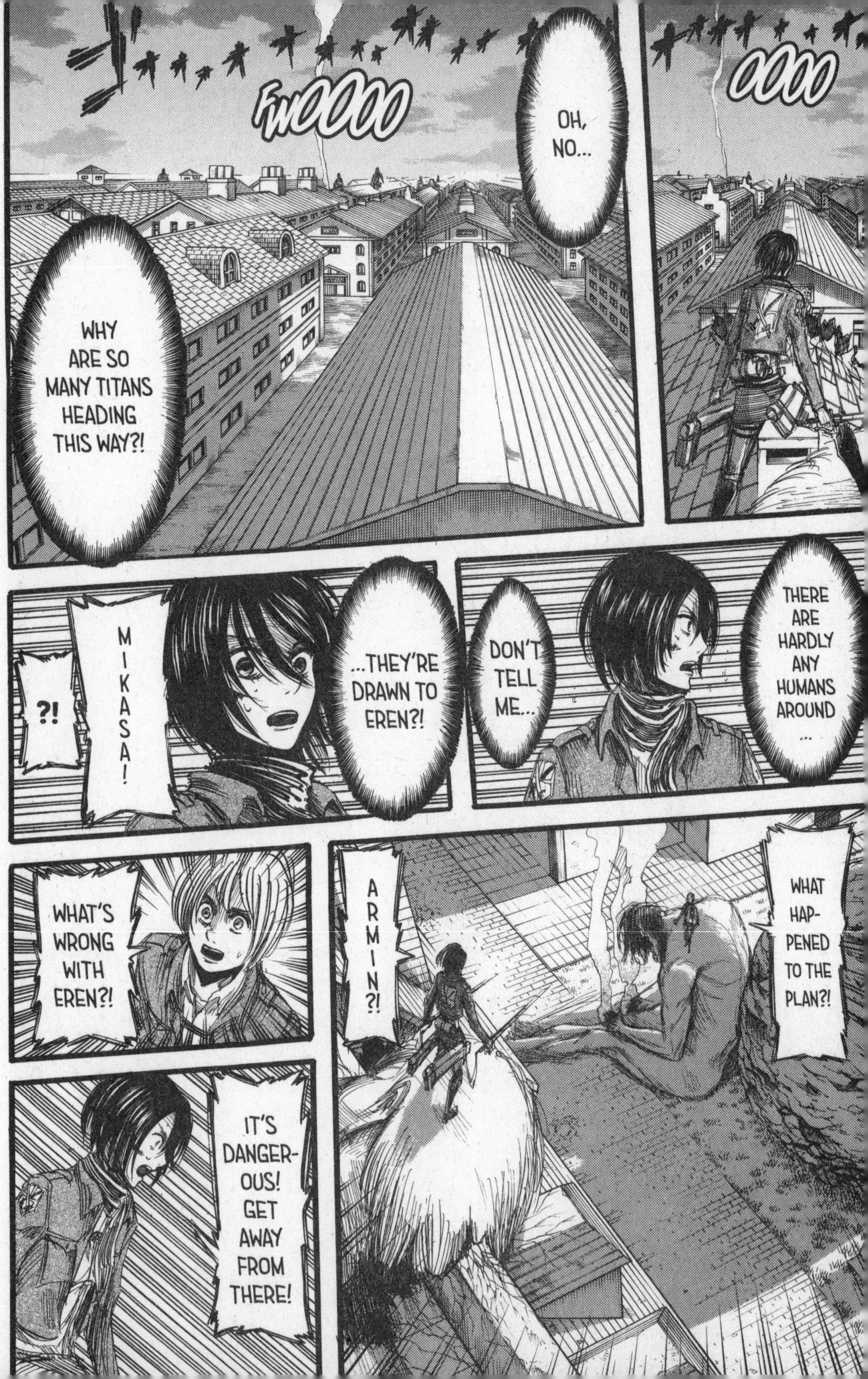
OOOO
OH, NO...
FWOOOO
WHY ARE SO MANY TITANS HEADING THIS WAY?!
THERE ARE HARDLY ANY HUMANS AROUND...
DON'T TELL ME...
...THEY'RE DRAWN TO EREN?!
MIKASA!
?!
WHAT HAPPENED TO THE PLAN?!
ARMIN?!
WHAT'S WRONG WITH EREN?!
IT'S DANGEROUS! GET AWAY FROM THERE!

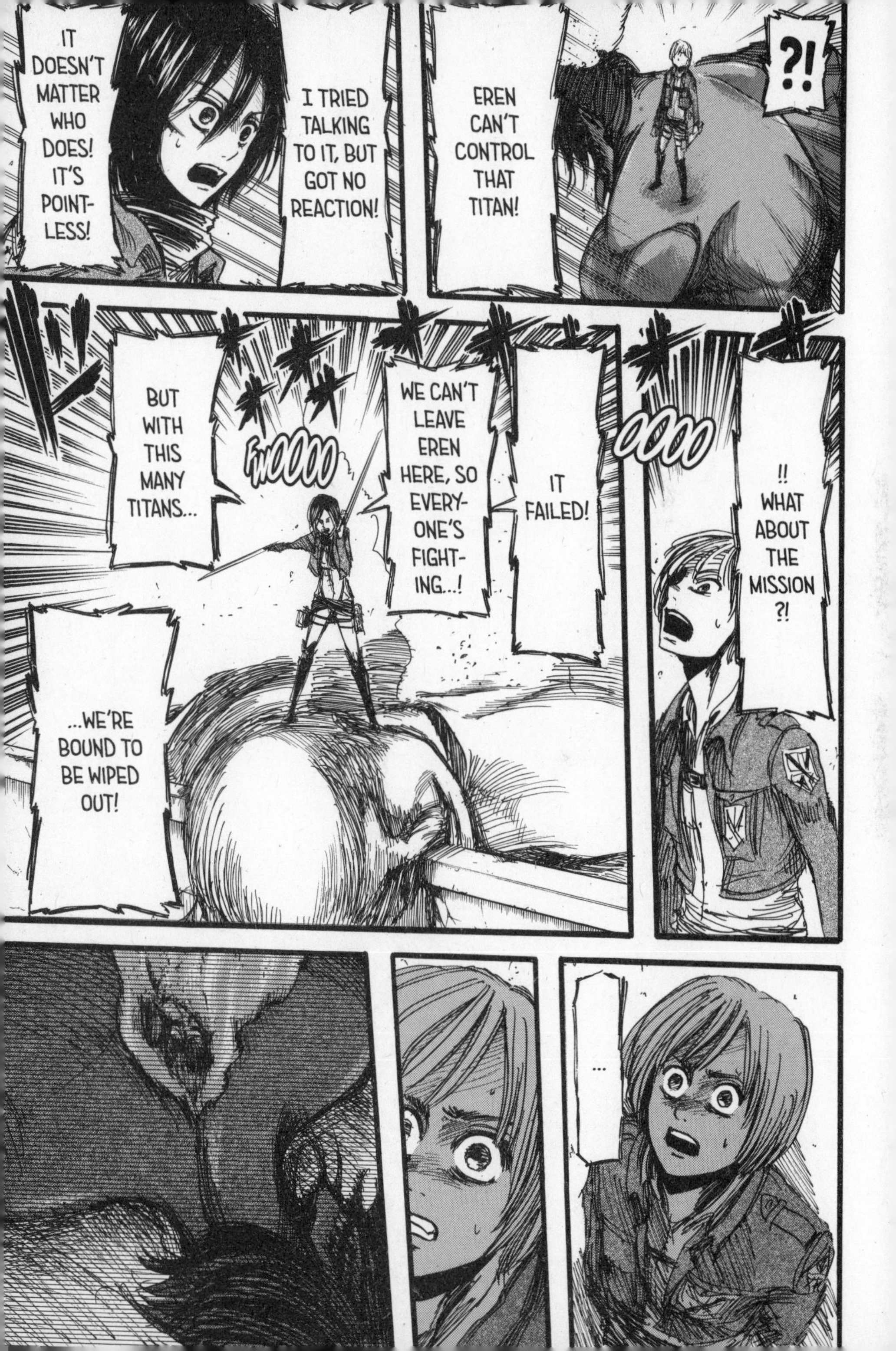
?!
EREN CAN'T CONTROL THAT TITAN!
I TRIED TALKING TO IT, BUT GOT NO REACTION!
IT DOESN'T MATTER WHO DOES! IT'S POINTLESS!
OOOO
!! WHAT ABOUT THE MISSION?!
IT FAILED!
WE CAN'T LEAVE EREN HERE, SO EVERYONE'S FIGHTING...!
FWOOOO
BUT WITH THIS MANY TITANS...
...WE'RE BOUND TO BE WIPED OUT!
...

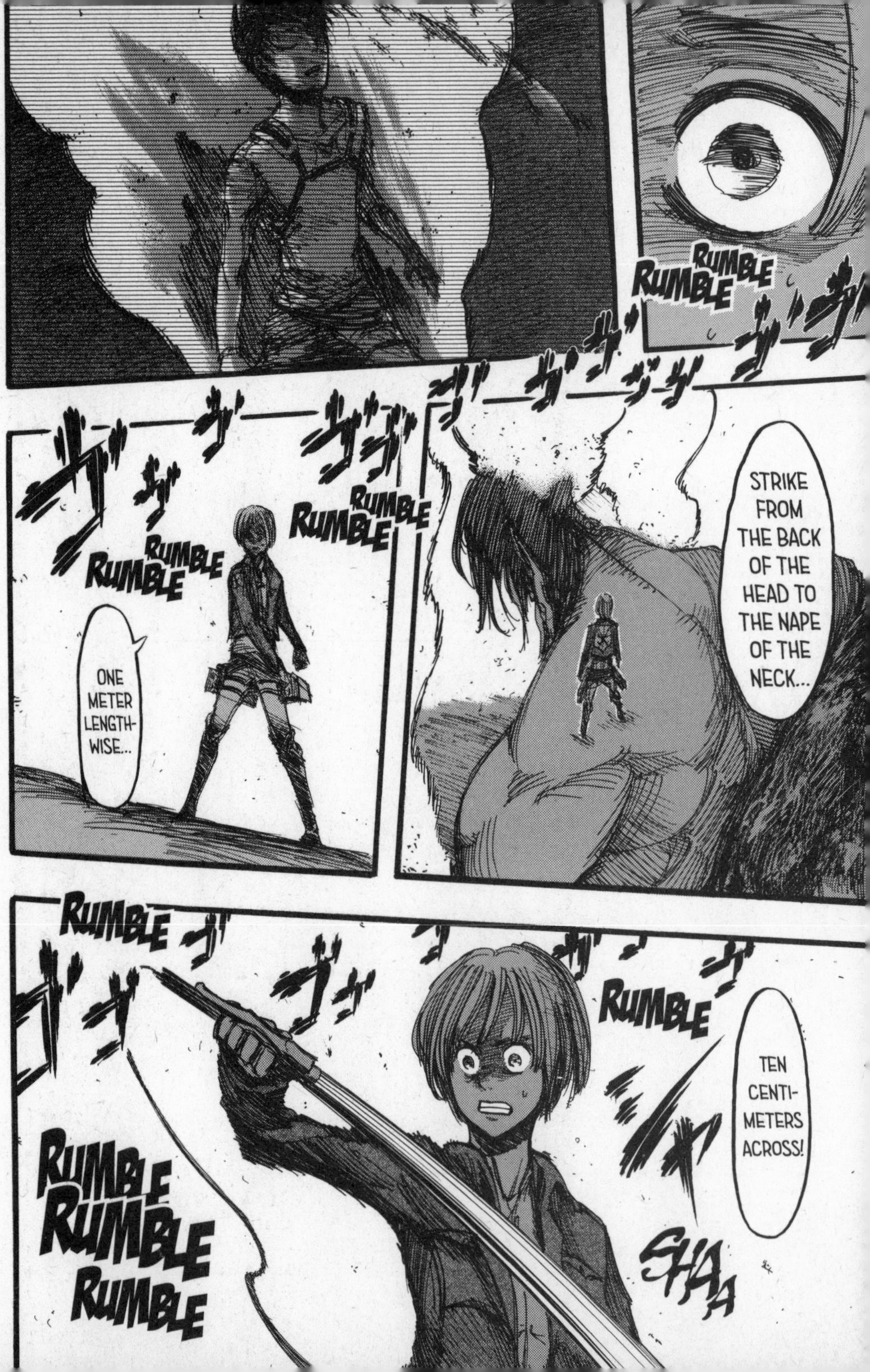
RUMBLE
RUMBLE
STRIKE FROM THE BACK OF THE HEAD TO THE NAPE OF THE NECK...
RUMBLE
RUMBLE
RUMBLE
RUMBLE
ONE METER LENGTH-WISE...
RUMBLE
TEN CENTI-METERS ACROSS!
SHAA
RUMBLE
RUMBLE
RUMBLE
RUMBLE

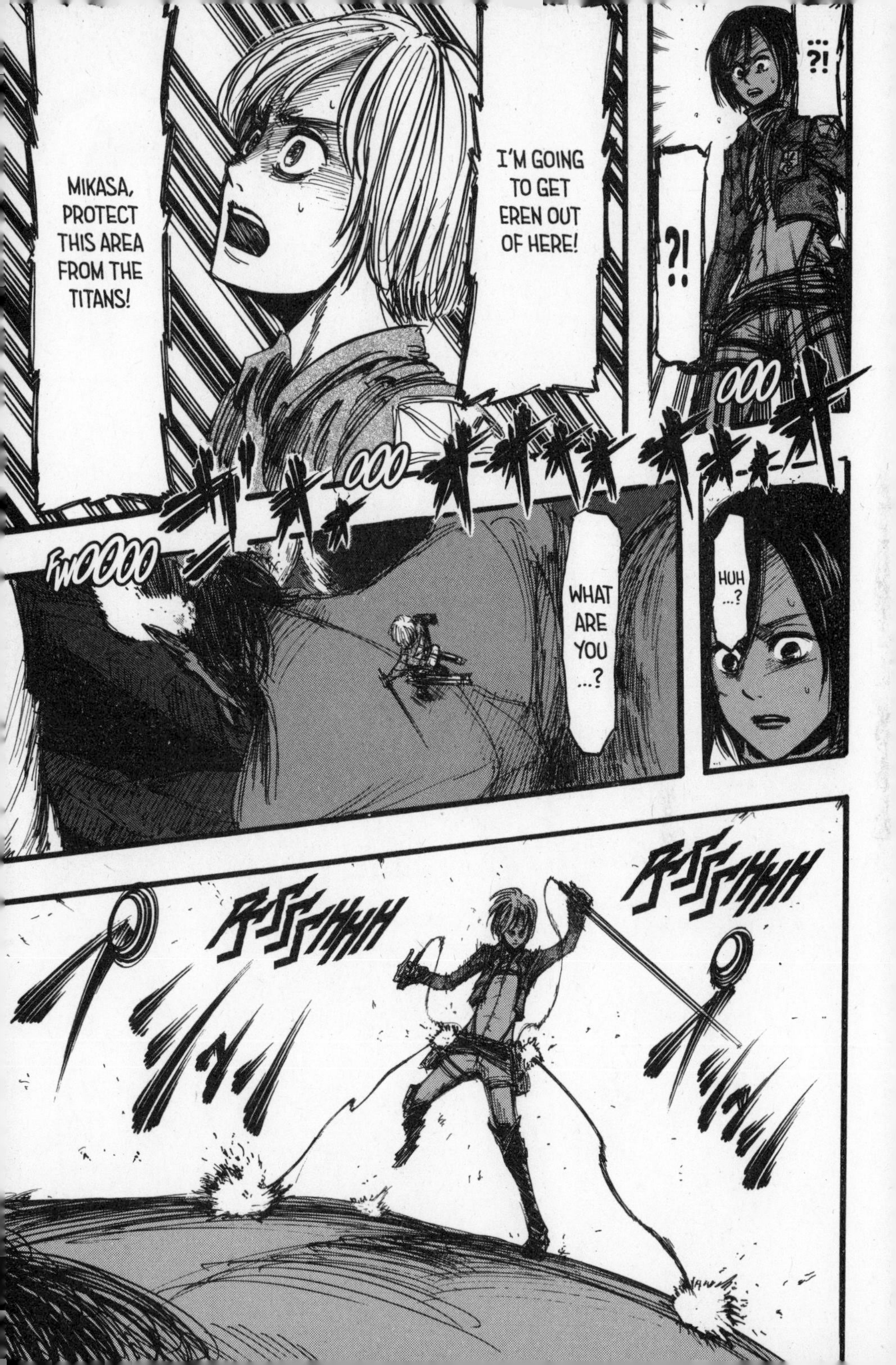
...
?!
I'M GOING TO GET EREN OUT OF HERE!
MIKASA, PROTECT THIS AREA FROM THE TITANS!
?!
OOO
OOO
FWOOOO
HUH ...?
WHAT ARE YOU ...?
RSSSHHH
RSSSHHH

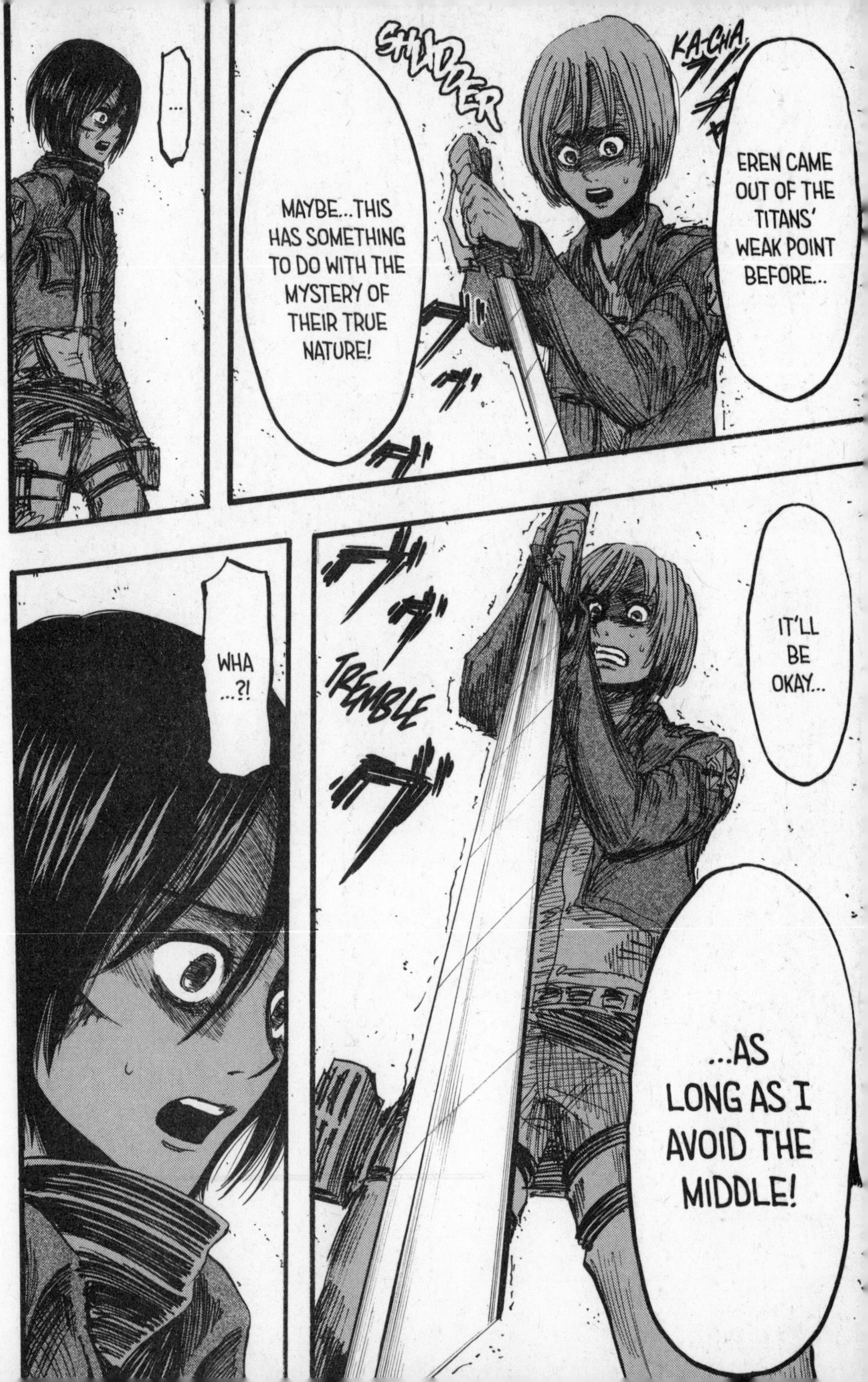
KA-CHA
EREN CAME OUT OF THE TITANS' WEAK POINT BEFORE...
SHUDDER
MAYBE...THIS HAS SOMETHING TO DO WITH THE MYSTERY OF THEIR TRUE NATURE!
...
IT'LL BE OKAY...
...AS LONG AS I AVOID THE MIDDLE!
TREMBLE
WHA ...?!

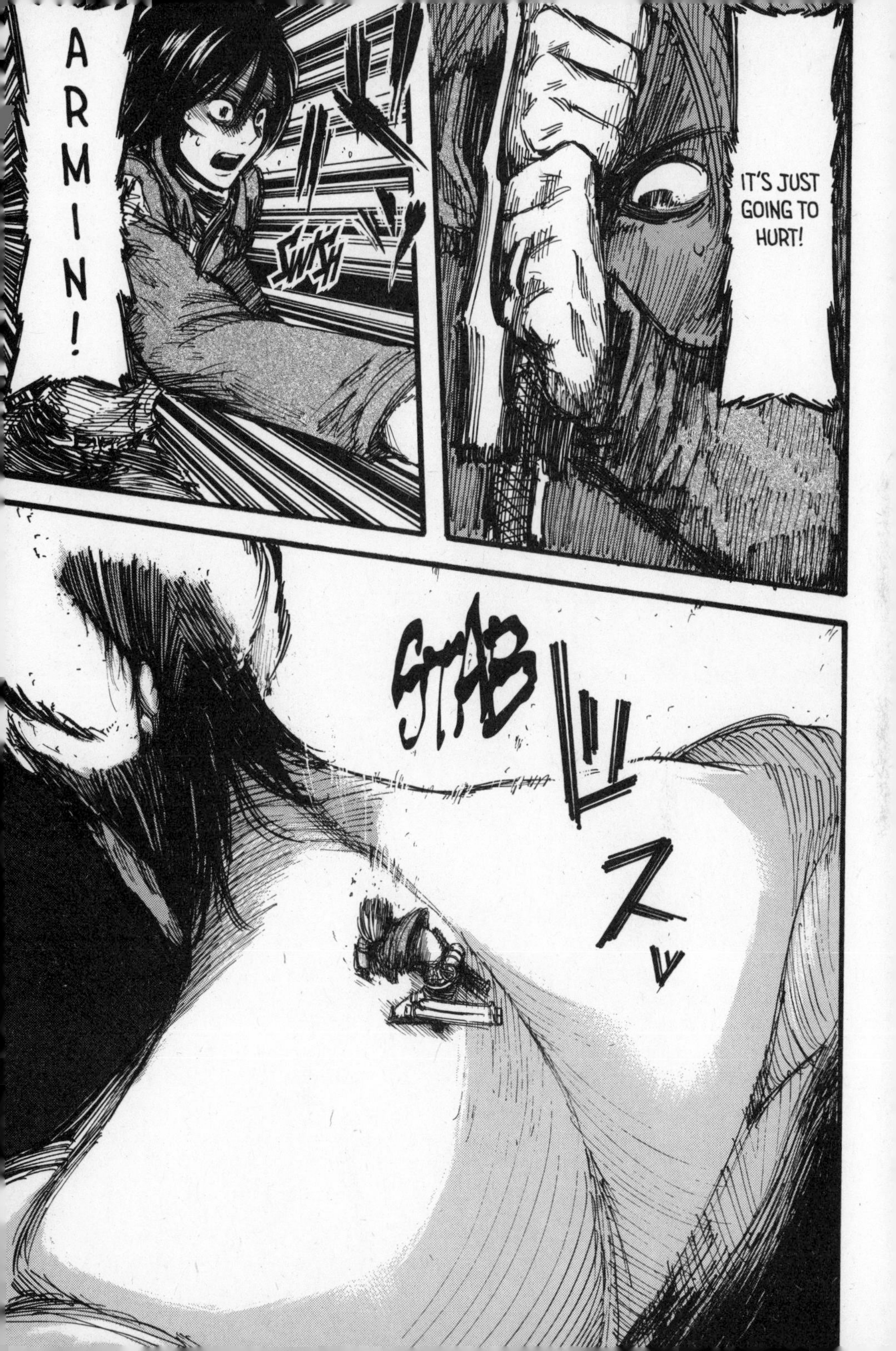
IT'S JUST GOING TO HURT!
ARMIN!
SWISH
STAB

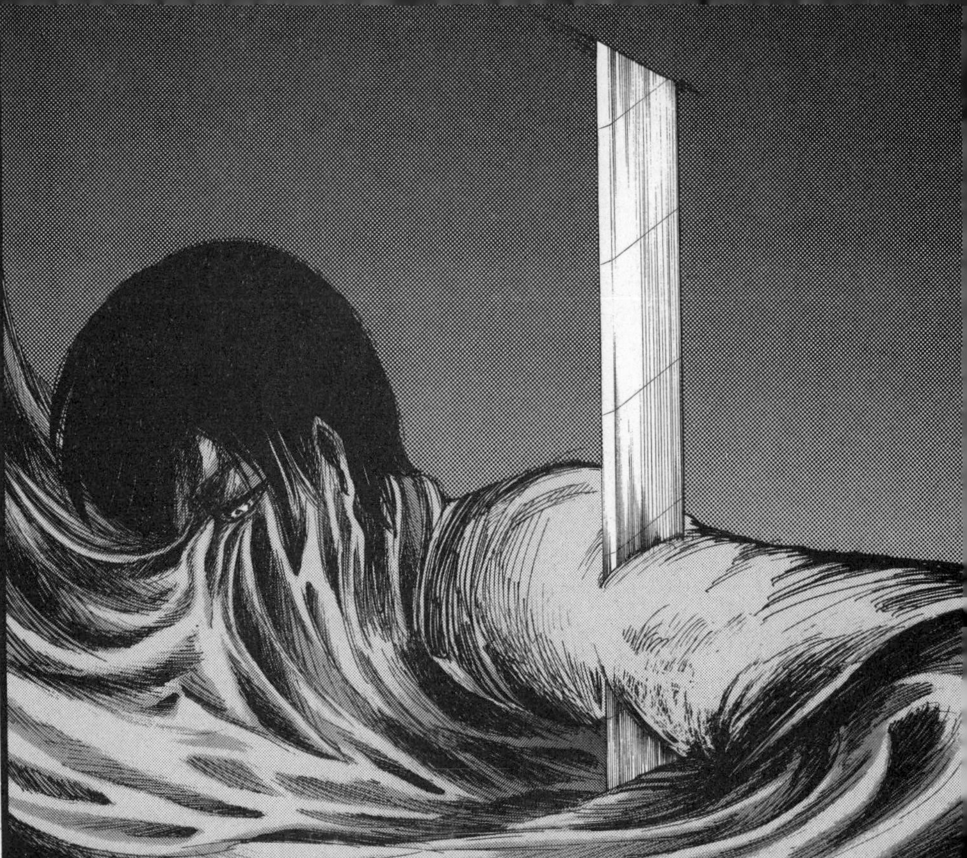
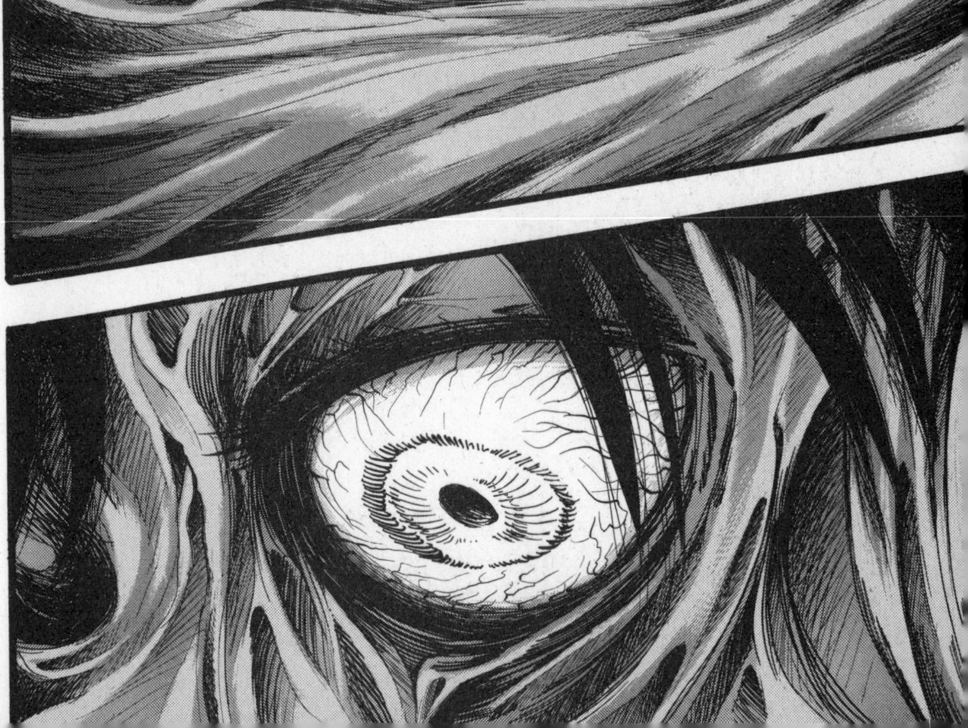

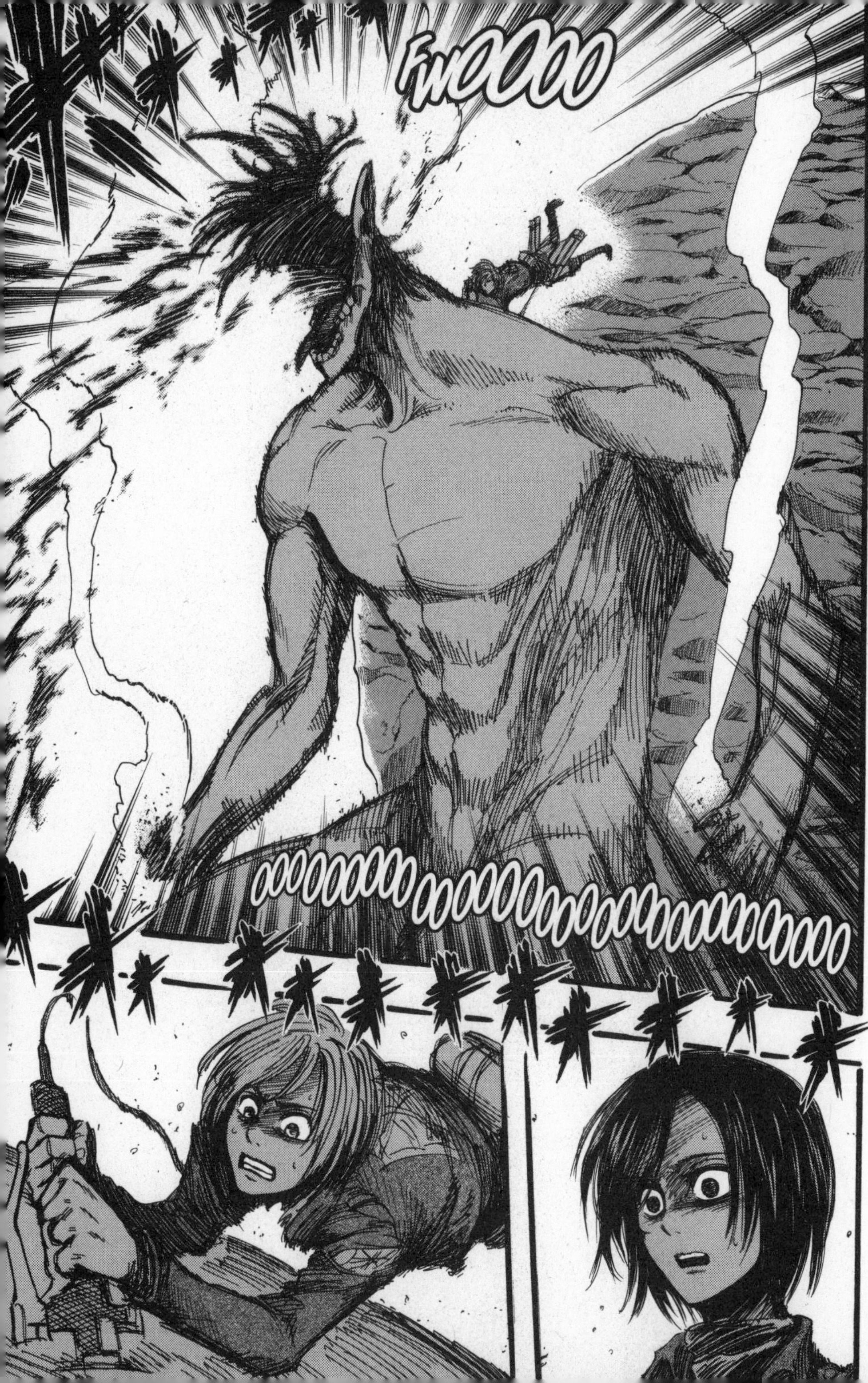
FWOOOO
OOOOOOOOOOOOOOOOOOOOOOOOOOOOOOOOOOO

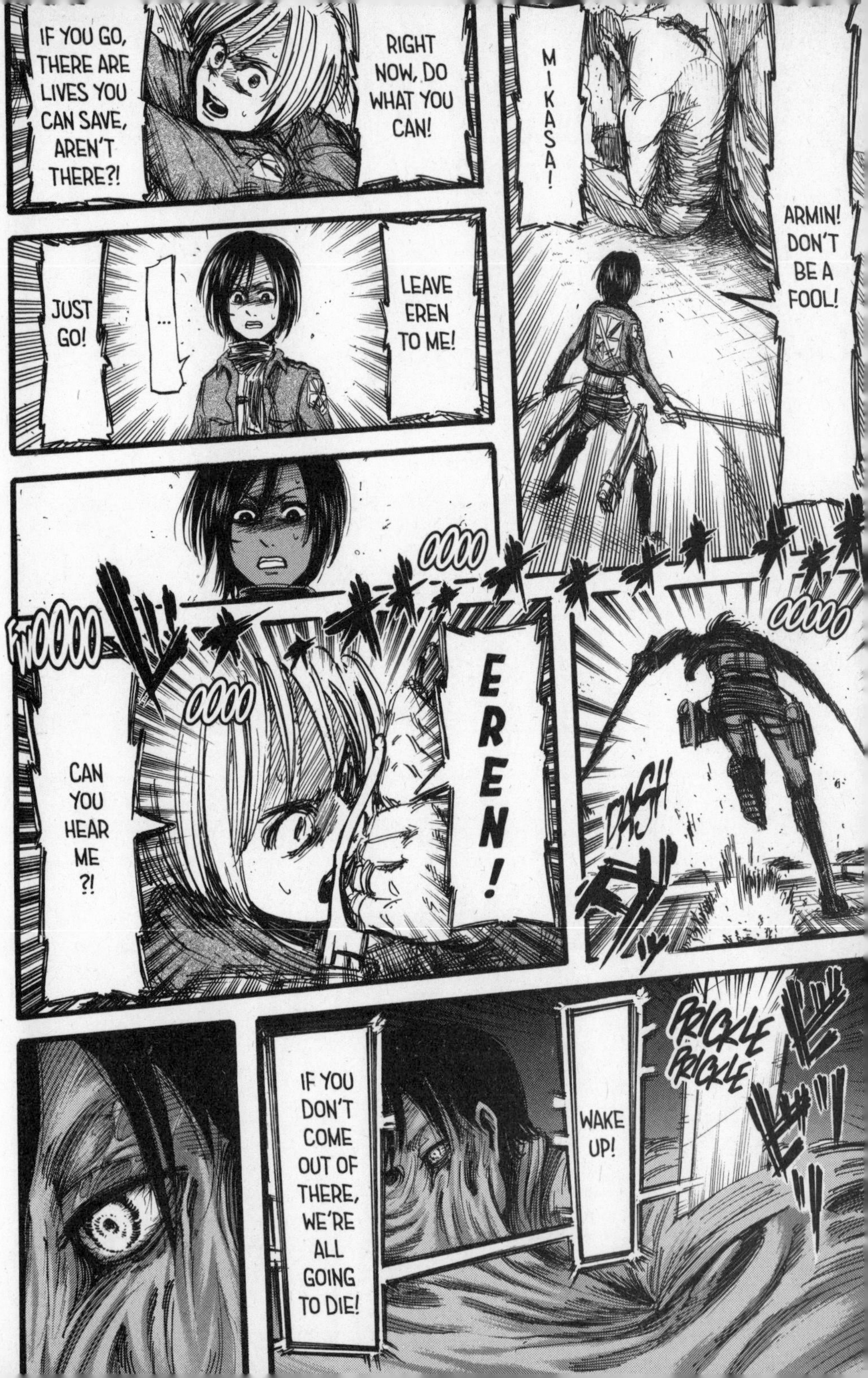
MIKASA!
ARMIN! DON'T BE A FOOL!
RIGHT NOW, DO WHAT YOU CAN!
IF YOU GO, THERE ARE LIVES YOU CAN SAVE, AREN'T THERE?!
LEAVE EREN TO ME!
...
JUST GO!
OOOO
OOOOO
DASH
EREN!
OOOO
FWOOOO
CAN YOU HEAR ME?!
PRICKLE PRICKLE
WAKE UP!
IF YOU DON'T COME OUT OF THERE, WE'RE ALL GOING TO DIE!

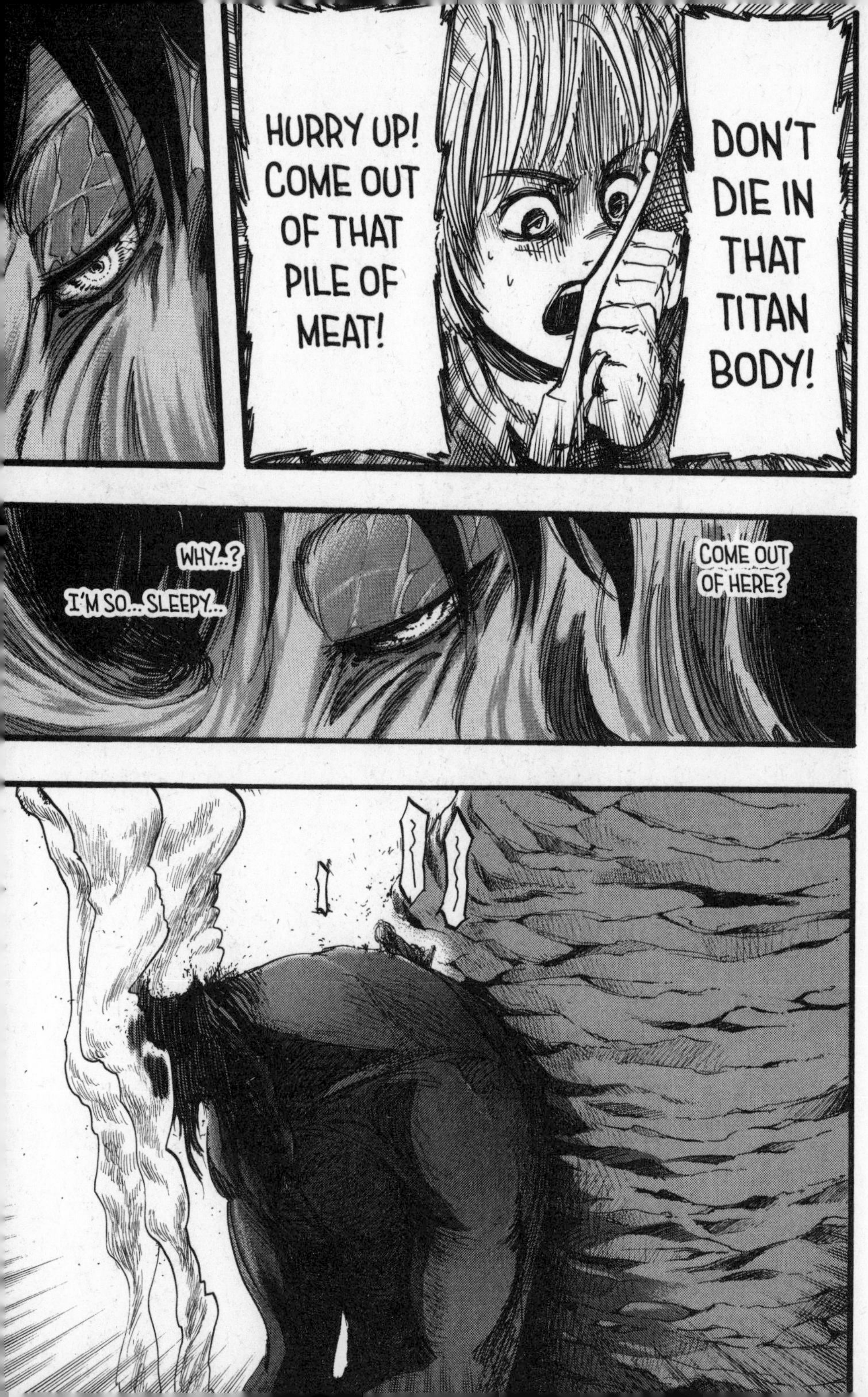
DON'T DIE IN THAT TITAN BODY!
HURRY UP! COME OUT OF THAT PILE OF MEAT!
COME OUT OF HERE?
WHY...?
I'M SO... SLEEPY...

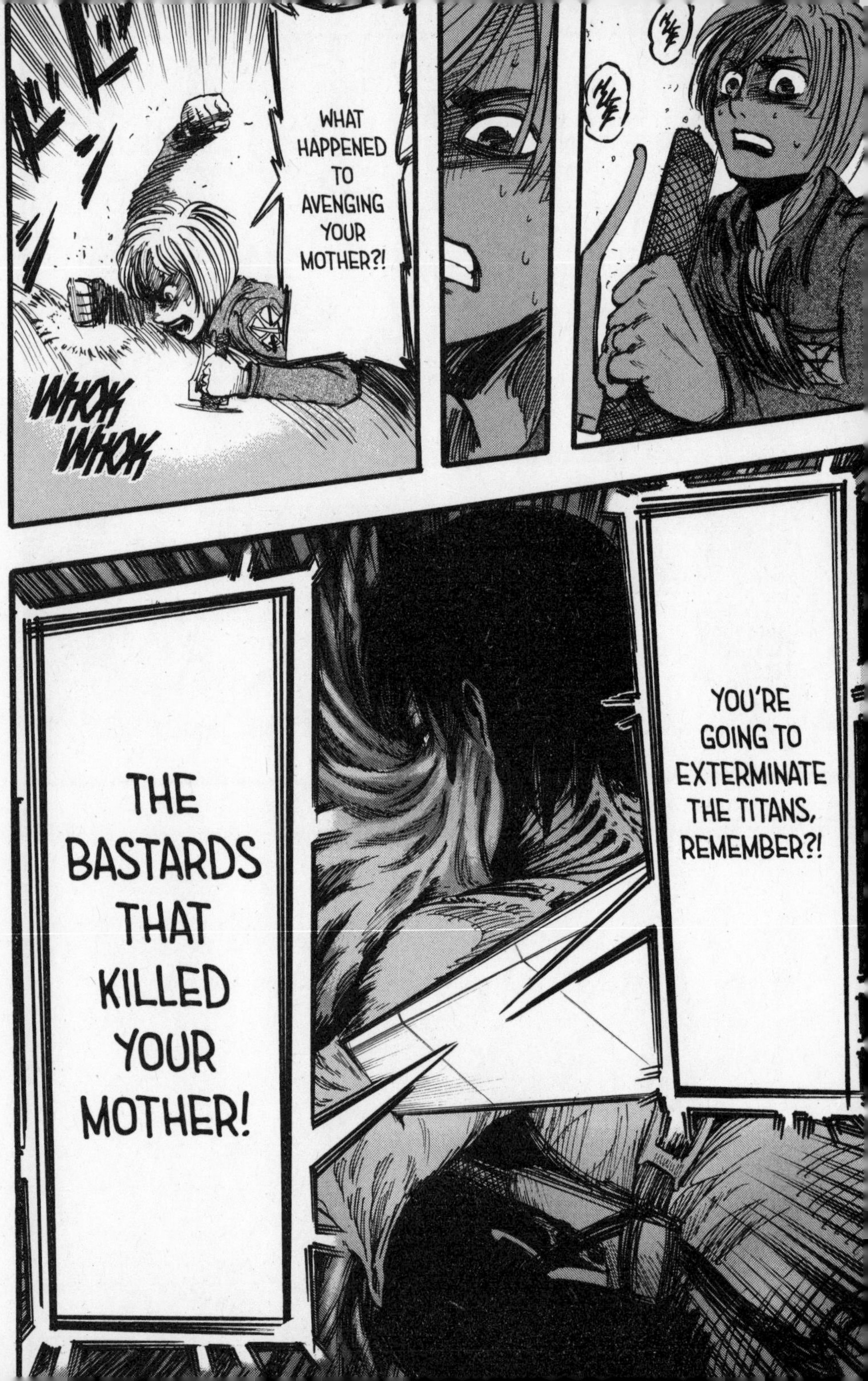
WHAT HAPPENED TO AVENGING YOUR MOTHER?!
WHOK WHOK
YOU'RE GOING TO EXTERMINATE THE TITANS, REMEMBER?!
THE BASTARDS THAT KILLED YOUR MOTHER!

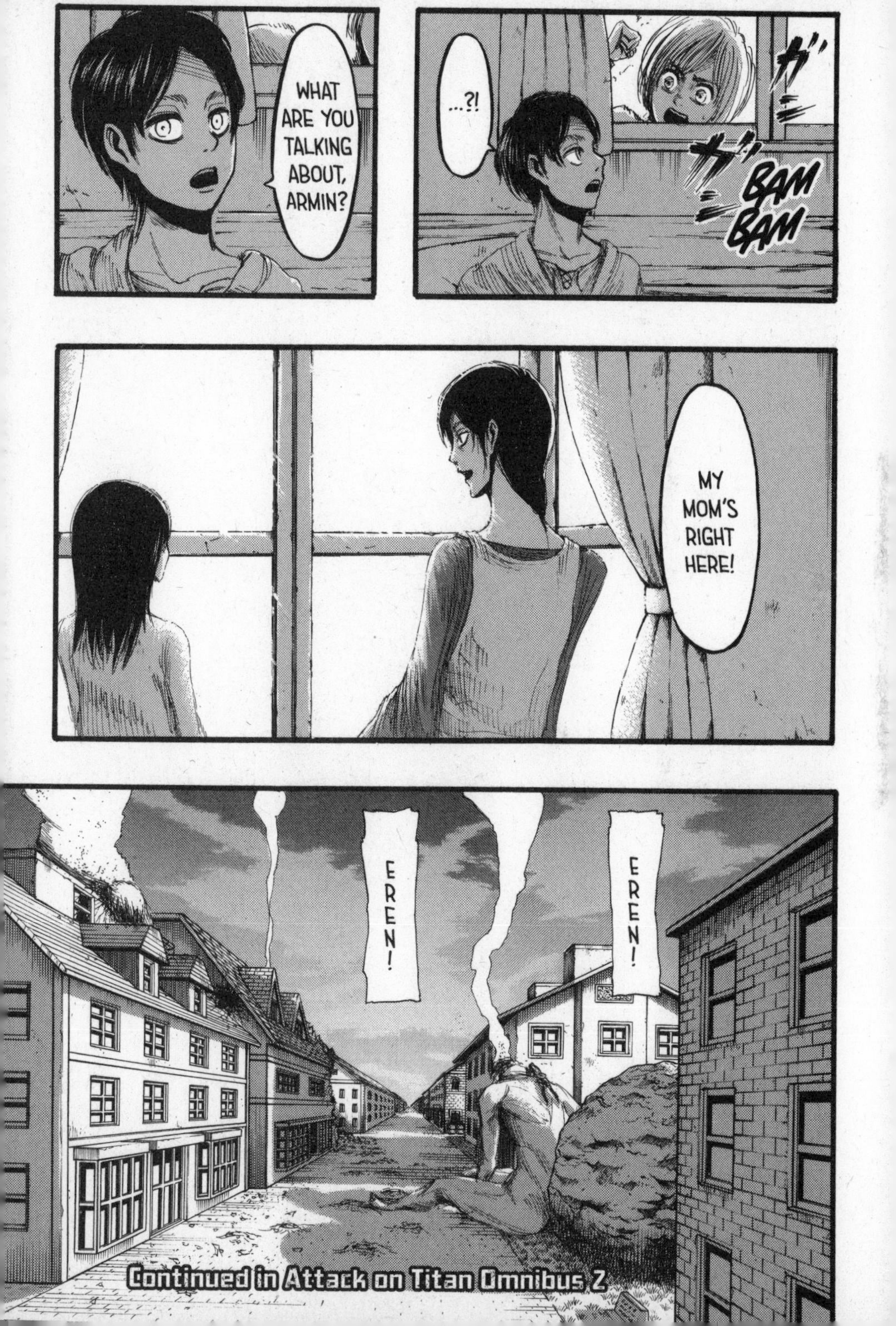
...?!
BAM BAM
WHAT ARE YOU TALKING ABOUT, ARMIN?
MY MOM'S RIGHT HERE!
EREN!
EREN!

Continued in Attack on Titan Omnibus 2

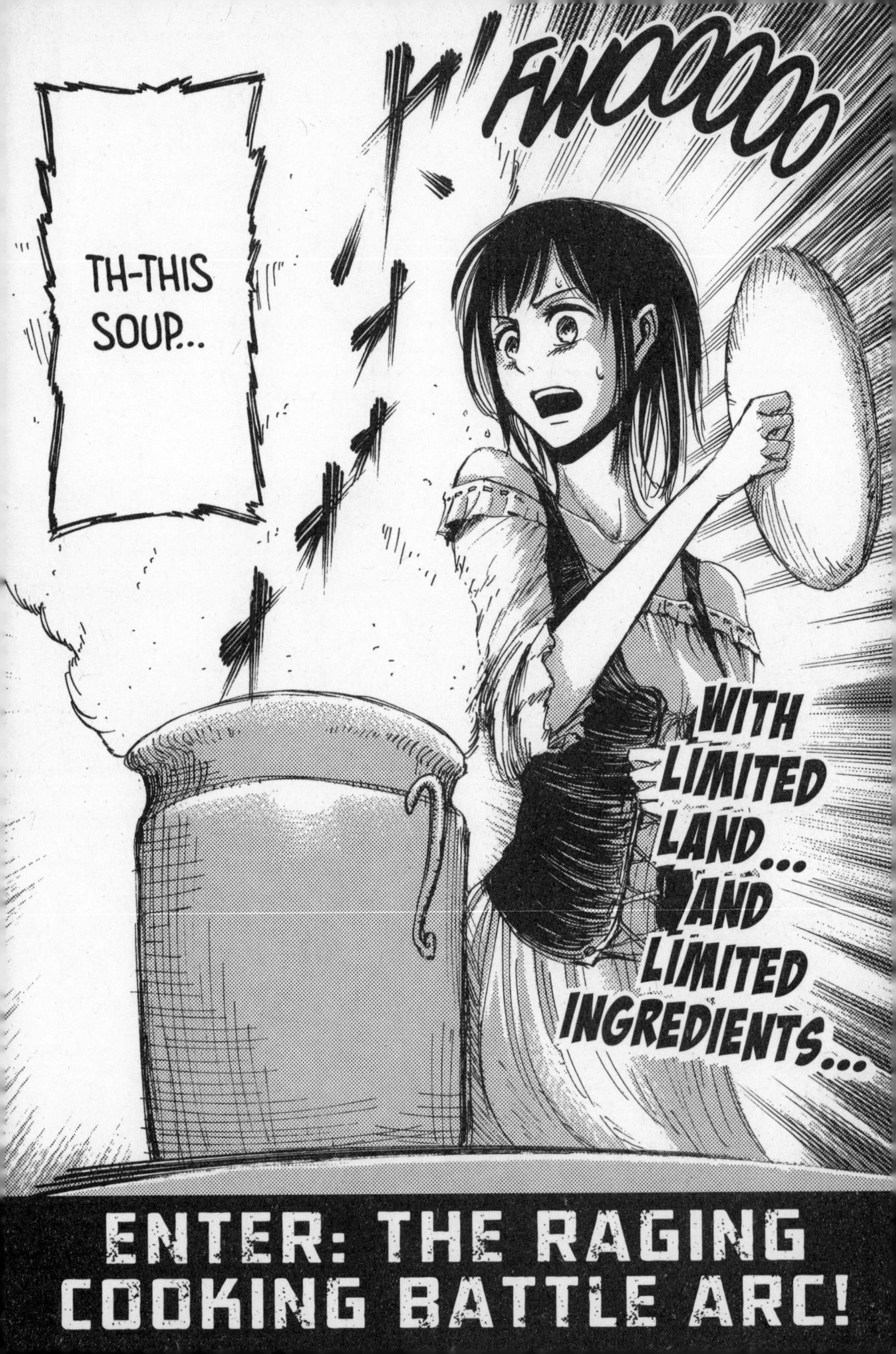
FWOOOOO
TH-THIS SOUP...
WITH LIMITED LAND... AND LIMITED INGREDIENTS...
ENTER: THE RAGING COOKING BATTLE ARC!

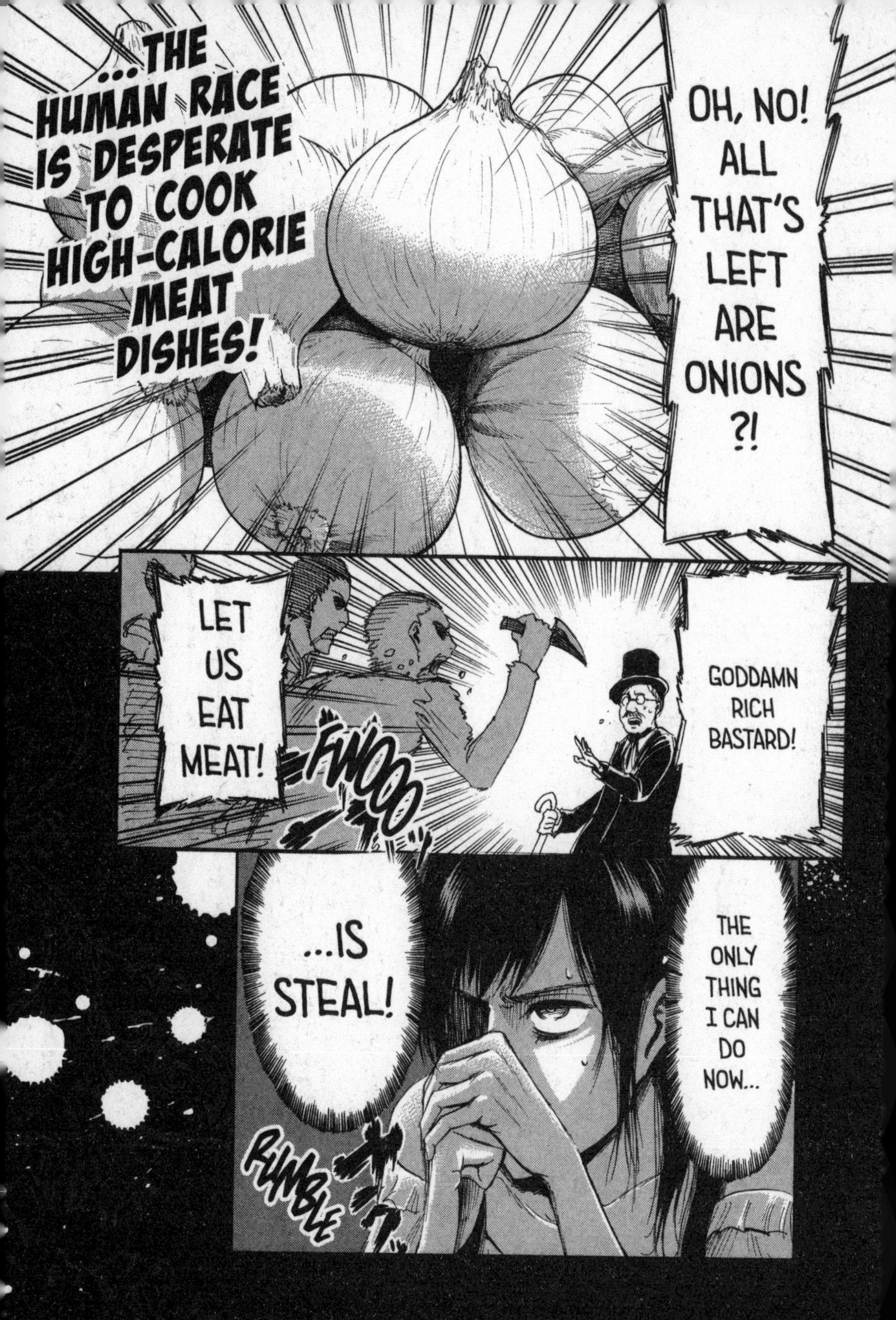
OH, NO! ALL THAT'S LEFT ARE ONIONS ?!
...THE HUMAN RACE IS DESPERATE TO COOK HIGH-CALORIE MEAT DISHES!
GODDAMN RICH BASTARD!
LET US EAT MEAT!
FWOOO
THE ONLY THING I CAN DO NOW...
...IS STEAL!
RUMBLE

*Not a real preview.

Preview of Volume 4!

ATTACK on TITAN

ATTACK on TITAN

One of CLAMP's biggest hits returns in this definitive, premium, hardcover 20th anniversary collector's edition!

CLAMP

₁ Chobits

20TH ANNIVERSARY EDITION

"A wonderfully entertaining story that would be a great installment in anybody's manga collection."
— Anime News Network

"CLAMP is an all-female manga-creating team whose feminine touch shows in this entertaining, sci-fi soap opera."
—Publishers Weekly

Poor college student Hideki is down on his luck. All he wants is a good job, a girlfriend, and his very own "persocom"—the latest and greatest in humanoid computer technology. Hideki's luck changes one night when he finds Chi—a persocom thrown out in a pile of trash. But Hideki soon discovers that there's much more to his cute new persocom than meets the eye.

KC/
KODANSHA
COMICS

The boys are back, in 400-page hardcovers that are as pretty and badass as they are!

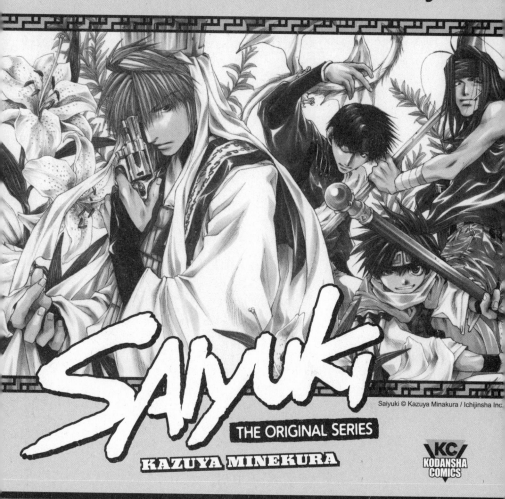

Saiyuki © Kazuya Minakura / Ichijinsha Inc.

SAIYUKI

THE ORIGINAL SERIES

KAZUYA MINEKURA

"AN EDGY COMIC LOOK AT AN ANCIENT CHINESE TALE." —YALSA

Genjo Sanzo is a Buddhist priest in the city of Togenkyo, which is being ravaged by yokai spirits that have fallen out of balance with the natural order. His superiors send him on a journey far to the west to discover why this is happening and how to stop it. His companions are three yokai with human souls. But this is no day trip — the four will encounter many discoveries and horrors on the way.

FEATURES NEW TRANSLATION, COLOR PAGES, AND BEAUTIFUL WRAPAROUND COVER ART!

Young characters and steampunk setting, like *Howl's Moving Castle* and *Battle Angel Alita*

Beyond the Clouds © 2018 Nicke / Ki-oon

A boy with a talent for machines and a mysterious girl whose wings he's fixed will take you beyond the clouds! In the tradition of the high-flying, resonant adventure stories of Studio Ghibli comes a gorgeous tale about the longing of young hearts for adventure and friendship!

THE SWEET SCENT OF LOVE IS IN THE AIR! FOR FANS OF OFFBEAT ROMANCES LIKE *WOTAKOI*

Sweat and Soap © Kintetsu Yamada / Kodansha Ltd.

In an office romance, there's a fine line between sexy and awkward... and that line is where Asako — a woman who sweats copiously — meets Koutarou — a perfume developer who can't get enough of Asako's, er, scent. Don't miss a romcom manga like no other!

A SMART, NEW ROMANTIC COMEDY FOR FANS OF *SHORTCAKE CAKE* AND *TERRACE HOUSE!*

A romance manga starring high school girl Meeko, who learns to live on her own in a boarding house whose living room is home to the odd (but handsome) Matsunaga-san. She begins to adjust to her new life away from her parents, but Meeko soon learns that no matter how far away from home she is, she's still a young girl at heart — especially when she finds herself falling for Matsunaga-san.

AUG - - 2023

A Kodansha Trade Paperback Original

Published in the United States by
Kodansha USA Publishing, LLC, New York.

Publication rights for this English edition arranged through
Kodansha Ltd., Tokyo.

First published in Japan in 2010 by Kodansha Ltd., Tokyo
as *Shingeki no Kyojin*, volumes 1, 2, and 3.

ISBN 978-1-64651-374-1

Original cover design by Takashi Shimoyama (Red Rooster)

Printed in the United States of America.

9 8 7 6 5

Translation: Sheldon Drzka
Lettering: Steve Wands
Additional Lettering: Evan Hayden
Editing: Tiff Joshua TJ Ferentini
Kodansha USA Publishing edition cover design by Adam Del Re
Kodansha USA Publishing edition logo design by Phil Balsman

Publisher: Kiichiro Sugawara

Director of Publishing Services: Ben Applegate
Associate Director of Operations: Stephen Pakula
Publishing Services Managing Editors: Alanna Ruse, Madison Salters
Production Managers: Emi Lotto, Angela Zurlo

KODANSHA.US

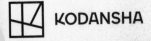
KODANSHA

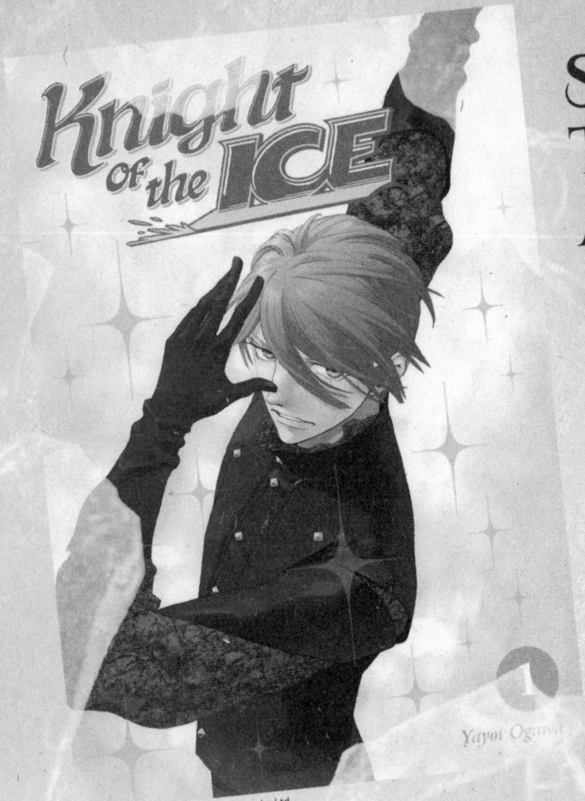
Knight of the ICE
1
Yayoi Ogawa

SKATING THRILLS AND ICY CHILLS WITH THIS NEW TINGLY ROMANCE SERIES!

Knight of the Ice ©Yayoi Ogawa/Kodansha Ltd.

A rom-com on ice, perfect for fans of *Princess Jellyfish* and *Wotakoi*. Kokoro is the talk of the figure-skating world, winning trophies and hearts. But little do they know... he's actually a huge nerd! From the beloved creator of *You're My Pet* (*Tramps Like Us*).

Chitose is a serious young woman, working for the health magazine *SASSO*. Or at least, she would be, if she wasn't constantly getting distracted by her childhood friend, international figure skating star Kokoro Kijinami! In the public eye and on the ice, Kokoro is a gallant, flawless knight, but behind his glittery costumes and breathtaking spins lies a secret: He's actually a hopelessly romantic otaku, who can only land his quad jumps when Chitose is on hand to recite a spell from his favorite magical girl anime!

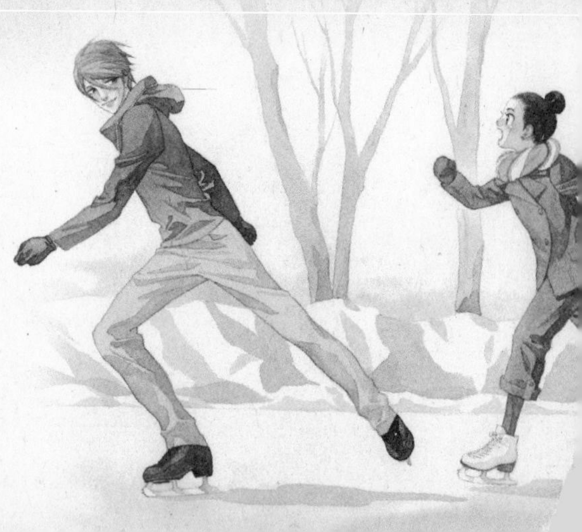

KC KODANSHA COMICS